Meets you **anywhere**
takes you **everywhere**

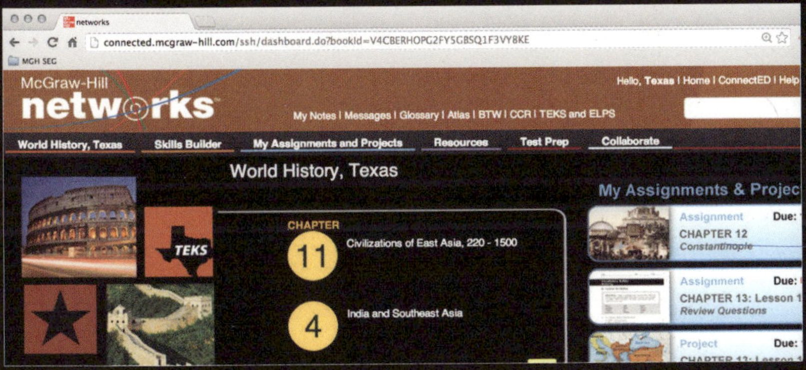

networks™

A Social Studies Learning System

To connect:

1. connected.mcgraw-hill.com
2. Enter your username and password from your teacher
3. Click on your book
4. Select your chapter and lesson, or explore the Resource Library

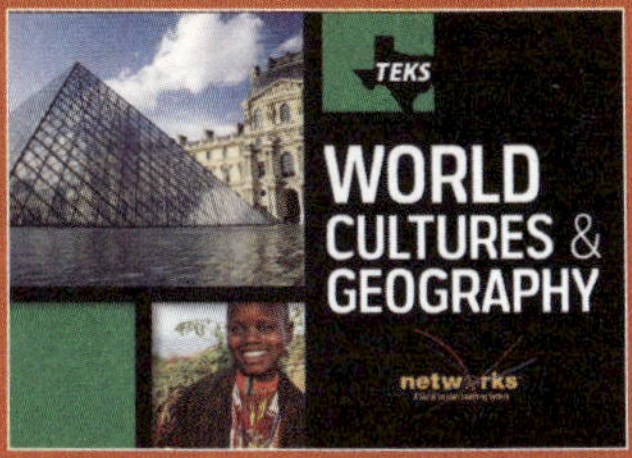

Connect with Social Studies in Networks and explore:

Events which shaped our lives and entire civilizations

People who commanded our attention and amassed empires

Places where our stories were written and almost unwritten

Clockwise from top left: Between takeoff and landing, all human space flights are under the watch of Mission Control at the Lyndon B. Johnson Space Center. George Washington is honored at the George Washington Masonic Museum. Texas is a major contributor to oil and natural gas production in the U.S.

networks™
A Social Studies Learning System

The range of human ingenuity and creativity can be seen in such wonders as the Sydney Opera House in Australia, the stilt fishing platforms which dot the coastline of Sri Lanka, and the Great Wall of China.

Experience a whole new world and discover:

Hidden histories and lost civilizations

Popular trade practices and ancient trade routes

Modern traditions and exotic customs

PHOTOS: (t)Kimberley Coole/Lonely Planet Images/Getty Images, (bl)Christian Kober/Robert Harding World Imagery/Getty Images, (br)sinopics/E+/Getty Images

Encounter heroes and villains and choose your allies wisely.

Meeting people is easy with Networks. Discover interactive profiles of important figures that shaped history and connect with modern news makers impacting your world now.

Get to know people from across time and around the world. Clockwise from top left: Nelson Mandela, Amelia Earhart, Ellen Ochoa, Josef Stalin, Franklin D. Roosevelt, Winston Churchill, Ronald Reagan.

PHOTOS: (t)Don Bayley/E+/Getty Images, (cl)McGraw-Hill Education, (inset)National Archives and Records Administration (NLS-WHPO-A-C584(12), (cr)Ingram Publishing, (bl)National Archives and Records Administration (NWDNS-111-SC-260486), (br)NASA

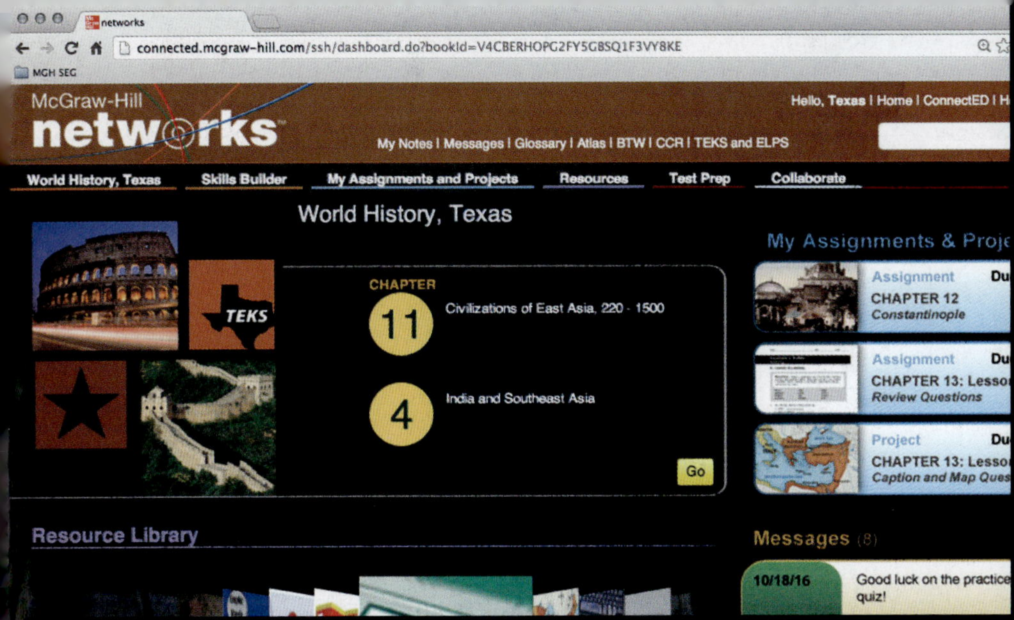

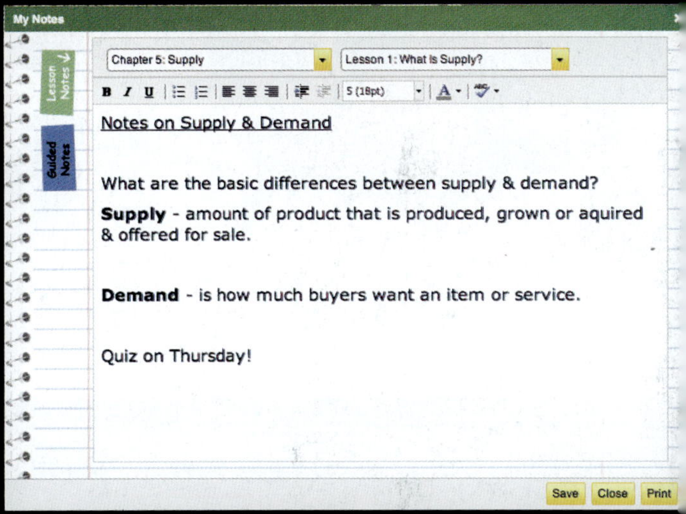

Clockwise from top left: Your Networks experience starts at your Student Learning Center dashboard. Tools such as My Notes, Messages, and My Planner help you be successful.

Make Networks yours.

Personalize your experience with Networks. Helpful embedded tools allow you to organize your work, take notes, message your teacher and classmates, and even turn your homework in — anytime, anywhere.

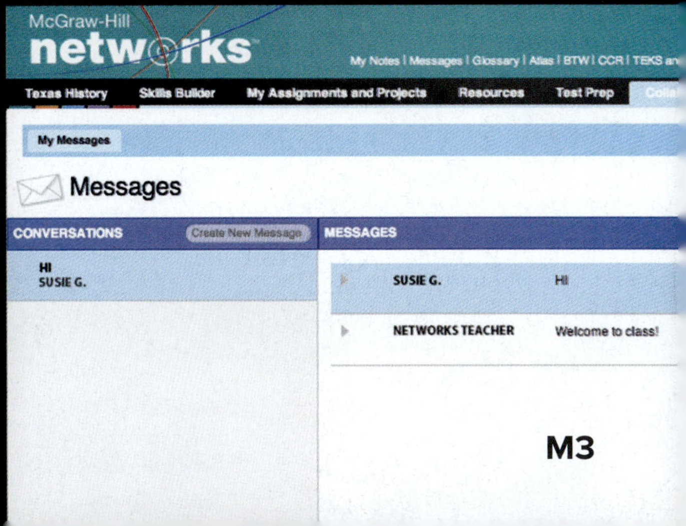

PHOTOS: McGraw-Hill Education

Your Social Studies course will come alive with infographics, audio lessons, short videos, and more.

Read. Listen. Watch.

Networks gives you more ways to learn what you need to know in Social Studies and to go deeper.

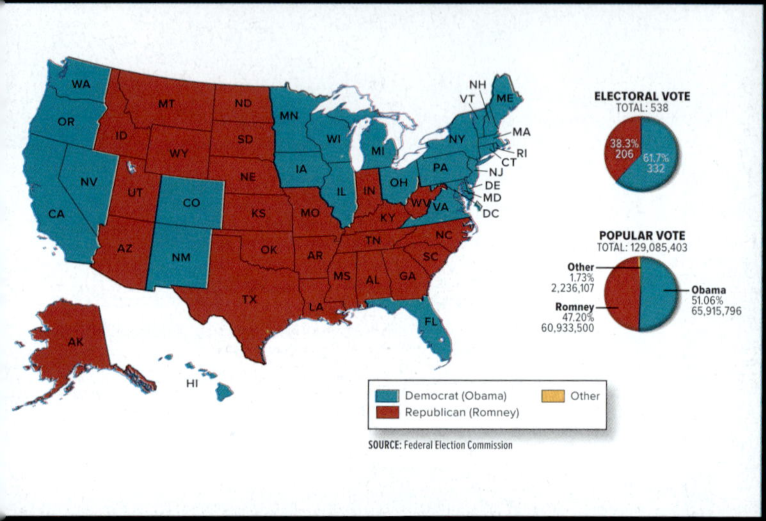

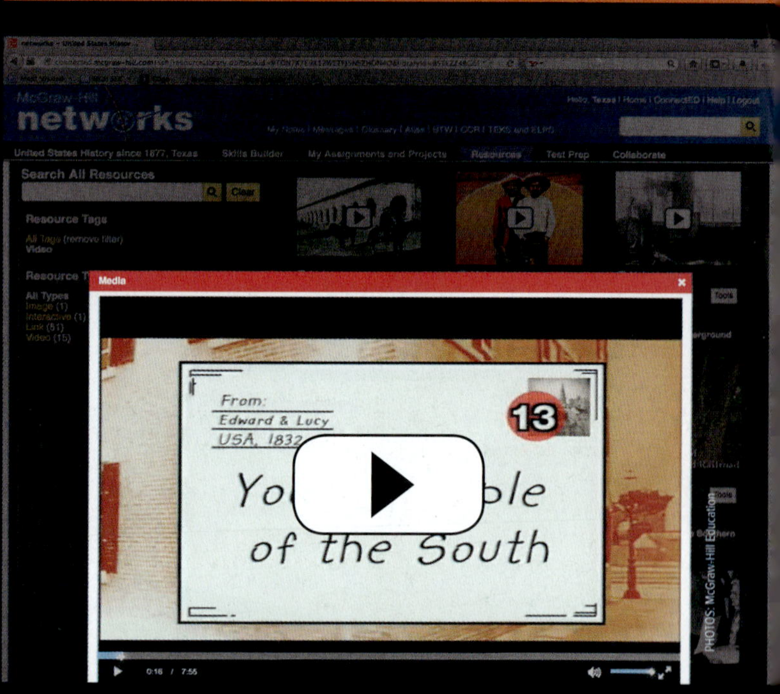

PHOTOS: McGraw-Hill Education

The Alamo: February and March, 1836

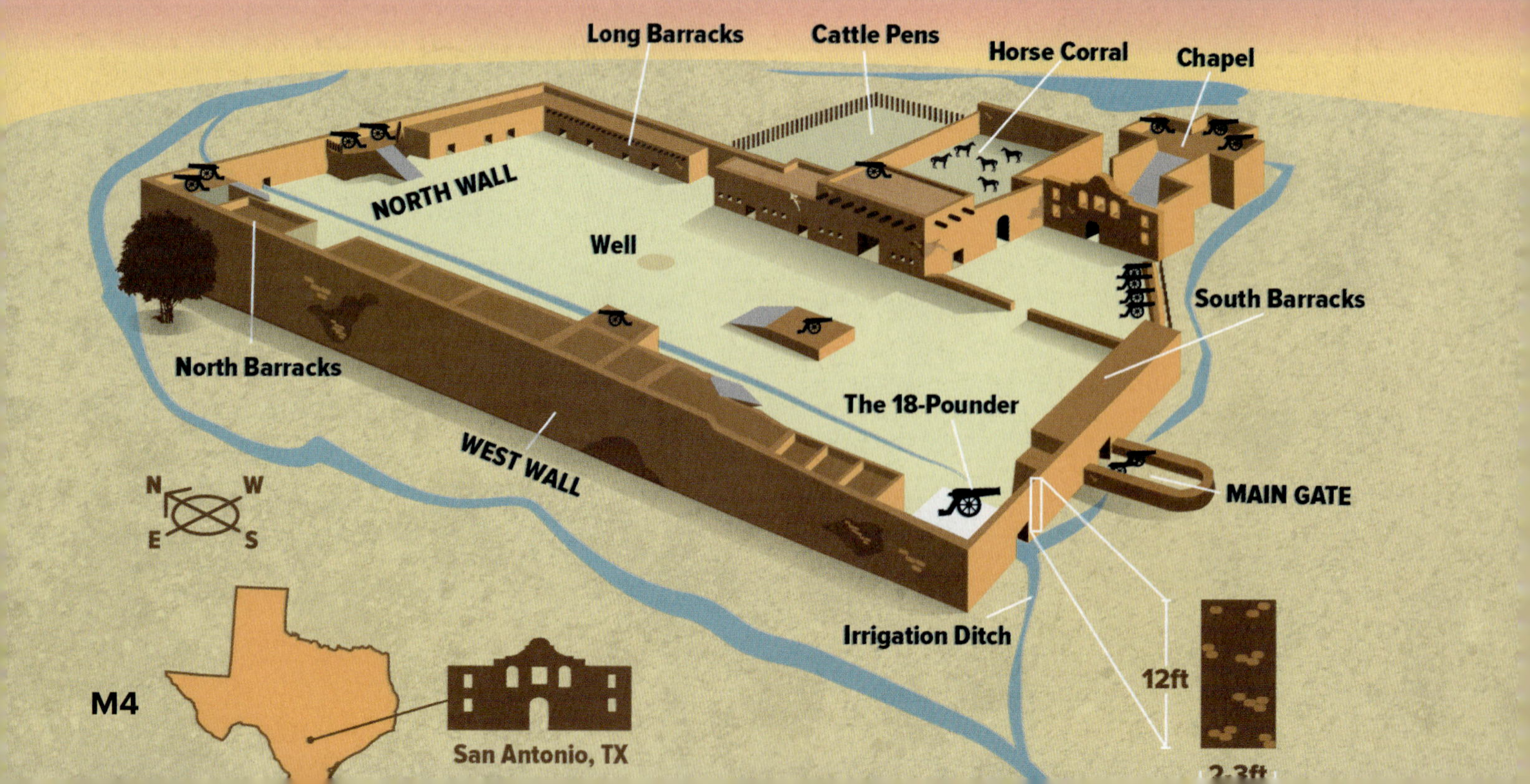

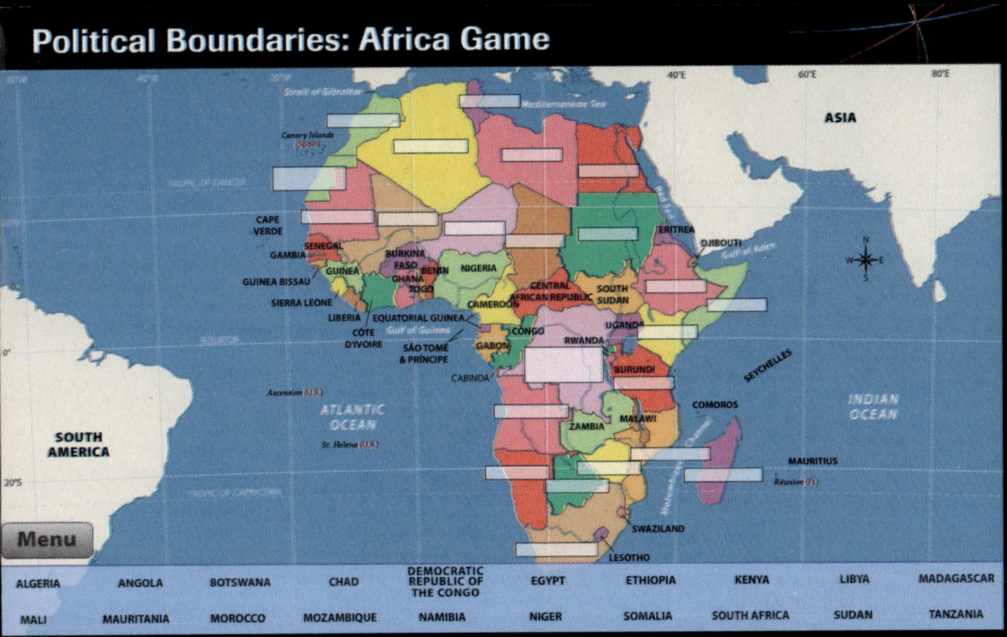

networks™
A Social Studies Learning System

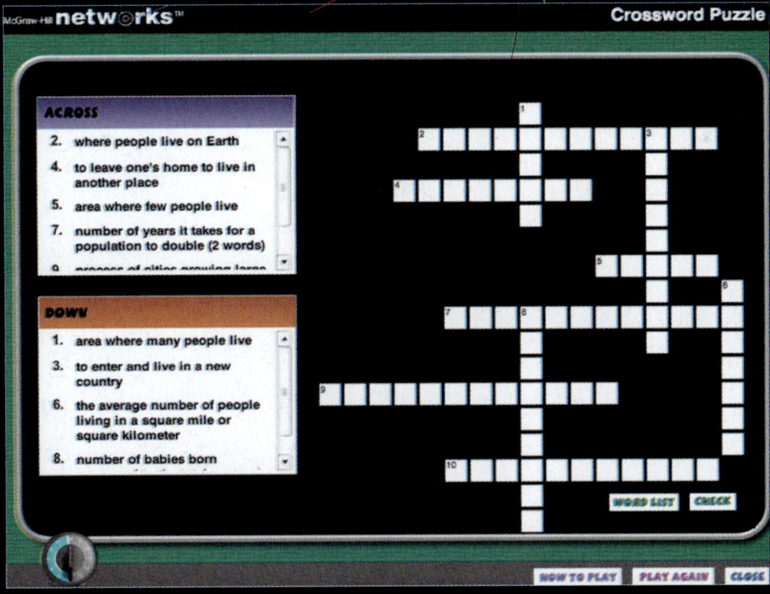

Find resources to help you make sense of what you are learning. Build your skills with interactive puzzles, drag n' drop maps, Foldables®, and more!

Experience.

Immerse yourself in videos, discover exciting games, and even keep organized with Foldables®.

PHOTOS: McGraw-Hill Education

FOLDABLES®

CHAPTER 13 The Republic of Texas

Summarizing Create the Foldable below and write the chapter title on the cover tab. Label the other 3 tabs with each lesson's title. Under the appropriate tabs, take notes and summarize the main ideas presented in each lesson. On the back of the Foldable, summarize the difference between Sam Houston's and Mirabeau Lamar's approach to dealing with the Native Americans.

Step 1
Begin with two sheets of lined paper.

Step 2
Stack the two sheets of paper and align them so one sheet is about an inch below the other sheet.

Step 3
Fold the bottom part of the stack up to create three equal tabs. Flip over. Staple at the fold and label as directed.

Join our Network!

Networks gives you the knowledge and insight you need to be successful in life. Learn from the past and gain an understanding of the world around you.

Go online now!
connected.mcgraw-hill.com

Clockwise from top left: The United States Capitol building is in Washington, D.C. In the United States, people aged 18 years and older have the right to vote.Wall Street, home of the New York Stock Exchange, is a hub of business activity.

networks™
A Social Studies Learning System

TEKS

WORLD HISTORY

networks™
A Social Studies Learning System

Jackson J. Spielvogel, Ph.D.

McGraw Hill Education

Bothell, WA • Chicago, IL • Columbus, OH • New York, NY

Cover Photo Credits: (t)Martin Child/Digital Vision/Getty Images, (c)Stephen Studd/Photographer's Choice/Getty Images, (bl)sinopics/E+/Getty Images, (br)DEA/G. DAGLI ORTI/ De Agostini/Getty Images

www.mheonline.com/networks

McGraw Hill Education

Send all inquiries to:
McGraw-Hill Education
8787 Orion Place
Columbus, OH 43240

ISBN: 978-0-07-660599-6
MHID: 0-07-660599-X

Printed in the United States of America.

2 3 4 5 6 7 8 9 QVS 19 18 17 16 15

Meets you anywhere, takes you everywhere. Networks™—A Social Studies Learning System. To connect: 1. connected.mcgraw-hill.com, 2. Enter your username and password from your teacher, 3. Click on your book, 4. Select your chapter and lesson, or explore the Resource Library.

Connect with Social Studies in Networks and explore:

- Events which shaped our lives and entire civilizations
- People who commanded our attention and amassed empires
- Places where our stories were written and almost unwritten

Clockwise from top left: Between takeoff and landing, all human space flights are under the watch of Mission Control at the Lyndon B. Johnson Space Center. George Washington is honored at the George Washington Masonic Museum. Texas is a major contributor to oil and natural gas production in the U.S.

AUTHORS AND CONSULTANTS

AUTHORS

Jackson Spielvogel, Ph.D., is associate professor emeritus of history at the Pennsylvania State University. He received his Ph.D. from the Ohio State University, where he specialized in Reformation history under Harold J. Grimm. His articles and reviews have been published in several scholarly publications. He is co-author (with William Duiker) of *World History*, published in 1994 (5th edition, 2007). Professor Spielvogel has won five major university-wide awards, and in 2000, he became the first winner of the Schreyer Institute's Student Choice Award for innovative and inspired teaching.

Contributing Author

Jay McTighe has published articles in a number of leading educational journals and has co-authored ten books, including the best-selling *Understanding By Design* series with Grant Wiggins. Jay also has an extensive background in professional development and is a featured speaker at national, state, and district conferences and workshops. He received his undergraduate degree from The College of William and Mary, earned a Masters degree from The University of Maryland and completed post-graduate studies at The Johns Hopkins University.

ACADEMIC CONSULTANTS

Karl E. Baughman, Ph.D.
Assistant Professor
Department of History
Stephen F. Austin State University
Nacogdoches, Texas

David Berger, Ph.D.
Ruth and I. Lewis Gordon Professor of Jewish History
Dean, Bernard Revel Graduate School
Yeshiva University
New York, New York

Michael C. Brose, Ph.D.
Associate Professor
Department of History
University of Wyoming
Laramie, Wyoming

Steven Cunha, Ph.D.
Professor
Department of Geography
Humboldt State University
Arcata, California

Tom Daccord
Educational Technology Specialist
Co-Director, EdTechTeacher
Boston, Massachusetts

Richard Golden, Ph.D.
Professor of History and Director of Jewish Studies Program
University of North Texas
Denton, Texas

Jamie Goodall, Ph.D.
Lecturer
Department of History
Ohio State University
Columbus, Ohio

Farid Mahdavi, Ph.D.
Lecturer
Department of History
San Diego State University
San Diego, California

Justin Reich
Educational Technology Specialist
Co-Director, EdTechTeacher
Boston, Massachusetts

Guy R. Welbon, Ph.D.
Associate Professor Emeritus
South Asia Studies and Religious Studies
University of Pennsylvania
Philadelphia, Pennsylvania

TEXAS ADVISORY BOARD

The Texas Teacher Advisory Board provided valuable feedback on the content and design of this program. We thank these teachers for their hard work, creative suggestions, and commitment to their discipline.

Mylynka Kilgore Cardona
University of Texas, Austin
Austin, Texas

Sean Clark
Fort Worth Independent School District
Fort Worth, Texas

Susan Gregurek
Spring Independent School District
Houston, Texas

Lisa Holtin
Conroe Independent School District
Conroe, Texas

Christine Hurley
Spring Independent School District
Houston, Texas

Linda Lancaster
Grapevine-Colleyville Independent School District
Grapevine, Texas

Dawn McGuffin Nixon
Educational Programs Coordinator, Williamson Museum
Georgetown, Texas
Cypress Fairbanks Independent School District, Retired
Cypress, Texas

Sam Pollard
Humble Independent School District
Humble, Texas

Gidget Tarwater
Conroe Independent School District
Conroe, Texas

Ann Urich
Spring Independent School District
Houston, Texas

Darlene Zavertnik
Conroe Independent School District
Conroe, Texas

REVIEWERS

TEACHER REVIEWERS

Elizabeth M. Bernard
Social Studies Teacher
Edgewood High School
Harford County Public Schools
Edgewood, Maryland

Christopher Bryant
Social Studies Teacher
Lake Forest High School
District 115
Lake Forest, Illinois

Penny Buckley
History Teacher
Sahuaro High School
Tucson Unified School District
Tucson, Arizona

Jennifer Lankau Chase
Teacher, AP World History and World History
Charles H. Milby High School
Houston Independent School District
Houston, Texas

Christine Conrad
Social Studies Department Chair
Olympia High School
Orange County Public Schools
Orlando, Florida

Stanley De Cusatis
Social Studies Teacher
Harford Technical High School
Harford County Public Schools
Belair, Maryland

Robin Depugh
Social Studies Teacher
Sahuaro High School
Tucson Unified School District
Tucson, Arizona

Dr. Jane Carter Eason
Secondary Social Studies Consultant
Richland County School District One
Columbia, South Carolina

Donny Funderburg
Teacher, Social Studies
Godley High School
Godley Independent School District
Godley, Texas

Nadia Gunter
Social Studies Teacher
R.T. Cream
Camden, New Jersey

Loyd Henderson
Social Studies Department Chair
Travelers Rest High School
Travelers Rest, South Carolina

William Hocking
Social Studies Department Chair 6–12
Mansfield High School
Mansfield Public Schools
Mansfield, Massachusetts

Scott E. Jones
Social Studies Teacher
Hazelwood West High School
Hazelwood School District
Hazelwood, Missouri

Lisa McBride
Social Studies Teacher
Owasso Mid High School
Owasso Public Schools
Owasso, Oklahoma

Andre' McConico
Social Studies Teacher
The Pathway School
Mobile County Public Schools
Mobile, Alabama

Donna A. Patch
Teacher, Social Studies/Director
Westside High School
Houston Independent School District
Houston, Texas

Chris Peek
Teacher, AP World History
Bellaire High School (Houston ISD)
Houston Independent School District
Bellaire, Texas

Julie Peterson
Social Studies Chair
Carbondale Community High School
District 165
Carbondale, Illinois

Jacalyn A. Roche
History Teacher
Waukegan High School
CUSD #60
Waukegan, Illinois

Heinz Schmidt
Teacher, Social Studies
Obra D. Tompkins High School
Katy Independent School District
Katy, Texas

Laura Snow
Social Studies Specialist, Retired
Escambia County School District
Pensacola, Florida

Gail S. Stockard
Teacher
Olympia High School
Orange County Public Schools
Orlando, Florida

Sharlene Vazquez
Teacher, Social Studies
Rivera High School
Brownsville Independent School District
Brownsville, Texas

PHOTO: Glow Images

CONTENTS

PHOTO: Scala/Art Resource, NY

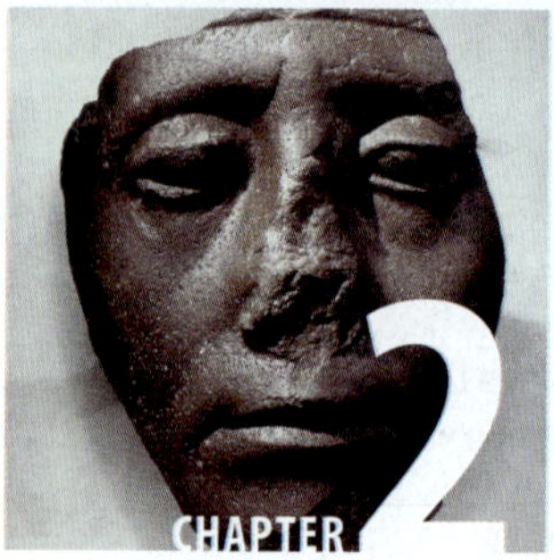

PHOTO: The Granger Collection, NYC, All rights reserved

PHOTO: Silvio Fiore/SuperStock/Getty Images

PHOTO: DEA / G. NIMATALLAH/De Agostini Picture Library/ Getty Images

Essential Questions

How can geography influence political organization? • How can cultural and political differences lead to conflict and change?

PHOTO: ©Dinodia Photos / Alamy

Essential Questions

How was early Indian culture influenced by religion and social structure? • How did ideas and events during the Mauryan and Gupta Empires affect India's development?

PHOTO: Keren Su/China Span/Getty Images

Essential Questions

How can differing philosophies influence a culture? • What factors can help a dynasty stay in power?

CONTENTS

PHOTO: The British Library/Photolibrary

PHOTO: Archives Charmet/Bridgman Art Library

PHOTO: Giraudon/Bridgeman Art Library

CONTENTS

PHOTO: Heini Schneebeli/Bridgeman Art Library

PHOTO: DEA / G. DAGLI ORTI/De Agostini Picture Library/ Getty Images

PHOTO: Leonardo da Vinci/The Bridgeman Art Library/Getty Images

PHOTO: North Wind Picture Archives/The Image Works

PHOTO: The Image Works.

The Age of Exploration, 1500–1800 377

Essential Question

What are the effects of political and economic expansion?

PHOTO: Sotheby / akg-images.

Conflict and Absolutism in Europe, 1550–1715 401

Essential Questions

What effect might social, economic, and religious conflicts have on a country? • How would the exercise of absolute power affect a country?

PHOTO: The Granger Collection, NYC, All rights reserved.

The Muslim Empires, 1450–1800 427

Essential Questions

What factors help unify an empire? • How can the creation of a new empire impact the people and culture of a region?

CONTENTS

PHOTO: CORBIS

The East Asian World, 1400–1800 447

Essential Questions

What factors help unify a kingdom or dynasty? • How can external forces influence a kingdom or dynasty?

PHOTO: The Granger Collection, NYC. All rights reserved

The Enlightement and Revolutions, 1550–1800 469

Essential Questions

Why do new ideas often spark change? • How do new ways of thinking affect the way people respond to their surroundings?

PHOTO: Scala/White Images / Art Resource, NY

The French Revolution and Napoleon, 1789–1815 497

Essential Questions

What causes revolution? • How does revolution change society?

PHOTO: Christie's Images/CORBIS.

Industrialization and Nationalism, 1800–1870 525

Essential Questions

How can innovation affect ways of life? • How does revolution bring about political and economic change?

PHOTO: The Granger Collection, NYC, All rights reserved.

Mass Society and Democracy, 1870–1914 557

Essential Questions

How can industrialization affect a country's economy? • How are political and social structures influenced by economic changes?

PHOTO: Bettmann/CORBIS

The Reach of Imperialism, 1800–1914 583

Essential Questions

What are the causes and effects of imperialism? • How do some groups resist control by others?

CONTENTS

PHOTO: Stringer/Fotosearch/Getty Images

Challenges and Transition in East Asia, 1800–1914 ... 609

Essential Questions

How can new ideas accelerate economic and political change? • How do cultures influence each other?

PHOTO: Rue des Archives/The Granger Collection, NYC

World War I and the Russian Revolution, 1914–1919 ... 631

Essential Questions

Why do politics often lead to war? • How can technology impact war?

PHOTO: Heinrich Hoffmann/Time & Life Pictures/Getty Images

The West Between the Wars, 1919–1939 ... 659

Essential Questions

What can cause economic instability? • How might political change impact society?

Nationalism Around the World, 1919–1939 681

Essential Questions

How can political control lead to nationalist movements? How does economic exploitation lead to nationalist movements?

World War II and the Holocaust, 1939–1945 709

Essential Questions

Why do political actions often lead to war? • How does war impact society and the environment?

The Cold War, 1945–1989 739

Essential Question

How does conflict influence political relationships?

CONTENTS

PHOTO: © Louise Gubb/Corbis SABA

Independence and Nationalism in the Developing World, 1945–1993

Essential Questions

How can political change cause conflict? • How can political relationships affect economic relationships?

PHOTO: ©Bettmann/Corbis

Life During the Cold War, 1945–1989

ESSENTIAL QUESTIONS

How does war result in change? • What challenges may countries face as a result of war?

PHOTO: ullstein bild / The Granger Collection, NYC. All rights reserved

A New Era Begins, 1989–Present

ESSENTIAL QUESTIONS

What motivates political change? • How can economic and social changes affect a country?

PHOTO: ©Phillipe Lissac/Godong/Corbis

FEATURES

BIOGRAPHY

Connections to TODAY...

Analyzing PRIMARY SOURCES

Thinking like a HISTORIAN

FEATURES

Political Cartoon

Skillbuilder

MAPS, CHARTS AND GRAPHS

MAPS, CHARTS AND GRAPHS

MAPS, CHARTS AND GRAPHS

Interactive Slide Shows

Chapter 1, Lesson 1	Art and Artifacts of Early Humans
Chapter 1, Lesson 1	Early Humans and their Environments
Chapter 1, Lesson 2	Learning to Domesticate Animals
Chapter 2, Lesson 2	Minoan Art
Chapter 3, Lesson 2	The Amarna Period of the New Kingdom
Chapter 3, Lesson 3	The Assyrian War Machine
Chapter 4, Lesson 5	Hellenistic Science
Chapter 7, Lesson 3	Roman Art
Chapter 7, Lesson 3	Roman Architecture
Chapter 8, Lesson 3	The Role of Monks
Chapter 9, Lesson 3	Islamic Sciences
Chapter 9, Lesson 3	Islamic Arts
Chapter 10, Lesson 1	The Code of Chivalry
Chapter 12, Lesson 3	High Middle Ages and Today
Chapter 14, Lesson 1	Native American Societies and their Environments
Chapter 14, Lesson 2	Inca Technology
Chapter 15, Lesson 2	Art of the Italian Renaissance
Chapter 15, Lesson 2	Art of the Northern European Renaissance
Chapter 18, Lesson 3	The Westernization of Russia by Peter the Great
Chapter 18, Lesson 4	Virtual Field Trip: Museum
Chapter 18, Lesson 4	Virtual Field Trip: Music
Chapter 18, Lesson 4	Virtual Field Trip: Theater
Chapter 19, Lesson 1	Ottoman Architecture and Arts
Chapter 19, Lesson 2	The Art of the Safavid
Chapter 20, Lesson 1	Chinese Art and Literature During the Ming and Qing Dynasties
Chapter 21, Lesson 2	The Enlightenment and the Arts
Chapter 22, Lesson 4	Napoleon's Final Days
Chapter 24, Lesson 1	Inventions of the Second Industrial Revolution
Chapter 24, Lesson 4	Modern Painting and Architecture
Chapter 29, Lesson 4	Modern Art of Latin America
Chapter 30, Lesson 4	The Holocaust

Interactive White Board Activities

Chapter 1, Lesson 1	Identifying Artifacts of Early Humans
Chapter 1, Lesson 2	Hunter-Gatherer and Farming Societies
Chapter 1, Lesson 3	Technology and Innovations in Sumer
Chapter 2, Lesson 1	Egyptian Pyramids
Chapter 2, Lesson 4	The Dynastic Cycle in Ancient China
Chapter 4, Lesson 4	Greek Philosophers
Chapter 5, Lesson 1	Four Stages of Life
Chapter 5, Lesson 2	The Four Noble Truths and the Eightfold Path
Chapter 5, Lesson 3	Indian Literature
Chapter 6, Lesson 1	Periods of Disorder
Chapter 6, Lesson 2	Political and Administrative Changes
Chapter 6, Lesson 3	Technological Advances
Chapter 7, Lesson 1	Roman Political Offices
Chapter 7, Lesson 2	From First Triumvirate to Dictatorship
Chapter 7, Lesson 2	Organization of the Roman Army
Chapter 8, Lesson 1	Features of Christianity
Chapter 8, Lesson 2	Reforms of Diocletian and Constantine
Chapter 8, Lesson 3	Church Hierarchy
Chapter 8, Lesson 5	The Byzantine and Catholic Divide
Chapter 9, Lesson 2	Styles of the Islamic Empire
Chapter 10, Lesson 3	Development of the English Law and Government
Chapter 11, Lesson 1	Science and Technology in China
Chapter 11, Lesson 2	Religion in Early China
Chapter 11, Lesson 4	The Conquests of Timur Lenk
Chapter 12, Lesson 1	Investiture Controversy
Chapter 12, Lesson 2	Effects of the Crusades
Chapter 12, Lesson 4	Nationalist Traditions in Europe
Chapter 13, Lesson 1	Africa's Geography
Chapter 14, Lesson 1	Toltec, Maya, and Aztec Political and Social Structure

Interactive White Board Activities (cont.)

Chapter 14, Lesson 2	Inca Political Structure
Chapter 15, Lesson 1	Renaissance Populations
Chapter 15, Lesson 2	The Liberal Arts
Chapter 15, Lesson 2	Humanism and Renaissance Art
Chapter 16, Lesson 1	Support for Lutheranism
Chapter 16, Lesson 2	The Protestant Reformation
Chapter 17, Lesson 1	The Treaty of Tordesillas
Chapter 17, Lesson 2	Triangular Trade
Chapter 17, Lesson 3	Economic Motives and their Effects
Chapter 18, Lesson 2	Tensions Between Kings and Parliament
Chapter 18, Lesson 3	Louis XIV's Policies
Chapter 19, Lesson 1	Political and Religious Structure in the Ottoman Empire
Chapter 19, Lesson 2	Decline of the Ottoman Empire
Chapter 19, Lesson 3	Decline of the Mogul Empire
Chapter 20, Lesson 1	Trade, the Economy, and Chinese Society 1400–1800
Chapter 20, Lesson 2	Feudal and Class Systems in Japan
Chapter 20, Lesson 3	The Korean Alphabet
Chapter 21, Lesson 1	Models of the Universe
Chapter 21, Lesson 3	Enlightened Absolutism
Chapter 21, Lesson 4	The Bill of Rights and Enlightenment Principles
Chapter 22, Lesson 1	The Three Estates
Chapter 22, Lesson 2	Governmental Groups
Chapter 22, Lesson 3	Napoleon's Domestic Policies
Chapter 23, Lesson 1	Industrial Capitalism and New Economic Classes
Chapter 23, Lesson 2	The Revolutions of 1848
Chapter 23, Lesson 3	Sweeping Changes
Chapter 23, Lesson 4	Revolutions in Latin America
Chapter 23, Lesson 5	Emotion Versus Reason
Chapter 24, Lesson 2	Urbanization in the Nineteenth Century
Chapter 25, Lesson 1	Colonial Takeover
Chapter 25, Lesson 1	Direct and Indirect Rule
Chapter 25, Lesson 2	The Suez Canal
Chapter 25, Lesson 3	Britain in India
Chapter 26, Lesson 1	The Opium War, the Treaty of Nanjing, and the British in China
Chapter 26, Lesson 2	Reform and Revolution
Chapter 26, Lesson 3	Economic Reforms of the Meiji Restoration
Chapter 27, Lesson 1	European Nationalism in 1914
Chapter 27, Lesson 4	The End of the War and Peace Negotiations
Chapter 28, Lesson 1	Effects of and Responses to the Great Depression
Chapter 28, Lesson 3	Nazi Racism and Nationalism
Chapter 29, Lesson 1	Modernizing Turkey and Iran
Chapter 29, Lesson 2	Resisting Colonial Rule in Kenya
Chapter 29, Lesson 4	Responding to the Great Depression
Chapter 30, Lesson 2	The European Theater, 1939–1941
Chapter 30, Lesson 3	Wartime Mobilization
Chapter 31, Lesson 1	The Cold War
Chapter 31, Lesson 2	China and the Superpowers
Chapter 31, Lesson 3	The Vietnam War
Chapter 32, Lesson 2	Iran, Iraq, and Afghanistan
Chapter 32, Lesson 3	African Independence Leaders
Chapter 32, Lesson 4	Events in Central and South America
Chapter 33, Lesson 1	European Domestic Politics, 1945–1985
Chapter 33, Lesson 2	The Soviet Leaders
Chapter 33, Lesson 3	Asian Economics
Chapter 34, Lesson 1	Transition from Communism
Chapter 34, Lesson 2	Post-Cold War Actions of World Leaders
Chapter 34, Lesson 4	Political Changes After the Cold War
Chapter 35, Lesson 1	Terrorist Attacks and the Impact of 9/11
Chapter 35, Lesson 2	Equality for Women
Chapter 35, Lesson 3	Regional Trade Blocs
Chapter 35, Lesson 4	Environmental Quiz Show

Interactive Time Lines

Chapter 1, Place and Time	The World: Prehistory–2300 B.C.
Chapter 2, Place and Time	The World: 3000 B.C.–200 B.C.
Chapter 2, Lesson 5	World Events During the Caral Period c. 2600–c. 2000 B.C.
Chapter 3, Place and Time	Near East 2300 B.C.–300 B.C.
Chapter 4, Place and Time	Greece, 1600 B.C.–100 B.C.
Chapter 4, Lesson 1	The Greek Dark Age
Chapter 4, Lesson 2	Development of Athenian Democracy
Chapter 5, Place and Time	Ancient India 1000 B.C.–A.D. 500
Chapter 6, Place and Time	Ancient China, 300 B.C.–A.D. 300
Chapter 6, Lesson 3	The Fall of the Han Empire
Chapter 7, Place and Time	Ancient Rome 600 B.C.–A.D. 500
Chapter 7, Lesson 1	The Punic Wars
Chapter 7, Lesson 2	Martyrs of the Roman Republic
Chapter 8, Place and Time	Europe A.D. 50–800
Chapter 9, Place and Time	The Arab Empire 600–1400
Chapter 10, Place and Time	Medieval Europe 800–1300
Chapter 11, Place and Time	East Asia 200–1400
Chapter 11, Lesson 1	Dynasties of China 500–1300
Chapter 11, Lesson 4	Southeast Asia 800–1500
Chapter 12, Place and Time	Europe 1000–1500
Chapter 12, Lesson 4	The Hundred Years' War
Chapter 13, Place and Time	Early Africa 500–1500
Chapter 14, Place and Time	The Americas 1200 B.C.–A.D. 1500
Chapter 15, Place and Time	Europe 1350–1600
Chapter 15, Lesson 1	The Italian Wars
Chapter 16, Place and Time	Europe 1517–1600
Chapter 16, Lesson 1	Christianity in Northern Europe
Chapter 17, Place and Time	The Age of Exploration 1500–1800
Chapter 17, Lesson 2	From Africa's Shores to America's Plantations
Chapter 17, Lesson 3	Spanish and Portuguese Settlement
Chapter 18, Place and Time	Europe 1550–1715
Chapter 18, Lesson 2	England Moves from Absolutism to Constitutional Monarchy
Chapter 19, Place and Time	The Muslim Empires 1450–1800
Chapter 19, Lesson 2	Ottoman and Safavid Conflicts
Chapter 20, Place and Time	East Asia 1400–1800
Chapter 21, Lesson 3	The Seven Years' War 1756–1763
Chapter 21, Lesson 4	The American Revolution 1775–1783
Chapter 22, Place and Time	France 1785–1815
Chapter 22, Lesson 2	The Reign of Terror
Chapter 23, Place and Time	Europe 1800–1870
Chapter 23, Lesson 3	Unification of Italy 1815–1870
Chapter 23, Lesson 3	Unification of Germany 1815–1871
Chapter 24, Place and Time	Europe 1870–1914
Chapter 25, Place and Time	Asia and Africa 1800–1914
Chapter 25, Lesson 2	Colonialism in South Africa
Chapter 26, Place and Time	East Asia 1800–1914
Chapter 26, Lesson 3	Japanese Expansion 1868–1910

INTERACTIVE SELF-CHECK QUIZZES

Each chapter has one Interactive Self-Check Quiz per lesson to provide a quick assessment of content knowledge.

Interactive White Board Activities (cont.)

Chapter 27, Place and Time	Europe and Russia 1914–1919
Chapter 27, Lesson 1	The Outbreak of World War I, 1914
Chapter 27, Lesson 3	The War in Europe and Russia 1914–1918
Chapter 27, Lesson 4	Final Years of World War I, 1917–1919
Chapter 28, Place and Time	Europe 1919–1939
Chapter 29, Place and Time	Africa and Asia 1919–1939
Chapter 30, Place and Time	Europe 1939–1945
Chapter 30, Lesson 5	The Final Months of WWII: D-Day to Victory in Asia
Chapter 31, Place and Time	U.S. and U.S.S.R. 1945–1975
Chapter 32, Place and Time	Africa and Asia 1945–1993
Chapter 33, Place and Time	Europe and the U.S. 1945–1989
Chapter 34, Place and Time	Eastern Europe 1989–Present
Chapter 34, Lesson 1	The Disintegration of Yugoslavia
Chapter 34, Lesson 4	U.S. Involvement in the Middle East
Chapter 35, Place and Tim	The World 1989–Present

Analyzing Primary Sources

Chapter 1, Place and Time	The World: Prehistory–2300 B.C.
Chapter 2, Place and Time	The World: 3000 B.C.–200 B.C.
Chapter 2, Lesson 1	Writing Systems in Ancient Egypt
Chapter 3, Place and Time	Near East 2300 B.C.–300 B.C.
Chapter 4, Place and Time	Greece, 1600 B.C.–100 B.C.
Chapter 5, Place and Time	Ancient India 1000 B.C.–A.D. 500
Chapter 6, Place and Time	Ancient China, 300 B.C.–A.D. 300
Chapter 7, Place and Time	Ancient Rome 600 B.C.–A.D. 500
Chapter 7, Lesson 3	Comparing Perspectives on Roman History
Chapter 8, Place and Time	Europe A.D. 50–800
Chapter 9, Place and Time	The Arab Empire 600–1400
Chapter 10, Place and Time	Medieval Europe 800–1300
Chapter 11, Place and Time	East Asia 200–1400
Chapter 11, Lesson 2	Who Were the Mongols?
Chapter 12, Place and Time	Europe 1000–1500
Chapter 12, Lesson 2	Were the Crusades Fought for Faith or Money?
Chapter 13, Place and Time	Early Africa 500–1500
Chapter 14, Place and Time	The Americas 1200 B.C.–A.D. 1500
Chapter 15, Place and Time	Europe 1350–1600
Chapter 16, Place and Time	Europe 1517–1600
Chapter 17, Place and Time	The Age of Exploration 1500–1800
Chapter 18, Place and Time	Europe 1550–1715
Chapter 19, Place and Time	The Muslim Empires 1450–1800
Chapter 20, Place and Time	East Asia 1400–1800
Chapter 22, Place and Time	France 1785–1815
Chapter 23, Place and Time	Europe 1800–1870
Chapter 24, Place and Time	Europe 1870–1914
Chapter 24, Lesson 1	Trade Unions and Their Opponents
Chapter 24, Lesson 4	Monet and Picasso
Chapter 25, Place and Time	Asia and Africa 1800–1914
Chapter 26, Place and Time	East Asia 1800–1914
Chapter 27, Place and Time	Europe and Russia 1914–1919
Chapter 28, Place and Time	Europe 1919–1939
Chapter 29, Place and Time	Africa and Asia 1919–1939
Chapter 30, Place and Time	Europe 1939–1945
Chapter 31, Place and Time	U.S. and U.S.S.R. 1945–1975
Chapter 32, Place and Time	Africa and Asia 1945–1993
Chapter 33, Place and Time	Europe and the U.S. 1945–1989
Chapter 34, Place and Time	Eastern Europe 1989–Present
Chapter 35, Place and Time	The World 1989–Present

Infographics

PRIMARY SOURCES AND POLITICAL CARTOONS

PRIMARY SOURCES AND POLITICAL CARTOONS

CHAPTER 23

CHAPTER 24

CHAPTER 25

CHAPTER 26

CHAPTER 27

CHAPTER 28

CHAPTER 29

PRIMARY SOURCES AND POLITICAL CARTOONS

CHAPTER 30

CHAPTER 31

CHAPTER 32

CHAPTER 33

CHAPTER 34

CHAPTER 35

HOW TO USE THE ONLINE STUDENT EDITION

TO THE STUDENT

Welcome to McGraw-Hill Education's **Networks** online student learning center. Here you will access your Online Student Edition as well as many other learning resources.

1 LOGGING ON TO THE STUDENT LEARNING CENTER

Using your internet browser, go to connected.mcgraw-hill.com.

Enter your username and password or

Create a new account using the redemption code your teacher gave you.

2 SELECT YOUR PROGRAM

Click your program to launch the home page of your Online Student Learning Center.

HOW TO USE THE ONLINE STUDENT EDITION

Using Your Home Page

1 HOME PAGE

To return to your home page at any time, click the Networks logo in the top left corner of the page.

2 QUICK LINKS MENU

Use this menu to access:

- My Notes (your personal notepad)
- Messages
- The online Glossary
- The online Atlas
- BTW (current events website for social studies)
- College and Career Readiness (CCR) materials
- TEKS and ELPS tool (provides location of TEKS and ELPS coverage)

3 HELP

For videos and assistance with the various features of the Networks system, click Help.

4 MAIN MENU

Use the menu bar to access:

- The Online Student Edition
- Skills Builder (for activities to improve your skills)
- Assignments and Projects
- Resource Library
- Test Prep
- Collaborate with Classmates

5 ONLINE STUDENT EDITION

Go to your Online Student Edition by selecting the chapter and lesson and then click Go.

6 ASSIGNMENTS

Go to your Online Student Edition by selecting the chapter and lesson and then click Go.

7 RESOURCE LIBRARY

Use the carousel to browse the Resource Library.

8 MESSAGES

Recent messages from your teacher will appear here. To view the full message, click the message or click See All.

Using Your Online Student Edition

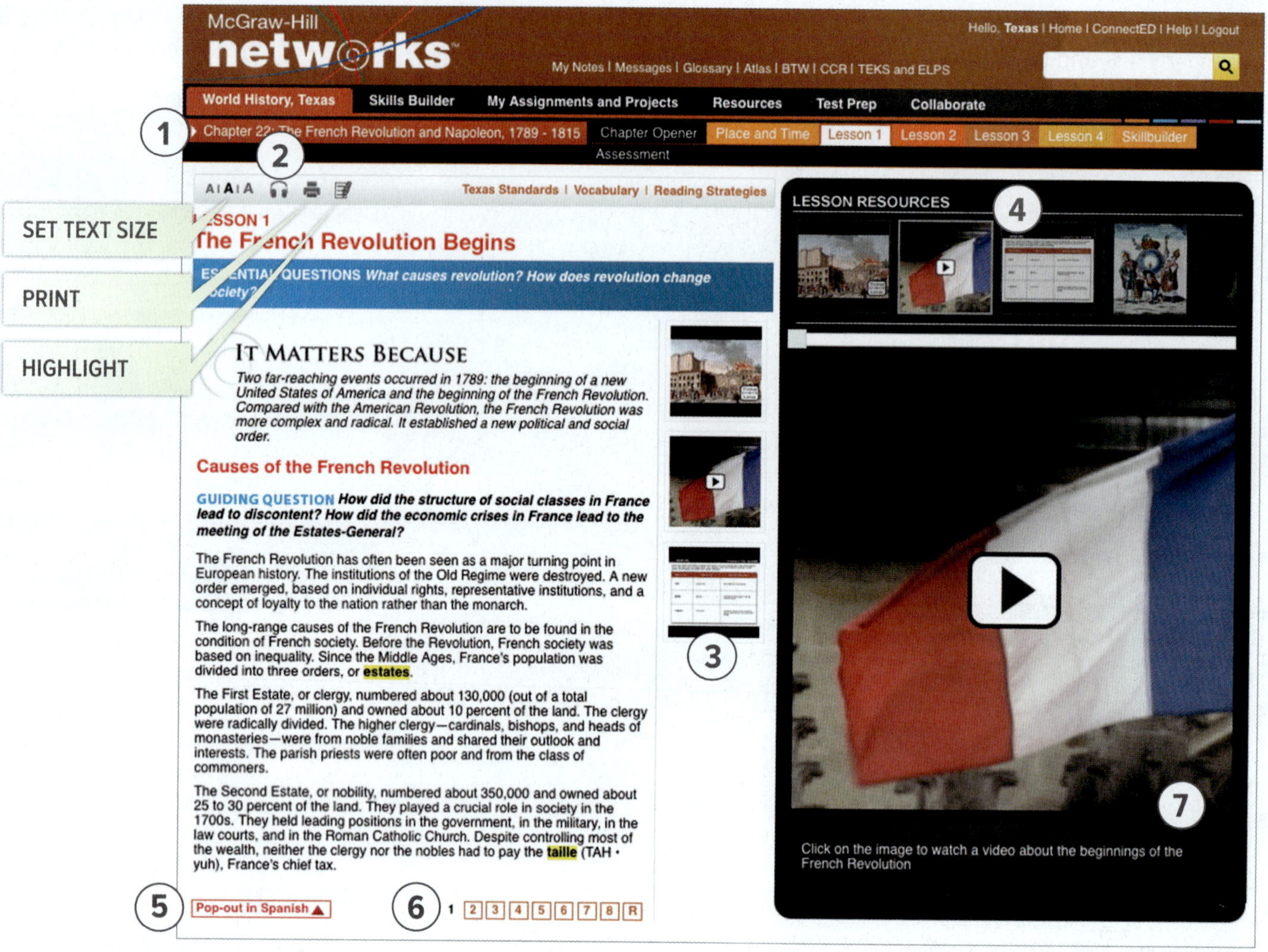

1 LESSON MENU

- Use the tabs to open the different lessons and special features in a chapter or unit.
- Clicking on the unit or chapter title will open the table of contents.

2 AUDIO EDITION

Click on the headphones symbol to have the page read to you. MP3 files for downloading each lesson are available in the Resource Library.

3 RESOURCES FOR THIS PAGE

Resources appear in the middle column to show that they go with the text on this page. Click the images to open them in the viewer.

4 LESSON RESOURCES

Use the carousel to browse the interactive resources available in this lesson. Click on a resource to open it in the viewer below.

5 SPANISH EDITION

If your program includes a Spanish edition, click here to open a window with the text in Spanish.

6 CHANGE PAGES

Click here to move to the next page in the lesson.

7 RESOURCE VIEWER

Click on the image that appears in the viewer to launch an interactive resource, including:

- Lesson Videos
- Interactive Photos and Slide Shows
- Interactive Maps
- Interactive Charts and Graphs
- Games
- Self-Check Quizzes for each lesson

HOW TO USE THE ONLINE STUDENT EDITION

Reading Support in the Online Student Edition

Your Online Student Edition contains several features to help improve your reading skills and understanding of the content.

1 LESSON VOCABULARY

Click Vocabulary to bring up a list of terms introduced in this lesson.

VOCABULARY POP-UP

Click on any term highlighted in yellow to open a window with the term's definition.

2 MY NOTES

Click My Notes to open the note-taking tool. You can write and save any notes you want in the Lesson Notes tab.

Click on the Guided Notes tab to view the Guided Reading Questions. Answering these questions will help you build a set of notes about the lesson.

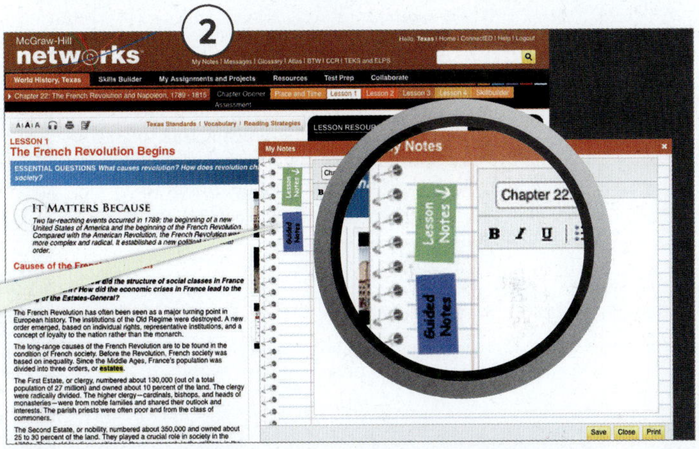

3 GRAPHIC ORGANIZER

Click Reading Strategies to open a note-taking activity using a graphic organizer.

Click the image of the graphic organizer to make it interactive. You can type directly into the graphic organizer and save or print your notes.

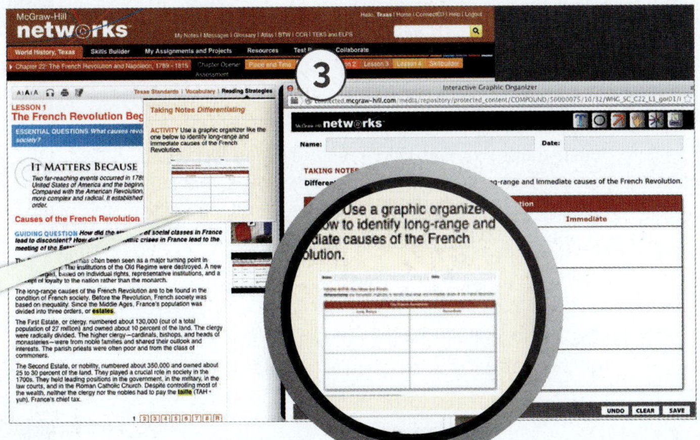

HOW TO USE THE ONLINE STUDENT EDITION

Using Interactive Resources in the Online Student Edition

Each lesson of your Online Student Edition contains many resources to help you learn the content and skills you need to know for this subject.

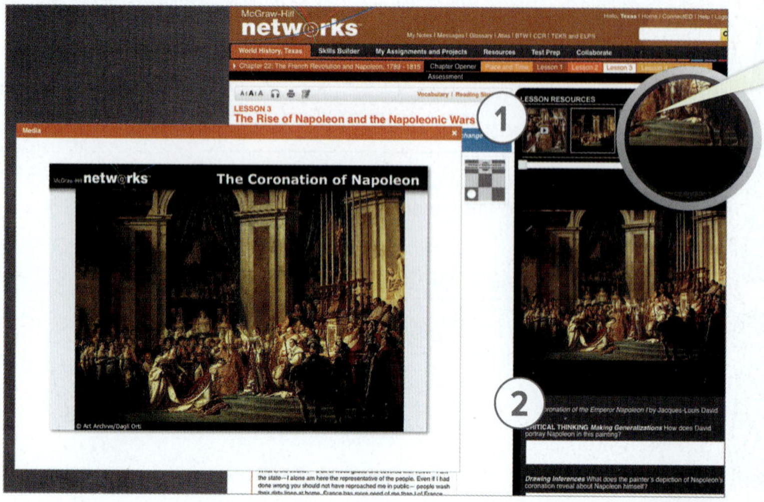

Networks provides many kinds of resources. This symbol shows that the resource is a slide show.

1 LAUNCHING RESOURCES

Clicking a resource in the viewer launches an interactive resource.

2 QUESTIONS AND ACTIVITIES

When a resource appears in the viewer, there are usually 1 or 2 questions or activities beneath it. You can type and save your answers in the answer boxes and submit them to your teacher.

3 INTERACTIVE MAPS

When a map appears in the viewer, click on it to launch the interactive map. You can use the drawing tool to mark up the map. You can also zoom in and turn layers on and off to display different information. Drag the scale onto the map to measure distances. Many maps have animations and audio as well.

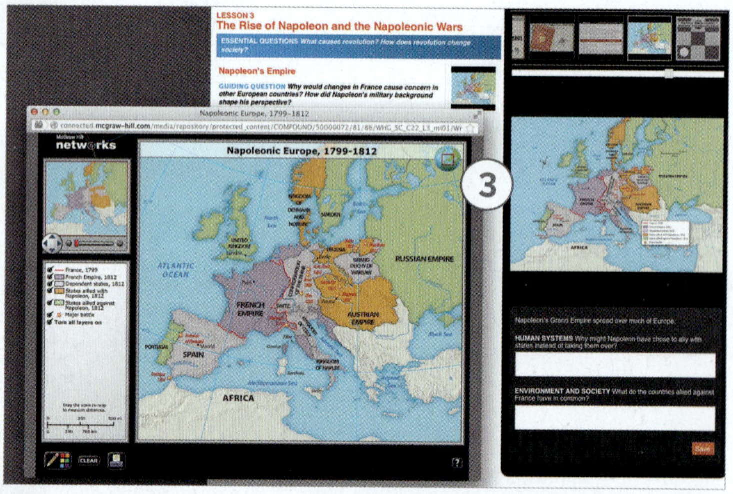

4 CHAPTER FEATURE

Each chapter begins with a feature called *Place and Time*. They include maps, primary sources, and a time line to help you understand the place and time of the chapter's events.

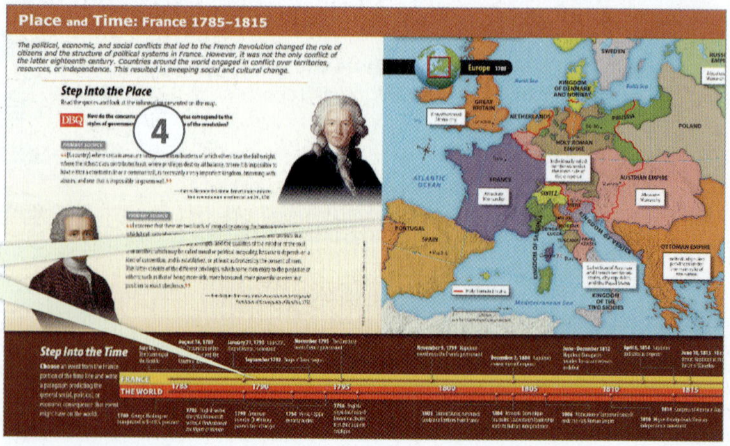

The map and time line are both interactive. You can click on the map and the time line for an interactive version.

Assessment

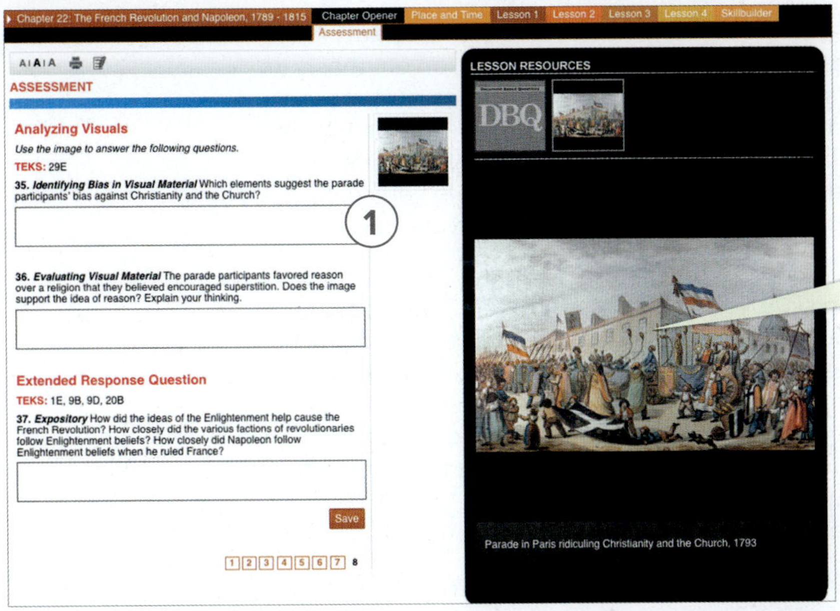

1 CHAPTER ASSESSMENT

At the end of each chapter is the assessment tab. Here you can test your understanding of what you have learned. You can type and save answers in the answer boxes and submit them to your teacher.

When a question uses an image or graph or map, it will appear in the viewer.

Finding Other Resources

There are hundreds of additional resources available in the Resource Library. Click the Resources tab to enter the library.

2 RESOURCE LIBRARY

Click the links to find collections of Primary Sources, Biographies, Skills Activities and the Reading Essentials and Study Guide.

You can search the Resource Library by keyword.

Click the star to mark a resource as a favorite.

A Guide For Students and Parents

Welcome to World History Studies and *World History*. This course provides an overview of human history from the earliest times to the present, with an emphasis on the study of significant people, events, and issues. You will trace the development of Western civilization as well as other civilizations around the world. You will be viewing and interpreting history from various perspectives, including historical, geographic, political, economic, and cultural. Together, these perspectives can help you come to understand how the past has led to our present and to appreciate your role in shaping our future.

The importance of the knowledge and skills you gain this year extends well beyond your classroom. As Americans we study history not only to learn names and dates but also to be prepared to live and prosper in a complex, interdependent world. Learning about the intellectual heritage of our civilization and other civilizations also helps us become better citizens. It sheds new light on our American values and institutions, such as patriotism, free enterprise, and democracy. We hope that this textbook will help you succeed as a student and an informed citizen.

The Texas Essential Knowledge and Skills (TEKS) for Social Studies

On the following pages, you will find the TEKS. These are the concepts and skills that you should learn and be able to demonstrate as you take the course. You may want to preview the TEKS with your parents or caregivers. Many of the names and terms may be unfamiliar to you at first, but you and your parents or caregivers can design a plan to help you gain proficiency. You may also choose to review these TEKS from time to time during the course of your study.

Mission Nuestra Senora de la purisima Concepcion de Acuna, San Antonio, Texas

PHOTO: McGraw-Hill Education

History

1 The student understands traditional historical points of reference in world history. The student is expected to:

A identify major causes and describe the major effects of the following events from 8000 BC to 500 BC: the development of agriculture and the development of the river valley civilizations

B identify major causes and describe the major effects of the following events from 500 BC to AD 600: the development of the classical civilizations of Greece, Rome, Persia, India (Maurya and Gupta), China (Zhou, Qin, and Han), and the development of major world religions.

C identify major causes and describe the major effects of the following important turning points in world history from 600 to 1450: the spread of Christianity, the decline of Rome and the formation of medieval Europe; the development of Islamic caliphates and their impact on Asia, Africa, and Europe; the Mongol invasions and their impact on Europe, China, India, and Southwest Asia.

D identify major causes and describe the major effects of the following important turning points in world history from 1450 to 1750: the rise of the Ottoman Empire, the influence of the Ming dynasty on world trade, European exploration and the Columbian Exchange, European expansion, and the Renaissance and the Reformation.

E identify major causes and describe the major effects of the following important turning points in world history from 1750 to 1914: the Scientific Revolution, the Industrial Revolution and its impact on the development of modern economic systems, European imperialism, and the Enlightenment's impact on political revolutions.

F identify major causes and describe the major effects of the following important turning points in world history from 1914 to the present: the world wars and their impact on political, economic, and social systems; communist revolutions and their impact on the Cold War; independence movements; and globalization.

▲ *Oil wells - west Texas*

---

2 The student understands how early civilizations developed from 8000 BC to 500 BC. The student is expected to:

A summarize the impact of the development of farming (Neolithic Revolution) on the creation of river valley civilizations.

B identify the characteristics of civilization.

C explain how major river valley civilizations influenced the development of the classical civilizations.

3 The student understands the contributions and influence of classical civilizations from 500 BC to AD 600 on subsequent civilizations. The student is expected to:

A describe the major political, religious/philosophical, and cultural influences of Persia, India, China, Israel, Greece, and Rome, including the development of monotheism, Judaism, and Christianity.

B explain the impact of the fall of Rome on Western Europe.

C compare the factors that led to the collapse of Rome and Han China.

---

4 The student understands how, after the collapse of classical empires, new political, economic, and social systems evolved and expanded from 600 to 1450. The student is expected to:

A explain the development of Christianity as a unifying social and political factor in medieval Europe and the Byzantine Empire.

B explain the characteristics of Roman Catholicism and Eastern Orthodoxy.

C describe the major characteristics of and the factors contributing to the development of the political/social system of feudalism and the economic system of manorialism.

D explain the political, economic, and social impact of Islam on Europe, Asia, and Africa.

▼ *San Jose Mission in San Antonio, Texas*

PHOTO: McGraw-Hill Education

E describe the interactions among Muslim, Christian, and Jewish societies in Europe, Asia, and North Africa.

F describe the interactions between Muslim and Hindu societies in South Asia.

G explain how the Crusades, the Black Death, the Hundred Years' War, and the Great Schism contributed to the end of medieval Europe.

H summarize the major political, economic, and cultural developments in Tang and Song China and their impact on Eastern Asia.

I explain the development of the slave trade.

J analyze how the Silk Road and the African gold-salt trade facilitated the spread of ideas and trade.

K summarize the changes resulting from the Mongol invasions of Russia, China, and the Islamic world.

---

5 The student understands the causes, characteristics, and impact of the European Renaissance and the Reformation from 1450 to 1750. The student is expected to:

A the political, intellectual, artistic, economic, and religious impact of the Renaissance.

B explain the political, intellectual, artistic, economic, and religious impact of the Reformation.

6 **The student understands the characteristics and impact of the Maya, Inca, and Aztec civilizations. The student is expected to:**

A compare the major political, economic, social, and cultural developments of the Maya, Inca, and Aztec civilizations and explain how prior civilizations influenced their development.

B explain how the Inca and Aztec empires were impacted by European exploration/colonization.

---

7 **The student understands the causes and impact of European expansion from 1450 to 1750. The student is expected to:**

A analyze the causes of European expansion from 1450 to 1750.

B explain the impact of the Columbian Exchange on the Americas and Europe.

C explain the impact of the Atlantic slave trade on West Africa and the Americas.

▼ *Pedernales River in Texas*

PHOTO: Photo by NPS

D explain the impact of the Ottoman Empire on Eastern Europe and global trade.

E explain Ming China's impact on global trade.

F explain new economic factors and principles that contributed to the success of Europe's Commercial Revolution.

---

8 The student understands the causes and the global impact of the Industrial Revolution and European imperialism from 1750 to 1914. The student is expected to:

A explain how 17th and 18th century European scientific advancements led to the Industrial Revolution.

B explain how the Industrial Revolution led to political, economic, and social changes in Europe.

C identify the major political, economic, and social motivations that influenced European imperialism.

D explain the major characteristics and impact of European imperialism.

E explain the effects of free enterprise in the Industrial Revolution.

9 The student understands the causes and effects of major political revolutions between 1750 and 1914. The student is expected to:

A compare the causes, characteristics, and consequences of the American and French revolutions, emphasizing the role of the Enlightenment, the Glorious Revolution, and religion.

B explain the impact of Napoleon Bonaparte and the Napoleonic Wars on Europe and Latin America.

C trace the influence of the American and French revolutions on Latin America, including the role of Simón Bolivar.

D identify the influence of ideas such as separation of powers, checks and balances, liberty, equality, democracy, popular sovereignty, human rights, constitutionalism, and nationalism on political revolutions.

---

10 The student understands the causes and impact of World War I. The student is expected to:

A identify the importance of imperialism, nationalism, militarism, and the alliance system in causing World War I.

B identify major characteristics of World War I, including total war, trench warfare, modern military technology, and high casualty rates.

C explain the political impact of Woodrow Wilson's Fourteen Points and the political and economic impact of the Treaty of Versailles, including changes in boundaries and the mandate system.

D identify the causes of the February (March) and October revolutions of 1917 in Russia, their effects on the outcome of World War I, and the Bolshevik establishment of the Union of Soviet Socialist Republics.

▼ *Cattle grazing in rural Texas.*

11 **The student understands the causes and impact of the global economic depression immediately following World War I. The student is expected to:**

A summarize the international, political, and economic causes of the global depression.

B explain the responses of governments in the United States, Germany, and the Soviet Union to the global depression.

---

12 **The student understands the causes and impact of World War II. The student is expected to:**

A describe the emergence and characteristics of totalitarianism.

B explain the roles of various world leaders, including Benito Mussolini, Adolf Hitler, Hideki Tojo, Joseph Stalin, Franklin D. Roosevelt, and Winston Churchill, prior to and during World War II.

C explain the major causes and events of World War II, including the German invasions of Poland and the Soviet Union, the Holocaust, Japanese imperialism, the attack on Pearl Harbor, the Normandy landings, and the dropping of the atomic bombs.

13 The student understands the impact of major events associated with the Cold War and independence movements. The student is expected to:

- **A** summarize how the outcome of World War II contributed to the development of the Cold War.
- **B** summarize the factors that contributed to communism in China, including Mao Zedong's role in its rise, and how it differed from Soviet communism.
- **C** identify the following major events of the Cold War, including the Korean War, the Vietnam War, and the arms race.
- **D** explain the roles of modern world leaders, including Ronald Reagan, Mikhail Gorbachev, Lech Walesa, and Pope John Paul II, in the collapse of communism in Eastern Europe and the Soviet Union.
- **E** summarize the rise of independence movements in Africa, the Middle East, and South Asia and reasons for ongoing conflicts.
- **F** explain how Arab rejection of the State of Israel has led to ongoing conflict.

---

14 The student understands the development of radical Islamic fundamentalism and the subsequent use of terrorism by some of its adherents. The student is expected to:

- **A** summarize the development and impact of radical Islamic fundamentalism on events in the second half of the 20th century, including Palestinian terrorism and the growth of al Qaeda.
- **B** explain the U.S. response to terrorism from September 11, 2001, to the present.

PHOTO: Index Stock/Alamy

Geography

15 The student uses geographic skills and tools to collect, analyze, and interpret data. The student is expected to:

A create and interpret thematic maps, graphs, and charts to demonstrate the relationship between geography and the historical development of a region or nation.

B analyze and compare geographic distributions and patterns in world history shown on maps, graphs, charts, and models.

---

16 The student understands the impact of geographic factors on major historic events and processes. The student is expected to:

A locate places and regions of historical significance directly related to major eras and turning points in world history.

B analyze the influence of human and physical geographic factors on major events in world history, including the development of river valley civilizations, trade in the Indian Ocean, and the opening of the Panama and Suez canals.

C interpret maps, charts, and graphs to explain how geography has influenced people and events in the past.

▼ *Houston Apollo moon rocket, Johnson Space Center*

Economics

17 The student understands the impact of the Neolithic and Industrial revolutions and globalization on humanity. The student is expected to:

A identify important changes in human life caused by the Neolithic Revolution and the Industrial Revolution.

B summarize the role of economics in driving political changes as related to the Neolithic Revolution and the Industrial Revolution.

C summarize the economic and social impact of 20th century globalization.

---

18 The student understands the historical origins of contemporary economic systems and the benefits of free enterprise in world history. The student is expected to:

A identify the historical origins and characteristics of the free enterprise system, including the contributions of Adam Smith, especially the influence of his ideas found in The Wealth of Nations.

B identify the historical origins and characteristics of communism, including the influences of Karl Marx.

▼ *Riverwalk in San Antonio*

C identify the historical origins and characteristics of socialism.

D identify the historical origins and characteristics of fascism.

E explain why communist command economies collapsed in competition with free market economies at the end of the 20th century.

F formulate generalizations on how economic freedom improved the human condition, based on students' knowledge of the benefits of free enterprise in Europe's Commercial Revolution, the Industrial Revolution, and 20th-century free market economies, compared to communist command communities.

Government

19 The student understands the characteristics of major political systems throughout history. The student is expected to:

A identify the characteristics of monarchies and theocracies as forms of government in early civilizations.

B identify the characteristics of the following political systems: theocracy, absolute monarchy, democracy, republic, oligarchy, limited monarchy, and totalitarianism.

20 The student understands how contemporary political systems have developed from earlier systems of government. The student is expected to:

A explain the development of democratic-republican government from its beginnings in the Judeo-Christian legal tradition and classical Greece and Rome through the English Civil War and the Enlightenment.

B identify the impact of political and legal ideas contained in the following documents: Hammurabi's Code, the Jewish Ten Commandments, Justinian's Code of Laws, Magna Carta, the English Bill of Rights, the Declaration of Independence, the U.S. Constitution, and the Declaration of the Rights of Man and of the Citizen.

C explain the political philosophies of individuals such as John Locke, Thomas Hobbes, Voltaire, Charles de Montesquieu, Jean Jacques Rousseau, Thomas Aquinas, John Calvin, Thomas Jefferson, and William Blackstone.

D explain the significance of the League of Nations and the United Nations.

Citizenship

21 The student understands the significance of political choices and decisions made by individuals, groups, and nations throughout history. The student is expected to:

A describe how people have participated in supporting or changing their governments.

B describe the rights and responsibilities of citizens and noncitizens in civic participation throughout history.

C identify examples of key persons who were successful in shifting political thought, including William Wilberforce.

▼ *The Alamo in San Antonio, Texas*

22 The student understands the historical development of significant legal and political concepts related to the rights and responsibilities of citizenship. The student is expected to:

A summarize the development of the rule of law from ancient to modern times.

B identify the influence of ideas regarding the right to a "trial by a jury of your peers" and the concepts of "innocent until proven guilty" and "equality before the law" that originated from the Judeo-Christian legal tradition and in Greece and Rome.

C identify examples of politically motivated mass murders in Cambodia, China, Latin America, the Soviet Union, and Armenia.

D identify examples of genocide, including the Holocaust and genocide in the Balkans, Rwanda, and Darfur.

E identify examples of individuals who led resistance to political oppression such as Nelson Mandela, Mohandas Gandhi, Oscar Romero, Natan Sharansky, Las Madres de la Plaza de Mayo, and Chinese student protestors in Tiananmen Square.

F assess the degree to which American ideals have advanced human rights and democratic ideas throughout the world.

Culture

23 The student understands the history and relevance of major religious and philosophical traditions. The student is expected to:

A describe the historical origins, central ideas, and spread of major religious and philosophical traditions, including Buddhism, Christianity, Confucianism, Hinduism, Islam, Judaism, Sikhism, and the development of monotheism.

B identify examples of religious influence on various events referenced in the major eras of world history.

24 The student understands the roles of women, children, and families in different historical cultures. The student is expected to:

A describe the changing roles of women, children, and families during major eras of world history.

B describe the major influences of women such as Elizabeth I, Queen Victoria, Mother Teresa, Indira Gandhi, Margaret Thatcher, and Golda Meir during major eras of world history.

---

25 The student understands how the development of ideas has influenced institutions and societies. The student is expected to:

A summarize the fundamental ideas and institutions of Eastern civilizations that originated in China and India.

B summarize the fundamental ideas and institutions of Western civilizations that originated in Greece and Rome.

C explain the relationship among Christianity, individualism, and growing secularism that began with the Renaissance and how the relationship influenced subsequent political developments.

D explain how Islam influences law and government in the Muslim world.

---

26 The student understands the relationship between the arts and the times during which they were created. The student is expected to:

A identify significant examples of art and architecture that demonstrate an artistic ideal or VISUAL principle from selected cultures.

B analyze examples of how art, architecture, literature, music, and drama reflect the history of the cultures in which they are produced.

C identify examples of art, music, and literature that transcend the cultures in which they were created and convey universal themes.

Science, Technology, and Society

27 The student understands how major scientific and mathematical discoveries and technological innovations affected societies prior to 1750. The student is expected to:

A identify the origin and diffusion of major ideas in mathematics, science, and technology that occurred in river valley civilizations, classical Greece and Rome, classical India, and the Islamic caliphates between 700 and 1200 and in China from the Tang to Ming dynasties.

B summarize the major ideas in astronomy, mathematics, and architectural engineering that developed in the Maya, Inca, and Aztec civilizations.

C explain the impact of the printing press on the Renaissance and the Reformation in Europe.

D describe the origins of the Scientific Revolution in 16th century Europe and explain its impact on scientific thinking worldwide.

E identify the contributions of significant scientists such as Archimedes, Copernicus, Eratosthenes, Galileo, Pythagoras, Isaac Newton, and Robert Boyle.

---

28 The student understands how major scientific and mathematical discoveries and technological innovations have affected societies from 1750 to the present. The student is expected to:

A explain the role of textile manufacturing and steam technology in initiating the Industrial Revolution and the role of the factory system and transportation technology in advancing the Industrial Revolution.

B explain the roles of military technology, transportation technology, communication technology, and medical advancements in initiating and advancing 19th century imperialism.

C explain the effects of major new military technologies on World War I, World War II, and the Cold War.

D explain the role of telecommunication technology, computer technology, transportation technology, and medical advancements in developing the modern global economy and society.

E identify the contributions of significant scientists and inventors such as Marie Curie, Thomas Edison, Albert Einstein, Louis Pasteur, and James Watt.

▼ *The San Antonio Botanical Gardens*

Social Studies Skills

29 The student applies critical-thinking skills to organize and use information acquired from a variety of valid sources, including electronic technology. The student is expected to:

- **A** identify methods used by archaeologists, anthropologists, historians, and geographers to analyze evidence.
- **B** explain how historians, when examining sources, analyze frame of reference, historical context, and point of view to interpret historical events.
- **C** explain the differences between primary and secondary sources and examine those sources to analyze frame of reference, historical context, and point of view.
- **D** evaluate the validity of a source based on language, corroboration with other sources, and information about the author.
- **E** identify bias in written, oral, and visual material.
- **F** analyze information by sequencing, categorizing, identifying cause-and-effect relationships, comparing, contrasting, finding the main idea, summarizing, making generalizations and predictions, drawing inferences and conclusions, and developing connections between historical events over time.
- **G** construct a thesis on a social studies issue or event supported by evidence.
- **H** use appropriate reading and mathematical skills to interpret social studies information such as maps and graphs.

30 The student communicates in written, oral, and visual forms. The student is expected to:

A use social studies terminology correctly.

B use standard grammar, spelling, sentence structure, and punctuation.

C interpret and create written, oral, and visual presentations of social studies information.

D transfer information from one medium to another.

---

31 The student uses problem-solving and decision-making skills, working independently and with others, in a variety of settings. The student is expected to:

A use a problem-solving process to identify a problem, gather information, list and consider options, consider advantages and disadvantages, choose and implement a solution, and evaluate the effectiveness of the solution.

B use a decision-making process to identify a situation that requires a decision, gather information, identify options, predict consequences, and take action to implement a decision.

▼ *Aerial view of highway in Dallas, Texas*

SCAVENGER HUNT

NETWORKS contains a wealth of information. The trick is to know where to look to access all the information in the book. If you complete this scavenger hunt exercise with your teachers or parents, you will see how the textbook is organized and how to get the most out of your reading and study time. Let's get started!

1. How many chapters and how many lessons are in this book?
2. Where do you find the glossary and the index? What is the difference between them?
3. Where can you find primary sources in the textbook?
4. If you want to quickly find all the maps, charts, and graphs about World War II, where do you look?
5. How can you find information about Constantine the Great?
6. Where can you find a graphic organizer that lists the causes of the French Revolution discussed in Chapter 22?
7. Where and how do you find the content vocabulary for Chapter 20, Lesson 3?
8. What are the online resources listed for Chapter 14, Lesson 2?
9. You want to read about the age of exploration. How will you find it?
10. What time period does Chapter 3 cover? How do you know?

The Rise of Civilization

Prehistory – c. 2300 B.C.

networks

There's More Online! about the rise of civilization.

CHAPTER 1

ESSENTIAL QUESTIONS
- *What do archaeology and anthropology teach us about prehistoric humans?*
- *What is a civilization, and how does one form?*

The Story Matters...

By 3000 B.C., the Sumerians had built cities and developed one of the world's first civilizations in an area known as Mesopotamia. Religion, one of the key elements of a civilization, was very important to the Sumerians. They believed that the gods ruled their cities and all aspects of their lives. Each Sumerian city had a great temple, known as a ziggurat, dedicated to the local god. There they left offerings, including carved figurines and statues such as this one. The figures were usually depicted in a pose of worship, with folded hands and wide eyes, symbolizing that they are eternally offering prayers to the gods.

◀ This Sumerian statue of a worshiping woman was created around 2450 b.c. It was carved from a type of mineral called alabaster and is from the city of Ur, one of the oldest known cities in Mesopotamia.

PHOTO: Scala/Art Resource, NY

CHAPTER 1

Place and Time: The World: PREHISTORY–c. 2300 B.C

The earliest hominids, humanlike creatures that walked upright, appeared in Africa at least 4 million years ago. Homo sapiens *developed there around 200,000 years ago, later migrating to Europe and Asia. Throughout the Paleolithic Age (from approximately 2,500,000 B.C. to 10,000 B.C.), early humans were primarily nomadic hunters using stone tools. Following the end of the last major Ice Age, human beings began to live in permanent settlements, to practice systematic agriculture, and to domesticate animals, paving the way for the first civilizations. Mesopotamia, a fertile land between the Tigris and Euphrates Rivers in what is today southern Iraq, is one of the areas where civilization first developed.*

Step Into the Place

Read the quotes and look at the information presented on the map.

DBQ **Analyzing Historical Documents** What are some of the early human behaviors that mark important stages in the development toward civilization?

PRIMARY SOURCE

"[Neanderthals] buried their dead—the first [early] humans known to have done so, and surely a significant event, though it tells us nothing for certain about the meaning that death may have had in Neanderthal culture, or the role of remembrance or respect. Some objects found associated with burials have been interpreted as grave goods, but no pattern of deliberate placing can be shown as yet, or any other clue to the possibility of ceremonies. Some skeletons show the marks of obvious injuries or illnesses suffered sometime before death, evidence that there must have been social care to support ailing or disabled individuals."

—Peter Andrews and Christopher Stringer, from *The Book of Life*, 2001

PRIMARY SOURCE

"Art did not have a linear evolution from clumsy and crude beginnings. . . . In the course of the Upper Paleolithic [period of cave art], there were doubtless numerous beginnings, pinnacles, and declines. But from the start there were very great artists and accomplished productions in certain regions, without the situation necessarily being the same everywhere at the same time. Our view of the beginnings of artistic creation and even of the psyche of these first modern humans has been changed by this [discovery of the Chauvet Cave]."

—Jean Clottes, from *The Dawn of Art: The Chauvet Cave*, 1996

Step Into the Time

Synthesizing Information
Choose an invention or development from the time line and explain its role in the human experience.

THE WORLD — 3,500,000 B.C. — 2,000,000 B.C. — 100,000 B.C.

- **before 3,500,000 B.C.** *Australopithecines* walk upright
- **c. 2,500,000 B.C.** Paleolithic Age begins
- **c. 2,500,000 B.C.** *Homo habilis* appears
- **c. 1,800,000 B.C.** Earliest stone tool industry
- **c. 1,700,000 B.C.** *Homo erectus* disperses
- **c. 500,000 B.C.** Paleolithic peoples make use of fire
- **after 200,000 B.C.** Neanderthals spread across Europe
- **c. 200,000 B.C.** *Homo sapiens sapiens* develops
- **c. 100,000 B.C.** Last major Ice Age begins

networks *There's More Online!*

MAP Explore the interactive version of this map on Networks.

TIME LINE Explore the interactive version of the time line on Networks.

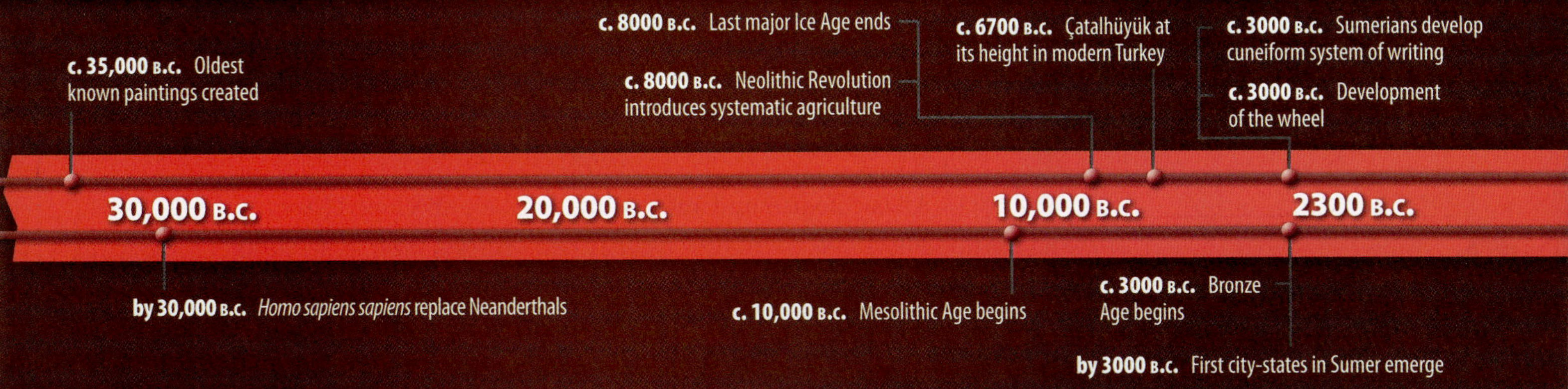

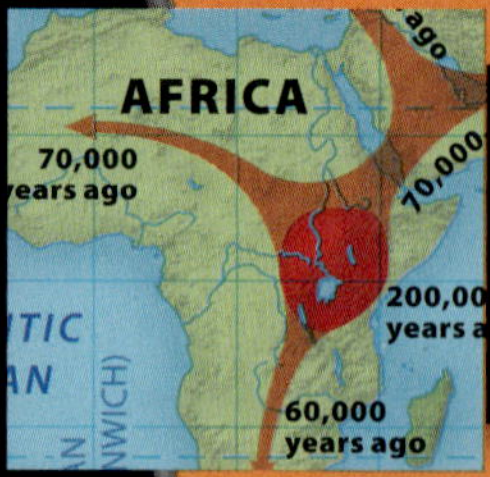

networks

There's More Online!

- BIOGRAPHY Louis and Mary Leakey
- BIOGRAPHY Lucy the Australopithecus
- GRAPHIC ORGANIZER Characteristics of the Paleolithic Age
- IMAGE Cave Painting at Lascaux
- INTERACTIVE SELF-CHECK QUIZ
- MAP Migration of Early Humans
- SLIDE SHOW Art and Artifacts of Early Humans
- VIDEO Early Humans

LESSON 1
Early Humans

ESSENTIAL QUESTION
What do archaeology and anthropology teach us about prehistoric humans?

IT MATTERS BECAUSE

Through studying and dating artifacts and fossils, anthropologists and archaeologists have revealed prehistory. This incomplete record shows how the earliest humans developed and how they adapted to make tools, use fire, and survive Ice Age conditions. Early humans also produced art that relates the human experience.

Reading HELPDESK

Academic Vocabulary
- **theory**
- **survive**

Content Vocabulary
- **archaeology**
- **anthropology**
- **hominid**
- ***Homo sapiens sapiens***
- **"out-of-Africa" theory**

TAKING NOTES:
Key Ideas and Details

Classifying Use a graphic organizer like the one below to list key facts about early humans.

Group	Qualities/ Advances	Time Period
Earliest Hominids		
Homo sapiens		
Homo sapiens sapiens		

TEKS Texas Essential Knowledge and Skills
29A identify methods used by archaeologists, anthropologists, historians, and geographers to analyze evidence

Prehistory

GUIDING QUESTION *How do we define and learn information about prehistory?*

Historians rely mostly on documents, or written records, to create their pictures of the past. However, no written records exist for the prehistory of humankind. In fact, *prehistory* means "the time before writing was developed." The story of prehistoric humans depends on archaeological and, more recently, biological evidence. Archaeologists and anthropologists use this information to create **theories** about our early past.

Archaeology and Anthropology

Archaeology is the study of past societies through analysis of what people left behind. Archaeologists dig up and examine artifacts—objects made by humans. Artifacts may be tools, weapons, art, and even buildings made by early humans.

Anthropology is the study of human life and culture. Culture includes what people wear, how they organize their society, and what they value. Anthropologists use artifacts and human fossils to create a picture of people's everyday lives. Fossils are rocklike remains of biological organisms such as a leaf imprint or a skeleton.

Archaeologists and anthropologists have developed scientific methods to carry out their work. They excavate sites, or carefully dig up land, at places around the globe to uncover fossil remains of early humans, ancient cities, burial grounds, and other objects. The examination and analysis of these remains give archaeologists a

PHOTO: Sisse Brimberg/National Geographic/Getty Images, Topham/The Image Works, ©Kenneth Garrett/National Geographic Stock, © Photolibrary RF Collection / SuperStock.

better understanding of ancient societies. By examining artifacts such as pottery, tools, and weapons, for example, these scientists learn about the social and military structures of a society. By analyzing bones, skins, and plant seeds, they are able to piece together the diets and activities of early people. One of the most difficult jobs is dating these finds.

Dating Artifacts and Fossils

Dating human fossils and artifacts helps scientists understand when and where the first humans lived. One method used to determine age is radiocarbon dating. All living things absorb a small amount of radioactive carbon, or C-14, from the atmosphere. After a living thing dies, it slowly loses C-14. By measuring the amount left in an object, a scientist can figure its age. This method is accurate for objects no more than about 50,000 years old. For objects dating back to 200,000 years ago, scientists can make relatively precise measurements using thermoluminescence. This measures the light given off by electrons trapped in the soil surrounding fossils and artifacts.

Microscopic and biological analyses of organic remains—such as blood, hairs, and plant tissues left on tools and weapons—give scientists still more information. Such analyses have shown that blood molecules may survive millions of years. This recent scientific discovery is especially useful in telling us more about humans, their use of tools, and the animals they killed. Ancient deoxyribonucleic acid (DNA) is providing new information on human evolution. The analysis of plant remains on stone tools yields evidence of the history of farming. All of these techniques give us insight into the lives of early peoples.

✓ READING PROGRESS CHECK

Explaining What have artifacts and fossils revealed about prehistory?

Connections to TODAY

Chocolate at Chaco Canyon

Located in what is now New Mexico, Chaco Canyon was the center of an ancestral Puebloan culture that flourished between A.D. 850 and 1250. In the 1970s, using traditional digging methods, archaeologists surveyed nearly 1,800 sites and collected more than 100,000 artifacts at Chaco Canyon. Recently, new scientific testing techniques have allowed archaeologists to learn more about how these artifacts were used. In 2008, using chemical analysis, scientists discovered cacao, or chocolate, residue in broken pieces of pottery. This is the earliest evidence of chocolate beverages in the American Southwest.

GEOGRAPHY CONNECTION

This map shows the "out-of-Africa" theory.

1. **THE WORLD IN SPATIAL TERMS** *From where did early humans migrate?*
2. **PLACES AND REGIONS** *What continent did early humans reach last? Why?*

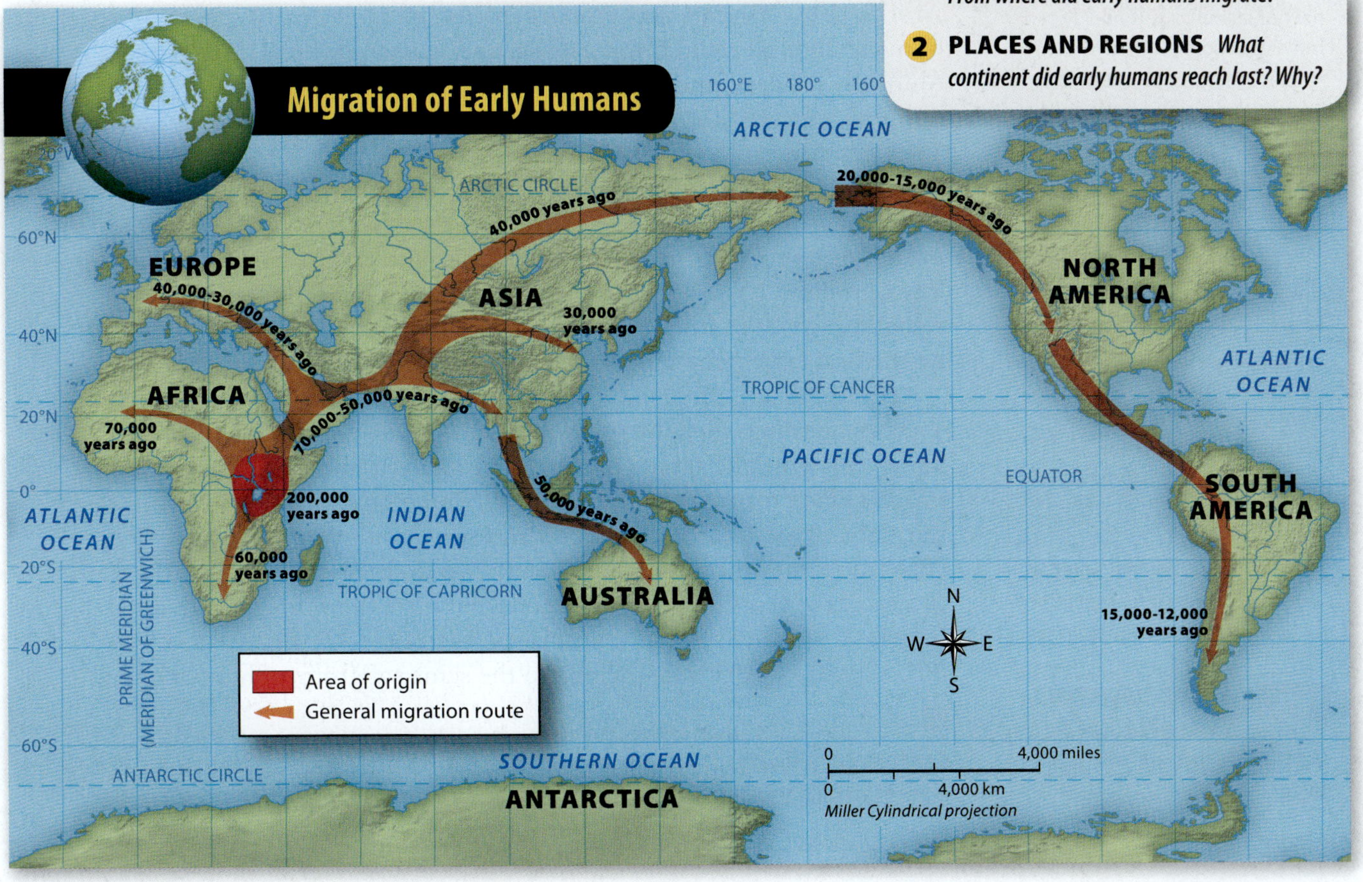

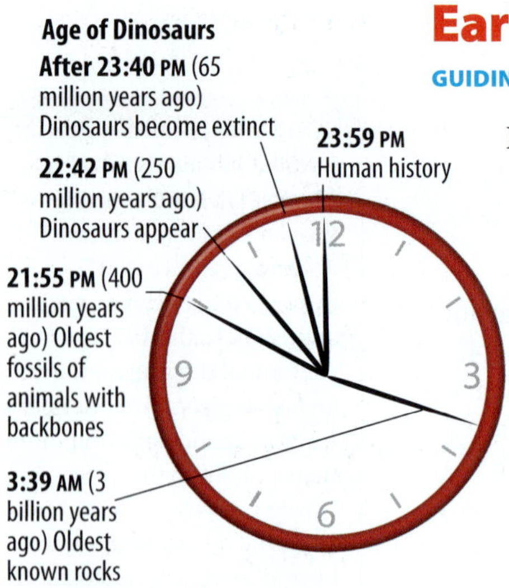

▲ If the approximately 4.6 billion years of Earth's history were squeezed into a single 24-hour day, each hour would last more than 190 million years. Each minute would last more than 3 million years; each second more than 50,000 years.

Analyzing PRIMARY SOURCES

Discovery at Olduvai Gorge

"[Mary] noticed a scrap of bone that . . . 'seemed to be part of a skull. . . . It had a hominid look. . . .' Mary then saw two large teeth set in the curve of a jaw, and her doubts vanished. 'It was a hominid skull . . . and there was a lot of it.' She . . . drove madly back to camp.

'I've got him! I've got him! I've got him!' she cried to Louis. . . . But Louis was groggy with the flu and could only manage a confused 'Got what? Are you hurt?' 'Him, the man! *Our* man,' she replied. 'The one we've been looking for.'"

—Richard Leakey, from *Ancestral Passions: The Leakey Family and the Quest for Humankind's Beginnings*

DBQ ***MAKING CONNECTIONS*** What type of bone did Mary Leakey find, and why was it so significant?

Early Development

GUIDING QUESTION *How did hominids develop?*

In recent decades, modern science has produced a clearer picture of how early humans developed. Pieces of the puzzle are still missing, however. When a new skull or skeleton is unearthed, scientists may find that they have to revise their ideas about the lives of prehistoric humans.

Hominids to *Homo Sapiens*

What is a **hominid**? A hominid is a humanlike creature that walked upright. The earliest hominids lived in Africa 4 million years ago. Called *Australopithecus* (aw • stray • loh • PIH • thuh • kuhs), or "southern ape," by its discoverer Donald Johanson, this hominid flourished in eastern and southern Africa.

Louis and Mary Leakey spent most of their lives searching for clues about early human life. Mary Leakey made a dramatic discovery of a skeleton at Olduvai Gorge in East Africa. Her discovery of a hominid in 1959 was the oldest at that time—about 1.8 million years old.

From 2.5 to 1.6 million years ago, a more advanced hominid developed with a somewhat larger brain. This hominid was named *Homo habilis*, meaning "handy human." *Homo habilis* may have used stone tools. Another hominid, *Homo erectus*, "upright human," emerged around 1.5 million years ago. Although other hominids walked on two legs, *Homo erectus* had arms and legs in modern human proportion. Remains in Asia show that *Homo erectus* was probably the first hominid to leave Africa.

Homo Sapiens Sapiens

Around 250,000 years ago, *Homo sapiens* emerged. *Homo sapiens*, "wise human," showed rapid brain growth and mastered fire. The first anatomically modern humans, ***Homo sapiens sapiens***, meaning "wise, wise human," appeared in Africa between 200,000 and 150,000 years ago. They probably spread out of Africa to other parts of the world about 100,000 years ago, replacing populations of earlier hominids in Europe and Asia. This is referred to as the **"out-of-Africa" theory**. One of the groups of hominids they encountered was known as the Neanderthals. They probably lived between 200,000 B.C. and 30,000 B.C. Neanderthal remains have been found in Europe and Turkey. Neanderthals seem to be the first early people to bury their dead.

By 30,000 B.C., *Homo sapiens sapiens* had replaced the Neanderthals. The Neanderthals died out, possibly as a result of conflicts with *Homo sapiens sapiens*. The spread of these first modern humans was a slow process. Over many thousands of years, *Homo sapiens sapiens* spread over the globe as they searched for food and new hunting grounds. In a whole generation, they may have moved only two to three miles. Over tens of thousands of years, this was enough to populate the world. Today, all humans—whether they are Europeans, Australian Aborigines (a • buh • RIHJ • nees), or Africans—belong to the same subgroup of human beings.

✓ READING PROGRESS CHECK

Contrasting How do the facts we know about *Homo sapiens sapiens* and Neanderthals tell different stories about how hominids developed?

The Paleolithic Age

GUIDING QUESTION *How did the first humans adapt to survive?*

One of the distinguishing features of the human species is the ability to make tools. The term *Paleolithic Age* is used to designate the early period of human history (approximately 2,500,000 B.C. to 10,000 B.C.) in which humans used simple stone tools. *Paleolithic* comes from Greek words meaning "old stone," and the Paleolithic Age is sometimes called the Old Stone Age.

For hundreds of thousands of years, humans relied on hunting and gathering for their daily food. Paleolithic peoples had a close relationship with their environment. They came to know what animals to hunt and what plants to eat. They gathered wild nuts, berries, fruits, wild grains, and green plants. Around the world, they hunted and ate various animals, including buffalo, horses, bison, and reindeer. In coastal areas, fish and shellfish provided a rich source of food.

The Paleolithic Way of Life

Early humans were able to sustain themselves through the use of stone tools. To make such tools, early people used very hard stones such as flint. They used one stone to chip away parts of another, creating an edge. Hand axes of various kinds—pointed tools with one or more cutting edges—were the most common. Hand axes eventually were set in wooden handles, making them easier to use. By attaching wooden poles to spear points and hardening the tips in fire, humans created spears to kill large animals. Over the years, Paleolithic hunters developed better tools. The invention of the bow and arrow made hunting much easier. Harpoons and fishhooks made of bone increased the catch of fish.

Because Paleolithic people were hunters and gatherers, they had to follow animal migrations and vegetation cycles. Paleolithic humans were nomads—people who move from place to place to **survive**. Archaeologists and anthropologists think these nomads probably lived in small groups of 20 or 30. Hunting depended on careful observation of animal behavior patterns and demanded group cooperation for success.

The main job of Paleolithic peoples was finding enough to eat. Both men and women were responsible for finding the food needed for survival. Paleolithic parents passed on their practices, skills, and tools to their children to ensure the survival of later generations. Because women bore and raised children, they probably stayed closer to camp. They played an important role in acquiring food by gathering berries, nuts, roots, and grains. Women taught the children which foods were edible. They trapped small animals and kept the camp safe. In the constant search for food, men had to travel far from camp to hunt herds of large animals. Because both men and women were responsible for finding and acquiring the food needed to sustain life, many scientists believe there was equality between them. It is likely that both men and women made decisions that affected the activities of the Paleolithic group.

Use of Fire

Another important result of the migration of early hominids was the use of fire. As early hominids moved from the tropics into colder regions, they needed to adjust to new climate conditions. Archaeologists have discovered the piled remains of ashes in caves that prove that Paleolithic people used fire systematically as long as 500,000 years ago. At a site in northern China,

theory hypothesis or unproved assumption

archaeology the study of past societies through an analysis of the items people left behind

anthropology the study of human life and culture based on artifacts and human fossils

hominid humans and other humanlike creatures that walk upright

Homo sapiens sapiens "wise, wise humans," a species that appeared in Africa between 150,000 and 200,000 years ago; they were the first anatomically modern humans

"out-of-Africa" theory also called the replacement theory; this theory refers to when *Homo sapiens sapiens* began spreading out of Africa to other parts of the world about 100,000 years ago and replacing populations of earlier hominids in Europe and Asia

survive to remain alive or in existence

▲ Around 35,000 years ago, Ice Age artists began to paint images in caves. The painting shown here was found in Lascaux Cave in southern France.

▶ **CRITICAL THINKING**

Analyzing Visuals What does this cave painting depict?

remnants of hearths, ashes, charcoal, and charred bones have been dated to 400,000 years ago.

Fire not only gave warmth but kept wild animals away from the campsite. Armed with spears, hunters used fire to flush out wild pigs for the kill. People gathered around the fire to trade stories and to cook. Cooked food tasted better, lasted longer, and was easier to chew and digest, so it seems likely that nutrition improved.

The Ice Ages

Having fire to create a source of heat was especially important when Ice Age conditions descended on the Paleolithic world. The most recent Ice Age began about 100,000 B.C. and ended about 8000 B.C. During this time, sheets of thick ice covered large parts of Europe, Asia, and North America. As sea levels went down, people migrated across land bridges that had not existed before.

Ice Age conditions posed a serious threat to human life, so the ability to adapt was crucial to human survival. The use of fire, for example, reminds us that early humans sometimes adapted not by changing themselves to better fit their environment but by changing the environment.

Paleolithic Art

Paleolithic peoples did more than just survive. The cave paintings of large animals found at Lascaux (la • SKOH) in southern France and Altamira in northern Spain bear witness to the cultural activity of Paleolithic peoples. The Chauvet cave discovered in southern France in 1994 contained more than 300 paintings of lions, oxen, owls, panthers, and other animals. Most of these are animals that Paleolithic peoples did not hunt, which indicates that they were painted for religious or decorative purposes.

Using stone lamps filled with animal fat to light the caves, early artists painted with fingers and twigs and even blew paint through hollow reeds. They mixed mineral ores with animal fat to make red, yellow, and black paint. A variety of realistically painted animals covers the caves. Few humans appear in these paintings, and when they do appear, they are drawn as sticklike figures. This has led some scholars to think the work was done for a magical or religious ritual to bring success in hunting.

✓ **READING PROGRESS CHECK**

Describing Describe how the Paleolithic way of life revolved around acquiring food.

LESSON 1 REVIEW TEKS

Reviewing Vocabulary

1. ***Applying*** Apply the "out-of-Africa" theory to explain the connection between early hominids such as Neanderthals and *Homo sapiens sapiens.*

Using Your Notes

2. ***Gathering Information*** Use your notes and other ideas from this lesson to describe early humans and their lives during the Paleolithic Age.

Answering the Guiding Questions

3. ***Summarizing*** How do we define and learn about prehistory?
4. ***Sequencing*** How did hominids develop?
5. ***Identifying Cause and Effect*** How did the first humans adapt to survive?

Writing Activity

6. **INFORMATIVE/EXPLANATORY** In one or more paragraphs, describe the work of archaeologists. Use precise nouns to name the subject of their work, where they perform their work, and the tools they use. Incorporate precise adjectives and adverbs to describe the processes or objects involved.

SKILLBUILDER

TEKS 29A

Analyzing Historical Evidence

Why Learn This Skill?

As you learn about history from this textbook and other sources, it is important to understand where this information comes from and how we have come to understand events and ideas that happened long ago. It is the work that archaeologists, anthropologists, and historians do in the field analyzing evidence that relates directly to what you learn in the classroom.

Learning the Skill

Historians, archaeologists, and anthropologists collect evidence in a variety of ways in order to piece together the story of the past. Archaeologists look at past societies by analyzing what people have left behind.

Ingram Publishing/age Fotostock

Anthropologists look at human life and culture, whether in the past or present day. And historians work with both of these disciplines to help create a larger picture of the political, economic, and cultural aspects of a particular place and time. When gathering evidence about ancient societies, writings can be difficult to find, or nonexistent, and so we have to piece together how ancient peoples lived, what they valued, and how they related to each other on the basis of artifacts left behind. Technology is also used to understand an artifact's date and function. When analyzing artifacts, it is helpful to use the basic questions of who, what, when, where, how, and why:

- Who created this artifact?
- What was it used for or what does it represent?
- When was it made?
- Where did this artifiact originate?
- How was it made or used?
- Why was it created or what was its purpose?

Sometimes, not all of these questions can be answered, and some may overlap, but any part that can provide answers will establish new information about a period in time.

Practicing the Skill

Read the following excerpt and fill in the table, below:

The Chauvet cave discovered in southern France in 1994 contained more than 300 paintings of lions, oxen, owls, panthers, and other animals. Most of these are animals that Paleolithic peoples did not hunt, which indicates that they were painted for religious or decorative purposes.

Using stone lamps filled with animal fat to light the caves, early artists painted with fingers and twigs and even blew paint through hollow reeds. They mixed mineral ores with animal fat to make red, yellow, and black paint. A variety of realistically painted animals covers the caves. Few humans appear in these paintings, and when they do appear, they are drawn as sticklike figures.

Who	
What	
When	
Where	
How/Why	

Applying the Skill

Locate an artifact either in this textbook or on the Internet on an archaeology site. As a class, go through the points of the table to better understand how that artifact fits into its particular time period. Also identify the methods used by archaeologists, anthropologists, or historians to analyze evidence.

PRIMARY SOURCES

The rise of civilization came hand in hand with the rise of religion. In the ancient period people began to look to religion to answer questions about where they came from and how to interpret the world around them. Read the following excerpts to explore what the ancient Babylonians, Israelites, and Egyptians believed about the creation of humanity.

Creation Accounts

PRIMARY SOURCE

The Babylonian story of the creation of humans is part of an epic poem titled *Enûma elish.*

As **Marduk** hears the words of the gods,
His heart prompts him to create ingenious things.
He conveys his idea to **Ea**,
Imparting the plan which he had conceived in his heart:
"Blood will I form and cause bone to be;
Then will I set up **lullû**,
'Man' shall be his name!
Yes, I will create lullû: Man!
Upon him shall the services of the gods be
imposed that they may be at rest."

PRIMARY SOURCE

The book of *Genesis* contains an Israelite account of the creation of humans.

Then God said, "Let us make man in our image,
in our likeness, and let them rule over the fish
of the sea and the birds of the air, over the live-
stock, over all the earth, and over all the
creatures that move along the ground."
So God created man in his own image, in the
image of God he created him; male and female
he created them...

Finally, the ancient Egyptians had several creation myths. In one account, Re, the ram-headed sun god, emerged from an egg that appeared on the surface of the ocean. Re later produced gods of air, earth, and heaven. Afterward, Re made humans and all other beings and objects on Earth. Re crosses through the underworld in his boat, carrying the spirits of Egyptians who have died. When Re reappears above the horizon at the beginning of each new day, the souls of the dead are reborn into new lives with him.

VOCABULARY

Marduk
ruler of the gods in Babylonian mythology

Ea
god of wisdom and magic; father of Marduk

lullû
humans

DBQ Analyzing Historical Documents

1. **Explaining** What is Marduk's plan based on the Babylonian gods' words?
2. **Identifying** "Genesis" means the beginning of something: In what way does the Israelite source describe a beginning?
3. **Analyzing** How does the Egyptian god Re represent the sun?
4. **Drawing Conclusions** What is the place of humans in the world in each of the three primary sources?

networks

There's More Online!

- CHART/GRAPH Culture and Civilization
- CHART/GRAPH Number of Farms in the U.S., 1940–2004
- IMAGE Bronze Age Tool
- IMAGE Çatalhüyük
- INTERACTIVE SELF-CHECK QUIZ
- MAP Spread of Systematic Agriculture
- SECONDARY SOURCE The Neolithic Revolution
- VIDEO The Neolithic Revolution

LESSON 2
The Neolithic Revolution

ESSENTIAL QUESTIONS

- *What do archaeology and anthropology teach us about prehistoric humans?*
- *What is a civilization, and how does one form?*

Reading HELPDESK

Academic Vocabulary

- **revolution**
- **role**

Content Vocabulary

- **systematic agriculture**
- **artisans**
- **culture**
- **civilization**
- **priests**

TAKING NOTES:

Key Ideas and Details

Identifying Use a graphic organizer like the one below to list major developments of the Neolithic Revolution.

Neolithic Revolution: Major Developments
1.
2.
3.
4.
5.

TEKS Texas Essential Knowledge and Skills

1A identify major causes and describe the major effects of the following events from 8000 BC to 500 BC: the development of agriculture and the development of the river valley civilizations

continued on the next page

It Matters Because

The development of systematic agriculture was a dramatic change, or revolution, during the Neolithic Age. The transition of humans from nomadic hunters to farmers and herders is part of the Neolithic Revolution. This revolution led to the development of traditional economies based on agriculture with limited trade.

The Development of Agriculture

GUIDING QUESTION *How did developments in the Neolithic period impact early human history?*

The end of the last Ice Age, around 8000 B.C., was followed by what is called the Neolithic Revolution—that is, the **revolution** that occurred in the Neolithic Age, the period of human history from around 8000 B.C. to 4000 B.C. The word *Neolithic* comes from Greek words meaning "new stone."

The name New Stone Age, however, is somewhat misleading. The real change in the Neolithic Revolution was the shift from the hunting of animals and the gathering of food to the development of agriculture. With the development of agriculture, animals were domesticated rather than hunted. In addition, rather than gathering food, people now grew and harvested food on a regular basis. Today we call this **systematic agriculture**.

Early humans had to move from place to place, following herds and finding plants. During the Neolithic Age, humans began planting crops, providing a regular food source. Domestication of animals, adapting them for human use, added a reliable source of meat, milk, and wool. Animals could also be used to do work. Growing crops and taming food-producing animals caused an agricultural revolution. Because there was enough food, humans had more control over their lives. Sufficient food also meant they could give up their nomadic ways of life and begin to live in settled communities. Some historians believe this revolution was the single most important development in human history.

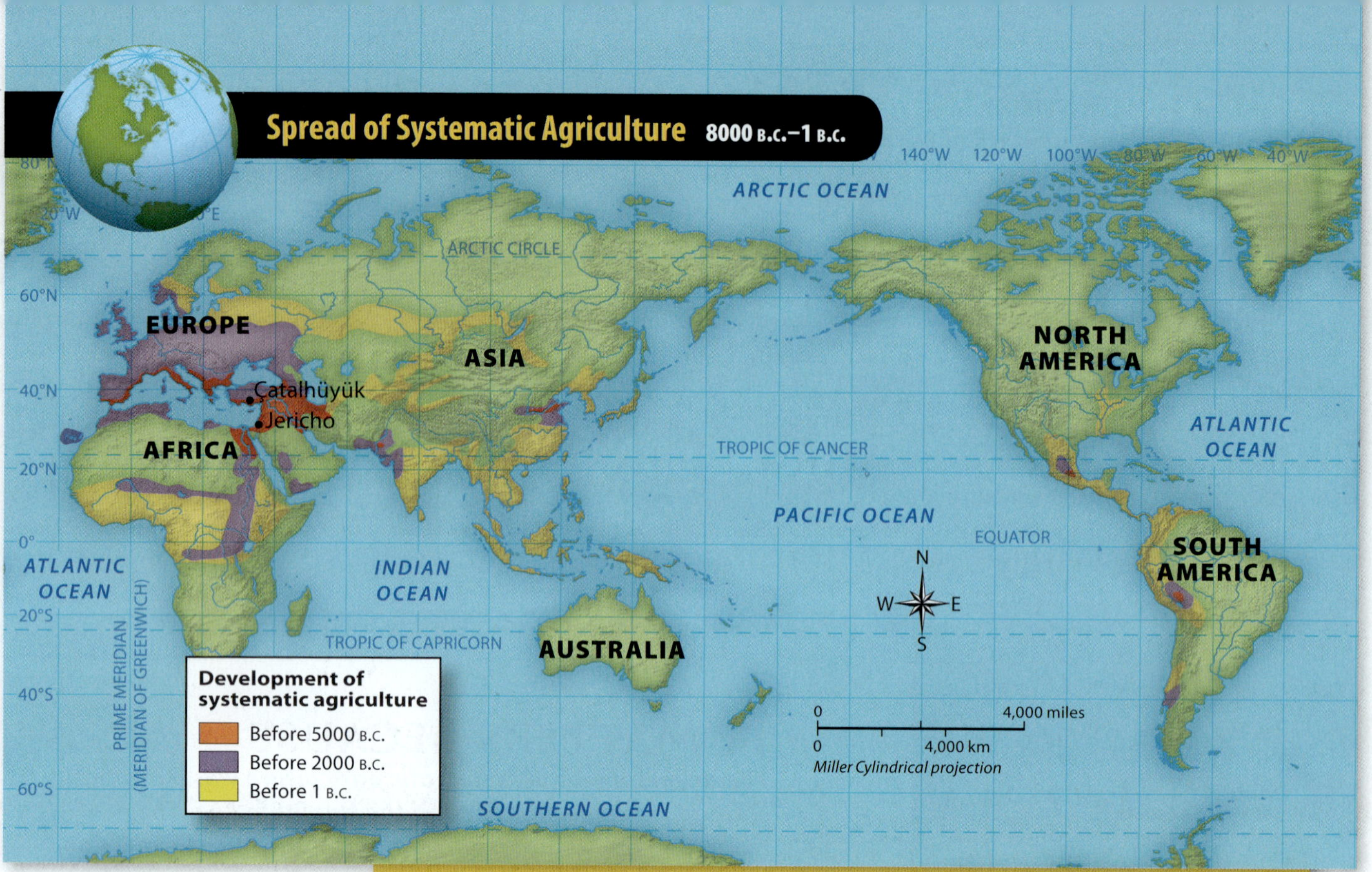

GEOGRAPHY CONNECTION

The Neolithic Revolution was the beginning of systematic agriculture.

1. **ENVIRONMENT AND SOCIETY** *What patterns do you see with the spread of systematic agriculture?*
2. **THE WORLD IN SPATIAL TERMS** *Where were the earliest farming villages located?*

revolution a sudden, complete change

systematic agriculture the keeping of animals and the growing of food on a regular basis

(continued from p. 11)

TEKS **Texas Essential Knowledge and Skills**

2A summarize the impact of the development of farming (Neolithic Revolution) on the creation of river valley civilizations

2B identify the characteristics of civilization

16B analyze the influence of human and physical geographic factors on major events in world history, including the development of river valley civilizations, trade in the Indian Ocean, and the opening of the Panama and Suez canals

17A identify important changes in human life caused by the Neolithic Revolution and the Industrial Revolution

17B summarize the role of economics in driving political changes as related to the Neolithic Revolution and the Industrial Revolution

19A identify the characteristics of monarchies and theocracies as forms of government in early civilizations

This shift to food producing from hunting and gathering was not as sudden as was once believed. During the Mesolithic Age ("Middle Stone Age," about 10,000 B.C. to 7000 B.C.), there was a gradual shift from the old food-gathering and hunting economy to a food-producing one. There was also a gradual taming of animals. Moreover, throughout the Neolithic period, hunting and gathering remained a way of life for many people.

Between 8000 B.C. and 5000 B.C., systematic agriculture developed in various parts of the world. In Southwest Asia, people began growing wheat and barley and domesticating pigs, cows, goats, and sheep by 8000 B.C. From there, farming spread into Southeastern Europe. By 4000 B.C., farming was well established in central Europe and the coastal regions of the Mediterranean Sea.

By 6000 B.C., the cultivation of wheat and barley had spread into the Nile Valley of Egypt. These crops soon spread up the Nile to other areas of Africa—Sudan and Ethiopia. In central Africa, a separate farming system emerged. There, people grew root crops called tubers, such as yams, and tree crops, such as bananas. Wheat and barley farming also moved eastward into India between 7000 B.C. and 5000 B.C.

By 5000 B.C., farmers in Southeast Asia were growing rice. From there, rice farming spread into southern China. By 6000 B.C., farming millet and domesticating dogs and pigs seem to have been established in northern China. In the Western Hemisphere, Mesoamericans—inhabitants of present-day Mexico and Central America—grew beans, squash, and maize. They also domesticated dogs and fowl in this period between 7000 B.C. and 5000 B.C.

▲ Aerial view of the archaeological site at Çatalhüyük in modern-day Turkey

Neolithic Farming Villages

Growing crops on a regular basis gave rise to more permanent settlements called Neolithic farming villages. These villages appeared in Europe, India, Egypt, China, and Mesoamerica. The oldest and biggest villages, however, were located in Southwest Asia. Jericho, near the Dead Sea, was in existence by 8000 B.C. Çatalhüyük (chah • tahl • hoo • YOOK) in modern Turkey was an even larger community, covering 32 acres (12.9 ha). Between 6700 B.C. and 5700 B.C., the city probably had 6,000 inhabitants. Their simple mud brick houses were built so close together that there were few streets. People walked on the roofs and entered their homes through holes in the rooftops.

Archaeologists have found a dozen products that were grown outside the city walls, including fruits, nuts, and wheat. Domesticated animals provided meat, milk, and hides. Scenes on the walls of the city's ruins show that the people also hunted. As a result of the steady food supply, Çatalhüyük had a food surplus. Specialization of labor began when not all villagers needed to farm. Some became **artisans**, or skilled workers, making goods to trade with neighboring people. These goods were bartered, or exchanged, not sold. This was the beginning of a traditional economy based on agriculture and some trade.

artisan a skilled worker who makes products such as weapons and jewelry

role a socially expected behavior pattern

Besides homes, Çatalhüyük had special buildings that were shrines containing figures of gods and goddesses. Statues of women giving birth or nursing a child have also been found there. Both the shrines and the statues point to the growing **role** of religion in the lives of Neolithic peoples.

Effects of the Neolithic Revolution

The Neolithic agricultural revolution caused dramatic changes that affected how people would live to the present day. When people began settling in villages or towns, they saw the need to build walls for protection and storehouses for goods. Storing surplus products encouraged trade. Trading encouraged more people to learn crafts. This led to the division of labor.

As artisans became more skilled, they made more refined tools. Flint blades were used to make sickles and hoes for farming. Eventually, many of the food plants still in use today began to be cultivated. Some plants, such as flax and cotton, were used to make yarn and cloth.

The development of agriculture also had a major effect on how men and women related to one another. Men became more active in farming and herding animals, jobs that took them away from the settlement. Instead of the whole family moving as in earlier times, women remained behind. They cared for children, wove cloth for clothes, and did other tasks that kept them in one place. As men took on more and more responsibility for obtaining food and protecting the settlement, they began to play a more dominant role in society.

The End of the Neolithic Age

Between 4000 B.C. and 3000 B.C., new developments began to affect some Neolithic towns. Even before 4000 B.C., craftspeople discovered that by heating metal-bearing rocks they could turn the metal into liquid. The liquid metal could be poured into molds, or casts, to make tools and weapons. The use of metals marked a new level of control over the environment.

Thinking Like a HISTORIAN

Interpreting Ancient Records

In interpreting a creation myth of the ancient Mesopotamians, historian Georges Roux observes, "To their deeply religious minds it offered a non-rational but nevertheless acceptable 'explanation' of the universe." What biases does Roux see expressed in this myth? What biases might Roux himself exhibit? In analyzing and evaluating the records of ancient cultures, historians must attempt to understand the biases they reflect as well as their own biases. Use the Internet or your school library to find an ancient text, such as the Code of Hammurabi or *The Epic of Gilgamesh,* and analyze and evaluate the cultural biases expressed in it.

▲ This socketed bronze hand axe was created around 1000 B.C.

▶ **CRITICAL THINKING**

Classifying Near the end of what age was this artifact created?

Copper was the first metal to be used in making tools. After 4000 B.C., artisans in western Asia discovered that combining copper and tin created bronze—a metal harder and more durable than copper.

The widespread use of bronze led to the Bronze Age from around 3000 B.C. to 1200 B.C. After about 1000 B.C., the use of iron tools and weapons became common in an era known as the Iron Age.

The Neolithic Age set the stage for major changes to come. As people mastered farming, some villages developed more complex and wealthier societies. To protect their wealth, they built armies and city walls. By the beginning of the Bronze Age, large numbers of people were concentrated in the river valleys of Mesopotamia, Egypt, India, and China. These farming villages led to the development of cities.

✓ **READING PROGRESS CHECK**

Locating Where and when did systematic agriculture develop?

Development of River Valley Civilizations

GUIDING QUESTION *How would you define civilization?*

culture the way of life a people follows

civilization a complex culture in which large numbers of people share a number of common elements such as social structure, religion, and art

Whether analyzing societies of the past or the present, anthropologists describe the **culture**—the way of life—of a people in a certain time and place. From earliest times, humans lived in small nomadic groups with simple cultures that helped them survive. When humans settled in permanent villages, their cultures became more complex. Gradually, more complex cultures developed into a new form of human society called civilization.

A **civilization** is a complex culture in which large numbers of human beings share a number of common elements. Historians have identified the basic characteristics of civilizations. Six of the most important characteristics are cities, government, religion, social structure, writing, and art.

The development of farming determined where people lived. The first civilizations developed in river valleys where physical geographic factors such as plentiful water and fertile land allowed people to carry on the large-scale farming that was needed to feed a large population. As food became abundant, more people would live in cities. New factors of human geography such as government, religion, social structures, and trade networks, soon emerged and began to shape civilization.

Economics determined many of the political changes that came with the Neolithic Revolution. Growing numbers of people made food production a central concern and led to more demanding practices, like irrigation. The organization and leadership required for such projects to succeed led to the growth of governments. Governments in early civilizations, usually led by a king, organized armies to protect their populations and made laws to regulate their subjects' lives.

Important religious developments also characterized the new urban civilizations. All of them developed religions to explain the forces of nature and their roles in the world. They believed that gods and goddesses were important to the community's success. To win their favor, **priests** supervised rituals aimed at pleasing them. This gave the priests special power and made them very important people. Rulers also claimed that their power was based on divine approval, and some rulers claimed to be divine.

priests in early urban civilizations, important and powerful people who supervised rituals aimed at pleasing gods and goddesses

A new social structure based on economic power also arose. Rulers and an upper class of priests, government officials, and warriors dominated society. Below this class was a large group of free people—farmers, artisans, and craftspeople. At the bottom was a slave class.

The demand of the upper class for luxury items, such as jewelry and pottery, encouraged artisans and craftspeople to create new products. As urban populations exported finished goods to neighboring populations in exchange for raw materials, organized trade began to grow. Because trade brought new civilizations into contact with one another, it often led to the transfer of new technology, such as metals for tools and new farming techniques, from one region to another. Competition for raw materials between neighboring groups also led to the first mass conflicts, or wars.

By and large, however, the early river valley civilizations developed independently. Each one was based on developments connected to the agricultural revolution of the Neolithic Age and the cities that this revolution helped produce. Taken together, the civilizations of Mesopotamia, Egypt, India, and China constituted nothing less than a revolutionary stage in the growth of human society.

SKILLS PRACTICE

The development of civilization was the result of many changes. Work with a partner to use each vocabulary term in this lesson in a sentence about the effects of the agricultural revolution.

Writing was an important feature in the life of these new civilizations. Above all, rulers, priests, merchants, and artisans used writing to keep accurate records. Of course, not all civilizations depended on writing to keep records. The Inca in Peru, for example, relied on well-trained memory experts to keep track of their important matters. Eventually, the earliest civilizations used writing for creative expression as well as for record keeping. This produced the world's first works of literature.

Significant artistic activity was another feature of the new civilizations. Architects built temples and pyramids as places for worship or sacrifice or for the burial of kings and other important people. Painters and sculptors portrayed stories of nature. They also depicted the rulers and gods they worshiped.

✓ **READING PROGRESS CHECK**

Gathering Information How did large-scale agriculture lead to new patterns of living in river valley civilizations?

LESSON 2 REVIEW TEKS

Reviewing Vocabulary

1. ***Identifying*** What are the six basic characteristics of *civilization?* 2B
2. ***Explaining*** Explain the relationship between *culture* and *civilization.* 2B

Using Your Notes

3. ***Synthesizing*** Use your notes and information in the lesson to explain how Çatalhüyük exemplifies major developments of the Neolithic Revolution. 17A

Answering the Guiding Questions

4. ***Identifying Cause and Effect*** How did developments during the Neolithic period impact early human history? 1A, 17A
5. ***Identifying Cause and Effect*** What led to the development of the river valley civilizations? 1A, 2A, 16B, 17A

Writing Activity

6. **NARRATIVE** In a single, well-developed paragraph, express your thoughts and feelings on what life would have been like as one in a large group of people in a river valley civilization. You may include reflections on place, occupation, social structure, and the role of religion.

networks

There's More Online!

- IMAGE Cuneiform Writing
- IMAGE The Standard of Ur
- IMAGE Ziggurat at Ur
- INTERACTIVE SELF-CHECK QUIZ
- MAP City of Ur, c. 2100 B.C.
- MAP Fertile Crescent, 1500–700 B.C.
- VIDEO Mesopotamia

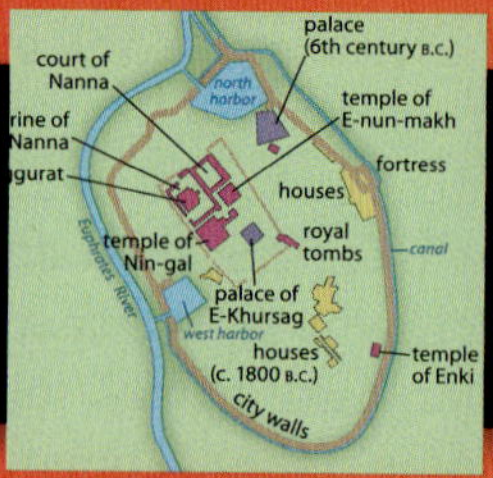

LESSON 3

Mesopotamia

ESSENTIAL QUESTIONS

- *What do archaeology and anthropology teach us about prehistoric humans?*
- *What is a civilization, and how does one form?*

It Matters Because

Mesopotamia was one area in which civilization began. The Tigris and Euphrates River valley supported agriculture and encouraged trade. Mesopotamians developed complex economic, political, and social structures. They invented a written language, built empires, and codified their laws.

Reading **HELP**DESK

Academic Vocabulary

- **transport**
- **invention**

Content Vocabulary

- **city-state**
- **ziggurat**
- **cuneiform**
- **polytheistic**
- **theocracy**

TAKING NOTES:

Key Ideas and Details

Categorizing Use a graphic organizer like the one below to record details about Mesopotamian civilization.

Mesopotamian Civilization	
Location/Place	City-States
Society	Achievements

TEKS Texas Essential Knowledge and Skills

2C explain how major river valley civilizations influenced the development of the classical civilizations

continued on the next page

The Fertile Crescent

GUIDING QUESTION *What role did the physical environment play in the development of Sumerian civilization?*

Fertile river valleys could support many people in permanent settlements. These farming villages grew into culture hearths, early centers of culture whose ideas and practices spread to surrounding areas. Highly organized societies then evolved in these regions.

The ancient Greeks spoke of the valley between the Tigris and Euphrates Rivers as Mesopotamia, the land "between the rivers." Mesopotamia was at the eastern end of the Fertile Crescent, an arc of land from the Mediterranean Sea to the Persian Gulf. Rich soil and abundant crops allowed the land to sustain an early civilization.

Mesopotamia had little rain, but over the years its soil had been enriched by layers of silt—material deposited by the two rivers. In late spring, the Tigris and Euphrates often overflowed their banks and deposited their fertile silt. This flooding was unpredictable. It depended on the melting of snows in the upland mountains where the rivers began. People in the valley could not predict the timing and size of the floods. Therefore, they learned to control the flow of the rivers. By using irrigation and drainage ditches, farmers were able to grow crops regularly. An abundance of food allowed many people to live together in cities, and civilization emerged.

Mesopotamian civilization refers to the achievements of people from three general areas: Assyria, Akkad, and Sumer. The Sumerians were the creators of the first Mesopotamian civilization.

READING PROGRESS CHECK

Analyzing How did people in the Fertile Crescent adapt their environment?

City-States of Ancient Mesopotamia

GUIDING QUESTION *How did religious beliefs influence the organization of Sumerian society?*

By 3000 B.C., the Sumerians had established a number of independent cities in southern Mesopotamia, including Eridu, Ur, and Uruk. As the cities expanded, they gained political and economic control over the surrounding countryside. They formed **city-states**, the basic units of Sumerian civilization.

city-state a state with political and economic control over the surrounding countryside

Sumerian cities were surrounded by walls. Uruk, for example, was encircled by a wall six miles (10 km) long, with defense towers located every 30 to 35 feet (9 to 10 m) along the wall. It is estimated that Uruk had a population of around 50,000 people by 2700 B.C., making it one of the largest city-states.

City dwellings, built of sun-dried bricks, included both the small houses of peasants and the larger buildings of the city officials, priests, and priestesses. Although Mesopotamia had little stone or wood for building purposes, it did have plenty of mud. Mud bricks, easily shaped by hand, were left to bake in the hot sun until they were hard enough to use for building. People in Mesopotamia were remarkably creative with mud bricks. They invented the arch and the dome, and they built some of the largest brick buildings in the world.

(continued from p. 16)

TEKS **Texas Essential Knowledge and Skills**

19A identify the characteristics of monarchies and theocracies as forms of government in early civilizations

19B identify the characteristics of the following political systems: theocracy, absolute monarchy, democracy, republic, oligarchy, limited monarchy, and totalitarianism

26C identify examples of art, music, and literature that transcend the cultures in which they were created and convey universal themes

continued on the next page

Religion and Rulers

In Mesopotamia, people looked to religion to answer their questions about life. To them, powerful spiritual beings—gods and goddesses—permeated all aspects of the universe. The Mesopotamians identified nearly 3,000 gods and goddesses. Their religion was **polytheistic** because of this belief in many gods. According to the beliefs of the Mesopotamians, humans were supposed to obey and serve the gods. By their nature, humans were inferior to the gods and could never be sure what the gods might do to them or for them.

polytheistic believing in many gods

The most prominent building in a Sumerian city was the temple dedicated to the chief god or goddess of the city. This temple was often built atop a massive stepped tower called a **ziggurat**. The Sumerians believed that gods and goddesses owned the cities. The people devoted much of their wealth to building temples and elaborate houses for the priests and priestesses who served the gods. The temples and related buildings served

ziggurat a massive stepped tower on which was built a temple dedicated to the chief god or goddess of a Sumerian city

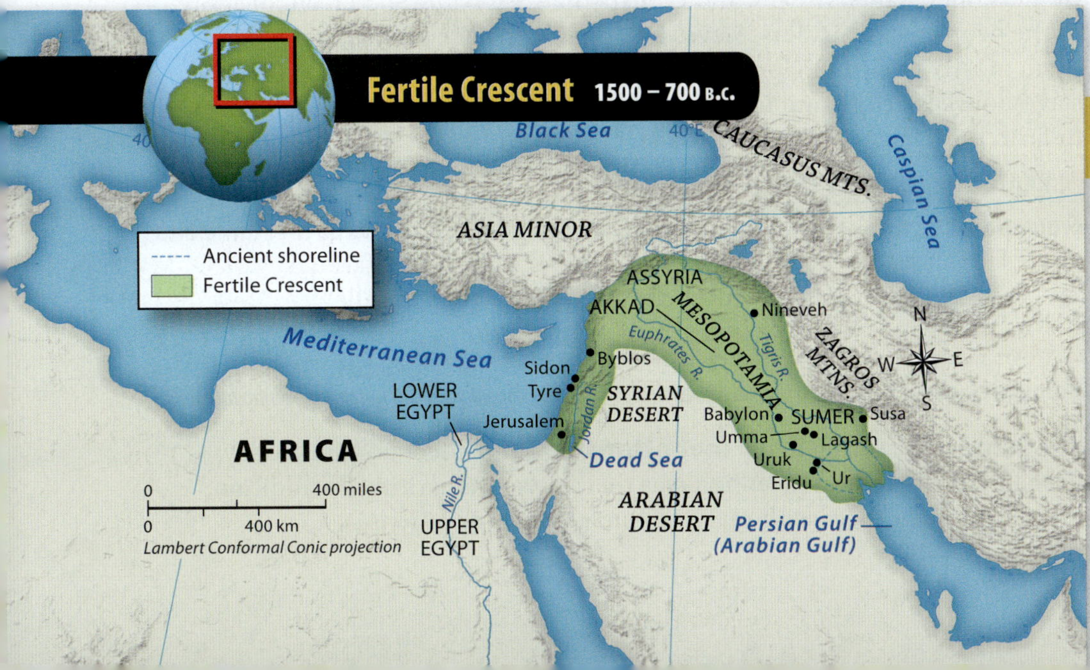

GEOGRAPHY CONNECTION

1. **PHYSICAL SYSTEMS** *Which landforms protected the cities from invasion?*
2. **THE USES OF GEOGRAPHY** *What rivers provided the fertile soil necessary for permanent settlements in Mesopotamia?*

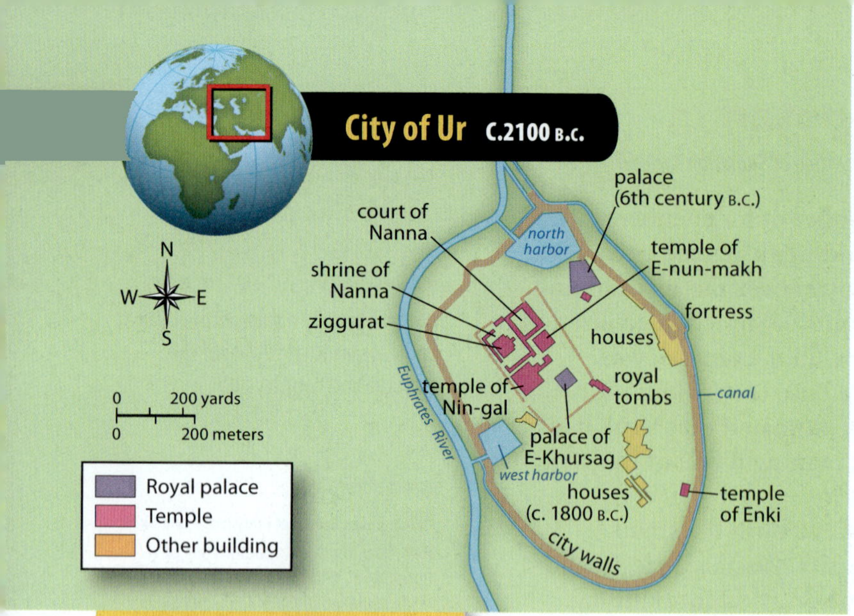

as the center of the city physically, economically, and even politically. The temples also served as storehouses for surplus food and crafts, which could then be distributed or traded.

The priests and priestesses who supervised the temples held a great deal of power. The Sumerians believed that the gods ruled the cities, making the state a **theocracy**—a government established by divine authority. Even when power passed into the hands of kings, Sumerians believed that these rulers derived their power from the gods and were the agents of the gods.

Regardless of their origins, kings held great power. They led armies, supervised the building of public works, and organized workers for the irrigation projects on which farming depended. The army, the government, and the priests and priestesses all aided the kings in their rule. As befitted their power, Sumerian kings and their families lived in large palaces.

GEOGRAPHY CONNECTION

1. **THE USES OF GEOGRAPHY** *Based on the map, to whom do you think the ziggurat was dedicated?*
2. **ENVIRONMENT AND SOCIETY** *What structures were built to manage the Euphrates River?*

theocracy a government established by divine authority

transport the moving of goods or people

(continued from p. 17)

TEKS **Texas Essential Knowledge and Skills**
27A identify the origin and diffusion of major ideas in mathematics, science, and technology that occurred in river valley civilizations, classical Greece and Rome, classical India, and the Islamic caliphates between 700 and 1200 and in China from the Tang to Ming dynasties

invention a new idea, method, or device

Economy and Society

Although the Sumerian city-states had a traditional economy based chiefly on farming, trade and industry became important as well. The peoples of Mesopotamia made woolen textiles and pottery, but they were particularly well known for their metalwork.

Copper, gold, and silver were already being used for jewelry and some tools. The Sumerians discovered that when tin is added to copper, it makes bronze. Bronze has a lower melting point, which makes it easier to cast than copper. Bronze is also a harder metal than copper and corrodes less.

The Sumerians bartered, or exchanged, wool, barley, dried fish, wheat, and metal goods for imported copper, tin, and timber. Sumerian traders traveled by land to the eastern Mediterranean in the west and by sea to India in the east. The invention of the wheel, around 3000 B.C., led to wheeled carts, making the **transport** of goods much easier.

Sumerian city-states contained three major social groups: nobles, commoners, and slaves. Nobles included royal and priestly officials and their families. Commoners worked for palace and temple estates and as farmers, merchants, fishers, and craftspeople. Probably 90 percent or more of the people were farmers. Slaves belonged to palace officials, who used them mostly in building projects. Temple officials most often used female slaves to weave cloth and to grind grain. Rich landowners also used slaves to farm their lands.

✓ READING PROGRESS CHECK

Evaluating Did the Sumerians have an advanced economy relative to their time and place? Explain your answer.

The Creativity of the Sumerians

GUIDING QUESTION *Based on their achievements, why do we consider the Sumerians to be innovative?*

The Sumerians created many **inventions** that still affect our lives today. Probably their greatest invention was their system of writing. In addition, historians credit them with many technological innovations.

Writing and Literature

Around 3000 B.C., the Sumerians created a **cuneiform** ("wedge-shaped") system of writing. Using a reed stylus (a tool for writing), they made wedge-shaped impressions on clay tablets, which were then baked or dried in the sun. After they dried, these tablets lasted a very long time. Several hundred thousand tablets have been found. They have been a valuable source of information for modern scholars.

cuneiform "wedge-shaped," a system of writing developed by the Sumerians using a reed stylus to create wedge-shaped impressions on a clay tablet

Mesopotamian peoples used writing primarily for record keeping. Cuneiform texts, however, were also used in schools to train scribes who served as copyists, teachers, and jurists. Men who began their careers as scribes became the leaders of their cities, temples, and armies. Scribes came to hold the most important positions in Sumerian society.

Writing was important because it allowed a society to keep records and to pass along knowledge from person to person and from generation to generation. Writing also made it possible for people to communicate ideas in new ways. This is especially evident in *The Epic of Gilgamesh*, an epic poem from Mesopotamia that records the exploits of a legendary king named Gilgamesh. Part man and part god, he befriends a hairy beast named Enkidu. Together, they set off to do great deeds. When Enkidu dies, Gilgamesh feels the pain of death and begins a search for the secret of immortality. His efforts fail, and Gilgamesh remains mortal, showing that "everlasting life" is only for the gods. The themes of *The Epic of Gilgamesh*, such as semidivine heroes, deeds of great warriors, and quests for immortality, would later appear in the writings of the classical civilization of Greece.

Technology, Science, and Mathematics

The Sumerians made several advances in technology, science, and mathematics. They developed the wagon wheel, for example, to help transport people and goods from place to place. The Sumerians were the first to make bronze out of copper and tin, creating finely crafted metalwork and weaponry. The Sumerians also made outstanding achievements in mathematics and in sciences like astronomy. In math, they devised a number system based on 60 and used geometry to measure fields and to erect buildings. In astronomy, the Sumerians charted the heavenly constellations. As the Sumerians encountered other civilizations through trade and conflict, these new ideas were slowly spread throughout Eurasia and North Africa.

✓ **READING PROGRESS CHECK**

Hypothesizing Given what you have learned about the Sumerians, develop a hypothesis on how or why they created a system of writing.

LESSON 3 REVIEW TEKS

Reviewing Vocabulary

1. ***Paraphrasing*** In your own words, explain what a ziggurat was and how it was used.

Using Your Notes

2. ***Gathering Information*** Use the notes you took and other information in this lesson to describe the city-states and society of Mesopotamia. **19A, 19B, 26C, 27A**

Answering the Guiding Questions

3. ***Drawing Conclusions*** What role did the physical environment play in the development of Sumerian civilization? **16B**
4. ***Analyzing*** How did religious beliefs influence the organization of Sumerian society?
5. ***Gathering Information*** Based on their achievements, why do scholars consider the Sumerians to be innovative? **26C, 27A**

Writing Activity

6. **ARGUMENT** In a fully developed paragraph, argue that *The Epic of Gilgamesh* either reflects aspects of Mesopotamian life or that it is a universal story with a universal theme. **26C**

CHAPTER 1 Assessment

TEKS

Directions: On a separate sheet of paper, answer the questions below. Make sure you read carefully and answer all parts of the questions.

Lesson Review

Lesson 1

1. ***Explaining*** How do scientists determine how old organic artifacts are?

2. ***Naming*** What were the earliest hominids called?

3. ***Describing*** When and where did the earliest hominids live? How did hominids change over long periods of time?

4. ***Explaining*** Explain the out-of-Africa theory.

5. ***Describing*** Which group of hominids was the first to bury its dead? Where have their remains been found?

6. ***Describing*** Describe the Paleolithic Age, including when it occurred.

7. ***Identifying*** What methods could archaeologists have used to determine that humans crossed into North America 20,000 years ago? **29A**

8. ***Identifying*** What is a method that anthropologists have used to determine the customs of early peoples? **29A**

Lesson 2

9. ***Identifying*** What important changes in human life were caused by the Neolithic Revolution? **1A, 17A**

10. ***Explaining*** What were Neolithic farming villages and where did they appear?

11. ***Describing*** Describe the living conditions of large Neolithic communities.

12. ***Interpreting*** Aside from homes, what other types of buildings were discovered in the Catalhüyükt community? What was their significance?

13. ***Analyzing*** How did the Neolithic Revolution change the dynamic between men and women?

14. ***Summarizing*** How did economic changes lead to political changes during the Neolithic Revolution? **17B**

15. ***Identifying*** What are the characteristics of monarchies and theocracies as forms of government in early river valley civilizations? **19A, 19B**

16. ***Identifying*** What are the characteristics of civilization? **2B**

17. ***Examining*** Why was writing an important feature of these new civilizations?

18. ***Identifying*** How did physical geographic factors, such as river valleys, and human geographic factors, such as the development of agriculture and cities, encourage the development of river valley civilizations? **1A, 2A, 16B**

Lesson 3

19. ***Explaining*** How did major river valley civilizations influence the development of the classical civilizations? **2C**

20. ***Describing*** Name and describe the religion of the Mesopotamians. How many gods and goddesses were identified in this religion?

21. ***Describing*** Describe the primary material used in building Mesopotamia's city dwellings.

Need Extra Help?

If You've Missed Question	1	2	3	4	5	6	7	8	9	10	11	12	13	14	15	16	17	18	19	20	21
Go to page	5	6	6	6	6	7	5	4	11	13	13	13	13	14	15	14	15	11	19	17	17

22. ***Sequencing*** When was the wheel invented and why was it significant for the Sumerians?

23. ***Describing*** Name and describe the system of writing created by the Sumerians.

24. ***Identifying*** What examples of Sumerian literature convey universal themes? **26C**

25. ***Identifying*** What were the mathematical, scientific, and technological innovations of the Sumerians? **27A**

26. ***Identifying*** How did the mathematical, scientific, and technological innovations of the Sumerians diffuse into other river valley civilizations? **27A**

Exploring the Essential Questions

27. ***Comparing and Contrasting*** What are the similarities in what archaeology and anthropology teach about prehistoric humans, and what are the differences?

28. ***Analyzing Cause and Effect*** How does a culture become a civilization? **2B**

Critical Thinking

29. ***Analyzing*** How did the use of fire help to ensure the survival of prehistoric peoples?

30. ***Analyzing Cause and Effect*** How did human geographic factors, such as the use of fire and metal-bearing rocks, influence tool and weapon making in the river valley civilizations? **16B**

31. ***Evaluating*** Why was literature one of Sumer's most significant achievements? **26C**

Social Studies Skills

32. ***Economics*** How did trade begin in Neolithic settlements? To what else did specialization lead? **17A**

33. ***Understanding Relationships Among Events*** Why are governments, such as monarchies or theocracies, an important feature of early civilizations? **19A, 19B**

34. ***Analyzing Cause and Effect*** How did the physical geographic factors of Mesopotamia contribute to the beginning of civilization? **16B**

35. ***Time, Chronology, and Sequencing*** Work with a partner to create an illustrated print or digital time line showing the development of humans from the earliest hominids to the river valley civilizations to the classical civilizations of Mesopotamia circa 3000 B.C. Your time line should contain visuals or multimedia elements such as photos of scientists or their finds, sketches, and maps. You may also include excerpts from primary sources. **2C**

36. ***Using Primary and Secondary Sources*** Discuss the tools and methods of archaeologists and anthropologists and the types of evidence they have used to formulate their theories about our prehistoric and historic ancestors through the time when civilizations arose in Mesopotamia.

37. ***Creating Charts*** Read a translation of one story from *The Epic of Gilgamesh* as well as another example of Sumerian literature (e.g., legends about Enmerkar or Lugalbanda, a creation myth, or a city lament). Create a chart that compares and contrasts how the two works convey universal themes. The chart should include quotations as well as interpretation and analysis. **26C**

Need Extra Help?

If You've Missed Question	22	23	24	25	26	27	28	29	30	31	32	33	34	35	36	37
Go to page	18	19	19	19	19	4	14	7	13	19	13	14	14	6	4	19

DBQ Analyzing Primary Sources

Use the text excerpt to answer the following questions.

Mary and Louis Leakey were among the first archaeologists to search for early humans in Africa. Mary recounts their 1959 field trip in *Disclosing the Past.*

PRIMARY SOURCE

> "But one scrap of bone that caught and held my eye was not lying loose on the surface but projecting from beneath. It seemed to be part of a skull, including a mastoid process (the bony projection below the ear). It had a hominid look, but the bones seemed enormously thick—too thick, surely. I carefully brushed away a little of the deposit, and then I could see parts of two large teeth in place in the upper jaw. They were hominid."
>
> —Mary Leakey, from *Disclosing the Past*

38. ***Identifying Perspectives*** How does Mary Leakey's account of her discovery of a new hominid species differ from her son Richard's account in Lesson 1?

39. ***Hypothesizing*** Why did Leakey carefully brush away the soil instead of just removing the skull?

Analyzing Visuals

Use the image of the artifact to answer the following questions.

40. ***Acquiring information*** When scientists study an artifact, they first record their observations. Examine this artifact closely. What is the artifact's color, size, shape, material, and state or condition? The metal used in this artifact came about due to a technological innovation. What do you think the artifact is made of? 27A

41. ***Speculating*** Next, scientists try to determine the purpose of the artifact. Examine this artifact closely. What are its possible purposes? Who might have used the artifact? How might you confirm or refute your ideas? 27A

Extended Response Question

42. ***Expository*** Choose a mathematical, scientific, or technological innovation of the Sumerians and write an essay that explains how this innovation diffused across time and place into other cultures or civilizations. Share what other cultures or civilizations used this innovation or versions of it. 27A

Need Extra Help?

If You've Missed Question	38	39	40	41	42
Go to page	6	6	5	5	19

The Spread of Civilization c.3100 B.C.–c.200 B.C.

ESSENTIAL QUESTIONS
- *How does geography affect the development of civilizations?*
- *In what ways do civilizations influence each other?*

networks

There's More Online! about the spread of civilization.

CHAPTER 2

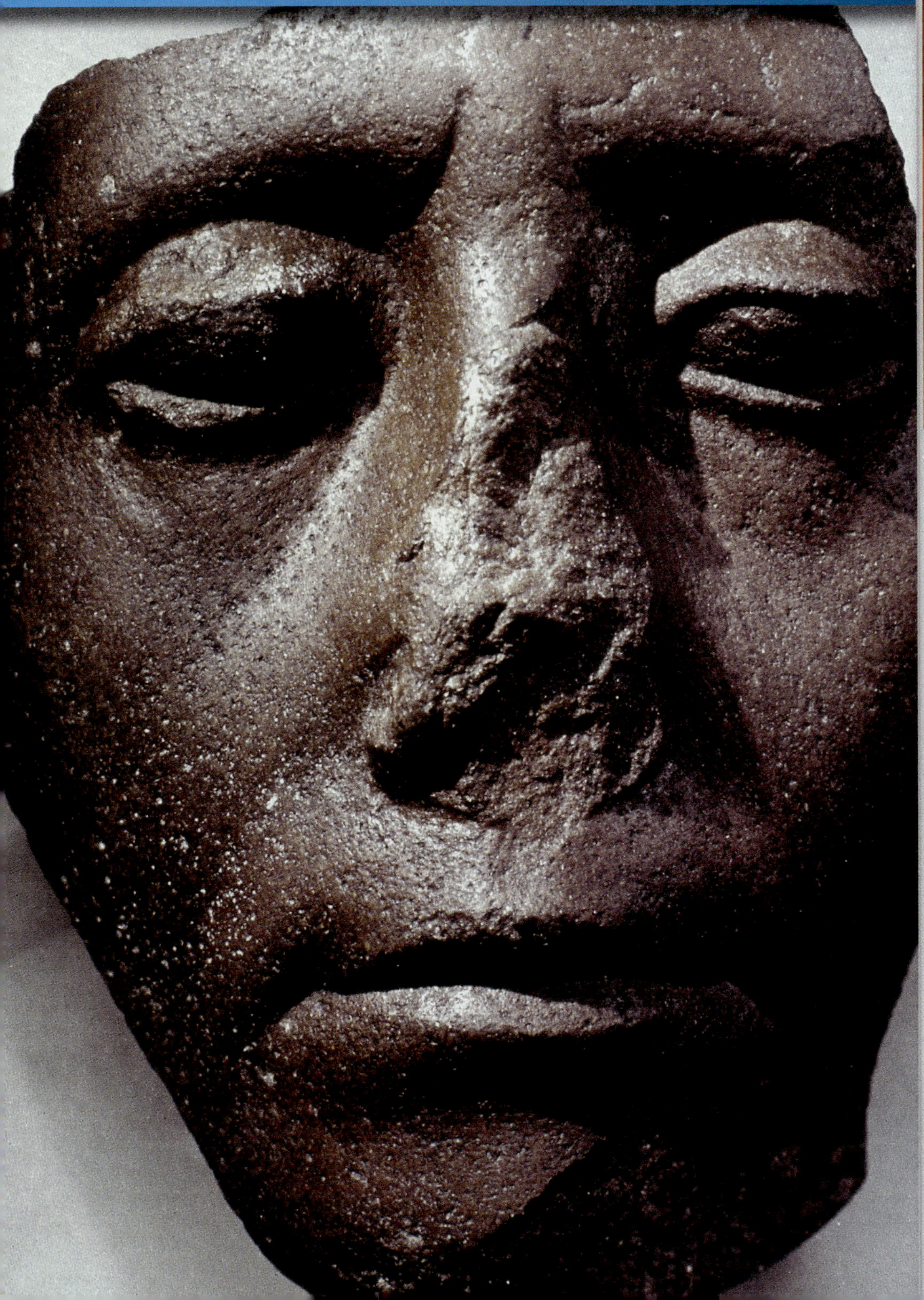

The Story Matters...

First developed in the river valleys of Mesopotamia, the key elements of civilization, including cities, governments, economies, organized religion, and writing systems, also emerged in other river valleys in Egypt, India, and China. With its fertile soil and natural barriers to invasion, Egypt developed a strong civilization, exhibited in its massive cultural achievements such as the pyramids. Its rulers, known as pharaohs, were worshiped as gods.

◀ Sesostris III, one of Egypt's rulers during the Middle Kingdom, was known for his military conquests. This stone head is notable because it shows a pharaoh looking careworn and human rather than idealized and god-like.

CHAPTER 2

Place and Time: The World 3000 B.C.–200 B.C.

Along with the rise of civilization in Mesopotamia, civilizations spread throughout the Mediterranean world, Asia, and the Americas. Egypt emerged along the Nile River, developing into a vast empire that had a largely stable monarchy, religion, languages, writing systems, and artistic tradition. The Phoenicians, Hittites and Israelites developed languages and extensive trade networks in the Mediterranean. Mohenjo Daro and Harappa fostered a flourishing early Indian culture. Governed by a succession of great dynasties, China developed cities along the Yellow River. Civilization later spread into Central and South America where the Olmec, Zapotec, and Chavin peoples farmed and built cities.

Step Into the Place

Read the quotes and look at the information presented on the map.

DBQ **Analyzing Secondary Sources** What are some defining characteristics of a civilization?

SECONDARY SOURCE

"At one time scholars believed that the civilization of ancient Egypt was the first in the history of the world and the progenitor of all others. We now know this to be untrue, but the ancient Egyptians retain one unique distinction: they were the first people on earth to create a nation-state. . . . [This state] served as the framework of a culture of extraordinary strength, assurance, and durability which lasted for 3,000 years and retained almost to the end its own unmistakable purity of style."

—Paul Johnson, from *The Civilization of Ancient Egypt*, 1999

SECONDARY SOURCE

"One of the greatest, if not the greatest, glory of the Phoenicians was the spread of the alphabet in the Mediterranean area. There is no doubt that the Phoenicians taught the alphabet to the Greeks, nor that the Phoenicians and Greeks were responsible for spreading it in the West. . . .

This is certain, and gives the Phoenicians an important role in the history of civilization."

—Sabatino Moscati, from *The World of the Phoenicians*, 1965

Step Into the Time

Integrating Information
Select several time line entries and explain how they demonstrate causes and effects of the spread of civilizations.

THE WORLD

3000 B.C. — 2500 B.C. — 2000 B.C.

- **c. 3100 B.C.** King Menes unites Upper and Lower Egypt
- **c. 3000 B.C.** Phoenician settlements emerge along the Mediterranean
- **c. 2800 B.C.** Minoan civilization established on island of Crete
- **c. 2700 B.C.** Egyptian Old Kingdom begins
- **c. 2540 B.C.** Great Pyramid of King Khufu constructed at Giza
- **c. 2500 B.C.** The Phoenicians and the Egyptians begin trade relations
- **c.2055 B.C.** Egyptian Middle Kingdom begins

networks
There's More Online!

- **MAP** Explore the interactive version of this map on Networks.
- **TIME LINE** Explore the interactive version of the time line on Networks.

Early Civilizations c.3000 B.C.–c.200 B.C.

c. 1600 B.C. Hittite kingdom flourishes in Asia Minor

c. 1350 B.C. Pharaoh Akhenaten briefly introduces monotheism to Egypt

c. 1100 B.C. Babylonian king Nebuchadnezzar I comes to power

c. 1000 B.C. King David establishes Jerusalem as the capital of the Kingdom of Israel

after 930 B.C. The 12 tribes of Israel separate into two kingdoms, Israel and Judah

721 or 722 B.C. Kingdom of Israel falls to Assyrians

612 B.C. Assyria falls to Chaldeans and Medes

1500 B.C. — **1000 B.C.** — **500 B.C.** — **200 B.C.**

c. 1200 B.C. Olmec civilization emerges in Mesoamerica

1045 B.C. Fall of the Shang dynasty in China, beginning of Zhou dynasty

c. 1050 B.C. King Saul establishes the Kingdom of Israel

c. 1000 B.C. Sanskrit writing comes into use in the Indus Valley

c. 900 B.C. Chavin civilization develops in South America

c. 500 B.C. Zapotec civilization emerges in central Mexico

256 B.C. Zhou dynasty ends in China

networks

There's More Online!

- BIOGRAPHY Menes
- IMAGE Canopic Jars
- IMAGE Horus
- IMAGE Pyramids at Giza
- INTERACTIVE SELF-CHECK QUIZ
- MAP Geography of Ancient Egypt
- PRIMARY SOURCE Class Mobility in Egyptian Society
- SECONDARY SOURCE Egyptian Education
- VIDEO The Rise of Egypt

LESSON 1

The Rise of Egypt

ESSENTIAL QUESTIONS

- *How does geography affect the development of civilizations?*
- *In what ways do civilizations influence each other?*

IT MATTERS BECAUSE

Egypt, like Mesopotamia, was one of the first river valley civilizations. Ancient Egyptian history included three long periods of stability and achievement interspersed with shorter periods of political disorder.

Geography and Religion

GUIDING QUESTION *What was the significance of geography to Egypt's development?*

The Nile River played an important role in Egyptian civilization. Egyptians wrote of their reliance on the great river in "Hymn to the Nile," praising it as the "creator of all good" in its ability to bring them food and other riches.

The Nile River begins in the heart of Africa and courses northward for more than 4,000 miles (6,436 km). It is the longest river in the world. Before it empties into the Mediterranean, the Nile splits into two **major** branches. This split forms a triangular territory called a delta. The Nile Delta region is called Lower Egypt; the land upstream, to the south, is called Upper Egypt.

The ancient Egyptians referred to the river's yearly flooding as the "miracle" of the Nile. The river rose in the summer from heavy rains in central Africa, reached its highest point in Egypt in early autumn, and left a deposit of mud that created an area of rich soil several miles wide on both sides of the river.

Farmers in the Nile Valley grew a surplus of food, which made Egypt prosperous. The river also served to unify Egypt. In ancient times, the Nile was the fastest way to travel through the land, making communication easier. North winds pushed sailboats south, and the Nile's current carried them north.

Egypt's natural barriers provided protection from invasion and a sense of security. These barriers included the deserts to the west and east; the Red Sea to the east; the cataracts, or rapids, on the southern part of the Nile; and the Mediterranean Sea to the north.

The regularity of the Nile floods and the relative isolation of the Egyptians created a feeling of security and changelessness. Unlike

Reading HELPDESK

Academic Vocabulary

- **major**
- **physical**

Content Vocabulary

- **dynasty**
- **pharaoh**
- **bureaucracy**
- **hieroglyphics**
- **hieratic script**

TAKING NOTES:

Key Ideas and Details

Classifying Use the following graphic organizer to identify people's social roles in Egyptian society.

Class	Social Roles

TEKS Texas Essential Knowledge and Skills

1A identify major causes and describe the major effects of the following events from 8000 BC to 500 BC: the development of agriculture and the development of the river valley civilizations

continued on p. 28

people in Mesopotamia, Egyptians faced life with a spirit of confidence in the stability of things. Ancient Egyptian civilization was characterized by a remarkable degree of continuity over thousands of years.

Religion , like physical geography, played a central role in the development of Egyptian civilization Religion provided the Egyptians with a sense of security and timelessness. They had no word for religion. For them, religious ideas represented an inseparable part of the entire world order. The Egyptians were polytheistic. They had a number of gods associated with heavenly bodies and natural forces. The Egyptian ruler took the title "Son of Re." The rulers were seen as an earthly form of Re, one of the sun god's names.

major great; significant in size or importance

dynasty a family of rulers whose right to rule is passed on within the family

✔ **READING PROGRESS CHECK**

Explaining What role did the Nile River play in the development of Egyptian civilization?

Egyptian Kingdoms

GUIDING QUESTION *What characterizes the divisions in the first two major periods in Egypt's history?*

Scholars divide Egyptian history into three major periods: the Old Kingdom, Middle Kingdom, and New Kingdom. These were periods of long-term stability marked by strong leadership, freedom from invasion, great building projects, and rich cultural activity. In between were the Intermediate periods, times of political disorder and invasion.

Egypt's history begins around 3100 B.C., when King Menes (MEE • NEEZ) united Upper and Lower Egypt into a single kingdom and created the first royal **dynasty**—a family of rulers whose right to rule is passed on within the family. From then on, the Egyptian ruler would be called "King of Upper and Lower Egypt." The crown was a double crown, indicating the unity of all Egypt.

The Old Kingdom

The Old Kingdom, which lasted from around 2700 B.C. to 2200 B.C., was an age of prosperity and splendor. The monarchs of the Old Kingdom were powerful rulers over a unified state. Among the various titles of Egyptian monarchs, that of **pharaoh**—originally meaning "great house" or "palace"—eventually became the most common.

Egyptian religion heavily influenced the development of kingship, as one tomb inscription noted,"What is the King of Upper and Lower Egypt? He is a god by whose dealings one lives, the father and mother of all men, alone by himself, without an equal." In obeying their pharaoh, subjects were helping to maintain a stable world order.

Egyptian pharaohs possessed absolute power; that is, they had complete, unlimited power to rule their people. Nevertheless, they had help in ruling. At first, members of the pharaoh's family provided this help. During the Old Kingdom, however, a government **bureaucracy**—an administrative organization with

GEOGRAPHY CONNECTION

1. **HUMAN SYSTEMS** *Why is the north called Lower Egypt and the south called Upper Egypt?*
2. **ENVIRONMENT AND SOCIETY** *Why are all cities shown on the map located along the Nile River?*

▲ Part of a complex at Giza, Khufu's Great Pyramid, right, was originally covered in white limestone and topped with a gold capstone.

▶ **CRITICAL THINKING**

Drawing Conclusions What message might a massive white and gold structure in the desert convey about Khufu?

pharaoh the most common of the various titles for ancient Egyptian monarchs; the term originally meant "great house" or "palace"

bureaucracy an administrative organization that relies on nonelective officials and regular procedures

physical relating to the body

(continued from p. 26)

TEKS **Texas Essential Knowledge and Skills**

16B analyze the influence of human and physical geographic factors on major events in world history, including the development of river valley civilizations, trade in the Indian Ocean, and the opening of the Panama and Suez canals

19A identify the characteristics of monarchies and theocracies as forms of government in early civilizations

27A identify the origin and diffusion of major ideas in mathematics, science, and technology that occurred in river valley civilizations, classical Greece and Rome, classical India, and the Islamic caliphates between 700 and 1200 and in China from the Tang to Ming dynasties

officials and regular procedures—developed. In time, Egypt was divided into 42 provinces, which were run by governors appointed by the pharaoh.

An example of the splendor of the Old Kingdom is the building of pyramids, one of the great achievements of Egyptian civilization. Pyramids were built as part of a larger complex of buildings dedicated to the dead—in effect, a city of the dead.

To preserve the **physical** body after death, the Egyptians practiced mummification, a process of slowly drying a dead body to prevent it from rotting. This process took place in workshops run by priests, primarily for the wealthy families who could afford it. Workers first removed the liver, lungs, stomach, and intestines and placed them in four special jars that were put in the tomb with the mummy. They then covered the corpse with a natural salt that absorbed the body's water. Later, they filled the body with spices and wrapped it with layers of linen soaked in resin. At the end of the process, which took about 70 days, a lifelike mask was placed over the head and shoulders of the mummy. The mummy was then sealed in a case and placed in its tomb.

Pyramids were tombs for the mummified bodies of pharaohs. The largest and most magnificent of all the pyramids was built under King Khufu (KOO • FOO). Constructed at Giza around 2540 B.C., the famous Great Pyramid of King Khufu covers 13 acres (5.3 ha), measures 756 feet (230 m) at each side of its base, and stands 481 feet (147 m) high. Speculation still surrounds the building of the Great Pyramid. Especially puzzling is how the builders achieved their amazing level of precision.

Guarding the Great Pyramid at Giza is a huge figure carved from rock, known as the Great Sphinx. This colossal statue is 240 feet (73 m) long and 66 feet (20 m) high. It has the body of a lion and a human head. Historians do not agree on the purpose of the Great Sphinx. Many Egyptians, however, believed that the mythical sphinx was an important guardian of sacred sites.

The Great Pyramid still stands as a visible symbol of the power of the Egyptian pharaohs of the Old Kingdom. No pyramid built later matched its size or splendor. The pyramid was not only the pharaoh's tomb but also an important symbol of royal power. It could be seen for miles and served to remind people of the glory, might, and wealth of the ruler who was a living god on Earth.

The Middle Kingdom

The Old Kingdom eventually collapsed, followed by a period of disorder that lasted about 150 years. Finally, a new dynasty gained control of all Egypt. The Middle Kingdom lasted from about 2055 B.C. to 1650 B.C. Egyptians later portrayed the Middle Kingdom as a golden age of stability.

As evidence of its newfound strength, Egypt began a period of expansion. It conquered Nubia to the south and built fortresses to protect the new frontier. Pharaohs also sent traders to Kush, Syria, Mesopotamia, and Crete.

One feature of the Middle Kingdom was a new concern of the pharaohs for the people. In the Old Kingdom, the pharaoh had been seen as a god-king far removed from his people. Now he was portrayed as the shepherd of his people and expected to build public works and provide for the public welfare.

✓ **READING PROGRESS CHECK**

Describing What was the pharaoh's role in the Old Kingdom?

Life in Ancient Egypt

GUIDING QUESTION *How was Egyptian society organized?*

Over a period of thousands of years, Egyptian society maintained a simple structure. It was organized like a pyramid, with the god-king at the top. The pharaoh was surrounded by an upper class of nobles and priests who ran the government and managed their own landed estates.

Below the upper class were merchants, artisans, scribes, and tax collectors. Merchants carried on an active trade up and down the Nile and in local markets. Egyptian artisans made a huge variety of well-built, beautiful goods: wooden furniture; gold, silver, and copper tools and containers; paper and rope made of papyrus; and linen clothing.

By far, the largest number of people in Egypt farmed the land. In theory, the pharaoh owned all the land but granted portions of it to his subjects. Large sections of land were held by nobles and the priests who supervised the numerous temples. Most of the lower classes were peasants who farmed the land of these estates. They paid taxes in the form of crops to the pharaoh, nobles, and priests; lived in small villages; and were forced to provide military service and labor for building projects.

Parents arranged marriages for their children (girls at age 12 and boys at age 14). The main purpose of marriage was to produce children, especially sons. Only sons could carry on the family name.

The husband was considered master of the house, but wives were well respected. Women's property and inheritance stayed in their hands, even in marriage. Most careers and public offices were closed to women, but some

ANALYZING PRIMARY SOURCES

Writing Systems in Ancient Egypt

Image of *Story of Sinuhe,* written in hieratic script on papyrus

The ancient Egyptians first developed a hieroglyphic script around 3000 B.C. Hieroglyphic writing uses a system of symbols or pictures to convey ideas or sounds. These complex symbols, often associated with Egyptian culture, are mainly found on tombs, monuments, and stone carvings. However, in everyday life, Egyptians used a much simpler form of hieroglyphics known as hieratic script. Hieratic script was generally used for keeping records or writing stories such as this excerpt from the Story of Sinuhe *written on papyrus. Sinuhe was an official who spent much of his life in exile in Syria, but he longed to return to Egypt.*

"O whatever god ordained this flight
Do thou [show] mercy and return me to the Residence!
Perhaps thou wilt let me see the place in which my heart dwells!
What is more important than that I should be buried in Egypt, since I was born there?
This is an appeal for help. May good fortune befall,
May God grant me peace, may he do thus to perfect the end of him whom he has afflicted, taking pity on him who he cast out to live Abroad!
Is he now appeased?
May he hear the prayer of one far away!
May he turn away his hand from him whom he sent roaming the earth,
Back to the place when he drew it forth!"

—*Story of Sinuhe,* from *Land of Enchanters,* 2001

DBQ Analyzing Historical Documents

1. ***Analyzing*** Why might the ancient Egyptians have used two different styles of script for different purposes?
2. ***Identifying Central Ideas*** How does Sinuhe feel about his exile? Who does he blame?

hieroglyphics "priest-carvings" or "sacred writings"; a complex system of writing that used both pictures and more abstract forms; used by the ancient Egyptians and Maya

hieratic script simplified version of hieroglyphics used in ancient Egypt for business transactions, record keeping, and the general needs of daily life

women operated businesses. Peasant women worked long hours in the fields and in the home. Upper-class women could become priestesses, and four queens became pharaohs.

✓ **READING PROGRESS CHECK**

Contrasting How would the life of a member of Egypt's lower class have differed from the life of a member of the upper class?

Egyptian Accomplishments

GUIDING QUESTION ***What were some of the cultural contributions of the ancient Egyptians?***

One system of writing in Egypt emerged around 3000 B.C. The Greeks later called this earliest Egyptian writing **hieroglyphics**, meaning "priest-carvings" or "sacred writings." This system of writing, which used pictures and more abstract forms, was complex. It appears in writing on temple walls and in tombs. A simplified version of hieroglyphics, known as **hieratic script**, was used for daily life. Hieroglyphs were at first carved in stone and later, hieratic script was written on papyrus, a paper made from the papyrus reed that grew along the Nile.

Pyramids, temples, and other monuments bear witness to the architectural and artistic achievements of the ancient Egyptians. Artists and sculptors were expected to follow particular formulas in style. For example, the human body was often portrayed as a combination of profile, semi-profile, and frontal view to accurately represent each part.

Egyptians also made advances in mathematics. As early as 3500 B.C., the Egyptians had developed a number system which allowed them to count indefinitely, and to make complex calculations necessary for their massive monuments. Egyptians were able to calculate area and volume and used geometry to survey flooded land. These concepts of geometry were later built upon by Hellenistic mathematicians after the conquest of Alexander the Great.

The Egyptians developed an accurate 365-day calendar by basing their year on the movements of the moon and on the bright star Sirius. Sirius rises in the sky just before the annual flooding of the Nile River, providing a standard date from which to calculate. The Romans later adopted this calendar in the first century B.C., and provided the basis for our current calendar developed in the sixteenth century A.D.

▼ These canopic jars held certain organs of mummified individuals. The tops were carved in the likeness of the sons of Horus, the god who ruled the universe.

✓ **READING PROGRESS CHECK**

Differentiating What were the different uses of hieroglyphic and hieratic script?

LESSON 1 REVIEW TEKS

Reviewing Vocabulary

1. ***Defining*** Write a paragraph describing the government of ancient Egypt in which you define the terms *dynasty, pharaoh,* and *bureaucracy.*

Using Your Notes

2. ***Identifying*** Use your graphic organizer to write a paragraph identifying people's roles in the upper, middle, and lower classes. What relationships existed among the classes?

Answering the Guiding Questions

3. ***Drawing Conclusions*** What was the significance of geography to Egypt's development?
4. ***Contrasting*** What characterizes the divisions in the first two major periods in Egypt's history?
5. ***Evaluating*** How was Egyptian society organized?
6. ***Interpreting Significance*** What were some of the cultural contributions of the ancient Egyptians?

Writing Activity

7. **INFORMATIVE/EXPLANATORY** Write an essay explaining the role of religious beliefs in ancient Egyptian life and social structure.

networks

There's More Online!

- BIOGRAPHY Solomon
- IMAGE City of David, Jerusalem
- IMAGE Phoenician Writing
- IMAGE Pottery from Phoenicia
- INTERACTIVE SELF-CHECK QUIZ
- MAP Hittite Empire, 1650 B.C. –1200 B.C.
- MAP The Phoenicians and Their Colonies, 1000 B.C.–700 B.C.
- SLIDE SHOW Minoan Art
- VIDEO Peoples in the Eastern Mediterranean

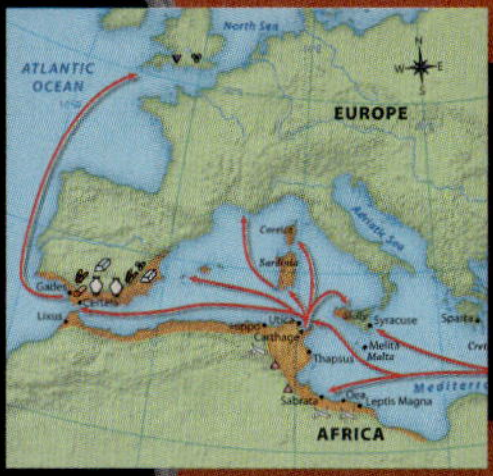

LESSON 2
Peoples in the Eastern Mediterranean

ESSENTIAL QUESTIONS
- *How does geography affect the development of civilizations?*
- *In what ways do civilizations influence each other?*

Reading HELPDESK

Academic Vocabulary
- **created**
- **domesticated**
- **technology**

Content Vocabulary
- **pastoral nomad**
- **monotheistic**

TAKING NOTES:
Key Ideas and Details

Organizing Use the following graphic organizer to name a major contribution to the region made by each culture of the eastern Mediterranean.

Culture	Contribution

TEKS Texas Essential Knowledge and Skills

1B identify major causes and describe the major effects of the following events from 500 BC to AD 600: the development of the classical civilizations of Greece, Rome, Persia, India (Maurya and Gupta), China (Zhou, Qin, and Han), and the development of major world religions

continued on p. 33

It Matters Because

After about 1200 B.C., there was no dominant power in western Asia. The Phoenicians emerged as the most important trading kingdom in the eastern Mediterranean area. While the Israelites did not create an empire, their religion, Judaism, had a significant influence on western civilization and the later religions of Christianity and Islam.

The Role of Nomadic Peoples

GUIDING QUESTION *What was the influence of nomadic peoples on civilized societies?*

On the fringes of the civilizations of Mesopotamia and Egypt lived nomadic peoples who depended on hunting and gathering, herding, and sometimes farming for their survival. Most important were the **pastoral nomads** who on occasion overran settled communities and then **created** empires. Pastoral nomads **domesticated** animals for food and clothing. They followed regular migratory routes to provide food for their animals. Pastoral nomads also carried products between civilized centers. In this way, nomads often passed on new **technology**, such as the use of bronze and iron, that helped strengthen civilizations. When overpopulation or drought disrupted the pastoral nomads' normal patterns, however, they often attacked the civilized communities to obtain relief.

One of the most significant group of nomadic peoples were those who spoke Indo-European languages. The term Indo-European does not refer to a specific ethnic group. It refers to a group of languages that have many similarities and are thought by most linguists to derive from a single parent tongue. Indo-European languages include Greek, Latin, and its derivatives such as Italian, French and Spanish, as well as Russian, Persian, Sanskrit, and Germanic languages such as English and German. The people who spoke the original language that fragmented into these modern languages are thought to have originated somewhere in the steppe region that stretches roughly from where the Ukraine is located today east to central Asia. There is much debate about where exactly they originated because linguists have to use

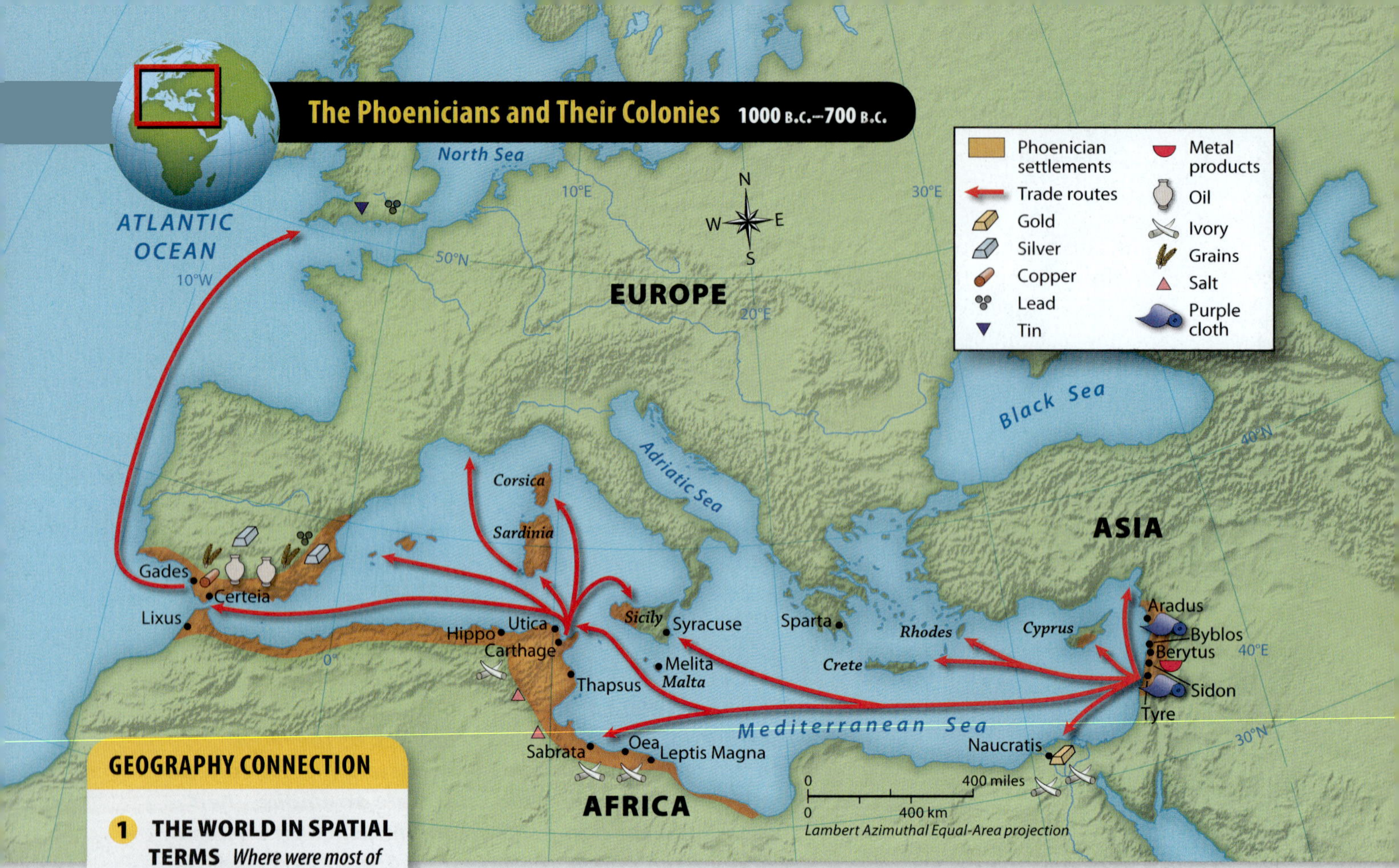

The Phoenicians and Their Colonies 1000 B.C.–700 B.C.

GEOGRAPHY CONNECTION

1. **THE WORLD IN SPATIAL TERMS** *Where were most of the Phoenician settlements located?*
2. **HUMAN SYSTEMS** *What goods did the Phoenicians obtain outside of the Mediterranean?*

pastoral nomad a person who domesticates animals for food and clothing and moves along regular migratory routes to provide a steady source of nourishment for those animals

created made or brought something new into existence

domesticated adapted to life with and to the advantage of humans

technology a manner of accomplishing a task using technical processes or knowledge

changes in language to trace the movement of people and cultures backward in time. There is much uncertainty, but between 4000 B.C. and 500 B.C, cultures using Indo-European languages developed all across Europe, in the Middle East, and as far east as Iran and northern India. There are many competing theories about the movement and mingling of peoples that spread the language group across such great distances.

Around 1750 B.C., a culture using an Indo-European language developed in Asia Minor. These people formed the Hittite kingdom that had its capital at Hattushash (Bogazkšy in modern Turkey). Between 1600 B.C. and 1200 B.C., the Hittites created an empire in western Asia and threatened the power of the Egyptians. The Hittites were the first Indo-Europeans to use iron. Iron weapons were stronger and cheaper to make because of the widespread availability of iron ore. Around 1200 B.C., invaders, known to historians only as the "Sea Peoples," destroyed the Hittite empire.

The end of the Hittite kingdom and the weakening of Egypt temporarily left no dominant powers in western Asia. This allowed a number of small kingdoms and city-states to emerge. The Phoenicians were one of these peoples.

✓ **READING PROGRESS CHECK**

Describing What activities characterized the pastoral nomads?

The Phoenicians

GUIDING QUESTION ***What were the cultural and economic accomplishments of the Phoenicians?***

The Phoenicians lived along the eastern coast of the Mediterranean Sea on a narrow band of land 120 miles (193 km) long. After the downfall of the Hittites and the Egyptians, the newfound political independence of the Phoenicians helped them expand their trade. Trade had long been the basis of their prosperity. The chief cities of the Phoenicians—Byblos, Tyre, and Sidon—were ports on the eastern Mediterranean. The Phoenicians produced a number of goods for foreign markets, including purple dye, glass, and lumber from the cedar forests of what is today modern Lebanon.

The Phoenicians built ships and became great international sea traders, eventually creating a trade empire. The Phoenicians charted new routes not only in the Mediterranean but also in the Atlantic Ocean, where they reached Britain and sailed south along the west coast of Africa. They set up a number of colonies in the western Mediterranean. Carthage, on the North African coast, was their most famous colony.

Phoenician culture is best known for its alphabet. The Phoenicians, who spoke a Semitic language, simplified their writing by using 22 different signs to represent the sounds of their speech. These 22 characters, or letters, could be used to spell out all the words in the Phoenician language. Although the Phoenicians were not the only people to invent an alphabet, theirs was important because it was eventually passed on to the Greeks. From the Greek alphabet came the Roman alphabet that we still use today.

✓ READING PROGRESS CHECK

Locating Where did the Phoenicians travel for trade?

▲ **Trade goods like this flask, used for storing oils, helped the Phoenicians build strong trade ties throughout the Mediterranean world.**

▶ CRITICAL THINKING

Analyzing How might a storage container indicate evidence of trade?

The Israelites

GUIDING QUESTION ***What was the lasting influence of the Israelites?***

To the south of the Phoenicians lived another group of Semitic-speaking people, known as the Israelites. They were a minor factor in the politics of the region. However, their religion—known today as Judaism—flourished and later influenced the religions of Christianity and Islam.

Much of the Israelites' history and religious beliefs eventually were written down in the Hebrew Bible, which is known to Christians as the Old Testament. According to tradition, Israelites were descendants of the patriarch Abraham. Their ancestors migrated from Mesopotamia to Canaan. They focused on grazing animals rather than on farming. Because of drought, the Israelites moved to Egypt, where they were enslaved until Moses led them out, probably in the latter part of the thirteenth century B.C.

According to the Hebrew Bible, the Israelites lived in the desert for forty years until they returned to Canaan. There, between 1200 B.C. and 1000 B.C., they organized in tribes and established a united kingdom known as Israel.

Under King David, who ruled from about 1000 B.C. to 970 B.C., the Israelites established control over all the land that came to be called Israel and made the city of Jerusalem its capital. David's youngest son, King Solomon, expanded the government and army and encouraged trade. He is best known for building the First Temple in Jerusalem, which the Israelites viewed as the symbolic center of their religion and of the Israelite kingdom itself. Under Solomon, ancient Israel reached the height of its power.

The Divided Kingdom

After Solomon's death, tension among Israel's tribes led to the creation of two separate kingdoms. The Kingdom of Israel was composed of the ten northern tribes and established its capital at Samaria. To the south, the Kingdom of Judah consisted of two tribes and had its capital at Jerusalem.

In 722 or 721 B.C., the Assyrians overran the Kingdom of Israel and sent

(continued from p. 31)

TEKS **Texas Essential Knowledge and Skills**

3A describe the major political, religious/philosophical, and cultural influences of Persia, India, China, Israel, Greece, and Rome, including the development of monotheism, Judaism, and Christianity

20A explain the development of democratic-republican government from its beginnings in the Judeo-Christian legal tradition and classical Greece and Rome through the English Civil War and the Enlightenment

20B identify the impact of political and legal ideas contained in the following documents: Hammurabi's Code, the Jewish Ten Commandments, Justinian's Code of Laws, Magna Carta, the English Bill of Rights, the Declaration of Independence, the U.S. Constitution, and the Declaration of the Rights of Man and of the Citizen

22B identify the influence of ideas regarding the right to a "trial by a jury of your peers" and the concepts of "innocent until proven guilty" and "equality before the law" that originated from the Judeo-Christian legal tradition and in Greece and Rome

continued on the next page

Analyzing PRIMARY SOURCES

Psalms

"By the rivers of Babylon we sat and wept when we remembered Zion. . . . How can we sing the songs of the Lord while in a foreign land? If I forget you, O Jerusalem, may my right hand forget [its skill]. May my tongue cling to the roof of my mouth if I do not remember you, if I do not consider Jerusalem my highest joy."

—Psalms 137: 1, 4–6

DBQ ***ANALYZING INFORMATION***

According to this passage from the Hebrew Bible, how did the people of Judah react to their captivity in Babylonia?

monotheistic believing in one God

(continued from p. 33)

TEKS **Texas Essential Knowledge and Skills**

23A describe the historical origins, central ideas, and spread of major religious and philosophical traditions, including Buddhism, Christianity, Confucianism, Hinduism, Islam, Judaism, Sikhism, and the development of monotheism

26C identify examples of art, music, and literature that transcend the cultures in which they were created and convey universal themes

27A identify the origin and diffusion of major ideas in mathematics, science, and technology that occurred in river valley civilizations, classical Greece and Rome, classical India, and the Islamic caliphates between 700 and 1200 and in China from the Tang to Ming dynasties

many Israelites to other parts of the Assyrian Empire. Most of these scattered Israelites (the "ten lost tribes") merged with neighboring peoples and gradually lost their identity.

The Kingdom of Judah managed to retain its independence for a while, but a new enemy, the Chaldeans (kal • DEE • uhnz), defeated Assyria, conquered the Kingdom of Judah, and completely destroyed Jerusalem in 586 B.C. Many people of Judah were sent as captives to Babylonia, inaugurating the period known as the Babylonian exile.

New conquerors, the Persians, allowed the people of Judah to return to Jerusalem and rebuild their city and Temple, ending the Babylonian captivity. The revived province of Judah was controlled by Persia until the conquests of Alexander the Great in the 300s B.C. The people of Judah survived, eventually becoming known as the Jews and giving their name to Judaism.

Judaism

The Jews are **monotheistic**, believing in one God, who is the Creator of the world and everything in it. Traditional Jews believe God is all powerful, all knowing, and present everywhere. God created nature but is not identified with it. The sun, the wind, and other natural phenomena are not gods, but God's creations to be admired but not worshiped. The growth of Judaism, as well as Christianity and Islam, each inspired by Judaism, influenced the development and spread of monotheism within the Western world.

"According to Jewish belief, the Creator is not removed from the life he created. God is just and good, and demands goodness from people. God is also 'compassionate, slow to anger, and rich in love.' God took an active interest in creation, promising the Israelites, "You will thrive and it will go well with you" if they kept his Torah, Judaism's foundational set of precepts. Through the Torah, each person can have a personal relationship with God."

Covenant

The covenant, and prophets are two unique aspects of Jewish religious tradition. Jews believe that during the exodus from Egypt, when Moses led his people out of bondage, God made a covenant, or contract, with them. God promised to protect them and they promised to follow his Torah, Judaism's foundational set of precepts. The most famous laws in the Torah are the Ten Commandments that Moses is said to have received at Mount Sinai.

The Ten Commandments established both religious and moral (concerned with the standards of right and wrong conduct) rules. The religious commandments required Israelites to worship only their God and not the gods of other peoples. They were forbidden to make images or statues for worship and were commanded not to use God's name in an offensive way. They were also required to observe a day of rest free from labor of any kind.

The commandments also established moral laws. They stressed proper family relationships by ordering children to respect their parents and by banning adultery. They outlawed murder and theft and prohibited false testimony.

The legal ideas in the Ten Commandments had important implications and a significant impact on the development of law in western civilization. First, the ancient Israelites believed that all people were equal before God's law. The laws against murder, theft, lying, and adultery applied equally to everyone regardless of class. Second, the Torah relied on witnesses to testify against those accused of crimes, and the commandment that one "shall not bear false witness against your neighbor" provided some protection against dishonest accusations.

Prophets

Jews also believe that God sent additional religious teachers, or prophets, to serve as his voice to his people. The age of prophecy, a time when the people were threatened or conquered by powerful neighbors, lasted from the 1000s B.C. to the 400s B.C. The prophets declared that faithlessness to God would bring catastrophe, but turning from evil would bring God's mercy. Later prophets embraced a concern for all humanity. All nations would find peace with the God of Israel.

The prophets also cried out against social injustice within the context of the Torah. They criticized violations of God's covenant, often attacking the wealthy, political elites. They condemned mistreatment of the poor, denounced excessive luxuries, and warned Israelites of punishments for their sins. They said that God's command was to live justly, to share with others, and to care for the poor and the unfortunate. These words influenced the development of social justice for Jews, Christians, and many others.

▲ This terra-cotta model found in Archanes, Crete, shows an example of a Minoan home with windows, columns, a lightwell, and balcony.

The religion of Israel was unique among the religions of western Asia and Egypt. Their belief in one God (monotheism) and their unique covenant relationship with God distinguished Israel from surrounding peoples. Judaism requires concern for all humanity because Jews believe that all people are made in God's image. The Jewish people's belief in one God distinguished the Jews from other peoples of Southwest Asia. Because Jews would not accept the gods of their conquerors or neighbors and because Jewish life was based on Jewish law and focused on the community, Jews were able to maintain their identity after the loss of Jewish independence. Other peoples resented the Jews' firm commitment to their faith.

The Impact of Judaism

The laws in the Ten Commandments had a major impact on future legal codes, especially because of their influence on the development of Christianity. Today, images of Moses are often associated with his status as great lawgiver. Famous artistic representations, such as Michelangelo's *Moses,* depict him as lawgiver carrying the two stone tablets of the Ten Commandments.

The concept of covenant and the Ten Commandments also helped shape political systems in the Western world. For example, the English political philosopher Thomas Hobbes (1588–1679) argued that the covenant provided a model for the proper relationship between kings and their subjects. He used the relationship between God and Israel to illustrate how an ideal ruler provides security in exchange for obedience.

Likewise, the Puritans who settled New England in the seventeenth century used the legal and political ideas in the Torah and Ten Commandments to organize some early European settlements in North America. Such examples have led some observers to argue that the spread of Jewish tradition has influenced the development of democratic-republican government in the Western world.

✓ READING PROGRESS CHECK

Differentiating What made the religion of Israel unique among the religions of western Asia and Egypt?

PHOTO: akg-images / John Hios

Judaism

Judaism is a monotheistic religion. In fact, Judaism was the first major religion to believe in one God. Jews trace their national and religious origins back to God's call to Abraham and the revelation of Torah to Moses at Mount Sinai. Jews believe that they have a convenant with God, who expects them to pursue justice and live ethical lives and will one day usher in an era of universal peace.

Over time Judaism has separated into branches, including Orthodox, Reform, Conservative, and Reconstructionist. Orthodox Jews are the most traditional of all the branches.

Menorah

Sacred Symbol

One of the oldest symbols of the Jewish people is the menorah, used in the celebration of Hanukkah, commemorating the rededication of the Temple of Jerusalem following the Maccabees' victory over the Syrian Greeks. Another important Jewish symbol is the Star of David, also known as the Magen David, or Shield of David. It has been popular since the 17th century.

This is the Star of David, also known as the Magen David.

Sacred Text

The Torah contains the five books of Moses, which tell the story of the origins of the Jews and explain Jewish laws. The remainder of the Hebrew Bible contains the writings of the prophets, Psalms (which are writings), and ethical and historical works.

"I am the Lord your God, who brought you out of the land of Egypt, out of the house of slavery. You shall have no other gods before me."

—Exodus 20:2-3

Sacred Site

The Western Wall is what remains of the structure surrounding the Second Jerusalem Temple, built after the Jews' return from the Babylonian captivity. It is considered the most sacred spot in Jewish religious tradition, in the holiest city for Judaism. Worldwide Jews pray facing Jerusalem morning, afternoon, and evening, and within Jerusalem, Jews face toward the Western Wall.

Worship and Celebration

The day-long Yom Kippur service ends with the blowing of the ram's horn (shofar). Yom Kippur is the holiest day in the Jewish calendar. During Yom Kippur, Jews do not eat or drink for 25 hours. The purpose is to reflect on the past year, repent for one's sins, and gain forgiveness from God. It falls in September or October, ten days after Rosh Hashanah, the Jewish New Year.

The Minoans

GUIDING QUESTION *How did the Minoans interact with other ancient civilizations?*

By 2800 B.C., another civilization in the eastern Mediterranean had been established on the island of Crete. Called the Minoan civilization, it flourished from 2700 B.C. to 1450 B.C. The Minoans were not Greek, but they influenced the peoples of the Greek mainland.

Arthur Evans, the English archaeologist who first discovered the civilization, named it after Minos, the legendary king of Crete, because some of its structures were similar to the labyrinth that King Minos was said to have built. At the beginning of the twentieth century, Evans discovered an enormous palace complex on Crete at Knossos (NAH • suhs). The remains of this complex revealed a rich culture, with Knossos as the center of a far-ranging sea empire based on trade. The ships of the Minoans took them to Egypt as well as southern Greece.

There, they traded finely crafted pottery and gold and silver jewelry from Crete for other goods. Trade also helped the Minoans improve the goods they produced: They drew inspiration from techniques and designs from objects from other lands. Although the Minoans built palaces on several sites in Crete, the palace at Knossos was the royal seat of the kings. This elaborate building included numerous private living rooms for the royal family and workshops for making decorated vases, ivory figurines, and jewelry. Even bathrooms, with elaborate drains, formed part of the complex. Rooms were decorated with brightly colored paintings showing sporting events and nature scenes. Storerooms held gigantic jars of oil, wine, and grain that were paid as taxes to the king.

The centers of Minoan civilization on Crete suffered a sudden and catastrophic collapse around 1450 B.C. Some historians believe that a tidal wave triggered by a powerful volcanic eruption on the island of Thera (THIHR • uh) was responsible for the devastation. Most historians, however, believe that the destruction was the result of invasion by mainland Greeks known as the Mycenaeans (my • suh • NE • uhnz).

✓ READING PROGRESS CHECK

Identifying What cultural artifacts did Minoans produce for trade with neighboring civilizations and for their own enjoyment?

SKILLS PRACTICE

Work with a partner to review the information in this lesson. As you review, point to pictures and maps in the text, use gestures to describe the movement of groups like pastoral nomads or Phoenician trades, and explain what you learned using the English words you know.

LESSON 2 REVIEW TEKS

Reviewing Vocabulary

1. ***Identifying Cause and Effect*** Write a paragraph explaining how domesticating livestock allowed civilizations to spread.

Using Your Notes

2. ***Comparing and Contrasting*** Use the graphic organizer to compare and contrast two cultures of the eastern Mediterranean and their contributions to world history.

Answering the Guiding Questions

3. ***Interpreting Significance*** What was the influence of nomadic peoples on civilized societies?
4. ***Drawing Conclusions*** What were the cultural and economic accomplishments of the Phoenicians?
5. ***Describing*** What were the lasting political and cultural influences of the Israelites? 3A
6. ***Making Connections*** How did the Minoans interact with other ancient civilizations?

Writing Activity

7. **NARRATIVE** Reflecting on the four ancient Mediterranean cultures—nomadic, Phoenician, Israelite, and Minoan—what similarities and differences did you observe? Write an essay that explains the key characteristics of these civilizations.

networks

There's More Online!

- ☑ CHART/GRAPH Indus Valley Trade
- ☑ IMAGE Animal Seal from Mohenjo Daro
- ☑ IMAGE Indus River Valley
- ☑ IMAGE Mohenjo Daro
- ☑ INTERACTIVE SELF-CHECK QUIZ
- ☑ MAP Indus Valley Civilization and Trade, c. 3000 B.C.–1500 B.C.
- ☑ MAP Monsoons in India
- ☑ PRIMARY SOURCE Poetry from Ancient India
- ☑ VIDEO The Indus Valley Civilization

Reading HELPDESK

Academic Vocabulary

- **primary**
- **reveal**

Content Vocabulary

- **monsoon**
- **Sanskrit**

TAKING NOTES:

Key Ideas and Details

Listing Use the following graphic organizer to list features of India's climate and geography that played a role in its development.

Features of India's climate and geography

TEKS Texas Essential Knowledge and Skills

1A identify major causes and describe the major effects of the following events from 8000 BC to 500 BC: the development of agriculture and the development of the river valley civilizations

continued on the next page

LESSON 3
The Indus Valley Civilization

ESSENTIAL QUESTIONS

- *How does geography affect the development of civilizations?*
- *In what ways do civilizations influence each other?*

IT MATTERS BECAUSE

The Indus River valley was the largest of the early river valley civilizations. Climate and an extensive river system supported agriculture, the development of cities, and widespread trade for Indian civilization.

The Impact of Geography

GUIDING QUESTION *What role did geography play in the development of the Indian subcontinent?*

India is a land of diversity. Today, about 110 languages and more than 1,000 dialects—varieties of language—are spoken in India. Diversity is also apparent in India's geography. The Indian subcontinent, shaped like a triangle hanging from the southern ridge of Asia, is composed of a number of core regions, including mountain ranges, river valleys, a dry interior plateau, and fertile coastal plains.

In the far north are the Himalaya, the highest mountains in the world. Directly south of the Himalaya is the rich valley of the Ganges (GAN • jeez) River, one of the chief regions of Indian culture. To the west is the Indus River valley, a relatively dry plateau that forms the backbone of the modern state of Pakistan. In ancient times, the Indus Valley enjoyed a more moderate climate and served as the cradle of Indian civilization.

South of India's two major river valleys—the valleys of the Ganges and the Indus—lies the Deccan Plateau, which extends from the Ganges Valley to the southern tip of India. The interior of the plateau is relatively hilly and dry. India's eastern and western coasts are lush plains. These plains have historically been among the most densely populated regions of India.

The **primary** feature of India's climate is the **monsoon**, a seasonal wind pattern in southern Asia. During the months of June through September, monsoon winds from the south and southwest blow across the Arabian Sea, part of the Indian Ocean. These summer monsoons carrying moisture-laden air cause heavy rainfall across the subcontinent, especially on the west coast near Mumbai.

During the cooler season, from October through February, the wind pattern reverses direction and blows from the north and northeast. Although this air is cooler and drier than the summer monsoons, the winter monsoons bring significant rainfall to the east coast of India.

The wettest place on earth is in the mountains of northeast India. Winds blow over the plains below, rise up the mountainside, cool, and release rain. Throughout history, Indian farmers have depended on the heavy rains brought by the southwest monsoons. If the rains come early or late, or too much or too little rain falls, crops are destroyed and thousands starve.

✓ READING PROGRESS CHECK

Locating Which regions in India are most affected by the monsoon? How does it affect them?

Indus Valley Civilization

GUIDING QUESTION *How advanced were the civilizations of the Indus Valley?*

As in Mesopotamia and Egypt, early civilization in India emerged in river valleys. Between 3000 B.C. and 1500 B.C., the valleys of the Indus River supported a civilization that extended hundreds of miles from the Himalaya to the Arabian Sea. Archaeologists have found the remains of more than a thousand settlements in this region. Two of the ruins were the sites of the cities of Harappa (huh • RA • puh) and Mohenjo Daro (moh • hehn • joh DAHR • oh). An advanced civilization flourished in these cities for hundreds of years. Historians call it the Harappan or Indus civilization.

At its height, Harappa had 35,000 inhabitants; Mohenjo Daro had about 35,000 to 40,000. Both cities were carefully planned. The broad main streets ran in a north-south direction and were crossed by smaller east-west roads.

primary most important

monsoon a seasonal wind pattern in southern Asia that blows warm, moist air from the southwest during the summer, bringing heavy rains, and cold, dry air from the northeast during the winter

(continued from p. 38)

TEKS **Texas Essential Knowledge and Skills**

2C explain how major river valley civilizations influenced the development of the classical civilizations

16B analyze the influence of human and physical geographic factors on major events in world history, including the development of river valley civilizations, trade in the Indian Ocean, and the opening of the Panama and Suez canals

continued on p. 41

GEOGRAPHY CONNECTION

1. **ENVIRONMENT AND SOCIETY** *What physical feature do both the Indus Valley civilization and Mesopotamia share?*
2. **THE USES OF GEOGRAPHY** *Why do you think the Indus Valley civilization traded with Babylon by sea instead of by land?*

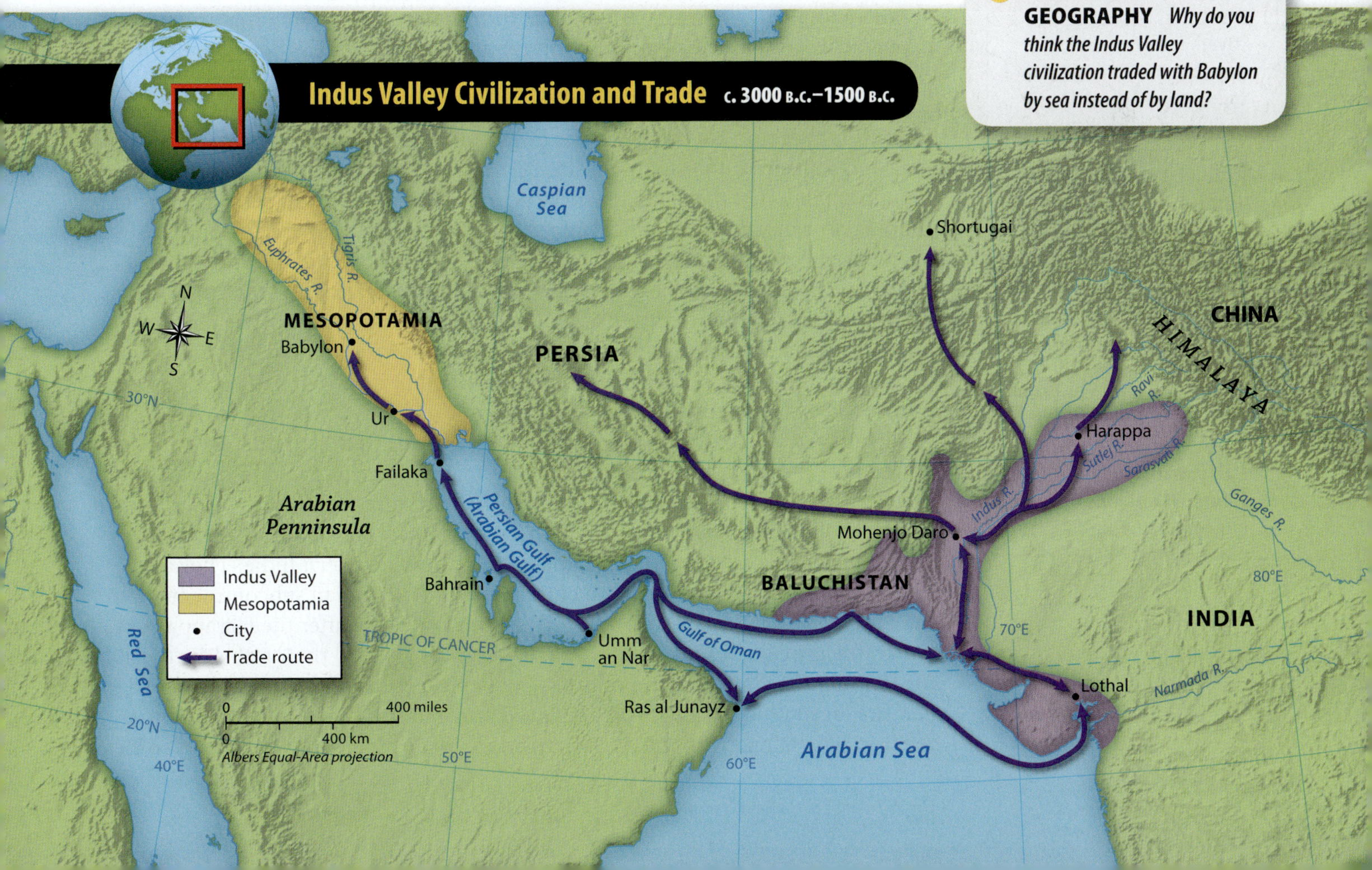

▲ Mohenjo Daro, located in present-day Pakistan, was at one time the largest city of the Indus Valley civilization. It covered about three square miles (five sq. km) and may have been home to up to 40,000 people.

Houses varied in size, some as high as three stories, but all followed the same plan—a square courtyard surrounded by rooms.

Public wells provided a regular supply of water for all the inhabitants. Bathrooms featured an advanced drainage system. Wastewater flowed out to drains located under the streets and then was carried to sewage pits beyond the city walls. A system of chutes took household trash from houses to street-level garbage bins. Only a well-organized government could have maintained such carefully structured cities.

As in Egypt and Mesopotamia, Harappan rulers based their power on a belief in divine assistance. Religion and political power were closely linked, as is indicated by the combination of the royal palace and the holy temple in the citadel, or fortress, at Harappa.

The Harappan economy was based on farming. The Indus River flooded every year, providing rich soil to grow wheat, barley, and peas. The Indus Valley civilization also carried on trade as far away as Mesopotamia. Sumerian textiles and food were traded for Indus Valley copper, lumber, precious stones, cotton, and various luxury goods.

✓ READING PROGRESS CHECK

Identifying Identify and discuss one feature of the Harappan (Indus) ruins that suggests that this civilization was particularly advanced.

Migration and Interaction

GUIDING QUESTION *Why did India's culture change after 1500 B.C.?*

How the Indus Valley civilization ended continues to be a mystery. Archaeologists have found signs of gradual decay in Indus Valley cities beginning around 1800 B.C. Floods, an earthquake, changes in climate, environmental changes from human settlements, and a change in the course of the Indus River weakened the once-flourishing civilization in the Indus River valley. Although theories about the end of the Indus Valley civilization abound, all agree that about 1500 B.C. there was a major shift in India's culture. Many historians explain this shift as the result of a foreign migration, while others cite other reasons including environmental changes.

Most western scholars contend that beginning in 2000 B.C. a group of Indo-European-speaking nomadic peoples began to move out of the steppes of central Asia and southward to Iran, the Indus River valley, and then into northern India. Linguists think that the language these people spoke was part of a sub-group of Indo-European languages called Indo-Aryan. For this reason, the people have been called Aryans by historians. Based on their study of language and cultural evidence, these scholars concluded that some Aryans migrated south over many centuries, crossed the Hindu Kush mountain range, and settled in the plains of northern India. Historians know very little about the origins and early culture of these Indo-Aryan speaking people. As they settled in northern India, they came into contact with the Indus Valley civilization.

Exactly how a new Indian civilization developed after the Indus Valley civilization collapsed is in dispute. The idea that Aryans migrated into India and that their culture replaced the culture of the Indus Valley people has been disputed by some scholars, many based in India. These scholars think that the Indo-European language group may have originated in or near northern India. They also think that a mingling of tribes and cultures within the Indian subcontinent led to the development of the new Indian civilization that came after the Harappans.

In the process of settling in India, the Aryans gave up their nomadic lifestyle for farming. The introduction of iron—probably from Southwest Asia, where it had first been used by the Hittites—played a role in this change. The creation of the iron plow, along with the use of irrigation, made it possible for farmers to clear

Connections to TODAY

Rivers in South Asia

The Indus and Ganges Rivers remain centers of population, commerce, and industry in the modern nations of India, Pakistan, and Bangladesh. The city of Kolkata (Calcutta) sits along a channel of the Ganges and supports a population of more than 15 million people. Its port provides an important site for the transfer of goods between land, river, and sea. The Ganges River also carries religious significance. It is the holiest river for Hindus. Every year, in January and February, millions of Hindu pilgrims bathe at sacred places along the Ganges, seeking to cleanse themselves of sin.

the dense jungle growth along the Ganges River and turn it into rich farmland.

The basic crops in the north were wheat, barley, and millet. Rice was most common in the fertile river valleys. In the south, grain and vegetables supplemented cotton and spices such as pepper, ginger, and cinnamon.

Although there is evidence of writing in the Indus Valley, no one has yet been able to translate those symbols. Like most nomadic peoples, the early Aryans had no written language. Around 1000 B.C., they started writing in **Sanskrit**, an Indo-European language. Having a written language enabled them to record the legends and religious rituals that had been passed down orally from earlier generations.

These early writings, the Vedas, **reveal** that between 1500 B.C. and 400 B.C., India was a world of many small kingdoms. Various leaders, known as rajas (princes), carved out small states. These kingdoms were often at war with one another as alliances shifted between them. Not until the fourth century B.C. did a leader establish a large Indian state.

Life in ancient India centered on the family, the most basic unit in society. The ideal was an extended family that had three generations—grandparents, parents, and children—living under the same roof. The family was basically patriarchal, because in most of India the oldest male held legal authority over the entire family unit.

As in other ancient civilizations, ancient Indian civilization gave males a place of prominence. Only males could inherit property, except in cases where there were no sons. Women could not serve as priests, and generally only males were educated. In upper-class families, young men began their education with a guru, or teacher, and then went on to study in one of the major cities. These young men were not supposed to marry until they completed 12 years of study. Although divorce was usually not allowed, husbands could take a second wife if the first was unable to bear children.

Children were an important product of marriage and were expected to take care of their parents as they grew older. Marriage, arranged by the parents, was common for young girls. Parents supported each daughter until marriage and then paid a dowry to the family of the man she married.

One of the practices known to have started in ancient India was the rare custom of suttee, considered early on to be a voluntary form of female suicide. The dead were placed on heaps of material called pyres, which were then set on fire. Suttee allowed a wife to throw herself on her dead husband's funeral pyre. While suttee was voluntary in theory, a Greek visitor reported that "those women who refused to burn themselves were held in disgrace." Suttee did not, however, have any basis in the Vedas or Upanishads. In later centuries, there were instances of forced suttee, and it was condemned over many centuries by Indian religious leaders until it was banned in 1829.

✓ **READING PROGRESS CHECK**

Synthesizing What were some characteristics of the new culture that emerged from interactions between the Aryans and the Dravidians?

▲ **Seal from Mohenjo Daro, most likely used as an amulet and a way to identify merchandise**

▶ **CRITICAL THINKING**

Drawing Conclusions What might have been the significance of the use of a seal in Harappan society?

Sanskrit the first writing system of the Aryans, developed around 1000 B.C.

reveal show; to make known

(continued from p. 39)

TEKS **Texas Essential Knowledge and Skills**

27A identify the origin and diffusion of major ideas in mathematics, science, and technology that occurred in river valley civilizations, classical Greece and Rome, classical India, and the Islamic caliphates between 700 and 1200 and in China from the Tang to Ming dynasties

LESSON 3 REVIEW *TEKS*

Reviewing Vocabulary

1. ***Describing*** Write a paragraph that describes Sanskrit and identifies the culture that invented it.

Using Your Notes

2. ***Determining Importance*** Use your graphic organizer to identify four important features of India's climate and geography.

Answering the Guiding Questions

3. ***Making Connections*** What role did geography play in the development of the Indian subcontinent?

4. ***Assessing*** How advanced were the civilizations of the Indus Valley?

5. ***Drawing Conclusions*** Why did India's culture change after 1500 B.C.?

Writing Activity

6. **INFORMATIVE/EXPLANATORY** Write an essay describing family structure and gender roles in ancient India.

networks

There's More Online!

- GRAPHIC ORGANIZER The Dynastic Cycle
- IMAGE Bronze Plate Carved with Pictographs from the Zhou Dynasty
- IMAGE Shang Dynasty Bronze Art
- IMAGE Zhou Dynasty Bronze Art
- INTERACTIVE SELF-CHECK QUIZ
- MAP Spread of Shang and Zhou Empires, c. 1750 B.C.–256 B.C.
- PRIMARY SOURCE The Analects of Confucius
- VIDEO The Rise of China

Reading HELPDESK

Academic Vocabulary

- **communicate**
- **cycle**

Content Vocabulary

- **aristocracy**
- **Dao**
- **filial piety**

TAKING NOTES:

Key Ideas and Details

Defining Use the following graphic organizer to write definitions of key concepts for early Chinese culture.

Concept	Definition
ancestor worship	
Mandate of Heaven	
filial piety	

TEKS Texas Essential Knowledge and Skills

1A identify major causes and describe the major effects of the following events from 8000 BC to 500 BC: the development of agriculture and the development of the river valley civilizations

continued on the next page

LESSON 4
The Rise of China

ESSENTIAL QUESTIONS

- *How does geography affect the development of civilizations?*
- *In what ways do civilizations influence each other?*

IT MATTERS BECAUSE

As in other regions, China's early civilizations followed the spread of agriculture along river valleys. As most of the rivers in China flow east to the Pacific Ocean, China's civilizations developed near the east coast.

The Impact of Geography

GUIDING QUESTION *How did China's physical geography influence the location of its early civilizations?*

Dating back more than 6,000 years, China has one of the world's oldest cultures. China also has the largest population of any nation and is made up of more than 50 ethnic groups that speak several languages and many dialects. The diversity of its people reflects the diversity of its land and climate.

The Huang He (HWAHNG • HUH), or Yellow River, stretches across China for more than 2,900 miles (4,666 km), carrying its rich yellow silt from Mongolia to the Pacific Ocean. The Chang Jiang (CHAHNG • JYAHNG), or Yangtze River, is longer, flowing for about 3,400 miles (5,470 km) across central China before emptying into the Yellow Sea. The cultivated valleys of these rivers emerged as one of the great food-producing areas of antiquity.

China is not just a land of fertile fields. Only 10 percent of the total land area is suitable for farming, compared with 19 percent of the United States. Much of the rest of the land in China consists of mountains and deserts on its northern and western frontiers.

This forbidding landscape is a dominant feature of Chinese life and has played an important role in Chinese history. Geographical barriers—mountains and deserts—isolated the Chinese people from peoples in other parts of Asia. In the frontier regions created by these barriers lived peoples of Mongolian, Indo-European, and Turkish backgrounds. The contacts of these groups with the Chinese were often marked by conflict. The northern frontier of China became one of the areas of conflict in Asia as Chinese armies tried to protect their land.

China's climates vary from region to region based on the elevation and the monsoons. In winter, monsoons blowing from the mountainous regions are cold and dry. In summer, the monsoons blow from the south across the seas, bringing rain. The dry season alternating with wet monsoons creates significant temperature differences in winter and summer.

✓ READING PROGRESS CHECK

Explaining What effect did China's mountains and deserts have on the development of its civilization?

The Shang Dynasty

GUIDING QUESTION ***What characterized China under the Shang dynasty?***

Historians of China have traditionally dated the beginning of Chinese civilization to the founding of the Xia (SHYAH) dynasty more than 4,000 years ago. Little is known about this dynasty, which was replaced by a second dynasty, the Shang.

China under the Shang dynasty (about 1750 B.C. to 1045 B.C.) was mostly a farming society ruled by an **aristocracy** whose major concern was war. An aristocracy is an upper class whose wealth is land-based and who passes power from one generation to the next.

Archaeologists have found evidence of impressive cities in Shang China. Shang kings may have had five different capital cities before settling Anyang (AHN • YAHNG), just north of the Huang He in north-central China. Excavations reveal huge city walls, royal palaces, and large royal tombs.

The Shang king ruled from the capital city, Anyang. His realm was divided into territories governed by aristocratic military leaders, called

(continued from p. 42)

TEKS **Texas Essential Knowledge and Skills**

1B identify major causes and describe the major effects of the following events from 500 BC to AD 600: the development of the classical civilizations of Greece, Rome, Persia, India (Maurya and Gupta), China (Zhou, Qin, and Han), and the development of major world religions

2C explain how major river valley civilizations influenced the development of the classical civilizations

continued on the next page

aristocracy an upper class whose wealth is based on land and whose power is passed on from one generation to another

GEOGRAPHY CONNECTION

1. **THE WORLD IN SPATIAL TERMS** *Which dynasty controlled the largest extent of China?*
2. **ENVIRONMENT AND SOCIETY** *What does the extent of the Zhou dynasty show about the importance of the Huang He?*

warlords, but the king had the power to choose or remove these leaders. The king also defended the realm and controlled large armies, which often fought on the fringes of the kingdom. The king's importance is evident in the ritual sacrifices that were undertaken at his death. Early Chinese kings were buried in royal tombs accompanied by the corpses of their faithful servants.

The royal family occupied the top of Shang society; the aristocracy came next. The aristocrats, the chief landowners, waged war and served as officials. The majority of people were peasants who farmed the aristocracy's land. In addition to the aristocrats and peasants, Shang society also included a small number of merchants and artisans, as well as slaves.

The Chinese believed in supernatural forces that could help the rulers in worldly affairs. To **communicate** with the gods, the priests made oracle bones. These were bones on which priests scratched questions asked by the rulers, such as: Will the king be victorious in battle? Heated metal rods were stuck into the bones, causing them to crack. The priests interpreted the shapes of the cracks as answers from the gods and recorded the answers on the bones.

The early Chinese believed in life after death. From this belief came the veneration of ancestors commonly known in the West as ancestor worship. The practice of burning replicas—exact copies—of physical objects to accompany the dead on their journey to the next world continues to this day in many Chinese communities. The early Chinese believed that it was important to treat the spirits of their ancestors well because the spirits could bring good or bad fortune to the living family members.

The Shang are perhaps best remembered for their mastery of bronze casting. Thousands of bronze objects have been found in tombs from the Shang period and are among the most admired creations of Chinese art.

DYNASTIC CYCLE

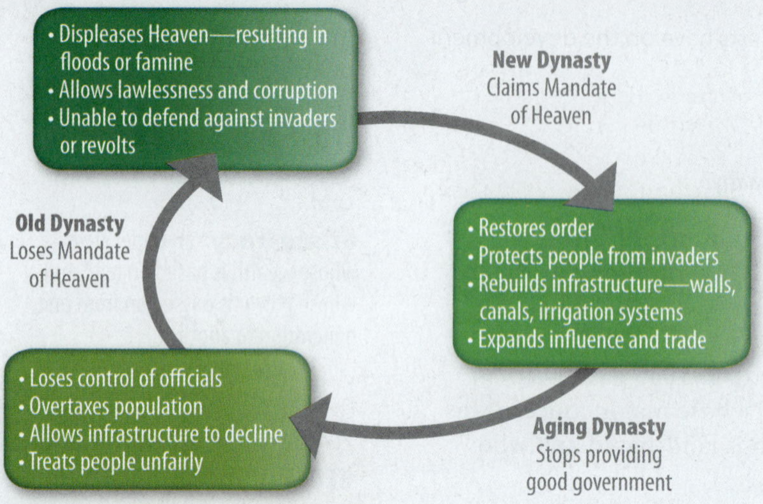

CHART

When the Zhou dynasty overthrew the Shang dynasty, they explained their right to rule as a Mandate of Heaven.

▶ CRITICAL THINKING

1. ***Explaining*** How does this dynastic cycle justify overthrowing a dynasty?
2. ***Drawing Conclusions*** What responsibilities does a ruler owe his people based on the Mandate of Heaven?

communicate to make known or share information about

✓ READING PROGRESS CHECK

Analyzing What effects did the early Chinese belief in the supernatural have on Chinese practices?

The Zhou Dynasty

GUIDING QUESTION *What contributed to the success and longevity of Zhou rule?*

According to legend, the last of the Shang rulers was a wicked tyrant who swam in ponds of wine. This decadence caused the ruler of the state of Zhou (JOH) to revolt against the Shang and establish a new dynasty. The Zhou dynasty, the longest lasting dynasty in Chinese history, ruled for almost 800 years (1045 B.C. to 256 B.C.).

The Zhou dynasty continued the political system of the rulers it had overthrown. At the head of the government was the Zhou king, who was served by an increasingly large and complex bureaucracy. The Zhou dynasty continued the Shang practice of dividing the kingdom into

(continued from p. 43)

TEKS **Texas Essential Knowledge and Skills**

16B analyze the influence of human and physical geographic factors on major events in world history, including the development of river valley civilizations, trade in the Indian Ocean, and the opening of the Panama and Suez canals

27A identify the origin and diffusion of major ideas in mathematics, science, and technology that occurred in river valley civilizations, classical Greece and Rome, classical India, and the Islamic caliphates between 700 and 1200 and in China from the Tang to Ming dynasties territories governed by officials. The officials of these territories were members of the aristocracy. They were appointed by the king and were subject to his authority. Like the Shang rulers, the Zhou king was in charge of defense and commanded armies throughout the country.

The Zhou dynasty claimed that it ruled China because it possessed the Mandate of Heaven. It was believed that Heaven,which was an impersonal law of nature, kept order in the universe through the Zhou king. The king was the link between Heaven and Earth. Thus, the king ruled by a mandate, or authority to command, from Heaven. The concept of the heavenly mandate became a basic principle of Chinese government.

The Mandate of Heaven, however, was double-edged. The king, who was chosen to rule because of his talent and virtue, was then responsible for ruling the people with goodness and efficiency. He was expected to rule according to the proper Way, called the **Dao** (DOW). It was the Zhou king's duty to keep the gods pleased to protect the people from natural disaster. If the king failed in his rule, he could be overthrown and replaced.

Dao "Way," the correct or divine way

This theory has political side effects. It sets forth a right of revolution to overthrow a corrupt ruler. It also makes clear that the king, though serving as a representative of Heaven, is not divine himself. In practice, each founder of a new dynasty would say that he had earned the Mandate of Heaven. Who could disprove it except by overthrowing the king?

cycle a series of events that recur regularly and usually lead back to the starting point

The Mandate of Heaven was closely tied to the pattern of dynastic **cycles**. From the beginning of Chinese history to A.D. 1912, China was ruled by a series of dynasties, all of which went through a cycle of change. A new dynasty would establish its power, rule successfully for many years, and then begin to lose power, giving rise to rebellions or invasion. When a new dynasty took over, the cycle began again.

After almost 800 years, the Zhou dynasty collapsed when the Zhou ruler was challenged by powerful states. In 403 B.C., civil war began an age known in Chinese history as the Period of the Warring States.

Warfare had also changed in China. Iron weapons, which were more powerful than bronze weapons, came into use. Soldiers on horseback, or cavalry, were armed with the powerful crossbow, a Chinese invention of the seventh century B.C. Eventually, one of the warring states—the Qin (CHIHN)—took control and created a new dynasty in 221 B.C.

During the Zhou dynasty, the basic features of Chinese economic and social life began to take shape. The Zhou continued the pattern of land ownership that had existed under the Shang. The peasants worked on lands owned by their lord. Each peasant family farmed an outer plot for its personal use and then joined with other families to work the inner one for their lord. A class of artisans and merchants lived in walled towns under the direct control of the local lord. Merchants did not operate freely but were considered the property of the local lord. There was also a slave class.

Few social institutions have been as closely identified with China as the family. As in most agricultural societies, in ancient China the family served as the basic economic and social unit. However, the family there took on an almost sacred quality as a symbol of the entire social order.

Working together on the land was an important factor of family life in ancient China. Farming required the work of many people, especially in growing rice, which had become the chief crop in the region of the Chang Jiang and the provinces to the south. Children were essential to the family because they worked in the fields. Later, sons were expected to take over the physical labor on the family plots and provide for their parents.

▼ The wealthy of the Zhou dynasty owned luxury items such as this bronze sculpture of a Mongolian boy from the late fifth or early fourth century B.C.

▲ This bronze plate is carved with pictographs telling the historical record of the Zhou emperor Zhouwuwang.

▶ **CRITICAL THINKING**

Analyzing What purpose did this Chinese script serve, and why might it have been cast in bronze?

filial piety the duty of family members to subordinate their needs and desires to those of the male head of the family

The concept of family in China focused on the idea of **filial piety**. Filial refers to a son or daughter. Filial piety, then, refers to the duty of members of the family to subordinate their needs and desires to those of the male head of the family. More broadly, the term describes a system in which every family member had his or her place.

As in other ancient civilizations, male supremacy was key to China's social system. Men provided for their families and worked the fields. They were the warriors, scholars, and government ministers. Women raised children and worked in the home. Some women, however, influenced politics at court, especially female members of the royal family.

The period from the sixth to the third centuries B.C. saw significant economic growth and technological change, especially in farming. Previously, farmers had depended on rain to water crops such as rice and millet. By the sixth century B.C., irrigation was in wide use. Changes in farming methods also increased food production. By the mid-sixth century B.C., land available for growing crops increased due to the use of iron in plowshares. Because of advances in farming tools and practices, China's population rose as high as 50 million people during the late Zhou period.

Improved farming methods were also a major factor in encouraging the growth of trade and manufacturing. One of the most important items of trade in China was silk. Chinese silk fragments from the period have been found throughout central Asia and as far away as Athens, Greece—clear indications of a far-reaching trade network.

A significant cultural contribution of ancient China was the creation of the Chinese written language. By Shang times, the Chinese had developed a simple script—an ancestor of today's complex written language. Its form was primarily pictographic and ideographic. Pictographs are characters that represent an object, like a mountain 山 or the sun 日. Ideographs are characters that combine two or more pictographs to represent an idea—the character *east* 東 symbolizes the sun rising behind the trees.

There was a sound associated with each Chinese character when read aloud. In other cultures, people eventually stopped using pictographs and ideographs and adopted phonetic symbols that represented speech sounds. The Chinese, too, eventually began to attach phonetic meanings to some of their symbols. However, although the Chinese language has evolved continuously over a period of 4,000 years, it has never entirely abandoned its original format.

✓ **READING PROGRESS CHECK**

Identifying Identify three important accomplishments of the Zhou dynasty.

LESSON 4 REVIEW TEKS

Reviewing Vocabulary

1. ***Identifying*** What was the Dao, and how did it affect the Zhou dynasty?

Using Your Notes

2. ***Describing*** Use your graphic organizer to help you write a paragraph describing the ancient Chinese practices of ancestor worship and filial piety.

Answering the Guiding Questions

3. ***Making Connections*** How did China's physical geography influence the location of its early civilizations? 16B

4. ***Analyzing Information*** What characterized China under the Shang dynasty?

5. ***Describing*** What contributed to the success and longevity of Zhou rule? 1B

Writing Activity

6. **INFORMATIVE/EXPLANATORY** Explain the role of religion in politics during the Shang and Zhou dynasties. What effects did religious beliefs have in these two political systems?

networks

There's More Online!

- IMAGE Gold Pendant from Chavin Culture
- IMAGE Olmec Stone Head
- IMAGE Teotihuacán
- INTERACTIVE SELF-CHECK QUIZ
- MAP Cultures of Mesoamerica and South America, 200 B.C.–A.D. 900
- SECONDARY SOURCE The Oldest City in the Americas
- SECONDARY SOURCE The Rise of the Olmec Civilization
- VIDEO Civilizations in the Americas

LESSON 5

Civilizations in the Americas

ESSENTIAL QUESTIONS

- *How does geography affect the development of civilizations?*
- *In what ways do civilizations influence each other?*

Reading HELPDESK

Academic Vocabulary

- **series**
- **estimate**

Content Vocabulary

- **obsidian**
- **ritual**

TAKING NOTES:

Key Ideas and Details

Locating Use the graphic organizer to provide the location and a notable characteristic of the following early American civilizations.

Civilization	Location	Characteristic
Olmec		
Zapotec		
Chavin		

It Matters Because

Archaeology tells us about the ancient societies that once existed in Mesoamerica. The first signs of civilization appeared around 1200 B.C. with the Olmec, whose culture influenced those that followed.

Early Civilizations in Mesoamerica

GUIDING QUESTION *What characterized the first Mesoamerican civilizations?*

Not until the late 1800s did archaeologists begin excavating ancient ruins found in Mesoamerica—a name used for areas of Mexico and Central America where ancient empires flourished. Detailed excavations revealed that the Maya once lived in this region. Later excavations told of an older society, the Olmec.

Archaeologists first discovered the Olmec society in the 1940s. They called these people the Olmec, or rubber people, because of the rubber trees that grew in the area where they lived. The Olmec, the first known civilization in Mesoamerica, appeared around 1200 B.C. They farmed along riverbanks in the hot, swampy lowlands along the coast of the Gulf of Mexico south of Veracruz. They traded with other peoples of Mesoamerica for jade and **obsidian** to make their tools, jewelry, and monuments.

The Olmec had large cities that were centers for their religious **rituals**. The oldest city was San Lorenzo, which contained pyramids and other stone monuments. In La Venta, a 30-foot- (9-m-) high pyramid towered above the city. Skilled Olmec artisans also carved a **series** of colossal stone heads, probably to represent their gods or rulers. These huge heads, 10 feet (3 m) high and weighing 20 tons (18 t), are especially remarkable because the Olmec had no metal tools. Carving them with instruments of stone must have taken a great deal of time.

Around 400 B.C., for reasons not yet fully understood, the Olmec civilization declined and eventually collapsed. However, some aspects of their tradition influenced later Mesoamerican societies. The Olmec played a ceremonial game on a stone ball court, a ritual that

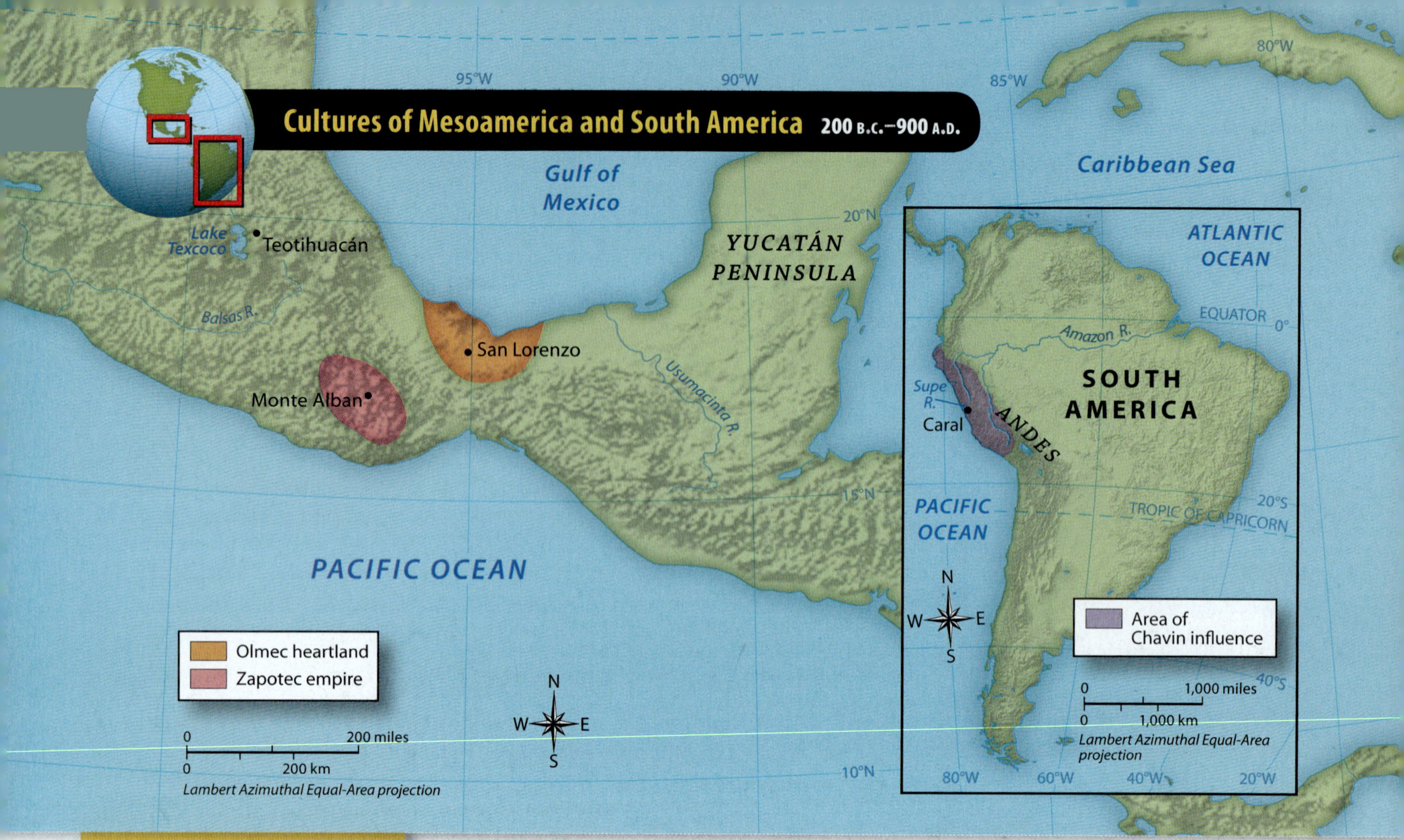

GEOGRAPHY CONNECTION

1. **HUMAN SYSTEMS** *How is the location of the Zapotec empire different from most early civilizations?*
2. **ENVIRONMENT AND SOCIETY** *What physical features may have prevented the Chavin from spreading across South America?*

obsidian a dark natural glass stone formed by lava

ritual a ceremony or a rite

series a group of related things or events

estimate to make a rough determination

the Maya people would later practice. The Maya also continued the Olmec fascination with a jaguarlike god and adopted the Olmec calendar and numerical system.

Around 500 B.C., the Zapotec peoples created a civilization that would flourish for several hundred years in the highlands overlooking the modern city of Oaxaca in central Mexico. Its center was Monte Alban. Like the Olmec sites, Monte Alban contains a number of temples and pyramids. However, they are located in much more awesome surroundings: a massive stone terrace atop a 1,200-foot- (365.8-m-) high mountain. Most of the **estimated** 20,000 people lived in terraces cut into the sides of the mountain.

An elite class of nobles and priests ruled over a population composed chiefly of farmers and artisans. Like the Olmec, the Zapotec devised a written language that has not been deciphered. Zapotec society survived for several centuries after the collapse of the Olmecs. However, Monte Alban was abandoned in the late eighth century A.D. It is unclear why.

The first major city in Mesoamerica was Teotihuacán (TAY • oh • TEE • wuh • KAHN), or Place of the Gods. This city was the capital of an early kingdom that arose around 250 B.C. and collapsed around A.D. 800. Located about 30 miles (48 km) northeast of Mexico City in a fertile valley, Teotihuacán occupied an area of 8 square miles (21 sq. km). It had as many as 200,000 inhabitants at its height. Along its main thoroughfare, known as the Avenue of the Dead, were temples and palaces. All of them, however, were dominated by a massive Pyramid of the Sun. This monument rose in four tiers to a height of more than 200 feet (60 m). Most of the people of Teotihuacán were farmers. Fertile soil made their valley one of the richest farming areas in Mesoamerica.

Teotihuacán was also a busy center for trade. In scores of workshops throughout the city, skilled artisans made tools, weapons, pottery, and jewelry. Especially famous were their obsidian tools. Obsidian, a volcanic glass, was prized in Mesoamerica. It was used in tools, as mirrors, and in the razor-sharp knives that were used in human and animal sacrifices. Archaeologists estimate that there were 400 obsidian workshops in the city. The goods made in Teotihuacán were shipped to Central America, Mexico, and southwestern North America. In return, the city's inhabitants received luxury items and the raw materials used in their crafts, such as shells and bird feathers. Sometime during the eighth century, for reasons yet unknown, the city's power declined. Eventually the ruling class left the city and around A.D. 800, the city was destroyed and abandoned.

✓ READING PROGRESS CHECK

Interpreting What does the existence of the massive Pyramid of the Sun in Teotihuacán suggest about this civilization?

Early Civilizations in South America

GUIDING QUESTION ***Who inhabited early South America?***

As in Mesoamerica, great civilizations flourished in early South America. The inhabitants of the city of Caral, and later the people of the Chavin culture, lived there before the Inca gained power in South America.

Complex societies first emerged in the coastal regions of modern-day Peru and Ecuador. In the Supe River valley of Peru, Caral is the oldest major city in the Americas. Appearing around 2500 B.C., it is believed to be 1,000 years older than the cities previously known in the Western Hemisphere. The city's stone buildings were used for official business, as apartment buildings, and as grand residences. The inhabitants of Caral also developed a sophisticated system of irrigation. They grew squash, beans, and tomatoes. Caral was abandoned between 2000 B.C. and 1500 B.C.

Around 900 B.C., the Chavin people in the coastal regions of modern-day Peru and Ecuador built a temple with stones gathered from nearby hills. Part of a larger ceremonial complex, the temple was surrounded by two pyramids and stone figures depicting different gods. The Chavin made objects of gold and silver. Their most impressive technological achievement was the building, around 300 B.C., of a solar observatory made up of thirteen stone towers on a hillside north of present-day Lima, Peru. There are even signs of a simple writing system. For unknown reasons, the Chavin culture declined around 200 B.C.

✓ READING PROGRESS CHECK

Summarizing What were some of the accomplishments of the Chavin people?

▼ This ceramic Chavin flute player, wearing a jaguar headdress, is most likely a religious leader.

▶ CRITICAL THINKING

Making Inferences This figure's facial tattoos and flute indicate he leads religious ceremonies. How might these items be connected to ceremonies?

PHOTO: Werner Forman/Art Resource, NY

LESSON 5 REVIEW TEKS

Reviewing Vocabulary

1. ***Explaining*** What is obsidian, and how was it incorporated into Mesoamerican culture?

Using Your Notes

2. ***Identifying*** Use your notes to write a paragraph identifying characteristics of the Olmec, Zapotec, and Chavin civilizations.

Answering the Guiding Questions

3. ***Analyzing Information*** What characterized the first Mesoamerican civilizations?
4. ***Assessing*** Who inhabited early South America?

Writing Activity

5. **INFORMATIVE/EXPLANATORY** Write an essay describing Mesoamerican civilizations. How did trade influence the development of Mesoamerican civilizations? Why might the reasons these civilizations declined be unknown?

CHAPTER 2 Assessment

TEKS

Directions: On a separate sheet of paper, answer the questions below. Make sure you read carefully and answer all parts of the questions.

Lesson Review

Lesson 1

1. ***Naming*** Where does the Nile River begin and what are its two major branches?

2. ***Interpreting*** What were the ancient Egyptians referring to with the "miracle" of the Nile?

3. ***Specifying*** Name two significant elements that helped create a sense of security and stability for the Egyptians.

4. ***Identifying Central Issues*** When did the Old Kingdom and the Middle Kingdom begin in Egypt, and how were these two periods similar?

5. ***Explaining*** Explain why the Egyptian ruler was called "King of Upper and Lower Egypt."

6. ***Describing*** How many provinces comprised Egypt and who ran them?

7. ***Summarizing*** What purpose did Pyramids serve as a part of Egyptian civilization?

8. ***Explaining*** How did the Egyptians preserve the physical body after death? How long did this process take?

9. ***Identifying*** What is the Great Sphinx and where is it located?

10. ***Explaining*** How did the Egyptians develop an accurate 365-day calendar?

Lesson 2

11. ***Explaining*** What does the term *Indo-European* refer to and which languages does it include?

12. ***Identifying*** Who were the first Indo-Europeans to use iron?

13. ***Naming*** Name the three chief cities of the Phoenicians and where they were located.

14. ***Explaining*** Explain the three main aspects of Jewish religious tradition.

15. ***Speculating*** What role might songs have played in early cultures before the advent of writing?

16. ***Identifying*** Why has the Hebrew Bible become relevant to so many different cultures? What universal themes does it represent? **26C**

17. ***Making Inferences*** What can you infer about the Minoan royal family's attitude toward art from the fact that there were workshops in the royal palace at Knossos?

Lesson 3

18. ***Analyzing Information*** How did physical geography and climate interact to influence the development of Indus Valley civilizations? **1A, 2C**

Lesson 4

19. ***Specifying*** What were three major activities of the Shang culture in China?

Lesson 5

20. ***Locating*** What was the oldest major city in the Americas? What notable buildings did it have?

Need Extra Help?

If You've Missed Question	1	2	3	4	5	6	7	8	9	10	11	12	13	14	15	16	17	18	19
Go to page	26	26	26	27	27	28	28	28	28	30	31	32	32	34	31	33	36	38	43

Exploring the Essential Questions

21 ***Interpreting Significance*** Working with a small group, find a large map or globe of the world showing at least six civilizations mentioned in this chapter. Analyze the common geographic features of these civilizations. Write an essay explaining your analysis, illustrated with photos of excavated sites and drawings of what you imagine those sites looked like when they were thriving.

22 ***Organizing*** Make a two-column chart with the heading "origin" on the left side and "spread" on the right. In the "origin" column list up to three technologies that were developed in one of the river valley civilizations. Then, in the "spread" column list how this technology spread to other areas and cultures. **27A**

Critical Thinking

23 ***Identifying Cause and Effect*** What is the legal and political impact of the Ten Commandments? **20B**

24 ***Describing*** What aspect of Judaism makes it unique when compared to other early religions? What later religions would be heavily influenced by Judaism? **1B, 3A**

25 ***Identifying and Explaining*** What is a dynasty? **19A**

26 ***Sequencing*** Describe the origins and eventual spread of Judaism as a major world religion. **23A**

27 ***Identifying Cause and Effect*** Give examples of how major ideas in mathematics that originated in Egypt spread to other cultures. **27A**

Social Studies Skills

28 ***Geography Skills*** How did mountains and deserts shape Egyptian civilization? **16B**

29 ***Describing*** How did the Israelites differ from all the other cultures of western Asia and Egypt in their religious and philosophical traditions? How does that difference still affect the world today? **23A**

30 ***Identifying/Explaining Continuity and Change*** What idea regarding an emperor's right to rule developed during the Zhou kingdom? Explain how the idea could possibly be used to overthrow a ruler. **1B**

31 ***Research Skills*** Research the origin of each of these. Explain how these ideas could been influenced by Jewish religious tradition: trial by a jury of your peers, innocent until proven guilty, equality before the law. **20A, 22B**

DBQ Analyzing Primary Sources

Use the document to answer the following questions.

The Arthrashastra was written during the last days of the Indus Valley civilization. It is a lengthy collection of advice to rulers on politics and economics.

PRIMARY SOURCE

"If a king is energetic, his subjects will be equally energetic. If he is reckless, they will not only be reckless likewise, but also eat into his works. . . . During the first one-eight part of the day, he shall post watchmen and attend to the accounts of receipts and expenditure; during the second part, he shall look to the affairs of both citizens and country people; during the third, he shall not only receive revenue in gold, but also attend to the appointments of superintendents; during the fifth, he shall correspond in writs with the assembly of his ministers, and receive the secret information gathered by his spies."

—from "The Duties of a King" (Book I, Chapter 19, of *The Arthrashastra*)

32 ***Drawing Conclusions*** People paid taxes based on how much they earned. With this in mind, what do you think "eat into his works" means?

33 ***Speculating*** What can you tell about the attitude of the author from the fact that he advises kings to meet with their spies? Was this advice probably good?

Need Extra Help?

If You've Missed Question	20	21	22	23	24	25	26	27	28	29	30	31
Go to page	49	25	31	35	34	27	33	30	26	33	45	34

Analyzing Visuals

Use the map to answer the following questions.

34 ***Analyzing Maps*** What major body of water contributed to the fertile Nile River valley and caused annual flooding of the area? **16B**

35 ***Analyzing Maps*** What two physical features formed natural barriers for the early Egyptian civilizations? **16B**

Extended Response Question

36 ***Informative/Explanatory*** Write an essay that compares the ways two ancient civilizations were structured. Compare and contrast the roles their people had and their degrees of hierarchy (class systems). Consider what these structures say about the civilizations' complexity. In your essay, be sure to use standard grammar, spelling, sentence structure, and punctuation. **30B**

Need Extra Help?

If You've Missed Question	32	33	34	35	36
Go to page	52	52	27	26	27

Early Empires in the Ancient Near East

c. 2300 B.C.–c. 300 B.C.

ESSENTIAL QUESTIONS • *How were empires of the ancient Near East governed?* • *How do empires rise, how are they maintained, and what causes them to fall?*

networks

There's More Online! about early empires in the ancient Near East.

CHAPTER 3

The Story Matters...

Around 2300 B.C., the first empires emerged in Mesopotamia. Sargon I, the ruler of the Akkadian Empire, expanded his territory by military conquest and maintained it by using local leaders as his governors. When the Akkadian Empire ultimately declined, the Babylonian Empire rose in its place. King Hammurabi maintained his empire through a strict system of justice. Eventually, the Babylonian Empire also fell into decay. The Egyptian, Assyrian, and Persian Empires rose and fell in similar patterns. The decline of these great empires can be traced to their inability to effectively govern or maintain order throughout their vast territories.

◀ Dating from 2300 B.C., this bronze sculpture is thought to be a portrait of Sargon I, ruler of Akkad. Sargon was the first great empire builder, conquering most of Mesopotamia, Syria, and modern-day Iran.

PHOTO: Silvio Fiore/SuperStock/Getty Images

CHAPTER 3

Place and Time: Near East 2300 B.C.–300 B.C.

The ancient Near East saw the rise and fall of great empires such as Akkad, Babylon, Egypt, Assyria, and Persia. Great leaders, supported by strong militaries, united many territories and peoples to create large empires. Each empire formed its own culture and unique traditions and ultimately evolved into a new society. Governments were maintained by complex systems of administrators who collected taxes and dispensed justice over wide territories. Abundant food production, due to the widespread use of irrigation, enabled the rise of magnificent cities, boasting high artistic and cultural achievements.

Step Into the Place

Read the quotes and look at the information presented on the map.

DBQ **Analyzing Historical Documents** What qualities do you think were required to be a successful ruler in the ancient Near East?

PRIMARY SOURCE

"I had in harness for the forces of my land more chariots and teams of horses than ever before. To Assyria I added land and to its people I added people. I brought contentment to my people [and] provided them with a secure abode.

Tilglath-pileser, exalted prince, the one whom the gods Ashur and Ninurta have continually guided wherever he wished [to go] and who pursued each and every one of the enemies of the god Ashur and laid low all the rebellious. . ."

—Tilglath-pileser I, King of Assyria c. 1100 B.C.

PRIMARY SOURCE

"195. If a son strike his father, his hands shall be hewn off.
196. If a man put out the eye of another man, his eye shall be put out.
197. If he break another man's bone, his bone shall be broken.
198. If he put out the eye of a freed man, or break the bone of a freed man, he shall pay one gold mina.
199. If he put out the eye of a man's slave, or break the bone of a man's slave, he shall pay one-half of its value.
200. If a man knock out the teeth of his equal, his teeth shall be knocked out.
201. If he knock out the teeth of a freed man, he shall pay one-third of a gold mina.
202. If any one strike the body of a man higher in rank than he, he shall receive sixty blows with an ox-whip in public."

—The Code of Hammurabi

PHOTO: (l)Middle Eastern / Brigeman Art Library/Getty Images, (r)©Corbis

Step Into the Time

Making Connections Research two leaders from the top portion of this time line and write a paragraph on their cultural contributions.

ANCIENT NEAR EAST

- **c. 2279 B.C.** Death of Sargon, founder of the Akkadian Empire
- **c. 2112 B.C.** Ur-Nammu becomes king of Sumerian city-state of Uruk
- **c. 1780 B.C.** Code of Hammurabi established in Babylonian kingdom
- **c. 1650 B.C.** Rise of Hyksos dynasty in Egypt

2300 B.C. — 1800

THE WORLD

- **c. 2300 B.C.** Minoan civilization flourishes on Crete
- **c. 1800 B.C.** Indus Valley civilization in Northwest India begins to decline
- **c. 1520 B.C.** Stonehenge monument completed in southern England

networks
There's More Online!

- ✓ **MAP** Explore the interactive version of this map on Networks.
- ✓ **TIME LINE** Explore the interactive version of the time line on Networks.

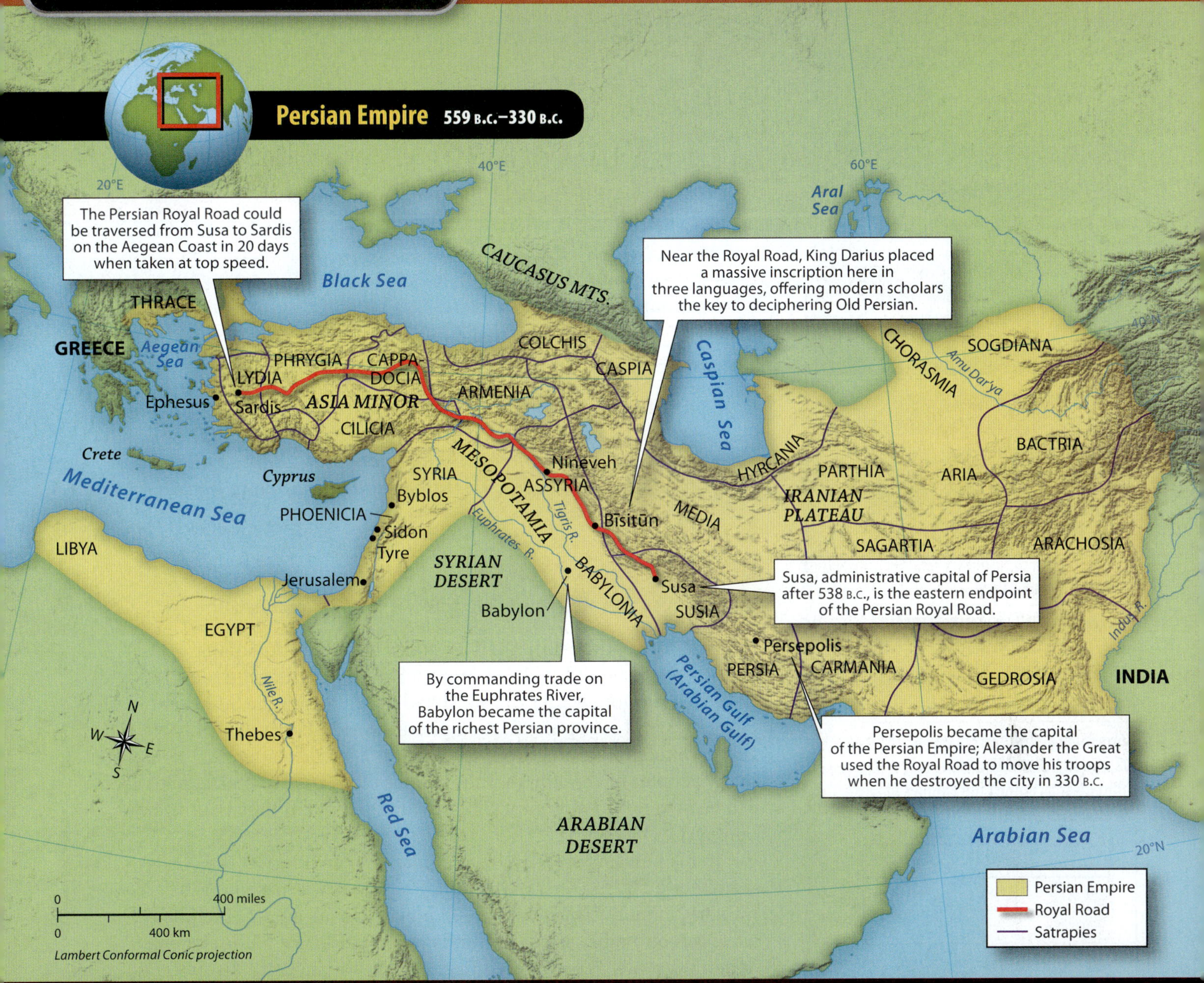

c. 1458 B.C. Death of Hatshepsut, female Egyptian pharaoh

c. 1353 B.C. Akhenaten (Amenhotep IV) becomes ruler of Egypt

c. 970 B.C. Solomon becomes king of Israel, expands empire into Syria and Mesopotamia

705 B.C. Sargon II, great Assyrian ruler, dies

628 B.C. Birth of Zoroaster, Persian religious reformer

539 B.C. Babylon falls to Cyrus "the Great," founder of Persian Empire

c. 331 B.C. Alexander the Great defeats the Persian king Darius III near Arbela

1300 | 800 | 300

c. 1150 B.C. San Lorenzo, oldest Olmec settlement, is founded in Mesoamerica

1045 B.C. Zhou dynasty rises in China, lasting around 800 years

753 B.C. City of Rome is founded on Italian Peninsula

551 B.C. Birth of philosopher Confucius in China

c. 500 B.C. Emergence of Maya civilization in Mesoamerica

c. 324 B.C. Rise of Candragupta Maurya in India, unites country under Mauryan Empire

netw◎rks

There's More Online!

- ☑ BIOGRAPHY Hammurabi
- ☑ BIOGRAPHY Sargon I
- ☑ CHART/GRAPH Hammurabi's Code
- ☑ IMAGE Akkadian Cylinder Seal
- ☑ IMAGE Babylonian Art
- ☑ IMAGE Hammurabi's Stela
- ☑ IMAGE Victory Stele of Naram-Sin
- ☑ INTERACTIVE SELF-CHECK QUIZ
- ☑ SECONDARY SOURCE The Rise of the Akkadian Empire under Sargon
- ☑ VIDEO Akkad and Babylon

Reading HELPDESK

Academic Vocabulary

- **successor**
- **method**

Content Vocabulary

- **empire**
- **patriarchal**

TAKING NOTES:

Key Ideas and Details

Comparing and Contrasting Use a graphic organizer like the one below to compare and contrast the empires of Akkad and Babylon.

	Akkad	Babylon
Time period		
Ruler(s)		
Achievement(s)		

TEKS Texas Essential Knowledge and Skills

2C explain how major river valley civilizations influenced the development of the classical civilizations

20B identify the impact of political and legal ideas contained in the following documents: Hammurabi's Code, the Jewish Ten Commandments, Justinian's Code of Laws, Magna Carta, the English Bill of Rights, the Declaration of Independence, the U.S. Constitution, and the Declaration of the Rights of Man and of the Citizen

LESSON 1

Akkad and Babylon

ESSENTIAL QUESTIONS

- *How were empires of the ancient Near East governed?*
- *How do empires rise, how are they maintained, and what causes them to fall?*

It Matters Because

As the number of Sumerian city-states grew and the city-states expanded, new conflicts arose. City-states fought each other for control of land and water. Located on flat land, the Sumerian city-states were also open to invasion by other groups.

Akkadian Empire

GUIDING QUESTION *What were the contributions of Sargon and the Akkadians?*

To the north of the Sumerian city-states were the Akkadians (uh • KAY • dee • uhnz). They spoke a Semitic language. Around 2340 B.C., Sargon, leader of the Akkadians, overran the Sumerian city-states and set up the first empire in world history. An **empire** is a large political unit or state, usually under a single leader, that controls many peoples or territories. Empires are often easy to create, but they can be difficult to maintain. The rise and fall of empires is an important part of history.

In his new empire, Sargon used the former rulers of the conquered city-states as his governors. His power was based on the military, namely his army of 5,400 men. Sargon's empire included all of Mesopotamia as well as lands westward to the Mediterranean. Sargon was later remembered in chronicles in ancient Mesopotamia as a king who "had no rival or equal, spread his splendor over all the lands, and crossed the sea in the east."

One of Sargon's **successors**, his grandson Naram-Sin, who ruled from 2260 B.C. to 2223 B.C., continued the greatness of the Akkadian empire. Like his grandfather, Naram-Sin waged numerous military campaigns. His successes led him to boast that he was "King of the Four Corners of the Universe," and he declared himself a god. The Akkadian empire, however, did not last. Attacks from neighbors caused the Akkadian empire to fall by 2150 B.C.

✓ **READING PROGRESS CHECK**

Explaining How did Sargon establish and rule his empire?

◀ Victory Stele of Naram-Sin, c. 2200 B.C.

▶ **CRITICAL THINKING**

Making Inferences Why do you think this monument was built? What or whom does it commemorate?

Babylonian Empire

GUIDING QUESTION *What was the significance of Hammurabi's codification of laws?*

The end of the Akkadian empire brought a return to independent city-states in Mesopotamia. Finally, after a long period of warfare among the city-states, a new empire arose.

Hammurabi's Rule

In 1792 B.C. Hammurabi (HA • muh • RAH • bee), a king from Babylon, which was a city-state south of Akkad, came to power. Using divide and conquer **methods**, he gained control of Sumer and Akkad, thus creating a new Mesopotamian kingdom with its capital at Babylon. After his conquests, Hammurabi called himself "the sun of Babylon, . . . the king who caused the four quarters of the world to render obedience." After his death in 1750 B.C., however, a series of weak kings was unable to keep the empire united, and it finally fell to new invaders.

The Code of Hammurabi

For centuries in Mesopotamia, laws had regulated people's relationships with one another. During his rule, Hammurabi laid out a set of laws known as the Code of Hammurabi. This collection of laws is one of the earliest examples of a written law code, and it carries ideas of both legal and political importance. The Code of Hammurabi was based on a system of strict justice. Penalties were severe, and they varied according to the social class of the victim. A crime against a noble by a commoner was punished more severely than the same offense against a member of the lower class. Moreover, the principle of retaliation (an eye for an eye, a tooth for a tooth) was a fundamental part of this system of justice.

The legal ideas in the Code of Hammurabi had a major impact on Mesopotamia and future legal codes. The largest category of laws in the code focused on marriage and the family. Parents arranged marriages for their children. After marriage, the two parties signed a marriage contract, which made the marriage legal.

Mesopotamian society was **patriarchal**; that is, men dominated the society. Hammurabi's code shows that women had far fewer rights in marriage than men had.A husband could divorce his wife if she failed to fulfill her duties, was unable

empire a large political unit or state, usually under a single leader, that controls many peoples or territories

successor one who follows, especially one who succeeds to a throne or an office

method a systematic plan for doing something

patriarchal dominated by men

Thinking Like a **HISTORIAN**

What defines an empire?

How would you define the word *empire*? How is it different from, or similar to, other terms like *dynasty, monarchy,* or *civilization*? The term first appears in reference to the rise of city-states in the major river valleys. But how or when does state-building become empire-building? Where did historians draw that line when they called Akkad the first empire? Use the Internet to find reliable sources to determine a concrete explanation of the term *empire*. Determine how it is different from other, similar terms. Then, make your case about whether you think Akkad was or was not an empire.

CHARTS/GRAPHS

HAMMURABI'S CODE

The Code of Hammurabi addresses a wide variety of topics.

▶ CRITICAL THINKING

1 ***Comparing*** What similarities do you find between Hammurabi's Code and laws in the United States?

2 ***Speculating*** Why do you think the code was carved onto a stele like this one?

Hammurabi's Code
If any one bring an accusation of any crime before the elders, and does not prove what he has charged, he shall, if it be a capital offense charged, be put to death.
If anyone is committing a robbery and is caught, then he shall be put to death.
If a man rent his boat to a sailor, and the sailor is careless, and the boat is wrecked or goes aground, the sailor shall give the owner of the boat another boat as compensation.
If a man wishes to separate from a woman who has borne him children, or from his wife who has borne him children, then he shall give that wife her dowry, and a part of the usufruct [right of use] of field, garden, and property, so that she can rear her children.
If a son strike his father, his hands shall be hewn off.
If a man put out the eye of another man, his eye shall be put out.
If a builder build a house for some one, and does not construct it properly, and the house which he built fall in and kill its owner, then that builder shall be put to death.

▲ *The Code of Hammurabi,* c. 1760 B.C., Louvre Museum, France

to bear children, or tried to leave home to engage in business. Even harsher, a wife who neglected her home or humiliated her husband could be drowned.

Fathers ruled their children as well. Obedience was expected: "If a son strike his father, his hands shall be hewn off." If a son committed a serious enough offense, his father could disinherit him. Hammurabi's laws clearly covered almost every aspect of people's lives.

Hammurabi's code also included ideas that held a political impact. The code took the duties of public officials seriously. Officials who failed to solve crimes had to make personal restitution to the victims or their families. Judges could be penalized for ruling incorrectly on a case.

Due to Hammurabi's connection with laws, images of him can be found in several government buildings in the United States. Hammurabi is one of the many "lawgivers" depicted in marble engravings in the United States Capitol building. There is also an engraving depicting the "great lawgivers of history", including Hammurabi, on an outside wall of the U.S. Supreme Court building.

✓ READING PROGRESS CHECK

Interpreting What was Hammurabi like as a conqueror and as a ruler?

LESSON 1 REVIEW TEKS

Reviewing Vocabulary

1. ***Applying*** Why could the word *empire* apply to Hammurabi's rule of Babylon?

Using Your Notes

2. ***Comparing and Contrasting*** How were Akkad and Babylon alike and different?

Answering the Guiding Questions

3. ***Assessing*** What were the contributions of Sargon and the Akkadians?

4. ***Evaluating*** What was the significance of Hammurabi's codification of laws?

Writing Activity

5. **ARGUMENT** In a well-developed essay, create and defend a thesis that states the degree or extent to which you agree or disagree with the laws of Hammurabi's code. Focus on at least three specific ideas in the code and support your thesis with observations, examples, explanations, facts, and, if applicable, anecdotes.

networks

There's More Online!

- ☑ BIOGRAPHY Akhenaten
- ☑ BIOGRAPHY Tutankhamen
- ☑ IMAGE Art from Meroë in Kush
- ☑ IMAGE Temple of Hatshepsut
- ☑ INTERACTIVE SELF-CHECK QUIZ
- ☑ MAP The Kingdoms of Egypt, Kush, and Axum, c. 1200 B.C.–A.D. 1400
- ☑ SECONDARY SOURCE The Hyksos Invasion of Egypt
- ☑ SLIDE SHOW The Amarna Period of the New Kingdom
- ☑ VIDEO Egypt and Kush

LESSON 2
Egypt and Kush

ESSENTIAL QUESTIONS
- *How were empires of the ancient Near East governed?*
- *How do empires rise, how are they maintained, and what causes them to fall?*

Reading HELPDESK

Academic Vocabulary
- **visible**
- **assume**

Content Vocabulary
- **chariot**
- **expedition**

TAKING NOTES:
Key Ideas and Details

Sequencing Use a graphic organizer like the one below to show major events and changes in Egypt and Kush between 1650 B.C. and A.D. 150.

TEKS Texas Essential Knowledge and Skills
23B identify examples of religious influence on various events referenced in the major eras of world history

IT MATTERS BECAUSE

After a period of disorder, new dynasties of pharaohs established the New Kingdom (c. 1550–1070 B.C.). The New Kingdom restored Egyptian greatness and created an empire that made Egypt the most powerful state in the ancient Near East. To the south of Egypt, a new kingdom known as Kush emerged.

Egypt: The New Kingdom

GUIDING QUESTION *What was distinctive about the New Kingdom in ancient Egypt?*

The Middle Kingdom came to an end around 1650 B.C. with the invasion of Egypt by a group of people from western Asia known as the Hyksos (HIHK • SAHS).

Influence of the Hyksos

The Hyksos used horse-drawn war **chariots** to overwhelm the Egyptian soldiers, who fought from donkey carts. For almost 100 years, the Hyksos ruled much of Egypt. The presence of the Hyksos was not entirely negative for Egypt, however.

The conquered Egyptians learned a great deal from their conquerors. From the Hyksos, the Egyptians learned to use bronze in the making of their farming tools and their weapons. The Egyptians also mastered many of the military skills of the Hyksos, especially the use of horse-drawn war chariots. Eventually, a new dynasty of pharaohs used the new weapons to drive out the Hyksos and reunite Egypt.

Height of the New Kingdom

It was the pharaoh Ahmose I who managed to defeat and expel the Hyksos from Egypt. He reunited Egypt and established the New Kingdom, which lasted from 1550 B.C. to 1070 B.C. Ahmose also launched the Egyptians along a new militaristic path. A more professional army was developed.

▲ Temple of Hatshepsut at Deir el-Bahri

▶ **CRITICAL THINKING**

Making Connections Who was Hatshepsut? What is the modern-day significance of this temple?

chariot a two-wheeled horse-drawn battle cart, also used in processions and races

visible capable of being seen

assume to take up or in; to take control of

During the period of the New Kingdom, Egypt created an empire and became the most powerful state in the ancient Near East. Thutmosis I expanded Egypt's border to the south by conquering the African kingdom of Nubia. Thutmosis III led 17 military campaigns into Canaan and Syria and even reached as far east as the Euphrates River. His forces occupied Canaan but allowed local native princes to rule. Egypt now pursued an active political and diplomatic policy.

The new Egyptian imperial state reached its height during the reign of Amenhotep III (c. 1412–1375 B.C.). The achievements of the empire were made **visible** in the construction of magnificent new buildings and temples. Especially famous were the temple centers at Karnak and Luxor and the 70-foot-high (21.33 m) statues of Amenhotep III in front of temples along the Nile.

By the end of his reign, Amenhotep III faced a growing military challenge from the Hittites. His son, Amenhotep IV, proved to be even less able to deal with this threat. In large part, this was because of a religious upheaval that he began in Egypt.

The pharaoh Amenhotep IV introduced the worship of Aten, god of the sun disk, as the sole god. He pursued the worship of Aten with great enthusiasm. Amenhotep changed his name to Akhenaten, "Servant of Aten," and closed the temples of other gods. He even set up a new capital called Akhetaten ("Horizon of Aten"), a new city located at modern Tell el-'Amârna, 200 miles (321.87 km) north of Thebes.

Akhenaten's attempt at religious change failed. In a society that had always been tolerant of many gods, Akhenaten's actions in destroying the old gods meant to many Egyptians the destruction of Egypt itself. Akhenaten's changes were soon undone after his death by the boy-pharaoh Tutankhamen, who restored the old gods. The Aten experiment failed to take hold. During the New Kingdom, an Egyptian queen even became pharaoh in her own right. This was Hatshepsut, who at first was regent for her stepson Thutmosis III but later **assumed** the throne herself. Hatshepsut's reign was a prosperous one, as is especially evident in her building activity. She built a great temple dedicated to herself at Deir el-Bahri, near Thebes.

PHOTO: Ary Diesendruck/Stone/Getty Images

As pharaoh, Hatshepsut sent out military **expeditions**, encouraged mining, and sent a trading expedition up the Nile. Hatshepsut's official statues sometimes show her clothed and bearded like a king. She was addressed as "His Majesty." That Hatshepsut was aware of her unusual position is evident from an inscription that she placed on one of her temples. It read: "Now my heart turns to and fro, in thinking what will the people say, they who shall see my monument in after years, and shall speak of what I have done."

▲ This painting in the tomb of Sennedjem depicts Sennedjem, who lived during the reign of Ramses II, worshiping Egyptian gods.

expedition a journey taken for a specific purpose

The Egyptian Empire Ends

The upheavals associated with Amenhotep's religious revolution led to a loss of Egypt's empire. Preoccupied with religious affairs, the pharaoh ignored foreign affairs and lost both Syria and Canaan. Under Ramses II, who reigned from c. 1279 B.C. to 1213 B.C., the Egyptians went back on the offensive. They regained control of Canaan but were unable to reestablish the borders of their earlier empire. New invasions in the 1200s B.C. by the "Sea Peoples," as the Egyptians called them, destroyed Egyptian power in Canaan and drove the Egyptians back within their old frontiers. The days of the Egyptian Empire ended. The New Kingdom collapsed in 1070 B.C.

For the next thousand years, Egypt was dominated periodically by Libyans, Nubians, Persians, and, finally, Macedonians after the conquest of Alexander the Great. In the first century B.C., the pharaoh Cleopatra VII tried to reestablish Egypt's independence. Her involvement with Rome led to her defeat and suicide, and Egypt became a province in Rome's empire.

✓ READING PROGRESS CHECK

Identifying Central Ideas What was the worship of Aten, and how did it affect Egypt?

SKILLS PRACTICE

Read the part of the text that explains the relationship between Egypt and Kush. Then, study the image of the gold plaque. Work with a partner to retell what you have read by describing the ways in which Egypt influenced its neighbors.

The Kingdom of Kush

GUIDING QUESTION *How did Kush emerge as a strong early African civilization?*

South of Egypt is an area known as Nubia. By 2000 B.C., a busy trade had arisen between Egypt and Nubia. Egyptian merchants traveled to Nubia to obtain ivory, ebony wood, frankincense (a fragrant tree resin), and leopard skins. Nubia was subject to Egyptian control for many centuries. However, the collapse of the New Kingdom enabled it to free itself and become the independent state of Kush around 1000 B.C.

In 750 B.C., Kush conquered Egypt. In 663 B.C., however, the Kushites, still using bronze and stone weapons, were overwhelmed by the Assyrians, who were armed with iron spears and swords. The Kushites, driven out of Egypt, returned to their original lands in the upper Nile valley.

The economy of Kush was based at first on farming; millet and other grain crops were grown along the banks of the river. Kush soon emerged, however, as one of the major trading states in the region with its center at the city of Meroë. Well-located at the point where a newly opened land route across the desert to the north crossed the Nile River, Meroë was also blessed with a large supply of iron ore. Having learned iron smelting from the Assyrians, the Kushites made iron weapons and tools that were sent abroad.

For the next several hundred years, Kush was a major trading empire that had links to other states throughout the region. In addition to its own quality iron products, Kush provided goods from Central and East Africa for the

▼ This gold plaque depicts a king from Meroë honoring an Egyptian god.

GEOGRAPHY CONNECTION

1. **HUMAN SYSTEMS** *How did the location of each kingdom contribute to its development?*
2. **ENVIRONMENT AND SOCIETY** *Why might trade have prospered in each kingdom?*

Roman Empire as well as Arabia and India. The major exports of Kush were ivory, gold, ebony, and slaves; in return, the Kushites received luxury goods, including jewelry and silver lamps from India and Arabia.

Not much is known about Kushite society. It seems likely that it was mostly urban. At first, state authorities probably controlled foreign trade, but the presence of extensive luxury goods in the numerous private tombs in the area indicates that at one time material prosperity was relatively widespread. This suggests that a fairly large merchant class carried on trading activities. Indeed, the merchants of Meroë built large houses with central courtyards. Like the Romans, they also built public baths. Kushite prosperity was also evident in the luxurious palaces of the Kushite kings. Like the Egyptian pharaohs, these kings were buried in pyramids, although theirs were considerably smaller than those of their Egyptian models.

The state of Kush flourished from about 250 B.C. to about A.D. 150 and then began to decline, possibly because of the rise of a new power in the region. Known as Axum, it was located in the highlands of modern-day Ethiopia. Axum owed its prosperity to its location along the Red Sea, on the trade route between India and the Mediterranean Sea.

✓ **READING PROGRESS CHECK**

Describing What was life like at different times in the kingdom of Kush?

LESSON 2 REVIEW TEKS

Reviewing Vocabulary

1. ***Determining Cause and Effect*** What is a chariot, and how did it affect the outcome of the Egyptian war with the Hyksos invaders?

Using Your Notes

2. ***Summarizing*** Summarize the major events that occurred in Egypt and Kush between 1650 B.C. and A.D. 150. As you do this, introduce some of the causes and effects of these events.

Answering the Guiding Questions

3. ***Making Generalizations*** What was distinctive about the New Kingdom in ancient Egypt?
4. ***Sequencing*** How did Kush emerge as a strong early African civilization?

Writing Activity

5. **NARRATIVE** Imagine yourself as a prosperous merchant in Meroë. Describe the items you trade, using the words that are most likely to make them desirable to a buyer. Do not limit yourself to adjectives—include figurative language such as metaphors, similes, descriptive adverbs, and precise nouns as appropriate.

SKILLBUILDER

TEKS 16A

Locating Ancient Places

Why Learn This Skill?

When thinking about different eras in history, inevitably certain places of historical significance will come to mind. In studying world history and geography, we can use the combination of places of significance and location to give us a snapshot of information about the era in general. Although this snapshot will not provide us with all the information we need, we can get a good idea about the geographic necessities and events that helped define an era.

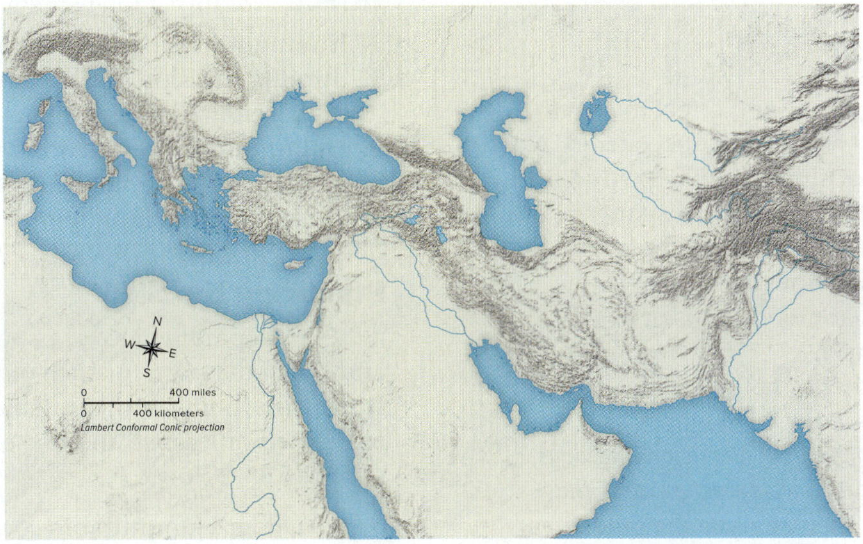

Learning the Skill

When locating places of historical significance directly related to major eras, it is important to use a map as one of your tools. However, you can also get a lot of information about why a place was significant to its time period from what you read. Ask yourself a few questions about location to help you understand a place's geographical and historical significance:

1. What are some of the defining characteristics of the historical period you are studying?
2. What needs to be present in the geography of this location in order to have these defining characteristics?
3. Why are all of these historical and geographic characteristics significant to world history?

Answering these questions will guide you in locating places of historical significance.

Knowing how the geography of an era influenced its growth will give you confidence in interpreting maps and passages in the textbook about the importance of geography.

Practicing the Skill

In the first few chapters of this textbook, you have learned the importance of ancient river valleys to civilization. These river valleys were necessary for establishing permanent agriculture, which in turn led to establishing civilizations. Beyond the earliest settlements, river valleys still played an important role in the historical significance of a region. Examine this map, which outlines river valleys in the ancient Near East. Select a particular river valley and then answer the questions in the "Learning the Skill" section, on the basis of what you see on the map and what you've learned so far in the textbook.

Applying the Skill

On the basis of what is going on in international news, select a location that you think future historians and geographers will consider significant to twenty-first century history. Either draw a map of the region or create bullet points indicating what should be highlighted on the map. Then write a paragraph addressing why you have chosen this location and what its historical and geographic significance is.

SKILLBUILDER

TEKS 29F

Understanding Cause and Effect

Why Learn This Skill?

It is important to understand how or why an event occurred in order to analyze information. What action or situation caused a particular event? What were the effects or consequences of that particular action or situation?

Learning the Skill

Understanding cause and effect involves considering how or why an event occurred. A cause is the action or situation that produces an event. An effect is the result or consequence of an action or situation. To identify cause-and-effect relationships, follow these steps:

- Identify two or more events or developments
- Decide whether or not one event causes the other. Look for "clue words" such as *because, led to, brought about, produced, as a result of, so that, since, therefore,* and *thus.*
- Identify and then analyze the outcomes of events.

Making a graphic organizer can help you identify and understand cause and effect. Read the passage below and examine the graphic organizer connected to it:

In 1792 B.C. Hammurabi, a king from Babylon, which was a city-state south of Akkad, came to power. Hammurabi had a well-disciplined army of foot soldiers who carried axes, spears, and copper or bronze daggers. He learned to divide his opponents and subdue them one by one. Using such methods, he gained control of Sumer and Akkad, thus creating a new Mesopotamian kingdom.

◄ *The Code of Hammurabi,* c. 1760 B.C., Louvre Museum, France

Cause
Hammurabi had a well-disciplined army of soldiers with axes, spears, and copper or bronze weapons. He also learned to divide his opponents.

↓

Effect
1. Hammurabi subdued his opponents through division and through weapons and the discipline of his army.
2. Hammurabi used his army to gain control of new land and create a new Mesopotamian kingdom.

Practicing the Skill

On a separate piece of paper, make a cause-and-effect diagram for each of the following statements. Some of the statements may have more than one cause and one effect. Write down your results below.

1. Under Hammurabi's code, a son found guilty of striking his father had his hand cut off.
2. Akhenaton's actions in destroying the old gods meant the destruction of Egypt itself. The upheavals associated with his religious revolution led to a loss of Egypt's empire.
3. The Kingdom of Kush, in the upper Nile valley, was a major trading state in the region. It was located where a land route across the desert to the north crossed the Nile River, and it also had a large supply of iron ore.

Applying the Skill

Read an account of a current event in your community as reported in a local newspaper. Determine at least one cause and one effect of that event and write these below. Show the cause-and-effect relationship in a chart.

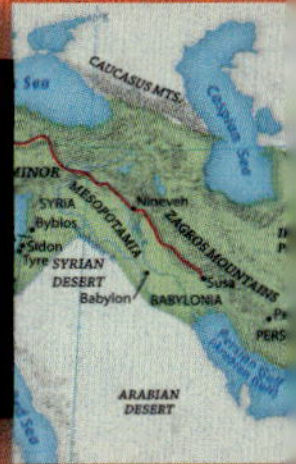

networks

There's More Online!

- ☑ BIOGRAPHY Cyrus
- ☑ IMAGE Ashurbanipal Hunting Lions
- ☑ IMAGE Darius I
- ☑ IMAGE Relief from Babylon's Ishtar Gate
- ☑ INTERACTIVE SELF-CHECK QUIZ
- ☑ MAP The Persian Empire, 500 B.C.
- ☑ PRIMARY SOURCE Zoroastrian Hymn to Ahuramazda
- ☑ SLIDE SHOW The Assyrian War Machine
- ☑ VIDEO Assyria and Persia

LESSON 3

Assyria and Persia

ESSENTIAL QUESTIONS

- *How were empires of the ancient Near East governed?*
- *How do empires rise, how are they maintained, and what causes them to fall?*

IT MATTERS BECAUSE

After 700 B.C., new empires arose in western Asia that covered vast stretches of the ancient world. The Assyrians were better at conquest than at ruling, and their empire lasted less than 100 years. The Persian Empire brought many years of peace to Southwest Asia, increasing trade and the general well-being of its people.

The Assyrian Empire

GUIDING QUESTION *What characterized the empire of the Assyrians?*

The first of the new empires was formed in Assyria, located on the upper Tigris River. The Assyrians were a Semitic-speaking people who exploited the use of iron weapons to establish an empire by 700 B.C. The Assyrian Empire included Mesopotamia, parts of the Plateau of Iran, sections of Asia Minor, Syria, Israel, and Egypt down to Thebes. In less than 100 years, however, internal strife and resentment of Assyrian rule began to tear the Assyrian Empire apart. In 612 B.C., the empire fell to a coalition of Chaldeans and Medes (people who lived in the east). Seven years later, the rest of the empire was finally divided between the two powers.

At its height, the Assyrian Empire was ruled by kings whose power was seen as absolute. Under their leadership, the Assyrian Empire became well organized. Local officials were directly responsible to the king. The Assyrians also developed an efficient system of communication to administer their empire more effectively. A network of staging posts was established throughout the empire that used relays of horses (mules or donkeys in the mountains) to carry messages. The system was so effective that a governor anywhere in the empire could send a question and receive an answer from the king within a week.

The Assyrians were good at conquering others. Through many years of practice, they developed effective military leaders and fighters. They were able to enlist and deploy troops numbering in

Reading HELPDESK

Academic Vocabulary

- **remarkable**
- **sought**
- **sustained**

Content Vocabulary

- **satrapy**
- **satrap**
- **monarchy**

TAKING NOTES:

Key Ideas and Details

Summarizing Use a graphic organizer like the one below to summarize the differences and similarities of the Assyrian and Persian Empires.

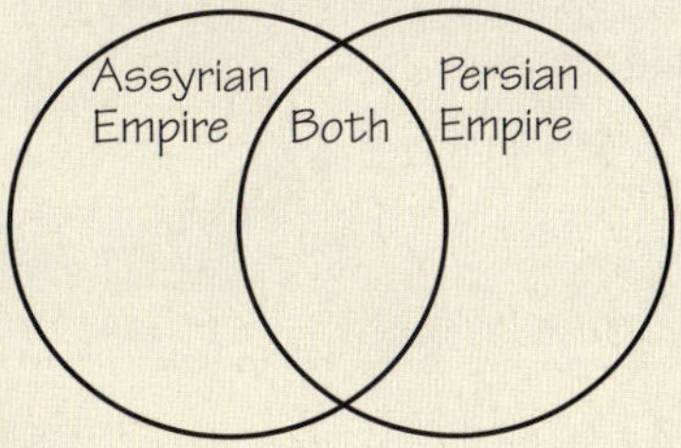

TEKS Texas Essential Knowledge and Skills

1B identify major causes and describe the major effects of the following events from 500 BC to AD 600: the development of the classical civilizations of Greece, Rome, Persia, India (Maurya and Gupta), China (Zhou, Qin, and Han), and the development of major world religions

continued on p. 67

Analyzing PRIMARY SOURCES

Assyrian Combat

"3,000 of their combat troops I felled with weapons. . . . Many I took alive; from some of these I cut off their hands to the wrist, from others I cut off their noses, ears, and fingers; I put out the eyes of many of the soldiers. . . . I burned their young men and women to death."

—Ashurbanipal, quoted in *The Might That Was Assyria*

DBQ ***IDENTIFYING POINT OF VIEW***
Do you think Ashurbanipal speaks with pride, remorse, or objectivity? Explain your answer.

the hundreds of thousands, although most campaigns were not on such a large scale. The Assyrian army was well organized and disciplined. A force of infantrymen was its core, joined by cavalrymen and horse-drawn war chariots that were used as platforms for shooting arrows. Moreover, the Assyrians had the first large armies equipped with iron weapons.

Another factor in the army's success was its ability to use different military tactics. The Assyrians could wage guerrilla warfare in the mountains and set battles on open ground, as well as lay siege to cities. They were especially known for their siege warfare. They used battering rams and siege towers to hammer at the city's walls. Then they would tunnel under them, making them collapse.

The Assyrians used terror as an instrument of warfare. They regularly laid waste to the land in which they were fighting. They smashed dams; looted and destroyed towns; set crops on fire; and cut down trees, particularly fruit trees. The Assyrians were also known for committing atrocities on their captives.

The culture of the Assyrian Empire was a mixture. The Assyrians took over much of Mesopotamian civilization. They saw themselves as guardians of Sumerian and Babylonian culture. One of the last Assyrian kings, Ashurbanipal, established one of the world's first libraries at Nineveh. This library has provided abundant information concerning ancient Southwest Asian civilizations.

✓ **READING PROGRESS CHECK**

Interpreting What factors helped the Assyrians assume and maintain power?

The Persian Empire

GUIDING QUESTION *What factors contributed to the success and ultimate fall of the Persian Empire?*

After the collapse of the Assyrian Empire, the Chaldean king Nebuchadnezzar (NEH • byuh • kuhd • NEH • zuhr) II made Babylonia the leading state in western Asia. He rebuilt Babylon as the center of his empire and gave it a reputation as one of the great cities of the ancient world. The city was most famous for its Hanging Gardens, known as one of the Seven Wonders of the

▼ This circa 650 B.C. relief of Ashurbanipal during a ceremonial lion hunt is from his palace at Nineveh.

▶ **CRITICAL THINKING**
Analyzing Visuals How are King Ashurbanipal, his servants, and the lions represented?

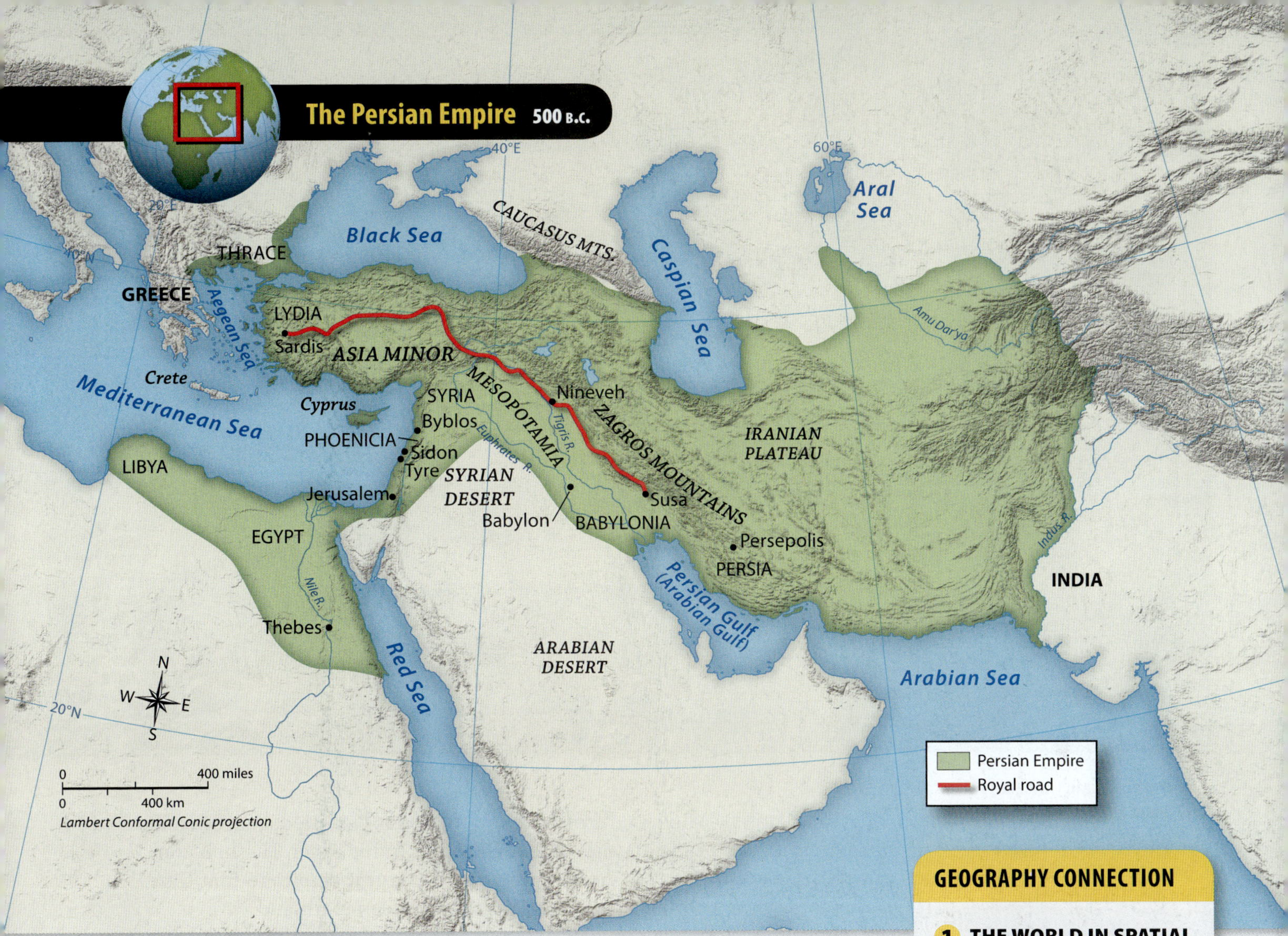

ancient world. However, the splendor of Chaldean Babylonia proved to be short-lived. Babylon fell to the Persians in 539 B.C.

The Rise of the Persian Empire

The Persians were Indo-Europeans who lived in what is today southwestern Iran. Primarily nomadic, the Persians were eventually unified by one family, the Achaemenids, leading to the development of the classical civilization of Persia. One member of this family, Cyrus, created a powerful Persian state that stretched from Asia Minor to India. Cyrus ruled from 559 B.C. to 530 B.C. In 539 B.C. he captured Babylon. His lenient treatment of Babylonia showed **remarkable** restraint. He also allowed the Jews held as captives by Babylon to return to Israel.

The people of his time called Cyrus "the Great." He demonstrated wisdom and compassion in the conquest and organization of his empire. He won approval by installing not only Persians but also native peoples as government officials in their own states. Unlike the Assyrian rulers, Cyrus had a reputation for mercy. Medes, Babylonians, and Jews all accepted him as their ruler. Cyrus had a genuine respect for other civilizations. For example, he used Assyrian, Babylonian, and Egyptian designs for building his palaces.

Cyrus's successors **sought** to extend the territory of the Persian Empire. His son Cambyses (kam • BY • SEEZ) successfully invaded Egypt. Then Darius

GEOGRAPHY CONNECTION

1. **THE WORLD IN SPATIAL TERMS** *Why was the Royal Road constructed? What accounts for its location?*
2. **PLACES AND REGIONS** *How do you think people traveled from Susa to Sardis before the Royal Road was built? Recreate the map with alternate routes. Explain what you have done.*

(continued from p. 65)

TEKS **Texas Essential Knowledge and Skills**

3A describe the major political, religious/philosophical, and cultural influences of Persia, India, China, Israel, Greece, and Rome, including the development of monotheism, Judaism, and Christianity

continued on the next page

remarkable worthy or likely to be noticed; being uncommon or extraordinary

sought made an attempt; tried

▲ An officer paying homage to King Darius I, shown here on his throne.

▶ CRITICAL THINKING
Evaluating What did King Darius accomplish during his reign?

(continued from p. 67)

TEKS **Texas Essential Knowledge and Skills**
19A identify the characteristics of monarchies and theocracies as forms of government in early civilizations
23A describe the historical origins, central ideas, and spread of major religious and philosophical traditions, including Buddhism, Christianity, Confucianism, Hinduism, Islam, Judaism, Sikhism, and the development of monotheism

satrapy one of the 20 provinces into which Darius divided the Persian Empire

satrap "protector of the Kingdom"; the governor of a province (satrapy) of the Persian Empire under Darius

sustained supported or held up

monarchy government by a sovereign ruler such as a king or queen

(duh • RY • uhs), who ruled from 521 B.C. to 486 B.C., added a new Persian province in western India that extended to the Indus River. He then conquered Thrace in Europe, creating the world's largest empire to that time. Contact with Greece led Darius to invade the Greek mainland.

Darius strengthened the Persian government. He divided the empire into 20 provinces, called **satrapies** (SAY • truh • pees). A governor, or **satrap**, literally a "protector of the kingdom," ruled each province. Each satrap collected taxes, provided justice, and recruited soldiers.

In addition to a centralized government, the Persian civilization was notable for efficient transportation and communication systems that **sustained** the empire. Officials easily traveled through the empire on well-maintained roads. The Royal Road stretched from Lydia in Asia Minor to Susa, the empire's chief capital. Like the Assyrians, the Persians set up way stations that provided shelter and supply, as well as fresh horses, for the king's messengers.

The Persian **monarchy** (a government ruled by a king or queen) of this vast administrative system. In the Persian monarchy the Persian king—the "Great King"—held an exalted position of tremendous authority, and he held the power of life and death over them. Government was centralized in the person of the king, who was supported in his rule by a large professional army and a bureaucratic administration of civil service officers. This method of governing proved effective and would influence empires created by the Greeks and Romans.

The Fall of the Persian Empire

After Darius, the Persian kings became isolated at their courts, surrounded by luxuries. As the kings increased taxes, loyalty to the empire declined. Persian kings were polygamous (having many wives) and had many children. Artaxerxes II, for example, who ruled in the fourth century B.C., had 115 sons. Of course, the sons had little real power. However, that made them even more willing to engage in plots to gain the throne. Of the nine rulers after Darius, six were murdered as a result of court intrigue. Struggles for the throne weakened the empire and led to its conquest by the Greek ruler Alexander the Great during the 330s B.C.

▼ This Zoroastrian tower, constructed near the end of the fifth century B.C., is located in modern Iran.

▶ **CRITICAL THINKING**

Making Inferences What might this tower have been used for?

Persian Religion

The religion of Zoroastrianism (zohr • uh • WAS • tree • uh • nih • zuhm) was one of Persia's major cultural, philosophical, and religious influences. According to tradition, Zoroaster, revered as a prophet of the "true religion," was born in 628 B.C. His teachings were recorded in the *Zend Avesta*, the sacred book of Zoroastrianism.

Like the Jews, Zoroastrians provide an early example of the development of monotheism. Prior to Zoroaster's time, Persians were polytheistic and worshipped many gods. Zoroaster reduced them to one: Ahuramazda, the supreme god who created all things. Though Ahuramazda was supreme, he was not unopposed. Zoroastrians believed that Ahuramazda, who was all good, was opposed by a spirit, Ahriman, that was all evil.

Zoroastrianism was influential in the development of the concepts of free will and a final judgment of humanity. Zoroaster taught that Ahuramazda, gave all humans the freedom to choose between right and wrong. Zoroaster also taught that Ahuramazda would triumph in the struggle between good and evil. At the end of the world, individuals would be judged. Those who had performed good deeds would achieve paradise, whereas those whohad performed evil deeds, would be thrown into an abyss to experience torment and misery.

✔ **READING PROGRESS CHECK**

Interpreting What was the relationship between the rise of the Persian state and Babylonia?

LESSON 3 REVIEW TEKS

Reviewing Vocabulary

1. ***Describing*** How did satraps and satrapies help Darius govern? 3A

Using Your Notes

2. ***Summarizing*** What did the Assyrian and Persian Empires have in common? How were they different?

Answering the Guiding Questions

3. ***Examining*** What characterized the empire of the Assyrians?

4. ***Identifying Cause and Effect*** What characteristics contributed to the success and ultimate fall of the Persian Empire? 1B

Writing Activity

5. **IDENTIFYING** Write a reflection on the rise and fall of the Persian Empire. How did the quality of its rulers influence the empire's success? How did the empire maintain itself and what happened to cause its decline?

CHAPTER 3 Assessment

TEKS

Directions: On a separate sheet of paper, answer the questions below. Make sure you read carefully and answer all parts of the questions.

Lesson Review

Lesson 1

1. ***Identifying*** Which civilization under what leader established the first empire in the world?

2. ***Identifying*** What was Hammurabi's Code? What is its legal and political impact? **20B**

3. ***Identifying Perspectives*** How were women viewed and treated under Hammurabi's code?

Lesson 2

4. ***Analyzing Cause and Effect*** Analyze the effects of the Hyksos invasion of Egypt, including how the invasion contained the seeds of the Hyksos eventual defeat by the Egyptians. **29F**

5. ***Specifying*** How did Ahmose I, Thutmosis I, and Thutmosis III contribute to Egypt's power?

6. ***Interpreting*** In what ways was it evident that Hatshepsut was aware of her unusual position?

7. ***Identifying Central Issues*** When and why did the Egyptian Empire end? When did the New Kingdom collapse?

8. ***Specifying*** Why did Egyptian merchants travel to Nubia?

9. ***Identifying*** What were the major exports of Kush and what did the Kushites receive in return from India and Arabia?

10. ***Comparing*** What did Kushite kings have in common with Egyptian pharaohs?

11. ***Identifying*** The state of Kush began to decline around 150 A.D. What was likely the cause?

Lesson 3

12. ***Making Inferences*** "The Assyrians were better at conquest than at ruling." Why is this so?

13. ***Identifying Perspectives*** How did the Assyrians see themselves in relation to Sumerian and Babylonian culture?

14. ***Stating*** Who made the city of Babylon the center of an empire? What happened to Babylon after his reign?

15. ***Exploring Issues*** Name three factors that helped in creating and sustaining the Persian Empire.

16. ***Describing*** Describe Cyrus's reputation with the people of his time. What did they call him?

Exploring the Essential Questions

17. ***Drawing Conclusions*** Work with a partner to create a large chart on poster board that lists reasons why the empires discussed in this chapter failed. Include visuals and primary sources to illustrate some of these reasons. Draw conclusions about why empires in general fail and what rulers might do to postpone the end.

18. ***Explaining*** Choose an empire of the ancient Near East and explain how it was governed.

Need Extra Help?

If You've Missed Question	1	2	3	4	5	6	7	8	9	10	11	12	13	14	15	16	17	18
Go to page	56	57	58	59	59	61	61	61	62	62	62	65	66	66	67	67	56	56

Critical Thinking

19. ***Making Connections*** How did the Egyptian shift to monotheism under Amenhotep IV influence events in the ancient Egyptian Empire? **23B**

20. ***Identifying Cause and Effect*** How did the rule of Cyrus the Great help develop the classical civilization of Persia? **1B**

21. ***Identifying Cause and Effect*** What effect did the Persian Royal Road have on the development of the classical civilization of Persia? **1B, 3A**

22. ***Interpreting Significance*** Who were the "Immortals," and what was the significance of their name?

23. ***Identifying Central Issues*** What major factor weakened the Persian Empire and eventually led to its conquest? Who became the next ruler?

24. ***Describing*** Where did Zoroastrianism originate? What is the central idea of Zoroastrianism? **23A**

25. ***Identifying/Explaining and Change*** Does the rise and fall of empires, from the Akkadians through the Persians, suggest that the only constant is change? Why or why not? Write a one-page essay to make your point and defend your argument.

26. ***Analyzing*** Analyze and describe the influences of the Persian religion of Zoroastrianism on the world. Make a three-column chart that lists the religious, philosophical, and cultural influences of the religion. **3A**

Social Studies Skills

27. ***Create and Analyze Arguments*** Do you think Hammurabi's Code sounds fair and just? Present an argument for why it is or is not just using specific examples.

28. ***Time, Chronology, and Sequencing*** In what chronological order did Hammurabi's kingdom, the Akkadian Empire, and independent city-states occur in Mesopotamia?

29. ***Identifying Cause and Effect*** Give three reasons why Kush was able to become a major trading empire.

30. ***Geography Skills*** How far did the Persian Empire stretch during the reign of Darius?

Need Extra Help?

If You've Missed Question	19	20	21	22	23	24	25	26	27	28	29	30
Go to page	60	67	68	67	68	69	56	69	57	56	61	68

DBQ Analyzing Primary Sources

Use the text excerpt to answer the following questions.

PRIMARY SOURCE

In about 440 B.C., Herodotus, a famous Greek historian, described the Persian postal system that had been perfected by Darius.

❝ There is nothing in the world which travels faster than the Persian couriers. The whole idea is a Persian invention, and works like this: riders are stationed along the road, equal in number to the number of days the journey takes—a man and a horse for each day. Nothing stops these couriers from covering their allotted stage in the quickest possible time—neither snow, rain, heat, nor darkness. The first, at the end of his stage, passes the dispatch to the second, the second to the third, and so on along the line, as in the Greek torch race. . . .❞

—from *The Histories,* translated by Aubrey de Sélincourt

31 ***Identifying*** What was Herodotus's opinion of the Persian postal system?

32 ***Hypothesizing*** What does the excerpt tell you about the general state of communication in the ancient world?

Analyzing Visuals

Use the map to answer the following questions.

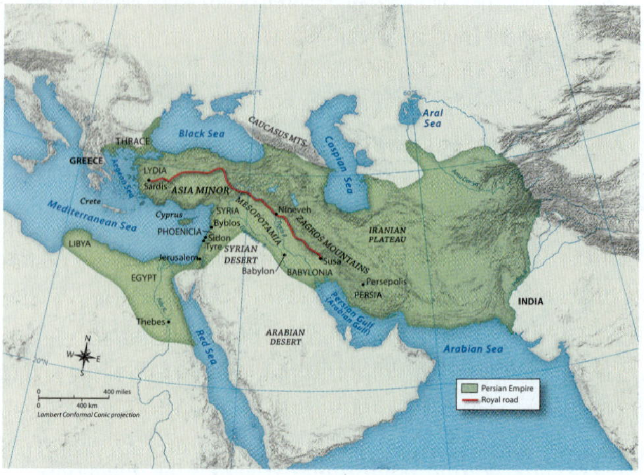

33 ***Analyzing Maps*** Which area shows where trade routes along the Persian Royal Road could move from a land route to a water route?

34 ***Analyzing Maps*** Which landform would prevent the Persian Royal Road from extending north?

Extended Response Question

35 ***Expository*** Compare the characteristics of a monarchy like the Persian Empire with other government structures you are familiar with. Write a comparison essay to compare the Persian monarchy with today's United States government. **19A**

Need Extra Help?

If You've Missed Question	31	32	33	34	35
Go to page	72	72	67	67	66

The Ancient Greeks

c. 1600 B.C.–c. 133 B.C.

ESSENTIAL QUESTIONS
- *How can geography influence political organization?*
- *How can cultural and political differences lead to conflict and change?*

networks

There's More Online! about the ancient Greeks.

CHAPTER 4

The Story Matters...

Ancient Greek culture first emerged around 1600 B.C. in Mycenae, which developed a powerful military and participated in a wide trading network. Over the next thousand years, Greek society organized itself into city-states—the most famous of which were Athens and Sparta—that served as centers of political, religious, and cultural life. In Athens during the mid-fourth century, Pericles developed a direct democracy, in which all male citizens played a direct role in government decision making.

◀ This bust depicts Pericles, an Athenian statesman, who organized the first direct democracy. Under his direction, Athens became the center of Greek culture.

PHOTO: DEA / G. NIMATALLAH/De Agostini Picture Library/ Getty Images

CHAPTER 4

Place and Time: Greece, 1600 B.C.–100 B.C.

Ancient Greek civilization marked a critical turning point in human history. Greek philosophers were the first to examine the world critically and rationally. They applied logic to philosophical, scientific, mathematical, and political questions. The Greeks developed a complex cultural tradition that included dramas, painting, sculpture, and architecture. In Athens, a democratic form of government emerged, which provided the foundation for various democratic governments today.

Step Into the Place

After reading the quotes and viewing the map, answer the following question.

DBQ **Analyzing Historical Documents** How did the Greeks perceive the role of the state and of its citizens?

PRIMARY SOURCE

“We have a form of government which does not emulate the practice of our neighbours: we are more an example to others than an imitation of them. Our constitution is called a democracy because we govern in the interests of the majority, not just the few. Our laws give equal rights to all in private disputes, but public preferment depends on individual distinction and is determined largely by merit rather than on rotation: and poverty is no barrier to office, if a man despite his humble condition has the ability to do some good to the city.”

—Pericles' funeral oration for Athenian dead, Thucydides, from *History of the Peloponnesian War,* 431 B.C.

PRIMARY SOURCE

“When several villages are united in a single community, perfect and large enough to be nearly or quite self-sufficing, the state comes into existence, originating in the bare needs of life, and continuing in existence for the sake of a good life. And therefore, if the earlier forms of society are natural, so is the state, for it is the end of them, and the nature is the end... Besides, the final cause and end of a thing is the best, and to be self-sufficing is the end and the best.

Hence it is evident that the state is a creation of nature, and that man is by nature a political animal.”

—Aristotle, from *Politics, Book I,* 350 B.C.

Step Into the Time

Making Connections Research one of the events or people from the time line and explain how it or their consequences are still felt today.

GREECE

- **1375 B.C.** Destruction of the Knossos palace on Crete
- **c. 1275 B.C.** Trojan War fought in western Anatolia (modern Turkey)

1600 B.C. — 1300 B.C.

THE WORLD

- **c. 1500 B.C.** Rise of Hinduism in India
- **1333 B.C.** King Tutankhamen, age 9, ascends the throne of Egypt

networks
There's More Online!

☑ **MAP** Explore the interactive version of this map on Networks.

☑ **TIME LINE** Explore the interactive version of the time line on Networks.

Greek City-States c. 500 B.C.

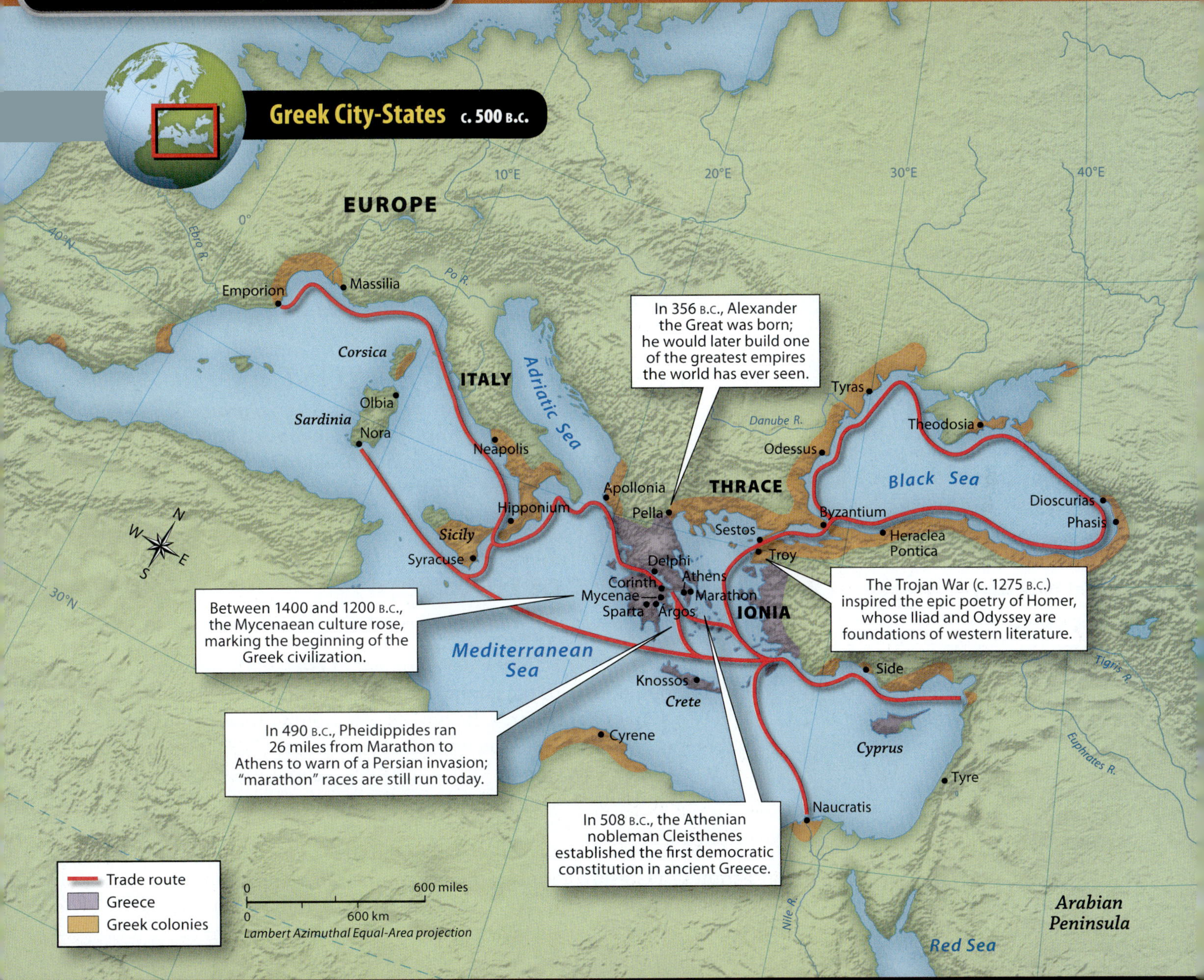

c. 1021 B.C. Israelite tribes unite under the kingship of Saul

814 B.C. Phoenicians found city of Carthage

776 B.C. First Olympic Games are held

c. 730 B.C. Sparta invades, occupies Messenia

721 B.C. Assyria conquers Israel

580 B.C. Birth of mathematician Pythagoras in Samos

c. 563 B.C. Siddhārtha Gautama, the Buddha, is born in India

509 B.C. Rome becomes a republic

479 B.C. Greeks successfully repel Persian invasion led by Xerxes

438 B.C. Dedication of the Parthenon in Athens

429 B.C. Death of Pericles, great Athenian statesman

335 B.C. Aristotle founds the Lyceum (academy) in Athens

218 B.C. Hannibal crosses the Alps in attempt to attack Rome

206 B.C. Han dynasty rises in China, defeats Qin army at the Battle of Wei

146 B.C. Romans conquer the last remnants of independent Greece

1000 B.C. | 700 B.C. | 400 B.C. | 100 B.C.

networks

There's More Online!

- BIOGRAPHY Homer
- IMAGE Greek Amphora from the Dark Age
- IMAGE Mycenaean Tholos Tomb
- IMAGE Scene from the *Iliad*
- IMAGE Statue of a Traveling Musician from the Dark Age
- INTERACTIVE SELF-CHECK QUIZ
- MAP Mycenaean Civilization
- SECONDARY SOURCE The Greek Arête
- TIME LINE The Dark Age in Greece
- VIDEO Poets and Heroes

LESSON 1

Poets and Heroes

ESSENTIAL QUESTIONS

- *How can geography influence political organization?*
- *How can cultural and political differences lead to conflict and change?*

Reading HELPDESK

Academic Vocabulary

- **isolate**
- **debated**

Content Vocabulary

- **epic poem**
- ***arete***

TAKING NOTES:

Key Ideas and Details

Comparing and Contrasting Use the following graphic organizer to compare and contrast two of Homer's epic poems.

the *Iliad* the *Odyssey*

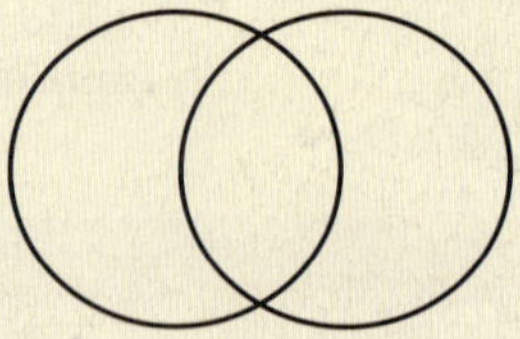

TEKS Texas Essential Knowledge and Skills

History. The student understands traditional historical points of reference in world history. The student is expected to:

1B identify major causes and describe the major effects of the following events from 500 BC to AD 600: the development of the classical civilizations of Greece, Rome, Persia, India (Maurya and Gupta), China (Zhou, Qin, and Han), and the development of major world religions

continued on the next page

IT MATTERS BECAUSE

The story of Greek civilization begins when a group of Greek-speaking Indo-European people moved into Greece around 1900 B.C. The Mycenaeans provided the inspiration for Homer's epics and paved the way for the political and cultural developments of Greece in the first millennium B.C.

The Impact of Geography

GUIDING QUESTION *How did the geography of Greece contribute to its development?*

Geography contributed to the development of **classical** Greek civilization. Compared with the landmasses of Mesopotamia and Egypt, Greece occupies a small area. It consists of a mountainous peninsula and numerous islands that encompass approximately 50,000 square miles (about 129,500 square km) of territory—about the size of the state of Louisiana. The mountains and the sea played especially significant roles in the development of Greek history.

Two peninsulas make up much of the Greek landmass. The Isthmus of Corinth connects the Peloponnesian peninsula to the mainland. About 80 percent of Greece is mountainous. Much of Greece consists of small plains and river valleys surrounded by mountain ranges from 8,000 to 10,000 feet (2,438 to 3,048 m) high. These mountains **isolated** Greeks from one another, causing different Greek communities to develop their own ways of life. Over a period of time, these communities became fiercely independent and only too willing to fight one another to gain advantage.

The sea also influenced the evolution of Greek society. The Aegean, Mediterranean, and Ionian Seas make up the eastern, southern, and western borders of Greece. Its location on a peninsula gives Greece a long seacoast dotted by bays and inlets that provided many harbors. Although Greece is small, it has an 8,500-mile (13,700-km) coastline. The ancient Greeks also lived on a number of islands to the west, south, and east of the Greek mainland. Surrounded by water, it was no accident that the Greeks became seafarers.

They sailed out into the Aegean Sea, the Mediterranean Sea, and the Black Sea, making contact with the outside world. Later they established colonies that spread Greek civilization throughout the Mediterranean world.

✓ READING PROGRESS CHECK

Making Connections What effect did Greece's mountainous geography have on the development of its culture?

Mycenae: The First Greek State

GUIDING QUESTION *What characterized the first Greek civilization of the Mycenaeans?*

The term *Mycenaean* comes from Mycenae (my • SEE • nee), a fortified site on the Greek mainland that was first discovered by the German archaeologist Heinrich Schliemann. Mycenae was part of a Mycenaean Greek civilization that flourished between 1600 B.C. and 1100 B.C.

The Mycenaean Greeks were part of the Indo-European family of peoples who spread into Europe and Asia. One of these groups entered Greece around 1900 B.C. and gradually gained control of the Greek mainland. Mycenaean civilization, which reached its high point between 1400 B.C. and 1200 B.C., was made of powerful monarchies. Each resided in a fortified palace center. Like Mycenae, these centers were built on hills and surrounded by gigantic stone walls. The monarchies in these various centers of power probably formed a loose alliance of independent states. While the royal families lived within the walls of these complexes, the

isolate to set apart from others

(continued from p. 76)

TEKS **Texas Essential Knowledge and Skills**
History. The student understands the contributions and influence of classical civilizations from 500 BC to AD 600 on subsequent civilizations. The student is expected to:

3A describe the major political, religious/philosophical, and cultural influences of Persia, India, China, Israel, Greece, and Rome, including the development of monotheism, Judaism, and Christianity

Culture. The student understands the relationship between the arts and the times during which they were created. The student is expected to:

continued on the next page

GEOGRAPHY CONNECTION

1. **HUMAN SYSTEMS** *How has Greece's geography affected settlement patterns?*
2. **PLACES AND REGIONS** *Using the map, discuss what might account for differences in the cultures of Mycenae and Troy.*

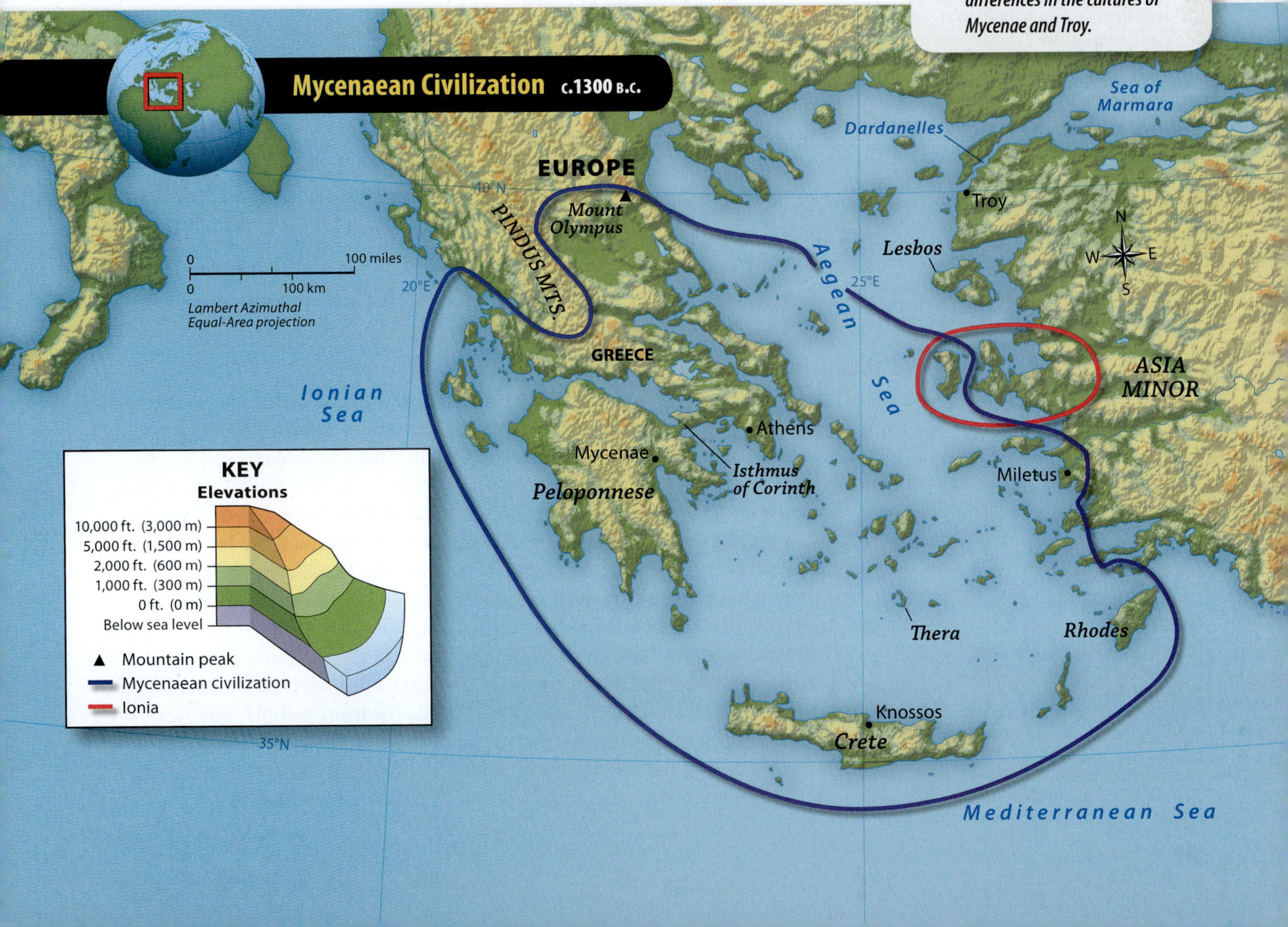

▲ Geometric patterns were typical of Greek pottery during the Dark Age. This amphora, or two-handled jar, decorated graves near the Dipylon gate in Athens.

▶ **CRITICAL THINKING**

Making Inferences What might you infer from this pottery about Greek life during the Dark Age?

debated discussed by considering opposing viewpoints

epic poem a long poem that tells the deeds of a great hero, such as the *Iliad* and the *Odyssey* of Homer

arete in early Greece, the qualities of excellence that a hero strives to win in a struggle or contest

(continued from p. 77)

TEKS **Texas Essential Knowledge and Skills**

26B analyze examples of how art, architecture, literature, music, and drama reflect the history of the cultures in which they are produced

26C identify examples of art, music, and literature that transcend the cultures in which they were created and convey universal themes

civilian populations lived scattered outside the walls. Among the noticeable features of these Mycenaean centers were the beehive-shaped tombs in which members of the royal families were buried.

The Mycenaeans were, above all, a warrior people who prided themselves on their heroic deeds in battle. Mycenaean wall murals often show war and hunting scenes.

Archaeological evidence also indicates that the Mycenaean monarchies developed an extensive commercial network. Mycenaean pottery has been found throughout the Mediterranean area, in Syria and Egypt to the east, and Sicily and southern Italy to the west. However, some historians believe that the Mycenaeans, led by Mycenae itself, also spread outward militarily, conquering Minoan Crete and making it part of the Mycenaean world.

The most famous of all their supposed military adventures is recounted in the poetry of Homer. According to Homer, Mycenaean Greeks, led by Agamemnon, king of Mycenae, sacked (plundered) the city of Troy on the northwestern coast of Asia Minor around 1250 B.C.

Did this event really occur? Ever since the excavations of Schliemann, begun in 1870, scholars have **debated** this question. Many believe that Homer's account of the attack on Troy is based on fact.

By the late thirteenth century B.C., Mycenaean Greece was showing signs of serious trouble. Mycenaean states fought one another, and major earthquakes caused widespread damage. In the twelfth century B.C., new waves of Greek-speaking invaders moved into Greece from the north. By 1100 B.C., Mycenaean civilization had collapsed.

✓ **READING PROGRESS CHECK**

Making Inferences What do the fortified palaces of the Mycenaean monarchs suggest about Mycenaean civilization?

Greeks in the Dark Age

GUIDING QUESTION ***What events occurred in ancient Greece during the Dark Age?***

After the collapse of Mycenaean civilization, Greece entered a difficult period in which the population declined and food production dropped. Historians call the period from approximately 1100 B.C. to 750 B.C. the Dark Age because few records of what happened exist. Not until 850 B.C. did the basis for a new Greece begin to form.

Changes of the Dark Age

During the Dark Age, many Greeks left the mainland and sailed across the Aegean Sea to various islands. Many went to the western shores of Asia Minor, a strip of territory that came to be called Ionia (or Ionian Greece), in modern-day Turkey.

Two other major groups of Greeks settled in established parts of Greece. The Aeolian Greeks of northern and central Greece colonized the large island of Lesbos and the territory near the mainland. The Dorians established themselves in southwestern Greece, especially in the Peloponnese, as well as on some of the southern Aegean islands.

There was a revival of some agriculture, trade, and economic activity during the Dark Age. The use of iron was central to this revival. Iron replaced bronze in weaponry, making weapons affordable for more people. Furthermore, iron farming tools helped reverse the decline in food production.

At some point in the eighth century B.C., the Greeks adopted the Phoenician alphabet to give themselves a new system of writing. By reducing all words to a combination of 24 letters, the Greeks made learning to read and write simpler. The work of Homer, one of the great poets of all time, appeared near the end of the Dark Age.

Homer: Poet of the Dark Age

The *Iliad* and the *Odyssey* were the first great epic poems of early Greece and would serve as major cultural influences throughout history. An **epic poem** is a long poem that tells the deeds of a great hero. The *Iliad* and the *Odyssey* were based on stories that had been passed down from generation to generation.

Homer used stories of the Trojan War to compose the *Iliad* and the *Odyssey.* The *Iliad* is not so much the story of the war itself, however, as it is the tale of the Greek hero Achilles (uh • KIH • leez) and how the anger of Achilles led to disaster. The *Odyssey* recounts the journeys of one of the Greek heroes, Odysseus, after the fall of Troy, and his ultimate return to his wife. It has long been considered Homer's other masterpiece.

Homer proved to be of great value to later Greeks. He did not so much record history; he created it, and it serves as a reflection of the warlike history of ancient Greek culture. The Greeks looked on the *Iliad* and the *Odyssey* as true history and as the works of one poet, Homer. These masterpieces gave the Greeks an ideal past with a cast of heroes. The epics came to be used as basic texts for the education of generations of Greek males. As one ancient Athenian stated, "My father was anxious to see me develop into a good man . . . and as a means to this end he compelled me to memorize all of Homer."

Homeric poetry taught the values of courage and honor. These values were relevant not just for ancient Greeks but for many cultures, making them **universal** themes. A hero strives for excellence, which the Greeks called ***arete*** (ahr • ah • TEE). *Arete* is won in a struggle or contest. Through his willingness to fight, the hero protects his family and friends, preserves his own honor and that of his family, and earns his reputation. Homer gave to later generations of Greek males, and males of later cultures, a model of heroism and honor.

PHOTO: Erich Lessing/Art Resource, NY

✓ READING PROGRESS CHECK

Identifying What important technological and cultural innovations occurred during Greece's Dark Age?

Analyzing PRIMARY SOURCES

The *Iliad*

"My mother Thetis, a moving silver grace,
Tells me two fates sweep me on to my death.
If I stay here and fight, I'll never return home,
But my glory will be undying forever.
If I return home to my dear fatherland
My glory is lost but my life will be long,
And death that ends all will not catch me soon."

—quote from Achilles in the *Iliad*

DBQ ***INTERPRETING*** What is the choice that Achilles faces in this passage?

▼ This statue shows a traveling musician and storyteller, or bard, like Homer.

LESSON 1 REVIEW TEKS

Reviewing Vocabulary

1. ***Defining*** Write a brief paragraph in which you identify Homer, define the epic, cite two examples of ancient Greek epic poems, and tell their universal themes. 26C

Using Your Notes

2. ***Summarizing*** Use your notes to summarize the similarities and differences between the *Iliad* and the *Odyssey,* including how they reflect the culture in which they were written and how they transcend the culture in which they were written. 3A, 26B, 26C

Answering the Guiding Questions

3. ***Making Connections*** How did the geography of Greece contribute to its development? 1B
4. ***Describing*** What characterized the first Greek civilization of the Mycenaeans?
5. ***Identifying*** What events occurred in ancient Greece during the Dark Age?

Writing Activity

6. **INFORMATIVE/EXPLANATORY** Write an essay in which you describe how the ancient Greek understanding of heroism influences the American understanding of heroism today. 3A

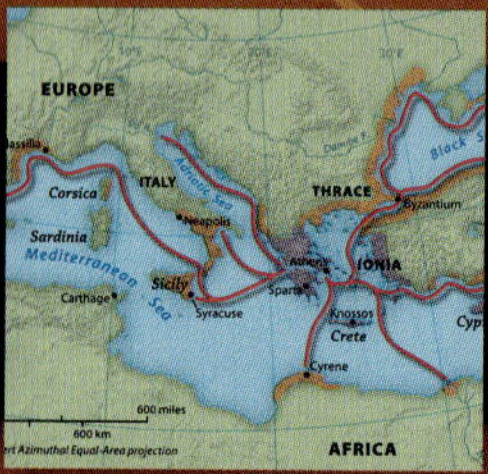

networks

There's More Online!

- BIOGRAPHY Cleisthenes
- GRAPHIC ORGANIZER Rise and Fall of Tyrants in Greek City-States
- IMAGE Acropolis
- IMAGE Spartan Helmet
- INTERACTIVE SELF-CHECK QUIZ
- MAP Greek Colonies and Trade, 750–550 B.C.
- PRIMARY SOURCE Plato's Observations on Greek Expansion
- TIME LINE The Development of Athenian Democracy
- VIDEO The Greek City-States

LESSON 2
The Greek City-States

ESSENTIAL QUESTIONS

- *How can geography influence political organization?*
- *How can cultural and political differences lead to conflict and change?*

Reading HELPDESK

Academic Vocabulary

- **assemble**
- **imply**

Content Vocabulary

- **polis**
- **agora**
- **tyrant**
- **oligarchy**
- **ephor**
- **acropolis**
- **phalanx**
- **democracy**
- **helot**

TAKING NOTES:

Key Ideas and Detail

Listing Use the following graphic organizer to list the goods that the Greeks exported to and imported from their colonies.

Exports	Imports

TEKS Texas Essential Knowledge and Skills

1B identify major causes and describe the major effects of the following events from 500 BC to AD 600: the development of the classical civilizations of Greece, Rome, Persia, India (Maurya and Gupta), China (Zhou, Qin, and Han), and the development of major world religions

continued on p. 83

IT MATTERS BECAUSE

In the course of the Dark Age, Greek villages gradually expanded and became independent city-states. The two most famous city-states were Sparta and Athens, whose rivalry would eventually lead to war.

Polis: The Center of Greek Life

GUIDING QUESTION *How were the city-states of ancient Greece organized?*

The city-state—or what the Greeks called a **polis**—became central to the development of classical civilization in Greece. By 750 B.C., the polis became the focus of Greek life. Our word *politics* is derived from the Greek word *polis*. In a physical sense, the polis was a town, a city, or even a village, along with its surrounding countryside. The town, city, or village served as the center of the polis where people could meet for political, social, and religious activities.

The central meeting place in the polis was usually a hill. At the top of the hill was a fortified area called an **acropolis** that served as both a fortress and religious center. Below the acropolis was an **agora**, an open area that served both as a place where people could **assemble** and as a market.

City-states varied greatly in size and population. Athens had a population of more than 300,000 by the fifth century B.C., but most city-states were much smaller, consisting of only a few hundred to several thousand people.

The polis was, above all, a community of people who shared a common identity and common goals. As a community, the polis consisted of citizens with political rights (adult males), citizens with no political rights (women and children), and noncitizens (including agricultural laborers, slaves, and resident aliens).

All male citizens had rights, such as the right to vote and participate in government, but these rights were coupled with responsibilities, like military service. The Greek philosopher Aristotle argued that a citizen did not belong just to himself or herself: "We must rather regard every citizen as belonging to the state." However, the loyalty that citizens had to their city-states had a negative side. City-states distrusted one another, and the division of Greece into fiercely patriotic, independent units helped bring about its ruin.

As the polis developed, so too did a new military system. IBy 700 B.C., the Greek military system had shifted from nobles on horseback to a system based on hoplites. Hoplites were heavily armed foot soldiers equipped with a round shield, a short sword, and a thrusting spear about nine feet long. Hoplites went into battle as a unit, marching shoulder to shoulder in a rectangular formation known as a **phalanx**. This close formation created a wall of shields to protect the hoplites. As long as they kept their order, it was difficult for enemies to harm them.

✓ **READING PROGRESS CHECK**

Defining How did the Greeks define the concept of citizenship?

Greek Expansion

GUIDING QUESTION *How did the Greeks spread their culture and political ideas throughout the Mediterranean?*

Between 750 B.C. and 550 B.C., large numbers of Greeks left their homeland to settle in distant lands. Overpopulation at home, a desire for good farmland, and the growth of trade were important factors in deciding to settle new places. Each Greek colony became a new polis, independent of the polis that had founded it.

Greek Colonies

Across the Mediterranean, new Greek colonies were established along the coastlines of southern Italy, southern France, eastern Spain, and northern Africa west of Egypt. At the same time, to the north, the Greeks set up colonies in Thrace, where they sought good farmland to grow grains. The Greeks also settled along the shores of the Black Sea, setting up cities on the Hellespont and the Bosporus straits. The most notable of these cities was Byzantium (buh • ZAN • shuhm), the site of what later became Constantinople and is now İstanbul. In establishing these colonies, the Greeks spread their culture and political ideas throughout the Mediterranean.

Colonization in these prime port locations also led to increased trade and industry. The Greeks on the mainland sent their pottery, wine, and olive oil to these areas. In return, they received grains and metals from the west,

polis the early Greek city-state, consisting of a city or town and its surrounding countryside

acropolis in early Greek city-states, a fortified gathering place at the top of a hill that was sometimes the site of temples and public buildings

agora in early Greek city-states, an open area that served as a gathering place and as a market

assemble to gather; to meet together

phalanx a wall of shields created by foot soldiers marching shoulder to shoulder in a rectangular formation

▼ **Ancient Athens was built near a rocky hill that could be easily fortified and defended. Temples and public buildings were located within the acropolis, shown at top.**

▶ **CRITICAL THINKING**

Drawing Conclusions Why were temples and public buildings located within the acropolis?

and fish, timber, wheat, metals, and slaves from the Black Sea region. The expansion of trade and industry created a new group of wealthy individuals in many of the Greek city-states. These men wanted political power but found it difficult to gain because of the power of the ruling aristocrats.

▲ The amphora, a jar to store wine, oil, and grain, came in all sizes. This black-figured amphora shows people gathering olives.

Tyranny in the City-States

The creation of this new group of rich men fostered the rise of tyrants in the seventh and sixth centuries B.C. Tyrants were not necessarily oppressive or wicked, as our word *tyrant* **implies**. Greek **tyrants** were rulers who seized power by force from the aristocrats.

Support for the tyrants came from the newly rich who were hungry for the social prestige and political influence that aristocrats had denied them. Poor peasants who were in debt to landholding aristocrats also supported the tyrants. Both the newly rich and the peasants were tired of aristocratic domination of their city-states.

The tyrants gained power and kept it by using hired soldiers. After they were in power, the tyrants tried to help the poor and launched public works projects. These efforts glorified the city but, more importantly, increased the tyrants' popularity. Despite their achievements, however, tyrants had fallen out of favor by the end of the sixth century B.C. Greeks believed in the rule of law, and tyranny was an insult to that ideal.

Tyranny played an important role in Greek history and in the development of classical Greek civilization. The rule of the tyrants ended the rule of the aristocrats in many city-states. The end of tyranny then allowed many new people to participate in government. In some Greek city-states, this led to the development of **democracy**, which is government by the people or rule of the many. Other city-states remained committed to government by an **oligarchy**, rule by the few. Democracy, a fundamental idea of Western civilization, remains one of the most lasting political influences of ancient Greece.

imply to express indirectly through reference or association

tyrant a ruler who seized power by force from the aristocrats, gained support from the newly rich and the poor, and maintained power by using hired soldiers and fighting tactics

democracy "the rule of many"; government by the people, either directly or through their elected representatives

oligarchy "the rule of the few"; a form of government in which a select group of people exercises control

helot in ancient Sparta, a captive person who was forced to work for the conqueror

READING PROGRESS CHECK

Identifying Which groups supported the rule of the tyrants?

Two Rival City-States

GUIDING QUESTION *What different systems of government did Sparta and Athens have?*

The differences in the Greek city-states can be understood by examining the two most famous and powerful city-states, Sparta and Athens.

Sparta

Like other Greek city-states, Sparta needed more land. Instead of starting new colonies, as some states did, the Spartans conquered the neighboring Laconians. Later, beginning around 730 B.C., the Spartans undertook the conquest of neighboring Messenia despite its larger size and population.

After their conquest, the Messenians and Laconians became serfs and were made to work for the Spartans. These captured people were known as helots, a name derived from a Greek word for "capture." To ensure control over the conquered **helots**, the Spartans made a conscious decision to create a military state.

Between 800 B.C. and 600 B.C., the lives of Spartans were rigidly organized and tightly controlled—thus, our word *spartan*, meaning "highly self-disciplined." Males spent their childhood learning military discipline. Then they enrolled in the army for regular military service at age 20.

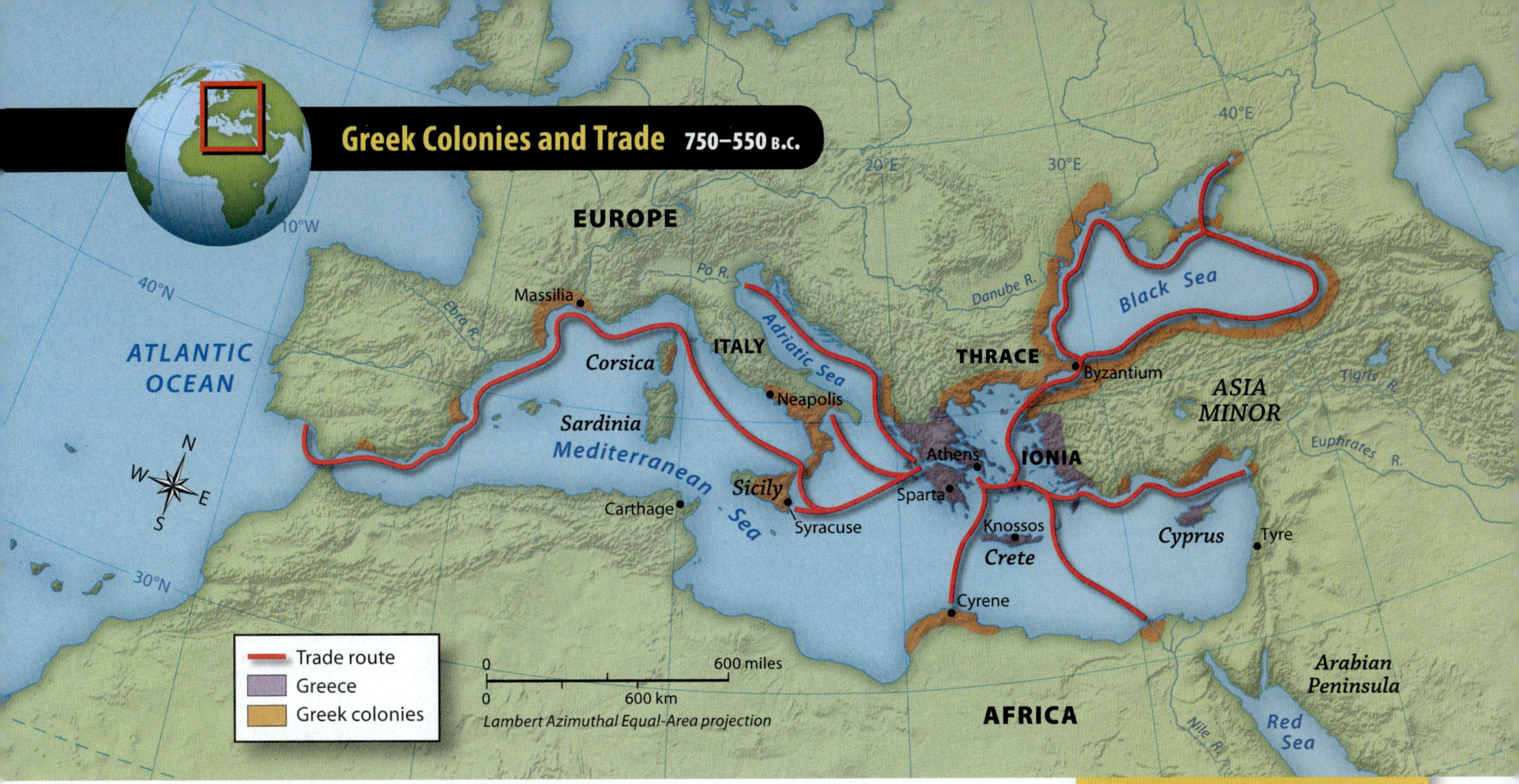

GEOGRAPHY CONNECTION

By the sixth century B.C., the Greeks used coins in trade. Each polis minted its own coins out of gold, silver, or bronze.

1. **HUMAN SYSTEMS** *Analyze the relationship between Greek trading routes and Greek colonies.*
2. **THE WORLD IN SPATIAL TERMS** *Use a modern map to list the countries where there were Greek colonies.*

Although allowed to marry, Spartan males continued to live in the military barracks until age 30. All meals were eaten in public dining halls with fellow soldiers. Meals were simple: the famous Spartan black broth consisted of a piece of pork boiled in animal blood, salt, and vinegar. A visitor who ate some of the black broth once remarked that he now understood why Spartans were not afraid to die. At 30, Spartan males were allowed to vote in the assembly (discussed later). They could live at home, but they stayed in the army until the age of 60.

While their husbands lived in the barracks, Spartan women lived at home. Because of this separation, Spartan women had greater freedom of movement and greater power in the household than was common elsewhere in Greece. Spartan women were expected to remain fit to bear and raise healthy children. Many Spartan women upheld the strict Spartan values, expecting their husbands and sons to be brave in war. The story is told of a Spartan mother who, as she handed her son his shield, told him to come back carrying his shield or being carried on it. In other words, he was not to drop his shield in retreat but to be victorious or to die bravely.

The Spartan government was an oligarchy headed by two kings, who led the Spartan army on its campaigns. A group of five men, known as the **ephors** (EH • fuhrs), were elected each year and were responsible for the education of youth and the conduct of all citizens. A council of elders, composed of the two kings and 28 citizens over the age of 60, decided on the issues that would be presented to an assembly made of male citizens. This assembly did not debate; it only voted on the issues.

To make their new military state secure, the Spartans turned their backs on the outside world. Foreigners, who might have brought in new ideas, were discouraged from visiting. Except for military reasons, Spartans were not allowed to travel abroad, where they might encounter ideas dangerous to the stability of the state. Likewise, Spartan citizens were discouraged from studying philosophy, literature, or the arts. The art of war was the Spartan ideal. All other arts were frowned upon.

(continued from p. 80)

TEKS **Texas Essential Knowledge and Skills**
3A describe the major political, religious/philosophical, and cultural influences of Persia, India, China, Israel, Greece, and Rome, including the development of monotheism, Judaism, and Christianity

continued on the next page

ephor one of the five men elected each year in ancient Sparta who were responsible for the education of youth and the conduct of all citizens.

▼ a Spartan helmet

(continued from p. 83)

TEKS **Texas Essential Knowledge and Skills**

19B identify the characteristics of the following political systems: theocracy, absolute monarchy, democracy, republic, oligarchy, limited monarchy, and totalitarianism

21A describe how people have participated in supporting or changing their governments

21B describe the rights and responsibilities of citizens and noncitizens in civic participation throughout history

24A describe the changing roles of women, children, and families during major eras of world history

25B summarize the fundamental ideas and institutions of Western civilizations that originated in Greece and Rome

Athens

By 700 B.C., Athens had become a unified polis on the peninsula of Attica. Early Athens was ruled by a king. By the seventh century B.C., however, Athens had become an oligarchy under the control of its aristocrats. These aristocrats owned the best land and controlled political life. There was an assembly of all the citizens, but it had few powers.

By the end of the 600s B.C., Athens faced political turmoil because of serious economic problems. Draco, a politician, codified the laws, adding harsh penalties, including slavery for debtors. Many Athenian farmers were sold into slavery when they were unable to pay their debts. There was an outcry to cancel the debts and to give land to the poor. Athens seemed on the verge of civil war.

The ruling Athenian aristocrats reacted to this crisis in 594 B.C. by giving full power to Solon, a reform-minded aristocrat. Solon canceled all land debts and freed people who had fallen into slavery for debts. He refused, however, to take land from the rich and to give it to the poor. Despite Solon's reforms, aristocrats were still powerful and poor peasants could not obtain land. Internal strife finally led to the very thing Solon had hoped to avoid—tyranny.

Peisistratus (pih • SIHS • truh • tuhs), an aristocrat, seized power in 560 B.C. He then aided Athenian trade as a way of pleasing the merchants. He also gave aristocrats' land to the peasants in order to gain the favor of the poor. The Athenians rebelled against Peisistratus's son, who had succeeded him, and ended the tyranny in 510 B.C. Two years later, with the backing of the Athenian people, Cleisthenes (KLYS • thuh • NEEZ), another reformer, gained the upper hand.

Cleisthenes created a new council of 500 that supervised foreign affairs, oversaw the treasury, and proposed the laws that would be voted on by the assembly. The Athenian assembly, composed of male citizens, was given final authority to pass laws after free and open debate. Because the assembly of citizens now had the central role in the Athenian political system, the reforms of Cleisthenes created the foundations for Athenian democracy.

✓ READING PROGRESS CHECK

Contrasting Identify and describe a major difference between Spartan and Athenian city-states.

LESSON 2 REVIEW *TEKS*

Reviewing Vocabulary

1. ***Analyzing Information*** What are the meanings of the terms *polis, acropolis,* and *agora?*

Using Your Notes

2. ***Identifying Central Issues*** Use your notes to list the goods that the Greeks exported to and imported from their colonies.

Answering the Guiding Questions

3. ***Analyzing*** How were the city-states of ancient Greece organized? **21B, 24A**

4. ***Identifying Cause and Effect*** How did the Greeks spread their culture and political ideas throughout the Mediterranean? **1B, 3A**

5. ***Contrasting*** What different systems of government did Sparta and Athens have? **19B**

Writing Activity

6. **PERSUASIVE** Write an essay in which you compare and contrast Sparta and Athens and argue for the superiority of one political and social system over the other. Be sure to explain what makes one system better than the other. **19B, 21A, 21B, 24A**

SKILLBUILDER

TEKS 15B

Analyzing Geographic Patterns in Maps

Why Learn This Skill?

This textbook is full of maps illustrating different empires and their defining events throughout history. There is a real potential to be overwhelmed by all the information they contain. Although they may seem very specific to a particular place and time, you can analyze them to get a bigger picture about general themes in world history. The ability to analyze and compare geographic patterns in world history through maps helps you to make connections and understand this bigger picture.

Learning the Skill

A pattern is something that occurs regularly and repeatedly, allowing you to identify a theme. There are certain elements you should look for when identifying, analyzing, and comparing geographic patterns on world history maps.

- Look for geographic elements, such as bodies of water or mountain ranges, around which patterns might occur.
- Look at the map title and key to identify what part of the world is being covered and who is involved.
- Think about maps you have viewed covering an earlier time period than the one you are currently viewing. Are there any similarities between maps beyond geographic location?

Practicing the Skill

In maps covering ancient world history, one pattern that emerges is of countries or city-states forming around strategically located bodies of water. Write out what geographic patterns you can identify on the map of the Greek Colonies and Trade, 750-550 B.C. Be sure to cover what geographic elements on the map make Greece distinctive and the role water plays in where the colonies and trade routes are located.

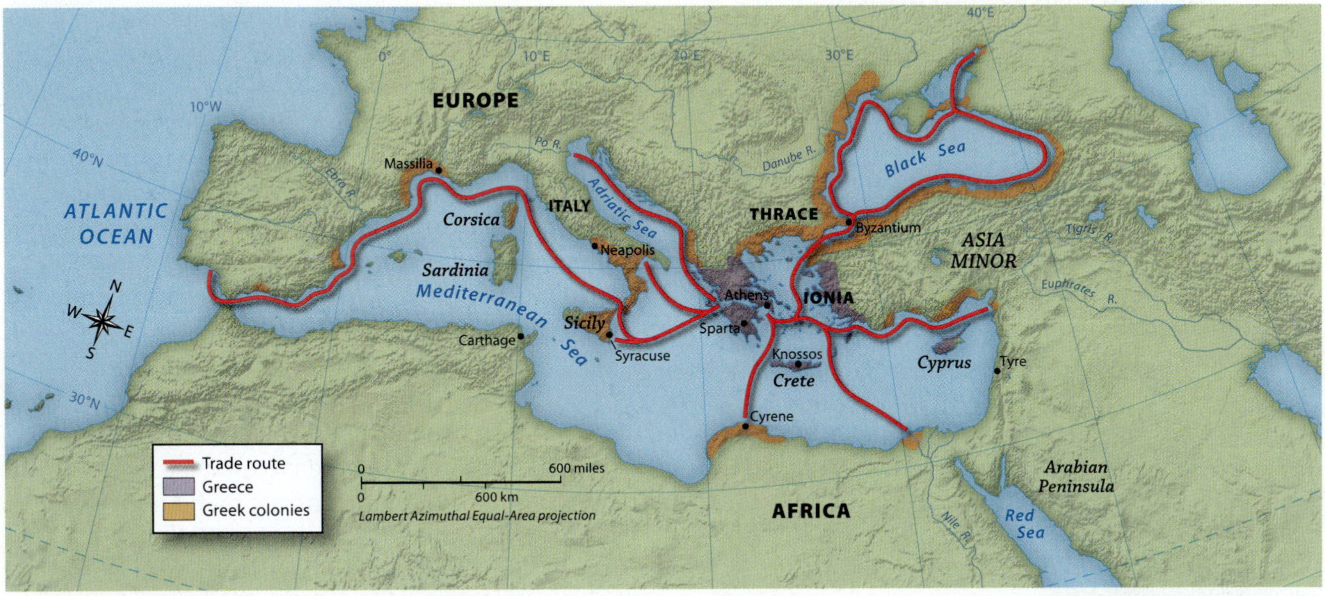

Applying the Skill

Now that you have analyzed the geographic patterns of the map on Greek Colonies and Trade, compare these patterns with a map on colonies or trade from an earlier period in time. Discuss with the class what patterns you can see emerging and whether you think these patterns will stay the same beyond the period of ancient history.

SKILLBUILDER

TEKS 29F

Making Comparisons

Why Learn This Skill?

When making comparisons, you identify the similarities and differences among two or more ideas, objects, or events.

Learning the Skill

Follow these steps to make comparisons and to contrast:

- Find two subjects that can be compared. They should be similar enough to have characteristics that are common to both. For example, it would be more appropriate to compare a Greek statue to an Egyptian statue than to an abstract modern painting.
- Determine which features they have in common that are suitable for comparison.
- Look for similarities and differences, or contrasts, within these areas.
- If possible, find information that explains the similarities and differences.

Practicing the Skill

The following passages discuss Spartan and Athenian models for raising children. Read both excerpts, and then answer the questions that follow.

◄ a Spartan helmet

Passage A

In Sparta, boys were trained to be soldiers. State officials examined all children at birth and decided whether or not they were fit to live. Those who were judged unfit were left in the open on a mountainside to die. Boys judged fit were put under control of the state at age seven. They lived in military-style barracks and were subjected to harsh discipline to make them tough. Their education stressed military training and obedience to authority.

Passage B

Athenian children were nurtured by their mothers until the age of seven when boys of the upper class were turned over to a male servant, known as a pedagogue. The pedagogue accompanied the child to school and was responsible for teaching his charge good manners. He could punish the child with a birch rod to improve discipline.

The purpose of an education for upper-class Athenian boys was to create a well-rounded person. A boy had three teachers. One taught reading, writing, and arithmetic; a second taught physical education; and a third taught music. Education ended at eighteen, when an Athenian male formally became a citizen.

1. Make a chart with one column labeled "Sparta" and one labeled "Athens." Compare how the two states raised children, then contrast by listing the differences.
2. How did the similarities and differences in raising male children suit the needs of each city-state?

Applying the Skill

Survey your classmates about an issue in the news. Summarize their opinions and compare the different results in a paragraph.

networks

There's More Online!

- ☑ BIOGRAPHY Pericles
- ☑ GRAPHIC ORGANIZER Causes and Effects of the Persian Wars
- ☑ IMAGE Ostrakon
- ☑ INFOGRAPHIC Pericles's Expansion of Athenian Democracy
- ☑ INTERACTIVE SELF-CHECK QUIZ
- ☑ MAP Peloponnesian War, 431–404 B.C.
- ☑ MAP Persian Wars, 499–479 B.C.
- ☑ SECONDARY SOURCE The Battle of Thermopylae
- ☑ VIDEO Classical Greece

Reading HELPDESK

Academic Vocabulary

- **classical**
- **strategy**

Content Vocabulary

- **Age of Pericles**
- **direct democracy**
- **ostracism**

TAKING NOTES:

Key Ideas and Details

Classifying Use the following graphic organizer to identify different groups in Athenian society and briefly describe their roles and rights.

Social Group	Roles and Rights
Adult male citizens	
Adult male foreigners	
Slaves	
Women citizens	

TEKS Texas Essential Knowledge and Skills

1B identify major causes and describe the major effects of the following events from 500 BC to AD 600: the development of the classical civilizations of Greece, Rome, Persia, India (Maurya and Gupta), China (Zhou, Qin, and Han), and the development of major world religions

continued on the next page

LESSON 3
Classical Greece

ESSENTIAL QUESTIONS

- *How can geography influence political organization?*
- *How can cultural and political differences lead to conflict and change?*

It Matters Because

Classical Greece is the name given to the period of Greek history from around 500 B.C. to the conquest of Greece by the Macedonian king Philip II in 338 B.C. This period was marked not only by a brilliant culture but also by a disastrous war among the Greeks, the Peloponnesian War.

The Challenge of Persia

GUIDING QUESTION *What did the Greek city-states do to defend themselves against Persian invaders?*

As the Greeks spread throughout the Mediterranean, they came into conflict with the Persian Empire to the east. By the mid-sixth century B.C., the Persian Empire controlled the Ionian Greek cities in western Asia Minor. In 499 B.C., these Ionian cities attempted a revolt, assisted by the Athenian navy. They were unsuccessful, but their attempt prompted the Persian ruler Darius to seek revenge. It is said that Darius ordered one of his slaves to say to him at every meal, "Sire, remember the Athenians."

In 490 B.C., the Persians landed on the plain of Marathon, only 26 miles (42 km) from Athens. There, an outnumbered Athenian army attacked and defeated the Persians decisively. The Persians returned to Asia. According to legend, news of Persia's defeat was brought by an Athenian runner named Pheidippides (fy • DIHP • uh • DEEZ), who raced from Marathon to Athens. With his last breath, he announced, "Rejoice! We win!" before dropping dead. Today's marathon race is based on this heroic story. Although the Battle of Marathon was a minor defeat to the Persians, to the Athenians, it proved that the Persians could be beaten and gave them new confidence in their city-state.

After Darius died in 486 B.C., Xerxes (ZUHRK • SEEZ) became the new Persian monarch. Xerxes vowed revenge and planned to invade Greece. In preparation for the attack, some of the Greek

GEOGRAPHY CONNECTION

1. **HUMAN SYSTEMS** *How did the strategy of the first Persian campaign differ from the second Persian campaign?*
2. **THE WORLD IN SPATIAL TERMS** *What do the locations of the major battles have in common? Why do they share this characteristic?*

(continued from p. 87)

TEKS **Texas Essential Knowledge and Skills**

3A describe the major political, religious/philosophical, and cultural influences of Persia, India, China, Israel, Greece, and Rome, including the development of monotheism, Judaism, and Christianity

19B identify the characteristics of the following political systems: theocracy, absolute monarchy, democracy, republic, oligarchy, limited monarchy, and totalitarianism

continued on p. 90

states formed a defensive league under the Spartans. The Athenians, however, followed a new military policy insisted on by Themistocles, one of the Athenian leaders, and built a navy. By the time the Persians invaded in 480 B.C., the Athenians had a fleet of about 200 vessels.

Xerxes led a massive invasion force into Greece. His forces included about 180,000 troops and thousands of warships and supply vessels. In spite of their differences, Athenians, Spartans, and other Greeks were united by a common goal of defeating the Persian invaders. The Greeks tried to delay the Persians at the pass of Thermopylae, along the main road into central Greece. A Greek force of about 7,000 held off the Persian army for two days. The 300 Spartans in the Greek army were especially brave. When told that Persian arrows would darken the sky in battle, one Spartan responded, "That's good news, we will get to fight in the shade." Unfortunately for the Greeks, a traitor told the Persians how to use a mountain path to outflank the Greek force.

The Athenians, threatened by Persian forces, abandoned their city. Near the island of Salamis, the outnumbered Greek fleet defeated the Persians. A few months later, early in 479 B.C., the Greeks formed the largest Greek army of the time and defeated the Persian army at Plataea (pluh • TEE • uh), northwest of Athens. The Greeks had won the war and were free to pursue their own destiny.

✓ **READING PROGRESS CHECK**

Identifying Central Issues What motivated Persian rulers to attack Greece?

The Athenian Empire

GUIDING QUESTION *Why was the expansion of Athenian democracy by Pericles a turning point in history?*

After the defeat of the Persians, Athens took over the leadership of the entire Greek world. In 478 B.C., the Athenians formed a defensive alliance against the Persians known as the Delian League. Its main headquarters was on the island of Delos. However, its chief officials, including the treasurers and commanders of the fleet, were Athenian. Under Athenian leadership, the Delian League pursued the attack against the Persian Empire, eventually liberating virtually all of the Greek states in the Aegean from Persian control. In 454 B.C., the Athenians moved the treasury of the league from the island of Delos to Athens on the mainland. By controlling the Delian League, Athens had created an empire.

Under Pericles, a dominant figure in Athenian politics between 461 B.C. and 429 B.C., Athens expanded its empire abroad while democracy flourished at home. This period of **classical** Athenian and Greek history, which historians have called the **Age of Pericles**, saw the height of Athenian power and brilliance.

The Age of Pericles

By creating a **direct democracy**, Pericles expanded the responsibilities and involvement of Athenian citizens in their government. In this system, every male citizen participated directly in government decision making by attending the assembly, where they voted on all major issues.

In the mid-fifth century B.C., the assembly consisted of about 43,000 male citizens older than 18 years old. Every 10 days, the assembly met on a hillside east of the Acropolis. Not all attended, and the number present seldom reached 6,000. The assembly passed all laws, elected public officials, and made decisions concerning war and foreign policy. Anyone could speak, but usually only respected leaders did so.

By making lower-class male citizens eligible for public office and by paying officeholders, Pericles made it possible for poor citizens to participate in civic affairs. Pericles believed that Athenian citizens were equal before the law and that they should be proud of their democracy. An assembly of citizens, active in self-government, would prove to be a central institution and a fundamental idea of Western civilization. This would prove to be the beginning of the development of democratic-republican government

Athenians devised the practice of **ostracism**. Members of the assembly could write on a pottery fragment (ostrakon) the name of a person they considered harmful. A person named by at least 6,000 members was banned from the city for 10 years. Athenians also had a system of justice called dikastaí, similar to a trial by jury of peers. In minor cases the dikastaí included up to 500 citizens, and up to 1500 citizens in major cases.

Under Pericles, Athens became the center of Greek culture. The power and prosperity of Athens allowed classical Greek civilization to further develop. Because warhad destroyed much of the city, Pericles began a great rebuilding program. New temples, like the Parthenon and statues signified Athens' greatness. Art, architecture, and philosophy flourished. Pericles proudly boasted that Athens had become the "school of Greece."

Daily Life in Classical Athens

By the fifth century B.C., Athens had the largest population of the Greek city-states. Before the plague in 430 B.C., there were about 300,000 people living in Athens and the surrounding area. About 43,000 of them were adult

Connections to TODAY

The Idea of Democracy

The theory and practice of democracy have undergone enormous changes since the Age of Pericles. One important difference lies in the form of government. Pericles promoted direct democracy in Athens. However, most modern democratic nations practice representative democracy. In a representative democracy, such as the United States or France, the citizens do not directly participate in a governing assembly. Instead, they elect political representatives to write laws and to govern. Another important change concerns restrictions on the right to political participation. In the twentieth century, most democratic nations extended that right to all adult citizens, regardless of race, class, or gender.

classical authoritative, traditional; relating to the literature, art, architecture, and ideals of the ancient Greek and Roman world

Age of Pericles the period between 461 B.C. and 429 B.C. when Pericles dominated Athenian politics and Athens reached the height of its power

direct democracy a system of government in which the people participate directly in government decision making through mass meetings

ostracism in ancient Athens, the process for temporarily banning ambitious politicians from the city by popular vote

▲ Built in the fifth century B.C., the "Maiden Porch" of the Erechtheum overlooks the city of Athens.

▶ **CRITICAL THINKING**

Making Inferences How might this porch have received its name?

SKILLS PRACTICE

Partner with another student. Listen carefully while your partner tells you about the daily life in classical Athens. When your partner is finished, summarize what he or she told you.

(continued from p. 88)

TEKS **Texas Essential Knowledge and Skills**

20A explain the development of democratic-republican government from its beginnings in the Judeo-Christian legal tradition and classical Greece and Rome through the English Civil War and the Enlightenment

21A describe how people have participated in supporting or changing their governments

21B describe the rights and responsibilities of citizens and noncitizens in civic participation throughout history

22B identify the influence of ideas regarding the right to a "trial by a jury of your peers" and the concepts of "innocent until proven guilty" and "equality before the law" that originated from the Judeo- Christian legal tradition and in Greece and Rome

24A describe the changing roles of women, children, and families during major eras of world history

continued on the next page

male citizens, meaning they had political power. Most residents of Athens were not citizens. Adult male foreigners living in Athens, numbering about 10,000, received the protection of the laws. Although they were noncitizens, foreigners were also subject to some of the responsibilities of citizens, such as military service.

Slavery was common in the ancient world. Slaves in Athens, who were not considered citizens, numbered around 100,000. Most often, slaves worked in the fields or in the home as cooks and maids. Some slaves were owned by the state and worked on public construction projects.

Economy and Society

The Athenian economy was largely based on farming and trade. Athenians grew grains, vegetables, and fruit for local use. Grapes and olive trees were cultivated for wine and olive oil, which were for local use and for export. Athenians raised sheep and goats for wool, milk, and dairy products.

Because of the number of people and the lack of fertile land, Athens had to import from 50 to 80 percent of its grain, a basic item in the Athenian diet. This meant that trade was highly important to the Athenian economy. The building of a port at nearby Piraeus (py • REE • uhs) helped Athens become the leading trade center in the fifth-century B.C. Greek world.

The family was an important institution in ancient Athens. It was composed of a husband, wife, and children, although Athenians also regarded other dependent relatives and even slaves as parts of their families. The family's primary role was to produce new citizens by having children.

Women were citizens who could take part in most religious festivals but otherwise were excluded from public life. They were expected to remain at home, out of sight in special quarters, unless attending funerals or festivals. If they left the house, women had to have a companion.

An Athenian woman was expected to be a good wife. Her chief obligation was to bear children, especially male children who would preserve the family line. She was also expected to take care of her family and her house. She either did the housework herself or supervised the slaves who did the work.

Women were strictly controlled. They could not own property beyond personal items. They always had a male guardian: if unmarried, a father; if married, a husband; if widowed, a son or male relative. Because they married at 14 or 15, girls learned their responsibilities early. Their mothers taught them how to run a home, including how to spin and weave cloth. Although many learned to read and to play musical instruments, girls did not have any formal education. Women did not work outside the home unless they were poor. Then they could work only at unskilled jobs.

✓ READING PROGRESS CHECK

Analyzing How did Pericles expand Athenians' involvement in their government?

The Great Peloponnesian War

GUIDING QUESTION ***How did Athens' growing power lead to conflict with Sparta?***

After the defeat of the Persians, the Greek world divided into two main camps: the Athenian Empire (Athens and the Delian League, which it controlled) and Sparta and its supporters (Peloponnesian League). Athens and Sparta had very different societies, and neither was able to tolerate the other's system. Sparta and its allies feared the growing Athenian Empire, and a series of disputes finally led to the outbreak of the Great Peloponnesian War in 431 B.C.

At the beginning of the war, both sides believed they had winning **strategies**. The Athenians planned to remain behind the city's protective walls and receive supplies from their colonies and navy. The Spartans and their allies surrounded Athens, hoping that the Athenians would send out their army to fight beyond the walls. Pericles knew, however, that the Spartan forces could beat the Athenians in open battles. The Athenians had a better navy, but the Spartans had a stronger army. Pericles also believed that Athens was secure behind its walls, so the Athenians stayed put.

In the first winter of the war, the Athenians held a public funeral to honor those who had died in combat. Pericles spoke about the greatness of Athens and the strength of its political system. In the second year of the war, a plague broke out in the overly crowded city of Athens. The plague killed more than a third of the people. Pericles himself died the following year (429 B.C.). Despite these severe losses, the Athenians fought on for about another 25 years.

A crushing blow to the Athenians came in 405 B.C., when their fleet was destroyed at Aegospotami (ee • guh • SPAH • tuh • mee) on the Hellespont. Within the next year, Athens surrendered. Its walls were torn down, the navy disbanded, and the Athenian Empire was destroyed. The great war was over, but the age of classical Greek culture and government was also.

The Great Peloponnesian War weakened the major Greek states and ruined any possibility of cooperation among them. During the next 67 years, Sparta, Athens, and Thebes (a new Greek power) struggled to dominate Greek affairs. In continuing their petty wars, the Greeks ignored the growing power of Macedonia to their north. This oversight would cost them their freedom.

READING PROGRESS CHECK

Contrasting What different strategies did Sparta and Athens adopt to fight the Peloponnesian War?

GEOGRAPHY CONNECTION

1. **PLACES AND REGIONS** *What geographical factors affected the ways in which city-states were allied?*
2. **ENVIRONMENT AND SOCIETY** *From a geographic standpoint, which side, Athens or Sparta, had an advantage in the war? Explain your answer.*

strategy a plan or method

(continued from p. 90)

TEKS **Texas Essential Knowledge and Skills**
25B summarize the fundamental ideas and institutions of Western civilizations that originated in Greece and Rome

LESSON 3 REVIEW TEKS

Reviewing Vocabulary

1. ***Analyzing Information*** What was the Age of Pericles, and how did it involve direct democracy? 19B, 21A, 21B, 25B

Using Your Notes

2. ***Organizing*** Use your notes to write a paragraph in which you describe the roles and rights of different groups in Athenian society. 21B, 24A

Answering the Guiding Questions

3. ***Explaining*** What did the Greek city-states do to defend themselves against Persian invaders?
4. ***Interpreting Significance*** Why was the expansion of Athenian democracy by Pericles a turning point in history? 1B, 3A, 20A, 25B
5. ***Analyzing Cause and Effect*** How did Athens' growing power lead to conflict with Sparta? 1B

Writing Activity

6. **DESCRIPTIVE** Describe the society and economy of classical Athens. What would daily life have been like for Athenians? 21A, 21B, 24A

networks

There's More Online!

- BIOGRAPHY Aristotle
- BIOGRAPHY Plato
- BIOGRAPHY Socrates
- CHART/GRAPH Olympian Gods
- IMAGE Greek Amphitheater
- IMAGE Parthenon
- INFOGRAPHIC Greek Myths and Theater
- INTERACTIVE SELF-CHECK QUIZ
- PRIMARY SOURCE Greek Religion in the *Iliad*
- VIDEO Classical Greek Culture

LESSON 4

Classical Greek Culture

ESSENTIAL QUESTIONS

- *How can geography influence political organization?*
- *How can cultural and political differences lead to conflict and change?*

Reading HELPDESK

Academic Vocabulary

- **method**
- **ethics**

Content Vocabulary

- **oracle**
- **tragedy**
- **philosophy**
- **Socratic method**

TAKING NOTES:

Key Ideas and Details

Differentiating Information Use a graphic organizer like the one below to understand the philosophies of Socrates, Plato, and Aristotle.

	Socrates	Plato	Aristotle
1. Views on the purpose of philosophy			
2. Views on human nature and the nature of the world			
3. Views on government			

TEKS Texas Essential Knowledge and Skills

1B identify major causes and describe the major effects of the following events from 500 BC to AD 600: the development of the classical civilizations of Greece, Rome, Persia, India (Maurya and Gupta), China (Zhou, Qin, and Han),

IT MATTERS BECAUSE

Classical Greece, especially Athens under Pericles' rule, witnessed a period of remarkable intellectual and cultural growth that became the main source of Western culture. Aristotle, Socrates, and Plato established the foundations of Western philosophy.

Greek Religion

GUIDING QUESTION *How was Greek religion an essential part of Greek society?*

Religion affected every aspect of Greek life. Greeks considered religion necessary to the well-being of the state. Temples dedicated to gods and goddesses were the major buildings in Greek cities.

Homer described the gods worshiped in the Greek religion. Twelve chief gods and goddesses were thought to live on Olympus, the highest mountain in Greece. Among the 12 were Zeus, the chief god and father of the gods; Athena, goddess of wisdom and crafts; Apollo, god of the sun and poetry; Artemis, the sister of Apollo, who was goddess of the moon and of the hunt; Ares, god of war; Aphrodite, goddess of love; and Poseidon, brother of Zeus and god of the seas and earthquakes.

Festivals developed as a way to honor the gods and goddesses. Certain festivals were held at special locations, such as those dedicated to the worship of Zeus at Olympia or to Apollo at Delphi. Numerous events, including athletic games, took place in honor of the gods at the Greek festivals. The first such games were held at the Olympic festival in 776 B.C. Today's Olympic games reflect the cultural influence of ancient Greece on the modern world.

The Greeks also had a great desire to learn the will of the gods. To do so, they made use of the **oracle**, a sacred shrine where a god or goddess was said to reveal the future through a priest or priestess. The most famous was the oracle of Apollo at Delphi. Here, a priestess, thought to be inspired by Apollo, listened to questions. Her responses were then interpreted by priests and given to the persons asking the questions.

The responses provided by the priests and priestesses were often puzzling and could be interpreted in more than one way. For example, Croesus (KREE • suhs), a king of Lydia known for his incredible wealth, sent messengers to the oracle at Delphi asking "whether he shall go to war with the Persians." The oracle replied that if Croesus attacked the Persians, he would destroy a mighty empire. Overjoyed to hear these words, Croesus made war on the Persians but was crushed. A mighty empire—that of Croesus—was destroyed!

Ancient Greek religion influenced most Greek drama and art. Although the ancient Greek religion is no longer practiced, it heavily influenced the Romans who adopted the Greek gods. Additionally, many stories and references to Greek gods appear in European and American literature.

oracle in ancient Greece, a sacred shrine where a god or goddess was said to reveal the future through a priest or priestess

(continued from p. 92)

TEKS **Texas Essential Knowledge and Skills**

3A describe the major political, religious/philosophical, and cultural influences of Persia, India, China, Israel, Greece, and Rome, including the development of monotheism, Judaism, and Christianity

25B summarize the fundamental ideas and institutions of Western civilizations that originated in Greece and Rome

continued on next page

✓ READING PROGRESS CHECK

Drawing Conclusions Was religion in Greece a public or private affair? Explain your answer.

Classical Greek Arts and Literature

GUIDING QUESTION *What groundbreaking art and literature were produced during the classical period in Greece?*

The arts of the Western world have been massively influenced by the standards set by the Greeks of the classical period. Classical Greek art was concerned with expressing eternal ideals. The subject matter of this art was the human being, presented as an object of great beauty. The classical style, with its ideals of reason, moderation, balance, and harmony in all things, was meant to civilize the emotions.

Architecture and Sculpture

In architecture, the most important form was the temple, dedicated to a god or goddess. At the center of Greek temples were walled rooms that housed both the statues of deities and treasuries in which gifts to the gods and goddesses were safeguarded. These central rooms were surrounded by a screen of marble columns that made Greek temples open structures rather than closed ones.

Some of the finest examples of Greek classical architecture were built in Athens in the fifth century B.C. The most famous building on the Acropolis, the Parthenon is regarded as the greatest example of the classical Greek temple. Built between 447 B.C. and 432 B.C., it is a reflection of the classical culture of the Greek city-states. Dedicated to Athena, the patron goddess of Athens, the Parthenon was an expression of the Athenians' pride in their city-state. Indeed, it was dedicated not only to Athena but also to the glory of Athens. The Parthenon exemplifies the principles of classical architecture: the search for calmness, clarity, and freedom from unnecessary detail.

Greek sculpture also developed a classical style. Lifelike statues of the male nude, the favorite subject of Greek sculptors, showed relaxed attitudes. Their faces were self-assured, their bodies flexible and smooth

▼ **The Parthenon in Athens was a temple dedicated to the Greek goddess Athena.**

▶ CRITICAL THINKING

Analyzing Visuals How does the Parthenon exemplify Greek classical architecture?

Analyzing PRIMARY SOURCES

The nature of mankind

"Many are the wonders, none is more wonderful than what is man. This it is that crosses the sea with the south winds storming and the waves swelling. . . . He it is again who wears away the Earth . . . as the ploughs wind across her from year to year. . . . A cunning fellow is man. His contrivances make him master of beasts of the field . . . and [he has taught himself] how to avoid the sharp frost . . . and pelting strokes of the rain. . . . Only against death can he call on no means of escape."

—Sophocles, from *Antigone*

DBQ ***DRAWING CONCLUSIONS***
What is the central point of this speech on the nature of human beings?

(continued from p. 93)

TEKS **Texas Essential Knowledge and Skills**

26A identify significant examples of art and architecture that demonstrate an artistic ideal or visual principle from selected cultures

26B analyze examples of how art, architecture, literature, music, and drama reflect the history of the cultures in which they are produced

26C identify examples of art, music, and literature that transcend the cultures in which they were created and convey universal themes

27A identify the origin and diffusion of major ideas in mathematics, science, and technology that occurred in river valley civilizations, classical Greece and Rome, classical India, and the Islamic caliphates between 700 and 1200 and in China from the Tang to Ming dynasties

muscled. Classical Greek sculptors did not seek to achieve realism, however, but rather a standard of ideal beauty. Polyclitus (PAH • lih • KLY • tuhs), a fifth-century sculptor, wrote down systematic rules for proportions that he illustrated in a work known as the *Doryphoros.* His theory maintained that the use of ideal proportions, based on mathematical ratios found in nature, could produce an ideal human form.

Drama

Drama as we know it in Western culture was created by the Greeks. Plays were presented in outdoor theaters as part of religious festivals. The first Greek dramas were **tragedies**, which were presented in a trilogy—a set of three plays—built around a common theme. The only complete trilogy we possess today, called the *Oresteia,* was composed by Aeschylus. This set of three plays relates the fate of Agamemnon, a hero of the Trojan War, and his family after his return from the war. In the plays, evil acts are shown to breed more evil acts and suffering. In the end, however, reason triumphs over the forces of evil.

Another great Athenian playwright was Sophocles, whose most famous play was *Oedipus Rex.* In this play, the oracle of Apollo foretells how Oedipus will kill his own father and marry his mother. Despite all attempts to prevent this, Oedipus does commit these tragic acts.

A third outstanding Athenian dramatist, Euripides, tried to create more realistic characters in real-life situations. Euripides was controversial. He questioned traditional values, portraying war as brutal and barbaric.

Greek tragedies dealt with universal themes still culturally relevant today. They examined problems such as the nature of good and evil, the rights of the individual, the nature of divine forces, and the nature of human beings. In the world of the Greek tragedies, striving to do the best thing may not always lead to success, but the attempt is a worthy endeavor. Greeks took great pride in their accomplishments and independence.

Greek comedy developed later than tragedy. Comedies were used to criticize politicians and intellectuals and were meant both to entertain and to provoke a reaction. Aristophanes, a good example of a Greek comedian, filled his plays with puns and satire.

The Writing of History

History, as we know it—a systematic analysis of past events—was created in the Western world by the Greeks. Herodotus (hih • RAH • duh • tuhs) wrote *History of the Persian Wars,* often seen as the first real history in Western civilization. Its central theme is the conflict between the Greeks and the Persians, which Herodotus viewed as a struggle between Greek freedom and Persian despotism. Herodotus traveled widely and questioned many people as a means of obtaining his information. He was a master storyteller.

Many historians today consider Thucydides (thoo • SIH • duh • DEEZ) the greatest historian of the ancient world. Thucydides was an Athenian general who fought in the Great Peloponnesian War and later wrote its history. Unlike Herodotus, he saw war and politics as caused by the activities of human beings, not gods. He examined the Peloponnesian War clearly and fairly, placing much emphasis on the accuracy of his facts. Thucydides also provided remarkable insight into the human condition. He believed that the study of history was of great value in understanding the present.

✓ READING PROGRESS CHECK

Identifying Central Issues What was an overarching goal of classical Greek artists and writers?

Greek Philosophy

GUIDING QUESTION *What were the philosophical ideas that came out of ancient Greece?*

Philosophy refers to an organized system of thought. The term comes from Greek roots that mean "love of wisdom." Early Greek philosophers focused on the development of critical or rational thought about the nature of the universe. Greek philosophy influenced scholars in the ancient world and continues to influence thinkers [or people] up to the present day.

Sophists

The Sophists were a group of traveling teachers in ancient Greece who rejected speculation. They argued that it was simply beyond the reach of the human mind to understand the universe. It was more important for individuals to improve themselves. The Sophists stressed the importance of rhetoric (the art of persuasive speaking necessary for winning debates and swaying audiences). This skill was especially valuable in democratic Athens.

Socrates

Socrates was a sculptor whose true love was philosophy. Because Socrates left no writings, we know about him only through what we have learned from the writings of his pupils, such as Plato. Socrates taught many pupils, but he accepted no pay. He believed that the goal of education was only to improve the individual.

Socrates used a teaching **method** that is still that is still used today and which carries his name. The **Socratic method** of teaching uses a question-and-answer format to lead pupils to see things for themselves by using their own reasoning skills. Socrates believed that all real knowledge is already present within each person. Only critical examination is needed to call it forth. This is the real task of philosophy, because, as Socrates said, "The unexamined life is not worth living." This belief in the individual's ability to reason was an important contribution of the Greeks.

Socrates questioned authority, which soon led him into trouble. Athens had had a tradition of free thought and inquiry, but defeat in the Peloponnesian War changed the Athenians. They no longer trusted open debate. Socrates was accused and convicted of corrupting the youth of Athens by teaching them to question and think for themselves. An Athenian jury sentenced him to die by drinking hemlock, a poison.

Plato

One of Socrates' students was Plato, considered by many the greatest philosopher of Western civilization. Unlike Socrates, Plato wrote a great deal. He was fascinated with the question of reality: How do we know what is real?

According to Plato, a higher world of eternal, unchanging Forms has always existed. These ideal Forms make up reality, and only a trained mind—the goal of philosophy—can become aware of or understand these Forms. To Plato, the objects that we perceive with our senses (trees, for example) are simply reflections of the ideal Forms (treeness). They (the trees) are but shadows. Reality is found in the Form (treeness) itself.

Plato explained his ideas about government in an influential work entitled *The Republic.* Plato had come to distrust the workings of democracy in Athens. To him, individuals could not achieve a good life unless they lived in a just and rational state. In Plato's ideal state, people were divided into three basic groups. At the top was an upper class of philosopher-kings. The second group were warriors, and the third group contained all the rest—people driven not by wisdom or courage but by desire. The third group were society's producers—artisans, tradespeople, and farmers. When each of these

Analyzing PRIMARY SOURCES

Thucydides on history

"And with regard to my factual reporting of the events of the war I have made it a principle not to write down the first story that came my way, and not even to be guided by my own general impressions; either I was present myself at the events which I have described or else I heard of them from eye-witnesses whose reports I have checked with as much thoroughness as possible."

—Thucydides, from the *History of the Peloponnesian War*

DBQ ***INTERPRETING*** How did Thucydides approach the study of history?

tragedy a form of drama that portrays a conflict between the protagonist and a superior force and having a protagonist who is brought to ruin or extreme sorrow, especially as a result of a fatal flaw

philosophy an organized system of thought, from the Greek for "love of wisdom"

method a systematic plan for doing something

Socratic method the method of teaching used by the Greek philosopher Socrates; it employs a question-and-answer format to lead pupils to see things for themselves by using their own reason

ethics moral principles; generally recognized rules of conduct

Analyzing PRIMARY SOURCES

Plato's *The Republic*

"Unless either philosophers become kings in their countries or those who are now called kings and rulers come to be sufficiently inspired with a genuine desire for wisdom; unless, that is to say, political power and philosophy meet together . . . there can be no rest from troubles . . . for states, nor for all mankind."

—Plato, from *The Republic, Book II*

DBQ ***DRAWING CONCLUSIONS***

How did Plato propose to create his ideal system of government?

▲ Aristotle argued that investigation and observation were the best ways to learn about the nature of the universe.

groups performed its appropriate role in society, society would function smoothly. Contrary to Greek custom, Plato also believed that men and women should have the same education and equal access to all positions.

Aristotle

Plato established a school in Athens that was known as the Academy, one of the first institutions of learning in Western civilization. His most famous pupil was Aristotle. Aristotle did not accept Plato's theory of ideal forms. He thought that by examining individual objects (trees), we could perceive their form (treeness). However, he did not believe that these forms existed in a separate, higher world of reality beyond material things. Rather, he thought of forms as a part of things themselves. (In other words, we know what treeness is by examining trees.)

Aristotle's interests, then, lay in analyzing and classifying things based on observation and investigation. Aristotle's line of inquiry formed the basis for the scientific method we use today—a method characterized by empirical observation, measurement, and experimentation. He defined entire categories of scientific study, such as logic, biology, and physics, and wrote about a range of subjects, including **ethics**, politics, poetry, and the sciences. Until the seventeenth century, science in the Western world was heavily influenced by Aristotle's ideas.

Like Plato, Aristotle wanted an effective form of government that would rationally direct human affairs. Unlike Plato, he did not seek an ideal state but tried to find the best form of government by analyzing existing governments. For his *Politics,* Aristotle discussed three good forms of government: monarchy, aristocracy, and constitutional government. He slightly favored constitutional government, which can be democratic, as the best form for most people.

✓ **READING PROGRESS CHECK**

Contrasting How did Plato and Aristotle differ in their opinions on government?

LESSON 4 REVIEW TEKS

Reviewing Vocabulary

1. ***Drawing Conclusions*** What is an oracle, and why was it important to the Greeks? 23B

Using Your Notes

2. ***Organizing Information*** Use your notes to explain the fundamental differences between the philosophies of Socrates, Plato, and Aristotle. 3A, 27A

Answering the Guiding Questions

3. ***Drawing Conclusions*** How was Greek religion an essential part of Greek society?
4. ***Evaluating*** What groundbreaking art and literature were produced during the classical period in Greece? 3A, 26A, 26C
5. ***Interpreting Significance*** What were the philosophical ideas that came out of ancient Greece? 27A

Writing Activity

6. **EXPOSITORY** Write several paragraphs on how Greek society centered around religion. Examine how religion affected all classes of people, society, art, literature, and politics. 23B, 26B

networks

There's More Online!

- BIOGRAPHY Alexander the Great
- BIOGRAPHY Philip II
- CHART/GRAPH Epicureanism and Stoicism
- IMAGE Alexander's Defeat of Darius III
- IMAGE Mosaic from Alexandria
- INTERACTIVE SELF-CHECK QUIZ
- MAP The Empire of Alexander the Great, 323 B.C.
- PRIMARY SOURCE The Legacy of Alexander the Great
- VIDEO Alexander and the Hellenistic Era

LESSON 5

Alexander and the Hellenistic Era

ESSENTIAL QUESTIONS

- *How can geography influence political organization?*
- *How can cultural and political differences lead to conflict and change?*

IT MATTERS BECAUSE

Under the leadership of Alexander the Great, Macedonians and Greeks united to invade and conquer the Persian Empire. In the conquered lands, Greeks and non-Greeks formed a new society in what is known as the Hellenistic era.

Macedonians Invade Greece

GUIDING QUESTION *How did the Macedonians and Greeks conquer the Persian Empire?*

The Greeks viewed their northern neighbors, the Macedonians, as barbarians. The Macedonians were rural people organized in groups, not in city-states like the Greeks. By the end of the fifth century B.C., however, Macedonia emerged as a powerful kingdom.

Philip and Alexander

In 359 B.C., Philip II came to the throne. He built a powerful army and turned Macedonia into the chief power of the Greek world. Philip was soon drawn into Greek affairs. A great admirer of Greek culture, he longed to unite all of Greece under Macedonia. Fearing Philip, the Athenians allied with a number of other Greek states and fought the Macedonians at the Battle of Chaeronea (KEHR • uh • NEE • uh), near Thebes, in 338 B.C. The Macedonian army crushed the Greeks.

Philip quickly brought an end to the freedom of the Greek city-states. He insisted that the Greek states form a league and then cooperate with him in a war against Persia. Before Philip could undertake his invasion of Asia, however, he was assassinated, leaving the task to his son Alexander.

Alexander the Great was only 20 years old when he became king of Macedonia. However, Philip had carefully prepared his son for kingship. By taking Alexander along with him on military campaigns, Philip taught Alexander the basics of military leadership. After his father's death, Alexander moved quickly to fulfill his father's dream—the invasion of the Persian Empire. He was

Reading HELPDESK

Academic Vocabulary

- **subsidizing**
- **founder**

Content Vocabulary

- **Hellenistic Era**
- **Epicureanism**
- **Stoicism**

TAKING NOTES:

Key Ideas and Details

Identifying Use a graphic organizer like the one below to summarize the accomplishments of Hellenistic scientists and philosophers.

Philosopher/ Scientist	Accomplishment/ Theory

TEKS Texas Essential Knowledge and Skills

3A describe the major political, religious/philosophical, and cultural influences of Persia, India, China, Israel, Greece, and Rome, including the development of monotheism, Judaism, and Christianity

continued on p. 99

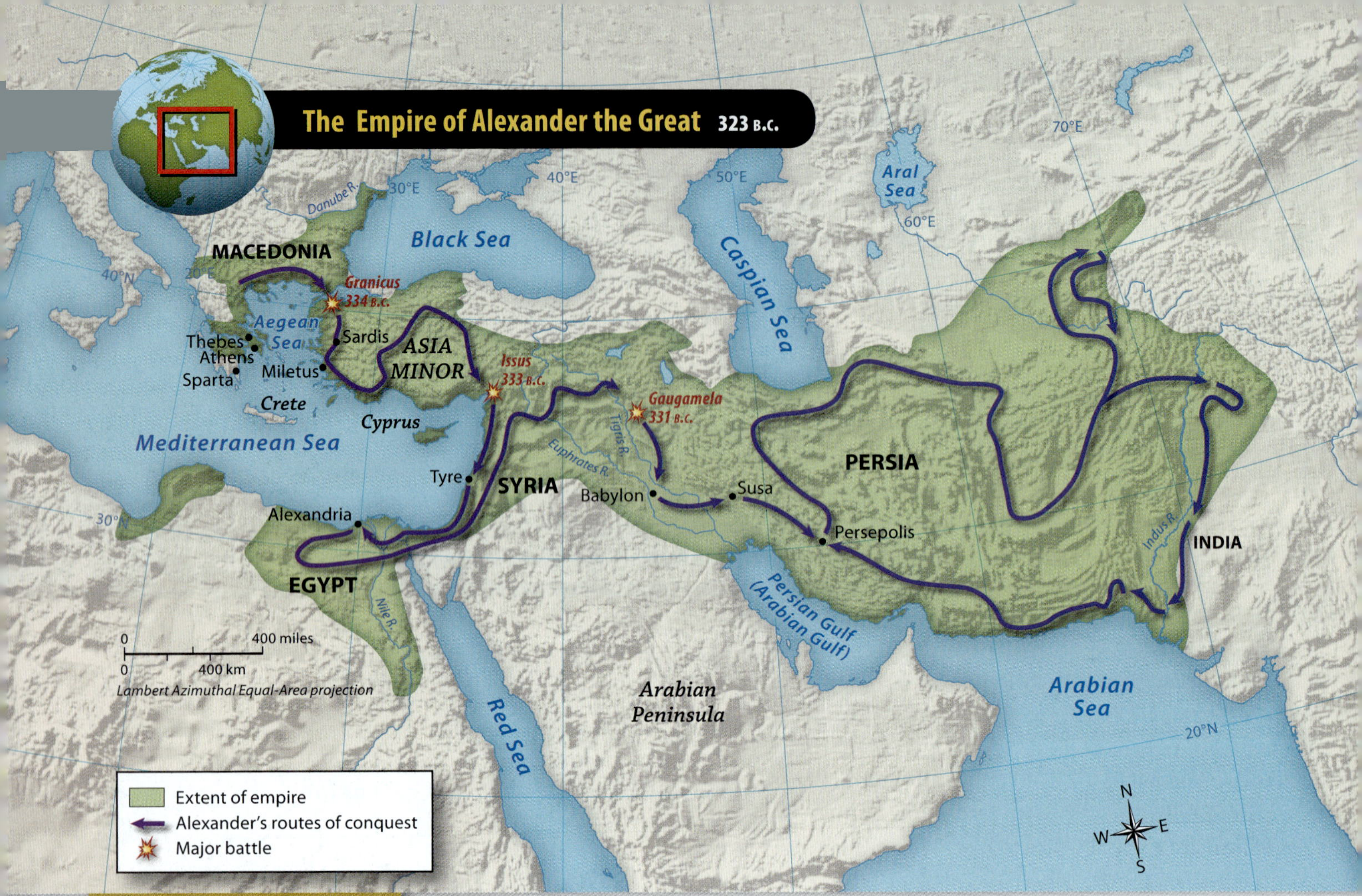

GEOGRAPHY CONNECTION

1. **ENVIRONMENT AND SOCIETY** *Does it appear that physical boundaries limited the extent of Alexander's empire? Explain your answer.*
2. **THE USES OF GEOGRAPHY** *Reproduce the map and draw modern-day country boundaries.*

motivated by the desire for glory and empire but also by the desire to avenge the Persian burning of Athens in 480 B.C.

Alexander's Conquests

Alexander was taking a chance in attacking the Persian Empire. Although weakened, it was still a strong state in the spring of 334 B.C. when Alexander entered Asia Minor with an army of some 37,000 men, both Macedonians and Greeks. The cavalry, which would play an important role as a striking force, numbered about 5,000.

By the next year, Alexander had freed the Ionian Greek cities of western Asia Minor from the Persians and defeated a large Persian army at Issus. He then turned south. By the winter of 332 B.C., Alexander had Syria and Egypt under his control. He built Alexandria as the Greek capital of Egypt. It became and remains today one of the most important cities in both Egypt and the Mediterranean world. It was also the first of a series of cities named after Alexander.

In 331 B.C., Alexander turned east and fought the decisive battle with the Persians at Gaugamela, not far from Babylon. Soon, Alexander controlled the rest of the Persian Empire. Over the next three years, he moved as far as modern Pakistan. In 326 B.C., he reached India, where the campaigning was hard. When his soldiers refused to go farther, he agreed to go home. He led his troops across the desert of today's southern Iran. Many were dying of thirst. At one point, some soldier found a little water and offered it to him. According to an ancient Greek writer, Alexander poured it onto the ground: "So extraordinary was the effect of this action that the water wasted by Alexander was as good as a drink for every man in the army."

SKILLS PRACTICE

During the discussion about Alexander the Great, listen for the main ideas about his conquests and his legacy and put them in your notes. As you write the main ideas, list supporting details below them.

Alexander returned to Babylon, planning more conquests. But in 323 B.C., exhausted from wounds, fever, and too much alcohol, he died. He was 32 years old.

▲ Portrait of Alexander the Great, circa 330 B.C.

Alexander's Legacy

Alexander's extraordinary success is explained by his leadership and military skills. He was a master of strategy and tactics, able to fight in all terrains and against all kinds of opponents. Brave and even reckless, he risked his own life, an example that inspired his soldiers to follow him. Alexander sought to imitate Achilles, the hero of Homer's *Iliad.* He kept a copy of the *Iliad*—and a dagger—under his pillow.

Alexander's legacy was enormous. He extended Greek and Macedonian rule over a vast area. Alexander's successors tried to imitate him, using force and claims of divine rule to create military monarchies. Although mainland Greeks remained committed to the ideals of the city-state, the creation of monarchies became part of Alexander's political legacy.

Alexander also left a cultural legacy as Greek language, architecture, literature, art, and religious diversity spread throughout parts of Asia and North Africa. Greek culture blended with aspects of Eastern culture to become a new Hellenistic culture.

✓ **READING PROGRESS CHECK**

Determining Cause and Effect How did the rule of Alexander the Great affect Greek culture?

The Hellenistic Era

GUIDING QUESTION ***What was the significance of Hellenistic cities as a result of Alexander the Great's conquests?***

Alexander created a new age, the **Hellenistic Era**. This new era is evidence of the impact of the classical civilization of Greece. The word *Hellenistic* is derived from Greek roots meaning "to imitate Greeks." It is a good way to describe an age that saw the expansion of the Greek language and ideas to the non-Greek world of Southwest Asia and beyond.

Hellenistic Era the age of Alexander the Great; period when the Greek language and ideas were carried to the non-Greek world

Hellenistic Kingdoms

Alexander's empire fell apart soon after his death. The most important Macedonian generals engaged in a struggle for power, and by 300 B.C., any hope of unity was dead Four Hellenistic kingdoms emerged as the successors to Alexander: Macedonia, Syria in the east, the kingdom of Pergamum in western Asia Minor, and Egypt. All were eventually conquered by the Romans.

Alexander the Great had planned to fuse Macedonians, Greeks, and Persians into his new empire by using Persians as officials and encouraging his soldiers to marry native women. The Hellenistic monarchs who succeeded him, however, relied only on Greeks and Macedonians to form the new ruling class. Even those from eastern regions who did advance to important government posts had learned Greek, for all government business was transacted in Greek.

In his conquests, Alexander had created a series of new cities and military settlements. Hellenistic kings did likewise. These new population centers varied in size from military settlements of only a few hundred men to cities with thousands of people. Alexandria, which Alexander had founded in Egypt, was the largest city in the Mediterranean region by the first century B.C.

(continued from p. 97)

TEKS **Texas Essential Knowledge and Skills**

27A identify the origin and diffusion of major ideas in mathematics, science, and technology that occurred in river valley civilizations, classical Greece and Rome, classical India, and the Islamic caliphates between 700 and 1200 and in China from the Tang to Ming dynasties

27E identify the contributions of significant scientists such as Archimedes, Copernicus, Eratosthenes, Galileo, Pythagoras, Isaac Newton, and Robert Boyle

Hellenistic rulers encouraged a spread of Greek colonists to Southwest Asia. Greeks (and Macedonians) provided not only new recruits for the army but also a pool of civilian administrators and workers. Architects, engineers, dramatists, and actors were all in high demand in the new Greek cities. The Greek cities of the Hellenistic Era became the chief agents in the spread of Greek culture in Southwest Asia—as far, in fact, as modern Afghanistan and India.

Hellenistic Arts and Literature

The Hellenistic Era was a period of considerable cultural accomplishment in many areas, especially science and philosophy. These achievements occurred throughout the Hellenistic world. Certain centers, however, stood out. Alexandria became home to poets, writers, philosophers, and scientists—scholars of all kinds. The library in Alexandria became the largest in ancient times, with more than 500,000 scrolls. The library encouraged the study of literature and language. There was also a museum that welcomed scholarly research.

▲ A Roman mosaic floor panel from Alexandria, Egypt

The founding of new cities and the rebuilding of old ones presented opportunities for Greek architects and sculptors. Hellenistic kings were very willing to spend money to beautify the cities within their states. The buildings characteristic of the Greek homeland—baths, theaters, and temples—lined the streets of these cities.

Both Hellenistic kings and rich citizens patronized sculptors. Thousands of statues were erected in towns and cities all over the Hellenistic world. Hellenistic sculptors maintained the technical skill of the classical period, but they moved away from the idealism of earlier classicism to a more emotional and realistic art. This is especially evident in the numerous statues of elderly women and young children.

subsidizing aiding or promoting with public money

The Hellenistic age also produced a great quantity of literature. Writing talent was held in high esteem, especially by Hellenistic leaders, who spent large amounts of money **subsidizing** writers. Unfortunately, very little of this literature has survived. Apollonius of Rhodes wrote the epic poem *Argonautica,* which tells the story of Jason's search for the Golden Fleece. Theocritus wrote short poems that expressed a love of nature and an appreciation of its beauty.

Athens remained the center of Greek theatre. A new type of comedy developed that sought only to entertain and to amuse and avoided political commentary. Menander was perhaps the most successful of these new playwrights.

Science, Mathematics and Technology

founder one who founds or establishes

Epicureanism the school of thought developed by the philosopher Epicurus in Hellenistic Athens; it held that happiness is the chief goal in life, and the means to achieve happiness was the pursuit of pleasure

The Hellenistic age witnessed considerable advances in the science of astronomy and in mathematics. One astronomer, Aristarchus (AR • uh • STAHR • kuhs) of Samos, developed the theory that the sun is at the center of the universe while the Earth rotates around the sun in a circular orbit. The prevailing view, in contrast, held that Earth was at the center of the universe. The new theory was not widely accepted at the time.

Eratosthenes (EHR • uh • TAHS • thuh • neez) was another important astronomer. He determined that Earth was round and calculated Earth's circumference at 24,675 miles (39,702 km), an estimate that was within 185 miles (298 km) of the actual figure. The mathematician Euclid wrote *Elements*, a textbook on plane geometry.

The most famous scientist of the Hellenistic era was Archimedes (AHR • kuh • MEE • deez) of Syracuse. He worked on the geometry of spheres and cylinders and also established the value of the mathematical constant pi. A practical inventor too, he may have devised the "Archimedes' screw," a machine used to pump water out of mines and to lift irrigation water. Archimedes' achievements inspired a number of stories. Supposedly, he discovered specific gravity by observing the water he displaced in his bath. He then became so excited by his realization that he jumped out of the water and ran home naked, shouting, "Eureka!" ("I have found it!").

Many of the works and ideas of these Greek scientists and mathematicians have been used up to modern times. Passed from Greece to ancient Rome, they have come to modern times by way of scientists and philosophers in the Arab world and from Europe over 500 years ago. As with the ideas of Plato and Aristotle, the ideas of these thinkers have become the foundation for much of Western thought.

Hellenistic Philosophy

Epicurus, the **founder** of **Epicureanism**, began a school in Athens at the end of the fourth century B.C. He believed that human beings were free to follow their own self-interest and make happiness their goal. The means to happiness was the pursuit of pleasure, the only true good. Epicurus did not speak of the pursuit of pleasure in a physical sense (which is what our word *epicurean* has come to mean). Instead, pleasure was freedom from emotional turmoil and worry. To achieve this, people had to free themselves from public activity.

Another school of thought was **Stoicism**. It became the most popular philosophy of the Hellenistic world and later flourished in the Roman Empire as well. Stoicism was the product of a teacher named Zeno. Zeno came to Athens and began to teach in a building known as the Painted Portico (the *Stoa Poikile*—hence, the word *Stoicism*).

Like Epicureans, Stoics wanted to find happiness, but they thought it could be found only by living in harmony with the will of God. Then they could bear whatever life offered (hence, our word *stoic*). Unlike Epicureans, Stoics did not want to separate themselves from the world. Public service was regarded as noble. The real Stoic was a good citizen.

✓ **READING PROGRESS CHECK**

Analyzing Information How are the arts and the sciences of the Hellenistic Age connected?

Analyzing PRIMARY SOURCES

Archimedes on water displacement

"[Archimedes] happened to go to the bath, and on getting into the tub observed that the more [he] sank into it the more water ran out over the tub... Without a moment's delay, and transported with joy, he jumped out of the tub and rushed home ... crying with a loud voice that he had found what he was seeking; for as he ran he shouted repeatedly in Greek, 'Eureka! Eureka!'"

—Vitruvius, from *De architectura*, Book IX

DBQ ***MAKING INFERENCES*** How does this description of Archimedes' discovery of the theory of water displacement illustrate the Hellenistic methods of scientific study?

Stoicism the school of thought developed by the teacher Zeno in Hellenistic Athens; it says that happiness can be achieved only when people gain inner peace by living in harmony with the will of God and that people should bear whatever life offers

LESSON 5 REVIEW TEKS

Reviewing Vocabulary

1. ***Analyzing Information*** What is a subsidy, and why is it important to cultural development?

Using Your Notes

2. ***Identifying*** Use your graphic organizer to write a paragraph on the theories or accomplishments of three major Hellenistic Era scientists or philosophers. 27A, 27E

3. ***Identifying*** Use your graphic organizer to write a paragraph identifying the theories or accomplishments of major Hellenistic Era scientists/inventors, mathematicians, or philosophers and describing the diffusion of these ideas. 27A, 27E

Answering the Guiding Questions

4. ***Drawing Conclusions*** How did the Macedonians and Greeks conquer the Persian Empire?

5. ***Evaluating*** What was the significance of Hellenistic cities as a result of Alexander the Great's conquests? 3A

Writing Activity

6. **ARGUMENT** Was the Hellenistic Era the most productive and inspired time in Greek history? Consider the following: politics, religion, art, literature/drama, architecture, science, mathematics, technology, and philosophy. Provide reasons and evidence and use precise terms in your argument. Anticipate and address any counterarguments.

CHAPTER 4 Assessment

TEKS

Directions: On a separate sheet of paper, answer the questions below. Make sure you read carefully and answer all parts of the questions.

Lesson Review

Lesson 1

1. ***Drawing Inferences*** What effect did geography have on how the Greeks related to each other and to the world? **1B**

2. ***Naming*** What was the first Greek state? Where was it located and during which period did it flourish?

3. ***Explaining*** What purpose did the beehive-shaped tombs serve in Mycenaean centers?

4. ***Drawing Conclusions*** Mycenaean pottery has been discovered throughout the Mediterranean area. What does this tell us about the Mycenaean monarchies?

5. ***Describing*** What did Homer write? What important purposes did his writings serve for later generations? How did his works both reflect and transcend classical Greek culture and convey universal themes? **3A, 26B, 26C**

6. ***Interpreting*** What period is known as the Dark Age? Where does its name come from?

7. ***Explaining*** Why was iron so important during the Dark Age?

8. ***Summarizing*** How did the Greeks simplify reading and writing in the eighth century B.C.?

Lesson 2

9. ***Describing*** By 750 B.C., the polis became the central focus of Greek life. Describe what this was and its significance to the people of the time.

10. ***Identifying Cause and Effect*** What were some of the reasons that Greeks began leaving their homeland between 750 B.C. and 550 B.C.? How did this affect their culture and political ideas?

11. ***Summarizing*** What happened to the Messenians and Laconians after the Spartans conquered them?

12. ***Describing*** What was life like for males in Sparta between 800 B.C. and 600 B.C.?

13. ***Explaining*** Why weren't Spartans allowed to travel abroad? What other restrictions were placed on the people of Sparta?

14. ***Making Connections*** How were the Spartan oligarchy and the Athenian democracy similar and different? **3A, 19B, 20A, 25B**

15. ***Specifying*** How did the Greeks participate in changing their government, and what were the rights and responsibilities of citizens? **21A, 21B**

Lesson 3

16. ***Explaining*** Explain the legend of Pheidippedes. How is it still relevant today?

Need Extra Help?

If You've Missed Question	1	2	3	4	5	6	7	8	9	10	11	12	13	14	15	16
Go to page	76	77	78	78	79	78	78	78	80	81	82	82	83	83	84	87

17 ***Identifying*** What common goal united the Athenians, Spartans, and other Greeks?

18 ***Describing*** What was the Delian League? What was its role in helping Athens create an empire?

19 ***Explaining*** Explain the role of the Athenian woman. What was her life like, including her obligations and the restrictions placed on her?

20 ***Summarizing*** In Greece, how did citizens participate in supporting their government? What were the rights and responsibilities of noncitizens, women, and families? **21A, 21B, 24A**

21 ***Exploring Issues*** How did the Greeks influence ideas such as "trial by jury," "innocent until proven guilty," or "equality before the law"? **22B**

Lesson 4

22 ***Explaining*** What were three ways the Greeks expressed their religious beliefs? How did religion influence various historical events? **3A, 23B**

23 ***Analyzing*** How did Greek art, architecture, or drama both reflect and transcend Greek culture and convey universal themes? **26A, 26B, 26C**

Lesson 5

24 ***Identifying Central Issues*** How did Alexander the Great plan to govern his new empire? After Alexander died, why did his empire fall apart? **3A**

25 ***Making Generalizations*** What were some of the innovations in mathematics, science, or technology during classical or Hellenistic Greece? Describe the diffusion of these ideas. **27A, 27E**

Exploring the Essential Questions

26 ***Analyzing Cause and Effect*** How can geography influence political organization? **1B**

27 ***Analyzing Cause and Effect*** How can cultural and political differences lead to conflict and change? **1B**

Critical Thinking

28 ***Analyzing Cause and Effect*** How did the culture of the Mycenaean Greeks spread throughout the Mediterranean world? **1B, 3A**

29 ***Collecting Information*** Where and how did the roots of democracy develop? **3A, 20A**

30 ***Analyzing Cause and Effect*** How did Alexander the Great help spread Greek culture into southwest Asia? **1B, 3A**

31 ***Making Generalizations*** Why do you think science and the arts, including architecture, literature, and drama, flourished during the Hellenistic Age? **26B**

32 ***Understanding Relationships*** Why did a civilization that celebrated harmony in its art and philosophy spend so much time on war over the centuries? Consider the influences of cultural ideals, literature, and colonization. Present your answer along with supporting reasons and evidence in the form of an essay. **26B**

Need Extra Help?

If You've Missed Question	17	18	19	20	21	22	23	24	25	26	27	28	29	30	31	32
Go to page	88	89	90	90	89	92	93	97	100	76	82	76	82	77	100	77

Social Studies Skills

33 ***Identifying Differing Interpretations*** How did Pericles create a direct democracy? What about ancient Athenian democracy is unlike democracy as we know it today? 3A, 19B

34 ***Comparing and Contrasting*** How were Herodotus and Thucydides similar or different in how they recorded history?

35 ***Time, Chronology, and Sequencing*** Work with a small group to create a multimedia presentation showing the evolution of Greece from Mycenaean forts to the Hellenistic period. Presentations could include visuals, video, and audio, including quotations, literary excerpts, and music, showing how Greece changed over time. 3A, 26B

DBQ Analyzing Primary Sources

Use the text excerpt to answer the following questions.

Plutarch was a Greek writer and priest of Apollo who lived about 400 years after Alexander the Great.

PRIMARY SOURCE

"Alexander did not follow Aristotle's advice to treat the Greeks as if he were their leader, and other peoples as if he were their master; to have regard for the Greeks as for friends and kindred, but to conduct himself toward other peoples as though they were plants or animals;. . . But Alexander desired to render all upon earth subject to one law of reason and one form of government and to reveal all men as one people, and to this purpose he made himself conform."

—from Plutarch's *Moralia*

36 ***Speculating*** Would the world have been better off if Alexander the Great had lived another 20 years? Why?

37 ***Understanding Historical Interpretation*** What does Lesson 5 say about Alexander's unfulfilled plans that confirms Plutarch's claim that he had planned to "reveal all men as one people"? 3A

Analyzing Visuals

Use the image of the artifact to answer the following questions.

38 ***Analyzing*** How does the amphora demonstrate the artistic ideals or visual principles of Greece? 26A

39 ***Identifying Central Issues*** How does the amphora convey universal themes? 26C

Extended Response Question

40 ***Explaining Continuity and Change*** Generate a list of philosophical or religious elements of ancient Greek culture that have influenced civilization. Write an essay that communicates information about one or more significant contributions and assess their long-lasting effects. Draw references where applicable to modern society. 3A

Need Extra Help?

If You've Missed Question	33	34	35	36	37	38	39	40
Go to page	89	94	77	104	99	82	82	92

India's First Empires

c. 1000 B.C.–A.D. 500

ESSENTIAL QUESTIONS

- *How was early Indian culture influenced by religion and social structure?*
- *How did ideas and events during the Mauryan and Gupta Empires affect India's development?*

networks

There's More Online! about India's first empires.

CHAPTER 5

The Story Matters...

Hinduism and Buddhism were vital to the development of Indian culture. Hinduism emerged after the Aryan migration into India between 1500 B.C. and 400 B.C. Buddhism evolved after the sixth century B.C. when Siddhārtha Gautama, who came to be known as the Buddha, began to spread his message throughout India. These religions came to influence the way Indians thought about government and social structures. Hinduism and Buddhism also inspired great works of literature and architecture. Some Buddhist temples, called stupas, were many stories tall, and others were carved into rock cliffs. These temples were often decorated with frescoes depicting the life of the Buddha.

◀ This fresco from the Ajanta caves in western India depicts the Bodhisattva, or Buddha-to-be. Depictions of scenes from the Buddha's life are a common theme in Buddhist art.

CHAPTER 5

Place and Time: Ancient India 1000 B.C.–A.D. 500

During this era, India was a civilization in transition. People began migrating to and settling in India. At the same time, empires rose and fell. The most significant arrivals were the Aryans, whose writings (the Vedas) became the foundation for Hinduism, the caste (varna) *system, and after 600 B.C., Buddhism. Trade played an important role in the early Indian empires. Buddhism spread throughout Asia via trade routes. By the beginning of the first century A.D., India traded with the eastern Mediterranean, Africa, and Asia, importing glass, copper, and wine and exporting pepper, pearls, and ivory. The Gupta Empire also established trade with China and encouraged domestic trade. As the Gupta wealth grew, so did the rich culture of the empire.*

Step Into the Place

After looking at the map and reading the sources, answer the following question.

DBQ **Analyzing Historical Documents** How did India in this time period interact with foreign powers?

PRIMARY SOURCE

“For India is a land of exceptional beauty, and since it is crossed by many rivers it is supplied with water over its whole area and produces two harvests each year. As a result it has such an abundance of the necessities of life that at all times it blesses its inhabitants with plentiful enjoyment of them. People say that because of the favorable climate in those parts the country has never endured famine or the destruction of crops. Also, it has an unbelievable profusion of elephants, which both in courage and bodily strength far surpass those of Libya, and likewise gold, silver, iron and copper; further, one can find within its borders great quantities of precious stones of every kind and of almost all other objects which contribute to luxury and wealth.”

—Diodorus Siculus, a Greek historian writing in the first century B.C., quoted in *The Making of Roman India*

PRIMARY SOURCE

“Everywhere, from the Sandy Desert, in all the countries of [central] India, the kings had been firm believers in [Buddhist] Law. When they make their offerings to a community of monks, they take off their royal caps, and along with their relatives and ministers, supply them with food with their own hands. That done, (the king) has a carpet spread for himself on the ground, and sits down on it in front of the chairman;—they dare not presume to sit on couches in front of the community [of monks].”

—Faxian's account of his travels in India, A.D. 402

PHOTO: Thomas J. Abercrombie/National Geographic/Getty Images

Step Into the Time

Intergrating Information

Research one of the capitals mentioned in the time line. Write an essay explaining how the capital's location played a role in its success or failure.

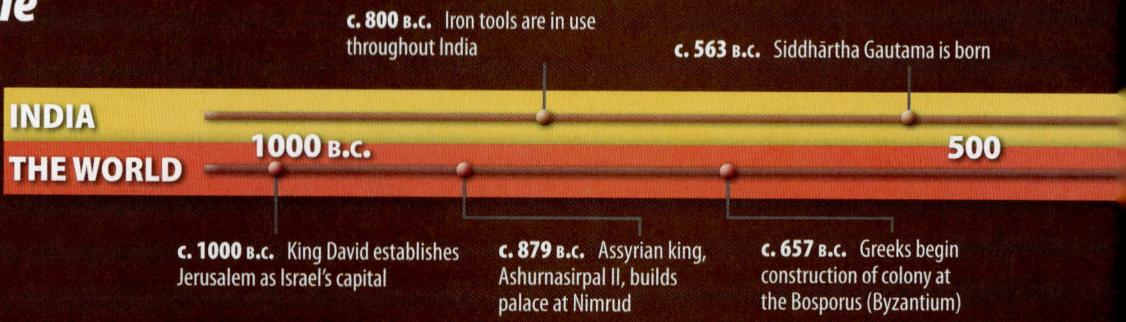

networks
There's More Online!

- **MAP** Explore the interactive version of this map on Networks.
- **TIME LINE** Explore the interactive version of the time line on Networks.

Trade in the Gupta Empire c. A.D. 320–540

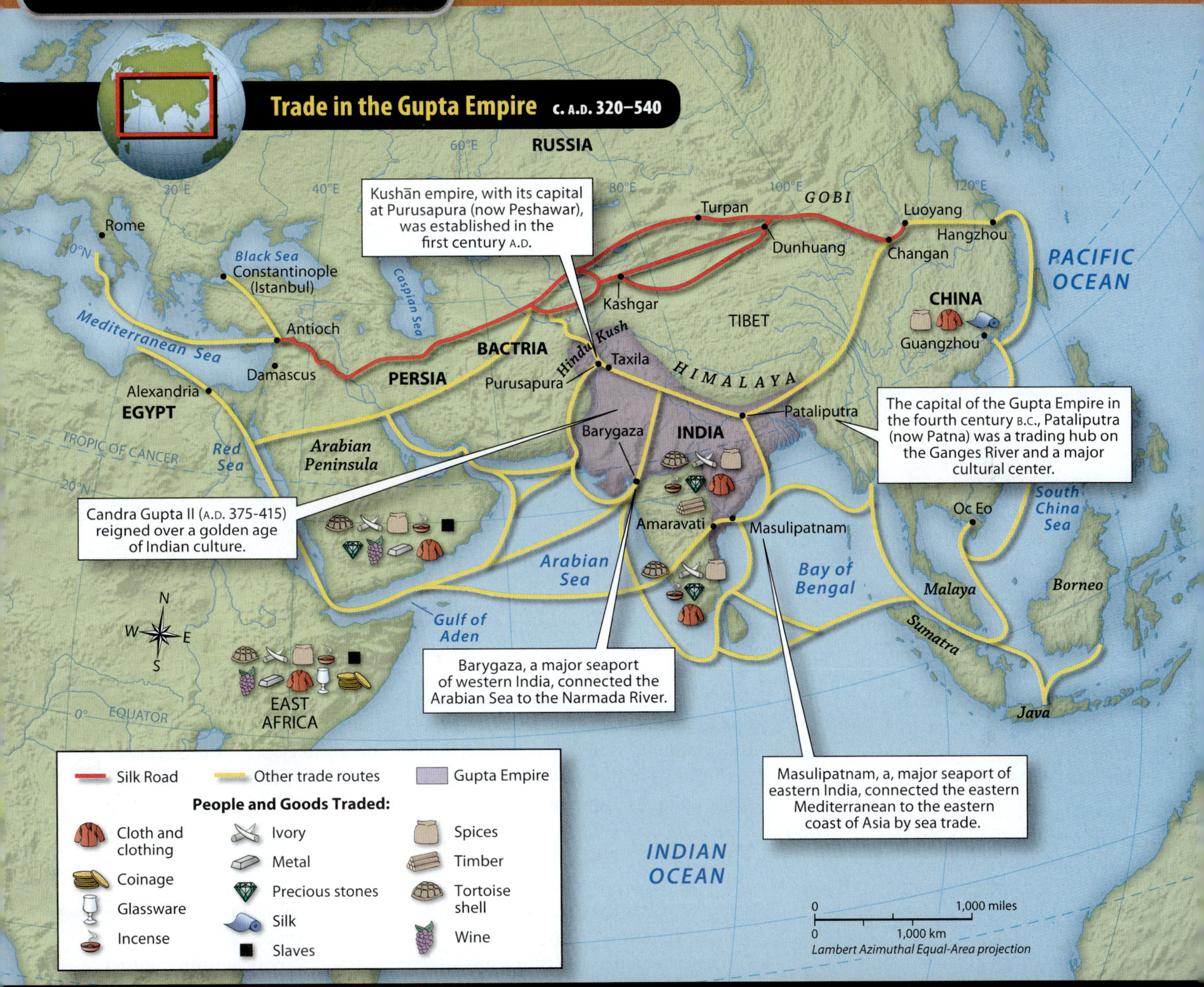

Time line

- **480 B.C.** Athenians demonstrate naval dominance in Battle of Salamis against Persia
- **327 B.C.** Alexander the Great attempts to invade India
- **c. 324 B.C.** Candragupta Maurya founds the Mauryan Empire
- **232 B.C.** Death of Aśoka, greatest of Mauryan rulers and Buddhist convert
- **207 B.C.** Shihuangdi, Qin emperor of China, buried at Xi'an
- **A.D. 1**
- **A.D. 78** Kushān empire is established in northwestern India
- **C. A.D. 250** Classic period begins in Maya civilization, Central America
- **A.D. 326** Constantine moves capital of Roman Empire to Byzantium
- **A.D. 380** Samudra Gupta, greatest ruler of the Gupta Empire, dies
- **A.D. 434** Attila the Hun leads army against Roman Empire
- **A.D. 450–500** Hun invasions threaten, then topple Gupta Empire
- **A.D. 481** Clovis I crowned King of the Franks, rules much of Gaul (France)
- **500**

networks

There's More Online!

- GRAPHIC ORGANIZER Hinduism: A Blending of Aryan and Dravidian Religious Practices
- IMAGE Brahma
- IMAGE Mohenjo Daro
- IMAGE Shiva
- IMAGE Temple of Vishnu
- INTERACTIVE SELF-CHECK QUIZ
- SECONDARY SOURCE Development of the Caste System in India
- VIDEO Origins of Hindu India

LESSON 1

Origins of Hindu India

ESSENTIAL QUESTIONS • *How was early Indian culture influenced by religion and social structure?* • *How did ideas and events during the Mauryan and Gupta Empires affect the development of India?*

IT MATTERS BECAUSE

Between 1500 B.C. and 400 B.C., the spread of the Aryans and their interaction with the indigenous Dravidians resulted in a new Indian culture. Two prominent features of this culture were a unique social class system and the Hindu religion.

Reading HELPDESK

Academic Vocabulary

- **emerge**
- **process**

Content Vocabulary

- ***varnas***
- **caste system**
- **Hinduism**
- **yoga**
- **reincarnation**
- **karma**
- **dharma**

TAKING NOTES:

Key Ideas and Details

Paraphrasing Use a graphic organizer like the one below to record key ideas about Hinduism and its origins.

varnas	
caste	
Brahman	
yoga	
chief Hindu gods	

TEKS Texas Essential Knowledge and Skills

1B identify major causes and describe the major effects of the following events from 500 BC to AD 600: the development of the classical civilizations of Greece, Rome, Persia, India (Maurya and Gupta), China (Zhou, Qin, and Han), and the development of major world religions

continued on the next page

Social Class in Ancient India

GUIDING QUESTION *What was the social structure of ancient India?*

As we have seen, life in ancient India centered on the family, the most basic unit in society. At the same time, the social structure of India came to reflect Aryan ideas of the ideal society. A set of social institutions and divisions **emerged** that has lasted in India, with some changes, down to the present day.

The Four *Varnas*

Vedic Aryans viewed a proper, ordered society as made up of four groups, which they called **varnas**. Here, *varna* ("color") meant "class" or "classification"; it did not refer to skin color. First among these varnas are the priests (Brahmins), second are the warrior-administrators *Kshatriyas* (KSHA • tree • uhz), and third are the "folk" *vaisya (VYSH • yuhz)*: the artisans, farmers, herdsman, and so on, who are the majority of the population. The fourth class or varna are the sudras (SOO • druhz), whose duty is to serve the other three classes. This view of society emphasizes rituals, Ksatriyas govern and protect, Vaisya cultivate, cook, weave, etc., and thus support the society materially and aesthetically. Sudras serve the needs of these three and thereby assure the stability and right functioning of the whole.

The Caste System

Over the centuries, a rigid and multiplex social structure developed across the Indian subcontinent. Eventually and to differing degrees, it

PHOTO: (l to r)©DEA / G NIMATALLAH/Age Fotostock America, ©Dinodia Photos / Alamy, Art Media / Heritage / The Image Works, R. u. S. Michaud / akg-images, The Bridgeman Art Library.

linked with the varna system. Based upon local traditions of ordering and ranking individuals from various families, lineages, tribes, occupations, and religious groupings, this scheme makes birth (*jati*) the key marker of a person's identity and place in society. And is what has come to be called the **caste system**, "caste" being the word casta used by Portuguese newcomers to western India in the late 15th and early 16th century to designate the fixed social groups into which individuals are born.

This so-called caste system was a major social and cultural institution of Indian civilization that influenced almost every aspect of daily life. It determined what jobs people could have, whom they could marry, and with whom they could socialize.

Associated with this system are beliefs about purity. Higher castes were considered more pure than lower castes, which were thought to be polluting to the higher-ranking castes. At the lowest level and so impure that they are entirely outside the caste system, were the so-called "Untouchables," who now more commonly refer to themselves as *dalit*, "the oppressed." They have traditionally performed the most polluting tasks such as collecting trash and disposing of the dead. Other Indians consider any contact with an Untouchable to be degrading, potentially leading to lower status.

READING PROGRESS CHECK

Identifying Central Issues What was the caste system, and what made it a unique social structure?

Central Ideas of Hinduism

GUIDING QUESTION *What are the origins, beliefs, and practices of Hinduism?*

Two of the world's major religions, Hinduism and Buddhism, originated in India. Both include fundamental ideas that were crucial in shaping the history of India and other Eastern civilizations.

emerge to manifest, to rise from an obscure or inferior position or condition

varnas the name given by Aryans in ancient India to a group of people in what was believed to be an ideal social structure of four groups

caste system a set of rigid categories in ancient India that determined a person's occupation and economic potential, as well as his or her position in society, based partly on skin color

(continued from p. 108)

TEKS **Texas Essential Knowledge and Skills**
3A describe the major political, religious/philosophical, and cultural influences of Persia, India, China, Israel, Greece, and Rome, including the development of monotheism, Judaism, and Christianity

continued on the next page

Hinduism the major Indian religious system, which had its origins in the religious beliefs of the Aryans who settled in India after 1500 B.C.

CHARTS/GRAPHS **CHANGES IN INDIA'S CIVILIZATION**

Social changes	Economic changes	Cultural changes
Aryan idea of four *varnas* lays basis for caste system	Shift back to farming and farming villages	Arts—Changes in materials, products, and pottery style
Varnas compare society to parts of the body, with all parts working together	Harappa and Mohenjo Daro deserted	Religion—Hinduism becomes dominant by 1000 B.C.
Chieftains, or rajas, ruled with the help of tribal councils and Brahmins	Less evidence of trade and luxury goods	Language—Four Vedas written in Sanskrit, an Indo-European language

By 1500 B.C., major changes had taken place in India. Mohenjo Daro, shown above, was abandoned around 1500 B.C.

CRITICAL THINKING

1. ***Determining Cause and Effect*** How did India's social structure change?
2. ***Summarizing*** What evidence is there of the changes described in the chart?

(continued from p. 109)

TEKS Texas Essential Knowledge and Skills
23A describe the historical origins, central ideas, and spread of major religious and philosophical traditions, including Buddhism, Christianity, Confucianism, Hinduism, Islam, Judaism, Sikhism, and the development of monotheism

yoga a method of training developed by the Hindus that is supposed to lead to oneness with Brahman

reincarnation the rebirth of an individual's soul in a different form after death

process progress, advance; a series of actions or operations leading to an end

karma in Hinduism, the force generated by a person's actions that determines how the person will be reborn in the next life

▼ **The sixth-century Vishnu Temple at Deogarh, India, is one of the oldest stone Hindu temples.**

▶ **CRITICAL THINKING**
Analyzing Visuals Who do you think is depicted on the relief panel? Why?

Early Practice

The origins of **Hindu** teachings and practices owe much to the religious practices of peoples calling themselves aryas, "noble," who first appear in northwest India sometime around 1500 B.C. What can be known of their religious thought is found in the Vedas ("Wisdom"), collections of hymns, speculation, and ritual instruction passed down orally for centuries by learned priests and not written down until modern times.

The oldest forms of Hindu teachings are based in the Vedic literature. One such teaching declared that ultimate reality is a single force that the wise called Brahman (a word that originally meant the power of a ritual to accomplish the objectives of the performer). From this premise, many concluded that the true reality of a person—the real "self" or "soul"—cannot be different from Brahman. The equation declaring that the real person or atman and the universal reality are one and the same is celebrated in late Vedic texts as a major religious discovery. From "knowing" this truth to experiencing it was said to require disciplined effort, or **yoga**. Meaning "yoking," yoga named both the taming and training of faculties required to realize the ultimate goal and the goal itself as a living realization of the union of individual and absolute.

Eventually Hindu teachings proposed that there are several yogas by which one may attain that realization, each suited to different personalities and aptitudes: a yoga of knowledge, a yoga of ritual practice, and a yoga of loyal devotion of *bhakti.* Cultivating the last-named yoga, the practitioner experiences the absolute as accessible, personal, lovable. This bhakti-yoga affirmed that the religious devotee followed a path as dignified and productive as the performance of austerities or the mastery of learned teachings.

And bhakti-yoga also became one mechanism by which devotees of various gods and goddesses that were originally quite outside the Vedic and Hindu cultural and historical universe were embraced as genuine participants in an increasingly complex set of Hindu traditions. Learned Hindus understood and accommodated diversity of religious teachings and practice and also comprehended those distinct traditions as being a part of a larger Hindu reality.

Principles of Hinduism

By the sixth century B.C., **reincarnation** or "rebirth," another widespread and important Hindu notion had appeared. It is the belief that the soul/self is reborn after death. Depending on the dedication and effort of the self, after some number of rebirths it will achieve its final goal of union with Brahman.

Central to the rebirth **process** is **karma**, action-and-consequence. According to the theory of karma, a person's intentional acts have inevitable consequences and determine the person's future condition in this life and in subsequent lives. This theory stresses personal responsibility and the importance of ethical action: One's current situation is not an accident but rather the consequence of previous actions. Through ethical action, one aspires to achieve the ultimate goal of union with the Absolute, in which the process of birth and rebirth finally is overcome. To varying degrees, Hindu teachings concerning karma and the process of birth and rebirth have significantly influenced many non-Hindus around the world.

Dharma—"order, truth, duty, law"—is probably the most important concept in Hindu teachings. It establishes that which is right and proper and supportive of good order. For individuals, dharma defines duty and right behavior. Duty will differ according to status. The oldest and possibly most influential statement of the nature of duty and responsibility is in the Bhagavad Gita. Preparing for battle in defense of righteousness, the warrior-hero Arjuna sees some friends, relatives, and former teachers in the opposing army. In despair, he appeals to his comrade, the god Krishna:

(continued from p. 109)

TEKS Texas Essential Knowledge and Skills
25A summarize the fundamental ideas and institutions of Eastern civilizations that originated in China and India

dharma in Hinduism, the divine law that rules karma; it requires all people to do their duty based on their status in society

PRIMARY SOURCE

"'When I see my family willing and ready to fight, Krishna, my limbs falter, my mouth goes dry. There is a trembling in my body and my hairs bristle....'

The Lord said, '...If you do not participate in this lawful battle, then you will give up your personal law and fame and incur guilt.'"

— from the Bhagavad Gita

▼ **Nataraja (The King of the Dance) is the dancing posture of the Hindu deity Shiva.**

Arjuna begins here to understand that he must act as a warrior. In short, he must perform his duty to protect righteousness (or Dharma) in the world. Doing his duty may involve killing, even killing friends and relatives fighting for the other side. Dharma makes possible all that is good in the world, so he must uphold Dharma, and protect those who follow Dharma, without regard to the consequences.

Within the Hindu concept of reincarnation, nothing was enjoyed or endured by accident or chance. Each person was responsible for their current situation, and must act in accordance with dharma to improve their condition in the future. And everyone has the same kind of opportunity. Everyone who acted according to the duties (dharma) of their station, would enjoy improved conditions in their future lives as they continued their journey toward a final union with Brahman.

✓ READING PROGRESS CHECK

Making Connections How do some of the principles of Hinduism reflect the social class structure that evolved from Aryan society?

LESSON 1 REVIEW TEKS

Reviewing Vocabulary

1. ***Contrasting*** What are karma and dharma, and how do they relate to Hinduism?
2. ***Listing*** What were the four *varnas?*

Using Your Notes

3. ***Synthesizing*** Use your notes to explain the relationship between the social structure and the prevailing religious beliefs of ancient India.

Answering the Guiding Questions

4. ***Classifying*** What was the social structure of ancient India?
5. ***Finding the Main Ideas*** What are the origins, beliefs, and practices of Hinduism?

Writing Activity

6. **INFORMATIVE/EXPLANATORY** In a well-developed paragraph, explain who the *Sudras* were and how they fit into the *varnas*. Be sure to cover ideas related to reincarnation, karma, and dharma.

networks

There's More Online!

- ☑ BIOGRAPHY Siddhārtha Gautama
- ☑ IMAGE Bodhi Tree
- ☑ IMAGE Buddha and His Disciples
- ☑ IMAGE Buddhist Shrine at Sarnath
- ☑ INTERACTIVE SELF-CHECK QUIZ
- ☑ PRIMARY SOURCE Life of Buddha
- ☑ PRIMARY SOURCE Sermon in the Deer Park
- ☑ SECONDARY SOURCE Buddhism and Hinduism
- ☑ VIDEO Buddhism

LESSON 2

Buddhism

ESSENTIAL QUESTIONS • *How was early Indian culture influenced by religion and social structure?* • *How did ideas and events during the Mauryan and Gupta Empires affect the development of India?*

Reading HELPDESK

Academic Vocabulary

- **devote**
- **rigid**

Content Vocabulary

- **Buddhism**
- **nirvana**

TAKING NOTES:

Key Ideas and Details

Categorizing Use a graphic organizer like the one below to identify those ideas, practices, and beliefs that Siddhārtha Gautama rejected and those that he accepted and/or taught.

Rejected	Accepted and/ or Taught

It Matters Because

Buddhism was the product of one man, Siddhārtha Gautama, whose simple message of achieving wisdom created a new spiritual philosophy in India. Buddhism became a rival to Hinduism in India and also spread to other regions of Asia.

Siddhārtha Gautama

GUIDING QUESTION *What are the origins of Buddhism?*

Buddhism began in the sixth or fifth century B.C. (There are different Buddhist traditions and divergent scholarly opinions concerning the date.) The new religion appeared in northern India and soon became a rival of Hinduism. The founder of Buddhism was Siddhārtha Gautama (sih • DAHR • tuh GOW • tuh • muh), known as the Buddha, or "Enlightened One."

Siddhārtha Gautama came from a small kingdom in the foothills of the Himalaya (in what is today part of southern Nepal). Born around 563 B.C., he was the son of a ruling princely family. The young and very handsome Siddhārtha was raised in the lap of luxury and lived a sheltered life. Like others of his class, he was also trained to be a warrior. At the age of 16, he married a neighboring princess and began to raise a family.

Siddhārtha appeared to have everything: wealth, a good appearance, a model wife, a child, and a throne that he would someday inherit. In his late twenties, however, Siddhārtha became aware of the pain of illness, the sorrow of death, and the effects of old age on ordinary people. He exclaimed, "Would that sickness, age, and death might be for ever bound!" He decided to spend his life seeking the cure for human suffering. He gave up his royal clothes, shaved his head, abandoned his family, and set off to find the true meaning of life.

At first, he tried to follow the example of the ascetics, people who practiced self-denial to achieve an understanding of ultimate reality. The abuse of his physical body did not lead him to a greater understanding of life, however. It led only to a close brush with death from not eating. He abandoned asceticism and turned instead to an intense period of meditation. As we have seen, in Hinduism, this was a way to find oneness with god. One evening, while sitting in meditation under a tree, Siddhārtha reached enlightenment as to the meaning of life. He spent the rest of his life preaching what he had discovered. The development of the religion of Buddhism begins with his teachings.

It is not certain that Siddhārtha Gautama ever intended to create a new religion or doctrine. In some ways, his ideas could be seen as an attempt to reform Hinduism. In his day, Hinduism had become complex and dependent on the Brahmins as keepers of religious secrets. Siddhārtha challenged people to be responsible for their own lives: "Do not accept what you hear by report.... Be lamps unto yourselves." He also advised, "Do not go by what is handed down, nor on the authority of your traditional teachings. When you know of yourselves: 'These teachings are not good...' then reject them."

In the Buddha's lifetime, many people went to him with questions. To inquiries concerning who he was, he responded that he was neither god nor angel. Rather, he would say, "I am awake." Importantly, he did not claim to be a being different from his questioners but simply a man who (unlike them) had awakened to the truth.

✓ READING PROGRESS CHECK

Describing How did Siddhārtha come to understand and teach the ideas that became Buddhism?

Buddhism a religious doctrine introduced in northern India in the sixth century B.C. by Siddhārtha Gautama, known as the Buddha, or "Enlightened One"

TEKS **Texas Essential Knowledge and Skills**
1B identify major causes and describe the major effects of the following events from 500 BC to AD 600: the development of the classical civilizations of Greece, Rome, Persia, India (Maurya and Gupta), China (Zhou, Qin, and Han), and the development of major world religions

continued on p. 115

▼ Stone relief carving of the Buddha from the second century B.C.

▶ CRITICAL THINKING

Analyzing Visuals How are the Buddha and his followers depicted?

PHOTO: ©Bettmann/CORBIS

BIOGRAPHY

Siddhārtha Gautama (c. 563–c. 483 B.C.)

Siddhārtha Gautama discovered the Middle Way—a path of moderation with worldwide appeal—through meditation. He achieved enlightenment and became the Buddha. Siddhārtha's teachings spread throughout India, as did artistic representations of him. Each region developed a different way of depicting the Buddha, but these representations often share some common traits. Images of the Buddha are symbolic, and they do not show him as he appeared in life. Additionally, the Buddha is often shown seated to signify his enlightenment, with a bump on his head to symbolize his intelligence, and with long earlobes to symbolize his spirituality.

▶ **CRITICAL THINKING**

Speculating Why are representations of the Buddha idealized or symbolic rather than realistic?

Central Ideas of Buddhism

GUIDING QUESTION ***What beliefs serve as the basis for Buddhist practices?***

The Buddha denied the abiding substantiality of the world we experience. That is, contrary to what we think, there are no abiding things. Without exception, all the objects of our ordinary experience are the result of causes. Therefore they are impermanent. The pain and sorrow that afflict us are due to our attachment to "things" in the world. If we renounce our desire for things, we will be freed from them and from the illusion that they exist substantially and are thus worth desiring and possessing. To give up the desire utterly is to attain *bodhi,* awakening or enlightenment. And enlightenment is the extinction (nirvana) of the fires of greed and desire.

Siddhārtha first shared this wisdom in a lecture he delivered in Sarnath, outside India's holy city of Varanasi. He began by advising his listeners to avoid extremes by following a Middle Way. The heart of this teaching is the Four Noble Truths:

1. All is suffering.
2. Suffering has a cause, which is desire.
3. Suffering can be overcome.
4. The way to end desire is to follow the Eightfold Path:
   - *Right view* knowing the Four Noble Truths.
   - *Right intention* resolving to attain Enlightenment.
   - *Right speech* speaking truthfully and with kindness.
   - *Right action* leading a moral life.
   - *Right livelihood* working in a responsible, harmless way.
   - *Right effort* ceaseless, unwavering striving to Enlightenment.
   - *Right mindfulness* controlling our thought.
   - *Right concentration* meditating to see the world as it is.

The Buddha accepted the notion of rebirth, but radicalized it. As everything is caused and impermanent, that which the ignorant see as permanent and substantial is in fact ceaselessly different from moment to moment. You and I are not abiding persons but processes of cause and effect. Again, it is when we are ignorant of this dynamic reality and treat the impermanent as though it were permanent that we desire and suffer.

▶ **The eight spokes of the dharmachakra ("wheel of law") represent the Eightfold Path that is central for all Buddhists.**

The Buddha did not so much reject the caste system as declare it irrelevant. No one was privileged or had an advantage in seeking Enlightenment (and, of course, no one is substantially or essentially different from anyone else). In the matter of religious practice, he did not reject devotion to the gods but rather taught that, though gods might have certain powers beyond those of humans, they too suffered from ignorant greed. And the Buddha discouraged the formation of a cult to himself and did not encourage the making of images.

In one regard, the Buddha did not step beyond the prejudices and restrictions of his own time and place: Initially he refused to admit women into the renunciant order, the monastic community of individuals who gave up life in the world in order exclusively to pursue the path to Enlightenment. But when he did allow the monastic ordination of women (five years after establishing the ordination of monks), he declared that women are as capable of attaining Enlightenment as men.

Traditions state that the Buddha died at age 80 in Kushinagar, which is located in present-day India's Uttar Pradesh state. After his death, his followers traveled throughout India, spreading his message. Temples sprang up throughout the countryside. Buddhist monasteries were also established to promote his teaching and to provide housing and training for monks dedicated to the simple life and the pursuit of wisdom. During the next centuries, Buddhism and Hinduism began to compete actively for followers.

✓ READING PROGRESS CHECK

Differentiating What is the difference between the Four Noble Truths and the Middle, or Eightfold, Path?

nirvana in Buddhism, ultimate reality, the end of the self and a reunion with the Great World Soul

rigid inflexibly set in opinion

(continued from p. 113)

TEKS **Texas Essential Knowledge and Skills**

3A describe the major political, religious/philosophical, and cultural influences of Persia, India, China, Israel, Greece, and Rome, including the development of monotheism, Judaism, and Christianity

23A describe the historical origins, central ideas, and spread of major religious and philosophical traditions, including Buddhism, Christianity, Confucianism, Hinduism, Islam, Judaism, Sikhism, and the development of monotheism

25A summarize the fundamental ideas and institutions of Eastern civilizations that originated in China and India

PHOTO: Prisma Bildagentur AG/Alamy

◀ **The Sarnath stupa was erected during the fifth and sixth centuries at the location where the Buddha delivered his first sermon.**

LESSON 2 REVIEW *TEKS*

Reviewing Vocabulary

1. ***Explaining*** In Buddhism, how might a person achieve nirvana? 23A

Using Your Notes

2. ***Interpreting*** Use your notes and other information from the lesson to explain how Siddhārtha created a new spiritual philosophy. 23A

Answering the Guiding Questions

3. ***Summarizing*** What are the origins of Buddhism? 23A
4. ***Identifying*** What beliefs serve as the basis for Buddhist practices? 23A

Writing Activity

5. **INFORMATIVE/EXPLANATORY** Use your own words to retell the life of the Buddha from birth to enlightenment. Put events in chronological order and incorporate transitional words and phrases to make the sequence clear. 23A

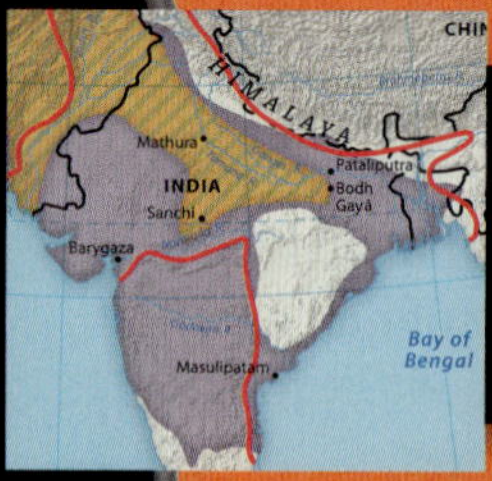

networks

There's More Online!

- BIOGRAPHY Aśoka
- BIOGRAPHY Candragupta Maurya
- BIOGRAPHY Faxian
- IMAGE Āryabhata
- INFOGRAPHIC Stupas
- INTERACTIVE SELF-CHECK QUIZ
- MAP Mauryan, Kushān, and Gupta Empires
- VIDEO The Mauryans and the Guptas

LESSON 3

The Mauryans and the Guptas

ESSENTIAL QUESTIONS • *How was early Indian culture influenced by religion and social structure?* • *How did ideas and events during the Mauryan and Gupta Empires affect the development of India?*

Reading HELPDESK

Academic Vocabulary
- **conversion**
- **welfare**

Content Vocabulary
- **Silk Road**
- **pilgrim**
- **Vedas**

TAKING NOTES:

Key Ideas and Details

Organizing Use a graphic organizer like the one below to record key facts about each of the three major empires of ancient India.

Empire	Facts

TEKS Texas Essential Knowledge and Skills

1B identify major causes and describe the major effects of the following events from 500 BC to AD 600: the development of the classical civilizations of Greece, Rome, Persia, India (Maurya and Gupta), China (Zhou, Qin, and Han), and the development of major world religions

continued on the next page

It Matters Because

While Hinduism and Buddhism spread through India, politically the land was fragmented. From around 1500 B.C. to 400 B.C., numerous small kingdoms challenged one another, preventing widespread, lasting peace. When these polities united – principally to confront invaders, three new Indian empires arose in the course of the millennium between the fourth century B.C. and the fifth century A.D., warring kingdoms prevented a lasting peace. However, when these kingdoms united to force out invaders, three new Indian empires emerged.

Three New Empires

GUIDING QUESTION *What led to the rise and fall of the Mauryan, Kushān, and Gupta Empires?*

After 400 B.C., India faced threats from invaders. First came the Persians, who extended their empire into western India. Then came the Greeks and Macedonians. After conquering Persia, Alexander the Great he swept into India in 327 B.C. Despite several victories, within a year his army refused to proceed further east, and Alexander withdrew. By weakening resistance in the northwest and stimulating new collaboration among small kingdoms in north central India, Alexander's raid played a role in the creation of the first pan-Indian empire: the Mauryas.

The Mauryan Empire

The new Indian state was founded by Candragupta Maurya (KUHN • druh • GUP • tuh MAH • oor • yuh), who ruled from 324 B.C. to 301 B.C. He drove out the foreign forces and established the capital of his new Mauryan Empire in northern India at Pataliputra, modern Patna, in the Ganges Valley.

The Mauryas established political influence in India through a well organized and highly centralized empire. The king divided his empire into provinces, ruled by governors whom he appointed.

Mauryan rule was also reinforced by a large army and a vast network of spies. A strong central government, large army, and secret police were all important parts of the Mauryan Empire.

According to Megasthenes, the Greek ambassador to the Mauryan court, Candragupta Maurya was afraid of assassination despite having a large army and a secret police. All food was tasted in his presence, and he made a practice of never sleeping two nights in a row in the same bed.

Aśoka (uh • SHOH • kuh), the grandson of Candragupta Maurya, is generally considered to be the greatest ruler in the history of India. After his **conversion** to Buddhism, Aśoka used Buddhist ideals to guide his rule and to shape Indian civilization. A large army and a vast network of spies also reinforced Mauryan rule. Aśoka's religious beliefs led him to set up hospitals for the **welfare** of both people and animals. Aśoka sponsored Buddhist missionaries who spread Buddhist traditions and ideas throughout India and eventually to China. This missionary effort had a major impact on China and, eventually, other countries, as well. One of the decrees of Aśoka read:

PRIMARY SOURCE

> “By order of the Beloved of the Gods [Aśoka]. Addressed to the officers in charge. . . . Let us win the affection of all men. All men are my children, and as I wish all welfare and happiness in this world and the next for my own children, so do I wish it for all men. . . . For that purpose many officials are employed among the people to instruct them in righteousness and to explain it to them.”
>
> —quoted in *Aśoka Maurya*, 1966

conversion the change from one belief or form to another

welfare something that aids or promotes well-being

(continued from p. 116)

TEKS **Texas Essential Knowledge and Skills**

3A describe the major political, religious/philosophical, and cultural influences of Persia, India, China, Greece, and Rome, including the development of monotheism, Judaism, and Christianity

continued on the next page

GEOGRAPHY CONNECTION

1. **PLACES AND REGIONS** *Which areas did the three empires have in common?*
2. **THE WORLD IN SPATIAL TERMS** *Locate the capital of the Mauryan and Gupta Empires. Why might each empire have chosen this location?*

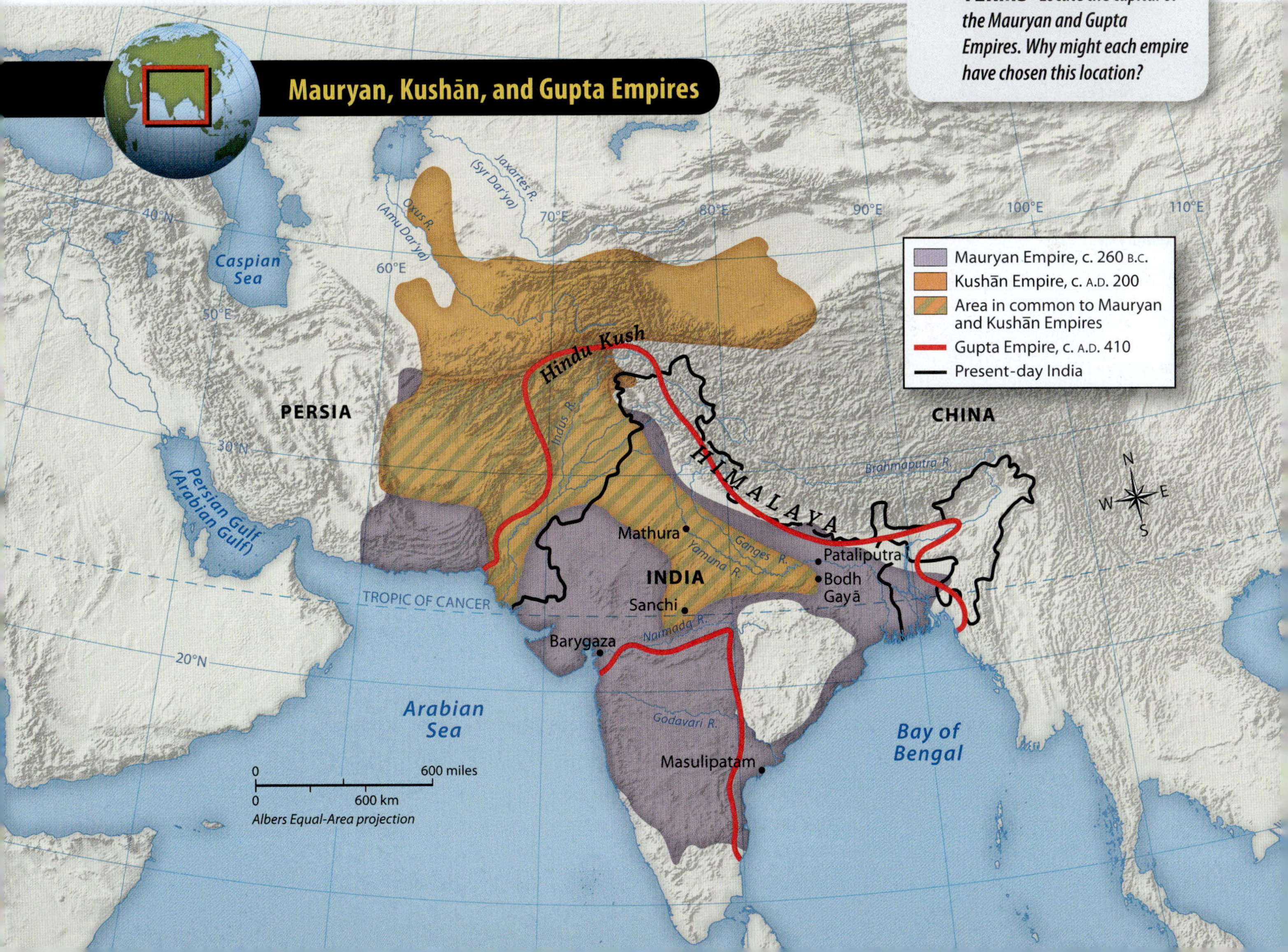

Aśoka was more than a kind ruler. His kingdom prospered as India's role in regional commerce expanded. India became a major crossroads in a trade network that extended from the rim of the Pacific to Southwest Asia and the Mediterranean Sea. After Aśoka's death in 232 B.C., the Mauryan Empire began to decline. In 183 B.C., the last Mauryan ruler was killed by one of his generals, who thereupon established the Sunga dynasty, which held sway over much of the former Maurya territory for 100 years.

The Kushān Empire

Silk Road a route between the Roman Empire and China, so called because silk was China's most valuable product

Following the decline of the Sungas in the mid-first century B.C., several kingdoms arose in north India. In the first century A.D., in Bactria (now Afghanistan) in the extreme northwest, the Kushans, nomadic warriors from Central Asia, established a kingdom that overspread and dominated north India for the next two centuries. In the rest of India, other kingdoms fought for control.

The Kushāns prospered from the trade that passed through their empire between the Mediterranean countries and the countries bordering the Pacific Ocean. Most of that trade was between the Roman Empire and China. It was shipped along the routes known as the **Silk Road**, so called because silk was China's most valuable product. One section of the Silk Road passed through the mountains northwest of India.

▲ This glass fish of Roman origin was traded to the Kushāns in the first century A.D.

In India, trade expanded rapidly in the first century A.D. Sailors learned to navigate the Indian Ocean, understanding ocean currents and seasonal monsoon winds. For the first time, goods could be shipped with some certainty from the Mediterranean to seaports on the west coast of India. From there, the goods could be carried overland to China.

Because of its location between influential cultures, the Kushān Empire was shaped by surrounding societies, but it maintained a distinctly Indian culture. The empire was in contact with China, Persia, and the Roman Empire. The Greek alphabet had reached Bactria to the west, and the Kushāns adapted it for their language. The Kushāns practiced both Hinduism and Buddhism, as well as Zoroastrianism from Persia. The Kushāns developed a calendar based on the sun and the moon, and their calendar is the basis of the Indian calendar used today.

The Empire of the Guptas

The Kushān kingdom came to an end in the third century A.D., when invaders from Persia overran it. In A.D. 320 a new state was created in the central Ganges Valley by a local prince named Candra Gupta, who was no relation to the earlier Candragupta Maurya. To achieve this goal, Candra Gupta made alliances with other powerful families in the Ganges area and located his capital at Pataliputra, the site of the decaying palace of the Mauryas.

His successor, his son Samudra Gupta, expanded the empire into surrounding areas. A court official wrote of Samudra Gupta that:

PRIMARY SOURCE

"He was dexterous in waging hundreds of various kinds of battles with only the strength of his... arms. The beauty of his charming body was enhanced by the multiplicity of... wounds, caused by the blows of battle axes, arrows, spears, spikes, barbed darts, swords, lances, javelins, iron arrows,... and many other weapons."

—quoted in *The Imperial Guptas*

(continued from p. 117)

TEKS **Texas Essential Knowledge and Skills**

23A describe the historical origins, central ideas, and spread of major religious and philosophical traditions, including Buddhism, Christianity, Confucianism, Hinduism, Islam, Judaism, Sikhism, and the development of monotheism

23B identify examples of religious influence on various events referenced in the major eras of world history

26B analyze examples of how art, architecture, literature, music, and drama reflect the history of the cultures in which they are produced

26C identify examples of art, music, and literature that transcend the cultures in which they were created and convey universal themes

continued on the next page

Eventually the Gupta Empire became the most influential political force in northern India. It also established loose control over central India, thus becoming the greatest state in India since the Mauryan Empire.

Under a series of efficient monarchs—especially Candra Gupta II, who reigned from A.D. 380 to 415—the Guptas created a golden age of Indian culture, shown in the flowering of Hindu and Buddhist arts. The Gupta Empire emerged as a classical civilization, a society that serves as a model of excellence and has lasting value and relevance.

The Gupta Empire actively engaged in trade with China, Southeast Asia, and the Mediterranean and also encouraged domestic trade in cloth, salt, and iron. Cities that were famous for their temples as well as for their prosperity rose along the main trade routes throughout India.

Much of the trade in the Gupta Empire was managed by the Gupta rulers, who owned silver and gold mines and vast lands. They earned large profits from their dealings. They lived in luxury, awakening to the sound of music and spending much time in dining with followers and guests. It was said that "the king and his companions drank wine out of ruby cups (padmaragsukti). Outside...lutes were strummed."

Much of their wealth came from religious trade as **pilgrims** (people who travel to religious places) from across India and as far away as China came to visit the major religious centers. Not surprisingly, many new Hindu and Buddhist temples and shrines were built during the Gupta era.

A Buddhist monk from China, Faxian (FAY • SYEN), visited India in search of documents about the teachings of the Buddha. Faxian's writings from the fifth century describe the Gupta rulers, their respect for Buddhism, and the prosperity of the empire. He said,

PRIMARY SOURCE

"The people are very well off, without poll-tax or official restrictions. Only those who till the royal lands return a portion of profit of the land [to the king]. If they desire to go, they go; if they like to stop, they stop."

—quoted in *A Source Book in Geography*

The good fortunes of the Guptas did not last. Beginning in the late fifth century A.D., invasions by nomadic Huns from the northwest gradually reduced the power of the empire. A military commander briefly revived the empire in the middle of the seventh century, but after his death, the empire collapsed. North India would not be reunited for hundreds of years.

READING PROGRESS CHECK

Comparing What did the three major empires have in common?

Indian Accomplishments

GUIDING QUESTION *What were the cultural contributions of ancient India?*

Few cultures in the world are as rich and varied as that of India. The country produced great works in almost all cultural fields, including literature, architecture, science, and mathematics.

Literature

The **Vedas** are India's oldest surviving literature. Their earliest material consists of hymns, songs praising divinities and stories. The Vedas were carefully transmitted orally by highly trained specialists over the centuries and were only written down

pilgrim a person who travels to a shrine or other holy place

(continued from p. 118)

TEKS **Texas Essential Knowledge and Skills**
27A identify the origin and diffusion of major ideas in mathematics, science, and technology that occurred in river valley civilizations, classical Greece and Rome, classical India, and the Islamic caliphates between 700 and 1200 and in China from the Tang to Ming dynasties

▼ **Sandstone fragment of a doorjamb from the doorway of an early Hindu temple from the Gupta period**

▶ CRITICAL THINKING

Drawing Conclusions What might this doorjamb fragment convey about the Gupta Empire?

PHOTO: The British Museum/Topham/The Image Works

Vedas the earliest known Indian literature, which contain religious chants and stories that were originally passed down orally from generation to generation and then recorded in Sanskrit after writing developed

in modern times. The *Mahabharata* (muh • HAH • BAH • ruh • tuh), one of India's two great epics, was compiled over many centuries from the fifth or sixth century B.C. India's other great epic, the *Ramayana* (rah • MAH • yuh • nuh), dates from at least the fourth century B.C. Both epics are attributed to individual authors, but were edited and re-edited over the centuries. Celebrating heroic, world-saving deeds, these epics preserve information about early Indian culture.

The *Mahabharata*, consisting of about 90,000 two-line stanzas, is the longest poem in any written language. Taking place around 1000 B.C., it describes a war between cousins for control of the kingdom. The poem also includes riddles about the meaning of life.

PRIMARY SOURCE

> "'What is the best of all things that are praised?'
> 'Skill.'
> 'What is the most valuable possession?'
> 'Knowledge.'
> 'What is not thought of until it departs?'
> 'Health.'
> 'What is the best happiness?'
> 'Contentment.'"
>
> —from the *Mahabharata*

The most famous section of the book, called the Bhagavad Gita (bah • guh • vad GEE • tuh), is a sermon by the god Krishna on the eve of a major battle. In this sermon, he sets forth one of the key points of Indian society: In taking action, one must not worry about success or failure. One should be aware only of the moral rightness of the act itself.

The *Ramayana*, written at about the same time, is much shorter than the *Mahabharata*. It is an account of the fictional ruler Rama. As a result of a palace plot, Rama is banished from the kingdom and forced to live in the forest. Later, he fights the demon-king of Ceylon, who had kidnapped his beloved wife Sita.

Like the *Mahabharata* and most works of the ancient world, the *Ramayana* is strongly imbued with religious and moral lessons that transcend the culture in which they were created. Rama is seen as the ideal hero and son, and a perfect ruler. Sita projects the supreme duty of wifely loyalty to her husband. To this day, the both works continue to inspire the people of India.

One of ancient India's most famous authors from the Gupta era was Kālidāsa. His poem, *The Cloud Messenger*, remains one of the most popular Sanskrit poems. In the poem, an exiled male earth spirit shares his grief and longing for his wife.

Analyzing PRIMARY SOURCES

The Cloud Messenger

> "Some months, divided from his spouse,
> Upon this mountain he had passed;
> His golden bracelet from his arm
> Already fallen, when at last, He
> saw a cloud embrace the fell....
>
> Before this tree-enlivening cloud
> With tears repressed and saddened heart,
> The servant of the king of kings
> Reflected long nor could depart:
> Not even a happy man unmoved
> Beholds a cloud before his face.
> Then how shall he who, far remote,
> Longs to enjoy the dear embrace?"
>
> —Kālidāsa, from *The Cloud Messenger*

DBQ ***MAKING CONNECTIONS*** What might account for this poem's enduring popularity in Indian culture?

Architecture

Some of the earliest examples of Indian architecture and sculpture date from the time of Aśoka, when Buddhism received much patronage and has become similar to a state religion. The desire to spread Buddhist teachings and to publicize Aśoka's accomplishments were major forces inspiring this art.

Three main kinds of art from this time deserve attention: carved stone pillars, Buddhist stupas (reliquary mounds), and rock-cut caves. Unfortunately, the number of these that survive and can be readily identified is not large. Aśoka had many large pillars erected throughout his domain at the frontier borders and at emerging Buddhist pilgrimage sites. As tall as 50 feed and weighing as much as 50 tons (45.4 t), the pillars followed traditions established centuries earlier by the Persians. Many bore inscriptions containing Aśoka's edicts and Buddhist teachings and were topped by carvings of lions or bulls. Only a handful of these pillars survive more or less undamaged.

Stupas were stylized burial mounds intended to house a relic, some remnant of the Buddha's body like a lock of hair, a bone fragment, or a tooth. Quite early, stupas became pilgrimage destinations for Buddhists. It is said that Aśoka ordered the building of the great stupa at Sanchi, and he also directed the construction of others as well. But at Sanchi and elsewhere, the growing reputation of stupas assured that they would regularly be renovated and enlarged. Doubtless many stupas that survive today are built around an early Aśokan stupa at their core.

Most of the architecture of Aśoka's time was built of brick and wood, perishable materials that, for the most part, have not survived. Aśoka's patronage of Buddhist rock-cut cave shrines was limited in scope; but examples are the simple, largely unadorned caves in the Barabar Hills near Bodhgaya in India's Bihar State.

SKILLS PRACTICE

Prepare a short five-sentence description of the accomplishments of early Indian civilization to share with your class. As you plan what you will say, think about the ideas and sentence types you will use. Connect similar ideas together in single sentences. Use connecting words, such as and, or, and but to combine the information.

Science, Mathematics, and Technology

Ancient Indians possessed an impressive amount of scientific knowledge, particularly in astronomy. Āryabhata, the most famous mathematician of the Gupta Empire, concluded that Earth revolves around the sun. Indians had also charted the stars and worked out that Earth was a sphere that rotated on its axis.

Their most important contribution was in the field of mathematics, including working with algebra. Āryabhata, was one of the first scientists known to have used algebra. Indian mathematicians also introduced the concept of zero and used a symbol (0) for it. Arab scholars would spread Indian ideas in science and mathematics throughout Southwest Asia, Europe, and beyond.

Technology in India saw some major developments. Metalworking, in particular, was highly developed. For example, the iron pillar of Qutub Minar in Delhi dates from the 300s A.D. The special method used to make the iron made it highly resistant to rust. Indian steel called "wootz" was adopted by Arab merchants and used in making strong "Damascus swords" in Southwest Asia.

After Arabs conquered parts of India in the eighth century A.D., Arab scholars adopted the Indian system. In turn, European traders borrowed it from the Arabs, and it spread through Europe in the 1200s. Today it is called the Indian Arabic numerical system.

▼ The Sanchi stupa was built in the third century B.C. to house a relic of the Buddha.

▶ **CRITICAL THINKING**

Defining How would you define *stupa* and *relic*?

PHOTO: Image Source/Getty Images

✓ **READING PROGRESS CHECK**

Synthesizing How did religion influence many of India's cultural contributions?

LESSON 3 REVIEW TEKS

Reviewing

1. ***Comparing and Contrasting*** How are the Vedas and the Bhagavad Gita similar and different? 26B

Using Your Notes

2. ***Describing*** Use your graphic organizer to briefly describe the three major ancient Indian empires. Include several key facts about each empire. 23A

Answering the Guiding Questions

3. ***Identifying Cause and Effect*** What led to the rise and fall of the Mauryan, Kushān, and Gupta Empires?

4. ***Summarizing*** What were the cultural contributions of ancient India? 26B, 27A

Writing Activity

5. **ARGUMENT** In an essay, argue that literature, architecture, or science and mathematics was the area of ancient India's greatest cultural contribution to the world. In addition to supporting your opinion, anticipate and respond to at least one opposing view. 26B, 27A

Hinduism

Hinduism is the oldest of the world's major living religions. It developed among the cultures in India as they spread out over the plains and forests of the subcontinent. It has no single founder or founding date. Hinduism is complex; it has numerous sects and many different divinities are honored. Among the more famous Hindu gods are Brahma, Vishnu, and Shiva, who represent, respectively, the creative, sustaining, and destructive forces in the universe. Major Hindu beliefs are reincarnation, karma, and dharma.

Hindus believe the universe contains several heavens and hells. According to the concept of rebirth or reincarnation, which is central to their beliefs, souls are continually reborn. In what form one is reborn is determined by the good and evil actions performed in his or her past lives. Those acts are karma. A soul continues in the cycle of rebirth until release is achieved.

Sacred Symbol

One important symbol of Hinduism is actually a symbol for a sound. "Om" is a sound that Hindus often chant during prayer, mantras, and rituals.

Sacred Text

The Vedas consist of hymns, prayers, and speculations composed in ancient Sanskrit. They are the oldest religious texts in an Indo-European language. The Rig Veda, Sama Veda, Yajur Veda, and Atharva Veda are the four great Vedic collections. Together, they make up one of the most significant and authoritative Hindu religious texts.

"Now, whether they perform a cremation for such a person or not, people like him pass into the flame, from the flame into the day, from the day into the fortnight of the waxing moon from the fortnight of the waxing moon into the six months when the sun moves north, from these months into the year, from the year into the sun, from the sun into the moon, and from the moon into the lightning. Then a person who is not human—he leads them to Brahman. This is the path to the gods, the path to Brahman. Those who proceed along this path do not return to this human condition."

—The Chandogya Upanishad 4:15.5

Sacred Site

Hindus believe that when a person dies his, or her soul is reborn. This is known as reincarnation. Many Hindus bathe in the Ganges and other sacred rivers to purify their souls and to be released from rebirth.

Worship and Celebration

Holi is a significant north Indian Hindu festival celebrating the triumph of good over evil. As part of the celebration, men, women, and children splash colored powders and water on each other. In addition to its religious significance, Holi also celebrates the beginning of spring.

WORLD RELIGIONS HANDBOOK

Buddhism

Siddhartha Gautama, known as the Buddha ("the Awakened") after his enlightenment at the age of 35, was born some 2,500 years ago in what is now Nepal. The Buddha's followers adhere to his teachings (dharma, meaning "divine law"), which aim to end suffering in the world. Buddhists call this goal Nirvana; and they believe that it can be achieved only by understanding the Four Noble Truths and by following the 4th Truth, which says that freedom from suffering is possible by practicing the Eightfold Path. Through the Buddha's teachings, his followers come to know the impermanence of all things and reach the end of ignorance and unhappiness.

Over time, as Buddhism spread throughout Asia, several branches emerged. The largest of these are Theravada Buddhism, the monk-centered Buddhism that is dominant in Sri Lanka, Burma, Thailand, Laos, and Cambodia; and Mahayana, a complex, more liberal variety of Buddhism that has traditionally been dominant in Tibet, Central Asia, Korea, China, and Japan.

Sacred Symbol

The dharmachakra ("wheel of the law") is a major Buddhist symbol. Among other things, it signifies the overcoming of obstacles. The eight spokes represent the Eightfold Path—right view, right intention, right speech, right action, right livelihood, right effort, right mindfulness, right concentration—that is central for all Buddhists.

Sacred Text

For centuries, the Buddha's teachings were transmitted orally. For Theravada Buddhists, the authoritative collection of Buddhist texts is the Tripitaka ("three baskets"). These texts were first written on palm leaves in a language called Pali. This excerpt from the *Dhammapada,* a famous text within the Tripitaka, urges responding to hatred with love:

"Never in this world is hate

Appeased by hatred.

It is only appeased by love—

This is an eternal law."

—Dhammapada 1.5

Sacred Site

Buddhists believe that Siddhartha Gautama achieved enlightenment beneath the Bodhi Tree in Bodh Gayā, India. Today, Buddhists from around the world flock to Bodh Gayā in search of their own spiritual awakening.

Worship and Celebration

The ultimate goal of Buddhists is to achieve Nirvana, the enlightened state in which individuals are free from ignorance, greed, and suffering. Theravada Buddhists believe that monks are most likely to reach Nirvana because of their lifestyle of renunciation, moral virtue, study, and meditation.

CHAPTER 5 Assessment

TEKS

Directions: On a separate sheet of paper, answer the questions below. Make sure you read carefully and answer all parts of the questions.

Lesson Review

Lesson 1

1. ***Summarizing*** What were the four varnas of ancient India, and what role did each group play in society? What was the fifth group? **23A, 25A**

2. ***Making Connections*** What does the word jati mean? How does it relate to religion? **23A, 25A**

3. ***Identifying*** What themes does the Bhagavad Gita express that remain relevant today? **26C**

4. ***Describing*** Who were the Untouchables, and how were they viewed in Indian society?

5. ***Explaining*** What was Brahman? How did it relate to the atman and to yoga?

6. ***Naming*** Name the three chief gods of Hinduism and explain their purpose.

7. ***Identifying*** What culturally transcendent universal themes can be found in early Hindu writings such as the Bhagavad Gita?

Lesson 2

8. ***Drawing Conclusions*** In what ways might Siddhārtha Gautama's ideas be understood as an attempt to reform Hinduism? **23A**

9. ***Describing*** What are the four Noble Truths of Buddhism? How many steps are on the Middle Path? **23A**

Lesson 3

10. ***Comparing*** Compare the Vedas of Ancient India and the Homeric Epics of Ancient Greece. How are these works similar? How do these examples of literature reflect the history of the ancient cultures in which they were produced? **26B**

11. ***Identifying*** The Kushans prospered from trade that passed through their empire. Where did most of this trade occur?

12. ***Sequencing*** Identify the causes of the end of the Kushan kingdom, and describe the effects of this end, including how these events initiated the development of the classical civilization of India. **1B**

13. ***Identifying Cause and Effect*** What eventually reduced the power of the Gupta empire?

14. ***Specifying*** Where does the earliest known Indian literature come from? How was it passed down from generation to generation?

15. ***Describing*** Describe the Mahabharata and its significance.

16. ***Explaining and Researching*** Explain the architectural innovations during this time, including the three main types of structures of early India. Research the technology used to engineer these architectural feats and how the use of this technology spread to other areas or cultures. Share your findings using digital presentation tools. Feature any relevant images. **27A**

17. ***Identifying*** Who was Aryabhata and what was he known for?

Need Extra Help?

If You've Missed Question	1	2	3	4	5	6	7	8	9	10	11	12	13	14	15	16	17
Go to page	108	109	111	109	110	111	111	113	114	118	118	119	119	120	120	119	117

18 ***Listing*** Who was Aśoka, and what were some of his accomplishments? **23A, 23B**

19 ***Making Inferences*** Why do you think Candra Gupta located the capital of the Gupta Empire at Pataliputra? **23A, 23B**

Exploring the Essential Questions

20 ***Identifying Perspectives*** Work with a partner to create a cause-and-effect chart showing the ways that ideas and events during the Mauryan, Kushān, and Gupta empires affected the development of India. Your chart should have three columns, the first labeled Empire, the second Origin, and the third Impact. You may use visuals and primary sources to enhance the entries on your chart. **23A, 23B**

21 ***Understanding Relationships Among Events*** Explain how Buddhism and Hinduism were major cultural influences in India, and identify at least three ways in which the culture of ancient India was influenced by religion. Consider issues related to social structure, art, and style of rule. Write a short essay linking the concepts you have chosen. **3A, 23A**

Critical Thinking

22 ***Identifying Cause and Effect*** What are the principles of dharma, karma, and reincarnation? How are they connected in Hinduism? **23A, 23B**

23 ***Identifying Perspectives*** In what way was Siddhartha Gautama unable to move beyond the social outlook of his day?

24 ***Identifying Perspectives and Differing Interpretations*** What role did women play in early Buddhism? How did this compare to other prominent contemporary cultures in different regions? Be sure to make reference to at least one religious text. **23A, 23B**

25 ***Interpreting*** According to Megasthenes, the Greek ambassador to the Mauryan court, Candragupta Maurya was afraid of assassination despite having a large army and secret police. What precautions did he take in regard to this fear and how might you interpret his behavior?

Social Studies Skills

26 ***Geography Skills*** Refer to a map of India and identify the location of the Kushān Empire. Explain how its location influenced events, specifically its trade prospects and its culture. **16C**

27 ***Creating Presentations*** With a partner, create an oral presentation that shares the ways Buddhism resembles Hinduism and the ways the two religions differ. Present summaries to peers, and have peers listen and review for bias in the presentations. Peers can provide feedback to the presenters on ways to limit any bias. **23A, 25A, 29E**

28 ***Synthesizing*** What role did religions play in ancient India? In what ways did a belief in reincarnation affect ancient Indian society? **23A**

29 ***Creating Charts*** Read a translation of two stories from The Bhagavad Gita, Vedas, Upanishads, or another Indian text. Create a chart that compares and contrasts how the two works convey universal themes. The chart should include quotations as well as interpretation and analysis. **23A**

30 ***Summarizing and Sequencing*** Work with a partner to create an illustrated print or digital time line showing the key events and figures in early Indian society from 1500 B.C. to the end of the Empire of the Guptas. Use the timeline to summarize the major political influences of India during this time range. Your time line should contain visuals or multimedia elements such as photos of art, architecture, and maps. You may also include excerpts from primary sources. **3A, 23A**

Need Extra Help?

If You've Missed Question	18	19	20	21	22	23	24	25	26	27	28	29	30
Go to page	118	116	109	110	115	115	116	117	110	110	110	106	116

DBQ Analyzing Primary Sources

Use the text excerpt to answer the following questions.

The Laws of Manu, an ancient document, is said to have been written by the Hindu god Brahma and given to his son Manu.

> “81. A barren [childless] wife may be superseded [replaced as primary wife] in the eighth year, she whose children all die in the tenth, she who bears only daughters in the eleventh, but she who is quarrelsome without delay.
>
> 148. In childhood female must be subject to her father, in youth to her husband, when her lord is dead to her sons; . . .
>
> 149. She must not seek to separate herself from her father, husband, or sons; by leaving them she would make both (her own and her husband's) families contemptible.”
>
> —from *The Laws of Manu*

31. ***Making Connections*** *The Laws of Manu* list several scenarios where a man is allowed to immediately divorce his wife. What conclusions can you make about the author of these laws? Why? **26B, 26C**

32. ***Interpreting*** What reason does *The Laws of Manu* consider to be good enough for a man to divorce his wife immediately? **26B, 26C**

Analyzing Visuals

Use the image below to answer the following questions

This photograph shows monks praying at the Bodhi tree at Mahabodhi Temple in Bodh Gaya, India. The Buddha is said to have attained enlightenment under the Bodhi tree.

33. ***Describing*** Write a paragraph describing the importance of meditation and the monastic tradition in Buddhism. Relate practice to specific aspects of the Buddha's teachings. **23A**

Extended Response Question

34. ***Expository*** Choose a mathematical, scientific, or architectural innovation of the ancient Indians. Write an essay about how this innovation diffused across time and place into other cultures or civilizations. Explain how other cultures or civilizations utilized this innovation, and share to what degree Indian innovations influenced neighboring cultures. **27A**

Need Extra Help?

If You've Missed Question	31	32	33	34
Go to page	126	126	114	120

The First Chinese Empires

221 B.C.–A.D. 220

ESSENTIAL QUESTIONS • *How can differing philosophies influence a culture?* • *What factors can help a dynasty stay in power?*

networks

There's More Online! about the first Chinese empires.

CHAPTER 6

The Story Matters...

The Chinese Empire was first unified by Qin Shihuangdi, who connected his provinces through a system of roads, a strong central government, and a common currency. Qin policies were influenced by Legalism, which held that society requires strict laws in order to function. An alternative way of thought, Confucianism held that people are basically good and only need compassionate rulers to guide them along the right path. The Han dynasty, which emerged after the collapse of the Qin, continued many of the Qin policies but adhered more to the teachings of Confucius than to Legalism.

◀ The Great Wall, one of the most recognizable landmarks of China, was begun as the *Wall of Ten Thousand Li* during the reign of emperor Qin Shihuangdi.

PHOTO: Glow Images

CHAPTER 6

Place and Time: Ancient China, 300 B.C.–A.D. 300

The period between 221 B.C. and A.D. 200 witnessed the emergence of a politically unified Chinese state. Chinese philosophy offered two opposing schools of thought to guide the process: Legalism and Confucianism. Qin rulers followed Legalism, which advocated the exercise of authoritarian state power. Han leaders preferred Confucianism, an ethical system that emphasized social harmony. In 136 B.C., Confucianism became the official state philosophy and has since strongly influenced Chinese culture.

Step Into the Place

After reading the quotes and looking at the map, answer the following question.

DBQ **Analyzing Historical Documents** How did Legalist and Confucian philosophies affect the ways in which the Qin and Han dynasties governed?

PHOTO: ©Wangwen/Age Fotostock America

PRIMARY SOURCE

"There is a saying, 'The dull cannot even see what has already happened, but the intelligent can see what is yet to sprout.' The people should not be consulted in the beginning; but they should join in in enjoying the results. . . . Laws exist to love the people; rites exist to make affairs go smoothly. Therefore, the sage does not stick to ancient laws if he can strengthen his state by changing them and does not keep ancient rituals if he can benefit the people by altering them."

—Legalist philosophy on government, from *The Book of Lord Shang*, before 338 B.C.

PRIMARY SOURCE

"The ancients honored the use of virtue and discredited the use of arms. Confucius said, 'If the people of far-off lands do not submit, then the ruler must attract them by enhancing his refinement and virtue. When they have been attracted, he gives them peace.'

At present, morality is discarded and reliance is placed on military force. Troops are raised for campaigns and garrisons are stationed for defense. It is the long-drawn-out campaigns and the ceaseless transportation of provisions that burden our people at home and cause our frontier soldiers to suffer from hunger and cold."

—a Confucian scholar's argument, from *The Debate on Salt and Iron at the Han Court*, 81 B.C.

Step Into the Time

Comparing and Contrasting Research two leaders from the time line. Use a Venn diagram to compare and contrast their contributions to society.

CHINA

- **221 B.C.** Beginning of Qin dynasty
- **213 B.C.** Qin emperor orders burning of nearly all books
- **210 B.C.** Qin Shihuangdi dies; end of Qin dynasty
- **202 B.C.** Liu Pang establishes Han dynasty
- **136 B.C.** Han ruler Wudi declares Confucianism the imperial ideology of China

300 B.C. — 200 B.C. — 100 B.C.

THE WORLD

- **218 B.C.** Rome begins Second Punic War with Carthage
- **c. 200 B.C.** Gauls, a Celtic people, settle in what is now Paris, France

networks
There's More Online!

- **MAP** Explore the interactive version of this map on Networks.
- **TIME LINE** Explore the interactive version of the time line on Networks.

Qin and Han Empires 221 B.C. – A.D. 220

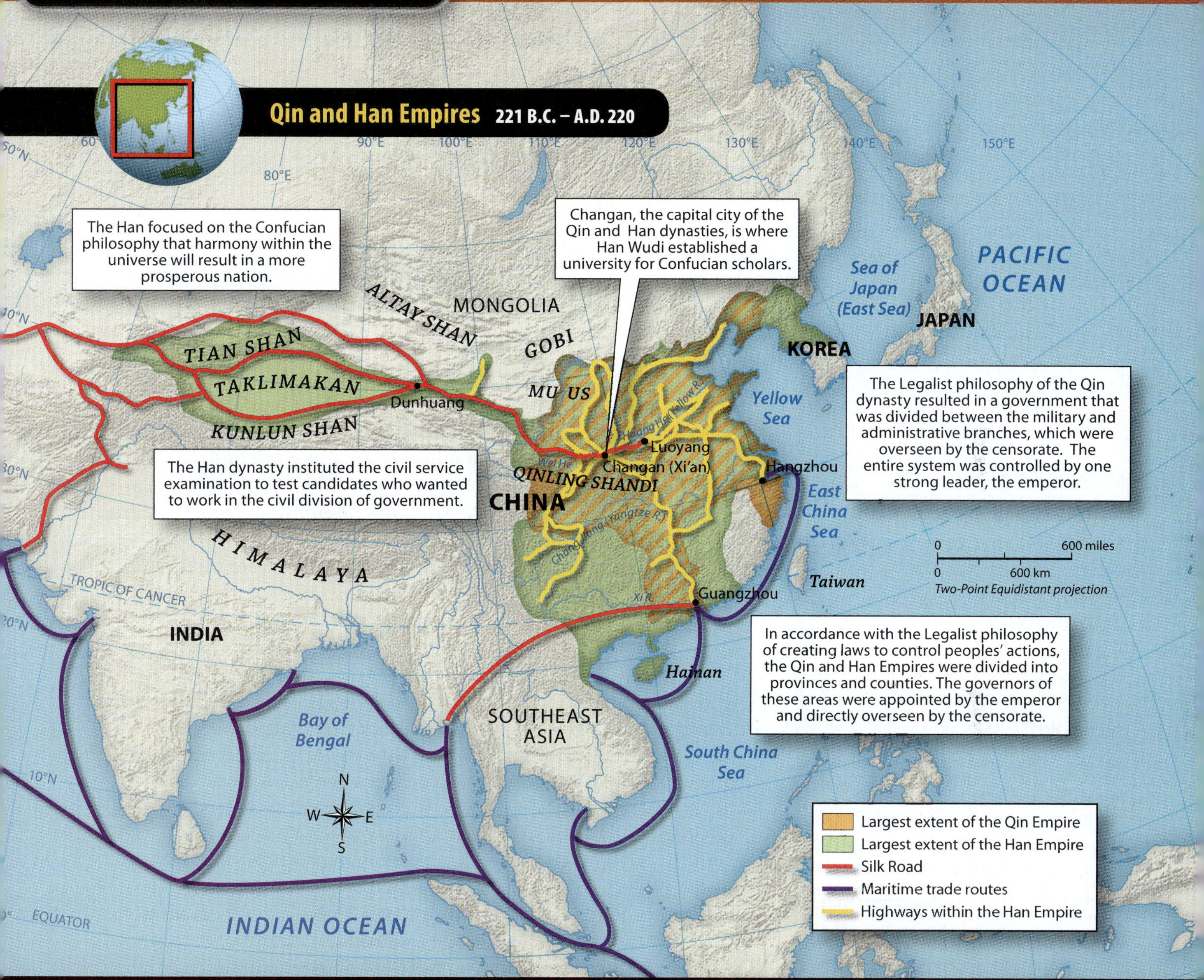

48 B.C. Egyptian civil war breaks out between Ptolemy XIII and Cleopatra

58 B.C. Julius Caesar invades Gaul, initiating Rome's Gallic Wars

A.D. 1

A.D. 73 Ban Chao, general and administrator, pacifies Xiongnu tribes

A.D. 77 Roman Pliny the Elder writes the first encyclopedia, *Historia Naturalis*

A.D. 79 Italy's Mount Vesuvius erupts, destroying Pompeii and Herculaneum

A.D. 100

A.D. 106 Female scholar, Ban Zhao, writes *Nujie* ("Lessons for Women")

A.D. 122 Roman emperor Hadrian begins building a wall across northern England

A.D. 190 Rebel armies attack Han dynasty capital

A.D. 200

A.D. c. 216 Greek physician and writer, Galen of Pergamum, dies

A.D. 220 Han general, Cao Cao, seizes control of Han government

A.D. 300

networks

There's More Online!

- BIOGRAPHY Confucius
- BIOGRAPHY Laozi
- IMAGE Confucius and His Disciples
- IMAGE Daoist Incense Burner
- IMAGE Qin Shihuangdi Orders the Burning of Books and the Execution of Scholars
- INTERACTIVE SELF-CHECK QUIZ
- PRIMARY SOURCE Analects of Confucius
- PRIMARY SOURCE Han Feizi on Legalism
- VIDEO Schools of Thought in Ancient China

LESSON 1

Schools of Thought in Ancient China

ESSENTIAL QUESTION

- *How can differing philosophies influence a culture?*

IT MATTERS BECAUSE

Between 500 B.C. and 200 B.C., toward the end of the Zhou dynasty, three major schools of thought about the nature of human beings and the universe emerged in China—Confucianism, Daoism, and Legalism. Although Hindus and Buddhists focused on freeing the human soul from the cycle of rebirth, Chinese philosophers were more concerned about the material world and creating a stable society.

Confucianism

GUIDING QUESTION *What were the basic tenets of Confucianism?*

As we have seen, the Zhou dynasty ruled China from 1122 B.C. to 256 B.C., the longest-lived dynasty in Chinese history. Like other dynasties, however, it also experienced a period of decline before its fall. During that decline, with all of its chaos, there emerged a philosopher who tried to answer one basic question: How do we restore order to this society?

Confucius was known to the Chinese as the First Teacher. Confucius is the Westernized form of Kongfuzi (KUNG • FOO • DZUH), meaning "Master Kung," as he was called by his followers. Confucius was born in 551 B.C. He hoped to get a job as a political adviser, but he had little success in finding a patron.

Upset by the violence and moral decay of his era, Confucius traveled round China in an attempt to spread his ideas and persuade political leaders to follow them. Few listened at the time, but a faithful band of followers revered him as a great teacher, recorded his sayings in the Analects, and spread his message widely. Until the twentieth century, almost every Chinese pupil studied his sayings, making the development of **Confucianism**, or the system of Confucian ideas, a widespread and influential force in Chinese culture.

The historical origins of Confucianism grew out of a chaotic period in China. Warfare and mass executions of men, women, and children were common. China was faced with restoring order. Confucius provided a set of ideas that eventually became widely accepted.

Reading HELPDESK

Academic Vocabulary

- **philosophy**
- **ethical**

Content Vocabulary

- **Confucianism**
- **Daoism**
- **Legalism**

TAKING NOTES:

Key Ideas and Details

Identifying Use the following graphic organizer to identify the three major schools of Chinese thought and an important principle of each.

School of Thought	Principle

TEKS Texas Essential Knowledge and Skills

1B identify major causes and describe the major effects of the following events from 500 BC to AD 600: the development of the classical civilizations of Greece, Rome, Persia, India (Maurya and Gupta), China (Zhou, Qin, and Han), and the development of major world religions

continued on the next page

Confucius's interest in **philosophy** was political and **ethical**, not spiritual. He believed that it was useless to speculate on spiritual questions. It was better to assume that there was an order in the universe. If humans would act in harmony with the universe, their own affairs would prosper.

Two central ideas stand out in the Confucian view of the Dao (Way): duty and humanity. The concept of duty meant that people had to subordinate their own interests to the broader needs of the family and the community. Everyone should be governed by the Five Constant Relationships: parent and child, husband and wife, older sibling and younger sibling, older friend and younger friend, and ruler and subject. Each person had a duty to the other. Parents should be loving, and children should revere their parents. Husbands should fulfill their duties, and wives should be obedient. The elder sibling should be kind, and the younger sibling respectful. The older friend should be considerate, and the younger friend deferential. Rulers should be benevolent, and subjects loyal. Showing the importance of family, Confucius said: "The duty of children to their parents is the fountains, whence all other virtues spring." The Confucian concept of duty was often expressed in the form of a "work ethic." If each individual worked hard to fulfill his or her duties, then the affairs of society as a whole would prosper as well.

As Confucius stated, "If there is righteousness in the heart, there will be beauty in the character. If there is beauty in the character, there will be harmony in the home. If there is harmony in the home, there will be order in the nation. If there is order in the nation, there will be peace in the world."

Confucius taught that humans are basically good. Above all, the ruler must set a good example. If the king followed the path of goodness, then subjects would respect him, and society would prosper. Confucius said, "Let him [the ruler] be filial and kind to all;—then they will be faithful to him.

Confucianism the system of political and ethical ideas formulated by the Chinese philosopher Confucius toward the end of the Zhou dynasty; it was intended to help restore order to a society that was in a state of confusion

philosophy an organized system of thought, from the Greek for "love of wisdom"

ethical conforming to accepted standards of conduct; moral

(continued from p. 130)

TEKS **Texas Essential Knowledge and Skills**
23A describe the historical origins, central ideas, and spread of major religious and philosophical traditions, including Buddhism, Christianity, Confucianism, Hinduism, Islam, Judaism, Sikhism, and the development of monotheism

▼ **This Qing dynasty drawing shows Confucius and his disciples.**

▶ **CRITICAL THINKING**
Analyzing Visuals Based on the image, how would you describe Confucius?

BIOGRAPHY

Confucius (551–479 B.C.)

Confucius was born in the small feudal state of Lu to a poor family. Early on, he distinguished himself as a devoted student. By the time he was 30, he was recognized as a classical scholar and a master of the six arts—ritual, music, archery, charioting, calligraphy, and arithmetic. He was the first teacher in China to promote education as a benefit to all human beings, not simply the aristocracy. Confucius believed that education built character. It involved constant self-improvement, a quest for self-knowledge, and devotion to public service. Confucius tried but failed to reform government policy concerning education. However, he became widely admired for his ideals and his efforts. At his death, Confucius had 3,000 followers.

CRITICAL THINKING

Drawing Conclusions Why might Confucius's ideas have met resistance in the government?

Let him advance the good and teach the incompetent;—then they will eagerly seek to be virtuous."

The second key element in the Confucian view of the Dao is humanity—compassion and empathy for others. Confucius said, "What you do not wish done to yourself, do not do to others." Confucius urged people to "measure the feelings of others by one's own," for "within the four seas all men are brothers." After his death in 479 B.C., his message spread widely throughout China.

Confucius was a harsh critic of his own times. He stressed a return to the values of the Golden Age of the early Zhou dynasty. Confucius saw it as an age of perfection. "When the Great Way was practiced, the world was shared by all alike."

Confucius, however, was not just living in the past. Many of his key ideas looked forward. Perhaps his most influential political idea was that government service should be open to all men of superior talent and not limited to those of noble birth. This concept of rule by merit was not popular with the aristocrats who held political offices based on their noble birth. Although Confucius's ideas did not have much effect in his lifetime, they eventually became the guiding principles for the Chinese Empire and fundamental ideas of Eastern civilization.

✓ READING PROGRESS CHECK

Making Connections What characterized the historical context to which Confucius responded?

Daoism

GUIDING QUESTION ***What was the system of ideas on which Daoism was based?***

Daoism was a system of ideas developed around the teachings of Laozi (LOW • DZUH). According to tradition, Laozi, or the Old Master, lived around the same time period as Confucius. Scholars do not know if Laozi actually existed. Nevertheless, the ideas people associate with him became influential in the fifth and fourth centuries B.C., and Daoism became a rival to Confucianism.

The chief ideas of Daoism are discussed in a short work known as *Tao Te Ching, or The Way of the Dao.* Scholars have argued for centuries over its meaning. Nevertheless, the basic ideas of Daoism, as interpreted by its followers, are straightforward. The fundamental idea of Daoism, like Confucianism, does not concern itself with the meaning of the universe. Rather, it sets forth proper forms of human behavior.

However, Daoism puts forth a point of view of life that is quite different from that of Confucianism. Followers of Confucius believe that it is the duty of human beings to work hard to improve life here on Earth. Daoists believe that the way to follow the will of Heaven is not through action but inaction: The best way to act in harmony with the universal order is not to interfere with the natural order.

Daoism a system of ideas based on the teachings of Laozi; teaches that the will of Heaven is best followed through inaction so that nature is allowed to take its course

PRIMARY SOURCE

"The universe is sacred. You cannot improve it. If you try to change it, you will ruin it. If you try to hold it, you will lose it".

—Laozi, from *Tao Te Ching*

▶ Bronze incense burner used in Daoist rituals, circa 206 B.C.–A.D. 9

✓ READING PROGRESS CHECK

Speculating What might be the consequences for a society of its members' following Daoism?

Legalism

GUIDING QUESTION *What were the beliefs behind the philosophy of Legalism?*

A third philosophy that of major political influence in China was **Legalism**. Unlike Confucianism or Daoism, Legalism proposed that human beings were evil by nature. Legalists were referred to as the "School of Law" because they rejected the Confucian view that government by "superior men" could solve society's problems. Instead, the fundamental idea of Legalism was to have for a system of impersonal laws.

The Legalists believed that a strong ruler was required to create an orderly society. Confucius had said, "Lead the people by virtue and restrain them by the rules of decorum [good taste], and the people will have a sense of shame, and moreover will become good." The Legalists believed that only harsh laws and stiff punishments would cause the common people to serve the interests of the ruler. To them, people were not capable of being good. Therefore, the ruler did not have to show compassion for the people.

✓ **READING PROGRESS CHECK**

Describing What are the characteristics of an ideal ruler according to Legalist philosophy?

◀ **Legalism was strictly followed during the Qin dynasty; opposition was not tolerated. This image shows Chinese books being burned and scholars being killed for their beliefs during the rule of Qin Shihuangdi.**

Analyzing PRIMARY SOURCES

Tao Te Ching

"Without going outside, you may know the whole world.
Without looking through the window, you may see the ways of heaven.
The farther you go, the less you know.

Thus the sage [wise man] knows without traveling;
He sees without looking;
He works without doing."

—Laozi, from *Tao Te Ching*

DBQ ***DRAWING CONCLUSIONS*** This passage presents a series of apparent contradictions. What do you think it means?

Legalism a popular philosophy developed in China toward the end of the Zhou dynasty; it proposes that human beings are evil by nature and can be brought to the correct path only by harsh laws

LESSON 1 REVIEW TEKS

Reviewing Vocabulary

1. ***Defining*** What are ethics, and how do they relate to Confucianism?

Using Your Notes

2. ***Comparing*** Use your notes to write a paragraph identifying the three major schools of thought in ancient China. What do these schools have in common?

Answering the Guiding Questions

3. ***Identifying Central Issues*** What were the basic tenets of Confucianism?

4. ***Finding the Main Idea*** What was the system of ideas on which Daoism was based?

5. ***Drawing Conclusions*** What were the beliefs behind the philosophy of Legalism?

Writing Activity

6. **ARGUMENT** Which ancient Chinese school of thought do you think provides the best guidance for government and society? Your essay should compare and contrast the three schools and make a compelling argument for the one that you believe would be most effective.

WORLD RELIGIONS HANDBOOK

Confucianism

Confucianism began more than 2,500 years ago in China. Although considered a religion, it is actually a philosophy. It is based upon the teachings of Confucius, which are grounded in ethical behavior and good government.

The teachings of Confucius focused on three areas: social philosophy, political philosophy, and education. Confucius taught that relationships are based on rank. Persons of higher rank are responsible for caring for those of lower rank. Those of lower rank should respect and obey those of higher rank. Eventually his teachings spread from China to other East Asian societies.

Sacred Teachings

Confucius was famous for his sayings and proverbs. These teachings were gathered into a book called the *Analects* after Confucius's death. Below is an example of Confucius's teachings:

Confucius said:

"To learn and to practice what is learned time and again is pleasure, is it not? To have friends come from afar is happiness, is it not? To be unperturbed when not appreciated by others is gentlemanly, is it not?"

Sacred Symbol

Yin-yang, associated with both Confucianism and Daoism, symbolizes the harmony offered by the philosophies. The light half represents *yang*, the creative, firm, strong elements in all things. The dark half represents *yin*, the receptive, yielding, weak elements. The two act together to balance one another.

Worship and Celebration

Confucianism does not have a god or clergy, but there are temples dedicated to Confucius, the spiritual leader. Those who follow his teachings see Confucianism as a way of life and a guide to ethical behavior and good government.

Sacred Site ▼

There are many temples associated with Confucianism. Among them is the temple at Qufu, a group of buildings dedicated to Confucius. It is located on Confucius's ancestral land. It is one of the largest ancient architectural complexes in China. Every year, followers gather at Qufu to celebrate the birthday of Confucius.

PHOTO: STR/Stringer/AFP/Getty Images

SKILLBUILDER

TEKS 29F

Sequencing

Why Learn This Skill?

When studying world history, it is important to recognize how a series of events can lead to things like a successful economy, the rise of a political leader, or the expansion of empire. Sequencing demonstrates how a continuous and connected set of ideas or events can lead to a particular result.

Learning the Skill

Focusing on sequence helps you to create order and organize the information you are gathering for analysis. In the same way that a time line shows history organized by dates, a sequencing chart or graph demonstrates the steps that lead to a particular result. When analyzing events through sequencing, it is helpful to think in terms of what happened first, what events or ideas followed, and what the final result was. You can also think of it in terms of beginning with a cause and ending up with an effect. These steps must be connected and continuous, though. If one step has nothing to do with another, it is not a sequence.

Practicing the Skill

In Confucianism, it is believed that fulfilling one's duties results in a prosperous society. Read the following graphic organizer to follow Confucius's sequence of ideas that leads from duty to prosperity, and then answer the questions below.

1. What does Confucius mean by "righteousness in the heart"?
2. What is meant by the sequence of ideas between boxes two and four, starting with an individual and ending with the world?
3. How does this chart demonstrate that sequencing can work for ideas, as well as events?

Sequencing a Concept in Confucianism

Individuals must work hard to fulfill their duties:

↓

"If there is righteousness in the heart, there will be harmony in the home."

↓

"If there is harmony in the home, there will be order in the nation."

↓

"In there is order in the nation, there will be peace in the world."

↓

Peace in the world.

Applying the Skill

Select a news item or current event to sequence. On a piece of paper, first identify the origin, or cause, of the event. Then create as many boxes as needed to sequence the event. The final panel should contain the result, or effect, of all the items previously listed.

networks

There's More Online!

- ☑ BIOGRAPHY Qin Shihuangdi
- ☑ IMAGE Great Wall of China
- ☑ IMAGE Terra-cotta Soldiers at the Tomb of Qin Shihuangdi
- ☑ INTERACTIVE SELF-CHECK QUIZ
- ☑ MAP Building the Great Wall
- ☑ PRIMARY SOURCE Peasant Revolts Against the Qin Dynasty
- ☑ PRIMARY SOURCE Qin Shihuangdi Describes His Dynasty
- ☑ VIDEO The Qin Unify China

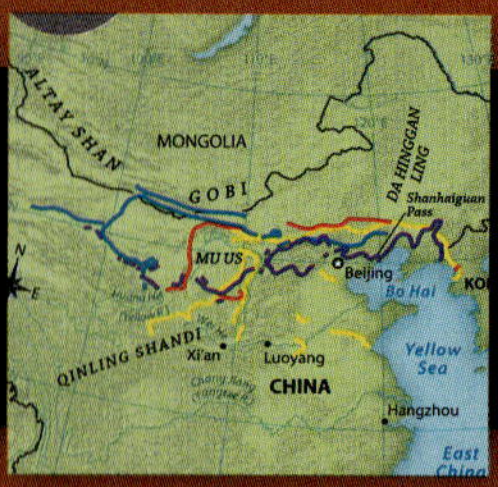

LESSON 2

The Qin Unify China

ESSENTIAL QUESTIONS

- *How can differing philosophies influence a culture?*
- *What factors can help a dynasty stay in power?*

It Matters Because

After more than 200 years of civil war, order was restored to China when the first Qin emperor unified the Chinese world. Although his dynasty was short-lived, Qin Shihuangdi made many important changes to a unified China during his brief rule. The Han dynasty that followed lasted more than 400 years.

Reading HELPDESK

Academic Vocabulary

- **individuality**
- **ideology**
- **instituted**

Content Vocabulary

- **regime**
- **censorate**

TAKING NOTES:

Key Ideas and Details

Listing Use the following graphic organizer to list how Qin Shihuangdi rose to power, what actions he took as ruler, and how his rule ended.

The Reign of Qin Shihuangdi	Attributes
Rise	
Rule	
Fall	

TEKS Texas Essential Knowledge and Skills

1B identify major causes and describe the major effects of the following events from 500 BC to AD 600: the development of the classical civilizations of Greece, Rome, Persia, India (Maurya and Gupta), China (Zhou, Qin, and Han), and the development of major world religions

continued on the next page

The Qin Dynasty

GUIDING QUESTION *How did Qin Shihuangdi unify the Chinese world?*

The Zhou Dynasty formed around 1000 B.C. and ruled a complex civilization that lasted hundreds of years. From approximately 400 B.C. to 221 B.C., however, China experienced a bloody civil war. Powerful states fought one another and ignored the authority of the Zhou kings. One state—that of Qin—gradually defeated its chief rivals. In 221 B.C., the Qin ruler declared the creation of a new dynasty.

Qin Shihuangdi

The ruler of the Qin dynasty was Qin Shihuangdi (CHIHN SHUH • HWAHNG • DEE), meaning "the First Qin Emperor." An ambitious person, he came to the throne in 246 B.C. at the age of 13. In 221 B.C., he defeated the last of his rivals and founded a new dynasty, with himself as emperor. The famous Chinese historian Sima Qian described Qin Shihuangdi as having "the chest of a bird of prey, the voice of a jackal, and the heart of a tiger."

Those were the qualities Qin Shihuangdi used to unite China and usher in the Qin era of classical China. He created a single monetary system and ordered the building of a system of roads throughout the entire empire. Many of these roads led out from his capital city of Xianyang (SHYEN • YAHNG), just north of modern-day Xi'an (SHEE • AHN). He reduced the powersof the landed aristocrats by dividing their estates among the peasants, who were now taxed directly by the state. In doing so, he eliminated possible rivals and gained tax revenues for the central government.

Qin Shihuangdi was equally aggressive in foreign affairs. His armies advanced to the south, extending the border of China to the edge of the Yuan (YOO • AHN) River, or Red River, in modern-day Vietnam. To supply his armies, he had a canal dug from the Chang Jiang in central China to what is now the modern city of Guangzhou (GWAHNG • JOH).

(continued from p. 136)

TEKS Texas Essential Knowledge and Skills

3A describe the major political, religious/philosophical, and cultural influences of Persia, India, China, Israel, Greece, and Rome, including the development of monotheism, Judaism, and Christianity

25A summarize the fundamental ideas and institutions of Eastern civilizations that originated in China and India

The Emperor's Army

Surprisingly, the emperor left behind a remarkable artistic legacy too, another sign of a classical civilization. In 1974 farmers digging a well about 35 miles (56 km) east of Xi'an discovered an underground pit near the burial mound of the First Qin Emperor. The pit contained a vast army made out of terra-cotta, or hardened clay. Chinese archaeologists believe that it was a re-creation of Qin Shihuangdi's imperial guard, meant to be with the emperor on his journey to the next world. The elaborate nature of this art clearly reflected the strong central power of the empire.

Archaeologists estimate that there are more than 6,000 figures in the first pit alone, along with horses, wooden chariots, and 7,000 bronze weapons. The figures are slightly larger than life-size. They were molded, fired, and painted in brilliant colors and then dressed in uniforms. To achieve **individuality** in the faces of the soldiers, 10 different head shapes were used, which were finished by hand. The project must have been enormously expensive and demonstrates the centralized nature of government in Qin China. It has been estimated that one-third of the national income may have been spent on preparations for the ruler's afterlife.

individuality a total character that distinguishes an individual from others

✓ READING PROGRESS CHECK

Describing What characteristics have been attributed to the emperor Qin Shihuangdi?

The Great Wall

GUIDING QUESTION ***What was the extent and purpose of the Great Wall in China?***

The Qin emperor's major foreign concern was in the north. In the area south of the Gobi, there resided a nomadic people known to the Chinese as the Xiongnu (SHYUNG • NOO), who had mastered the art of riding on horseback. Mounted on their horses, they ranged far and wide in search of pastures. The Xiongnu were organized loosely into tribes and moved with the seasons from one pasture to another with their flocks of cattle, sheep, or goats. The Xiongnu had mastered the art of fighting on horseback. The historian Sima Qian remarked:

PRIMARY SOURCE

"The little boys start out by learning to ride sheep and shoot birds and rats with a bow and arrow, and when they get a little older they shoot foxes and hares, which are used for food. Thus all the young men are able to use a bow and act as armed cavalry in time of war."

—quoted in *Records of the Grand Historian: Han Dynasty, Volume 2*

When the Xiongnu challenged Chinese communities near the northern frontier, a number of states constructed walls to keep out the nomads. Warriors on horseback, however, had definite advantages over the infantry troops of the Chinese.

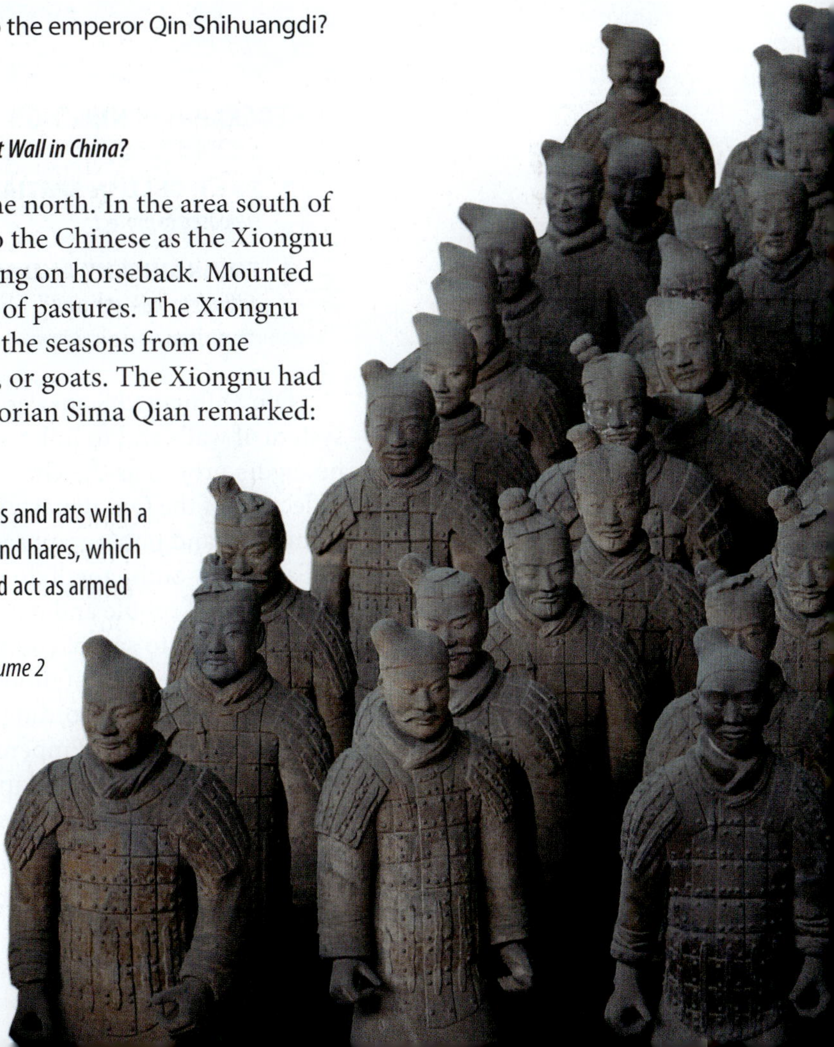

▼ These close to life-size terra-cotta soldiers guarded the tomb of Qin Shihuangdi.

▶ CRITICAL THINKING

Analyzing Visuals What features of the soldiers are individualized?

GEOGRAPHY CONNECTION

1. **THE WORLD IN SPATIAL TERMS** *Which border of the Chinese empires was the wall supposed to protect?*
2. **ENVIRONMENT AND SOCIETY** *What physical features of the environment made it difficult to build the wall?*

▲ Emperor Qin Shihuangdi

Qin Shihuangdi's answer to the problem was to strengthen the existing system of walls and to link them together to create Today we know Qin Shihuangdi's project as the Great Wall of China, and it serves as an architectural reflection of the Qin dynasty's defensive needs. However, the wall that we know from films and photographs was not built until 1,500 years later. Some of the walls built by Shihuangdi do remain, but most of them were built of loose stone, sand, or piled rubble and disappeared long ago.

This is not to say, of course, that the wall was not a massive project. It required the efforts of thousands of laborers. Many of them died while working there and, according to legend, are now buried within the wall. With his wall, the First Qin Emperor had some success in fighting off the nomads, but the victory was only temporary. Over the next 2,000 years, China's northern frontier became one of the great areas of conflict in Asia.

✓ **READING PROGRESS CHECK**

Identifying What practices of the Xiongnu made them especially difficult to combat?

Politics of the Qin Dynasty

GUIDING QUESTION ***What were the policies of the Qin dynasty and why did the dynasty fall?***

The Qin dynasty dramatically changed the political face of classical China. Legalism was adopted as the official **ideology** of the **regime**. Those who opposed the policies of the new regime were punished or even executed. Books presenting ideas opposed to the official views were publicly burned.

The ideas of Legalism led to a number of important political and administrative changes. Some of them were major political influences and survived the Qin dynasty. These ideas and institutions served as models for future dynasties. In the first place, unlike the Zhou dynasty, the Qin dynasty ruled a highly centralized state. The central bureaucracy was divided into three divisions: the civil division, the military division, and the **censorate**. The censorate was an influential institution that included inspectors who checked on government officials to make sure they were doing their jobs. This oversight became standard procedure for future Chinese dynasties.

Below the central government were two levels of administration: provinces and counties. Unlike under the Zhou, these officials did not inherit their positions but were appointed and dismissed by the emperor. The censors, who reported directly to the emperor, kept a close watch over the officials. Those found guilty of wrongdoing were executed.

By ruthlessly gathering control over the empire into his own hands, Qin Shihuangdi hoped to establish a rule that "would be enjoyed by his sons and grandsons for 10,000 generations." In fact, he was to be his dynasty's only ruler. The First Qin Emperor had angered many Chinese. Landed aristocrats and Confucian intellectuals, as well as the common people, groaned under the censorship of speech, harsh taxes, and forced labor projects **instituted** by the ruler. Sima Qian said of Qin Shihuangdi:

PRIMARY SOURCE

> "He killed men as though he thought he could never finish, he punished men as though he were afraid he would never get around to them all, and the whole world revolted against him."
>
> — Sima Qian, *Records of the Grand Historian*

The emperor died in 210 B.C., and his dynasty was overthrown four years later. The fall of the Qin dynasty was followed by a period of civil war, but it did not last long. A new dynasty soon arose, the Han.

✓ **READING PROGRESS CHECK**

Explaining How did Shihuangdi use the censorate to centralize government authority?

Connections to TODAY

The Great Wall of China

The Great Wall remains an important cultural symbol to many Chinese people. It is also a major tourist attraction that draws thousands of Chinese and foreign visitors every day. The Great Wall is not one wall but many that were built over the course of several centuries. The best-preserved section runs roughly 5,500 miles (8,850 km) through the countryside. In 1987 the United Nations Educational, Scientific, and Cultural Organization (UNESCO) designated the Great Wall a World Heritage Site. This designation means that UNESCO considers the Wall to have "outstanding universal value."

ideology a set of beliefs

regime the government in power

censorate part of the Chinese bureaucracy that made sure government officials were doing their jobs

instituted put into action

LESSON 2 REVIEW TEKS

Reviewing Vocabulary

1. ***Describing*** What is a regime? What policies did Qin Shihuangdi's regime institute?

Using Your Notes

2. ***Sequencing Information*** Use your notes to write a paragraph describing the rise, rule, and fall of Emperor Qin Shihuangdi.

Answering the Guiding Questions

3. ***Determining Cause and Effect*** How did Qin Shihuangdi unify the Chinese world?
4. ***Analyzing Information*** What was the extent and purpose of the Great Wall in China?
5. ***Making Connections*** What were the policies of the Qin dynasty and why did the dynasty fall?

Writing Activity

6. **INFORMATIVE/EXPLANATORY** Write an essay in which you describe the Great Wall of China and its purpose. What is the symbolic significance of such an endeavor? What does the Wall suggest about the formation of China's national identity?

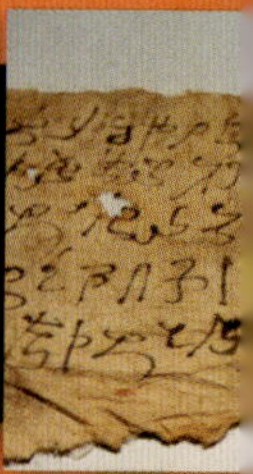

networks

There's More Online!

- BIOGRAPHY Han Wudi
- BIOGRAPHY Liu Pang
- IMAGE Civil Service Exam
- IMAGE Han Dynasty Bronze Art
- IMAGE Paper Created During the Han Dynasty
- INTERACTIVE SELF-CHECK QUIZ
- PRIMARY SOURCE Destruction of Luoyang
- PRIMARY SOURCE Fighting South of the Ramparts
- TIME LINE Fall of the Han Empire
- VIDEO The Han Dynasty

LESSON 3

The Han Dynasty

ESSENTIAL QUESTIONS
- *How can differing philosophies influence a culture?*
- *What factors can help a dynasty stay in power?*

Reading HELPDESK

Academic Vocabulary
- **ensure**
- **maintain**

Content Vocabulary
- **civil service**
- **martial**

TAKING NOTES:
Key Ideas and Details

Displaying Use the following graphic organizer to display the structure of the central and local governments under the Han dynasty.

Central Government Divisions	
Local Government Divisions	

TEKS Texas Essential Knowledge and Skills

1B identify major causes and describe the major effects of the following events from 500 BC to AD 600: the development of the classical civilizations of Greece, Rome, Persia, India (Maurya and Gupta), China (Zhou, Qin, and Han), and the development of major world religions

3A describe the major political, religious/philosophical, and cultural influences of Persia, India, China, Israel, Greece, and Rome, including the development of monotheism, Judaism, and Christianity

continued on p. 143

It Matters Because

The fall of the Qin dynasty was followed by a period of civil war, but it did not last long. One of the greatest and most long-lasting dynasties in Chinese history—the Han dynasty—emerged in 202 B.C. The Han dynasty, and the Qin before it, made contributions to culture and technology that have endured to the present.

The Han Dynasty

GUIDING QUESTION *How did the Han dynasty refine the political structures of the Qin dynasty?*

The founder of the Han (HAHN) dynasty, Liu Pang (LYOO BAHNG), was of peasant origin but became known by his title of Han Gaozu—Exalted Emperor of Han. Under his strong rule and that of his successors, the new dynasty quickly established its control over the empire and began the Han era of classical Chinese civilization.

Political Structures

The first Han emperor had expressed his desire to discard the harsh policies of the Qin dynasty. He did abandon the use of cruel and unusual punishments that had been part of the Legalistic approach to law enforcement. Confucian principles continued to prove politically influential in China. These, rather than Legalism, soon became the basis for the creation of a new state philosophy. However, Han Gaozu and his successors found it convenient to keep some of the practices of the First Qin Emperor, including the division of the central government into three ministries—the military, civil service, and censorate. The Han rulers also kept the system of local government that divided the empire into provinces and counties.

Most importantly, when the Han rulers took over, they looked to Confucianism for guidance. The Han rulers continued the Qin system of choosing government officials on the basis of merit rather than birth. To create a regular system for new officials, the Han dynasty introduced the **civil service** examination and established a school to train these candidates. This system for officials developed in classical

China influenced Chinese civilization for 2,000 years. Students were expected to learn the teachings of Confucius, as well as Chinese history and law. By creating a group of well-trained officials well versed in Confucian thought, the system **ensured** the influence of Confucianism on government for a long time.

civil service the administrative service of a government, not including the armed forces, in which appointments are determined by competitive examination

China under the Han dynasty was a vast civilization. The population increased rapidly—by some estimates rising from about 20 million to more than 60 million at the height of the dynasty. The large size of the population created a growing need for a large and efficient bureaucracy to **maintain** the state in proper working order.

In addition to providing a strong central government, the Han emperors also continued to expand the Chinese Empire. Han rulers, especially Han Wudi (HAHN WOO • DEE), **Martial** Emperor of Han, added the southern regions below the Chang Jiang into the empire. Part of what is now northern Vietnam, along the South China Sea coast, became part of the empire. Han armies also went westward into Central Asia, extending the Chinese boundary there. Han Wudi also had to deal with the Xiongnu, the nomads beyond the Great Wall to the north. His armies drove the Xiongnu back, and after he died in 87 B.C., China experienced almost another 150 years of peace.

▲ Chinese city officials taking an examination to demonstrate their knowledge of Confucian texts

▶ **CRITICAL THINKING**

Contrasting What are some differences between ancient Chinese and modern civil service examinations?

Society in the Han Empire

Although the Han period was prosperous, free peasants began to suffer. Land taxes on land-owning farmers were fairly light, but there were other demands on them, including military service and forced labor of up to one month per year. Then, too, as the population tripled, the average size of the individual farm plot was reduced to about one acre (0.4 ha) per person—barely enough for survival.

As time went on, many poor peasants were forced to sell their land and to become tenant farmers, paying up to half of the annual harvest in rent. Once again, aristocrats owned thousands of acres. These powerful nobles could bully free farmers into becoming tenant farmers.

The Han did, however, increase the importance of the family in the Chinese system of life. The First Qin Emperor had tried to weaken the family, seeing family loyalty as a threat to a strong monarch. But the efforts of the Qin to weaken the family system ran into heavy opposition, and the Han, reinforced by the ideas of Confucianism, renewed the emphasis on the family. Under the Han, the family system began to take on the character that it would have until the twentieth century. The family was not only the basic economic unit, it was also the basic social unit for education and training in morals.

ensure to make sure, certain, or safe

maintain to keep in an existing state; to preserve from failure or decline

martial relating to, or suited for, war or a warrior

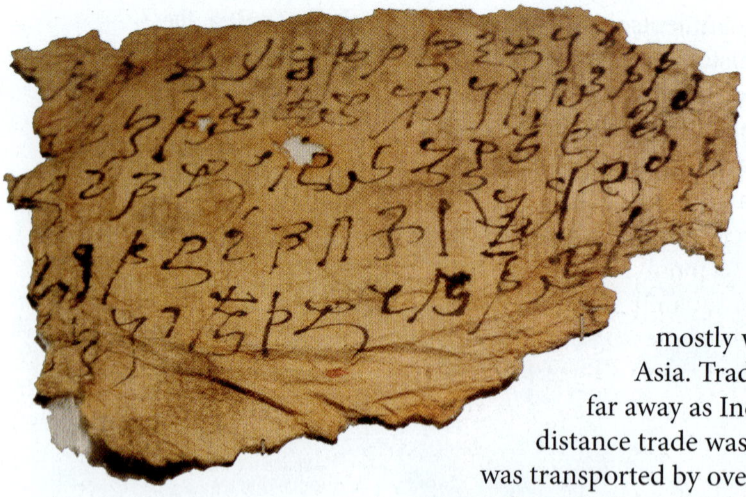

▲ This paper fragment was located in an ancient Chinese burial ground. It is dated from A.D. 25 to 420.

▶ **CRITICAL THINKING**

Drawing Conclusions How did the Chinese benefit from the development of paper?

Although the economic problems in the countryside helped lead to the eventual downfall of the dynasty, in general the Han era was one of great prosperity. There was a major expansion of trade and manufacturing. Much of this activity was directed by the state. The government owned shipyards, manufactured weapons, and controlled mining and the operation of granaries. The government also participated in foreign trade, mostly with neighboring areas in Central and Southeast Asia. Trade relations were even established with countries as far away as India and off the Mediterranean. Some of the long-distance trade was carried by sea through southern ports, but more was transported by overland caravans on the Silk Road and other similar routes through the vast deserts and plateaus that led westward into Central Asia.

Technology and Culture

New technology added to the economic prosperity of the Han era. Much progress was made in areas such as textile manufacturing, water mills for grinding grain, and iron casting. Iron-casting technology led to the invention of steel. In addition, paper was developed under the Han dynasty. The art of papermaking spread eastward from China beginning in the seventh century A.D. First India and then the Arab world developed the technique. Paper was shipped from the Arab cities of Baghdad, Damascus, and Cairo to the West, but Europeans did not begin their production of paper until the twelfth century.

With the invention of the rudder and fore-and-aft rigging, ships could sail into the wind. This made it possible for Chinese merchant ships carrying heavy cargoes to travel throughout the islands of Southeast Asia and India, leading to a major expansion of trade in the Han period.

The Han dynasty was also known for its influential cultural achievements. The key works of the Confucian school were made into a set of Confucian classics, which became required reading for generations of Chinese schoolchildren. This literature directly reflected the Han devotion to Confucian ideals. These classics introduced children to the forms of behavior that they would need as adults.

During the Han dynasty, the writing of history became the chief form of literary effort. The major histories of the Han period, written by Sima Qian and Ban Gu, scaptured Chinese culture of the time and influenced future dynastic histories. These works combined political and social history with biographies of key figures.

✓ READING PROGRESS CHECK

Contrasting What school of thought did the Han dynasty embrace over the Qin dynasty's Legalism, and what difference did it make for China's social and political structure?

Thinking Like a HISTORIAN

The Development of Paper

Try to imagine the world without paper. Paper has been the basic material for communication and the spread of information for centuries. People may not have recognized the significance of paper, however, when it was first invented. It took hundreds of years for the technology to travel westward to Central Asia and Europe. It was only after the invention of the printing press in the 1450s that demand increased significantly. In the 1800s, people learned to make paper from wood pulp instead of cotton rags to accommodate rising demand. Today, we find paper increasingly replaced by electronic methods of communication. What impact do you think the rise of electronic communication will have on the modern world?

Fall of the Han Empire

GUIDING QUESTION ***What factors contributed to the fall of the Han dynasty?***

Over a period of time, the Han Empire began to fall into decay. As weak rulers amused themselves with the pleasures of court life, the power of the central government began to decline. The great noble families filled the gap, amassing huge landed estates and forcing free farmers to become their tenants. Official corruption and the concentration of land in the hands of the wealthy led to widespread peasant unrest. The population of the empire had been estimated at 60 million in China's first census in the year A.D. 2. Two hundred years later, it had declined to less than 20 million. Then, too, nomadic raids continued in the north. At one point, a group of marauders reached the gates of the capital city.

By A.D. 170, wars, intrigues at the court, and peasant uprisings brought the virtual collapse of the Han dynasty. In A.D. 190 rebel armies sacked the Han capital. The final blow came in A.D. 220, when a general seized control. He was unable to maintain his power, however. China again plunged into civil war, made worse by invasions of northern tribal peoples. The Han empire achieved the lasting greatness of a classical civilization. The next great dynasty would not arise for 400 years.

READING PROGRESS CHECK

Making Inferences Why did the population of China decline during the last two centuries of Han rule?

SKILLS PRACTICE

Working with a partner, take turns asking and answering questions about the technological achievements of the Han dynasty.

(continued from p. 140)

TEKS Texas Essential Knowledge and Skills

3C compare the factors that led to the collapse of Rome and Han China

21A describe how people have participated in supporting or changing their governments

25A summarize the fundamental ideas and institutions of Eastern civilizations that originated in China and India

PHOTO: Panorama Media/Age Fotostock America

◀ **Han dynasty bronze chariot**

▶ CRITICAL THINKING

Analyzing Visuals What might you infer about life during the Han dynasty from this artifact?

LESSON 3 REVIEW TEKS

Reviewing Vocabulary

1. ***Identifying*** What is civil service, and how does it relate to the system of government during the Han dynasty?

Using Your Notes

2. ***Organizing Information*** Use your notes to describe the structure of the central and local governments under the Han dynasty.

Answering the Guiding Questions

3. ***Comparing and Contrasting*** How did the Han dynasty refine the political structures of the Qin dynasty?

4. ***Identifying Cause and Effect*** What factors contributed to the fall of the Han dynasty?

Writing Activity

5. **INFORMATIVE/EXPLANATORY** What were the technological innovations and cultural achievements of the Han dynasty? How did they contribute to the empire's strength and success?

CHAPTER 6 Assessment

TEKS

Directions: On a separate sheet of paper, answer the questions below. Make sure you read carefully and answer all parts of the questions.

Lesson Review

Lesson 1

1. ***Specifying*** Summarize the two central ideas of the Confucian view of the right way to live? **3A, 23A, 25A**

2. ***Identifying Perspectives*** What were Confucius's views on spirituality? What did he believe was the best way for human affairs to prosper?

3. ***Defining*** What is the highest form of action in Daoism?

4. ***Naming*** What are the Five Constant Relationships of the Dao?

5. ***Explaining*** How was the Confucian concept of duty often expressed?

6. ***Summarizing*** What is considered Confucius's most significant political idea? What made this idea unpopular?

7. ***Identifying Central Issues*** What were the two vastly different ways Confucianism and Legalism thought rulers should act to bring order to the chaos of society? **3A**

8. ***Describing*** Despite their rival teachings, what is the commonality Daoism and Confucianism both share?

Lesson 2

9. ***Naming*** What were Qin Shihuangdi's greatest accomplishments?

10. ***Exploring Issues*** What purpose has Qin Shihuangdi's buried terra-cotta army served for modern-day researchers? What does it reveal about how the emperor chose to spend his country's money?

11. ***Identifying*** Who were the Xiongnu? Describe their way of life.

12. ***Summarizing*** How did the Qin dynasty dramatically change Chinese politics? What were the consequences for those who opposed the new views?

13. ***Specifying*** How was the central bureaucracy of the Qin dynasty divided?

14. ***Explaining*** What were the two levels of administration below the central government? How did officials come to gain their positions?

15. ***Describing*** How did the censorate keep officials in check?

16. ***Sequencing*** How long after the emperor's death did it take for his dynasty to collapse? What became of the new dynasty?

Need Extra Help?

If You've Missed Question	1	2	3	4	5	6	7	8	9	10	11	12	13	14	15	16
Go to page	131	131	132	131	131	132	133	132	136	136	136	139	139	139	139	139

Lesson 3

17 ***Identifying*** Which practices did Han Gaozu keep from the First Qin Emperor?

18 ***Finding the Main Idea*** How did Han Gaozu's decision to keep the Qin system of a merit-based bureaucracy help the Han dynasty switch from Legalism to Confucianism?

19 ***Explaining*** Under the Han, what was the family's role in the Chinese system of life?

20 ***Identifying*** Name the technology and cultural achievements of the Han era.

21 ***Speculating*** How far did China's borders extend at the peak of the Han empire? Would the empire have expanded if the Han philosophy had been Daoist rather than Confucian? Why or why not?

22 ***Explaining*** How long did the Han empire last? Why did it fall?

Exploring the Essential Question

23 ***Defending*** With a partner, play the roles of Qin Shihuangdi and Han Gaozu in a debate on "The Best Way to Run an Empire." Write out ahead of time what points you will make. Identify the strengths of your rule and the philosophy behind it and the weaknesses of your opponent's rule and the philosophy behind it. Use at least two primary sources. You may also use visuals if you like. Rehearse the debate. Then hold it in front of the class; record it if possible.

Critical Thinking

24 ***Evaluating*** Explain how architecture, art, and literature were each lasting influences on the early Chinese civilizations. Give an example of each and tell how it reflects the history of the culture in which it was produced. **26B**

25 ***Interpreting*** Explain how the origin of Confucianism occurred at an unlikely time, considering its philosophies. **23A**

26 ***Assessing*** Write a paragraph to explain how Confucianism spread to other empires in China. **23A**

Social Studies Skills

27 ***Create and Analyze Arguments*** Do you agree with Laozi that "The farther you go, the less you know"? Why or why not?

28 ***Economics*** What were some new technologies developed during the Han dynasty that caused the civilization to rise? What effect did they have on China's prosperity? **1B**

29 ***Understanding Relationships Among Events*** Explain why the idea of civil service in the Han dynasty was a major political influence. **3A**

30 ***Compare and Contrast*** Describe why Confucianism is not a major world religion, even though the ideals have influenced many and the lasted centuries. Compare Confucianism to another world religion. **1B**

Need Extra Help?

If You've Missed Question	17	18	19	20	21	22	23	24	25	26	27	28	29	30
Go to page	140	140	141	142	141	142	140	142	130	140	133	142	140	134

DBQ Analyzing Primary Sources

Use the document to answer the following questions.

Sima Qian was the grand historian of the Han court. He recorded a proposal by Qin Shihuangdi's prime minister that was made into law.

PRIMARY SOURCE

"I humbly propose that all historical records but those of Qin be burned . . . If thirty days after the issuing of this order the owners of these books have still not had them destroyed, they should have their faces tattooed and be condemned to hard labor at the Great Wall. The only books which need not be destroyed are those dealing with medicine, divination [foretelling the truth], and agriculture."

—Prime Minister Li Si, quoted in *The Records of the Grand Historian*

31. ***Drawing Conclusions*** What does Li Si's proposal tell you about the Legalists' point of view?

32. ***Making Inferences*** Why were books about medicine and agriculture not destroyed?

Analyzing Visuals

Use the map to answer the following questions.

33. ***Analyzing Visuals*** What part of the wall existed during the time when the dynasty was under the rule of Legalism?

34. ***Analyzing Visuals*** What part of the wall existed during the time when the dynasty was under the rule of Confucianism?

Extended Response Question

35. ***Expository*** Write an article tied to the concept of keeping your country at peace. Use what you have learned about the first Chinese empires to identify three actions and attitudes that could help keep a country from war and write a conclusion.

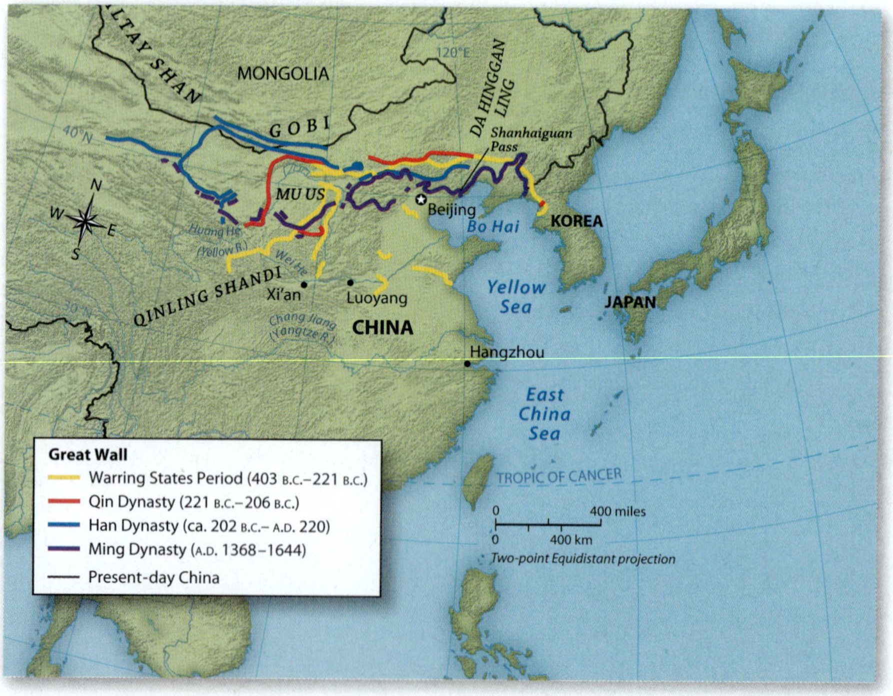

Need Extra Help?

If You've Missed Question	31	32	33	34	35
Go to page	139	139	138	138	130

The Romans

600 B.C.–A.D. 500

ESSENTIAL QUESTIONS

- *How do different types of political organizations emerge?*
- *How can new ideas lead to social and political change?*

networks

There's More Online! about the Romans.

CHAPTER 7

The Story Matters...

The myth of Rome's origin begins with twin brothers Romulus and Remus vying for control of the land along the Tiber River. It ends with Romulus becoming patriarch of a new civilization. Historically, however, Roman civilization developed over a long time. It began as a republic but ultimately became an empire ruled by an emperor. This empire grew as a result of its military prowess and was maintained by the common language of Latin, strong leaders, and a vast system of roads. At its height, the Roman Empire expanded into Europe, Asia, and Africa, spreading not only its political control but its culture.

◄ Much can be learned about Roman society from its art. This fresco, found in a home in Pompeii, was preserved beneath layers of volcanic ash after the eruption of Mount Vesuvius in A.D. 79. Based on the clothing and accessories in the fresco, it can be deduced that Roman women of the upper class were educated.

CHAPTER 7

Place and Time: Ancient Rome 600 B.C.–A.D. 500

From a small village in central Italy, Rome gradually expanded its control over the entire Mediterranean region and much of Western Europe. For centuries Rome was ruled as a republic, but over time elected leaders were replaced by emperors. The Latin language connected a vast empire and gave voice to Roman philosophy, oratory, and political debate. As the Roman Empire grew to encompass a large part of Western Europe and western Asia, its superiority was maintained through technological advances in both civil engineering and military organization.

Step Into the Place

Read the excerpts and examine the map.

DBQ **Analyzing Historical Documents** Given the size of their empire and the distances involved, how do you think the Romans maintained control over subject peoples and spread their culture? TEKS 27A

PRIMARY SOURCE

“In great buildings as well as in other things the rest of the world has been outdone by us Romans. If, indeed, all the buildings in our City are considered in the aggregate, and supposing them—so to say—all thrown together in one vast mass, the united grandeur of them would lead one to imagine that we were describing another world, accumulated in a single spot.”

—Pliny the Elder, from *Natural History*, C.A.D. 79

PRIMARY SOURCE

“Anyone who goes out of his way to examine the general organization of their army will realize that the Romans have acquired an empire of such an extent as a reward for their prowess, not as a gift of fate. . . . Whenever they invade hostile territory they always build a fortified camp before they engage the enemy in battle. . . . It is as if a city is created at a single stroke, complete with market place, artisans' quarter, and council hall where the centurions and military tribunes can pass judgment on whatever disputes are brought before them.”

—Flavius Josephus, from *History of the Jewish War*, A.D. 75–79

Step Into the Time

Making Connections
Research one event from the time line and explain what made it pivotal to Rome's history.

ROME

- **509 B.C.** Last of the Roman kings driven out, Republic is proclaimed
- **396 B.C.** Successful Roman siege of Veii deals fatal blow to Etruscans
- **287 B.C.** Hortensian Law grants plebeians the full right to pass laws
- **216 B.C.** Carthage defeats much larger Roman army at Battle of Cannae

600 B.C. — 300 B.C.

THE WORLD

- **586 B.C.** Babylonian king Nebuchadnezzar II captures Jerusalem
- **458 B.C.** First performance of Aeschylus' trilogy of plays, the *Oresteia*, in Athens
- **323 B.C.** Alexander the Great dies
- **276 B.C.** Mathematician Eratosthenes measures circumference of Earth

networks
There's More Online!

- MAP Explore the interactive version of this map on Networks.
- TIME LINE Explore the interactive version of the time line on Networks.

133 B.C. Tiberius Gracchus attempts agrarian reform, is assassinated

49 B.C. Julius Caesar crosses Rubicon, takes military control of Rome

27 B.C. Octavian is declared Augustus Caesar, Roman Empire begins

A.D. 80 Dedication of Roman Colosseum, seating up to 50,000

A.D. 306 Constantine becomes emperor, later converts to Christianity

A.D. 410 Rome is sacked and pillaged by the Visigoths under Alaric

A.D. 1 — **A.D. 300** — **A.D. 500**

A.D. 57 First mention of Japan, found in Chinese records

A.D. 105 Invention of paper in China

C. A.D. 146 Hereditary monarchy begins in the ancient Korean kingdom of Koguryo

C. A.D. 250 Maya classical period begins in Mesoamerica

A.D. 380 Candra Gupta II ascends to the throne in India

networks

There's More Online!

- BIOGRAPHY Hannibal
- CHART/GRAPH Effects of Geography on the Rise of Rome
- CHART/GRAPH Twelve Tables of Rome, 450 B.C.
- IMAGE Hannibal Crossing the Alps
- IMAGE Roman Patrician
- INFOGRAPHIC Roman Law
- INTERACTIVE SELF-CHECK QUIZ
- MAP Punic Wars, 264 B.C.–146 B.C.
- TIME LINE The Punic Wars
- VIDEO The Rise of Rome

LESSON 1

The Rise of Rome

ESSENTIAL QUESTIONS

- *How do different types of political organizations emerge?*
- *How can new ideas lead to social and political change?*

Reading HELPDESK

Academic Vocabulary

- **virtually**
- **institution**

Content Vocabulary

- **republic**
- **patrician**
- **plebeian**
- **consul**
- **praetor**

TAKING NOTES:

Key Ideas and Details

Identifying Use a graphic organizer like the one below to identify contributing factors to the rise of Rome.

Factors Contributing to the Rise of Rome

TEKS Texas Essential Knowledge and Skills

1B identify major causes and describe the major effects of the following events from 500 BC to AD 600: the development of the classical civilizations of Greece, Rome, Persia, India (Maurya and Gupta), China (Zhou, Qin, and Han), and the development of major world religions

continued on the next page

IT MATTERS BECAUSE

Roman history is the story of the Romans' conquest of the area around Rome, then of Italy, and finally of the entire Mediterranean world. The Romans were conquerors, but they also governed, using republican forms that have been passed down to modern democratic societies.

The Land and Peoples of Italy

GUIDING QUESTION *What was the significance of Rome's central location and geographic features?*

Italy is a peninsula extending about 750 miles (1,207 km) from north to south. It is not very wide, averaging about 120 miles (193 km) across. The Apennine (A • puh • NYN) mountain range forms a ridge running from north to south, dividing west from east. Italy has some fairly large fertile plains that are ideal for farming. Most important are the Po River valley in the north; the plain of Latium, on which the city of Rome is located; and the region of Campania, to the south of Latium.

As in other early civilizations, geography played an important role in the development of Rome. The Apennines are less rugged than the mountain ranges of Greece and did not divide the Italian Peninsula into many small isolated communities. Italy also had more land for farming than did Greece, enabling it to support a large population.

The location of the city of Rome was especially favorable to its early settlers. Located about 18 miles (29 km) inland on the Tiber River, Rome had a route to the sea. However, it was far enough inland to be relatively safe from pirates. It could be easily defended because of its position, built on seven hills. In addition, it was situated where the Tiber River could be easily crossed. Thus, it became a natural crossing point for north-south traffic in western Italy. Geography played a major role in the early development and expansion of Roman civilization.

The Italian Peninsula is an important crossroads between the western and eastern Mediterranean Sea due to the way the land juts into the sea. After the Romans had established their Mediterranean empire, governing it was made easier because of Italy's central location.

Indo-European peoples moved into Italy during the period from about 1500 B.C. to 1000 B.C. Historians know very little about these peoples, but they do know that one such Indo-European group was the Latins, who lived in the region of Latium. These people spoke Latin, which, like Greek, is an Indo-European language.

The Latins were herders and farmers who lived in settlements consisting of huts on the tops of Rome's seven hills. After about 800 B.C., other people also began settling in Italy—the two most notable being the Greeks and the Etruscans.

The Greeks came to Italy in large numbers during the age of Greek colonization (750 B.C.–550 B.C.). They settled in southern Italy and then slowly moved around the coast and up the peninsula. They also occupied the eastern two-thirds of Sicily, an island south of the Italian Peninsula. The Greeks had much influence on the people of Rome. They cultivated olives and grapes, passed on their alphabet, and provided the Romans with artistic and cultural models through their sculpture, architecture, and literature.

The early development of Rome, however, was influenced most by the Etruscans, who were located north of Rome in Etruria. After 650 B.C., they expanded into north-central Italy and came to control Rome and most of Latium. The Etruscans found Rome a village but launched a building program that turned it into a city. The Romans borrowed ideas from the Etruscans, such as Etruscan dress—the toga and short cloak. The Roman army also borrowed its organization from the Etruscans.

READING PROGRESS CHECK

Describing Name three early peoples of Rome and describe their relationship to Rome.

(continued from p. 150)

TEKS **Texas Essential Knowledge and Skills**

3A describe the major political, religious/philosophical, and cultural influences of Persia, India, China, Israel, Greece, and Rome, including the development of monotheism, Judaism, and Christianity

19B identify the characteristics of the following political systems: theocracy, absolute monarchy, democracy, republic, oligarchy, limited monarchy, and totalitarianism

continued on the next page

▲ **This fresco from the fifth century B.C. of an Etruscan musician is part of a banquet scene found in the Tomb of the Leopards, a large underground burial chamber at Tarquinia, Italy.**

The Roman Republic

GUIDING QUESTION ***What were the political and military structures of Rome during the Republic?***

Roman tradition maintains that early Rome (753 B.C.–509 B.C.) was under the control of seven kings and that two of the last three kings were Etruscan. Historians know for certain that Rome did fall under Etruscan influence during this time. In 509 B.C., the Romans overthrew the last Etruscan king and established a **republic**. In a republic, the leader is not a monarch, and some citizens have the right to vote. This was the beginning of a new era in Rome's history.

republic a form of government in which the leader is not a king and certain citizens have the right to vote

War and Conquest

At the beginning of the republic, Rome was surrounded by enemies. For the next 200 years, the city was engaged in almost continuous warfare. In 338 B.C., Rome crushed the Latin states in Latium. During the next 50 years, the Romans waged a fierce struggle against people from the central Apennines, some of whom had settled south of Rome. Rome was again victorious. The conquest gave the Romans control over a large part of the Italian Peninsula.

It also brought them into direct contact with the Greek communities of southern Italy. Soon, the Romans were at war with these Greek cities. By

PHOTO: Etruscan/Bridgeman Art Library/Getty Images

264 B.C., they had overcome the Greeks and completed their conquest of southern Italy. After defeating the remaining Etruscan states to the north over the next three years, Rome had conquered **virtually** all of Italy.

virtually almost entirely; nearly

To rule Italy, the Romans devised the Roman Confederation. Under this system, Rome allowed some peoples—especially Latins—to have full Roman citizenship. Most of the remaining communities were made allies. They remained free to run their own local affairs but were required to provide soldiers for Rome. The Romans made it clear that loyal allies could improve their status and become Roman citizens. The Romans made the conquered peoples feel they had a real stake in Rome's success.

(continued from p. 151)

TEKS **Texas Essential Knowledge and Skills**

20A explain the development of democratic-republican government from its beginnings in the Judeo-Christian legal tradition and classical Greece and Rome through the English Civil War and the Enlightenment

21A describe how people have participated in supporting or changing their governments

21B describe the rights and responsibilities of citizens and noncitizens in civic participation throughout history

22B identify the influence of ideas regarding the right to a "trial by a jury of your peers" and the concepts of "innocent until proven guilty" and "equality before the law" that originated from the Judeo- Christian legal tradition and in Greece and Rome

25B summarize the fundamental ideas and institutions of Western civilizations that originated in Greece and Rome

Successful Strategies

Romans believed that their early ancestors were successful because of their sense of duty, courage, and discipline. The Roman historian Livy, writing in the first century B.C., provided a number of stories to teach Romans the virtues that had made Rome great. His account of Cincinnatus (SIHN • suh • NA • tuhs), a simple farmer who was chosen as a dictator, or temporary ruler, to save Rome from attack, is one such example. Livy wrote:

PRIMARY SOURCE

> "A mission from the city found him at work on his land—digging a ditch, maybe, or ploughing. Greetings were exchanged, and he was asked . . . to put on his toga and hear the Senate's instructions. . . . He told his wife Racilla to run to their cottage and fetch his toga. . . . Wiping the grimy sweat from his hands and face he put it on; at once the envoys from the city saluted him, with congratulations, as Dictator."
>
> —**Livy, *The Early History of Rome***

After Cincinnatus led the army to victory, he resigned as dictator and returned to his farm.

Looking back today, how can we explain Rome's success in gaining control of the entire Italian Peninsula? First, the Romans were good diplomats. They were shrewd in extending Roman citizenship and allowing states to run their own internal affairs. Although diplomatic, they could be firm, and even cruel when necessary, crushing rebellions without mercy.

Second, the Romans excelled in military matters. They were not only accomplished soldiers but also persistent ones. The loss of an army or a fleet did not cause them to quit but instead spurred them on to build new armies and new fleets. In addition, they were brilliant strategists. As they conquered, the Romans built colonies—fortified towns—throughout Italy. By building roads to these towns and thus connecting them, the Romans could move troops quickly throughout their conquered territory.

institution an organization for the promotion of a cause

Finally, in law and politics, as in conquest, the Romans were practical. They did not try to build an ideal government but instead created political **institutions** in response to problems, as the problems arose.

Roman Political Structure

patrician a social class of wealthy, powerful landowners, they formed the ruling class in the Roman Republic

plebeian in the Roman Republic, a social class made up of minor landholders, craftspeople, merchants, and small farmers

The Romans had been ruled by kings under the Etruscans. As a result, they distrusted kingship and devised a very different system of government.

Early Rome was divided into two groups or orders—the **patricians** and the **plebeians** (plih • BEE • uhns). The patricians were wealthy landowners who became Rome's ruling class. Less wealthy landowners, craftspeople, merchants, and small farmers were all part of a larger group called plebeians. Men in both orders were citizens who paid taxes, owed military service, and could vote. Only patricians, however, could be elected to governmental offices.

The chief executive officers of the Roman Republic were the **consuls** and **praetors** (PREE • tuhrz). Two consuls, chosen every year, ran the government and led the Roman army into battle. The praetor was in charge of civil law—laws that applied to Roman citizens. As Rome's territory expanded, another praetor was added to judge cases in which one or both people were noncitizens. The Romans also had a number of officials who had special duties, such as supervising the treasury.

The Roman Senate came to hold an especially important position in the Roman Republic. It was a select group of about 300 patricians who served for life. At first, the Senate's only role was to advise government officials. By the third century B.C., however, the Senate's advice had the force of law.Though Rome was never a traditional democracy, the development of the Roman Senate from an advisory council to a governing body served as an example of a form of democratic-republican government. Many modern republics today call their legislative body a senate, demonstrating the lasting impression made by this Roman institution on future republican governments.

The Roman Republic had several people's assemblies in addition to the Senate. By far the most important of these was the centuriate assembly. The centuriate assembly elected the chief officials, such as consuls and praetors, and passed laws. Because it was organized by classes based on wealth, the wealthiest citizens always had a majority. The council of the plebs was the assembly for plebeians only, and it came into being as a result of the struggle between the social orders in Rome.

TWELVE TABLES OF ROME 450 B.C.

Table I	**Proceedings Preliminary to a Trial** 9. If both parties are present, sunset shall be the time limit of the proceedings.
Table II	**Trial**
Table III	**Execution of Judgment** 1. Thirty days shall be allowed by law for payment of confessed debt and for settlement of matters adjudged in court.
Table IV	**Paternal Power**
Table V	**Inheritance and Guardianship**
Table VI	**Ownership and Possession**
Table VII	**Real Property**
Table VIII	**Torts or Delicts**
Table IX	**Public Law** 6. For anyone whomsoever to be put to death without a trial and unconvicted . . . is forbidden.
Table X	**Sacred Law**
Table XI	**Supplementary Laws**
Table XII	**Supplementary Laws** 5. Whatever the people ordain last shall be legally valid.

TABLE

The Twelve Tables, a set of laws on public display in Rome, established and protected certain rights for both patricians and plebeians in the Roman Republic.

1. ***Making Inferences*** Why would it be important to record and display the laws for citizens to see?

2. ***Comparing and Contrasting*** What similarities exist between the laws in the table and the laws in the United States?

The Struggle of the Orders

There was often conflict between the patricians and plebeians in the early Roman Republic. The children of patricians and plebeians were forbidden to marry each other. Plebeians resented this situation, especially considering they served in the Roman army that protected the Republic. Plebeians thought that they deserved both political and social equality with the patricians.

The conflict between the patricians and plebeians, also known as the struggle of the orders, dragged on for hundreds of years. Ultimately, it led to success for the plebeians. The council of the plebs, which was a popular assembly for plebeians only, was created in 471 B.C. New officials, known as tribunes of the plebs, were given the power to protect the plebeians. In the fourth century B.C., plebeians were permitted to marry patricians and to become consuls. Finally, in 287 B.C., the council of the plebs received the right to pass laws for all Romans.

By 287 B.C., all male Roman citizens were now supposedly equal under the law. In reality, however, a few wealthy patrician and plebeian families formed a new senatorial ruling class that came to dominate the political offices. The Roman Republic had not become a democracy.

Roman Law

One of Rome's chief gifts to the Mediterranean world of its day and to later generations was its system of law. Rome's first code of laws was the Twelve Tables, which was adopted in 450 B.C. This code was a product of a simple farming society and proved inadequate for later Roman needs. From the Twelve Tables,

consul a chief executive officer of the Roman Republic; two were elected each year to run the government and to lead the army into battle

praetor an official of the Roman Republic in charge of enforcing civil law

▲ The Roman Forum, lined with markets and shops, was a site where public meetings, courts, and gladiatorial games took place in Rome. It also was the site of the Curia, or senate house.

the Romans developed a more sophisticated system of civil law. This system applied only to Roman citizens, however.

As Rome expanded, legal questions arose that involved both Romans and non-Romans, as well as citizens and noncitizens. The Romans found that although some of their rules of civil law could be used in these cases, special rules were often needed. These rules gave rise to a body of law known as the Law of Nations. The Romans came to identify the Law of Nations with natural law, or universal law based on reason. This enabled them to establish standards of justice that applied to all people.

These standards of justice included fundamental ideas of Western civilization still recognized today. A person was regarded as innocent until proved otherwise. People accused of wrongdoing were allowed to defend themselves before a judge. A judge, in turn, was expected to weigh evidence carefully before arriving at a decision. These principles lived on long after the fall of the Roman Empire.

✓ READING PROGRESS CHECK

Interpreting How did the rule of law develop to include some standards of justice that are still used today?

Roman Expansion

GUIDING QUESTION ***What military conquests did the Romans carry out during the Republic?***

After their conquest of Italy, the Romans found themselves face to face with a strong power in the Mediterranean—the state of Carthage. The Phoenicians had founded Carthage around 800 B.C. on the coast of North Africa. By the third century B.C., Carthage had an enormous trading empire in the western Mediterranean, including the coast of northern Africa, southern Spain, Sardinia, Corsica, and western Sicily. With its control of western Mediterranean trade, Carthage was the largest and richest state in the area.

The presence of Carthaginians in Sicily, an island close to the Italian coast, made the Romans fearful. In 264 B.C. the two powers began a lengthy struggle for control of the western Mediterranean.

The First Punic War

Rome's first war with Carthage began in 264 B.C. It is called the First Punic War, after the Latin word for "Phoenician": punicus. The war started when the Romans sent an army to Sicily. The Carthaginians, who thought of Sicily as part of their empire, considered this an act of war. Both sides determined to conquer Sicily.

The Romans—a land power—realized that they could not win the war without a navy and built a large fleet. After a long struggle, a Roman fleet defeated the Carthaginian navy off the coast of Sicily, and the war came to an end. In 241 B.C., Carthage gave up all rights to Sicily and paid a fine to the Romans. Sicily became the first Roman province.

Carthage vowed revenge, however, and added new lands in Spain to make up for the loss of Sicily. The Romans encouraged one of Carthage's Spanish allies to revolt against Carthage. In response, Hannibal, the greatest

PHOTO: akg / Bildarchiv Steffens/

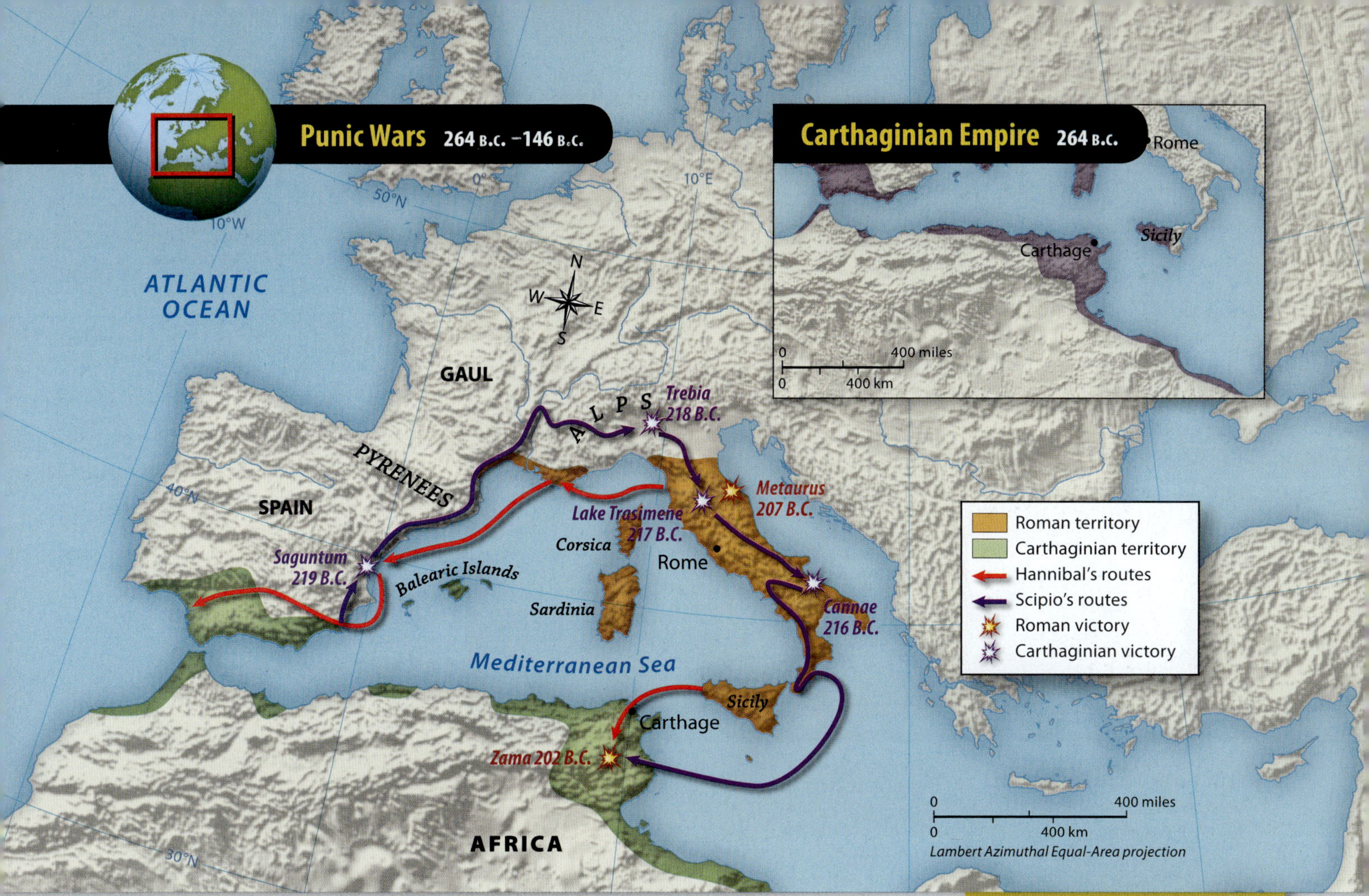

of the Carthaginian generals, struck back, beginning the Second Punic War, which lasted from 218 B.C. to 201 B.C. Hannibal had been raised to fight the Romans. When he was only nine years old, his father, a Carthaginian general, took him to a temple in Carthage and made him swear that he would always hate the Romans.

The Second Punic War

Hannibal decided that the Carthaginians would bring the war to Rome. Hannibal entered Spain, moved east, and crossed the Alps with an army of about 46,000 men, a large number of horses, and 37 battle elephants. The Alps took a toll on the Carthaginian army; most of the elephants did not survive. The remaining army, however, posed a real threat.

In 216 B.C., the Romans decided to meet Hannibal head-on. It was a serious mistake. At Cannae (KA • nee), Hannibal's force devastated a Roman army, killing as many as 40,000 men. Then, some of the southern Italian cities rebelled against Roman rule and went over to Hannibal's side. Rome seemed on the brink of disaster but refused to give up and raised yet another army.

Rome gradually recovered. Although Hannibal remained free to roam in Italy, he had neither the men nor the equipment to attack the major cities. The Romans began to reconquer some of the Italian cities that had been taken by Hannibal. They also sent troops to Spain, and by 206 B.C., they had pushed the Carthaginians out of Spain.

In a brilliant military initiative, Rome invaded Carthage rather than fight Hannibal in Italy. This strategy forced the Carthaginians to recall Hannibal from Italy. At the Battle of Zama in 202 B.C., the Romans, led by

GEOGRAPHY CONNECTION

From 264 B.C. to 146 B.C., the Romans fought the Carthaginians in the Punic Wars.

1. **ENVIRONMENT AND SOCIETY** *What natural barriers did the Romans and Carthaginians have to cross to fight these wars?*
2. **MOVEMENT** *Why might Hannibal have chosen to cross the Alps to get to Rome?*

▲ This drawing depicts Hannibal and his army crossing the Alps during the Second Punic War.

▶ **CRITICAL THINKING**
Analyzing Information Based on this image and the map on the Punic Wars, why might this event be seen as a remarkable moment in ancient history?

Scipio Africanus, crushed Hannibal's forces, ending the war. Carthage lost Spain, which became a Roman province. Rome had become the dominant power in the western Mediterranean.

The Romans pursued Hannibal for years, catching up with him in Bithynia, near the Black Sea. To avoid capture, Hannibal took poison after remarking, "Let us relieve the Romans of the fear which has so long afflicted them, since it seems to tax their patience too hard to wait for an old man's death."

More Conquests

Fifty years later, the Romans fought their third and final battle with Carthage, the Third Punic War. For years, a number of prominent Romans, especially the conservative politician Cato, had called for the complete destruction of Carthage. Cato ended every speech he made to Senate with the words, "Furthermore, I think Carthage must be destroyed." In 146 B.C., it was indeed destroyed. For 10 days, Roman soldiers burned and demolished the city. The inhabitants—50,000 men, women, and children—were sold into slavery. The territory of Carthage became a Roman province called Africa.

During its struggle with Carthage, Rome also battled the Hellenistic states in the eastern Mediterranean. The Fourth Macedonian War ended in 148 B.C., and Macedonia was made a Roman province. Two years later, Greece was placed under the control of the Roman governor of Macedonia. In 129 B.C., Pergamum became Rome's first province in Asia. Rome was now master of the entire Mediterranean Sea.

✓ **READING PROGRESS CHECK**

Synthesizing Why did Rome find it necessary to wage three Punic Wars?

LESSON 1 REVIEW TEKS

Reviewing Vocabulary

1. ***Drawing Conclusions*** What were the two main social classes in Rome?

Using Your Notes

2. ***Assessing*** What were the main factors that led to the rise of Rome?

Answering the Guiding Questions

3. ***Explaining*** What was the significance of Rome's central location and geographic features?
4. ***Analyzing*** What were the political and military structures of Rome during the Republic?
5. ***Listing*** What military conquests did the Romans carry out during the Republic?

Writing Activity

6. **INFORMATIVE/EXPLANATORY** In a fully developed paragraph, explain how the term *republic* or *republican government* applies to Rome during the years of its rise. Use details from the lesson to support your definition by explaining who Rome's leaders were and what rights people had.

networks

There's More Online!

- BIOGRAPHY Antony
- BIOGRAPHY Cleopatra
- BIOGRAPHY Gracchus Brothers
- GRAPHIC ORGANIZER Struggle Between Marius and Sulla
- IMAGE Assassination of Julius Caesar
- IMAGE Julius Caesar Crossing the Rubicon
- INTERACTIVE SELF-CHECK QUIZ
- VIDEO Cleopatra

LESSON 2

From Republic to Empire

ESSENTIAL QUESTIONS

- *How do different types of political organizations emerge?*
- *How can new ideas lead to social and political change?*

Reading HELPDESK

Academic Vocabulary

- **financial**
- **instability**

Content Vocabulary

- **triumvirate**
- **dictator**
- **imperator**

TAKING NOTES:

Key Ideas and Details

Sequencing Use a graphic organizer like the one below to sequence the major events that led Rome from a republic to an empire.

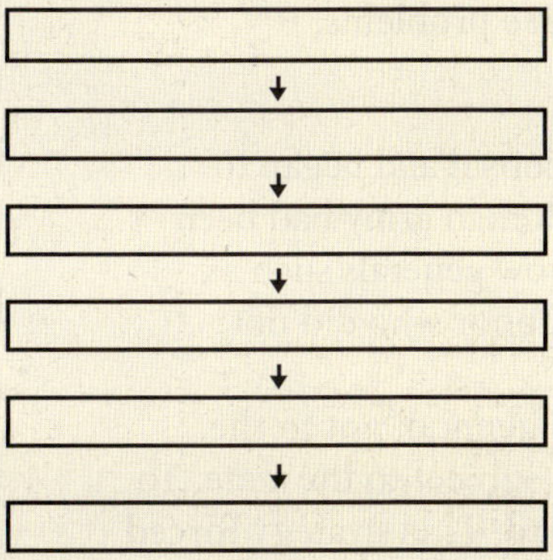

It Matters Because

Early in the days of the Roman Republic, farmers fulfilled their duty to Rome by serving in the army. As Rome grew, the landed aristocracy became more powerful, and the ideals of the republic changed. By 129 B.C., Rome stood supreme over the Mediterranean Sea, but the process of creating an empire had weakened the internal stability of Rome. This led to a series of crises that plagued Rome for the next hundred years.

The Decline of the Roman Republic

GUIDING QUESTION *How did political and social unrest lead to civil wars in Rome?*

By the second century B.C., the Senate had become the real governing body of the Roman state. Members of the Senate were drawn mostly from the landed aristocracy. They remained senators for life and held the chief offices of the republic. The Senate directed the wars of the third and second centuries B.C. and took control of both foreign and domestic policy, including **financial** affairs.

Growing Unrest

The Senate and political offices were increasingly controlled by a small circle of wealthy and powerful families. Of course, these aristocrats formed only a tiny minority of the Roman people. The backbone of the Roman state and army had always been the small farmers. Over a period of time, however, many farmers of small amounts of land were unable to compete with large wealthy landowners and lost their lands. By taking over state-owned land and by buying out small peasant farmers, these landed aristocrats had developed large estates that used slave labor. Thus, the rise of large estates led to a decline in the number of small citizen farmers. As a result, many of these small farmers drifted to the cities, especially Rome, forming a large class of landless poor.

▲ **This woodcut depicts a wealthy Roman in the garden of his villa.**

▶ **CRITICAL THINKING**
Drawing Conclusions What does this image depict about the life of a wealthy Roman? Do you think it is accurate?

Some aristocrats tried to remedy this growing economic and social crisis. Two brothers, Tiberius and Gaius Gracchus (GRA • kuhs), came to believe that the basic cause of Rome's problems was the decline of the small farmer. To help the landless poor, they had the council of the plebs pass land-reform bills that called for the government to take back public land held by large landowners and to give it to landless Romans.

Many senators, themselves large landowners whose estates included large areas of public land, were furious. A group of senators took the law into their own hands and killed Tiberius in 133 B.C. His brother Gaius later suffered the same fate. The attempts of the Gracchus brothers to bring reforms had opened the door to more **instability** and more violence. Changes in the Roman army soon brought even worse problems.

financial relating to the management of funds

instability the quality or state of being liable to change or alteration

A New Role for the Army

In 107 B.C., a Roman general named Marius became consul and began to recruit his armies in a new way. For a long time, the Roman army had been made of men who were landholders of small farms. Now generals such as Marius recruited volunteers from the urban and rural poor who did not own any property.

These volunteers swore an oath of loyalty to the general, not to the Roman state, creating a new type of army no longer subject to the state. To recruit these men, a general would promise them land. This strategy forced generals to become involved in politics to get laws passed that would provide the land they needed for their veterans. Marius left a powerful legacy. He had created a new system of military recruitment that placed great power in the hands of the individual generals.

SKILLS PRACTICE

When you hear a new academic vocabulary word, be sure to use it. For example, you can use it in sentences you write and in discussions with your classmates. Practice using the academic vocabulary words *financial* and *instability* by writing a sentence containing each of these words.

Lucius Cornelius Sulla was the next general to take advantage of the new military system. The Senate had given him command of a war in Asia Minor. When the council of the plebs tried to transfer command to Marius, a civil war broke out. Sulla won and seized Rome itself in 82 B.C., conducting a reign of terror to wipe out all opposition. Then Sulla restored power to the hands of the Senate and eliminated most of the powers of the popular assemblies.

Sulla hoped that he had created a firm foundation to restore a traditional Roman republic governed by a powerful Senate. His real legacy was quite different from what he had intended, however. His example of using an army to seize power would prove most attractive to ambitious men.

TEKS Texas Essential Knowledge and Skills

1B identify major causes and describe the major effects of the following events from 500 BC to AD 600: the development of the classical civilizations of Greece, Rome, Persia, India (Maurya and Gupta), China (Zhou, Qin, and Han), and the development of major world religions

3A describe the major political, religious/philosophical, and cultural influences of Persia, India, China, Israel, Greece, and Rome, including the development of monotheism, Judaism, and Christianity

21A describe how people have participated in supporting or changing their governments

25B summarize the fundamental ideas and institutions of Western civilizations that originated in Greece and Rome

✓ **READING PROGRESS CHECK**

Making Inferences Rome had always had people who were not citizens and did not own land. Why was a large class of landless poor a source of growing unrest now?

The End of the Republic

GUIDING QUESTION ***What characterized the actions of the First Triumvirate?***

For the next fifty years, from 82 B.C. to 31 B.C., Roman history was characterized by two particularly important features: competition for power by a number of individuals and the civil wars caused by their conflicts. The Roman historian Sallust observed:

PRIMARY SOURCE

"But when our country had grown great through toil . . . when great kings had been vanquished in war . . . when Carthage, the rival of Rome's sway, had perished root and branch, then Fortune began to grow cruel. . . . Hence the lust for power first, then for money, grew upon them; these were, I may say, the root of all evils. For avarice destroyed honour, integrity, and all other noble qualities. . . . Ambition drove many men to become false; to have one thought locked in the breast, another ready on the tongue; to value friendships and enmities not on their merits but by the standard of self-interest."

—from *Sallust*, J. C. Rolfe, trans., 1921

triumvirate a government by three people with equal power

Three powerful individuals—Crassus, Pompey, and Julius Caesar—came to hold enormous military and political power. The concentration of all Rome's power between just three men would have great consequences for Roman civilization. Crassus was known as the richest man in Rome. Pompey had returned from a successful command in Spain as a military hero. Julius Caesar also had a military command in Spain. In 60 B.C., Caesar joined with Crassus and Pompey to form the First Triumvirate. A **triumvirate** is a government by three people with equal power.

▼ In this engraving, Julius Caesar is shown crossing the Rubicon with his troops, disobeying the Roman Senate's orders to enter Rome only as a citizen.

The First Triumvirate

The combined wealth and power of these three men was enormous and enabled them to dominate the political scene and to achieve their basic aims. Pompey received a

▲ This nineteenth-century painting by Friedrich Heinrich Feuger depicts the assassination of Julius Caesar by members of the Roman Senate.

command in Spain, Crassus was given a command in Syria, and Caesar was granted a special military command in Gaul, which is modern-day France. When Crassus was killed in battle in 53 B.C., however, only two powerful men were left. During his time in Gaul, Caesar had gained both fame and military experience. As a military leader, Caesar had always been willing to face great personal danger. Moreover, he now had an army of seasoned veterans who were loyal to him.

Fearing Caesar's popularity, leading senators decided that rule by Pompey alone would be least harmful to their cause. They voted for Caesar to lay down his command and return as a private citizen to Rome. Such a step was intolerable to Caesar, as it would leave him totally vulnerable to his enemies. Caesar chose to keep his army and moved into Italy by illegally crossing the Rubicon, the river that formed the southern boundary of his province. The phrase related to this action, "crossing the Rubicon," means to take a decisive action that cannot be taken back. According to his ancient biographer, Caesar said to his troops, "Even now we could turn back; but once we cross that tiny bridge, then everything will depend on armed force." Caesar marched on Rome, starting a civil war between his forces and those of Pompey and his allies. The defeat of Pompey's forces left Caesar in complete control of the Roman government.

Caesar was officially made **dictator**, or absolute ruler, in 47 B.C. This position was usually temporary, used only in emergencies, but Caesar was made dictator for life in 44 B.C. Realizing the need for reforms, Caesar gave land to the poor and increased the Senate to 900 members. By filling the Senate with his supporters and increasing the number of senators, he weakened the Senate's power.

Caesar granted citizenship to a number of people in the provinces who had helped him. He also reformed the calendar by introducing the Egyptian solar year of 365 days. (With later changes in 1582, it became the basis of our own calendar.) Caesar planned much more in the way of building projects and military campaigns to the east but was not able to carry them out. In 44 B.C., a group of leading senators who resented his growing power assassinated him, believing that the old republican system would now return. In truth, however, they had set the stage for another civil war that delivered the death blow to the republic.

Analyzing PRIMARY SOURCES

The Death of Cleopatra

"Antony was the first to commit suicide, by the sword. Cleopatra threw herself at Octavian's feet. . . . It was not her life she was after . . . but a portion of her kingdom. When she realized this was hopeless . . . she took advantage of her guard's carelessness to get herself into . . . the royal tomb. Once there, she put on the royal robes . . . and lay down in a richly perfumed coffin beside her Antony. Then she applied poisonous snakes to her veins and slipped into death as though into a sleep."

—Florus, from *Epitome of Roman History*

DBQ ***DRAWING CONCLUSIONS***
Did Cleopatra's death have any political effect? If so, what?

The Second Triumvirate

A new struggle for power followed the death of Caesar. Three men—Octavian, Caesar's heir and grandnephew; Antony, Caesar's ally and assistant; and Lepidus, who had been commander of Caesar's cavalry—joined forces to form the Second Triumvirate. Within a few years after Caesar's death, however, only two men divided the Roman world between them. Octavian took the west; Antony, the east.

The empire of the Romans, large as it was, was still too small for two masters. Octavian and Antony soon came into conflict. Antony allied himself with the Egyptian queen Cleopatra VII, with whom, like Caesar before him, he fell deeply in love. At the Battle of Actium in Greece in 31 B.C., Octavian's forces smashed the army and the navy of Antony and Cleopatra. Both fled to Egypt, where they committed suicide a year later.

Octavian, at the age of 32, stood supreme over the Roman world. The civil wars had ended. So had the republic. The period beginning in 31 B.C. and lasting until A.D. 14 witnessed the foundations of the Roman Empire.

✓ **READING PROGRESS CHECK**

Comparing and Contrasting How were the events and personalities of the Second Triumvirate similar to and different from those of the First Triumvirate?

The Beginning of the Roman Empire

GUIDING QUESTION ***What factors led to the beginning of the Roman Empire?***

In 27 B.C., Octavian proclaimed the "restoration of the Republic." He knew that only traditional republican forms would satisfy the Senate. At the same time, Octavian was aware that the republic could not be fully restored. Although he gave some power to the Senate, Octavian in fact became the first Roman emperor.

In 27 B.C., the Senate awarded Octavian the title of Augustus—"the revered one," a fitting title in view of his power, which previously had been reserved for gods. Augustus proved to be highly popular. No doubt people were glad the civil wars had ended. At the same time, his continuing control of the army was the chief source of Augustus's power. The Senate gave Augustus the title **imperator**, or commander in chief. The English word *emperor* comes from *imperator*.

Augustus maintained a standing army of 28 legions, or about 151,000 men. A legion was a military unit of about 5,000 troops. Only Roman citizens could be legionnaires—members of a legion. Noncitizens, or subject peoples, could serve as auxiliary forces, which numbered around 130,000 under Augustus. Augustus also set up a praetorian guard of roughly 9,000 men who had the important task of guarding the emperor.

While claiming to have restored the republic, Augustus began a new system for governing the provinces. Under the Roman Republic, the Senate had appointed the governors of the provinces. During the empire, certain provinces were given to the emperor, who assigned deputies known as legates to govern them. The Senate still chose the governors of the remaining provinces. However, the power of Augustus enabled him to overrule the senatorial governors and establish unity in imperial policy.

Augustus also stabilized the frontiers of the Roman Empire. He conquered the central and maritime Alps and then expanded Roman control of the Balkan peninsula up to the Danube River. His attempt to conquer Germany failed, however, when three Roman legions led by the Roman

BIOGRAPHIES

Julius Caesar (c.100 B.C.–44 B.C.)

When the Senate could no longer rule the complex republic that was Rome, Julius Caesar not only became a permanent dictator but also held the most exalted position to date in Rome. Caesar's actions helped end the republic and begin the empire.

Augustus (63 B.C.–A.D. 14)

Significantly influenced by his great-uncle, Julius Caesar, Augustus also began his rule of Rome at a time of political chaos. As Rome's first emperor, Augustus tried to maintain what had been best in republican rule, yet his power depended in large part on his army.

▶ **CRITICAL THINKING**

Comparing How were Julius Caesar and Augustus alike in their actions?

dictator an absolute ruler

imperator commander in chief; the Latin origin of the word *emperor*

▶ The Temple of Vespasian in Pompeii, Italy, was one of many temples dedicated to the worship of the emperor. This relief, depicting an animal sacrifice, appears on an altar in the temple.

▶ **CRITICAL THINKING**

Drawing Conclusions Why did Augustus encourage religious devotion to the emperor?

general Varus were massacred by a group of Germanic warriors. These defeats in Germany taught Augustus that Rome's power was not unlimited. This knowledge devastated him. According to legend, for months he would beat his head on a door, shouting, "Varus, give me back my legions!"

Augustus was very concerned about the social health of the Roman state. He believed that the civil wars of the first century had weakened the strength of public religion, which he considered a pillar of a strong state. Thus, he rebuilt many ruined temples and built new ones to honor the Roman gods. Augustus also encouraged the development of a new religious cult dedicated to the emperor. Upon his death, Augustus was declared a god by the Senate.

The Augustan Age was a lengthy one. Augustus died in A.D. 14 after dominating the Roman world for 45 years. He had created a new order while maintaining traditional values, perhaps fitting for a leader whose favorite phrase was "Make haste slowly." By the time of his death, the Republic was only a memory. Rome would now be ruled by emperors.

✓ **READING PROGRESS CHECK**

Explaining Why did the Senate appear to endorse the shift to empire?

LESSON 2 REVIEW TEKS

Reviewing Vocabulary

1. ***Summarizing*** What happened after Augustus was named imperator of Rome?

Using Your Notes

2. ***Sequencing*** What were the major events, in chronological order, that led Rome from a republic to an empire?

Answering the Guiding Questions

3. ***Identifying Cause and Effect*** How did social and political unrest lead to civil wars in Rome?

4. ***Drawing Conclusions*** What characterized the actions of the First Triumvirate?

5. ***Identifying Cause and Effect*** What factors led to the beginning of the Roman Empire?

Writing Activity

6. **INFORMATIVE/EXPLANATORY** Describe one of the shifts in power or power struggles that occurred in Rome between the time the republic began to decline and the death of Augustus. Use precise nouns, strong verbs, and a variety of modifiers, including adjectives, adverbs, and adjective and adverb phrases, to make clear the prevailing political atmosphere of divisiveness, plotting, and threat.

networks

There's More Online!

- CHART/GRAPH Terms from Roman Mythology
- IMAGE Colosseum
- IMAGE Roman Aqueduct
- INTERACTIVE SELF-CHECK QUIZ
- MAP Roman Empire Trade and Expansion
- PRIMARY SOURCE Ode by Horace
- PRIMARY SOURCE Policies of Trajan and Hadrian
- SLIDE SHOW Roman Art and Architecture
- VIDEO Trade in Imperial Rome

LESSON 3

The Early Roman Empire

ESSENTIAL QUESTIONS

- *How do different types of political organizations emerge?*
- *How can new ideas lead to social and political change?*

IT MATTERS BECAUSE

Augustus created a new order that began the Roman Empire. The period from his death in A.D. 14 until A.D. 180 is called the Early Empire. During this period, the Roman Empire reached the height of its power and prosperity.

Reading HELPDESK

Academic Vocabulary

- **whereas**
- **primary**
- **guaranteed**

Content Vocabulary

- **paterfamilias**
- ***insulae***

TAKING NOTES:

Key Ideas and Details

Differentiating Use a graphic organizer like the one below to record what you consider to be positive aspects, or achievements, and negative aspects, or problems, of the early Roman Empire.

Positive	Negative

Emperors of the Early Empire

GUIDING QUESTION *What elements defined the early Roman Empire?*

Augustus's new political system allowed the emperor to select his successor from his natural or adopted family. The first four emperors after Augustus came from his family. They were Tiberius, Caligula, Claudius, and Nero. During their reigns, these emperors took over more and more of the responsibilities that Augustus had given to the Senate. As the emperors grew more powerful, many became more corrupt.

Nero, for example, had people killed if he wanted them out of the way, including his own mother. Without troops, the senators were unable to oppose his excesses, but the Roman legions finally revolted against him. Nero, abandoned by his guards, committed suicide after allegedly uttering these final words: "What an artist the world is losing in me."

After Nero's death, a civil war broke out in A.D. 69. It soon became obvious that the Roman Empire had a major flaw. Without a system for selecting a new emperor, emperors could be made and deposed by the Roman legions.

At the beginning of the second century, a series of five so-called good emperors came to power. They were Nerva, Trajan, Hadrian, Antoninus Pius, and Marcus Aurelius. These emperors continued a period of peace and prosperity known as the Pax Romana—the Roman Peace.

The Pax Romana lasted for almost 200 years. The rulers during this period treated the ruling classes with respect, ended arbitrary executions, maintained peace in the empire, and supported domestic

PHOTO: (l to r)©Sylvain Sonnet/Corbis, ©Dave Bartruff/CORBIS, Author's Image/PunchStock, Erich Lessing/Art Resource, NY.

TEKS Texas Essential Knowledge and Skills

1B identify major causes and describe the major effects of the following events from 500 BC to AD 600: the development of the classical civilizations of Greece, Rome, Persia, India (Maurya and Gupta), China (Zhou, Qin, and Han), and the development of major world religions

3A describe the major political, religious/philosophical, and cultural influences of Persia, India, China, Israel, Greece, and Rome, including the development of monotheism, Judaism, and Christianity

23B identify examples of religious influence on various events referenced in the major eras of world history

24A describe the changing roles of women, children, and families during major eras of world history

26A identify significant examples of art and architecture that demonstrate an artistic ideal or visual principle from selected cultures

26B analyze examples of how art, architecture, literature, music, and drama reflect the history of the cultures in which they are produced

26C identify examples of art, music, and literature that transcend the cultures in which they were created and convey universal themes

27A identify the origin and diffusion of major ideas in mathematics, science, and technology that occurred in river valley civilizations, classical Greece and Rome, classical India, and the Islamic caliphates between 700 and 1200 and in China from the Tang to Ming dynasties

policies generally helpful to the empire. Although they were absolute rulers, they were known for their tolerance. By adopting capable men as their sons and successors, the first four "good emperors" reduced the chances of succession problems.

Under the emperors of the Pax Romana, the powers of the emperor continued to expand at the expense of the Senate's powers. Officials appointed and directed by the emperor took over the running of the government. These emperors also created new social programs. Trajan, for example, provided state funds to assist poor parents in the raising and educating of their children. The "good emperors" were widely praised for their building programs. Trajan and Hadrian were especially active in building public works—aqueducts, bridges, roads, and harbor facilities—throughout the provinces and in Rome.

The Empire Expands

Rome expanded further during the period of the Early Empire. Although Trajan extended Roman rule into Dacia (Romania), Mesopotamia, and the Sinai Peninsula, his successors realized that the empire was too large to be easily governed. Hadrian withdrew Roman forces from much of Mesopotamia. To protect the frontier, he strengthened the fortifications along a line connecting the Rhine and Danube Rivers. He also built a 74-mile- (118-km-) long wall—Hadrian's Wall—across northern Britain to keep out the Picts and the Scots.

By the end of the second century, it became apparent that it would be more and more difficult to defend the empire. Roman forces were located in permanent bases behind the frontiers. When one frontier was attacked, however, troops were drawn from other frontiers, leaving the latter frontiers open to attack.

At its height in the second century, the Roman Empire, like the Han empire in China at the same time, was one of the greatest states the world had ever seen. The Roman Empire covered about three and a half million square miles (9.1 million square km) and had a population that has been estimated at more than 50 million people.

The emperors and the imperial government provided a degree of unity throughout the empire. At the same time, the Romans gave much leeway to local customs. The privileges of Roman citizenship were granted to many people in the provinces. In A.D. 212, the emperor Caracalla gave Roman citizenship to every free person in the empire.

The administration of the Roman Empire depended greatly on cities and towns. A provincial governor's staff was not large, so local officials acted as Roman agents, performing many government duties, especially taxation. Most cities were not large by modern standards. Provincial cities resembled each other with their temples, markets, and public buildings. These cities were important in the spread of Roman culture, Roman law, and the Latin language. Latin was the language of the western part of the empire, **whereas** Greek was used in the East as a result of Alexander the Great's earlier conquests. Roman culture spread and freely mixed with Greek culture. The result has been called Greco-Roman civilization.

whereas although

This Roman aqueduct, spanning the Gard River, brought water to the French city of Nîmes on its upper level while the lower level served as a road. ▶

▶ **CRITICAL THINKING**

Drawing Conclusions How would such an invention enable the growth and success of a city?

Economy and Society

The Early Empire was a period of much prosperity, with internal peace leading to high levels of trade. Merchants from all over the empire came to the chief Italian ports of Puteoli (pyu • TEE • uh • ly) on the Bay of Naples and Ostia at the mouth of the Tiber. Trade went beyond the Roman frontiers as well and even included silk goods from China. Large quantities of grain were imported to feed the people of Rome. Luxury items poured in to satisfy the desires of the wealthy.

Despite the active trade and commerce, however, farming remained the chief occupation of most people and the underlying basis of Roman prosperity. Large landed estates, called latifundia (la • tuh • FUHN • dee • uh), dominated farming in southern and central Italy. These estates mostly used slaves to raise sheep and cattle on a large scale. Small peasant farms continued to exist in northern Italy.

An enormous gulf separated rich and poor in Roman society. The upper classes lived lives of great leisure and luxury in their villas and on their vast estates. Small farmers often became dependent on the huge estates of their wealthy neighbors. In the cities, many poor citizens worked in shops and markets. Thousands of unemployed depended on the emperor's handouts of grain to survive.

✓ **READING PROGRESS CHECK**

Demonstrating Describe the Roman Empire at its height by discussing its extent, its challenges, its administration, and its cities.

Roman Arts and Science

GUIDING QUESTION *How did the Romans spread Greco-Roman arts and culture throughout the empire, and what were their characteristics?*

After they conquered Greece, the Romans began to adopt many aspects of Greek culture. By adapting Greek styles, the Romans spread Greco-Roman civilization throughout their empire.

Art, Architecture, and Technology

In a reflection of the Greek influence on ancient Roman culture, the Romans adopted many features of the Greek style of art during the third and second centuries B.C.. They developed a taste for Greek statues, which they placed in public buildings and in their houses. Reproductions of Greek statues became popular when the supply of original works ran low. Although Greek sculptors aimed for an ideal appearance in their figures, Roman sculptors produced more realistic works that included even unattractive physical details.

The Romans excelled in architecture, a highly practical art. Although they continued to use Greek styles such as colonnades and rectangular buildings, the Romans also used curved forms such as the arch, the vault, and the dome. The Romans were the first people in antiquity to use concrete on a massive scale. Using concrete along with the new architectural forms made it possible for the Romans to construct huge buildings undreamed of by the Greeks. In order to emphasize the usefulness of Roman

▲ This Roman road, lined with Corinthian columns and still paved with its original granite stones, is located in Jerash, in modern-day Jordan.

▶ **CRITICAL THINKING**

Drawing Inferences How might the vast network of roads have contributed to the prosperity of the Early Empire?

architecture, Frontinus, Emperor Trajan's aqueduct commissioner, wrote, "Will anybody compare the idle Pyramids, or those other useless though much renowned works of the Greeks with these aqueducts, with these many indispensable structures?"

The remarkable engineering skills of the Romans were also put to use constructing roads, bridges, and aqueducts. The Romans built a network of some 50,000 miles (80,450 km) of roads throughout the empire. In Rome, almost a dozen aqueducts kept a population of 1 million supplied with water. Public baths and even some homes of the wealthy were supplied with freshwater while dirty water was flushed out through an extensive network of lead or clay pipes. Although the Roman technologies of sewers and drainage were mostly lost during the Middle Ages, they reemerged throughout Europe during the population boom and **urbanization** of the 1700s and 1800s.

Mathematics

Like their alphabet, the Romans borrowed their numerical system from the Etruscans, who may have originally created the numerical system based on tally marks. Roman numerals used letters to represent numbers, however, there was not an individual letter for each number. Using a limited number of symbols for specific values (I, V, X, L, C, D, M), addition and subtraction were used in order to express each number. Romans used an abacus, a type of counting frame, in order to carry out complex mathematical problems, as long numbers could become quite cumbersome. Although they are not commonly used today, Roman numerals continue to find use in recording book volumes or the production year of movies.

Science

Greek thought heavily influenced Roman science. Romans, like Pliny the Elder (A.D. 23 – A.D. 79), compiled the works of Greek thinkers into encyclopedic volumes. These Roman summaries of Greek science and thought became the standard for scientific knowledge in Europe, North Africa, and much of Southwest Asia until the scientific revolution of the seventeenth and eighteenth centuries.

Greek thought also inspired Roman medicine. For example, because so many doctors who had studied medicine were Greek, Julius Caesar attempted to lure them to Rome with promises of Roman citizenship during the first century B.C. Galen of Pergamum (A.D. 129 – A.D. 200) is considered to be the greatest physician and medical writer of the ancient period. Starting out as a doctor for gladiators in Pergamum, he later became a court physician for the emperor Marcus Aurelius. Combining Greek medical knowledge with his own experiments, Galen expanded Roman understandings of anatomy and medicine by dissecting animals, as Roman law did not allow the dissection of people.

One of Galen's most lasting contributions to science was his development of the Greek theory of humors. Galen believed that four different bodily fluids, called humors, were the key to medicine. He believed these humors should exist in equal measures in the human body and that, when unbalanced, they could harm a person's temperament and health. This theory of humors proved to be enduring. From ancient Rome it spread into the Arab world and medieval Europe and continued to dominate the understanding of the body until the advent of modern medicine in the nineteenth century.

Literature

Although there were many talented writers, the high point of Latin literature was reached in the Age of Augustus. Indeed, the Augustan Age has been called the golden age of Latin literature.

The most distinguished poet of the Augustan Age was Virgil, who wrote his masterpiece, the *Aeneid* (ih • NEE • uhd), in Rome's honor. In the poem, the character of Aeneas is portrayed as the ideal Roman whose virtues are duty, piety, and faithfulness. Aeneas fulfilled his purpose by establishing the Romans in Italy and initiating their mission to rule the world. The poem was also meant to express that Rome's gift was the art of ruling. Although heavily influenced by Greek literature, Virgil's *Aeneid* reflected Roman historical values and traditions.

Another prominent Augustan poet was Horace, a friend of Virgil's. A sophisticated writer, he pointed out some of the follies and vices of his age. In the *Satires*, Horace directs attacks against dissatisfaction and greed: "How does it happen, Maecenas, that no-one lives content with the lot that either choice has granted him or that chance has thrown in his way...?"

The most famous Latin prose work of the golden age was written by the historian Livy, whose masterpiece was *The Early History of Rome*. In 142 books, of which only 35 survive, Livy traced Roman history to 9 B.C. Livy saw history in terms of moral lessons. His stories transcend Roman culture, revealing the character of its chief figures and demonstrated the virtues that had made Rome great.

✓ **READING PROGRESS CHECK**

Examining In what ways were the Romans remarkable builders, and how did their buildings help create and spread Greco-Roman culture?

ANALYZING PRIMARY SOURCES

Comparing Perspectives on Roman History

Intellectuals of Rome's imperial age looked to the past for inspiration, often comparing contemporary leaders with figures from Rome's glorious past. Livy was among Rome's greatest historians, and Virgil one of its greatest poets. Both were contemporaries of Augustus, who used art and literature to enhance his reputation. Both writers—and Augustus himself—criticized contemporary Roman morality and called for a revival of early Roman virtues. Virgil and Livy also suggested ways in which the Roman government could improve itself.

"Let others fashion from bronze more lifelike, breathing images— / for so they shall—and evoke living faces from marble; / others excel as orators, others track with their instruments / the planets circling in heaven and predict when stars will appear. / But, Romans, never forget that government is your medium! / Be this your art: —to practise men in the habit of peace, / generosity to the conquered, and firmness against aggressors."

—Virgil, from the *Aeneid*

"The subjects to which I would ask each of my readers to devote his earnest attention are these—the life and morals of the community; the men and the qualities by which through domestic policy and foreign war dominion was won and extended. Then as the standard of morality gradually lowers, let him follow the decay of the national character, observing how at first it slowly sinks, then slips downward more and more rapidly, and finally begins to plunge into headlong ruin, until he reaches these days, in which we can bear neither our diseases nor their remedies."

—Livy, from the Preface to *The History of Rome*

DBQ Analyzing Historical Documents

1. ***Drawing Conclusions*** Why were the Romans interested in their own history?
2. ***Analyzing Information*** According to Virgil and Livy, how should the Roman government approach foreign policy?

SKILLBUILDER

Interpreting Maps

Why Learn This Skill?

Maps not only tell us where we are; they also are capable of letting us know where we've been. When we take the time to interpret them, maps have stories to tell. History texts are filled with maps to help explain how geography has influenced people and events in the past.

Learning the Skill

There are many layers to uncover when interpreting a map. The first step is to take note of specific geographic features, such as seas, rivers, mountains, and deserts. These features tell us a lot about what the people had to work with in the region the map covers. For instance, people in mountainous regions might live in isolated communities because it was difficult to get around. Likewise, geographic features can tell us about events in the area covered. If a city was located in a strategic position with access to a waterway, you could interpret that this was an area many groups would want to control and there likely were battles over the location.

Beyond that first step, looking to keys or items called out on the map provides you with additional information for its interpretation. A map key is the little box to the side of the actual map that contains symbols, dates, or other information about the people, place, or time period being covered. Keys can highlight natural resources, battles, empire expansion, or the loss of land, all of which point to what angle you can take in interpreting the map.

Practicing the Skill

With most topics in world history, maps are necessary to help paint the complete picture. This is especially true with the Roman Empire, since the people and events discussed are scattered over such a large area of the Mediterranean world and beyond. Maps help students interpret the full scale of the Roman Empire, including its military, economy, culture, and how its leaders kept the vast empire together. Study the map "Roman Empire: Trade and Expansion," being sure to study its geographic location, as well as all the elements called out on the map and in the map key. Then answer the questions to help you interpret the map.

1. The Romans traded a variety of items. What does this tell you about the resources available in the empire?

2. How might expansion play a role in gaining these resources?

Applying the Skill

Using the map of the Roman Empire, create five more questions about it and write five more answers for your questions. These questions should be specific enough to help you interpret how the geography of the Roman Empire has influenced both people and events. Utilize any labeled geographic features, the call-outs on the map, and the map key. Your questions should be complex enough that one-word answers won't work. (In other words, don't ask which body of water Italy is next to. Ask what role that body of water plays in Rome's quest for empire.)

Life in the Roman World

GUIDING QUESTION *What was the family and social structure of the ancient Romans, and how did they live?*

At the heart of the Roman social structure stood the family, headed by the **paterfamilias**—the dominant male. The household also included the wife, sons with their wives and children, unmarried daughters, and slaves.

paterfamilias in the Roman social structure, the dominant male head of the household, which also included his wife, sons and their wives and children, unmarried daughters, and slaves

Family Life and Women's Roles

Unlike the Greeks, the Romans raised their children at home. All Roman upper-class children—boys and girls—were expected to learn to read. Teachers were often Greek slaves because upper-class Romans had to learn Greek to prosper in the empire.

Roman boys learned reading and writing, moral principles and family values, law, and physical training to prepare them to be soldiers. At age 16, childhood ended for Roman males. At a special ceremony, a young Roman exchanged his purple-edged toga for a plain white toga, which was the toga of manhood.

▲ This detail from a Roman stele depicts a teacher with two of his students.

▶ **CRITICAL THINKING**

Comparing and Contrasting How is this classroom scene similar to or different from one found today?

Some parents in upper-class families provided education for their daughters by hiring private tutors or sending the girls to **primary** schools. However, at the age when boys were entering secondary schools, girls were entering into marriage.

primary most important

Like the Greeks, Roman males believed that the weakness of females made it necessary for women to have male guardians. The paterfamilias had that responsibility. When he died, his sons or nearest male relatives assumed the role of guardian. Fathers also arranged the marriages of their daughters.

For females, the legal minimum age for marriage was 12, although 14 was a more common age. For males, the legal minimum age was 14, although most men married later. Traditionally, Roman marriages were meant to be for life, but divorce was introduced in the third century B.C. and became fairly easy to obtain. Either husband or wife could ask for a divorce.

By the A.D. 100s, changes were occurring in the Roman family. The paterfamilias no longer had absolute authority over his children. He could not sell his children into slavery or have them put to death. The husband's absolute authority over his wife also disappeared. Women were no longer required to have guardians.

Upper-class Roman women in the Early Empire had considerable freedom and independence. They had the right to own, inherit, and sell property. Unlike Greek wives, Roman wives were not segregated from males in the home. Outside their homes, upper-class women could attend races, the theater, and the amphitheater; however, they had to sit in separate female sections. When they went out, women of rank were still accompanied by maids and companions. Women could not participate in politics but influenced politics through their husbands.

Slavery and Slave Revolts

Slavery was common throughout the ancient world, but no people had more slaves or relied so much on slave labor as the Romans did. After the Roman conquest of the Mediterranean, large numbers of foreign peoples who had been captured in wars were brought back to Italy as slaves.

Greek slaves were in much demand as tutors, musicians, doctors, and artists. Roman businessmen would employ them as shop assistants or craftspeople. Slaves of all nationalities were used as household workers such as cooks, valets, waiters, cleaners, and gardeners. Slaves built roads and public buildings and farmed the large estates of the wealthy. The conditions under which these slaves lived were often pitiful.

One Roman writer argued that it was cheaper to work slaves to death and then to replace them than it was to treat them well. Some slaves revolted against their owners and even murdered them, causing some Romans to live in great fear of their slaves. The murder of a master by a slave might mean the execution of all the other household slaves.

The most famous slave revolt in Italy occurred in 73 B.C. Led by the gladiator Spartacus, the revolt broke out in southern Italy and involved 70,000 slaves. Spartacus managed to defeat several Roman armies before being trapped and killed in 71 B.C. The Romans crucified—put to death by nailing to a cross—6,000 of Spartacus's followers.

Living Conditions in Rome

At the center of the colossal Roman Empire was Rome. Truly a capital city, Rome had the largest population of any city in the empire—close to 1 million by the time of Augustus. People from all over the empire resided there. For anyone with ambitions, Rome was the place to be.

Rome boasted public buildings unequaled anywhere in the empire. Its temples, markets, baths, theaters, governmental buildings, and amphitheaters gave parts of the city an appearance of grandeur and magnificence. On the other hand, Rome was an overcrowded and noisy city. Because of the congestion, cart and wagon traffic was banned from the streets during the day. However, the noise from the traffic at night often made sleep difficult. Walking in Rome at night was also dangerous. Although Augustus had organized a police force, people were assaulted or robbed. They could also be soaked by filth thrown out of the upper-story windows of Rome's massive apartment buildings.

insulae Roman apartment blocks constructed of concrete with wooden-beam floors

A large gulf existed between rich and poor. The rich had comfortable villas, while the poor lived in apartment blocks called ***insulae***, which might be six stories high. Constructed of concrete walls with wooden-beam floors, these buildings were usually poorly built and often collapsed. Fire was a constant threat in the insulae where stoves, torches, candles, and lamps were used for heat and light. Once they started, fires were extremely difficult to put out. The famous fire of A.D. 64, which Nero was falsely accused of starting, destroyed a large part of the city.

Although it was the center of a great empire, Rome had serious problems. Beginning with Augustus, the emperors provided food for the city poor. About 200,000 people received free grain, much of it imported from Egypt. Even so, conditions remained grim for the poor.

Large-scale entertainment was provided for the inhabitants of Rome. The poet Juvenal said of the Roman masses, "But nowadays, with no vote . . . , their motto is 'couldn't care less.' Time was when their [vote] elected generals, heads of state, commanders of legions: but now . . . there's only two things that concern them: bread and circuses."

Public spectacles were provided by the emperor as part of the great religious festivals celebrated by the state. The festivals included three major types of entertainment. At the Circus Maximus, horse and chariot races attracted hundreds of thousands. Dramatic performances were held in theaters. The most famous of all the public spectacles, however, were the gladiatorial shows.

✓ READING PROGRESS CHECK

Evaluating Why were slaves important in Rome, and what were their lives like?

Religion in the Roman World

GUIDING QUESTION *What characterized Roman religion?*

The Romans believed that the observance of proper ritual by state priests brought them into a right relationship with the gods. This **guaranteed** peace and prosperity. Indeed, the Romans believed that their success in creating an empire meant that they had earned the favor of the gods. As the politician Cicero claimed in the first century B.C., "We have overcome all the nations of the world, because we have realized that the world is directed and governed by the gods."

guaranteed assured the fulfillment of a condition

At the same time, the Romans were tolerant of other religions. They allowed the worship of native gods and goddesses throughout their provinces. They even adopted some of the local gods. Under Julius Caesar, Jews, believers in a monotheistic religion, were permitted to practice Judaism, seeing it as an ancient religion that supported social stability. This tolerance preserved monotheism within the Western world, making room for the development of Christianity.

Augustus brought back traditional festivals and ceremonies to revive the Roman state religion, which had declined during the turmoil of the late Roman Republic. The official state religion focused on the worship of a number of gods and goddesses, including Jupiter, Juno, Minerva, and Mars. In addition, beginning with Augustus, emperors were often officially made gods by the Roman Senate, thus bolstering support for the emperors.

✓ READING PROGRESS CHECK

Making Inferences What can you infer about the Romans' attitudes toward their gods?

The ruins of the Colosseum in Rome, which seated around 50,000 spectators to various combats ▶

Author's Image/PunchStock

LESSON 3 REVIEW TEKS

Reviewing Vocabulary

1. ***Stating*** What were *insulae* and what social class used them?

Using Your Notes

2. ***Exploring Issues*** In what ways was the Early Empire a period of greatness, and in what ways was the Early Empire riddled with problems?

Answering the Guiding Questions

3. ***Making Generalizations*** What elements defined the early Roman Empire?
4. ***Gathering Information*** How did the Romans spread Greco-Roman arts and culture, and what were their characteristics?
5. ***Explaining*** What was the family and social structure of the ancient Romans, and how did they live?
6. ***Summarizing*** What characterized Roman religion?

Writing Activity

7. **Personal Writing** Write an essay in which you agree or disagree, in full or in part, with the idea that life would have been good for a Roman citizen living in Rome during the days of the Early Empire. Include accurate facts from "Living Conditions in Rome," as well as what you know about the privileges of Roman citizenship. Use your sense of the world at that time to supplement and explain your personal feelings about life in the greatest city of the great Roman Empire.

Assessment

TEKS

Directions: On a separate sheet of paper, answer the questions below. Make sure you read carefully and answer all parts of the questions.

Lesson Review

Lesson 1

1. ***Describing*** How did geography play an important role in the development of Rome?

2. ***Identifying*** Who were the Latins? Where did they live?

3. ***Identifying*** Name a few of the ways that Greek culture influenced Rome.

4. ***Identifying*** Which group had the largest influence on the early development of Rome?

5. ***Identifying Cause and Effect*** What political change occurred in 509 B.C. after the Romans overthrew the last Etruscan king?

6. ***Explaining*** How did the Roman Confederation affect the Latins?

7. ***Explaining*** What three virtues did Romans believe made their early ancestors successful? How were these virtues passed down?

8. ***Naming*** Name three key points that help us explain Rome's success in gaining control of the entire Italian Peninsula.

9. ***Speculating*** What power did the council of the plebs receive in 287 B.C.? Why do you think this power did not lead to its intended goal of equality under the law? **22B**

10. ***Identifying*** Name the two groups that comprised early Rome and explain each of their roles.

11. ***Describing*** Who were the chief executive officers of the Roman Republic? Which area of government did each of them oversee?

12. ***Explaining*** Explain why the representative body of people was part of the development of the Roman democratic-republican government, and how the Roman Senate influenced future democratic-republican governments, as an institution and in governing practices. **1B, 3A, 20A**

13. ***Explaining*** How was the centuriate assembly organized? How did this affect the passing of laws?

14. ***Explaining*** Explain the struggle of the orders. How long did this last and what was the outcome?

15. ***Evaluating*** What about the Law of Nations makes it unique for its time? How might the principles of the Law of Nations apply today?

Need Extra Help?

If You've Missed Question	1	2	3	4	5	6	7	8	9	10	11	12	13	14	15
Go to page	150	151	151	151	151	152	152	152	153	152	153	153	153	153	154

Lesson 2

16. ***Identifying Cause and Effect*** What were the consequences of the rise of large estates?

17. ***Identifying*** Who were Tiberius and Gaius Gracchus?

18. ***Explaining*** Who was Marius, and what change did he make in how Roman soldiers were recruited? **21A**

19. ***Interpreting*** How did Augustus change the system for governing Roman provinces? What were the effects? **1B**

Lesson 3

20. ***Analyzing*** When was the golden age of Latin literature, and how did its writers differ in their style and outlook? **3A**

21. ***Theorizing*** What did the custom of marrying off girls at a very young age reflect about Roman society? **24A**

Exploring the Essential Questions

22. ***Synthesizing*** With a small group, create a word web of key aspects of the republic and the empire. Start with one circle labeled "Roman Republic" and one labeled "Roman Empire." For each circle, draw four circles beyond it. Label them "politics," "society," "culture," and "religion." Add circles with the ideas and individuals involved. Fill another ring of circles beyond these with details. Add lines connecting circles where aspects of the republic overlap those of the empire. You may include artwork, maps, and primary sources in your web. **3A**

Critical Thinking

23. ***Describing*** How did ancient Rome influence the development of monotheism? **3A**

24. ***Interpreting*** Explain the meaning of the legal concept "innocent until proven guilty." What body of law acknowledged this concept in ancient Rome? What is the impact of this concept today? **22B, 25B**

25. ***Analyzing*** What were the rights and responsibilities of citizens and noncitizens in the Roman Republic, including civic participation? **21B**

26. ***Drawing Inferences*** How did references to the Roman gods affect the science of astronomy? **23B, 25B**

27. ***Drawing Conclusions*** How was American law influenced by the Roman Empire? **25B**

Social Studies Skills

28. ***Identifying Perspectives and Differing Interpretations*** People took steps to salvage the Roman Republic but actually helped lead to its end. What are two examples of actions that were intended to save the republic but had the opposite effect?

29. ***Create and Analyze*** Explain the major characteristics of the republican form of government as it existed in ancient Rome. **19B**

Need Extra Help?

If You've Missed Question	16	17	18	19	20	21	22	23	24	25	26	27	28	29
Go to page	157	151	151	151	151	151	151	171	154	154	170	153	157	151

30 ***Understanding Relationships Among Events*** What was the Pax Romana? How did the emperors keep people in the provinces from rebelling?

31 ***Creating and Using Charts*** Make a chart with three columns and two rows. Label the three columns Science, Technology, and Mathematics. In the first row, write how each idea had Roman origins. In the second row, explain how each idea spread to other cultures. **27A**

32 ***Presentation Skills*** Research an example of architecture from the ancient Rome. Explain how the structure reflects Roman culture and visual principles. Present your conclusions to the class, along with a picture of the architecture you have chosen. **26A, 26B**

DBQ Analyzing Primary Sources

Use the document to answer the following questions.

In A.D. 64, a fire swept through Rome, burning for nearly a week and destroying much of the city. Years later, the historian Tacitus described the fire in his *Annals.*

PRIMARY SOURCE

"A disaster followed, whether accidental or treacherously [betraying trust] contrived by the emperor [Nero], is uncertain, as authors have given both accounts, worse, however, and more dreadful than any which have ever happened to this city by the violence of fire. . . . And no one dared to stop the mischief, because of incessant [constant] menaces from a number of persons who forbade the extinguishing of the flames, because again others openly hurled brands [burning torches], and kept shouting that there was one who gave them authority."

—Tacitus, from *The Annals*

33 ***Examining*** What universal theme is conveyed in the prose, and how does the writing transcend the culture? **26B**

34 ***Making Inferences*** How does this text reflect the history of Roman culture?

Analyzing Visuals

Use the artwork to answer the following questions.

35 ***Analyzing Visuals*** Which of the following does the artwork reflect about ancient Roman culture? **26B**

A the importance of law
B the importance of learning
C the worship of gods
D the structure of family

36 ***Drawing Conclusions*** What does this image tell us about the importance of learning in ancient Rome? **26A**

Extended Response Question

37 ***Expository*** If you lived roughly 2,000 years ago and your country was conquered by the Romans, what would be the pluses and minuses of Roman rule? Research at least one Roman province and write an article about what life would have been like for native peoples.

Need Extra Help?

If You've Missed Question	30	31	32	33	34	35	36	37
Go to page	163	165	165	165	170	169	169	150

The Byzantine Empire and Emerging Europe

A.D. 50–800

ESSENTIAL QUESTIONS • *How can religion impact a culture?* • *What factors lead to the rise and fall of empires?*

networks

There's More Online! about the Byzantine Empire and emerging Europe.

CHAPTER 8

The Story Matters...

On Christmas Day in the year 800, as the Frankish ruler Charlemagne attended mass in St. Peter's in Rome, Pope Leo III placed a crown on his head and those assembled hailed him as "emperor of the Romans." The spiritual leader of Christendom had acknowledged a Germanic king as the heir to the Roman Empire. Charlemagne's coronation symbolized the joining of Roman, Christian, and Germanic cultures, the three elements that were combined to form the new medieval civilization emerging in Europe.

◄ Created in twelfth-century France, this stained glass image expresses Charlemagne's identity as the ideal Christian ruler. The pictorial glass of Gothic cathedrals served an important function for a largely illiterate public.

PHOTO: French School/The Bridgeman Art Library/Getty Images.

CHAPTER 8

Place and Time: Europe A.D. 50–800

Between A.D. 600 and 800, Christianity became the dominant religion of Western Europe. When the Christian faith appeared in the Roman province of Judaea around A.D. 50, Rome's power was at its height. Persecuted sporadically during its first centuries, Christianity grew until by A.D. 391, it became the state religion of the Roman Empire. Arising within the Roman world, the Christian faith was spread later by missionaries to peoples outside the empire's borders. As Christianity grew, the Church developed a governing structure based on the authority of bishops and the pope in Rome. Other Christian institutions arising during these early centuries were the religious communities known as monasteries.

Step Into the Place

Read the quotations and look at the information presented on the map.

DBQ **Analyzing Historical Documents** In what different ways was the authority of the Church spread during this period?

PRIMARY SOURCE

"[The seventh-century Irish missionary Aidan] always traveled on foot unless compelled by necessity to ride; and whatever people he met on his walks, whether high or low, he stopped and spoke to them. If they were heathen, he urged them to be baptized; and if they were Christians, he strengthened their faith. . . . He cultivated peace and love, purity and humility; he was above anger and greed, and despised pride and conceit. . . . He used his priestly authority to check the proud and powerful."

—Bede, from *A History of the English Church and People,* A.D. 731–732

PRIMARY SOURCE

"No war ever undertaken by the Frank[s] [under Charlemagne] was carried on with such persistence and bitterness, or cost so much labor, because the Saxons, like almost all the tribes of Germany, were a fierce people, given to the worship of devils, and hostile to our religion. . . . Accordingly war was begun against them, and was waged for thirty-three successive years with great fury. . . . They were sometimes so much weakened and reduced that they promised to renounce the worship of devils, and adopt Christianity, but they were no less ready to violate these terms than prompt to accept them. . . . "

—Einhard, from *Life of Charlemagne,* A.D. 830–833

Step Into the Time

Synthesizing Information

Select three events from the time line and show how they strengthened the power of the Christian Church during this period.

EUROPE

A.D. 64 Great Fire of Rome is followed by Nero's persecution of Christians

313 Constantine issues Edict of Milan

325 Council of Nicaea defines Christian belief

50 — 100 — 200 — 300

THE WORLD

A.D. 70 Destruction of the Jewish Temple in Jerusalem

220 Final collapse of China's Han dynasty

c. 250 Classic Maya period begins in Mexico and Central America

networks
There's More Online!

☑ **MAP** Explore the interactive version of this map on Networks.

☑ **TIME LINE** Explore the interactive version of the time line on Networks.

391 Theodosius I bans paganism; makes Christianity the state religion

476 Last Roman emperor deposed; fall of the Western Roman Empire

c. 500 Frankish king Clovis converts to Christianity

c. 520 Benedict establishes his rules for Christian monasteries

590 Gregory I becomes pope; broadens secular power of papacy

800 Charlemagne is crowned emperor of the Romans

400 — 500 — 600 — 700 — 800

c. 380 Candra Gupta II comes to the throne of India's Gupta Empire

c. 500 Mexican city of Teotihuacán reaches its height

604 Prince Shōtoku Taishi introduces Confucianism to Japan

711 Muslims invade Spain

762 Baghdad is founded as capital of Muslim empire

794 Japanese capital moves from Nara to Heian-kyo (modern Kyōto)

networks

There's More Online!

- ☑ BIOGRAPHY Constantine
- ☑ IMAGE Early Christian Catacombs
- ☑ IMAGE Mural from a Jewish Synagogue in the Roman City of Dura-Europos
- ☑ INTERACTIVE SELF-CHECK QUIZ
- ☑ MAP Spread of Christianity, A.D. 325
- ☑ MAP World Religions Today
- ☑ PRIMARY SOURCE Christianity in Rome
- ☑ VIDEO Christianity

LESSON 1
The First Christians

ESSENTIAL QUESTION *How can religion impact a culture?*

It Matters Because

A new civilization came into being in western Europe after the collapse of the Western Roman Empire. This new civilization—European civilization—was formed by the coming together of three major elements: the Germanic people who moved in and settled the Western Roman Empire, the legacy of the Romans, and the Christian Church.

Reading HELPDESK

Academic Vocabulary

- **transformation**
- **structure**

Content Vocabulary

- **prefect**
- **clergy**
- **laity**

TAKING NOTES:

Key Ideas and Details

Contrasting As you read, use a table like the one below to contrast the Roman state religion with Christianity.

Roman State Religion	Christianity

TEKS Texas Essential Knowledge and Skills

1B identify major causes and describe the major effects of the following events from 500 BC to AD 600: the development of the classical civilizations of Greece, Rome, Persia, India (Maurya and Gupta), China (Zhou, Qin, and Han), and the development of major world religions

continued on the next page

Judaism in the Roman Empire

GUIDING QUESTION *How did a movement within Judaism lead to development of a new faith?*

In the period immediately preceding the Roman conquest of 63 B.C., the Jewish people enjoyed independence. By A.D. 6, however, Judaea (joo • DEE • uh), which embraced the lands of the old Jewish kingdom of Judah, had been made a Roman province placed under the direction of an official called a **prefect**, later known as a procurator.

A wide variety of Jewish groups developed and vied for influence under the Romans. Unrest was widespread in Judaea, and Roman rule influenced developments within Judaism. The priestly Sadducees (SA • juh • SEEZ) probably favored cooperation with Rome. The scholarly Pharisees (FAR • uh • SEEZ) held that close observance of religious law would protect them from Roman influences. The Essenes lived apart from society, sharing goods in common. Like many other Jews, they waited for God to save Israel from oppression. The Zealots, however, called for the violent overthrow of Roman rule. In fact, a Jewish revolt began in A.D. 66, only to be crushed by the Romans four years later. The Jewish Temple in Jerusalem was destroyed, and Roman power once more stood supreme.

A few decades before the revolt, a Jewish teacher named Jesus traveled and preached throughout Judaea and neighboring Galilee. These teachings began a new movement within Judaism.

☑ **READING PROGRESS CHECK**

Summarizing How did the Jews differ about how to respond to Roman rule?

◀ Early Christians were forced to worship in catacombs such as this one in Salzburg, Austria.

▶ **CRITICAL THINKING**

Drawing Conclusions Why did early Christians worship in catacombs?

The Rise of Christianity

GUIDING QUESTIONS *What are the beliefs that define Christianity? How did Christianity spread throughout the Roman Empire and what were the consequences?*

After reports spread that Jesus had overcome death, the movement gained additional support throughout Judaea and Galilee and led to the development of a new monotheistic faith. Known as Christianity, it was heavily influenced by the culture of ancient Israel.

prefect in the Roman Empire, an official in charge of a province

The Teachings of Jesus

Jesus believed that his mission was to complete the salvation that God had promised to Israel throughout its history. He stated: "Do not think that I have come to abolish the Law or the Prophets; I have not come to abolish them but to fulfill them." Jesus, then, adhered to the entire Law and emphasized those elements that called for the **transformation** of the inner person: "So in everything, do to others what you would have them do to you, for this sums up the Law and the Prophets."

transformation conversion; change in character or condition

Citing verses from the Hebrew Bible, Jesus said, "Love the Lord your God with all your heart and with all your soul and with all your mind and with all your strength. This is the first commandment. The second is this: Love your neighbor as yourself." Jesus shared these and related ethical concepts with other prominent Jewish teachers. He gave them particularly eloquent and influential expression. The concepts—humility, charity, and love toward others—later influenced the value system of Western civilization.

Jesus's preaching stirred controversy. Some people saw him as a potential revolutionary who might lead a revolt against Rome. His opponents finally turned him over to Roman authorities. The prefect Pontius Pilate ordered Jesus's crucifixion. After the death of Jesus, his followers proclaimed that he had risen from death and had appeared to them. They believed Jesus to be the Messiah (anointed one), the long-expected deliverer who would save Israel from its foes and inaugurate an age of peace, prosperity, and monotheism.

(continued from p. 178)

TEKS **Texas Essential Knowledge and Skills**

1C identify major causes and describe the major effects of the following important turning points in world history from 600 to 1450 the spread of Christianity, the decline of Rome and the formation of medieval Europe; the development of Islamic caliphates and their impact on Asia, Africa, and Europe; the Mongol invasions and their impact on Europe, China, India, and Southwest Asia

3A describe the major political, religious/philosophical, and cultural influences of Persia, India, China, Israel, Greece, and Rome, including the development of monotheism, Judaism, and Christianity

continued on the next page

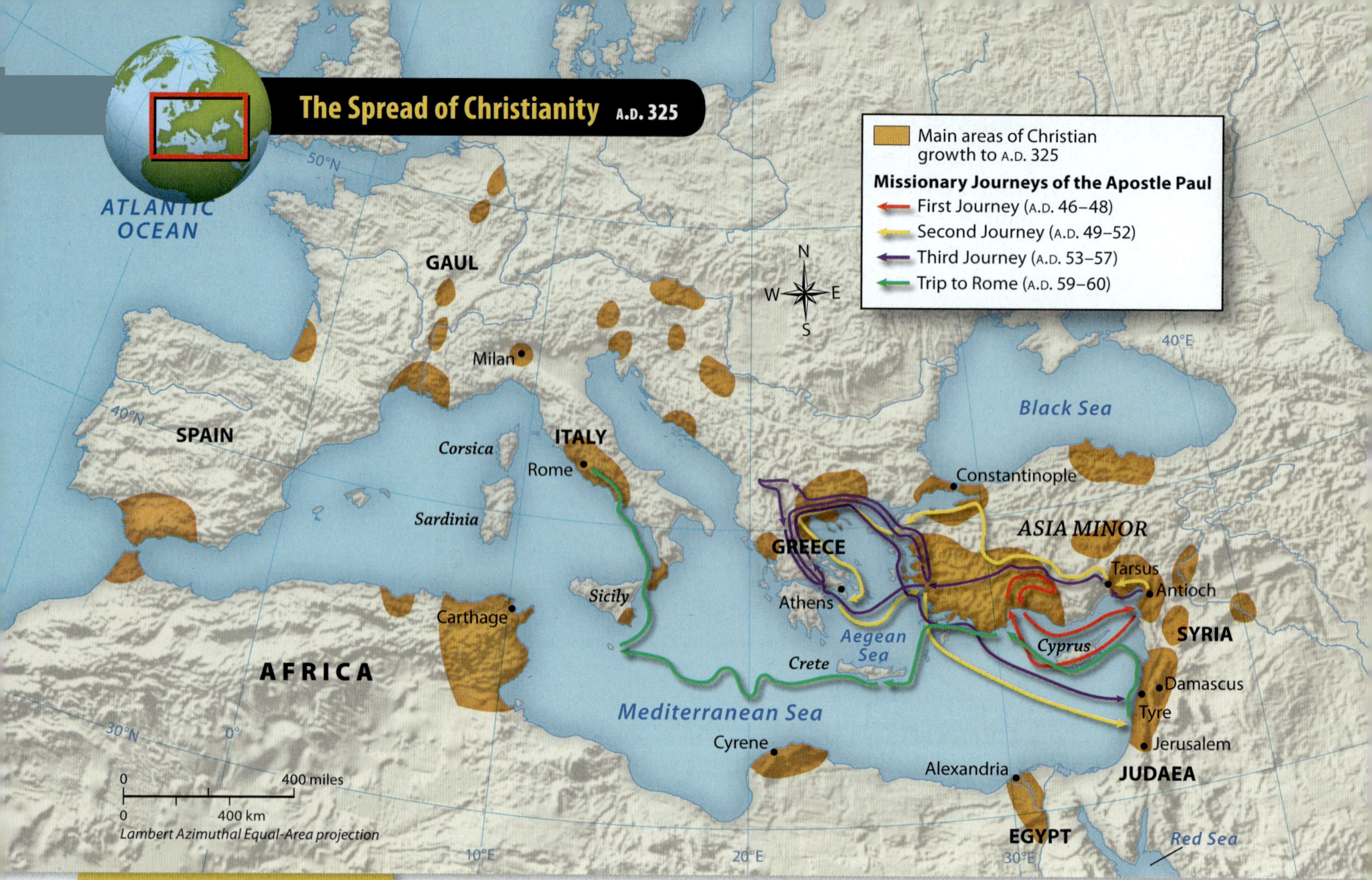

GEOGRAPHY CONNECTION

Christianity had begun to spread throughout Europe and the Mediterranean by A.D. 325.

1. **HUMAN SYSTEMS** *What cities did Paul pass through on his second journey?*
2. **ENVIRONMENT AND SOCIETY** *Based on the map, how do you think Christianity was spread?*

(continued from p. 179)

TEKS Texas Essential Knowledge and Skills

4A explain the development of Christianity as a unifying social and political factor in medieval Europe and the Byzantine Empire

23A describe the historical origins, central ideas, and spread of major religious and philosophical traditions, including Buddhism, Christianity, Confucianism, Hinduism, Islam, Judaism, Sikhism, and the development of monotheism

23B identify examples of religious influence on various events referenced in the major eras of world history

continued on the next page

Christianity Spreads Through the Empire

Prominent apostles, or leaders, arose in early Christianity. The recognized leader was Simon Peter, a Jewish fisherman who had become a follower of Jesus during Jesus's lifetime. Another major apostle was Paul, a highly educated Jewish Roman citizen who joined the movement later. Paul took the message of Jesus to Gentiles—non-Jews—as well as to Jews.

At the center of Paul's message was the belief that Jesus was the Savior, the Son of God who had come to Earth to save humanity. Paul taught that Jesus's death made up for the sins of all humans. By accepting Jesus as Christ (from *Christos,* the Greek term for Messiah) and Savior, people could be saved from sin and reconciled to God.

These central ideas of early Christianity were passed on orally through preaching. Paul and other followers of Jesus also wrote letters, or epistles, outlining and developing Christian beliefs. Also, some of Jesus's disciples, or followers, may have preserved some of the sayings of Jesus in writing. Later, between A.D. 40 and A.D. 100, these accounts became the basis of the written Gospels—the "good news" concerning Jesus. These writings give a record of Jesus's life and teachings, and they form the core of the New Testament, the second part of the Christian Bible. This same Christian Bible has become the most published book in the world and has endured into the present day, conveying universal themes to a variety of cultures around the globe.

By A.D. 100, the early missionaries had established Christian churches in most of the major cities of the eastern empire and in some places in the western part of the empire. Most early Christians came from the Jews and the Greek-speaking populations of the east. In the second and third centuries, however, Christianity had spread among an increasing number of Latin-speaking people.

Roman Persecution

The basic values of Christianity differed markedly from those of the Greco-Roman world. In spite of that, the Romans at first paid little attention to the Christians, whom they regarded as simply another sect of Judaism. However, the Roman attitude toward Christianity began to change.

The Romans tolerated the religions of other peoples unless these religions threatened public order or public morals. Many Romans came to view Christians as harmful to the Roman state because Christians refused to worship the state gods and emperors. The Romans saw the Christians' refusal to do so as an act of treason, punishable by death. The Christians, however, believed there was only one God. To them, the worship of state gods and the emperors meant worshiping false gods and endangering their own salvation. Jews, who also refrained from such worship, had been allowed to follow "the laws of their fathers," but this exemption was not extended to the new religion.

The Roman government began persecuting (harassing to cause suffering) Christians during the reign of Nero (A.D. 54– A.D. 68). The emperor blamed the Christians for the fire that destroyed much of Rome in A.D. 64, and subjected them to cruel deaths. In contrast, in the second century, persecution of Christians diminished, allowing this new monotheistic faith to develop. By A.D. 180, Christians still represented a small minority, but one of considerable strength.

▲ **Relief carving of the apostle Peter being taken prisoner by Roman authorities**

▶ **CRITICAL THINKING**

Describing According to the Christian tradition, who was Peter?

Roman Empire Adopts Christianity

The occasional persecution of Christians by the Romans in the first and second centuries had not stopped the growth of Christianity. It had, in fact, served to strengthen Christianity in the second and third centuries by causing it to become more organized. Influenced by the Roman institutions under which they lived, missionaries used the Roman language and organizational structures to spread their message. Fear of persecution meant that only the most committed would follow the faith.

Crucial to this change was the emerging role of the bishops, who began to assume more control over church communities. The Christian church was creating a new **structure** in which the **clergy**, or church leaders, had distinct functions separate from the **laity**, or the regular church members.

Christianity grew quickly in the first century. It took root in the second century, and by the third century, it had spread widely. Why was Christianity able to attract and maintain so many followers?

First, the Christian message had much to offer the Roman world. The Roman state-based religion was impersonal and existed for the good of Rome. Christianity was personal and offered salvation and eternal life to individuals. Christianity gave life a meaning and purpose beyond the simple material things of everyday reality.

Second, Christianity seemed familiar. It was viewed by some as similar to other mystery religions, offering immortality as the result of the

structure an arrangement in a definite pattern of organization

clergy church leaders

laity regular church members

(continued from p. 180)

TEKS **Texas Essential Knowledge and Skills**

26C identify examples of art, music, and literature that transcend the cultures in which they were created and convey universal themes

BIOGRAPHY

Constantine (c. A.D. 280–337)

After Diocletian abdicated the throne, he did not pick Constantine to be the next emperor. In response, Constantine engaged in a civil war to win the throne. He attributed his eventual success to his belief in Christianity. In 313 Constantine and the Eastern emperor Licinius issued the Edict of Milan, which granted freedom of religion to Christians and all others within the Roman Empire. Under the rule of Constantine, Christianity began to grow into a world religion.

CRITICAL THINKING

Making Inferences Why might it have been valuable to Constantine to claim divine aid in his victory over his rival?

sacrificial death of a savior-god. At the same time, it offered more than the other mystery religions did. Jesus had been a human figure to whom it was easy to relate. Moreover, Christianity did not require painful or expensive initiation rites as other mystery religions did. Initiation was by baptism—a purification by water—by which one entered into the Christian community.

Finally, Christianity fulfilled the human need to belong. Christians formed communities bound to one another. In these communities, people could express their love by helping one another and offering assistance to the poor and the sick. Christianity satisfied the need to belong in a way that the huge Roman Empire could never provide, and developed a unifying social element that would endure into medieval Europe.

Christianity proved attractive to all classes, but especially to the poor and powerless. Eternal life is promised to all—rich, poor, aristocrats, slaves, men, and women. As Paul stated in his letters to the Colossians and the Galatians, "And [you] have put on the new self. . . . Here there is no Greek or Jew . . . barbarian, Scythian, slave or free, but Christ is all, and is in all." Although Christianity did not call for revolution, it stressed a sense of spiritual equality for all people—a revolutionary idea at the time.

The Christian Church became more organized in the third century. Some emperors began new persecutions, but their schemes failed. The last great persecution was by Diocletian (DY • uh • KLEE • shuhn) at the beginning of the fourth century. Even he had to admit, however, what had become obvious in the course of the third century: Christianity and its followers were too strong to be blotted out by force.

In the fourth century, Christianity prospered and found a powerful supporter in Emperor Constantine. According to the traditional story, before the battle, Constantine saw a vision of the Christian cross with the words, "In this sign you shall conquer." Having won the battle, Constantine was convinced of the power of the Christian God. Although he was not baptized until the end of his life, in A.D. 313 Constantine issued the Edict of Milan, which proclaimed official tolerance of Christianity. Then, under Theodosius the Great, who ruled from A.D. 378 to A.D. 395, the Romans adopted Christianity as the official religion of the Roman Empire.

✓ READING PROGRESS CHECK

Analyzing Prior to the adoption of Christianity in the empire, why did the Romans charge some Christians with treason?

LESSON 1 REVIEW TEKS

Reviewing Vocabulary

1. ***Making Inferences*** How do you think the division of the Christian church into clergy and laity in response to Roman persecution helped them spread their beliefs? **1B, 1C, 3A, 23A, 23B**

Using Your Notes

2. ***Contrasting*** Use your notes to contrast the differences between the Roman state religion and Christianity. **3A, 23A**

Answering the Guiding Questions

3. ***Drawing Conclusions*** How did a new movement within Judaism lead to the development of a new faith? **1B, 3A, 23B**
4. ***Identifying*** What are the beliefs that define Christianity? **23A**
5. ***Assessing*** How did Christianity spread throughout the Roman Empire, and what were the consequences? **1C**

Writing Activity

6. **INFORMATIVE/EXPLANATORY** Research why Romans thought Christianity, a monotheistic religion, was dangerous to their empire. Compare these arguments to the doctrine and practices of Christians at that time. Present your findings in an essay. **1B, 3A, 23A**

Christianity

Christianity claims more members than any of the other world religions. It dates its beginning to the death of Jesus in A.D. 33 in what is now Israel. It is based on the belief in one God and on the life and teachings of Jesus. Christians believe that Jesus, who was born a Jew, is the son of God and is fully divine and human. Christians regard Jesus as the Messiah (Christ), or savior, who died for humanity's sins. Christians feel that people are saved and achieve eternal life by faith in Jesus.

The major forms of Christianity are Roman Catholicism, Eastern Orthodoxy, and Protestantism. In 1054, disputes over doctrine and the leadership of the Christian Church caused the church to divide into the Roman Catholic Church, headed by the Bishop of Rome, also known as the Pope, and the Eastern Orthodox Churches, led by patriarchs. Protestant churches emerged in the 1500s in an era known as the Reformation. Protestants disagreed with some Catholic doctrines and were critical of the Pope's authority. Despite their different theologies, all three forms are united in their belief in Jesus as savior.

Sacred Symbol

Christians believe that Jesus died for their sins. His death redeemed those who follow his teachings. The statue Christ the Redeemer, located in Rio de Janeiro, Brazil, stands at the top of a mountain over-looking the city. The placement of the statue and its depiction of Jesus's arms outreached symbolize this fundamental belief of redemption.

Worship and Celebration

Christians celebrate many events commemorating the life and death of Jesus. Among the most widely known and observed are Christmas, Good Friday, and Easter. Christmas is often commemorated by attending church services to celebrate the birth of Jesus.

Sacred Text

The Christian Bible is the spiritual text for all Christians and is considered to be inspired by God. This excerpt, from Matthew 5:3–12, is from Jesus' Sermon on the Mount. It depicts his moral teachings.

"Blessed are the poor in spirit, for theirs is the kingdom of heaven.
Blessed are those who mourn, for they shall be comforted.
Blessed are the meek, for they shall inherit the earth.
Blessed are those who hunger and thirst for
righteousness, for they shall be satisfied.
Blessed are the merciful, for they shall obtain mercy.
Blessed are the pure in heart, for they shall see God.
Blessed are the peacemakers, for they shall be
called sons of God.
Blessed are those who are persecuted for
righteousness' sake, for theirs is the kingdom of heaven.
Blessed are you when men revile you and
persecute you and utter all kinds of evil
against you falsely on my account.
Rejoice and be glad, for your reward is great
in heaven, for so men persecuted the prophets
who were before you."

Sacred Site

The Gospels affirm that Bethlehem was the birthplace of Jesus. Consequently, it holds great importance to Christians. The Church of the Nativity is located in the heart of Bethlehem. It houses the spot where Christians believe Jesus was born and many Christians travel there to view it.

SKILLBUILDER

TEKS 29F

Categorizing

Why Learn This Skill?

Studying world history means studying a series of patterns in order to gain an understanding and come to conclusions about specific themes during particular time periods and general themes that cover all of world history. Categorizing information can help you recognize those patterns.

Learning the Skill

Analyzing information by categorizing means breaking down what you read into smaller parts. You can then see how these smaller parts are organized and relate to each other in order to help you manage and organize information. Categorizing can be especially useful in helping you recognize meanings that might not be obvious at first glance. Likewise, categorizing can help you take smaller parts and put them together to recognize a pattern and find evidence to identify something larger, such as an idea or conclusion.

Practicing the Skill

Categorizing helps you break down and organize ideas for analysis. There are some points to consider when dividing items or ideas into different categories:

1. What are you categorizing? For instance, are you breaking information down by subject matter, type of object, location, or point of view, among other things?
2. How much should you categorize? Are there smaller bits of information to help you break down your categories even further?
3. What is the purpose of the categorization? Breaking your information into categories should help you identify the parts of something greater.

You can find examples of this skill throughout this textbook. In fact, you could see this textbook as one major exercise in categorizing. It takes the general theme of world history and then breaks it down to see how different periods in history relate to each other and to the theme of world history as a whole. You can even recognize subtle meanings and connections, on the basis of which lessons fall under which chapters. Take a look at how Chapter 8 is organized:

The Byzantine Empire and Emerging Europe, A.D. 50-800

Lesson 1: The First Christians
Lesson 2: Decline and Fall of Rome
Lesson 3: The Early Christian Church
Lesson 4: The Age of Charlemagne
Lesson 5: The Byzantine Empire

The lessons are a part of the larger category, which is the chapter. How do the lesson titles demonstrate a pattern within the category that is Chapter 8?

Applying the Skill

Read through Lesson 1 of Chapter 8 to learn about the development of early Christianity. Take the information from that lesson and categorize it into different periods of indifference, persecution, and acceptance by leaders in the Roman Empire.

PHOTO: ©Christel Gerstenberg/Corbis

networks
There's More Online!
- BIOGRAPHY Diocletian
- GRAPHIC ORGANIZER Succession of Roman Emperors
- IMAGE Constantine's Arch
- IMAGE The Tetrarchs
- INTERACTIVE SELF-CHECK QUIZ
- MAP Migrations Into the Roman Empire, A.D. 200–500
- MAP The Roman Empire Under the Tetrarchs, A.D. 293–311
- VIDEO The Fall of Rome

LESSON 2
Decline and Fall of Rome

ESSENTIAL QUESTIONS • *How can religion impact a culture?* • *What factors lead to the rise and fall of empires?*

Reading HELPDESK

Academic Vocabulary
- **military**
- **collapse**

Content Vocabulary
- **plague**
- **inflation**

TAKING NOTES:
Key Ideas and Details

Determining Cause and Effect
As you read, use a table like the one below to describe the events that led to the decline and fall of the Roman Empire.

Decline	Fall

TEKS Texas Essential Knowledge and Skills
1B identify major causes and describe the major effects of the following events from 500 BC to AD 600: the development of the classical civilizations of Greece, Rome, Persia, India (Maurya and Gupta), China (Zhou, Qin, and Han), and the development of major world religions

continued on the next page

IT MATTERS BECAUSE

In A.D. 410, the Visigoths sacked Rome. After ruling the Mediterranean world for hundreds of years, the Roman Empire in the west declined and then fell. The Germanic peoples were only one factor in Rome's collapse.

The Decline of Rome

GUIDING QUESTIONS *What political factors led to the decline of the Roman Empire? How did economic and social reforms by Diocletian and Constantine affect the Roman Empire?*

During the reign of Marcus Aurelius, the last of the five "good emperors," a number of catastrophes struck Rome. To many Romans, these natural disasters seemed to portend an ominous future for Rome. New problems arose soon after the death of Marcus Aurelius in A.D. 180. A period of conflict, confusion, and civil war followed.

Problems and Upheavals

In the course of the third century, the Roman Empire came near collapse. Following a series of civil wars, a **military** government under the Severan rulers, restored order. Septimius Severus told his sons "enrich the soldiers and ignore everyone else," setting the tone for the new dynasty. After the Severan rulers, there was more disorder. For almost 50 years, from A.D. 235 to A.D. 284, the Roman throne was occupied by whomever had the military strength to seize it. During this period, there were 22 emperors, most of whom died violently.

At the same time, the empire was troubled by a series of invasions, no doubt encouraged by the internal turmoil. In the east, the Sassanid (suh • SAH • nuhd) Persians made inroads into Roman territory. Germanic tribes poured into the Balkans, Gaul, and Spain.

Invasions, civil wars, and plague almost caused an economic **collapse** in the third century. A labor shortage created by **plague**—an epidemic disease—affected both military recruiting and the economy. There was a decline in trade and small industry. Farm production declined as crops were ravaged by invaders or the defending Roman army. Armies were needed more than ever, but financial strains made it

(continued from p. 185)

TEKS Texas Essential Knowledge and Skills

1C identify major causes and describe the major effects of the following important turning points in world history from 600 to 1450 the spread of Christianity, the decline of Rome and the formation of medieval Europe; the development of Islamic caliphates and their impact on Asia, Africa, and Europe; the Mongol invasions and their impact on Europe, China, India, and Southwest Asia

3B explain the impact of the fall of Rome on Western Europe

3C compare the factors that led to the collapse of Rome and Han China

difficult to enlist and pay more soldiers. By the mid-third century, the state had to hire Germans to fight. These soldiers did not understand Roman traditions and had little loyalty to either the empire or the emperors.

Reforms by Diocletian and Constantine

At the end of the third and the beginning of the fourth centuries, the Roman Empire gained a new lease on life through the efforts of two emperors, Diocletian and Constantine. These emperors' reforms caused The the empire changed to develop into a new state: the Late Roman Empire, which included a new governmental structure, a rigid economic and social system, and a new state religion—Christianity.

Believing that the empire had grown too large for a single ruler, Diocletian, who ruled from A.D. 284 to A.D. 305, divided it into two parts, east and west. Each part was then also halved and ruled by individual rulers. This new system was called the tetrarchy (rule by four). Despite the appearance of four-man rule, Diocletian's military power enabled him to hold ultimate authority.

military relating to the armed forces or to soldiers, arms, or war

collapse to break down completely; to suddenly lose force or effectiveness

plague an epidemic disease

Constantine, who ruled from A.D. 306 to A.D. 337, continued and even expanded the policies of Diocletian, in hopes of slowing the effects of Rome's decline. Constantine's biggest project was the construction of a new capital city in the east, on the site of the Greek city of Byzantium on the shores of the Bosporus. The city, eventually renamed Constantinople (now İstanbul, Turkey), was developed for defensive reasons. Its strategic location provided protection of the eastern frontier. Constantinople, the "New Rome," became the center of the Eastern Roman Empire and one of the great cities of the world. Constantine enriched the city with a forum, large palaces, and a vast amphitheater.

Diocletian's and Constantine's political and military reforms enlarged two institutions—the civil service and the army. A hierarchy of officials exercised control at the various levels of government. The army was enlarged to 500,000 men, including German units. Mobile units could be quickly moved to support frontier troops where the borders were threatened.

inflation a rapid increase in prices

The expansion of the bureaucracy and the army created a demand for more revenues. The population was not growing, however, so the tax base could not pay for them. Roman money, or currency, began to lose value.

Both rulers devised new economic and social policies to deal with these financial burdens. Like their political policies, the new economic and social policies were all based on coercion and loss of individual freedom. To fight **inflation**, Diocletian issued a price edict in 301 that set wage and price controls for the empire. Despite severe penalties, it failed to work.

To ensure the tax base and to keep the empire going despite the labor shortage, the emperors issued edicts forcing workers to remain in their vocations. Hence, jobs, such as bakers and shippers, became hereditary. The fortunes of free farmers also declined. Soon they found themselves bound to the land by landowners, who took advantage of depressed conditions to enlarge their estates.

In general, the economic and social policies of Diocletian and Constantine were based on control and coercion. Although temporarily successful, such policies in the long run stifled the very vitality the Late Empire needed to revive its sagging fortunes.

▼ The Arch of Constantine in the Forum in Rome was erected by Constantine to commemorate his victory at the Battle of Milvian Bridge in A.D. 312

✓ **READING PROGRESS CHECK**

Determining Cause and Effect What were the effects of the political and military reforms of Diocletian and Constantine?

GEOGRAPHY CONNECTION

Diocletian divided the Roman Empire into four prefectures.

1. **THE WORLD IN SPATIAL TERMS** *How would establishing four different capitals help protect Rome?*
2. **HUMAN SYSTEMS** *Compare and contrast the territories controlled by the emperors and the caesars.*

The End of the Western Roman Empire

GUIDING QUESTION ***How did the migration of Germanic tribes contribute to the fall of the Roman Empire?***

Constantine had reunited the Roman Empire and restored a semblance of order. After his death, however, the empire continued to divide into western and eastern parts as fighting erupted on a regular basis between elements of the Roman army backing the claims of rival emperors. By A.D. 395, the western and eastern parts of the empire became virtually two independent states. In the course of the fifth century, the empire in the east remained intact under the Roman emperor in Constantinople. At the same time, the administrative structure of the empire in the west collapsed and was replaced by an assortment of Germanic kingdoms. The process was a gradual one, beginning with the movement of Germans into the empire.

Until the fourth century, the empire had proved capable of absorbing the Germans without harm to its political structure. In the late fourth century, the Huns, a fierce tribe of nomads from the steppes of Asia, moved in to displace many Germanic tribes, like the Visigoths. These Visigoths crossed into Roman territory, and at first became Roman allies, but soon revolted. At Adrianople in A.D. 378, the Visigoths defeated the Roman army.

Increasing numbers of Germans now crossed the frontiers. In A.D. 410 the Visigoths sacked Rome and then moved into Spain and Gaul. The Vandals poured into southern Spain and Africa and ravaged Rome in A.D. 455. By the middle of the fifth century, the western provinces of the Roman Empire had

Thinking Like a HISTORIAN

Historiography

Why did Rome decline and fall? Writing in the rationalist, skeptical eighteenth century, the historian Edward Gibbon attributed the decline of Rome to "the triumph of barbarism and religion." Other historians, both before and after Gibbon, have offered a wide variety of other causes for the fall of the Roman Empire. As historians write history, they critically examine a variety of sources, which can still lead them to different conclusions. Use the Internet to find reliable sources presenting different theories for the decline and fall of Rome. Identify which theories seem the most plausible to you.

been taken over by Germanic peoples who were in the process of creating independent kingdoms.

In A.D. 476 Odoacer, a military leader of German origin, deposed the Roman emperor, the boy Romulus Augustulus. To many historians, the deposition of Romulus signaled the end of the Roman Empire in the west. Of course, this is only a symbolic date because much of direct imperial rule had already been lost in the course of the fifth century.

The fall of the Western Roman Empire allowed the establishment of new, mostly rural, Germanic kingdoms. Although eventually unified religiously through the growing Catholic Church, the divided Western kingdoms would lose the unified transportation, educational, and commercial institutions of the Roman Empire. Much like the fall of Han China, Rome endured a series of weak rulers whose abuse of power and decadent lifestyles led to peasant unrest and dissatisfaction within the military. These rulers were unable to stop the influx of outside invaders, and soon both Rome and the capital of Han China were sacked by foreign raiders. Ultimately, neither Rome nor Han China was able to stem the tide of collapse, and both empires deteriorated into divided kingdoms for several centuries.

Many theories have been proposed by historians to explain the decline and fall of the Roman Empire. They include the following:

- Christianity's emphasis on a spiritual kingdom weakened Roman military virtues.
- Traditional Roman values declined as non-Italians gained prominence in the empire.
- Lead poisoning through leaden water pipes and cups caused a mental decline in the population.
- Plague wiped out one-tenth of the population.
- Rome failed to advance technologically due to slavery.
- Rome could not create a workable political system.

There may be an element of truth in each of these theories, but history is an intricate web of relationships, causes, and effects. No single explanation can sufficiently explain the fall of a great empire. The Roman army in the west was not able to fend off the hordes of people moving into Italy and Gaul, and the Western Roman Empire collapsed. A series of German kingdoms replaced the Western Roman Empire. In contrast, the Eastern Roman Empire, which would survive for another thousand years, was able to withstand invaders.

✓ **READING PROGRESS CHECK**

Understanding Historical Interpretation Why do many historians date the fall of the Roman Empire at A.D. 476?

LESSON 2 REVIEW TEKS

Reviewing Vocabulary

1. ***Making Inferences*** How did plague help lead to an economic collapse in the third century? 1C

Using Your Notes

2. ***Analyzing Cause and Effect*** Use your notes to identify the causes of the decline and fall of the Roman Empire. 1C

Answering the Guiding Questions

3. ***Identifying Central Issues*** What political factors led to the decline of the Roman Empire? 1C
4. ***Drawing Conclusions*** How did economic and social reforms by Diocletian and Constantine affect the Roman Empire? 1B
5. ***Making Connections*** How did the migrations of Germanic tribes contribute to the fall of the Roman Empire? 1C

Writing Activity

6. **ARGUMENT** Look at the theories that explain the decline and fall of the Roman Empire. Choose one and write an essay explaining why you think this reason was or was not a significant factor in the fall of the Roman Empire. 1C

networks

There's More Online!

- IMAGE Abbey at Whitby
- IMAGE Franks Casket
- IMAGE Illuminated Manuscript
- IMAGE Layout of a Monastery
- IMAGE Monastery in Northumberland
- INTERACTIVE SELF-CHECK QUIZ
- MAP Early Centers of Christianity and Monastic Learning
- PRIMARY SOURCE Gregory I Describing the Role of the Pope
- SLIDE SHOW The Role of Monks
- VIDEO The Rise of the Papacy

Reading HELPDESK

Academic Vocabulary

- **pursue**
- **conversion**

Content Vocabulary

- **bishopric**
- **monk**
- **monasticism**
- **missionary**
- **nun**
- **abbess**

TAKING NOTES:

Key Ideas and Details

Organizing As you read, use a Venn diagram like the one below to identify similarities and differences between monks and nuns.

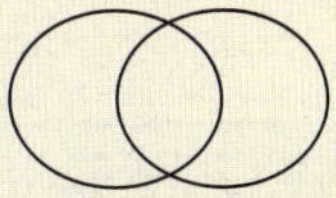

TEKS Texas Essential Knowledge and Skills

1B identify major causes and describe the major effects of the following events from 500 BC to AD 600: the development of the classical civilizations of Greece, Rome, Persia, India (Maurya and Gupta), China (Zhou, Qin, and Han), and the development of major world religions

continued on the next page

LESSON 3

The Early Christian Church

ESSENTIAL QUESTION *How can religion impact a culture?*

It Matters Because

By the end of the fourth century, Christianity had become the supreme religion of the Roman Empire. As the official Roman state fell apart, the Church played an increasingly important role in the growth of the new European civilization.

Organization of the Early Church

GUIDING QUESTION *How was the Christian Church organized by the fourth century?*

By the fourth century, the Christian Church had developed a system of government. Priests led local Christian communities called parishes. These priests also met the social needs of their parishes, as the church often was the center of village social life. A group of parishes formed a **bishopric**, or diocese, headed by a bishop. These bishoprics were joined together under the direction of an archbishop.

The bishops of four great cities—Rome, Jerusalem, Alexandria, and Antioch—held positions of special power in church affairs. The churches in these cities all believed that they had been founded by the original apostles sent out by Jesus. Soon, however, one of them—the bishop of Rome—claimed even more that he was the leader of the western Christian church. According to church tradition, Jesus had given the keys to the kingdom of heaven to Peter, who was considered the chief apostle and the first bishop of Rome. Later bishops of Rome were viewed as Peter's successors. They came to be known as popes (from the Latin word *papa,* meaning "father") of the Catholic Church, as it is now called.

Western Christians came to accept the pope as head of the church in the fourth and fifth centuries, but people did not agree on how much power the pope should have. In the sixth century, a strong pope, Gregory I, known as Gregory the Great, strengthened the power of the papacy and the Roman Catholic Church. This characteristic of Roman Catholicism would have important consequences in its relationship with the Christians in the Eastern Roman Empire.

bishopric a group of Christian communities, or parishes, under the authority of a bishop

As pope, Gregory I, who reigned from A.D. 590 to A.D. 604, took control of Rome and its surrounding territories (later called the Papal States), thus giving the papacy a source of political power. Gregory also extended papal authority over the Christian church in the west. He was especially active in converting the non-Christian peoples of Germanic Europe to Christianity. His chief instrument was the monastic movement.

✓ **READING PROGRESS CHECK**

Analyzing How did Pope Gregory I increase the power of the Roman Catholic Church?

The Monks and Their Missions

GUIDING QUESTIONS *What role did monks and monasteries play in the early Catholic Church? How did the Catholic Church affect the emerging medieval European civilization?*

monk a man who separates himself from ordinary human society in order to dedicate himself to God; monks live in monasteries headed by abbots

monasticism practice of living the life of a monk

pursue to follow up or proceed with

A **monk** was one who sought to live a life cut off from ordinary human society in order to pursue an ideal of total dedication to God. The practice of living the life of a monk is known as **monasticism**. At first, Christian monasticism was based on the model of the solitary hermit who gives up all civilized society to **pursue** a spiritual life.

These early monks, however, soon found it difficult to live alone. Their feats of holiness attracted followers on a wide scale. As the monastic ideal spread, a new form of monasticism based upon living together in a community became the chief form. The monastic community came to be seen as the ideal Christian society that could provide a moral example to the rest of society.

Benedict, who founded a monastic house for which he wrote a set of rules, established the basic form of monastic life in the western Christian church. The Benedictine rule came to be used by other monastic groups and was crucial to the growth of monasticism in the western Christian world.

Benedict's rule divided each day into a series of activities with primary emphasis upon prayer and manual labor. Physical work was required of all monks for several hours a day because idleness was "the enemy of the soul." At the heart of community practice was prayer, the proper "Work of God." This included private meditation and reading, and all monks gathered together seven times a day for prayer and chanting of psalms. Life in the monastery was a communal one. Monks ate, worked, slept, and worshiped together.

(continued from p. 189)

TEKS **Texas Essential Knowledge and Skills**

1C identify major causes and describe the major effects of the following important turning points in world history from 600 to 1450 the spread of Christianity, the decline of Rome and the formation of medieval Europe; the development of Islamic caliphates and their impact on Asia, Africa, and Europe; the Mongol invasions and their impact on Europe, China, India, and Southwest Asia

4A explain the development of Christianity as a unifying social and political factor in medieval Europe and the Byzantine Empire

continued on the next page

▶ **The Franks Casket, which was likely created in a monastery in Northumbria, England, in the first half of the 8th century A.D., includes the depiction of both pagan and Christian stories.**

▶ **CRITICAL THINKING**

Drawing Conclusions Why did a casket that was created at a Christian monastery contain images of pagan legends?

PHOTO: Erich Lessing/Art Resource, NY

Each Benedictine monastery was strictly ruled by an abbot, or "father" of the monastery, who had complete authority over it. Unquestioning obedience to the will of the abbot was expected of each monk. Each Benedictine monastery held lands that enabled it to be a self-sustaining community. Within the monastery, however, monks were to fulfill a vow of poverty.

Monasticism was an important force in the new European civilization. Monks became the new heroes of Christian civilization, and their dedication to God became the highest ideal of Christian life. They were the social workers of their communities: Monks provided schools for the young, hospitality for travelers, and hospitals for the sick. Monasteries also became centers of learning. Monks passed on the legacy of the ancient world to European civilization.

By the ninth century, the work required of Benedictine monks was the copying of manuscripts. Many monasteries contained a scriptorium, or writing room, where monks copied not only the works of early Christianity, such as the Bible, but also the works of Latin classical authors. Monks also developed new ways of producing books. Their texts were written on pages made of parchment or sheepskin rather than papyrus. They were then bound in covers decorated with jewels and precious metals. The use of parchment made books very expensive. The making of manuscripts was a crucial factor in the preservation of the ancient legacy. Virtually 90 percent of the ancient Roman works that we have today exist because they were copied by monks.

The monks were also important in spreading Christianity to the entire European world. English and Irish monks were particularly enthusiastic **missionaries** who undertook the **conversion** of non-Christian peoples, especially in German lands.

Women, too, played an important role in the monastic missionary movement. Like monks, women, called **nuns**, also began to withdraw from the world to dedicate themselves to God. Nuns lived in convents headed by **abbesses**. Many of the abbesses belonged to royal houses, especially in Anglo-Saxon England. For example, in the kingdom of Northumbria, Abbess Hilda founded the monastery of Whitby in A.D. 657.

Nuns of the seventh and eighth centuries were especially active in the spread of Christianity. Nuns in England provided books and money for missionary activities. Groups of nuns established convents in newly converted German lands. A nun named Leoba established the first convent in Germany.

READING PROGRESS CHECK

Describing What was the Benedictine rule?

missionary a person sent out to carry a religious message

conversion the change from one belief or form to another

nun a woman who separates herself from ordinary human society in order to dedicate herself to God; nuns live in convents headed by abbesses

abbess the head of a convent

(continued from p. 190)

TEKS **Texas Essential Knowledge and Skills**

4B explain the characteristics of Roman Catholicism and Eastern Orthodoxy

23A describe the historical origins, central ideas, and spread of major religious and philosophical traditions, including Buddhism, Christianity, Confucianism, Hinduism, Islam, Judaism, Sikhism, and the development of monotheism

▼ **Bishop Aidan founded a monastery in Lindisfarne in 635. The ruins of Lindisfarne Priory in England remain partially intact.**

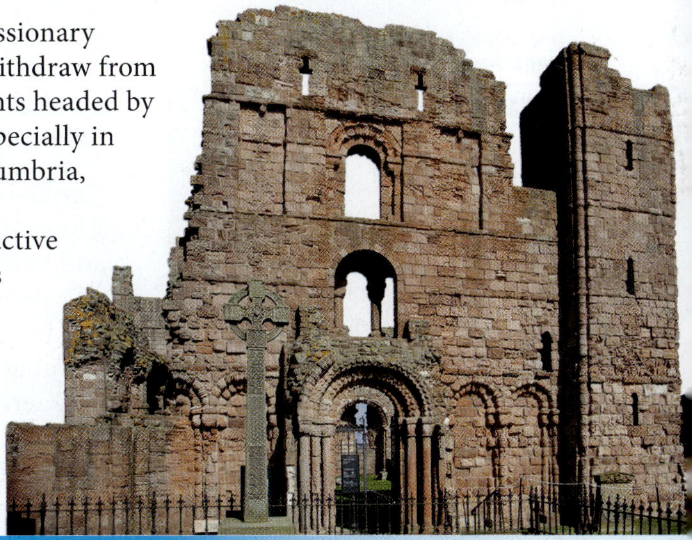

LESSON 3 REVIEW TEKS

Reviewing Vocabulary

1. ***Identifying*** What rules did Benedict set up for those who practiced monasticism? 4B

Using Your Notes

2. ***Comparing*** Use your notes to identify similarities between monks and nuns. 1C

Answering the Guiding Questions

3. ***Organizing*** How was the Christian Church organized by the fourth century? 1B, 4B, 23B

4. ***Drawing Conclusions*** What role did monks and monasteries play in the early Catholic Church? 4B

5. ***Making Connections*** How did the Catholic Church affect the emerging medieval European civilization? 4A

Writing Activity

6. **NARRATIVE** Pretend that you have just joined a medieval monastic community. Write an essay describing your daily life and your duties. Use outside sources to supplement information from the text. 4B

networks

There's More Online!

- ☑ BIOGRAPHY Charlemagne
- ☑ BIOGRAPHY Charles Martel
- ☑ CHART/GRAPH Germanic Law
- ☑ IMAGE Charlemagne's Coronation
- ☑ IMAGE Clovis's Conversion
- ☑ IMAGE Illuminated Manuscript from the Court School of Charlemagne
- ☑ INTERACTIVE SELF-CHECK QUIZ
- ☑ MAP Frankish Kingdom
- ☑ MAP Territory of the Germanic Peoples, A.D. 500
- ☑ VIDEO The Anglo Saxons

Reading HELPDESK

Academic Vocabulary

- **excluded**
- **ensure**

Content Vocabulary

- **wergild**
- **ordeal**

TAKING NOTES:

Key Ideas and Details

Determining Importance As you read, use a table like the one below to identify the contributions of the rulers discussed in the lesson.

Clovis	Charlemagne

TEKS Texas Essential Knowledge and Skills

1C identify major causes and describe the major effects of the following important turning points in world history from 600 to 1450 the spread of Christianity, the decline of Rome and the formation of medieval Europe; the development of Islamic caliphates and their impact on Asia, Africa, and Europe; the Mongol invasions and their impact on Europe, China, India, and Southwest Asia

continued on the next page

LESSON 4

The Age of Charlemagne

ESSENTIAL QUESTIONS • *How can religion impact a culture?* • *What factors lead to the rise and fall of empires?*

It Matters Because

Although Christianity was becoming the dominant religion in Europe during the Early Middle Ages, Germanic tribes became the dominant political force. Ultimately a new empire emerged that was linked to the idea of a lasting Roman Empire.

The New Germanic Kingdoms

GUIDING QUESTIONS *How did the Germanic kingdoms influence the transformation of the Roman world? What was the significance of Clovis's conversion to Christianity?*

The Germanic peoples had begun to move into the lands of the Roman Empire by the third century. The Visigoths occupied Spain and Italy until the Ostrogoths, another Germanic tribe, took control of Italy in the fifth century. By A.D. 500, the Western Roman Empire had been replaced by a number of states ruled by German kings. The merging of Romans and Germans took different forms in the various Germanic kingdoms.

Both the kingdom of the Ostrogoths in Italy and the kingdom of the Visigoths in Spain retained the Roman structure of government. However, a group of Germanic warriors came to dominate the considerably larger native populations and eventually **excluded** Romans from holding power.

Roman influence was even weaker in Britain. When the Roman armies abandoned Britain at the beginning of the fifth century, the Angles and Saxons, Germanic tribes from Denmark and northern Germany, moved in and settled there. Eventually, these peoples became the Anglo-Saxons.

The Kingdom of the Franks

Only one of the German states proved long lasting—the kingdom of the Franks. The Frankish kingdom was established by Clovis, a strong military leader who around A.D. 500 became the first Germanic ruler to convert to Catholic Christianity. At first, Clovis had refused the pleas of his Christian wife to adopt Christianity as his religion. According to Gregory of Tours, a sixth-century historian, Clovis had remarked to his wife, "Your God can do nothing."

During a battle with another Germanic tribe, however, Clovis's army faced certain destruction. Clovis was reported to have cried out, "Jesus Christ…if you will give me victory over my enemies… I will believe in you and I will be baptized in your name." After he uttered these words, the enemy began to flee. Clovis soon became a Christian.

Clovis found that his conversion to Christianity won him the support of the Roman Catholic Church, as the Christian church in Rome was now known. Not surprisingly, the Catholic Church was eager to gain the friendship of a major ruler in the Germanic states.

By 510, Clovis had established a powerful new Frankish kingdom that stretched from the Pyrenees in the southwest to German lands—modern-day France and western Germany. He defeated the many Germanic tribes surrounding him and unified the Franks as a people. After Clovis's death, his sons followed Frankish custom and divided his newly created kingdom among themselves. The once-united Frankish kingdom came to be divided into three major areas.

exclude to bar from inclusion or participation in

(continued from p. 192)

TEKS Texas Essential Knowledge and Skills

4A explain the development of Christianity as a unifying social and political factor in medieval Europe and the Byzantine Empire

24A describe the changing roles of women, children, and families during major eras of world history

Germanic Society

Over time, Germans and Romans intermarried and began to create a new society. As they did, some of the social customs of the Germanic people came to play an important role. The crucial social bond among the Germanic peoples was the family, especially the extended family of husbands, wives, children, brothers, sisters, cousins, and grandparents. The German family structure was quite simple. Males were dominant and made all the important decisions. A woman obeyed her father until she

GEOGRAPHY CONNECTION

The Germanic peoples migrated throughout Europe.

1. **THE WORLD IN SPATIAL TERMS** *Which Germanic peoples came from around the Black Sea?*
2. **HUMAN SYSTEMS** *Which Germanic peoples moved into the British Isles?*

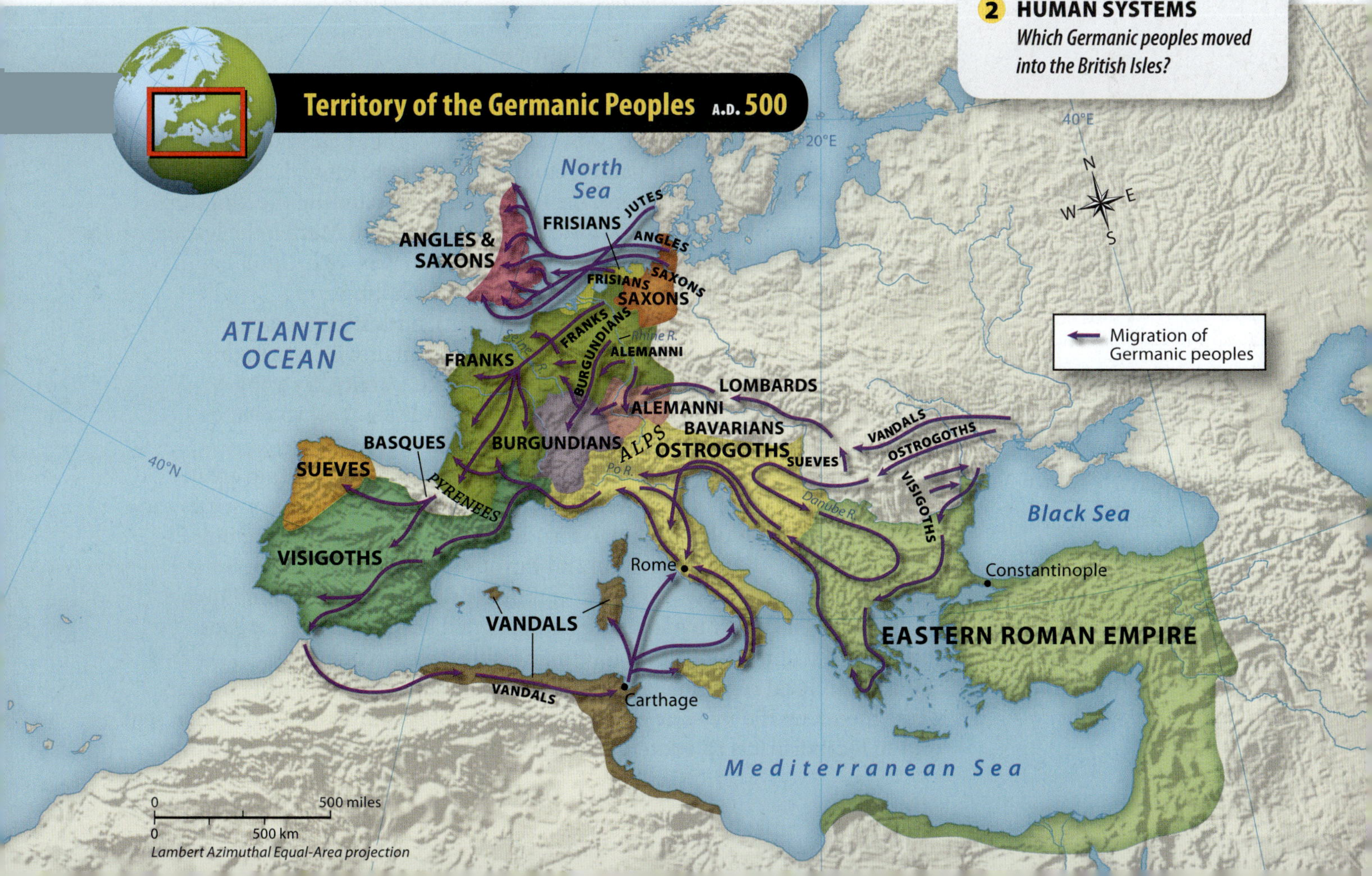

married and then fell under the legal domination of her husband. This extended family worked the land together and passed it down to future generations. The family also provided protection, which was much needed in the violent atmosphere of the time.

The German concept of family affected the way Germanic law treated the problem of crime and punishment. In the Roman system, as in the United States legal system, a crime such as murder was considered an offense against society or the state. Thus, a court would hear evidence and arrive at a decision. Germanic law, on the other hand, was personal. An injury by one person against another could mean a blood feud, and the feud could lead to savage acts of revenge.

wergild "money for a man"; the value of a person in money, depending on social status; in Germanic society, a fine paid by a wrongdoer to the family of the person he or she had injured or killed

ordeal a means of determining guilt in Germanic law, based on the idea of divine intervention: if the accused person was unharmed after a physical trial, he or she was presumed innocent

To avoid bloodshed, a new system developed, based on a fine called **wergild** (WUHR • gihld). Wergild was the amount paid by a wrongdoer to the family of the person he or she had injured or killed. Wergild, which means "money for a man," was the value of a person in money. The value varied according to social status. An offense against a member of the nobility, for example, cost considerably more than an offense against an ordinary person or a slave. Germanic laws were now established by custom, not at the whim of a king or codified like Roman law.

One means of determining guilt in Germanic law was the **ordeal**. The ordeal was based on the idea of divine intervention. All ordeals involved a physical trial of some sort, such as holding a red-hot iron. It was believed that divine forces would not allow an innocent person to be harmed. If the accused person was unharmed after a physical trial, or ordeal, he or she was presumed innocent.

✓ **READING PROGRESS CHECK**

Contrasting What is a difference between the Roman and Germanic systems of justice?

The Carolingian Empire

GUIDING QUESTION ***What impact did Charlemagne have on the Frankish kingdom?***

During the A.D. 600s and A.D. 700s, the Frankish kings had gradually lost their power to the mayors of the palace, chief officers of the king's household. One of them, Pepin, finally took the logical step of assuming the kingship for himself and his family. Pepin was the son of Charles Martel, the leader who defeated the Muslims at the Battle of Tours in A.D. 732. Upon Pepin's death in A.D. 768, his son became the new Frankish king.

This powerful ruler is known to history as Charles the Great, or Charlemagne. He was a determined and decisive man who was highly intelligent and curious. Charlemagne was a fierce warrior, a strong statesman, and a pious Christian. Although possibly unable to read or write, he was a wise patron—supporter—of learning.

During his long rule, from A.D. 768 to A.D. 814, Charlemagne greatly expanded the Frankish kingdom and created what came to be known as the Carolingian (KAR • uh • LIN • jee • uhn) Empire. At its height, this empire covered much of western and central Europe. Not until Napoleon Bonaparte's time in the 1800s would an empire its size be seen again in Europe.

The administration of the empire depended both on Charlemagne's household staff and on counts (German nobles) who acted as the king's chief local representatives. In order to limit the counts' powers, Charlemagne set up the *missi dominici* (messengers of the lord king)—two men sent out to local districts to **ensure** that the counts carried out the king's wishes.

SKILLS PRACTICE

Read about the Carolingian Empire. With a partner, retell what you have read in your own words. When you do not know a word you want to use, think of a synonym. If you cannot think of a synonym, use a definition or description to tell your partner what you mean.

Carolingian Renaissance

Charlemagne had a strong desire to promote learning in his kingdom. His efforts led to an intellectual revival sometimes called the Carolingian Renaissance, or rebirth. Monasteries played a central role in this cultural renewal. The efforts of the monks who copied the Bible and the works of classical Latin authors led to the preservation of thousands of Greek and Roman manuscripts.

The monasteries in the Carolingian Empire, many of which had been founded by Irish and English missionaries, played a central role in this cultural renewal. As we have seen, monks in the writing rooms copied the Bible and the works of classical Latin authors. Their work was a crucial factor in the preservation of the ancient legacy. About eight thousand manuscripts survive from Carolingian times.

▲ An early example of an illuminated manuscript produced at the Court School of Charlemagne during the Carolingian Renaissance

▶ **CRITICAL THINKING**

Making Inferences Why do you think monks elaborately decorated handwritten copies of the Bible?

Charlemagne as Roman Emperor

As Charlemagne's power grew, so too did his prestige as the most powerful Christian ruler. One monk even described Charlemagne's empire as the "kingdom of Europe." In A.D. 800, Charlemagne acquired a new title—emperor of the Romans. Charlemagne's coronation as Roman emperor—over 300 years after the Western Roman Empire's collapse—showed the strength of the idea of an enduring Roman Empire.

The coronation also symbolized the joining of Roman, Christian, and Germanic elements. A Germanic king had been crowned emperor of the Romans by the pope, the spiritual leader of Western Christendom. Christianity was triumphant in Europe. The Germanic peoples had settled new kingdoms in Europe, all of which adopted the faith of Christianity. This faith would serve as a unifying political factor as it gave kingdoms across the continent common religious rituals, traditions, and standards for behavior. Christianity blended the cultures of the Germanic peoples and ancient Rome into the culture of medieval Europe. This common faith would help the nations of medieval Europe bridge the divides of language, culture, and distance.

Here at the beginning of a new era was Charlemagne. He had created an empire that stretched from the North Sea in the north to Italy in the south and from France in western Europe to Vienna in central Europe. By focusing on Europe rather than the Mediterranean world, Charlemagne's empire differed significantly from the empire of Rome. A new civilization had emerged. As one author has argued, Charlemagne could be seen as the as the "father of Europe."

ensure to make sure

✓ **READING PROGRESS CHECK**

Explaining What was the importance of the *missi dominici?*

LESSON 4 REVIEW TEKS

Reviewing Vocabulary

1. ***Identifying*** What was the difference between wergild and the ordeal?

Using Your Notes

2. ***Determining Importance*** Use your notes to identify why Charlemagne and Clovis were considered important leaders. 1C, 4A, 23B

Answering the Guiding Questions

3. ***Making Connections*** How did Germanic kingdoms influence the transformation of the Roman world in terms of the roles of women and families and the legal system? 24A
4. ***Drawing Conclusions*** What was the significance of Clovis's conversion to Christianity? 4A
5. ***Identifying Central Issues*** What impact did Charlemagne have on the Frankish kingdom?

Writing Activity

6. **ARGUMENT** Write a persuasive essay about whether or not the wergild was a good way to punish wrongdoers.

networks

There's More Online!

- BIOGRAPHY Belisarius
- BIOGRAPHY John of Damascus
- BIOGRAPHY Justinian
- BIOGRAPHY Theodora
- IMAGE Mosaic of Justinian
- IMAGE Rebecca at the Well
- INTERACTIVE SELF-CHECK QUIZ
- MAP Byzantine Empire, 750–1025
- VIDEO The Byzantine Empire

LESSON 5

The Byzantine Empire

ESSENTIAL QUESTIONS • *How can religion impact a culture?* • *What factors lead to the rise and fall of empires?*

IT MATTERS BECAUSE

In the fourth century, a separation between the western and eastern parts of the Roman Empire began to develop. In the fifth century, the Germanic tribes moved into the western part of the empire and helped create a new European civilization. Meanwhile, the Eastern Roman Empire, with Constantinople as its capital, continued to exist and develop into a new empire.

Reading HELPDESK

Academic Vocabulary

- **legal**
- **enormous**

Content Vocabulary

- **patriarch**
- **icon**
- **idolatry**

TAKING NOTES:

Key Ideas and Details

Determining Cause and Effect As you read, use a diagram like the one below to identify the causes of a powerful Byzantine Empire.

Powerful Byzantine Empire

TEKS Texas Essential Knowledge and Skills

3A describe the major political, religious/philosophical, and cultural influences of Persia, India, China, Israel, Greece, and Rome, including the development of monotheism, Judaism, and Christianity

4A explain the development of Christianity as a unifying social and political factor in medieval Europe and the Byzantine Empire

continued on the next page

Eastern Roman Empire and Justinian

GUIDING QUESTION *How did the Eastern Roman Empire evolve into the Byzantine Empire?*

When he became emperor of the Eastern Roman Empire, Justinian (A.D. 527–A.D. 565) was determined to reestablish the Roman Empire in the entire Mediterranean world.

By A.D. 552, Justinian appeared to have achieved his goals. He had restored the Roman Empire in the Mediterranean. But these conquests were fleeting; in a matter of years after Justinian's death the western section of the Mediterranean had been lost again, never to be recovered by the empire.

Justinian's most important contribution was his codification of Roman law, issued between A.D. 529 and A.D. 534, entitled *The Body of Civil Law*. This codification of Roman law became the basis of imperial law in the Eastern Roman Empire until its end in A.D. 1453. More importantly, however, because it was written in Latin (it was, in fact, the last product of eastern Roman culture to be written in Latin, which was soon replaced by Greek) it was also used in the West.

After its rediscovery in the West, the Body of Civil Law became the foundation for the revival and study of Roman law in medieval universities. As a result, the political and legal ideas contained in Justinian's Code of Law have left their impact on some parts of the world. The political idea of the emperor as the source of authority and all law made an impact on the kings of European states in the Middle Ages. Legally, the code has been used as a resource, especially in civil law. Indeed, the Body of Civil Law became the basis for much of the legal system in parts of Europe, Japan, and in the state of Louisiana.

legal relating to law; founded on law

✓ **READING PROGRESS CHECK**

Assessing What was the significance of *The Body of Civil Law?*

From Roman to Byzantine Empire

GUIDING QUESTIONS *How did the Eastern Roman Empire evolve into the Byzantine Empire? What were the cultural contributions of the Byzantine Empire?*

(continued from p. 196)

TEKS **Texas Essential Knowledge and Skills**

4B explain the characteristics of Roman Catholicism and Eastern Orthodoxy

20B identify the impact of political and legal ideas contained in the following documents: Hammurabi's Code, the Jewish Ten Commandments, Justinian's Code of Laws, Magna Carta, the English Bill of Rights, the Declaration of Independence, the U.S. Constitution, and the Declaration of the Rights of Man and of the Citizen

26B analyze examples of how art, architecture, literature, music, and drama reflect the history of the cultures in which they are produced

Justinian's accomplishments had been spectacular, but the Eastern Roman Empire was left with serious problems: too much territory to protect far from Constantinople, an empty treasury, a decline in population after a plague, and renewed threats to its frontiers. In the first half of the seventh century, the empire was faced with attacks from the Persians to the east and the Slavs to the north. The empire survived, only to face new threats.

The most serious challenge to the Eastern Roman Empire came from the rise of Islam, which unified the Arab tribes and created a powerful new force that swept through the east. The defeat of an eastern Roman army at Yarmuk in A.D. 636 meant the loss of the provinces of Syria and Palestine. Problems also arose, however, along the northern frontier, especially in the Balkans. In A.D. 679 the Bulgars defeated the eastern Roman forces and took the lower Danube valley, creating a strong Bulgarian kingdom.

By the beginning of the eighth century, the Eastern Roman Empire was a much smaller state, consisting only of the eastern Balkans and Asia Minor, but these external challenges had produced important internal changes. By the eighth century, this smaller Eastern Roman Empire had become what historians call the Byzantine Empire, a civilization with its own unique character that lasted until A.D. 1453.

enormous huge; vast; immense

The Byzantine Empire was both a Greek and a Christian state. Increasingly, Latin fell into disuse as Greek became both the common language and the official language of the Byzantine Empire. The Byzantine Empire was also a Christian state. The empire was built on the Christian faith that was shared in a profound way by almost all its citizens. An **enormous** amount of artistic talent was poured into the construction of churches, church ceremonies, and church decoration to honor this faith.

patriarch the head of the Eastern Orthodox Church, originally appointed by the Byzantine emperor

The emperor occupied a crucial position in the Byzantine state. Portrayed as chosen by God, he was crowned in sacred ceremonies, and his subjects were expected to prostrate themselves in his presence. His power was considered absolute. Because the emperor appointed the head of the church (known as the **patriarch**), he also exercised control over both church and state. The Byzantines believed that God had commanded their state to preserve the true Christian faith. Emperor, church, and state officials were all bound together in service to this ideal. It can be said that spiritual values of Christianity held the Byzantine state together both socially and politically.

After the destruction caused by riots in A.D. 532, Emperor Justinian had rebuilt Constantinople and given it the appearance it would keep for almost a thousand years. With a population estimated in the hundreds of thousands, Constantinople was the largest city in medieval Europe. It viewed itself as the center of an empire and a special Christian city.

Until the twelfth century, Constantinople was the greatest center of commerce in Europe during the Middle Ages. The city was the chief center for the exchange of products between West and East , which contributed to its rapid growth.

Analyzing PRIMARY SOURCES

The Justinian Code

“The maxims of law are these: to live honestly, to hurt no one, to give every one his due.”

—The Institutes of Justinian, A.D. 527–A.D. 565

DBQ ***DRAWING CONCLUSIONS*** How do these maxims compare with the rule of law in the modern United States?

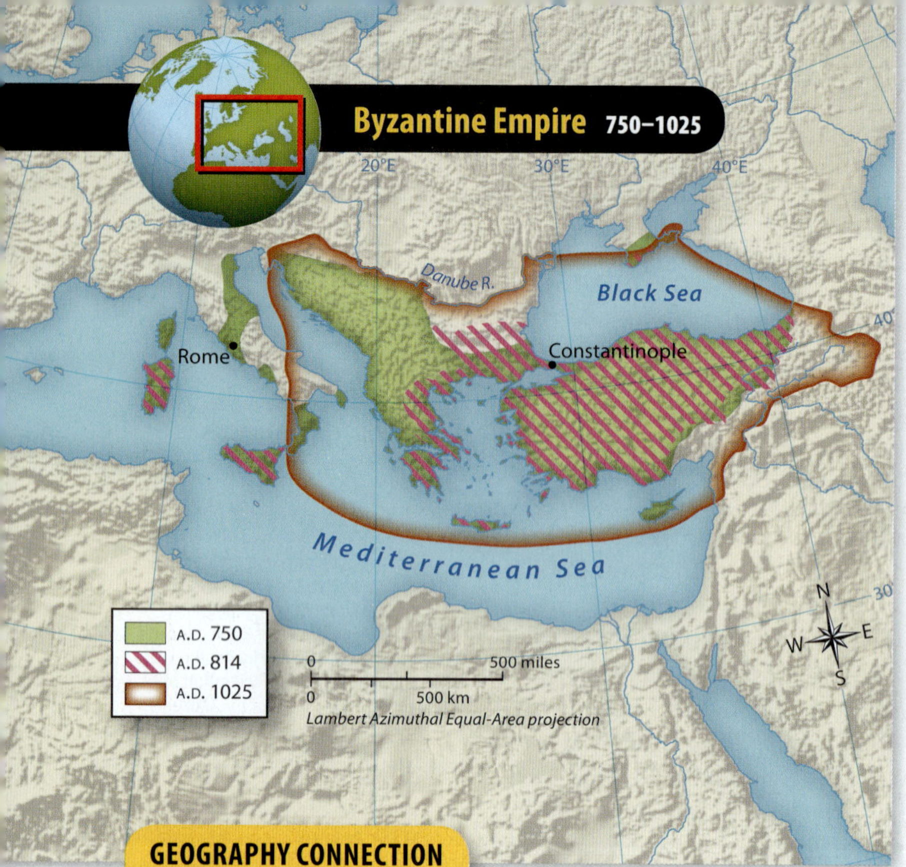

GEOGRAPHY CONNECTION

The size of the Byzantine Empire changed from A.D. 750–A.D. 1025.

1. **THE WORLD IN SPATIAL TERMS** *In what year did the Byzantine Empire cover the least amount of territory?*
2. **HUMAN SYSTEMS** *What areas had the Byzantine Empire acquired by A.D. 1025?*

Much of Constantinople's appearance in the Early Middle Ages was due to Justinian's program of rebuilding in the sixth century. The city was dominated by an immense palace complex and a huge amphitheater known as the Hippodrome, the site of chariot races that were an important part of Byzantine culture. In a reflection of the spiritual nature of Byzantine culture, hundreds of churches dotted the city, including the magnificent cathedral Hagia Sophia. No residential district was particularly fashionable because palaces, tenements, and slums existed alongside one another. Justinian added many new buildings. His public works projects included roads, bridges, walls, public baths, law courts, schools, churches, and colossal underground reservoirs to hold the city's water supply.

✔ **READING PROGRESS CHECK**

Contrasting How was the Byzantine Empire different from the Roman Empire?

New Heights and New Problems

GUIDING QUESTIONS *What role did the Christian Church play in the Byzantine Empire? What threats did the Byzantine Empire face in the eleventh century?*

By A.D. 750, the Byzantine Empire consisted only of Asia Minor, some lands in the Balkans, and the coastal areas of Italy. Byzantium recovered and not only endured; it even expanded due to the efforts of a new dynasty of Byzantine emperors known as the Macedonians.

The Macedonian Emperors

This line of emperors, who ruled from A.D. 867 to A.D. 1081, managed to beat off its external enemies and to go on the offensive. The empire was expanded to include Bulgaria in the Balkans, the islands of Crete and Cyprus, and Syria. By A.D. 1025, the Byzantine Empire was the largest it had been since the seventh century.

The Macedonian emperors also fostered a burst of economic prosperity by expanding trade relations with western Europe, especially by selling silks and metalworks. Thanks to this prosperity, the city of Constantinople flourished. Foreign visitors continued to be astounded by its size, wealth, and physical surroundings. To them, it was the stuff of legends and fables.

The Macedonian dynasty of the tenth and eleventh centuries had restored much of the power of the Byzantine Empire. However, its incompetent successors soon undid most of the gains. Power struggles between ambitious military leaders and aristocratic families led to political and social disorder in the late eleventh century.

Schisms

The Byzantine Empire had also been troubled by the growing split between the Catholic Church of the West and its own Eastern Orthodox Church. Trouble began in A.D. 730 when the Byzantine emperor Leo III outlawed the use of **icons**

icons pictures of religious images

as **idolatry**. Resistance ensued, especially from monks, such as John of Damascus, who wrote defenses of the use of holy images, an art form that reflects the spiritual focus of Byzantine culture. Roman Catholic popes also condemned this act. Late in the eighth century, the Byzantine emperors reversed their stand allowing icons, but the damage between the churches due to the Iconoclast controversy was done.

The Eastern Orthodox Church was unwilling to accept the pope's claim that he was the sole head of the church. In 1054 Pope Leo IX and the Patriarch Michael Cerularius, head of the Byzantine church, formally excommunicated each other—each took away the other's right of church membership. This began a schism, or separation, between the two great branches of Christianity that has not been completely healed.

Because of this break between the Eastern and Western Churches, Eastern Orthodoxy developed distinctive characteristics as it continued under the leadership of its patriarchs within the Byzantine Empire. Unlike the Roman Catholic Church, the Patriarch of Constantinople, although holding a special honor and authority within the Church, does not wield the same authority and power as the Pope in Rome does for Catholics. With a strong devotion to its **iconography**, Eastern Orthodoxy also developed a distinctive artistic and architectural character different from the West. Today, Eastern Orthodox Christians represent the second largest Christian denomination after Roman Catholicism, with the majority living in Eastern Europe, Russia, and the Middle East.

The Byzantine Empire faced threats from abroad as well. The greatest challenge came from the advance of the Seljuk Turks who had moved into Asia Minor—the heartland of the empire and its main source of food and manpower. In A.D. 1071 a Turkish army defeated Byzantine forces at Manzikert. As a result, Emperor Alexus I turned to Europe for military aid to fight the Turks. This problem would lead to Byzantine involvement in the Crusades and help bring about the downfall of the Byzantine Empire.

▲ **John of Damascus, depicted at center, played an important role in the Iconoclast controversy.**

▶ **CRITICAL THINKING**

Analyzing What role did John of Damascus play in the schism between Catholic and Eastern Orthodox churches?

idolatry the worship of religious images

PHOTO: The Art Gallery Collection/Alamy

✓ **READING PROGRESS CHECK**

Determining Cause and Effect What effects did the expansion of trade have on the Byzantine Empire?

LESSON 5 REVIEW TEKS

Reviewing Vocabulary

1. ***Inferring*** How did the use of icons lead to a schism between the Catholic Church and the Eastern Orthodox Church? 4B, 23B

Using Your Notes

2. ***Determining Cause and Effect*** Use your notes to identify why a powerful Byzantine Empire developed. 1B

Answering the Guiding Questions

3. ***Identifying Central Issues*** How did the Eastern Roman Empire evolve into the Byzantine Empire? 4A
4. ***Drawing Conclusions*** What were the cultural contributions of the Byzantine Empire? 23B, 26B
5. ***Analyzing*** What role did the Christian church play in the Byzantine Empire? 4A, 23B, 26B
6. ***Making Connections*** What threats did the Byzantine Empire face in the eleventh century?

Writing Activity

7. **INFORMATIVE/EXPLANATORY** Write a brochure advertising the public works projects built by Justinian in the sixth century. Include details about what projects were built and how they were expected to improve the city. 26B

CHAPTER 8 Assessment

TEKS

Directions: On a separate sheet of paper, answer the questions below. Make sure you read carefully and answer all parts of the questions.

Lesson Review

Lesson 1

1. ***Specifying*** How did the Zealots react to Roman rule? What was this reaction?

2. ***Describing*** How did Jesus's teachings form religious and philosophical traditions that influenced the development and spread of a major world religion? **1B, 23A**

3. ***Explaining*** How were the teachings of early Christianity passed on?

4. ***Describing*** Why did the spread of Christianity lead to Roman persecution, and what was the effect of this persecution? **1C, 3A, 23A**

5. ***Speculating*** What role might songs have played in the spread of Christianity? **26C**

6. ***Identifying*** Name three reasons that Christianity was able to attract so many followers.

7. ***Summarizing*** Who became the first Christian emperor? How did he help fuel Christianity?

8. ***Identifying*** What about the Christian Bible has made it a work of literature relevant to many different cultures thousands of years after it was written? **26C**

Lesson 2

9. ***Identifying*** What changes were made to the Roman Empire in attempts to slow its decline? **1B**

10. ***Describing*** What led to the development of the "New Rome"?

11. ***Identifying*** What are some of the major reasons given by historians for the decline of Rome? What effect did this event have on Europe? **1C, 3B**

12. ***Explaining*** How did certain jobs, such as bakers and shippers, become hereditary?

13. ***Identifying Central Issues*** What were the economic and social policies of Diocletian and Constantine based on? Why were these policies not successful in the end?

14. ***Summarizing*** Who was Odoacer? How did he help signal the end of the Roman Empire in the west?

Lesson 3

15. ***Explaining*** Who was Gregory the Great? What did he achieve during his reign?

16. ***Explaining*** What role did monks and monasteries play in early Christianity? **4B, 23A**

17. ***Explaining*** What were the characteristics of Eastern Orthodoxy? **4B**

Need Extra Help?

If You've Missed Question	1	2	3	4	5	6	7	8	9	10	11	12	13	14	15	16	17
Go to page	178	179	180	181	180	181	182	180	185	185	188	186	186	188	189	190	189

Lesson 4

18. ***Describing*** What was the role of women during the era of Charlemagne? **24A**

19. ***Explaining*** Why was Clovis's conversion to Christianity significant? How did Christianity come to serve as a unifying political force? **4A**

20. ***Defining*** What was a wergild and how did it play into the new judicial system?

21. ***Describing*** What were the roles of families during this era of Charlemagne? **24A**

Lesson 5

22. ***Identifying*** What were the influences and impacts of the political and legal ideas contained in Justinian's Code of Laws? **20B**

23. ***Explaining*** How did Christianity serve as a unifying social and political factor in the Byzantine Empire? **4A**

Exploring the Essential Questions

24. ***Analyzing Cause and Effect*** How does a religion such as Christianity have social and political impacts on culture? **4A**

25. ***Analyzing Cause and Effect*** How do social and political factors impact empires?

Critical Thinking

26. ***Describing*** How did Rome influence the development of Judaism, and, in turn, how did Judaism influence the development of Christianity? **3A**

27. ***Explaining*** What characteristics of Roman Catholicism made the religion more appealing to followers than the Roman state-based religion? **4B**

28. ***Explaining*** Why might some historians refer to Charlemagne as the "father of Europe"? **4A**

29. ***Describing*** How did Germanic tribes transform the Roman world?

Social Studies Skills

30. ***Identifying Perspectives*** What similar experiences led rulers Constantine and Clovis to embrace Christianity? **1C, 4A**

31. ***Economics*** What role did Constantinople play in medieval Europe's economy until the twelfth century?

32. ***Identifying Perspectives*** With a partner, choose a work of medieval or Byzantine art and reproduce it on a color copier. Using sticky notes, annotate the artwork by explaining how it reflects the history of the culture that produced it. **26B**

33. ***Identifying Perspectives*** Choose a work of medieval or Byzantine architecture and reproduce it on a color copier or create a three-dimensional model of it. Use labels to explain how it reflects the history of the culture that produced it. **26B**

Need Extra Help?

If You've Missed Question	18	19	20	21	22	23	24	25	26	27	28	29	30	31	32	33
Go to page	194	193	194	194	196	198	178	185	178	181	195	192	192	197	197	197

DBQ Analyzing Primary Sources

Use the text excerpt to answer the following questions.

One of the most influential and long-serving Byzantine leaders, Justinian became emperor of Byzantium in A.D. 527. Justinian is probably best remembered for his work with Byzantium's legal system.

PRIMARY SOURCE

"The maxims of law are these: to live honestly, to hurt no one, to give every one his due."

—Justinian, from The Institutes of Justinian, A.D. 527–A.D. 565

34 ***Comparing*** Justinian unified church and state. Which world religion seems to be reflected in Justinian's view of the law? **20B**

35 ***Making Connections*** Which region influenced Justinian's legal ideas and which regions were influenced by them? **3A, 20B**

Analyzing Visuals

Use the map above to answer the following questions.

36 ***Locating*** What mountain chain separated the Burgundians and Ostrogoths?

37 ***Examining*** What Germanic peoples migrated to northern Africa?

Extended Response Question

38 ***Expository*** Write a short essay in which you compare and contrast the factors that led to the collapse of Rome and Han China. Offer conclusions regarding the fall of these two empires in your essay. **3C**

Need Extra Help?

If You've Missed Question	34	35	36	37	38
Go to page	196	196	194	194	185

Islam and the Arab Empire

600–1400

ESSENTIAL QUESTIONS • *How can religion influence the development of an empire?* • *How might religious beliefs affect society, culture, and politics?*

networks

There's More Online! about Islam and the Arab Empire.

CHAPTER 9

The Story Matters...

As Muslim armies spread Islam beyond the Arabian Peninsula from the seventh century onward, the new faith came into contact with older civilizations. Under the caliphates, Muslim scholars helped to both preserve and advance the work of the ancient Greeks in philosophy, science, mathematics, and other areas of thought. Islamic thinkers also made significant original contributions to the sciences. The *Canon of Medicine* by the eleventh-century Persian philosopher and scientist Ibn Sīnā was one of the most influential works in medical history.

◄ Known to Europeans as Avicenna, Ibn Sīnā remained a medical authority in both the Islamic world and the West for centuries after his death. Of unknown date, this dignified French portrait of Ibn Sīnā, although an imagined likeness, reflects the respect with which he was regarded by Europeans.

PHOTO: Imaginary portrait of Avicenna (Ibn Sina) (c.992-1037) (oil on canvas), French School/Bibliotheque de la Faculte de Medecine, Paris, France/Archives Charmet/Bridgeman Images

CHAPTER 9

Place and Time: The Arab Empire 600–1400

Islam began on the Arabian Peninsula with the preaching of Muhammad early in the seventh century. By the time of Muhammad's death, his followers, known as Muslims, controlled much of the peninsula. A little more than a century later, Arab expansion extended from the Atlantic coasts of Spain and Morocco to the border of India. Within this vast area, a new civilization arose that combined cultural elements from a variety of sources, including ancient Greek and Roman thought, as well as Arab, Turkish, and Persian artistic traditions. This Islamic civilization was centered in great cities, such as Damascus, Baghdad, Cairo, and Córdoba.

Step Into the Place

Read the quotes and look at the information presented on the map.

DBQ **Analyzing Historical Documents** What generalizations can you make about Islamic civilization?

PRIMARY SOURCE

"By the time I was ten I had mastered the [Quran] and a great deal of literature, so that I was marveled at for my aptitude. . . .

[After studying elementary logic with a tutor] I took to reading texts by myself; I studied the commentaries, until I had completely mastered the science of Logic. . . .

I now occupied myself with mastering the various texts and commentaries on natural science and metaphysics, until all the gates of knowledge were open to me. Next I desired to study medicine, and proceeded to read all the books that have been written on this subject. . . . I also undertook to treat the sick, and methods of treatment derived from practical experience revealed themselves to me such as baffle description. At the same time I continued between whiles to study and dispute on law, being now sixteen years of age."

—Ibn Sīnā (Avicenna), from his autobiography, 980–1037

PRIMARY SOURCE

"People who grow up in villages and uncivilized (thinly populated) cities and who have an innate desire for scientific activity, cannot find scientific instruction in those places. For scientific instruction is something technical, and there are no crafts among the inhabitants of the desert. These people, therefore, must travel and seek scientific instruction in cities where (civilization) is highly developed, as is the case with all crafts."

— Ibn Khaldūn, from *The Muqaddimah*, c. 1375

Step Into the Time

Drawing Conclusions

Select several events from the time line and use them to draw a conclusion about the Arab Empire.

600 — 700 — 800 — 900

ISLAMIC EMPIRE

- **622** Muhammad moves to Yathrib (modern Madinah)
- **661** Umayyad caliph moves Muslim capital to Damascus
- **756** Córdoba becomes Muslim capital in Spain
- **762** Baghdad is founded as capital of Abbasid empire
- **786** Hārūn al-Rashīd becomes Abbasid caliph

THE WORLD

- **604** Prince Shōtoku Taishi introduces Confucianism to Japan
- **755** Chinese general An Lushan starts civil war in Tang China
- **794** Japanese capital is moved from Nara to Heian-kyo (modern Kyōto)
- **800** Charlemagne is crowned Roman emperor by the pope
- **867** Basil I founds Macedonian dynasty of the Byzantine Empire

networks *There's More Online!*

- **MAP** Explore the interactive version of this map on Networks.
- **TIME LINE** Explore the interactive version of the time line on Networks.

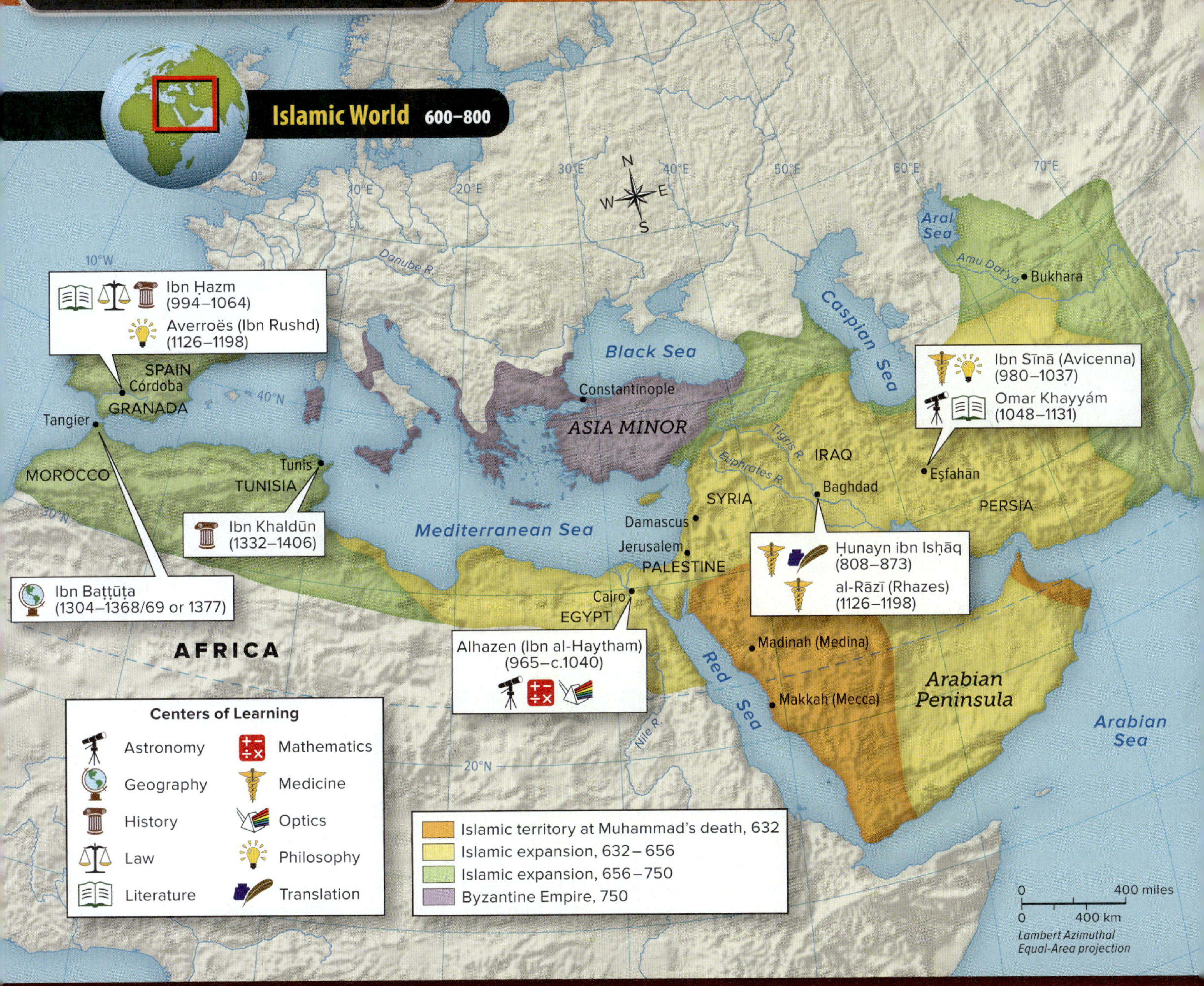

973 Fatimid dynasty establishes Cairo as their capital

1048 Persian poet and astronomer Omar Khayyám is born

1169 Ibn-Rushd begins his commentaries on the Greek philosopher Aristotle

1238 Construction begins on Alhambra palace in Granada, Spain

1382 Ibn-Khaldūn teaches at university in Cairo

1000 1100 1200 1300 1400

907 Tang dynasty collapses in China

1066 Normans invade England

1206 Mongols are unified under Genghis Khan

1260 Chartres Cathedral, an example of Gothic architecture, is consecrated

c. 1370 Chaucer composes *The Canterbury Tales*

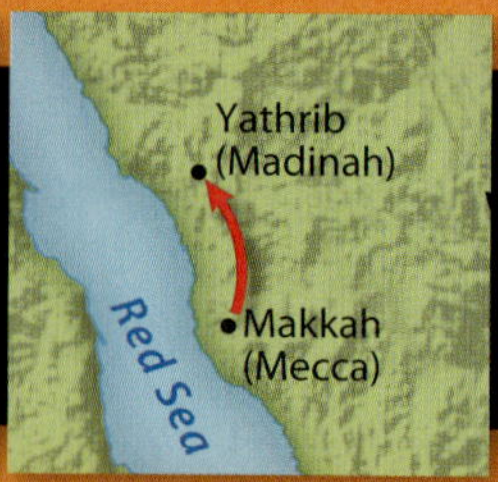

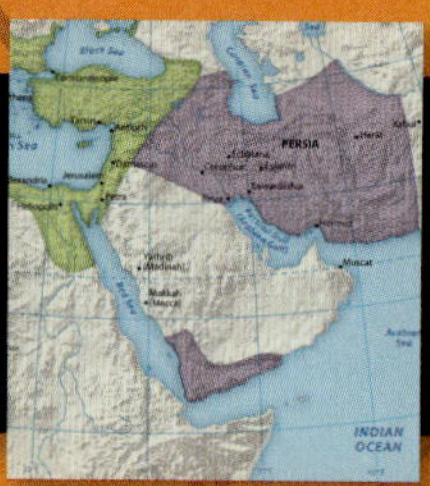
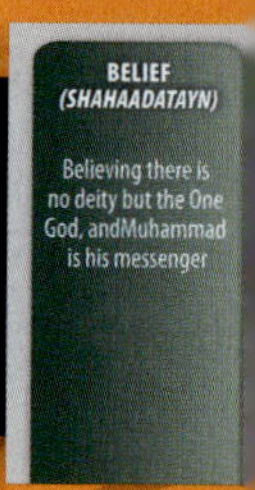

networks

There's More Online!

- ☑ CHART/GRAPH Five Pillars of Islam
- ☑ CHART/GRAPH Islamic Terminology
- ☑ IMAGE The Kaaba at Makkah
- ☑ INTERACTIVE SELF-CHECK QUIZ
- ☑ MAP Muhammad's Journey from Makkah to Yathrib
- ☑ MAP Southwest Asia in Muhammad's Time
- ☑ PRIMARY SOURCE The Quran
- ☑ VIDEO The Beginnings of Islam

LESSON 1

The First Muslims

ESSENTIAL QUESTIONS

- *How can religion influence the development of an empire?*
- *How might religious beliefs affect society, culture, and politics?*

It Matters Because

Early Arabs were nomads who believed in many gods. In the seventh century, Muhammad founded the Islamic religion on the Arabian Peninsula. Over 1,000 years after Islam began, the cultural, artistic, and scientific contributions of Muslims continue to enrich our daily lives.

Reading HELPDESK

Academic Vocabulary

- **revelations**
- **Islam**
- **submission**

Content Vocabulary

- **sheikh**
- **Allah**
- **Quran**
- **Muslim**
- ***Hijrah***
- **bedouin**
- **hajj**
- **Five Pillars of Islam**
- ***shari'ah***

TAKING NOTES:

Key Ideas and Details

Contrasting As you read, use a table like the one below to contrast the beliefs of early Arabs with the religion of Islam.

Early Arabic beliefs	Islam

TEKS Texas Essential Knowledge and Skills

1B identify major causes and describe the major effects of the following events from 500 BC to AD 600: the development of the classical civilizations of Greece, Rome, Persia, India (Maurya and Gupta), China (Zhou, Qin, and Han), and the development of major world religions

continued on the next page

The Arabs

GUIDING QUESTION *Why did communities on the Arabian Peninsula prosper economically?*

Western Asia has witnessed some of the most powerful civilizations in history, beginning with the Sumerians and continuing with the Assyrians, the Babylonians, the Persians, and the brief conquests of Alexander the Great. In the seventh century, another force—the Arabs—arose in the Arabian Peninsula and spread their influence throughout Western Asia and beyond.

Like the Israelites and the Assyrians, the Arabs were a Semitic-speaking people. They lived in the Arabian Peninsula, a desert land sorely lacking in rivers and lakes. The Arabs were nomads who, because of their hostile surroundings, moved constantly to find water and food for their animals.

Survival in such a harsh environment was not easy, and the Arabs organized into tribes to help one another. Each tribe was ruled by a **sheikh** (SHAYK) who was chosen from one of the leading families by a council of elders. Although each tribe was independent, all the tribes were loosely connected to one another.

The Arabs lived as farmers and sheepherders on the oases and rain-fed areas of the Arabian Peninsula. After the camel was domesticated in the first millennium B.C., the Arabs populated more of the desert. They also expanded the caravan trade into these regions. Towns developed along the routes as the Arabs became major carriers of goods between the Indian Ocean and the Mediterranean, where the Silk Road ended.

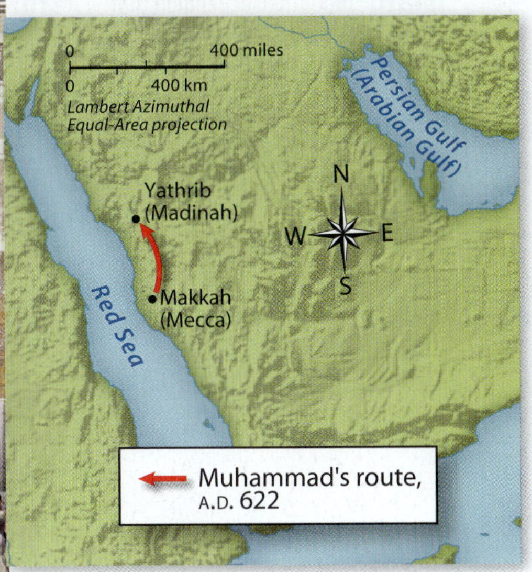

◀ **The Kaaba, located at Makkah, is the holiest shrine of the Islamic faith. Muhammad traveled from Makkah to Yathrib in A.D. 622. He returned to Makkah in A.D. 630.**

▶ **CRITICAL THINKING**

Transferring Calculate the distance Muhammad traveled in A.D. 622.

Early Arabs were polytheistic—they believed in many gods. The Arabs recognized a supreme god named **Allah** (*Allah* is Arabic for "God"), but they also believed in other tribal gods. Allah was symbolized by a sacred stone, and each tribe had its own stone. All tribes, however, worshiped a massive black meteorite, the Black Stone, which had been placed in a central shrine called the Kaaba (KAW • buh). This shrine is in the city of Makkah (Mecca), which is located in the Arabian Peninsula.

The Arabian Peninsula took on a new importance when political unrest in Mesopotamia and Egypt made the usual trade routes in Southwest Asia too dangerous to travel. A safer route through Makkah to present-day Yemen and then by ship across the Indian Ocean became popular. Camel caravans transported highly prized frankincense and myrrh along this route. The journey was long and camels had to stop more than 60 times.

Communities along this route prospered from the increased trade. Tensions arose, however, as increasingly wealthy merchants showed little concern for the welfare of poor people and slaves.

✓ **READING PROGRESS CHECK**

Summarizing Why was it necessary for previously nomadic Arab tribes to organize?

The Life of Muhammad

GUIDING QUESTION ***What was the significance of Gabriel's messages to Muhammad according to Islamic teachings?***

Into this world of tension stepped a man named Muhammad. Born in Makkah to a merchant family, he was orphaned at five. He grew up to become a caravan manager and married a rich widow named Khadija. Over time, Muhammad became troubled by the growing gap between the generosity of most Makkans and the greediness of the wealthy elite and began to visit the hills to meditate. During one of these visits, Muslims believe, Muhammad received **revelations** from God. According to Islamic teachings, the angel Gabriel gave the messages to Muhammad. Gabriel told Muhammad to recite what he heard. Muhammad had a knowledge of the Jewish and Christian monotheistic traditions and came to believe that Allah had already revealed himself through Moses and Jesus—and thus

sheikh the ruler of an Arabic tribe, chosen from one of the leading families by a council of elders

Allah Arabic for *God*; the supreme god of Islam

revelation a divine truth

(continued from p. 206)

TEKS **Texas Essential Knowledge and Skills**

4D explain the political, economic, and social impact of Islam on Europe, Asia, and Africa

16A locate places and regions of historical significance directly related to major eras and turning points in world history

23A describe the historical origins, central ideas, and spread of major religious and philosophical traditions, including Buddhism, Christianity, Confucianism, Hinduism, Islam, Judaism, Sikhism, and the development of monotheism

25D explain how Islam influences law and government in the Muslim world

26B analyze examples of how art, architecture, literature, music, and drama reflect the history of the cultures in which they are produced

26C identify examples of art, music, and literature that transcend the cultures in which they were created and convey universal themes

Islam monotheistic religion that emerged in the Arabian Peninsula during the seventh century

submission act of submitting to the control or authority of another

Muslim a person who believes in Islam

Quran the holy scriptures of the religion of Islam

Hijrah the journey of Muhammad and his followers to Madinah in 622, which became year 1 of the official calendar of Islam

bedouin a nomadic Arab who lives in the Arabian, Syrian, or North African deserts

hajj a pilgrimage to Makkah, one of the requirements of the Five Pillars of Islam

SKILLS PRACTICE

As you read about the early development of the religion of Islam, write the vocabulary words for this lesson on flashcards. On the back of each flashcard, draw a picture to help you remember what the word means.

through the Jewish and Christian teachings . He believed, however, that the final revelations of Allah were now being given to him.

Out of these revelations developed the religion of Islam. The revelations were eventually written down, and became the holy book of **Islam,** called the **Quran.** The word *Islam* means "peace through **submission** to the will of Allah." Those who practice the religion of Islam are called **Muslims**. According to Islam, there is only one God, Allah, and Muhammad is God's prophet. The **Quran** contains the ethical guidelines and laws by which the followers of Allah are to live. The Quran not only reflects the Arab culture from which it was derived, it also transcends it and continues to guide modern-day Muslims throughout the world.

Muhammad returned home after receiving the revelations and reflected on his experience. His wife urged him to follow Gabriel's message, and she became the first convert to Islam. Muhammad then set out to convince the people of Makkah of the truth of the revelations. Many were surprised at Muhammad's claims to be a prophet. The wealthy feared that his attacks on corrupt society would upset the established social and political order. After three years of preaching, he had only 30 followers.

Muhammad became discouraged by the persecution of his followers, as well as by the Makkans' failure to accept his message. In A.D. 622 he and some of his closest supporters left Makkah and moved north to the rival city of Yathrib, later renamed Madinah (Medina; "city of the prophet"). The journey of Muhammad and his followers to Madinah is known as the ***Hijrah*** (HIH • jruh). The year the journey occurred became year 1 in the official calendar of Islam, still in use today.

Muhammad, who had been invited to Madinah by a number of prominent residents, soon began to win support from people there as well as from Arabs in the desert, known as **Bedouin**. The initial spread of Islam into Madinah was successful as Muhammad formed the first community of practicing Muslims from these groups.

Muslims saw no separation between political and religious authority. Submission to the will of Allah meant submission to his prophet, Muhammad. For this reason, Muhammad soon became both a religious and a political leader. His political and military skills enabled him to put together a reliable military force to defend himself and his followers.

In A.D. 630 Muhammad returned to Makkah with 10,000 men. The city quickly surrendered, and most of the townspeople converted to Islam. During a visit to the Kaaba, Muhammad declared it a sacred shrine of Islam. Two years after his triumphal return to Makkah, just as Islam was spreading through the Arabian Peninsula, Muhammad died. All Muslims are strongly encouraged to make a pilgrimage to Makkah, known as the **hajj** (HAJ), if possible.

✓ **READING PROGRESS CHECK**

Identifying What is the significance of the city of Makkah to early Islam?

The Teachings of Muhammad

GUIDING QUESTION *What beliefs and ways of life shape the religious traditions of Islam?*

Like Christianity and Judaism, Islam is a monotheistic religion. Allah is the all-powerful being who created the universe and everything in it. Islam emphasizes salvation and offers the hope of an afterlife. Those who desire to achieve life after death must subject themselves to Allah's will.

An important religious tradition that separates Christianity and Islam is the Islamic beliefthat its first preacher was not divine. Muhammad is considered a prophet, similar to Moses, but he was also a man like other men. Muslims believe that because humans rejected Allah's earlier messengers, Allah sent his final revelation through Muhammad. At the heart of Islam is the Quran. The Quran consists of 114 chapters and is the sacred book of Islam. It is also a guidebook for ethics and a code of law combined.

Islam is a direct and simple faith, stressing the need to obey the will of Allah. This means practicing the central acts of worship known as the **Five Pillars of Islam**: belief, prayer, charity, fasting, and pilgrimage. Muslims believe that there is no deity but the one God, and Muhammad is his messenger (belief). They perform prescribed prayers five times each day (prayer) and give part of their wealth to the poor (charity). During Ramadan, Muslims refrain from food and drink from dawn to sunset (fasting). Finally, believers are expected to make a pilgrimage to Makkah at least once in their lifetimes (pilgrimage). The faithful who follow the law are guaranteed a place in an eternal paradise.

Believers are expected to follow sound principles for behavior. In addition to the acts of worship called the Five Pillars, Muslims must practice traditions of honesty and justice in dealing with others. Muslims are forbidden to gamble, eat pork, drink alcoholic beverages, or engage in dishonest behavior. Family life is based on marriage.

▲ The Quran is the sacred text of Islam.

Islam is not just a set of religious beliefs but a way of life as well. After Muhammad's death, Muslim scholars developed a law code known as the ***shari'ah*** (shuh • REE • uh). It provides believers with a set of laws to regulate their daily lives. It is based on scholars' interpretations of the Quran and the example set by Muhammad in his life. It regulates all aspects of Muslim life, including family life, business practice, government, and moral conduct. The *shari'ah* does not separate religious matters from civil or political law. It continues to influence law and politics in many parts of the Muslim world, especially in Southwest Asia and northern Africa.

Five Pillars of Islam acts of worship every Muslim must perform; this includes belief, prayer, charity, fasting, and pilgrimage

shari'ah a law code drawn up by Muslim scholars after Muhammad's death; it provided believers with a set of practical laws to regulate their daily lives

✓ READING PROGRESS CHECK

Comparing and Contrasting What similarities and differences exist between the belief systems of Islam and Christianity?

PHOTO: Art Archive/Museum of Islamic Art, Cairo/Dagli Orti

LESSON 1 REVIEW TEKS

Reviewing Vocabulary

1. ***Identifying*** What is the significance of *shari'ah* in the lives of Muslims?

Using Your Notes

2. ***Contrasting*** Use your notes to contrast the differences between the beliefs of early Arabs and the religion of Islam.

Answering the Guiding Questions

3. ***Drawing Conclusions*** Why did communities on the Arabian Peninsula prosper economically?
4. ***Evaluating*** What was the significance of Gabriel's messages to Muhammad according to Islamic teachings?
5. ***Analyzing*** What beliefs and ways of life shape the religious traditions of Islam?

Writing Activity

6. **NARRATIVE** Imagine that you are a former bedouin who now lives in Makkah after the introduction of Islam. Write a letter to your bedouin cousin describing how your life has changed since your move to the city.

networks

There's More Online!

- ☑ BIOGRAPHY Abū Bakr
- ☑ CHART/GRAPH Early Caliphs
- ☑ CHART/GRAPH The Split in Islam
- ☑ IMAGE Artwork Sponsored by Hārūn al-Rashīd
- ☑ IMAGE Battle of Tours
- ☑ IMAGE Hārūn al-Rashīd
- ☑ INTERACTIVE SELF-CHECK QUIZ
- ☑ MAP Spread of Islam, 632–1000
- ☑ VIDEO Islamic Science

LESSON 2

The Arab Empire and the Caliphates

ESSENTIAL QUESTIONS

- *How can religion influence the development of an empire?*
- *How might religious beliefs affect society, culture, and politics?*

Reading HELPDESK

Academic Vocabulary

- complex

Content Vocabulary

- caliph
- jihad
- Shia
- Sunni
- cosmopolitan
- vizier
- sultan
- caliphate

TAKING NOTES:

Key Ideas and Details

Categorizing Information As you read, use a table like the one below to identify the characteristics of the Umayyads, Abbasids, and Seljuk Turks.

Umayyads	Abbasids	Seljuk Turks

TEKS Texas Essential Knowledge and Skills

1B identify major causes and describe the major effects of the following events from 500 BC to AD 600: the development of the classical civilizations of Greece, Rome, Persia, India (Maurya and Gupta), China (Zhou, Qin, and Han), and the development of major world religions

continued on the next page

It Matters Because

The successors to Muhammad were known as caliphs, rulers who became the secular and spiritual leaders of the Islamic community. As the empire grew, caliphs became more like kings or emperors, which was an indication of the strength and power of the growing Arab Empire.

Creation of an Arab Empire

GUIDING QUESTIONS *Why was there tension over who should rule the empire after the death of Muhammad? How did Muhammad's successors help expand the Arab Empire after his death?*

Muhammad had been accepted as the political and religious leader of the Islamic community. The death of Muhammad left his followers with a problem: Muhammad had never named a successor. Although he had several daughters, he had left no son. In a male-oriented society, who would lead the community of the faithful?

Muhammad's death led to the development of the Islamic **caliphate**. Shortly after Muhammad's death, some of his closest followers chose Abū Bakr (uh • BOO BA • kuhr), a wealthy merchant and Muhammad's father-in-law, to be their leader. Abū Bakr had been Muhammad's companion on the journey to Madinah in A.D. 622. There Abū Bakr had functioned as Muhammad's chief adviser and also led the public prayers during Muhammad's final illness. In A.D. 632 Abū Bakr was named **caliph** (KAY • luhf), the religious and political successor to Muhammad.

Under Abū Bakr's leadership, the Islamic movement and the caliphate grew. He suppressed tribal political and religious uprisings, thereby uniting the Muslim world. Muhammad had overcome military efforts by the early Makkans to defeat his movement. Muhammad's successors expanded their territory and the reach of Islam through conquest.

One important duty in the Quran is for Muslims to wage **jihad** (jih • HAHD)—which literally means "striving in the way of God." It refers to a Muslim's duty to work for the triumph of Islam in the world, and within themselves (by avoiding sin and acting righteously). Muslim understanding of the term has changed over time, but for much of Islam's early history jihad meant armed struggle against non-believers. It was also used to justify war within Islam when Muslims disagreed with one another.

The term is controversial today because many Muslim terrorists use it to justify their actions. Many argue jihad requires Muslims to be perpetually at war with non-Muslims until Islam conquers the world, but other scholarly traditions within Islam disagree. They view jihad as a set of principles to help decide when war is necessary to protect or advance the faith.

The duty of jihad played a role in the decisions of early Muslim leaders to attack neighboring kingdoms and build the Arab empire. Unified under Abū Bakr, the Arabs began to turn the energy they had once directed toward each other against neighboring peoples. At Yarmūk in A.D. 636, the Arab army defeated the Byzantine army and four years later, they took control of the Byzantine province of Syria in Southwest Asia. By A.D. 642, Egypt and other areas of northern Africa had been added to the new Arab Empire. To the east, the Arabs had conquered the entire Persian Empire by A.D. 650.

The Arabs, led by a series of brilliant generals, had put together a large, dedicated army that traveled long distances and crossed mountains and harsh terrain. The courage of the Arab soldiers was enhanced by the belief that Muslim warriors were assured a place in paradise if they died in battle.

Early caliphs ruled their far-flung empire from Madinah. After Abū Bakr died, problems arose over who should become the next caliph. There were no clear successors to Abū Bakr, and the first two caliphs to rule after his death were assassinated. In A.D. 656 Ali, Muhammad's son-in-law and one of the first converts to Islam, was chosen to be caliph, but he was also assassinated after ruling for five years.

In the conquered territories of Asia and North Africa there were peacefull interactions among Muslim, Christian, and Jewish societies. Muslim

caliph a successor of Muhammad as spiritual and temporal leader of the Muslims

jihad "struggle in the way of God"

(continued from p. 210)

TEKS **Texas Essential Knowledge and Skills**

1C identify major causes and describe the major effects of the following important turning points in world history from 600 to 1450 the spread of Christianity, the decline of Rome and the formation o medieval Europe; the development of Islamic caliphates and their impact on Asia, Africa, and Europe; the Mongol invasions and their impact on Europe, China, India, and Southwest Asia

continued on the next page

GEOGRAPHY CONNECTION

Islam expanded throughout the Middle East and Mediterranean from A.D. 632–1000.

1. **HUMAN SYSTEMS** *What impact did the Battle of Tours have on the spread of Islam?*
2. **ENVIRONMENT AND SOCIETY** *What do you think prevented Islam from spreading further south into Africa?*

administrators sometimes allowed local officials to continue to govern. Both Christian and Jewish communities were given some autonomy. They could practice their religions, run their own schools, impose taxes on their communities, and enforce their own laws relating to marriage, divorce, and inheritance. Following the concept of dhimmitude, however, they were also subjected to regulations in order to make them aware that they had been subdued by their conquerors. Those who chose not to convert were required to be loyal to Muslim rule and to pay special taxes. Other regulations that were sometimes imposed included a ban on riding horses, carrying weapons, building or repairing places of worship, and engaging in religious practices in public. Sometimes Christians and Jews were also required to wear special clothes or badges to indicate their second class status within Muslim society.

✓ **READING PROGRESS CHECK**

Making Generalizations What was Abū Bakr's chief success as caliph and to what did it contribute?

caliphate the office or dominion of a caliph

(continued from p. 211)

TEKS **Texas Essential Knowledge and Skills**

4D explain the political, economic, and social impact of Islam on Europe, Asia, and Africa

4E describe the interactions among Muslim, Christian, and Jewish societies in Europe, Asia, and North Africa

23A describe the historical origins, central ideas, and spread of major religious and philosophical traditions, including Buddhism, Christianity, Confucianism, Hinduism, Islam, Judaism, Sikhism, and the development of monotheism

25D explain how Islam influences law and government in the Muslim world

The Umayyads

GUIDING QUESTION ***What internal struggles led to revolts against the Umayyads?***

In A.D. 661 the general Mu'āwiyah (moo • AH • wee • uh), the governor of Syria and one of Ali's chief rivals, became caliph. He was known for one outstanding virtue: The used force only when absolutely necessary. As he said, "I never use my sword when my whip will do, nor my whip when my tongue will do."

Mu'āwiyah moved quickly to make the **caliphate**, hereditary in his own family. In doing this, he established the Umayyad (oo • MY • uhd) dynasty. He then moved the capital of the Arab Empire from Madinah to Damascus, in Syria.

Umayyad Conquests

At the beginning of the eighth century, the Arabs carried out new attacks at both the eastern and western ends of the Mediterranean world. Arab armies moved across North Africa and conquered and converted the Berbers, a pastoral people who lived along the Mediterranean coast. The forces of the caliphate could now threaten Europe at both its western and eastern ends.

Around A.D. 710, combined Berber and Arab forces crossed the Strait of Gibraltar and occupied southern Spain in Europe. By A.D. 725, most of Spain had become a Muslim state with its center at Córdoba. In 732, however, Arab forces were defeated at the Battle of Tours in Gaul (now France).

In A.D. 717 another Muslim force had launched an attack on Constantinople with the hope of defeating the Byzantine Empire. The Byzantines survived, however, by destroying the Muslim fleet, although the Byzantine Empire was weakened by this second siege of Constantinople. Arab expansion in Europe had come to a halt.

By A.D. 750, the Arab advance had finally come to an end, but not before the southern and eastern Mediterranean parts of the old Roman Empire had been conquered. Arab power also extended to the east in Mesopotamia and Persia and northward into central Asia.

The Umayyad dynasty at Damascus now ruled an enormous empire. Expansion had brought great wealth and new ethnic groups into the fold of Islam, as well as contact with other civilizations. As a result, the new Arab Empire would be influenced by Byzantine and Persian cultures.

▼ **Charles Martel defeated the army of 'Abd ar-Raḥmān at the Battle of Tours.**

▶ **CRITICAL THINKING**

Analyzing What was the significance of the Battle of Tours?

A Split in Islam

In spite of Umayyad successes, internal struggles threatened the empire's stability. Many Muslims of non-Arab background, such as Persians and Byzantines, did not like the way local administrators favored the Arabs. Financial troubles further weakened the Umayyad dynasty. Also, since the empire was so vast, it was difficult to rule from a capital that was far from the frontiers. These distant regions began to develop their own power, which was hostile to the caliphate.

An especially important revolt took place in what is now Iraq early in the Umayyad period. It was led by Hussein (hoo • SAYN), second son of Ali—the son-in-law of Muhammad. Hussein encouraged his followers to rise up against Umayyad rule in A.D. 680. He set off to do battle, but his soldiers defected, leaving him with an army of 72 warriors against 10,000 Umayyad soldiers. Hussein's tiny force fought courageously, but all died.

The struggle over who should rightfully rule in Islam led to a split of Islam into two groups. The **Shia** (SHEE • AH) Muslims accept only the descendants of Ali as the true rulers of Islam. The **Sunni** (SU • NEE) Muslims did not all agree with Umayyad rule but accepted the Umayyads as caliphs. This political split led to the development of two branches of Muslims that persist to the present. The Sunnis are a majority in the Muslim world, but most of the people in Iraq and neighboring Iran consider themselves to be Shia.

✓ READING PROGRESS CHECK

Describing How did the caliphate become a dynasty, and what factors threatened that dynasty?

▲ Hārūn al-Rashīd was the fifth Abbasid caliph.

▶ CRITICAL THINKING

Evaluating Why was the period of Hārūn al-Rashīd's rule referred to by some as a golden age?

The Abbasid Dynasty and the Seljuk Turks

GUIDING QUESTION *What changes did the Abbasid rulers bring to the world of Islam?*

Resentment against Umayyad rule grew among non-Arab Muslims over the favoritism shown to Arabs. The Umayyads also helped bring about their demise by corrupt behavior. Abū al-ʿAbbās, a descendant of Muhammad's uncle, overthrew the Umayyad dynasty in A.D. 750. Abū al-ʿAbbās established a new caliphate ruled by the Abbasid (uh • BA • suhd) dynasty, which lasted until 1258.

Abbasid Rule

In A.D. 762 the Abbasids built a new capital city at Baghdad, on the Tigris River, far to the east of the Umayyad capital at Damascus. Baghdad's location took advantage of river traffic in the Persian Gulf and the caravan route from the Mediterranean to central Asia.

The move eastward increased Persian influence and encouraged a new cultural outlook. Under the Umayyads, warriors had been seen as the ideal citizens. Under the Abbasids, judges, merchants, and government officials were the new heroes. The Abbasid rulers tried to break down the distinctions between Arab and non-Arab Muslims. This change opened Islamic culture to the influence of the civilizations they had conquered. All Muslims, regardless of ethnic background, could now hold both civil and military offices. Many Arabs began to intermarry with conquered peoples, impacting the social structure and creating a **cosmopolitan** culture in southwest Asia and Egypt.

The best known of the caliphs of the time was Hārūn al-Rashīd (ha • ROON ahl•rah • SHEED), whose reign is often described as the golden age of the Abbasid caliphate. Hārūn al-Rashīd was known for his charity, and he also lavished support on artists and writers.

This was a period of growing prosperity in the Muslim world. The Arabs had conquered many of the richest provinces of the Roman Empire, and they now controlled the trade routes to the East. Baghdad became the center of a large trade empire that helped spread products and knowledge from the Islamic world to Asia, Africa, and Europe. For example, from Persia the knowledge of planting sugarcane and building windmills spread west along the trade routes.

Under the Abbasids, the caliph began to act more regally. The bureaucracy

Shia a Muslim group that accepts only the descendants of Muhammad's son-in-law Ali as the true rulers of Islam

Sunni a Muslim group that accepts only the descendants of the Umayyads as the true rulers of Islam

cosmopolitan a place or area that contains several different cultures and groups

complex having many intricate parts

vizier a high government official in ancient Egypt or in Muslim countries

assisting the caliph grew more **complex**. A council headed by a prime minister, known as a **vizier**, advised the caliph. During council meetings, the caliph sat behind a screen listening to the council's discussions and then whispered his orders to the vizier.

Decline and Division

Despite its prosperity, all was not well in the empire of the Abbasids. There was much fighting over the succession to the caliphate. When Hārūn al-Rashīd died, his two sons fought to succeed him, almost destroying the city of Baghdad.

Vast wealth gave rise to financial corruption. Members of Hārūn al-Rashīd's clan were given large sums of money from the state treasury. His wife was reported to have spent vast sums on a pilgrimage to Makkah.

The shortage of qualified Arabs for key positions in the army and the civil service also contributed to the decline of the Abbasids. Caliphs began to recruit officials from among non-Arabs, such as Persians and Turks. These people were trained to serve the caliphs, but gradually they dominated the army and the bureaucracy.

Eventually, rulers of the provinces of the Abbasid Empire began to break away and establish independent dynasties. Spain had established a separate caliphate when a prince of the Umayyad dynasty fled there in A.D. 750. Morocco became independent, and a new dynasty under the Fatimids was established in Egypt, with its capital at Cairo, in A.D. 973. The Muslim Empire was now politically divided.

Seljuk Turks

The Fatimid dynasty in Egypt soon became the dynamic center of Islamic civilization. From their position in the heart of the Nile delta, the Fatimids played a major role in trade from the Mediterranean to the Red Sea. They created a strong army by hiring nonnative soldiers. One such group was the Seljuk (SEHL • JOOK) Turks.

The Seljuk Turks were a nomadic people from central Asia. They had converted to Islam and prospered as soldiers for the Abbasid caliphate. As the Abbasids grew weaker, the Seljuk Turks grew stronger, moving gradually into Iran and Armenia. By the eleventh century, they had taken over the eastern provinces of the Abbasid Empire.

sultan "holder of power," the military and political head of state under the Seljuk Turks and the Ottomans

In 1055 a Turkish leader captured Baghdad and took command of the empire. His title was **sultan**—or "holder of power." The Abbasid caliph was still the chief religious authority, but, after they captured Baghdad, the Seljuk Turks held the real military and political power of the state.

✓ **READING PROGRESS CHECK**

Analyzing How did the prosperous Abbasid dynasty become politically divided?

LESSON 2 REVIEW TEKS

Reviewing Vocabulary

1. ***Making Inferences*** What is the significance of Abū Bakr's being named caliph?

Using Your Notes

2. ***Identifying*** Use your notes to identify the characteristics of the Umayyads, Abbasids, and Seljuk Turks.

Answering the Guiding Questions

3. ***Evaluating*** Why was there tension over who should rule the empire after the death of Muhammad?
4. ***Making Generalizations*** How did Muhammad's successors help expand the Arab Empire after his death?
5. ***Drawing Conclusions*** What internal struggles led to revolts against the Umayyads?
6. ***Assessing*** What changes did the Abbasid rulers bring to the world of Islam?

Writing Activity

7. **ARGUMENT** Imagine you are Mu'āwiyah and have just become caliph. Write a speech that outlines how you will rule and why you believe the caliphate should be hereditary.

Islam

Followers of Islam, known as Muslims, believe in one god, whom they call Allah. The spiritual founder of Islam, Muhammad, began his teachings in Makkah (Mecca) in A.D. 610. Eventually the religion spread throughout much of Asia, including parts of India to the borders of China, along with a substantial portion of Africa. According to Muslims, the Quran, their holy book, contains the direct word of God, revealed to their prophet Muhammad sometime between A.D. 610 and A.D. 632. Muslims believe that God created Nature, and without his intervention there would be nothingness. God serves four functions: creation, sustenance, guidance, and judgment.

Central to Islamic beliefs are the Five Pillars. These are an affirmation of the belief in Allah and Muhammad as his prophet and include: group prayer; tithing, or the giving of money to charity; fasting during Ramadan; and a pilgrimage to Makkah once in a lifetime if physically and financially able. Within Islam, there are two main branches: Sunni and Shia.

▲ Sacred Site

Makkah is a sacred site for all Muslims. One of the Five Pillars of Islam states that all who are physically and financially able must make a hajj, or pilgrimage, to the holy city once in their lives. Practicing Muslims are also required to pray facing Makkah five times a day.

Sacred Text

The sacred text of Islam is the Quran. Preferably, it is written and read only in Arabic, but translations have been made into many languages. The excerpt below is a verse repeated by all Muslims during their five daily prayers.

In the Name of Allah, the Compassionate, the Merciful,
Praise be to Allah, the Lord of the World,
The Compassionate, the Merciful,
Master of the Day of Judgment,
Only You do we worship, and only You
Do we implore for help.
Lead us to the right path,
The path of those you have favored
Not those who have incurred
Your wrath or
Have gone astray.

—The Quran

Sacred Symbol

Islam is often symbolized by the crescent moon. It is an important part of Muslim rituals, which are based on the lunar calendar.

Worship and Celebration

Ramadan is a month-long celebration commemorating the time during which Muhammad received the Quran from Allah. It is customary for Muslims to fast from dawn until sunset all month long. Muslims believe that fasting helps followers focus on spiritual rather than bodily matters and creates empathy for one's fellow men and women. Ramadan ends with a feast known as Eid-al-Fitr, or Feast of the Fast.

SKILLBUILDER

TEKS 31B

Making Decisions

Why Learn This Skill?

A decision is a choice you make from among two or more alternatives. For instance, when choosing which elective class to take, how will you decide? What if you are equally interested in taking computer graphics and band? Following the steps below will help you make more thoughtful decisions.

Learning the Skill

In making a decision follow these steps:

- **Identify the situation** Define the problem. Ask: Why do I have to make a decision on this matter?
- Gather information What are the reasons behind the situation?
- Identify the options Ask: What are the alternatives? How can I deal with this situation in a different way?
- Predict consequences Consider the possible outcomes. What are the positive or negative effects.
- Take action and make a decision Use all the information gathered to make a decision. Then implement your decision.

Practicing the Skill

Read the following passage from the text; then using the steps in the decision-making process, answer the questions that follow.

"Muhammad had been accepted as the political and religious leader of the Islamic community. The death of Muhammad left his followers with a problem: Muhammad had never named a successor. Although he had several daughters, he had left no son. In a male-oriented society, who would lead the community of the faithful?

"Shortly after Muhammad's death, some of his closest followers chose Abū Bakr (uh • BOO BA • kuhr)*, a wealthy merchant and Muhammad's father-in-law, to be their leader. Abū Bakr had been Muhammad's companion on the journey to Madinah in* A.D. *622. There Abū Bakr had functioned as Muhammad's chief adviser and also led the public prayers during Muhammad's final illness. In* A.D. *632 Abū Bakr was named caliph* (KAY • luhf)*, the religious and political successor to Muhammad.*

"Under Abū Bakr's leadership, the Islamic movement grew. He suppressed tribal political and religious uprisings, thereby uniting the Muslim world."

Answer these questions below:

1. What situation or problem did Muhammad's followers face?
2. What information can you gather about the situation from reading the text?
3. What were the options or choices that Muhammad's followers had?
4. Why was Abū Bakr considered a possible successor? What positive or negative consequences were expected?
5. What decision was made?

Applying the Skill

Read print or online newspapers for articles about an event that affects your community, such as a decision of whether to tear down a historic landmark to build a new shopping mall. Following the five steps in the decision-making process, research the information and options that led to the decision. Predict the consequences that you think will come out of this decision. If a decision has not yet been made on your event, continue the decision-making process. What decision would you implement? Create a multimedia presentation on your community event and the decision-making process that went into it.

networks

There's More Online!

- BIOGRAPHY Ibn-Rushd
- BIOGRAPHY Ibn Sīnā
- IMAGE Umayyad Mosque
- INFOGRAPHIC Baghdad: Center of Trade and Culture
- INTERACTIVE SELF-CHECK QUIZ
- MAP Trade in Southwest Asia, 737–1212
- PRIMARY SOURCE One Thousand and One Nights
- SLIDE SHOW Islamic Arts
- SLIDE SHOW Islamic Sciences
- VIDEO The Islamic Golden Age

Reading HELPDESK

Academic Vocabulary

- **eroded**
- **commentary**

Content Vocabulary

- **bazaar**
- **dowry**
- **astrolabe**
- **arabesques**
- **minaret**
- **muezzin**

TAKING NOTES:

Key Ideas and Details

Categorizing Information As you read, use a table like the one below to identify the characteristics of the upper class, slaves, and women in the Islamic world.

Upper Class	Slaves	Women

TEKS Texas Essential Knowledge and Skills

4D explain the political, economic, and social impact of Islam on Europe, Asia, and Africa

24A describe the changing roles of women, children, and families during major eras of world history

26A identify significant examples of art and architecture that demonstrate an artistic ideal or visual principle from selected cultures

continued on p. 219

LESSON 3
Islamic Civilization

ESSENTIAL QUESTIONS

- *How can religion influence the development of an empire?*
- *How might religious beliefs affect society, culture, and politics?*

IT MATTERS BECAUSE

An extensive trade network brought prosperity to the Islamic world. Muslim scholars made great advances in the areas of mathematics and the natural sciences. Islamic art and architecture incorporated innovative, geometric decorations.

Prosperity in the Islamic World

GUIDING QUESTION *What factors allowed both urban and rural areas to flourish after the eighth century within the Arab Empire?*

Despite internal struggles, this was one of the most prosperous periods in the history of the Middle East. The Arabs carried on extensive trade both by ship and by camel caravans, which traveled from Morocco in the far west to the countries beyond the Caspian Sea. From south of the Sahara came gold and slaves; from China, silk and porcelain; from eastern Africa, gold and ivory; from Spain, iron and metals; and from Southeast Asia and India, sandalwood and spices. Within the empire, Egypt contributed grain; Iraq provided linens, dates, and precious stones; and western India supplied textiles. The development of banking and the use of coins made it easier to exchange goods.

With flourishing trade came exposure to different goods and the rise of prosperous cities. While the Abbasids were in power, the Asian city of Baghdad, the Abbasid capital known as the City of Peace, was probably the greatest city in the empire and one of the greatest cities in the world. After the rise of the Fatimids in the African country of Egypt, however, the focus of trade shifted to Cairo. Another great trading city was the Asian city of Damascus in modern-day Syria. Such an increase in overall trade made Asian and African cities like Baghdad, Cairo, and Damascus the centers of cultural, administrative, and economic activity for their regions.

The **bazaar**, or covered market, was a crucial part of every Muslim city or town. The bazaar was an important trading center, where goods from all the known world were for sale. Customers could compare prices and seek the best bargains. To make sure of high standards, bazaars had

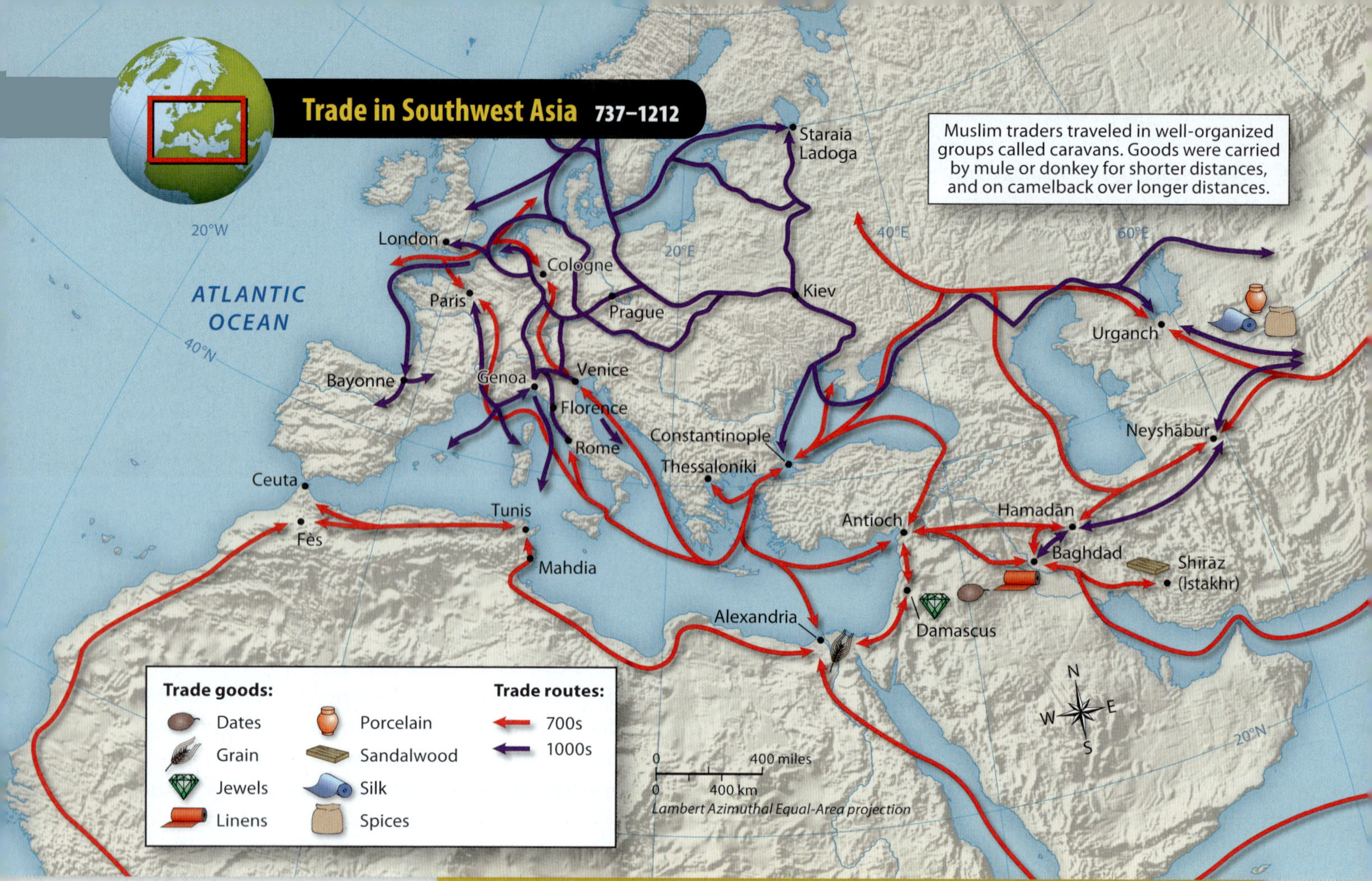

GEOGRAPHY CONNECTION

Trade helped expand the reach of Islam throughout multiple regions.

1. **THE WORLD IN SPATIAL TERMS** *What trade city was known for its sandalwood?*
2. **HUMAN SYSTEMS** *Through what cities would a merchant traveling from Damascus to Cologne be likely to pass?*
3. **THE WORLD IN SPATIAL TERMS** *How would you compare the trade goods from Shiraz to those of Alexandria? What does your comparison lead you to believe about these places?*

market inspectors who enforced rules. The bazaar also housed many craftspeople's shops, as well as services like laundries and bathhouses.

The Arab Empire was more urbanized than most other areas of the known world at the time. Nevertheless, a majority of people still lived in the country, making their living by farming or herding animals. During the early stages of the empire, most of the farmland was owned by independent peasants. Later, wealthy landowners began to amass large estates. Some lands were owned by the state or the court and were farmed by slave labor.

✓ READING PROGRESS CHECK

Drawing Conclusions Why would conducting trade by both caravans and ships be lucrative for the Arab Empire?

Islamic Society

GUIDING QUESTION *How were the principles of Islam reflected in the social structure of the Arab Empire?*

To be a Muslim is not simply to worship Allah but also to live one's life according to Allah's teachings as revealed in the Quran. This also included social life.

Connections to TODAY

Bazaars in the Islamic World

Many bazaars still exist throughout the Islamic world today. Perhaps the most celebrated is İstanbul's *Kapalıçarşı* (Turkish for "covered bazaar"), or Grand Bazaar, which was built 550 years ago by the Ottoman sultan Mehmed II after his conquest of Constantinople. As the centuries passed, the foundation of the modern Turkish banking system was established in the Grand Bazaar. Today this huge commercial complex has more than 3,600 businesses. It is a frequent first stop for foreign visitors to İstanbul. More than 500,000 people pass daily through the Grand Bazaar when it is open for business.

Social Structure

According to Islam, all Muslim people are equal in the eyes of Allah. The doctrine, however, was not translated into social reality. There was a fairly well-defined upper class that consisted of ruling families, senior officials, nomadic elites, and the wealthiest merchants. Even ordinary merchants, however, enjoyed a degree of respect that merchants did not receive in Europe, China, or India.

Non-Muslims were not considered equal to Muslims in the Islamic world. As in the other early civilizations, slavery was widespread. Because Muslims could not be slaves in Islamic society, most of their slaves came from Africa or from non-Islamic populations elsewhere in Asia, resulting in a significant impact on societies in these places. Many had been captured in war.

Slaves often served in the army. This was especially true of slaves recruited from the Turks of central Asia. Many military slaves were freed. Some even came to exercise considerable power.

Many slaves, especially women, were used as domestic servants. These slaves were sometimes permitted to purchase their freedom. Islamic law made it clear that slaves should be treated fairly, and it was considered a good act to free them.

The Role of Women

The Quran granted women spiritual equality with men. Believers, men and women, were to be friends and protectors of one another. Women had the right to the fruits of their work and to own and inherit property although the Quran did state that if an inheritance was shared, men were to inherit twice that of women. Islamic teachings accounted for differences between men and women in the family and social order. Both had duties and responsibilities. As in most societies of the time, men were dominant in Muslim society.

Every woman had a male guardian, be it father, brother, or other male relative. Parents or guardians arranged marriages for their children. The Quran allowed Muslim men to have more than one wife, but no more than four. Most men, however, were unable to afford more than one, because they were required to pay a **dowry** (a gift of money or property) to their brides. Women enjoyed certain privileges, like the right to freely enter into marriage, and the right of divorce under some circumstances. Adultery was forbidden to both men and women.

After the spread of Islam, older, pre-Islamic customs slowly **eroded** the rights enjoyed by early Muslim women. For example, some women were secluded and kept from social contacts with males outside their families. The custom of requiring women to cover virtually all parts of their bodies when appearing in public was common in the cities and is still practiced today in many Islamic societies. It should be noted, however, that these customs owed more to traditional Arab practice than to the Quran. Despite the restrictions, the position of women in Islamic society was better than it had been in former times, when women had often been treated like slaves.

✓ READING PROGRESS CHECK

Contrasting In what ways were the lives of early Muslim men and women different?

Philosophy, Science, and History

GUIDING QUESTION *What were the major contributions of Islamic scholars?*

During the first few centuries of the Arab Empire, the ancient Greek philosophers were largely unknown in Christian Europe. The Arabs,

(continued from p. 217)

TEKS **Texas Essential Knowledge and Skills**

26B analyze examples of how art, architecture, literature, music, and drama reflect the history of the cultures in which they are produced

27A identify the origin and diffusion of major ideas in mathematics, science, and technology that occurred in river valley civilizations, classical Greece and Rome, classical India, and the Islamic caliphates between 700 and 1200 and in China from the Tang to Ming dynasties

bazaar a covered market in Islamic cities

dowry a gift of money or property paid at the time of marriage, either by the bride's parents to her husband or, in Islamic societies, by a husband to his wife

erode to diminish or destroy by degrees

however, were aware of Greek philosophy and were translating works by Plato and Aristotle into Arabic. It was through the Muslim world that Europeans recovered the works of Aristotle and other Greek philosophers. In the twelfth century, the Arabic translations were translated into Latin, making them available to the West. This process was aided by papermaking, which was introduced from China in the although the Quran did state that if an inheritance was shared, men were to inherit twice that of women 700s. By the end of the century, paper factories were found in Baghdad. Booksellers and libraries soon followed.

commentary an explanatory treatise

Islamic civilization contributed more intellectually to the West than translations. When Aristotle's works arrived in Europe in the second half of the twelfth century, they were accompanied by commentaries written by outstanding Arabic philosophers. One such philosopher was Ibn-Rushd (IH • buhn • RUSHT). He lived in Córdoba and wrote a **commentary** on virtually all of Aristotle's surviving works. Islamic scholars also made contributions to mathematics and the natural sciences that were passed on to the West. The Muslims adopted and passed on the numerical system of India, including the use of the zero. In Europe, it became known as the Arabic system, which we use today. A ninth-century Arab mathematician developed the mathematical discipline of algebra, which is taught in schools today and can be applied to fields like medicine, economics, and engineering.

astrolabe an instrument used by sailors to determine their location by observing the positions of stars

Islamic scholars also made significant contributions to major scientific ideas and technological advances. In astronomy, Muslims set up an observatory at Baghdad to study the positions of the stars. They knew that Earth was round, and they named many stars. They also perfected a technological instrument called the **astrolabe**, an instrument used by sailors to determine their location. The spread of the use of the astrolabe into Europe made it possible for Europeans to sail to the Americas.

Additionally, Muslim scholars developed medicine as a field of scientific study. Al-Razi was known as the best doctor of his time in the tenth century in Baghdad. He wrote numerous works to educate others in the medical knowledge of his day. Also well known was the philosopher and scientist,Ibn Sīnā (IH • buhn SEE • nuh). He wrote a medical encyclopedia that, among other things, stressed the contagious nature of certain diseases. Ibn Sīnā showed how diseases could be spread by contaminated water supplies. He was one of many Arabic scholars whose work was translated into Latin and was spread westward, aiding the growth of intellectual life in Europe in the 1100s and 1200s.

▼ The Great Mosque of Damascus, or the Umayyad Mosque, was built originally between A.D. 705 and 715.

▶ CRITICAL THINKING

Drawing Conclusions Why is this mosque also called the Umayyad Mosque?

Islamic scholars also took an interest in writing history. Ibn-Khaldūn (IH • buhn KAL • DOON) was the most prominent Muslim historian of the age. In his most famous work, *Muqaddimah (Introduction to History)*, he argued for a cyclical view of history. Civilizations, he believed, go through regular cycles of birth, growth, and decay. He tried to find a scientific basis for the political and social factors that determine the course of history.

✓ READING PROGRESS CHECK

Identifying Which innovations and ideas of Muslim scholars could still be used today?

Literature, Art, and Architecture

GUIDING QUESTION *How did the arts convey the ideals of spiritual glory in Islam?*

Islam brought major changes to the culture of Southwest Asia, including its literature. Though Muslims regarded the Quran as their greatest literary work, pre-Islamic traditions continued to influence writers. One of the most familiar works of Middle Eastern literature is the *Rubaiyat* (ROO • bee • AHT) of Omar Khayyám (KY • YAHM). We know little of the life and poetry of this twelfth-century Persian poet, mathematician, and astronomer, but we know that he composed his poetry orally. His simple, direct poetry was recorded later by friends or scribes.

Islamic art is a blend of Arab, Turkish, and Persian traditions, reflecting the history of these three cultures. Most decorations on Islamic art consisted of Arabic letters, natural plants, and abstract figures. These decorations were repeated over and over in geometric patterns called **arabesques** that completely covered the surfaces of objects. The Hadith, an early collection of Muhammad's sayings, warns against any attempt to imitate God by creating pictures of living beings. As a result, no representations of figures, including Muhammad, appear in Islamic religious art.

arabesques geometric patterns repeated over and over to completely cover a surface with decoration

The best expression of Islamic architecture is found in the way Muslim mosques represent the spirit of Islam. A significant example of this architecture that demonstrates the Islamic artistic ideal is the Great Mosque of Sāmarrā' in present-day Iraq. It was the world's largest mosque at the time it was built (A.D. 848 to A.D. 852), covering 10 acres (more than 40,000 square m). The most famous section of this mosque, its **minaret**, is nearly 90 feet (27 m) tall and has an unusual outside spiral staircase. The **muezzin** (moo • EH • zuhn), or crier, calls the faithful to prayer five times each day from the minaret.

▲ This tile mosaic covers a wall in the Zaytouna Great Mosque in Morocco.

minaret the tower of a mosque from which the muezzin calls the faithful to prayer five

muezzin the crier who calls the Muslim faithful to prayer from the minaret of a mosque

Because the Muslim religion unites spiritual and political power, palaces were built to reflect this unity and the glory of Islam. Beginning in the eighth century with the castles of Syria, Islamic rulers built large brick palaces with protective walls, gates, and baths. Designed around a central courtyard surrounded by two-story arcades and massive gate-towers, Islamic castles resembled fortresses. The finest example of the Islamic palace is the Alhambra in Granada, Spain. Built in the fourteenth century, every inch of the castle's surface is decorated in floral and abstract patterns. Much of the decoration is finely carved plasterwork that looks like lace. The Alhambra is an excellent expression of Islamic art blending with architecture, reflecting the social impact of Islam on Europe through cultural expression.

PHOTO: akg-images/Gerard Degeorge

✓ **READING PROGRESS CHECK**

Assessing How was Islamic art influenced by Arab, Persian, and Turkish traditions?

LESSON 3 REVIEW TEKS

Reviewing Vocabulary

1. ***Explaining*** Why was the bazaar an important part of a Muslim city or town?

Using Your Notes

2. ***Identifying*** Use your notes to identify characteristics of the upper class, slaves, and women in the Islamic world.

Answering the Guiding Questions

3. ***Evaluating*** What factors allowed both urban and rural areas to flourish after the eighth century within the Arab Empire?
4. ***Making Generalizations*** How were the principles of Islam reflected in the social structure of the Arab Empire?
5. ***Drawing Conclusions*** What were the major contributions of Islamic scholars?
6. ***Assessing*** How did the arts convey the ideals of spiritual glory in Islam?

Writing Activity

7. **INFORMATIVE/EXPLANATORY** Write an essay explaining how Muslim artists incorporated their Islamic beliefs into their art when they designed mosques and palaces.

CHAPTER 9 Assessment

TEKS

Directions: On a separate sheet of paper, answer the questions below. Make sure you read carefully and answer all parts of the questions.

Lesson Review

Lesson 1

1. ***Describing*** What was Makkah known for before the development of Islam?

2. ***Explaining*** Explain the role of the sheikh. How were they chosen?

3. ***Identifying*** What is the *hajj*?

4. ***Describing*** What is *shari'ah*? **1B**

5. ***Explaining*** Explain the early Arab belief in Allah before the development of Islam.

6. ***Identifying*** What was the Black Stone, and what purpose did it serve the early Arab tribes?

7. ***Summarizing*** According to Islamic teachings, how did Muhammad receive revelations from God? **1B**

8. ***Describing*** Where were Muhammad's revelations recorded? **1B**

Lesson 2

9. ***Identifying*** Who was Abu Bakr? What was his relation to Muhammad?

10. ***Identifying Cause and Effect*** What belief enhanced the courage of Muslim soldiers during warfare?

11. ***Explaining*** Explain the concept of dhimmitude and how this concept was applied in territory that had been conquered by Muslims in the A.D. 600s. **4E**

12. ***Describing*** Describe the main issue that drove Islam to split into two groups. Be sure to name the two groups. **1B**

13. ***Summarizing*** How did the Umayyads help bring about their own demise?

14. ***Identifying Cause and Effect*** What factors eventually led to the decline of the Abbasids?

Lesson 3

15. ***Explaining*** What new development made it easier to exchange goods during this time?

16. ***Describing*** Describe the unique physical appearance of Islamic cities during this era.

17. ***Explaining*** How did the teachings of the Quran play a role in social life?

18. ***Describing*** Where was the Islamic advance halted in Eastern Europe? Where was the Islamic advance halted in Western Europe? Why might these events be considered turning points in history? **16A**

19. ***Describing*** What was one of the warnings given by Muhammad in the Hadith regarding art? Describe how this became a central idea of Islam and influenced Muslim art. **23A**

Exploring the Essential Questions

20. ***Describing*** Write an essay describing how the religion of Islam influenced the development of the Arab Empire. Use a time line to show the development of the Arab Empire. Give several examples of how Islam affected Arab society, culture, and politics. Include two other forms of media to illustrate some of these examples, such as primary source quotes and photos. **1B, 23A**

Need Extra Help?

If You've Missed Question	1	2	3	4	5	6	7	8	9	10	11	12	13	14	15	16	17	18	19	20
Go to page	207	206	208	209	207	207	207	208	210	211	211	213	213	214	217	217	219	212	212	212

21 ***Identifying*** Identify how the religious beliefs of Muslims affected their society, culture, and politics. Explain how the development of Islamic caliphates impacted life in Asia, and Africa.

Critical Thinking

22 ***Interpreting Significance*** What are the Five Pillars of Islam? Describe how these are central ideas of Islam. **23A**

23 ***Analyzing*** Why do you think it was common that palaces built by Islamic rulers often resembled fortresses? **26A, 26B**

24 ***Describing*** How did Muhammad contribute to the change of Middle Eastern religious traditions, including the spread of monotheism? **23A**

Social Studies Skills

25 ***Describing*** Describe the societal problems in Makkah that concerned Muhammad. How did Muhammad's beliefs become his solution to these problems?

26 ***Describing*** What were the beliefs of early Arabs? What changed as a result of Muhammad's teachings? What remained the same? **23A**

27 ***Describing*** How did the Arab Empire interact with Christian and Jewish societies in Asia and North Africa after the Islamic conquests?

28 ***Identifying*** Identify and describe two important Islamic works of literature. Explain the similarities and differences between the two works.

29 ***Explaining*** Make a chart with three columns and three rows. Title the columns, "Asia," "Europe" and "Africa." Title the rows, "Political," "Economic," and "Social." Fill out the chart to explain the political, economic, and social impact of Islam on Europe, Asia, and Africa. **4D**

30 ***Presentation Skills*** Make a presentation that analyzes the origin of the astrolabe and the spread of the concept as a major idea in science and technology. Include information about how the astrolabe represents Islamic influence on the world. **27A**

Analyzing Primary Sources

Use the document to answer the following questions.

31 ***Analyzing*** What is the relationship between the Quran and *shari'ah*?

32 ***Interpreting Visuals*** Interpret the social studies content that is tied to this visual. How is the page from the Quran an example of art that reflects Islamic culture? **26B, 30C**

Need Extra Help?

If You've Missed Question	21	22	23	24	25	26	27	28	29	30	31	32
Go to page	209	209	221	208	207	207	211	221	210	220	220	220

Analyzing Visuals

Use the map to answer the following question

33 ***Analyzing Maps*** What territories had been conquered by Muslims by A.D. 656? **1C**

34 ***Analyzing*** What statement can you make about Muslim expansion that includes all the information in the table? **15A, 15B**

Extended Response Question

35 ***Expository*** Write a short essay about the origin of a major idea in mathematics that occurred during the Islamic Empire and explain how it was diffused throughout other civilizations. **27A**

Need Extra Help?

If You've Missed Question	33	34	35
Go to page	224	224	220

Medieval Kingdoms in Europe 800–1300

networks

There's More Online! about medieval kingdoms in Europe.

CHAPTER 10

ESSENTIAL QUESTIONS
- *How can changes to political systems impact economic activities?*
- *How is society influenced by changes in political and economic systems?*

The Story Matters...

Charlemagne's Carolingian Empire began to fall apart as a result of internal divisions and external threats from invaders such as Muslims, Vikings, and Magyars. The need for security encouraged the growth of a feudal society dominated by powerful landowning nobles. Opposing this tendency were ambitious rulers such as King Henry II of England, who applied his restless energy, military skill, and cool ruthlessness to rebuilding royal power.

◀ Created between 1280 and 1300, this detail comes from an illustration in an Anglo-French chronicle showing Henry II seated on his throne. Painted a century after Henry's death, this stylized image is not a portrait of the king, who was thickset and wore his hair closely cropped.

CHAPTER 10

Place and Time: Medieval Europe 800–1300

Charlemagne created a strong monarchy, but it did not long survive his death in 814. His grandsons Lothair, Louis the German, and Charles the Bald first fought for control of the Carolingian Empire and then split it into three parts. Invasions by Muslims, Magyars, and Vikings throughout the ninth and tenth centuries produced varying responses in different parts of Europe. In France, these invasions weakened the power of the monarchy and strengthened the nobility. By contrast, the strong English response to Viking invasion eventually united the country. Throughout Europe, however, the need for security encouraged the growth of feudalism, one of the defining institutions of medieval society.

Step Into the Place

Read the quotes and look at the information presented on the map.

DBQ **Analyzing Historical Documents** What different responses did European communities and rulers make to invasions?

PRIMARY SOURCE

“Louis [the German] hurled his men on the troops which Lothair [shown right] had stationed to resist him, slew many of them and put the rest to flight. . . .

Meanwhile Danish pirates sailed down the Channel and attacked Rouen, plundered the town with pillage, fire and sword, slaughtered or took captive the monks and the rest of the population, and laid waste all the monasteries and other places on the banks of the Seine, or else took large payments and left them thoroughly terrified.”

—from *The Annals of Saint-Bertin*, 841

PRIMARY SOURCE

“In the year of the Lord’s incarnation [885], (the thirty-seventh of king Alfred’s life), the Viking army split up into two bands: one band set out for [the East Frankish kingdom], and the other, coming to Britain, entered Kent and besieged the city which in English is called Rochester, situated on the eastern bank of the river Medway. The Vikings immediately constructed a strong fortification for themselves in front of its entrance, but they were unable to capture the city because the citizens defended themselves courageously until King Alfred [shown left] arrived, bringing them relief with a large army. Thereupon the Vikings, abandoning their fortress, . . . fled quickly to their ships. . . .”

—from Asser’s *Life of King Alfred*, 884

Step Into the Time

Contrasting Research two events from the time line and contrast what they show about the development of European kingdoms in the early Middle Ages.

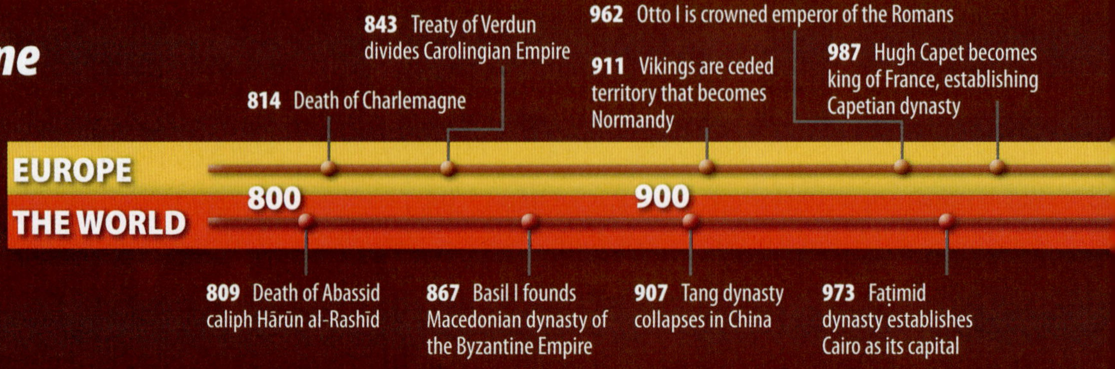

networks
There's More Online!

- **MAP** Explore the interactive version of this map on Networks.
- **TIME LINE** Explore the interactive version of the time line on Networks.

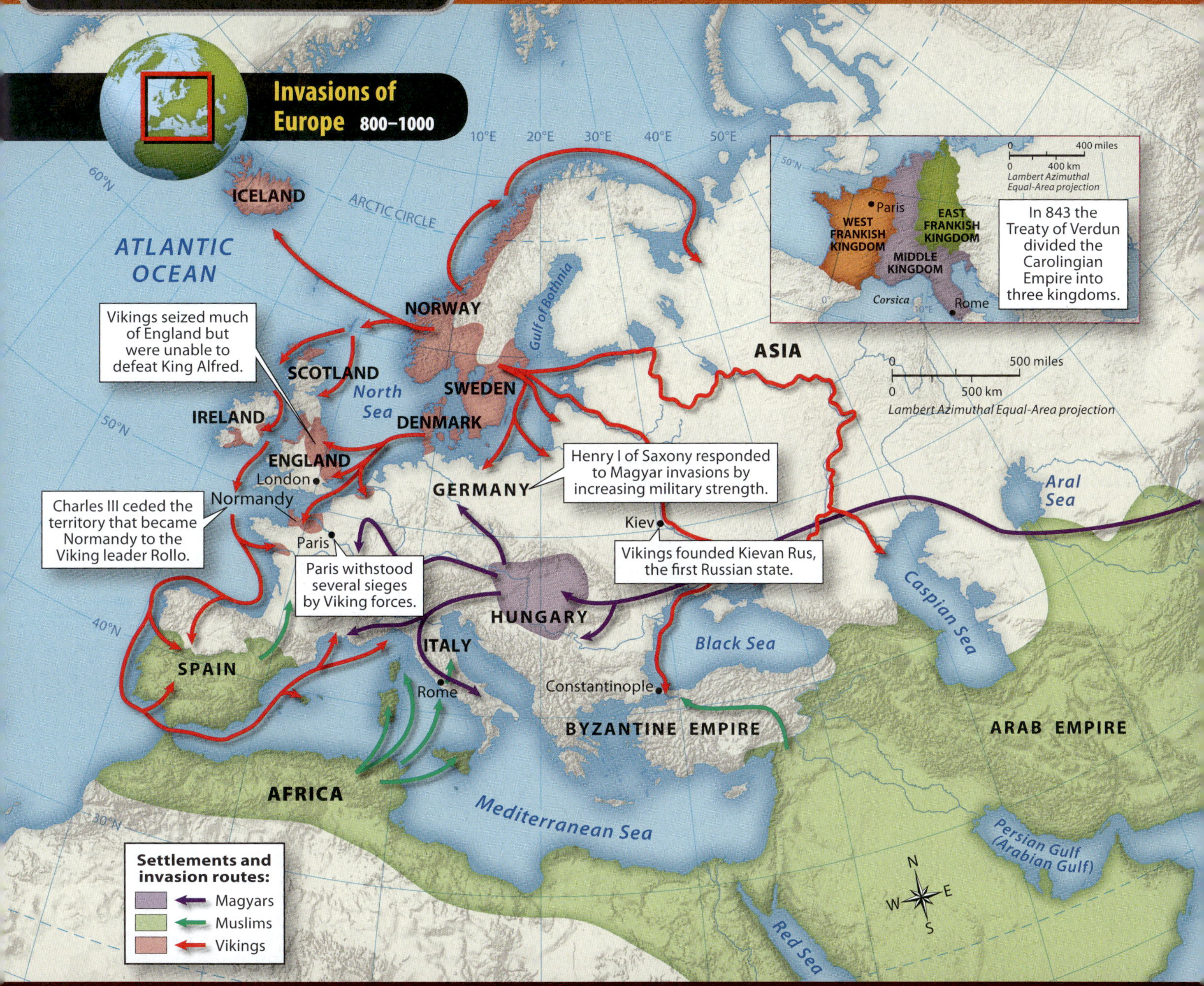

1000 — **1100** — **1200** — **1300**

- **1001** Muslim ruler Maḥmūd of Ghazna invades India
- **1048** Persian poet and astronomer Omar Khayyám is born
- **1054** Kievan Rus state is fragmented by civil war
- **1066** Normans invade England
- **1099** First Crusade captures Jerusalem
- **1170** Thomas à Becket is murdered
- **1206** Mongols become unified under Genghis Khan
- **1215** King John is forced to sign Magna Carta
- **1240** Mali ruler Sundiata destroys Ghana capital of Kumbi
- **c. 1275** Marco Polo reaches court of Kublai Khan
- **1295** King Edward I summons the Model Parliament

networks

There's More Online!

- BIOGRAPHY Eleanor of Aquitaine
- CHART/GRAPH Feudalism Terminology
- GRAPHIC ORGANIZER Feudal and Manorial Relationships
- IMAGE Knights in a Tournament
- IMAGE Medieval Castle
- INTERACTIVE SELF-CHECK QUIZ
- MAP Invasions of Europe, 800–1000
- SLIDE SHOW The Code of Chivalry
- VIDEO Feudalism

LESSON 1

Feudalism

ESSENTIAL QUESTIONS

- *How can changes to political systems impact economic activities?*
- *How is society influenced by changes in political and economic systems?*

Reading HELPDESK

Academic Vocabulary

- **enabled**
- **contract**

Content Vocabulary

- **feudalism**
- **vassal**
- **knight**
- **fief**
- **feudal contract**
- **chivalry**

TAKING NOTES:

Key Ideas and Details

Categorizing As you read, use a table like the one below to identify the ideals of chivalry.

Ideals of Chivalry

TEKS Texas Essential Knowledge and Skills

1C identify major causes and describe the major effects of the following important turning points in world history from 600 to 1450 the spread of Christianity, the decline of Rome and the formation o medieval Europe; the development of Islamic caliphates and their impact on Asia, Africa, and Europe; the Mongol invasions and their impact on Europe, China, India, and Southwest Asia

continued on the next page

It Matters Because

The Carolingian Empire was weakened inside and out after Charlemagne's death. Local nobles became more important as people turned to them for the protection that the empire could no longer provide. The result was feudalism.

The End of the Carolingian Empire

GUIDING QUESTION *What internal and external factors after Charlemagne's death weakened kingdoms in Europe?*

The Carolingian Empire began to fall apart soon after Charlemagne's death in 814. Less than 30 years later, it was divided among his grandsons into three major sections: the west Frankish lands, the eastern Frankish lands, and the Middle Kingdom. Local nobles gained power while the Carolingian rulers fought each other. Invasions in different parts of the old Carolingian world added to the process of disintegration.

In the ninth and tenth centuries, Western Europe was beset by a wave of invasions. The most far-reaching attacks of the time came from the Norsemen, or Northmen, of Scandinavia, also called the Vikings. They were a Germanic people, whose great love of adventure and search for spoils of war and new avenues of trade may have led them to invade other areas of Europe.

In the ninth century, Vikings sacked villages and towns, destroyed churches, and easily defeated small local armies. The Vikings were warriors, and they were superb shipbuilders and sailors. Long and narrow with beautifully carved, arched prows, the Viking dragon ships each carried about 50 men. The ships' construction **enabled** them to sail up European rivers and to attack places far inland. By the mid-ninth century, the Vikings had begun to build various European settlements.

Beginning in 911, the ruler of the west Frankish lands gave one band of Vikings land at the mouth of the Seine River, forming a region of France that came to be known as Normandy. The Frankish policy of settling the Vikings and converting them to Christianity was a deliberate one. As a result of their conversion to Christianity, the Vikings soon became a part of European civilization.

✓ READING PROGRESS CHECK

Identifying What factors helped the Vikings invade Europe successfully?

enable to make possible

(continued from p. 228)

TEKS **Texas Essential Knowledge and Skills**

4C describe the major characteristics of and the factors contributing to the development of the political/social system of feudalism and the economic system of manorialism

24A describe the changing roles of women, children, and families during major eras of world history

The Development of Feudalism

GUIDING QUESTION *Why did the collapse of governments lead to the new political and social order known as feudalism?*

The Vikings posed a threat to the safety of people in Europe. As organized governments such as the Carolingian Empire were torn apart, people began to turn to local landed aristocrats, or nobles, to protect them. To survive, it became important to find a powerful lord who could offer protection in return for service. This led to the formation of a new political and social order in medieval Europe known as **feudalism**. One of the major characteristics of feudalism was the idea of vassalage.

feudalism political and social order that developed during the Middle Ages when royal governments were no longer able to defend their subjects; nobles offered protection and land in return for service

Knights and Vassals

In Germanic society, warriors swore an oath of loyalty to their leaders and fought in battles for them. The leaders, in turn, took care of the warriors' needs. By the eighth century, a man who served a lord in a military capacity was known as a **vassal**.

vassal under feudalism, a man who served a lord in a military capacity

The Frankish army had originally consisted of foot soldiers dressed in coats of mail—armor made of metal links or plates—and armed with swords. Horsemen had been throwers of spears. In the eighth century, however, larger horses and the stirrup were introduced. Now horsemen were armored in coats of mail because the larger horses could carry the weight. With stirrups to keep them on their horses, they wielded long lances that enabled them to act as battering rams. For almost 500 years, warfare in Europe was dominated by heavily armored cavalry, or **knights**, as they came to be called. The knights had great social prestige and formed the backbone of the European aristocracy.

knight under feudalism, a member of the heavily armored cavalry

CHART

Feudalism and manorialism involved a web of obligations.

1. ***Contrasting*** How did the obligations of serfs differ from those of lords and knights?
2. ***Interpreting*** Which social group resided in Leeds Castle (below)?

FEUDAL AND MANORIAL RELATIONSHIPS

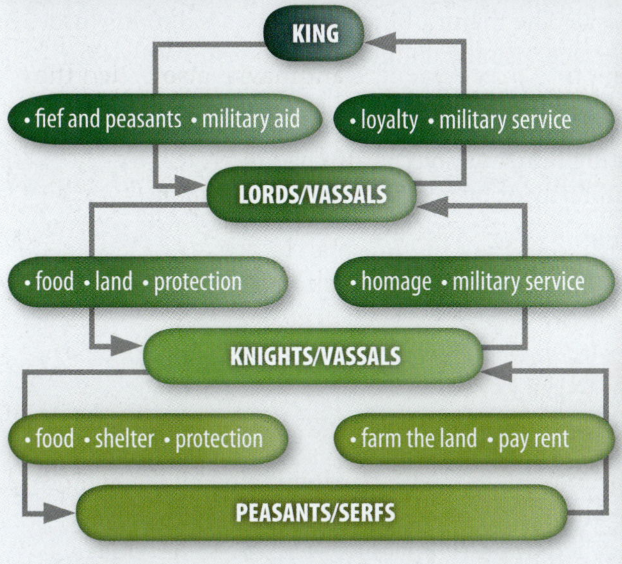

▲ In tournaments, such as this one featuring the Duke of Anhalt, knights fought one another.

It was expensive to have a horse, armor, and weapons. It also took more time and practice to learn to use these instruments skillfully. With the breakdown of royal governments, the more powerful nobles took control of large areas of land. When these lords wanted men to fight for them, they granted each vassal a piece of land that supported the vassal and his family. In the Early Middle Ages, when wealth was based primarily on land, it was the best gift a lord could give to a vassal.

The Feudal Contract

In feudal society, loyalty to one's lord was the chief virtue. The relationship between lord and vassal was made official by a ceremony::

PRIMARY SOURCE

"The man should put his hands together as a sign of humility, and place them between the two hands of his lord as a token that he vows everything to him and promises faith to him; and the lord should receive him and promise to keep faith with him. Then the man should say: 'Sir, I enter your homage and faith and become your man by mouth and hands, and I swear and promise to keep faith and loyalty to you against all others.'"

—from *A Source Book for Mediaeval History*

fief under feudalism, a grant of land made to a vassal; the vassal held political authority within his fief

By the ninth century, the grant of land made to a vassal had become known as a **fief** (FEEF). Vassals who held fiefs came to hold political authority within them. As the Carolingian world fell apart, the number of separate, powerful lords and vassals increased, leading to the formation of medieval Europe. Instead of a single government, many different people now maintained order.

Feudalism became increasingly complicated. The vassals of a king, who were great lords, might also have vassals who would owe them military service in return for a grant of land taken from their estates. Those vassals, in turn, might likewise have vassals. At that level, the vassals would be simple knights with barely enough land to provide them income.

feudal contract under feudalism, the unwritten rules that determined the relationship between a lord and his vassal

contract a binding agreement between two or more people or parties

The lord-vassal relationship bound together greater and lesser landowners. It was an honorable relationship between free men and implied no sense of servitude. Feudalism came to be characterized by a set of unwritten rules—known as the **feudal contract**—that determined the relationship between a lord and his vassal. The major obligation of a vassal to his lord was to perform military service, usually about 40 days a year. When summoned, a vassal had to appear at his lord's court to give advice.

Under this **contract**, the lord also had responsibilities to his vassals. He supported a vassal by granting him land, but he also had to protect his vassal by defending him militarily or by taking his side in a dispute.

✓ **READING PROGRESS CHECK**

Analyzing Why was land the most important gift a lord could give a vassal?

The Nobility of the Middle Ages

GUIDING QUESTION *How was European feudal society structured?*

In the Middle Ages, European feudal society was dominated by men whose chief concern was warfare. In this culture of warfare vassals prepared to fight for their lords when called upon. The nobles were the kings, dukes, counts, barons, and even bishops who had large landed estates and considerable political power in society. They formed an aristocracy, or nobility, that consisted of people who held political, economic, and social power.

Great lords and ordinary knights came to form a common group within the aristocracy. They were all warriors, and the institution of knighthood united them all. However, there were also social divisions among them based on extremes of wealth and landholdings.

Trained to be warriors but with no adult responsibilities, young knights had little to do but fight. In the twelfth century, tournaments—contests in which knights could demonstrate their fighting skills—began to appear. By the late twelfth century, the joust—individual combat between two knights—had become the main part of the tournament.

In the eleventh and twelfth centuries, under the influence of the Catholic Church, **chivalry**, an idea of civilized behavior, gradually evolved among the nobility. Chivalry was a code of ethics that knights were supposed to uphold. In addition to their oath to defend the Church and defenseless people, knights were expected to treat captives as honored guests instead of putting them in dungeons. A knight was expected to treat aristocratic women with tenderness and respect.

Although women could legally hold property, most remained under the control of men—of their fathers until they married and of their husbands if they married. Still, aristocratic women had many opportunities to play important roles.

Because the lord was often away at war or court, the lady of the castle had to manage the estate, including large numbers of officials and servants. Care of the financial accounts alone took considerable knowledge. The lady of the castle was also responsible for overseeing the food supply and maintaining all the other supplies needed for the household.

Women were expected to be subservient to their husbands, but there were many strong women who advised, and even dominated, their husbands. Perhaps the most famous of these was the remarkable Eleanor of Aquitaine. Heiress to the duchy of Aquitaine in southwestern France, she was married at the age of 15 to King Louis VII of France. The marriage was not a happy one, and Louis had their marriage annulled. Eleanor married again, only eight weeks later, to Duke Henry of Normandy, who soon became King Henry II of England. She and Henry had eight children (five were sons). Two of her sons—Richard and John—became kings of England.

✓ **READING PROGRESS CHECK**

Summarizing List three features of chivalry.

chivalry in the Middle Ages, the ideal of civilized behavior that developed among the nobility; it was a code of ethics that knights were supposed to uphold

Thinking Like a HISTORIAN

Chivalry in the Middle Ages

"More than a code of manners in war and love," observed historian Barbara Tuchman, "chivalry was a moral system governing the whole of noble life. That it was about four parts in five illusion made it no less governing for all that." How accurate was her assessment? Was chivalry only an ideal—largely ignored in practice by medieval knights? What effect, for example, did chivalry have on actual warfare during the Middle Ages? How did it affect the status of medieval women? Use the Internet to find reliable sources presenting different views on the extent to which chivalry was actually practiced in the Middle Ages.

LESSON 1 REVIEW TEKS

Reviewing Vocabulary

1. ***Making Connections*** How did the introduction of larger horses lead to the use of heavily armored knights? 1C

Using Your Notes

2. ***Identifying*** Use your notes to identify the ideals of chivalry.

Answering the Guiding Questions

3. ***Drawing Conclusions*** What internal and external factors after Charlemagne's death weakened kingdoms in Europe? 1C
4. ***Inferring*** Why did the collapse of governments lead to the new political and social order known as feudalism? 1C, 4C
5. ***Making Generalizations*** How was European feudal society structured? 4C, 29F

Writing Activity

6. **NARRATIVE** Imagine you are a minor lord in the Middle Ages. Write a letter to a friend explaining your day-to-day responsibilities. Be sure to include both your responsibilities to a greater lord and to your vassals. 1C, 4C

networks

There's More Online!

- IMAGE Medieval Covered Market
- IMAGE Medieval Guilds
- IMAGE Peasant Ploughing a Field
- IMAGE Peasants' Wheel of Life
- INTERACTIVE SELF-CHECK QUIZ
- MAP Medieval Centers of Trade, After 1100
- PRIMARY SOURCE Charter of the Medieval Town of Lorris, France
- VIDEO Peasants, Trade, and Cities

LESSON 2

Peasants, Trade, and Cities

ESSENTIAL QUESTIONS

- *How can changes to political systems impact economic activities?*
- *How is society influenced by changes in political and economic systems?*

Reading **HELP**DESK

Academic Vocabulary

- **technology**
- **crucial**

Content Vocabulary

- ***carruca***
- **serf**
- **patrician**
- **manor**
- **bourgeoisie**

TAKING NOTES:

Key Ideas and Details

Describing As you read, use a table like the one below to describe the factors that led to the growth of cities in Europe.

Factors Leading to the Growth of Cities

TEKS Texas Essential Knowledge and Skills

1C identify major causes and describe the major effects of the following important turning points in world history from 600 to 1450 the spread of Christianity, the decline of Rome and the formation o medieval Europe; the development of Islamic caliphates and their impact on Asia, Africa, and Europe; the Mongol invasions and their impact on Europe, China, India, and Southwest Asia

continued on the next page

IT MATTERS BECAUSE

During the High Middle Ages, new farming methods enabled Europe's population to grow. Many serfs worked the land under the manorial system. The revival of trade led to a money economy and the growth of cities.

The New Agriculture

GUIDING QUESTION *How did new farming methods benefit Europe in the Middle Ages?*

In the Early Middle Ages, Europe had a relatively small population. In the High Middle Ages, however, population increased dramatically—nearly doubling between 1000 and 1300 from approximately 38 million to 74 million people.

What caused this huge increase? For one thing, Europe was more settled and peaceful after the invasions of the Early Middle Ages had stopped. Food production after 1000 also increased because the climate changed during the High Middle Ages, resulting in improved growing conditions.

Changes in **technology** also aided the growth of farming. The Middle Ages witnessed an explosion of labor-saving devices. People harnessed the power of water and wind to do jobs once done by human or animal power. Many of these new devices were made from iron, which was mined in various areas of Europe. Iron was **crucial** in making the ***carruca***, a heavy, wheeled plow with an iron plowshare. Unlike earlier plows, this plow, drawn by six or eight oxen, easily turned over heavy clay soils.

Use of the *carruca* also led to the growth of farming villages, where people worked together. Because iron was expensive, an entire community had to buy a *carruca*. Likewise, one family could not afford a team of animals, so villagers shared their beasts.

Shifting from a two-field to a three-field crop rotation also increased food production. In the Early Middle Ages, peasants divided their land into two fields. They planted one field and allowed the other to lie fallow, or unplanted, to regain its fertility.

Now, lands were divided into three parts. Peasants planted one field in the fall with grains, such as rye and wheat, that they harvested in summer. They planted the second field in spring with grains, such as oats and barley, and vegetables, such as peas and beans, that they harvested in fall. They allowed the third field to lie fallow. This way, only one-third, rather than one-half, of the land lay fallow at any time. This practice of rotating crops kept the soil fertile, while allowing people to grow more crops.

technology the science or study of the practical or industrial arts; applied sciences

crucial essential; important

carruca a heavy, wheeled plow with an iron plowshare

✓ **READING PROGRESS CHECK**

Making Connections What factors led to population growth in the High Middle Ages?

(continued from p. 232)

TEKS **Texas Essential Knowledge and Skills**

4C describe the major characteristics of and the factors contributing to the development of the political/social system of feudalism and the economic system of manorialism

24A describe the changing roles of women, children, and families during major eras of world history

The Manorial System

GUIDING QUESTION ***What was life like for nobles and peasants under the economic system of manorialism?***

Landholding nobles were a military elite whose ability to be warriors depended on having the leisure time to pursue the arts of war. Landed estates, located on the fiefs given to a vassal by his lord and worked by peasants, gave the economic support that made the economic system of manorialism possible.

A **manor** was an agricultural estate that a lord ran and peasants worked. Increasing numbers of free peasants became **serfs**, or peasants legally bound to the manor. Serfs had to give labor services, pay rents, and be subject to the lord's control. By 800, probably 60 percent of western Europeans were serfs.

manor in medieval Europe, an agricultural estate that a lord ran and peasants worked

serf in medieval Europe, a peasant legally bound to the land who had to provide labor services, pay rents, and be subject to the lord's control

A serf's labor services included working the lord's land, which made up one-third to one-half of the cultivated land scattered throughout the manor. Peasants used the rest of the estate's land to grow food for themselves. Serfs usually worked about three days a week for their lords and paid rents by giving the lords a share of every product they raised. Serfs also paid the lords for the use of the manor's common pasturelands, streams, ponds, and woodlands.

Lords had a variety of legal rights over the serfs on their estates. Serfs could not leave the manor without the lord's permission. Lords often had political authority on their lands, which gave them the right to try peasants in their own courts. Even with these restrictions, however, serfs were not slaves. The land assigned to serfs to support themselves usually could not be taken away, and their responsibilities to the lord remained fairly fixed. It was also the lord's duty to protect his serfs, giving them the safety to farm the land.

▲ **A peasant and his oxen from early thirteenth-century France.**

The life of peasants in Europe was simple. Their cottages had wood frames surrounded by sticks, with the spaces between sticks filled with straw and rubble and then plastered over with clay. Roofs were simply thatched. The houses of poorer peasants consisted of a single room. Others had at least two rooms—a main room for cooking, eating, and other activities and another room for sleeping. There was little privacy in a medieval household.

The seasons of the year largely determined peasant activities. Each season brought a new round of tasks. Harvest time in August and September was especially hectic. A good harvest of grains for making bread was crucial to survival in the winter months. A new cycle of labor began in October, when peasants worked the ground for the planting of winter crops. In November came the slaughter of excess livestock because there was usually not enough

SKILLS PRACTICE

As you learn about the the revival of trade and cities, list vocabulary terms you hear during class instruction and discussion. To help you learn vocabulary, think of other words that have similar meanings. Think of these words when you hear or see the new vocabulary word.

food to keep the animals alive all winter. The meat would be salted to preserve it for winter use. In February and March, the land was plowed for the planting of spring crops—oats, barley, peas, and beans. Early summer was a fairly relaxed time, although there was still weeding and sheepshearing to be done.

In every season, the serfs worked not only their own land but also the lords' lands. They also tended the small gardens next to their dwellings, where they grew the vegetables that made up part of their diet. The basic staple of the peasant diet, and of the medieval diet in general, was bread. Women made the dough for the bread. The loaves were usually baked in community ovens, which the lord owned. Highly nutritious, peasant bread contained not only wheat and rye but also barley, millet, and oats. These ingredients gave the bread a dark appearance and a heavy, hard texture.

✓ **READING PROGRESS CHECK**

Summarizing How were serfs legally bound to the land?

The Revival of Trade

GUIDING QUESTION ***How did the revival of trade result in a commercial revolution during the Middle Ages?***

Medieval Europe was an agricultural society in which most people lived in small villages. In the 1000s and 1100s, however, Europe experienced a revival of trade and an associated growth of towns and cities.

The revival of trade in Europe was gradual. Italian cities, such as Venice, developed a mercantile fleet (a fleet of trading ships) and became major trading centers in the Mediterranean. The towns in Flanders, an area along the coast of present-day Belgium and northern France, were ideally located for northern European traders. Merchants from surrounding areas came to Flanders for woolen cloth. In the thirteenth century, a medieval trade association, the Hanseatic League, developed in the Baltic and North Sea region. The Hanseatic League was an alliance of more than 100 northern European cities that banded together for mutual trade protection and economic opportunity.

▲ **Merchants sell their wares in a medieval covered market.**

By the 1100s, a regular trade had developed between Flanders and Italy. To encourage trade, the counts of Champagne, in northern France, initiated a series of annual trade fairs. Northern European merchants brought furs, woolen cloth, tin, hemp, and honey to trade for cloth and swords from northern Italy and the silks, sugar, and spices of the East. As trade increased, so did the demand for gold and silver coins. Slowly, a money economy—an economic system based on money rather than barter—emerged. New trading companies and banking firms were set up to manage the exchange and sale of goods. These new practices were part of the rise of commercial capitalism, an economic system in which people invested in trade and goods for profit.

✓ **READING PROGRESS CHECK**

Classifying Why were the towns of Flanders busy trading centers?

The Growth of Cities

GUIDING QUESTION ***What spurred the growth of cities in the Middle Ages?***

The revival of trade led to a revival of cities. Towns had greatly declined in the Early Middle Ages, especially in Europe north of the Alps. Old Roman cities had continued to exist, but they had dwindled in size and population.

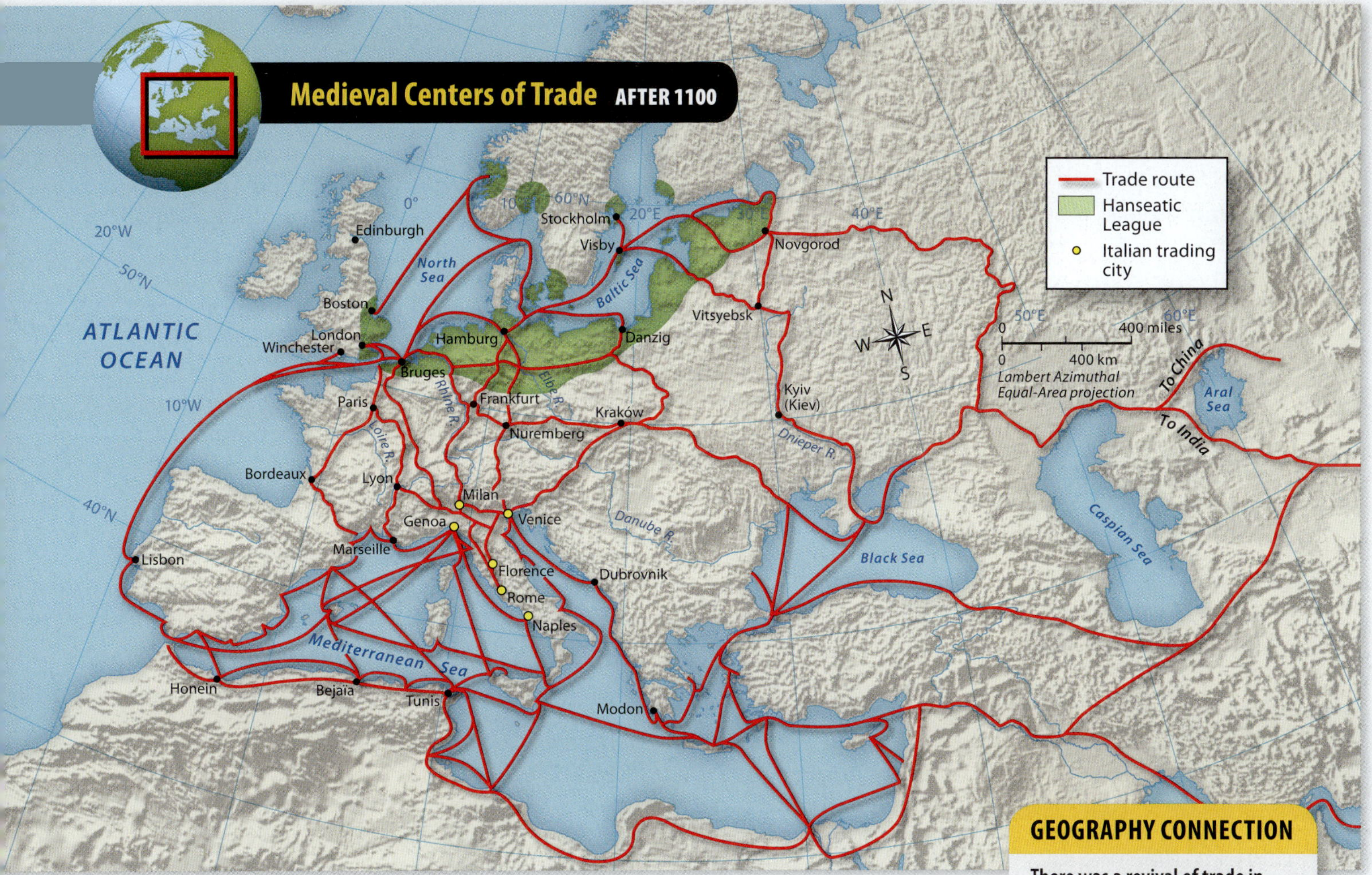

With the revival of trade, merchants began to settle in the old Roman cities. They were followed by craftspeople or artisans—people who had developed skills and saw a chance to make goods that the merchants could sell. In the eleventh and twelfth centuries, the old Roman cities came alive with new populations and growth.

Many new cities or towns were also founded, especially in northern Europe. Usually a group of merchants built a settlement near a castle because it was located along a trade route or river and because the lords of the castle would offer protection. If the settlement prospered and expanded, new walls were built to protect it.

The merchants and artisans of these new cities later came to be called burghers, or **bourgeoisie**, from the German word *burg*, meaning "a walled enclosure." Medieval cities were small in comparison with either ancient cities or modern cities. A large medieval trading city would have about 5,000 inhabitants.

Most towns were often part of a lord's territory and were therefore subject to his authority. However, townspeople needed freedom to trade. They wanted their own unique laws and were willing to pay for them. Lords and kings, in turn, saw that they could also make money and sold to the townspeople the liberties they wanted.

By 1100, townspeople had numerous rights from local lords. These included the right to buy and sell property, freedom from military service to the lord, a written law that guaranteed townspeople their freedom, and the right for an escaped serf to become a free person after living a year and a day in the town.

GEOGRAPHY CONNECTION

There was a revival of trade in Europe in the Middle Ages.

1. **THE WORLD IN SPATIAL TERMS** *What cities were located within the Hanseatic League?*
2. **ENVIRONMENT AND SOCIETY** *Why were many trade cities located along bodies of water?*

bourgeoisie the middle class, including merchants, industrialists, and professional people

Over time, medieval cities developed their own governments for running the affairs of the community. Only males who had been born in the city or who had lived there for some time were citizens. In many cities, these citizens elected the city council members, who served as judges and city officials and who passed laws. Elections were rigged so that only **patricians**—members of the wealthiest and most powerful families—were elected to public office.

patrician a wealthy, powerful landowner

Medieval cities were surrounded by stone walls. Walls were expensive to build, so the cities were tightly filled. They had narrow, winding streets, and houses were crowded against one another, with the second and third stories built out over the streets.

The physical environment of medieval cities was not pleasant. Often dirty, cities smelled from animal and human waste. Air pollution was also a fact of life. Smoke from wood fires or from the burning of cheap grades of coal filled the air.

▲ **Emblems of different medieval guilds in Umbria, Italy.**

▶ **CRITICAL THINKING**

Analyzing Visuals Why would guilds use symbols in addition to words? Can you identify the glovemaker, armorer, and barber?

Considerably more men than women lived in medieval cities. Women were expected to supervise the household, prepare meals, raise the children, and manage the family's finances. Often, they helped their husbands in their trades, and some women developed their own trades to earn extra money. Sometimes, when a master craftsman died, his widow carried on his trade. It was thus possible for women in medieval towns to lead quite independent lives.

With the revival of trade, cities and towns became important centers for manufacturing a wide range of goods such as cloth, metalwork, shoes, and leather goods. Many craft activities were carried on in houses located in the narrow streets of medieval cities. From the 1000s on, craftspeople began to organize themselves into guilds, or business associations. Guilds played a leading role in the economic life of cities. By the 1200s, there were guilds for almost every craft, such as tanners and bakers, and separate guilds for specialized groups of merchants, such as dealers in silk, spices, or wool. Craft guilds directed almost every aspect of the production process. They set the standards for the quality of the articles produced and even fixed the price at which the finished goods could be sold. Guilds also determined the number of people who could enter a specific trade.

✓ **READING PROGRESS CHECK**

Making Generalizations What role did guilds play in the economic life of towns and cities?

LESSON 2 REVIEW TEKS

Reviewing Vocabulary

1. ***Inferring*** Why do you think citizens allowed patricians to fix elections in medieval cities?

Using Your Notes

2. ***Making Connections*** What events during the Middle Ages led to a growth of cities? 1C

Answering the Guiding Questions

3. ***Identifying*** How did new farming methods benefit Europe in the Middle Ages? 1C
4. ***Explaining*** What was life like for nobles and peasants under the economic system of manorialism? 4C
5. ***Making Generalizations*** How did the revival of trade result in a commercial revolution during the Middle Ages? 1C, 29F
6. ***Drawing Conclusions*** What spurred the growth of cities in the Middle Ages? 1C

Writing Activity

7. **ARGUMENT** Imagine you are a trader doing business at the beginning of the money economy. Write a letter addressed to other traders convincing them to convert from bartering to a money system. 1C

networks

There's More Online!

- BIOGRAPHY Louis IX
- BIOGRAPHY Otto I
- BIOGRAPHY Philip II Augustus
- BIOGRAPHY William of Normandy
- IMAGE Seal on the Magna Carta
- IMAGE King John Signs the Magna Carta
- INTERACTIVE SELF-CHECK QUIZ
- MAP Europe, 1160
- PRIMARY SOURCE Magna Carta
- VIDEO The Growth of European Kingdoms

LESSON 3

The Growth of European Kingdoms

ESSENTIAL QUESTIONS

- *How can changes to political systems impact economic activities?*
- *How is society influenced by changes in political and economic systems?*

It Matters Because

The domination of society by the nobility reached its high point between 1000 and 1300—the High Middle Ages. At the same time, monarchs began extending their power. This frequently led to conflict between kings and nobles.

Reading HELPDESK

Academic Vocabulary

- **challenge**
- **document**

Content Vocabulary

- **common law**
- **Magna Carta**
- **Parliament**
- **estate**

TAKING NOTES:

Key Ideas and Details

Identifying As you read, use a table like the one below to identify important events during the High Middle Ages.

England	France	Holy Roman Empire

TEKS Texas Essential Knowledge and Skills

1C identify major causes and describe the major effects of the following important turning points in world history from 600 to 1450 the spread of Christianity, the decline of Rome and the formation of medieval Europe; the development of Islamic caliphates and their impact on Asia, Africa, and Europe; the Mongol invasions and their impact on Europe, China, India, and Southwest Asia

continued on p. 239

England in the High Middle Ages

GUIDING QUESTION *How did society and the legal system in England evolve after 1066?*

Angles and Saxons, Germanic peoples from northern Europe, had invaded England early in the fifth century. King Alfred the Great had united various kingdoms in the late ninth century, and since then, England had been ruled by Anglo-Saxon kings.

The Norman Conquest

On October 14, 1066, an army of heavily armed knights under William of Normandy landed on the coast of England and soundly defeated King Harold and his foot soldiers at the Battle of Hastings. William was then crowned king of England. Norman knights received parcels of land, which they held as fiefs, from the king. All nobles swore an oath of loyalty to William as sole ruler of England.

The Norman ruling class spoke French, but the marriage of the Normans with the Anglo-Saxon nobility gradually merged Anglo-Saxon and French into a new English language. The Normans also took over existing Anglo-Saxon institutions, like the office of sheriff. William took a census known as the Domesday Book, the first census taken in Europe since Roman times and included people, manors, and farm animals. William also developed more fully the system of taxation and royal courts begun by earlier Anglo-Saxon kings.

Henry II and the Church

The power of the English monarchy was enlarged during the reign of Henry II, from 1154 to 1189. Henry increased the number of criminal cases tried in the king's court and also devised means for taking property

BIOGRAPHY

William of Normandy (1028–1087)

Known to history as "the Conqueror," William, Duke of Normandy, proved adept at seizing political opportunities. After the death of England's king Edward the Confessor in 1066, Harold the Saxon took the English throne. Claiming Edward had designated him to be England's next king, William and his Norman troops invaded England. According to the *Anglo-Saxon Chronicle*, "William came upon [Harold] by surprise before his people were marshaled. Nevertheless the king fought very hard against him with those men who wanted to support him, and there was a great slaughter on either side. . . . And the French had possession of the place of slaughter, just as God granted them . . ."

▶ CRITICAL THINKING

Analyzing What does William's seizure of the English throne show about the transfer of royal power in the Middle Ages?

common law a uniform system of law that developed in England based on court decisions and on customs and usage rather than on written law codes; replaced law codes that varied from place to place

challenge a summons that is often stimulating, inciting, or threatening

cases from local courts and moving them to the royal courts. By expanding the power of the royal courts, Henry expanded the king's overall power. In addition, because the royal courts were now found throughout England, a body of **common law**—law that was common to the whole kingdom—was created and began to replace law codes that varied from place to place.

Henry was less successful at imposing royal control over the Church. He claimed the right to punish clergymen in royal courts. Thomas à Becket, archbishop of Canterbury and the highest-ranking English cleric, claimed that only Roman Catholic Church courts could try clerics. An angry king publicly expressed the desire to be rid of Becket: "Who will free me from this turbulent priest?" Four knights took the **challenge**, went to Canterbury, and murdered the archbishop in the cathedral. Faced with public outrage, Henry backed down in his struggle with the Church.

The Magna Carta

Many English nobles resented the ongoing growth of the king's power and rebelled during the reign of King John. At Runnymede in 1215, John was forced by the nobles to put his seal on a **document** called the **Magna Carta**, or the Great Charter. This document gave written recognition to the feudal custom that the relationship between king and vassals was based on mutual rights and obligations. The ideas contained in the Magna Carta continue to impact governments in the present day. Politically, it gives strength to the idea that the power of a government is limited, not absolute. Legally, the Magna Carta limits the king's power to punish people outside the rule of law. Punishments for crimes cannot be random and must be based on laws.

In the thirteenth century, during the reign of Edward I, an important institution in the development of representative government (one of the basic institutions of modern democratic governments)—the **Parliament**—also emerged. It was composed of two knights from every county, two people from every town, and all the nobles and bishops throughout England. Eventually, nobles and church lords formed the House of Lords; knights and townspeople, the House of Commons. The Parliaments of Edward I granted taxes, discussed politics, and passed laws.

✓ READING PROGRESS CHECK

Understanding Why was 1066 a turning point in European history?

France in the High Middle Ages

GUIDING QUESTION *Why was the reign of King Philip II Augustus a turning point in the French monarchy?*

In 843 the Carolingian Empire was divided into three sections. The western section formed the core of the kingdom of France. In 987 after the last Carolingian king died, the west Frankish nobles made Hugh Capet their king, establishing the Capetian (kuh • PEE • shuhn) dynasty of French kings. Although called kings, the Capetians had little real power, controlling only the area around Paris. Many of the great dukes of France were more powerful than their king.

The reign of Philip II Augustus, who reigned from 1180 to 1223, was a turning point in the French monarchy, expanding its income and power. Philip fought wars against the English to take control of the French territories of Normandy, Maine, Anjou, and Aquitaine. Philip's successors continued to add lands to the royal domain.

Much of the thirteenth century was dominated by the reign of Louis IX. Deeply religious, he was later made a saint by the Catholic Church. Louis was known for trying to bring justice to his people by hearing their complaints in person. Philip IV, called Philip the Fair, ruled from 1285 to 1314. He made the monarchy stronger by expanding the royal bureaucracy. Indeed, by 1300, France was the largest and best-governed monarchy in Europe. Philip IV also created a French parliament by meeting with members of the three **estates**, or orders—the clergy (First Estate), the nobles (Second Estate), and the townspeople and peasants (Third Estate). The meeting, held in 1302, began the Estates-General, the first French parliament.

READING PROGRESS CHECK

Questioning Why was the reign of Philip II Augustus important to the growth of the French monarchy?

(continued from p. 237)

TEKS **Texas Essential Knowledge and Skills**

4D explain the political, economic, and social impact of Islam on Europe, Asia, and Africa

4E describe the interactions among Muslim, Christian, and Jewish societies in Europe, Asia, and North Africa

4K summarize the changes resulting from the Mongol invasions of Russia, China, and the Islamic world

20B identify the impact of political and legal ideas contained in the following documents: Hammurabi's Code, the Jewish Ten Commandments, Justinian's Code of Laws, Magna Carta, the English Bill of Rights, the Declaration of Independence, the U.S. Constitution, and the Declaration of the Rights of Man and of the Citizen

The Holy Roman Empire

GUIDING QUESTION *Why did the lands of Germany and Italy not become united during the Middle Ages?*

In the tenth century, the powerful dukes of the Saxons became kings of the eastern Frankish kingdom, which came to be known as Germany. The best-known Saxon king of Germany was Otto I. Otto was a patron of German culture and brought the Church under his control. In return for protecting the pope, Otto I was crowned emperor of the Romans in 962. The title had not been used since the time of Charlemagne. Otto's creation of a new Roman Empire in the hands of the Germans had long-range consequences for Europe.

As leaders of a new Roman Empire, the German kings attempted to rule both German and Italian lands. Two of these kings, Frederick I and Frederick II, instead of building a strong German kingdom, tried to create a new kind of empire. Frederick I planned to get his chief revenues from Italy. He considered Italy the center of a "holy empire," as he called it—hence the name Holy Roman Empire.

Frederick's attempt to conquer northern Italy led to severe problems. The pope opposed him, fearing that he wanted to include Rome and the Papal States as part of his empire. The cities of northern Italy, which had become used to their freedom, were also unwilling to become his subjects. An alliance of these northern Italian cities and the pope defeated the forces of Frederick I in 1176.

The struggle between popes and German emperors had dire consequences for the Holy Roman Empire. By spending their time fighting in Italy, the emperors left Germany in the hands of powerful German lords. These nobles ignored the emperor and created their own independent kingdoms. This made the German monarchy weak and incapable of main-taining a strong monarchical state.

In the end, the German Holy Roman Emperor had no real power over either the German states or the Italian states. Unlike France and England, neither Germany nor Italy created a national monarchy in the Middle Ages. Both Germany and Italy consisted of many small independent states and territories.

READING PROGRESS CHECK

Making Connections What is the origin of the term Holy Roman Empire?

document an original or official paper that gives proof of or support to

Magna Carta the "Great Charter" of rights, which King John was forced to sign by the English nobles at Runnymede in 1215

Parliament in thirteenth-century England, the representative government that emerged; it was composed of two knights from every county, two people from every town, and all the nobles and bishops throughout England

estate a social or political class

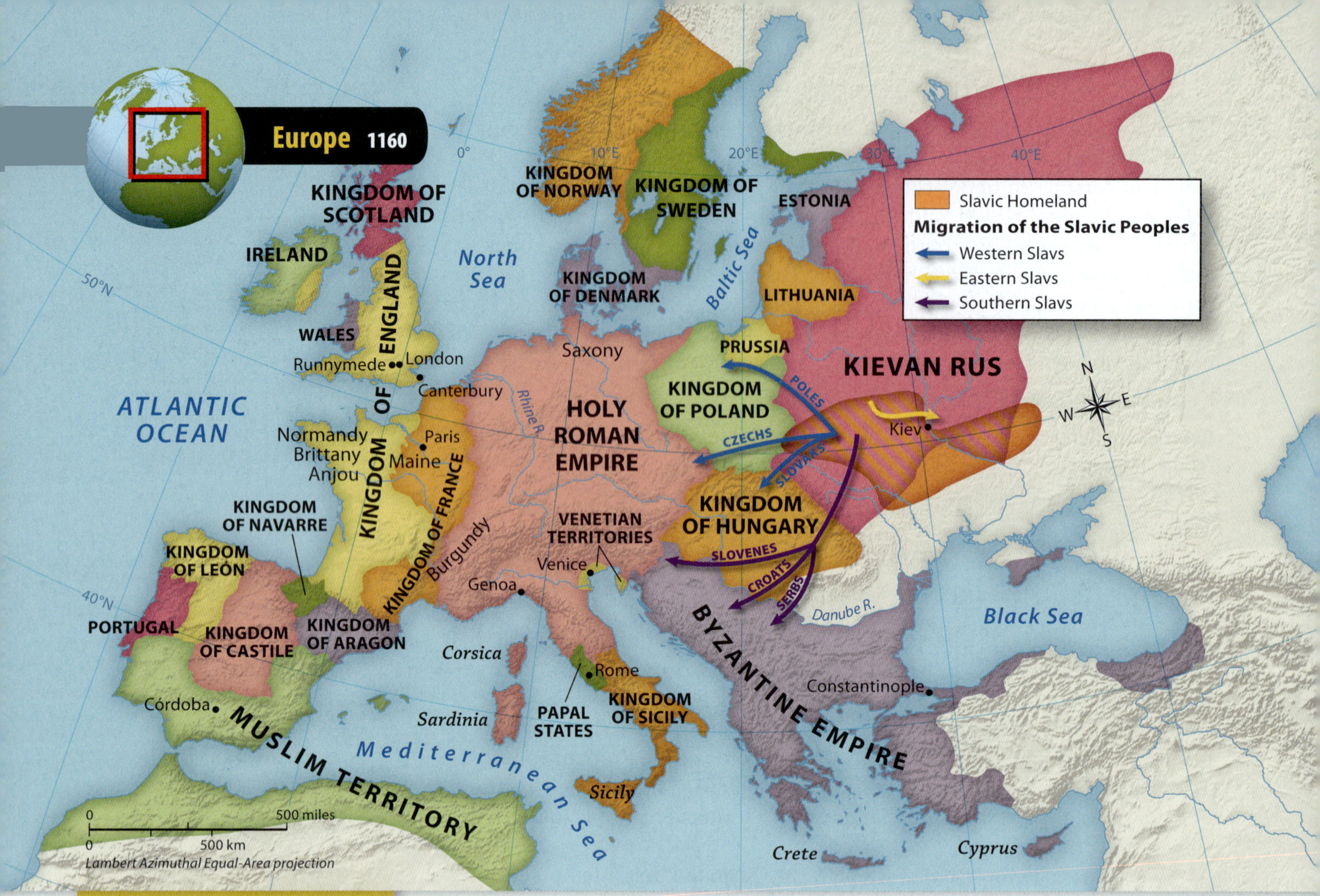

GEOGRAPHY CONNECTION

The Slavic people migrated into Central and Eastern Europe.

1. **THE WORLD IN SPATIAL TERMS** *In what country is most of the Slavic homeland located?*
2. **HUMAN SYSTEMS** *What are some possible reasons for the migration of the Slavic peoples?*

Spain and the Umayyad Caliphate

GUIDING QUESTION *What was the impact of Muslim rule on Europe?*

After its conquest by the Umayyad Caliphate in 725, most of Spain had become a Muslim province called Al-Andalus. Muslim rule over much of Spain would last for centuries. Consequently, the Islamic caliphates had an impact on the social, cultural, and political development of this part of Europe.

Non-Muslim groups in the caliphate, which included Christians and Jews, were allowed to continue practicing their religions. Additionally, they had their own courts and could hold minor positions in government. However, as elsewhere in the caliphate, Christians and Jews were ruled under the concept of *dhimmitude*. This meant they were subject to a special tax and other regulations meant to remind them that they lived under Muslim rule. As a consequence many people, especially in the southern part of Spain, converted to Islam.

Islamic rule also significantly impacted Spanish culture. For example, modern-day Andalusia in the southernmost region of Spain gets its name from the Islamic term "Al-Andalus." Similarly, although it has been believed that the Spanish language derives solely from Latin, Arabic influence can be found in various words such as *algebra* or *azúcar*—meaning sugar. Most recognizable, however, would be Islam's architectural influence, notably the palace of Seville. Slender columns, cupolas, and open spaces characterized Moorish architecture.

Politically, the majority of Spain was under the rule of the caliphate or the Emir (Duke) of Córdoba for centuries. However, pockets of Christian resistance remained, particularly in the northern regions of the Iberian Peninsula. Historians count the *Reconquista*—or the Christian re-conquest of Spain—as beginning as early as 718 A.D. with a victory of Christian forces over the forces of the Umayyad Caliphate. By 929 A.D., Spain had divided into a collection of Christian kingdoms in the north and Muslim emirates in the south. The *Reconquista* would continue for another 500 years.

◀ Brothers Cyril and Methodius devising the Cyrillic alphabet.

✓ READING PROGRESS CHECK

Drawing Conclusions What was the political impact of Islam on medieval Spain?

Central and Eastern Europe

GUIDING QUESTION ***Which Slavic peoples formed new kingdoms in eastern and central Europe?***

The Slavic peoples were originally a single people in central Europe. Gradually, they divided into three major groups: the western, southern, and eastern Slavs.

Slavic Europe

The western Slavs eventually formed the Polish and Bohemian kingdoms. German monks had converted both the Czechs in Bohemia and the Slavs in Poland to Christianity by the tenth century. The non-Slavic kingdom of Hungary was also converted. The Poles, Czechs, and Hungarians (Magyars) all accepted Western Christianity and became part of the Roman Catholic Church and its Latin culture.

The eastern Slavic peoples of Moravia were converted to Orthodox Christianity by two Byzantine missionary brothers, Cyril and Methodius, who began their activities in 863. The Slavic peoples had no written language. Cyril developed the Cyrillic alphabet so that he could create a Christian Bible and liturgy in the Slavic language.

The southern Slavic peoples included the Croats, the Serbs, and the Bulgarians. Most of them embraced Eastern Orthodoxy, although the Croats came to accept the Roman Catholic Church. The acceptance of Eastern Orthodoxy by many southern and eastern Slavic peoples meant that their cultural life was linked to the Byzantine state.

Kievan Rus and Mongol Rule

Eastern Slavic peoples had also settled in present-day Ukraine and Russia. There, in the late eighth century, they encountered Swedish Vikings who moved into their lands in search of plunder and new trade routes. The native peoples were eventually dominated by the Vikings, whom they called "the Rus" (from which *Russia* is derived).

One Viking leader, Oleg, settled in Kiev (present-day Kyiv) at the beginning of the tenth century and created the Rus state known as the Principality of Kiev. Oleg also opened trade with the Byzantines, increasing the prosperity of the Rus. His successors extended their control over the eastern Slavs and expanded Kiev, until it included the territory between the Baltic and Black Seas and the Danube and Volga Rivers. By marrying Slavic wives, the Viking ruling class was gradually assimilated into the Slavic population.

The growth of the principality of Kiev attracted Byzantine missionaries. One Rus ruler, Vladimir, married the Byzantine emperor's sister and officially accepted Eastern Orthodox Christianity for himself and his people in 988. Orthodox Christianity became the religion of the state. By adopting Orthodox Christianity, Vladimir tied Russia politically and culturally to the Byzantine Empire.

Kievan Rus reached its high point in the first half of the eleventh century. This was largely due to the prosperous trade route between the Baltic and Black Seas. However, civil wars and new invasions brought an end to the first Russian state in 1169, fragmenting the region into a collection of minor states. This disunity, coupled with devastating cavalry tactics, allowed the Mongols to invade and conquer Russia in the thirteenth century.

The Mongolian invasion had a significant impact on Europe. The first effect was largely negative. The shock and brutality of the invasion resulted in a loss of population as Mongolians forces destroyed cities and refugees fled their advance. However, as time passed, the Mongolian invasions had some positive results. For instance, the Mongolians introduced several Eastern inventions, like gunpowder, to Europe. Trade, too, increased under Mongol rule. Finally, Mongolian rule led to an eventual unification of Russia. One subject Russian prince, Alexander Nevsky of Novgorod, defeated a German invading army in northwestern Russia in 1242. The leader of the western Mongol Empire rewarded Nevsky with the title of Grand Prince. His descendants became princes of Moscow and eventually leaders of all Russia.

✓ READING PROGRESS CHECK

Making Connections How was the Viking ruling class gradually assimilated into the Slavic population?

LESSON 3 REVIEW TEKS

Reviewing Vocabulary

1. ***Making Inferences*** What was the benefit of common law over local law codes? 1C

Using Your Notes

2. ***Identifying*** Use your notes to identify important events in England, France, and the Holy Roman Empire during the High Middle Ages. 1C

Answering the Guiding Questions

3. ***Making Generalizations*** How did society and the legal system in England evolve after 1066? 1C, 29F
4. ***Explaining*** Why was the reign of King Philip II Augustus a turning point in the French monarchy? 1C
5. ***Drawing Conclusions*** Why did the lands of Germany and Italy not become united during the Middle Ages? 1C
6. ***Identifying*** Which Slavic peoples formed new kingdoms in eastern and central Europe? 1C

Writing Activity

7. **ARGUMENT** Look at the structure of the English Parliament compared to the French Estates-General. Write an essay explaining which parliamentary system would be better at defending the interests of townspeople and peasants. 1C

SKILLBUILDER

TEKS 15B

Understanding Geographic Distributions and Patterns: Charts

Why Learn the Skill?

There is much more to geography than just studying a map. We can also learn a great deal about how geography relates to events, ideas, and people in history by analyzing and comparing data in graphic organizers such as charts. Analyzing and comparing information in charts can lead you to make conclusions about relationships among those events, ideas, and people.

Learning the Skill

There are times when the amount of information on a map can be overwhelming. Sometimes it needs to be broken down into small bits of information, and that is when a chart can come in handy. This can be applied to the concepts of geographic distribution and geographic patterns. Geographic distribution is how something is spread out over a particular area, and we see it illustrated in maps in many different ways, such as in how populations spread from one continent to another, the growth of trade in a region, and the distribution of world religions. Geographic patterns relate to how people, places, things, or events are grouped together or related to one another. When you look for and find a pattern, you are able to draw conclusions and make connections. Using charts is also a manageable way to take information about geographic distributions and patterns and compare them to another region or period in time.

Practicing the Skill

When studying a subject such as the Medieval Kingdoms of Europe, there is a lot of information to process. A great way to help break down, analyze, and compare this information is to put it in chart form. The following chart is a synopsis of information about the distribution of religions in Europe, covered in Lesson 3. Review the chart and then answer the questions.

Roman Catholic Church	Eastern Orthodox Church
France	Moravia
England	Serbs
Holy Roman Empire	Bulgarians
Polish Kingdom	Kievan Rus
Bohemian Kingdom	
Kingdom of Hungary	

1. By analyzing and comparing the distribution of kingdoms and people in the chart, what was the background of many of the people of the Eastern Orthodox Church?
2. Analyze and compare the pattern of peoples adopting the beliefs of the Roman Catholic Church shown in the chart. Why do you think it was also called the Western Catholic Church?

Applying the Skill

Geographic distributions and patterns are subjects that come up regularly when talking about current events. Using a national newspaper or news website, locate two charts that illustrate a geographic distribution or geographic patterns in a region. Look for information about population percentages, land ownership, border disputes, or patterns of settlement and analyze how the geographic distributions or patterns have affected the issue covered in the news. Compare the information in the two charts to analyze whether both charts relay the same information.

CHAPTER 10 Assessment

TEKS

Directions: On a separate sheet of paper, answer the questions below. Make sure you read carefully and answer all parts of the question.

Lesson Review

Lesson 1

1. ***Explaining*** How was the Carolingian Empire divided after Charlemagne's death?

2. ***Identifying*** Why were Vikings able to expand throughout Europe? **1C**

3. ***Identifying Cause and Effect*** How did the Vikings influence a new political and social order in Europe? What was the new order called? **4C**

4. ***Making Connections*** What was a vassal? How did it relate to feudalism? **4C**

5. ***Summarizing*** What was considered the chief virtue in a feudal society? How did one become a vassal?

6. ***Describing*** What was the feudal contract? What did this contract require? **4C**

7. ***Explaining*** Explain the joust and how it became popular during this time.

8. ***Explaining*** Explain the role of women during this time. What rights did they have? **24A**

Lesson 2

9. ***Summarizing*** What factors contributed to the huge increase in Europe's population during the High Middle Ages?

10. ***Contrasting*** How was the life of a serf different from the life of a free peasant? What were serfs' duties to their lords? What restrictions did the lord have in his treatment of the serfs? **4C**

11. ***Explaining*** How did serfs pay rents? What else were they required to pay for? **4C**

12. ***Summarizing*** How was trade revived in Europe in the 1000s and 1100s? **1C**

13. ***Identifying*** By 1100, what rights did townspeople have from local lords?

Lesson 3

14. ***Drawing Conclusions*** What did King William of Normandy accomplish during his reign? What effect did this have on the monarchy in England?

15. ***Summarizing*** What was Henry II's answer to dealing with the archbishop of Canterbury, Thomas a Becket, after Becket claimed that only Roman Catholic Church courts could try clerics? How did this affect Henry's struggle with the Church?

Need Extra Help?

If You've Missed Question	1	2	3	4	5	6	7	8	9	10	11	12	13	14	15
Go to page	228	228	229	229	230	230	231	231	232	233	233	234	235	237	238

16 ***Explaining*** How did Muslim rule affect language in Spain? **1C, 4D**

17 ***Explaining*** Why were the Mongols able to conquer Russian lands quickly? How did the Mongolian invasion impact Russia? **1C, 4K**

Exploring the Essential Questions

18 ***Analyzing*** With a partner, create a multimedia presentation describing the changes in the political system in Western Europe from the time of Charlemagne through the development of feudalism. **1C, 4C, 30C**

Critical Thinking

19 ***Identifying Central Issues*** Explain the impact of the political and legal ideas contained in the Magna Carta. **20B**

20 ***Interpreting*** How did the merging of the Normans with the Anglo-Saxons impact language, and what does that indicate about the culture of the blended society?

21 ***Identifying Cause and Effect*** Describe the quests of German kings Frederick I and Frederick II, and explain the impact on Germany as compared to England and France.

22 ***Making Inferences*** Explain how religious conversion brought life to a written Slavic language. What inferences can you make about literacy and the spread of religious beliefs?

23 ***Identifying Cause and Effect*** How did the Umayyad Caliphate impact Spain culturally? What was the political impact of the Umayyad conquest of Spain? **1C, 4D**

24 ***Identifying Central Issues*** How did the presence of Islamic caliphates impact non-Muslim groups, such as Christians and Jews? **4E**

25 ***Drawing Conclusions*** What was the Reconquista, and how did it affect the political status of Spain in respect to Islamic presence? **1C, 4D, 4E**

Social Studies Skills

26 ***Identifying Cause and Effect*** What helped support population growth during the High Middle Ages?

27 ***Identifying Continuity and Change*** What influence did French kings have after the last Carolingian king died, and how did it change over time? Be sure to name what kings brought about the changes.

28 ***Summarizing*** Write a paragraph describing the advances in agriculture made between 1000 and 1300.

29 ***Creating Presentations*** Work with a partner to create a multimedia presentation showing three or more photographs or images that reflect medieval Europe culture, economy, or political structure. Explain the significance of the images in the context of medieval society.

Need Extra Help?

If You've Missed Question	16	17	18	19	20	21	22	23	24	25	26	27	28	29
Go to page	240	243	228	238	237	239	241	240	240	241	232	238	232	233

DBQ Analyzing Primary Sources

Use the document to answer the following questions.

A chivalrous knight pledged loyalty and service to the church, his lord, women, and the weak. The knight was expected to observe church doctrine, to protect his lord, to deal with women honorably, and to use his military skill to protect the weak.

30 ***Identifying Perspectives*** What part of the pledge does the above image represent?

31 ***Hypothesizing*** Are there any modern equivalents of chivalry? Give some examples. 29F

Analyzing Visuals

Use the image of the artifact to answer the following question.

This image from an early thirteenth-century French manuscript, *"Miracles of Our Lady,"* shows a peasant, his plough, and his oxen.

32 ***Identifying*** What technological advance allowed for the use of faster draft animals to plow fields?

Extended Response Question

33 ***Expository*** Research and write about the important elements of the life of the two Byzantine missionary brothers, Cyril and Methodius. Include details of the lasting impact they had. Be sure to name your sources. 4A

Need Extra Help?

If You've Missed Question	30	31	32	33
Go to page	230	230	232	241

Civilizations of East Asia

220–1500

ESSENTIAL QUESTIONS

- *What qualities define power struggles and stable periods of rule?*
- *How can invasion change the lives of people in conquered lands?*

networks

There's More Online! about civilizations of East Asia.

CHAPTER 11

Lesson 1
China Reunified

Lesson 2
The Mongols and Chinese Culture

Lesson 3
Early Japan and Korea

Lesson 4
India and Southeast Asia

The Story Matters...

This period saw the appearance of classical civilizations in China and Japan. China was unified for the first time since the fall of the Han under the Sui, Tang, and Song dynasties. Empress Wu rose to power during the Tang dynasty and strengthened the civilian bureaucracy. During Japan's Heian period, major cultural, political, and social institutions evolved, such as the position of the emperor and the samurai class. In India, the traditional religions of Buddhism and Hinduism were challenged by factors such as the eastward expansion of Islam.

◄ Created with watercolor on paper, this portrait of Wu Zhao, who was an effective empress during the early Tang dynasty, conveys the sharp intelligence with which she rose to power.

PHOTO: Archives Charmet/Bridgman Art Library

CHAPTER 11

Place and Time: East Asia 200–1400

The final collapse of China's Han Empire brought centuries of disorder, which ended when the Sui dynasty briefly reunited China in 581. By contrast, the succeeding Tang dynasty, which took power in 618, ruled for nearly three centuries, expanding Chinese territory and leaving major legacies in trade, government, and culture. The Tang capital, Chang'an (modern Xi'an), was connected by a network of land and sea routes to the rest of Asia and the world beyond. Exotic luxury goods and everyday staples reached Chang'an by local market roads, long-distance highways, the caravan routes known as the Silk Road, and by ships via canals and the sea. Ideas also traveled along the trade routes, including those of Buddhism, which reached Tang China from India and Central Asia.

Step Into the Place

Read the quotes and look at the information presented on the map.

DBQ **Analyzing Historical Documents** How did foreign trade affect Chinese society during the Tang dynasty period?

PRIMARY SOURCE

"I should humbly like to let you know that while crossing the Indus I had lost a load of sacred texts. I now send you a list of those texts annexed to this letter. I request you to send them to me if you get the chance. I am sending some small objects as presents. Please accept them. The road is long and it is not possible to send much. Do not disdain it."

—Chinese Buddhist monk Xuanzang, from a letter to the Indian Buddhist Iñanāprabha, 654

PRIMARY SOURCE

"Ever since the Western horsemen began raising smut and dust,
Fur and fleece, rank and rancid, have filled Hsien and Lo.
Women [shown left] make themselves Western matrons by the study of
Western makeup; Entertainers present Western tunes, in their devotion to
Western music."

—Yüan Chen, from a poem, late eighth century

Step Into the Time

Drawing Conclusions
Research two events from the time line and draw conclusions about the influence of China during this period.

EAST ASIA

- **220** Final collapse of China's Han empire
- **581** Sui dynasty briefly reunites China
- **604** Prince Shōtoku Taishi introduces Confucianism to Japan

200 — 400 — 600

THE WORLD

- **c. 250** Classic Maya period begins in Mexico and Central America
- **c. 500** Mexican city of Teotihuacán reaches its height
- **c. 540** Gupta Empire comes to an end in India

networks
There's More Online!

- ☑ **MAP** Explore the interactive version of this map on Networks.
- ☑ **TIME LINE** Explore the interactive version of the time line on Networks.

Trade Routes 220–1300s

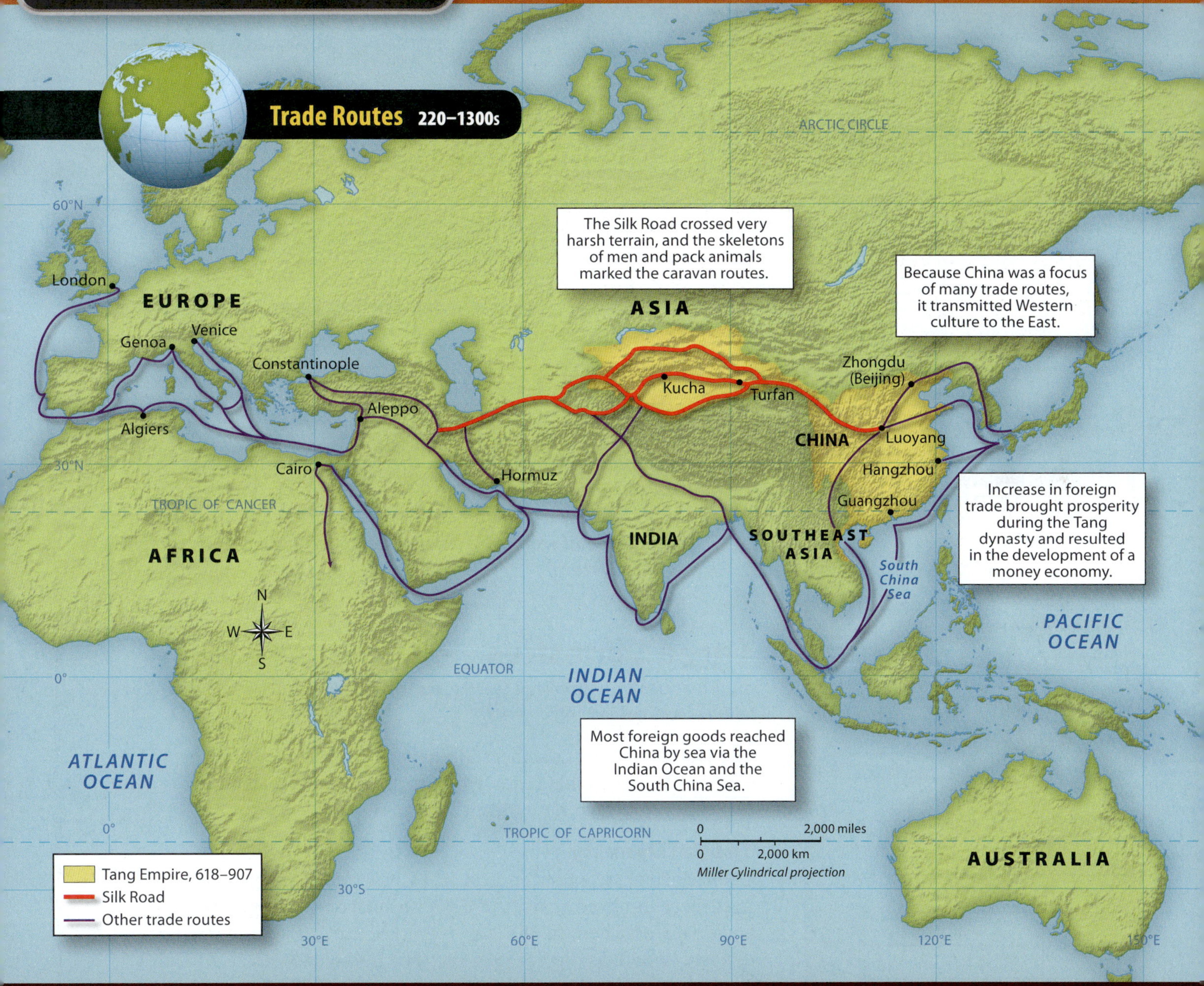

668 With Chinese support, Silla dynasty unifies Korea

762 Baghdad is founded as capital of Arab Empire

800 Charlemagne is crowned emperor by the pope in Rome

907 Tang dynasty collapses in China

960 Song dynasty is established

1066 Normans invade England

1099 First Crusade captures Jerusalem

1122 Emperor Henry V and Pope Calixtus II agree to Concordat of Worms

1206 Mongols become unified under Genghis Khan

1215 King John is forced to sign Magna Carta

c. 1275 Venetian traveler Marco Polo reaches court of Kublai Khan

1279 Kublai Khan completes conquest of China

800 — 1000 — 1200 — 1400

networks

There's More Online!

- BIOGRAPHY Marco Polo
- BIOGRAPHY Sui Yangdi
- BIOGRAPHY Wu Zhao
- IMAGE Hangzhou
- IMAGE Marco Polo Crossing Asia on the Silk Road
- INTERACTIVE SELF-CHECK QUIZ
- MAP Three Dynasties in China, 581–1279
- TIME LINE Dynasties of China
- VIDEO Marco Polo

LESSON 1
China Reunified

ESSENTIAL QUESTIONS
- *What qualities define power struggles and stable periods of rule?*
- *How can invasion change the lives of people in conquered lands?*

Reading HELPDESK

Academic Vocabulary
- **period**
- **complexity**

Content Vocabulary
- **scholar-gentry**
- **dowry**

TAKING NOTES:
Key Ideas and Details

Contrasting As you read, use a table like the one below to identify the characteristics of the Sui, Tang, and Song dynasties.

Sui	Tang	Song

TEKS Texas Essential Knowledge and Skills

1C identify major causes and describe the major effects of the following important turning points in world history from 600 to 1450 the spread of Christianity, the decline of Rome and the formation of medieval Europe; the development of Islamic caliphates and their impact on Asia, Africa, and Europe; the Mongol invasions and their impact on Europe, China, India, and Southwest Asia

continued on the next page

IT MATTERS BECAUSE

In 581 the Sui dynasty unified China for the first time in hundreds of years. Over the next several centuries, with only a brief period of disorder in the 900s, three dynasties brought progress and stability to China. During this period, China invented block printing and gunpowder, participated in increased foreign trade, and restored a merit-based civil service system.

Three Dynasties

GUIDING QUESTION *How did the Sui, Tang, and Song dynasties bring order to China between periods of chaos and instability?*

The Han dynasty is considered to have set the standard for the Chinese dynasties that followed. In fact, the Chinese word for someone who is Chinese means "a man of Han."

The Sui Dynasty

The Han dynasty ended in 220, and China fell into chaos. For the next three hundred years, the Chinese suffered through disorder and civil war. Then, in 581, a new empire was set up under a dynasty known as the Sui (SWAY). The Sui dynasty (581–618) did not last long, but it unified China once again under the authority of the emperor.

Sui Yangdi, the second emperor of the dynasty, completed the Grand Canal, built to link the two great rivers of China, the Huang He (Yellow River) and the Chang Jiang (Yangtze River). The new canal linked north and south, making it easier to ship rice from the south to the north.

Sui Yangdi was a cruel ruler. He used forced labor to build the Grand Canal, which he used to keep an eye on his empire. This practice, together with high taxes, his extravagant and luxurious lifestyle, and military failures, caused a rebellion. The emperor was murdered, and his dynasty came to an end.

The Tang Dynasty

A new dynasty, the Tang (TAHNG), soon emerged. It would last for nearly three hundred years, from 618 until 907. The early Tang rulers created a more stable economy by giving land to the peasants and breaking up the large estates to reduce the power of their owners. They also restored the civil service examination to serve as the chief method of recruiting officials for the civilian bureaucracy.

Young men prepared to take the civil service examination by memorizing all the Confucian classics. They had little free time. Even after many years of education, only about one in five students managed to pass the exam and receive a position in the civil service.

In working hard to restore the power of China in East Asia, the Tang rulers had a major impact on Eastern Asia. They brought peace to northwestern China and expanded China's control into the area north of the Himalaya—known as Tibet. China claimed to be the greatest power in East Asia. Neighboring states, including Korea, offered tribute to China. The Chinese imperial court also set up diplomatic relations with the states of Southeast Asia. The Tang dynasty also oversaw economic developments, such as increased trade with the West and Japan.

Like the Han, however, the Tang sowed the seeds of their own destruction. Tang rulers were unable to prevent plotting and government corruption. One emperor was especially unfortunate. Emperor Tang Xuanzong (SHWAHN • DZUNG) is remembered for his devotion to a commoner's daughter, Yang Guifei. To entertain her, he kept hundreds of dancers and musicians at court.

Finally, the emperor's favorite general led a bloody revolt. The army demanded that someone be held accountable for the war and strife in the country. For this reason, the emperor invited his true love to hang herself from a nearby tree.

(continued from p. 250)

TEKS **Texas Essential Knowledge and Skills**

4H summarize the major political, economic, and cultural developments in Tang and Song China and their impact on Eastern Asia

4J analyze how the Silk Road and the African gold-salt trade facilitated the spread of ideas and trade

23A describe the historical origins, central ideas, and spread of major religious and philosophical traditions, including Buddhism, Christianity, Confucianism, Hinduism, Islam, Judaism, Sikhism, and the development of monotheism

24A describe the changing roles of women, children, and families during major eras of world history

25A summarize the fundamental ideas and institutions of Eastern civilizations that originated in China and India

continued on the next page

GEOGRAPHY CONNECTION

China unified under the Sui Dynasty.

1. **THE WORLD IN SPATIAL TERMS** *Which dynasty covered the least amount of territory?*
2. **ENVIRONMENT AND SOCIETY** *Why do you think the Silk Road avoided the Taklimakan desert?*

▶ A view of Hangzhou, China, from Marco Polo's *Livres des Merveilles*

▶ CRITICAL THINKING

Analyzing Visuals Describe the economic activity taking place at Hangzhou.

(continued from p. 251)

TEKS **Texas Essential Knowledge and Skills**

27A identify the origin and diffusion of major ideas in mathematics, science, and technology that occurred in river valley civilizations, classical Greece and Rome, classical India, and the Islamic caliphates between 700 and 1200 and in China from the Tang to Ming dynasties

During the eighth century, the Tang dynasty weakened and became prey to rebellions. Tang rulers hired Uighurs (WEE • gurz), a northern tribal group of Turkic-speaking people, to fight for them. Continued unrest, however, led to the collapse of Tang rule in 907.

The Song Dynasty

In 960 a new dynasty known as the Song (SUNG) rose to power. The Song ruled during a period of prosperity and cultural achievement, from 960 to 1279. From the start, political developments in Song China included trouble northern neighbors. These groups crossed into northern China and occupied large parts of Chinese territory. Because of this threat, Song rulers were forced to move the imperial court south to Hangzhou (HAHNG • JOH). The Song also lost control over Tibet.

The Song dynasty could never overcome the challenge from the north. During the 1200s, the Mongols—a nomadic people from the Gobi—carried out wars of conquest and built a vast empire. Within 70 years, the relative weakness of the Song dynasty allowed the Mongols to gain control of China. As we shall see, the Mongols overthrew the Song and created a new Mongol dynasty in China.

The impact of the Song dynasty on Eastern Asia was profound. Social progress was matched by economic progress, including the first use of paper currency and a large increase in farm production, leading to an increase in population. Its astronomers developed new instruments, while its inventors applied new technologies to warfare, navigation, and printing.

SKILLS PRACTICE

Create a summary to deliver to the class that compares and contrasts the Sui, Tang, and Song dynasties. Use connecting words to combine ideas in your summary. Use words such as *also* and *like* to connect similar ideas. Connect contrasting ideas with words such as *but* and *although*. When describing events, connect your ideas with words such as *first* and *next* to show the order in which they occurred.

✓ READING PROGRESS CHECK

Summarizing What were the reasons for the collapse of the three dynasties?

Government and the Economy

GUIDING QUESTION ***How did the Chinese government and economy develop and change over the time period of the three dynasties?***

The era of the Sui, Tang, and Song dynasties lasted nearly 700 years. During that **period**, a mature political system based on principles first put into practice during the Qin and Han dynasties gradually emerged in China. The Tang and Song dynasties restored the merit-based selection of civil servants. This civil service examination, an important institution of Eastern civilization,

period an interval of time

gave China a government staffed by a literate bureaucracy. Beyond the capital, government was based on provinces, districts, and villages. Confucian ideals were still the cement that held the system together.

During the long period between the Sui and Song dynasties, the Chinese economy grew in size and **complexity**. Agriculture flourished, and manufacturing and trade grew dramatically.

complexity the state of being complex or of having many intricate parts

China was still primarily a farming society. In the long period of civil war, aristocratic families had taken control of most of the land, and the majority of peasants had become serfs or slaves. The Song government, however, worked to weaken the power of the large landholders and help poor peasants obtain their own land. These changes were major economic developments. The reform efforts and improved farming techniques led to an abundance of food.

In Chinese cities, technological developments added new products and stimulated trade. For example, during the Tang dynasty, the Chinese began to make steel for swords by mixing cast iron and wrought iron in a blast furnace. The introduction of cotton made it possible to make new kinds of clothes.

Chinese inventors of this era developed major ideas in science. The invention of gunpowder occurred during the Tang dynasty. It was used to make explosives and a primitive flamethrower called a fire-lance. The fire-lance could spit out a mixture of flame and projectiles that could travel 40 yards (36.6 m).

The Chinese also made important advancements in mathematics. Early Chinese developed a sophisticated number system. Perhaps the most major idea in mathematics from China occuring in the 1200s. Chinese inventors of this era developed major ideas in science.

The changing nature of trade was also a major economic development. State officials had controlled most long-distance trade. By the time of the Song, private merchants were active in. Guilds began to appear, along with a new money economy, which is an economic system based on money rather than barter. The use of paper money began in the 700s and 800s. With the increased flow of paper money, banking began to develop.

Long-distance trade by land and by sea expanded. Trade had declined between the 300s and 500s as a result of the collapse of the Han dynasty and the Roman Empire. The revival of trade under the Tang dynasty was a major economic development. The unification of much of Southwest Asia under the Arabs increased trade, as well.

▼ This Tang dynasty statue shows a foreign trader riding a camel on the Silk Road.

The Silk Road was renewed and thrived as caravans carried goods between China and Southwest Asia and South Asia. The Silk Road facilitated trade by providing a reliable and safe land route for merchants and caravans to traverse long distances. The Silk Road was more than a trading route, however. It also facilitated the spread of ideas. Merchants carried their religions with them along the route, and contributed to the exchange of ideas in mathematics and technology. Three religions—Buddhism, Christianity, and Islam—spread along the Silk Road. Technical knowledge from China—including the secrets of printing, drilling wells, and making iron, gunpowder, paper, and silk—reached the West along the Silk Road.

Trade with regions near China, such as Japan and Korea, also increased during the Tang and Song dynasties. As a result of trade, Changan, with a population of about two million, became the wealthiest city in the world. Changan was filled with temples and palace, and its markets were filled with goods from all over Europe, Africa, and Asia.

✓ PROGRESS CHECK

Making Connections What principles from former dynasties did the Sui, Tang, and Song use to shape the government?

Chinese Society

GUIDING QUESTION *How did Chinese society evolve during the period of the three dynasties?*

Economic developments such as increased trade had an impact on Chinese society. For wealthier city dwellers, the Tang and Song eras were an age of prosperity. There was probably no better example than the Song capital of Hangzhou. In the late thirteenth century, the Italian merchant Marco Polo described the city to European readers as one of the largest and wealthiest cities on Earth. "So many pleasures may be found," he said, "that one fancies himself to be in Paradise."

For rich Chinese during this period, life offered many pleasures. There were new forms of entertainment, such as playing cards and chess, which was brought from India. The paddlewheel boat and horseback riding, which was made possible by the introduction of the stirrup, made travel easier. The invention of block printing in the eighth century provided new ways to communicate.

The vast majority of the Chinese people still lived off the land in villages. Changes were taking place in the countryside, however. Before, there had been a great gulf between wealthy landowners and poor peasants. A more complex mixture of landowners, free peasants, sharecroppers, and landless laborers now emerged.

scholar-gentry in China, a group of people who controlled much of the land and produced most of the candidates for civil service

Most significant was the rise of the landed gentry. This group controlled much of the land and at the same time produced most of the candidates for the civil service. The **scholar-gentry**, as this class was known, replaced the old landed aristocracy as the political and economic elite of Chinese society.

Few Chinese women had any power. An exception was Wu Zhao (WOO JOW), known as Empress Wu. The concubine of the second Tang emperor, she then became empress of China and ruled for half a century.

dowry a gift of money or property paid at the time of marriage, either by the bride's parents to her husband or, in Islamic societies, by a husband to his wife

As in other parts of the world, female children were considered less desirable than male children. When a girl married, her role was to become part of her husband's family. In addition, a girl's parents were expected to provide a **dowry**—money, goods, or property—to her husband when she married. Poor families often sold their daughters to wealthy villagers. Men held the dominant roles in families.

✓ READING PROGRESS CHECK

Identifying Which group replaced the landed aristocracy as the elite in Chinese society? Why?

LESSON 1 REVIEW TEKS

Reviewing Vocabulary

1. ***Making Inferences*** Why were the landed gentry that replaced the old aristocracy known as scholar-gentry?
2. ***Identifying*** How did the dowry contribute to female children being less desirable than male children? 24A

Using Your Notes

3. ***Contrasting*** Use your notes to identify the characteristics of the Sui, Tang, and Song dynasties. 1C, 4H, 25A

Answering the Guiding Questions

4. ***Drawing Conclusions*** How did the Sui, Tang, and Song dynasties bring order to China between periods of chaos and instability? 4H, 25A
5. ***Evaluating*** How did the Chinese government and economy develop and change over the time period of the three dynasties? 4H, 25A
6. ***Summarizing*** How did Chinese society evolve during the period of the three dynasties? 4H, 23A

Writing Activity

7. **ARGUMENT** Do you think an exam system is a good way to identify potential candidates for the civil service? Explain your answer. 4H, 25A

networks

There's More Online!

- ☑ BIOGRAPHY Genghis Khan
- ☑ BIOGRAPHY Kublai Khan
- ☑ IMAGE Genghis Khan Enthroned
- ☑ IMAGE Landscape Painting
- ☑ IMAGE Life in Genghis Khan's Army
- ☑ IMAGE Printing Technology
- ☑ INTERACTIVE SELF-CHECK QUIZ
- ☑ MAP Mongol Empire, 1294
- ☑ PRIMARY SOURCE Du Fu
- ☑ PRIMARY SOURCE Li Bo
- ☑ VIDEO Genghis Khan

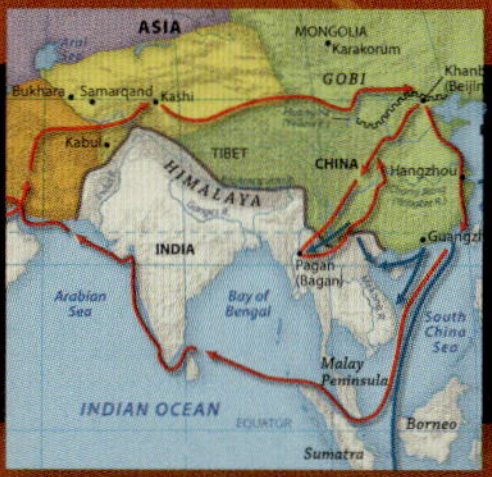

LESSON 2

The Mongols and Chinese Culture

ESSENTIAL QUESTIONS

- *What qualities define power struggles and stable periods of rule?*
- *How can invasion change the lives of people in conquered lands?*

Reading **HELP**DESK

Academic Vocabulary

- **acquired**
- **available**
- **vision**

Content Vocabulary

- **khanate**
- **neo-Confucianism**
- **porcelain**

TAKING NOTES:

Key Ideas and Details

Categorizing As you read, create a time line like the one below that illustrates events in the Mongols' rise to power.

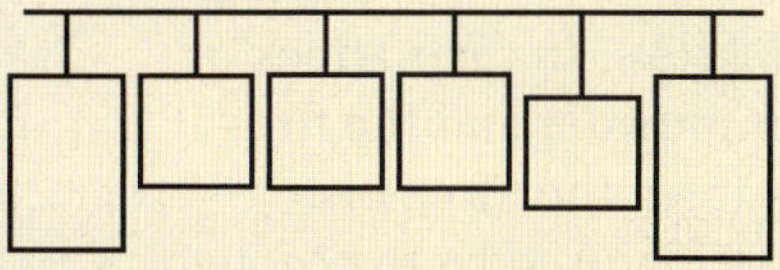

TEKS Texas Essential Knowledge and Skills

1C identify major causes and describe the major effects of the following important turning points in world history from 600 to 1450 the spread of Christianity, the decline of Rome and the formation of medieval Europe; the development of Islamic caliphates and their impact on Asia, Africa, and Europe; the Mongol invasions and their impact on Europe, China, India, and Southwest Asia

continued on the next page

IT MATTERS BECAUSE

The Mongols were a pastoral people who swept out of the Gobi in the early thirteenth century to seize control over much of the known world. Their empire included creating a new Chinese dynasty. At the time of the Mongol invasion, art and literature in China were in the middle of a golden age.

The Mongols

GUIDING QUESTIONS *How did the Mongols create the world's largest land empire? What effect did the Mongol invasion of the Arab Empire have on Islamic civilization?*

The formation of the Mongol Empire was a turning point in world history. Due largely to their military prowess, the Mongols rose to power in Asia with stunning speed. The Mongols were a pastoral people from the region of modern-day Mongolia who were organized loosely into clans. Temüjin (TEHM • yuh • juhn), born during the 1160s, gradually unified the Mongols. In 1206, he was elected Genghis Khan—strong ruler—at a massive meeting somewhere in the Gobi. From that time on, he devoted himself to conquest.

The army that Genghis Khan unleashed on the world was not unusually large; it totaled fewer than 130,000 in 1227. It was the Mongols' military tactics, which were devastatingly effective, that allowed them to invade and conquer so many foreign lands. Mongol armies were almost entirely made up of archers mounted on horseback. Their ability to move quickly around a battlefield set them apart from their enemies.

The impact of the Mongolian invasions was felt across most of Asia and much of Europe where their conquests resulted in the largest land empire in history. To rule the new Mongol Empire, Genghis Khan set up a capital city at Karakorum. Mongol armies traveled both to the west and to the east. Some went as far as central Europe.

After the death of Genghis Khan in 1227, the empire began to change. Following Mongol custom, upon the death of the ruling

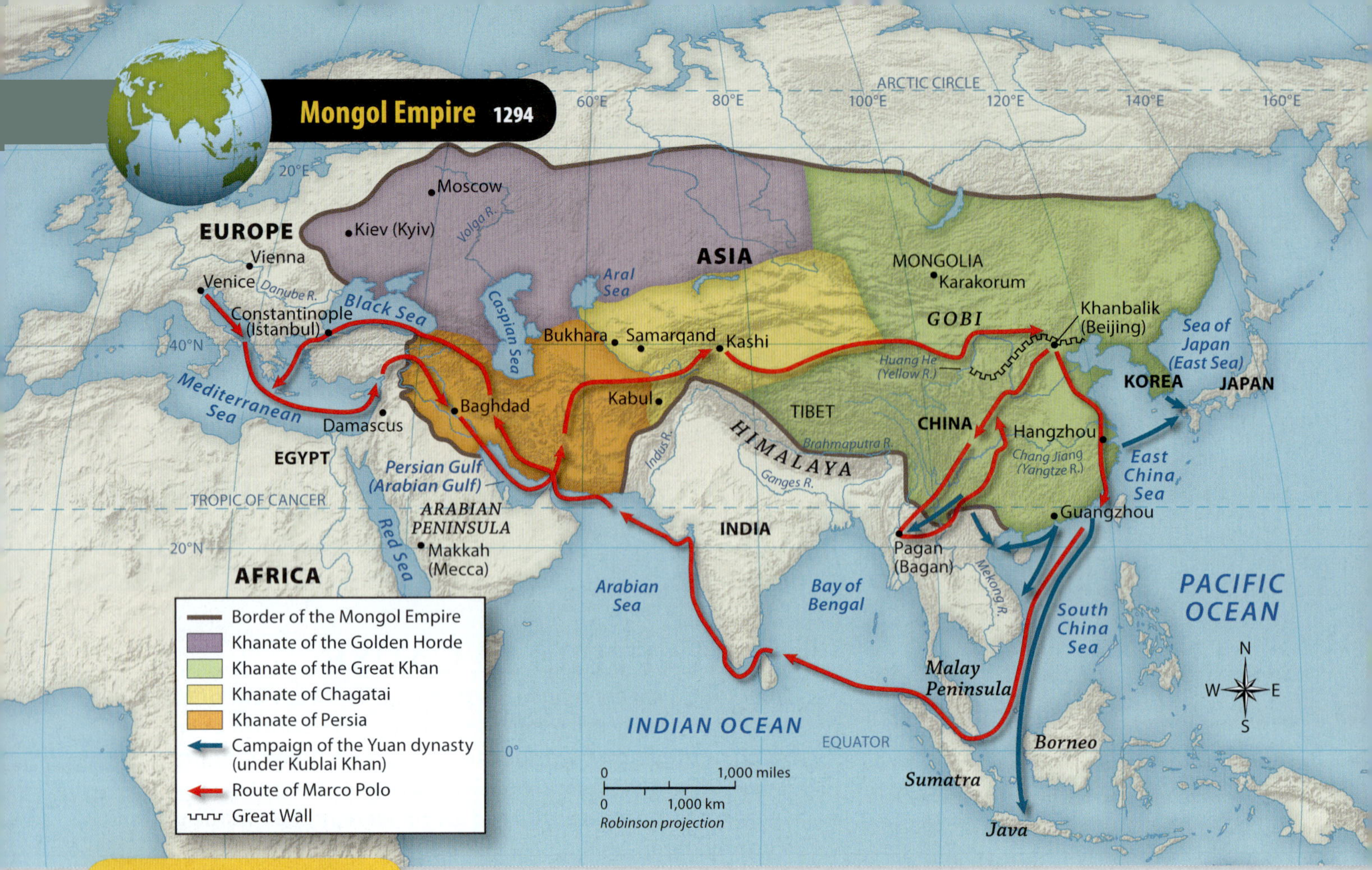

GEOGRAPHY CONNECTION

The Mongol Empire stretched from East Asia into Europe.

1. **THE WORLD IN SPATIAL TERMS** *Which Khanate was located partially in Europe?*
2. **ENVIRONMENT AND SOCIETY** *What prevented Kublai Khan from taking control of Japan?*

(continued from p. 255)

TEKS **Texas Essential Knowledge and Skills**

4H summarize the major political, economic, and cultural developments in Tang and Song China and their impact on Eastern Asia

4K summarize the changes resulting from the Mongol invasions of Russia, China, and the Islamic world

23A describe the historical origins, central ideas, and spread of major religious and philosophical traditions, including Buddhism, Christianity, Confucianism, Hinduism, Islam, Judaism, Sikhism, and the development of monotheism

continued on the next page

khan, his heirs divided the territory. The once-united empire of Genghis Khan was split into several separate territories called **khanates**, each under the rule of one of his sons. It may be that only the death of Genghis Khan kept the Mongols from attacking western Europe.

In 1231 the Mongols attacked Persia and defeated the Abbasids at Baghdad in 1258. The weakness of the Abbasid Caliphate allowed the Mongols to conquer much of Southwest Asia. With Baghdad conquered, the caliphate lost any real authority and the center of Islamic power shifted to the Mamluk dynasty based in Cairo, Egypt. The caliph would exist only as a figurehead until the early 1500s. Mongol invasions also paved the way for the future Islamic Ottoman, Safavid, and Mogul dynasties.

Mongol forces attacked the Song dynasty in the 1260s. In their attack on the Chinese, the Mongols encountered the use of gunpowder and the fire-lance. These inventions came too late to save China from the Mongols, however. By the early fourteenth century, foreigners employed by the Mongol rulers of China had introduced the use of gun-powder and firearms into Europe. These technologies had a major impact on Europe.

In 1279 one of Genghis Khan's grandsons, named Kublai Khan (KOO • bluh KAHN), completed the conquest of the Song and set up a new Chinese dynasty, the Yuan (YWAHN). The effects of the Mongol invasion of China were seen far and wide. Kublai Khan, who ruled China until his death in 1294, established his capital at Khanbalik—the city of the Khan—later known by the Chinese name Beijing.

Under the leadership of the talented Kublai Khan, the Yuan, or Mongol, dynasty continued to expand the empire. Mongol armies advanced into

Vietnam, and Mongol fleets were launched against Java and Sumatra and twice against the islands of Japan. Only parts of Vietnam were conquered, however, and then only for a while. The other campaigns failed. On one occasion, a massive storm destroyed the Mongol fleet that attacked Japan, killing thousands.

The Mongols had more success in ruling China. Mongol rulers adapted to the Chinese political system and made use of Chinese bureaucrats. Culturally, the Mongols were quite different from the Chinese and became a separate class with their own laws.

The Mongol invasions of China resulted in profound changes. The Mongols overthrew the Song dynasty, leaving China ruled by a foreign power for the first time. While Mongols adapted to the Chinese political system, they ended civil service exams. Mongols and Chinese lived by different laws. The Mongols welcomed merchants into court, and trade flourished.

Over time, the Mongol dynasty won the support of many Chinese people. Some came to respect the stability and prosperity that the Mongols brought. By bringing the entire Eurasian landmass under a single rule, the Mongols increased trade, especially along the Silk Road. This new trade had a major impact on Europe. The capital at Khanbalik was a magnificent city, and foreign visitors, such as Marco Polo, were impressed by its splendor. An effect of these foreign visits was to generate new interest in trade between Europe and China. This interest eventually contributed to the discovery of the Americas.

The Mongol dynasty eventually fell victim to the same problems that had plagued other dynasties: too much spending on foreign conquests, corruption at court, and growing internal instability. In 1368 Zhu Yuanzhang (JOO YWAHN • JAHNG), the son of a peasant, put together an army, ended the Mongol dynasty, and set up the Ming dynasty.

✓ READING PROGRESS CHECK

Summarizing Why were Mongol rulers successful in ruling China?

Religion and Government

GUIDING QUESTION *How did the role of religion in Chinese government change between the Han and Yuan dynasties?*

Confucian principles became the basis for Chinese government during the Han dynasty. By the time of the Sui and Tang dynasties, Buddhism and Daoism rivaled the influence of Confucianism.

Buddhism and Daoism

Buddhism was brought to China in the first century by merchants and missionaries from India. At first, only merchants and intellectuals were intrigued by the new ideas. However, as a result of the insecurity that prevailed after the collapse of the Han dynasty, both Buddhism and Daoism became more attractive to many people. Both beliefs gained support among the ruling classes. Daoism was a rival system of ideas to Confucianism.

The growing popularity of Buddhism continued into the early Tang dynasty. Early Tang rulers lent their support to Buddhist monasteries that were set up throughout the country. Buddhists even became advisers at the imperial court. Ultimately, though, Buddhism lost favor at court.

Analyzing **PRIMARY SOURCES**

Marco Polo on Khanbalik

"The streets are so straight and wide that you can see right along them from end to end and from one gate to the other. And up and down the city there are beautiful palaces, and many great and fine hostelries, and fine houses in great numbers."

—Marco Polo, Italian traveler

DBQ ***USING CONTEXT CLUES*** How do you think Khanbalik was different from Italian cities of the time?

khanate one of several separate territories into which Genghis Khan's empire was split, each under the rule of one of his sons

(continued from p. 256)

TEKS **Texas Essential Knowledge and Skills**

25A summarize the fundamental ideas and institutions of Eastern civilizations that originated in China and India

26A identify significant examples of art and architecture that demonstrate an artistic ideal or visual principle from selected cultures

26B analyze examples of how art, architecture, literature, music, and drama reflect the history of the cultures in which they are produced

acquired came into possession or control of

neo-Confucianism a revised form of Confucianism that evolved as a response to Buddhism and held sway in China from the late Tang dynasty to the end of the dynastic system in the twentieth century

available ready for immediate use; accessible

Buddhism was criticized for being a foreign religion. Like Christian monasteries in Europe during the Middle Ages, Buddhist monasteries had **acquired** thousands of acres of land and serfs. With land came corruption. The government reacted strongly. During the later Tang period, it destroyed countless Buddhist temples and monasteries and forced more than 260,000 monks and nuns to return to secular life.

Buddhists taught that the material world was not real, but an illusion. By teaching this, Buddhism was denying the very essence of Confucian teachings—the need for devotion to family and hard work. These were virtues that the Chinese state had reason to support.

Neo-Confucianism

From the Song dynasty to the end of the dynastic system in the twentieth century, official support went to a revived Confucianism, which became the heart of the state government. This new doctrine, called **neo-Confucianism**, served as a Confucian response to Buddhism and Daoism. It teaches that the world is real, not an illusion, and that fulfillment comes from participation in the world.

Neo-Confucianists divide the world into a material world and a spiritual world. Humans live in the material world but are also linked with the Supreme Ultimate. The goal is to move beyond the material world to reach union with the Supreme Ultimate. Humans do this through careful study of the moral principles that rule the universe.

READING PROGRESS CHECK

Explaining Why was neo-Confucianism embraced by the state government?

ANALYZING PRIMARY SOURCES

Who Were the Mongols?

When news of the Mongol conquests in Asia reached Europe, emissaries traveled to Mongol territories to learn about them. The historian Matthew Paris, relying on a mixture of facts and embellishments, painted an alarming picture. Marco Polo, writing about his travels, offered a different perspective.

"Special ambassadors [reported] that a monstrous . . . race of men had taken possession of the extensive, rich lands of the east. . . . If [the Saracens] themselves could not withstand the attacks of such people, nothing remained to prevent their devastating the countries of the West. . . . [Regarding their] cruelty . . . there can be no infamy [great enough]. . . . The Tartar[s] . . . fed upon their [victim's] carcasses . . . and left nothing but the bones for the vultures."

—Matthew Paris, quoted in *Storm from the East*

"Their style of conversation is courteous; they . . . have an air of good breeding, and eat their victuals with particular cleanliness. To their parents they show the utmost reverence. . . . The order . . . of all ranks of people, when they present themselves before his majesty, ought not to pass unnoticed. When they approach . . . him they show their respect . . . by assuming a humble, placid, and quiet demeanor."

—Marco Polo, quoted in *Genghis Khan and Mongol Rule*

DBQ Analyzing Historical Documents

1. ***Drawing Conclusions*** What effect would Matthew Paris's description of Mongols have on Europeans?

2. ***Contrasting*** In what way does Marco Polo's description add a dimension to the Mongols that is missing from Paris's description?

Chinese Culture: Tang to Mongol Dynasties

GUIDING QUESTION ***What spurred the golden age of literature and art in China?***

The period between the Tang and Ming dynasties was in many ways the great age of Chinese literature. The invention of printing during the Tang dynasty helped to make literature more readily **available** and more popular among the educated elite. Art, especially landscape painting and ceramics, flourished during this period.

Poetry

Historians view this period as the great age of poetry in China, and this literature reflected the history of Chinese culture. At least 48,000 poems were written by some 2,200 authors. Poetry was expected to represent Confucian ideals, to encourage high moral ideals and served as a means of self-expression. Chinese poems celebrated the beauty of nature, the changes of the seasons, and the joys of friendship.

Li Bo (LEE BWAW) and Du Fu (DOO FOO) were two of the most popular poets during the Tang era. Li Bo was a free spirit whose writing often centered on nature. He wrote probably the best-known poem in China, "Quiet Night Thoughts," which has been memorized by schoolchildren for centuries.

Painting and Ceramics

During the Song and Mongol dynasties, landscape painting was a major cultural development. Influenced by Daoism, artists went into the mountains to find the Dao, or Way, in nature. Chinese artists demonstrated ideals and principles from their culture through their art. Rather than depicting the realistic shape of a specific mountain, for example, they tried to portray the idea of "mountain." Empty spaces were left in the paintings because in the Daoist **vision**, one cannot know the whole truth. Daoism also influenced the portrayal of humans as insignificant in the midst of nature. Chinese artists painted people as tiny figures fishing in small boats or wandering up a hillside trail, living in but not dominating nature.

Tang artisans perfected the making of **porcelain**—a ceramic made of fine clay baked at very high temperatures. Porcelain-making techniques did not reach Europe until the eighteenth century.

✓ **READING PROGRESS CHECK**

Identifying What factor made forms of art such as painting and ceramics available to more Chinese people than literature?

▲ This painting is titled *Spring Dawn Over Elixir Terrace.*

▶ **CRITICAL THINKING**

Analyzing Visuals Describe how Daoism influenced the artist's rendering of this scene.

vision the way of seeing or believing

porcelain a ceramic made of fine clay baked at very high temperatures

LESSON 2 REVIEW TEKS

Reviewing Vocabulary

1. ***Identifying*** How did neo-Confucianism serve as a response to Buddhism and Daoism? 23A, 23B, 25A

Using Your Notes

2. ***Sequencing*** Use your notes to identify events that show the Mongols' rise to power. 1C, 4K

Answering the Guiding Questions

3. ***Drawing Conclusions*** How did the Mongols create the world's largest land empire? 1C

4. ***Evaluating*** What effect did the Mongol invasion of the Arab Empire have on Islamic civilization? 1C, 4K

5. ***Contrasting*** How did the role of religion in Chinese government change between the Han and Yuan dynasties? 23A, 23B, 25A

6. ***Analyzing*** What spurred the golden age of literature and art in China? 26A, 26B

Writing Activity

7. **INFORMATIVE/EXPLANATORY** Imagine you are a merchant traveling with Marco Polo. Write a letter to merchants in Europe describing China under the Mongols. Be sure to include explanations of items that could be used as trade goods. 1C, 4K

networks

There's More Online!

- BIOGRAPHY Minamoto Yoritomo
- CHART/GRAPH Influence of Buddhism on Early Korea
- CHART/GRAPH Korean Kingdoms
- GRAPHIC ORGANIZER Reforms of Shōtoku Taishi
- IMAGE Scene from Tale of Genji
- IMAGE Silla Dynasty Artwork
- INFOGRAPHIC Japanese and European Feudalism
- INTERACTIVE SELF-CHECK QUIZ
- MAP Korean Kingdoms
- VIDEO Dark Ages Japan

LESSON 3
Early Japan and Korea

ESSENTIAL QUESTIONS
- *What qualities define power struggles and stable periods of rule?*
- *How can invasion change the lives of people in conquered lands?*

Reading **HELP**DESK

Academic Vocabulary
- **revenue**
- **code**

Content Vocabulary
- **samurai**
- **Bushido**
- **shogun**
- **daimyo**
- **Shinto**
- **Zen**
- **archipelago**

TAKING NOTES:

Key Ideas and Details

Categorizing As you read, use a chart like the one below to identify characteristics of life in early Japan.

Life in Early Japan	
Role of Women	Religion and Culture

TEKS Texas Essential Knowledge and Skills

3A describe the major political, religious/philosophical, and cultural influences of Persia, India, China, Israel, Greece, and Rome, including the development of monotheism, Judaism, and Christianity

23A describe the historical origins, central ideas, and spread of major religious and philosophical traditions, including Buddhism, Christianity, Confucianism, Hinduism, Islam, Judaism, Sikhism, and the development of monotheism

continued on the next page

It Matters Because

Early Japan was unified by a noble family that gave rise to a line of emperors. Over time, power passed from the hands of the emperor to powerful aristocratic families and then to military leaders called shoguns. Finally, centralized power in Japan disappeared altogether. Korea's history during this period is one of a struggle for independence against the neighboring Chinese.

Early Japan

GUIDING QUESTIONS *How did Japan's geography affect its economy and culture? What influenced the rise and fall of central rule in medieval Japan?*

Japan's history has been marked by power struggles between rulers and independent families. Geography has also played an important role in the development of Japanese history.

Chinese and Japanese societies have historically been very different. One of the reasons for these differences is geography. Whereas China is located on a vast continent, Japan is a mountainous **archipelago**, or chain of many islands. The population is concentrated on four main islands: Hokkaidō, the main island of Honshū, and the two smaller islands of Kyūshū and Shikoku. Japan's total land area is approximately 146,000 square miles (378,000 square km)—about the size of Montana.

Like China, much of Japan is mountainous. Only about 11 percent of the total land area can be farmed. The mountains are volcanic in origin. Volcanic soils are very fertile, which has helped Japanese farming. The area, however, is prone to earthquakes. In 1923 an earthquake nearly destroyed the entire city of Tokyo.

The fact that Japan is an island nation has also affected its history. Because of their geographical isolation, the Japanese developed a number of unique qualities. These qualities contributed to the Japanese belief that they had a destiny separate from that of the peoples on the continent.

The ancestors of present-day Japanese settled in the Yamato Plain near the location of the modern cities of Ōsaka and Kyōto in the first centuries A.D. Their society was made up of clans. The people were divided between a small aristocratic class (the rulers) and a large population of rice farmers, artisans, and household servants. The local ruler of each clan protected the people in return for a share of the annual harvest. Eventually, one ruler of the Yamato clan (named for the Yamato Plain) achieved supremacy over the others and became, in effect, ruler of Japan.

In the early seventh century, Shōtoku Taishi, a Yamato prince, tried to unify the various clans so that the Japanese could more effectively resist invasion from China. To do this, Prince Shōtoku sent representatives to the Tang capital of China to learn how the Chinese organized their government. He then began to create a centralized system of government, based roughly on the Chinese political model.

▲ **The Heiji Insurrection of 1159 was one of the first samurai battles.**

▶ **CRITICAL THINKING**

Comparing and Contrasting Compare and contrast the clothing and weaponry of the samurai with those of European knights.

Prince Shōtoku wanted a centralized government under a supreme ruler. His objective was to limit the powers of the aristocrats and enhance the Yamato ruler's (his own) authority. Thus, the ruler was portrayed as a divine figure and the symbol of the Japanese nation.

Shōtoku Taishi's successors continued to make reforms based on the Chinese model. The territory of Japan was divided into administrative districts, and the senior official of each district was selected from among the local nobles. As in China, the rural village was the basic unit of government. A new tax system was set up. Now all farmland technically belonged to the state. All taxes were to be paid directly to the central government rather than to local aristocrats.

(continued from p. 260)

TEKS **Texas Essential Knowledge and Skills**

24A describe the changing roles of women, children, and families during major eras of world history

26B analyze examples of how art, architecture, literature, music, and drama reflect the history of the cultures in which they are produced

The Nara Period

After Shōtoku Taishi's death in 622, political power fell into the hands of the Fujiwara clan. A Yamato ruler was still emperor. He was, however, strongly influenced by the Fujiwara family. In 710 a new capital was established at Nara. The emperor now used the title "Son of Heaven."

Though the reforms begun by Prince Shōtoku continued during this period, Japan's central government could not overcome the power of the aristocrats. These powerful families were able to keep the taxes from the lands for themselves. Unable to gain tax **revenues**, the central government steadily lost power and influence.

archipelago a chain of islands

revenue the yield of sources of income that a nation or state collects and deposits into its treasury for public use

The Heian Period

In 794 the emperor moved the capital from Nara to nearby Heian-kyo, on the site of present-day Kyōto. The emperor continued to rule in name, but actual power remained in the hands of the Fujiwara clan. In fact, the government was returning to the decentralized system that had existed before the time of Shōtoku Taishi. Powerful families whose wealth was based on the ownership of tax-exempt farmland dominated the rural areas.

With the decline of central power, local aristocrats took justice into their own hands. They turned to military force, and a new class of military servants emerged whose purpose was to protect the security and property of their employers. Called the **samurai** ("those who serve"), these warriors fought on horseback, clad in helmet and armor, and carried a sword and a bow. Like knights in Europe, the samurai were supposed to live by a strict warrior **code**, known in Japan as **Bushido** ("the way of the warrior").

samurai "those who serve;" Japanese warriors similar to the knights of medieval Europe

code a system of principles or rules

Bushido "the way of the warrior;" the strict code by which Japanese samurai were supposed to live

The Kamakura Shogunate

By the end of the twelfth century, rivalries among Japanese aristocratic families had led to almost constant civil war. Finally, a powerful noble named Minamoto Yoritomo defeated several rivals and set up his power near the modern city of Tokyo.

To strengthen the state, he created a more centralized government under a military leader known as the **shogun** (general). In this new system—called the shogunate—the emperor remained ruler in name only, and the shogun exercised the actual power. The Kamakura shogunate, founded by Yoritomo, lasted from 1192 to 1333.

Although the shogunate was a military government, it was unprepared when Mongol ruler Kublai Khan sent 23,000 troops to invade Japan in 1274. The Mongols were winning until a storm sank their fleet. In 1281, Kublai Khan sent nearly 150,000 troops. Fighting from behind stone walls they had built, the Japanese forced the Mongols to retreat. A typhoon (violent storm) then devastated the Mongol fleet. The wars strained the political system. In 1333, several powerful families overthrew the Kamakura shogunate.

shogun "general," a powerful military leader in Japan

Collapse of Central Rule

The power of the local aristocrats grew during the fourteenth and fifteenth centuries. Heads of noble families, now called **daimyo** (DY • mee • oh), or "great names," controlled vast landed estates that owed no taxes to the government. As family rivalries continued, the daimyo relied on the samurai for protection, and political power came into the hands of a loose coalition of noble families.

By 1500, Japan was close to chaos. A disastrous civil war known as the Onin War (1467–1477) led to the virtual destruction of the capital city of Kyōto. Central authority disappeared. Powerful aristocrats in rural areas seized control over large territories, which they ruled as independent lords. Their rivalries caused almost constant warfare.

daimyo "great names;" head of noble families in Japan who controlled vast landed estates and relied on samurai for protection

Shinto "the Sacred Way" or "the way of the Gods;" the Japanese state religion; among its doctrines are the divinity of the emperor and the sacredness of the Japanese nation

Zen a sect of Buddhism that became popular with Japanese aristocrats and became part of the samurai's code of behavior; under Zen Buddhism, there are different paths to enlightenment

✓ **READING PROGRESS CHECK**

Summarizing At the conclusion of the twelfth century, what ended Japan's civil war?

Life in Early Japan

GUIDING QUESTION *What was life like in early Japan?*

Early Japan was mostly a farming society. Its people took advantage of the limited amount of farmland and abundant rainfall to grow wet rice. Trade in Japan was slow to develop. Barter was used until the twelfth century.

Manufacturing began to develop during the Kamakura period. Markets appeared in large towns, and industries such as the making of paper and porcelain emerged. Trade between regions also grew. Goods were carried in carts, on boats, or on human backs. Foreign trade, mainly with Korea and China, began during the eleventh century. Japan shipped raw materials, paintings, swords, and other manufactured items in return for silk, porcelain, books, and copper coins.

The Role of Women

In early Japan, women may have had a certain level of equality with men. An eighth-century law code, for example, guaranteed the inheritance rights of women. In addition, wives who were abandoned could divorce and

▲ Three-part woodblock illustration from *The Tale of Genji*

▶ **CRITICAL THINKING**

Drawing Conclusions Why was prose fiction such as *The Tale of Genji* written primarily by women?

remarry. Later practices, however, show that women were considered to be subordinate to men. A husband could divorce his wife if she did not produce a son or if she committed adultery, talked too much, was jealous, or had a serious illness.

Although women did not possess the full legal and social rights of men, they played an active role at various levels of society. Aristocratic women were prominent at court. Some women gained more prominent roles through their artistic or literary talents. Women often appear in the paintings of the period along with men. The women are doing the spring planting, threshing and hulling rice, and acting as salespersons and entertainers.

Religion and Culture

Early Japanese people worshiped spirits, called kami, whom they believed resided in trees, rivers, and mountains. The Japanese also believed that the spirits of their ancestors were present in the air around them. In Japan, these beliefs evolved into a religion called **Shinto** ("the Sacred Way" or "the Way of the Gods"), which is still practiced today. Over time, Shinto became a state doctrine linked to a belief in the divinity of the emperor and the sacredness of the Japanese nation.

Shinto, however, did not satisfy the spiritual needs of all the Japanese people. Some turned to Buddhism, , a major religious influence from China. During the A.D. 500s, Buddhist monks brought this religion from China to Japan. Among the aristocrats in Japan, one sect, known as **Zen**, became the most popular. Zen beliefs about self-discipline became part of the samurai warrior's code. The two main schools of Zen teach that nirvana either comes by instantaneous enlightenment or through a long process of meditation.

During much of the history of early Japan, aristocratic men believed that prose fiction was merely "vulgar gossip" and was thus beneath them. Consequently, from the ninth to the twelfth centuries, women were the most productive writers of prose fiction in Japanese. From this tradition appeared one of the world's great novels, *The Tale of Genji,* written by court author Murasaki Shikibu. Her novel traces the life of nobleman Genji as he moves from youthful adventures to a life of compassion in his later years. An aristocratic woman, Sei Shonagon, also wrote *The Pillow Book,* which told of her activities as a court lady.

Connections to TODAY

Genji in Modern Japanese Culture

Over the ten centuries since it was written, *The Tale of Genji* has had a huge impact on Japanese culture. In Japanese fine arts in recent years, Lady Murasaki's novel has inspired a modern-dance adaptation, a symphony, and an opera. Popular culture treatments of *Genji* include several film versions, a television series, *mangas* (comic book) adaptations aimed at different audiences, video games, and even a robot. Robotic specialists at Kyoto University created a kimono-clad robotic figure of Lady Murasaki with a built-in MP3 player that plays *The Tale of Genji.*

SKILLS PRACTICE

Work with a partner to review the content vocabulary words archipelago, Bushido, and daimyo. Take turns asking questions about these new concepts using words you already know. Start each question with the words *who, what, when,* or *where.*

In Japanese art and architecture, landscape serves as an important means of expression. The landscape surrounding the Golden Pavilion in Kyōto displays a harmony of garden, water, and architecture.

✓ READING PROGRESS CHECK

Explaining Why were Shinto and Buddhism important to the development of Japanese culture?

The Emergence of Korea

GUIDING QUESTION ***How was Korea influenced by China and Japan?***

The Korea Peninsula, only slightly larger than the state of Minnesota, is relatively mountainous. Its closeness to both China and Japan has greatly affected its history. Indeed, no society in East Asia was more strongly influenced by the Chinese model than Korea.

In 109 B.C., the northern part of the Korea Peninsula came under Chinese control. The Koreans, however, drove them out in the A.D. 200s. Eventually, three separate kingdoms emerged: Koguryo in the north, Paekche (PAK • chuh) in the southwest, and Silla in the southeast. Each of the kingdoms was governed by the combination of a hereditary monarch and powerful aristocratic families. From the fourth to the seventh centuries, the three kingdoms were bitter rivals. In this period the beliefs and traditions of Buddhism spread to Korea. It quickly became the state religion of each kingdom. After 527, Silla kings adopted Buddhist names and sponsored the building of many Buddhist temples. As the Silla kingdom became more allied with the Chinese, the monarchy turned to Confucian ideals.

Gradually, with the support of the Tang dynasty of China, the kingdom of Silla gained control of the peninsula. After the king of Silla was assassinated, Korea sank into civil war. Finally, in the early tenth century, a new dynasty called Koryo (the root of the modern word *Korea*) arose in the north. This kingdom adopted Chinese political institutions in order to unify its territory and remained in power for four hundred years.

In the thirteenth century, the Mongols seized the northern part of Korea. By accepting Mongol authority, the Koryo dynasty managed to remain in power. Mongol rule led to much suffering for the Korean people, especially the thousands of peasants and artisans who were forced to build ships for Kublai Khan's invasion of Japan. After the collapse of the Mongol dynasty in China, the Koryo dynasty broke down.

▼ **This gilded bronze dragon head was constructed in the Silla kingdom in the eighth or ninth century.**

✓ READING PROGRESS CHECK

Identifying How did the kingdom of Silla gain control of the Korean peninsula?

LESSON 3 REVIEW TEKS

Reviewing Vocabulary

1. ***Identifying*** What did Bushido mean to the samurai?

Using Your Notes

2. ***Categorizing*** Use your notes to identify the characteristics of life in early Japan. 24A, 26A

Answering the Guiding Questions

3. ***Drawing Conclusions*** How did Japan's geography affect its economy and culture?
4. ***Evaluating*** What influenced the rise and fall of central rule in medieval Japan?
5. ***Describing*** What was life like in early Japan? 3A, 23A, 23B, 24A, 26A
6. ***Analyzing*** How was Korea influenced by China and Japan? 3A

Writing Activity

7. **INFORMATIVE/EXPLANATORY** Write an essay describing how China influenced the culture, economy, and governments of Japan and Korea. 3A, 23A,23B

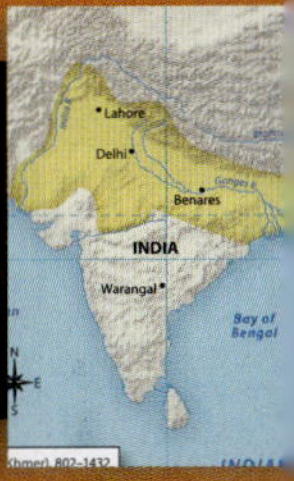

networks

There's More Online!

- BIOGRAPHY Timur Lenk
- CHART/GRAPH Impact of Religions on India
- GRAPHIC ORGANIZER Societies in Southeast Asia
- IMAGE Angkor Wat
- IMAGE Mahabodhi Temple
- INTERACTIVE SELF-CHECK QUIZ
- MAP India and Southeast Asia, 1200
- TIME LINE States of Southeast Asia
- VIDEO Angkor Wat

LESSON 4

India and Southeast Asia

ESSENTIAL QUESTIONS
- *What qualities define power struggles and stable periods of rule?*
- *How can invasion change the lives of people in conquered lands?*

Reading HELPDESK

Academic Vocabulary
- **retain**
- **traditional**

Content Vocabulary
- **Theravada**
- **Mahayana**

TAKING NOTES:
Key Ideas and Details

Contrasting As you read, use a table like the one below to identify the characteristics of the states of Southeast Asia.

Vietnam	Angkor, Thai, and Burma	The Malay World

TEKS Texas Essential Knowledge and Skills

1B identify major causes and describe the major effects of the following events from 500 BC to AD 600: the development of the classical civilizations of Greece, Rome, Persia, India (Maurya and Gupta), China (Zhou, Qin, and Han), and the development of major world religions

continued on p. 267

IT MATTERS BECAUSE

After the Gupta Empire collapsed, Muslim conquerors moved into India, eventually taking control of nearly all of the subcontinent. Unlike most of the other regions of Asia, Southeast Asia was never unified under a single government.

India after the Guptas

GUIDING QUESTION *How did Buddhism, Hinduism, and Islam influence the development of India?*

For hundreds of years, Buddhism **retained** widespread acceptance among the Indian people. The teachings of the Buddha came to be interpreted in different ways, however. People did not always agree on the meaning of the Buddha's teachings, resulting in a split among Buddhists in India.

One group believed that they were following the original teachings of the Buddha. They called themselves the school of **Theravada**, "the teachings of the elders." The development of Theravada began with a view of Buddhism as a way of life. This school insists that an understanding of oneself is the chief way to gain nirvana, or release from the "wheel of life." Theravada stressed transforming oneself through moral conduct and meditation.

Another view of Buddha and his teachings emerged in North India. This was **Mahayana**, "the Great Vehicle." Not strictly a school but rather a way of understanding the Buddha and his path, the Mahayana perspective was broad and embracing. Where Theravada and other similar schools held that only the solitary monk could successfully pursue nirvana, Mahayana Buddhists taught that the way to enlightenment was open to everyone. Unsatisfied with any single depiction of the Buddha, they sought to understand every aspect of the teacher and every implication of his teachings. In the process, they produced fresh interpretations and generated new practices—including devotional rituals—that extended beyond those supported by the more austere Theravada.

BIOGRAPHY

Timur Lenk (1330s–1405)

A cunning, ruthless opportunist, Timur Lenk began his career of conquest with a revolt against a ruler to whom he had vowed allegiance. Timur was a tireless military campaigner who personally led his armies. He put down revolts by destroying whole cities and massacring their populations. With the loot derived from his conquests, Timur built beautiful structures, including his celebrated tomb, the Gūr-e Amīr ("Tomb of the Commander"), in his capital of Samarqand, which became the economic and cultural center of Central Asia.

▶ **CRITICAL THINKING**

Speculating Why might Timur Lenk have become a legendary figure?

But, eventually, neither Mahayana nor the Theravada Buddhism remained popular in Indian. By the seventh century, Theravada was declining, and Mahayana was losing appeal in the face of a reinvigorated Hinduism. And alter Buddhism's appeal would also be challenged by a new arrival: Islam.

Despite their decline in India, though, both schools of Buddhism found success abroad. Carried by monks to China, Korea, Southeast Asia, and Japan, the practice of Buddhism has remained active in all four areas to the present.

The Eastward Expansion of Islam

In the early eighth century, Islam became popular in the northwestern part of the Indian subcontinent and had a major impact on Indian civilization. This impact is still evident today in the division of the subcontinent into mostly Hindu India and two Islamic states, Bangladesh and Pakistan.

One reason for Islam's success was the state of political disunity in India when it arrived. The Gupta Empire had collapsed, and no central authority had replaced it. India was divided into about 70 states, which fought each other constantly.

When the forces of the Islamic caliphate reached India in the early eighth century, they did little more than move into the frontier regions. At the end of the tenth century, however, a new phase of Islamic expansion took place when a group of rebellious Turkish slaves founded a new Islamic state known as Ghazna (Ghaznī), located in what is now Afghanistan.

When the founder of the new state died in 997, his son, Mahmūd of Ghazna, succeeded him. Mahmūd, an ambitious man, began to attack neighboring Hindu kingdoms to the southeast. Before his death in 1030, he was able to extend Islamic rule throughout the upper Indus Valley and as far south as the Indian Ocean.

Resistance against these advances into northern India was led by the Rajputs, who were Hindu warriors. They fought bravely, but their infantry supported by elephants were no match for the cavalry of the invaders, which could strike with great speed. Mahmūd's successors continued their advances. By 1200, Muslim power had reached over the entire plain of northern India, creating a new Muslim state known as the sultanate of Delhi. In the fourteenth century, this state extended its power into the Deccan Plateau.

The Turkish and Mongolian Invasion of India

During the latter half of the fourteenth century, the sultanate of Delhi began to decline. Near the end of the century, a new military force crossed the Indus River from the northwest. These invaders, of mixed Mongol and Turkish heritage, raided the capital of Delhi. They soon withdrew, but not before making a major impact. As many as 100,000 Hindu prisoners were massacred before the gates of the city. It was India's first meeting with Timur Lenk (Tamerlane).

Timur Lenk was the ruler of a state based in Samarqand. Born sometime during the 1330s, Timur Lenk seized power in 1369 and immediately launched a program of conquest, bringing much of Central Asia under his control. He also briefly invaded the western part of India. After his brief foray into northern India, he turned to the west. He died in 1405 in the midst of a military campaign.

The death of Timur Lenk removed a major menace from India. Nevertheless, members of his dynasty, known as the Timurids, continued to rule a few parts of India. At the beginning of the sixteenth century, Babur, a descendant of Timur Link on his father's side and the Mongol conqueror Genghis Khan on his mother's side, conquered northern India and established the

retain to keep in possession or use

Theravada "the teachings of the elders," a school of Buddhism that developed in India; its followers view Buddhism as a way of life

Mahayana a school of Buddhism that developed in northwest India, stressing the view that nirvana can be achieved through devotion to the Buddha; its followers consider the Buddha a divine figure

PHOTO: Tim Graham/Getty Images

Mogul Empire, an Islamic state. These Islamic rulers, descendants of nomadic Turks and Mongols, would shape life in India for hundreds of years.

✓ **READING PROGRESS CHECK**

Outlining Briefly explain the arrival and expansion of Islam in India through the 1300s.

Indian Society and Culture

GUIDING QUESTION ***How did Islam and Hinduism exist together in Indian society and culture?***

The imposition of Islamic rule by Mahmūd of Ghazna and his successors created a level of general tension in Indian society. The life of the typical Indian, however, remained about the same as it had been for the past several hundred years.

The Muslim rulers in India viewed themselves as foreign conquerors. They tried to maintain a strict separation between the Muslim ruling class and the Hindu population. Like rulers elsewhere at this time, many Muslim rulers in India were intolerant of other faiths. However, they generally used peaceful means to encourage people to convert to Islam. Still, some could be fierce when their religious zeal was aroused. Said one, "I forbade the infliction of any severe punishment on the Hindus in general, but I destroyed their idol temples and raised mosques in their place."

Most Muslim rulers realized that there were simply too many Hindus to convert them all. They reluctantly accepted the need to tolerate religious differences. Nevertheless, Muslim rulers did impose many Islamic customs on Hindu society. Overall, theinteractions between Muslims and Hindus were those between conqueror and conquered, a relationship marked by dislike rather than understanding.

Between 500 and 1500, most Indians lived on the land and farmed their own tiny plots. These peasants paid a share of their harvest each year to a landlord, who in turn sent part of the payment to the local ruler. In effect, the landlord worked as a tax collector for the king, who in theory owned all the land in his state. Although the vast majority of Indians were peasants, reports by foreign visitors between 500 and 1500 indicate that many people lived in the cities. It was here where the landed elites and rich merchants lived, often in conditions of considerable wealth.

Rulers naturally had the most wealth. One maharaja (great king) of a small state in southern India, for example, had more than 100,000 soldiers in his pay, along with 900 elephants and 20,000 horses. Another ruler kept a thousand high-caste women to sweep his palace. Each carried a broom and a brass basin holding a mixture of cow dung and water. One observer said,

PRIMARY SOURCE

"When the King goes from one house to another, or to a house of prayer, he goes on foot, and these women go before him with their brooms and basins in their hands, plastering the path where he is to tread."

—from *The Book of Duarte Barbosa*

Agriculture was not the only source of wealth in India. Since ancient times, India's location had made it a center for trade between Southwest Asia and East Asia. It was also a source for other goods shipped throughout the world.

(continued from p. 265)

TEKS **Texas Essential Knowledge and Skills**

1C identify major causes and describe the major effects of the following important turning points in world history from 600 to 1450 the spread of Christianity, the decline of Rome and the formation of medieval Europe; the development of Islamic caliphates and their impact on Asia, Africa, and Europe; the Mongol invasions and their impact on Europe, China, India, and Southwest Asia

continued on the next page

Connections to TODAY

Conflict in the Kashmir

Conflicts between Hindus and Muslims remain a problem in modern India and Pakistan. For example, the Kashmir region is predominantly Muslim and ruled by the secular Indian government, which is predominantly Hindu. A "Line of Control" divides the region with Indian and Pakistani military forces on either side of the division. Intermittent violence and cross-border firings in the Kashmir raise global concerns because India and Pakistan are both nuclear weapons states.

traditional established; customary

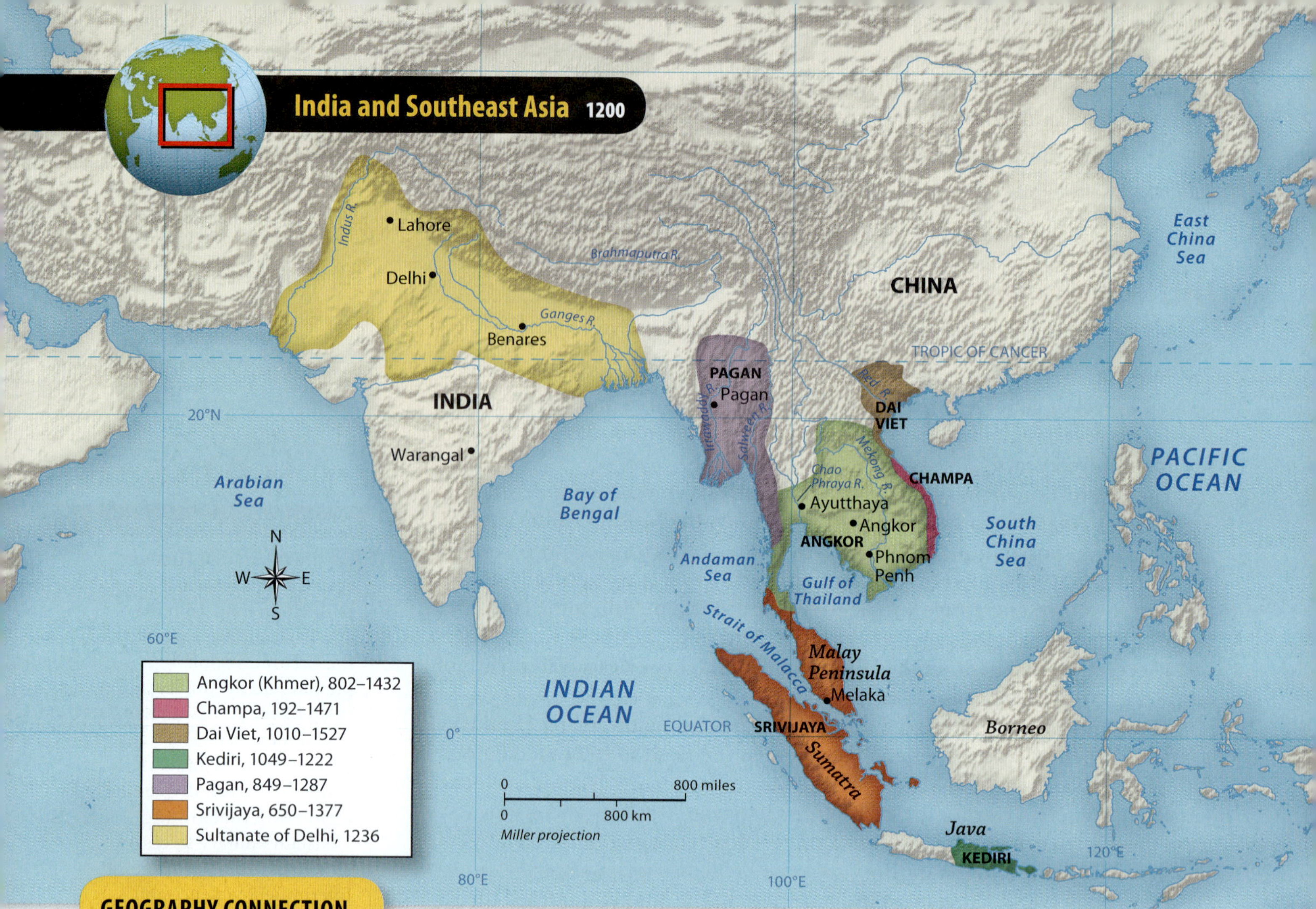

GEOGRAPHY CONNECTION

Southeast Asia was home to many different cultures.

1. **ENVIRONMENT AND SOCIETY** *Why did Southeast Asia contain so many cultures and kingdoms?*
2. **HUMAN SYSTEMS** *According to the map, which kingdom lasted the longest?*

(continued from p. 267)

TEKS **Texas Essential Knowledge and Skills**

4F describe the interactions between Muslim and Hindu societies in South Asia

23A describe the historical origins, central ideas, and spread of major religious and philosophical traditions, including Buddhism, Christianity, Confucianism, Hinduism, Islam, Judaism, Sikhism, and the development of monotheism

25A summarize the fundamental ideas and institutions of Eastern civilizations that originated in China and India

continued on the next page

Internal trade within India probably declined during this period, primarily because of the fighting among the many states of India. However, the level of foreign trade remained high, especially in the south and along the northwestern coast. Both areas were located along the **traditional** trade routes to Southwest Asia and the Mediterranean Sea region.

Between 500 and 1500, Indian artists and writers built on the achievements of their predecessors while making innovations in all fields of creative endeavor, both secular and religious. Here, we examine two such fields: architecture and prose literature.

During this period, Hindu religious architecture in India developed from modest temples built of perishable materials like wood and brick to increasingly grand and complex structures of stone. Different styles developed in north and south India. Usually a temple consisted of a central shrine topped by a tower and set in a protective compound. An entry porch and one or more halls for worshippers would lead to the main shrine. Among the most famous examples of Hindu temple art in this period are the temples at Khajuraho in present Madhya Pradesh. Of 80 temples built there from the tenth to the twelfth centuries, twenty major temples survive. All are built upon substantial stone bases, elevating them and making them even more impressive. These and other Hindu temples were considered to be dwelling places of the divinities and images of the entire universe.

The use of prose in fiction was well established in India by the sixth and seventh centuries. This is truly astonishing in light of the fact that the novel did not appear in Japan until the tenth or eleventh century and in Europe until the seventeenth century. One of the greatest masters of Sanskrit prose was Dandin, a seventh-century author. In *The Adventures of the Ten Princes*, he created a fantastic world, fusing history and fiction. His powers of observation, details of everyday life, and humor give his writing much vitality.

✓ **READING PROGRESS CHECK**

Summarizing What were the two major sources of wealth in India?

(continued from p. 268)

TEKS **Texas Essential Knowledge and Skills**

26A identify significant examples of art and architecture that demonstrate an artistic ideal or visual principle from selected cultures

26B analyze examples of how art, architecture, literature, music, and drama reflect the history of the cultures in which they are produced

Formation of States in Southeast Asia

GUIDING QUESTION ***What geographic factors led to the development of distinct cultures in Southeast Asia? What fueled the growth of the states in Southeast Asia?***

Between 500 and 1500, a number of organized states developed throughout Southeast Asia. When the peoples of the region began to form states, they used models from China and India. At the same time, they adapted these models to their own needs and created their own unique states.

Between China and India lies the region that today is called Southeast Asia. It has two major parts. One is the mainland region, extending southward from the Chinese border down to the tip of the Malay Peninsula. The other is an extensive archipelago, or chain of islands, most of which is part of present-day Indonesia and the Philippines. Ancient mariners called the area the "golden region" or "golden islands." Located between India and China, Southeast Asia contains a mixture of races, cultures, and religions.

Mainland Southeast Asia consists of several north-south mountain ranges. Between these ranges are fertile river valleys that run in a southerly or southeasterly direction. The mountains are densely forested and often infested with malaria-bearing mosquitoes. Thus, the people living in the river valleys were often cut off from one another and had only limited contact with the people living in the mountains.

These geographical barriers might help explain why Southeast Asia is one of the few regions in Asia that was never unified under a single government. The geographical barriers encouraged the development of separate, distinctive cultures within Southeast Asia.

Vietnam

The Vietnamese were one of the first peoples in Southeast Asia to develop their own state and their own culture. After the Chinese finally conquered Vietnam in 111 B.C., they tried for centuries to make Vietnam part of China. However, Chinese officials were often frustrated by the Vietnamese.

The Vietnamese clung to their own identity. In the tenth century, they finally overthrew Chinese rule. Chinese influence remained, however. Vietnamese rulers realized the advantages of taking over the Chinese model of centralized government. The new Vietnamese state, which called itself Dai Viet, adopted state Confucianism. Following the Chinese model, the rulers called themselves emperors and adopted Chinese court rituals. They also introduced the civil service examination as a means of recruiting government officials on the basis of merit instead of heredity.

The state of Dai Viet became a dynamic force on the Southeast Asian mainland. As its population grew, it expanded southward. Several centuries of bitter warfare with its southern neighbor, Champa, ended in Vietnamese victory by 1500.

Analyzing PRIMARY SOURCES

Chinese official describing the Vietnamese

"The people are like birds and beasts; they wear their hair tied up and go barefoot, while for clothing they simply cut a hole in a piece of cloth for their head or they fasten their garments on the left side. It is useless to try to change them."

—Chinese official, *The Birth of Vietnam*

DBQ ***ANALYZING*** How did the Chinese view the Vietnamese?

Angkor, Thai, and Burma

In the ninth century, the kingdom of Angkor arose in the region that is present-day Cambodia. The kingdom was formed when a powerful figure named Jayavarman united the Khmer (kuh • MEHR) people and established a capital at Angkor Thom. In 802, Jayavarman was crowned as god-king of his people. For several hundred years, Angkor—or Khmer empire—was the most powerful state in mainland Southeast Asia.

Angkor faced enemies on all sides. To the east were the Vietnamese and the kingdom of Champa. To the west was the Burmese kingdom of Pagan. In 1432, the Thai from the north destroyed the Angkor capital. The Angkor ruling class fled to the southeast, where they set up a new capital near Phnom Penh, the capital of present-day Cambodia.

The Thai had first appeared in the 500s as a frontier people in China. Beginning in the eleventh or twelfth century, Thai groups began moving southward. This process was encouraged by the Mongol invasion of China in the mid-1200s. After destroying the Angkor capital, the Thai set up their capital at Ayutthaya (AH • yoo • TY • uh), where they remained as a major force in the region for the next 400 years. Although they converted to Buddhism and borrowed Indian political practices, they created a unique blend that evolved into the modern-day culture of Thailand.

The Thai were also threatened from the west by the Burmese peoples, who had formed their society along the Salween and Irrawaddy Rivers. The Burmese were pastoral peoples, but they adopted farming soon after their arrival in Southeast Asia. In the eleventh century, they founded the first great Burmese state, the kingdom of Pagan. Like the Thai, they converted to Buddhism and adopted Indian political institutions and culture.

▲ This bronze Buddha is from fifteenth-century Thailand.

During the next two centuries, Pagan became a major force in the western part of Southeast Asia. It played an active role in regional sea trade. Attacks by the Mongols in the late 1200s helped cause its decline.

The Malay World

In the Malay Peninsula and the Indonesian archipelago, a different pattern emerged. For centuries, this area had been tied to the trade that passed from East Asia into the Indian Ocean. The area had never been united under a single state. The vast majority of the people were of Malay background, but the peoples were divided into many separate communities.

It was not until the late 1200s that a strong state, the new kingdom of Majapahit, emerged in the region. In the mid-fourteenth century, Majapahit incorporated most of the archipelago and perhaps even parts of the mainland under a single rule. Majapahit did not have long to enjoy its status, however. By the 1400s, a new state was beginning to emerge in the region.

After the Muslim conquest of northern India, Muslim merchants—either Arabs or Indian converts—settled in port cities in the region and began to convert the local population. Around 1400, an Islamic state began to form in Melaka, a small town on the western coast of the Malay Peninsula. Melaka soon became the major trading port in the region and a chief rival to Majapahit. From Melaka, Muslim traders and the Muslim faith moved into the interior of the peninsula. Eventually, almost the entire population of the region was converted to Islam and became part of the sultanate of Melaka.

✓ READING PROGRESS CHECK

Identifying Why did China have difficulty making Vietnam a part of China?

Life in Southeast Asia

GUIDING QUESTION *Which economic activities contributed to the development of societies in Southeast Asia?*

The states of Southeast Asia can be divided into two groups: agricultural and trading societies. States such as Vietnam, Angkor, and Pagan drew most of their wealth from the land. Others, such as the sultanate of Melaka, supported themselves chiefly through trade. Trade through Southeast Asia expanded after the emergence of states in the area and reached even greater heights after the Muslim conquest of northern India. The rise in demand for spices also added to the growing volume of trade. As the wealth of Europe and Southeast Asia increased, demand grew for the products of East Asia.

At the top of the social ladder in most Southeast Asian societies were the hereditary aristocrats. They held both political power and economic wealth. Most aristocrats lived in the major cities. Angkor Thom, for example, had royal palaces and parks, a huge parade ground, and many temples.

Beyond the major cities lived the rest of the population, which consisted of farmers, fishers, artisans, and merchants. In most Southeast Asian societies, the majority of people were probably rice farmers who lived at a subsistence level and paid heavy rents or taxes to a landlord or local ruler.

Most of the societies in Southeast Asia gave greater rights to women than did their counterparts in China and India. Women worked side by side with men in the fields and often played an active role in trading activities.

Chinese culture made an impact on Vietnam. In many other areas of Southeast Asia, Indian cultural influence prevailed. The most visible example of this influence was in architecture, and the most famous and beautiful temple is Angkor Wat. Its architectural techniques demonstrate the ideals and principles of its culture. The temple is a blend of local and Indian culture, and the architecture reflects the history of the region's combined culture.

Monks, merchants, and cultural influence from India spread Hinduism and Buddhist ideas into Southeast Asia in the first millennium A.D. In all Southeast Asian societies, as in China and Japan, old beliefs were blended with those of the new faiths. Buddhism also spread to Southeast Asia. Monks spread Theravada Buddhism in Burma in the eleventh century. From Burma, Theravada spread rapidly to other areas of Southeast Asia.

✓ **READING PROGRESS CHECK**

Identifying Which countries influenced the cultural development of Southeast Asia?

LESSON 4 REVIEW TEKS

Reviewing Vocabulary

1. ***Identifying*** How did living on an archipelago affect the culture of the early Malays in Southeast Asia?

Using Your Notes

2. ***Contrasting*** Use your notes to identify the characteristics of the nations of Southeast Asia. 23A

Answering the Guiding Questions

3. ***Drawing Conclusions*** How did Buddhism, Hinduism, and Islam influence the development of India? 1B, 23A, 23B
4. ***Explaining*** How did Islam and Hinduism exist together in Indian society and culture? 4F
5. ***Analyzing*** What geographic factors led to the development of distinct cultures in Southeast Asia?
6. ***Determining Causes and Effects*** What fueled the growth of the states in Southeast Asia?
7. ***Summarizing*** Which economic activities contributed to the development of societies in Southeast Asia?

Writing Activity

8. **INFORMATIVE/EXPLANATORY** Write an essay explaining the various religions that existed in India in the time period discussed in this lesson and describe how they influenced the culture of India. 1B, 4F, 23A, 23B, 25A

CHAPTER 11 Assessment

Directions: On a separate sheet of paper, answer the questions below. Make sure you read carefully and answer all parts of the questions.

Lesson Review

Lesson 1

1. ***Summarizing*** What were the major political developments of the Tang and Song dynasties? Be sure to use social studies terminology correctly in your answer. **4H, 30A**

2. ***Summarizing*** What were the major economic developments of the Tang and Song dynasties? **4H**

3. ***Analyzing*** How did the Silk Road facilitate trade and the spread of ideas? **4J, 23A, 27A**

4. ***Describing*** Describe the roles of women in Tang dynasty China. **24A**

5. ***Identifying*** What were the primary advancements in mathematics, science, and technology during the Tang and Song dynasties? How did the knowledge of these advancements spread to other areas outside China? **27A**

6. ***Summarizing*** What were the major economic developments in Song era China? What were the major economic developments in Tang era China? **4H**

Lesson 2

7. ***Identifying*** How did the Mongols become a world power? How did the Mongol invasion impact China and the Islamic world? **1C**

8. ***Summarizing*** Which attributes or behaviors of the Mongol dynasty led to diminished power and eventually ended its reign? **1C**

9. ***Summarizing*** What were the major cultural developments of the Tang to Ming dynasties particularly in literature and art? **4H, 26A, 26B**

10. ***Describing*** How did neo-Confucianism spread and influence events in world history? **23A, 23B, 25A**

Lesson 3

11. ***Describing*** What are the major political, religious, and philosophical influences of China on Japan? **3A, 23A, 23B**

12. ***Describing*** What was the role of women in early Japan, including their role in the field of literature? How might historians use a frame of reference in examining information related to this topic? **24A, 26B, 29B, 29C**

13. ***Describing*** Describe how Japanese Shinto beliefs were connected to the political structure in Japan and how similarly Buddhist beliefs also became integrated with the Japanese political structure, especially the samurai warrior. **23A**

14. ***Describing*** Between 109 B.C. and the thirteenth century, how was China's relationship to Korea both adversarial and collaborative? **3A, 23A**

Lesson 4

15. ***Identifying*** How was Islam introduced to India? What was the political impact of Islam in India at this time? **1C**

16. ***Identifying*** How did the Mongol invasions eventually impact India? **1C**

Need Extra Help?

If You've Missed Question	1	2	3	4	5	6	7	8	9	10	11	12	13	14	15	16
Go to page	252	252	253	254	253	251	255	257	259	258	261	252	263	264	266	266

17 ***Identifying*** How did the Mongol invasions impact China and the Islamic world? **4K**

18 ***Summarizing*** How did ruling Muslims interact with Indian Hindus, and what kind of a relationship was theirs? **4F, 23A**

Exploring the Essential Question

19 ***Using Mathematical Skills*** With a partner, create a political map showing the changes in boundaries and governments in China from 960–1279. Clearly label the map and use mathematical skills to scale the map and create a legend displaying distances, important dates, invasions, and changes in governments. In writing, give details about the causes of the various changes and discuss the qualities that defined the times of struggles between rulers as well as periods of stable rule. **1C, 29H**

Critical Thinking

20 ***Identifying*** Despite being prosperous, what problems did the Song Dynasty experience from the beginning? Explain what happened as a result. **1C**

21 ***Hypothesizing*** After Chinese society shifted from two main groups of either wealthy landowners or poor peasants to multiple groups consisting of landowners, free peasants, sharecroppers, and landless laborers, how do you think the distribution of wealth shifted as well as the balance of knowledge and skills?

22 ***Analyzing causes and effects*** What effect did attempts by the Mongols to invade Japan have on the Japanese government? What factors helped prevent Mongols from conquering Japan?

23 ***Comparing and Contrasting*** Compare key principles of Buddhism with Confucianism and explain why during the Song dynasty a new doctrine called neo-Confucianism arose.

24 ***Analyzing effects*** How did the Vietnamese resist Chinese influence? What element of Chinese rule did the Vietnamese adopt? **3A, 23A**

25 ***Drawing Conclusions*** Based on the geographic elements and cultural identities of Southeast Asia, why did smaller, unique states develop independently from Chinese or Indian regimes?

26 ***Describing*** What influences of other cultures can be seen in Thailand and Burma? **3A, 23A**

Social Studies Skills

27 ***Using Social Studies Terminology*** What was the Grand Canal in China built to link? Use social studies terminology correctly to give directional details. **30A**

28 ***Interpreting Written Information*** After the Mongols conquered China, what aspects of Chinese life did not change? **30C**

29 ***Explaining Using a Frame of Reference*** Using knowledge about the effect of guns in warfare, what might historians speculate would have happened to the Song Dynasty had handguns been invented in the 12th century rather than the 13th century? **29B, 29C**

Need Extra Help?

If You've Missed Question	17	18	19	20	21	22	23	24	25	26	27	28	29
Go to page	267	267	250	252	254	262	257	269	269	269	250	257	252

30 ***Analyzing Information*** Compare and contrast the prominent artistic and literary mediums during a Chinese golden age of literature and art, which took place between the Tang and Ming dynasties and between the Song and Mongol dynasties. Which art forms had ties to religious beliefs, and which were more accessible or less accessible to the general public? Explain your comparisons. **29F**

31 ***Analyzing Information*** Analyze the events tied to rulers and regimes in early Japan beginning with the Nara Period through the Onin War in 1467. How did each event in the sequence connect to the next?

DBQ Analyzing Primary Sources

Read the excerpt from Du Fu, a Chinese writer who returns home after a rebellion has left the capital city in ruins, and answer the questions that follow.

PRIMARY SOURCE

"The capital is taken. The hills and streams are left, And with spring in the city the grass and trees grown dense. Mourning the times, the flowers trickle their tears; Saddened with parting, the birds make my heart flutter. The army beacons have flamed for three months; A letter from home would be worth ten thousand in gold. My white hairs have I anxiously scratched ever shorter; But such disarray! Even hairpins will do no good."

—from "Spring Prospect"

32 ***Explaining Primary and Secondary Sources*** Is this excerpt a primary or secondary source? Explain. **29C**

33 ***Examining Point of View*** What is the writer's point of view regarding nature? How does the excerpt reflect the culture that produced it? **26B, 29C, 30C**

Analyzing Visuals

Use the image to answer the following questions.

This photograph displays the Mahabodhi Temple in Bodhgaya, India, where the Buddha is reputed to have achieved enlightenment. It is surrounded by stone railings that feature Hindu gods.

34 ***Identifying*** What artistic ideals or visual principles are demonstrated in this architectural example? **26A**

35 ***Analyzing*** How does this architectural example reflect the history of the South Asian culture? **26B**

Extended Response Question

36 ***Expository*** Choose one of the Southeast Asian states and explain how the politics, economics, culture, and religion were influenced by China or India. **3A, 4H, 23B, 25A**

Need Extra Help?

If You've Missed Question	30	31	32	33	34	35	36
Go to page	259	261	259	259	268	268	269

Crusades and Culture in the Middle Ages

1000–1500

ESSENTIAL QUESTIONS
- *How did the Church influence political and cultural changes in medieval Europe?*
- *How did both innovations and disruptive forces affect people during the Middle Ages?*

networks

There's More Online! about the Crusades and culture in the Middle Ages.

CHAPTER 12

The Story Matters...

During the Middle Ages, a new culture developed in Europe that was shaped by Christian values and was controlled by the Church. Nowhere was this combination of Christian values and Church control more evident than in the brief, triumphant, and tragic career of Joan of Arc. A French peasant girl whose religiously inspired leadership helped her country recover from the disasters of the Hundred Years' War, she was later tried as a heretic and burned at the stake.

◀ Produced within a century of Joan of Arc's death in 1431, this illustration from an illuminated manuscript on the lives of famous women shows Joan with her standard, the banner she carried to inspire her troops.

PHOTO: Giraudon/Bridgeman Art Library

CHAPTER 12

Place and Time: Europe 1000–1500

During the Middle Ages, the Christian Church dominated Europe, affecting every aspect of medieval life. Throughout this period, strong popes often engaged in a power struggle with equally aggressive secular rulers. A focus of the conflict was the appointment of Church officials, known as the investiture controversy. Secular rulers, such as King Henry IV of Germany, wanted lay investiture, the power to choose Church officials. Pope Gregory VII, fearing that the Church would become more political than religious, fought this lay investiture, which resulted in a long struggle with Henry.

Step Into the Place

Read the quotes and look at the information presented on the map.

DBQ What historical methods would a historian use to analyze these primary sources? How would a historian explain Pope Gregory VII's and Henry IV's points of view? In your answer, be sure to use standard grammar, spelling, sentence structure, and punctuation.

PRIMARY SOURCE

"**1.** That the Roman church was established by God alone.
2. That the Roman pontiff [the pope] alone is rightly called universal.
9. That all princes shall kiss the foot of the pope alone. . . .
12. That he has the power to depose emperors. . . .
18. That his decree can be annulled by no one, and that he can annul the decrees of anyone.
19. That he can be judged by no one. . . .
24. That by his command or permission subjects may accuse their rulers."

—Pope Gregory VII, from *Dictatus Papae* [The Pope's Proclamation], 1075

PRIMARY SOURCE

"Henry, king not by usurpation, but by the holy ordination of God, to Hildebrand [Gregory VII], not pope, but a false monk. . . . You have mistaken our humility for fear, and have dared to make an attack upon the royal and imperial authority which we received from God. You have threatened to take it away, as if we had received it from you, and as if the empire and kingdom were in your disposal and not in the disposal of God. . . . You have attacked me, who, unworthy as I am, have yet been anointed to rule among the anointed of God, and who, according to the teachings of the fathers, can be judged by no one save God alone, and can be deposed for no crime except infidelity."

—Henry IV, from a letter to Pope Gregory VII, 1076

Step Into the Time

Research an event from the time line and explain how it produced a cultural change.

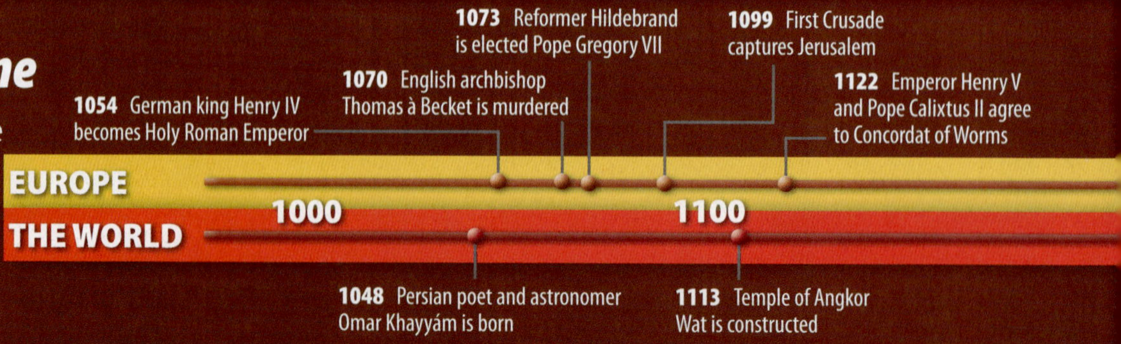

networks
There's More Online!

- **MAP** Explore the interactive version of this map on Networks.
- **TIME LINE** Explore the interactive version of the time line on Networks.

1184 First Inquisition is established by Pope Lucius III

1215 King John is forced to sign Magna Carta

1340 Height of *Reconquista*, Alfonso XI defeats Muslims at battle of Rio Salado

1478 Spanish Inquisition is established by Pope Sixtus IV and Ferdinand and Isabella of Spain

1492 Fall of Granada, last Muslim stronghold in Spain

1200 — 1300 — 1400 — 1500

1206 Genghis Khan unifies Mongols

1200 Zhu Xi, major figure in neo-Confucian revival, dies

c. 1275 Marco Polo reaches court of Kublai Khan

1240 Mali ruler Sundiata destroys Ghana capital of Kumbi

1325 The Aztec establish Tenochtitlán as their capital

1398 Muslim conqueror Timur Lenk invades India

after 1438 Pachacuti expands Inca Empire

1492 Columbus reaches the West Indies

networks

There's More Online!

- BIOGRAPHY Bernard of Clairvaux
- BIOGRAPHY Francis of Assisi
- BIOGRAPHY Hildegard of Bingen
- BIOGRAPHY Pope Gregory VII
- CHART/GRAPH Religious Orders
- IMAGE Trial from the Inquisition
- INTERACTIVE SELF-CHECK QUIZ
- PRIMARY SOURCE Account of the Inquisition
- PRIMARY SOURCE Writings of Hildegard of Bingen
- VIDEO St. Francis of Assisi

LESSON 1
Medieval Christianity

ESSENTIAL QUESTIONS

- *How did the Church influence political and cultural changes in medieval Europe?*
- *How did both innovations and disruptive forces affect people during the Middle Ages?*

Reading HELPDESK

Academic Vocabulary

- **pursue**
- **remove**

Content Vocabulary

- **lay investiture**
- **interdict**
- **sacrament**
- **heresy**
- **relics**

TAKING NOTES:

Key Ideas and Details

Categorizing As you read, use a table like the one below to identify the characteristics of the Cistercian, Dominican, and Franciscan religious orders.

Cistercians	Franciscans	Dominicans

TEKS Texas Essential Knowledge and Skills

1C identify major causes and describe the major effects of the following important turning points in world history from 600 to 1450 the spread of Christianity, the decline of Rome and the formation of medieval Europe; the development of Islamic caliphates and their impact on Asia, Africa, and Europe; the Mongol invasions and their impact on Europe, China, India, and Southwest Asia

continued on the next page

It Matters Because

The Catholic Church reached the height of its political power in the thirteenth century under Pope Innocent III. Religious enthusiasm spread and new monastic orders emerged. By the High Middle Ages, the Catholic Church had become a dominant and forceful presence in Europe.

The Papal Monarchy

GUIDING QUESTION *How did the political power of the Catholic Church change between the papacies of Pope Gregory VII and Pope Innocent III?*

Since the fifth century, the popes of the Catholic Church had claimed supremacy over the affairs of the Church. They had also gained control of territories in central Italy that came to be known as the Papal States. This control kept the popes involved in political matters, often at the expense of their spiritual duties.

At the same time, the Church became involved in the feudal system. Chief officials of the Church, such as bishops and abbots, came to hold their offices as grants from nobles. As vassals, they were obliged to carry out feudal services, including military duties. Lords often chose their vassals from other noble families for political reasons. Thus, the bishops and abbots they chose were often worldly figures who cared little about their spiritual duties.

Reform of the Papacy

By the eleventh century, Church leaders realized the need to be free from the lords' interference in the appointment of Church officials. When an individual became a Church official in the Middle Ages, he was given a ring and a staff. These objects symbolized the spiritual authority with which the Church granted, or invested, the official. Secular, or lay, rulers usually chose nominees to Church offices and gave them the symbols of their office, a practice known as **lay investiture**. Pope Gregory VII decided to fight this practice.

Elected pope in 1073, Gregory was convinced that he had been chosen by God to reform the Church. To **pursue** this aim, Gregory claimed that he—the pope—was truly God's "vicar on earth" and that the pope's authority extended over all the Christian world, including its rulers. Gregory believed that only by eliminating lay investiture could the Church regain its freedom. Then the Church would be able to appoint clergy and run its own affairs. If rulers did not accept this, the pope would **remove** them.

Gregory VII soon found himself in conflict with Henry IV, Holy Roman Emperor and king of Germany, over these claims. For many years, German kings had appointed high-ranking clerics, especially bishops, as their vassals to use them as administrators. Without them, the king could not hope to maintain power over the German nobles.

In 1075 Pope Gregory issued a decree forbidding high-ranking clerics from receiving their investiture from lay leaders:

PRIMARY SOURCE

"We decree that no one of the clergy shall receive the investiture with a bishopric or abbey or church from the hand of an emperor or king or of any lay person."

—*Pope Gregory VII,* from a papal decree, 1075

Henry, however, had no intention of obeying a papal decree that challenged the heart of his administration.

The struggle between Henry IV and Gregory VII, known as the Investiture Controversy, was one of the great conflicts between church and state in the High Middle Ages. It dragged on until a new German king and a new pope reached a compromise known as the Concordat of Worms in 1122. Under this agreement, a bishop in Germany was first elected by Church officials. After election, the new bishop paid homage to the king as his lord. The king in turn invested him with the symbols of temporal (earthly) office. A representative of the pope, however, then invested the new bishop with the symbols of his spiritual office.

The Church Supreme

Pope Gregory VII also tried to improve the Church's ability to provide spiritual guidance to the faithful. Twelfth-century popes did not give up the reform ideals of Pope Gregory VII, but they were even more inclined to strengthen papal power and build a strong administrative system. During the papacy of Pope Innocent III in the thirteenth century, the Catholic Church reached the height of its political power. Pope Innocent III had a strong belief in papal supremacy.

To achieve his political ends, Innocent used the spiritual weapons at his command. His favorite was the **interdict**. An interdict forbids priests from giving the **sacraments** (Christian rites) of the Church to a particular group of people. The goal was to cause the people under interdiction, who were deprived of the comforts of religion, to exert pressure against their ruler. For example, with an interdict, Pope Innocent III forced the king of France, Philip Augustus, to take back his wife after Philip had tried to have his marriage annulled.

✓ READING PROGRESS CHECK

Explaining Why was the Concordat of Worms an important turning point for the Catholic Church?

lay investiture the practice by which secular rulers both chose nominees to church offices and gave them the symbols of their office

pursue to follow up or proceed with

remove to eliminate

interdict a decree by the pope that forbade priests from giving the sacraments of the Church to the people

sacrament a Christian rite

(continued from p. 278)

TEKS **Texas Essential Knowledge and Skills**

4A explain the development of Christianity as a unifying social and political factor in medieval Europe and the Byzantine Empire

4B explain the characteristics of Roman Catholicism and Eastern Orthodoxy

24A describe the changing roles of women, children, and families during major eras of world history

Analyzing PRIMARY SOURCES

Pope Innocent III on papal supremacy

"As God, the creator of the universe, set two great lights in the firmament of heaven, the greater light to rule the day, and the lesser light to rule the night, so He set two great dignities in the firmament of the universal church, . . . the greater to rule the day, that is, souls, and the lesser to rule the night, that is, bodies. These dignities are the papal authority and the royal power. And just as the moon gets her light from the sun, and is inferior to the sun . . . so the royal power gets the splendor of its dignity from the papal authority."

—Pope Innocent III, 1198

DBQ ***INTERPRETING*** How does the Pope characterize royal power?

New Religious Orders

GUIDING QUESTION *What effects did the new religious orders formed after 1098 have on medieval Europe?*

In the late 1000s and early 1100s, a wave of religious enthusiasm seized Europe. This movement led to a rise in the number of monasteries and the emergence of new monastic orders, a key aspect of Roman Catholicism.

Cistercians

One of the most important new orders of the Middle Ages was the Cistercian (sis • TUHR • shuhn) order. It was founded in 1098 by a group of monks who were unhappy with the lack of discipline at their own Benedictine monastery. Cistercian monasticism spread rapidly from southern France into the rest of Europe.

The Cistercians were strict. They ate a simple diet, and each had only a single robe. All decorations were eliminated from their churches and monastic buildings. More time for prayer and manual labor was gained by spending fewer hours at religious services.

The Cistercians played a major role in developing a new, activistic spiritual model for twelfth-century Europe. Benedictine monks spent hours inside the monastery in personal prayer, but the Cistercians took their religion to the people outside the monastery. More than any other person, Bernard of Clairvaux embodied the new spiritual ideal of Cistercian monasticism: "Arise, soldier of Christ, I say arise! Shake off the dust and return to the battle. You will fight more valiantly after your flight, and you will conquer more gloriously."

▲ Hildegard of Bingen as depicted on the middle panel of the Hildegard Altarpiece

Women in Religious Orders

In a reflection of new roles for women in religious life, the number of women joining religious houses also grew dramatically. In the High Middle Ages, most nuns were from the ranks of the landed aristocracy. Convents were convenient for families who were unable or unwilling to find husbands for their daughters, for aristocratic women who did not choose to marry, or for widows.

Female intellectuals found convents a haven for their activities. Most learned women of the Middle Ages, especially in Germany, were nuns. This was certainly true of Hildegard of Bingen, who became abbess of a religious house for females in western Germany. Hildegard was also one of the first important women composers. She was an important contributor to the body of music known as Gregorian chant. Her work is remarkable because she succeeded at a time when music, especially sacred music, was almost exclusively the domain of men.

► Some European rulers were very spiritual, such as King Louis IX of France, shown here on a pilgrimage to Nazareth in the thirteenth century.

► **CRITICAL THINKING**
Identifying Why did kings take pilgrimages to holy shrines?

Franciscans and Dominicans

In the 1200s, two new religious orders emerged that had a strong impact on the lives of ordinary people. They were the Franciscans and the Dominicans.

The Franciscans were founded by Francis of Assisi. Francis was born to a wealthy Italian merchant family in Assisi. After having been imprisoned during a local war, he had a series of dramatic spiritual experiences. These experiences led him to abandon all worldly goods and to live and preach in poverty, working and begging for his food. His simplicity, joyful nature, and love for others soon attracted a band of followers, all of whom took vows of absolute poverty, agreeing to reject all property and live by working and begging for their food.

The Franciscans became very popular. They lived among the people, preaching repentance and aiding the poor. Their calls for a return to the simplicity and poverty of the early Church, reinforced by example, were especially effective. The Franciscans also undertook missionary work, first throughout Italy and then to all parts of Europe and the Muslim world.

▲ Francis of Assisi before Pope Honorius III

▶ **CRITICAL THINKING**

Identifying Identify Francis of Assisi and Pope Honorius III. How were you able to make these determinations?

The Dominican order was founded by a Spanish priest, Dominic de Guzmán. Dominic wanted to defend Church teachings from **heresy**—the denial of basic Church doctrines. The spiritual revival of the High Middle Ages led to the emergence of heresies within the Church. Adherents of these movements were called heretics. Heretical movements became especially widespread in southern France. Dominic believed that a new religious order of men who lived in poverty and could preach effectively would best be able to attack heresy.

The Inquisition

The Church created a court called the Inquisition, or Holy Office, to deal with heretics. This court developed a regular procedure to find and try heretics. The Dominicans became especially well known for their roles as examiners of people suspected of heresy.

heresy the denial of basic Church doctrines

Those who confessed to heresy performed public penance and received punishment, such as flogging. Beginning in 1252, the Inquisition added the element of torture to extract confessions. Those who did not confess but were still considered guilty and those who had done penance for heresy and then relapsed were subject to execution by the state. Thirteenth-century Christians believed the only path to salvation was through the Church. To them, heresy was a crime against God and humanity, so using force to save souls from damnation was the right thing to do.

✓ **READING PROGRESS CHECK**

Making Connections What led to the creation of the Cistercian order? Explain how it was different from the Benedictine order.

Analyzing PRIMARY SOURCES

On an abbey's relics

"There is kept there a thing more precious than gold, … the right arm of St. Oswald … This we have seen with our own eyes and have kissed, and have handled with our own hands.…"

—from *The Chronicle of Hugh Candidus.*

DBQ ***READING CLOSELY*** What relic is described by this monk?

relic bones or other objects connected with saints; considered to be worthy of worship by the faithful

Religion in the High Middle Ages

GUIDING QUESTION *How did religion influence the daily lives of people in the High Middle Ages?*

The Catholic Church of the High Middle Ages was a crucial part of ordinary people's lives from birth to death. Its rites were practiced in similar ways throughout western and northern Europe during the medieval period. These practices, and the use of the old Roman language of Latin in its rituals also helped to make Roman Catholic Christianity a unifying social factor in medieval Europe.

The sacraments of the Roman Catholic Church, such as baptism, marriage, and the Eucharist (Communion), were seen as means for receiving God's grace and were necessary for salvation. Since only the clergy could administer these rites, people depended on them to achieve salvation. Ordinary people also venerated saints—men and women who, because of their holiness, were believed to have achieved a special position in heaven. Many saints are figures from the Christian bible, such as Jesus's apostles. Others are figures central to the religious history of a certain area. Because it was believed that saints could ask for favors before the throne of God for people who prayed to them, saints were very popular with all Christians.

Emphasis on the role of the saints was closely tied to the use of **relics**, usually bones of saints or objects connected with saints. Relics were considered worthy of worship because they were believed to provide a link between the earthly world and God. It was deemed that relics could heal people or produce other miracles.

Medieval Christians also believed that a pilgrimage to a holy shrine produced a spiritual benefit. The greatest shrine, but the most difficult to reach, was the Holy City of Jerusalem. On the continent, two pilgrim centers were especially popular in the High Middle Ages: Rome, which contained the relics of Peter and Paul, and the Spanish town of Santiago de Compostela, supposedly the site of the tomb of the apostle James.

▶ The reliquary, or casket, of St. Maur was made at the request of the Benedictine monastery in Florennes, Belgium, in the thirteenth century.

▶ **CRITICAL THINKING**
Interpreting Why might reliquaries have been ornate?

PHOTO: Isifa/Getty Images News/Getty Images

✓ READING PROGRESS CHECK

Inferring Why were relics important to Christians living in Europe during the Middle Ages?

LESSON 1 REVIEW TEKS

Reviewing Vocabulary

1. ***Identifying*** How did the pope use interdicts to achieve his goals? 1C, 4A

Using Your Notes

2. ***Categorizing*** Use your notes to identify the characteristics of the medieval religious orders. 4B

Answering the Guiding Questions

3. ***Drawing Conclusions*** How did the political power of the Catholic Church change between the papacies of Pope Gregory VII and Pope Innocent III? 4A, 4B

4. ***Evaluating*** What effects did the new religious orders formed after 1098 have on medieval Europe? 23B, 4B

5. ***Analyzing*** How did religion influence the daily lives of people in the High Middle Ages? 4A, 23B

Writing Activity

6. INFORMATIVE/EXPLANATORY Describe the power struggle between secular and religious authorities. How did the Church exercise political power in the Middle Ages? How did secular leaders attempt to challenge this authority? 4A, 1C

networks

There's More Online!

- ☑ GRAPHIC ORGANIZER The Effects of the Crusades
- ☑ IMAGE Crusading Armies Fighting Alongside their Kings
- ☑ IMAGE Sacking of Constantinople
- ☑ IMAGE Siege of Jerusalem
- ☑ INFOGRAPHIC The Crusades
- ☑ INTERACTIVE SELF-CHECK QUIZ
- ☑ MAP The Crusader States
- ☑ MAP The Crusades, 1095–1204
- ☑ PRIMARY SOURCE The Siege of Jerusalem
- ☑ VIDEO The Crusades

LESSON 2

The Crusades

ESSENTIAL QUESTIONS

- *How did the Church influence political and cultural changes in medieval Europe?*
- *How did both innovations and disruptive forces affect people during the Middle Ages?*

Reading HELPDESK

Academic Vocabulary

- **proceed**
- **libel**

Content Vocabulary

- **Crusades**
- **infidel**

TAKING NOTES:

Key Ideas and Details

Categorizing As you read, use a table like the one below to identify each of the Crusades and the result of each.

Crusade	Result

TEKS Texas Essential Knowledge and Skills

4D explain the political, economic, and social impact of Islam on Europe, Asia, and Africa

4E describe the interactions among Muslim, Christian, and Jewish societies in Europe, Asia, and North Africa

4G explain how the Crusades, the Black Death, the Hundred Years' War, and the Great Schism contributed to the end of medieval Europe

23B identify examples of religious influence on various events referenced in the major eras of world history

It Matters Because

From the eleventh to the thirteenth centuries, European Christians carried out a series of military expeditions to regain the Holy Land from the Muslims. These expeditions are known as the Crusades.

The Early Crusades

GUIDING QUESTION *What were the religious, political, and economic motivations behind the Crusades?*

The **Crusades** started when the Byzantine emperor Alexius I Comnenus asked for help against the Seljuk Turks. The Seljuk Turks were Muslims who had taken control of Asia Minor. Pope Urban II, who responded to the request, saw an opportunity to provide leadership for a great cause. That cause was rallying Europe's warriors to free Jerusalem and the Holy Land from people whom Christians viewed as **infidels**, or unbelievers—the Muslims.

At the Council of Clermont in southern France near the end of 1095, Urban II asked Christians to take up their weapons and join in a holy war. The pope promised: "All who die . . . shall have immediate remission [forgiveness] of sins." The enthusiastic crowd cried out: "It is the will of God, it is the will of God."

Warriors of western Europe, particularly France, formed the first crusading armies. These knights were mostly motivated by religious fervor, but some sought adventure and welcomed the chance to fight. Others saw a chance to gain wealth and a possible title. Italian merchants also sought new trade in Byzantine and Muslim lands.

After asking for help, the Byzantines became doubtful. Alexius I and his daughter, Anna Comnena (who was also the Byzantines' only female historian), were fearful that the western crusading armies,which would have to go through Byzantine lands to reach their objective, might prove harmful to the Byzantine Empire.

Regardless, the First Crusade began as three organized bands of mostly French warriors made their way to the East. The crusading

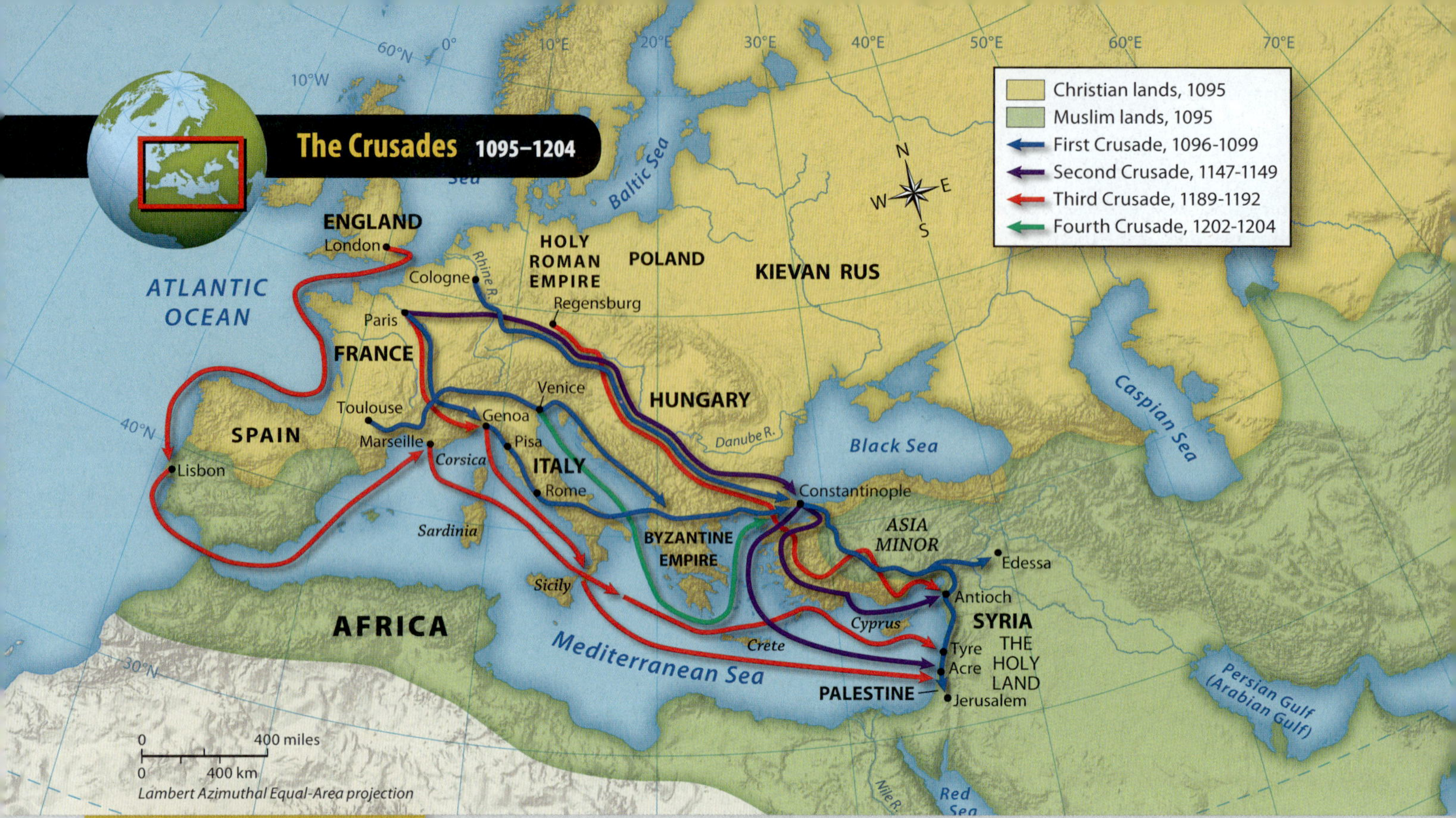

GEOGRAPHY CONNECTION

There were four Crusades from 1096 to 1204.

1. **THE WORLD IN SPATIAL TERMS** *Which Crusades did not go through Constantinople?*
2. **HUMAN SYSTEMS** *Why did all the Crusades go through an Italian city?*

army, which included thousands of men in cavalry and infantry, captured Antioch in 1098. The crusaders **proceeded** down the Palestinian coast, avoiding the well-defended coastal cities, and reached Jerusalem in June 1099. The Holy City was taken amid a horrible massacre of its inhabitants.

After further conquests, the crusaders organized four Latin crusader states in the East. One of these was the kingdom of Jerusalem under Godfrey de Bouillon, one of the Frankish leaders of the First Crusade. Godfrey, however, rejected the title of king, protesting that it belonged only to God. Surrounded by Muslims, these crusader kingdoms depended on Italian cities for supplies. Some Italian port cities, such as Genoa, Pisa, and especially Venice, grew rich and powerful in the process.

It was not easy, however, for the crusader kingdoms to maintain themselves in the East. By the 1140s, the Muslims had begun to strike back. The fall of one of the Latin kingdoms to the Muslims led to calls for another crusade, especially from the monastic leader Bernard of Clairvaux.

PRIMARY SOURCE

"Now, on account of our sins, the sacrilegious enemies of the cross have begun to show their faces. . . . What are you doing, you servants of the cross? . . . Will you cast pearls before swine?"

—*Bernard of Clairvaux*

Bernard managed to enlist two powerful rulers, King Louis VII of France and Emperor Conrad III of Germany, in a Second Crusade. This campaign, however, was a total failure.

In 1187 Jerusalem fell to Muslim forces under Saladin. Saladin had made himself sultan of Egypt in 1169 and then become leader of the Muslim offensive against the Christian kingdom of Jerusalem. After Saladin's success, three European rulers then agreed to lead a Third Crusade: German emperor Frederick Barbarossa, English king Richard I (Richard the Lionhearted), and French king Philip II Augustus.

Crusades military expeditions carried out by European Christians in the Middle Ages to regain the Holy Land from the Muslims

infidel an unbeliever; a term applied to the Muslims during the Crusades

proceed to advance or move along a course

Some members of the Third Crusade arrived in the East by 1189, only to encounter problems. Frederick drowned in a local river. The English and French arrived by sea and captured the coastal cities but were unable to move inland. After Philip returned home, Richard negotiated a settlement with Saladin that permitted Christian pilgrims free access to Jerusalem.

✓ **READING PROGRESS CHECK**

Summarizing How many early Crusades were there? What was the common factor?

The Later Crusades

GUIDING QUESTION *How did the Crusades affect Europe and Southwest Asia?*

About six years after Saladin's death in 1193, Pope Innocent III initiated the Fourth Crusade. As it headed east, the crusading army became involved in a fight over the Byzantine throne. The Venetian leaders of the Crusade used the situation to weaken their greatest commercial competitor, the Byzantine Empire. In 1204 the crusaders sacked Constantinople, adding to the division between the Eastern Orthodox Church and the Catholic Church. Western forces also set up a new Latin empire of Constantinople.

Not until 1261 did a Byzantine army recapture the city, but the Byzantine Empire was no longer a great Mediterranean power. It now comprised the city of Constantinople and its surrounding lands, as well as part of Asia Minor. The empire limped along for another 190 years, until its weakened condition enabled the Ottoman Turks to conquer it in 1453.

Despite failures, the crusading ideal continued. In Germany in 1212, a youth known as Nicholas of Cologne announced that God had inspired him to lead a "children's crusade" to the Holy Land. Thousands of young people

ANALYZING PRIMARY SOURCES

Were the Crusades Fought for Faith or Money?

Among the pope's audience in 1095 was a French monk, Peter the Hermit, who became a tireless recruiter for the First Crusade. By 1204, however, crusaders were attacking fellow Christians for plunder. The second passage describes a French abbot stealing valuable relics from Constantinople.

"In every admonition and sermon, with all the persuasion of which he was capable, he urged setting out on the journey as soon as possible. In response to his constant admonition and call, bishops, abbots, clerics, and monks set out; next, most noble laymen, and princes... then, all the common people...indeed, every class of the Christian profession, nay, also, women and those influenced by the spirit of penance—all joyfully entered upon this expedition...."

—from the chronicle of Albert of Aix during the First Crusade

"While the victors were rapidly plundering the conquered city, which was theirs by right of conquest, the abbot Martin began to cogitate about his own share of the booty...lest he alone should remain empty-handed, while all the others became rich... But, since he thought it not meet to handle any booty of worldly things...he began to plan how he might secure some portion of the relics of the saints, of which he knew there was a great quantity in the city."

—from Gunther's *Historia Constantinopolitana*, a chronicle of the Fourth Crusade

DBQ Analyzing Historical Documents

1. ***Analyzing Information*** What inspired the men and women recruited by Peter the Hermit to join the crusade? Write your answer in the form of an oral presentation, such as a TV news broadcast.

2. ***Drawing Conclusions*** What is Gunther's opinion of Abbot Martin?

joined Nicholas and made their way down the Rhine and across the Alps to Italy, where the pope told them to go home. Most tried to do so. At about the same time, a group of about 20,000 French children headed to Marseille, where two shipowners agreed to take them to the Holy Land. Seven ships filled with youths left the port. Two of the ships went down in a storm. The other five sailed to North Africa, where the children were sold into slavery.

The next Crusades of adult warriors were hardly more successful. The last two major Crusades were organized by the king of France, Louis IX. After his defeat by Baybars, the sultan of Egypt, Louis tried again but died of the plague without any conquests.

libel a written or oral defamatory statement or representation that conveys an unjustly unfavorable impression

Did the Crusades have much effect on European civilization? Historians disagree. Clearly, the Crusades benefited the Italian port cities. Even without the Crusades, however, Italian merchants would have increased trade with the Eastern world.

The Crusades had some unfortunate side effects on the interactions among Christian and Jewish societies in Europe. The first widespread attacks on the Jews began in the context of the Crusades. Some Christians argued that to fight the Muslims while the Jews, whom they blamed for Jesus's death, ran free at home was unthinkable. The Jews of medieval Europe came to be subjected to periodic **libels**, attacks, and expulsions.

▼ A medieval fighter uses a trebuchet (catapult) during a fourteenth-century siege.

▶ **CRITICAL THINKING**

Describing What was it like to live in a medieval city that was under siege?

Perhaps the greatest impact of the Crusades was political. They eventually helped to break down feudalism. As kings levied taxes and raised armies, nobles joining the Crusades sold their lands and freed their serfs. As nobles lost power, the kings created stronger central governments. Taxing trade with the East also provided kings with new sources of wealth. This paved the way for the development of true nation-states and contributed to the end of medieval Europe. By the mid-1400s, three strong nation-states—Spain, England, and France—had emerged in Europe.

✓ **READING PROGRESS CHECK**

Monitoring Was the Fourth Crusade successful? Explain your answer.

LESSON 2 REVIEW TEKS

Reviewing Vocabulary

1. ***Making Inferences*** Why did the Christians believe that Jerusalem was controlled by infidels? 4B, 4E, 23B
2. ***Summarizing*** What was the cause of the libels against Jews in medieval Europe? 4E

Using Your Notes

3. ***Identifying*** Use your notes to identify each Crusade and the result of each.

Answering the Guiding Questions

4. ***Drawing Conclusions*** What were the religious, political, and economic motivations behind the Crusades? 4A, 4D
5. ***Evaluating*** How did the Crusades affect Europe and Southwest Asia? 4D

Writing Activity

6. **NARRATIVE** Imagine you were a crusader under German emperor Frederick Barbarossa. Write a letter back home explaining the death of Frederick and your reactions to it.

networks

There's More Online!

- ☑ BIOGRAPHY Anselm of Canterbury
- ☑ BIOGRAPHY Geoffrey Chaucer
- ☑ BIOGRAPHY Roger Bacon
- ☑ BIOGRAPHY Thomas Aquinas
- ☑ IMAGE Canterbury Tales
- ☑ IMAGE University of Paris
- ☑ INTERACTIVE SELF-CHECK QUIZ
- ☑ PRIMARY SOURCE Troubador Poetry
- ☑ SLIDE SHOW Universities of the High Middle Ages and Today
- ☑ VIDEO Marriage in Dark Ages Europe

LESSON 3
Culture of the Middle Ages

ESSENTIAL QUESTIONS
- *How did the Church influence political and cultural changes in medieval Europe?*
- *How did both innovations and disruptive forces affect people during the Middle Ages?*

Reading HELPDESK

Academic Vocabulary
- **technical**
- **corporation**

Content Vocabulary
- **theology**
- **scholasticism**
- **vernacular**
- ***chanson de geste***

TAKING NOTES:
Key Ideas and Details

Contrasting As you read, use a table like the one below to compare the Romanesque style of architecture with the Gothic style of architecture.

Romanesque	Gothic

TEKS Texas Essential Knowledge and Skills

20C explain the political philosophies of individuals such as John Locke, Thomas Hobbes, Voltaire, Charles de Montesquieu, Jean Jacques Rousseau, Thomas Aquinas, John Calvin, Thomas Jefferson, and William Blackstone

26A identify significant examples of art and architecture that demonstrate an artistic ideal or visual principle from selected cultures

continued on the next page

It Matters Because

During the High Middle Ages, Europe witnessed a surge in architectural innovations and an intellectual revival. Beautiful cathedrals appeared across Europe, and the intellectual revival gave rise to Europe's first universities.

Architecture

GUIDING QUESTION *How did innovations change the architecture of churches and cathedrals in the High Middle Ages?*

The eleventh and twelfth centuries witnessed a dramatic building of churches in Europe. These cathedrals were built in the Romanesque style, which was a deliberate return to the architectural principles of Rome. Romanesque churches normally followed the basilica shape of churches built in the late Roman Empire.

Romanesque builders replaced the basilica's flat wooden roof with a long, round, arched vault made of stone or with a cross vault, in which two barrel vaults intersected. The builder used the cross vault to create a church plan in the shape of a cross. Because stone roofs were extremely heavy, these churches required massive pillars and walls to hold them up. This left little space for windows, so Romanesque churches were dark inside.

A significant example of architectural style that demonstrates the artistic ideal of the High Middle Ages was a new style, called Gothic, which appeared in the twelfth century and was brought to perfection in the thirteenth. The Gothic cathedral remains one of the greatest artistic triumphs of the High Middle Ages. Two basic innovations made Gothic cathedrals possible.

One innovation was the replacement of the round barrel vault with a combination of ribbed vaults and pointed arches. Builders could now make Gothic churches higher, giving a sense of upward movement, as if the building is reaching to God.

Another **technical** innovation was the flying buttress—a heavy, arched support made of stone built onto the outside of the walls. Flying buttresses made it possible to distribute the weight of the

▲ Saint-Étienne-du-Mont Church, a Gothic cathedral in Paris, France

church's vaulted ceilings outward and down. This eliminated the heavy walls needed in Romanesque churches to hold the weight of the massive barrel vaults. Gothic cathedrals were built, then, with relatively thin walls filled with stained glass windows.

These windows depict religious scenes and scenes from daily life. The colored glass windows create a play of light inside the cathedral that varies with the sun at different times of the day. The Gothic cathedral, with its towers soaring toward heaven, bears witness to an age when most people believed in a spiritual world.

✓ READING PROGRESS CHECK

Visualizing Imagine visiting a Romanesque church and then a Gothic church on a warm and sunny day. How might you describe your experience?

Universities

GUIDING QUESTION ***How did universities reflect the intellectual revival that occurred in Europe during the High Middle Ages?***

technical of or pertaining to a technique

corporation a business organization that has a separate legal entity with all the rights and responsibilities of an individual, including the right to buy and sell property, enter into legal contracts, and sue and be sued

The university of today, with faculty, students, and degrees, was a product of the High Middle Ages. The word *university* comes from the Latin word *universitas*, meaning "**corporation**" or "guild."

The first European university appeared in Bologna (buh • LOH • nyuh), Italy. The University of Paris was the first university in northern Europe. In the late 1300s, many students and masters (teachers) left Paris and started a university at Oxford, England. By 1500, Europe had 80 universities.

Students began their studies with the traditional liberal arts—grammar, rhetoric, logic, arithmetic, geometry, music, and astronomy. Teachers lectured by reading from a basic text and adding explanations. After four to six years, students took oral examinations to earn a bachelor of arts degree and later a master of arts. After about ten more years, students earned a doctor of law, medicine, or theology.

theology the study of religion and God

scholasticism a medieval philosophical and theological system that tried to reconcile faith and reason

The most highly regarded subject was **theology**—the study of religion and God. The study of theology was strongly influenced by a philosophical system known as **scholasticism**. Scholasticism tried to reconcile faith and reason—to show that faith was in harmony with reason. Its chief task was to harmonize Christian teachings with the works of the Greek philosophers. Aristotle reached his conclusions by rational thought, not by faith, and his ideas sometimes contradicted Church teachings. In his major work, the *Proslogion*, Anselm of Canterbury, a monastic theologian, made one of the first attempts in the eleventh century to demonstrate how the truths of faith are compatible with reason, reflecting the highly religious culture of medieval Europe. In fact, Anselm made an argument to prove by reason the existence of God.

In the 1200s, Thomas Aquinas (uh • KWY • nuhs) made the most famous attempt to reconcile Aristotle with the doctrines of Christianity. Aquinas is best known for his *Summa Theologica* ("summa" was a summary of all knowledge on a topic). His masterpiece followed a logical method of scholarly investigation. Aquinas first posed a question such as, "Does God exist?" He then cited opposing opinions before coming to his own conclusions. He believed that truths arrived at through reason or faith could not conflict with each other. Reason, without faith, could only reveal truths about the physical world, not spiritual truths. The political philosophy of Aquinas held that humans, by using reason, could arrive at natural law, which is part of God's eternal law, and determine what is inherently good or evil. Further, Aquinas believed that reason could help define when war was "just" or righteous. In order to have a "just war,"

(continued from p. 287)

TEKS **Texas Essential Knowledge and Skills**

26B analyze examples of how art, architecture, literature, music, and drama reflect the history of the cultures in which they are produced

26C identify examples of art, music, and literature that transcend the cultures in which they were created and convey universal themes

according to Aquinas, it must be waged for a good purpose rather than pursuit of wealth or power. Moreover, a proper institution of authority such as the state must be the one to wage war. Finally, peace must always be the central motive.

In the late 1260s, at the request of Pope Clement IV, the English philosopher Roger Bacon wrote *Opus Majus*, an encyclopedia advocating a reformation of all sciences, including logic, mathematics, physics, experimentation, and philosophy. Bacon emphasized the importance of mathematics for the study of philosophy.

▲ From Chaucer's *The Canterbury Tales*

✓ READING PROGRESS CHECK

Summarizing What degrees could students obtain by going to university?

Vernacular Literature

GUIDING QUESTION ***Why was the development of vernacular literature important during the High Middle Ages?***

Latin was the universal language of medieval civilization. However, in the twelfth century, much new literature was being written in the **vernacular**—the language of everyday speech in a particular region, such as Spanish, French, English, or German. A market for vernacular literature appeared in the twelfth century when educated people at courts and in the cities took an interest in new sources of entertainment.

vernacular the language of everyday speech in a particular region

chanson de geste a type of vernacular literature, this heroic epic was popular in medieval Europe and described battles and political contests

Perhaps the most popular vernacular literature of the twelfth century was troubadour poetry, which was chiefly the product of nobles and knights. This poetry told of the love of a knight for a lady, who inspires him to become a braver knight and a better poet.

Another type of vernacular literature was known as the ***chanson de geste***, or heroic epic. The earliest and finest example of such literature is *The Song of Roland*, which appeared around 1100 and was written in French. The chief events described in heroic epic poems are battles in which knights fight courageously for their kings and lords. Its martial theme of bravery in the face of defeat transcends medieval culture.

In the fourteenth century, the English author Geoffrey Chaucer used the English vernacular in his famous work *The Canterbury Tales*. This work consists of a collection of stories told by a group of 29 pilgrims, representing a range of English society, as they journeyed to the tomb of Saint Thomas á Becket at Canterbury, England.

Connections to TODAY

Gothic Architecture

Grand Gothic cathedrals, such as Chartres and Notre Dame, influenced American architecture. The American Gothic revival produced St. Patrick's Cathedral in New York City and university campuses such as Yale and Princeton.

✓ READING PROGRESS CHECK

Identifying What were two popular types of vernacular literature in the twelfth century?

LESSON 3 REVIEW TEKS

Reviewing Vocabulary

1. ***Identifying*** What was the goal of scholasticism? 23B

Using Your Notes

2. ***Contrasting*** Use your notes to contrast churches built in the Romanesque style of architecture with churches built in the Gothic style. 26A, 26B

Answering the Guiding Questions

3. ***Drawing Conclusions*** How did innovations change the architecture of churches and cathedrals in the High Middle Ages? 26A, 26B

4. ***Analyzing*** How did universities reflect the intellectual revival that occurred in Europe during the High Middle Ages? 23B

5. ***Evaluating*** Why was the development of vernacular literature important during the High Middle Ages? 26B, 26C

Writing Activity

6. **INFORMATIVE/EXPLANATORY** Write an essay comparing and contrasting the curriculum of modern universities with the curriculum of universities in the High Middle Ages. 29F

networks

There's More Online!

- BIOGRAPHY John Hus
- CHART/GRAPH Results of the Hundred Years' War
- IMAGE The Black Death
- IMAGE The Great Schism
- INFOGRAPHIC Disasters of the Fourteenth Century
- INTERACTIVE SELF-CHECK QUIZ
- MAP The Hundred Years' War
- PRIMARY SOURCE Black Death
- PRIMARY SOURCE Great Schism
- TIME LINE Hundred Years' War
- VIDEO The Late Middle Ages

Reading HELPDESK

Academic Vocabulary

- **period**
- **consequence**

Content Vocabulary

- **anti-Semitism**
- **new monarchy**
- **taille**

TAKING NOTES:

Key Ideas and Details

Categorizing As you read, use a chart like the one below to identify the impact of the Black Death.

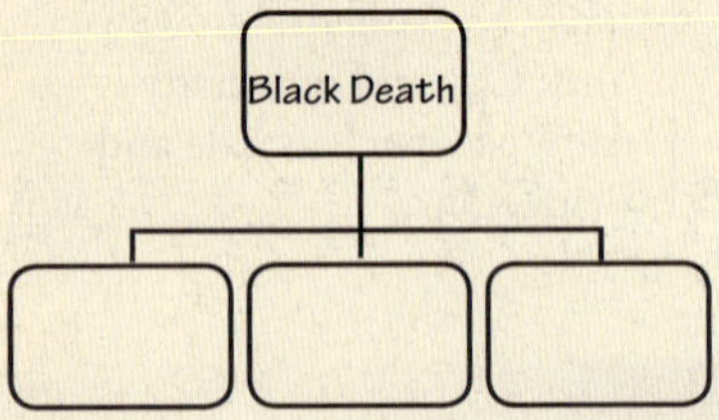

TEKS Texas Essential Knowledge and Skills

4E describe the interactions among Muslim, Christian, and Jewish societies in Europe, Asia, and North Africa

4G explain how the Crusades, the Black Death, the Hundred Years' War, and the Great Schism contributed to the end of medieval Europe

23B identify examples of religious influence on various events referenced in the major eras of world history

LESSON 4
The Late Middle Ages

ESSENTIAL QUESTIONS

- *How did the Church influence political and cultural changes in medieval Europe?*
- *How did both innovations and disruptive forces affect people during the Middle Ages?*

It Matters Because

Medieval European society reached its high point in the 1200s. However, much changed in the 1300s when a series of disastrous forces overwhelmed Europe. The Black Death spread, killing more than one-third of the population. People's faith was undermined when the Great Schism rocked the Catholic Church. Then, the Hundred Years' War started. Recovery began in the 1400s, and rulers responded by establishing their "new" monarchies.

The Black Death

GUIDING QUESTION *What social and economic effects did the Black Death have on Europe?*

Toward the end of the thirteenth century, noticeable changes in weather patterns were occurring as Europe entered a **period** that has been called a "little ice age." A drop in overall temperatures led to shorter growing seasons and bad weather conditions. Between 1315 and 1317, heavy rains in northern Europe destroyed harvests and caused food shortages, resulting in extreme hunger and starvation. The Great Famine expanded to other parts of Europe as well. Famine might have led to chronic malnutrition and in turn to higher susceptibility to disease because malnourished people are less able to resist infection. This might help explain the high mortality of the great plague known as the Black Death, the most devastating natural disaster in European history.

Bubonic plague was the most common form of the Black Death. It was spread by black rats infested with fleas carrying a deadly bacterium. Italian merchants brought the plague with them from Kaffa, on the Black Sea, to the island of Sicily in October 1347. The plague had spread to southern Italy and southern France by the end of 1347. Usually, the path of the Black Death followed trade routes. In 1348 and 1349, the plague spread through France, the Low Countries (modern Belgium, Luxembourg, and the Netherlands), and Germany. It ravaged England in 1349 and expanded to northern Europe and Scandinavia. Eastern Europe and Russia were affected by 1351.

Out of a total European population of 75 million, possibly more than one-third of the population died of the plague between 1347 and 1351. Especially hard hit were Italy's crowded cities, where 50 to 60 percent of the people died. In England and Germany, entire villages disappeared.

People did not know what caused the plague. Many believed that God sent it as punishment for their sins or that the devil caused it. Extreme reactions led to **anti-Semitism**, or hostility toward Jews, who were sometimes falsely accused of causing the plague by poisoning town wells.

The death of so many people had economic **consequences**. Trade declined, and a shortage of workers caused a dramatic rise in the price of labor. At the same time, the decline in the number of people lowered the demand for food, resulting in falling prices. Landlords were now paying more for labor while incomes from rents were declining. Some peasants bargained with their lords to pay rent instead of owing services. This change freed them from serfdom, an institution that had been declining throughout the High Middle Ages, ultimately contributing to the end of the medieval Europe.

period an interval of time

anti-Semitism hostility toward or discrimination against Jews

consequence the effect or result of an action

✓ **READING PROGRESS CHECK**

Identifying What did many people believe caused the plague?

Decline of Church Power

GUIDING QUESTION *How did the Great Schism and other crises lead to the decline of Church power?*

The popes reached the height of their power in the 1200s. In the 1300s, the Church encountered a series of problems. These problems led to a decline in the Church's power.

GEOGRAPHY CONNECTION

The Black Death spread throughout Europe.

1. **THE WORLD IN SPATIAL TERMS** *What was the last part of Europe to be affected by the plague?*
2. **IDENTIFYING GEOGRAPHICAL METHODS:** *Why would geographers focus on trade routes in studying the plague?*

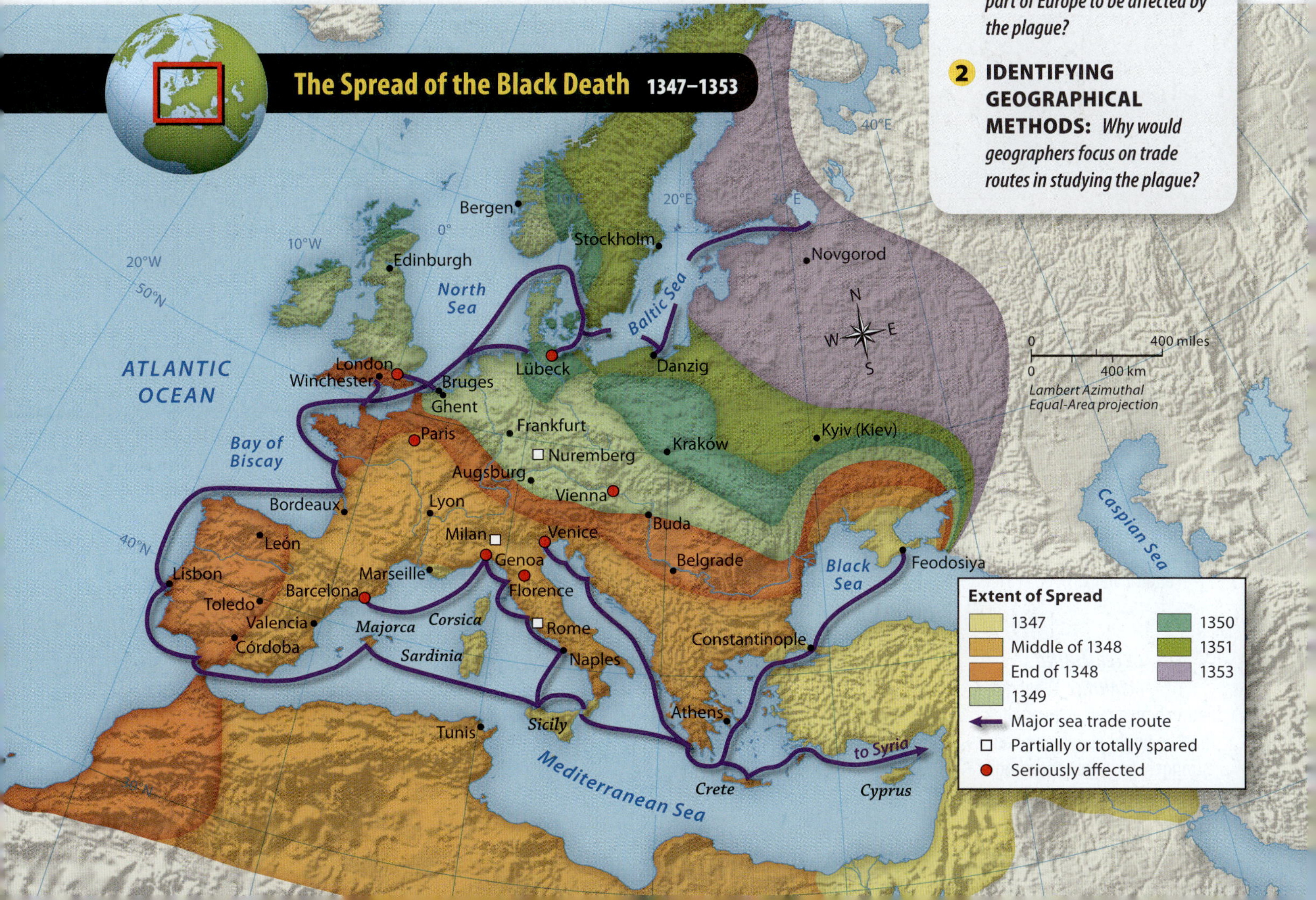

The Popes at Avignon

European kings had begun to reject papal claims of supremacy by the end of the 1200s. The struggle between Pope Boniface VIII and King Philip IV of France had serious consequences for the papacy.

Philip claimed the right to tax the clergy. Boniface argued that taxing the clergy required the pope's consent, because popes were supreme over both Church and state. Philip rejected the pope's position and sent French forces to Italy to bring Boniface back to France for trial. The pope escaped but died soon afterward. Philip then engineered the election of a Frenchman, Clement V, as pope in 1305. Clement took up residence in Avignon (a • VEEN • YOHN), in southern France. From 1305 to 1377, the popes lived in Avignon.

Sentiments against the papacy grew during this time. Many believed that the pope as bishop of Rome should reside in Rome, not in Avignon. The splendor in which the pope and cardinals were living in Avignon also led to criticism. At last, Pope Gregory XI, perceiving the disastrous decline in papal prestige, returned to Rome in 1377.

The Great Schism

Gregory XI died soon after his return to Rome. When the cardinals met to elect a new pope at the behest of the citizens of Rome, they elected an Italian, Pope Urban VI. Five months later, a group of French cardinals declared the election invalid and chose a Frenchman as pope. This pope returned to Avignon.

Because Urban remained in Rome, there were now two popes, beginning the Great Schism of the Church. Lasting from 1378 to 1417, the Great Schism divided Europe. France and its allies supported the pope in Avignon; England and its allies supported the pope in Rome.

In addition to creating political conflict, the Great Schism damaged the Church. The pope was believed to be the true leader of Christendom. When each line of popes denounced the other as the Antichrist (one who opposes Christ), people's faith in both the papacy and the Church were undermined. The situation became worse when an effort to resolve the problem in 1409 resulted in the simultaneous reign of three popes. A Church council finally met at Constance, Switzerland, and ended the schism in 1417. The competing popes either resigned or were deposed. A new pope, acceptable to all, was then elected.

Meanwhile, these crises in the Catholic Church led to calls for reform. John Wyclif in England and John Hus in Bohemia called for an end to clerical corruption and to excessive papal power within the Church. Hus was accused of heresy by the Council of Constance and burned at the stake in 1415. In response, the Bohemians led a revolutionary upheaval in Bohemia that was not crushed until 1436. Hus's ideas would later have an impact on the German monk Martin Luther.

By the early 1400s, then, the Church had lost much of its political power. The pope could no longer assert supremacy over the state. Although Christianity remained central to medieval life, the papacy and the Church had lost much of their authority as people lost faith in the papacy. The Great Schism contributed to the end of medieval Europe and ultimately laid the groundwork for the Protestant Reformation of the sixteenth century.

✓ READING PROGRESS CHECK

Summarizing Why were popes living in Avignon criticized?

Analyzing PRIMARY SOURCES

On the popes at Avignon

"Here reign the successors of the poor fishermen of Galilee; they have strangely forgotten their origin. I am astounded . . . to see these men loaded with gold and clad in purple, boasting of the spoils of princes and nations."

—Petrarch, Italian poet, in a letter to a friend

DBQ ***DETERMINING MEANING*** What did Petrarch mean when he wrote that the popes at Avignon had "strangely forgotten their origin"?

◀ French manuscript illumination of the siege of Orléans, 1428–1429

▶ **CRITICAL THINKING**

Identifying Who won the battle of Orléans?

The Hundred Years' War

GUIDING QUESTION *Why was the Hundred Years' War a turning point in warfare, and what were its consequences?*

Plague, economic crisis, and the decline of the Catholic Church were not the only problems of the late Middle Ages. War and political instability must also be added to the list. The Hundred Years' War was the most violent struggle during this period.

Trouble began over the duchy of Gascony in France. England possessed it, and France wanted it. King Edward III of England was also the duke of Gascony and a vassal to the French king. However, when King Philip VI of France seized the duchy in 1337, Edward declared war on Philip, thus beginning the Hundred Years' War.

This war between England and France began in a burst of knightly enthusiasm. Trained to be warriors, knights viewed battle as a chance to show their fighting abilities. The Hundred Years' War proved to be an important turning point in the nature of warfare, however. Peasant foot soldiers, not knights, won the chief battles of the war.

France's heavily armed noble cavalrymen viewed foot soldiers as social inferiors. The English also used heavily armed cavalry, but they relied more on large numbers of peasants, paid to be foot soldiers. English soldiers were armed with pikes, or heavy spears, and longbows, which had greater striking power, longer range, and more rapid speed of fire than the crossbow (formerly the weapon of choice).

The first major battle of the Hundred Years' War occurred in 1346 at Crécy. The larger French army followed no battle plan and attacked in a disorderly fashion. The English archers devastated them.

The Battle of Crécy was not decisive, however. The English did not have enough resources to conquer all of France. Nevertheless, they continued to try. The English king, Henry V, achieved victory at the Battle of Agincourt in 1415. The French knights who attacked Henry's forces across a muddy field were disastrously defeated, and 1,500 French nobles died in battle.

The seemingly hopeless French cause now fell into the hands of Charles, heir to the French throne. Quite unexpectedly, a French peasant woman saved the timid monarch. The daughter of prosperous peasants, Joan of Arc was a deeply religious person. She claimed to have visions and believed that saints had commanded her to free France. Though only 17, Joan's sincerity and simplicity persuaded Charles to allow her to accompany a French army to Orléans. Apparently inspired by Joan's faith, the French armies found new confidence and seized Orléans.

Analyzing PRIMARY SOURCES

On the English victory at Crécy

"[With their longbows] the English continued to shoot into the thickest part of the crowd, wasting none of their arrows. They impaled or wounded horses and riders, who fell to the ground in great distress, unable to get up again without the help of several men."

—Froissart, from *Chronicles*

DBQ ***READING CLOSELY*** What is meant by the phrase "wasting none of their arrows"?

BIOGRAPHY

Henry V (1387–1422)

Shakespeare's famous plays have popularized the tradition of Henry's wild youth that ended abruptly when he became king. If there was any truth in the legends, King Henry V must have undergone an extraordinary change, because as a ruler he displayed such consistent prudence, skill, and leadership in his conduct of domestic affairs and the invasion of France, that he is often offered as an example of an ideal medieval king. Henry was also deeply religious. Dying of a fever at the age of 34, he expressed the wish to go on a crusade to Jerusalem.

▶ **CRITICAL THINKING**
Describing What were the leadership qualities of Henry V?

Joan had brought the war to a turning point but did not live to see its end. The English captured her in 1430, turning her over to the Inquisition on charges of witchcraft. At the time, it was thought that either God or the devil inspired such visions. Although the war dragged on for another two decades after Joan was condemned to death, English defeats at Normandy and Aquitaine led to a French victory by 1453. Also important to French success was the cannon, a new weapon made possible by the invention of gunpowder.

The Hundred Years' War ultimately contributed to the end of medieval Europe. The steady defeat of knights with the use of longbow and pike, and later gunpowder as evidenced by French success with the cannon, reduced the importance of knights in warfare. This, in turn, reduced the overall need for knights in battle and thus lessened their importance to the feudal order that supported their existence. With the decline of feudalism, medieval Europe would give way to a new political order dominated by monarchs.

✓ **READING PROGRESS CHECK**

Identifying What event sparked the Hundred Years' War?

Political Recovery

GUIDING QUESTION ***What kind of political recovery occurred in Europe in the 1400s?***

In the 1300s, European rulers faced serious problems. Many hereditary monarchies or dynasties in Europe were unable to produce male heirs. The founders of new dynasties had to fight for their positions when groups of nobles supported opposing candidates for the kingship. Rulers found themselves with financial problems as well.

In the 1400s, however, recovery set in as a number of new rulers in Europe attempted to reestablish the centralized power of monarchies. Some historians have spoken of these reestablished states as the **new monarchies**. This term applies especially to the monarchies of France, England, and Spain as they existed at the end of the 1400s.

new monarchy in the fifteenth century, government in which power had been centralized under a king or queen, i.e., France, England, and Spain

taille an annual direct tax, usually on land or property, that provided a regular source of income for the French monarchy

France

The Hundred Years' War left France exhausted. However, the war had also developed a strong degree of French national feeling toward a common enemy. The kings used that spirit to reestablish royal power.

The development of a strong French state was greatly advanced by King Louis XI, who ruled from 1461 to 1483. Known by many as the Spider because of his devious ways, Louis strengthened the use of the **taille**—an annual direct tax usually on land or property—as a permanent tax imposed by royal authority. This tax gave Louis a sound, regular source of income. To curb the power of the great French nobles, Louis relied on support from the lower nobility and middle class. He added Anjou, Maine, Provence, and other regions to his kingdom. By consolidating power and by promoting industry and commerce, he created the foundations of a strong monarchy.

England

The Hundred Years' War had also strongly affected the English. The cost of the war and losses in manpower strained the economy. At the end of the war, England faced even greater turmoil when civil conflicts—known as the Wars of the Roses—erupted. Noble factions fought to control the monarchy until 1485, when Henry Tudor established a new dynasty.

As the first Tudor king, Henry VII worked to create a strong royal government. Henry ended the wars of the nobles by abolishing their private armies. He was also very thrifty. By not overburdening the nobles and the middle class with taxes, Henry won their support.

Spain

Spain, too, experienced the growth of a strong national monarchy at the end of the 1400s. During the Middle Ages, Christian rulers in Spain fought to regain their lands from the Muslims. Several independent Christian kingdoms emerged in the course of the long reconquest of the Iberian Peninsula. Among them were Aragon and Castile.

When Isabella of Castile married Ferdinand of Aragon in 1469, it was a major step toward unifying Spain. Though Castile and Aragon remained distinct kingdoms, Isabella and Ferdinand worked together to strengthen royal power. Both believed religious unity was necessary for political unity, pursuing a policy of strict conformity to Catholicism. This policy meant forced conversions of both Jews and Muslims. In 1492 they took the drastic step of expelling from Spain all Jews who did not convert.

After their final loss in 1492 to the armies of Ferdinand and Isabella, Muslims were given the choice of converting to Christianity or going into exile. Even after the forced conversions and expulsions, converted Jews and Muslims were pursued by the Inquisition, tortured and killed to ensure the orthodoxy of their conversion to Christianity. Over the centuries of the Spanish Inquisition, tens of thousands were burned at the stake. Ferdinand and Isabella, the "most Catholic" monarchs, had largely achieved their goal of religious uniformity. To be Spanish was to be Catholic.

SKILLS PRACTICE

After reading about developments in France, England, and Spain, work with a partner to make sure you understand everything you have read. Take turns asking and answering questions about the methods kings and queens of these nations used to increase their power.

Central and Eastern Europe

Unlike France, England, and Spain, the Holy Roman Empire did not develop a strong monarchical authority. Germany was a land of hundreds of states, most of which acted independently of the German ruler. After 1438, the position of Holy Roman emperor was held by the Hapsburg dynasty, who ruled the Austrian lands along the Danube.

In Eastern Europe, rulers found it difficult to centralize their states. Religious differences troubled the area as Roman Catholics, Eastern Orthodox Christians, and other groups, including Mongols and Muslims, confronted one another.

Since the 1200s, Russia had been under Mongol domination. But by 1480, Ivan III had thrown off the yoke of the Mongols. The next ruler of Muscovy, Ivan IV, was recognized as the legitimate ruler and czar of Russia by the Orthodox Church.

✓ READING PROGRESS CHECK

Monitoring What type of government had France, England, and Spain developed by the end of the 1400s?

LESSON 4 REVIEW TEKS

Reviewing Vocabulary

1. ***Analyzing*** How did the use of the taille help strengthen the power of Louis XI?

Using Your Notes

2. ***Categorizing*** Use your notes to identify the effects of the Black Death. 4G

Answering the Guiding Questions

3. ***Drawing Conclusions*** What social and economic effects did the Black Death have on Europe? 4G
4. ***Evaluating*** How did the Great Schism and other crises lead to the decline of Church power? 4G
5. ***Inferring*** Why was the Hundred Years' War a turning point in warfare, and what were its consequences? 4G
6. ***Making Generalizations*** What kind of political recovery occurred in Europe in the 1400s?

Writing Activity

7. **INFORMATIVE/EXPLANATORY** Write a newspaper obituary for Joan of Arc. The obituary should either be from a French or an English perspective. Include details about her life, and describe what her death means to the perspective you are writing from.

CHAPTER 12 Assessment

TEKS

Directions: On a separate sheet of paper, answer the questions below. Make sure you read carefully and answer all parts of the questions.

Lesson Review

Lesson 1

1. ***Assessing*** Explain the characteristics of Roman Catholicism as it had developed in the High Middle Ages. 4B

2. ***Contrasting*** Describe the similarities between the Franciscans and Dominicans, as well as the impact they had in their time.

3. ***Describing*** Describe the new roles for and experiences of women in the late 1000s and early 1100s in Europe due to the increase in religious orders. Which women often entered religious life?

4. ***Identifying*** Who was Hildegard of Bingen? Describe why she is significant.

5. ***Explaining*** Why did pilgrimages become an important part of Christianity in the High Middle Ages? What difficulties faced medieval pilgrims? 4B

Lesson 2

6. ***Explaining*** How did the Crusades contribute to the end of medieval Europe? 4G

7. ***Evaluating*** Where do historians stand on how the Crusades affected European economics and trade? Explain the possible reasons why. 4G

8. ***Identifying*** What methods would geographers use to create maps depicting the routes Europeans took during the Crusades? 29A

Lesson 3

9. ***Drawing Inferences*** What did Europeans build much of during the eleventh and twelfth centuries? Describe characteristics of the work and make an inference about why Europeans focused on these types of structures. 26A, 26B, 29F

10. ***Analyze Information*** Summarize the university experience initiated in Bologna, Italy during the 1300s including the key subjects of study. Draw inferences about the importance of theology as a subject of study and the philosophical system of scholasticism. Why did scholars explore the connection between faith and reason? 29F

11. ***Explaining*** How did Thomas Aquinas connect Greek philosophy, doctrines of Christianity, and his personal investigations into one significant piece of work? Explain why according to Aquinas natural law was also God's law. 20C

12. ***Analyzing*** How does the vernacular literature of the *chanson de geste* reflect the history of the culture in which it was produced? 26B

Lesson 4

13. ***Identifying Cause and Effect*** What might have caused people to be vulnerable to the plague in Europe in the 1300s? How did it spread so widely?

14. ***Drawing Conclusions*** How did French kings benefit from the Hundred Years' War?

15. ***Analyze Information*** Compare the situations in France and England following The Hundred Years' War. What did each country's governing powers do to stabilize their nations? 29F

Exploring the Essential Question

16. ***Synthesizing*** With a partner, create a word web showing how the Church influenced political and cultural changes in medieval Europe. The middle circle should be labeled Church and two circles should be attached to it and labeled Political Change and Cultural Change. From these two circles, draw more branches and circles in which you will include examples. 23B

Need Extra Help?

If You've Missed Question	1	2	3	4	5	6	7	8	9	10	11	12	13	14	15	16
Go to page	282	281	280	280	283	286	284	282	287	288	288	289	290	293	294	282

17 ***Drawing Conclusions*** Create a time line showing major disruptive forces and innovations in Europe during the Middle Ages. Give a written or oral explanation of how the actions of the Church, disruptive forces, and innovations affected people of that time. **4G**

Critical Thinking

18 ***Explaining*** Explain the ways in which Christianity acted as a unifying social and political factor in medieval Europe. **4A**

19 ***Assessing*** How did the Black Death contribute to the end of medieval European feudalism and society? **4G**

20 ***Understanding Historical Interpretation*** Explain how the Hundred Years' War contributed to the end of medieval Europe and set the stage for monarchical nation-states. **4G**

21 ***Making Generalizations*** The Byzantine Empire was situated between Europe and Asia Minor. When Muslim influence from Asia Minor spread east to the Byzantine Empire, the emperor asked Pope Urban II for support. Based on what you have learned, make a generalization about the spread of Islam and Christian reactions to a call for protection. **4D**

22 ***Speculating*** Choose an issue from the Middle Ages—the Plague, conflicts, such as The Hundred Years' War or the Crusades—and speculate how use of modern technological or scientific innovations might have changed outcomes, altered events. Would there have been more loss of life or less? Would conflicts or diseases ended sooner or lasted longer? Point to information you have learned to support your answer.

23 ***Making Connections*** What commonalities can you identify between two or more of the notable female figures of the Middle Ages, such as Hildegard of Bingen, abbess and composer, Anna Comnena, historian of Byzantine and daughter of the emperor, Joan of Arc, French soldier and devout Christian, and Isabella of Castile.

Social Studies Skills

24 ***Understanding Relationships Among Events*** Why did the Jews of medieval Europe become the victims of libels, attacks, and expulsions during the Crusades? **4E**

25 ***Time, Chronology, and Sequencing*** Trace the development of universities in Europe from their inception until 1500.

DBQ Analyzing Primary Sources

Use the image to answer the following questions.

During the Inquisition, heritics underwent varying forms of punishment.

26 ***Speculating*** What form of punishment does the woodcut show? Explain what might have led Inquisitors to inflict this type of punishment. **23B**

27 ***Understanding Historical Interpretation*** Consider the woodcut's depiction of punishment during the Inquisition. With a classmate, discuss the methods historians use to analyze evidence, such as this woodcut, and form opinions about past events. How might a historian analyze this visual in respect to the artist's point of view? **29A, 29B**

Need Extra Help?

If You've Missed Question	17	18	19	20	21	22	23	24	25	26	27
Go to page	292	283	290	294	283	290	280	286	288	281	281

PHOTO: akg-images

28 ***Interpreting*** How did the Inquisition reinforce the authority of the Catholic Church? **4B, 23B**

Analyzing Visuals

Use the image to answer the following questions.

This picture shows a royal entourage en route to the Council of Constance in 1414. The Council of Constance ended the Great Schism.

29 ***Interpreting*** Why did French cardinals claim that the election of pope Urban VI was illegitimate?

30 ***Analyzing Visuals*** Write a short essay explaining the impact of the Great Schism on the Roman Catholic Church and medieval European politics and society in general. **4G**

Extended-Response Question

31 ***Argument*** What political impact did the Crusades have in Europe? **4G**

32 ***Exploring Issues*** Prepare a presentation on a notable work of medieval vernacular literature. Look for ways in which your selection reflects the culture in which it was produced. Also make note of any universal themes you find. **26B, 26C**

Need Extra Help?

If You've Missed Question	28	29	30	31	32
Go to page	281	292	292	286	289

Kingdoms and States of Medieval Africa

500–1500

ESSENTIAL QUESTION *How does geography affect society, culture, and trade?*

networks

There's More Online! about kingdoms and states of medieval Africa.

CHAPTER 13

Lesson 1
African Society and Culture

Lesson 2
Kingdoms and States of Africa

The Story Matters...

Hundreds of cultures developed across Africa, each shaped by the diverse geography of the continent. In West Africa, south of the vast desert of the Sahara, a series of great trading empires rose and fell between A.D. 500 and 1500. During this same period, the Yoruba people established a group of small kingdoms in the savannas and forests to the south of these empires. One of these kingdoms was Ife.

◀ Created sometime between the twelfth and fifteenth centuries, this sensitive terra-cotta sculpture presumably depicts one of the rulers of Ife (in what is today southwestern Nigeria).

CHAPTER 13

Place and Time: Early Africa 500–1500

Land and sea trade routes kept Africa linked to the rest of the world. Caravans across the Sahara encouraged the development of Ghana, Mali, and Songhai, the trading empires of West Africa. East African ports such as Sofala, Kilwa, and Mogadishu participated in the seaborne trade that crisscrossed the Indian Ocean. Driven by the seasonal monsoon winds, ships carried goods back and forth between East Africa, the Persian Gulf region, and the west coast of India. Many of the merchants and sailors on these ships were Arabs, and as a result, a culture and language developed, called Swahili, which combined African and Arab elements.

Step Into the Place

Read the quotes and look at the information presented on the map. TEKS 4D, 16B

DBQ **Analyzing Historical Documents** How did the location of the East African cities lead to their success as trading ports?

PRIMARY SOURCE

"The land of Zanj [Arab term for *East Africa*] produces wild leopard skins. The people wear them as clothes, or export them to Muslim countries. They are the largest leopard skins and the most beautiful for making saddles. . . . They also export tortoise-shell for making combs, for which ivory is likewise used. . . . It is from this country that come [elephant] tusks weighing fifty pounds and more. They usually go to Oman, and from there are sent to China and India. This is the chief trade route, and if it were not so, ivory would be common in Muslim lands."

—Abu'l-Hasan Ali al-Musudi, from *Meadows of Gold*, 943

PRIMARY SOURCE

"A little boat keeps near the shore, a larger vessel ventures out to the deep sea."

—Swahili proverb

PHOTO: Sonia Halliday Photographs/Alamy

Step Into the Time

Determining Cause and Effect

Select two events from the time line that appear to have a cause-effect relationship.

AFRICA

8th century Arabs begin to settle East African coast

after 800 Ghana Empire flourishes

500 — 700

THE WORLD

668 With Chinese support, Silla dynasty unifies Korea

800 Charlemagne is crowned Roman emperor by the pope

networks
There's More Online!

- **MAP** Explore the interactive version of this map on Networks.
- **TIME LINE** Explore the interactive version of the time line on Networks.

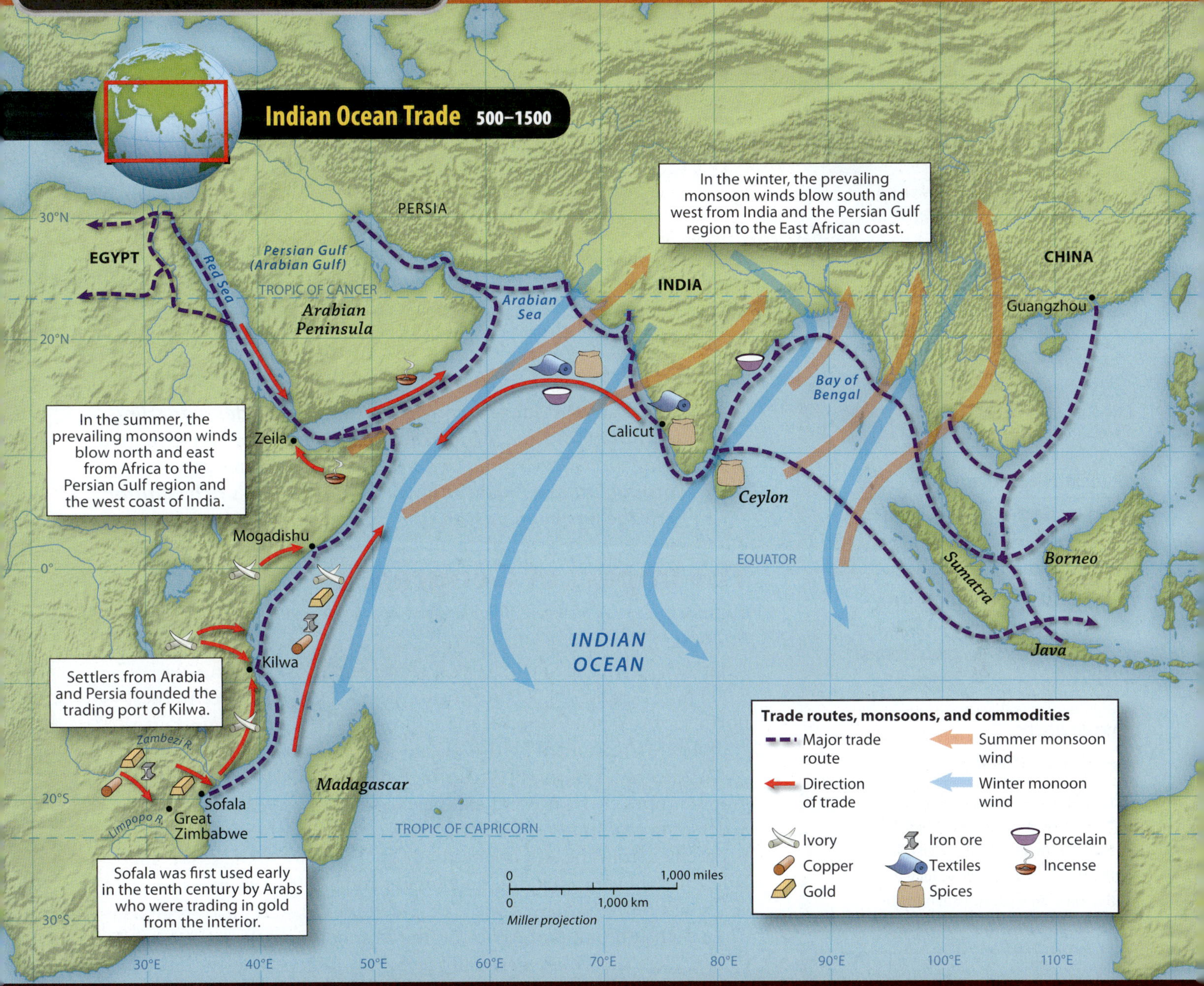

10th century Muslims found East African ports of Kilwa, Sofala, and Mogadishu

1009 Songhai ruler converts to Islam

1076 Berbers seize Ghana capital of Kumbi

1240 Mali ruler Sundiata Kieta destroys Kumbi

1324 Mali ruler Mansu Mūsā makes pilgrimage to Makkah

1352 Arab traveler Ibn Battuta visits Mali Empire

1464 Sunni Ali becomes ruler of Songhai

900 — 1100 — 1300 — 1500

907 Tang dynasty collapses in China

1066 Normans invade England

1206 Mongols become unified under Genghis Khan

1325 Aztec establish Tenochtitlán as their capital

1398 Timur Lenk invades India

1453 Constantinople falls to Ottoman forces

1492 Columbus reaches the West Indies

networks

There's More Online!

- CHART/GRAPH Common Features of Kilwa, Mombasa, and Mogadishu
- CHART/GRAPH Influences on African Religions
- IMAGE Christian Church in Axum
- IMAGE Great Rift Valley
- IMAGE Griot Tradition
- IMAGE Wood Carving from Benin
- INTERACTIVE SELF-CHECK QUIZ
- MAP Climate Zones and Geography of Africa

LESSON 1

African Society and Culture

ESSENTIAL QUESTION

How does geography affect society, culture, and trade?

IT MATTERS BECAUSE

Earth's second-largest continent, Africa, includes a dazzling array of landforms. African societies were based on extended family units, with most people living in rural villages. Through unique music and storytelling, Africa's rich cultural heritage has been passed from one generation to the next.

Reading HELPDESK

Academic Vocabulary

- **so-called**
- **founding**

Content Vocabulary

- **plateau**
- **savanna**
- **lineage groups**
- **matrilineal**
- **patrilineal**
- **diviner**
- **griot**

TAKING NOTES:

Key Ideas and Details

Identifying Cause and Effect As you read, use a table like the one below to identify the four different climate zones of Africa, what percentage of Africa each zone covers, and how the climate has affected farming.

Climate Zone				
Percentage of Africa				
Farming				

TEKS Texas Essential Knowledge and Skills

1C identify major causes and describe the major effects of the following important turning points in world history from 600 to 1450 the spread of Christianity, the decline of Rome and the formation of medieval Europe; the

continued on the next page

The Impact of Geography

GUIDING QUESTION *How have Africa's landforms and climate zones influenced its farming and herding?*

After Asia, Africa is Earth's largest continent. It stretches nearly 5,000 miles (around 8,000 km) from the Mediterranean Sea in the north to the Cape of Good Hope in the south. Africa is almost completely surrounded by two oceans and two seas.

As diverse as it is vast, Africa includes several distinct geographic zones. Africa's Mediterranean coast is mostly mountainous. South of the mountains lies Earth's largest desert, the Sahara. It stretches from the Atlantic to the Indian Ocean. To the east is the Nile River. Beyond that, the Red Sea separates Africa from Asia.

South of the Sahara, Africa is divided into several major regions. The **so-called** hump of Africa, in the west, juts into the Atlantic Ocean. Here the Sahara gradually gives way to grasslands in the interior and to tropical jungles along the coast.

Far to the east is a very different terrain of snow-capped mountains, upland **plateaus** (high, flat areas), and lakes. A distinctive feature is the Great Rift Valley, where mountains loom over deep canyons. Much of this region is grassland populated by wild animals. Farther south lies the Congo basin, with its dense vegetation watered by the mighty Congo River. The tropical rain forests of this region fade gradually into the hills, plateaus, and deserts of the south.

Africa includes four distinct climate zones. A mild climate zone stretches across the northern coast and southern tip of Africa. Moderate rainfall, warm temperatures, and fertile land produce abundant crops that can support large populations.

Deserts form another climate zone, covering about 40 percent of Africa. The Sahara in the north and the Kalahari in the south are the two largest deserts. A third climate zone is the rain forest that stretches along the Equator and covers about 10 percent of the continent. Heavy rains and warm temperatures produce dense forests where little farming or travel is possible. **Savannas** exist both north and south of the rain forest. They cover perhaps 40 percent of Africa's land area. The savannas get enough rainfall for farming and herding, but the rain is unreliable.

READING PROGRESS CHECK

Identifying What are Africa's four climate zones?

African Society

GUIDING QUESTION *How did values and customs help shape societies in medieval Africa?*

Early African societies, including those of Ghana, Mali, and Songhai, had many characteristics in common. African towns often began as fortified villages and slowly grew into larger communities. They were government and trade centers, with markets filled with goods from faraway regions.

so-called commonly named; popularly termed

plateau a relatively high, flat land area

savanna broad grassland dotted with small trees and shrubs

(continued from p. 302)

TEKS **Texas Essential Knowledge and Skills** development of Islamic caliphates and their impact on Asia, Africa, and Europe; the Mongol invasions and their impact on Europe, China, India, and Southwest Asia

continued on the next page

GEOGRAPHY CONNECTION

Africa's geographical and climatic zones affect the way its people live.

1. **ENVIRONMENT AND SOCIETY** *How do you think Africa's climate and geography would affect settlement patterns?*
2. **HUMAN SYSTEMS** *How would Africa's climate and geography affect trade with Europe or the Middle East?*

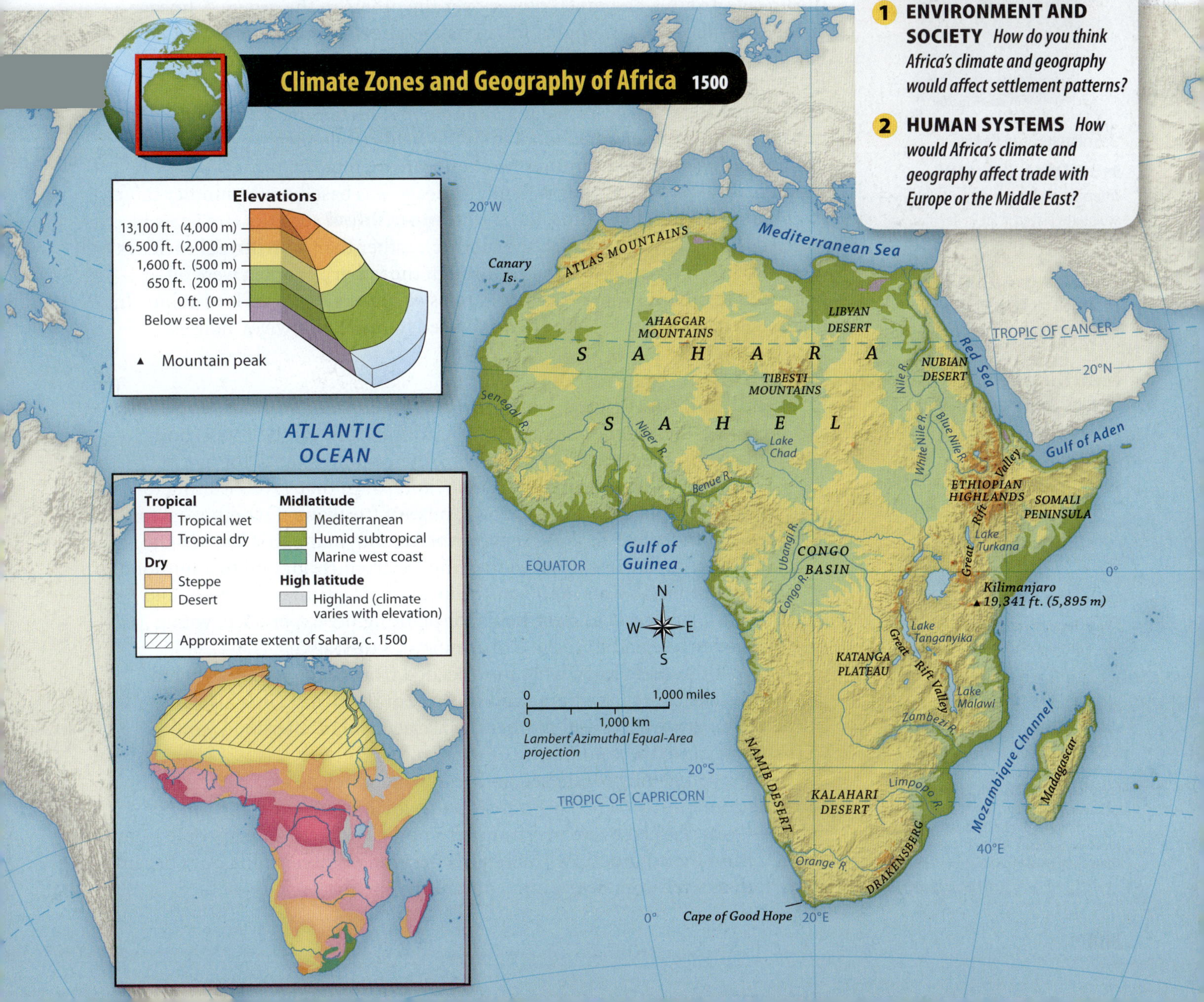

▲ Sculpture of an Ife king

▶ **CRITICAL THINKING**

Inferring What role do you think these sculptures played in life in Ife?

lineage groups an extended family unit that has combined into a larger community

matrilineal tracing lineage through the mother rather than the father

patrilineal tracing the lineage through the father

(continued from p. 303)

TEKS **Texas Essential Knowledge and Skills**

4D explain the political, economic, and social impact of Islam on Europe, Asia, and Africa

4I explain the development of the slave trade

23A describe the historical origins, central ideas, and spread of major religious and philosophical traditions, including Buddhism, Christianity, Confucianism, Hinduism, Islam, Judaism, Sikhism, and the development of monotheism

continued on the next page

African towns were home to artisans of metalwork, woodwork, pottery, and other crafts, as well as to farmers.

Most African societies did not have written languages, so much of our knowledge of them comes from descriptions recorded by foreign visitors, such as the Arab traveler Ibn Battuta. Although filled with information, visitors' reports were skewed as outside perspectives. Also, visitors usually came into contact only with the wealthy and the powerful. Their accounts tell little about ordinary people's lives.

Family and Lineage

Most Africans, including those in the east, west, and south, lived in small rural villages. Identity was determined by their membership in an extended family and a lineage group. At the basic level was the extended family, made up of parents, children, grandparents, and other family dependents. They lived in small round dwellings made of packed mud with thatched roofs of plant material such as straw. These family units assumed roles in larger communities known as **lineage groups**.

Lineage groups were the basic building blocks of African society. All members of a lineage group could claim to be descended from a real or legendary common ancestor. As in China, the elders—leading members of the lineage group—had much power over the others in the group. A lineage group provided mutual support for all its members. Members of extended families and lineage groups were expected to take care of one another.

Women were usually subordinate to men. In some cases, they were valued for their work or for having children and increasing the size of the lineage group. Women often worked in the fields while men tended cattle or hunted. In some communities, women were merchants.

In many African societies, a family's lineage was based on the mother rather than the father. In other words, these were **matrilineal** societies (societies in which descent is traced through the mother), rather than **patrilineal** societies (societies in which descent is traced through the father). Women were often permitted to inherit property and hold roles of social or political leadership. In these societies, husbands were often expected to move into wives' houses.

Education

In a typical African village, a process existed for educating young people and preparing them to become part of the community. By the 1400s, both boys and girls in the Congo were raised by their mothers until the age of six. They learned language, family history, and songs that gave meaning to their lives. At age six, girls went to the "house of the women" and boys went to the "house of the men." In these separate places, boys and girls learned the roles they should play in society as they moved from childhood to adulthood.

Fathers then took over their sons' education. Boys learned to hunt and fish, to grow plants, and to clear fields for planting. By experience, young men learned to live and to survive in the natural world.

Girls continued to learn what they needed from their mothers, including how to take care of the home and to work in the fields. Girls also learned to be good wives and mothers. Marriage and motherhood would be their entry into the community of women.

Finally, young people reached an age at which they were expected to enter the community fully. This transition—which occurred at the time of puberty—was marked by an initiation ceremony in which young people were isolated from the community. Young girls became women; young boys became men. Both entered completely into community life.

Slavery

Europeans did not introduce slavery to Africa. In fact, it had been practiced there since ancient times. Moreover, slavery was not unique to Africa, but common throughout the world.

North African Berber groups may have raided villages south of the Sahara for captives. The captives were then taken north and sold throughout the Mediterranean region. As Islam does not allow Muslims to be slaves, many non-Muslim Africans were used as slaves in the Arab and Turkish empires. The sale and use of captives for forced labor was common in African societies farther south and along the east coast of Africa as well. It is estimated that between 10 million and 18 million Africans were enslaved and transported to Arab territories from about A.D. 650 to the late 1800s when European powers took control of most of Africa. The slave trade in Africa has never completely ended, however, and still exists today in parts of Mauritania and Sudan.

✓ **READING PROGRESS CHECK**

Summarizing What was the role of lineage groups in African society?

Religious Beliefs

GUIDING QUESTION *What part did religious beliefs play in medieval African societies?*

Early African religious beliefs varied from place to place. Most African societies shared some common religious ideas, including a belief in a single creator god. Some Yoruba peoples in Nigeria believed that their chief god sent his son Oduduwa down from heaven in a canoe to create the first humans. Sometimes, the creator god was joined by a group of lesser gods. The Ashanti people of Ghana believed in the supreme being Nyame, whose sons were lesser gods. Ashanti gods could not always be trusted, so humans needed to appease them to avoid their anger. Some peoples believed that the creator god had lived on Earth but left in disgust at human behavior. However, the god was also merciful and could be pacified by proper behavior.

Ritual was a way to communicate with the gods. It was usually carried out by a special class of **diviners**, people who were believed to have the power to foretell events, usually by working with supernatural forces. The king employed many diviners to guarantee a bountiful harvest and to protect his interests and those of his subjects.

Another key element in African religion was the importance of ancestors. Each lineage group could trace itself back to a **founding** ancestor or a group of ancestors. Ritual ceremonies were dedicated to ancestors because the ancestors were believed to be closer to the gods. They had the power to influence the lives of their descendants.

African religious beliefs and traditions were challenged, though not necessarily replaced, by the arrival of Islam. Islam swept across northern Africa in the wake of the conquests of the caliphate. Consequently, much of North Africa converted to Islam. Islam was slower to spread through the lands south of the Sahara. The process likely began as a result of trade, as merchants introduced Muslim beliefs to the trading states of Mali, Ghana, and Songhai. At first, conversion took place on an individual basis. The first rulers to convert were the royal family of Gao. These conversions demonstrated the political impact of Islam. By the end of the 1400s, much of the population south of the Sahara had accepted Islam. In some ways, the beliefs of Islam were in conflict with African beliefs and customs. Over time, Islamic laws, customs, and beliefs were combined with native traditions to create a unique brand of Africanized Islam.

(continued from p. 304)

TEKS **Texas Essential Knowledge and Skills**

24A describe the changing roles of women, children, and families during major eras of world history

26B analyze examples of how art, architecture, literature, music, and drama reflect the history of the cultures in which they are produced

SKILLS PRACTICE

Write a sentence for each vocabulary word in this lesson. Leave a blank space where the vocabulary word should be in the sentence. Switch papers with a partner and complete the sentences about early African society.

diviner a person who is believed to have the power to foretell events

founding originating; beginning

Connections to TODAY

Griots and Oral Traditions

The tradition of the griot continues to be a vital part of West African culture. In countries such as Gambia and Senegal, these storytellers still act as oral historians and genealogists. Today's griots are also popular entertainers who put on shows, appear on television, and record CDs. Modern griots often mix traditional stories and modern commentary.

The process was even more gradual in East Africa. Islam was first brought to East Africa by Muslim traders from Arabia, but it did not gain many converts there until the twelfth and thirteenth centuries. It had even less success in areas of Ethiopia, where, beginning in the fourth century, Christianity had been adopted by the rulers of the state of Axum. As Muslim states slowly moved inland, they became involved in a conflict with Axum that ultimately led to Axum's collapse.

✓ **READING PROGRESS CHECK**

Identifying What role did ancestors play in African religion?

African Culture

GUIDING QUESTIONS ***How did values and customs help shape societies in medieval Africa? What part did religious beliefs play in medieval African societies?***

In early Africa, including in the kingdoms of Ghana, Mali, and Songhai, the arts—whether painting, literature, or music—were a means of serving religion. A work of art was meant to express religious conviction. For example, wood-carvers throughout Africa made remarkable masks and statues. The carvings often represented gods, spirits, or ancestral figures and were believed to embody the spiritual powers of the subjects.

In the thirteenth and fourteenth centuries, metalworkers produced handsome bronze and iron statues at Ife (EE • feh), the capital of the Yoruba people, in what is now Nigeria. The Ife sculptures may have influenced artists in Benin in West Africa, who produced equally impressive works in bronze during the same period. The Benin sculptures include bronze heads, many of kings, and figures of various types of animals.

Like wood carving and sculpture, African music and dance often served a religious purpose. African dance was a way to communicate with the spirits. It was "the great popular art of the African people." With its strong rhythmic beat, African music would come to influence modern Western music.

African music also had a social purpose. In the absence of written language, the words to songs transmitted folk legends and religious traditions from generation to generation. Storytelling, usually by priests or a special class of storytellers known as **griots** (GREE • OHZ), served the same purpose. Such storytellers were oral historians and genealogists who kept alive a people's history. For example, the epic of Sundiata, which tells the story of the first Mali king, was passed down by griots.

griot a special class of African storytellers who help keep alive a people's history

✓ **READING PROGRESS CHECK**

Determining Importance Why was music and storytelling important in African societies?

LESSON 1 REVIEW

TEKS

Reviewing Vocabulary

1. ***Identifying*** What special powers did diviners claim to have? How did kings use diviners?

Using Your Notes

2. ***Identifying Cause and Effect*** Use your notes and knowledge of geography to explain how Africa's climatic zones and food production capabilities might have influenced the way African people have lived.

Answering the Guiding Questions

3. ***Inferring*** How have Africa's landforms and climate zones influenced its farming and herding?
4. ***Making Connections*** How did values and customs help shape societies in medieval Africa?
5. ***Analyzing*** What part did religious beliefs play in medieval African societies?

Writing Activity

6. **NARRATIVE** Describe a day in the life of a young African teenage boy or girl living in the savanna in medieval times. Include details about this person's surroundings, living situation, parental education, a religious activity, and an activity involving learning about his or her history.

Indigenous Religions

There are many varieties of religious belief that are limited to particular ethnic groups. These local religions are found in Africa as well as isolated parts of Japan, Australia, and the Americas.

Most local religions reflect a close relationship with the environment. Some groups teach that people are a part of nature, not separate from it. Animism is characteristic of many indigenous religions. Natural features are sacred, and stories about how nature came to be are an important part of religious heritage. Although many of these stories have been written down in modern times, they were originally transmitted orally.

Africa

The continent of Africa is home to a variety of local religions. Despite their differences, most African religions recognize the existence of one creator in addition to spirits that inhabit all aspects of life. Religious ceremonies are often celebrated with music and dance.

Japan

Shinto, founded in Japan, is the largest indigenous religion. It dates back to prehistoric times and has no formal doctrine. The gods are known as kami. Ancestors are also revered and worshiped. Its four million followers often practice Buddhism in addition to practicing Shinto.

Australia

The Australian Aboriginal religion has no deities. It is based upon a belief known as the Dreaming, or Dreamtime. Followers believe that ancestors sprang from the Earth and created all people, plant, and animal life. They also believe that these ancestors continue to control the natural world.

Native Americans

The beliefs of most Native Americans center on the spirit world; however, the rituals and practices of individual groups vary. Most Native Americans believe in a Great Spirit who, along with other spirits, influences all aspects of life. These spirits make their presence known primarily through acts of nature.

The rituals, prayers, and ceremonies of Native Americans are often centered on health and good harvest and hunting. Rituals used to mark the passage through stages of life, including birth, adulthood, and death, are passed down as tribal traditions. Religious ceremonies often focus on important points in the agricultural and hunting seasons. Prayers, which are offered in song and dance, also concentrate on agriculture and hunting themes as well as health and well-being.

Totem poles were popular among the Native American peoples of the Northwest Coast. They were often decorated with mythical beings, family crests, or other figures, and placed outside homes.

SKILLBUILDER

TEKS 31A

Problem Solving

Why Learn This Skill?

Whether it's in or outside of the classroom, there will always be problems present that need to be solved. Having a specific process to help you tackle these problems can make it a lot more manageable to deal with.

Learning the Skill

It is useful to have a process, or set of steps, when trying to manage a problem. World history is influenced by problems faced and decisions made. Understanding the process used to solve problems is a good strategy to use when trying to understand historical concepts and themes. Of course, it's also an excellent strategy to use in your day-to-day life. Read the points below to see the steps in the problem-solving process:

- Identify a problem: What is the issue that needs to be solved?
- Gather information: What are the factors that led to this becoming a problem?
- List and consider options: What steps could be taken to solve this problem on the basis of the information gathered?
- Consider advantages and disadvantages: Would one option work better than another?
- Choose and implement a solution: On the basis of the previous steps, apply the solution that works best.
- Evaluate the effectiveness of the solution: Did the process lead to the correct decision? Were there outcomes that weren't anticipated?

Keep in mind that sometimes you might have to go back to a previous step if it seems like you are heading toward a dead end rather than a solution.

Practicing the Skill

Read this excerpt about early African kingdoms and then answer the questions below.

"Most African societies did not have written languages, so much of our knowledge of them comes from descriptions recorded by foreign visitors, such as the Arab traveller Ibn Battuta. Although filled with information, visitors' reports were skewed as outside perspectives. Also, visitors usually came into contact only with the wealthy and the powerful. Their accounts tell little about ordinary people's lives."

1. What problem can you identify from this paragraph?
2. What are the factors contributing to this problem?
3. What are some options for solving this problem?
4. What advantages and disadvantages are there to each of these options?
5. What solution would you propose to deal with this problem?
6. How effective do you think this solution would be? Why?

Applying the Skill

Using the steps outlined above, identify a problem in your community that you feel needs a solution. List each of the steps above, and if possible implement your solution and evaluate its effectiveness. Did the process lead you to a useful solution?

networks

There's More Online!

- BIOGRAPHY Mansa Mūsā
- BIOGRAPHY Muhammad Ture
- BIOGRAPHY Sundiata Keita
- BIOGRAPHY Sunni Ali
- CHART/GRAPH Northern and Southern African Kingdoms
- INFOGRAPHIC Coastal Trade in Africa
- INTERACTIVE SELF-CHECK QUIZ
- MAP The Bantu Migration
- PRIMARY SOURCE Ibn Battuta
- VIDEO The Kingdom of Mali

LESSON 2
Kingdoms and States of Africa

ESSENTIAL QUESTION

How does geography affect society, culture, and trade?

Reading HELPDESK

Academic Vocabulary
- factor
- administrative
- security

Content Vocabulary
- subsistence farming
- stateless society

TAKING NOTES:
Key Ideas and Details

Organizing As you read, use a table like the one below to compare and contrast East, West, and South Africa.

	Economy	Politics	Society
East			
West			
South			

TEKS Texas Essential Knowledge and Skills

4D explain the political, economic, and social impact of Islam on Europe, Asia, and Africa

4J analyze how the Silk Road and the African gold-salt trade facilitated the spread of ideas and trade

16B analyze the influence of human and physical geographic factors on major events in world history, including the development of river valley civilizations, trade in the Indian Ocean, and the opening of the Panama and Suez canals

It Matters Because

As African civilizations developed, great trading states arose. Traveling across the desert and over the wide Indian Ocean, traders from these states helped make their people rich and powerful. Trade not only resulted in a transfer of ivory, gold, and other valuable merchandise but also in a transfer of cultures, spreading religions, languages, and new ideas.

The Kingdom of Ghana

GUIDING QUESTION *How did gold help create a strong economy in the kingdom of Ghana?*

Ghana, the first great trading state in West Africa, emerged as early as A.D. 500. The kingdom of Ghana was located in the upper Niger River valley, a grassland region between the Sahara and the tropical forests along the West African coast. (The modern state of Ghana, located in the forest region to the south, takes its name from this early state.) Most people in the area were farmers living in villages under the authority of a local ruler. Together, the villages made up the kingdom of Ghana.

The kings of Ghana were strong rulers who governed without written laws. They played active roles in running the kingdom, and their wealth was vast. Al-Bakri wrote of the Ghanaian king's court:

PRIMARY SOURCE

"He sits in audience or to hear grievances against officials in a domed pavilion around which stand ten horses covered with gold-embroidered materials. Behind the king stand ten pages holding shields and swords decorated with gold, and on his right are the sons of the vassal kings' of his country wearing splendid garments and their hair plaited with gold."

—Al-Bakri, an eleventh-century Muslim traveler to Ghana, quoted in *The Human Record: Sources of Global History: To 1700*

To protect their kingdom and enforce their wishes, Ghanaian kings relied on a well-trained regular army of thousands of men.

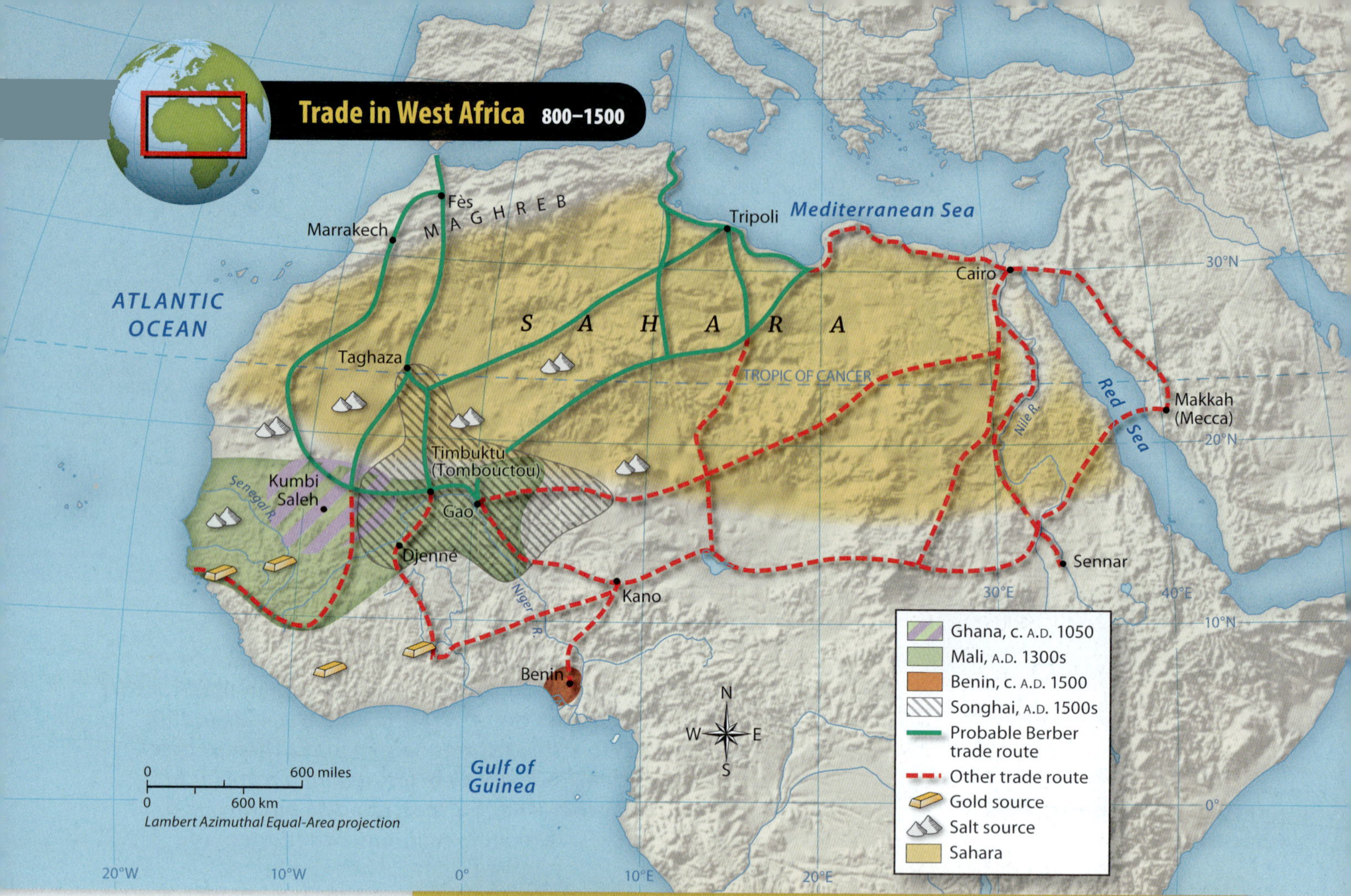

GEOGRAPHY CONNECTION

Berbers used several trade routes to cross the vast Sahara.

1. **HUMAN SYSTEMS** *How did the various resources shown on the map make these African kingdoms wealthy?*
2. **ENVIRONMENT AND SOCIETY** *What do the western African cities shown on the map have in common?*

Ghana had an abundance of gold. The heartland of the state was located near one of the richest gold-producing areas in all of Africa. Ghana's gold made it the center of an enormous trade empire. By the eighth and ninth centuries, Muslim merchants carried on much of this trade. These merchants had established trade networks throughout the world of Islam, opening up Africa south of the Sahara to a much wider marketplace. Muslim merchants bought goods from Ghanaian traders and then sold the goods to Berbers, who carried them across the desert.

Muslim merchants from North Africa brought to Ghana metal goods, textiles, horses, and salt. Salt was a highly desired item for the Ghanaians. It was used to preserve food and to improve food's taste. Salt was also important because people needed extra salt to replace what their bodies lost in the hot climate. Ghanaians traded their abundant gold for products brought from North Africa. Other Ghanaian exports, including ivory, hides, and slaves, were carried to the markets of the Mediterranean and beyond.

More than just trade goods were exchanged through the gold and salt trade. Berbers from North Africa and Ghanaians from south of the Sahara had different religions, customs, and ideas. The gold-salt trade provided an opportunity for these two cultures to interact peacefully. This interaction facilitated the spread of new forms of technology and new ideas about religion and science.

Berber camel caravans became known as the "fleets of the desert," and they carried much of the trade across the Sahara. Camels were a crucial **factor** in trans-Saharan trade. They were well-adapted to desert conditions and could drink large quantities of water at one time. Accompanied by guards, the caravan of as many as 100 camels moved at a rate of about three miles (4.8 km) per hour. A caravan might take 40 to 60 days to reach its destination.

factor a contributing part

✓ READING PROGRESS CHECK

Monitoring What role did the Berbers play in African trade?

The Kingdom of Mali

GUIDING QUESTION ***What contributed to the success of the kingdom of Mali?***

Ghana flourished for several hundred years. Weakened by wars, it collapsed during the 1100s. In its place rose new trading states in West Africa. The greatest was the kingdom of Mali, established in the mid-1200s by Sundiata Keita.

Considered the founder of his nation, Sundiata defeated Ghana and captured its capital in 1240. He united the people of Mali and created a strong government. Extending from the Atlantic coast inland to the famous trading city of Timbuktu (TIHM • BUHK • TOO), present-day Tombouctou, Mali built its wealth and power on the gold and salt trade. Most of its people, however, were farmers who grew grains such as sorghum, millet, and rice. The farmers lived in villages with local rulers, who served as both religious and **administrative** leaders. The ruler was responsible for sending tax revenues from the village to the kings of Mali.

administrative relating to the execution of public affairs, as distinguished from policy making

One of the richest and most powerful kings was Mansa Mūsā (*mansa* means "king"), who ruled from 1312 to 1337. Mansa Mūsā doubled the size of the kingdom of Mali. He created a strong central government and divided the kingdom into provinces ruled by governors whom he appointed. After he felt secure, he decided—as a devout Muslim—to make a pilgrimage to Makkah.

A king was no ordinary pilgrim. Thousands of servants and soldiers joined Mansa Mūsā on this journey. Hundreds of camels carrying gold, food, clothing, and supplies accompanied the people.

Everywhere he went, Mansa Mūsā lavished gold gifts on his hosts and bought hundreds of items with gold. By putting so much gold into circulation in such a short time, he caused its value to fall. The caravan's route took it through Egypt, and one observer reported, "Gold was at a high price in Egypt until they came in that year.... its value fell and it cheapened in price and has remained cheap till now."

No doubt, Mansa Mūsā's great pilgrimage left people with an image of him as a great ruler of a powerful and prosperous kingdom. Mansa Mūsā also left another legacy. Earlier rulers had already converted to Islam, but Mansa Mūsā was inspired to make Timbuktu a center of Islamic learning and culture. In Timbuktu, he built mosques and libraries. He brought scholars to the city to study the Quran.

Timbuktu became recognized as one of the intellectual capitals of the Muslim world. The city attracted religious leaders, scholars, and artists from all over the Middle East and Africa. As many as 20,000 students may have attended the famous University of Sankore.

Thinking Like a HISTORIAN

What makes a commodity valuable?

The ancient West African peoples who lived along the Niger and other rivers could easily pan for gold. However, that gold was less valuable to them than salt, a resource that they lacked but needed to preserve and season their food. To the Muslim merchants from North Africa, "trading salt for gold was a dream come true." Use the Internet to find reliable sources about how the differing values placed on commodities contributed to the growth of West African trading empires such as Ghana.

▲ **Mansa Mūsā is shown seated on his throne in this map of Africa from the Catalan Atlas of 1375.**

▶ **CRITICAL THINKING**

Analyzing Visuals What information is included on this fourteenth-century map?

Mansa Mūsā proved to be the last powerful ruler of Mali. By 1359, civil war divided Mali. Within another hundred years, a new kingdom—that of Songhai—was beginning to surpass Mali.

✓ READING PROGRESS CHECK

Identifying What were Mansa Mūsā's accomplishments?

The Kingdom of Songhai

GUIDING QUESTION *What were the key factors in the kingdom of Songhai's rise to power?*

Like the Nile, the Niger River floods, providing a rich soil for raising crops and cattle. East of Timbuktu, the Niger makes a wide bend. The Songhai established themselves south of that river bend.

In 1009 a ruler named Kossi converted to Islam and established the Dia dynasty. This first Songhai state benefited from the Muslim trade routes linking Arabia, North Africa, and West Africa. An era of prosperity ensued with Gao as the chief trade center.

Under the leadership of Sunni Ali, who created a new Sunni dynasty in 1464, Songhai began to expand. Sunni Ali spent much of his reign on horseback and on the march as he led his army in one military campaign after another. His armies both defended Songhai territory from attacks by outsiders and conquered new territories.

Two of Sunni Ali's conquests, Timbuktu and Djenné, gave Songhai control of the trading empire—especially trade in salt and gold—that had made Ghana and Mali so prosperous. Also, the Songhai, like its predecessors, used the shells of cowries as a medium of exchange.

Sunni Ali controlled not only the military but also the government of Songhai. Among his most important administrative accomplishments was uniting rural and city dwellers, who often had differing interests, under a single government.

The Songhai Empire reached the height of its power during Muhammad Ture's reign. A military commander and devout Muslim, Muhammad Ture overthrew the son of Sunni Ali and seized power in 1493, thus creating the new Askia dynasty. *Askia* means "usurper."

Muhammad Ture continued Sunni Ali's policy of expansion, creating an empire that stretched a thousand miles along the Niger River. He was also an able administrator who divided Songhai into provinces and appointed a governor to be in charge of each one. Muhammad Ture maintained the peace and **security** of his kingdom with a navy and soldiers on horseback. The chief cities of the empire prospered as never before from the expanding salt and gold trade.

security freedom from danger or invasion; safety

Under Askia Dawud, or Daud (1549–1582), Songhai became the largest empire in African history. After his reign, Songhai entered a period of slow decline. Near the end of the 1500s, that decline quickened when the forces of the sultan of Morocco occupied much of Songhai. One observer wrote, "From that moment on, everything changed. Danger took the place of security, poverty of wealth. Peace gave way to distress, disaster, and violence." By 1600, the Songhai Empire was a remnant of its former glorious self.

✓ **READING PROGRESS CHECK**

Identifying What were the key factors in Songhai's rise to power?

Societies in East Africa

GUIDING QUESTIONS ***How did Bantu migration affect culture in different areas of Africa? How did Indian Ocean trade affect societies in East Africa?***

In eastern Africa, several states and societies, many influenced by Islam, took root. Some became extremely wealthy through trade.

Migration of the Bantus

South of Axum, along the shores of the Indian Ocean and inland from the mountains of Ethiopia, lived a mixture of peoples. Some lived by hunting and food gathering, while others raised livestock.

In the first millennium B.C., farming peoples who spoke dialects of the Bantu (BAN • TOO) family of languages began to move from the Niger River region into East Africa. They moved slowly as small communities.

Recent archaeological work has provided insight into Bantu society. Their communities were based on **subsistence farming**—growing crops for personal use, not for sale. Millet and sorghum were the primary crops, along with yams, melons, and beans. Iron and stone tools were used to farm the land. Men hunted or traded locally in salt, copper, and iron ore. Women tilled fields and cared for children.

subsistence farming the practice of growing just enough crops for personal use, not for sale

The Bantus spread iron-smelting techniques and the knowledge of high-yield crops such as yams and bananas across Africa. Sometime after A.D. 1000, descendants of a Bantu group established the prosperous city of Great Zimbabwe, which dominated the trade route to the coast.

Indian Ocean Trade and Ports

On the eastern fringe of Africa, the Bantu-speaking peoples began to take part in the regional sea trade up and down the eastern coast. The physical geography of the Indian Ocean made it an ideal avenue for trade as seasonal monsoon winds allowed for brisk sailing between markets of East Africa and India.

Human geography played its role in the development of trade across the Indian Ocean. The spread of Islam to East Africa resulted in an increase in regional trade. Through the influence and efforts of Muslim merchants, the

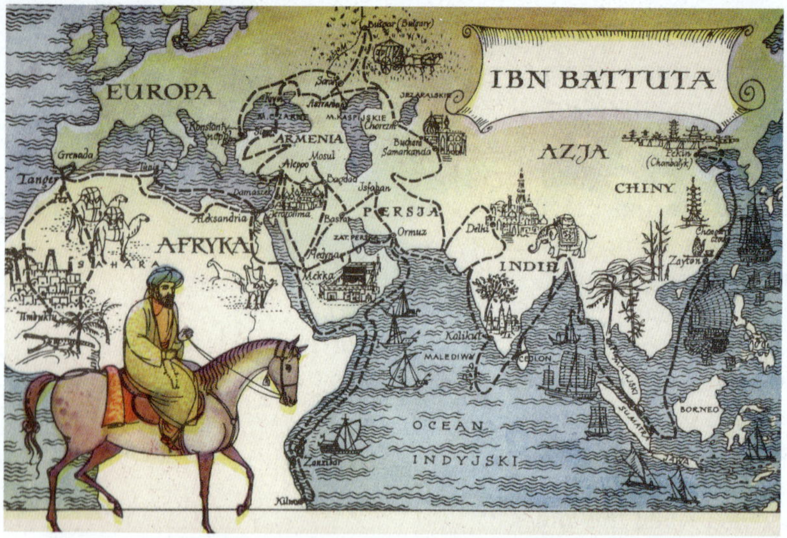

▲ A map of Ibn Battuta's journeys in the fourteenth century

▶ CRITICAL THINKING

Interpreting Significance To what parts of the world did Ibn Battuta travel? Why were his travels significant?

eastern coast of Africa became a part of the trading network along the Indian Ocean. Beginning in the eighth century, Muslims from the Arabian Peninsula and the Persian Gulf began to settle in port cities along the coast. The result was the formation of a string of trading ports that included Mogadishu (MOH • guh • DEE • shoo), Mombasa, and Kilwa in the south, settled by Arab traders.

In the fourteenth century in Kilwa, two monumental buildings were constructed of coral cut from the cliffs along the shore. One was the Great Mosque of Kilwa. Even grander was the Husuni Kubwa palace, an enormous cliff-top building with more than 100 rooms.

Arab traveler Ibn Battuta, who lived in the fourteenth century, was among those who visited the cities of Kilwa, Mogadishu, and Mombasa. One of the most widely traveled people of his time period, Battuta traveled as many as 75,000 miles (120,700 km), visiting almost all Muslim countries and even reaching China. He recorded his impressions about the places he visited.

No stranger to architectural wonders, Battuta called Kilwa, which he visited in 1331, "one of the most beautiful and well-constructed towns in the world." Kilwa's splendor did not last long. After a decline, in 1505 the Portuguese sacked the city and destroyed its major buildings.

Located just north of the Equator, Mogadishu was established in the tenth century. This trading port enjoyed hundreds of years of prosperity but declined in the sixteenth century. Mombasa, located on the coast of present-day Kenya, arose in the eleventh century. Like Mogadishu and Kilwa, Mombasa played a key role in trade across the Indian Ocean.

As time passed, a mixed African-Arabian culture, eventually known as Swahili (swah • HEE • lee), began to emerge throughout the coastal area. Intermarriage was common among the ruling groups. Gradually, the Muslim religion and Arabic architectural styles became part of a society that was still largely African.

The term *Swahili* (from *sahel*, meaning "coast" in Arabic, and thus "peoples of the coast") was also applied to the major language used in the area. The Swahili language arose as a result of trade between people from Arab lands and the Bantu people who lived along Africa's eastern coast. The language incorporated words from both Bantu and Arabic. It enabled these two groups of people without a common language to communicate and to trade. As Arab trade in ivory and slaves spread north and west, the Swahili language spread there, too. Today Swahili is the national language of Kenya and Tanzania.

✓ READING PROGRESS CHECK

Identifying How did the arrival of Arab traders influence life in eastern Africa?

Societies in South Africa

GUIDING QUESTION *In what way were states in southern Africa different than those in the north?*

stateless societies a group of independent villages organized into clans led by a local ruler or clan head without any central government

In the southern half of the African continent, states formed more slowly than in the north. Until the eleventh century, most of the peoples in this region lived in what are sometimes called **stateless societies**. A stateless society was a group of independent villages that were organized by clans and ruled by a local chieftain or clan head.

Beginning in the eleventh century, in some parts of southern Africa, these independent villages gradually began to consolidate. Out of these groups came the first states. In the grassland regions south of the Zambezi River, a mixed economy of farming, cattle herding, and trade had developed over a period of many centuries. Villages were usually built inside walls to protect the domestic animals from wild animals at night. Beginning in the eleventh century, some of these villages in southern Africa gradually united.

From about 1300 to about 1450, Zimbabwe (zihm • BAH • bwee) was the wealthiest and most powerful state in the region. It prospered from the gold trade with the Swahili trading communities on the eastern coast of Africa. Indeed, Zimbabwe's gold ended up in the court of Kublai Khan.

The ruins of Zimbabwe's capital, known as Great Zimbabwe, illustrate the kingdom's power and influence. Modern visitors generally agree that the ruins are the most impressive archaeological site in southern Africa.

Great Zimbabwe was well placed to benefit from trade between the coast and the interior. The town sits on a hill overlooking the Zambezi River and is surrounded by stone walls. Ten thousand residents would have been able to live in the area enclosed by the walls. Artifacts found at the site include household implements, ornaments made of gold and copper, and porcelain imported from China. The massive walls of Great Zimbabwe are unusual. The local people stacked granite blocks together without mortar to build the walls.

The Great Enclosure, whose exact purpose is not known, dominated the site. It was an oval space surrounded by a wall 800 feet long, 17 feet thick, and 32 feet high (about 244 m long, 5 m thick, and 10 m high). Near the Great Enclosure were smaller walled enclosures that contained round houses built of a mud-like cement on stone foundations. In the valley below was the royal palace, surrounded by a high stone wall.

Most of the king's wealth came from two sources: the ownership of cattle and the king's ability to levy heavy taxes on the gold that passed through the kingdom en route to the coast. By the middle of the fifteenth century, however, the city was abandoned, possibly because of damage to the land through overgrazing or natural disasters such as droughts and crop failures. With the decline of Zimbabwe, the focus of economic power began to shift northward.

▲ **Trees grow amid the ruins of Great Zimbabwe where thousands of people once lived.**

▶ **CRITICAL THINKING**

Hypothesizing Why was Great Zimbabwe abandoned?

PHOTO: Dennis Johnson/Lonely Planet Images

✓ **READING PROGRESS CHECK**

Identifying In what type of society did most peoples in southern Africa live until the eleventh century?

LESSON 2 REVIEW TEKS

Reviewing Vocabulary

1. ***Describing*** What is subsistence farming? What early African group of people used this type of farming?

Using Your Notes

2. ***Comparing*** Use your notes to compare the economic, political, and social characteristics of West, East, and South Africa.

Answering the Guiding Questions

3. ***Identifying*** How did gold help create a strong economy in the kingdom of Ghana? 4J
4. ***Analyzing*** What contributed to the success of the kingdom of Mali? 16B
5. ***Synthesizing*** What were the key factors in the kingdom of Songhai's rise to power?
6. ***Summarizing*** How did the human geography of the Bantu migration affect culture in different areas of Africa? 16B
7. ***Analyzing Cause and Effect*** How did Indian Ocean trade affect societies in East Africa?
8. ***Contrasting*** In what way were states in southern Africa different than those in the north?

Writing Activity

9. **INFORMATIVE/EXPLANATORY** Explain how geography influenced the societies in East Africa. 16B

CHAPTER 13 Assessment

TEKS

Directions: On a separate sheet of paper, answer the questions below. Make sure you read carefully and answer all parts of the questions.

Lesson Review

Lesson 1

1. ***Explaining*** Explain the development of the slave trade in medieval Africa. **4I**

2. ***Contrasting*** How were matrilineal societies different from patrilineal societies? **24A**

3. ***Naming*** From where does much of our knowledge of early African societies come? What traveler is known for his recorded descriptions of African societies?

4. ***Identifying*** What is a griot? What purpose do they serve in west African culture?

5. ***Describing*** Describe the four climate zones in African and name natural features that exist across the zones. Do you think that humans struggle to live in or near any of the zones?

6. ***Analyze Information*** Compare the basic foundations of Yoruba and Ashanti spiritual beliefs, including their idea of human origins and characteristics of gods. **29F**

7. ***Making Connections*** Why might artistic works have a tie to religious beliefs? Select a form of artwork and explain how that particular artwork in African kingdoms of Ghana, Mali, or Songhai conveyed a spiritual value or concept.

Lesson 2

8. ***Summarizing*** Summarize how the powerful king of Mali, Mansa Mūsā, both enhanced the kingdom of Mali, as well as hindered its economy. State whether his contributions outweigh any negative aspects of his reign.

9. ***Identifying*** What allowed Ghana to become a wealthy state? Who benefited the most?

10. ***Describing*** What led to the fall of the Songhai Empire?

11. ***Analyzing*** How did the arrival of Islam in East Africa influence trade in the Indian Ocean? **16B**

12. ***Identifying*** Trading in East Africa during the 14th century led to wealthy merchants and impressive cities, such the city of Kilwa. Provide an example of how natural geography was utilized in the construction of impressive buildings or palaces.

13. ***Describing*** Describe the organization of "stateless societies" in southern Africa before the 11th century. What happened to shift this structure at the start of the 11th century?

Exploring the Essential Question

14. ***Analyzing and Comparing*** With a partner, choose two of the ancient kingdoms of Africa. Create a multimedia presentation that analyzes and compares the geographic distributions and patterns of each kingdom. Include at least one map and interpret the geography and climate of the kingdom, and explain how geography and climate affected society, culture, trade, and the settlement patterns of people. If possible, include at least one primary source. **16C**

Need Extra Help?

If You've Missed Question	1	2	3	4	5	6	7	8	9	10	11	12	13	14
Go to page	305	304	314	306	302	305	309	311	309	313	314	314	314	309

Critical Thinking

15 ***Making Connections*** Consider the family structure and values in African society, such as lineage groups and identifying founding ancestors. Make a connection to African religious beliefs, including ritual ceremonies dedicated to ancestors. Describe the ties between the two aspects of African society.

16 ***Explaining*** In what ways did Islam impact the economy of Ghana and North Africa? **4D**

17 ***Interpreting*** What qualified Ibn Battuta to make judgments about the African cities he visited, such as Kilwa in eastern Africa? Why might his accounts be skewed in one way or another?

18 ***Analyzing*** How did physical geographic features impact trade in the Indian Ocean? **16B**

19 ***Explaining*** How was the kingdom of Axum affected by the arrival of Islam in East Africa? **4D**

20 ***Describing*** What does education in medieval African society tell you about the roles of children at this time? **24A**

Social Studies Skills

21 ***Analyze*** What geographic feature guided the settlement pattern of the Songhai that helped the kingdom thrive? Explain why.

22 ***Identifying Cause and Effect*** How did the conquests of the caliphate in North Africa impact Africa south of the Sahara? **1C**

23 ***Explaining Continuity and Change*** What was the social impact of Islam on the people of Africa? **4D**

24 ***Explaining*** Discuss with a partner how historians would use records and artifacts to analyze the ruins of Zimbabwe's former capital, known as Great Zimbabwe. What information might historians continue to seek in order to understand more about the past? **29B**

25 ***Create Presentations*** Choose a king or significant leader from early African kingdoms. Gather additional research about the individual and create visuals that help communicate key details about his role, accomplishments, and society's culture. Leave the presentation open-ended for classmates to do further inquiry on aspects of the figure that are most appealing. **30C**

Need Extra Help?

If You've Missed Question	15	16	17	18	19	20	21	21	23	24	25
Go to page	304	305	304	313	306	304	312	305	305	315	311

DBQ Analyzing Primary Sources

Use the map to answer the following questions.

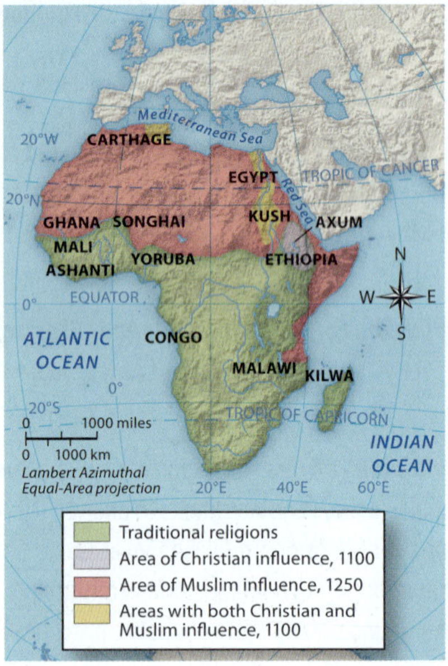

In some areas, African traditional religion fused with Islam or Christianity. Today in the Congo, half the people are Roman Catholic, and the rest belong to sects that have blended two or more belief systems.

26. ***Describing Movement*** Describe the spread of Islam in early African kingdoms, states, or societies. To which kingdoms had Islam reached by 1250? **23A**

27. ***Describing Location*** What were the religious differences among East, West, and South Africa? Where did Christianity spread? **23A**

28. ***Making Inferences*** If more than half of the people living in the Congo today are Roman Catholic, what inferences can you make about the spread of Christianity after 1250?

Analyzing Visuals

Use the image to answer the following questions.

This map depicts the gold and salt trade of West Africa between 800 and 1500 A.D.

29. ***Analyzing*** How did the Berbers facilitate the gold-salt trade? **4J**

30. ***Analyzing*** Analyze the expansive gold-salt trade route and explain how this trade facilitated the spread of ideas. **4J**

31. ***Hypothesizing*** Looking at the Berber and other trade routes included on the map, what does the distance of each route and number of cities along the routes tell you about the experiences of traders?

32. ***Analyzing*** In order to understand more about the challenges and time involved in traveling along a trade route, what additional information would enhance this map?

Extended Response Question

33. ***Informative/Explanatory*** How were African religious beliefs affected by Islam? **4D**

Need Extra Help?

If You've Missed Question	26	27	28	29	30	31	32	33
Go to page	305	305	318	310	310	310	318	305

Pre-Columbian America

300–1550

ESSENTIAL QUESTIONS • *In what ways were civilizations in early Mesoamerica and South America complex?* • *How were civilizations in early Mesoamerica and South America influenced by previous cultures?*

networks

There's More Online! about pre-Columbian America.

CHAPTER 14

The Story Matters...

Between 2000 B.C. and A.D. 1500, new civilizations arose in several regions of the Western Hemisphere. In fertile Mesoamerica (present-day Mexico and Central America), a series of cultures, including the Olmec, Maya, Toltec, and Aztec, built great cities that nurtured rich traditions. At their peak around A.D. 900, the Maya had a stable government, a written language, and a calendar. The Maya also created great works of architecture, painting, pottery, and sculpture.

◀ This Maya mask, constructed of jade with inlaid mother of pearl eyes, was made between the seventh and tenth centuries near the city of Palenque, in modern-day Mexico. The mask is a striking example of the skill of Maya craftspeople in representing the stylized human form.

CHAPTER 14

Place and Time: The Americas 1200 B.C.–A.D. 1500

In Mesoamerica and South America, new civilizations emerged beginning in the second millennium B.C. As the older civilizations, such as the Olmec, the first-known civilization in Mesoamerica, and the Chavin, an early South American civilization, declined, a series of new civilizations took their places. From their religious beliefs to their farming and building methods to their calendars, later civilizations, such as the Aztec and Inca, shared many characteristics with the earlier ones. It is believed that these cultural traits and customs were disseminated throughout the region by both conquest and trade.

Step Into the Place

Interpret the chart and look at the information presented on the map. Consider how geography influenced people and events in the region's past.

DBQ Explain the features of early Mesoamerican and South American society that remained the same throughout several civilizations? Which features changed?

	Agriculture	Religion	Architecture	Calendar and Writing
Olmec	• raised fields • drainage canals	• jaguar-god • human sacrifice	• monumental pyramids	• astronomical calendar • hieroglyphics
Zapotec	• slash-and-burn farming	• several gods • human sacrifice	• cities with temples and plazas	• solar and ritual calendars • hieroglyphics
Chavin	• potatoes, peanuts, and yams	• gods with human and feline traits	• platform temples • adobe and cut stone	• no calendar system • no written language
Maya	• slash-and-burn farming • swamp drainage • terracing and irrigation	• worship of Quetzalcoatl • human sacrifice	• monumental pyramids	• ritual, solar, "long count" calendars • hieroglyphics
Aztec	• *chinampas,* artificial islands for farming	• many gods • worship of Huitzilopochtli • human sacrifice	• Tenochtitlán island city with canals and causeways	• ritual and civil calendars • written language
Inca	• terracing • irrigation • drainage canals	• many gods • human sacrifice	• massive stone structures without mortar • 19,000 miles of roads	• 12-month calendar • no written language; *quipu,* knotted strings to record expenses and trade

Step Into the Time

Research a civilization from the time line and write a paragraph describing the reasons for its fall.

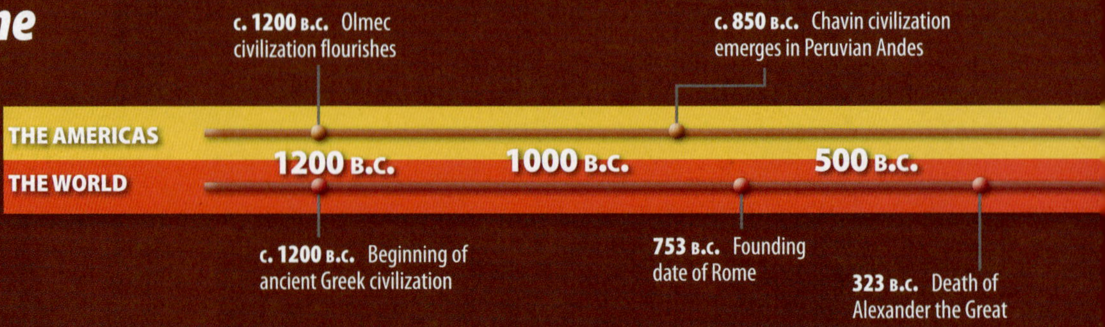

networks *There's More Online!*

- **MAP** Explore the interactive version of this map on Networks.
- **TIME LINE** Explore the interactive version of the time line on Networks.

Cultures of the Americas

Time Line

A.D. 1 — **A.D. 500** — **1000** — **1500**

- **202 B.C.– A.D. 220** Han dynasty rules in China
- **c. A.D. 250** Classic Maya period begins in Mexico and Central America
- **A.D. 320** Gupta dynasty rules in India
- **A.D. 323** Deach of Alexander the Great
- **A.D. 476** Last Roman emperor deposed; fall of the Western Roman Empire
- **8th century** Kingdom of Ghana emerges in Africa
- **c. A.D. 900** Toltecs burn city of Teotihuacán
- **A.D. 1325** The Aztec establish Tenochtitlán as their capital
- **after A.D. 1438** Pachacuti expands Inca Empire
- **A.D. 1453** Constantinople falls to Ottoman forces
- **A.D. 1521** Tenochtitlan is demolished; end of Aztec Empire
- **A.D. 1533** Inca capital Cuzco falls to the Spanish

LESSON 1

The Peoples of North America and Mesoamerica

ESSENTIAL QUESTIONS • *In what ways were civilizations in early Mesoamerica and South America complex?* • *How were civilizations in early Mesoamerica and South America influenced by previous cultures?*

networks

There's More Online!

- BIOGRAPHY Pacal the Great
- BIOGRAPHY Topiltzin
- IMAGE Pyramid of Kukulcan
- IMAGE Teotihuacán
- INTERACTIVE SELF-CHECK QUIZ
- MAP Tenochtitlán
- PRIMARY SOURCE Anasazi Legend
- SLIDE SHOW North American Societies and their Environments
- VIDEO Early North Americans

Reading HELPDESK

Academic Vocabulary

- **consist**
- **area**

Content Vocabulary

- **longhouse**
- **clan**
- **tepee**

TAKING NOTES:

Key Ideas and Details

Organizing As you read, use a table like the one below to organize information on the Maya, Toltec, and Aztec.

	Politics and Society	Religion and Culture
Maya		
Toltec		
Aztec		

TEKS Texas Essential Knowledge and Skills

6A compare the major political, economic, social, and cultural developments of the Maya, Inca, and Aztec civilizations and explain how prior civilizations influenced their development

27B summarize the major ideas in astronomy, mathematics, and architectural engineering that developed in the Maya, Inca, and Aztec civilizations

It Matters Because

Across the Atlantic Ocean from the great civilizations of the Old World, new civilizations were in the process of being formed. Most of these early peoples in the Americas lived by hunting and fishing or by food gathering. By 1200 B.C., the first organized societies started in Central America.

The Peoples of North America

GUIDING QUESTION *Who were the early peoples of North America?*

During the last Ice Age, a natural land bridge connected the Asian and North American continents. Early hunters used this land bridge when they followed herds of bison and caribou into North America. These hunters became the first people to live in North America.

Eastern Woodlands

Around 1000 B.C., farming villages appeared in the Eastern Woodlands, the land in eastern North America from the Great Lakes to the Gulf of Mexico. People here grew crops but also continued to gather wild plants for food. Best known are the Hopewell peoples in the Ohio River valley, who extended their culture along the Mississippi River. The Hopewell people, known as the Mound Builders, built large, elaborate earth mounds that were used as tombs or for ceremonies. Some were built in the shapes of animals.

The shift to full-time farming in approximately A.D. 700 led to a prosperous culture in the Mississippi River valley. This Mississippian culture grew corn, squash, and beans together to provide plants with nutrients, support, and shade.

Cities began to appear, and some of them contained 10,000 people or more. At the site of Cahokia (kuh • HOH • kee • uh), near the modern city of East St. Louis, Illinois, archaeologists found a burial mound more than 98 feet (30 m) high. It had a base larger than the base of the Great Pyramid in Egypt. Between A.D. 850 and 1150, Cahokia flourished and served as the seat of government. For reasons unknown, Cahokia collapsed during the 1200s.

PHOTO: (l to r)©Goodshoot/Fotosearch, ©Werner Forman/CORBIS, Mary Evans Picture Library/The Image Works, ©Jose Fuste Raga/Corbis.

North American and Mesoamerican Cultural Centers 900 B.C.–A.D. 1500

GEOGRAPHY CONNECTION

1. **THE WORLD IN SPATIAL TERMS** *Why do you think more culture groups were located in the south than in the north?*
2. **PLACES AND REGIONS** *List the major Mesoamerican civilizations and suggest reasons for where their cities were situated.*

To the northeast of the Mississippian culture were people known as the Iroquois (IHR • uh • KWOY). The Iroquois lived in villages that **consisted** of **longhouses** surrounded by wooden fences for protection. Each longhouse, built of wooden poles covered with sheets of bark, was 150 to 200 feet (46 to 61 m) in length and housed about a dozen families.

Iroquois men hunted deer, bear, caribou, and small animals such as rabbits and beaver. They were warriors who protected the community. Women owned the dwellings, gathered wild plants, and grew crops. The most important crops were the "three sisters"—corn, beans, and squash. Women also cooked, made baskets, and cared for the children.

Wars were common, especially among groups of Iroquois who lived in much of present-day Pennsylvania, New York, and parts of southern Canada. Legend holds that sometime during the 1500s, the Iroquois peoples were nearly torn apart by warfare. Deganawida, an elder of one Iroquois group, appeared and preached the need for peace.

One who listened was Hiawatha, a member of the Onondaga (AH • nuhn • DAW • guh) group. From the combined efforts of Deganawida and Hiawatha came the Great Peace, which created an alliance of five groups called the Iroquois League.

A council of representatives, a group of 50 Iroquois leaders known as the Grand Council, met regularly to settle differences. Representatives were chosen in a special way. Each Iroquois group was made up of **clans**, or groups of related families. The women of each clan singled out a well-respected woman as the clan mother. The clan mothers then chose the male members of the Grand Council. Much was expected of these men—patience and firmness, but also a tenderness for their people and calm deliberation.

consist to be composed of or made up of

longhouse Iroquois house about 150 to 200 feet (46 to 61 m) long built of wooden poles covered with sheets of bark and housing about a dozen families

clan a group of related families

▲ Cliff Palace at Mesa Verde National Park, Colorado, is one of many cliff dwellings built by the Anasazi.

tepee a circular tent made by stretching buffalo skins over wooden poles

area a geographic region

Great Plains and Southwest

West of the Mississippi River basin, the Plains Indians cultivated beans, corn, and squash along the river valleys of the eastern Great Plains. Every summer, the men left their villages to hunt buffalo, a very important animal to the Plains culture. Hunters would work together to frighten a herd of buffalo, causing them to stampede over a cliff.

The buffalo served many uses for Plains peoples. They ate the meat, used the skins for clothing, and made tools from the bones. By stretching buffalo skins over wooden poles, they made circular tents called **tepees**. Tepees provided excellent shelter; they were warm in winter and cool in summer.

The Southwest covers the territory of present-day New Mexico, Arizona, Utah, and Colorado. Conditions are dry, but there is sufficient rain in some **areas** for farming. The Anasazi (AH • nuh • SAH • zee) peoples established an extensive farming society there.

Between A.D. 500 and 1200, the Anasazi used canals and earthen dams to garden in the desert. They were skilled at making baskets and pottery. Using stone and adobe (sun-dried brick), they built pueblos, or multistoried structures that housed many people.

At Chaco Canyon in northwestern New Mexico, they built an elaborate center for their civilization. At the heart of Chaco Canyon was Pueblo Bonito, a large complex that contained some 800 rooms housing more than 1,000 people. However, persistent droughts led the Anasazi to abandon it.

The Anasazi culture did not die. In southern Colorado, a large community formed at Mesa Verde (MAY • suh VEHR • dee) (today, a national park). Groups of Anasazi built a remarkable series of buildings in the recesses of the cliff walls. However, in the late 1200s, the Anasazi abandoned the settlement due to a prolonged drought.

✓ **READING PROGRESS CHECK**

Making Connections How did the shift to farming contribute to the development of various cultures in North America?

The Maya

GUIDING QUESTION *What made the Maya one of the most sophisticated civilizations of the early Americas?*

Signs of civilization in Mesoamerica—a name we use for areas of Mexico and Central America that were civilized before the Spaniards arrived—appeared around 1200 B.C. On the Yucatán Peninsula, one of the most sophisticated civilizations in the Americas arose. This was the civilization of the Maya, which flourished between A.D. 300 and A.D. 900.

The Maya built splendid temples and pyramids and developed a complicated calendar that was as accurate as any in existence in the world at that time. Maya civilization included much of Central America and southern Mexico.

Sometime around A.D. 800, the Maya civilization in the central Yucatán Peninsula began to decline. Why did this happen? Explanations include invasion, internal revolt, a volcanic eruption, or overuse of the land that led to reduced crop yields.

Whatever the case, Maya cities were abandoned and covered by dense jungle growth. They were not rediscovered until the nineteenth and twentieth centuries.

Political and Social Structures

Maya cities were built around a central pyramid topped by a shrine to the gods. Nearby were other temples, palaces, and a sacred ball court. Some scholars believe that more than 100,000 inhabitants might have lived in urban centers such as Tikal in present-day Guatemala.

Maya civilization was composed of city-states, each governed by a hereditary ruling class. These Maya city-states were often at war with each other. Ordinary soldiers who were captured in battle became slaves. Captured nobles and war leaders were used for human sacrifice.

In the powerful city-state of Palenque (pah • LEHNG • kay), the ruler Pacal claimed to be descended from the gods, as did other Maya rulers. These rulers were supported by nobles and a class of scribes who might also have been priests. Maya society also contained peasants and townspeople who worked as skilled artisans, officials, and merchants.

Most of the Maya peasants were farmers. They lived on tiny plots or on terraced hills in the highlands. Houses were built of adobe and thatch. There was a fairly clear-cut division of labor. Men did the fighting and hunting; women provided the homemaking and raising of children. Women also made cornmeal, the basic food of much of the population. The Maya also cultivated cacao trees, the source of chocolate, which was used as a beverage by the upper classes.

Religion and Culture

Crucial to Maya civilization was its spiritual perspective. For the Maya, all of life was in the hands of divine powers. The name of their supreme god was Itzamna (eet • SAWM • nuh), or "Lizard House." Gods were ranked in order of importance. Some, such as the jaguar god of night, were evil rather than good. The Maya were likely influenced by the prior civilization, the Olmec. This influence was especially seen in the practice of building step pyramids and in shared traits of ceremonial rituals.

Like other ancient civilizations in Mesoamerica, the Maya practiced human sacrifice to appease the gods. Human sacrifices were also used for special ceremonial occasions. The Maya created a sophisticated writing system based on hieroglyphs, or pictures. Unfortunately, the Spanish conquerors of the sixteenth century had little respect for the Maya language and made no effort to decipher it.

The Maya developed major ideas in architectural engineering that allowed them to incorporate religious ideas into their built structures. For example, pyramids sometimes cast shadows in significant shapes and reflected religious beliefs.

The Maya wrote on bark, folding it like an accordion, then covering the outside with thin plaster. Four of these books have survived. Maya hieroglyphs remained a mystery for centuries. Then, scholars discovered that many passages contained symbols that recorded dates in the Maya calendar. This calendar, known as the Long Count, was based on cycles of creation and destruction.

▼ **The design of the Maya pyramid of Kukulcan was shaped by celestial events. For example, during the spring and fall equinoxes (when the days and nights are of equal length), the stepped sides of the pyramid show a snake-like pattern.**

▶ **CRITICAL THINKING**

Drawing Conclusions Why might the Maya have constructed a pyramid to show solar events?

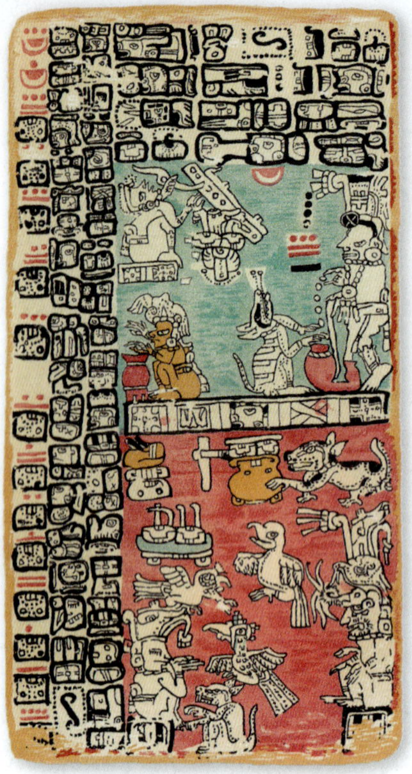

▲ This page from the Codex Troano, a Maya calendar, depicts gods and symbolic creatures.

The Maya used two different systems for measuring time. One was based on a solar calendar of 365 days, divided into 18 months of 20 days each and an extra 5 days at the end. The other was based on a sacred calendar of 260 days, divided into 13 weeks of 20 days. Only trained priests could read and use this calendar. These priests also used mathematics for astronomical and religious purposes. Maya numerals were based on the number 20 and included a symbol for zero—a concept developed independently from European and Asian cultures.

Many Maya hieroglyphics record important events in Maya history. One of the most important collections of Maya hieroglyphs is located at Palenque. There, archaeologists discovered a royal tomb covered with hieroglyphs that record the accomplishments of the great ruler Pacal.

✓ **READING PROGRESS CHECK**

Drawing Conclusions How did the belief system of the Maya affect their daily life?

The Toltec

GUIDING QUESTION ***What contributions did the Toltec make to early Mesoamerican culture?***

Around A.D. 1000, new peoples rose to prominence in central Mexico. Most significant were the Toltec. The Toltec empire reached its high point between A.D. 950 and 1150. The center of the empire was Tula, which was built on a high ridge about 43.5 miles (70 km) northwest of present-day Mexico City. The Toltec irrigated their fields with water from the Tula River and grew a number of crops, including beans, maize, and peppers. This agriculture enabled Tula to support a population of 40,000 to 60,000 people.

The Toltec were a warlike people. Their empire included much of northern and central Mexico. They also extended their conquests into the Maya lands of Guatemala and the northern Yucatán. The Toltec controlled the upper Yucatán Peninsula from Chichén Itzá for centuries.

The Toltec were also builders who constructed pyramids and palaces. They brought metalworking to Mesoamerica and were the first people in the region to work in gold, silver, and copper.

The Toltec empire began to decline around 1125 as a result of fighting among different groups in Tula. Around 1170, the city was sacked and much of it burned. There was no single ruling group for nearly 200 years until the Aztec Empire emerged. The prior Toltec civilization influenced the Aztec Empire's building styles and artwork.

✓ **READING PROGRESS CHECK**

Identifying What caused the decline of the Toltec empire?

The Aztec

GUIDING QUESTION ***How did the Aztec continue the tradition of building successful civilizations in Mesoamerica?***

The origins of the Aztec are uncertain. Sometime during the twelfth century, they began a long migration that brought them to the Valley of Mexico. They eventually established a capital at Tenochtitlán (tay • NAWCH • teet • LAHN), now Mexico City.

According to their legends, when the Aztec arrived in the Valley of Mexico, other peoples drove them into a snake-infested region. However, the Aztec survived, strengthened by their belief in a sign. Huitzilopochtli (wee • tsee • loh • POHKT • lee), their god of war and of the sun, had told them that when they saw an eagle perched on a cactus growing out of a rock, their journey would end.

In 1325 under attack by another people, they were driven into the swamps and islands of Lake Texcoco (tehs • KOH • koh). On one island, they saw an eagle standing on a prickly pear cactus on a rock. There they built Tenochtitlán (or "place of the prickly pear cactus"):

PRIMARY SOURCE

"Now we have found the land promised to us. We have found . . . peace for the weary Mexican people. Now we want for nothing."

—quoted in *500 Nations*

For the next 100 years, the Aztec constructed temples, other public buildings, and houses. They built roadways of stone across Lake Texcoco to the north, south, and west, linking the islands to the mainland.

The Aztec at Tenochtitlán formed a Triple Alliance with two other city states, Tetzcoco and Tlacopan. This alliance enabled the Aztec to dominate an empire that included much of today's Mexico, from the Gulf of Mexico to the Pacific Ocean and as far south as the Guatemalan border. This alliance lasted until the reign of Montezuma and the arrival of Spanish in the 1500s.

The new Aztec kingdom was not a centralized state but a collection of semi-independent territories that local lords governed. The Aztec ruler supported these rulers in return for tribute, goods or money paid by conquered peoples to their conquerors.

Political and Social Structures

By 1500, as many as four million Aztec lived in the Valley of Mexico and the surrounding valleys of central Mexico. Like all great empires in ancient times, the Aztec state was authoritarian. The monarch, who claimed lineage with the gods, held all power. A council of lords and government officials assisted the Aztec ruler.

The nobility, the elite of society, held positions in the government. Noble male children were sent to temple schools, which stressed military training. When they became adults, males would select a career in the military service, the government bureaucracy, or the priesthood. As a reward for their services, nobles received large estates from the government. The rest of the population consisted of indentured workers, slaves, and commoners. Indentured workers were landless laborers who contracted to work on the nobles' estates. Sold in the markets, male and female slaves worked in wealthy households.

▼ This image depicts Aztec priests discovering the location to build Tenochtitlán.

Most people were commoners, many of whom were farmers. The Aztec built *chinampas,* swampy islands crisscrossed by canals. The practical architectural engineering of these canals provided irrigation for crops and easy travel to markets. Aztec merchants were active traders. Especially in Tenochtitlán and other large cities, merchants exported and traded goods made by Aztec craftspeople from imported raw materials. When the Spanish arrived, they were astonished to find city markets that were considerably larger and better stocked than any markets in Spain.

From infancy, boys and girls in Aztec society had very different roles. The midwife who attended the birth of a male infant said, "You must understand that your home is not here where you have been born, for you

▲ The Codex Cospi is an Aztec calendar. Like the Maya calendar, it was created by priests.

▶ **CRITICAL THINKING**

Comparing and Contrasting How were the the Codex Troano and Codex Cospi similar? How were they different?

are a warrior." To a female infant, the midwife said, "As the heart stays in the body, so you must stay in the house." Though not equal to men, Aztec women could own and inherit property and enter into contracts, something not often allowed in other world cultures at the time. Most women worked in the home, weaving textiles and raising children. However, some were trained as priestesses.

Religion and Culture

Like other peoples in Central America and around the world, the Aztec had a polytheistic religion, believing in many gods. There was a supreme god, called Ometeotl, who represented the all-powerful forces of the heavens. Historians believe the Olmec influenced Aztec building styles and ceremonies.

Another important god was Quetzalcoatl, who had a more direct impact on the lives of the people. According to Aztec tradition, Quetzalcoatl had left his homeland in the Valley of Mexico in the tenth century, promising to return in triumph. When the Aztec first saw Spanish explorers in the 1500s, they believed that representatives of Quetzalcoatl had returned.

Aztec religion was based on a belief in an unending struggle between the forces of good and evil throughout the universe. This struggle created and destroyed four worlds, or suns. People believed they were now living in the time of the fifth sun, a world destined to be destroyed by earthquakes. To postpone the day of reckoning, the Aztec practiced human sacrifice, which they believed would appease the sun god Huitzilopochtli.

Religion had a significant influence on Aztec art and architecture. At the center of Tenochtitlán was the sacred district, dominated by a massive pyramid dedicated to Huitzilopochtli. Aztec architecture blended religious themes with the pyramid's traditional step-pyramid design. At the top was a platform containing shrines to the gods and an altar for performing human sacrifices.

The Aztec also made advances in astronomy, which is evident in their sun calendar. It contained pictographs that showed days, months, and larger cosmic cycles. Like those of the Maya, Aztec priests not only computed the calendar but also observed the movements of the stars and planets to gain knowledge of the future. The Aztec developed major ideas in mathematics, such as a number system based on units of 20.

✓ **READING PROGRESS CHECK**

Understanding Relationships What factors indicate that the Aztec had an advanced civilization?

LESSON 1 REVIEW TEKS

Reviewing Vocabulary

1. ***Describing*** Where was Cahokia located, and how was it important to the Hopewell peoples? What did archaeologists find at the site? Be specific.

Using Your Notes

2. ***Comparing and Contrasting*** Use your notes to compare and contrast the three great Mesoamerican civilizations. 6A, 27B

Answering the Guiding Questions

3. ***Listing*** Who were the early peoples of North America?
4. ***Identifying*** What made the Maya one of the most sophisticated civilizations of the early Americas? 27B
5. ***Summarizing*** What contributions did the Toltec make to early Mesoamerican culture? 6A
6. ***Analyzing*** How did the Aztec continue the tradition of building successful civilizations in Mesoamerica? 27B

Writing Activity

7. **INFORMATIVE/EXPLANATORY** How were the Maya, Toltec, and Aztec civilizations influenced by geography? Be specific. 27B

networks

There's More Online!

- BIOGRAPHY Huayna Capac
- IMAGE Inca Ice Maiden
- IMAGE Moche Arts
- IMAGE Nazca Lines
- IMAGE Quipu
- IMAGE Terraced Farming
- INFOGRAPHIC The Inca Trail
- INTERACTIVE SELF-CHECK QUIZ
- MAP Civilizations in South America, A.D. 700–1530
- SLIDE SHOW Inca Technology
- VIDEO The Inca

LESSON 2

Early South American Civilizations

ESSENTIAL QUESTIONS • *In what ways were civilizations in early Mesoamerica and South America complex?* • *How were civilizations in early Mesoamerica and South America influenced by previous cultures?*

Reading HELPDESK

Academic Vocabulary

- **instruct**
- **resident**

Content Vocabulary

- **maize**
- ***quipu***

TAKING NOTES:

Key Ideas and Details

Organizing As you read, use a pyramid diagram like the one below to show the hierarchy of the Inca political organization.

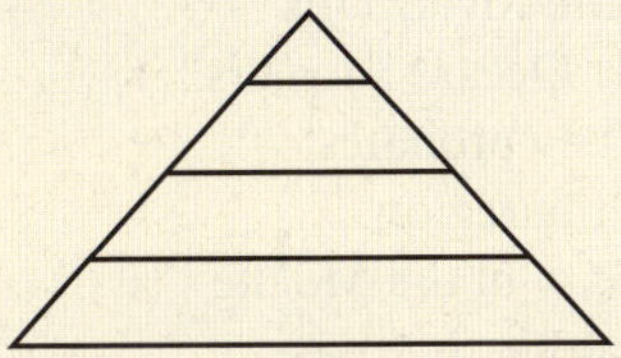

TEKS Texas Essential Knowledge and Skills

6A compare the major political, economic, social, and cultural developments of the Maya, Inca, and Aztec civilizations and explain how prior civilizations influenced their development

27B summarize the major ideas in astronomy, mathematics, and architectural engineering that developed in the Maya, Inca, and Aztec civilizations

IT MATTERS BECAUSE

The Nazca and Moche cultures, which existed in South America before the Inca, built stone buildings and sophisticated irrigation systems. Later, the Inca created a spectacular, well-organized empire. The Inca Empire was still flourishing when the Spanish arrived in the sixteenth century.

The Nazca

GUIDING QUESTION *What characteristics defined the early civilizations of South America?*

As in Mesoamerica, great civilizations flourished in early South America. The people of the Nazca and Moche cultures lived before the Inca gained power. While not much is known about these cultures, the cities, buildings, and artifacts these peoples left behind provide some clues.

Beginning around 200 B.C., the Nazca culture appeared in southern Peru. At its height, the Nazca culture covered more than 200 miles of territory. They prospered until approximately A.D. 600.

Nazca culture preserved some aspects of Chavin culture, especially its style of pottery. However, the Nazca, unlike the Chavin, did not build great temples. The Nazca might have practiced their religion outdoors, as suggested by ancient formations known as the Nazca Lines. These are grooves etched into the rocky soil of southern Peru in the images of animals, especially birds, as well as humans and geometric shapes, including triangles, trapezoids, and spirals. The images are so large, however, that their shapes can only be seen from the air. Although many theories have been presented, the exact significance of these lines remains unknown.

READING PROGRESS CHECK

Identifying How do the structures and artifacts the Nazca left behind provide clues about their civilization?

GEOGRAPHY CONNECTION

1. **THE WORLD IN SPATIAL TERMS** *Estimate in miles the length of the Inca Empire.*
2. **HUMAN SYSTEMS** *How did physical geography affect the settlement patterns of early South American cultures?*

SKILLS PRACTICE

While reading about the Moche and Inca, look at the photos and boldface words. Do they remind you of anything you have seen, done, or heard before?

The Moche

GUIDING QUESTION *What characteristics defined the early civilizations of South America?*

Around A.D. 300, another civilization developed near the Pacific coast not far south of the border of Ecuador. At Moche (MOH • cheh), a major urban center arose amid irrigated fields in the valley of the Moche River. This river flows from the foothills of the Andes into the Pacific Ocean. Farmers in the area grew **maize**, peanuts, potatoes, and cotton. They probably supplied much of the food for peoples living throughout the region.

maize corn

Moche was the capital of a powerful state. The authority of the Moche rulers might have extended as far as 400 miles (644 km) along the coast. The people of Moche had no written language, but their pottery gives us some idea of their interests. Among other things, the pottery indicates that the people at Moche, like those in Central America, led lives centered on warfare. Moche paintings and pottery frequently portray warriors, prisoners, and sacrificial victims.

After the collapse of the Moche civilization in the eighth century, a period of decline set in until a new power arose about 300 years later. The kingdom of Chimor dominated the area for nearly four centuries. Then, it was destroyed by a people who created a more spectacular empire—the Inca.

✓ READING PROGRESS CHECK

Inferring Why was it important for the urban center at Moche to be in a river valley?

The Inca

GUIDING QUESTIONS ***How did the Inca develop their successful empire? What were the main attributes of Inca culture?***

In the late 1300s, the Inca (IHNG • kuh) were only a small community in the area of Cuzco (KOOS • koh), a city located at 11,000 feet (3,353 m) in the mountains of southern Peru. In the 1440s, however, under the leadership of the ruler Pachacuti, the Inca launched a campaign of conquest that eventually brought the entire region under Inca control.

Pachacuti created a highly centralized state. The capital of Cuzco was transformed from a city of mud and thatch into an imposing city of stone. The city's most impressive structure was a temple dedicated to the sun.

▲ This Inca agricultural terrace is still in use in Pisac, Peru.

Political and Social Structures

Pachacuti and his immediate successors, Topa Inca and Huayna Capac Inca—*Inca* means "ruler"—extended the boundaries of the Inca Empire as far as Ecuador, central Chile, and the edge of the Amazon basin. The empire included perhaps 12 million people.

Like the civilizations of the Aztec and the Maya, the Inca state was built on war. All young men were required to serve in the Inca army. With some 200,000 members, the army was the largest and best armed in the region. Because the Inca, like other people in the early Americas, did not make use of the wheel, supplies were carried on the backs of llamas.

After an area was placed under Inca control, the local inhabitants were **instructed** in the Quechua (KECH • uh • wuh) language. Control of new territories was carefully regulated. A noble of high rank was sent to govern the new region. Local leaders could keep their posts as long as they were loyal to the Inca ruler. To encourage loyalty, the children of local leaders were taken as hostages to the Inca capital, where they were educated in Inca ways before returning home.

instruct to teach or to train

ANALYZING PRIMARY SOURCES

Enforcing Inca Laws

Most of our knowledge of Inca practices is based on narratives written after Pizarro's conquest. Garcilaso de la Vega, born in Cuzco, was the son of a Spanish conqueror and an Inca princess. Bernabé Cobo, a Spanish Jesuit missionary, went to Cuzco in 1599 and stayed there for most of his adult life.

"The Incas [made laws] always with the intention of applying them to anyone who dared to break them. . . . [According to one Inca ruler] He who kills another . . . condemns himself to death. . . . Thieves are in no wise to be permitted; . . . wherefore it is only right that thieves should be hanged. . . . Judges who secretly take gifts from litigants and suitors should be regarded as thieves, and as such punished with death."

—Garcilaso de la Vega, from *Royal Commentaries of the Incas*, 1609

"Justice was not equal and common to all. . . . [O]ther kinds of punishment were given to the higher-born and rich than those given to the humble and poor. The practice originated in the belief that to an Inca of royal blood a more public reprimand was by far a greater punishment than death was for a plebeian. . . . Crimes which, when common people were in question, were punished with death, were, when persons of the noble Inca family were involved, only punished with public reprehension."

—Bernabé Cobo, quoted in *The Last of the Incas*

DBQ Analyzing Historical Documents

1. ***Contrasting*** In what way do these accounts of Inca justice differ?
2. ***Identifying Central Ideas*** How might you account for the difference between their accounts?

resident one who resides in a place

To create a well-organized empire, Pachacuti divided it into four quarters, with each ruled by a governor. In turn, the quarters were divided into provinces, each also ruled by a governor. Those chosen to be governors were usually related to the royal family. Each province was supposed to contain about 10,000 **residents**. At the top of the entire system was the emperor, who was believed to be descended from Inti, the sun god.

Forced labor was another important feature of the state. All Inca subjects were responsible for labor service, usually for several weeks each year. Laborers, often with their entire communities, were moved according to need from one part of the country to another to take part in building projects. Forced laborers probably built the buildings and monuments of the capital city of Cuzco.

Inca society was highly regimented. So, too, were marriage and the lives of women. Men and women were required to select a marriage partner from within their immediate tribal groups. After marriage, women were expected to care for the children and to weave cloth. Some young girls were chosen to serve as priestesses in temples.

Economics and Culture

The Inca economy was based on high-altitude agriculture. In the mountains, they used terraced farms, watered by irrigation systems that carried precise amounts of water into the fields. These were planted with corn, potatoes, and other crops suited to high altitudes. The farmers' houses, built of stone or adobe with thatched roofs, were located near the fields.

The Inca also established extensive trade networks for long-distance trade. This trade, however, was organized by government officials and not by independent merchants. Food products, textiles, and pottery were the major articles that were exchanged.

The Inca were great builders, the best engineers among Native American peoples. They built a system of some 24,800 miles (around 40,000 km) of roads extending from the border of modern-day Colombia to a point south of modern-day Santiago, Chile. Two major roadways extended in a north-south direction—one through the Andes and the other along the coast with connecting routes between them.

Rest houses, located a day's walk apart, and storage depots were placed along the roads. Various types of bridges, including some fine, premodern examples of suspension bridges, were built over ravines and waterways. The roads were used chiefly for official and military purposes. Government permission was needed to use them. Trained runners carried messages rapidly from one way station to another, enabling information to travel up to 140 miles

PHOTO: Adalberto Rios Szalay/Sexto Sol/Getty Images

▶ Machu Picchu was created by the Inca Empire during its height.

▶ **CRITICAL THINKING**

Drawing Conclusions What do the ruins of Machu Picchu suggest about the civilization of the Inca?

in a single day. Most people walked the roads, but rulers and other high officials were carried in litters (covered couches used for carrying passengers).

The buildings and monuments of the capital city of Cuzco were the wonder of early European visitors. These structures were built of close-fitting stones without mortar—the better to withstand the frequent earthquakes in the area. The Inca were influenced by the prior Tiwaniku civilization in building design and engineering. When the Inca conquered the area inhabited by this civilization, they were impressed enough to employ Tiwaniku masons and architects.

Nothing demonstrates the Inca feats of architectural engineering more than the ruins of the abandoned city of Machu Picchu (MAH • CHOO PEE • CHOO). Machu Picchu, elevation 8,000 feet (2,400 m), was built on a lofty hilltop surrounded by mountain peaks far above the Urubamba River. Machu Picchu was hardly a city, containing only about 200 buildings. The buildings were placed harmoniously in their natural setting, creating a place of incredible beauty. In one part of Machu Picchu, a long stairway leads to an elegant stone known to the Inca as the "hitching post of the sun." Carved from the mountain, this "hitching post" might have been used as a solar observatory. During the sun festivals held in June and December, the people of Machu Picchu gathered here to chant and say prayers to Inti.

The Inca had no writing system. Instead, they kept records using a system of knotted strings called the **quipu**. The *quipu* system represents the development of mathematics in Inca civilization. The *quipu* enabled the Inca to record the number of men who went to war and goods that were exchanged. The system was so precise that it allowed such mathematical computations as multiplication and division of both integers and fractions. The Inca number system was based on units of 10.

quipu a system of knotted strings used by the Inca people for keeping records

The lack of a fully developed writing system, however, did not prevent the Inca from attaining a high level of cultural achievement. Since the *quipu* could only be a record of things that could be counted, Inca wise men turned historical events into stories, which were told to young people as a way of passing down their history.

The Inca had a well-developed tradition of court theater, consisting of tragic and comic works. Plays often involved the recounting of valiant deeds and other historical events. Actors were not professionals—they were members of the nobility. Poetry was also recited, often accompanied by music played on reed instruments.

Like the Maya and Aztec, the Inca made astronomical observations. They created two calendars based on the path of the sun, one of which was based on a year of 365 days.

✓ **READING PROGRESS CHECK**

Making Connections How did the Inca use technology to support their empire?

Comparing the Maya, Aztec, and Inca Civilizations

GUIDING QUESTION *What are the similarities between the political, economic, social, and cultural developments of the Maya, Inca, and Aztec civilizations?*

These three pre-Columbian civilizations shared many traits. All three had a similar political structure ruled by a monarch. An aristocracy in each empire supported the monarchy. All three empires developed decentralized states. In

SKILLBUILDER

TEKS 29H

Math and Social Studies

Why Learn This Skill?

It's nearly impossible to learn about history without learning about other disciplines as well. The studies of art, literature, geography, and science are all closely connected with history. Although it might not seem quite as logical a connection as these other disciplines, the study of mathematics can also be connected to history.

Learning the Skill

There are a couple of different approaches when thinking about how mathematical skills can be used to interpret social studies information.

1. You can look at how different civilizations in history have utilized mathematical skills to achieve cultural significance. For instance, you can consider how the ancient Egyptians used mathematics to construct their pyramids. Or you can look at how civilizations like the Phoenicians or the Chinese used mathematics to help them navigate their ships, or how thinkers in the Islamic civilizations used math to calculate a lunar calendar.
2. You can use hands-on mathematical skills to interpret the information you encounter in your history text. For instance, you can use math to calculate and understand latitude and longitude on maps. Math can also help you understand the number systems, engineering feats, and calendars of civilizations. You can also take statistics from history to construct graphs and analyze percentages.

Understanding basic mathematical concepts will help you with both of these approaches and will provide you with the context to interpret the information you are reading in this world history text.

Practicing the Skill

Read the following three excerpts illustrating how the Inca Empire incorporated mathematical skills into running a successful empire. Then answer the questions that follow, interpreting information in the excerpts on the basis of your knowledge of mathematics.

To create a well-organized empire, Pachacuti divided it into four quarters, with each ruled by a governor. In turn, the quarters were divided into provinces, each also ruled by a governor.

The Inca were great builders, the best engineers among Native American peoples. They built a system of some 24,800 miles (around 40,000 km) of roads extending from the border of modern-day Colombia to a point south of modern-day Santiago, Chile.

Like the Maya and Aztec, the Inca made astronomical observations. They created two calendars based on the path of the sun, one of which was based on a year of 365 days.

1. The conquests of the Inca leader Pachacuti greatly expanded the Inca Empire and there were millions of people living within it. Mathematically, why do you think he divided his empire into quarters and provinces?
2. The Inca Empire was in a mountainous area of the world. What is the significance of the Inca's engineering a major road system throughout their borders?
3. What is the mathematical significance of the Inca's making observations relating to astronomy?

Applying the Skill

Gathering statistics from information provided is one way to use mathematical skills to interpret social studies information. World history textbooks are filled with graphic organizers such as charts and graphs. Using a newspaper or an online news source, take statistics from a current event and create a chart or graph that might be found in a future world history book covering the events of today.

the case of the Maya, the empire was a collection of city-states. Each city-state had a measure of self-government, though all were loyal to the empire. The Aztec and Inca, on the other hand, pieced together empires based on territories they had conquered. Each territory maintained a degree of self-government but, like the Maya, was loyal to the central authority.

The Maya, Aztec, and Inca empires had many similar economic developments. All three empires developed strong agricultural economies. Staple crops, such as corn or potatoes, grew in abundance. This reliable food supply allowed the empires to focus on priorities other than food production, such as trade, warfare, and construction projects.

Each empire developed a strong trade network. In the case of the Inca, the state controlled the network, including merchants' access to major roads. The Maya and Aztec trade networks were different, however. In these empires, merchants traded their goods independent of the government. These networks sometimes created thriving economic centers, such as the Aztec market in Tenochtitlán.

Social developments in the Maya, Aztec, and Inca empires also followed similar patterns. All three empires developed highly militarized societies. In a militarized society, most young men are trained to be soldiers, and fighting in combat is a social obligation. In all three societies, warfare with neighboring groups was common. With conflict playing such a major role in daily life, their societies needed to prioritize military training and discipline.

Forced labor was another social factor that appeared in more than one society. The Aztec and the Inca both used forced labor. This labor was likely used to build many of the empires' large religious buildings and monuments.

Cultural developments in the three empires were also similar. Religion fundamentally shaped each culture. Temples were numerous, and rituals were frequent. Often, religious observances had violent qualities. Violence was especially frequent in the religious practices of the Maya and the Aztec. Human sacrifice was a major development in these cultures. In both cultures, sacrifices were meant to appease a god. Human sacrifice occurred in Inca culture, as well, though it was likely less common.

A visitor to these empires could not miss the importance of religion in these places. Pyramids such as Kukulcan in the Maya Empire or those in Tenochtitlán rose to great heights and would have been unmistakable landmarks of local culture.

▲ **This *quipu* was made circa 1430–1532. The number and position of the knots and the color of the string represented information such as population figures and the size of the harvest.**

PHOTO: ©Werner Forman/CORBIS

✓ **READING PROGRESS CHECK**

Comparing Compare the major economic developments of the Maya, Aztec, and Inca civilizations.

LESSON 2 REVIEW TEKS

Reviewing Vocabulary

1. ***Describing*** How did the Inca use the *quipu* in place of a formal system of writing? 27B

Using Your Notes

2. ***Organizing*** Use your notes to describe the organization of the Inca government.

Answering the Guiding Questions

3. ***Analyzing*** What characteristics defined the early civilizations of South America? 27B
4. ***Drawing Conclusions*** How did the Inca develop their successful empire?
5. ***Finding the Main Idea*** What were the main attributes of Inca culture? 27B, 29F

Writing Activity

6. **INFORMATIVE/EXPLANATORY** How did geography influence how the Inca road system and Machu Picchu were built? How do these feats of engineering point to the complexity of the Inca culture? 27B

CHAPTER 14 Assessment

TEKS

Directions: On a separate sheet of paper, answer the questions below. Make sure you read carefully and answer all parts of the questions.

Lesson Review

Lesson 1

1. ***Identifying*** What construction feat by the Hopewell people was comparable to an Egyptian construction feat? Describe the Hopewell structure.

2. ***Specifying*** With what aspect of climate did the Anasazi people struggle, and what specific areas of their society did this climate issue impact?

3. ***Explaining*** What prior civilizations influenced the development of the Maya and the Aztec? In what ways were these civilizations an influence? **6A**

4. ***Summarizing*** What were the major ideas in astronomy developed by the Maya and the Aztec? **27B**

5. ***Summarizing*** What major ideas in mathematics did the Maya and the Aztec develop? **27B**

6. ***Summarizing*** What major architectural engineering ideas did the Maya and the Aztec develop and execute? **27B**

Lesson 2

7. ***Identifying Cause and Effect*** How did the Moche's main economic activity—farming—lend itself to stability and growth in one location?

8. ***Explaining*** How did the Tiwaniku civilization influence the Inca? **6A**

9. ***Summarizing*** What major ideas did the Inca contribute to the field of astronomy? **27B**

10. ***Summarizing*** Summarize the major ideas the Inca contributed to mathematics. **27B**

11. ***Summarizing*** What were the major ideas in architectural engineering developed by the Inca? **27B**

12. ***Comparing*** How do the political and economic developments of the Maya, the Aztec, and the Inca compare? **6A**

13. ***Comparing*** How do the social and cultural developments of the Maya, the Aztec, and the Inca compare? **6A**

Exploring the Essential Question

14. ***Constructing a Thesis*** Write an essay about the Maya, Aztec, or Inca by constructing a thesis that states what made the civilization complex. Use primary or secondary sources as evidence to support your reasons. These sources can be text excerpts, photographs, drawings, or maps. **29G**

Critical Thinking

15. ***Draw Inferences*** What inferences can you make about the personal qualities and viewpoints of the Iroquois leader Deganawida and Hiawatha of the Onondaga?

16. ***Speculating*** What might you speculate about the transfer of religious beliefs from one generation to another within the Aztec community? For example, how did the concept of the four worlds or suns and appeasement through human sacrifice continue to persist?

17. ***Hypothesizing*** Make a hypothesis about the purpose and value of the Nazca Lines. What information is yet needed to solve their mystery?

18. ***Analyzing*** Analyze the relationship between a culture's artistic products and primary social structures by considering the Moche pottery artifacts.

19. ***Finding the Main Idea*** What was the Triple Alliance? What purpose did it serve? **29F**

20. ***Comparing*** How was the Aztec nobility similar to the nobility of medieval Europe?

Need Extra Help?

If You've Missed Question	1	2	3	4	5	6	7	8	9	10	11	12	13	14	15	16	17	18	19	20
Go to page	322	324	324	328	326	325	330	333	333	333	333	335	335	335	323	328	329	330	335	327

21 ***Drawing Conclusions*** Draw conclusions about the fact that several early civilizations explored the concept of time keeping with a calendar and drafted their versions of a calendar. Why did different groups seek to establish related formats for this aspect of life?

22 ***Using Reading Skills*** Using your reading skills to interpret social studies information, how were the Inca able to conquer and govern a large empire in South America? **29H**

23 ***Synthesizing*** Synthesize information about Inca transportation engineering, style of territorial takeover, leadership election, laws regarding marriage and forced labor to summarize the style of governing within the Inca empire.

Social Studies Skills

24 ***Geography Skills*** What geographical features allowed the Moche economy to flourish?

25 ***Finding the Main Idea*** Describe the economy of the Inca. **29F**

26 ***Interpreting Social Studies Information*** How did the Inca emperor ensure that newly conquered territories were loyal to him? **29H**

27 ***Geography Skills*** How did the Inca adapt their farming efforts to their geographical conditions?

28 ***Create Presentations*** Use maps within the chapter or gathered from external resources to create a visual presentation showing locations for several early civilizations. Include symbols and a map key that tells information about civilizations' cities, populations, and resources at a glance. Make sure the content on the map fits under a time period or time range and label the map with that time period.

DBQ Analyzing Primary Sources

Use the document to answer the following questions.

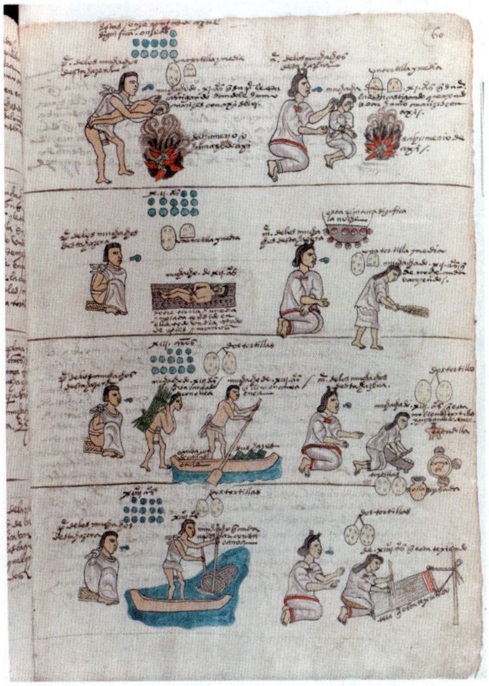

The above illustration from an Aztec book shows parents teaching their children. From sources such as this, historians know that boys learned basic tasks from their fathers, went to school to study, and learned to be warriors. Girls learned from their mothers how to take care of the home and children.

29 ***Analyzing*** Knowing that the blue dots represent one year, at what age would Aztec boys learn how to fish?

30 ***Synthesizing*** How does the different educational focus of Aztec boys and girls reflect the different roles of Aztec men and women?

Need Extra Help?

If You've Missed Question	21	22	23	24	25	26	27	28	29	30
Go to page	333	332	331	330	332	331	332	330	337	332

Analyzing Visuals

Use the chart to answer the following questions.

The Peoples of North America	Hopewell	• Known as Mound Builders • Shifted to full-time farming from gathering wild plants • Cahokia was a huge city of the Hopewell.
	Iroquois	• Hunters, gatherers, and farmers • Formed an alliance of five groups called the Iroquois League with a Grand Council
	Plains Indians	• Lived in river valleys in the eastern Great Plains • Hunters and gatherers • Hunted buffalo
	Anasazi	• Farmers who used canals to grow crops in the desert • Made baskets and pottery and built pueblos—buildings with many stories for homes
The Peoples of Mesoamerica (present-day Mexico and Central America)	Maya	• Made up of city-states governed by hereditary rulers • Society made of nobles, scribes, peasants, and townspeople • Created a calendar and number system, wrote in hieroglyphs
	Toltec	• Lived in central Mexico • Tula was the center of the empire. • Farmers, warriors, builders, and first metalworkers
	Aztec	• Capital was Tenochtitlán (present-day Mexico City). • Formed Triple Alliance with other city-states • Made advances in astronomy, created a calendar, had a number system

As the great civilizations of the Old World thrived, new ones were forming in the Americas. This chart shows the characteristics of some of these civilizations.

31 ***Interpreting Charts*** How did geography influence the economic and architectural practices of the Anasazi? **16C**

32 ***Explaining the influence of geography*** How did geography influence the dietary and economic practices of many early American civilizations? **16C**

33 ***Constructing Arguments*** Review the content in the chart and what you know about successful civilizations in North and South America to make an argument for or against hunter-gather practices as a means to a thriving, powerful society.

34 ***Ask and Answer Questions*** Use the chart to ask and answer questions about the early civilizations and the complexity of each society's roles and government.

Extended Response

35 ***Expository*** Create a print or digital visual presentation that traces the rise and decline of the early South American civilizations in chronological order. Use print and digital sources to provide written captions that identify geographical locations, causes for the rise and decline, and the effects of the rise and decline. **30C, 30D**

Need Extra Help?

If You've Missed Question	31	32	33	34	35
Go to page	324	338	338	338	320

The Renaissance in Europe

1350–1600

ESSENTIAL QUESTIONS

- *How can trade lead to economic prosperity and political power?*
- *How can ideas be reflected in art, sculpture, and architecture?*

networks

There's More Online! about the Renaissance in Europe.

CHAPTER 15

Lesson 1
The Italian States

Lesson 2
Ideas and Art of the Renaissance

The Story Matters...

The word *renaissance* means "rebirth." What was reborn during this period? One of the most enduring innovations of Renaissance culture was a new view of human beings. This outlook, embodied in the intellectual movement known as humanism, celebrated the extraordinary individual. The Italian artist Leonardo da Vinci, who was also an architect, inventor, and mathematician, was seen by those around him as a model of this humanist ideal.

◄ Depicting Mary, Jesus's mother in Christian tradition, Leonardo's painting *Virgin of the Rocks* shows the influence of Renaissance humanism in portraying a realistic form, but also takes it a step further to depict human perfection.

PHOTO: Leonardo da Vinci/The Bridgeman Art Library/Getty Images

CHAPTER 15

Place and Time: Europe 1350–1600

The Renaissance began in northern Italy in the late fourteenth century and then spread throughout Europe. Renaissance culture developed in the unique political, social, and economic environment of Italy's small, independent states. Located on major trade routes, cities such as Milan and Florence were ideal places to receive and spread ideas. Florence, controlled by the Medici family, was perhaps the most influential city. Its scholars, writers, artists, and architects defined the culture of the Renaissance.

Step Into the Place

Read the quotes and review the information presented on the panorama of Renaissance Florence.

DBQ **Analyzing Historical Documents** Why do you think the Medici family spent large amounts of money on the patronage of the arts in Florence?

PRIMARY SOURCE

"Lorenzo [de' Medici, shown at right] showed the same favor to poetry in the vernacular, to music, architecture, painting, sculpture, and to all the arts of mind and hand, so that the city [of Florence] overflowed with all these exquisite things. And these arts flourished all the more because Lorenzo, a universal man, could pass judgment and distinguish among men, so that they competed with one another to please him."

—Francesco Guicciardini, from *History of Florence*

PRIMARY SOURCE

"In the time of the elder Lorenzo de' Medici, Lorenzo the Magnificent, truly a golden age for men of talent, there flourished an artist called Alessandro . . . Botticelli.

. . . [Botticelli] carried out many works in the house of the Medici for Lorenzo the Magnificent, notably a life-size Pallas [Athena] on a shield wreathed with fiery branches, and a St Sebastian [a painting created for Florence's Santa Maria Maggiore church]. . . . As an old man, Botticelli found himself so poor that if Lorenzo de' Medici . . . and then his friends and other worthy men who loved him for his talent had not come to his assistance, he would have almost died of hunger."

—Giorgio Vasari, from *The Lives of the Artists*

Step Into the Time

Determining Cause and Effect Research one or more publications from the time line. Write a short essay explaining how the publication(s) increased political unrest in Italy and around the world.

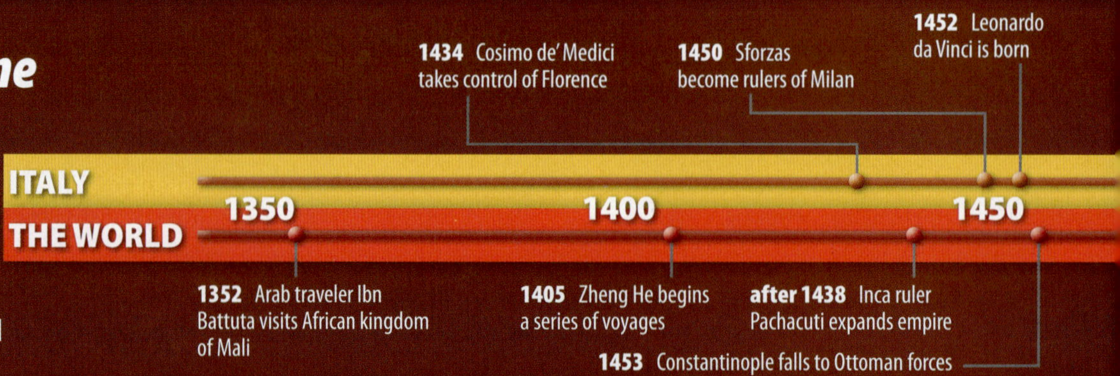

networks
There's More Online!

- ☑ **MAP** Explore the interactive version of this map on Networks.
- ☑ **TIME LINE** Explore the interactive version of the time line on Networks.

Panorama of Florence c. 1500

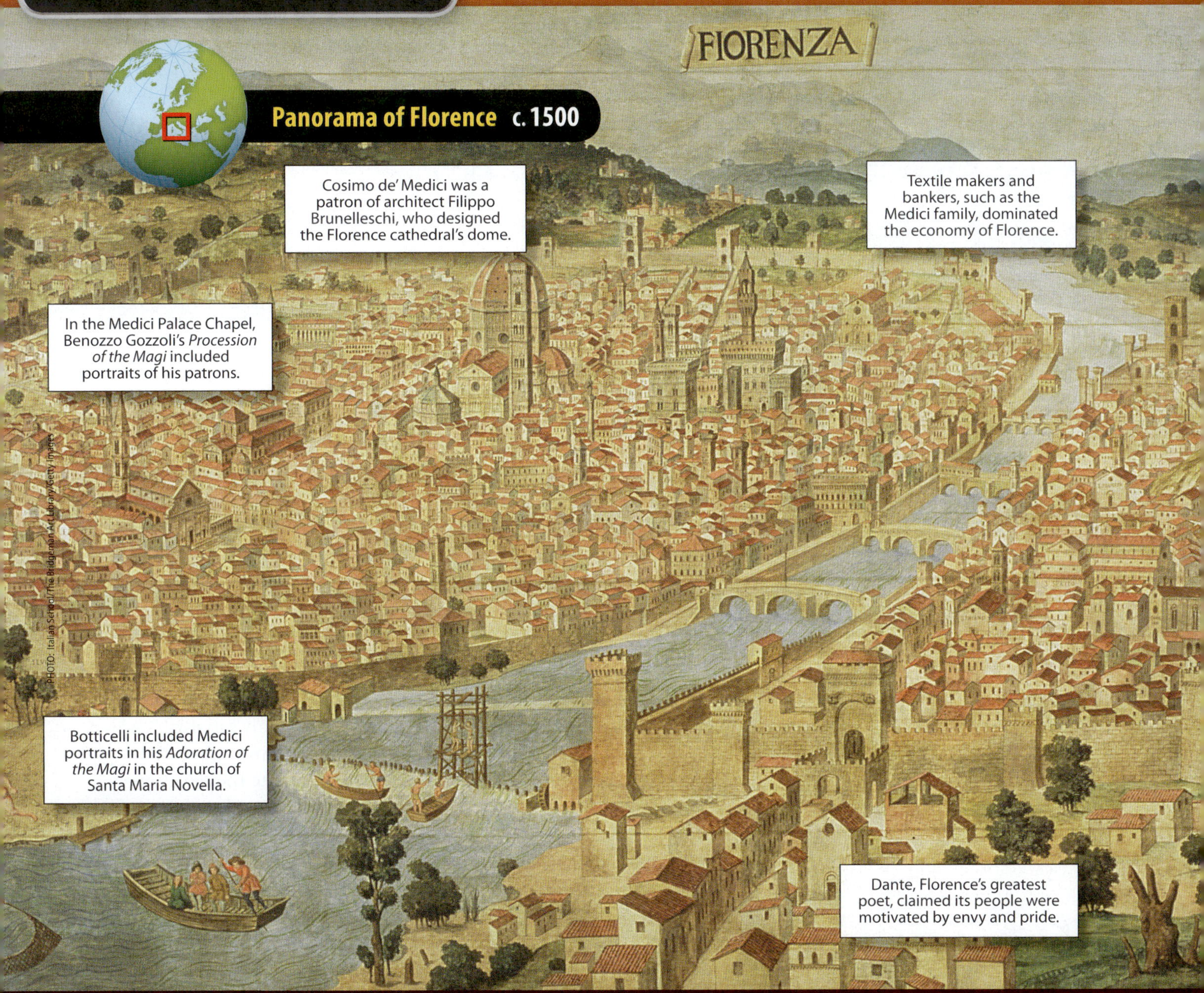

PHOTO: Italian School/The Bridgeman Art Library/Getty Images

- **1455** Gutenberg Bible becomes the earliest book printed from moveable type in Europe
- **1492** Lorenzo de' Medici dies
- **1492** Columbus reaches the West Indies
- **1494** French king Charles VIII leads an army into Italy
- **1498** Portuguese expedition under Vasco da Gama reaches India
- **1500**
- **1513** Machiavelli's *The Prince* is completed
- **1520** Süleyman I becomes Ottoman sultan
- **1527** German troops of Charles I pillage Rome
- **1530** Bābur, first Mogul emperor of India, dies at Agra
- **1550**
- **1558** Elizabeth I becomes queen of England
- **1559** Italian Wars end
- **1571** Christian forces defeat Ottomans in naval battle at Lepanto
- **1600**

networks

There's More Online!

- BIOGRAPHY Lorenzo de' Medici
- BIOGRAPHY Niccolò Machiavelli
- IMAGE Procession of the Magi
- INTERACTIVE SELF-CHECK QUIZ
- MAP Italy, 1500
- PRIMARY SOURCE The Book of the Courtier
- TIME LINE Italian Wars
- VIDEO The Renaissance

LESSON 1

The Italian States

ESSENTIAL QUESTION

How can trade lead to economic prosperity and political power?

It Matters Because

The Renaissance served as a bridge between the Middle Ages and modern times. Beginning in the prosperous states of Italy, the Renaissance marked the emergence of a new urban culture that was largely spread by trade. This culture had a more worldly outlook than that of the Middle Ages.

Reading HELPDESK

Academic Vocabulary

- **dominate**
- **decline**

Content Vocabulary

- **mercenary**
- **burgher**
- **republic**

TAKING NOTES:

Key Ideas and Details

Identifying Use a graphic organizer like this one to identify the major principles of Machiavelli's work, *The Prince*.

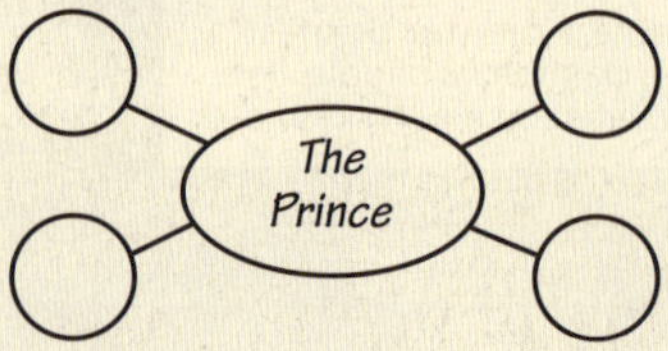

TEKS Texas Essential Knowledge and Skills

1D identify major causes and describe the major effects of the following important turning points in world history from 1450 to 1750: the rise of the Ottoman Empire, the influence of the Ming dynasty on world trade, European exploration and the Columbian Exchange, European expansion, and the Renaissance and the Reformation

continued on the next page

The Major Italian States

GUIDING QUESTIONS *What contributed to the rise of the Italian states during the Renaissance? How did Machiavelli's work influence political power in the Western world?*

In the late Middle Ages, Italy was much more urban than the rest of Europe, and a thriving trade network was based in Italy's many cities. The energy that trade gave to Italy's urban environment encouraged an exchange of ideas that helped stimulate the development of Renaissance culture.

During the Middle Ages, Italy had failed to develop a centralized monarchical state. This made it possible for a number of city-states in northern and central Italy to remain independent and offer patronage to artists and thinkers. By early in the fifteenth century, five major territorial states had come to **dominate** the peninsula. These were the city-states of Milan, Venice, and Florence, the Papal States centered on Rome, and the Kingdom of Naples. Because of their economic power, these states played crucial roles in the development of the Renaissance .

Italy had prospered from a flourishing trade. Italian cities such as Venice had taken the lead in establishing merchant fleets and trading with the Byzantine and Islamic civilizations to the east. Italian trading ships had also moved into the western Mediterranean and then north along the Atlantic seaboard. These ships exchanged more than just goods with merchants in England and the Netherlands. The ideas of the Renaissance, developed in Italy, spread north along trade routes to the rest of Europe. Additionally, Byzantine scholars fled to Italy after the fall of Constantinople in 1453, bringing new forms of thought

PHOTO: (l to r) ©SuperStock/SuperStock; Italian School/The Bridgeman Art Library/Getty Images; ©Massimo Listri/CORBIS; ©Art Archive, The/SuperStock and texts with them. These events further fueled the development of the Renaissance.

Economics and Politics in the Major Italian States

Each of the five major territorial states dominated the economic and political life of its region. Milan, Venice, and Florence were located in northern Italy. One of the richest city-states, Milan stood at the crossroads of the main trade routes from Italian coastal cities to the Alpine passes. In the fourteenth century, members of the Visconti family established themselves as dukes of Milan. They extended their power over the surrounding territory of Lombardy. The last Visconti ruler of Milan died in 1447. Francesco Sforza (SFAWRT • sah) led a band of **mercenaries**—soldiers who fought primarily for money. Sforza conquered the city and became its duke. The Visconti and Sforza rulers built a strong centralized state. Using an efficient tax system, the Sforzas generated huge revenues for the government.

Another major northern Italian city-state, Venice, served as a commercial link between Asia and Western Europe. The city drew traders from around the world. Officially, Venice was a **republic** with an elected leader called a doge (DOHJ). In reality, a small group of wealthy

(continued from p. 342)

TEKS **Texas Essential Knowledge and Skills**

5A explain the political, intellectual, artistic, economic, and religious impact of the Renaissance

continued on the next page

dominate to influence or control

mercenary a soldier who fights primarily for pay

republic a form of government in which the leader is not a king and certain citizens have the right to vote

GEOGRAPHY CONNECTION

1. **PLACES AND REGIONS** *Which of the five dominant Italian states did not have a seacoast?*
2. **HUMAN SYSTEMS** *How could traders from landlocked states gain access to the sea?*

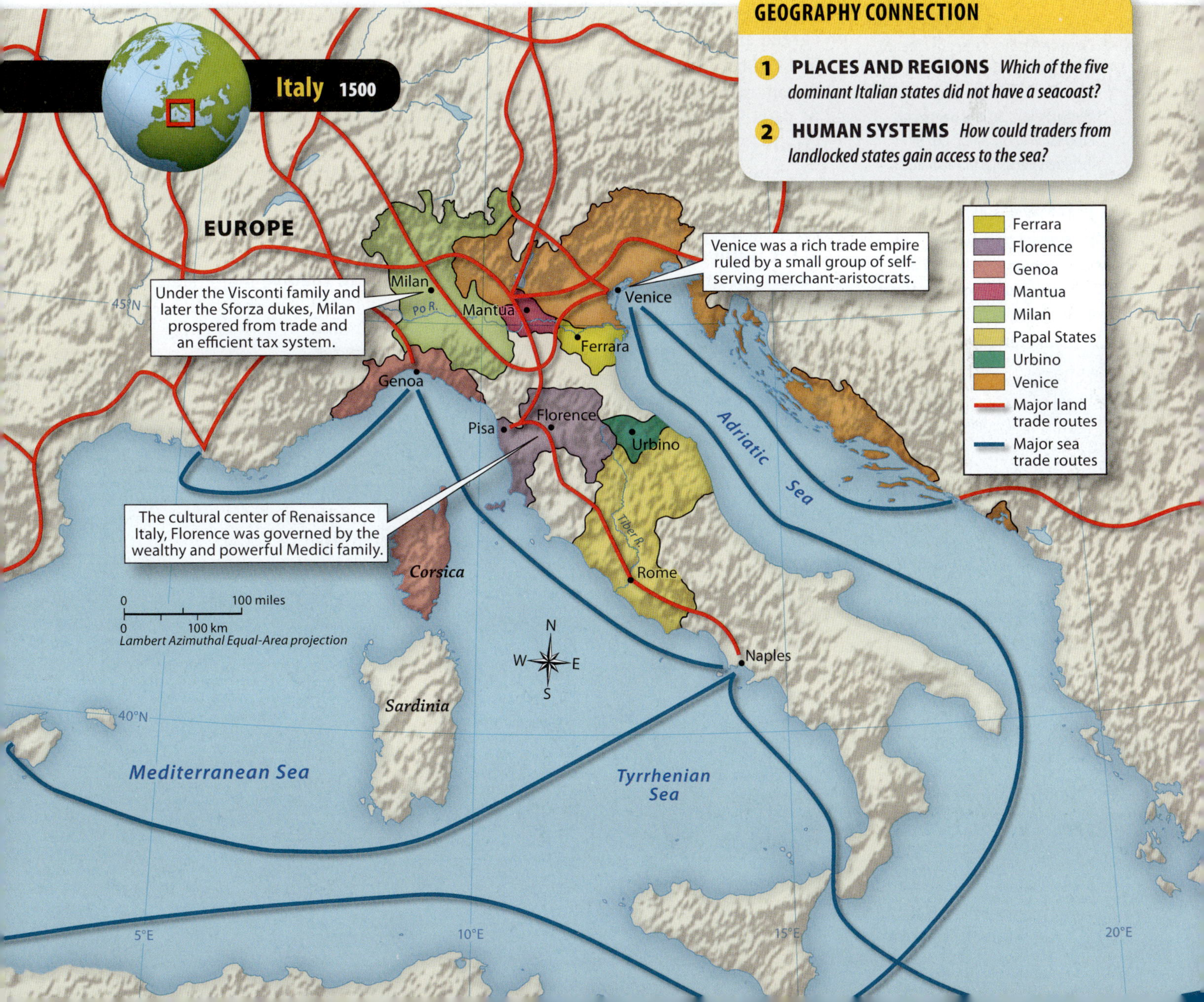

(continued from p. 343)

TEKS **Texas Essential Knowledge and Skills**

19B identify the characteristics of the following political systems: theocracy, absolute monarchy, democracy, republic, oligarchy, limited monarchy, and totalitarianism

24A describe the changing roles of women, children, and families during major eras of world history

merchant-aristocrats ran the government of Venice for their benefit. Venice's trade empire was tremendously profitable and made the city-state an international power.

The republic of Florence dominated the northern Italian region of Tuscany. During the fourteenth century, a small, wealthy group of merchants established control of the Florentine government. They waged a series of successful wars against their neighbors and established Florence as a major city-state.

In 1434 Cosimo de' Medici (MEH • duh • chee) took control of the city. The wealthy Medici family ran the government from behind the scenes. Using their wealth and personal influence, Cosimo, and later his grandson Lorenzo de' Medici, dominated the city when Florence was the cultural center of Italy.

decline a change to a lower state or level

As the Italian states grew wealthier, the power of the Church began to **decline** slightly. Some church doctrines, such as the sinfulness of usury, or charging borrowers a fee on money loaned to them, were openly ignored. Many Italian leaders borrowed and loaned money without fear of reprisal.

During the late 1400s, Florence experienced an economic decline. Most of its economy was based on the manufacturing of cloth. Increased competition from English and Flemish cloth makers drove down profits.

During this time, a Dominican preacher named Girolamo Savonarola began condemning the excesses of the Medici family. The people of Florence agreed and sided with Savonarola. The Medici, and a French invasion of Italy in 1494 resulted in their exile from Florence. The Florentines soon tired of Savonarola's strict rules, and his attacks on the Church angered the pope. In 1498 Savonarola was accused of heresy and sentenced to death. The Medici family returned to power in Florence.

The two other dominant centers in Renaissance Italy were the Papal States and the Kingdom of Naples. Located in central Italy, Rome was the capital of the Papal States. These territories were officially under the control of the Catholic Church at this time. By contrast, the Kingdom of Naples, which dominated southern Italy, was the only one of the five major states ruled by a hereditary monarch.

▼ **Piero de' Medici, father of Lorenzo, hired Benozzo Gozzoli in 1459 to paint frescoes in the chapel of the Medici Palace. In this part of his *Procession of the Magi*, Gozzoli included portraits of the Medici, such as Lorenzo (shown as a young king on horseback).**

▶ **CRITICAL THINKING**

Drawing Conclusions Why do you think Gozzoli included portraits of the Medici?

Income from trade and more efficient government gave these Italian states the wealth necessary to build strong, centralized states. These developments in Italy foreshadowed developments in much of the rest of Europe. States such as England, France, and Spain would develop stronger trade networks and much stronger governments, centered on a king or queen. The growth of strong monarchial states in the rest of Europe would lead to trouble for the Italian states.

The Italian Wars

The riches of Italy attracted the French king, Charles VIII. He led an army of 30,000 men into Italy in 1494. The French occupied the Kingdom of Naples. Northern Italian states turned for help to the Spanish, who gladly agreed to send soldiers to Italy. For the next 30 years, the French and the Spanish battled in Italy as they sought to dominate the region.

A turning point in this struggle came in 1527. On May 5, thousands of troops arrived at the city of Rome. This army belonged to Charles I, king of Spain and ruler of the Holy Roman Empire. It included mercenaries from different countries. They had not been paid for months. When they yelled, "Money! Money!" their leader responded, "If you have ever dreamed of pillaging a town and laying hold of its treasures, here now is one, the richest of them all, queen of the world."

The next day the invading forces smashed the gates and pushed into the city. The troops went berserk in a frenzy of bloodshed and looting. The terrible sack of Rome in 1527 by the armies of Charles I left the Spanish a dominant force in Italy. The Italian Wars would continue for another quarter-century, ending only in 1559.

Machiavelli on Power

Political power fascinated the people of the Italian Renaissance. No one gave better expression to this interest than Niccolò Machiavelli (MA • kee • uh • VEH • lee). His book *The Prince* is one of the most influential works on political power in the Western world.

Machiavelli's central thesis in *The Prince* is the issue of how to get—and keep—political power. He dedicated his study of practical politics to the grandson of Lorenzo de' Medici. Machiavelli offered him rules on how to govern. In the Middle Ages, many writers on political power had emphasized the duty of rulers to follow Christian moral principles. Machiavelli, however, rejected this popular approach. He believed that morality was unrelated to politics.

From Machiavelli's point of view, a prince's attitude toward power must be based on an understanding of human nature. He believed human beings were motivated by self-interest. He said, "...this is to be asserted in general of men, that they are ungrateful, fickle, false, cowardly, covetous, and as long as you succeed they are yours entirely." Based on such an assessment, therefore, political activity should not be restricted by moral principles. A prince acts on behalf of the state. According to Machiavelli, for the state's sake, a leader must do good when possible but be ready to do evil when necessary. Machiavelli abandoned morality as the basis for analyzing political activity and argued that the ends justify the means. His views have had a profound influence on later political leaders. His influence on politics has continued to the present day.

✓ **READING PROGRESS CHECK**

Explaining Why might Machiavelli have argued that political activity should not be restricted by moral principles?

Analyzing PRIMARY SOURCES

Machiavelli on Trust

"Everyone realizes how praiseworthy it is for a prince to honor his word and to be straightforward rather than crafty in his dealings; none the less, contemporary experience shows that princes who have achieved great things have been those who have given their word lightly, who have known how to trick men with their cunning, and who, in the end, have overcome those abiding by honest principles."

—Niccolò Machiavelli, from *The Prince*

DBQ ***INTERPRETING*** What does Machiavelli use as the basis for his argument about how a prince should act?

▲ This portrait of Baldassare Castiglione was painted by the Renaissance artist Raphael in 1516.

Renaissance Society

GUIDING QUESTION *How was society characterized during the Renaissance?*

In the Middle Ages, society had been divided into three social classes: the clergy, the nobility, and the peasants and townspeople. Although this social order continued into the Renaissance, some changes became evident.

The Nobility

During the Renaissance, nobles, or aristocrats, continued to dominate society. Making up only a tiny portion of the population in most countries, nobles held important political posts and served as advisers to the king.

Nobles were expected to fulfill certain ideals in Renaissance society. The characteristics of a perfect Renaissance noble were expressed in *The Book of the Courtier,* written by the Italian diplomat Baldassare Castiglione (kahs • teel • YOH • nay) and published in 1528. One of the key ideals of the Renaissance was the well-developed individual. In Castiglione's interpretation, this ideal became the social goal of the aristocracy. A noble was born, not made. He must have character, grace, and talent. The noble had to be a warrior but also needed a classical education and an interest in the arts. Finally, a noble had to follow certain standards of conduct. What was the purpose of these standards?

PRIMARY SOURCE

"The aim of the perfect Courtier . . . is so to win . . . the favor and mind of the prince whom he serves that he may be able to tell him . . . the truth about everything he needs to know . . . and that when he sees the mind of his prince inclined to a wrong action, he may dare to oppose him . . . so as to dissuade him of every evil intent and bring him to the path of virtue."

—Baldassare Castiglione, from *The Book of the Courtier*

Thus, the aim of the perfect noble, by Renaissance standards, was to serve his prince in an effective and honest way. Nobles would aspire to Castiglione's principles for hundreds of years while they continued to dominate European social and political life.

Peasants and Townspeople

During the Renaissance, peasants still constituted the vast majority of the total European population. Serfdom continued to decrease with the decline of the manorial system. By 1500, especially in Western Europe, more and more peasants became legally free.

At the top of urban society were the patricians. With their wealth from trade, industry, and banking, they dominated their communities. Below them were the **burghers**—the shopkeepers, artisans, guild masters, and guild members. Below the burghers were the workers, who earned low wages, and the unemployed. Both of the latter groups lived miserable lives and made up a significant portion of the urban population.

burgher a member of the middle class who lived in a city or town

During the late 1300s and the 1400s, urban poverty increased dramatically throughout Europe. One rich merchant, who had little sympathy for the poor, wrote:

PRIMARY SOURCE

"Those that are lazy in a way that does harm to the city, and who can offer no just reason for their condition, should either be forced to work or expelled from the [city]. The city would thus rid itself of that most harmful part of the poorest class."

—quoted in *Renaissance Europe: Age of Recovery and Reconciliation*

Family and Marriage

The family bond was a source of great security during the Renaissance. Parents carefully arranged marriages to strengthen business or family ties. In upper-class families, parents often worked out the details when their children were only two or three years old. These marriage contracts included a dowry, a sum of money that the wife's family gave to the husband upon marriage.

The father-husband was at the center of the Italian family. He managed all finances, since his wife had no share in his wealth. He also made the decisions that determined the paths of his children's lives.

The mother's chief role was to supervise the household and raise her children, which might include their moral education. For example, the fifteenth-century Florentine noblewoman Alessandra Strozzi wrote a letter to one of her grown sons commending him for acting charitably to the son of an enemy:

PRIMARY SOURCE

"You gave Brunetto's son food to eat and clothes to wear, and you gave him shelter and money and sent him back here; out of the seven acts of mercy you have performed three."

—quoted in *Selected Letters of Alessandra Strozzi*

Children's role within the family was to be subservient to the authority of their fathers. Males became adults when they left home, reached a certain age—which varied from place to place—or were emancipated (legally freed) by their fathers. Women never became legal adults while the father lived unless they were emancipated.

✓ READING PROGRESS CHECK

Contrasting How does Castiglione's view of the responsibilities of a ruling class differ from Machiavelli's?

▼ Raphael's *Marriage of the Virgin* (1504) presents biblical figures in a contemporary Renaissance setting.

▶ CRITICAL THINKING

Synthesizing What view of the role of marriage in Renaissance society does the composition of this work present?

LESSON 1 REVIEW TEKS

Reviewing Vocabulary

1. ***Comparing*** Write a paragraph comparing a republic to a monarchical state. Give examples of each type of government from Renaissance Italy. 5A, 19B

Using Your Notes

2. ***Summarizing*** Use your graphic organizer identifying the major principles of Machiavelli's work to write a paragraph summarizing his political views. 5A, 19B

Answering the Guiding Questions

3. ***Identifying Cause and Effect*** What contributed to the rise of the Italian states during the Renaissance? 1D

4. ***Making Connections*** How did Machiavelli's work influence political power in the Western world? 5A

5. ***Identifying Central Issues*** How was society characterized during the Renaissance?

Writing Activity

6. **INFORMATIVE/EXPLANATORY** Write a paragraph explaining how trade encouraged the development of the Renaissance. 5A

networks

There's More Online!

- ☑ **BIOGRAPHY** Michelangelo
- ☑ **IMAGE** Gilded Door at the Baptistry of Florence
- ☑ **INFOGRAPHIC** Gutenberg and the Spread of Literacy
- ☑ **INTERACTIVE SELF-CHECK QUIZ**
- ☑ **PRIMARY SOURCE** The Book of the City of Ladies
- ☑ **SLIDE SHOW** Art of the Italian Renaissance
- ☑ **SLIDE SHOW** Art of the Northern European Renaissance
- ☑ **VIDEO** Leonardo Da Vinci

LESSON 2
Ideas and Art of the Renaissance

ESSENTIAL QUESTION

• How can ideas be reflected in art, sculpture, and architecture?

Reading HELPDESK

Academic Vocabulary

- **attain**
- **core**
- **style**
- **circumstance**

Content Vocabulary

- **humanism**
- **fresco**
- **vernacular**
- **perspective**

TAKING NOTES:

Key Ideas and Details

Organizing Use a chart like the following one to identify how Renaissance education was affected by humanism.

Area:
Effect:
Effect:
Effect:

TEKS Texas Essential Knowledge and Skills

1D identify major causes and describe the major effects of the following important turning points in world history from 1450 to 1750: the rise of the Ottoman Empire, the influence of the Ming dynasty on world trade, European exploration and the Columbian Exchange, European expansion, and the Renaissance and the Reformation

continued on the next page

It Matters Because

Renaissance humanism focused European culture on the individual, marking a major change from the religion-centered view of the Middle Ages. The goal of the humanists was to educate the whole person, much as modern educators seek to do. Today's liberal arts curriculum began during the Renaissance.

Italian Renaissance Humanism

GUIDING QUESTION *How did humanism help define the Italian Renaissance?*

Secularism and an emphasis on the individual characterized the Renaissance. These characteristics are most noticeable in the intellectual and artistic accomplishments of the period. A key intellectual movement of the Renaissance was **humanism**.

Development of Humanism

Humanism was based on the study of the classics, the literature of ancient Greece and Rome. Humanists studied grammar, rhetoric, poetry, moral philosophy, and history. Today these subjects are called the humanities.

Humanists studied grammar, rhetoric, poetry, moral philosophy, and history. Today these subjects are called the humanities. Humanism was based on the study of the classics, the literature of ancient Greece and Rome. Even though much of the Greek and Roman source material had been lost in the west after the fall of Rome, humanist scholars of the Renaissance were able to obtain copies of these works because Byzantine and Arab scholars had preserved them.

The humanists approached the classics in new ways. In the Middle Ages, writers had quoted the surviving classical texts in order to give authority to their religious writings. The humanists had a different goal. They wanted to use classical values to revitalize their culture. The humanists also felt a different relationship with the writers of antiquity. They saw the ancient Greek and Roman writers as their intellectual equals.

Francesco Petrarch (PEE • TRAHRK) is often called the father of Italian Renaissance humanism. He did more than any other individual in the fourteenth century to foster its development. He looked for forgotten Latin manuscripts and set in motion a search for similar manuscripts in monastic libraries throughout Europe. Petrarch also began the humanist emphasis on using pure classical Latin. This meant Latin as it was used by the ancient Romans, rather than medieval Latin. Humanists used the works of two Roman writers as models—Cicero for prose and Virgil for poetry.

Fourteenth-century humanists such as Petrarch had described the intellectual life as one of solitude. They rejected family and a life of action in the community. In contrast, humanists in the early fifteenth century took a new interest in civic life. They believed that intellectuals had a duty to live an active civic life and to put their study of the humanities to the state's service. It is no accident that they served as secretaries in the Italian states and to princes and popes.

humanism an intellectual movement of the Renaissance based on the study of the humanities, which included grammar, rhetoric, poetry, moral philosophy, and history

Vernacular Literature

The humanist emphasis on classical Latin led to its widespread use in the writings of scholars, lawyers, and religious writers. However, some writers wrote in the **vernacular**, the local spoken language. People in different parts of Italy spoke different Italian dialects. In the fourteenth and fifteenth centuries, the literary works of Dante (DAHN • tay) Alighieri and Christine de Pizan helped make vernacular literature popular.

vernacular the language of everyday speech in a particular region

In a reflection of literature's shift to vernacular language during the Renaissance, Dante wrote his masterpiece, the *Divine Comedy*, in the dialect of his native Florence, which would later become the Italian language. The *Divine Comedy* is a long poem describing the soul's journey to **attain** Paradise. Dante defended his use of the vernacular in the *Divine Comedy*, arguing that if he had written in Latin, only scholars would have understood him.

attain to gain or achieve

PRIMARY SOURCE

"The Latin could only have explained them to scholars; for the rest would have not understood it. Therefore, as among those who desire to understand them there are many more illiterate than learned, [it follows that the Latin would not have fulfilled this behest as well as the vulgar tongue, which is understood both by the learned and the unlearned.]"

—Dante Alighieri, from *De vulgari eloquentia* ("Of Literature in the Vernacular")

(continued from p. 348)

TEKS **Texas Essential Knowledge and Skills**

5A explain the political, intellectual, artistic, economic, and religious impact of the Renaissance

25C explain the relationship among Christianity, individualism, and growing secularism that began with the Renaissance and how the relationship influenced subsequent political developments

26A identify significant examples of art and architecture that demonstrate an artistic ideal or visual principle from selected cultures

26B analyze examples of how art, architecture, literature, music, and drama reflect the history of the cultures in which they are produced

continued on the next page

PHOTO: SuperStock.

◀ **In this painting by Domenico di Michelino, Dante stands outside the walls of Florence and holds a copy of his *Divine Comedy*.**

▶ **CRITICAL THINKING**

Making Connections How does this painting reflect Renaissance humanism's emphasis on the individual?

BIOGRAPHY

Gutenberg (c. 1400–1468)
Johannes Gutenberg was born in Mainz, Germany. Beginning in the 1440s, and borrowing from several existing technologies, he developed a method of printing using blocks of movable type set on a mechanical press. This process took more than a decade, and Gutenberg borrowed heavily to finance his printing press. In 1455 the Gutenberg Bible became the earliest book printed from movable type in Europe.

▶ **CRITICAL THINKING**
Drawing Conclusions Why might Gutenburg have chosen the Bible as a first project for his printing press?

Another writer who used the vernacular was Christine de Pizan, an Italian who lived in France and wrote in French. She is best known for her works written in defense of women. In *The Book of the City of Ladies*, written between 1404 and 1405, she denounced the many male writers who had argued that women, by their very nature, are unable to learn. Women, de Pizan argued, could attain learning as well as men if they could attend the same schools, since "a woman's nature is clever and quick enough to learn speculative sciences as well as to discover them, and likewise the manual arts..."

✓ **READING PROGRESS CHECK**

Explaining How did the Renaissance contribute to the rediscovery of classical civilization and the development of vernacular literature?

Renaissance Education

GUIDING QUESTION ***How was education during the Renaissance shaped by humanism?***

The humanist movement had a profound effect on education in the fourteenth and fifteenth centuries. Education during this time became increasingly secular—less focused on religion. Renaissance humanists believed that education could change human beings. They wrote books on education and opened schools based on their ideas.

At the **core** of humanist schools were the liberal studies. These form the basis of today's liberal arts. According to the humanists, students should learn history, ethics, public speaking, grammar, logic, poetry, mathematics, astronomy, and music. Humanists believed that liberal studies enabled individuals to reach their full potential. The purpose of a liberal education was to produce individuals who follow a path of virtue and wisdom. These individuals should also possess rhetorical skills so they could persuade others to take this same path.

core basic or essential part

Humanist educators thought that education was a practical preparation for life. Its aim was to create well-rounded citizens, not great scholars. Humanist education was also considered necessary for preparing the sons of aristocrats for leadership roles. Following the classical ideal of a sound mind in a sound body, humanist educators also emphasized physical education. Students learned the skills of javelin throwing, archery, and dancing. They ran, wrestled, hunted, and swam. The few female students who attended humanist schools studied the classics and were encouraged to know some history as well as how to ride, dance, sing, play the lute, and appreciate poetry.

The development of printing affected not only education, but eventually all aspects of Renaissance culture. Beginning in the mid-fifteenth century, the use of movable type was pioneered by the German printer Johannes Gutenberg (GOO • tehn • BURG). This innovation started a revolution that has affected how knowledge is distributed ever since. As the number of printing presses multiplied, the effects of new technology were felt in every area of European life. The printing of books encouraged scholarly research and stimulated an ever-expanding reading public's desire to gain knowledge.

✓ **READING PROGRESS CHECK**

Identifying Central Ideas What was the focus of education for the Renaissance humanists?

(continued from p. 349)

TEKS **Texas Essential Knowledge and Skills**
26C identify examples of art, music, and literature that transcend the cultures in which they were created and convey universal themes
27C explain the impact of the printing press on the Renaissance and the Reformation in Europe

Italian Renaissance Art

GUIDING QUESTION *How did humanism influence the works of Renaissance artists and authors?*

Renaissance artists sought to imitate nature. They wanted viewers to be convinced of the reality of their subjects. At the same time, these artists were developing a new, human-focused worldview. To emphasize this, many artists painted the human body. The style and techniques of the Renaissance would have a lasting impact on the artistic world of the West.

fresco painting done on fresh, wet plaster with water-based paints

perspective artistic techniques used to give the effect of three-dimensional depth to two-dimensional surfaces

style having a distinctive quality or form

New Techniques in Painting

The works of the fourteenth-century Italian painter Giotto anticipated some of the innovations of the Renaissance. His style focused on depicting human beings and their realities and dramas.

However, the Renaissance period in art truly began with Tommaso di Giovanni, called Masaccio (muh • ZAH • chee • OH). His frescoes are the first masterpieces of Early Renaissance (1400–1490) art. A **fresco** is a painting done on fresh, wet plaster with water-based paints. Human figures in medieval paintings look flat, but Masaccio's figures have depth and "come alive." By mastering the laws of **perspective**, Masaccio could create the illusion of three dimensions, leading to a new, realistic **style**. One of his most famous works is *The Tribute Money,* which depicts the story of the life of Peter, a Christian saint. It is one of many frescoes Masaccio was commissioned to paint in the Brancacci Chapel in Florence.

Other fifteenth-century Florentine painters used and modified this new, or Renaissance, style. Especially important were two major developments. One development stressed the technical side of painting. This included understanding the laws of perspective and the organization of outdoor space and light through geometry. The second development was the investigation of movement and human anatomy. Realistic portrayal of the individual, especially the human nude, became one of the chief aims of Italian Renaissance art.

Sculpture and Architecture

The Renaissance produced equally stunning advances in sculpture and architecture. Like painters, Renaissance sculptors and architects sought to express a human-centered world. The sculptor Donatello studied the statues of the Greeks and Romans. His works included a realistic, free-standing marble figure of George, a Christian saint.

The buildings of classical Rome inspired the work of architect Filippo Brunelleschi (BROO • nuh • LEHS • kee). A significant example of architecture that demonstrates this return to classical artistic ideals is his design of the church of San Lorenzo in Florence. The classical columns and rounded arches in the church's interior design create an open environment that does not overwhelm the worshiper, as Gothic cathedrals might, thus serving human—not divine—needs. Likewise, he rediscovered the classical principles of linear-perspective construction, which were reflective of the culture of the Renaissance. These principles helped Renaissance artists create realistic imagery.

▼ **Architect Filippo Brunelleschi's technical achievements mark the design and construction of the dome for the Cathedral of Florence as one of the major artistic landmarks of the Renaissance.**

▶ **CRITICAL THINKING**

Drawing Conclusions Why might an architect be an appropriate model for the humanist ideal of the universal Renaissance person?

▲ The first casual portrait, Leonardo's *Mona Lisa* revolutionized art.

▶ **CRITICAL THINKING**

Making Inferences Why would portraiture be a natural development for a Renaissance culture shaped by humanism?

High Renaissance Masters

The final stage of Italian Renaissance painting flourished from about 1490 to 1520. Called the High Renaissance, this period is associated with Leonardo da Vinci, Raphael Sanzio, and Michelangelo Buonarroti and their works.

Leonardo da Vinci was the model "Renaissance man." He was an artist, scientist, inventor, and visionary. Leonardo mastered the art of realistic painting, even dissecting human bodies to better understand their workings. However, he wanted to go beyond such realism to create idealized forms that captured the perfection of nature in the individual. Leonardo could not express his vision of perfection fully in a realistic style.

At age 25, Raphael Sanzio was already one of Italy's best painters. He was admired for his numerous madonnas (paintings of Mary, the mother of Jesus). Raphael is also well known for his frescoes in the Vatican Palace. His *School of Athens* is a classic example of Renaissance art, transcending his own culture. It demonstrates reveals a world of balance, harmony, and order—the underlying visual principles of classical Greek and Roman art.

Michelangelo Buonarroti, an accomplished painter, sculptor, and architect, was another master of the High Renaissance. Fiercely driven by his desire to create, he worked with great passion and energy on a remarkable number of projects. Michelangelo's figures on the ceiling of the Sistine Chapel in Rome depict an ideal type of human being with perfect proportions. The beauty of this idealized human being is meant to be a reflection of divine beauty—the more beautiful the body, the more godlike the figure.

✓ **READING PROGRESS CHECK**

Specifying In what ways did Italian artists use the ideas of the humanist movement in their works?

The Northern Artistic Renaissance

GUIDING QUESTION *How did the works of northern European artists differ from those of Italian artists?*

Like the Italian artists, the artists of northern Europe sought to portray their world realistically. However, their approach was different from that of the Italians. This was particularly true of the artists of the Low Countries (present-day Belgium, Luxembourg, and the Netherlands).

circumstance a determining condition

Circumstance played a role in the differences. The large wall spaces of Italian churches had encouraged the art of fresco painting. Italian artists used these spaces to master the technical skills that allowed them to portray humans in realistic settings. In the north, the Gothic cathedrals of the Middle Ages, with their stained glass windows, did not allow enough space for frescoes. Instead, northern European artists painted illustrations for books and wooden panels for altarpieces. Great care was needed to depict each object on a small scale.

The most important northern school of art in the 1400s was in Flanders, one of the Low Countries. Flemish artists turned to universal secular themes depicting daily life, as in Robert Campin's *Merode Altarpiece*. Campin, one of the earliest Flemish masters of painting, used shadows to create depth and the smallest details to reflect reality. The Flemish painter Jan van Eyck (EYEK) was among the first to use and perfect the technique of oil painting. He used a varnish made of linseed oil and nut oils mixed with resins. This medium enabled van Eyck to use a wide variety of brilliant colors. With his oil paints, he could create striking realism in fine details, as in his painting *Giovanni*

SKILLS PRACTICE

Think about the important and interesting details in the development of Renaissance art. Use these details to explain the history of Renaissance art to the class.

Arnolfini and His Bride. Like other Northern Renaissance artists, however, van Eyck imitated nature not by using perspective, as the Italians did, but by simply observing reality and portraying details as best he could.

By 1500, artists from the north had begun to study in Italy and to be influenced by what artists were doing there. One German artist who was greatly affected by the Italians was Albrecht Dürer. He made two trips to Italy and absorbed most of what the Italians could teach on the laws of perspective. Like the Italian artists of the High Renaissance, Dürer tried to achieve a standard of ideal beauty that was based on a careful examination of the human form. He did not reject the use of minute details typical of northern artists. However, he did try to fit those details more harmoniously into his works in accordance with Italian artistic theories.

✓ **READING PROGRESS CHECK**

Contrasting What was a key difference between the northern European artists and the Italian artists?

▼ **This central panel of the *Merode Altarpiece* by Flemish artist Robert Campin (c. 1378–1444) shows the Annunciation, when the archangel Gabriel told Mary she was to be the mother of Jesus.**

▶ **CRITICAL THINKING**

Making Connections For the people who first saw this painting, what effect might have been created by the placement of this religious scene in an everyday setting?

PHOTO: © Francis G. Mayer/CORBIS.

LESSON 2 REVIEW TEKS

Reviewing Vocabulary

1. ***Explaining*** Write a paragraph explaining why vernacular literature eventually became the preferred way to produce books. 26B

Using Your Notes

2. ***Explaining*** Using your chart on the effects of humanism on a Renaissance education, write a brief paragraph explaining these effects. 5A

Answering the Guiding Questions

3. ***Finding the Main Idea*** How did humanism help define the Italian Renaissance? 5A

4. ***Evaluating*** How was education during the Renaissance shaped by humanism? 5A

5. ***Making Connections*** How did humanism influence the works of Renaissance artists and authors? Give specific examples. 5A

6. ***Contrasting*** How did the works of northern European artists differ from the works of Italian artists? 5A

Writing Activity

7. **INFORMATIVE/EXPLANATORY** Write a paragraph describing one of the works of art in the lesson. Pay particular attention to how the image is representative of the humanist movement of the Renaissance. Be sure to use descriptive words that will help your reader visualize the work of art. 5A

SKILLBUILDER

TEKS 15B, 29A

Understanding Geographic Distributions and Patterns: Models

Why Learn This Skill?

Geographers, to analyze evidence in a variety of ways, can use geographic distributions and patterns of populations, resources, and trade, along with other subjects. One such way is through their use of models. It's important to understand how to interpret models so you can get the most out of your own analysis.

Learning the Skill

Models are useful tools to analyze and compare geographic distributions and patterns that show how a typical city is laid out. Models like the concentric zone model, the sector model, or the multiple nuclei model present you with a basic outline for understanding urbanization in the period of history you are studying. These models provide the basic outline of zones within a city and explain their use. Using one of the models on this page as an example, you can create a model of the city you live in or that is nearest to you. Some of the areas you should look for when creating your model include: city center, business areas, neighborhoods, industrial areas, transportation options.

Geographers use all of these aspects within a model to analyze and compare geographic distributions and patterns. Creating and analyzing models is a useful exercise for students of history, too.

Practicing the Skill

The concentric zone model is used by geographers to illustrate how a typical city is laid out. This model is based on the idea that land is most valuable at the center of a city because competition for that land is the most high. Following this same idea, the areas on the edge of town are the least settled. Examine the concentric zone model and then answer the questions that follow.

1. Why do you think the zone of independent workers' homes is closer to the central business district than those of wealthier residences?
2. How do you think access to transportation affects where individuals settle in the city?
3. Why do you think the central business district is located in the heart of the city, rather than in another location?

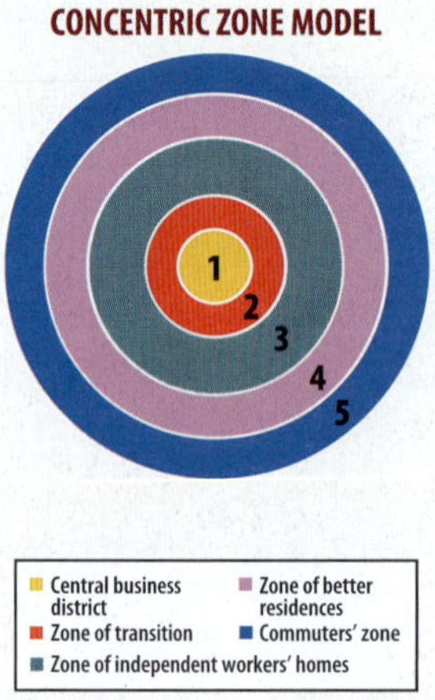

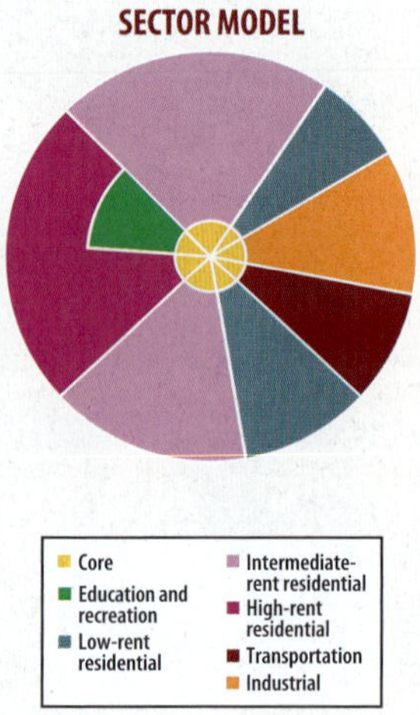

Applying the Skill

Analyze how your city, town, or village is organized. Does it fit with the concentric zone model, or is it organized in a different way? Compare the locations of businesses, residences, and green spaces. Are they clumped together in certain areas, or are they spread out across a larger area? Write a paragraph with your conclusions, explaining how your hometown does or doesn't fit with the model, including observations about distributions and patterns.

SKILLBUILDER

TEKS 16A

Locating Turning Points in History

Why Learn This Skill?

Geographic factors are crucial to understanding major events in history. If we can't put time and place together, we can't get the full picture of an event's significance.

Learning the Skill

Turning points in history occur when major periods of change or events change the way people live or look at the world. Turning points can include:

- revolutions
- exploration
- discoveries
- the rise and fall of empires
- social and religious change (such as disease, urbanization, industrialization, the introduction of new religions, new technology)

Location is an influential and motivating factor when it comes to turning points in history, as these events or ideas can affect a particular region or a larger part of the world. When attempting to locate places of historical significance in which turning points occurred, ask yourself these questions:

- In what area of the world did the turning point occur? Was it in one particular region, or was it widespread?
- What is special or different about the geography of the location where the turning point occurred?
- Can you recognize a pattern between different turning points that occurred in the same area?

Practicing the Skill

Examine this map of Europe and the Mediterranean world, noting the various cities included on it. Each of these cities holds historical significance by being a part of at least one turning point in history.

1. Most of the cities on the map are located around seas or major rivers. What general conclusion can you reach about the role of access to major waterways and turning points in history?
2. On the basis of your answer to question 1, how might seas and rivers affect turning points in history?
3. After examining this map, use areas called out to identify at least two turning points in history that could be illustrated on this map.

Applying the Skill

Using your knowledge of current events, select a region of the world and a significant current event happening there. Write a paragraph explaining how that significant event could become a turning point in history for students reading about it in the future. Be sure to explain how location plays a role in a turning point in history. (Use the examples included in the bulleted list under "Learning the Skill" for guidance, if needed.)

CHAPTER 15 Assessment

TEKS

Directions: On a separate sheet of paper, answer the questions below. Make sure you read carefully and answer all parts to the question.

Lesson Review

Lesson 1

1. ***Analyzing*** How did the lack of a single strong ruler benefit Italy during the Renaissance? How might Italy have evolved, if it had been ruled by one powerful monarch?

2. ***Determining Cause and Effect*** How did consumers' demand for goods affect the power of the Italian states and the power of the Catholic Church? **5A**

3. ***Sequencing*** Explain the sequence of key events telling the Medici family's rise to power, decline of power, and return to power.

4. ***Drawing Conclusions*** How did the fact that other countries in Europe had strong rulers affect Italy's fate? Compare and contrast the king of Spain's treatment of Italy with that of the king of France.

5. ***Explaining*** Explain the importance of the family bond and marriage contracts during the Renaissance.

6. ***Summarizing*** Summarize Machiavelli's theory for political leadership.

7. ***Explaining*** Explain how the increase in wealth for the Italian states during the Renaissance impacted the position of the Church. **5A**

Lesson 2

8. ***Explaining*** Explain the significance of the use of the vernacular, including Dante's work.

9. ***Assessing*** Why is Christine de Pizan's argument for women's intelligence so convincing?

10. ***Contrasting*** What were fresco artists able to convey that medieval painters could not? How does their accomplishment embody characteristics of humanism? **5A**

11. ***Identifying*** What stages did Leonardo da Vinci go through in learning to paint the human form? What goal did he share with other High Renaissance artists like Raphael and Michelangelo? **5A**

Exploring the Essential Questions

12. ***Analyzing Cause and Effect*** How did the humanist movement influence the arts in the European Renaissance? How do you think Renaissance art, in turn, reinforced the humanist worldview? **5A, 1D**

13. ***Explaining*** Describe in a paragraph the role of trade in the development of the Renaissance. Reference specific Renaissance ideas and political structures in your answer. **1D, 5A**

Critical Thinking

14. ***Speculating*** Speculate how Renaissance ideas spread through the trade of goods.

15. ***Synthesizing*** How did the work of architects, such as Filippo Brunelleschi's church of San Lorenzo in Florence, synthesize Renaissance ideals in its design? **26A**

16. ***Identifying Continuity and Change*** How did Early Renaissance artists learn to create more realistic art than their predecessors? **5A**

Need Extra Help?

If You've Missed Question	1	2	3	4	5	6	7	8	9	10	11	12	13	14	15	16
Go to page	342	345	344	345	347	345	344	349	350	351	352	350	342	342	351	351

17 ***Argument*** Explain how the Renaissance was a rebirth. Analyze the ways in which it imitated and differed from the cultures that inspired it. **5A, 1D**

18 ***Making Connections*** What was the relationship among individualism, Christianity, and increasing secularism during and after the Renaissance, and how might this new cultural mindset have impacted future political movements? **25C**

19 ***Theorizing*** Theorize about the areas of study within the humanist tradition as a basis for education of a well-rounded individual. Suggest how the concept reflected Renaissance society's values.

20 ***Comparing and Contrasting*** Compare the humanist viewpoint in the 14th century with that of the viewpoint of humanists in the 15th century. Explain how adopting the later viewpoint might alter a scholar's life.

21 ***Constructing Arguments*** Construct an argument in favor of or opposed to humanist educational philosophy, including treatment of male and female students.

Social Studies Skills

22 ***Identifying Cause and Effect*** Why did Florence enjoy a flourishing of the arts in the fifteenth century? **5A**

23 ***Geography Skills*** Look at the map in Lesson 1 and locate the cities of Milan, Florence, Venice, Rome, and Naples. Which of these cities appear most accessible to trade routes? What other advantages did their locations provide?

24 ***Comparing*** Compare the viewpoints of Baldassare Castiglione and Machiavelli. How might both viewpoints compete with one another but also blend?

25 ***Economics*** How could urban poverty increase while the Italian states grew wealthier?

26 ***Drawing Conclusions*** Draw conclusions about Italy's economic decline when competition from English and Flemish cloth makers drove down prices.

27 ***Identifying Cause and Effect*** Explain the importance of the printing press in Renaissance culture, making sure to specifically address its application in education. **27C**

28 ***Synthesizing*** Work with a partner to create a multimedia presentation showing three pieces of art that reflect ideas that shaped the Renaissance. Provide a photo or reproduction of each piece of art, an audio analysis of its features, and a written explanation of how it was shaped by Renaissance ideas. Primary sources may also be used. **5A, 30C**

29 ***Analyzing Models*** View the image from the Skillbuilder page in this chapter. Analyze and compare the geographic distributions shown in the models. **15B**

Need Extra Help?

If You've Missed Question	17	18	19	20	21	22	23	24	25	26	27	28	29
Go to page	342	348	348	348	348	349	343	346	346	352	350	348	354

DBQ Analyzing Primary Sources

Use the text excerpt to answer the following questions.

Filippo Brunelleschi was the first architect since the ancient Greeks to successfully design and construct a large dome. A few years later, one of his students, Leon Battista Alberti, praised the dome:

PRIMARY SOURCE

"Within, one breathes the perpetual freshness of spring. Outside there may be frost, fog or wind, but in this retreat, closed to every wind, the air is quiet and mild. What a pleasant refuge from the hot blasts of summer and autumn! And if it is true that delight resides where our senses receive all that they can demand of nature, how can one hesitate to call this temple a nest of delights?"

—quoted in *Brunelleschi's Dome: How a Renaissance Genius Reinvented Architecture*

30. ***Drawing Conclusions*** Alberti was one of Brunelleschi's students. How might this relationship have influenced Alberti's opinion? **5A**

31. ***Making Connections*** Medieval architects were anonymous. Brunelleschi became famous throughout Italy. What humanist principle does this shift in attitude reflect? **5A**

32. ***Analyzing*** What language did the speaker use that points to the focus of the human experience on earth—part of Renaissance values—versus the unreachable divine presence?

Analyzing Visuals

Use the image of the artifact to answer the following questions.

33. ***Drawing Conclusions*** Why might the artist have chosen to include members of the Medici family in his painting? **5A**

34. ***Synthesizing*** Would a wealthy family have themselves painted into a work of art today? **5A**

Extended Response Question

35. ***Expository*** In a short essay, describe the social and political structure in Renaissance Italian states. In your closing paragraph, compare and contrast the political structure of Italian states with modern nation-states. **5A, 19B**

Need Extra Help?

If You've Missed Question	30	31	32	33	34	35
Go to page	358	358	358	358	358	342

The Reformation in Europe

1517–1600

ESSENTIAL QUESTIONS • *What conditions can encourage the desire for reform?* • *How can reform influence society and beliefs?*

networks

There's More Online! about the Reformation in Europe.

CHAPTER 16

Lesson 1
The Protestant Reformation

Lesson 2
The Spread of Protestantism

The Story Matters...

The Protestant Reformation is the name given to the religious reform movement that divided western Christianity into Catholic and Protestant groups. Martin Luther's bold attempts to reform the Church led to new forms of Christianity. Although Luther did not see himself as a rebel, the spread of Protestantism ignited decades of bloody religious conflict and ended a thousand years of domination by the Catholic Church.

◀ Based on an earlier portrait, Charles Wagstaff's nineteenth-century engraving depicts Martin Luther, whose studies and determination drove him to defy the power of the Church and the Holy Roman Empire in order to assert his religious principles.

CHAPTER 16

Place and Time: Europe 1517–1600

In the sixteenth century, Europe was undergoing rapid change as economies expanded, cities grew, and a recent invention, the printing press, helped spread new ideas. New ideas appeared in the movement known as the Reformation, which began in Germany with Martin Luther's protest against what he saw as abuses within the Catholic Church. The Reformation movement he started soon spread throughout Europe. In Switzerland, John Calvin created a center of Reformation thought in Geneva. King Henry VIII made himself head of the Protestant Church of England.

Step Into the Place

Read the quotes and look at the information presented on the map.

DBQ How was the struggle between Protestantism and the Catholic Church a war of ideas?

PRIMARY SOURCE

"Unless I am convicted by Scripture and plain reason—I do not accept the authority of popes and councils, for they have contradicted each other—my conscience is captive to the Word of God. I cannot and I will not recant anything, for to go against conscience is neither right nor safe. Here I stand, I cannot do otherwise. God help me. Amen."

—Martin Luther, before the Diet of Worms in 1521

PRIMARY SOURCE

"Now, in order that true religion may shine on us, we ought to hold that it must take its beginning from heavenly doctrine and that no one can get even the slightest taste of right and sound doctrine, unless he be a pupil of Scripture."

—John Calvin, from *Institutes of the Christian Religion*

Step Into the Time

Organize the European events on the time line into two groups: (1) actions by Protestants and (2) reactions by the Catholic Church.

EUROPE

- **October 31, 1517** Martin Luther displays his Ninety-five Theses
- **1521** Church excommunicates Luther; Edict of Worms outlaws him within the Holy Roman Empire
- **1534** Act of Supremacy begins creation of Church of England
- **1536** John Calvin publishes *Institutes of the Christian Religion*
- **1540** Catholic Church recognizes the Society of Jesus, or Jesuits

1510 — 1525 — 1540

THE WORLD

- **1520** Ferdinand Magellan sails into the Pacific Ocean
- **1526** Afonso I, king of Congo, attempts to restrict Portuguese slave trade
- **1529** Ottoman siege of Vienna fails
- **1542** Bartolomé de Las Casas writes his *Short Account of the Destruction of the Indies*

networks
There's More Online!

- ☑ **MAP** Explore the interactive version of this map on Networks.
- ☑ **TIME LINE** Explore the interactive version of the time line on Networks.

1545 Council of Trent begins; concludes in 1563

1554 Catholic ruler Mary I begins persecution of Protestants in England

1555 Peace of Augsburg divides Christianity in Germany

1562 Teresa of Ávila founds reformed Carmelite Convent

1555 | **1570** | **1585** | **1600**

1549 Jesuit missionary Francis Xavier arrives in Japan

1566 Ottoman Sultan Süleyman I dies

1570 Mogul emperor Akbar begins new capital at Fatehpur Sikri; abandoned in 1586

1587 "Lost Colony" of Roanoke founded in Virginia

1588 ʿAbbās becomes Shah of Persian Ṣafavid Dynasty

networks

There's More Online!

- BIOGRAPHY Charles V
- BIOGRAPHY Desiderius Erasmus
- BIOGRAPHY Martin Luther
- IMAGE The True Church and the False Church
- INFOGRAPHIC Martin Luther and the Ninety-Five Theses
- INTERACTIVE SELF-CHECK QUIZ
- TIME LINE Christianity in Northern Europe
- VIDEO The Protestant Reformation

LESSON 1

The Protestant Reformation

ESSENTIAL QUESTION

What conditions can encourage the desire for reform?

Reading **HELP**DESK

Academic Vocabulary

- **fundamental**
- **external**
- **valid**

Content Vocabulary

- **Christian humanism**
- **salvation**
- **indulgence**
- **Lutheranism**

TAKING NOTES:

Key Ideas and Details

Determining Cause and Effect Use a graphic organizer like this one to identify steps that led to the Reformation.

Step
Step
Step
Reformation

TEKS Texas Essential Knowledge and Skills

1D identify major causes and describe the major effects of the following important turning points in world history from 1450 to 1750: the rise of the Ottoman Empire, the influence of the Ming dynasty on world trade, European exploration and the Columbian Exchange, European expansion, and the Renaissance and the Reformation

continued on the next page

IT MATTERS BECAUSE

The humanist ideas of the Renaissance, in addition to perceived worldly and corrupt practices in the Catholic Church, gave rise to a widespread call for Church reform. The Protestant faith that resulted gave new direction to European history and culture by fragmenting Western Christianity and reshaping political power.

Prelude to Reformation

GUIDING QUESTION *How did Christian humanism and Desiderius Erasmus pave the way for the Protestant Reformation in Europe?*

A German priest and professor named Martin Luther began the Protestant Reformation in the early 1500s. Prior developments, such as widespread intellectual changes during the preceding century, had already set the stage for religious change.

Christian Humanism

During the second half of the fifteenth century, the new classical learning that was part of Italian Renaissance humanism spread to northern Europe, leading to the development ofa movement called **Christian humanism**, or Northern Renaissance humanism. The major goal of this movement was the reform of the Catholic Church. The Christian humanists believed in the ability of human beings to reason and improve themselves. They thought that if people read the classics, and especially the **fundamental** teachings of Christianity in the Bible, they would become more sincerely religious. An effect of this religious feeling would be a reform of the Church and society.

The best-known Christian humanist was Desiderius Erasmus (ih • RAZ • muhs). Erasmus believed that Christianity should show people how to live good lives on a daily basis, not just provide beliefs that might help them be saved. He also thought that the Catholic Church needed to return to the simpler days of early Christianity. Stressing the inwardness of religious feeling, Erasmus thought the **external** forms of medieval religion, such as pilgrimages, fasts, and relics, were not all that important.

Erasmus wanted to educate people in the works of Christianity and worked to criticize the abuses in the Church. In his 1509 satire *The Praise of Folly*, Erasmus humorously criticized society's moral and religious state and called for a simpler, purer faith. In this passage, he satirizes what he views as the folly of clergy who encourage the practice of visiting the shrines of saints:

PRIMARY SOURCE

"[They] attribute strange virtues to the shrines and images of saints and martyrs, and so would make their credulous proselytes believe, that if they pay their devotion to St. Christopher in the morning, they shall be guarded and secured the day following from all dangers and misfortunes: if soldiers, when they first take arms, shall come and mumble over such a set prayer before the picture of St. Barbara, they shall return safe from all engagements."

—from *The Praise of Folly*

▲ A portrait of Erasmus, painted in 1523 by Hans Holbein the Younger.

Erasmus sought reform within the Catholic Church, not a break from it. His ideas, however, prepared the way for the Reformation. As people of his day said, "Erasmus laid the egg that Luther hatched."

Need for Reform

Erasmus and the Christian humanists were not the only ones calling for reform. Records from the era show that ordinary people, humanists, and some Church leaders were critical of the Church. For example, from 1450 to 1520, a series of Renaissance popes were viewed as more concerned with worldly interests. Church officials were viewed as using their church offices to advance their careers and their wealth. At the same time, many ordinary parish priests appeared to their parishioners as ignorant of their spiritual duties. People wanted to know how to save their souls, but many parish priests appeared unwilling or unable to offer them advice or instruction.

While the leaders of the Church were failing to meet their responsibilities, ordinary people desired meaningful religious expression and assurance of their **salvation**, or acceptance into heaven. As a result, for some, the process of obtaining salvation became almost mechanical.

According to Church practice at that time, venerating a relic, such as a scrap of a saint's clothing, could gain someone an **indulgence**. An indulgence was a document sold by the Church and signed by the pope or another church official that released the bearer from all or part of the punishment for sin. Making pilgrimages to view relics grew popular as a way to acquire indulgences and, therefore, salvation.

As more people sought certainty of salvation through veneration of relics, collections of such objects grew. Frederick III, also known as Frederick the Wise, Luther's prince, had amassed more than 5,000 relics. Some people believed the indulgences attached to them could reduce time spent in purgatory by 1,443 years. The Church also sold indulgences.

Other people sought certainty of salvation in the popular mystical movement known as the Modern Devotion. The Modern Devotion downplayed Church practices and stressed the need to follow the teachings of Jesus. This deepening of religious life was done within the Catholic Church. It also helps explain the tremendous impact of Luther's ideas.

✓ READING PROGRESS CHECK

Identifying Central Issues Why, according to Erasmus, other Christian humanists, and other critics, did the Church need reform?

(continued from p. 362)

TEKS **Texas Essential Knowledge and Skills**

5B explain the political, intellectual, artistic, economic, and religious impact of the Reformation

23B identify examples of religious influence on various events referenced in the major eras of world history

27C explain the impact of the printing press on the Renaissance and the Reformation in Europe

Christian humanism a movement that developed in northern Europe during the Renaissance, combining classical learning and individualism with the goal of reforming the Catholic Church

fundamental basic or essential

external outward or observable

salvation the state of being saved (that is, going to heaven) through faith alone or through faith and good works

indulgence a release from all or part of punishment for sin by the Catholic Church, reducing time in purgatory after death

Martin Luther

GUIDING QUESTION *What role did Martin Luther and his ideas play in the Reformation?*

▲ This image depicts Luther publicly displaying his Ninety-five Theses.

▶ **CRITICAL THINKING**
Interpreting Significance How might art be a useful weapon in a war of ideas such as the Protestant Reformation?

Martin Luther was a monk in the Catholic Church and a professor at the University of Wittenberg, in Germany, where he lectured on the Bible. Through his study of the Bible, Luther arrived at an answer to a problem that had bothered him since he had become a monk. He wanted to know about the certainty of salvation.

Catholic teaching had stressed that faith and good works were needed to gain personal salvation. In Luther's opinion, human beings were powerless in the sight of an almighty God and could never do enough good works to earn salvation. Through his study of the Bible, Luther came to believe that humans are not saved through their good works but through their faith in God. This idea, called justification by faith alone, became the chief teaching of the Protestant Reformation. Because Luther had arrived at his understanding of salvation by studying the Bible, the Bible became for Luther, as for all later Protestants, the only **valid** source of religious truth.

valid well-grounded or justifiable

The Ninety-five Theses

Luther was greatly upset by the widespread selling of indulgences. Especially offensive in his eyes was the monk Johann Tetzel, who the Church had authorized to sell indulgences to raise money to build St. Peter's Basilica in Rome. Tetzel told the faithful that their purchases would free the souls of their loved ones from purgatory. His slogan was: "As soon as coin in the coffer [money box] rings, the soul from purgatory springs." This enraged Luther, who believed that indulgences did not forgive sins but only soothed the conscience.

On October 31, 1517, Luther, angered by the Church's practices, made his Ninety-five Theses public, perhaps by posting them on the door of the Castle Church in Wittenberg. The act of posting may be a legend, but posting topics to discuss was a common practice of the time. In any case, his theses were a stunning attack on abuses in the sale of indulgences and had an impact on the course of religion all over Europe. The recent invention of the printing press made possible the printing of. thousands of copies of the Ninety-five Theses. They soon were printed and spread to all parts of Germany.

A Break With the Church

By 1520, Luther began to move toward a more definite break with the Catholic Church. He called on the German princes to overthrow the papacy in Germany and establish a reformed German church.

Luther also attacked the Church's system of sacraments. In his view, they were the means by which the pope and the Catholic Church had destroyed the real meaning of the Gospel for a thousand years. He kept only two sacraments—baptism and the Eucharist, which is also known as Communion. Luther also called for the clergy to marry. This went against the long-standing requirement of the Catholic Church that its clergy remain celibate, or unmarried.

Through all these calls for change, Luther continued to emphasize his new doctrine of salvation. It is faith alone, he said, and not good works, that justifies and brings salvation through Jesus.

Unable to accept Luther's ideas, the pope excommunicated him in January 1521, excluding him from Church membership. He was also summoned to appear before the imperial diet—or legislative assembly—of the Holy Roman Empire, which was called into session in the city of Worms by the newly elected emperor Charles V. The emperor believed he could convince Luther to change his ideas. However, Luther refused.

The young emperor was outraged. "A single friar who goes counter to all Christianity for a thousand years," he declared, "must be wrong." By the Edict of Worms, Martin Luther was made an outlaw within the empire. His works were to be burned, and Luther was to be captured and delivered to the emperor. However, Frederick III, the elector (or prince) of Saxony, was unwilling to see his subject killed. He sent Luther into hiding and then protected him when Luther returned to Wittenberg at the beginning of 1522.

The Rise of Lutheranism

During the next few years, Luther's religious movement became a revolution. Luther was able to gain the support of many of the German rulers among the approximately three hundred states that made up the Holy Roman Empire. These German rulers, motivated as much by politics and economics as by any religious feeling, quickly took control of the Catholic churches in their territories, forming state churches supervised by the government. The political leaders, not the Roman pope, held the last word. As part of the development of these state-dominated churches, Luther also set up new religious services to replace the Catholic mass. These services consisted of Christian Bible readings, preaching the word of God, and song. Luther also married a former nun, Katharina von Boren, providing a model of married and family life for the new Protestant ministers. Luther's doctrine soon became known as **Lutheranism** and the churches as Lutheran churches. Lutheranism was the first Protestant faith.

▲ Summoned to the imperial assembly at Worms, Luther refused to change his ideas.

▶ CRITICAL THINKING

Predicting Consequences If Luther had agreed to change his ideas, what do you think would have been the consequences for the development of Protestantism? Explain.

A series of crises soon made it apparent, however, that spreading the word of God was not an easy task for Luther. The Peasants' War was Luther's greatest challenge. In June 1524, German peasants revolted against their lords and looked to Luther to support their cause. Instead, Luther supported the lords. To him, the state and its rulers were called by God to maintain the peace necessary to spread the Gospel, the first four books of the New Testament in the Christian Bible. It was the duty of princes to stop all revolts. By the following spring, the German princes had crushed the peasant revolts. Luther found himself even more dependent on state authorities for the growth of his reformed church.

Lutheranism the religious doctrine that Martin Luther developed; it differed from Catholicism in the doctrine of salvation, which Luther believed could be achieved by faith alone, not by good works; Lutheranism was the first Protestant faith

✓ READING PROGRESS CHECK

Interpreting How did Luther's ideas lead to a break with the Church and to a new faith?

▲ A portrait by Lucas Cranach the Younger depicting Frederick III, Elector of Saxony. He sent Luther into hiding to protect him.

Political Impact of the German Reformation

GUIDING QUESTION *Why was the Holy Roman Empire forced to seek peace with the Lutheran princes?*

From its beginning, the fate of Luther's movement was tied closely to political affairs. Charles V, the Holy Roman emperor, ruled an immense empire consisting of Spain and its colonies, the Austrian lands, Bohemia, Hungary, the Low Countries, the duchy of Milan in northern Italy, and the kingdom of Naples in southern Italy.

Religious authorities primarily saw the Reformation as a challenge to Church power. Rulers such as Charles also saw the Reformation as a force that disrupted the political and social order. Charles hoped to preserve his empire's unity by keeping it Catholic and under the control of his dynasty, the Hapsburgs. However, a number of problems cost him his dream and his health. These same problems helped Lutheranism survive by giving Lutherans time to organize before facing Catholic forces.

The chief political concern of Charles V was his rivalry with the king of France, Francis I. Their conflict over a number of disputed territories led to a series of wars that lasted more than 20 years. Invasions by Ottoman Turks forced Charles to send forces into the eastern part of his empire as well.

Finally, the internal political situation in the Holy Roman Empire was not in Charles's favor. Germany was a land of several hundred territorial states. Although all owed loyalty to the emperor, many rulers of the German states supported Luther as a way to assert their authority and dislike of papal control. By the time Charles V brought military forces to Germany, the Lutheran princes were well organized. Unable to defeat them, Charles was forced to seek peace.

An end to religious warfare in Germany came in 1555 with the Peace of Augsburg. This agreement formally accepted the division of Christianity in Germany. The German states were now free to choose between Catholicism and Lutheranism. Lutheran states would have the same legal rights as Catholic states. Subjects did not choose their religion. German rulers determined that for them.

SKILLS PRACTICE

Discuss the development of Protestantism with a partner. Make sure to use words from the lesson in your discussion such as *fundamental, external, valid, indulgence, salvation,* and *Christian humanism*.

✓ READING PROGRESS CHECK

Evaluating How were the goals of Charles and the Holy Roman Empire at odds with the desires of Lutheran princes?

PHOTO: SuperStock / SuperStock

LESSON 1 REVIEW TEKS

Reviewing Vocabulary

1. ***Analyzing*** Write a paragraph that reports on indulgences by telling what they were, what people did to get them, who might buy or sell them, when or how they were given, and why they were considered desirable.

Using Your Notes

2. ***Gathering Information*** Use your notes on the steps leading to the Reformation and other insights you gathered while reading the lesson to explain that Luther did not start the Reformation on his own.

Answering the Guiding Questions

3. ***Identifying Cause and Effect*** How did Desiderius Erasmus and Christian humanism pave the way for the Protestant Reformation in Europe?
4. ***Assessing*** What role did Martin Luther and his ideas play in the Reformation?
5. ***Drawing Conclusions*** Why was the Holy Roman Empire forced to seek peace with the Lutheran princes?

Writing Activity

6. **NARRATIVE** Write a narrative paragraph based on the events surrounding Luther's possible posting of his Ninety-five Theses on the church door at Wittenberg. Be sure to use chronological order to present the events, and try to introduce literary techniques of conflict, characterization, and setting to strengthen your narrative.

SKILLBUILDER

TEKS 29F

Summarizing Information

Why Learn This Skill?

Imagine you have been assigned a chapter on the Renaissance for a midterm. After taking a short break, you discover that you cannot recall important information. What can you do to avoid this problem?

When you read a long selection, it is helpful to take notes. Summarizing information—reducing large amounts of information to a few key phrases—can help you remember the main ideas and important facts.

Learning the Skill

To summarize information, follow these guidelines when you read:

- Distinguish the main ideas from the supporting details. Use the main ideas in the summary.
- Use your own words to describe the main ideas. Do not copy the selection word for word.
- Summarize the author's opinion if you think it is important.
- If the summary is almost as long as the reading selection, you are including too much information. The summary should be very short.

Practicing the Skill

Read the selection below, and then answer the questions that follow.

"For the next 30 years, the French and Spanish made Italy their battleground as they fought to dominate the country. A decisive turning point in their war came in 1527. On May 5, thousands of troops belonging to the Spanish king Charles I arrived at the city of Rome along with mercenaries from different countries. They had not been paid for months. When they yelled, 'Money! Money!' their leader responded, 'If you have ever dreamed of pillaging a town and laying hold if its treasures, here now is one, the riches of them all, queen of the world.' "

The next day the invading forces smashed down the gates and pushed their way into the city. The terrible sack of Rome in 1527 by the armies of the Spanish king Charles I ended the Italian wars and left the Spanish a dominant force in Italy.

1. What are the main ideas of these paragraphs?
2. What are the supporting details of the main ideas?
3. Write a brief summary of two or three sentences that will help you remember what the paragraph is about.

▲ Charles I, king of Spain, was also Holy Roman Emperor.

Applying the Skill

Read and summarize an article from an online news source or a newspaper. Have a classmate ask you questions about the article. How much were you able to remember after summarizing the information?

PRIMARY SOURCES

The Reformation brought about Protestantism, a new way for Christians to think about their relationship with God and the church. But within Protestantism, not everyone agreed on doctrine. In 1529, Martin Luther and Ulrich Zwingli, two major figures of the Reformation, debated over the sacrament of the Lord's Supper, also known as Holy Eucharist or Communion.

Reformation Debate

LUTHER: Although I have no intention of changing my mind, which is firmly made up, I will nevertheless present the grounds of my belief and show where the others are in error. . . . Your basic **contentions** are these: In the last analysis you wish to prove that a body cannot be in two places at once, and you produce arguments about the unlimited body which are based on natural reason. I do not question how Christ can be God and man and how the two natures can be joined. For God is more powerful than all our ideas, and we must submit to his word. Prove that Christ's body is not there where the **Scripture** says, "This is my body!" God is beyond all mathematics and the words of God are to be **revered** and carried out in awe. It is God who commands, "Take, eat, this is my body." I request, therefore, valid scriptural proof to the contrary.

ZWINGLI: I insist that the words of the Lord's Supper must be **figurative.** This is ever apparent, and even required by the article of faith; "taken up into heaven, seated at the right hand of the Father." Otherwise, it would be absurd to look for him in the Lord's Supper at the same time that Christ is telling us that he is in heaven. One and the same body cannot possibly be in different places. . . .

LUTHER: I call upon you as before: your basic contentions are shaky. Give way, and give glory to God!

ZWINGLI: And we call upon you to give glory to God and to quit begging the question! The issue at stake is this: Where is the proof of your position?

LUTHER: It is your point that must be proved, not mine. But let us stop this sort of thing. It serves no purpose.

ZWINGLI: It certainly does! It is for you to prove that the passage in John 6 speaks of a physical meal.

LUTHER: You express yourself poorly. . . . You're going nowhere.

VOCABULARY

contention
point made in an argument

Scripture
passage from the Bible

revered
honored or respected

figurative
describing something in terms normally used for another

DBQ Analyzing Historical Documents

1. **Citing Text Evidence** Do you think that Martin Luther's beliefs about communion could be changed? Cite text evidence to support your answer.
2. **Analyzing** What is the basis for the disagreement between Luther and Zwingli?
3. **Drawing Conclusions** Was a conclusion reached in the debate presented between Luther and Zwingli?

networks

There's More Online!

- BIOGRAPHY John Calvin
- BIOGRAPHY John of Leiden
- BIOGRAPHY Thomas More
- BIOGRAPHY Ulrich Zwingli
- INTERACTIVE SELF-CHECK QUIZ
- PRIMARY SOURCE Decrees of the Council of Trent
- PRIMARY SOURCE *Institutes of the Christian Religion*
- TIME LINE Henry VIII and the Church of England
- VIDEO The Spread of Protestantism

LESSON 2
The Spread of Protestantism

ESSENTIAL QUESTION *How can reform influence society and beliefs?*

Reading HELPDESK

Academic Vocabulary
- **community**
- **publish**

Content Vocabulary
- **justification**
- **predestination**
- **annul**
- **ghetto**

TAKING NOTES:
Key Ideas and Details

LISTING Use a graphic organizer like this one to list the characteristics of the Reformation in Switzerland and England.

Switzerland	England

TEKS Texas Essential Knowledge and Skills

1D identify major causes and describe the major effects of the following important turning points in world history from 1450 to 1750: the rise of the Ottoman Empire, the influence of the Ming dynasty on world trade, European exploration and the Columbian Exchange, European expansion, and the Renaissance and the Reformation

continued on the next page

It Matters Because

Different forms of Protestantism emerged in Europe during the 1500s. Calvinism challenged Lutheranism with new ideas about salvation, England's Henry VIII created a national church, and Anabaptists challenged both Catholics and other Protestants with ideas about separation of church and state. In response to Protestantism, the Catholic Church also underwent a reformation.

Protestantism in Switzerland

GUIDING QUESTION *Why did Calvinism become an important form of Protestantism by the mid-sixteenth century?*

By permitting German states to choose between Catholicism and Lutheranism, the Peace of Augsburg officially ended Christian unity in the Holy Roman Empire. Previously, however, divisions had appeared within Protestantism. One of these new groups arose in Switzerland.

Ulrich Zwingli was a priest in the Swiss city of Zürich. The city council of Zürich, strongly influenced by Zwingli, began to introduce religious reforms. All paintings and decorations were removed from the churches and replaced by whitewashed walls. A new church service consisting of Scripture reading, prayer, and sermons replaced the Catholic mass.

As Zwingli's movement began to spread to other cities in Switzerland, he sought an alliance with Luther and the other German reformers. The German and Swiss reformers saw the need for unity to defend themselves against Catholic authorities, but they could not agree on certain Christian rites.

In October 1531, war broke out between the Protestant and Catholic states in Switzerland. Zürich's army was routed, and Zwingli was found wounded on the battlefield. His enemies killed him, cut up his body, burned the pieces, and scattered the ashes. The leadership of Protestantism in Switzerland passed to John Calvin.

publish to print for distribution

justification process of being justified, or deemed worthy of salvation, by God

predestination belief that God has determined in advance who will be saved (the elect) and who will be damned (the reprobate)

annul declare invalid

(continued from p. 369)

TEKS **Texas Essential Knowledge and Skills**

5B explain the political, intellectual, artistic, economic, and religious impact of the Reformation

20C explain the political philosophies of individuals such as John Locke, Thomas Hobbes, Voltaire, Charles de Montesquieu, Jean Jacques Rousseau, Thomas Aquinas, John Calvin, Thomas Jefferson, and William Blackstone

As a reformer and convert to Protestantism, Calvin had fled his native France for the safety of Switzerland. In 1536 he **published** his *Institutes of the Christian Religion,* a summary of his understanding of Protestant thought. Because of the recent invention of the printing press, Calvin's work and the writings of other Protestant leaders could be distributed widely, helping spread Protestant ideas. Publication of Calvin's work immediately gained him a reputation as one of the new leaders of Protestantism.

Like Luther, Calvin believed that faith alone was sufficient for **justification**, the process of being deemed worthy of salvation by God. However, Calvin's belief in the all-powerful nature of God led him to other ideas, such as **predestination**. This meant that God had selected some people to be saved and others to be damned. Although Calvin stressed that no one could ever be absolutely certain of salvation, his followers did not always heed this warning. The belief in predestination gave later Calvinists the firm conviction that they were doing God's work on Earth. Calvinism became a dynamic and activist faith.

In a reflection of his political philosophy, Calvin created a type of theocracy, or government by divine authority, in the Swiss city of Geneva. Calvin believed church teachings were the foundation of government functions, though he did not believe the church should control the state. He did hold, however, that a government lost its divine right to rule if it rejected the teachings of God.

For Calvin, It was the responsibility of church and state to work together for the benefit of the people. Additionally, in order to limit the abuse of power, Calvin believed that different responsibilities of government should be divided among different government bodies. This is perhaps a foreshadowing of the concept of a separation of powers.

✔ **READING PROGRESS CHECK**

Describing How did divisions in Protestantism take place in Switzerland?

Reformation in England

GUIDING QUESTION ***What made the English Reformation different from the Reformation in the rest of Europe?***

The English Reformation was rooted in politics. King Henry VIII wanted to divorce his wife, Catherine of Aragon, with whom he had not yet had a son and heir. The pope was unwilling to **annul** the king's marriage, so Henry turned to England's highest church courts. These courts ruled in May 1533 that the king's first marriage was "null and absolutely void." At the beginning of June, Henry's new wife, Anne, was made queen. Three months later their child, the future Queen Elizabeth I, was born.

In 1534 at Henry's request, Parliament finalized England's break with the pope and the Catholic Church. The Act of Supremacy of 1534 declared that the king was "the only supreme head on earth of the [new] Church of England." The king now had control over religious doctrine, clerical appointments, and discipline. Thomas More, a Christian humanist and devout Catholic, opposed the king's action and was beheaded.

Henry used his new powers to close monasteries. He sold their lands and possessions to landowners and merchants. The English nobility had disliked papal control of the Church, and now they had a financial interest in the new order. Additionally, the king received a boost to his treasury. In most matters of doctrine, however, Henry stayed close to Catholic teachings.

When the king died in 1547, he was succeeded by Edward VI, his

▲ This gold half sovereign shows Henry VIII as king and head of the Church of England.

nine-year-old son by his third wife. During the brief reign of King Edward VI, church officials who favored Protestant doctrines moved the Church of England, or the Anglican Church, in a Protestant direction. New acts of Parliament gave clergy the right to marry and created a Protestant church service. Before he turned 16, Edward died of tuberculosis.

The rapid changes in doctrine and policy during Edward's reign aroused opposition. When Henry VIII's daughter Mary I came to the throne in 1553, England was ready for a reaction. Mary was a Catholic who wanted to restore England to Roman Catholicism, but her efforts had the opposite effect. Among other actions, she ordered the burning of almost 300 Protestants as heretics, earning her the nickname "Bloody Mary." As a result of her policies, England was even more committed to Protestantism by the end of Mary's reign.

▲ This image shows the execution of Thomas Cranmer, Protestant Archbishop of Canterbury, which was ordered by Mary I in 1556.

▶ CRITICAL THINKING

Drawing Conclusions Why would Protestants want to circulate images of events such as the execution of Cranmer?

✓ READING PROGRESS CHECK

Identifying Cause and Effect What caused the Protestant Reformation in England, and what resulted from it?

Anabaptists

GUIDING QUESTION *Why did both Catholics and Protestants consider Anabaptists dangerous radicals?*

Reformers such as Luther had allowed the state to play an important, if not dominant, role in church affairs. However, some people strongly disliked giving such power to the state. These were radicals known as Anabaptists. Most Anabaptists believed in the complete separation of church and state. Not only was government to be kept out of the realm of religion, it was not supposed to have any political authority over "real" Christians. Anabaptists refused to hold political office or bear arms because many took literally the biblical commandment "Thou shall not kill."

To Anabaptists, the true Christian church was a voluntary **community** of adult believers who had undergone spiritual rebirth and then had been baptized. This belief in adult baptism separated the Anabaptists from Catholics and other Protestants, who baptized infants.

community a group of people with common interests and characteristics living together within a larger society

Anabaptists also believed in following the practices and the spirit of early Christianity. They considered all believers to be equal. Anabaptists based this belief on the accounts of early Christian communities in the New Testament of the Bible. Each Anabaptist church chose its own minister, or spiritual leader. Because all Christians were considered to be priests, any member of the community was eligible to be a minister—though women were often excluded.

Their political beliefs, as much as their religious beliefs, caused the Anabaptists to be regarded as dangerous radicals who threatened the very fabric of sixteenth-century society. The chief thing other Protestants and Catholics could agree on was the need to persecute Anabaptists.

Many of the persecuted Anabaptists settled in Münster, a city in Westphalia in modern-day Germany, in the 1530s. Under John of Leiden, the city became a sanctuary for Anabaptists. In 1534 an army of Catholics and other Protestants surrounded the city. Then in 1535, they captured it, torturing and killing the Anabaptist leaders.

✓ READING PROGRESS CHECK

Discussing What beliefs did the Anabaptists have that alarmed the other Protestants and Catholics?

Reformation and Society

GUIDING QUESTION *How did the Reformation affect European society?*

The Protestant Reformation had an impact on the development of education in Europe. Protestant teachers employed humanist methods, though Protestant schools were aimed at a much wider audience than the humanist schools, which were mostly for the elite. Martin Luther urged the cities and villages of German states to provide schools paid for by the public. Protestants in Germany then established secondary schools, where teaching in Greek and Latin was combined with religious instruction.

The Protestant Reformation had an economic impact as well. The seizing of Catholic monasteries and their assets in various Protestant states often resulted in a brief flood of wealth for their rulers. Additionally, Protestants–Calvinists especially– were not as concerned with laws and rules regarding the lending of money. This opened the door for small changes in personal lending and investment.

To some extent, Protestantism also modified the traditional view of marriage. Protestants had abolished monasticism and the celibacy requirement for their clergy. Traditional understanding of the roles of husband as the ruler and wife as the obedient servant and bearer of children remained unchanged. Calvin and Luther saw this role of women as part of the divine plan.

Other traditional features of European society were unaffected by the Reformation. Anti-Semitism, which is hostility or discrimination against Jews, remained common in Europe after the Reformation. Martin Luther expected Jews to convert to Lutheranism. When they resisted, he recommended that Jewish houses of worship should be destroyed. The Catholic Church was no more tolerant. In Italy's Papal States, which were controlled by the popes, Jews who would not convert were forced to live in segregated areas called **ghettos**.

Analyzing PRIMARY SOURCES

Luther on Marriage

"The rule remains with the husband, and the wife is compelled to obey him by God's command. He rules the home and the state, wages war, defends his possessions, tills the soil, builds, plants, etc. The woman on the other hand is like a nail driven into the wall."

—Martin Luther, from *Lectures on Genesis*

DBQ ***INTERPRETING*** What might Luther mean by comparing a woman to a nail in the wall?

ghetto formerly a district in a city in which Jews were required to live

✓ **READING PROGRESS CHECK**

Analyzing What was Luther's view about women's role in society?

Catholic Reformation

GUIDING QUESTION *What prompted the Catholic Reformation during the sixteenth century?*

The situation in Europe did not appear favorable for the Catholic Church. Lutheranism had become rooted in Germany and Scandinavia, and Calvinism had taken hold in Switzerland, France, the Netherlands, and Eastern Europe. In England, the split from Rome had resulted in the creation of a national church. However, the Catholic Church was revitalized in the sixteenth century. It found new strength and regained much that it had lost to the Protestant Reformation. Three elements supported this Catholic Reformation, which is also called the Counter-Reformation. The first was the establishment of a new religious order, the Jesuits. The second was the reform of the papacy. The third element was the Council of Trent.

A Spanish nobleman, Ignatius of Loyola, founded the Society of Jesus, or Jesuits. Pope Paul III recognized Loyola's small group of followers as a religious order in 1540. All Jesuits took a special vow of absolute obedience to the pope, making them an important instrument for papal policy. Jesuits used education to spread their message and established schools. Jesuit missionaries were very successful in restoring Catholicism to parts of Germany and eastern Europe and in spreading it to other parts of the world.

Later in the century, a Spanish nun, Teresa of Ávila, promoted the reform of the Carmelite order. The Carmelites were one of the four major religious orders founded in the Middle Ages who took a vow of complete poverty. In 1562 Teresa founded a small convent at Ávila where the nuns followed a very strict way of life.

Reform of the papacy was another important element in the Catholic Reformation. The participation of Renaissance popes in dubious financial transactions and in Italy's politics and wars had encouraged corruption. It took the jolt of the Protestant Reformation to change the Catholic Church.

Pope Paul III saw the need for reform. He took the bold step of naming a Reform Commission in 1535 to determine the Church's ills. The commission blamed the Church's problems on the popes' corrupt policies.

Pope Paul III also called the Council of Trent. Beginning in March 1545, a group of cardinals, archbishops, bishops, abbots, and theologians met off and on for 18 years in the city of Trent near the northern border of modern-day Italy.

The final decrees of the Council reaffirmed traditional Catholic teachings in opposition to Protestant beliefs. Both faith and good works were declared necessary for salvation. The seven sacraments, the Catholic view of the Eucharist, and clerical celibacy were all upheld. Belief in purgatory and in the use of indulgences was strengthened, although the selling of indulgences was forbidden. The Roman Catholic Church now possessed a clear body of doctrine. It was unified under the pope's supreme leadership. Catholics were now more confident as defenders of their faith.

✓ READING PROGRESS CHECK

Exploring Issues What were the three key elements of the Catholic Reformation, and why were they so important to the Catholic Church in the sixteenth century?

BIOGRAPHY

Teresa of Ávila (1515–1582)

Displeased with the relaxed lifestyle at the Carmelite convent at Ávila, Teresa began thinking of ways to return the order to its former strict way of life. In her reforms, she required nuns to meditate and practice penance. With Pope Pius IV's approval, she opened the first convent of the Carmelite Reform in 1562. She went on to found 16 more convents throughout Spain.

▶ CRITICAL THINKING

Drawing Conclusions How did Teresa of Ávila combine the spiritual and the practical in her life?

LESSON 2 REVIEW TEKS

Reviewing Vocabulary

1. ***Explaining*** Explain why England's King Henry VIII needed the pope to annul his marriage to Queen Catherine of Aragon.

Using your Notes

2. ***Distinguishing*** Use your notes to identify the characteristics of the Protestant Reformation in Switzerland and England.

Answering the Guiding Questions

3. ***Explaining*** Why did Calvinism become an important form of Protestantism by the mid-sixteenth century?

4. ***Contrasting*** What made the English Reformation different from the Reformation in the rest of Europe?

5. ***Analyzing*** Why were Anabaptists considered by both Catholics and Protestants to be dangerous radicals?

6. ***Finding the Main Idea*** How did the Reformation affect European society?

7. ***Making Connections*** What prompted the Catholic Reformation during the sixteenth century?

Writing Activity

8. INFORMATIVE/EXPLANATORY Explain how political and economic issues played a role in the Protestant Reformation in Europe.

CHAPTER 16 Assessment

TEKS

Directions: On a separate sheet of paper, answer the questions below. Make sure you read carefully and answer all parts of the question.

Lesson Review

Lesson 1

1. ***Contrasting*** How did humanism contradict medieval attitudes toward Christianity?

2. ***Identifying*** What was the Modern Devotion?

3. ***Contrasting*** How did Martin Luther's attitude toward good works contradict Erasmus's philosophy of Christ?

4. ***Describing*** Describe the practice of indulgences, and explain how the Church used the practice to raise funds. **1D**

5. ***Drawing Conclusions*** What was the political impact of the Reformation on the Holy Roman Empire? **5B, 23B**

6. ***Describing*** How did Luther modify religious services?

7. ***Assessing*** Why did it take 38 years from the time Luther wrote his Ninety-five Theses until Lutheranism was accepted at the Peace of Augsburg?

Lesson 2

8. ***Drawing Conclusions*** How is the concept of predestination tied to the dynamic growth of the Calvinist faith?

9. ***Identifying Central Issues*** What were the Anabaptists' core beliefs?

10. ***Summarizing*** What role did the Bible play in Protestant faiths? In the Roman Catholic faith?

11. ***Identifying*** What was the Council of Trent?

12. ***Explaining*** Explain how King Henry VIII used his political influence over religious authorities.

Exploring the Essential Questions

13. ***Sequencing*** Work with a small group to create a time line showing at least six events in the Reformation and the Catholic Reformation. Label each event explaining how it influenced society and beliefs. Include visuals such as portraits, drawings of events, and maps. **5B, 23B**

14. ***Analyzing*** What conditions in Catholicism caused Martin Luther's desire for reform?

Critical Thinking

15. ***Analyzing*** Why was Christian humanism an outgrowth of Renaissance ideals?

16. ***Sequencing*** What led the Holy Roman Emperor, Charles V, to seek peace in Germany?

17. ***Evaluating*** The political system developed by John Calvin was an example of a theocracy. What were the characteristics of the system, and what kind of political impact did it have on the Reformation? **5B, 19B, 20C**

18. ***Identifying Central Issues*** How did violence play a role in opposing religious views and conflicts during this time?

19. ***Contrasting*** In what ways did the vows of the Carmelite order contrast with previous papal lifestyles?

20. ***Making Inferences*** Make an inference about the geographical location of Reformation efforts in Germany, Switzerland, and England and the notable Catholic figures of Ignatius Loyola and Teresa Avila from Spain.

Need Extra Help?

If You've Missed Question	1	2	3	4	5	6	7	8	9	10	11	12	13	14	15	16	17	18	19	20
Go to page	362	363	364	364	366	365	366	370	371	370	372	370	370	364	362	366	370	369	373	369

21. ***Identifying Cause and Effect*** What was the effect of Jesuit missionary work?

22. ***Drawing Conclusions*** Explain the impact that the printing press had on the Reformation in Europe. **27C**

23. ***Defending*** Describe how the Reformation was a turning point in world history. **1D**

Social Studies Skills

24. ***Identifying Perspectives*** What were Protestants protesting against?

25. ***Understanding Relationships Among Events*** Why did the German peasants expect Luther to support their revolt?

26. ***Identifying Cause and Effect*** One can never predict all the effects of one's actions. How does the experience of Queen Mary I as she tried to restore Catholicism as the sole religion of England illustrate this?

27. ***Understanding Relationships Among Events*** What benefits, if any, did the revolt against the Catholic Church lead to for Catholicism? **1D**

28. ***Research Skills*** Refer to Foxe's Book of Martyrs and its account of the Reformation in England. Then write a short report to explain how it is a reflection of the history of the Reformation. Include in your report how this work could have influenced events in England.

29. ***Identifying Cause and Effect*** One of the economic impacts of the Reformation was the monetary gain of landowners in England who received land formerly owned by Catholic missions. Explain how this kind of action impacts English society as a whole. **5B**

30. ***Creating Presentations*** Make a visual presentation to demonstrate an example of the intellectual impact of the Reformation. **5B**

31. ***Geography Skills*** Create a map that includes key Italian Renaissance sites, as well as Northern European cities where Christian reform efforts took place. Include sites of Christian humanism, German Reformation, Protestantism in Switzerland, Reformation in England, and the Catholic Counter-Reformation. Label key cities and identify political borders. **16A**

DBQ Analyzing Primary Sources

Use the document to answer the following questions.

Teresa of Ávila wrote several books, including a treatise on prayer called *The Interior Castle,* addressed to the nuns in her convent. The excerpt is from the epilogue to *The Interior Castle.*

PRIMARY SOURCE

"In return for my strong desire to aid you in serving Him, my God and my Lord, I implore you, whenever you read this, to praise His Majesty fervently in my name and to beg Him to prosper His Church, to give light to the Lutherans, to pardon my sins and to free me from purgatory, where perhaps I shall be, by the mercy of God, when you see this book (if it is given to you after having been examined by theologians). If these writings contain any error, it is through my ignorance; I submit in all things to the teachings of the holy Catholic Roman Church, of which I am now a member, as I protest and promise I will be both in life and death."

32. ***Analyzing Primary Sources*** What is Teresa's opinion of her religion?

33. ***Making Inferences*** Why does Teresa pray for God to give light to the Lutherans?

Need Extra Help?

If You've Missed Question	21	22	23	24	25	26	27	28	29	30	31	32	33
Go to page	373	364	365	369	365	371	372	370	370	372	369	375	375

Analyzing Visuals

Use the artwork to answer the following question.

34 ***Analyzing Visuals*** The art shows the execution of a Protestant Archbishop of Canterbury, an event that was order by Mary I of England. What does the picture explain about the political impact of the Reformation? Choose the correct answer. **5B**

A The Reformation was mainly a political issue that did not involve most citizens.

B Mary I's efforts to restore Catholicism to England were working.

C Former religious leaders were becoming violent toward the Church of England.

D Former religious leaders no longer had influence in society.

Extended Response Question

35 ***Expository*** Discuss the links between politics and religion during the fifteenth and sixteenth centuries. Explain which political, economic, and social factors led to religious reform. **1D**

Need Extra Help?

If You've Missed Question	34	35
Go to page	376	364

The Age of Exploration

1500–1800

ESSENTIAL QUESTION *What are the effects of political and economic expansion?*

networks

There's More Online! about the age of exploration.

CHAPTER 17

The Story Matters...

During the Age of Exploration that began in the late fifteenth century, European explorers made voyages in search of wealth, new lands, and converts for Christianity. They found all of these things and more, including civilizations undreamed of by Europeans. They also established the first global trading empires. One of these European explorers was Amerigo Vespucci, an Italian navigator who made several voyages to the Western Hemisphere.

◀ Reading of Vespucci's voyages, a German mapmaker proposed using a form of the name Amerigo for the newly found lands. In 1507 he published the first map with the name "America" on the still unknown lands of the Western Hemisphere. This portrait of Vespucci appeared in a geographical work published in 1673.

CHAPTER 17

Place and Time: The Age of Exploration 1500–1800

The Age of Exploration led to great cultural and economic changes, both in Europe and throughout the world. The European explorers of the fifteenth and sixteenth centuries pioneered new trade routes that would link regions previously isolated. New global political and economic relations developed, and a new interconnected world began to emerge. However, this large-scale European expansion often had negative side effects for the indigenous peoples, including war, disease, and cultural devastation.

Step Into the Place

Read the quotes and look at the information presented on the map.

DBQ **Analyzing Historical Documents** What different motivations affected European explorers of this time?

PRIMARY SOURCE

"And [the Portuguese explorer Vasco da Gama] told [the Indian ruler of Calicut]. . . [kings of Portugal] had annually sent out vessels to make discoveries in the direction of India, . . . not because they sought for gold or silver, for of this they had such abundance that they needed not what was to be found in this country. He further stated that the captains sent out traveled for a year or two, until their provisions were exhausted, and then returned to Portugal. . ."

—from *Journal of the First Voyage of Vasco da Gama,* 1497–1499

PRIMARY SOURCE

"[Hernán Cortés] said to [the Aztec ruler] Montezuma through our interpreter, half laughing: 'Señor Montezuma, I do not understand how such a great Prince and wise man as you are has not come to the conclusion, in your mind, that these idols of yours are not gods, but evil things that are called devils'. . .

Montezuma replied half angrily. . .'Señor [Cortés], . . . we consider [our gods] to be very good, for they give us health and rains and good seed times and seasons and as many victories as we desire, and we are obliged to worship them and make sacrifices, and I pray you not to say another word in their dishonour.'"

—from *The Discovery and Conquest of Mexico,* Bernal Díaz del Castillo, 1552–1568

PHOTO: (l to r) Master of Saldana/Bridgeman Art Library/Getty Images, Pedro Barretto de Resende/The Bridgeman Art Library/Getty Images

Step Into the Time

Demonstrating Understanding Choose an event from the time line and explain how it shows a consequence of the European voyages of discovery.

EUROPE AND THE AMERICAS

- **1500** Pedro Cabral of Portugal reaches South America
- **1519** Hernán Cortés of Spain arrives in Mexico; by 1521 he has conquered the Aztec Empire
- **1520** Commanding a Spanish fleet, Ferdinand Magellan sails into the Pacific Ocean
- **1533** Francisco Pizarro of Spain conquers the Inca Empire
- **1538** Fewer than 500 Native Americans survive on Hispaniola
- **1608** Samuel de Champlain of France founds Quebec

1500 — 1550 — 1600

THE WORLD

- **1520** Süleyman I takes control of the Ottoman Empire.
- **circa 1526** West African ruler Afonso I attempts to restrict slave trade
- **1590** Toyotomi Hideyoshi takes control of Japan

networks *There's More Online!*

- **MAP** Explore the interactive version of this map on Networks.
- **TIME LINE** Explore the interactive version of the time line on Networks.

European Voyages of Discovery 1500–1800

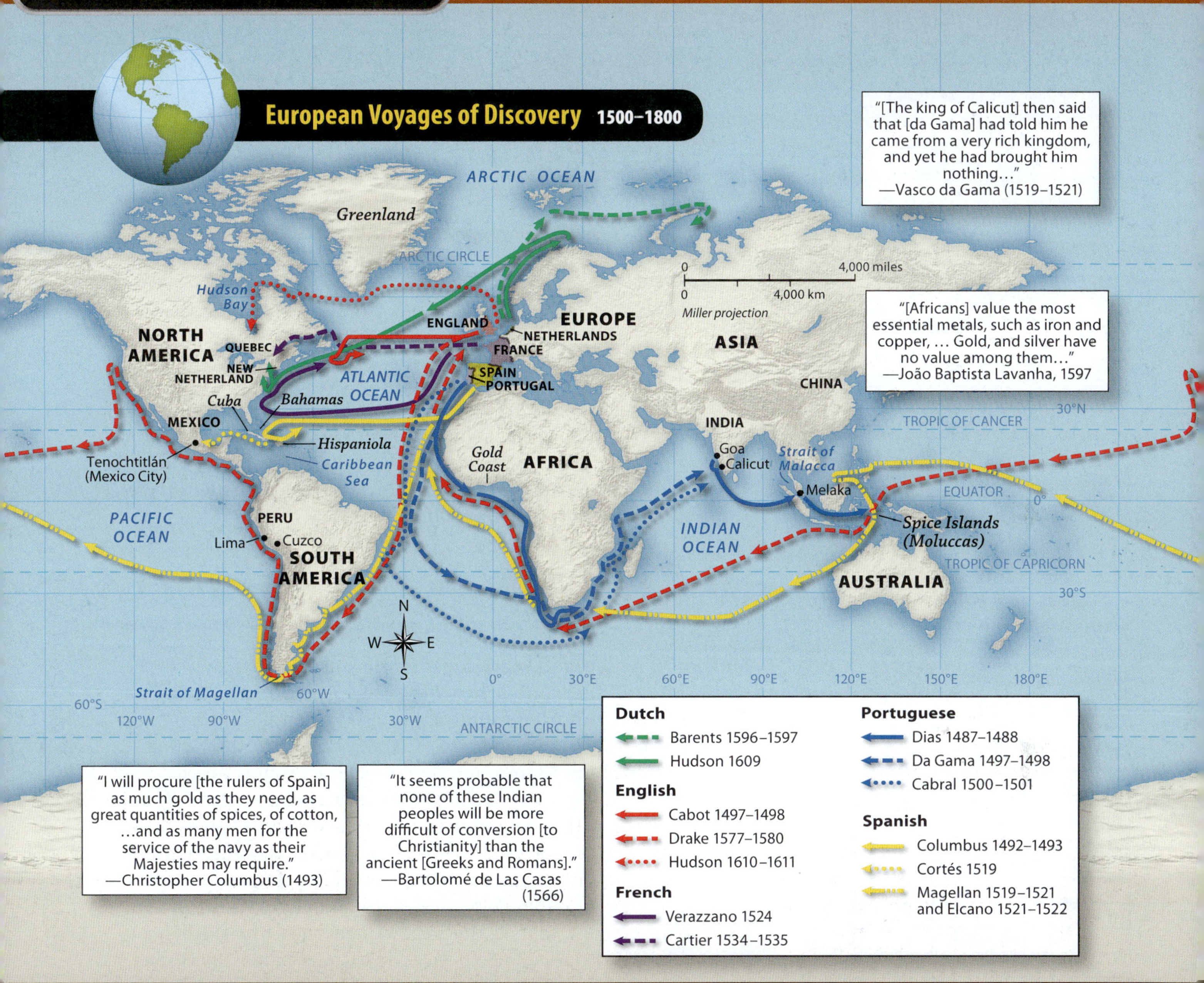

1650 · **1700** · **1750** · **1800**

1612 Tokugawa Shogunate begins closing of Japan to foreign missionaries

1632 Building of Taj Mahal begins

1644 End of China's Ming Dynasty; succeeded by Qing Dynasty

1664 England seizes New Netherland colony from the Dutch and renames it New York

1687 Ottoman Sultan Süleyman II comes to power

1707 Decline of Mogul empire in India begins

1736 End of Safavid rule in Iran

1740 War of Austrian Succession begins

1756 Seven Years' War between Britain and France begins

1787 Northwest Ordinance bans slavery in the Northwest Territory of the United States

networks

There's More Online!

- BIOGRAPHY Christopher Columbus
- BIOGRAPHY Hernán Cortés
- IMAGE Aztec Warriors Defend Tenochtitlán
- INFOGRAPHIC Spanish Conquest of the Aztec and Inca
- INTERACTIVE SELF-CHECK QUIZ
- PRIMARY SOURCE Letter from Hernán Cortés
- PRIMARY SOURCE Rights Granted to Columbus by Spain
- VIDEO Columbus' Voyage

Reading HELPDESK

Academic Vocabulary
- **overseas**

Content Vocabulary
- **caravel**
- **colony**
- **conquistador**

TAKING NOTES:
Key Ideas and Details

Summarizing Use a graphic organizer like this one to identify which European nations and individuals explored which region(s).

Nation	Explorer	Region(s)

TEKS Texas Essential Knowledge and Skills

1D identify major causes and describe the major effects of the following important turning points in world history from 1450 to 1750: the rise of the Ottoman Empire, the influence of the Ming dynasty on world trade, European exploration and the Columbian Exchange, European expansion, and the Renaissance and the Reformation

continued on the next page

LESSON 1

European Exploration and Expansion

ESSENTIAL QUESTION
What are the effects of political and economic expansion?

It Matters Because

European explorers traveled east and west driven by a variety of motives, including desire for wealth, political ambition, religious zeal, and the call of adventure. These connections between Europe and the rest of the world were crucial to forming the modern world.

Motives and Means

GUIDING QUESTION *What were the motivations behind European exploration of distant lands?*

For almost a thousand years, most Europeans had remained in their small region of the world. Then, between 1500 and 1800, European explorers used improved sailing ships to travel and explore the rest of the world. First Portugal and Spain, and then later the Netherlands, England, and France, reached to new economic heights through their travels and resulting trading activity. At the end of the fifteenth century, they set out on a remarkable series of **overseas** journeys. What caused them to undertake such dangerous voyages?

European explorers had long been attracted to Asia. In the late thirteenth century, Marco Polo traveled from Venice with his father and uncle to the Chinese court of the great Mongol ruler Kublai Khan (KOO • bluh KAHN). Marco Polo wrote an account of his experiences, entitled *The Travels,* fascinating many Europeans who read the book. In the fourteenth century, conquests by the Ottoman Turks reduced the ability of Westerners to travel by land to the East. This was one of the major causes of European exploration: gaining access to Asia by sea.

Economic motives were one of the major causes of European expansion. Merchants, adventurers, and state officials had high hopes of expanding trade, especially for the spices of the East. The spices, which were needed to preserve and flavor food, were very expensive after Arab middlemen shipped them to Europe. Europeans also had hopes of finding precious metals.

It has been said that "Gold, glory, and God" were the key motives for European expansion. This statement suggests another reason for the overseas voyages: religious zeal. Many people shared the belief of Hernán Cortés, the Spanish conqueror of Mexico, that they must ensure that indigenous people were "introduced into and instructed in the holy Catholic Faith."

Spiritual and secular affairs were connected in the sixteenth century. Many Europeans wanted to convert indigenous people to Christianity, but grandeur, glory, and a spirit of adventure also played a major role in European expansion.

New sailing technology made the voyages of discovery possible. Europeans had now reached a level of ship design that enabled them to make long-distance voyages beyond Europe. The Portuguese invented a ship, called the **caravel**, that was faster than previous models. It made long voyages of exploration possible and lowered the cost of transport. The caravel's design included a large cargo hold. It used triangular, or lateen, sails, taken from Arab designs, which allowed it to sail against the wind.

European explorers also had more accurate maps because of advances in cartography, the art and science of mapmaking. Sailors used the astrolabe, an invention of Greek astronomers, to plot their latitude using the sun or stars. The magnetic compass, invented in China, also helped sailors chart a course across the ocean.

Another factor assisting European explorers was their increasing knowledge of wind patterns of the Atlantic Ocean. The winds, ocean currents, and climate influenced the journeys of the early sailing vessels that depended on them. The Atlantic, Pacific, and Indian Oceans have spiraling currents, called gyres, that result from global winds and other forces. The winds blowing south and west in the North Atlantic, known as the trade winds, and the winds blowing from the west to the east, known as westerlies, were studied and utilized to the explorers' benefit.

✓ **READING PROGRESS CHECK**

Explaining What does the phrase "Gold, glory, and God" mean?

A Race for Riches

GUIDING QUESTION *How were Spain and Portugal able to take the lead in discovering new lands?*

During the fifteenth century, European explorers sailed into the world in new directions. Portuguese ships took the lead when they sailed southward along the West African coast.

Portuguese Explorers

Beginning in 1420, under the sponsorship of Prince Henry the Navigator, Portuguese fleets began probing southward along the western coast of Africa. There, they discovered a new source of gold. The southern coast of West Africa became known to Europeans as the Gold Coast.

Portuguese sea captains heard reports of a route to India around the southern tip of Africa. In 1488 Bartholomeu Dias reached the tip, later called the Cape of Good Hope, and returned. Next, Vasco da Gama went around Africa and cut across the Indian Ocean to the coast of India. In May 1498, he arrived off the port of Calicut. After da Gama returned to Portugal, he made a large profit from the cargo of spices he obtained in India.

overseas beyond or across the sea

caravel a small, fast, maneuverable ship that had a large cargo hold and usually three masts with lateen sails

(continued from p. 380)

TEKS **Texas Essential Knowledge and Skills**

5A explain the political, intellectual, artistic, economic, and religious impact of the Renaissance

6B explain how the Inca and Aztec empires were impacted by European exploration/colonization

7A analyze the causes of European expansion from 1450 to 1750

7F explain new economic factors and principles that contributed to the success of Europe's Commercial Revolution

▼ A Portuguese caravel

▲ An engraving from 1592 shows the harbor of Lisbon full of ships coming from and going to Portugal's overseas colonies.

▶ **CRITICAL THINKING**

Analyzing What does this image suggest about Portugal's role in international trade at the end of the sixteenth century?

Portuguese fleets returned to the area to take control of the spice trade from the Muslims. The Portuguese Admiral Afonso de Albuquerque (AL • buh • KUR • kee) established a port at Goa, India. Later, Albuquerque sailed into Melaka, a thriving spice trade port on the Malay Peninsula. By taking over Melaka, the Portuguese destroyed Arab control of the spice trade and gained a stopping place on the long journey to the Moluccas, then known as the Spice Islands.

A Portuguese treaty signed with the local Moluccan ruler established Portuguese control of the spice trade. The Portuguese had a limited empire of trading posts on the coasts of India and China. They did not have the power, people, or the desire to colonize these regions.

Spanish Explorers

Educated Europeans knew the world was round but had no idea of its circumference, the size of the Asian continent, or that another continent was located to the west between Europe and Asia. While the Portuguese sailed south along the coast of Africa, then east through the Indian Ocean, the Spanish sailed west across the Atlantic Ocean to find the route to Asia.

Christopher Columbus believed he could reach Asia by sailing west instead of east around Africa. Columbus persuaded Queen Isabella of Spain to finance an exploratory expedition. In October 1492, he reached the Americas, where he explored the coastline of Cuba and the island of Hispaniola in the Caribbean.

Columbus believed he had reached Asia. After three voyages, he had still not found a route through the outer islands to what he believed was the Asian mainland. In his four voyages, Columbus reached all the major Caribbean islands and Honduras in Central America—all of which he called the Indies.

Another important explorer funded by Spain was Ferdinand Magellan. In September 1519, he set sail from Spain in search of a sea passage through the Americas. In October 1520, Magellan passed through a waterway along the tip of South America, later called the Strait of Magellan, into the Pacific Ocean. The fleet reached the Philippines, but indigenous people there killed Magellan. Although only one of Magellan's ships returned to Spain, as the leader of the expedition, he is remembered as the first person to sail completely around the globe.

Connections to TODAY

Mapping Ocean Winds

A contemporary use of ocean winds is to drive wind turbines producing electricity. To harness this resource, scientists first need to identify areas in the oceans that have strong winds, using data from NASA satellites. Then, scientists can prepare maps that indicate potential sites for wind farms.

New Lands to Explore

Spain and Portugal each feared that the other would claim some of its newly discovered territories. They resolved their concerns over control of the Americas with the Treaty of Tordesillas, signed in 1494. The treaty called for a boundary line extending from north to south through the Atlantic Ocean and the easternmost part of the South American continent. Unexplored territories east of the line would be controlled by Portugal, and those west of the line by Spain. This treaty gave Portugal control over its route around Africa, and it gave Spain rights to almost all of the Americas.

Soon, government-sponsored explorers from many European countries joined the race to the Americas. A Venetian seaman, John Cabot, explored the New England coastline of the Americas on behalf of England in 1497. The Portuguese sea captain Pedro Cabral landed in South America in 1500,

SKILLBUILDER

TEKS 29A, 29B, 29C, 29D

Analyzing Primary and Secondary Sources

Why Learn This Skill?

Suppose for a moment that a devastating tornado has struck a nearby town. On television that night, a reporter interviews an eyewitness. The eyewitness begins to cry as she describes the destruction of her own home and neighborhood. The next day, there is a newspaper account that describes the tornado's path. Is one of these accounts of the same event more accurate than the other?

Learning the Skill

To determine the accuracy and evaluate the validity of an account, historians must analyze its source. There are two main types of sources—**primary** and **secondary.**

Primary sources are produced by eyewitnesses to events. Diaries, letters, autobiographies, interviews, artifacts, and paintings are primary sources. Because primary sources convey personal experiences, they often include the emotions and opinions of participants in an event.

Secondary sources use information gathered from others. Newspapers, textbooks, and biographies are secondary sources. Secondary sources, written later, help us to understand events in a larger context or time frame.

To determine reliability of a source, consider the type of source you are using. For a primary source, determine who the author is and when the material was written. An account written during or immediately after an event is often more reliable than one written years later. For a secondary source, look for good documentation. Researchers should cite their sources in footnotes and bibliographies.

For both types of sources you also need to evaluate the author. Is this author biased? What background and authority does he or she have? Finally, compare two accounts of the same event. If they disagree, you should question the reliability of the material and conduct further research to determine which can be corroborated with other reliable sources.

Practicing the Skill

Read the following excerpts, and answer the questions:

"Finally the two groups met . . . When all was ready Montezuma placed his feet, shod in gold-soled, gem-studded sandals, on the carpeted pavement and . . . advanced to an encounter that would shape both his own destiny and that of his nation. . . . Montezuma had servants bring forward two necklaces of red shells hung with life-size shrimps made of gold. These he placed around Cortés's neck."

—from Cortés by William Weber Johnson, 1975

"When we had arrived at a place not far from the town, the monarch raised himself in his sedan. . . . Montezuma himself was sumptuously attired, had on a species of half boot, richly set with jewels, and whose soles were made of solid gold. . . . Montezuma came up to Cortés, and hung about his neck a chaste necklace of gold, most curiously worked with figures all representing crabs."

—from an account by Conquistador Bernal Díaz del Castillo, 1519

1. What is the general topic of the two sources?
2. Identify the primary source.
3. Is one account more reliable than the other? If so, why? How do you know?

Applying the Skill

Find two accounts of a recent event or a historical event. Analyze and evaluate the reliability and validity of each. Be sure to document how you reached your conclusions about the reliability and validity of the sources.

Religion was an important feature of Aztec life. Prayers, legends, and ceremonies at great temples (some of which included human sacrifices to deities) were all part of Aztec religious practices. The Spanish, after their arrival in Mexico in 1519, were shocked by Aztec religious rituals and worked to convert the Aztec to Christianity. Read the following passages to learn more about Aztec and Spanish viewpoints about religion and Aztec society.

VOCABULARY

vassals
people in a subordinate position

precipitated
threw down

Moctezuma
the Aztec king in 1520

remonstrated
vocally protested

temporal
relating to earthly life

DBQ Analyzing Historical Documents

1. **Explaining** Why did King Ahuizotl pray to the god Huitzilopochtli?
2. **Identifying Points of View** How did Cortés's background influence his actions in the Aztec temple?
3. **Synthesizing** On what points do Ahuizotl and Cortés agree in their description of Aztec religious beliefs?
4. **Recognizing Bias** Consider the question "What was the role of religion in Aztec society?" How would an Aztec have answered that question differently than a Spaniard? Which answer do you think would have been most similar to your own answer to the question?

The Role of Religion in Aztec Society

PRIMARY SOURCE

The Aztec king Ahuizotl, who ruled from 1486 to 1502, offered the following prayer to the god Huitzilopochtli while celebrating a successful military campaign.

"O almighty, powerful lord of All Created Things,
You who give us life, and whose **vassals** and slaves we are,
Lord of the Day and of the Night, of the Wind and the Water,
Whose strength keeps us alive! I give you infinite thanks
For having brought me back to your city of Mexico
With the victory which you granted me.
I have returned. . . .
Since you did not frown upon my extreme youth
Or my lack of strength or the weakness of my chest,
You have subjected those remote and barbarous nations
To my power. You did all of these things! All is yours!
All was won to give you honor and praise!
Therefore, O powerful and heroic Huitzilopochtli,
You have brought us back to this place which was only water
Before, which was enclosed by our ancestors,
And where they built our city."

PRIMARY SOURCE

Spanish conquistador Hernán Cortés wrote the following description of a temple in the Aztec capital in a 1520 letter to the Spanish king, Charles V.

"Three halls are in this grand temple, which contain the principal idols; these are of wonderful extent and height, and admirable workmanship, adorned with figures sculpted in stone and wood; leading from the halls are chapels with very small doors. . . . In these chapels are the images of idols, although as I have before said, many of them are also found on the outside; the principal ones, in which the people have greatest faith and confidence, I **precipitated** from their pedestals, and cast them down the steps of the temple, purifying the chapels in which they had stood, as they were all polluted with human blood, shed ill the sacrifices. In the place of these I put images of Our Lady and the Saints, which excited not a little feeling in **Moctezuma** and the inhabitants, who at first **remonstrated,** declaring that if my proceedings were known throughout the country, the people would rise against me; for they believed that their idols bestowed on them all **temporal** good, and if they permitted them to be ill-treated, they would be angry and without their gifts, and by this means the people would be deprived of the fruits of the earth and perish with famine. . . ."

which established Portugal's claim to the region later named Brazil. Amerigo Vespucci (veh • SPOO • chee), a Florentine, went along on several voyages. His letters describing the lands he saw led to the use of the name America (after Amerigo) for the new lands.

✓ **READING PROGRESS CHECK**

Interpreting How were the first explorations of Spain and Portugal similar and different?

The Spanish Empire

GUIDING QUESTION *What were the results of Spanish and Portuguese conquests in the Americas?*

The Spanish conquerors of the Americas—known as **conquistadors**—were individuals whose firearms, organizational skills, and determination brought them extraordinary success. With their resources, the Spanish were able to establish an overseas empire that was quite different from the Portuguese trading posts.

conquistador a leader in the Spanish conquest of the Americas

Conquest of the Aztec

For a century, the Aztec ruled much of central Mexico from the Gulf of Mexico to the Pacific coast. Most local officials accepted the authority of the Aztec king in the capital Tenochtitlán, which was located at the site of modern-day Mexico City.

In 1519 a Spanish force under the command of Hernán Cortés landed at Veracruz, on the Gulf of Mexico. Cortés marched to Tenochtitlán with a small number of troops—550 soldiers and 16 horses. As he went, he made alliances with city-states that had tired of the oppressive rule of the Aztec. Particularly important was the alliance with Tlaxcala. In November, Cortés arrived at Tenochtitlán and was welcomed by the Aztec monarch Montezuma (Moctezuma). The Aztec were astounded to see the unfamiliar sight of men on horseback with firearms, cannons, and steel swords. These weapons gave the Spaniards a great advantage in fighting the Aztec.

▲ Aztec warriors defending Tenochtitlán against the Spanish

▶ **CRITICAL THINKING**

Drawing Conclusions How did the differences between Aztec and Spanish methods of waging war affect the outcome of the Spanish invasion?

PRIMARY SOURCE

"We arrived at a broad causeway, when we saw many towns and villages built in the lake, and other large towns on the land, with the level causeway running in a straight line to [Tenochtitlán]. We were astounded and told one another that the majestic towers and houses, all of massive stone and rising out of the waters, were like enchanted castles we had read of in books. Indeed, some of our men even asked if what we saw was not a dream."

— Bernal Díaz del Castillo, from *The True History of the Conquest of New Spain*

Eventually, tensions arose between the Spaniards and the Aztec. The Spanish took Montezuma hostage and began to pillage the city. In the fall of 1520, one year after Cortés had first arrived, the local population revolted and drove the invaders from the city. Many of the Spaniards were killed.

In the end, contact with Europeans proved disastrous for the Aztec empire. With no natural immunity to European diseases, many Aztec fell sick and died, especially from smallpox carried to the Americas by the Spaniards. Meanwhile, Cortés received fresh soldiers from his new allies in city-states such as Tlaxcala. After four months, the Aztec surrendered.

The forces of Cortés leveled pyramids, temples, and palaces and used the stones to build Spanish government buildings and churches. They filled in Aztec canals to make roads. The magnificent city of Tenochtitlán was no more. During the 30 years after the fall of the Aztec Empire, the Spanish expanded their control to all of Mexico.

Conquest of the Inca

When the first Spanish expeditions arrived in the central Andes of South America, they encountered a flourishing empire ruled by the Inca. In early 1531, Francisco Pizarro landed on the Pacific coast of South America with only a small band of about 180 men. Like Cortés, Pizarro brought steel weapons, gunpowder, and horses. The impact these Europeans would have on the Inca empire would be grim.

The Spanish also brought smallpox. Like the Aztec, the Inca had no immunities to European diseases. Smallpox soon devastated entire villages. Even the Inca emperor was a victim.

When the emperor died, both of his sons claimed the throne. This led to a civil war. Taking advantage of the situation, Pizarro captured Atahuallpa, the new emperor. With their stones, arrows, and light spears, Inca warriors provided little challenge to Spanish technology.

After executing Atahuallpa, Pizarro, his soldiers, and their Inca allies sacked Cuzco, the Inca capital. By 1535, Pizarro had established a new capital at Lima for a new **colony** of the Spanish Empire.

colony a settlement of people living in a new territory, linked with the parent country by trade and direct government control

✓ READING PROGRESS CHECK

Comparing and Contrasting How were the conquests of the Aztec and the Inca similar and different?

European Rivals

GUIDING QUESTION *Which other European countries explored and settled in the Americas?*

By the end of the sixteenth century, several new European rivals—the Dutch, French, and English—had begun to challenge the Portuguese and the Spanish for colonial dominance. Motivated by the promise of gold and other precious goods, these countries sent explorers to the Americas to search for new sources of wealth and trade opportunities.

The Dutch formed the West India Company. Although it made some temporary inroads in Portuguese Brazil and the Caribbean, the company lacked the resources and power to maintain these gains.

In the early seventeenth century, Dutch settlements were established on the North American continent and named New Netherland. The colony extended from the mouth of the present-day Hudson River as far north as present-day Albany, New York. This settlement and others never flourished because of the West India Company's commercial goals. Fur trading, with its remote outposts, did not encourage settlement.

After 1660, the Dutch commercial empire in the Americas fell to its rivals, the English and the French. In 1664 the English seized the colony of New Netherland from the Dutch and renamed it New York. The Dutch West India Company soon went bankrupt.

GEOGRAPHY CONNECTION

1. **ENVIRONMENT AND SOCIETY** On which waterways did the early Dutch and French fur trappers depend?
2. **PLACES AND REGIONS** How did the pattern of English settlement differ from that of the Dutch and the French?

During the seventeenth century, the French colonized parts of what is now Canada, then named New France, and Louisiana. In 1608 Samuel de Champlain founded Quebec, the first permanent French settlement in the Americas. When New France became a royal province in 1663, with its own governor, military commander, and soldiers, the population grew and the colony developed. Meanwhile, English settlers were founding Virginia and the Massachusetts Bay Colony.

By the end of the seventeenth century, the English had established control over most of the eastern seaboard of North America. They had also set up sugar plantations on several Caribbean islands. Nevertheless, compared to the enormous Spanish empire in Latin America, the North American colonies were of minor importance to the English economy.

✓ READING PROGRESS CHECK

Locating Where were the earliest settlements of the Dutch, French, and English in the Americas?

LESSON 1 REVIEW TEKS

Reviewing Vocabulary

1. ***Identifying*** Write a paragraph explaining why the caravel was an important development for European explorers. 1D, 7A

Using Your Notes

2. ***Summarizing*** Use your graphic organizer on European exploration to write a paragraph summarizing the major explorers and the regions each nation explored. 1D

Answering the Guiding Questions

3. ***Analyzing Cause and Effect*** What were the motivations behind European exploration of distant lands? 1D, 7A, 7F, 23B
4. ***Making Connections*** How were Spain and Portugal able to take the lead in discovering new lands? 1D, 7A
5. ***Analyzing Cause and Effect*** What were the results of Spanish and Portuguese conquests in America? 1D, 6B
6. ***Naming*** Which other European countries explored and settled in the Americas? 1D

Writing Activity

7. **INFORMATIVE/EXPLANATORY** Write an essay explaining how the Spanish succeeded in conquering much of the Americas. Identify the various factors that enabled them to overthrow such long-standing and extensive empires as the Aztec and the Inca. 1D, 6B

networks

There's More Online!

- ☑ BIOGRAPHY King Afonso I
- ☑ CHART/GRAPH Age of Exploration Economic Concepts
- ☑ INTERACTIVE SELF-CHECK QUIZ
- ☑ PRIMARY SOURCE Grant for Encomienda
- ☑ PRIMARY SOURCE King Afonso's Letter to the King of Portugal
- ☑ TIME LINE From Africa's Shores to America's Plantations
- ☑ VIDEO The First Global Economic Systems

LESSON 2

The First Global Economic Systems

ESSENTIAL QUESTION

What are the effects of political and economic expansion?

Reading HELPDESK

Academic Vocabulary

- **culture**
- **export**
- **regime**

Content Vocabulary

- **mercantilism**
- **plantations**
- **Middle Passage**

TAKING NOTES:

Key Ideas and Details

Identifying Use a graphic organizer like this one to note how plants, animals, and diseases moved between Europe, Africa, and Asia and the Americas as a result of the Columbian Exchange.

Europe, Africa, and Asia	⟷	The Americas

TEKS Texas Essential Knowledge and Skills

1D identify major causes and describe the major effects of the following important turning points in world history from 1450 to 1750: the rise of the Ottoman Empire, the influence of the Ming dynasty on world trade, European exploration and the Columbian Exchange, European expansion, and the Renaissance and the Reformation

continued on the next page

IT MATTERS BECAUSE

As the number of European colonies grew in the 1500s and 1600s, so did the volume and area of European trade, beginning a process that led to a world economy. An Atlantic slave trade also brought as many as 10 million enslaved Africans to the Americas between 1500 and the late 1800s. Species of plants and animals, along with diseases, spread between the continents. These exchanges had a lasting effect on the world's peoples.

The Commercial Revolution

GUIDING QUESTION *What economic theories were put into practice during the age of exploration?*

Many Italian city-states grew rich from trade during the early Renaissance. Not every European power benefited from this trade, however. The Italians and Ottomans controlled key trade routes. Thus, in the 1400s, other European powers who also sought spices, silk, and other goods from Asia began in earnest to look for alternative trade routes. The resulting 300-year-long age of exploration reshaped the world economy. The economic impact of the Renaissance was so fundamental that it is called the Commercial Revolution. This economic revolution saw the rapid expansion of European economies and the building of vast international trading empires.

The economic factors that contributed to the Commercial Revolution included trade, exploration, colonization, and new financial practices. To find new trade routes, European states sent one ship after another down the coast of Africa or across the Atlantic. These explorations opened European eyes to economic opportunities in faraway lands. New lands held new trade partners or valuable resources. Soon, European powers established colonies in every continent they visited. These colonies were the outposts of new trading networks that made European powers rich during the Commercial Revolution. The flow of wealth was so great that new financial practices emerged to manage the money, including new kinds of banking, accounting, and insurance.

The new economic principle of **mercantilism** also contributed to the success of the Commercial Revolution. Mercantilists believed that the prosperity of a nation depends on a large supply of bullion, or gold and silver. The fastest route to a large supply of gold and silver was to extract it from one's colonies. Spain was especially good at this, claiming vast wealth from the Americas.

The other method was to earn the gold and silver through having a favorable balance of trade. The balance of trade is the difference in value between what a nation imports and hat it **exports** over time. Imports are goods brought into a country; exports are goods shipped out of a country. When the balance is favorable, the exported goods are of greater value than the imported goods.

To encourage exports, governments stimulated the growth of industries and trade. They granted subsidies to new industries. Subsidies are payments made to support enterprises a government thinks are beneficial. Governments also improved transportation systems by building roads, bridges, and canals. They placed high tariffs, or taxes, on foreign goods to keep the balance of trade favorable. Tariffs make foreign goods less attractive because they raise the price of imports. European colonies were considered to be important as sources of raw materials and were viewed as markets for exports of manufactured goods.

The Commercial Revolution provided the benefits of free enterprise for many Europeans. Individuals began to open companies and attempt to profit from new discoveries. New job opportunities arose, and although many workers had an economic freedom that they did not have before, many workers also suffered from the pitiful wages they received. Trade also provided new goods for purchase, which eventually improved the European standard of living.

✓ **READING PROGRESS CHECK**

Drawing Inferences How might mercantilism have encouraged colonial expansion abroad?

culture the customary beliefs, social forms, and material traits of a racial, religious, or social group

regime a government in power

mercantilism a set of principles that dominated economic thought in the seventeenth century; it held that the prosperity of a nation depended on a large supply of gold and silver

export to send a product or service for sale to another country

(continued from p. 388)

TEKS **Texas Essential Knowledge and Skills**

4I explain the development of the slave trade

7B explain the impact of the Columbian Exchange on the Americas and Europe

7C explain the impact of the Atlantic slave trade on West Africa and the Americas

18F formulate generalizations on how economic freedom improved the human condition, based on students' knowledge of the benefits of free enterprise in Europe's Commercial Revolution, the Industrial Revolution, and 20th-century free market economies, compared to communist command communities

GOLD IMPORTS TO SPAIN IN THE SIXTEENTH CENTURY

CHARTS/GRAPHS

Period	Gold Imports (In grams)
1503–1510	4,965,180
1511–1520	9,153,220
1521–1530	4,889,050
1531–1540	14,466,360
1541–1550	24,957,130
1551–1560	42,620,080
1561–1570	11,530,940
1571–1580	9,429,140
1581–1590	12,101,650
1591–1600	19,451,420
Total	153,564,170

Source: Earl J. Hamilton, *American Treasure and the Price Revolution in Spain, 1501–1650*

Gold and silver from the Americas increased Spain's economic power.

▸ **CRITICAL THINKING**

1. ***Analyzing*** About how many times greater were gold imports in 1551–1560 than they had been at the beginning of the century?

2. ***Identifying*** How does this pattern of change show mercantilist goals?

PHOTO: Giraudon/The Bridgeman Art Library

SKILLS PRACTICE

Visuals such as pictures, charts, maps, and graphs can help you better understand the lesson. How does the picture of items of Dutch trade help you understand the impact of the Columbian Exchange?

plantation a large agricultural estate

The Columbian Exchange

GUIDING QUESTION *How did the Columbian Exchange affect the Americas and Europe?*

A major goal of European exploration was to gain wealth. European nations sought to increase their wealth by exploiting sources of precious metals and raw materials in their colonies. They also tried to build wealth by increasing exports of goods from producers at home to colonial markets overseas. All of this economic activity created an immense trade network. The resulting exchange of plants and animals between Europe and the Americas is known as the Columbian Exchange. This name recognizes the explorer Christopher Columbus's key role in bringing Europe into contact with the Americas. This complex process had far-reaching results, both good and bad, on peoples around the world.

Colonization and trade drove the Columbian Exchange, which had an immense impact on Europe and the Americas. Colonists established **plantations** to grow sugar, cotton, vanilla, and other crops introduced to the Americas. Colonists established ranches where they raised livestock brought from Europe. Much of what the colonists grew and raised was exported to Europe. Europeans brought such plants and animals as wheat, citrus fruit, honeybees, horses, and cattle to the Americas. Horses altered the lifestyles of Native Americans on the Great Plains, allowing them to travel faster and farther and hunt more effectively. Agricultural products native to the Americas, such as potatoes, cocoa, corn, tomatoes, and tobacco, were shipped to Europe.

The exchange of plants and animals between Europe and the Americas transformed economic activity on both sides of the Atlantic. Potatoes, for example, became a basic food staple in some areas of Europe. There was a rapid increase in population because potato plants produced more food per acre than foods that had been grown there before. Elsewhere in the world, new food crops from the Americas not only supported population growth but also changed tastes and created new markets. For example, the export of American crops such as maize and sweet potatoes to China encouraged a population explosion during the Qing dynasty, which began in 1644.

Some aspects of the Columbian Exchange proved deadly. With no immunity to European diseases, the native peoples of Mexico and Central and South America, such as the Aztec and the Inca, were ravaged by smallpox, measles, and typhus. Many of them died. Hispaniola, for example, had a population of 250,000 when Columbus arrived in 1492. By 1538, fewer than 500 Native Americans had survived. In Mexico, the population dropped from 25 million in 1500 to 1 million in 1630. Similar devastation occurred elsewhere in the region. In North America, entire communities of Native Americans died in epidemics of smallpox and other diseases brought by European settlers.

▼ Turkey and citrus fruits show the range of Dutch trade.

Colonization had other negative effects, such as the *encomienda* granted by Spain to Spanish settlers. This was the right to use Native Americans as laborers on plantations. The holders of an *encomienda* were supposed to protect the Native Americans, but they often abused them.

✓ **READING PROGRESS CHECK**

Evaluating How did the introduction of European livestock, foods, and diseases affect people in the Americas?

European Rivals in the East

GUIDING QUESTION *How did the nature of European exploration change by the seventeenth century?*

The Spanish and Portuguese were not the only European trading powers. The Dutch, English, and French also expanded their activities into Asia. The first Dutch fleet had arrived in India in 1595. Shortly after, the Dutch formed the East India Company and gradually pushed the Portuguese out of the spice trade in Southeast Asia. The Dutch domination of the spice trade led to massive profits for Dutch merchants. These profits helped make the seventeenth century a Golden Age for the Dutch as they surpassed the Spanish and Portuguese in world trade.

The English soon followed. During the first half of the seventeenth century, the English presence in India steadily increased. By 1650, the British had established a number of trading posts. From them, English ships carried Indian-made cotton goods to the East Indies. There they were bartered for spices, which were shipped back to England.

English success in India attracted rivals. While the Dutch focused on the spice trade, the French established forts along the coast of India. British efforts, however, limited the French, who were soon restricted to a handful of small territories on the southeastern coast of the subcontinent. During the Seven Years' War, the British forced the French to withdraw completely from India. The British East India Company then began to expand, ultimately giving it complete control of India.

✓ **READING PROGRESS CHECK**

Drawing Conclusions How was the Dutch form of mercantilism different from that of Portugal or Spain?

The Atlantic Slave Trade

GUIDING QUESTION *How did European expansion affect Africa and the slave trade?*

European expansion led to a dramatic increase in the development of the slave trade. Traffic in enslaved people was not new. As in other areas of the world, slavery had been practiced in Africa since ancient times. However, the demand for enslaved Africans increased with the European settlement of the Americas in the 1490s and the planting of sugarcane there.

Plantations were established in the 1500s along the coast of Brazil and on Caribbean islands to grow sugarcane. Growing cane sugar demands many laborers. Already devastated by European diseases, the surviving population of Native Americans could not supply the labor needed. So enslaved Africans were shipped to the Americas to relieve a labor shortage on plantations.

In 1518 a Spanish ship carried the first enslaved Africans directly from West Africa to the Americas. During the next two centuries, the trade in enslaved people grew dramatically. It became part of the triangular trade that connected Europe, Africa, and the American continents.

The triangular trade functioned as follows: European merchant ships carried European manufactured goods, such as guns and cloth, to West Africa where they were traded for enslaved people. The enslaved Africans were then sent to the Americas and sold. European merchants then bought tobacco, molasses, sugar, and raw cotton in the Americas and shipped them back to Europe.

As a result of this triangular trade, as many as 10 million enslaved Africans were brought to the Americas between the early sixteenth century and the late nineteenth century. Their journey from Africa to the Americas became known as the **Middle Passage**, the middle portion of the triangular

Middle Passage the forced voyage of enslaved Africans across the Atlantic Ocean to the Americas trade route. Many enslaved Africans died on the journey. Those who survived often died from diseases to which they had little or no immunity.

Death rates were higher for newly arrived enslaved Africans than for those born and reared in the Americas. The new generation gradually developed at least a partial immunity to many diseases. Slaveholders, however, rarely encouraged enslaved people to have children. Many slaveholders, especially on islands in the Caribbean, believed that buying a new enslaved person was less expensive than rearing a child from birth to working age.

Sources of Enslaved Africans

Before Europeans arrived in the fifteenth century, most enslaved persons in Africa were prisoners of war. Europeans first bought enslaved people from African merchants at slave markets in return for gold, guns, or other European goods. Local slave traders first obtained their supplies of enslaved persons from nearby coastal regions. As demand grew, they had to move farther inland to find their victims. Local rulers became concerned about the impact of the slave trade on their societies. King Afonso of Congo (Bakongo) attempted to describe the extent of the crisis in his country.

PRIMARY SOURCE

“[W]e cannot reckon how great the damage is, since the [slave traders] are taking every day our natives, sons of the land and the sons of our noblemen and vassals and our relatives,. . . [S]o great, Sir, is the corruption and licentiousness that our country is being completely depopulated. . . .”

—Afonso of Congo, from a letter to the king of Portugal, 1526

▲ The growing demand for labor in the Americas fueled the slave trade in Africa. In this image, caravans of enslaved Africans are led by local slave traders.

Europeans and other Africans, however, generally ignored such protests. Local rulers who traded in enslaved people viewed the slave trade as a source of income. Many sent raiders into defenseless villages.

Impact of the Atlantic Slave Trade

The slave trade was a tragedy for the victims and their families. Its broader effects varied from region to region. The slave trade depopulated some areas and deprived many African communities of their youngest and strongest men and women. Coastal or near-coastal African chiefs and their followers, armed with guns acquired from the trade in enslaved people, increased raids and wars on neighboring peoples. Some Europeans lamented what they were doing to traditional African societies. One Dutch slave trader remarked:

PRIMARY SOURCE

“From us they have learned . . . strife, quarrelling, drunkenness, trickery, theft, . . . unbridled desire for what is not one’s own, misdeeds unknown to them before, and . . . the accursed lust for gold.”

—From *Africa in History: Themes and Outlines*

The slave trade had a devastating effect on some African states. The case of Benin (buh • NEEN) in West Africa is a good example. A brilliant and creative society in the sixteenth century, Benin was pulled into the slave trade. As the population declined and warfare increased, the people of Benin lost faith in their gods, their art deteriorated, and human sacrifice became more common.

African culture had a major impact on colonies where enslaved people were sent. In places such as Brazil and throughout the Caribbean, African culture blended with indigenous customs to create a vibrant new culture. In

the United States, African culture did not blend with local customs in the same way, and yet African culture still had an influence.

The use of enslaved Africans remained largely acceptable to European society. Not until the Society of Friends, known as the Quakers, began to condemn slavery in the 1770s did feelings against slavery begin to build in Europe. Even then, it was not until the French Revolution in the 1790s that the French abolished slavery. The British abolished slavery throughout the empire in 1833. Despite these reforms, slavery continued in the newly formed United States until the Civil War of the 1860s.

GEOGRAPHY CONNECTION

1. **THE WORLD IN SPATIAL TERMS** *Which part of Africa was the greatest source of enslaved people? Why?*
2. **HUMAN SYSTEMS** *What is the connection between the slave trade and the triangular trade?*

READING PROGRESS CHECK

Determining Cause and Effect How did epidemics among the Native American populations contribute to an increase in the trade of enslaved Africans?

LESSON 2 REVIEW TEKS

Reviewing Vocabulary

1. ***Summarizing*** Write a paragraph explaining the function of colonies in increasing the wealth of European nations. 1D, 7A

Using Your Notes

2. ***Organizing*** Use your graphic organizer on the Columbian Exchange to list the plants, animals, and diseases that were exchanged among Europe and Africa and the Americas. 1D

Answering the Guiding Questions

3. ***Identifying Central Issues*** Which economic theory was put into practice during the age of exploration? 1D, 7A
4. ***Drawing Conclusions*** How did the Columbian Exchange affect the Americas and Europe? 1D, 7B
5. ***Making Generalizations*** How did European exploration change by the seventeenth century? 1D
6. ***Making Connections*** How did European expansion affect Africa and the slave trade? 1D, 4I, 7C

Writing Activity

7. **INFORMATIVE/EXPLANATORY** Write a paragraph describing the effects, both positive and negative, of European trade on the Americas. Be sure to refer to specific ideas and specific events. 1D, 7B, 7C

networks

There's More Online!

- CHART/GRAPH Value of Silver Mined at Potosí
- GRAPHIC ORGANIZER Social Classes in Colonial Latin America
- IMAGE Jesuit Mission in Argentina
- INTERACTIVE SELF-CHECK QUIZ
- PRIMARY SOURCE Society in Colonial Latin America
- PRIMARY SOURCE The Encomienda System
- TIME LINE Spanish and Portuguese Settlement
- VIDEO Conquest of the Inca

LESSON 3
Colonial Latin America

ESSENTIAL QUESTION
What are the effects of political and economic expansion?

It Matters Because

The colonization of Latin America by Portugal and Spain lasted from the early sixteenth century to the early nineteenth century. The Latin American colonies—rich in gold, silver, and other natural resources—proved to be very profitable for the two European nations. However, colonization led to many changes for both the indigenous peoples and the outsiders who settled there. The interactions of indigenous peoples, enslaved Africans, and the European colonists led to the formation of new social classes. The Catholic Church also had a great influence.

Reading HELPDESK

Academic Vocabulary
- **labor**
- **draft**

Content Vocabulary
- ***peninsulare***
- **creole**
- ***encomienda***
- **mestizo**
- **mulatto**
- ***mita***

TAKING NOTES:
Key Ideas and Details

Organizing Information Use a graphic organizer like this one to summarize the political, social, and economic characteristics of colonial Latin America.

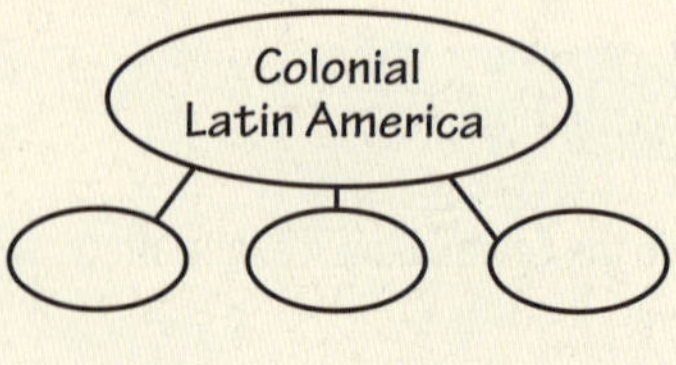

TEKS Texas Essential Knowledge and Skills

1D identify major causes and describe the major effects of the following important turning points in world history from 1450 to 1750: the rise of the Ottoman Empire, the influence of the Ming dynasty on world trade, European exploration and the Columbian Exchange, European expansion, and the Renaissance and the Reformation

Colonial Empires in Latin America

GUIDING QUESTION *What were the social characteristics of colonial Latin America?*

In the sixteenth century, Spain and Portugal imposed their rule on the new lands they had conquered. Spain established an enormous colonial empire that included most of South America and parts of Central America and North America. At the same time, Portugal became the ruler of Brazil. Within the lands of Central and South America, a new civilization arose, which we call Latin America. This name comes from its principal languages, Spanish and Portuguese, both derived from Latin.

Social Classes

European colonies imitated the culture and social patterns of their parent countries. Colonial Latin America was divided by social classes that were based on status. At the top were **peninsulares**, Spanish and Portuguese officials born in Europe. They were called *peninsulares* because they came from the Iberian Peninsula, the part of Europe containing Spain and Portugal. The *peninsulares* held all the important government positions. Below the *peninsulares* were the **creoles**, descendants of Europeans born in Latin America.

The creoles resented the *peninsulares*, who retained power and regarded the creoles as second-class citizens.

Beneath the *peninsulares* and creoles were numerous multiracial groups. The Spanish and Portuguese in Latin America lived with Native Americans and Africans. Many Native Americans were forced to work in mines and on plantations. Because they were not able to do all the work that was required, however, enslaved Africans were also used for labor. Over a period of three centuries, as many as 8 million Africans were brought to Latin America.

Spanish rulers permitted intermarriage between Europeans and Native Americans. Their offspring became known as the **mestizos**. In addition, the offspring of Africans and Europeans—called **mulattoes**—became another social group. Other groups emerged as a result of unions between mestizos and mulattoes and between Native Americans and Africans. The coexistence of these various groups produced a unique multiracial society in Latin America.

The *peninsulares* and creoles considered all these multiethnic groups to be socially inferior. However, over a period of time, mestizos grew in status due to their increasing numbers. Some mestizos became artisans and merchants in cities, and others became small-scale farmers or ranchers. The groups at the very bottom of the social scale were the Africans and conquered Native Americans.

peninsulare a person born on the Iberian Peninsula; typically, a Spanish or Portuguese official who resided temporarily in Latin America for political and economic gain and then returned to Europe

creole a person of European descent born in Latin America and living there permanently

mestizo a person of mixed European and Native American descent

mulatto a person of mixed African and European descent

GEOGRAPHY CONNECTION

1. **THE WORLD IN SPATIAL TERMS** *What river formed part of the border of New Spain?*
2. **PLACES AND REGIONS** *What country had colonies to the east of the line set by the Treaty of Tordesillas?*

labor people with all their abilities and efforts

encomienda a system of labor the Spanish used in the Americas; Spanish landowners had the right, as granted by Queen Isabella, to use Native Americans as laborers

mita a labor system that the Spanish administrators in Peru used to draft native people to work

draft to select for some purpose; to conscript

Economic Foundations

One source of wealth for the Portuguese and Spanish came from resource extraction, or the removal of natural resources from the land. The most important resource extraction was the mining of gold and silver. The abundant supply of those precious metals exported from Latin American colonies financed Spain's wars and stimulated further colonization.

Farming became a more enduring source of prosperity as Spanish and Portuguese landowners created immense estates. However, colonial farming practices also damaged the environment as a result of deforestation, overgrazing, and overcultivation of single export crops.

To maintain a supply of **labor**, the Spanish continued to make use of the ***encomienda*** system. In this system, Spanish landowners forced Native Americans to pay taxes and provide labor. In return, the landowners were expected to protect them and ensure they were instructed in the Catholic faith. In Peru, the Spanish used an arrangement known as the ***mita***, which allowed authorities to **draft** indigenous labor to work in the silver mines.

▲ A silver mine in Brazil

▶ **CRITICAL THINKING**

Evaluating How would Europeans find workers to mine silver?

This system of landowners and dependent peasants became a feature of Latin American society, and it could be an extremely damaging one. The harsh working conditions under the system contributed to a drastic decline in the Native American population. It was the population decline among Native Americans that spurred the importation of enslaved Africans. Catholic priest Bartolomé de Las Casas (bar • to • lo • MAY day lahs CAH • sahs) spoke out against the *encomienda* and its effects on the indigenous peoples.

PRIMARY SOURCE

“[T]he Spaniards, from the beginning . . . were no more solicitous of promoting the preaching of the Gospel of Christ to [the Native Americans], than if they had been dogs or beasts, . . . laying many heavy [burdens] upon them, daily afflicting and persecuting them, that they might not have so much time and leisure at their own disposal, as to attend their preaching and divine service; for they looked upon that to be an impediment to their getting gold.”

—Bartolomé de Las Casas, from *A Brief Account of the Destruction of the Indies*, 1534

Trade provided another avenue for profit. Besides gold and silver, other products shipped to Europe were sugar, tobacco, diamonds, and animal hides. In turn, the Europeans supplied their colonists with manufactured goods. Spain and Portugal regulated the trade of their colonies to keep other European nations out. By the beginning of the eighteenth century, however, the British and French were too powerful to be kept out of these lucrative markets.

✓ **READING PROGRESS CHECK**

Drawing Conclusions What were the two key factors in determining status in colonial Latin America?

State and Church

GUIDING QUESTION *How did Portugal and Spain govern their colonies to promote economic gain and exert their authority?*

The Portuguese and Spanish colonial empires in Latin America lasted more than 300 years. Communication and travel between the Americas and Europe were difficult, making it impossible for the European monarchs to keep a close watch on their overseas empires. As a result, colonial officials in Latin America took liberties in carrying out imperial policies.

Beginning in the mid-sixteenth century, the Portuguese monarchy attempted to assert its control over Brazil by creating the position of governor-general. The governor-general (later called a viceroy) headed a bureaucracy that governed the colony. Such an official was in the colony as a representative of the monarch. But it was not a perfect system. At best, the governor-general had only loose control over the lesser officials who governed the districts into which Brazil was divided.

To rule his American empire, the Spanish king also appointed viceroys. The first was established for New Spain (Mexico) in 1535. Another viceroy was appointed for Peru in 1543. In the eighteenth century, two additional viceroyalties (colonies ruled by a viceroy) were added. Spaniards held all major government positions.

From the beginning of their conquest of the Americas, religion influenced the colonization efforts of the Spanish and Portuguese, whose rulers were determined to Christianize the indigenous peoples.
This policy gave the Catholic Church great influence upon the society and culture of the Americas.

Catholic missionaries—especially the Dominicans, Franciscans, and Jesuits—fanned out to different parts of the Spanish Empire. To make their efforts easier, the missionaries brought Native Americans together into villages, or missions. There, they could be converted, taught trades, and encouraged to grow crops.

Missions enabled missionaries to control the lives of the Native Americans and make them docile subjects of the empire. The Jesuits established more than 30 missions in the region of Paraguay. Well-organized, the Jesuits made their missions into profitable businesses.

Along with the missions, the Catholic Church also built cathedrals, hospitals, and schools in the colonies. These schools gave the Native American students a basic education in the Spanish or the Portuguese language and grammar while preparing them for a religious education.

The Catholic Church provided an outlet other than marriage for women. Women could enter convents and become nuns. Women in religious orders—many of them of aristocratic background—often lived well. Many nuns worked outside their convents by running schools and hospitals. Indeed, one of these women, the Mexican nun Juana Inés de la Cruz (WAHN • ah ee • NAYS de la KROOS), wrote poetry and prose and urged that women be educated.

✓ READING PROGRESS CHECK

Applying What role did the Catholic Church play in the colonization of Latin America?

BIOGRAPHY

Juana Inés de la Cruz (1651–1695)

Juana Inés de la Cruz was a Mexican poet and scholar. In 1664 she was invited to the Spanish court and later had her knowledge tested by scholars. She became a nun in 1667, largely in order to focus on her studies. At the Convent of Santa Paula in Mexico, in addition to reading and writing poetry, she served as an archivist and accountant. She became the unofficial poet of the court in the 1680s and was renowned in Mexico and Spain.

▶ CRITICAL THINKING

Analyzing What freedoms did becoming a nun afford Juana Inés de la Cruz?

LESSON 3 REVIEW TEKS

Reviewing Vocabulary

1. ***Summarizing*** Explain how the social status of mestizos changed over time.

Using Your Notes

2. ***Identifying*** Using your graphic organizer of characteristics of colonial Latin America, summarize the political and economic features. 23B

Answering the Guiding Questions

3. ***Applying*** What were the social characteristics of colonial Latin America? 23B

4. ***Analyzing*** How did Portugal and Spain govern their colonies to promote economic gain and exert their authority?

Writing Activity

5. INFORMATIVE/EXPLANATORY Indigenous populations of colonial Latin America were forced to work for years under the *encomienda* and *mita* systems. Write three paragraphs that explain how these systems were the result of economic and political expansion. 1D

CHAPTER 17 Assessment

TEKS

Directions: On a separate sheet of paper, answer the questions below. Make sure you read carefully and answer all parts of the questions.

Lesson Review

Lesson 1

1. ***Describing*** What events and new economic factors first caused Europeans' interest in exploration and expansion in Asia and the Middle East, starting in the thirteenth century? **1D, 7A, 7F**

2. ***Summarizing*** Summarize the aspirations of European exploration.

3. ***Explaining*** How did Portuguese exploration, including their geographic route, result in expanded trade control and access to prized resources in the spice trade?

4. ***Identifying Cause and Effect*** Why didn't the Portuguese have access to the territory that is present-day Latin and North America?

5. ***Categorizing*** What effects were Europeans trying to achieve through exploration and expansion in North America in the sixteenth and seventeenth centuries? Who were some of the explorers, and where did they travel? **1D**

Lesson 2

6. ***Explaining*** What is the principle of mercantilism? What did the governments of European nations do to encourage exports and favorable trade balances that led to the Columbian Exchange and the success of Europe's Commercial Revolution? **7B, 7F**

7. ***Drawing Conclusions*** Why would countries want to use their colonies as sources for raw materials, such as minerals or crops?

8. ***Explaining*** Why did the slave trade develop? Be sure to describe the rise of the internal slave trade in medieval Africa, as well as the development of the Atlantic slave trade, and its impact on Africa and the Americas. **4I, 7C**

9. ***Defining and Explaining*** What was the Middle Passage, and why was it often devastating for Africans?

10. ***Identifying*** Name several plants or agricultural products native to the Americas, and name several plants, insects, or agricultural products brought to the Americas by Europeans.

11. ***Identifying Cause and Effect*** How did the potato impact European populations?

Lesson 3

12. ***Analyzing*** How did religion influence colonization in Latin America? **23B**

13. ***Analyzing*** Why would education efforts by colonists work against native groups' abilities to retain their culture?

14. ***Describing*** Describe the background and social status of the group known as *mestizos*.

15. ***Specifying*** What natural resources did Spain find in Latin America? What did the Spanish government use these resources for?

Need Extra Help?

If You've Missed Question	1	2	3	4	5	6	7	8	9	10	11	12	13	14	15
Go to page	380	380	381	382	380	389	390	391	392	390	390	396	397	394	396

Exploring the Essential Questions

16 ***Interpreting Significance*** How did a new European economic principle—mercantilism—change the world during the 1500s through the 1800s? **7F**

17 ***Analyzing Effects*** What were the effects of European cultural expansion during the 1500s through the 1800s? **1D, 7B**

18 ***Analyzing Effects*** What were the effects of European political expansion during the 1500s through the 1800s? **1D, 4I**

Critical Thinking

19 ***Analyzing Effects*** What was one effect of the introduction of the horse to the Americas in the Columbian Exchange? **7B**

20 ***Identifying Central Issues*** In both the case of Spanish forces under Cortés and Spanish forces under Pizarro, what elements led to Spanish victories and territory control?

21 ***Speculating*** Why do you think some Spanish settlers abused the Native Americans who worked for them?

22 ***Analyzing Effects*** Due to distance and communication limitations, European monarchs could not closely monitor overseas empires. Therefore, colonial officials carried out policies. What was the effect of this type of arrangement?

23 ***Analyzing*** What were the main advantages of the Portuguese caravel?

24 ***Making Generalizations*** How did the human condition improve during the Commercial Revolution? Form generalizations on how economic freedom contributed to these improvements. **7F, 18F**

Social Studies Skills

25 ***Economics*** What is a country's balance of trade? What makes a trade balance favorable?

26 ***Geography Skills*** How would Columbus have used the ocean winds in his voyages to the Americas and home? Be specific.

27 ***Making Inferences*** Why do the people of Brazil speak Portuguese instead of Spanish? What event between Portugal and Spain ensured this outcome? **1D**

28 ***Speculating*** If the instant communication of today had been available when European nations were exploring the world, how do you think it would have affected events?

29 ***Creating Maps*** Work with a partner to create a map that shows places where the political and economic expansion of European states had negative effects on the indigenous peoples and/or the environment. Include visuals and primary sources from some of the people and places involved. Be prepared to draw conclusions about the effects of European expansion. **1D, 6B, 7C**

30 ***Creating Arguments*** Explain the origin and the outcomes of Europe's Commercial Revolution. What factors contributed to its development? Present your answers along with supporting reasons and evidence in the form of an essay. **1D, 7F, 18F**

Need Extra Help?

If You've Missed Question	16	17	18	19	20	21	22	23	24	25	26	27	28	29	30
Go to page	389	394	394	390	385	391	397	381	388	389	381	384	390	388	388

31 ***Creating Maps*** With a partner, research Magellan's voyage that went from Spain to the Pacific Ocean and to the Philippines. Create a map that shows a well-researched route.

DBQ Analyzing Historical Documents

Use the text excerpt to answer the following questions.

Bartolomé de Las Casas took part in the Spanish colonization of the Americas. Shocked by the Spanish soldiers' treatment of the local people, he became a priest and worked in their defense.

PRIMARY SOURCE

> "For God's sake and man's faith in him, is this the way to impose the yoke of Christ on Christian men? Is this the way to remove wild barbarism from the minds of barbarians? Is it not, rather, to act like thieves, cut-throats, and cruel plunderers and to drive the gentlest of people headlong into despair? The Indian race is not that barbaric, nor are they dull-witted or stupid, but they are easy to teach and very talented in learning all the liberal arts . . . "
>
> —from Bartolomé de Las Casas, *In Defense of the Indians,* 1550

32 ***Synthesizing*** Does Las Casas approve of the behavior of his countrymen in the Americas? Does he think the Spanish soldiers are good Christians?

33 ***Drawing Conclusions*** Las Casas calls the Indians "the gentlest of people." Why then does he (or any European) also call them barbarians?

Analyzing Visuals

Use the image of the artifact to answer the following questions.

34 ***Analyzing*** What is the artist's tone or attitude toward Cortés and how does the artist convey this tone?

35 ***Evaluating*** Is Cortes portrayed as a hero or a villain? Do you agree with this portrayal—why or why not? 6B

Extended Response Question

36 ***Expository*** Write a short essay that explains how exploration endeavors were a reflection of the time's innovations and scientific understandings.

Need Extra Help?

If You've Missed Question	31	32	33	34	35	36
Go to page	379	400	400	400	400	380

Conflict and Absolutism in Europe

1550–1715

ESSENTIAL QUESTIONS
- *What effect might social, economic, and religious conflicts have on a country?*
- *How would the exercise of absolute power affect a country?*

networks

There's More Online! about conflict and absolutism in Europe.

CHAPTER 18

The Story Matters...

In seventeenth–century Europe, absolutism was a reaction to instability. In England, the desire of King James II to practice his Catholic faith openly was opposed by Parliament, ending in the creation of a constitutional monarchy under the joint rule of William III and Mary II. Mary's life mirrors the conflicts of her time. Raised as a Protestant, she reluctantly overthrew her own Catholic father, James II.

◀ Painted in 1677, years before Mary became queen, court painter Sir Peter Lely's portrait of her already conveys a regal pride and self-assurance.

PHOTO: Sotheby / akg-images.

CHAPTER 18

Place and Time: Europe 1550–1715

During the sixteenth and seventeenth centuries, Europe was the scene of conflicts fueled by religious differences, along with political and economic rivalries. In some European nations, these conflicts led to the absolute power of a single ruler; in others, a constitutional monarchy developed. The cultural response by writers and artists of this period often reflected a spiritual search and an examination of the human condition.

Step Into the Place

Read the quotations and look at the information presented on the map.

DBQ **Analyzing Historical Documents** Explain why Parliament would be threatened if the king in England took actions like those attributed to Louis XIV.

PRIMARY SOURCE

"Whereas the late King James the Second [right image], by the assistance of diverse evil counselors, judges and ministers employed by him, did endeavor to subvert and extirpate the Protestant religion and the laws and liberties of this kingdom;. . .

That the freedom of speech and debates or proceedings in Parliament ought not to be impeached or questioned in any court or place out of Parliament;. . ."

—from the English Bill of Rights, 1689

PRIMARY SOURCE

"Louis XIV [left image] took great pains to be well informed of all that passed everywhere; in the public places, in the private houses, in society and familiar intercourse. His spies and tell-tales were infinite. He had them of all species; many who were ignorant that their information reached him; others who knew it; others who wrote to him direct, sending their letters through channels he indicated; and all these letters were seen by him alone, and always before everything else; others who sometimes spoke to him secretly in his cabinet, entering by the back stairs."

—Duc de Saint-Simon, from Memoirs, 1694–1723

Step Into the Time

Determining Cause and Effect

Choose an event from the European portion of the time line and predict its long-term political, social, or cultural consequences.

EUROPE

- **1555** Peace of Augsburg divides Christianity in Germany
- **1562** French Wars of Religion begin
- **1588** England defeats the Spanish Armada
- **1598** Henry IV issues the Edict of Nantes; ends Wars of Religion

1550 — 1575 — 1600

THE WORLD

- **1566** Ottoman Sultan Süleyman I dies
- **1588** Shāh 'Abbās becomes ruler of Persian Ṣafavid dynasty
- **1598** Rurik dynasty ends in Russia; Romanovs succeed in 1613
- **1603** Tokugawa shogunate begins in Japan

networks *There's More Online!*

- **MAP** Explore the interactive version of this map on Networks.
- **TIME LINE** Explore the interactive version of the time line on Networks.

1618 Start of the Thirty Years' War

1623 Shakespeare's *First Folio* is published

1630 English found Massachusetts Bay Colony

1644 China's Ming dynasty is overthrown; Qing dynasty succeeds

1661 Louis XIV begins absolutist rule in France

1680 Pueblo Rebellion temporarily overthrows Spanish rule in New Mexico

1682 La Salle claims Mississippi Valley for France

1690 John Locke publishes *Two Treatises of Government*

1697–1698 Peter the Great visits the West

1707 Death of Aurangzeb, last great Mogul emperor

1715 Louis XIV dies

1625 1650 1675 1700 1725

networks

There's More Online!

- ☑ BIOGRAPHY Elizabeth I
- ☑ BIOGRAPHY Philip II of Spain
- ☑ CHART The Thirty Years' War
- ☑ IMAGE The Thirty Years' War
- ☑ INFOGRAPHIC The Voyage of the Spanish Armada
- ☑ INTERACTIVE SELF-CHECK QUIZ
- ☑ PRIMARY SOURCE The Treaty of Westphalia
- ☑ PRIMARY SOURCE Account of a Witchcraft Trial in 1628
- ☑ VIDEO The Spanish Armada

LESSON 1
Europe in Crisis

ESSENTIAL QUESTION
What effect might social, economic, and religious conflicts have on a country?

Reading HELPDESK

Academic Vocabulary
- **conflict**
- **policy**

Content Vocabulary
- **heretic**
- **inflation**
- **armada**

TAKING NOTES:
Key Ideas and Details

Monitoring As you read, complete the chart by filling in key details for each topic.

	Spain	England	France
Government			
Religion			
Conflicts			

TEKS Texas Essential Knowledge and Skills

23B identify examples of religious influence on various events referenced in the major eras of world history

24B describe the major influences of women such as Elizabeth I, Queen Victoria, Mother Teresa, Indira Gandhi, Margaret Thatcher, and Golda Meir during major eras of world history

It Matters Because

During the sixteenth and seventeenth centuries, conflicts between Protestants and Catholics in many European nations resulted in wars for religious and political control. Social and economic crises also contributed to instability during these centuries.

Spain's Conflicts

GUIDING QUESTION *What roles did France and Spain play in religious conflicts?*

By 1560, Calvinism and Catholicism had become highly militant, or combative, religions. They were aggressive in winning converts and in eliminating each other's authority. Their struggle was the chief cause of the religious wars that plagued Europe in the sixteenth century. However, economic, social, and political forces also played an important role in these conflicts.

Spain's Militant Catholicism

The greatest supporter of militant Catholicism in the second half of the 1500s was King Philip II. He was the son of Charles V—the Holy Roman Emperor, King of Spain, and Archduke of Austria. Charles V's brother, Ferdinand I, succeeded him as Holy Roman Emperor. Philip II inherited the kingdoms of Milan, Naples, Sicily, the Netherlands, and Spain and its empire in the Americas from Charles V. Philip, who reigned from 1556 to 1598, ushered in an age of Spanish greatness. To strengthen his control, Philip insisted on strict conformity to Catholicism and strong monarchial authority. He also had the powerful Spanish navy at his command.

Around 1500, Catholic kingdoms in Spain had reconquered Muslim areas there and expelled Spanish Jews. Muslims were forced to convert or go into exile. Spain saw itself as a nation chosen by God to save Catholic Christianity from Protestant **heretics**. Philip II, the "Most Catholic King," championed Catholic causes. His actions led to

PHOTO: (l to r) English School/The Bridgeman Art Library/Getty Images, The Print Collector/Age Fotostock, SuperStock/Getty Images.

spectacular victories and defeats. Spain's leadership of a Holy League against the Turks resulted in a stunning victory over the Turkish fleet in the Battle of Lepanto in 1571. Philip was not so fortunate in his other **conflicts**.

heretic one who does not conform to established doctrine

conflict opposition; a fight, battle, or war

Resistance From the Netherlands

One of the richest parts of Philip's empire, the Spanish Netherlands, consisted of 17 provinces (modern-day Netherlands and Belgium). Philip's attempts to strengthen his control in this region caused resentment and opposition from the nobles of the Netherlands. Philip also tried to crush Calvinism in the Netherlands. When violence erupted in 1566, Philip sent 10,000 troops to crush the rebellion.

Philip faced growing resistance from the Dutch in the northern provinces led by William the Silent, the prince of Orange. The struggle dragged on until 1609 when a 12-year truce finally ended the war. The northern provinces began to call themselves the United Provinces of the Netherlands and became the core of the modern Dutch state. In fact, the seventeenth century has often been called the golden age of the Dutch Republic by scholars because the United Provinces held center stage as one of Europe's great powers.

Protestantism in England

Elizabeth Tudor ascended the English throne in 1558. During her reign, the small island kingdom became the leader of the Protestant nations of Europe and laid the foundations for a world empire. Intelligent, careful, and self-confident, Elizabeth moved quickly to solve the difficult religious problemshe inherited from her Catholic half-sister, Queen Mary Tudor. Elizabeth

GEOGRAPHY CONNECTION

Spain's Philip II ruled the world's largest empire at the time.

1. **HUMAN SYSTEMS** *How might the distribution of Philip's empire have made it difficult to administer?*
2. **PLACES AND REGIONS** *Why was Philip's relationship with the Holy Roman Emperor important?*

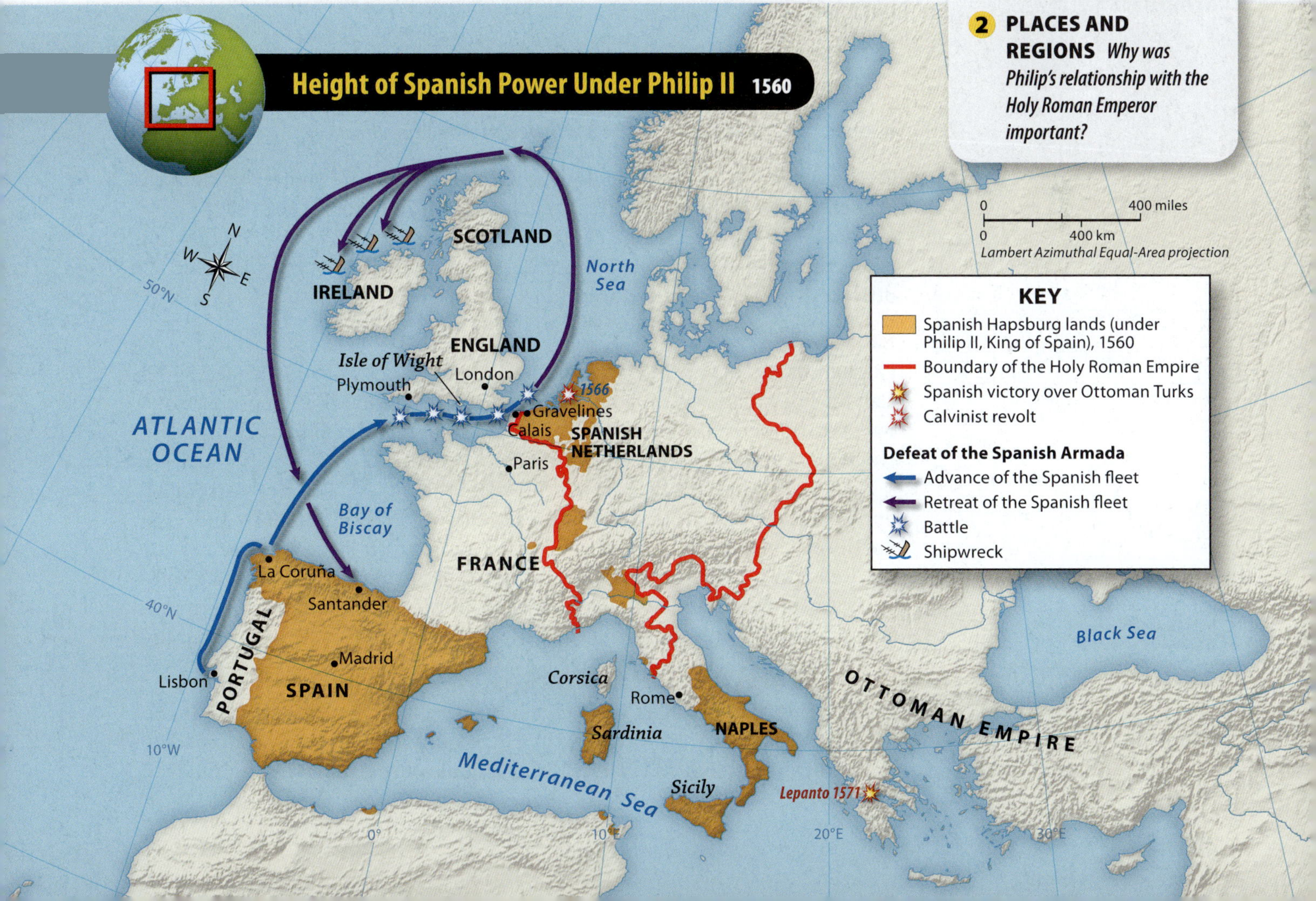

▲ Queen Elizabeth I of England

policy an overall plan embracing the general goals and acceptable procedures of a governmental body

armada a fleet of warships

repealed the laws favoring Catholics. A new Act of Supremacy named Elizabeth as "the only supreme governor" of both church and state. The Church of England under Queen Elizabeth followed a moderate Protestantism that kept most people satisfied.

Elizabeth was also moderate in her foreign **policy**. She tried to keep Spain and France from becoming too powerful by balancing power. If one nation seemed to be gaining in power, England would support the weaker nation. The queen feared that war would be disastrous for England and for her own rule; however, she could not escape a conflict with Spain.

Defeat of the Spanish Armada

In 1588, Philip II made preparations to send an **armada**—a fleet of warships—to invade England. A successful invasion of England would mean the overthrow of Protestantism. The fleet that set sail had neither the ships nor the manpower that Philip had planned to send.

The hoped-for victory never came. The armada was battered by the faster English ships and sailed back to Spain by a northern route around Scotland and Ireland where it was pounded by storms.

By the end of Philip's reign in 1598, Spain was not the great power that it appeared to be. Spain was the most populous empire in the world, but it was bankrupt. Philip II had spent too much on war. His successor spent too much on his court. The armed forces were out of date, and the government was inefficient. Spain continued to play the role of a great power, but the real power in Europe had shifted to England and France.

✓ **READING PROGRESS CHECK**

Drawing Conclusions Why might the overthrow of Protestantism in England have been important to Philip II?

The French Wars of Religion

GUIDING QUESTION *What fueled the French civil wars of the sixteenth century?*

Of the sixteenth-century religious wars, none was more shattering than the French civil wars known as the French Wars of Religion (1562–1598). Religious conflict was at the center of these wars. The Catholic French kings persecuted Protestants throughout the country, but the persecution did little to stop the spread of Protestantism.

Huguenots

Huguenots (HYOO • guh • nahts) were French Protestants influenced by John Calvin. They made up only about 7 percent of the total French population, but 40 to 50 percent of the nobility became Huguenots. This made the Huguenots a powerful political threat to the Crown.

An extreme Catholic party—known as the ultra-Catholics—strongly opposed the Huguenots. Having the loyalty of parts of northern and northwestern France, they could pay for and recruit large armies.

Religion was the most important issue, but other factors played a role in the ensuing French civil wars. Towns and provinces were willing to assist the nobles in weakening the growing power of the French monarchy.

Henry IV and the Edict of Nantes

For 30 years, battles raged in France between the Catholics and the Huguenots. In 1589, Henry of Navarre, the Huguenot political leader, succeeded to the throne as Henry IV. He realized that as a Protestant he would never

PHOTO: The Print Collector/Age Fotostock

be accepted by Catholic France. Therefore, he converted to Catholicism. When Henry IV was crowned king in 1594, the fighting in France finally came to an end.

To solve the religious problem, Henry IV issued the Edict of Nantes in 1598. The edict recognized Catholicism as the official religion of France. It also gave the Huguenots the right to worship and to enjoy all political privileges such as holding public offices. This edict appeased both Catholics and Huguenots.

SKILLS PRACTICE

Read about the crises in Europe during the 1600s and 1700s with a partner. Help each other with any words or sentences that are difficult. If needed, ask the teacher for help.

✓ **READING PROGRESS CHECK**

Identifying What was the purpose of the Edict of Nantes?

Crises in Europe

GUIDING QUESTION *How was Europe affected by social and economic crises in the seventeenth century?*

In addition to political upheaval and religious warfare, severe economic and social crises plagued Europe in the sixteenth and seventeenth centuries. One major economic problem was **inflation**, or rising prices. A growing population in the sixteenth century increased the demand for land and food and drove up prices for both.

inflation a rapid increase in prices

Economic and Social Crises

By 1600, an economic slowdown had begun in parts of Europe. Spain's economy, grown dependent on imported silver, was failing by the 1640s. Its mines were producing less silver. Its fleets were subject to pirate attacks. Also, the loss of Muslim and Jewish artisans and merchants hurt the economy. Italy, the financial center of Europe in the Renaissance, was also declining economically.

Population figures in the 1500s and 1600s reveal Europe's worsening conditions. The 1500s were a period of growing population, possibly due to a warmer climate and increased food supplies. Europe's population probably increased from 60 million in 1500 to 85 million by 1600. By 1620, the population had leveled off. It had begun to decline by 1650, especially in central and southern Europe. Warfare, plague, and famine all contributed to the population decline and to the creation of social tensions. One source of tension involved the witchcraft trials.

The Witchcraft Trials

A belief in witchcraft, or magic, had been part of traditional village culture for centuries. The religious zeal that led to the Inquisition and the hunt for heretics was extended to concern about witchcraft. During the sixteenth and seventeenth centuries, an intense hysteria affected the lives of many Europeans. Perhaps more than a hundred thousand people were charged with witchcraft. As more and more people were brought to trial, the fear of witches grew, as did the fear of being accused of witchcraft.

Common people—usually the poor and those without property—were the ones most often accused of witchcraft. More than 75 percent of those accused were women. Most of them were single or widowed and over 50 years old.

Under intense torture, accused witches usually confessed to a number of practices. For instance, many said that they had sworn allegiance to the devil and attended sabbats, nightly gatherings at which they feasted and danced. Others admitted to casting evil spells.

▲ A public execution of accused witches in England

By 1650, the witchcraft hysteria had begun to lessen. As governments grew stronger, fewer officials were willing to disrupt their societies with trials of witches. In addition, attitudes were changing. People found it unreasonable to believe in the old view of a world haunted by evil spirits.

✓ READING PROGRESS CHECK

Identifying What sources of social tension existed in Europe during the sixteenth and seventeenth centuries?

The Thirty Years' War

GUIDING QUESTION *What were the causes and effects of the Thirty Years' War?*

▲ A villager is attacked by a soldier during the Thirty Years' War.

Religious disputes continued in Germany after the Peace of Augsburg in 1555. One reason for the disputes was that the peace settlement had not recognized Calvinism. By the 1600s, Calvinism had spread through Europe.

Religion played an important role in the outbreak of the Thirty Years' War, called the "last of the religious wars." However, political and territorial motives were also evident. Beginning in 1618 in the Holy Roman Empire, the war first involved the struggle between Catholic forces, led by the Hapsburg Holy Roman emperors, and Protestant (primarily Calvinist) nobles in Bohemia. As Denmark, Sweden, France, and Spain entered the war, the conflict became more political. For instance, France, directed by the Catholic Cardinal Richelieu, fought against the Holy Roman Empire and Spain in an attempt to gain European leadership.

All major European powers except England were involved in the plundering and destruction of Germany during the Thirty Years' War. The Peace of Westphalia officially ended the war in 1648 and gave Sweden, France, and their allies new territories. Sweden's acquisitions in the Baltic Sea region increased its power in northern Europe. The peace settlement also divided the more than 300 states of the Holy Roman Empire into independent states, each with the freedom to determine their own religion and conduct foreign policy. The Holy Roman Empire ceased to be a political entity. Another 200 years would pass before German unification.

✓ READING PROGRESS CHECK

Stating Was the original motivation for the Thirty Years' War political or religious? State evidence.

LESSON 1 REVIEW TEKS

Reviewing Vocabulary

1. ***Identifying*** Explain why King Philip II viewed Protestants as heretics and why that view may have met with conflict.

Using Your Notes

2. ***Comparing and Contrasting*** Use your notes to choose one of the topics discussed in the lesson. Write several sentences comparing how the government, religion, or conflicts affected each power.

Answering the Guiding Questions

3. ***Applying*** What roles did England and Spain play in religious conflicts?
4. ***Identifying Cause and Effect*** What fueled the French civil wars of the sixteenth century?
5. ***Examining*** How was Europe affected by social and economic crises in the seventeenth century?
6. ***Identifying Cause and Effect*** What were the causes and effects of the Thirty Years' War?

Writing Activity

7. **INFORMATIVE/EXPLANATORY** In two or three paragraphs, compare Elizabeth I of England and King Philip II of Spain in terms of their personalities as rulers, their relationship to religion, and their foreign policy. Use descriptive language. 24B

networks

There's More Online!

- BIOGRAPHY John Locke
- BIOGRAPHY Oliver Cromwell
- BIOGRAPHY William and Mary
- CHART/GRAPH The Petition of Right and the English Bill of Rights
- INTERACTIVE SELF-CHECK QUIZ
- PRIMARY SOURCE Leviathan
- PRIMARY SOURCE Two Treatises of Government
- TIME LINE England: Absolutism to Constitutional Monarchy
- VIDEO John Locke

LESSON 2
War and Revolution in England

ESSENTIAL QUESTION

What effect might social, economic, and religious conflicts have on a country?

IT MATTERS BECAUSE

The seventeenth century was a period of great social and political change in England. These changes raised important questions about how to balance the power of government with the need to maintain order. England's answers eventually formed the basis of many modern democracies, including that of the United States.

Reading HELPDESK

Academic Vocabulary

- **commonwealth**
- **restoration**
- **convert**

Content Vocabulary

- **divine right of kings**
- **Puritans**
- **Cavaliers**
- **Roundheads**
- **natural rights**

TAKING NOTES:

Key Ideas and Details

Summarizing As you read, use a chart like the one below to identify which conflicts were prompted by religious concerns.

Conflicts in England	Results

TEKS Texas Essential Knowledge and Skills

19B identify the characteristics of the following political systems: theocracy, absolute monarchy, democracy, republic, oligarchy, limited monarchy, and totalitarianism

continued on the next page

Revolutions in England

GUIDING QUESTION *How did disagreements over rule between the Stuarts and Parliament lead to the English Civil War? What were the causes and effects of the Glorious Revolution?*

In addition to the Thirty Years' War, a series of rebellions and civil wars rocked Europe in the seventeenth century. By far the most famous struggle was the civil war in England known as the English Revolution. The war was between king and Parliament to determine what role each should play in governing England. It would take another revolution later in the century to finally reach a resolution.

The Stuarts and Divine Right

The Tudor dynasty ended with the death of Queen Elizabeth I in 1603. The Stuart line of rulers began when the king of Scotland, Elizabeth's cousin, ascended the English throne and became James I.

James believed that he received his power from and was only responsible to God. This is called the **divine right of kings**. Parliament did not think much of the divine right of kings. It had come to assume that the monarch and Parliament ruled England together.

Religion was an issue as well. The **Puritans**—Protestants in England inspired by Calvinist ideas—did not like the king's strong defense of the Church of England. While they were members of the Church of England, the Puritans wished to make the church more Protestant. Many of England's gentry, mostly well-to-do landowners, had become Puritans. The Puritan gentry formed an important

divine right of kings the belief that the king gets his power from God and not from his subjects

Puritans English Protestants who believed that the Church of England needed further reform and sought to simplify and regulate forms of worship

Cavaliers supporters of King Charles I in the English Civil War

Roundheads supporters of Parliament in the English Civil War

▲ Oliver Cromwell, Lord Protector of England during the Commonwealth

(continued from p. 409)

TEKS **Texas Essential Knowledge and Skills**

20A explain the development of democratic-republican government from its beginnings in the Judeo-Christian legal tradition and classical Greece and Rome through the English Civil War and the Enlightenment

continued on the next page

part of the House of Commons, the lower house of Parliament. It was not wise to alienate them.

The conflict that began during the reign of James came to a head during the reign of his son, Charles I. Charles, like his father, believed in the divine right of kings. In 1628, Parliament passed a Petition of Right. The petition placed limits on the king's ability to tax, imprison citizens without cause, quarter troops, and institute martial law. Although Charles initially accepted this petition, he later ignored it after realizing the limits it put on his power.

Charles also tried to impose more ritual on the Church of England. Thousands of Puritans went to America rather than accept his policy. Thus the struggles of the English Reformation influenced American history.

Civil War and Commonwealth

Complaints grew until England slipped into a civil war in 1642 between the supporters of the king (the **Cavaliers** or Royalists) and the parliamentary forces (called the **Roundheads**). Parliament proved victorious, due largely to the New Model Army of Oliver Cromwell, who was a military genius.

The New Model Army chiefly consisted of more extreme Puritans, known as the Independents. These men believed they were doing battle for God. As Cromwell wrote, "This is none other but the hand of God; and to Him alone belongs the glory." Some credit is due to Cromwell. His soldiers were well-disciplined and trained in the new military tactics of the 1600s.

The victorious New Model Army lost no time in taking control. Cromwell purged Parliament of any members who had not supported him. What was left—the so-called Rump Parliament—had Charles I executed on January 30, 1649. The execution of the king horrified much of Europe. Parliament next abolished the monarchy and the House of Lords and declared England a **commonwealth**, a type of republic.

Cromwell found it difficult to work with the Rump Parliament and finally dispersed it by force, exclaiming, "I have been forced to do this. I have sought the Lord, night and day, that He would slay me, than put upon me the doing of this work." After destroying both king and Parliament, Cromwell set up a military dictatorship.

The Restoration

Cromwell ruled until his death in 1658. The army, realizing how unpopular it had become, restored the monarchy in 1660 in the person of Charles II, the son of Charles I.

The **restoration** of the Stuart monarchy, known as the Restoration period, did not mean, however, that the work of the English Revolution was undone. Parliament kept much of the power it had won and continued to play an important role in government. The principle that Parliament must give its consent to taxation was also accepted. Charles, however, continued to push his own ideas, some of which were clearly out of step with many of the English people.

Charles was sympathetic to Catholicism. Moreover, his brother James, heir to the throne, did not hide the fact that he was a Catholic. Parliament's suspicions about their Catholic leanings were therefore aroused when Charles took the bold step of suspending the laws that Parliament had passed against Catholics and Puritans after the restoration of the monarchy. Parliament would have none of it and forced the king to back down. Driven by a strong anti-Catholic sentiment, Parliament then passed a Test Act, specifying that only Anglicans (members of the Church of England) could hold military and civil offices.

commonwealth a nation, state, or other political unit founded on law and united by agreement for and by the people

restoration a bringing back to a former position or condition

Arousing more suspicion, on his deathbed Charles II had decided to **convert** to Catholicism. After Charles died without a son, James II became king in 1685. James was an open and devout Catholic. He named Catholics to high positions in the government, army, navy, and universities. Religion once more became a cause of conflict between king and Parliament.

Parliament objected to James's policies but stopped short of rebellion. Members knew he was an old man and his Protestant daughters, Mary and Anne, born to his first wife, would succeed him. However, in 1688, James and his second wife, a Catholic, had a son. Now the possibility of a Catholic monarchy loomed large.

A Glorious Revolution

A group of English nobles invited the Dutch leader, William of Orange, to invade England. In their invitation, they informed William that most of the kingdom's people wanted a change. The invitation put William and his wife Mary, the daughter of James II, in a difficult position. It would be appalling for Mary to rise up against her father. However, William, a foe of France's Catholic king Louis XIV, welcomed this opportunity to fight France with England's resources.

William began making preparations to invade England in early 1688. It was not until early October that James realized William's intentions. In November 1688, William's forces landed at Torbay and began their march toward London. James responded by sending forward his army. Following the desertion of many of his soldiers and the defection of his daughter Anne and her husband, James retreated to London. There he made plans for his wife and son to flee to France where James later joined them.

With almost no bloodshed, England had undergone a "Glorious Revolution." The issue was not if there would be a monarchy but who would be monarch.

In January 1689, Parliament offered the throne to William and Mary. They accepted it, along with a Bill of Rights, which contained many of the same ideas as the Petition of Right. The Bill of Rights set forth Parliament's right to make laws and to levy taxes. It also made it impossible for kings to oppose or to do without Parliament by stating that standing armies could be raised only with Parliament's consent. The rights of citizens to keep arms and to have a jury trial were also confirmed. The Bill of Rights helped create a system of government based on the rule of law and a freely elected Parliament. This bill laid the foundation for a limited, or constitutional, monarchy.

Another important action of Parliament was the Toleration Act of 1689. This act granted Puritans, but not Catholics, the right of free public worship. It did mark a turning point in English history because few English citizens would ever again be persecuted for religion.

By deposing one king and establishing another, Parliament had destroyed the divine-right theory of kingship. William was, after all, king by the grace of Parliament, not by the grace of God. Parliament had asserted its right to be part of the government. Parliament did not have complete control of the government, but it now had the right to participate in affairs of state. Over the next century, Parliament would gradually prove to be the real authority in the English system of constitutional monarchy.

✓ **READING PROGRESS CHECK**

Identifying Central Issues In what important way was the monarchy of William and Mary different from the previous Stuart monarchy?

Analyzing PRIMARY SOURCES

The English Bill of Rights

"...King James the Second having abdicated the government and the throne being thereby vacant, his Highness the prince of Orange (who it hath pleased Almighty God to make the glorious instrument of delivering this kingdom from popery and arbitrary power) did (by the advice of the Lords Spiritual and Temporal and divers principal persons of the Commons) cause letters to be written to the Lords Spiritual and Temporal...in order to such an establishment as that their religion, laws and liberties might not again be in danger of being subverted..."

—from English Bill of Rights

DBQ ***ANALYZING*** This document states James II abdicated the government. What does this mean, and how do the events of the Glorious Revolution support or not support this statement?

convert to change from one belief to another

(continued from p. 410)

TEKS **Texas Essential Knowledge and Skills**

20B identify the impact of political and legal ideas contained in the following documents: Hammurabi's Code, the Jewish Ten Commandments, Justinian's Code of Laws, Magna Carta, the English Bill of Rights, the Declaration of Independence, the U.S. Constitution, and the Declaration of the Rights of Man and of the Citizen

20C explain the political philosophies of individuals such as John Locke, Thomas Hobbes, Voltaire, Charles de Montesquieu, Jean Jacques Rousseau, Thomas Aquinas, John Calvin, Thomas Jefferson, and William Blackstone

21A describe how people have participated in supporting or changing their governments

▲ Title page from *Leviathan*, by Thomas Hobbes, 1651

natural rights rights with which all humans are born, including the rights to life, liberty, and property

Legal and Political Thought

GUIDING QUESTION *How did the English Revolution influence political thought?*

Concerns with order and power were reflected in English legal and political thought. William Blackstone, a judge and professor of law, wrote *Commentaries on the Laws of England*, arguing that political stability could be achieved by a revived emphasis on English common law. Two English political thinkers, Thomas Hobbes and John Locke, provided their own responses to the English revolutions of the seventeenth century.

Thomas Hobbes was alarmed by the revolutionary upheavals in England. In 1651, he published the political work *Leviathan* to try to deal with the problem of disorder. Hobbes argued that before organized society, humans were guided not by reason and moral ideals but by a ruthless struggle for self-preservation. To save themselves from destroying one another, people made a social contract and agreed to form a state. Hobbes called the state "that great LEVIATHAN . . . to which we owe . . . our peace and defense." People in the state agreed to be governed by an absolute ruler with unlimited power in order to suppress rebellion and to preserve order.

John Locke viewed the exercise of political power quite differently. His *Two Treatises of Government*, published in 1690, argued against the absolute rule of one person. Unlike Hobbes, Locke believed that before society was organized, humans lived in a state of equality and freedom rather than in a state of war. As a result, all humans had certain **natural rights**—rights with which they were born. These included rights to life, liberty, and property.

Like Hobbes, however, Locke believed people found it difficult to protect their natural rights. Thus, they agreed to establish a government to ensure the protection of their rights and to judge those who violated them. Government would protect the rights of the people, and the people would act reasonably. However, if a government broke the contract—for example, if a monarch failed to protect citizens' natural rights—the people would be within their rights to alter or remove and form a new government.

To Locke, *people* meant the landholding aristocracy. He was not an advocate of democracy, but his ideas proved important in the eighteenth century. These ideas were used to support demands for constitutional government, the rule of law, and the protection of rights. Locke's ideas can be found in both the American Declaration of Independence and the United States Constitution.

✓ **READING PROGRESS CHECK**

Drawing Inferences Did Hobbes or Locke have more trust in self-governance? Why?

PHOTO: North Wind Picture Archives

LESSON 2 REVIEW TEKS

Reviewing Vocabulary

1. ***Defining*** Outline the differences between the Roundheads and the Cavaliers.

Using Your Notes

2. ***Discussing*** Using your notes, describe the conflicts that occurred in England.

Answering the Guiding Questions

3. ***Evaluating*** How did disagreements over rule between the Stuarts and Parliament lead to the English Civil War?
4. ***Identifying Cause and Effect*** What were the causes and effects of the Glorious Revolution? 20A
5. ***Synthesizing*** How did the English Revolution influence political thought? 20C

Writing Activity

6. **ARGUMENT** Write a paragraph arguing either Locke's or Hobbes's position. Be sure to include specific ideas. You may use any of the material in the chapter to illustrate your argument.

SKILLBUILDER

TEKS 29F

Making Generalizations

Why Learn This Skill?

Generalizations are broad statements or principles derived from specific facts. Look at the table to see some facts about Michigan and Florida.

Average monthly temperature (°F)

	January	April	July	October
Grand Rapids, Michigan	22	46.3	71.4	50.9
Vero Beach, Florida	61.9	71.7	81.8	75.2

One generalization that can be made from these facts is that Florida is warmer than Michigan. Generalizations are useful when you want to summarize large amounts of information and when detailed information is not required.

Predictions can be made from generalizations. For example, from the table we can predict that the average temperature in Michigan next January will be in the 20s, and that the average temperature in Florida in December will probably be in the 50s.

Learning the Skill

Steps for making a valid generalization:

- **Identify the subject matter.** The example above compares Michigan to Florida.
- **Gather related facts and examples.** Each fact is about the climate of Michigan or Florida.
- **Identify similarities among these facts.** In each of the examples, the climate of Florida is more moderate than the climate of Michigan.
- **Use these similarities to form a general statement about the subject.** You can state either that Florida is warmer than Michigan or that Michigan is colder than Florida.
- **Determine whether there are other factors that could affect your prediction.** These factors could change your generalizations for the future. There will be wide ranges of temperatures in both states, but one can predict with some certainty that Florida will always be warmer than Michigan.

Practicing the Skill

Europe experienced economic crises and political upheaval from 1560 to 1650. Read the following excerpt from the text, then identify valid and invalid generalizations about what you have read.

"By the beginning of the seventeenth century, an economic slowdown had begun in some parts of Europe. Spain's economy, which had grown dependent on imported silver, was seriously failing by the decade of the 1640s. Italy, once the financial center of Europe in the age of the Renaissance, was also declining economically."

Identify each of the following generalizations as valid or invalid on the basis of the information presented:

1. Multiple factors can contribute to inflation.
2. Less dependency on the importing of silver would have helped Spain's economy.

Now from the valid generalizations above, and what you know of current world events, can you predict any changes in the European economy?

Applying the Skill

Over the next two weeks, read opinions and editorials (op/eds) from online news sources such as *The Washington Post* or *The Huffington Post.* Write a list of generalizations about the source's or publication's position on issues that have been discussed, either national or local. Then during the third week, determine a new issue and predict the publication's position on that issue.

PRIMARY SOURCES

Written in 1689, the English Bill of Rights is an influential document. In the United Kingdom, it followed the precedent set by the Magna Carta in limiting the powers of the government and in protecting the rights of the people. It inspired later documents, like the Bill of Rights in the United States, and is an important part of the formation of modern democratic-republican government.

The English Bill of Rights

An act declaring the rights and liberties of the subject and settling the succession of the crown. Whereas the lords spiritual and temporal and commons assembled at Westminster lawfully, fully, and freely representing all the estates of the people of this realm did upon the thirteenth day of February in the year of our Lord one thousand six hundred eighty-eight [nine] present unto their majesties . . . William and Mary prince and princess of Orange . . . a certain declaration in writing made by the said lords and commons in the words following viz [namely]:

Whereas the late king James the second, by the assistance of **divers** evil counsellors, judges and ministers employed by him did endeavor to subvert and **extirpate** the Protestant religion and the laws and liberties of this kingdom. By assuming and exercising a power of dispensing with and suspending of laws and the execution of laws without consent of parliament. . . . By levying money for and to the use of the crown by pretence of **prerogative** for other time and in other manner than the same was granted by parliament. By raising and keeping a standing army within this kingdom in time of peace without consent of parliament and quartering soldiers contrary to law. . . . By violating the freedom of election of members to serve in parliament. . . . And excessive bail hath been required of persons committed in criminal cases to elude the benefit of the laws made for the liberty of the subjects. And excessive fines have been imposed. And illegal and cruel punishments inflicted . . . And thereupon the said lords spiritual and temporal and commons . . . do . . . declare that the pretended power of suspending of laws or the execution of laws by regal authority without consent of parliament is illegal. That levying money for or to the use of the crown . . . without grant of parliament for longer time or in other manner than the same is or shall be granted is illegal. That it is the right of the subjects to petition the king and all commitments and protections for such petitioning are illegal. That the raising or keeping a standing army within the kingdom in time of peace unless it be with consent of parliament is against law. . . . That election of members of parliament ought to be free. . . . That excessive bail ought not to be required nor excessive fines imposed nor cruel and unusual punishments inflicted. . . . The said lords . . . do resolve that William and Mary, prince and princess of Orange, be declared king and queen of England, France, and Ireland. . . .

VOCABULARY

divers
various

extirpate
to destroy

prerogative
a special right or privilege given because of one's rank or position

DBQ Analyzing Historical Documents

1. **Defending** The document states that King James II "raised a standing army . . . and quartered soldiers contrary to law." What was unlawful about these actions?
2. **Recognizing Bias** How does the author's point of view affect the tone of the document?
3. **Determining Meaning** How did the English Bill of Rights settle "the succession of the crown"?

networks

There's More Online!

- BIOGRAPHY Frederick William
- BIOGRAPHY Louis XIV
- BIOGRAPHY Peter the Great
- CHART/GRAPH Characteristics of an Absolute Monarch
- INFOGRAPHIC Versailles: A Palace Fit for the Sun King
- INTERACTIVE SELF-CHECK QUIZ
- MAP Expansion of Russia, 1505–1725
- SLIDE SHOW The Westernization of Russia by Peter the Great
- VIDEO Louis XIV and Versailles

LESSON 3
Absolutism in Europe

ESSENTIAL QUESTION
How does the exercise of absolute power affect a country?

Reading HELPDESK

Academic Vocabulary
- **stability**
- **emerge**
- **authority**

Content Vocabulary
- **absolute monarchy**
- **absolutism**
- **boyar**
- **czar**

TAKING NOTES:
Key Ideas and Details

Summarizing Information As you read, complete a chart like the one below summarizing the accomplishments of European leaders.

	Reforms
Louis XIV	
Frederick William	
Peter the Great	

TEKS Texas Essential Knowledge and Skills
19B identify the characteristics of the following political systems: theocracy, absolute monarchy, democracy, republic, oligarchy, limited monarchy, and totalitarianism

It Matters Because

In reaction to the crises of the seventeenth century, several European nations turned to absolute monarchy, with France's Louis XIV as its epitome. He waged many military campaigns and was extravagant. While Prussia, Austria, and Russia were emerging as great European powers under their monarchs' leadership, Spain was declining in power.

France Under Louis XIV

GUIDING QUESTION *Why is the reign of Louis XIV regarded as the best example of absolutism in the seventeenth century?*

One response to the crises of the seventeenth century was to seek more **stability** by increasing the power of the monarch. The result was what historians have called absolutism.

Absolutism is a system in which a ruler holds total power. **Absolute monarchy**, therefore, is a form of monarchy in which the power of the monarch is not limited by laws or a constitution. In seventeenth-century Europe, absolutism was tied to the idea of the divine right of kings. This means that absolute monarchs supposedly received their power from God and were responsible to no one except God. They had the ability to make laws, levy taxes, administer justice, control officials, and determine foreign policy.

The reign of Louis XIV has long been regarded as the best example of absolutism in the seventeenth century. French culture, language, and manners reached into all levels of European society. French diplomacy and wars dominated the political affairs of Europe. The court of Louis XIV was imitated throughout Europe.

Richelieu

French history for the 50 years before Louis XIV was a period of struggle as governments fought to avoid the breakdown of the state. Louis XIII and Louis XIV were only boys when they came to the throne. The government was left in the hands of royal ministers. In France, two ministers, Cardinal Richelieu with Louis XIII and Cardinal Mazarin with Louis XIV, played important roles in preserving the **authority** of the monarchy.

stability the state of being stable; strong enough to endure

absolutism a political system in which a ruler holds total power

authority power; person in command

Cardinal Richelieu (RIH • shuh • loo), Louis XIII's chief minister, strengthened the monarchy's power. Because the Huguenots were seen as a threat to the king, Richelieu took away their political and military rights. He did preserve their religious rights. Richelieu also set up a network of spies to uncover and crush conspiracies by nobles, executing the conspirators.

Louis in Power

After his minister Cardinal Mazarin died in 1661, Louis XIV took over supreme power. The new king, at the age of 23, stated his desire to be a real king and the sole ruler of France. Well aware of her son's love of fun and games and his affairs with the maids, Louis's mother laughed at him. Louis was serious, however. He kept a strict routine and also fostered the myth of himself as the Sun King—the source of light for all of his people.

One key to Louis's power was his control of the central policy-making machinery of government. The royal court that Louis established at Versailles (vuhr • SY) served three purposes. The royal council was the personal household of the king. In addition, the chief offices of the state were located there. Finally, Versailles was the place powerful subjects came to find favors and offices for themselves.

The greatest danger to Louis's rule came from the highest nobles and royal princes. They believed they should play a role in the government. Instead, Louis removed them from the royal council. It was the king's chief administrative body, which supervised the government. At the same time, Louis enticed the nobles and royal princes to come to his court, where he kept them busy with court life and out of politics.

Louis's government ministers were to obey his every wish. Said Louis, "I had no intention of sharing my authority with them." Thus, Louis had complete authority over the traditional areas of royal power: foreign policy, the church, and taxes. Although Louis had absolute power over nationwide policy making, his power was limited at the local level. Nobles, local officials, and town councils had more influence than the king in the daily operation of local governments. As a result, the king bribed important people in the provinces to see that his policies were carried out.

Desiring to maintain religious harmony as part of the monarchical power in France, Louis pursued an anti-Protestant policy aimed at converting the Huguenots to Catholicism. Early in his reign, Louis ordered the destruction of Huguenot churches and the closing of their schools. As many as 200,000 Huguenots fled to England, the United Provinces, and the German states.

The cost of building palaces, maintaining his court, and pursuing his wars made finances a crucial issue for Louis XIV. He was most fortunate in having the services of Jean-Baptiste Colbert (kohl • BEHR) as controller-general of finances.

Colbert sought to increase France's wealth and power by following mercantilism. To decrease imports and increase exports, he granted subsidies to new industries. To improve communications and the transportation of goods within France, he built roads and canals. To decrease imports directly, Colbert raised tariffs on foreign goods and created a merchant marine to carry French goods.

To increase his royal power, Louis developed a standing army numbering 400,000 in time of war. He wished to achieve the military glory befitting the Sun King and ensure that his Bourbon dynasty dominated Europe. To achieve his goals, Louis waged four wars between 1667 and 1713. Many nations formed coalitions to prevent him from dominating Europe.

Analyzing PRIMARY SOURCES

Louis XIV to his Chancellor (1661)

"[Up] to this moment I have been pleased to entrust the government of my affairs to the late Cardinal. It is now time that I govern them myself. You [secretaries and ministers of state] will assist me with your counsels when I ask for them. . . . I request and order you to seal no orders except by my command. . . . I order you not to sign anything, not even a passport . . . without my command; to render account to me personally each day and to favour no one."

—Louis XIV, quoted in *Princes and Peoples*

DBQ ***INTERPRETING*** How do Louis XIV's instructions to his Chancellor exemplify absolutism?

Through his wars, Louis added some territory and set up a member of his own dynasty on the throne of Spain.

Legacy of Louis XIV

In 1715, the Sun King died. He left France surrounded by enemies and many of the French people in poverty. On his deathbed, the 76-year-old monarch seemed remorseful when he told his successor (his great- grandson), "You are about to become a great king. Do not imitate me either in my taste for building or in my love of war. Live in peace with the nations. . . . Strive to relieve the burdens of your people in which I have been so unfortunate as to fail."

Did Louis mean it? We do not know. In any event, his successor probably did not remember this advice; Louis's great-grandson was only five years old.

✓ **READING PROGRESS CHECK**

Classifying How was the monarchy of Louis XIV characteristic of absolutism?

▲ *Triumph of King Louis XIV of France driving the Chariot of the Sun preceded by Aurora,* by Joseph Werner

The Spread of Absolutism

GUIDING QUESTION *How did Prussia and Austria emerge as great powers in seventeenth- and eighteenth- century Europe?*

Although absolutism largely failed in Spain, it was more successful in central and eastern Europe. After the Thirty Years' War, there were more than 300 German states. Of these, Prussia and Austria **emerged** in the seventeenth and eighteenth centuries as two great European powers.

emerge to become manifest; to become known

The Decline of Spain

At the beginning of the seventeenth century, Spain was the most populous empire in the world. To most Europeans, Spain seemed the greatest power of the age. Reality was quite different, however.

The reign of Philip IV came closest to the practice of absolute monarchy. A program of political reform sought to centralize the government of Spain in the hands of the monarchy. However, unlike Louis XIV in France, the king was unable to curtail the power of the Spanish nobles. Expensive military campaigns led to revolts and the decline of Spain as a great power.

The Emergence of Prussia

Frederick William the Great Elector laid the foundation for the Prussian state. Realizing that Prussia was a small, open territory with no natural frontiers for defense, Frederick William built a large and efficient standing army. He had a force of 40,000 men, which made the Prussian army the fourth-largest in Europe.

To maintain the army and his own power, Frederick William set up the General War Commissariat to levy taxes for the army and oversee its growth. The Commissariat soon became an agency for civil government as well. The new bureaucratic machine became the elector's chief instrument to govern the state. Many of its officials were members of the Prussian landed aristocracy, or the Junkers, who also served as officers in the army.

In 1701, Frederick William's son Frederick officially gained the title of king. Elector Frederick III became King Frederick I.

The New Austrian Empire

The Austrian Hapsburgs had long played a significant role in European politics as emperors in the Holy Roman Empire. By the end of the Thirty

GEOGRAPHY CONNECTION

Prussia and Austria emerged as great European powers during the seventeenth and eighteenth centuries.

1. **PHYSICAL SYSTEMS** *What geographical features might account for Austria's expansion to the north and east?*
2. **HUMAN SYSTEMS** *What problems might Prussia have encountered in governing its territories?*

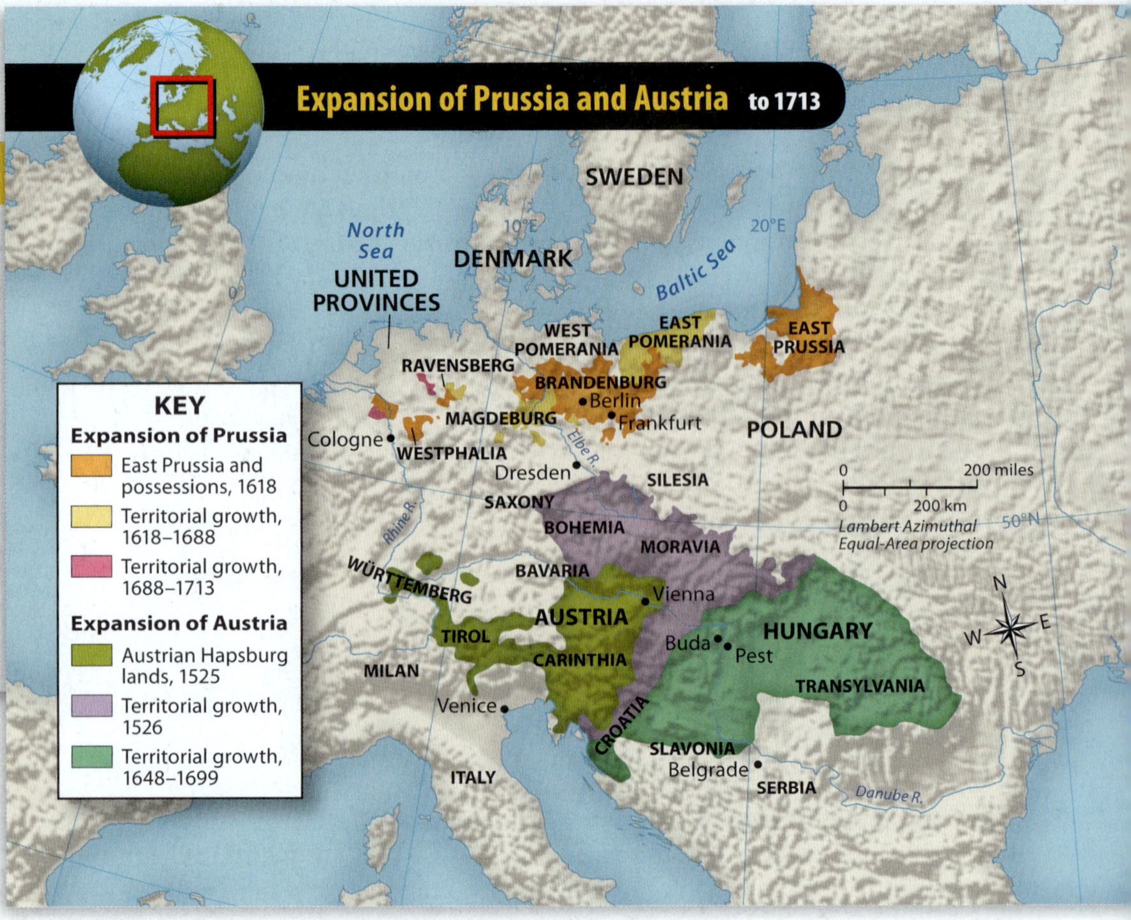

Years' War, their hopes of creating an empire in Germany had been dashed. In the seventeenth century, however, the Hapsburgs created a new empire in eastern and southeastern Europe.

The core of the new Austrian Empire was the traditional Austrian lands in present-day Austria, the Czech Republic, and Hungary. After the defeat of the Turks at Vienna in 1683, Austria took control of all of Hungary, Transylvania, Croatia, and Slavonia. By the beginning of the eighteenth century, the Austrian Hapsburgs had gained a sizable new empire.

The Austrian monarchy, however, never became a highly centralized, absolutist state, chiefly because it was made of so many different national groups. The Austrian Empire remained a collection of territories held together by the Hapsburg emperor, who was archduke of Austria, king of Bohemia, and king of Hungary. Each of these areas had its own laws and political life. No common sentiment tied the regions together other than the ideal of service to the Hapsburgs.

✓ READING PROGRESS CHECK

Comparing How was the role of the military significant in Prussia and Austria?

Peter the Great

ESSENTIAL QUESTION *How did Russia emerge as a powerful state under Peter the Great?*

A new Russian state emerged in the fifteenth century under the principality of Muscovy and its grand dukes. In the sixteenth century, Ivan IV became the first ruler to take the title of **czar**, the Russian word for *caesar*.

Ivan expanded the territories of Russia eastward. He also crushed the power of the Russian nobility, or **boyars**. He was known as Ivan the

czar Russian for *caesar*; the title used by Russian emperors

boyar a Russian noble

Terrible because of his ruthless deeds, including stabbing his son to death in a heated argument. When Ivan's dynasty ended in 1598, a period of anarchy, the Time of Troubles, followed. This period ended when the *zemsky sobor*, or national assembly, chose Michael Romanov as the new czar in 1613.

The Romanov dynasty lasted until 1917. One of its most prominent members was Peter the Great, who became czar in 1689. Like other Romanov czars who preceded him, Peter was an absolute monarch who claimed the divine right to rule.

After becoming czar, Peter visited the West. Determined to Westernize Russia, he was eager to borrow European technology. Modernization of the army and navy was crucial to make Russia a great power. Peter employed Russians and Europeans as officers. He drafted peasants for 25-year stints of service to build a standing army of 210,000 soldiers. By Peter's death in 1725, Russia was a great military power and an important European state.

Peter began to introduce Western customs, practices, and manners into Russia. He ordered the first Russian book of etiquette to teach Western manners. Men had to shave their beards and shorten their coats. Upper-class women were allowed to remove their traditional face-covering veils.

Along with making Russia into a great state and military power, Peter wanted to open a "window to the West," meaning a port with ready access to Europe. This could be achieved only on the Baltic Sea, which Sweden, the most important power in northern Europe, controlled. Peter acquired the lands he sought after a long war with Sweden. On the Baltic in 1703, Peter began construction of a new city, St. Petersburg, a base for the new Russian navy and a window to the West. St. Petersburg became Russia's most important port and remained the Russian capital until 1918.

To impose the rule of the central government more effectively, Peter divided Russia into provinces. He hoped to create a "police state," a well-ordered community governed by law. However, few bureaucrats shared his concept of honest service and duty to the state. Peter's personality created an atmosphere of fear. He wrote to one administrator, "According to these orders act, act, act. I won't write more, but you will pay with your head if you interpret orders again." Peter wanted the impossible—that his administrators be slaves and free persons at the same time.

✓ READING PROGRESS CHECK

Stating In what ways did Peter the Great modernize both the culture and the military of Russia?

BIOGRAPHY

Peter the Great (1672–1725)

As czar, Peter protected the interests of Russia's ruling class by creating a Table of Ranks, which modified the status of nobility. He also changed the rules so that the property of all landowners became hereditary instead of dependent on their service to the czar. In his appointments, Peter chose the most talented candidates, regardless of their level in society.

▶ CRITICAL THINKING

Drawing Conclusions How might Peter's policy make those he appointed more loyal to him?

LESSON 3 REVIEW TEKS

Reviewing Vocabulary

1. ***Defining*** Write a paragraph that relates the term *czar* to the term *absolutism* by giving two examples of czars and telling how they ruled absolutely.

Using Your Notes

2. ***Identifying*** Use your notes to write a paragraph that summarizes the reforms of absolutist rulers.

Answering the Guiding Questions

3. ***Constructing Arguments*** Why is the reign of Louis XIV regarded as the best example of absolutism in the seventeenth century?
4. ***Comparing*** How did Prussia and Austria emerge as great powers in seventeenth- and eighteenth-century Europe?
5. ***Identifying Cause and Effect*** How did Russia emerge as a powerful state under Peter the Great?

Writing Activity

6. **ARGUMENT** Write a paragraph that proves or disproves this thesis: Although absolutism was destructive in France, it had some positive effects in Russia. 19B

networks

There's More Online!

- BIOGRAPHY Artemisia Gentileschi
- BIOGRAPHY El Greco
- BIOGRAPHY Miguel de Cervantes
- BIOGRAPHY William Shakespeare
- IMAGE The Globe Theater
- INTERACTIVE SELF-CHECK QUIZ
- PRIMARY SOURCE All Citizens are Soldiers
- PRIMARY SOURCE As You Like It
- VIDEO Shakespeare

LESSON 4

European Culture After the Renaissance

ESSENTIAL QUESTION

What effect might social, economic, and religious conflicts have on a country?

Reading HELPDESK

Academic Vocabulary

- **decline**
- **creative**
- **drama**

Content Vocabulary

- **Mannerism**
- **baroque**

TAKING NOTES:

Key Ideas and Details

Summarizing Use the following graphic organizer to identify one major figure and his or her country of origin in each of these areas of cultural expression: painting, architecture, music, and literature.

Medium	Artist	Country of Origin
Painting		
Architecture		
Music		
Literature		

TEKS Texas Essential Knowledge and Skills

5B explain the political, intellectual, artistic, economic, and religious impact of the Reformation

continued on the next page

It Matters Because

The religious and political conflicts of seventeenth-century Europe were reflected in the art, music, and literature of the time. Art produced during the Mannerist and baroque movements aroused the emotions, and the literature spoke of the human condition.

Art After the Renaissance

GUIDING QUESTION *How did art movements change in Europe after the Renaissance?*

The artistic movements of Mannerism and the baroque began in Italy and spread through Europe. The art produced during these movements reflected the tension of religious upheaval and the spirituality of religious revival central to the period.

Mannerism

The artistic Renaissance came to an end when a new movement, called **Mannerism**, emerged in Italy in the 1520s and 1530s. The Reformation's revival of religious values brought much political turmoil. Especially in Italy, the worldly enthusiasm of the Renaissance **declined** as people grew more anxious and uncertain and wished for spiritual experience.

Mannerism in art reflected this new environment by deliberately breaking down the High Renaissance principles of balance, harmony, and moderation. The rules of proportion were deliberately ignored as elongated figures were used to show suffering, heightened emotions, and religious ecstasy.

Mannerism spread from Italy to other parts of Europe and perhaps reached its high point in the work of El Greco, "the Greek." El Greco studied the elements of Renaissance painting in Venice. He also wrote many works on painting. From Venice, El Greco moved to Rome. His career as a painter stalled there possibly because he had criticized Michelangelo's artistic abilities. When he moved to Spain, El Greco met with success.

In El Greco's paintings, the figures are elongated or contorted and he sometimes used unusual shades of yellow and green against an eerie background of stormy grays. The mood of his works reflects well the tensions created by the religious upheavals of the Reformation.

Baroque Art

Mannerism eventually was replaced by a new movement—the **baroque**. This movement began in Italy at the end of the sixteenth century and eventually spread to the rest of Europe and Latin America. It was eagerly adopted by the Catholic reform movement as shown in the richly detailed buildings at Catholic courts, especially those of the Hapsburgs in Madrid, Prague, Vienna, and Brussels.

Baroque artists tried to bring together the classical ideals of Renaissance art and the spiritual feelings of the sixteenth-century religious revival. In large part, though, baroque art and architecture reflected a search for power. Baroque churches and palaces were magnificent and richly detailed. Kings and princes wanted others to be in awe of their power.

Perhaps the greatest figure of the baroque period was the Italian architect and sculptor Gian Lorenzo Bernini, who completed Saint Peter's Basilica in Vatican City, Rome. Saint Peter's Basilica is the church of the popes and a major pilgrimage site.

Action, exuberance, and dramatic effects mark the work of Bernini in the interior of Saint Peter's. For instance, his *Throne of Saint Peter* is a highly decorated cover for the pope's medieval wooden throne. It is considered by many to be Bernini's crowning achievement in Saint Peter's Basilica. The throne seems to hover in midair, held by the hands of the four great theologians of the early Catholic Church. Above the chair, rays of heavenly light drive a mass of clouds and angels toward the spectator.

The baroque painting style was known for its use of dramatic effects to arouse the emotions as shown in the work of another important Italian artist of the baroque period, Caravaggio. Similar to other baroque painters, Caravaggio used dramatic lighting to heighten emotions, to focus details, and to isolate the figures in his paintings. His work placed an emphasis on everyday experience. He shocked some of his patrons by depicting religious figures as common people in everyday settings, rather than in a traditional, idealized style.

Mannerism an artistic movement that emerged in Italy in the 1520s and 1530s; it marked the end of the Renaissance by breaking down the principles of balance, harmony, and moderation

decline a change to a lower state or level

baroque an artistic style of the seventeenth century characterized by complex forms, bold ornamentation, and contrasting elements

(continued from p. 420)

TEKS **Texas Essential Knowledge and Skills**

26A identify significant examples of art and architecture that demonstrate an artistic ideal or visual principle from selected cultures

26B analyze examples of how art, architecture, literature, music, and drama reflect the history of the cultures in which they are produced

26C identify examples of art, music, and literature that transcend the cultures in which they were created and convey universal themes

▼ ***The Beheading of St. John the Baptist*** **by Caravaggio, 1607–1608**

▶ CRITICAL THINKING

Interpreting Significance How is this biblical scene depicted and how might this style indicate a change in a way of thinking?

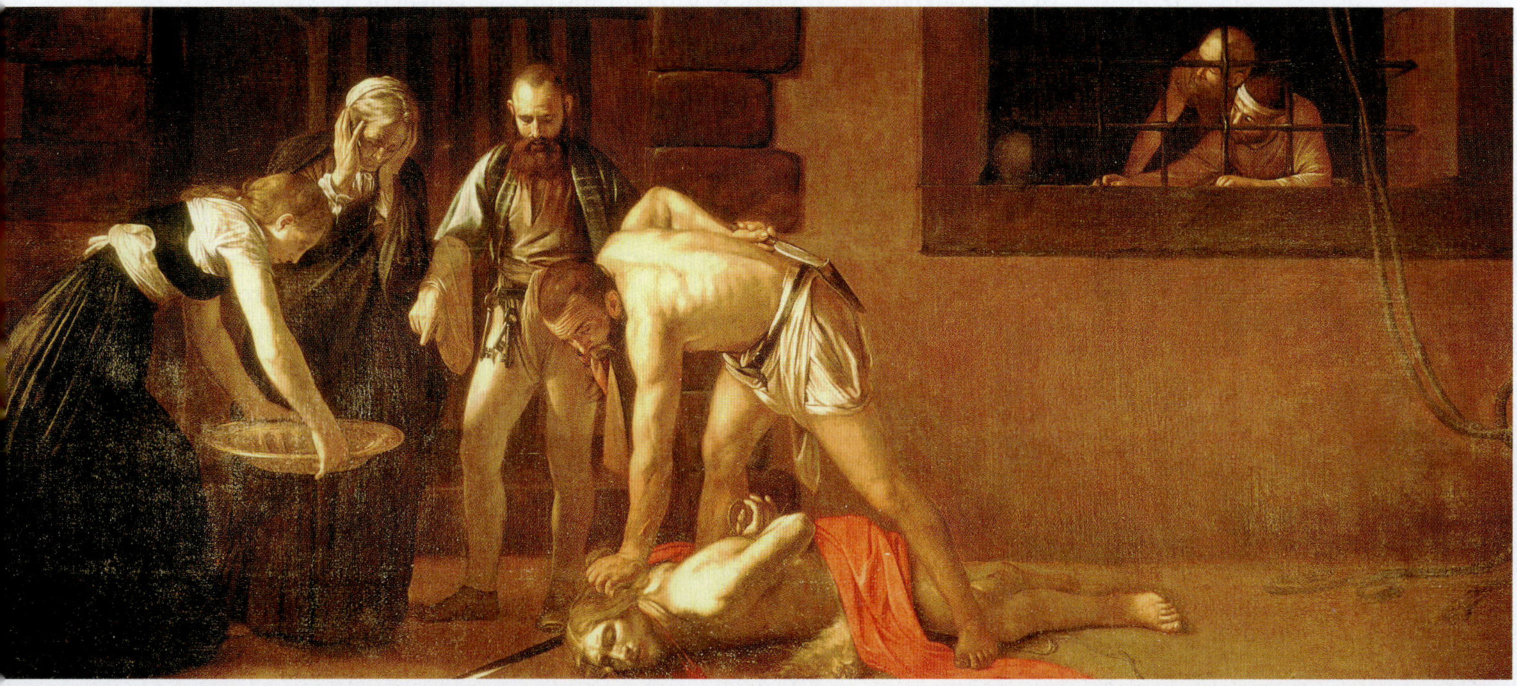

PHOTO: Sylvain Grandadam/Age Fotostock

Artemisia Gentileschi is less well-known than the male artists who dominated the seventeenth-century art world in Italy but is prominent in her own right. Born in Rome, she studied painting with her father. In 1616 she moved to Florence and began a successful career as a painter. At the age of 23, she became the first woman to be elected to the Florentine Academy of Design. She was known internationally in her day as a portrait painter, but her fame now rests on a series of pictures of Hebrew Bible heroines.

The baroque style of art did not just flourish in Italy. Peter Paul Rubens embodied the baroque movement in Flanders (the Spanish Netherlands). A scholar and a diplomat as well as an artist, Rubens used his classical education and connections with noble patrons to depict the human form in lavish and extravagant images, much like the court life he experienced during the baroque period. This example and others show that the baroque style transcended the culture in which it was created.

Baroque Music

In the first half of the eighteenth century, two composers—Johann Sebastian Bach and George Frideric Handel—perfected the baroque musical style and composed some of the world's most enduring music. Baroque music reflected the history of European culture at the close of the Reformation. Music was growing in complexity and reflected both religious and secular influences.

Bach, a renowned organist as well as a composer, spent his entire life in Germany. While he was music director at the Church of Saint Thomas in Leipzig, he composed his *Mass in B Minor* and other works that gave him the reputation of being one of the greatest composers of all time.

Handel was a German who spent much of his career in England. Handel wrote much secular music, but he is probably best known for his religious music. Handel's *Messiah* has been called a rare work that appeals immediately to everyone and yet is a masterpiece of the highest order.

✓ READING PROGRESS CHECK

Identifying Cause and Effect How did the Mannerist and baroque styles in art reflect the religious conflicts and revivals of their time?

Golden Age of Literature

GUIDING QUESTION *What characterized the Golden Age of literature in England and Spain?*

In both England and Spain, writing for the theater reached new heights between 1580 and 1640. Other forms of literature flourished as well.

England's Shakespeare

A cultural flowering took place in England in the late sixteenth and early seventeenth centuries. The period is often called the Elizabethan era, because so much of it fell within the reign of Queen Elizabeth I. Of all the forms of Elizabethan literature, none expressed the energy of the era better than **drama**. Of all the English dramatists, none is more famous than William Shakespeare.

When Shakespeare appeared in London in 1592, Elizabethans already enjoyed the stage. The theater was a very successful business. London theaters ranged from the Globe, a circular, unroofed structure holding 3,000 people, to the Blackfriars, a roofed structure that held only 500.

The Globe Theatre's admission charge of one or two pennies enabled even the lower classes of London to attend performances. The higher prices of the Blackfriars filled the audience with more well-to-do patrons. Because Elizabethan audiences for a single performance varied greatly, playwrights wrote works that were meant to please nobles, lawyers, merchants, and vagabonds alike.

drama a composition that tells a story, usually involving conflicts and emotions, through action and dialogue and typically designed for the theater

▶ CRITICAL THINKING

Drawing Conclusions How did the location and purpose of theaters like the Globe bring different classes together?

▼ **The Globe Theatre in London was surrounded by other theaters holding entertainments such as plays, bear baitings, and sword-fighting displays.**

William Shakespeare was a "complete man of the theater." Although best known for writing plays, he was also an actor and shareholder in the chief theater company of the time, the Lord Chamberlain's Men, which performed at the Globe.

Shakespeare has long been viewed as a universal genius. A master of the English language, he brought many new words into common usage. Shakespeare also wrote over 150 sonnets, a type of poetry popular during the Elizabethan era. He had a keen insight into human psychology. In his tragedies, comedies, and histories, Shakespeare showed a remarkable understanding of the human condition.

Spain's Cervantes and Vega

One of the crowning achievements of the golden age of Spanish literature was the work of Miguel de Cervantes (suhr • VAN • teez). His novel *Don Quixote* has been hailed as one of the greatest literary works of all time.

In the two main characters of this famous work, Cervantes presented the dual nature of the Spanish character. The knight, Don Quixote from La Mancha, is the visionary so involved in his lofty ideals that he does not see the hard realities around him. To him, for example, windmills appear to be our-armed giants. In contrast, the knight's fat and earthy squire, Sancho Panza, is a realist. Each of these characters finally comes to see the value of the other's perspective. The readers of *Don Quixote* are left with the conviction that both visionary dreams and the hard work of reality are necessary to the human condition.

The theater was also one of the most **creative** forms of expression during Spain's golden period of literature. The first professional theaters were created in Seville and Madrid. Soon, every large town had a public playhouse, including Mexico City in the Americas. Touring companies brought the latest Spanish plays to all parts of the Spanish Empire.

Beginning in the 1580s, the standard for playwrights was set by Lope de Vega. He wrote an extraordinary number of plays, perhaps 1,500 in all. Almost 500 of them survive to this day. Vega's plays are thought to be witty, charming, action-packed, and realistic. Lope de Vega made no apologies for the fact that he wrote his plays to please his audiences and to satisfy public demand. He remarked once that if anyone thought he had written his plays for the sake of fame, "undeceive him and tell him that I wrote them for money."

✓ READING PROGRESS CHECK

Explaining Why was the theater so popular in England, Spain, and the Spanish Empire between 1580 and 1640?

Analyzing PRIMARY SOURCES

Don Quixote on the Windmills

"[F]or you can see over there, good friend Sancho Panza, a place where stand thirty or more monstrous giants with whom I intend to fight a battle and whose lives I intend to take; and with the booty we shall begin to prosper. For this is a just war, and it is a great service to God to wipe such a wicked breed from the face of the earth."

—Miguel de Cervantes, from *Don Quixote*

DBQ ***CONTRASTING*** How do Don Quixote's motives for attacking the windmills show a contrast?

creative imaginative

LESSON 4 REVIEW TEKS

Reviewing Vocabulary

1. ***Defining*** Write a paragraph defining Mannerism and the baroque in art. Be sure to describe the characteristics of each style. **26A**
2. ***Comparing*** Write a paragraph that defines the term *drama* and compares the qualities of drama to those of a novel, such as Cervantes' *Don Quixote*.

Using Your Notes

3. ***Identifying*** Use your notes to write a paragraph identifying one major figure in each of the following areas of cultural expression: painting, architecture, music, and literature. Briefly describe each figure's work.

Answering the Guiding Questions

4. ***Identifying Central Issues*** How did art movements change in Europe after the Renaissance? **5B, 26A**
5. ***Drawing Conclusions*** What characterized the Golden Age of literature in England and Spain?

Writing Activity

6. **INFORMATIVE/EXPLANATORY** Write a paragraph evaluating the effects of religious and political turmoil on sixteenth- and seventeenth-century art. Be sure to discuss specific artists. **5B, 26A**

CHAPTER 18 Assessment

TEKS

Directions: On a separate sheet of paper, answer the questions below. Make sure you read carefully and answer all parts of the questions.

Lesson Review

Lesson 1

1. ***Identifying*** What was King Philip II of Spain's religion? How did his religious beliefs influence his political actions? **23B**

2. ***Identifying*** What contributed to Spain going bankrupt?

3. ***Summarize*** How did Henry IV's crowning as king and the Edict of Nantes bring peace and balance to the people of France?

4. ***Describing*** What were the major influences of Queen Elizabeth I during her reign over England? **24B**

5. ***Summarize*** How was Germany affected by the Thirty Years' War?

Lesson 2

6. ***Summarizing*** Summarize the actions of Oliver Cromwell up until the Restoration period. How might you characterize his style of rule?

7. ***Identifying*** In the late 1680s, how did the personal life of James II, brother of Charles I, potentially change the course of history in England?

8. ***Identifying*** What are the political and legal ideas contained in the English Bill of Rights? What is the impact of these ideas? **20B**

9. ***Analyzing*** How did Parliament end the idea of divine-right theory of kingship in England? What implications did this have for England's future?

10. ***Identifying*** What was the political philosophy of William Blackstone? What did he write? **20C**

11. ***Comparing*** Compare the political philosophies of Thomas Hobbes and John Locke. **20C**

Lesson 3

12. ***Stating*** What are the characteristics of absolutism, and how was absolutism reflected in 17th century monarchies? **19B**

13. ***Identifying*** What effect did Louis XIV's absolute monarchy have on his country and his people?

14. ***Explaining*** How did Louis XIV's controller-general of finances, Jean-Baptiste Colbert, improve France's financial status after Louis XIV's actions had done much to deplete France's wealth?

15. ***Stating*** What inspired Frederick William to build a large standing army in Prussia? What was the result of this strong military presence?

16. ***Describing*** Describe the efforts of Peter the Great to Westernize Russia. How did his reign change Russia?

Lesson 4

17. ***Interpreting*** Consider the evolution and change from one prevailing art style to another—High Renaissance to Mannerism to Baroque—and explain how one style's elements are connected to the next, providing examples. Offer a viewpoint on why artistic movements shift.

18. ***Identifying*** Who was Artemisia Gentileschi? Briefly describe how her work demonstrates the artistic ideals of the period. **26A**

Need Extra Help?

If You've Missed Question	1	2	3	4	5	6	7	8	9	10	11	12	13	14	15	16	17	18
Go to page	404	406	406	406	408	410	410	414	411	412	412	415	415	416	417	418	420	422

19 ***Analyzing*** What kind of audience did the Globe Theatre attract? How did Shakespeare's dramas reflect the culture of the period? **26B**

20 ***Analyzing*** Give an example of baroque music that both reflects the history of the culture in which it was produced and continues to hold meaning for audiences today. **26B, 26C**

Exploring the Essential Question

21 ***Explaining*** Work with a partner to create a large chart on poster board that lists political, economic, and religious conflicts in at least four European countries and shows the effects of those conflicts on each country and its culture. Include visuals such as sketches, maps, and photos of art. **23B**

Critical Thinking

22 ***Comparing*** In respect to religious harmony in their countries, compare Elizabeth I's decisions when she took the throne in England to Henry IV's actions in France when he took the throne in France.

23 ***Speculate*** Speculate on the strength of the arguments against many women accused of witchcraft during the Inquisition in the 16th and 17th centuries.

24 ***Assessing*** Write a paragraph explaining how the English Civil War transformed the political front in England and laid part of the groundwork for the development of democratic systems of government. **20A**

25 ***Constructing Arguments*** Select a specific example of literature from the Golden Age of Literature in England and Spain. Then, write an argument in which you argue its relevance in today's society. Remember to consider universal themes presented in these works and whether or not it holds meaning across time and cultures. **26C**

26 ***Analyzing*** What influenced the artistic movement known as Mannerism? How is this influence reflected in works of the movement? **5B**

Social Studies Skills

27 ***Understanding Relationships Among Events*** What were the effects of religious wars on Europe in the sixteenth and seventeenth centuries? How did the concept of heresy contribute to the issue? **23B**

28 ***Compare and Contrast*** What were the roles of the English nobility, Parliament, and religion in the Glorious Revolution? **23B**

29 ***Identifying Cause and Effect*** What impact did Peter the Great have on Russia?

DBQ Analyzing Primary Sources

In 1589 King James VI of Scotland wrote, anonymously, a book in which he defended the divine right of kings to absolute power. Read the excerpt from King James VI, and answer the questions that follow.

PRIMARY SOURCE

"And as ye see it manifest that the king is over-lord of the whole land, so is he master over every person that inhabiteth the same, having power over the life and death of every one of them; for although a just prince will not take the life of any of his subjects without a clear law, yet the same laws whereby he taketh them are made by himself or his predecessors; and so the power flows always from himself . . . ."

—from *True Law of Free Monarchies*

30 ***Interpreting*** What protection does James I claim subjects have against execution by their ruler?

31 ***Drawing Conclusions*** Why does the king say that all kings are overlords of their whole lands?

Need Extra Help?

If You've Missed Question	19	20	21	22	23	24	25	26	27	28	29	30	31
Go to page	422	422	404	406	407	411	422	420	404	411	418	425	425

Analyzing Visuals

Use the image to answer the following questions.

This painting, *The Beheading of John the Baptist,* was painted by the famous Italian artist Caravaggio. It depicts the moments before the important biblical figure was beheaded.

32 ***Interpreting*** What technique does the painter use to show the emotions of the people in the painting? How does this reflect the history of the culture in which this painting was created? **26B**

33 ***Analyzing Visuals*** What universal theme about emotions or religion does this painting reflect?

34 ***Drawing Inferences*** Draw an inference about the figures in the painting watching the main scene.

Extended Response Question

35 ***Expository*** Write an essay contrasting absolute monarchies and constitutional, or limited, monarchies. What are the differences between each type of monarchy? How did the type of monarchy a country had affect the satisfaction of its people? The essay should include an introduction, at least three paragraphs, and a conclusion that supports your main idea. Use information gathered from primary and secondary sources to provide examples to support your answer. **9B, 20B**

Need Extra Help?

If You've Missed Question	32	33	34	35
Go to page	426	426	426	404

The Muslim Empires

1450–1800

ESSENTIAL QUESTIONS • *What factors help unify an empire?* • *How can the creation of a new empire impact the people and culture of a region?*

networks

There's More Online! about the Muslim empires.

CHAPTER 19

The Story Matters...

Three Muslim empires, each united by the Islamic religion and its ruling dynasty, reached the height of their power at different times between 1450 and 1800. The Ottoman Empire dominated the eastern Mediterranean, threatening Europe. The Mogul Empire ruled most of what is now India and Pakistan. Centered in Persia between its two Muslim rivals was the Ṣafavid Empire. All three empires created brilliant cultures, as shown in this vivid painting of the Mogul ruler Akbar.

◄ Akbar was powerful as well as physically and mentally energetic. A tireless soldier, he conquered much of India. Although unable to read, he fostered a brilliant culture at his court.

CHAPTER 19

Place and Time: The Muslim Empires 1450–1800

Each dedicated to extending Muslim power, the Ottoman, Ṣafavid, and Mogul dynasties were also alike in establishing what historians refer to as "gunpowder empires." Their success as conquerors was based on their mastery of the technology of firearms. These empires were also similar in sharing the influence of Persian culture in literature and the arts and in gaining strength from a growing world economy.

Step Into the Place

Read the quotes and look at the information presented on the map.

DBQ **Analyzing Historical Documents** Compare the ruling styles of Akbar and Süleyman I. Predict the strengths and weaknesses of each style.

PRIMARY SOURCE

"His Imperial Majesty [Akbar] does not let a month or year pass without devising good regulations or without providing the source of tranquility to the world through his far-seeing wisdom that mirrors truths, earthly and divine. At this time he cast his eyes far and wide to arrange better the conditions of the army and peasantry and secure the extension of the empire and enlargement of the Imperial resources, and instituted [for that purpose] wonderful regulations and firm rules."

—Abu-l-Fazl 'Allāmī, from *Akbarnama,* 1574–1575

PRIMARY SOURCE

"The Sultan's [Süleyman I] headquarters were crowded by numerous attendants, including many high officials . . . In all that great assembly no single man owed his dignity to anything but his personal merits and bravery; no one is distinguished from the rest by his birth, and honour is paid to each man according to the nature of the duty and offices which he discharges. . . . The Sultan himself assigns to all their duties, . . . pays no attention to wealth or the empty claims of rank, and takes no account of any influence or popularity which a candidate may possess; he only considers merit, and scrutinizes the character, natural ability, and disposition of each."

—Ogier Ghislain de Busbecq, from *The Turkish Letters,* 1555–1562

Step Into the Time

Determining Cause and Effect Choose an event from the time line and predict what consequences it may have had for the expansion of one of these Muslim empires.

THE MUSLIM EMPIRES

- **April 6, 1453** Ottomans, led by Mehmed II, lay siege to Constantinople
- **1519** Mogul ruler Bābur crosses Khyber Pass into India
- **1526** Ottomans defeat Hungarians at Mohács
- **1556** Akbar, grandson of Bābur, takes over Mogul Empire
- **1571** Christian alliance destroys Ottoman fleet at Battle of Lepanto

1450 | 1500 | 1550

THE WORLD

- **1464** The Sunni dynasty in Africa begins
- **1517** Martin Luther writes Ninety-Five Theses
- **1533** Francisco Pizarro conquers the Inca Empire
- **1534** Act of Supremacy makes Henry VIII head of the new Church of England

networks
There's More Online!

- **MAP** Explore the interactive version of this map on Networks.
- **TIME LINE** Explore the interactive version of the time line on Networks.

The Muslim Empires at Their Heights 1699–1722

1588 Rule of Shāh 'Abbās begins, leading to peak of the Ṣafavid dynasty

1600 Victory at battle of Sekigahara establishes Tokugawa control of Japan

1628 Akbar's grandson Shāh Jahān assumes control of India

1653 Oliver Cromwell begins reign as Lord Protector of England

1683 Ottomans unsuccessfully besiege Vienna

1715 Louis XV of France comes to the throne

1739 Delhi, in Mogul India, is destroyed by Persians

1757 British forces, led by Sir Robert Clive, defeat the Moguls

1762 Catherine the Great begins 34-year reign in Russia

1776 Thomas Jefferson writes the Declaration of Independence

1600 | 1650 | 1700 | 1750 | 1800

networks

There's More Online!

- ☑ BIOGRAPHY Mehmed II
- ☑ IMAGE The Sacking of Constantinople
- ☑ INTERACTIVE SELF-CHECK QUIZ
- ☑ MAP Expansion of the Ottoman Empire to 1699
- ☑ PRIMARY SOURCE The Siege of Constantinople
- ☑ SLIDE SHOW Ottoman Architecture and Arts
- ☑ VIDEO The Rise and Expansion of the Ottoman Empire

LESSON 1
The Rise and Expansion of the Ottoman Empire

ESSENTIAL QUESTIONS • *What factors help unify an empire?* • *How can the creation of a new empire impact the people and culture of a region?*

Reading HELPDESK

Academic Vocabulary
- **successor**
- **domain**

Content Vocabulary
- **janissary**
- **gunpowder empire**
- **sultan**
- **grand vizier**
- **harem**
- **pasha**
- **ulema**

TAKING NOTES:
Key Ideas and Details

Organizing Create a chart like this one to show the structure of the Ottoman society. List the groups in order of importance.

Class	Description

IT MATTERS BECAUSE

At its peak in the sixteenth century, the Ottoman Empire consisted of lands in western Asia, North Africa, and Europe. The Ottomans contributed new designs to world art, as seen in their magnificent mosques. They also practiced religious tolerance with their subjects.

Rise of the Ottoman Turks

GUIDING QUESTION *How did the Ottoman Turks establish power and expand their empire?*

In the late thirteenth century, a new group of Turks, under their leader Osman, began to build power in Anatolia, in the chaos created by the Mongolian invasions. As they expanded, the Osman Turks founded the Ottoman dynasty. In the fourteenth century, the Ottoman Turks moved into the Balkans, and built a strong military by developing an elite guard called **janissaries**, children enslaved from the local Christian population and converted to Islam. The janissaries were trained as foot soldiers or administrators and they served the sultan, or Ottoman leader.

As knowledge of firearms spread during this period, the Ottomans began to master the new technology. With the janissaries, the Ottomans defeated the Serbs at the Battle of Kosovo in 1389. During the 1390s, they advanced northward and annexed Bulgaria.

Fall of the Byzantine Empire

In their expansion westward, the Ottomans came to control the Bosporus and the Dardanelles. These two straits (narrow water passageways), separated by the Sea of Marmara, connect the Black Sea and the Aegean Sea, which leads to the Mediterranean Sea. The Byzantine Empire had controlled this area for centuries.

Under Mehmed II, the Ottomans moved to end the Byzantine Empire. With 80,000 troops fighting against only 7,000 defenders, Mehmed laid siege to Constantinople.

The attack began on April 6, 1453, as the Ottomans bombarded Constantinople with massive cannons hurling stone balls weighing up to 1,200 pounds (545 kg) each. The Byzantines fought desperately for almost two months to save Constantinople. Finally, on May 29, the walls were breached, and Ottoman soldiers poured in. The Byzantine emperor died in the final battle, and an atrocious three-day sack of the city began. The Byzantine Empire was now gone, and Eastern Europe would be forever changed.

The capture of Constantinople marked an important turning point for the Turks, who now linked the European and Asian parts of their empire. Mehmed II renamed the city Istanbul. The effect of Ottoman control of this important crossroads was enormous, as Europeans now looked for alternative trading routes to Asia. These explorations led Europeans to Africa and the Americas, forever changing global trade and power.

Expansion of the Ottoman Empire

From their new capital at İstanbul, the Ottoman Turks controlled the Balkans and the Anatolian Peninsula. From 1514 to 1517, Sultan Selim I conquered Mesopotamia, Egypt, and Arabia—the original heartland of Islam. Through these conquests, Selim I was now in control of several of Islam's holy cities. These cities included Jerusalem, Makkah (Mecca), and Madinah (Medina). Selim declared himself the new caliph, or defender of the faith and **successor** to Muhammad.

Ottoman forces advanced westward along the African coast almost to the Strait of Gibraltar. They also began to expand into other parts of Europe, back into the Balkans, and the Romanian territory of Walachia. The Hungarians, however, stopped their advance up the Danube Valley.

Under Süleyman I, whose reign began in 1520, the Ottomans advanced anew up the Danube, seized Belgrade, and won a major victory over the Hungarians in 1526 at the Battle of Mohács (MOH • hach). They then conquered most of Hungary and moved into Austria. Advancing to Vienna, they were defeated in 1529. They moved into the western Mediterranean until the Spanish destroyed a large Ottoman fleet at Lepanto in 1571. Although halted, the Ottomans still controlled a significant portion of eastern Europe, removing self-rule for centuries and introducing Islam into the predominantly Christian territories.

During the first half of the seventeenth century, the Ottoman Empire in eastern Europe remained a "sleeping giant." Occupied with internal problems, the Ottomans kept the status quo. However, in the second half of the seventeenth century, they again went on the offensive, laying siege to Vienna. Repulsed by a European army, the Ottomans retreated and were pushed out of Hungary. Although they retained the core of their empire, the Ottoman Turks would never again be a threat to central Europe.

✓ **READING PROGRESS CHECK**

Explaining What was the role of the janissaries in the rise of the Ottoman Empire?

Life Under Ottoman Rule

GUIDING QUESTION *How was the Ottoman Empire ruled under a sultan? What were society and culture like in the Ottoman Empire?*

Like the Muslim empires in Persia and India, the Ottoman Empire is often labeled a "**gunpowder empire**." Gunpowder empires were formed by outside conquerors who unified their conquered regions. Such an empire's success was largely based on its mastery of firearms.

Analyzing **PRIMARY SOURCES**

Mehmed II on Constantinople

"When he saw what a large number had been killed, and the ruin of the buildings, and the wholesale ruin and destruction of the City, he was filled with compassion and repented not a little at the destruction and the plundering. Tears fell from his eyes as he groaned deeply and passionately: What a city we have given over to plunder and destruction."

—Kritovoulos, from *The History of Mehmed the Conqueror*, 1453

DBQ ***DRAWING CONCLUSIONS*** Why did the Ottomans need to capture Constantinople?

janissary a soldier in the elite guard of the Ottoman Turks

successor one who follows, especially one who takes over a throne, title, estate, or office

TEKS Texas Essential Knowledge and Skills

1C identify major causes and describe the major effects of the following important turning points in world history from 600 to 1450 the spread of Christianity, the decline of Rome and the formation o medieval Europe; the development of Islamic caliphates and their impact on Asia, Africa, and Europe; the Mongol invasions and their impact on Europe, China, India, and Southwest Asia

continued on p. 433

gunpowder empire an empire formed by outside conquerors who unified the regions that they conquered through their mastery of firearms

sultan "holder of power"; the military and political head of state under the Seljuk Turks and the Ottomans

domain place where one has absolute ownership of land or other property

harem "sacred place"; the private domain of an Ottoman sultan, where he and his wives resided

grand vizier the Ottoman sultan's chief minister who carried the main burdens of the state and who led the council meetings

pasha an appointed official of the Ottoman Empire who collected taxes, maintained law and order, and was directly responsible to the sultan's court

ulema a group of religious advisers to the Ottoman sultan; this group administered the legal system and schools for educating Muslims

The Imperial Sultans

At the head of the Ottoman system was the **sultan**, who was the supreme authority in a political and a military sense. As the empire expanded, the status and prestige of the sultan increased. The position took on the trappings of imperial rule. A centralized administrative system was adopted, and the sultan became increasingly isolated from his people.

The position of the sultan was hereditary. A son, although not necessarily the eldest, always succeeded the father. This practice led to struggles over succession upon the death of individual sultans. The losers in these struggles were often executed. The private **domain** of the sultan was called the **harem** ("sacred place"). Here, the sultan and his wives resided. When a son became a sultan, his mother became known as the queen mother and acted as a major adviser to the throne. This tradition often gave considerable power to the queen mother in the affairs of state.

The sultan controlled his bureaucracy through an imperial council that met four days a week. The **grand vizier**, a chief minister who carried the main burdens of the state, led the meetings of the council. During the council meetings, the sultan sat behind a screen, overhearing the proceedings, and then privately indicated his desires to the grand vizier.

The empire was divided into provinces and districts, each governed by officials. They were assisted by bureaucrats known as **pashas**, who had been trained in a palace school for officials in İstanbul. The sultan gave land to the senior officials. They were then responsible for collecting taxes and supplying armies for the empire from this landed area.

The Topkapi ("iron gate") Palace in İstanbul was the center of the sultan's power. The palace was built in the fifteenth century by Mehmed II. Like Versailles in France, it had an administrative purpose but also served as the private residence of the ruler and his family.

Ottoman Society

Like most Turkic-speaking peoples in the Anatolian Peninsula and throughout western Asia, the Ottomans were Sunni Muslims. Ottoman sultans had claimed the title of caliph since the early sixteenth century. In theory, they were responsible for guiding the flock and maintaining Islamic law. In practice, the sultans gave their religious duties to a group of religious advisers known as the **ulema**. This group administered the legal system and schools for educating Muslims. Islamic law and customs were applied to all Muslims in the empire.

Non-Muslims made up a significant minority within the empire. Non-Muslims paid a tax, but they were allowed to practice their religion or to convert to Islam. Most people in the European areas of the empire remained Christian. In some areas, however, such as present-day Bosnia, large numbers of non-Muslims converted to the Islamic faith.

The subjects of the Ottoman Empire were divided by occupation. In addition to the ruling class, there were four main occupational groups: peasants, artisans, merchants, and pastoral peoples. Peasants farmed land

▼ **The Topkapi Palace overlooks the Bosporus and Sea of Marmara, part of an essential trade route connecting the Aegean and Black Seas.**

▶ **CRITICAL THINKING**
Interpreting Significance What was the symbolic importance of where the Topkapi Palace was located?

that the state leased to them. Ultimate ownership of all land resided with the sultan. Artisans were organized according to craft guilds. Each guild provided financial services, social security, and training to its members. Outside the ruling elite, merchants were the most privileged class in Ottoman society. They were largely exempt from government regulations and taxes.

Technically, women in the Ottoman Empire were subject to the same restrictions as women in other Muslim societies. However, their position was somewhat better. As applied in the Ottoman Empire, Islamic law was more tolerant in defining the legal position of women. This relatively tolerant attitude was probably due to Turkish traditions that regarded women as almost equal to men. For instance, women were allowed to own and inherit property. They could not be forced into marriage and, in certain cases, were permitted to seek divorce. Women often gained considerable power within the palace. In a few instances, they served as senior officials.

(continued from p. 431)

TEKS Texas Essential Knowledge and Skills

1D identify major causes and describe the major effects of the following important turning points in world history from 1450 to 1750: the rise of the Ottoman Empire, the influence of the Ming dynasty on world trade, European exploration and the Columbian Exchange, European expansion, and the Renaissance and the Reformation

7D explain the impact of the Ottoman Empire on Eastern Europe and global trade

26B analyze examples of how art, architecture, literature, music, and drama reflect the history of the cultures in which they are produced

Architecture and the Arts

The Ottoman sultans were enthusiastic patrons of the arts. Artists came from all over the world to compete for the sultans' generous rewards. They produced pottery; rugs, silk, and other textiles; jewelry; and arms and armor. All of these adorned the palaces of the rulers.

By far the greatest contribution of the Ottoman Empire to world art was in architecture, especially the magnificent mosques of the last half of the sixteenth century. The Ottomans modeled their mosques after Constantinople's Byzantine church of Hagia Sophia by creating a prayer hall with an open central area under one large dome. This new style of architecture reflected the merger of Turkish and Byzantine cultures within this rapidly growing multiethnic empire.

In the mid-sixteenth century, the greatest of all Ottoman architects, Sinan, began building the first of his 81 mosques. One of Sinan's masterpieces was the Süleymaniye Mosque in İstanbul. Each of his mosques was topped by an imposing dome, and often the entire building was framed with four towers, or minarets.

The sixteenth century also witnessed the flourishing of textiles and rugs. The Byzantine emperor Justinian had introduced silk cultivation to the West in the sixth century. Under the Ottomans, the silk industry resurfaced. Factories produced silks for wall hangings and especially court costumes. Rugs were a peasant industry. The rugs were made of wool and cotton in villages from different regions.

READING PROGRESS CHECK

Explaining What aspects of Ottoman life did the sultan control?

SKILLS PRACTICE

After the class discussion, summarize the lesson with a partner by taking turns explaining to each other how the Ottomans defeated the Byzantine Empire.

LESSON 1 REVIEW TEKS

Reviewing Vocabulary

1. ***Describing*** Write a paragraph describing the relationship between the sultan and the grand vizier.

Using Your Notes

2. ***Explaining*** Use your graphic organizer on Ottoman society to identify how the upper classes were supported by the lower classes.

Answering the Guiding Questions

3. ***Evaluating*** How did the Ottoman Turks establish power and expand their empire?
4. ***Assessing*** How was the Ottoman Empire ruled under the sultan?
5. ***Summarizing*** What were society and culture like in the Ottoman Empire?

Writing Activity

6. **NARRATIVE** Write a paragraph on Ottoman expansion or warfare from the point of view of a janissary in the Ottoman army.

networks

There's More Online!

- BIOGRAPHY Shāh 'Abbās
- BIOGRAPHY Süleyman I
- IMAGE Süleymaniye Mosque
- INTERACTIVE SELF-CHECK QUIZ
- MAP Ṣafavid Empire, 1501–1722
- SLIDE SHOW Ṣafavid Arts
- TIME LINE Ottoman and Ṣafavid Conflicts
- VIDEO The Ottomans and the Ṣafavids

LESSON 2

The Ottomans and the Ṣafavids

ESSENTIAL QUESTIONS • *What factors help unify an empire?*
• *How can the creation of a new empire impact the people and culture of a region?*

Reading HELPDESK

Academic Vocabulary

- **administrator** • **conform**

Content Vocabulary

- **shah** • **orthodoxy**
- **anarchy**

TAKING NOTES:

Key Ideas and Details

Comparing and Contrasting Use the Venn diagram to compare and contrast the Ottoman and Ṣafavid Empires.

Ottoman Empire   Ṣafavid Empire

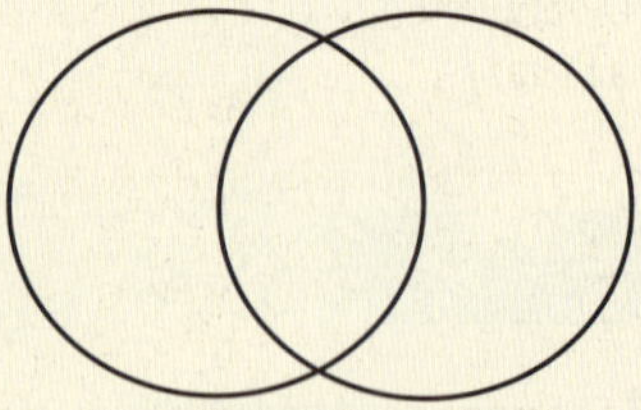

TEKS Texas Essential Knowledge and Skills

24A describe the changing roles of women, children, and families during major eras of world history

25D explain how Islam influences law and government in the Muslim world

IT MATTERS BECAUSE

The Ṣafavid Empire was the shortest lived of the three Muslim empires but was nonetheless influential. The Shia faith, declared as the state religion, unified the empire but also brought it into conflict with the Ottomans, who were Sunni Muslims.

Problems in the Ottoman Empire

GUIDING QUESTION *What led to the disintegration of the Ottoman Empire?*

The Ottoman Empire reached its high point under Süleyman I, known as the empire's greatest ruler. Süleyman (1520–1566) was also a great military leader, who led his army on 13 major military campaigns. He doubled the size of the Ottoman Empire. Europeans called him the "Grand Turk" and the "Magnificent."

To his own subjects, however, Süleyman was known as the "Lawgiver." Eager to provide justice for his subjects, he reorganized the government, regulated the laws of the empire, and saw that they were properly enforced. However, it might also have been during Süleyman's rule that problems began to occur. Having executed his two most able sons on suspicion of treason, Süleyman was succeeded by his only surviving son, Selim II (the Sot, or "the drunken sultan").

The problems of the Ottoman Empire did not become visible until 1699, when the empire began to lose some of its territory. However, signs of internal disintegration had already appeared in the early 1600s.

After the death of Süleyman, sultans became less involved in government. They allowed their ministers to exercise more power. The training of officials declined, and senior positions were increasingly assigned to the sons or daughters of elites. Members of the elite soon formed a privileged group seeking wealth and power. Earlier, the sultans had regarded members of the ruling class as the "sultan's slaves." Now the sultan became the servant of the ruling class. Moreover, the central bureaucracy lost its links with rural areas. Local officials became corrupt, taxes increased, and palace intrigue grew. Constant wars depleted the imperial treasury.

Another sign of change within the empire was a growing wealth and the impact of Western ideas and customs. Officials and merchants began to imitate the lifestyles of Europeans. They wore European clothing and bought Western furniture and art objects. During the sixteenth and early seventeenth centuries, coffee and tobacco were introduced into polite Ottoman society. Cafes, where both were consumed, began to appear in the major cities.

Some sultans attempted to counter this by outlawing such goods as coffee and tobacco. One sultan patrolled the streets ofİstanbul at night, ordering the immediate execution of subjects he caught in illegal acts. Their bodies were left on the streets as an example to others.

The Ottoman Empire had economic problems reaching back to the closure of trade routes through its territories. The economy was also troubled by inflation and the trade imbalance between the empire and Europe. The Ottomans did not invest in manufacturing. Their guilds had strict price regulations and could not compete with inexpensive manufactured goods from Europe. This declining economy left little money for military expansion.

▲ The Süleymaniye Mosque in İstanbul, built between 1550–57

▶ **CRITICAL THINKING**

Interpreting Significance Why is it significant that the mosque design was inspired by the Byzantine church of Hagia Sophia?

✓ **READING PROGRESS CHECK**

Determining Cause and Effect How did some sultans respond to the influence of Western ideas in the Ottoman Empire?

The Ṣafavid Empire

GUIDING QUESTION ***What was the source of conflict between the Ottomans and the Ṣafavids?***

After the empire of Timur Lenk (Tamerlane) collapsed in the early fifteenth century, the area extending from Persia into central Asia fell into anarchy. At the beginning of the sixteenth century, however, a new dynasty known as theṢafavids (sah • FAH • weedz) took control. Unlike many of their Islamic neighbors who were Sunni Muslims, the Ṣafavids became ardent Shias.

The Ṣafavid dynasty was founded by Shāh Esmā'īl (ihs • MAH • eel), who, in 1501, used his forces to seize much of Iran and Iraq. He then called himself the **shah**, or king, of a new Persian state. Esmā'īl sent Shia preachers into the Anatolian Peninsula to convert members of Turkish tribes in the Ottoman Empire. The Ottoman sultan tried to halt this activity, but Esmā'īl refused to stop. Esmā'īl also ordered the massacre of Sunni Muslims when he conquered Baghdad in 1508.

shah king (used in Persia and Iran)

Alarmed by these activities, the Ottoman sultan, Selim I, advanced against the Ṣafavids in Persia. With their muskets and artillery, the Ottomans won a major battle near Tabrīz. However, a few years later, Esmā'īl regained Tabrīz.

During the following decades, the Ṣafavids tried to consolidate their rule throughout Persia and in areas to the west. The Ṣafavids were faced with the problem of integrating various Turkish peoples with the settled Persian-speaking population of the urban areas. The Shia faith was used as a unifying force. Esmā'īl made conversion to the Shia faith mandatory for the largely Sunni population. Many Sunnis were killed or exiled. Like the Ottoman sultan, the shah claimed to be the spiritual leader of all Islam.

BIOGRAPHY

Shāh 'Abbās (1571–1629)

Also called 'Abbās the Great, Shāh 'Abbās came to the throne in 1588. He organized a permanent army and drove the Ottoman and Uzbek armies out of Persia. He moved the Persian capital from Kazvin to Eşfahān, where he established trade relationships with European ambassadors. Shāh 'Abbās showed tolerance in religion but punished corrupt government officials severely. He was also a notable patron of the arts.

▶ **CRITICAL THINKING**

Summarizing What made the rule of Shāh 'Abbās successful?

In the 1580s, the Ottomans went on the attack. They placed Azerbaijan under Ottoman rule and controlled the Caspian Sea with their fleet. This forced the new Şafavids shah, 'Abbās, to sign a peace treaty in which he lost much territory in the northwest. The capital of the Şafavids was moved from the northwestern city of Kazvin to the more centrally located city of Eşfahān. Eşfahān became one of the world's largest cities with a population of 1 million.

Under Shāh 'Abbās, who ruled from 1588 to 1629, the Şafavids reached the high point of their glory. Similar to the Ottoman Empire, **administrators** were trained to run the kingdom. Shāh 'Abbās also strengthened his army, which he outfitted with the latest weapons. In the early seventeenth century, Shāh 'Abbās moved against the Ottomans and returned Azerbaijan to the Şafavids.

After the death of Shāh 'Abbās in 1629, the Şafavid dynasty gradually lost its vigor. Most of 'Abbās's **successors** lacked his talent and political skills. Eventually, however, the power of Shia religious elements began to increase at court and in Şafavid society at large.

Intellectual freedom marked the height of the empire. However, the pressure to **conform** to traditional religious beliefs, called religious **orthodoxy**, increased. For example, Persian women had considerable freedom during the early empire. That changed as they were now forced into seclusion and required to wear a veil. Treatment of non-Muslims deteriorated as well.

In the early eighteenth century, the Şafavid dynasty collapsed. The Turks took advantage of the situation to seize territories along the western border. Persia sank into a long period of political and social **anarchy**.

✓ **READING PROGRESS CHECK**

Analyzing What was the role of religion during the rule of Shāh Esmāʾīl?

Life under the Şafavids

GUIDING QUESTION *What was life like under the Şafavids?*

Persia under the Şafavids was a mixed society. The combination of Turkish and Persian elements affected virtually all aspects of Şafavid society.

As Shia Islam was the state religion, the Şafavid rulers were eagerly supported by Shias. Shahs were more available to their subjects than were rulers elsewhere. "They show great familiarity . . . even to their own subjects, eating and drinking with them pretty freely," remarked one visitor.

Strong-minded shahs firmly controlled the power of the landed aristocracy. In addition, appointment to senior positions in the bureaucracy was based on merit rather than birth. For example, Shāh 'Abbās hired foreigners from neighboring countries for positions in his government.

The Şafavid shahs played an active part in trade and manufacturing activity. Across the empire, bazaars in regional capitals provided citizens with access to a variety of goods and merchandise. Merchants came from across Central Asia to trade in the Şafavid region.

The bazaar was the heart of their commerce. Many bazaars were enclosed and had high vaulted ceilings that covered narrow rows of stalls. Specific sections housed similar types of goods for shoppers' convenience. Spaces for manufacturing, storage, and merchants' offices stood alongside shops. Caravansaries attached to the bazaar received trains of camels or mules loaded with goods. In the caravansary, newly arrived trade goods were sold wholesale. In the bazaar, they were sold retail.

administrator one who manages the affairs of a government or a business

conform to adhere to rules or standards; to fit in

orthodoxy traditional beliefs, especially in religion

anarchy political disorder; lawlessness

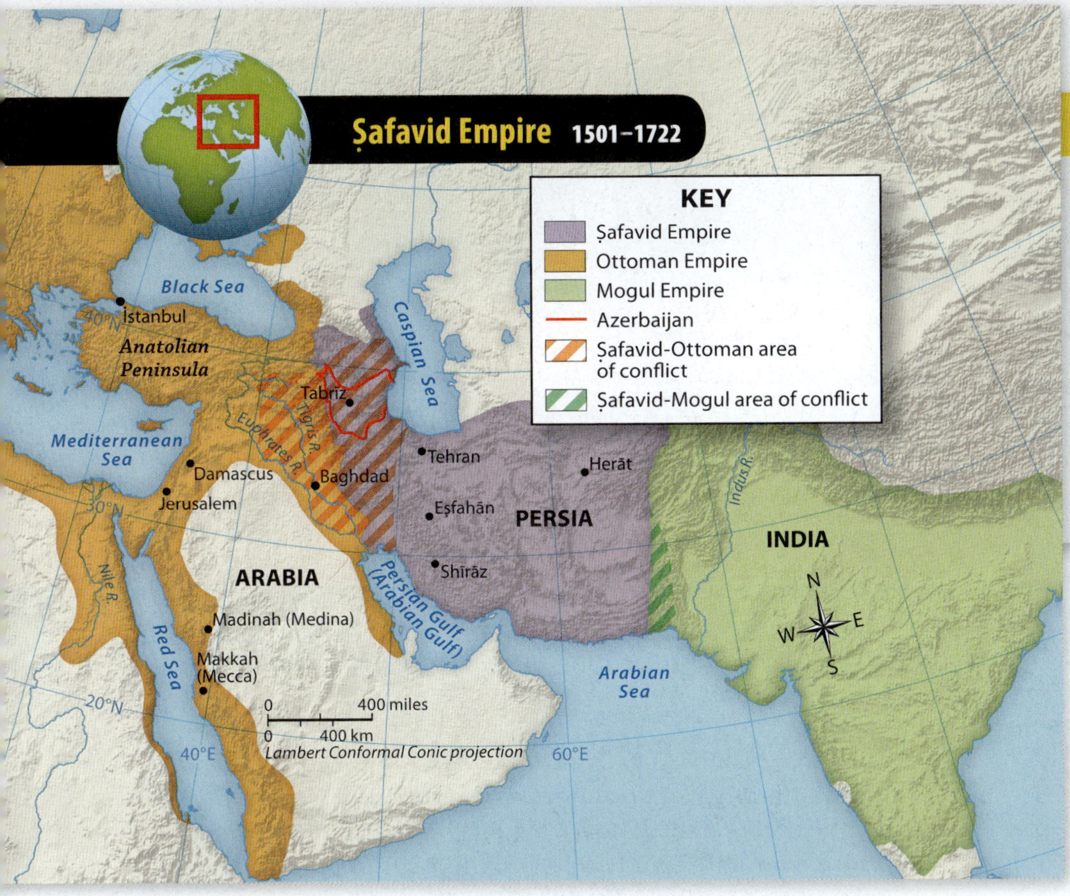

GEOGRAPHY CONNECTION

Differences between the Ṣafavids and the Ottomans led to conflict.

1. **PLACES AND REGIONS** *Which rivers flowed through the area disputed by the Ottomans and Ṣafavids?*
2. **THE WORLD IN SPATIAL TERMS** *Why would Tabrīz be a likely spot for a battle?*

Despite its trading activity, Ṣafavid Persia was probably not as prosperous as its neighbors to the east and west—the Moguls and the Ottomans. Hemmed in by European sea power to the south and the land power of the Ottomans to the west, the Ṣafavids found trade with Europe difficult.

In terms of culture, knowledge of science, medicine, and mathematics under the Ṣafavids was equal to that of other societies in the region. Persia also witnessed an extraordinary flowering of the arts during the reign of Shāh ʿAbbās. Silk weaving and carpet weaving flourished, stimulated by the great demand for Persian carpets in the West. Persian painting enjoyed a long tradition. Riza-i-Abbasi, the most famous artist of this period, created exquisite works. Soft colors and flowing movement dominated the features of Ṣafavid painting.

✓ READING PROGRESS CHECK

Differentiating What is the difference between a bazaar and a caravansary?

LESSON 2 REVIEW TEKS

Reviewing Vocabulary

1. ***Identifying*** Provide an example of a Persian shah and explain his duties and achievements.

Using Your Notes

2. ***Comparing*** Using your Venn diagram, discuss the similarities between the Ottoman and Ṣafavid empires.

Answering the Guiding Questions

3. ***Explaining*** What led to the disintegration of the Ottoman Empire?
4. ***Interpreting*** What was the source of the conflict between the Ottomans and the Ṣafavids?
5. ***Summarizing*** What was life like under the Ṣafavids?

Writing Activity

6. **ARGUMENT** Write a paragraph that supports or refutes this statement: Süleyman I was a cruel leader who was more interested in expanding his empire than in protecting or providing for his subjects.

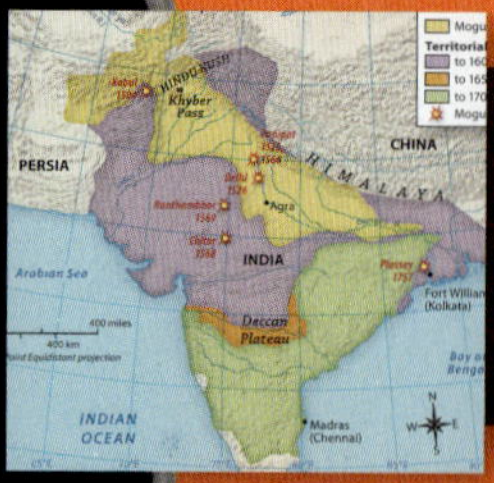

networks

There's More Online!

- BIOGRAPHY Akbar
- BIOGRAPHY Aurangzeb
- CHART/GRAPH Mogul Trade
- CHART/GRAPH Mogul Methods of Rule
- IMAGE Mogul Architecture
- IMAGE Mogul Painting
- INFOGRAPHIC Taj Mahal
- INTERACTIVE SELF-CHECK QUIZ
- MAP Mogul Empire, 1530–1707
- VIDEO The Mogul Empire

Reading HELPDESK

Academic Vocabulary

- **intelligent**
- **authority**
- **principle**

Content Vocabulary

- **zamindars**
- **suttee**

TAKING NOTES:

Key Ideas and Details

Identifying Use a chart like this one to identify Akbar's accomplishments.

	Akbar's Accomplishments
Political	
Military	
Cultural	

TEKS Texas Essential Knowledge and Skills

1B identify major causes and describe the major effects of the following events from 500 BC to AD 600: the development of the classical civilizations of Greece, Rome, Persia, India (Maurya and Gupta), China (Zhou, Qin, and Han), and the development of major world religions

continued on p. 440

LESSON 3
The Mogul Empire

ESSENTIAL QUESTIONS • *What factors help unify an empire?* • *How can the creation of a new empire impact the people and culture of a region?*

It Matters Because

Although they were not natives of India, the Moguls established a new dynasty by uniting the country under a single government with a common culture that blended Persian and Indian influences. The Mogul Empire reached its high point under the reign of Shāh Akbar.

The Mogul Dynasty

GUIDING QUESTION *How were the Moguls able to bring almost all of India under one rule?*

In 1500 the Indian subcontinent was still divided into a number of Hindu and Muslim kingdoms. The Moguls, who were descendants of the Mongols and not natives of India, established a new dynasty and brought a new era of unity to the region. They came from the mountainous region north of the Indus River valley. Their founder, Bābur, was descended from both Timur Lenk and Genghis Khan. Bābur had inherited a part of Timur Lenk's empire in an upland river valley of the Syr Dar'ya. As a youth, he led a group of warriors who seized Kabul in 1504. Thirteen years later, Bābur's forces crossed the Khyber Pass into India.

Bābur's forces were far smaller than those of his enemies, but with advanced weapons, including artillery, he captured Delhi. Establishing his power in the plains of North India, Bābur continued his conquests there until his death in 1530 at the age of 47.

Bābur's grandson Akbar was only 14 when he took the throne. **Intelligent** and industrious, by 1605 Akbar had brought Mogul rule to most of India. How was Akbar able to place almost all of India under his rule? By using heavy artillery, Akbar's armies were able to overpower the stone fortresses of their rivals. The Moguls also were successful negotiators. Akbar's conquests created the greatest Indian empire since the Mauryan dynasty. The empire appeared highly centralized but was actually a collection of semi-independent states held together by the power of the emperor.

Akbar was probably the greatest of the conquering Mogul monarchs, but he is best known for the humane character of his rule. Like all Mogul rulers, Akbar was born a Muslim, but he showed a keen interest in other religions and tolerated Hindu practices. Akbar put his policy of religious tolerance into practice by taking a Hindu princess as one of his wives.

Akbar was also tolerant in his administration of the government. The upper ranks of the government bureaucracy were filled with nonnative Muslims, but many of the lower-ranking officials were Hindus. It became common practice to give the lower-ranking officials plots of farmland for their temporary use. These local officials, known as **zamindars**, kept a portion of the taxes paid by the peasants in lieu of a salary. They were then expected to forward the rest of the taxes from the lands under their control to the central government. Zamindars came to exercise considerable power and **authority** in their local districts.

The Akbar era was a time of progress, at least by the standards of the day. Indian peasants were required to pay about one-third of their annual harvest to the state, but the system was applied justly. When bad weather struck in the 1590s, taxes were reduced or suspended. Thanks to a long period of peace and political stability, trade and manufacturing flourished.

The era was an especially prosperous one in the area of foreign trade. Indian goods, notably textiles, tropical food products and spices, and precious stones, were exported in exchange for gold and silver. Arab traders handled much of the foreign trade because the Indians, like their Mogul rulers, did not care for travel by sea.

Akbar died in 1605 and was succeeded by his son Jahāngīr (juh • HAHN • gihr). During the early years of his reign, he continued to strengthen the central government's control over his vast empire. Eventually, however, his grip began to weaken when he fell under the influence of one of his wives, Persian-born Nūr Jahān. As Jahāngīr slowly lost interest in governing, he gave more authority to Nūr Jahān. The empress used her position to enrich her own family. She arranged the marriage of her niece to her husband's third son and successor, Shāh Jahān.

During his reign from 1628 to 1658, Shāh Jahān maintained the political system established by earlier Mogul rulers. He also expanded the boundaries of the empire through successful campaigns in the Deccan Plateau. Shāh Jahān's rule, however, was marred by his failure to deal with growing domestic problems. He had inherited a nearly empty treasury. His military campaigns and expensive building projects put a heavy strain on the imperial finances and compelled him to raise taxes. The peasants were even more deprived as a result of these taxes. The majority of Jahān's subjects lived in poverty.

Shāh Jahān's troubles worsened with his illness in the mid-1650s. It was widely reported that he had died. Such news led to a struggle for power among his sons. The victorious son, Aurangzeb, had his brother put to death and imprisoned his father. Aurangzeb then had himself crowned emperor in 1658.

Aurangzeb is one of the most controversial rulers in the history of India. During his reign, the empire reached its greatest physical size. He had expanded it along nearly all of its boundaries. Constant warfare and religious intolerance, however, made his subjects resentful.

As a man of high **principle,** Aurangzeb attempted to eliminate many of what he considered to be India's social evils. He forbade the custom of

Analyzing Primary Sources

Jahāngīr on Akbar

“In his actions and his movements, Akbar was not as ordinary men. The glory of God was manifest in him. He knew no fear and was always ready to risk his life in battle. With exquisite courtesy, he charmed all those that approached him.”

—quoted in *A Brief History of India*

DBQ ***DRAWING CONCLUSIONS***
How do the qualities Jahāngīr attributes to his father explain Akbar's success as a ruler?

intelligent having a high degree of understanding and mental capacity

zamindar a local official in Mogul India who received a plot of farmland for temporary use in return for collecting taxes for the central government

▼ Officials pay homage to Akbar in the *Akbarnama* (*History of Akbar*).

authority power; person in command

principle a fundamental law or idea; when said of people (e.g., someone is highly principled), it means a devotion to high codes or rules of conduct

suttee the Hindu custom of cremating a widow on her husband's funeral pyre

suttee, which required a wife to throw herself on her dead husband's funeral pyre and was practiced by many Hindus, and he put a stop to the levying of illegal taxes. He tried to forbid gambling and drinking as well.

Aurangzeb was a devout Muslim and adopted a number of measures that reversed the Mogul policies of religious tolerance. For instance, he prohibited the building of new Hindu temples and forced Hindus to convert to Islam. Aurangzeb's policies led to Hindu outcries and a number of revolts against imperial authority.

After Aurangzeb's death in 1707, there were many contenders for the throne. Their reigns were short-lived, however. India was increasingly divided and vulnerable to attack from abroad. In 1739, Delhi was sacked by the Persians, who left it in ashes.

✓ **READING PROGRESS CHECK**

Contrasting What were some differences between the rules of Shāh Jahān and Aurangzeb?

Life in Mogul India

GUIDING QUESTION ***What was life like in Mogul society?***

The Moguls were foreigners in India. In addition, they were Muslims ruling a largely Hindu population. The resulting blend of influences on the lives of ordinary Indians could be complicated. The treatment of women serves as a good example.

Women had long played an active role in Mogul tribal society. Mogul rulers often relied on female relatives for political advice. To a degree, these Mogul attitudes toward women affected Indian society. Women from aristocratic families frequently received salaries and were allowed to own land.

At the same time, the Moguls placed certain restrictions on women under their interpretations of Islamic law. These practices generally were adopted by Hindus. The practice of isolating women, for example, was followed by many upper-class Hindus.

In other ways, however, Hindu practices remained unchanged by Mogul rule. The custom of suttee continued in spite of efforts by the Moguls to abolish it. Child marriage also remained common.

The Mogul era saw the emergence of a wealthy nobility and a prosperous merchant class. During the late eighteenth century, this prosperity was shaken by the decline of the Moguls and the arrival of the British. However, many prominent Indians had trading ties with foreigners.

A new and beautiful architectural style emerged, which reflected the merger of Persian and Indian cultural influences within Mogul India. This style is best symbolized by the Taj Mahal, which Shāh Jahān built in Agra in the mid-seventeenth century. The project lasted more than twenty years. To finance it, the government raised land taxes, driving many Indian peasants into complete poverty.

The Taj Mahal is widely considered to be the most beautiful building in India, if not in the entire world. The building is monumental in size and boasts nearly blinding brilliance yet delicate lightness.

Another major artistic achievement of the Mogul period was in painting. Like architecture, painting in Mogul India resulted from the blending of two cultures: Persian and Indian. Akbar established a state workshop for artists, mostly Hindus, who worked under the guidance of Persian masters to

(continued from p. 438)

TEKS **Texas Essential Knowledge and Skills**

1C identify major causes and describe the major effects of the following important turning points in world history from 600 to 1450 the spread of Christianity, the decline of Rome and the formation o medieval Europe; the development of Islamic caliphates and their impact on Asia, Africa, and Europe; the Mongol invasions and their impact on Europe, China, India, and Southwest Asia

23A describe the historical origins, central ideas, and spread of major religious and philosophical traditions, including Buddhism, Christianity, Confucianism, Hinduism, Islam, Judaism, Sikhism, and the development of monotheism

24A describe the changing roles of women, children, and families during major eras of world history

25D explain how Islam influences law and government in the Muslim world

26B analyze examples of how art, architecture, literature, music, and drama reflect the history of the cultures in which they are produced create the Mogul school of painting. Much like all of Mogul culture, the "Akbar style" combined Persian with Indian motifs. It included the portrayal of humans in action, a charac-teristic not usually seen in Persian art.

✓ **READING PROGRESS CHECK**

Explaining What rights were enjoyed and what restrictions were imposed on upper-class women during the Mogul Empire?

The Development of Sikhism

GUIDING QUESTION ***What is the significance of Gurus to the Sikh religious tradition?***

According to Sikh (pronounced "Sik-kh", with a short "i" sound) tradition, during the rule of Bābur a man named Nanak (1469–1539) had a religious vision at the age of twenty-nine or thirty. Nanak (NA • nahk) lived in the Punjab (PUHN–JAB), a region of South Asia that was ruled by the Moguls. The Punjab was an especially diverse environment with Muslims, Hindus, Buddhists, and Jains living in the region. Guru Nanak had a vision in which God revealed that everyone is a child of God and all faiths are different paths towards the same Creator.

Nanak then travelled widely, preaching a monotheistic message that emphasized devotion to a formless, infinite One (or single God) that can be found in everyone and in all of nature. Guru Nanak taught that God is formless, all-powerful, all-loving, and without fear or hate towards anyone. One can achieve unity with God through service to humanity, meditation, and honest labor. Nanak prohibited discrimination on the basis of caste, race, religion, or gender. His direct teaching style and focus on equality drew many followers who became known as Sikhs, from a Punjabi word meaning "disciple."

Nanak is regarded as the first Guru (GUR • oo), or spiritual leader in the Sikh tradition. His teachings and those of his successors were compiled by the fifth Guru, Guru Arjan (1563–1606), into a holy book called the Adi Granth. Guru Arjan also built Darbar Sahib (later known at the Golden Temple), an important Sikh house of worship, in the city of Amritsar, Punjab.

Nine Gurus followed Nanak until the Tenth Guru, Guru Gobind Singh (1666–1708), appointed the Sikh holy text and the community as his successors. Along with passing his authority to the holy book, now known as the Guru Granth Sahib, Singh also established the Khalsa, a community of initiated Sikhs. All initiated Sikhs display the signs of the Khalsa (KAL • suh), popularly called the "five Ks." These are: 1) Kesh, uncut hair covered by a special turban; 2) Kanga, comb for the hair; 3) Kirpan, a short ceremonial sword; 4) Kara, a metal bracelet; and 5) Kachera, traditional underwear.

Sikhs initially experienced hostility and persecution from Mogul officials. Slowly, however, Sikhs built a strong religious and economic community and, in the middle of the eighteenth century, created an independent kingdom in the Punjab.

Today, Sikhism is the world's fifth-largest religion with more than 20 million followers in India and Pakistan. Worldwide, there are an additional 2 million Sikhs, including more than 200,000 estimated to be living the United States. Sikhism favors moral living, careful study and intellectual achievement, hard work, charity, and equality of all humans regardless of class or beliefs.

✓ **READING PROGRESS CHECK**

Describing How did the Sikh religion spread?

Sikhism

Vaisakhi is a significant Punjabi and Sikh festival in April. Sikhs celebrate Vaisakhi as the day Guru Gobind Singh, the 10th Guru, established the Khalsa, the community of people who have been initiated into the Sikh religion. In Punjab, Vaisakhi is celebrated as the New Year and the beginning of the harvest season.

Sacred Symbol

One of the sacred symbols of the Sikhs is the *khanda*. It is composed of four traditional Sikh weapons.

Sikhism emerged in the mid-1400s in the Punjab, a region of northwest India. Sikhism is a distinct and independent religion that arose out of the teachings of Guru Nanak. Sikh tradition says that Guru Nanak's teachings were revealed directly to him by God. Sikhs believe in one God who is formless, all-powerful, all-loving, and without fear or hate towards anyone. One can achieve unity with God through service to humanity, meditation, and honest labor.

Sikhism is the world's fifth-largest religion with 27 million followers. Most Sikhs live in India and Pakistan, though over 2 million live elsewhere around the world.

Central Symbol

Ek Onkar is one of the central Sikh symbols. It represents the belief that there is one God for all people, regardless of religion, gender, race, or culture.

Sacred Text

The primary sacred text for Sikhs is the Guru Granth Sahib. Compiled from the mid-1500s through the 1600s, it includes contributions from Sikh Gurus and from some persons also claimed as saints by Hindus and Muslims, such as Namdev, Ravidas, and Kabir.

"Enshrine the Lord's Name within your heart.
The Word of the Guru's Bani prevails
throughout the world, through this Bani, the
Lord's name is obtained."

—Guru Amar Das, page 1066

Sikh men often wear long beards and cover their heads with turbans.

Sacred Site

Darbar Sahib (also known as the Golden Temple) is located in Amritsar, Punjab. It is one of the most popular Sikh houses of worship because of its historical significance.

Europeans Come to India

GUIDING QUESTION *What led to the decline of the Mogul Empire?*

▲ The Taj Mahal in Agra is a classic example of Mogul architecture.

The arrival of the British hastened the decline of the Mogul Empire. By 1650, British trading forts had been established at Surat, Fort William (which was renamed Calcutta and is now the city of Kolkata), and Madras (Chennai). British ships carried Indian-made cotton goods to the East Indies, where they were traded for spices.

British success in India attracted rivals, especially the French. The French established their own forts, many of them along the coast. For a brief period, the French went on the offensive, even capturing the British fort at Madras.

The British were saved by the military genius of Sir Robert Clive, an aggressive British empire builder. Clive served as the chief representative in India of the East India Company, a private company that acted on behalf of the British Crown. Clive's forces ultimately restricted the French to a few small territories.

While fighting the French, Clive was also consolidating British control in Bengal. The Indian ruler of Bengal had attacked Fort William in 1756. He had imprisoned the British garrison in the "Black Hole of Calcutta," an underground prison. Due to the intense heat in the crowded space, only 23 people (out of 146) survived.

In 1757 Clive led a small British force of about 3,000 to victory over a Mogul-led army more than 10 times its size in the Battle of Plassey in Bengal. As part of the spoils of victory, the failing Mogul court gave the East India Company the power to collect taxes from lands in the area around Calcutta.

Britain's rise to power in India, however, was not a story of constant success. The arrogance and incompetence of many East India Company officials offended their Indian allies. Such behavior also alienated the local population, who were taxed heavily to meet the East India Company's growing expenses.

In the late eighteenth century, the East India Company moved inland from the bustling coastal cities. British expansion brought great riches to individual British merchants. British officials also became wealthy as they found they could obtain money from local rulers by selling trade privileges. The British were in India to stay.

✓ **READING PROGRESS CHECK**

Summarizing How did Sir Robert Clive increase the power of the British in India?

LESSON 3 REVIEW TEKS

Reviewing Vocabulary

1. ***Explaining*** Describe the duties and rewards of a zamindar in the Mogul system of governing.

Using Your Notes

2. ***Summarizing*** Describe the rule of Akbar using the information compiled in your graphic organizer.

Answering the Guiding Questions

3. ***Identifying*** How were the Moguls able to bring almost all of India under one rule?

4. ***Analyzing*** What was life like in Mogul society?

5. ***Identifying Cause and Effect*** What led to the decline of the Mogul Empire?

Writing Activity

6. **INFORMATIVE/EXPLANATORY** Using descriptive terms, write a paragraph on the reasons for the decline of the Mogul Empire beginning with Shāh Jahān.

CHAPTER 19 Assessment

TEKS

Directions: On a separate sheet of paper, answer the questions below. Make sure you read carefully and answer all parts of the questions.

Lesson Review

Lesson 1

1. ***Describing*** What elite force comprised the Ottoman military? How did they serve the Ottoman state?
2. ***Identifying*** Why was the Ottoman Empire often called a "gunpowder empire"?
3. ***Describing*** How did the Mongolian invasions indirectly lead to the rise of the Ottoman Empire? **1C, 1D**
4. ***Describing*** Describe key positions in the Ottoman system of rule including the sultan, grand vizier, and pashas.
5. ***Explaining*** What impact did the Ottoman Empire have on eastern Europe? **7D**
6. ***Explaining*** What name did the Ottomans give Constantinople after they crushed the Byzantine Empire?
7. ***Summarizing*** How did the Ottoman Turks draw upon Byzantine architectural style?

Lesson 2

8. ***Compare and Contrast*** How did Islam impact law in the Şafavid Empire? **25D**
9. ***Analyzing*** What impact did the Shia faith of the Şafavids have on the empire?
10. ***Explaining*** Explain why, despite trading activities, Safavid Persia had difficulty attaining greater success through trading.

Lesson 3

11. ***Describing*** How did the Mongolian invasions impact India? **1C**
12. ***Identifying*** What are the origins and central ideas of Sikhism? How did the Mogul Empire impact the development of Sikhism? **23A**
13. ***Identifying*** During the Mogul Dynasty in India, what Indian products were valued as items of trade by Arab traders, and what was received in exchange for the goods?
14. ***Interpreting*** How might you interpret the historical information that shows that the Moguls as Muslim rulers caused only minor shifts in cultural practices of Indians, who were mainly Hindus?
15. ***Naming*** Which cultural influences did the Moguls bring together as they developed a new architecture style and create structures, such as the Taj Mahal?

Exploring the Essential Questions

16. ***Identifying*** Work with a partner to identify the factors that unified the Ottoman, Şafavid, and Mogul Empires at their heights. Create a three-circle Venn diagram and record factors that are independent to each empire as well as those they have in common.
17. ***Describe*** Assume the role of a specific inhabitant of either the Ottoman Empire or the Mogul Empire during a specific year in its history. Use details about the Ottoman or Mogul Empire to describe how its rule would have impacted this person's life at that time such as Hungary in 1526 or 1550, or Istanbul in 1650. **1D**

Critical Thinking

18. ***Evaluating*** In what ways were family relations significant to the rule and leadership within the Ottoman system of rule and who acquired power by way of family line?
19. ***Assessing*** Write a paragraph that explains how Mogul Akbar-style painting reflects the culture in which it was produced. **26B**
20. ***Interpreting*** From what you've read and learned, was there religious tolerance within Ottoman society for those who practiced a religion other than Islam? Explain why or why not.

Need Extra Help?

If You've Missed Question	1	2	3	4	5	6	7	8	9	10	11	12	13	14	15	16	17	18	19	20
Go to page	430	431	430	432	431	431	433	435	435	437	438	441	439	440	440	430	430	432	440	432

21 ***Constructing Arguments*** Write an argument in which you identify the most significant effect the rise of the Ottoman Empire had and support it with evidence. **1D**

22 ***Identifying Central Issues*** Describe the religious issues within the Şafavid Empire in the 1500s.

23 ***Making Connections*** How did British military leader Sir Robert Clive impact France's presence and future in India?

Social Studies Skills

24 ***Compare and Contrast*** How did the role of women change under Şafavid and Mogul rule? **25D**

25 ***Identifying Cause and Effect*** What impact did the rise of the Ottoman Empire have on global trade? Identify a series of causes and effects in your response. **7D**

26 ***Using Geography Skills*** Generate a map showing the Ottoman efforts to pursue European lands and indicate the push back from Hungary and other European countries, such as Spain, that blockaded the Ottomans from stretching into European territory.

27 ***Analyzing Information*** Create a time line showing key events of the recounting of the conflicts between the Ottomans and Şafavid empire, the rise of the Şafavid empire, and points along its decline. **29F**

28 ***Creating Presentations*** Choose two significant architectural structures that were designed and built during this era. Research and write about the design, method of construction, and purpose for the people who lived during its construction. Share similarities and differences between the two structures. Use illustration, computer graphics, photographic images, or a combination of these options within your presentation. **30C**

DBQ Analyzing Primary Sources

Use the document to answer the following questions.

Sir John Chardin, a Frenchman, took two six-year trips through the Şafavid Empire, one during the reign of Shāh Abbās II and one after the death of Shāh Abbās II. Chardin described the changes between his two trips.

PRIMARY SOURCE

> "Counting from that time to this, the riches seemed to be half diminished, with so little an interval as twelve years time only. Even the coin itself was altered. There was no such thing as good silver to be seen. The grandees being impoverished, exacted upon the people and peeled them of their fortunes. The people, to ward against the impressions of the great, were become cheats and sharpers, and from thence all the ill tricking ways that could be were introduced into the art of trade and commerce. There are too many examples throughout the world which show that even the fertility of the soil and the plenty of a country depends on the good order of a just and moderate government, and exactly regulated according to the laws."
>
> —from *Sir John Chardin's Travels in Persia*

29 ***Identifying Perspectives*** What changes in money and trade did Chardin observe during his two trips through the Şafavid Empire? Does his perception of when the dynasty lost its vigor agree with that of Lesson 2?

30 ***Making Inferences*** What does Chardin's final sentence imply about his opinion of the Şafavid Empire during his second trip?

31 ***Theorizing*** What can you theorize about opportunities for production and sale of goods, if so many people lived from cheating?

Need Extra Help?

If You've Missed Question	21	22	23	24	25	26	27	28	29	30	31
Go to page	430	436	443	436	430	430	434	433	445	445	445

Analyzing Visuals

Use the image to answer the following questions.

This image shows the Süleymaniye Mosque, also known as the "Blue Mosque," in Istanbul. The Ottoman Turks built it between 1550 and 1557.

32 ***Identifying*** Which culture influenced the Blue Mosque's large central dome and open floor plan, also present in the Hagia Sophia?

33 ***Analyzing Visuals*** How does the architecture of the Blue Mosque reflect the history of the culture in which it was produced? **26B**

34 ***Making Generalizations*** Based on this significant architectural construction by the Ottoman Turks, make a generalization about this society's intermix of religion, government, and large-scale regime construction projects.

Extended Response Question

35 ***Expository*** Write an essay that compares and contrasts the ways in which each of the three Muslim Empires—Ottoman, Şafavid, and Mogul—rose to power and ruled over vast territories. The essay should include an introduction, at least three paragraphs, and a conclusion that supports your main idea. Use information gathered from primary and secondary sources to support your answer. **1D**

Need Extra Help?

If You've Missed Question	32	33	34	35
Go to page	433	433	433	430

The East Asian World

1400–1800

ESSENTIAL QUESTIONS • *What factors help unify a kingdom or dynasty?* • *How can external forces influence a kingdom or dynasty?*

networks

There's More Online! about the East Asian world.

CHAPTER 20

The Story Matters...

In 1644 Manchu invaders from north of China founded the Qing dynasty. The Manchu were the most successful foreign conquerors in Chinese history and the Qing dynasty would rule China until 1911. Rulers such as Kangxi believed they were meant to restore China's greatness, and for two centuries they succeeded. It was during the Qing dynasty that Europeans gained their first in-depth look at the brilliance of Chinese civilization.

◀ This portrait shows Kangxi at about the age of 60, near the end of his reign. Although he was eager to learn about the science and technology of the West, he also feared the problems that contact with Europeans might bring to China.

PHOTO: CORBIS

CHAPTER 20

Place and Time: East Asia 1400–1800

Strong rulers dominated East Asia between 1400 and 1800. Under the Ming and Qing dynasties, China flourished politically, economically, and culturally. At the end of the sixteenth century, powerful Japanese leaders reunified Japan and established the Tokugawa shogunate. The renowned Yi dynasty in Korea struggled to maintain its independence from China and Japan. In Southeast Asia, mainland and island kingdoms adopted different styles of ruling, depending on their religion and culture. Throughout East Asia, the arrival of European missionaries and merchants represented a social and cultural challenge.

Step Into the Place

Read the quotes and look at the information presented on the map.

DBQ **Analyzing Historical Documents** Draw a conclusion about the concerns East Asian governments had about contact with Europeans.

PRIMARY SOURCE

"Since I discovered on the Southern Tour of 1703 that there were [Christian] missionaries wandering at will over China, I had grown cautious and determined to control them more tightly: to bunch them in the larger cities and in groups that included men from several different [European] countries, to catalogue their names and residences, and to permit no new establishments without my express permission. For with so many Westerners coming to China it has been hard to distinguish the real missionaries from other white men pretending to be missionaries."

—quoted in *Emperor of China: Self-portrait of K'ang-hsi* [Kangxi]

PRIMARY SOURCE

"**1.** Japanese ships are strictly forbidden to leave for foreign countries.

2. No Japanese is permitted to go abroad. If there is anyone who attempts to do so secretly, he must be executed. . . .

3. If any Japanese returns from overseas after residing there, he must be put to death. . . .

7. If there are any Southern Barbarians [Europeans] who propagate the teachings of the priests, or otherwise commit crimes, they may be incarcerated in the prison. . . ."

—Tokugawa Iemitsu, from Closed Country Edict of 1635

Step Into the Time

Demonstrating Understanding Research one or more publications from the time. Write a short essay explaining how the publication(s) influenced society

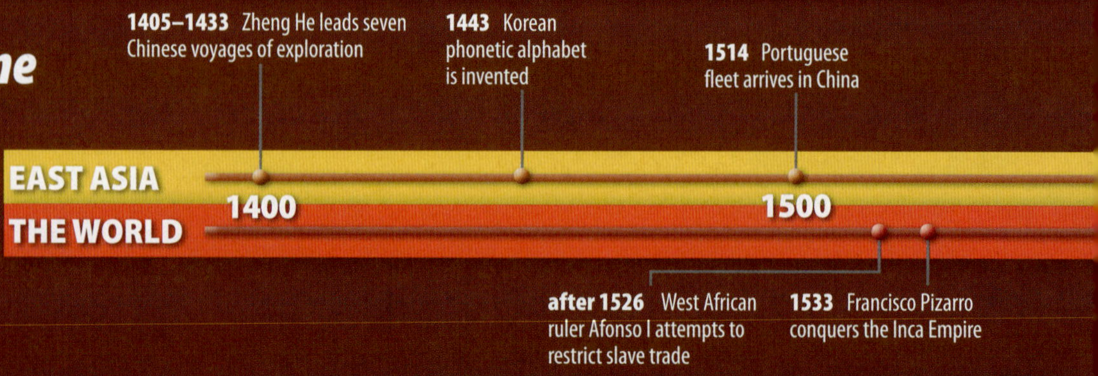

networks
There's More Online!

- ☑ **MAP** Explore the interactive version of this map on Networks.
- ☑ **TIME LINE** Explore the interactive version of the time line on Networks.

Trade Centers and Trade Routes in Southeast Asia 1770

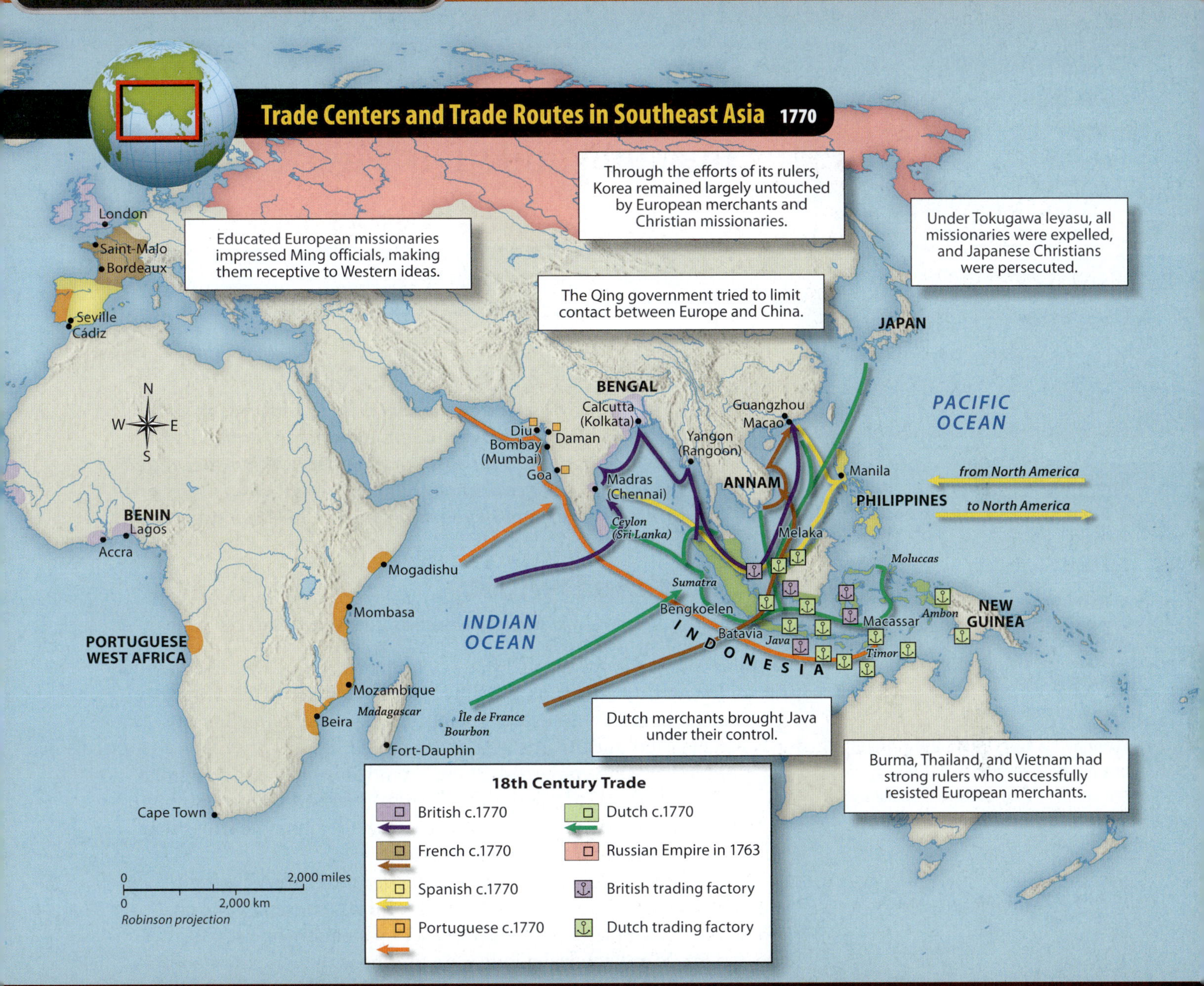

- **1603** Tokugawa shogunate begins in Japan
- **1619** Dutch establish fort at Batavia on Java
- **1644** China's Ming dynasty is overthrown; Qing dynasty succeeds
- **1661** Kangxi, the greatest Qing emperor, comes to the throne
- **1679** Matsuo Bashō writes his first haiku in Japan
- **1791** Cao Xueqin's novel *The Dream of the Red Chamber* is published in China
- **1793** Lord Macartney leads British trade mission to China

1600 | **1700** | **1800**

- **1555** Peace of Augsburg divides Christianity in Germany
- **1566** Ottoman sultan Süleyman I dies
- **1618** Thirty Years' War begins
- **1623** Shakespeare's First Folio is published
- **1661** Louis XIV begins absolutist rule in France
- **1664** England seizes Dutch New Netherland colony
- **1707** Aurangzeb, the last great Mogul emperor, dies

networks

There's More Online!

- BIOGRAPHY Kangxi
- BIOGRAPHY Qianlong
- BIOGRAPHY Yong Le
- CHART/GRAPH Culture in China
- INTERACTIVE SELF-CHECK QUIZ
- MAP The Great Wall of China
- MAP Voyages of Zheng He
- PRIMARY SOURCE Qianlong's Letter to King George III
- SLIDE SHOW Art and Literature During the Ming and Qing Dynasties
- VIDEO The Ming Dynasty

LESSON 1

The Ming and Qing Dynasties

ESSENTIAL QUESTIONS • *What factors help unify a kingdom or dynasty?* • *How can external forces influence a kingdom or dynasty?*

Reading HELPDESK

Academic Vocabulary

- **series**
- **perspective**

Content Vocabulary

- **queue**
- **clan**
- **porcelain**
- **isolationist**

TAKING NOTES:

Key Ideas and Details

Comparing and Contrasting Use a graphic organizer like this one to compare and contrast the achievements of the Ming and Qing dynasties.

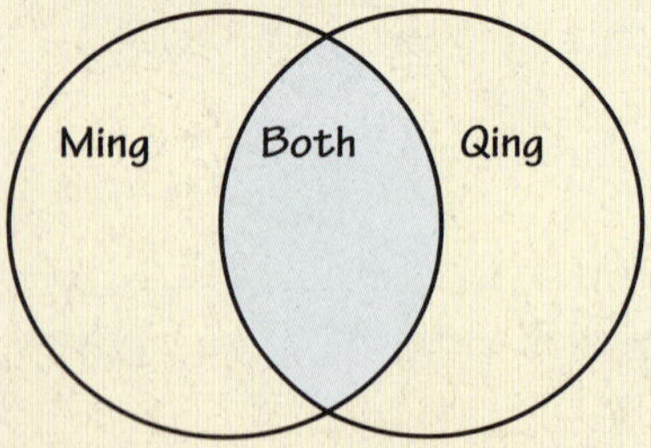

TEKS Texas Essential Knowledge and Skills

1D identify major causes and describe the major effects of the following important turning points in world history from 1450 to 1750: the rise of the Ottoman Empire, the influence of the Ming dynasty on world trade, European exploration and the Columbian Exchange, European expansion, and the Renaissance and the Reformation

continued on the next page

IT MATTERS BECAUSE

The Ming dynasty began a new era of greatness in China, bringing effective government, expansion, and cultural advancements. Under the Qing dynasty, which succeeded the Ming, China continued to prosper, but Qing limits on foreign trade would eventually harm China economically.

The Ming Dynasty

GUIDING QUESTION *What were the achievements of the Ming dynasty?*

The Mongol dynasty in China was overthrown in 1368. The founder of the new dynasty took the title of Ming Hong Wu (the Ming Martial Emperor). This was the beginning of the Ming dynasty, which lasted until 1644.

Under Ming emperors, China extended its rule into Mongolia and central Asia. Along the northern frontier, the Chinese strengthened the Great Wall and made peace with the nomadic tribes that had troubled them for many centuries.

At home, Ming rulers ran an effective government using a centralized bureaucracy staffed with officials chosen by the civil service examination system. They set up a nationwide school system. Manufactured goods were produced in workshops and factories in vastly higher numbers. New crops were introduced, which greatly increased food production. The Ming rulers also renovated the Grand Canal, making it possible to ship grain and other goods from southern to northern China. The Ming dynasty truly began a new era of greatness in Chinese history.

Ming Hong Wu ruled from 1368 until 1398. After his death, his son Yong Le became emperor. In 1406 Yong Le began construction of the Imperial City in Beijing (BAY • JIHNG). In 1421 he moved the capital from Nanjing to Beijing. The Imperial City was created to convey power and prestige. It is an immense complex of palaces and temples surrounded by six and one-half miles of walls. Because it was off-limits to commoners, it was known as the Forbidden City.

During his reign, Yong Le also sent a **series** of naval voyages into the wider world. Led by the court official Zheng He (JUHNG • HUH), seven voyages were made between 1405 and 1433. These voyages explored the coasts of western India, Southeast Asia, and East Africa, returning with items unknown in China and with information about the outside world.

series a group of related things or events

In 1514 a Portuguese fleet arrived off the coast of China. It was the first direct contact between the Chinese Empire and Europe since the journeys of Marco Polo. At the time, the Ming government thought little of their arrival. China was at the height of its power, and from the **perspective** of the emperor, the Europeans were only an unusual form of barbarian. To the Chinese ruler, the rulers of all other countries were simply "younger brothers" of the Chinese emperor, who was seen as the Son of Heaven.

perspective viewpoint

China had goods the Western world wanted, such as silk, porcelain, and cotton. The Ming dynasty had little interest in European goods, except for the silver from Spanish and Portuguese mines in the New World. The Ming dynasty used silver as its primary means of exchange and demand for it in China was high. This demand led to a system of exchange that had a significant impact on global trade. The demand for silver in China was so great, for instance, that the majority of silver mined in the New World went directly to Ming dynasty markets.

Ming dynasty emperors had mixed attitudes toward trade and exploration. While Emperor Yong Le encouraged trade and exploration, most Ming emperors were inward looking and **isolationist**. As many Ming emperors withdrew their support for trade outside China many European states and merchants took their place. This allowed Europeans to gain a trading foothold in east Asia.

isolationist a national policy of abstaining from political or economic relations with other countries

In addition to material trade was the exchange of ideas. Christian missionaries made the long voyage to China on European merchant ships. Many of them were highly educated men who brought along instruments, such as clocks, that impressed Chinese officials and made them more receptive to Western ideas.

Both sides benefited from this early cultural exchange. Chinese scholars marveled at their ability to read better with European eyeglasses. Christian missionaries were impressed with the teachings of Confucius, the printing and availability of books, and Chinese architecture.

(continued from p. 450)

TEKS **Texas Essential Knowledge and Skills**

7E explain Ming China's impact on global trade

26C identify examples of art, music, and literature that transcend the cultures in which they were created and convey universal themes

After a period of prosperity and growth, the Ming dynasty gradually began to decline. Government corruption rose and. high taxes, caused in part by this corruption, led to peasant unrest. Crop yields declined because of harsh weather. In the 1630s, a major epidemic greatly reduced the population in many areas. The suffering caused by the epidemic helped spark a peasant revolt began in central China and then spread to the rest of the country. In 1644 peasant forces occupied the capital of Beijing, and the last Ming emperor committed suicide in the palace gardens.

The overthrow of the Ming dynasty created an opportunity for the Manchus. They were a farming and hunting people who lived northeast of the Great Wall in the area known today as Manchuria. The forces of the Manchus conquered Beijing, and Li Zicheng's army fell. The victorious Manchus then declared the creation of a new dynasty called the Qing (CHIHNG), meaning "pure." This dynasty, created in 1644, remained in power until 1911.

▼ A section of the Imperial City in Beijing, China

✓ **READING PROGRESS CHECK**

Evaluating Explain the importance of three achievements of the Ming dynasty.

The Qing Dynasty

GUIDING QUESTION *How did the Qing dynasty adapt to become successful?*

queue the braided pigtail that was traditionally worn by Chinese males

When some Chinese resisted their new rulers and seized the island of Taiwan, the Manchu government prepared to attack them. To identify the rebels, the government ordered all males to adopt Manchu dress and hairstyles. They had to shave their foreheads and braid their hair into a pigtail called a **queue**. Those who refused were assumed to be rebels and were executed: "Lose your hair or lose your head."

Gradually accepted as legitimate rulers, the Qing flourished under a series of strong early rulers who pacified the country, corrected serious social and economic ills, and restored peace and prosperity. The Qing maintained the Ming political system but faced one major problem: The Manchus were ethnically and culturally different from their subject population. The Qing rulers dealt with this reality in two ways.

First, the Qing tried to preserve their distinct identity within Chinese society. The Manchus, only 2 percent of the population, were defined legally as distinct from everyone else in China. The Manchu nobility maintained large landholdings and received revenues from the state treasury. Second, the Qing dealt with this problem by bringing Chinese into the imperial administration to win their support. Chinese held more than 80 percent of lower posts, but a much smaller share of the top positions.

Kangxi (KAHNG • SHEE), who ruled from 1661 to 1722, was perhaps the greatest of the emperors who ruled China during the Ming and Qing dynasties. A person with political skill and a strong character, Kangxi took charge of the government while still in his teens and reigned for 61 years.

Kangxi rose at dawn and worked until late at night. He wrote: "One act of negligence may cause sorrow all through the country, and one moment of negligence may result in trouble for thousands of generations." Kangxi calmed the unrest along the northern and western frontiers by force. As a patron of the arts and letters, he gained the support of scholars in China.

In 1689, during Kangxi's reign, China and Russia signed the Treaty of Nerchinsk. Beginning in the 1620s, Russian traders had pushed eastward into land under China's protection in search of trade routes and goods. The treaty stopped Russia's push east, ended the frontier wars, and established trade between the two empires. This gave the Russians a special status with the Qing. Other European powers were limited to trade at certain ports.

Also during Kangxi's reign, the efforts of Christian missionaries reached their height. The emperor was quite tolerant of the Christians. Several hundred officials became Catholics, as did an estimated 300,000 ordinary Chinese. Ultimately, however, the Christian effort was undermined by squabbling among the Western religious orders. After the death of Kangxi, his successor began to suppress Christian activities.

✓ **READING PROGRESS CHECK**

Categorizing Explain how Kangxi exemplifies the adaptability of the Qing leaders.

Europeans in China

GUIDING QUESTION *How did the changing economy affect society during the Ming and Qing dynasties?*

Under Qianlong (CHEE • UHN • LUNG), who ruled from 1736 to 1795, the Qing dynasty experienced the greatest period of prosperity and reached its greatest physical size. It was during this great reign, however, that the first signs of decay appeared. Why did this happen?

As the emperor grew older, he fell under the influence of destructive elements at court. Corrupt officials and higher taxes led to unrest in rural areas. Population growth also exerted pressure on the land and led to economic hardship. In central China, unhappy peasants launched a revolt, the White Lotus Rebellion (1796–1804). The revolt was suppressed, but the expenses of war weakened the Qing dynasty.

Unfortunately for China, the Qing dynasty was declining just as Europe was seeking more trade. At first, the Qing government sold trade privileges to the Europeans, but to limit contacts between Europeans and Chinese, the Qing confined all European traders to a small island just outside Guangzhou. Traders could reside there only between October and March and deal only with a limited number of Chinese firms licensed by the government.

At first, the British accepted this system. By the end of the eighteenth century, however, some British traders had begun to demand access to additional cities, as Russian traders already enjoyed, along the Chinese coast. Likewise, the Chinese government was under pressure from its own merchants to open China to British manufactured goods.

Britain had an unfavorable, or negative, trade balance with China. That is, Britain imported more goods from China than it exported to the country. For years, Britain had imported tea, silk, and **porcelain** from the Chinese. To pay for these imports, Britain had sent Indian cotton to China, but this did not cover the entire debt, and the British had to pay for their imports with silver. The British sent ever-increasing quantities of silver to China, especially in exchange for tea, which was in great demand by the British.

In 1793 a British mission led by Lord George Macartney visited Beijing to seek more liberal trade policies. However, Emperor Qianlong responded that China had no need of "your country's manufactures."

✓ READING PROGRESS CHECK

Constructing a Thesis How did the Qing dynasty adapt to the presence of Europeans?

SKILLS PRACTICE

Review the lesson text looking for connecting words such as *and, but, because, also,* and ranking numbers. Classify these words by the type of connection they show such as comparison, sequence, or cause. For example, in the sentence "Crop yields declined because of harsh weather" the word *because* would be classified as a connecting word showing cause.

porcelain a ceramic material made of fine clay baked at very high temperatures

GEOGRAPHY CONNECTION

China expanded its borders during the Ming and Qing dynasties.

1. **THE WORLD IN SPATIAL TERMS** ***How large was the Qing Dynasty in comparison to the Ming?***
2. **HUMAN SYSTEMS** ***How did the location of the rebellion of Li Zicheng help the Qing conquest of Ming China?***

Economy and Daily Life

GUIDING QUESTION *How did the changing economy affect society during the Ming and Qing dynasties?*

Between 1500 and 1800, China remained a mostly agricultural society. Nearly 85 percent of the people were small farmers. Nevertheless, the Chinese economy was changing.

The first change for China involved an increase in population, from less than 80 million in 1390 to more than 300 million at the end of the 1700s. The increase had several causes. These included a long period of stability under the early Qing dynasty and improvements in the food supply due to a faster growing species of rice from Southeast Asia.

The population increase meant that less land was available for each family. The imperial court tried to make more land available by limiting the amount wealthy landowners could hold. By the eighteenth century, however, almost all the land that could be was already being farmed. Rural land shortages led to unrest and revolts.

Another change in this period was a steady growth in manufacturing and increased trade between provinces. Taking advantage of the long era of peace and prosperity, merchants and manufacturers expanded their trade in silk, porcelain, cotton goods, and other products.

▲ Emperor Qianlong, in full ceremonial armor

Despite the growth in trade and manufacturing, China did not develop the same attitude toward business that was emerging in Europe. Middle-class merchants and manufacturers in China were not as independent as those in Europe, The government controlled commercial activity and also saw business as inferior to farming. Due to Confucian ideals, merchants bought land rather than reinvesting their profits in their businesses.

Chinese society was organized around the family. The family was expected to provide for its members' needs, including the education of children, support of unmarried daughters, and care of the elderly. At the same time, all family members were expected to sacrifice their individual needs to benefit the family as a whole. This was based on Confucian ideals.

The ideal family unit in Qing China was the extended family, in which generations lived under the same roof. When sons married, their wives, no longer considered members of their original families, lived with them in the husband's family home. Unmarried daughters also remained in the house, as did parents and grandparents. Chinese society held the elderly in high regard. Aging parents knew they would be cared for in their homes by their children.

clan a group of related families

Beyond the extended family was the **clan**, which consisted of dozens, or even hundreds, of related families. These families were linked by a clan council of elders and common social and religious activities. This system made it possible for wealthier families to help poorer relatives.

Women were considered inferior to men in Chinese society. Only males could have a formal education and pursue a career in government or scholarship. Within the family, Chinese women often played strong roles. Nevertheless, the wife was clearly subordinate to the husband. Legally, she could not divorce her husband or inherit property. The husband could divorce his wife if she did not produce sons. He could also take a second wife. Husbands were expected to support their wives and children.

A feature of Chinese society that restricted the mobility of women was the practice of foot binding. Scholars believe it began among the wealthy and was later adopted by all classes. Bound feet were a status symbol. Women who had bound feet were more marriageable than those who did not; thus, there was a status incentive as well as an economic incentive. An estimated one-half to two-thirds of the women in China bound their feet.

The process, begun in childhood, was very painful. Women who had their feet bound could not walk; they were carried. Not all clans looked favorably on foot binding. Women who worked in the fields or in occupations that required mobility did not bind their feet.

✓ **READING PROGRESS CHECK**

Summarizing How did population increases cause unrest?

Chinese Art and Literature

GUIDING QUESTION ***What artistic advancements did China experience during the Ming and Qing dynasties?***

During the late Ming and the early Qing dynasties, traditional culture in China reached new heights. The Ming economic expansion increased standards of living, providing many Chinese with money to purchase books. Also, new innovations in paper manufacturing encouraged the growth of printing throughout China.

During the Ming dynasty, a new form of literature arose that evolved into the modern Chinese novel. Works in this literary form were quite popular, especially among well-to-do urban dwellers.

One Chinese novel, *The Golden Lotus,* is considered by many to be the first realistic social novel. *The Golden Lotus* depicts the corrupt life of a wealthy landlord in the late Ming period who cruelly manipulates those around him for sex, money, and power.

The Dream of the Red Chamber, by Cao Xueqin, is generally considered even today to be China's most distinguished popular novel. Published in 1791, it tells of the tragic love between two young people caught in the financial and moral disintegration of a powerful Chinese clan.

During the Ming and the early Qing dynasties, China experienced an outpouring of artistic brilliance. In architecture, the most outstanding example is the Imperial City in Beijing. The decorative arts also flourished in this period. Perhaps the most famous of all the arts of the Ming Era was blue-and-white porcelain. Europeans admired the beauty of this porcelain and collected it in great quantities. Different styles of porcelain were produced during the reign of individual emperors.

✓ **READING PROGRESS CHECK**

Identifying Relate advances in literature to economic advances during the period.

Analyzing PRIMARY SOURCES

Women in China

"How sad it is to be a woman! Nothing on earth is held so cheap. . . . No one is glad when a girl is born: By *her* the family sets no store."

—Fu Hsüan, from "Woman"

DBQ ***READING CLOSELY*** Based on what you've read, does this seem like a fair assessment of the role of women in China?

▲ Porcelain vase from the Ming Dynasty, fifteenth century

LESSON 1 REVIEW TEKS

Reviewing Vocabulary

1. ***Summarizing*** Write a paragraph explaining how the queue functioned as an effective political tool during the Qing dynasty.

Using Your Notes

2. ***Comparing and Contrasting*** Use your notes on the Ming and Qing dynasties to write a paragraph comparing and contrasting their achievements.

Answering the Guiding Questions

3. ***Listing*** What were the achievements of the Ming dynasty?
4. ***Synthesizing*** How did the Qing dynasty adapt to become successful?
5. ***Summarizing*** How did the changing economy affect society during the Ming and Qing dynasties? 1D, 7E
6. ***Summarizing*** What artistic advancements did China experience during the Ming and Qing dynasties? 26B, 26C

Writing Activity

7. **INFORMATIVE/EXPLANATORY** Write a paragraph that evaluates the positive and negative features of the traditional family-centered values of Chinese society.

networks

There's More Online!

- BIOGRAPHY Matsuo Basho
- BIOGRAPHY Oda Nobunaga
- BIOGRAPHY Tokugawa Ieyasu
- BIOGRAPHY Toyotomi Hideyoshi
- CHART/GRAPH Japan's Isolation
- CHART/GRAPH Japan's Three Great Unifiers
- IMAGE Edo
- IMAGE Kabuki Theater
- IMAGE Samurai
- INTERACTIVE SELF-CHECK QUIZ
- VIDEO The Samurai

LESSON 2
The Reunification of Japan

ESSENTIAL QUESTIONS • *What factors help unify a kingdom or dynasty?* • *How can external forces influence a kingdom or dynasty?*

Reading **HELP**DESK

Academic Vocabulary

- **process**
- **community**

Content Vocabulary

- **daimyo**
- **hans**
- **hostage system**
- **eta**

TAKING NOTES:

Key Ideas and Details

Categorizing Use a graphic organizer like this one to categorize key elements of Japanese society and culture during the Tokugawa era.

TEKS Texas Essential Knowledge and Skills

26C identify examples of art, music, and literature that transcend the cultures in which they were created and convey universal themes

It Matters Because

From the sixteenth century to the eighteenth century, Japan was unified through efforts of powerful leaders. It imposed restrictive social systems and enforced cultural isolation, while trade and industry increased.

Political Changes in Japan

GUIDING QUESTION *What changes took place in Japan after its political unification?*

At the end of the fifteenth century, Japan was in chaos. The centralized power of the shogunate had collapsed. **Daimyo**, heads of noble families, controlled their own lands and warred with their neighbors. Soon, however, a dramatic reversal would unify Japan.

The **process** of unification began in the late sixteenth century with three powerful political figures. The first was Oda Nobunaga (oh • dah noh • boo • nah • gah). Nobunaga seized the imperial capital of Kyōto and placed the reigning shogun under his control. By 1582 he had unified the central part of present-day Japan.

Nobunaga was succeeded by Toyotomi Hideyoshi (toh • yoh • toh • mee hee • day • yoh • shee), a farmer's son who had become a military commander. Hideyoshi located his capital at Ōsaka. By 1590 he had persuaded most of the daimyo on the Japanese islands to accept his authority.

After Hideyoshi's death in 1598, Tokugawa Ieyasu (toh • kuh • gah • wah ee • yah • soo), the powerful daimyo of Edo (modern-day Tokyo), took control of Japan. Ieyasu took the title of shogun in 1603. The Tokugawa rulers completed the restoration of central authority that had begun with Nobunaga and Hideyoshi. The Tokugawa shoguns remained in power at their capital of Edo until 1868. Tokugawa rule brought a period of peace known as the "Great Peace."

As the three great commanders were unifying Japan, the first Europeans began to arrive. Portuguese traders landed on the islands in 1543. In a few years, Portuguese ships began stopping regularly at Japanese ports to take part in the regional trade between Japan, China, and Southeast Asia.

At first, the visitors were welcomed. The Japanese were fascinated by tobacco, clocks, eyeglasses, and other European goods. Nobunaga and Hideyoshi found the new firearms helpful in defeating their enemies and unifying the islands.

The first Jesuit missionary, Francis Xavier, arrived in 1549. The Jesuits converted a number of local daimyo. By the end of the sixteenth century, thousands of Japanese had become Christians. However, after the Jesuits destroyed local shrines, Hideyoshi issued an edict in 1587 prohibiting Christian activities within his lands.

European merchants were the next to go. Only a small Dutch **community** was allowed to remain in Japan. Dutch ships were permitted to dock at Nagasaki harbor only once each year and could remain for only two to three months.

daimyo "great names"; heads of noble families in Japan who controlled vast landed estates and relied on samurai for protection

process a series of actions or steps leading to an end

community a group of people with common interests and characteristics living together within a larger society

hans approximately 250 domains into which Japan was divided under the Tokugawa

✓ **READING PROGRESS CHECK**

Interpreting How did the rule of Japan shift from the rule of the daimyo to the rule of the three great commanders?

The Tokugawa Era

GUIDING QUESTION *What forms of art flourished under Tokugawa rule?*

Major political and economic change took place under the Tokugawa. Since the fourteenth century, many upper-class Japanese, influenced by Confucianism, had considered trade and industry beneath them. Under the Tokugawa rulers, however, trade and industry began to flourish.

Tokugawa Rule

The Tokugawa rulers established control of the feudal system that had governed Japan for more than 300 years. As before, the state was divided into about 250 separate territories called **hans**, or domains. Each was ruled by a daimyo. In theory, the daimyo were independent because they were able to support themselves from taxes on their lands. In actuality, the shogunate controlled the daimyo by a **hostage system**.

In this system, the daimyo were required to maintain two residences—one in their own lands and one in Edo, where the shogun's court was located. When the daimyo was absent from his residence in Edo, his family was forced to stay home there as a kind of insurance for the daimyo's loyalty to the shogun.

During this long period of peace—known as the "Great Peace"—brought by Tokugawa rule, the samurai who had served the daimyo gradually ceased to be a warrior class. Many became managers on the daimyo's lands.

Economy and Society

By 1750, Edo had a population of more than one million and was one of the largest cities in the world. Banking flourished, and paper money became the normal medium of exchange in business transactions. A Japanese merchant class emerged and began to play a significant role in Japan. What effect did these economic changes have on Japanese peasants who made up most of the population?

Some farm families benefited by exploiting the growing demand for cash crops (crops grown for sale). Most peasants, however, experienced

▲ Eighteenth-century Japanese samurai armor

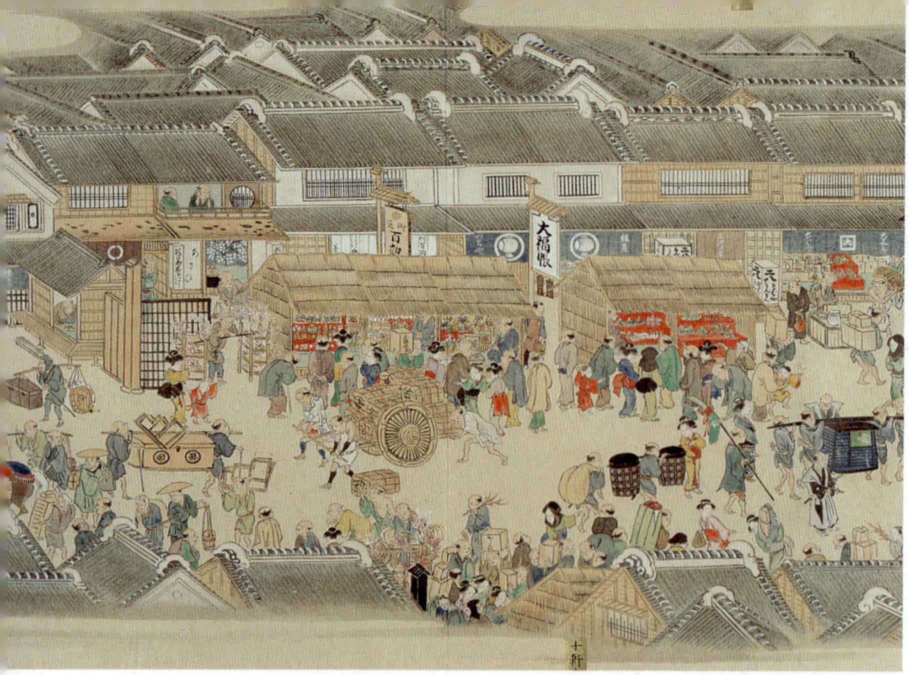

▲ Detail from a scroll depicting an *Excellent View of Our Prosperous Age,* from the Edo period

▶ **CRITICAL THINKING**
Analyzing Information How does this street scene in Edo depict Japanese prosperity?

hostage system a system used by the shogunate to control the daimyo in Tokugawa Japan; the family of a daimyo lord was forced to stay at their residence in the capital whenever the lord was absent from it

eta Japan's outcast class, whose way of life was strictly regulated by the Tokugawa

declining profits and rising costs and taxes. Many were forced to become tenants or to work as hired help. When rural conditions became desperate, some peasants revolted.

Social changes influenced by Confucian doctrines also marked the Tokugawa Era. During this era, Japan's class system became rigid. Rulers established strict legal distinctions among the four main classes: warriors, peasants, artisans, and merchants. Intermarriage between any of these classes was forbidden.

The emperor and imperial court families were at the top of the political and social structure. Next came the warrior class—the shogun, daimyo, samurai, and *ronin*. The shogun was supreme ruler below the emperor and distributor of the national rice crop. The local daimyo received land and rice from the shogun in exchange for military service. Samurai received rice from the daimyo in exchange for their services as advisers and government officials. Finally, the *ronin* were warriors who traveled the countryside seeking jobs.

Below the warriors were the farmers, artisans, and merchants. Farmers produced rice and held a privileged position in society but were often poor. The artisan class included craftspeople such as sword makers and carpenters. Merchants, who distributed basic goods, were at the bottom of the social hierarchy because they profited from others' labor.

Below these classes were Japan's outcasts, the ***eta***. The Tokugawa enacted severe laws to regulate the places of residence, the dress, and even the hairstyles of the *eta*.

Especially in the samurai class where Confucian values were highly prized, the rights of females were restricted. Male heads of households had broad authority over property, marriage, and divorce.

Among the common people, women were also restricted. Parents arranged marriages, and a wife had to move in with her husband's family. A wife who did not meet the expectations of her husband or his family was likely to be divorced. Still, women were generally valued among the common people for their roles as child bearers and homemakers.

Literature and Arts

In the Tokugawa Era, a new set of cultural values began to appear, especially in the cities. It included the rise of popular literature written by and for the people. The best example of the new urban fiction is from Ihara Saikaku, considered one of Japan's greatest writers. Saikaku's greatest novel, *Five Women Who Loved Love*, tells of a search for love by five women.

Much popular literature of the Tokugawa Era was lighthearted, but poetry remained a more serious form of literature. Matsuo Bashō, the greatest Japanese poet, wrote exquisite poetry about nature in the seventeenth century.

A new world of entertainment in the cities gave rise to Kabuki in the theater. Early Kabuki dramas dealt with the world of teahouses and dance halls in the cities. Government officials, fearing that these subjects onstage might corrupt people's moral standards, forbade women to appear on stage. Thus a new profession was created—male actors who portrayed female characters on stage.

Art also reflected the changes in Japanese culture under the Tokugawa Era. The shogun's order that all daimyo and their families have residences in Edo sparked an increase in building. Nobles competed to erect the most magnificent mansions with lavish and beautiful furnishings.

Japanese art was enriched by ideas from other cultures. The Japanese studied Western medicine, astronomy, languages, and painting styles. In turn, Europeans wanted Japanese ceramics, which were prized as highly as the ceramics of the Chinese.

✓ READING PROGRESS CHECK

Summarizing Summarize the social structure that developed during the Tokugawa shogunate.

▼ Kabuki actors performing a play called *Soga Monogatari*

▶ CRITICAL THINKING

Comparing and Contrasting How does Kabuki theater appear similar to or different from Western theater?

PHOTO: Utagawa Hirosada/Bridgeman Art Library/Getty Images

LESSON 2 REVIEW

Reviewing Vocabulary

1. ***Explaining*** Write a paragraph explaining how the hostage system helped the shogunate control the daimyo.

Using Your Notes

2. ***Describing*** Use your notes to write a paragraph describing Japanese society and culture under the Tokugawa shogunate. 26B, 26C

Answering the Guiding Questions

3. ***Identifying*** What changes took place in Japan under the Tokugawa shogunate?

4. ***Identifying*** What forms of art flourished under Tokugawa rule? 26B, 26C

Writing Activity

5. ***NARRATIVE*** Write a narrative paragraph presenting an imaginary episode during the introduction of European goods to Japan. Present vivid details of the event in clear chronological order.

networks

There's More Online!

- BIOGRAPHY Yi Songgye
- CHART/GRAPH Melaka, the Moluccas, and the Strait of Malacca
- IMAGE Dutch Fort at Batavia
- IMAGE Korean Art
- INTERACTIVE SELF-CHECK QUIZ
- MAP Southeast Asian Kingdoms and Political Systems, 1500
- MAP Spice Island Trading Posts
- PRIMARY SOURCE Japan's Invasion of Korea
- VIDEO Religion in Southwest Asia

Reading HELPDESK

Academic Vocabulary

- **archipelago**
- **network**
- **impose**

Content Vocabulary

- **isolationist**
- **mainland states**
- **bureaucracy**

TAKING NOTES:

Key Ideas and Details

Organizing As you read, use a chart like the one below to list and organize information about the kingdoms of Korea and Southeast Asia.

Korea	
Mainland states: Burma, Thailand, and Cambodia	
Vietnam	
Indonesian archipelago	
Malay Peninsula	

LESSON 3

The Kingdoms of Korea and Southeast Asia

ESSENTIAL QUESTIONS • *What factors help unify a kingdom or dynasty?* • *How can external forces influence a kingdom or dynasty?*

It Matters Because

Beginning in the fourteenth century, the powerful Yi dynasty created a stable state in Korea. In Southeast Asia, Muslim merchants, attracted to the growing spice trade, established a workable trade network. In the sixteenth century, however, the Portuguese seized control of the spice trade, eventually attracting English and Dutch competition.

Korea: The Hermit Kingdom

GUIDING QUESTION *What characterized Korea's culture in the sixteenth and seventeenth centuries?*

The Yi dynasty in Korea began in 1392 when Yi Sŏng-gye (YEE • sung • jay), a renowned military strategist, ascended the throne by overthrowing the Koryo dynasty. Lasting for five centuries, the Yi dynasty was one of the world's longest-lasting monarchies.

From their capital at Hanseong (modern-day Seoul), Yi rulers consolidated their rule of Korea by adopting the Chinese example of a strong bureaucratic state. They patterned their society after the Chinese to the north but maintained their distinctive identity.

One distinctive Korean characteristic was its alphabet—Hangul. The first Korean and Japanese writing systems developed from Chinese characters, or symbols. Unlike Chinese, which uses thousands of symbols, the Korean Hangul is phonetically based. One symbol stands for each sound, similar to the English alphabet. Hangul is still largely the standard writing system in present-day Korea.

The Yi dynasty also experienced serious problems. During the late sixteenth and early seventeenth centuries, internal conflicts within the royal court weakened the dynasty. Japanese and Chinese invasions also devastated Korea.

A Japanese force under Toyotomi Hideyoshi invaded Korea in the late sixteenth century. Hideyoshi wanted to use Korea as the transit route for his conquest of China. Korean forces defeated the Japanese invaders, but victory came at a high price. Korean farmlands were devastated, and villages and towns were burned. The Japanese also killed or kidnapped skilled workers.

Korea was still recovering from the Japanese invasions when the Manchus attacked in the 1620s and 1630s. Korea recovered, however, and then began to experience a long period of peace.

In response to these events, the Korean rulers sought to limit contact with foreign countries and tried to keep the country isolated from the outside world. The country remained largely untouched by European merchants and Christian missionaries. Due to its **isolationist** practices, Korea received the name "Hermit Kingdom."

isolationist a policy of national isolation by abstention from alliances and other international political and economic relations

✓ READING PROGRESS CHECK

Explaining Why was Korea called the "Hermit Kingdom"?

Kingdoms in Southeast Asia

GUIDING QUESTION ***What factors influenced the emerging kingdoms in Southeast Asia beginning in the sixteenth century?***

In 1500 mainland Southeast Asia was a relatively stable region. Throughout the region, from Burma in the west to Vietnam in the east, kingdoms with unique ethnic, linguistic, and cultural characteristics were being formed.

Nevertheless, conflicts erupted among the emerging states on the Southeast Asian mainland. One such conflict, over territory between the Thai and the Burmese, was bitter until a Burmese army sacked the Thai capital in 1767. The Thai then created a new capital at Bangkok, farther to the south.

GEOGRAPHY CONNECTION

Southeast Asia had a variety of kingdoms in the 1500s.

1. **HUMAN SYSTEMS** *Why was Islam present on the Indonesian islands?*
2. **THE WORLD IN SPATIAL TERMS** *What was the main style of kingship on the mainland?*

Across the mountains to the east, the Vietnamese had begun their "March to the South." By the end of the fifteenth century, they had subdued the rival state of Champa on the central coast. The Vietnamese then gradually took control of the Mekong Delta from the Khmer—the successor of the old Angkor kingdom. By 1800, the Khmer monarchy had virtually disappeared.

archipelago a chain of islands

network an interrelated or interconnected group or system

The situation was different in the Malay Peninsula and the Indonesian **archipelago**. Muslim merchants, who were attracted to the growing spice trade, gradually entered the area. The creation of an Islamic trade **network** had political results as new Islamic states arose along the spice route. The major impact of this trade network, however, came in the fifteenth century with the new Muslim sultanate at Melaka. Melaka owed its new power to its strategic location on the Strait of Malacca and to the rapid growth of the spice trade itself. Within a few years, Melaka had become the leading power in the region.

Religious beliefs changed in Southeast Asia during the period from 1500 to 1800. Particularly in the non-mainland states and the Philippines, Islam and Christianity began to attract converts. Buddhism advanced on the mainland, becoming dominant from Burma to Vietnam. Traditional beliefs, however, survived and influenced the new religions.

The political systems in Southeast Asian states evolved into four main types. Buddhist kings, Javanese kings, Islamic sultans, and Vietnamese emperors adapted foreign models of government to suit their particular local circumstances.

mainland states part of the continent, as distinguished from peninsulas or offshore islands

bureaucracy an administrative organization that relies on nonelective officials and regular procedures

The Buddhist style of kingship became the chief form of government in the **mainland states** of Burma, Thailand, Laos, and Cambodia. In the Buddhist model, the king was considered superior to other human beings and served as the link between human society and the universe.

The Javanese style of kingship was rooted in the political traditions of India and shared many characteristics of the Buddhist system. Like Buddhist rulers, Javanese kings were believed to have a sacred quality. They maintained the balance between the sacred world and the material world. The royal palace was designed to represent the center of the universe. Its shape was like rays spreading outward to the corners of the Javanese realm.

Islamic sultans ruled on the Malay Peninsula and in the small coastal states of the Indonesian archipelago. In the Islamic pattern, the head of state was a sultan. Viewed as a mortal, he still possessed some special qualities. He was a defender of the faith and staffed his **bureaucracy** (nonelected government officials) mainly with aristocrats.

▼ This print depicts the port of Batavia (now Jakarta) on the island of Java in the Dutch East Indies.

▶ **CRITICAL THINKING**

Identifying Central Issues Why did the Dutch East India Company establish its headquarters at Batavia?

In Vietnam, kingship followed the Chinese model. Like the Chinese emperor, the Vietnamese emperor ruled according to the teachings of Confucius. Confucius believed that a ruler should treat subjects with love and respect. The ruler was seen as an intermediary between heaven and Earth. The emperor was appointed by heaven to rule by his talent and virtue.

✓ **READING PROGRESS CHECK**

Drawing Conclusions How did religion influence the forms of government in the kingdoms of Southeast Asia?

Europeans and the Spice Trade

GUIDING QUESTION *How did the arrival of Europeans affect Southeast Asia beginning in the sixteenth century?*

Since ancient times, spices had been highly valued. They were used as flavorings, medicines, and food preservers. After bad harvests and in winter, meat preserved with salt and pepper kept many people from starving. Ginger, cloves, cinnamon, and nutmeg were also in high demand. European countries competed to find a sea route to the Indies. In particular, that hunt was for Melaka, the fabled gateway to the Spice Islands. Portugal found that gateway.

When Vasco da Gama and his crew came ashore at Calicut in 1498, they shouted, "For Christ and spices!" Most important were the spices. In 1511 the Portuguese seized Melaka and soon occupied the Moluccas. Known to Europeans as the Spice Islands, the Moluccas were the main source of spices that first attracted the Portuguese to the Indian Ocean. The Portuguese, however, lacked the military and financial resources to **impose** their authority over broad areas. They set up small settlements along the coast and used them as trading posts during travel to and from the Spice Islands.

impose to establish or apply

The situation changed with the arrival of the English and Dutch (Netherlands) traders, who were better financed than the Portuguese. The shift in power began in the early 1600s when the Dutch seized a Portuguese fort in the Moluccas and gradually pushed the Portuguese out of the spice trade.

During the next 50 years, the Dutch occupied most Portuguese coastal forts along the trade routes throughout the Indian Ocean. They drove the English traders out of the spice market. England was left with a single port on the southern coast of Sumatra.

✓ **READING PROGRESS CHECK**

Drawing Conclusions If the mainland states had been rich in spices like the Moluccas were, would they have faced the same fate? Explain your answer.

LESSON 3 REVIEW TEKS

Reviewing Vocabulary

1. ***Describing*** Write a paragraph about the trading networks in the mainland states and archipelagos of Southeast Asia.

Using Your Notes

2. ***Explaining*** Use your notes to write a paragraph describing the governments of Korea and Southeast Asia.

Answering the Guiding Questions

3. ***Making Generalizations*** What characterized Korea's culture in the sixteenth and seventeenth centuries?
4. ***Identifying the Central Issues*** How did Korea and the kingdoms of Southeast Asia respond to contact with foreign nations?
5. ***Identify Cause and Effect*** How did the arrival of Europeans affect Southeast Asia between the sixteenth and eighteenth centuries?

Writing Activity

6. **INFORMATIVE/EXPLANATORY** Write a paragraph comparing and contrasting Portuguese and Dutch activities in the spice trade in Southeast Asia. Be sure to link to specific facts and dates.

SKILLBUILDER

TEKS 29F

Making Inferences and Drawing Conclusions

Why Learn This Skill?

While driving, you hear a news report about a fire downtown. As you approach downtown, traffic is very heavy. You cannot see any smoke, but you infer that the traffic is caused by the fire.

To infer means to evaluate information and arrive at a conclusion. When you make inferences, you draw conclusions that are not stated directly.

Learning the Skill

Follow the steps below to help make inferences and draw conclusions:

- Read carefully to determine the main facts and ideas.
- Write down the important facts.
- Consider any information you know that relates to this topic.
- Determine how your own knowledge adds to or changes the material.
- What inferences can you make about the material that are not stated in the facts that you gathered from your reading?
- Use your knowledge and reason to develop conclusions about the facts.
- If possible, find specific information that proves or disproves your inference.

Practicing the Skill

Read the passage below, then answer the questions that follow.

"In 1511, the Portuguese seized Melaka and soon occupied the Moluccas. Known to Europeans as the Spice Islands, the Moluccas were the chief source of the spices that had originally attracted the Portuguese to the Indian Ocean.

The Portuguese, however, lacked the military and financial resources to impose their authority over broad areas. Instead, they set up small settlements along the coast, which they used as trading posts or as way stations en route to the Spice Islands.

The situation changed with the arrival of the English and Dutch traders, who were better financed than were the Portuguese. The shift in power began in the early 1600s, when the Dutch seized a Portuguese fort in the Moluccas and drove out the Portuguese.

During the next fifty years, the Dutch occupied most of the Portuguese coastal forts along the trade routes throughout the Indian Ocean. The aggressive Dutch traders also drove the English traders out of the spice market, reducing the English influence to a single port on the southern coast of Sumatra."

1. What events does the writer describe?
2. What facts are presented?
3. What can you infer about the Dutch traders during this period?
4. What conclusion can you make about the spice market, other than those specifically stated by the author?

Applying the Skill

Locate a political cartoon from a news source or magazine. Share the cartoon with the class by cutting it out, printing a copy, or creating a whiteboard projection. List three valid inferences based on the work.

SKILLBUILDER

TEKS 29G, 29H, 30A, 30B, 30C

Writing a Report

Why Learn This Skill?

You have learned about taking notes, making outlines, and finding sources for researching a paper. Now how do you put all those skills together to actually write a report?

Learning the Skill

Use the following guidelines to help you create a written presentation of social studies information:

- **Select an interesting thesis.** As you identify possible topics, focus on resources that are available. Do preliminary research to determine whether your topic is too broad or too narrow. For example, writing about Japan in the nineteenth century is very broad. There is too much information to research and write about. Narrowing it down to one event in the nineteenth century, such as the Treaty of Kanagawa, is much more practical. If, however, you cannot find enough information about your topic, it is probably too narrow. Use appropriate reading skills to interpret the information you find.
- **Write a thesis statement.** The thesis defines what you want to prove, discover, or illustrate in your report.
- **Prepare and do research on your topic.** Make a list of main idea questions, and then do research to answer those questions. Prepare note cards on each main idea question, listing the source information.
- **Organize your information.** Use an outline or another kind of organizer. Then follow your outline or organizer in writing a rough draft of your report.
- **Create a written presentation of your information.** Include an introduction, main body, and conclusion. The introduction briefly presents the topic and gives your topic statement. The main body should follow your outline to develop the important ideas in your argument. The conclusion summarizes and restates your findings. Be sure to use social studies terminology correctly in your draft.
- **Revise the first draft.** Before writing the final draft of your report, wait one day and then reread and revise your first draft. Edit for standard grammar, spelling, sentence structure, and punctuation.

PHOTO: Hero/Corbis/Glow Images

Practicing the Skill

Suppose you are writing a report on the decline of the Qing dynasty. Answer the following questions about the writing process.

1. What is a possible thesis statement?
2. What are three main idea questions?
3. What are three possible sources of information?
4. What are the next two steps in the process of writing a report?

Applying the Skill

Review the thesis, questions, and resources you came up with for the report on the Qing dynasty. Using this information, continue your research on this topic, organize your information, and write a short report.

CHAPTER 20 Assessment

TEKS

Directions: On a separate sheet of paper, answer the questions below. Make sure you read carefully and answer all parts of the questions.

Lesson Review

Lesson 1

1. ***Identifying*** Why was China important to world trade? What effect did China's Ming Dynasty have on world trade? **1D, 7E**

2. ***Analyzing*** What are some examples of literature that reflect the Chinese culture from this period? **26B**

3. ***Stating*** What was the Confucian ideal regarding families in China? What specific needs were families expected to meet?

4. ***Comparing and Contrasting*** How were the Ming and Qing dynasties similar in their treatment of the Europeans? How were they different?

5. ***Describing*** What was the Imperial City, and how was it viewed by different groups in society?

Lesson 2

6. ***Explaining*** Explain the Japanese feudal system under Tokugawa rule that included a structure of hans, daimyos, and the hostage system.

7. ***Identifying*** What political leaders brought about Japanese reunification? What did each accomplish?

8. ***Drawing Conclusion*** What aspects of Japan's geography made it fairly easy to prohibit Europeans from entering the country?

9. ***Describing*** Describe the rigid class system during the Tokugawa Era in Japan.

Lesson 3

10. ***Making Connections*** What were the causes and effects of Korea's isolationist policy in the seventeenth century?

11. ***Identifying*** Identify and name the groups and/or regions that comprised Southeast Asia around the sixteenth century.

12. ***Exploring Issues*** How did the political systems of Southeast Asian kingdoms change from the sixteenth to the eighteenth centuries?

13. ***Analyze Information*** Explain the interest in spices and the sequence of European traders on the Molucca islands.

Exploring the Essential Question

14. ***Gathering Information*** Write an essay explaining how external factors influenced east Asian kingdoms and dynasties between 1400 and 1800. Include several examples from each lesson and discuss factors that had both negative and positive influences.

Critical Thinking

15. ***Defining*** How would you define "dynasty"?

16. ***Analyzing Causes*** What circumstances might bring about the emergence of a new political dynasty in a country?

Need Extra Help?

If You've Missed Question	1	2	3	4	5	6	7	8	9	10	11	12	13	14	15	16
Go to page	450	455	454	450	455	457	456	456	457	461	461	461	462	450	450	450

17 ***Identifying Central Issues*** What challenges would be faced by a new dynasty that differed in religion or ethnicity from the people it was now ruling?

18 ***Analyzing*** What characteristics might make a dynasty successful?

19 ***Evaluating*** Beginning with the arrival of Portuguese traders in China in 1514 and ending with British traders in 1793, evaluate the viewpoints of the Chinese toward European explorers and traders.

20 ***Drawing Inferences*** Draw an inference about the motivations behind allowing only men to perform on stage in Kabuki theater.

21 ***Identifying Central Issues*** The Southeast Asian states had similar but distinct political systems. What main concept appeared to belong to Buddhist kingship, Javanese Islamic sultans, and Vietnamese emperors?

22 ***Making Comparisons and Contrasts*** Compare the religious influences in Southeast Asia with the religious influences in China or Japan during this period. Which area had greater variety and which had greater continuity of religious philosophy?

23 ***Making Connections*** Consider the motivations of Europeans to have a successful spice trade. Make a connection between the impact of the spice trade on European economies and relationships with one another with a modern issue that involves multiple countries and potentially across continents.

Social Studies Skills

24 ***Identifying Cause and Effect*** How did the Manchus, a small percentage of the population, maintain power over a much larger group of Chinese subjects?

25 ***Identifying Perspectives*** How did the Japanese treatment of and attitude toward Europeans change after Europeans first arrived on Japan's shores?

26 ***Comparing*** Compare the artistic and literary output of the Tokugawa Era in Japan.

27 ***Analyzing Information by Sequencing*** What kinds of conflicts developed among the mainland states of Southeast Asia? Construct a time line that shows these conflicts. Then, analyze this sequenced information to respond to the following question: What were some of the reasons for these conflicts? Give two examples. **29F**

28 ***Transfer Information*** View photographs of the Imperial Palace included within your textbook, online, or within other resources. Research architectural information related to the image and create a blueprint sketch that shares data about the height, width, or other measurements or values related to a structure. You might consider creating a collage instead of an illustration or using paints to communicate the data. **30D**

29 ***Geography Skills*** Produce maps that show the routes of Europeans who undertook journeys for the spice trade. Verify the information by referencing additional materials. Include a map key that indicates distance traders may have traveled.

Need Extra Help?

If You've Missed Question	17	18	19	20	21	22	23	24	25	26	27	28	29
Go to page	450	450	451	458	462	460	465	451	457	458	460	451	465

DBQ Analyzing Primary Sources

Use the document to answer the following questions.

Lord George Macartney was the British ambassador to China when Qianlong was emperor. In 1793 he visited Qianlong's palace.

PRIMARY SOURCE

"[The buildings are]. . . furnished in the richest manner, with pictures of the Emperor's huntings and progresses; with stupendous vases of jasper and agate; with the finest porcelains and japan, and with every kind of European toys and sing-songs; with spheres, orreries [models of the solar system], clocks and musical automatons of such exquisite workmanship, and in such profusion, that our presents must shrink from the comparison. . ."

—quoted in *The Fall of Imperial China*

30. ***Analyzing*** How does Macartney's description of the court depict the economy of China under the Qing dynasty?

31. ***Drawing Inferences*** What does Macartney's statement that "our presents must shrink from the comparison" reveal about his likely success in improving Britain's negative trade balance with China?

Analyzing Visuals

Use the cartoon to answer the following questions.

32. ***Interpreting Visual Images*** What is the attitude of the Europeans toward the Chinese?

33. ***Explaining the Influence of Geography*** What is the attitude of the Chinese toward the Europeans? Does the cartoonist suggest that this meeting is positive or negative?

Extended Response Question

34. ***Expository Analysis of Sequenced Information*** What kinds of relationships did China, Japan, Korea, and Southeast Asia have with Europe in the sixteenth century? Construct a time line of interactions among these countries. Then, analyze this sequenced information to respond in writing to the following questions: How did these relationships change over time? What can you conclude from these patterns about what causes countries to become allies and what causes conflict? 29F

PHOTO: ©Chris Hellier/Corbis

Need Extra Help?

If You've Missed Question	30	31	32	33	34
Go to page	468	468	468	468	450

The Enlightenment and Revolutions

1550–1800

ESSENTIAL QUESTIONS • *Why do new ideas often spark change?* • *How do new ways of thinking affect the way people respond to their surroundings?*

networks

There's More Online! about the Enlightenment and revolutions.

CHAPTER 21

The Story Matters...

The Scientific Revolution led to the Enlightenment, a major European intellectual movement that applied reason to all human experience. The English mathematician Sir Isaac Newton was a key figure in the Scientific Revolution. His fundamental scientific insight, that the physical world operated according to natural laws discovered through scientific investigation, influenced every area of Enlightenment thought.

◀ This engraving was based on a portrait of Newton by Sir Godfrey Kneller. The poet Alexander Pope summed up Newton's contribution to human understanding: "Nature and Nature's laws lay hid in night: / God said, Let Newton be! and all was light."

CHAPTER 21

Place and Time: Europe and the World 1550–1800

The seventeenth and eighteenth centuries witnessed the Scientific Revolution and the Enlightenment. Philosophers and scientists produced new theories about the structure of the universe and humankind's relationship to it. As European powers explored the world and expanded their colonial empires, conflicts erupted. This first age of global warfare culminated in the Seven Years' War, fought in Europe, North America, and India.

Step Into the Place

Read the quotes and look at the information presented on the map.

DBQ **Analyzing Historical Documents** How would you generalize the attitude of the Enlightenment toward a conflict between colonial empires, such as the Seven Years' War? Reference specific primary sources in your answer.

PRIMARY SOURCE

"Though . . . politics [cannot] be founded on any thing but the consent of the people . . . in the noise of war, which makes so great a part of the history of mankind, this consent is little taken notice of: and therefore many have mistaken the force of arms for the consent of the people, and reckon conquest as one of the originals of government. But conquest is as far from setting up any government, as demolishing an [sic] house is from building a new one in the place.... Without the consent of the people, [one] can never erect a new one."

—John Locke, from *Two Treatises of Government*, 1690

Step Into the Time

Making Connections
Choose several events from the time line and use them to write a paragraph summarizing the key interests of Enlightenment thinkers.

EUROPE

- **1610** Galileo Galilei publishes *The Starry Messenger*
- **1637** René Descartes publishes *Discourse on Method*

THE WORLD

1550 — 1600

- **1562** Beginning of Akbar's reign in India
- **1588** Shāh 'Abbās comes to power in Persia
- **1603** Tokugawa shogunate begins in Japan
- **1607** Founding of Jamestown Colony in Virginia
- **1632–53** Construction of Taj Mahal

networks
There's More Online!

- **MAP** Explore the interactive version of this map on Networks.
- **TIME LINE** Explore the interactive version of the time line on Networks.

1690 John Locke publishes *Two Treatises of Government*

1740 War of Austrian Succession begins

1751 Denis Diderot begins to publish *Encyclopedia*

1762 Jean-Jacques Rousseau publishes *The Social Contract*

1756 Seven Years' War breaks out in North America, Europe, and India

1763 War in Europe and War in India ends

1776 Adam Smith publishes *The Wealth of Nations*

1786 Reign of Frederick the Great of Prussia ends

1796 Reign of Catherine the Great of Russia ends

1650 — 1700 — 1750 — 1800

1661 Kangxi, the greatest Qing emperor, comes to the throne

1691 Sor Juana Inés de la Cruz writes her self-defense

1728 Vitus Bering explores sea between Siberia and North America

c. 1787 Zulu ruler Shaka is born

1788 U.S. Constitution is ratified

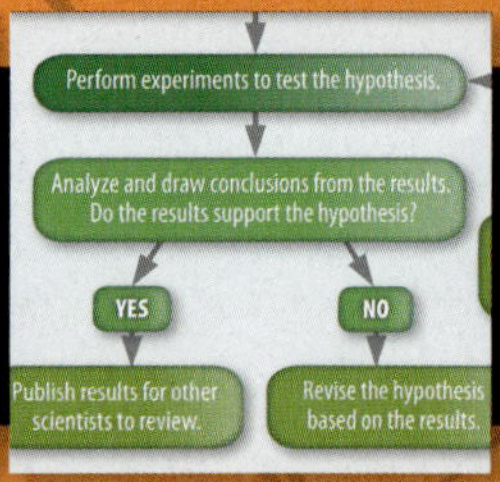

networks

There's More Online!

- BIOGRAPHY Francis Bacon
- BIOGRAPHY Galileo Galilei
- BIOGRAPHY Isaac Newton
- CHART/GRAPH Intellectuals of the Scientific Revolution
- GAME Terms from the Scientific Revolution
- GRAPHIC ORGANIZER The Scientific Method
- INTERACTIVE SELF-CHECK QUIZ
- PRIMARY SOURCE Meditations on First Philosophy
- VIDEO Galileo

LESSON 1
The Scientific Revolution

ESSENTIAL QUESTIONS • *Why do new ideas often spark change?* • *How do new ways of thinking affect the way people respond to their surroundings?*

Reading **HELP**DESK

Academic Vocabulary

- **philosopher**
- **sphere**

Content Vocabulary

- **geocentric**
- **heliocentric**
- **universal law of gravitation**
- **rationalism**
- **scientific method**
- **inductive reasoning**

TAKING NOTES:

Key Ideas and Details

Summarizing Use a table like this one to list the contributions of Copernicus, Kepler, Galileo, and Newton to a new concept of the universe.

Copernicus	
Kepler	
Galileo	
Newton	

TEKS Texas Essential Knowledge and Skills

1E identify major causes and describe the major effects of the following important turning points in world history from 1750 to 1914: the Scientific Revolution, the Industrial Revolution and its impact on the

continued on the next page

It Matters Because

Of all the changes that swept Europe in the sixteenth and seventeenth centuries, the most widely influential was the Scientific Revolution. This revolution often is associated with the various scientific and technological changes made during this time. However, the Scientific Revolution was also about changes in the way Europeans looked at themselves and their world.

Causes of the Scientific Revolution

GUIDING QUESTION *What developments were the foundation of the Scientific Revolution?*

In the Middle Ages, many educated Europeans took great interest in the world around them. However, these "natural philosophers," as medieval scientists were known, did not make observations of the natural world. Instead they relied on a few ancient authorities—especially Aristotle—for their scientific knowledge. During the fifteenth and sixteenth centuries, a number of changes occurred that caused the natural philosophers to abandon their old views.

Renaissance humanists had mastered Greek as well as Latin. These language skills gave them access to newly discovered works by Archimedes and Plato. These writings made it obvious that some ancient thinkers had disagreed with Aristotle and other accepted authorities of the Middle Ages.

Other developments also encouraged new ways of thinking. Technical problems that required careful observation and accurate measurements, such as calculating the amount of weight that ships could hold, served to stimulate scientific activity. Then, too, the invention of new instruments, such as the telescope and microscope, made fresh scientific discoveries possible. Above all, the printing press helped spread new ideas quickly and easily.

Mathematics played a key role in the scientific achievements of the time. It was promoted in the Renaissance by the rediscovery of the works of ancient mathematicians. Moreover, mathematics was seen as the key to navigation, military science, and geography.

Renaissance thinkers also believed that mathematics was the key to understanding the nature of things in the universe. Nicolaus Copernicus, Johannes Kepler, Galileo Galilei, and Isaac Newton were all great mathematicians who believed that the secrets of nature were written in the language of mathematics. After studying, and sometimes discarding, the ideas of the ancient mathematicians, these intellectuals developed new theories that became the foundation of the Scientific Revolution.

(continued from p. 472)

TEKS **Texas Essential Knowledge and Skills**
development of modern economic systems, European imperialism, and the Enlightenment's impact on political revolutions

27D describe the origins of the Scientific Revolution in 16th century Europe and explain its impact on scientific thinking worldwide

continued on the next page

✓ **READING PROGRESS CHECK**

Drawing Conclusions Why might new inventions such as the telescope and microscope change the way people saw the world?

Scientific Breakthroughs

GUIDING QUESTIONS ***What role did scientific breakthroughs play during the Scientific Revolution? What obstacles did participants in the Scientific Revolution face?***

The effects of the Scientific Revolution are seen in a variety of sciences and technologies throughout the world. Discoveries in astronomy led to a new conception of the universe, advanced medical knowledge departed from ancient standards, and a new field called chemistry emerged.

The Ptolemaic System

Ptolemy, who lived in the A.D. 100s, was the greatest astronomer of antiquity. Using Ptolemy's ideas, as well as those of Aristotle and of Christianity, **philosophers** of the Middle Ages constructed a model of the universe known later as the Ptolemaic (TAH • luh • MAY • ihk) system. This system is **geocentric** because it places Earth at the center of the universe.

In the Ptolemaic system, the universe is seen as a series of concentric **spheres**—one inside the other. Earth is fixed, or motionless, at the center. The heavenly bodies—pure orbs of light—are embedded in the crystal-like, transparent spheres that rotate about Earth. The moon is embedded in the first sphere, Mercury in the second, Venus in the third, and the sun in the fourth. The rotation of the spheres makes these heavenly bodies rotate about Earth and move in relation to one another.

The tenth sphere in the Ptolemaic system is the "prime mover." This sphere moves itself and gives motion to the other spheres. Beyond the tenth sphere is Heaven, where God resides. God was at one end of the universe, then, and humans were at the center.

philosopher a person who seeks wisdom or enlightenment; a scholar or a thinker

geocentric Earth-centered; a system of planetary motion in which the sun, moon, and other planets revolve around the Earth

sphere any of the concentric, revolving, spherical transparent shells in which, according to ancient astronomy, the stars, sun, planets, and moon are set

heliocentric sun-centered; the system of the universe in which the Earth and planets revolve around the sun

Copernicus and Kepler

In May 1543, Nicolaus Copernicus, a native of Poland, published his famous book, *On the Revolutions of the Heavenly Spheres.* Copernicus, a mathematician, thought that his **heliocentric**, or sun-centered, conception of the universe offered a more accurate explanation than did the Ptolemaic system. In his system, the sun, not Earth, was at the center of the universe. The planets revolved around the sun. The moon, however, revolved around Earth. Moreover, according to Coper-nicus, the apparent movement of the sun around Earth was caused by the rotation of Earth on its axis and its journey around the sun.

Johannes Kepler, a German mathematician, took the next step in destroying the Ptolemaic system. Kepler used detailed astronomical data to arrive at his laws of planetary motion. His observations confirmed that the

▼ **Diagram of the Copernican system, Andreas Cellarius, 1660**

▶ **CRITICAL THINKING**

Analyzing Information How does this diagram illustrate the workings of the universe?

(continued from p. 473)

TEKS **Texas Essential Knowledge and Skills**
27E identify the contributions of significant scientists such as Archimedes, Copernicus, Eratosthenes, Galileo, Pythagoras, Isaac Newton, and Robert Boyle

sun was at the center of the universe and also added new information. In his first law, Kepler showed that the planets' orbits around the sun were not circular, as Copernicus had thought. Rather, the orbits were elliptical (egg-shaped), with the sun toward the end of the ellipse instead of at the center. This finding, known as Kepler's First Law, contradicted the circular orbits and crystal-like spheres that were central to the Ptolemaic system.

Galileo's Discoveries

Scientists could now think in terms of planets revolving around the sun in elliptical orbits. Important questions remained unanswered, however. Of what are the planets made? How does one explain motion in the universe? An Italian scientist answered the first question. As the first European to make regular observations of the heavens using a telescope, mathematician Galileo Galilei made a series of remarkable discoveries: mountains on Earth's moon, four moons revolving around Jupiter, and sunspots.

Galileo's observations seemed to destroy another aspect of the Ptolemaic conception. Heavenly bodies had been seen as pure orbs of light. They now appeared to be composed of material substance, just as Earth was.

Galileo's discoveries, published in *The Starry Messenger* in 1610, did more to make Europeans aware of the new view of the universe than did the works of Copernicus and Kepler. But in the midst of his newfound fame, Galileo found himself under suspicion by the Catholic Church. The Church ordered him to abandon the Copernican idea, which threatened the Church's entire conception of the universe. In the Copernican view, humans were no longer at the center of the universe; God was no longer in a specific place.

In spite of the Church's position, by the 1630s and 1640s, most astronomers had accepted the heliocentric idea of the universe. However, motion in the universe had not been explained. The ideas of Copernicus, Kepler, and Galileo had yet to be tied together. An Englishman—Isaac Newton—would make this connection; he is considered the greatest genius of the Scientific Revolution.

▲ **Galileo appears before officials in the Vatican in 1663.**

▶ **CRITICAL THINKING**
Interpreting Significance Why would the Church be concerned that Galileo's ideas contradicted its worldview?

Newton's View of the Universe

Born in 1642, Isaac Newton attended Cambridge University and later became a professor of mathematics there. His major work was *Mathematical Principles of Natural Philosophy,* known simply as the *Principia*, from a shortened form of its Latin title.

In the *Principia*, Newton defined the three laws of motion that govern the planetary bodies, as well as objects on Earth. Crucial to his whole argument was the **universal law of gravitation**. This law explains why the planetary bodies continue their elliptical orbits about the sun. The law states, in mathematical terms, that every object in the universe is attracted to every other object by a force called gravity. This one universal law, mathematically proved, could explain all motion in the universe.

Newton's ideas created a new picture of the universe. It was now seen as one huge, regulated, uniform machine that worked according to natural laws. Newton's concept dominated the modern worldview until Albert Einstein's concept of relativity gave a new picture of the universe.

universal law of gravitation one of Newton's three rules of motion; it explains that planetary bodies continue in elliptical orbits around the sun because every object in the universe is attracted to every other object by a force called gravity

Breakthroughs in Medicine and Chemistry

The teachings of Galen, a Greek physician in the A.D. 100s, dominated medicine in the Late Middle Ages. Relying on animal, rather than human, dissection to picture human anatomy, Galen was wrong in many instances.

A revolution in medicine began in the sixteenth century. During this time Andreas Vesalius and William Harvey added to the understanding of human anatomy. By dissecting human bodies at the University of Padua, Vesalius accurately described the individual organs and general structure of the human body. William Harvey showed that the heart—not the liver, as Galen had thought—was the beginning point for the circulation of blood. He also proved that the same blood flows through the veins and arteries and makes a complete circuit through the body.

The French scientist Blaise Pascal experimented with how liquids behaved under pressure. This led him to the principle known as Pascal's Law. He applied this principle to the development of tools such as the syringe and the hydraulic press.

Robert Boyle was one of the first scientists to conduct controlled experiments in chemistry. His work on the properties of gases led to Boyle's Law, which states that the volume of a gas varies with the pressure exerted on it. In the eighteenth century, Antoine Lavoisier invented a system for naming chemical elements still used today. Many people consider him the founder of modern chemistry.

Women's Contributions

Although scholarship was considered the exclusive domain of men, there were women who contributed to the Scientific Revolution. Margaret Cavendish, a philosopher, and Maria Winkelmann, an astronomer, helped advance science through their work.

Margaret Cavendish came from an English aristocratic family and was tutored on subjects considered suitable for girls of proper upbringing—music, dancing, reading, and needlework. She was not formally educated in the sciences. However, Cavendish wrote a number of works on scientific matters, including *Observations Upon Experimental Philosophy*. In this work, Cavendish was especially critical of the growing belief that humans, through science, were the masters of nature:

PRIMARY SOURCE

"We have no power at all over natural causes and effects. . . for man is but a small part, his powers are but particular actions of Nature, and he cannot have a supreme and absolute power."

—from *Observations Upon Experimental Philosophy*

Cavendish published under her own name at a time many female writers had to publish anonymously. Her contribution to philosophy is widely recognized today; however, many intellectuals of the time did not take her work seriously.

In Germany, many of the women who were involved in science were astronomers. These women had received the opportunity to become astronomers from working in family observatories where their fathers or husbands trained them. Between 1650 and 1710, women made up 14 percent of all German astronomers.

The most famous female astronomer in Germany was Maria Winkelmann. She received training in astronomy from a self-taught astronomer. When she married Gottfried Kirch, Prussia's foremost astronomer, she became his assistant and began to practice astronomy.

Connections to TODAY

Women in Science

The important position of women in the sciences today can be traced back to the Enlightenment's ideas about human equality and natural rights. The careers of Enlightenment-era women like Margaret Cavendish and the astronomer Caroline Herschell (1750–1848), who was a pioneer in the study of nebulae and star clusters, gained acceptance for the female scientists who would follow them. For example, half of the engineers operating the Large Hadron Collider, a powerful particle accelerator, are women.

rationalism a system of thought expounded by René Descartes based on the belief that reason is the chief source of knowledge

scientific method a systematic procedure for collecting and analyzing evidence that was crucial to the evolution of science in the modern world

inductive reasoning the doctrine that scientists should proceed from the particular to the general by making systematic observations and carefully organized experiments to test hypotheses or theories, a process that will lead to correct general principles

Winkelmann made some original contributions to astronomy, including the discovery of a comet. When her husband died, Winkelmann applied for a position as assistant astronomer at the Berlin Academy. She was highly qualified, but as a woman—with no university degree—she was denied the post. Members of the Berlin Academy feared that they would set a bad example by hiring a woman.

✓ **READING PROGRESS CHECK**

Speculating Why might changes in the way people saw the universe change the questions they asked about the natural world?

Philosophy and Reason

GUIDING QUESTION ***How did the Scientific Revolution change people's worldview?***

New conceptions of the universe brought about by the Scientific Revolution strongly influenced the Western view of humankind.

Descartes and Rationalism

Nowhere is this more evident than in the work of the seventeenth-century French philosopher René Descartes (day • KAHRT), who brought a philosophical perspective to the natural sciences. He began by considering the doubt and uncertainty that seemed to be everywhere in the confusion of the seventeenth century. He ended with a philosophy that largely dominated Western thought until the twentieth century.

The starting point for Descartes's new system was doubt. In his most famous work, *Discourse on Method,* written in 1637, Descartes decided to set aside all that he had learned and to begin again. One fact seemed to him to be beyond doubt—his own existence.

Descartes emphasized the importance of his own mind, accepting only those things that his reason said were true. From his first principle—"I think, therefore I am"—Descartes used his reason to arrive at a second principle. He argued that because "the mind cannot be doubted but the body and material world can, the two must be radically different."

From this idea came the principle of the separation of mind and matter (and of mind and body). Descartes's idea that mind and matter were completely separate allowed scientists to view matter as dead or inert. That is, matter was something that was totally detached from the mind and that could be investigated independently by reason. Descartes has rightly been called the father of modern **rationalism**. This system of thought is based on the belief that reason is the chief source of knowledge.

Bacon and the Scientific Method

During the Scientific Revolution, people became concerned about how they could best understand the physical world. The result was the creation of the **scientific method**—a systematic procedure for collecting and analyzing evidence. The scientific method was crucial to the evolution of science in the modern world.

The person who developed the scientific method was not a scientist, but an English philosopher with few scientific credentials. Francis Bacon believed that scientists should not rely on the ideas of ancient authorities. Instead, they should learn about nature by using **inductive reasoning**—proceeding from the particular to the general. Knowledge of the natural world should be achieved through observation and experimentation.

Before beginning this reasoning, scientists try to free their minds of opinions that might distort the truth. Then they start with detailed facts and

Analyzing **PRIMARY SOURCES**

Discourse on Method

"But I immediately became aware that while I was thus disposed to think that all was false, it was absolutely necessary that I who thus thought should be something; and noting that this truth *I think, therefore I am,* was so steadfast and so assured . . . I concluded that I might without scruple accept it as being the first principle of the philosophy I was seeking."

—René Descartes, from *Discourse on Method*

DBQ ***ANALYZING INFORMATION*** What is the first principle of Descartes's philosophy?

proceed toward general principles. From observing natural events, scientists propose hypotheses, or possible explanations, for the events. Then systematic observations and carefully organized experiments to test the hypotheses would lead to correct general principles.

Bacon was clear about what he believed his scientific method could accomplish. He stated that "the true and lawful goal of the sciences is none other than this: that human life be endowed with new discoveries and powers." He was much more concerned with practical matters than pure science. Bacon wanted science to benefit industry, agriculture, and trade. He said, "I am laboring to lay the foundation, not of any sect or doctrine, but of human utility and power."

Bacon believed this "human power" could be used to "conquer nature in action." The control and domination of nature became an important concern of science and the technology that accompanied it.

✓ READING PROGRESS CHECK

Describing What did Bacon believe was the purpose of the scientific method?

SKILLS PRACTICE

During a class discussion about the development of the scientific method, write down key words that are used to describe the thinkers who developed it and the ways in which it changed the way we think about the world. After the discussion, work with a partner to write sentences using these words to demonstrate you understand their meanings.

THE SCIENTIFIC METHOD

CHARTS/GRAPHS

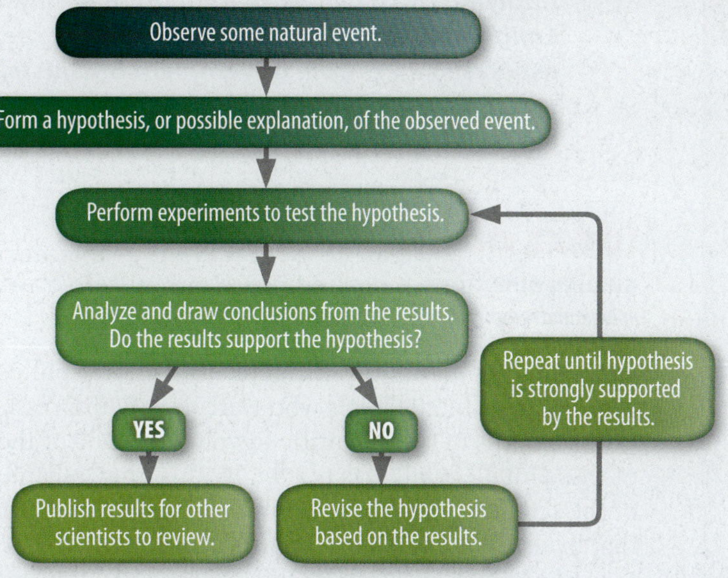

Bacon's method began a systematic approach to collecting and analyzing evidence that today is known as the scientific method.

▶ CRITICAL THINKING

1. ***Explaining*** What do scientists do when the results of their experiments disagree with their proposed explanation?
2. ***Analyzing*** How does the scientific method help to arrive at a true explanation of a natural event?

LESSON 1 REVIEW TEKS

Reviewing Vocabulary

1. ***Making Connections*** Write a paragraph explaining how the scientific method exemplified the new emphasis on reason.

Using Your Notes

2. ***Summarizing*** Use your graphic organizer on Copernicus, Kepler, Galileo, and Newton to write a paragraph summarizing how each contributed to a new concept of the universe.

Answering the Guiding Questions

3. ***Identifying Central Issues*** What developments were the foundation of the Scientific Revolution? 27D
4. ***Identifying Cause and Effect*** What role did scientific breakthroughs play during the Scientific Revolution?
5. ***Identifying*** What obstacles did participants in the Scientific Revolution face? 25C
6. ***Drawing Conclusions*** How did the Scientific Revolution change people's worldview? 1C

Writing Activity

7. **EXPLANATORY** Write a paragraph analyzing the passage from Descartes's *Discourse on Method* from this lesson. Explain how his rationalism relates to the inductive reasoning used in the scientific method.

networks

There's More Online!

- BIOGRAPHY Adam Smith
- BIOGRAPHY Montesquieu
- BIOGRAPHY Voltaire
- CHART/GRAPH The Philosophes
- IMAGE The 18th-Century Salon
- INTERACTIVE SELF-CHECK QUIZ
- PRIMARY SOURCE The Social Contract
- PRIMARY SOURCE Vindication of the Rights of Woman
- SLIDE SHOW Enlightenment Arts
- VIDEO The Enlightenment

Reading HELPDESK

Academic Vocabulary

- **generation**
- **arbitrary**

Content Vocabulary

- **philosophe**
- **separation of powers**
- **deism**
- **laissez-faire**
- **social contract**
- **salons**
- **rococo**

TAKING NOTES:

Key Ideas and Details

Summarizing As you read, use a diagram like the one below to list some of the concepts introduced by intellectuals during the Enlightenment.

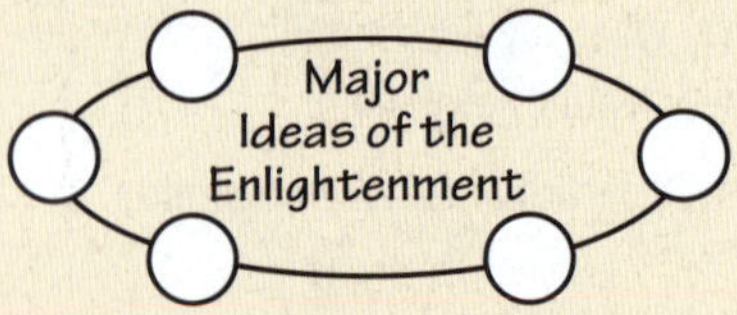

TEKS Texas Essential Knowledge and Skills

9D identify the influence of ideas such as separation of powers, checks and balances, liberty, equality, democracy, popular sovereignty, human rights, constitutionalism, and nationalism on political revolutions

continued on the next page

LESSON 2
The Ideas of the Enlightenment

ESSENTIAL QUESTIONS • *Why do new ideas often spark change?* • *How do new ways of thinking affect the way people respond to their surroundings?*

It Matters Because

Applying the scientific method to their physical world, Enlightenment thinkers, or philosophes, reexamined all aspects of life—from government and justice to religion and women's rights. They created a movement that influenced the entire Western world.

Ideas of the Philosophes

GUIDING QUESTIONS *What role did philosophes play in the Enlightenment? How did the belief in logic and reason promote the beginnings of the social sciences?*

The Enlightenment was an eighteenth-century philosophical movement of intellectuals who were greatly impressed with the achievements of the Scientific Revolution. One of the favorite words of these intellectuals was *reason*. By this, they meant the application of the scientific method to an understanding of all life. They hoped that by using the scientific method, they could make progress toward a better society than the one they had inherited. *Reason, natural law, hope, progress*—these were common words to the thinkers of the Enlightenment. The ideas of the Enlightenment would become a force for reform and eventually revolution.

The intellectuals of the Enlightenment were especially influenced by the ideas of two seventeenth-century Englishmen—John Locke and Isaac Newton. In his *Essay Concerning Human Understanding*, Locke argued that every person was born with a tabula rasa, or blank mind. Locke's ideas suggested that people were molded by the experiences that came through their senses from the surrounding world. Enlightenment thinkers began to believe that if environments were changed and people were exposed to the right influences, then they could be changed to create a new, and better, society.

The ideas of Isaac Newton also influenced eighteenth-century intellectuals. Newton believed that the physical world and everything in it was like a giant "world machine," operating according to natural laws that could be uncovered through systematic investigation.

The Enlightenment thinkers reasoned that if Newton was able to discover the natural laws that governed the physical world, then by applying his scientific methods, they would be able to discover the natural laws that governed human society. If all institutions would then follow these natural laws, the result would be an ideal society.

The Role of Philosophy

The intellectuals of the Enlightenment were known by the French word **philosophe** (FEE • luh • ZAWF), meaning "philosopher." Not all philosophers were French, however, and few were philosophers in the strict sense of the term. They were writers, professors, journalists, economists, and above all, social reformers. They came chiefly from the nobility and the middle class.

Most leaders of the Enlightenment were French, although the English had provided the philosophical inspiration for the movement. It was the French philosophes who affected intellectuals elsewhere and created a movement that influenced the entire Western world.

To the philosophes, the role of philosophy was to change the world. The use of reason and a spirit of rational criticism were to be applied to everything, including religion and politics. In the first half of the eighteenth century, three individuals dominated the intellectual landscape—Montesquieu (MAHN • tuhs • KYOO), Voltaire, and Diderot (dee • DROH).

Montesquieu

Charles-Louis de Secondat, the baron de Montesquieu, was a French noble. His famous work *The Spirit of the Laws* (1748) was a study of governments. In it, Montesquieu tried to find the natural laws that govern the social and political relationships of human beings.

Montesquieu stated that England's government had three branches: the executive (the monarch), the legislative (Parliament), and the judicial (the courts of law). The government functioned through a **separation of powers**. In this separation, the executive, legislative, and judicial powers of the government limit and control each other in a system of checks and balances. By preventing any one person or group from gaining too much power, this system provides the greatest freedom and security for the state.

The system of checks and balances through separation of powers was Montesquieu's most lasting contribution to political thought. Translation of his work into English made it available to American philosophes, who worked these democratic-republican principles into the United States Constitution.

Voltaire

The greatest figure of the Enlightenment was François-Marie Arouet, known simply as Voltaire. A Parisian, Voltaire came from a prosperous middle-class family. His numerous writings during the eighteenth century brought him both fame and wealth.

Voltaire was well known for his criticism of Christianity. He often challenged the actions of the Church, one of the most powerful institutions of the time. He had a strong belief in religious toleration, fighting against religious intolerance in France. Voltaire championed **deism**, an eighteenth-century religious philosophy based on reason and natural law. Deism built on the idea of the Newtonian world machine. In the Deists' view, a mechanic (God) had created the universe. To Voltaire and most other philosophes, the universe was like a clock. God, the clockmaker, had created it, set it in motion, and allowed it to run without his interference and according to its own natural laws.

(continued from p. 478)

TEKS **Texas Essential Knowledge and Skills**

18A identify the historical origins and characteristics of the free enterprise system, including the contributions of Adam Smith, especially the influence of his ideas found in The Wealth of Nations

20A explain the development of democratic-republican government from its beginnings in the Judeo-Christian legal tradition and classical Greece and Rome through the English Civil War and the Enlightenment

20C explain the political philosophies of individuals such as John Locke, Thomas Hobbes, Voltaire, Charles de Montesquieu, Jean Jacques Rousseau, Thomas Aquinas, John Calvin, Thomas Jefferson, and William Blackstone

continued on the next page

philosophe French for "philosopher"; applied to all intellectuals during the Enlightenment

separation of powers a form of government in which the executive, legislative, and judicial branches limit and control each other through a system of checks and balances

deism an eighteenth-century religious philosophy based on reason and natural law

▼ **Voltaire helped spread Enlightenment ideas through his writings.**

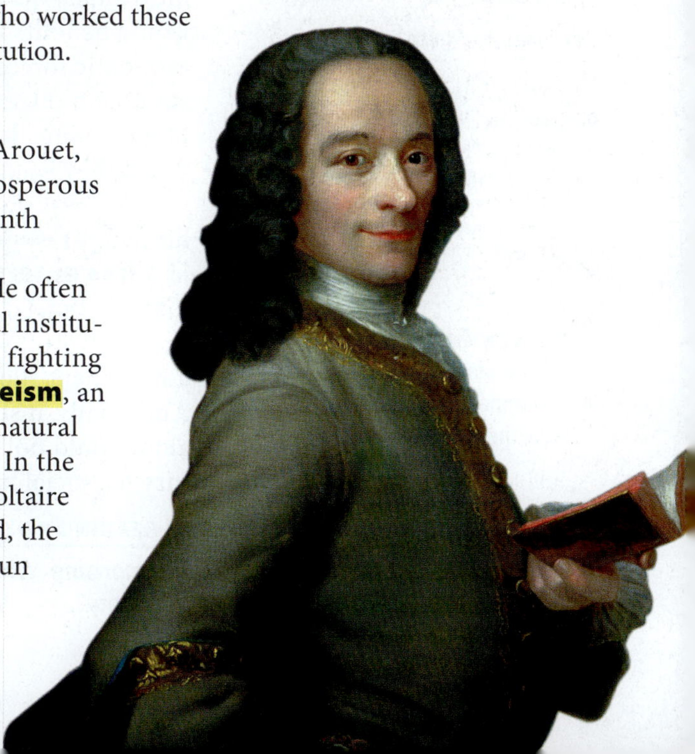

PHOTO: French School / Bridgeman / Getty Images

▲ The press room of a print shop, from Diderot's *Encyclopedia*, 1751

▶ **CRITICAL THINKING**

Drawing Conclusions How did both printing and the *Encyclopedia* contribute to the promotion of Enlightenment ideas?

Diderot

Denis Diderot went to the University of Paris. His father hoped Denis would pursue a career in law or the Church. He did neither. Instead, he became a writer, covering many subjects. Diderot's most famous contribution to the Enlightenment was the *Encyclopedia, or Classified Dictionary of the Sciences, Arts, and Trades*, a 28-volume collection of knowledge that he edited. Published between 1751 and 1772, the purpose of the *Encyclopedia*, according to Diderot, was to "change the general way of thinking."

The *Encyclopedia* became a weapon against the old French society. Many of its articles attacked religious superstition and supported religious toleration. Others called for social, legal, and political reforms. Sold to doctors, clergymen, teachers, and lawyers, the *Encyclopedia* spread Enlightenment ideas.

✓ **READING PROGRESS CHECK**

Identifying Central Issues What are two ways in which philosophes sought to change the world?

(continued from p. 479)

TEKS **Texas Essential Knowledge and Skills**

21C identify examples of key persons who were successful in shifting political thought, including William Wilberforce

24A describe the changing roles of women, children, and families during major eras of world history

25C explain the relationship among Christianity, individualism, and growing secularism that began with the Renaissance and how the relationship influenced subsequent political developments

26A identify significant examples of art and architecture that demonstrate an artistic ideal or visual principle from selected cultures

26B analyze examples of how art, architecture, literature, music, and drama reflect the history of the cultures in which they are produced

26C identify examples of art, music, and literature that transcend the cultures in which they were created and convey universal themes

New Social Sciences

GUIDING QUESTION ***How did the belief in logic and reason promote the beginnings of the social sciences?***

The philosophes, as we have seen, believed that Newton's methods could be used to discover the natural laws underlying all areas of human life. This led to what we would call the social sciences—areas such as economics and political science.

The Physiocrats and Scottish philosopher Adam Smith have been viewed as the founders of the modern social science of economics. The Physiocrats, a French group, were interested in identifying the natural economic laws that governed human society. They maintained that if individuals were free to pursue their own economic self-interest, all society would benefit. The state, then, should not interrupt the free play of natural economic forces by imposing regulations on the economy. Instead, the state should leave the economy alone. This doctrine became known by its French name, **laissez-faire** (LEH • SAY • FEHR), meaning "to let (people) do (what they want)."

The best statement of laissez-faire was made in 1776 by Adam Smith in his famous work, *The Wealth of Nations*. Like the Physiocrats, Smith believed in a **free enterprise system**—the state should not interfere in economic matters. Indeed, Smith gave to government only three basic roles. First, it should protect society from invasion (the function of the army). Second, the government should defend citizens from injustice (the function of the police). And finally, it should keep up certain public works that private individuals alone could not afford—roads and canals, for example—but which are necessary for social interaction and trade.

✓ **READING PROGRESS CHECK**

Summarizing What roles did Adam Smith believe the government should fulfill in society?

laissez-faire the concept that the state should not impose government regulations but should leave the economy alone

generation a group of individuals born and living at the same time

The Spread of Ideas

GUIDING QUESTIONS *How did Enlightenment ideas influence society and culture?*

By the late 1760s, a new **generation** of philosophes had come to maturity. Ideas about liberty and the condition of women were spread through an increasingly literate society.

The Social Contract

The most famous philosophe of the later Enlightenment was Jean-Jacques Rousseau (ru • SOH). In his *Discourse on the Origins of the Inequality of Mankind*, Rousseau argued that people had adopted laws and government in order to preserve their private property. In the process, they had become enslaved by government and needed to regain their freedom.

In his major work, *The Social Contract*, published in 1762, Rousseau presented his concept of the **social contract**. Through a social contract, an entire society agrees to be governed by its general will. Individuals who wish instead to follow their own self-interests must be forced to abide by the general will. "This means nothing less than that [they] will be forced to be free," said Rousseau. Thus, liberty is achieved by being forced to follow what is best for "the general will" because the general will represents what is best for the entire community.

Unlike many Enlightenment thinkers, Rousseau believed that emotions, as well as reason, were important to human development. He sought a balance between heart and mind, between emotions and reason.

Women's Rights

For centuries, male intellectuals had argued that the nature of women made them inferior to men and made male domination of women necessary. By the eighteenth century, however, female thinkers began to express their ideas about improving the condition of women. Mary Wollstonecraft, an English writer, advanced the strongest statement for the rights of women. Many see her as the founder of the modern European and American movements for women's rights.

In *A Vindication of the Rights of Women*, Wollstonecraft identified two problems with the views of many Enlightenment thinkers. She noted that the same people who argued that women must obey men also said that government based on the **arbitrary** power of monarchs over their subjects was wrong. Wollstonecraft pointed out that the power of men over women was equally wrong.

Wollstonecraft further argued that the Enlightenment was based on an ideal of reason in all human beings. Therefore, because women have reason, they are entitled to the same rights as men. Women, Wollstonecraft declared, should have equal rights in education, as well as in economic and political life. The concept of women's rights had emerged.

The Growth of Reading

Of great importance to the Enlightenment was the spread of its ideas to the literate elite of European society. The growth of both publishing and the reading public during the eighteenth century was noticeable. Books had previously been aimed at small groups of the educated elite. Now many books were directed at the new reading public of the middle classes, which included women and urban artisans. Especially appealing to these readers were the works of novelists who began to use realistic social themes. The English writer Henry Fielding wrote novels about people without morals who survive by their wits. Fielding's best-known work is *The History of Tom Jones, a Foundling*, which describe the adventures of a young scoundrel.

BIOGRAPHY

William Wilberforce (1759–1833)

Combining the Enlightenment ideals of human rights and his Christian faith, William Wilberforce was one of the leading English abolitionists and a Member of Parliament for twenty-eight years. His firm belief in human rights and his persistence shifted political thought in Great Britain. Beginning in 1787 and continuing until Britain banned the slave trade in 1807, Wilberforce headed the campaign for its abolition within Parliament. Even after Wilberforce resigned from Parliament in 1826 because of his health, he continued to campaign for the complete abolition of slavery throughout the entire British Empire. Three days after Wilberforce died in 1833, Parliament announced the abolition of slavery in all British-held territories.

social contract the concept that an entire society agrees to be governed by its general will and all individuals should be forced to abide by it since it represents what is best for the entire community

▲ Mary Wollstonecraft was an advocate of women's rights.

arbitrary at one's discretion; random

An important aspect of the growth of publishing and reading in the eighteenth century was the development of magazines and newspapers for the general public. The first daily newspaper was printed in London in 1702. Newspapers were relatively cheap and were even provided free in many coffeehouses. Coffeehouses also served as gathering places for the exchange of ideas.

▲ An eighteenth-century coffeehouse in London

▶ **CRITICAL THINKING**

Constructing Arguments Do the coffeehouses of today serve the same purpose as early ones? Why or why not?

Enlightenment ideas were also spread through the salon. **Salons** were the elegant drawing rooms of the wealthy upper class's great urban houses. Invited guests gathered in these salons and took part in conversations that were often centered on the new ideas of the philosophes. The salons brought writers and artists together with aristocrats, government officials, and wealthy middle-class people. The women who hosted the salons were in a position to sway political opinion and helped spread the ideas of the Enlightenment.

salons the elegant urban drawing rooms where, in the eighteenth century, writers, artists, aristocrats, government officials, and wealthy middle-class people gathered to discuss the ideas of the philosophes

Christianity, Individualism, and Growing Secularism

The Enlightenment saw the growth of **secularism**—the principle that religion should not play a role in government, education, or other parts of society. The roots of secularism can be found in the thought of ancient philosophers and in the humanist movement that began during the Renaissance. While humanist thinkers were Christians, they emphasized the development of the individual rather than the authority of religion. Enlightenment thinkers further developed this concept, emphasizing the importance of an individual's ability to reason over strict obedience to religious dogma.

This changing relationship among Christianity, individualism, and secularism is made evident in political developments of the Enlightenment. Many Enlightenment thinkers emphasized the ability of individuals to be self-governing, an idea that they applied to both the authority of monarchs and church officials. This would greatly influence the development of the "separation of church and state" concept. It would also influence important political movements like the American and French Revolutions.

✓ **READING PROGRESS CHECK**

Evaluating How did Mary Wollstonecraft use the Enlightenment ideal of reason to advocate rights for women?

Enlightenment and the Arts

GUIDING QUESTION ***How did Enlightenment ideas influence society and culture?***

The ideas of the Enlightenment also had an impact on the world of culture. Eighteenth-century Europe witnessed both traditional practices and important changes in art, music, and literature.

Architecture and Art

The palace of Louis XIV at Versailles, in France, had made an enormous impact on Europe as other European rulers also built grand residences. These palaces were modeled more on the Italian baroque style of the 1500s and 1600s than on the late seventeenth-century French classical style of Versailles. One of the greatest architects of the eighteenth century was Balthasar Neumann. Neumann's two masterpieces are the Church of the Fourteen Saints in southern Germany and the Residence, the palace of the prince bishop of Würzburg. In these buildings, secular and spiritual become one, as lavish and fanciful ornament, light, bright colors, and elaborate detail greet the visitor. The baroque and neoclassical styles that had dominated seventeenth-century art continued into the eighteenth century. By the 1730s, however, a new artistic style, known as **rococo**, had spread all over Europe. Unlike the baroque style, which stressed grandeur and power, rococo emphasized grace,

rococo an artistic style that replaced baroque in the 1730s; it was highly secular, emphasizing grace, charm, and gentle action

PHOTO: Bettman / Corbis

charm, and gentle action. Rococo made use of delicate designs colored in gold with graceful curves. The rococo style was highly secular, reflecting the Enlightenment culture of the time. Its lightness and charm spoke of the pursuit of pleasure, happiness, and love.

Rococo's appeal is evident in the work of Antoine Watteau. In his paintings, gentlemen and ladies in elegant dress reveal a world of upper-class pleasure and joy. Underneath that exterior, however, is an element of sadness. The artist suggests such sadness in his paintings by depicting the fragility and passing nature of pleasure, love, and life, connecting universal themes across class and culture. One of his masterpieces, the *Embarkation for Cythera*, demonstrates this artistic ideal of French rococo.

▲ *The Swing,* by Jean-Honore Fragonard, 1767

Music

Eighteenth-century Europe produced some of the world's most enduring music. Two geniuses of the second half of the eighteenth century, Franz Joseph Haydn and Wolfgang Amadeus Mozart, were innovators who wrote classical music rather than the baroque music of Bach and Handel. Haydn spent most of his adult life as musical director for wealthy Hungarian princes. Visits to England introduced him to a world in which musicians wrote for public concerts rather than princely patrons, demonstrating how music and its production were reflective of the culture. This "liberty," as he called it, led him to write two great works, *The Creation* and *The Seasons, each conveying universal themes of beginnings and everyday life.*

Mozart was truly a child prodigy. He gave his first harpsichord concert at age six and wrote his first opera at twelve. His failure to get a regular patron to support him financially made his life miserable. Nevertheless, he wrote music passionately. His works *The Marriage of Figaro*, *The Magic Flute*, and *Don Giovanni* are three of the world's greatest operas, transcending time and cultures. Haydn remarked to Mozart's father, "Your son is the greatest composer known to me . . . "

✓ **READING PROGRESS CHECK**

Making Inferences How do Haydn's interests as a composer reflect the influence of Enlightenment ideas?

LESSON 2 REVIEW TEKS

Reviewing Vocabulary

1. ***Explaining*** Write a paragraph explaining what Montesquieu meant by the phrase *separation of powers* and where he saw this principle applied.

Using Your Notes

2. ***Summarizing*** As you read, use your graphic organizer to list some of the main ideas introduced during the Enlightenment.

Answering the Guiding Questions

3. ***Identifying*** How did Enlightenment thinkers use the ideas of the Scientific Revolution?
4. ***Questioning*** What role did the philosophes play in the Enlightenment?
5. ***Understanding Relationships*** How did the belief in logic and reason promote the beginnings of the social sciences?
6. ***Interpreting*** How did Enlightenment ideas influence society and culture?

Writing Activity

7. **NARRATIVE** Write a paragraph giving your personal opinion of the ideas of one of the intellectuals discussed in this lesson. Explain why you agree or disagree with that person's work. Be sure to give specific details of the chosen topic as part of your response.

networks

There's More Online!

- BIOGRAPHY Catherine the Great
- BIOGRAPHY Frederick II
- BIOGRAPHY Maria Theresa
- CHART/GRAPH Rulers of Prussia, Austria, and Russia, 1714–1796
- GRAPHIC ORGANIZER Austrian Succession, 1658–1740
- INTERACTIVE SELF-CHECK QUIZ
- MAP The Seven Years' War
- PRIMARY SOURCE Treaty of Paris
- TIME LINE The Seven Years' War
- VIDEO Catherine the Great

LESSON 3

Enlightened Absolutism and the Balance of Power

ESSENTIAL QUESTIONS

- *Why do new ideas often spark change?*
- *How do new ways of thinking affect the way people respond to their surroundings?*

Reading HELPDESK

Academic Vocabulary

- **rigid**
- **eventually**

Content Vocabulary

- **enlightened absolutism**
- **successors**

TAKING NOTES:

Key Ideas and Details

Describing Use a graphic organizer like the one below to list details that help show the political philosophies of Frederick II, Joseph II, and Catherine II.

Ruler	Details That Show Political Philosophy
Frederick II	
Joseph II	
Catherine II	

TEKS Texas Essential Knowledge and Skills

19B identify the characteristics of the following political systems: theocracy, absolute monarchy, democracy, republic, oligarchy, limited monarchy, and totalitarianism

26C identify examples of art, music, and literature that transcend the cultures in which they were created and convey universal themes

IT MATTERS BECAUSE

Enlightenment ideas had an impact on the politics of eighteenth-century Europe. While they liked to talk about enlightened reforms, most rulers were more interested in the power and stability of their nations. Their desire for balancing power, however, could also lead to war. The Seven Years' War became global as war broke out in Europe, India, and North America.

Enlightenment and Absolutism

GUIDING QUESTION *How were European rulers guided by Enlightenment thought?*

Enlightenment thought influenced European politics in the eighteenth century. The philosophes believed in natural rights for all people. These rights included equality before the law; freedom of religious worship; freedom of speech; freedom of the press; and the rights to assemble, hold property, and pursue happiness. To establish and preserve these natural rights, most philosophes believed that people needed to be governed by enlightened rulers. Enlightened rulers must allow natural rights and nurture the arts, sciences, and education. Above all, they must obey and enforce the laws fairly for all subjects. Only strong monarchs could bring about the enlightened reforms society needed.

Most monarchs who ruled during this period were absolute monarchs. **Absolute monarchy** is a form of monarchy where the power of the monarch is not limited by laws or a constitution. Many historians once assumed that a new type of monarchy, **enlightened absolutism**, emerged in the later eighteenth century. In this system, rulers tried to govern by Enlightenment principles while maintaining their royal powers. Did Europe's rulers actually follow the advice of the philosophes and become enlightened? To answer this question, we examine three states—Prussia, Austria, and Russia.

enlightened absolutism a system in which rulers tried to govern by Enlightenment principles while maintaining their full royal powers

Two able Prussian kings, Frederick William I and Frederick II, made Prussia a major European power in the eighteenth century. Frederick William I maintained a highly efficient bureaucracy of civil service workers.

They observed the supreme values of obedience, honor, and, above all, service to the king. As Frederick William asserted: "One must serve the king with life and limb, … and surrender everything except salvation. The latter is reserved for God. But everything else must be mine."

Frederick William's other major concern was the army. By the end of his reign in 1740, he had doubled the army's size. Although Prussia was a small state, it had the fourth-largest army after France, Russia, and Austria. The Prussian army, because of its size and its good reputation, was the most important institution in the state.

Members of the nobility, who owned large landed estates with many serfs, were the officers in the Prussian army. These officers, too, had a strong sense of service to the king or state. As Prussian nobles, they believed in duty, obedience, and sacrifice.

Frederick II, or Frederick the Great, who ruled from 1740 to 1786, was one of the best educated monarchs of the time. He was well versed in Enlightenment ideas and was also a dedicated ruler. He, too, enlarged the Prussian army by actively recruiting the nobility into civil service. Frederick kept a strict watch over the bureaucracy.

rigid inflexible, unyielding

For a time, Frederick seemed quite willing to make enlightened reforms. He abolished the use of torture except in treason and murder cases. He also granted limited freedom of speech and press, as well as greater religious toleration. However, Frederick kept Prussia's serfdom and **rigid** social structure intact and avoided any additional reforms.

▲ Maria Theresa, empress of Austria, and some of her children

The Austrian Empire had become one of the great European states by the start of the eighteenth century. It was hard to rule, however, because it was a sprawling empire composed of many nationalities, languages, religions, and cultures. Empress Maria Theresa, who inherited the throne in 1740, worked to centralize and strengthen the state. While not open to the philosophes' calls for reform, she did work to improve the condition of the serfs.

Her son, Joseph II, believed in the need to sweep away anything standing in the path of reason: "I have made Philosophy the lawmaker of my empire." Joseph abolished serfdom and eliminated the death penalty. He established the principle of equality of all before the law and enacted religious reforms, including religious toleration.

Joseph's reform program largely failed, however. He alienated the nobles by freeing the serfs. He alienated the Catholic Church with his religious reforms. Even the serfs were unhappy because they could not understand the drastic changes. Joseph realized his failure when he wrote his own epitaph for his gravestone: "Here lies Joseph II who was unfortunate in all his enterprises." His **successors** undid almost all of Joseph II's reforms.

In Russia, Peter the Great was followed by six weak successors who were often put in power and deposed by the palace guard. A group of nobles murdered the last of these six successors, Peter III. His German wife emerged as ruler of all the Russians.

Catherine II, or Catherine the Great, ruled Russia from 1762 to 1796. She was an intelligent woman who was familiar with the works of the philosophes and seemed to favor enlightened reforms. She considered the idea of a new law code that would recognize the principle of equality of all people in the eyes of the law.

successor one that follows, especially one who takes over a throne, title, estate, or office

eventually in the end

In the end, however, Catherine did nothing because she knew that her success depended on the support of the Russian nobility. Her policy of favoring the landed nobility led to worse conditions for the Russian peasants and **eventually** to rebellion. Led by an illiterate Cossack (a Russian warrior), Yemelyan Pugachov, the rebellion spread across southern Russia but soon collapsed. Catherine took stronger measures against the peasants. Rural reform was halted, and serfdom was expanded into newer parts of the empire.

Catherine proved to be a worthy successor to Peter the Great in her policies of territorial expansion. Russia spread southward to the Black Sea by defeating the Turks under Catherine's rule. To the west, Russia gained about 50 percent of Poland's territory, with the remainder split between Prussia and Austria. The Polish state disappeared until after World War I.

▲ Catherine II (Catherine the Great) was a strong Russian ruler.

Of the rulers under discussion, only Joseph II sought truly radical changes based on Enlightenment ideas. Both Frederick II and Catherine II liked to talk about enlightened reforms. They even attempted some, but their priority was maintaining the existing system.

In fact, all three of these enlightened absolutists—Frederick, Joseph, and Catherine—were guided primarily by their interest in the power and welfare of their state. When they did manage to strengthen their position as rulers, they did not undertake enlightened reforms to benefit their subjects. Rather, their power was used to collect more taxes and thus to create armies, to wage wars, and to gain even more power.

The philosophes condemned war as a foolish waste of life and resources. Despite their words, the rivalry among states that led to costly struggles remained unchanged in eighteenth-century Europe. Europe's states were chiefly guided by their rulers' self-interest.

The eighteenth-century monarchs were concerned with the balance of power. This concept meant that states should have equal power in order to prevent any one from dominating the others. Large armies created to defend a state's security, however, were often used to conquer new lands as well. As Frederick II of Prussia said, "The fundamental rule of governments is the principle of extending their territories." This rule led to two major wars in the eighteenth century.

✓ **READING PROGRESS CHECK**

Comparing Describe two similarities between the reigns of Frederick II of Prussia and Catherine the Great of Russia.

The Seven Years' War

GUIDING QUESTION *How did changing alliances in Europe lead to the Seven Years' War and how was the war carried out on a global scale?*

The stage was set for the Seven Years' War when, in 1740, a major war broke out over the succession to the Austrian throne. When the Austrian emperor Charles VI died without a male heir, his daughter, Maria Theresa, succeeded him. King Frederick II of Prussia took advantage of the confusion surrounding the succession of a woman to the throne by invading Austrian Silesia, a piece of land that he hoped to add to Prussia. By this action, Frederick refused to recognize the legitimacy of the empress of Austria. France then entered the war against Austria, its traditional enemy. In turn, Maria Theresa allied with Great Britain.

The War of the Austrian Succession (1740–1748) was fought in three areas of the world. In Europe, Prussia seized Silesia while France occupied some Austrian territory. In Asia, France took Madras (today called Chennai) in India from the British. In North America, the British captured the French fortress of Louisbourg at the entrance of the St. Lawrence River.

By 1748, all parties were exhausted and agreed to the Treaty of Aix-la-Chapelle. The treaty guaranteed the return of all occupied territories but Silesia to their original owners. Prussia's refusal to return Silesia meant yet another war, for Maria Theresa refused to accept the loss. She rebuilt her army while working diplomatically to separate Prussia from its chief ally, France. In 1756 Maria Theresa achieved what was soon labeled a diplomatic revolution.

SKILLS PRACTICE

Working with a partner, take turns reading the text under the Seven Years' War heading. Ask your partner for help if you do not know a word or understand something in the lesson.

The War in Europe

French-Austrian rivalry had been a fact of European diplomacy since the late sixteenth century. However, two new rivalries now replaced the old one: the rivalry of Britain and France over colonial empires and the rivalry of Austria and Prussia over Silesia.

France abandoned Prussia and formed an alliance with Austria. Russia, which saw Prussia as a major threat to Russian goals in central Europe, joined the new alliance with France and Austria. In turn, Britain allied with Prussia. This diplomatic revolution of 1756 led to another worldwide war. The war had three major areas of conflict: Europe, India, and North America.

Europe witnessed the clash of the two major alliances: the British and Prussians against the Austrians, Russians, and French. The superb army and military skill of Frederick the Great of Prussia enabled him at first to defeat the Austrian, French, and Russian armies. Under attack from three different directions, however, his forces were gradually worn down.

Frederick faced disaster until Peter III, a new Russian czar who greatly admired Frederick, withdrew Russian troops from the conflict. This withdrawal created a stalemate and led to the desire for peace. The European war ended in 1763. All occupied territories were returned to their original owners, except Silesia. Austria officially recognized Prussia's permanent control of Silesia.

GEOGRAPHY CONNECTION

Changing alliances led to the Seven Years' War in Europe.

1. **PLACES AND REGIONS** *Identify the countries that belonged to each of the two European alliances.*
2. **THE WORLD IN SPATIAL TERMS** *In which countries did most of the battles take place?*

The War in India

The struggle between Britain and France that took place in the rest of the world had more decisive results. Known as the Great War for Empire, it was fought in India and North America. The French had returned Madras to Britain after the War of the Austrian Succession, but the struggle in India continued. The British ultimately won out, not because they had better forces but because they were more persistent. With the Treaty of Paris in 1763, the French withdrew and left India to the British.

The War in North America

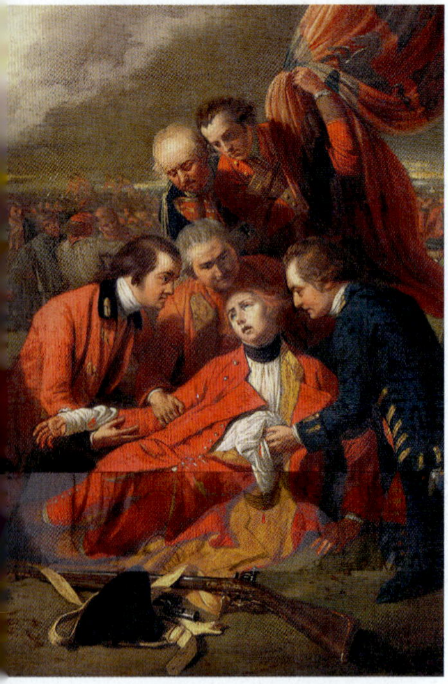

▲ This painting by Benjamin West shows the death of the British General James Wolfe.

The greatest conflicts of the Seven Years' War took place in North America. On the North American continent, the French and British colonies were set up differently. The French government administered French North America (Canada and Louisiana) as a vast trading area. It was valuable for its fur, leather, fish, and timber, but its colonies were thinly populated.

British North America consisted of thirteen prosperous colonies on the eastern coast of what is now the United States. Unlike the French colonies, the British colonies were more populated, containing more than one million people by 1750.

The British and French fought over two main areas in North America. One consisted of the waterways of the Gulf of St. Lawrence, which were protected by the fortress of Louisbourg and by forts that guarded French Quebec. The other area they fought over was the unsettled Ohio River valley. The French scored a number of victories at first. British fortunes were revived, however, by the efforts of William Pitt the Elder, Britain's prime minister. Pitt was convinced that the French colonial empire would have to be destroyed for Britain to create its own colonial empire.

A series of British victories soon followed. In 1759 British forces under General Wolfe defeated the French under General Montcalm on the Plains of Abraham, outside Quebec. Both generals died in the battle. The British went on to seize Montreal, the Great Lakes area, and the Ohio River valley. The French were forced to make peace. By the Treaty of Paris, the French transferred Canada and the lands east of the Mississippi to England. Spain, an ally of the French, transferred Spanish Florida to British control. In return, the French gave their Louisiana territory to the Spanish. By 1763, Great Britain had become the world's greatest colonial power.

✓ **READING PROGRESS CHECK**

Explaining Explain the involvement of Great Britain and France in the Seven Years' War.

LESSON 3 REVIEW TEKS

Reviewing Vocabulary

1. ***Identifying*** Write a paragraph defining the term ***enlightened absolutism***. Discuss one example of an eighteenth-century monarch and explain how he or she fulfilled or failed to fulfill this ideal. 19B

Using Your Notes

2. ***Evaluating*** Use your graphic organizer to write a paragraph evaluating the degree to which Frederick II, Joseph II, and Catherine II did or did not embrace Enlightenment ideas.

Answering the Guiding Questions

3. ***Making Connections*** How were European rulers guided by Enlightenment thought?

4. ***Identifying Cause and Effect*** How did changing alliances in Europe lead to the Seven Years' War and how was the war carried out on a global scale?

Writing Activity

5. **NARRATIVE** Narrate a series of events that helps tell the story of both the War of the Austrian Succession and the Seven Years' War. Use transitional words and phrases to show a clear sequence.

networks

There's More Online!

- BIOGRAPHY George Washington
- BIOGRAPHY Thomas Jefferson
- CHART/GRAPH Powers of the U.S. Federal Government
- INTERACTIVE SELF-CHECK QUIZ
- MAP Land Claims After the American Revolution, 1783
- PRIMARY SOURCE The Articles of Confederation
- PRIMARY SOURCE The Declaration of Independence
- TIME LINE The American Revolution
- VIDEO John Hancock

LESSON 4
The American Revolution

ESSENTIAL QUESTIONS • *Why do new ideas often spark change?* • *How do new ways of thinking affect the way people respond to their surroundings?*

Reading HELPDESK

Academic Vocabulary
- **amendment**
- **guarantee**

Content Vocabulary
- **federal system**

READING STRATEGY:
Key Ideas and Details

Summarizing As you read, use a chart like the one below to identify important elements of the government created by the American colonists.

TEKS Texas Essential Knowledge and Skills

1E identify major causes and describe the major effects of the following important turning points in world history from 1750 to 1914: the Scientific Revolution, the Industrial Revolution and its impact on the development of modern economic systems, European imperialism, and the Enlightenment's impact on political revolutions

continued on p. 491

IT MATTERS BECAUSE

The ideas of the Enlightenment clearly made an impact on the colonies in North America. In response to unfair taxation and other issues, the colonists revolted against British rule, formed their own army, and declared their independence. Many Europeans saw the American Revolution as the embodiment of the Enlightenment's political dreams.

Britain and the American Revolution

GUIDING QUESTION *What were the causes of and influences on the American Revolution?*

The United Kingdom of Great Britain came into existence in 1707, when the governments of England and Scotland were united. The term *British* came to refer to both the English and the Scots.

In 1688 the Glorious Revolution resulted in a Bill of Rights that affirmed Parliament's right to make laws. As a result, the monarch and Parliament shared power. The monarch chose ministers, who were responsible to the Crown. These ministers set policy and guided Parliament. Parliament's power to make laws, levy taxes, and pass the budget indirectly influenced the monarch's ministers.

In 1714 a new dynasty was established when the last Stuart ruler, Queen Anne, died without an heir. The crown was offered to her nearest relatives, Protestant rulers of the German state of Hannover. The first Hanoverian king, George I, did not speak English. Neither the first nor the second George knew the British system well, so their chief ministers were allowed to deal with Parliament.

In the meantime, growing trade and industry led to an ever-increasing middle class that favored the expansion of trade and of Britain's world empire. They found a spokesman in William Pitt the Elder, who became head of the cabinet in 1757. He expanded the British Empire by acquiring Canada and India in the Seven Years' War.

▲ *The Declaration of Independence, 4 July, 1776*, by John Trumbull

▶ **CRITICAL THINKING**
Drawing Inferences What does this painting reveal about the process of the colonial break with Great Britain?

In North America, then, Britain controlled Canada as well as the thirteen colonies on the eastern coast of what is now the United States. The British colonies were well populated, containing more than 1 million people by 1750. They were also prosperous.

In theory, the British Board of Trade, the Royal Council, and Parliament controlled the colonies. In actuality, the colonies had legislatures that often acted independently. Merchants in port cities such as Charleston, New York, and Boston did not want the British government to run their affairs.

The American Revolution Begins

After the Seven Years' War, British leaders wanted to get new colonial revenues from the colonies. These revenues would then be used to cover war costs. These would also pay for the expenses of maintaining an army to defend the colonies.

In 1765 Parliament imposed the Stamp Act on the colonies. The act required certain printed materials, such as legal documents and newspapers, to carry a stamp showing that a tax had been paid to Britain. Opposition was widespread and often violent. The act was repealed in 1766, ending the immediate crisis, but the cause of the dispute was not resolved.

Crisis followed crisis in the 1770s. To counteract British actions, the colonies organized the First Continental Congress, which met in Philadelphia in September 1774. Members urged colonists to take up arms and organize militias.

Fighting finally erupted between colonists and the British army in April 1775 in Lexington and Concord, Massachusetts. Meeting soon afterward, the Second Continental Congress set up an army, called the Continental Army. George Washington served as its commander in chief.

Analyzing PRIMARY SOURCES

Declaration of Independence

"We hold these truths to be self-evident; that all men are created equal; that they are endowed by their Creator with certain inalienable rights; that among these are life, liberty and the pursuit of happiness; that to secure these rights, governments are instituted among men, deriving their just powers from the consent of the governed . . ."

—from the Declaration of Independence

DBQ ***PARAPHRASING*** Rewrite the excerpt from the Declaration of Independence in your own words.

The Declaration of Independence

More than a year passed before the colonies declared independence from the British Empire. On July 4, 1776, the Second Continental Congress approved the Declaration of Independence written by Thomas Jefferson. This stirring political document, inspired by many Enlightenment ideas, formally began the American Revolution.

The Declaration of Independence contains important legal and political ideas. It states that "...all men are created equal, that they are endowed by their Creator with certain unalienable Rights, that among these are Life, Liberty and the pursuit of Happiness." In simple terms, this forms a legal foundation for the principles of equality before the law and individual rights. The impact of these legal ideas is immense. Unlike later governing documents of the United States, the Declaration of Independence includes broad statements supporting equality and human rights. Today, the Declaration of Independence continues to influence human and property rights movements all over the world.

In its opening line, the Declaration of Independence spelled out that the United States was a new nation, ready to interact with other nations on an equal footing. Politically, the writers of the Declaration of Independence were asserting that a government existed only because of popular sovereignty—or the right to govern through the consent of the people. Additionally, the Declaration firmly states that a government that fails to uphold the ideals of liberty could be justifiably overthrown by the people. These political ideas expressed in the Declaration of Independence inspired revolutionaries in Latin America, France, and other parts of Europe just decades after the American Revolution. Today they continue to influence revolutionaries and political reformers across the globe.

(continued from p. 489)

TEKS **Texas Essential Knowledge and Skills**

9D identify the influence of ideas such as separation of powers, checks and balances, liberty, equality, democracy, popular sovereignty, human rights, constitutionalism, and nationalism on political revolutions

20B identify the impact of political and legal ideas contained in the following documents: Hammurabi's Code, the Jewish Ten Commandments, Justinian's Code of Laws, Magna Carta, the English Bill of Rights, the Declaration of Independence, the U.S. Constitution, and the Declaration of the Rights of Man and of the Citizen

20C explain the political philosophies of individuals such as John Locke, Thomas Hobbes, Voltaire, Charles de Montesquieu, Jean Jacques Rousseau, Thomas Aquinas, John Calvin, Thomas Jefferson, and William Blackstone

Thomas Jefferson

Thomas Jefferson, the author of the Declaration of Independence, was an American revolutionary, Founding Father, and politician. He was heavily influenced by Enlightenment thinkers John Locke, Francis Bacon, and Isaac Newton. As a supporter of the Enlightenment, Jefferson distrusted a strong central government, favoring republicanism and having a strong belief in religious freedom and the separation of church and state. Jefferson authored the Virginia Statute for Religious Freedom in 1777, which the Virginia legislature adopted as law in 1786. Jefferson's republican political principles and his views on religious freedom would profoundly influence the formation of the U.S. Constitution in 1787.

As a Founding Father of the United States, Jefferson's popularity carried him from governor of Virginia to Secretary of State, Vice President, and eventually the third President of the United States (1801–1809). Although a strong presidential figure instrumental in doubling the size of the United States with the Louisiana Purchase in 1803, Jefferson also set a standard of presidency that emphasized a weak executive power. Thomas Jefferson's political writings continue to influence American politics today.

British Defeat

Support from foreign countries was important to the colonies' cause. These nations were eager to gain revenge for earlier defeats at the hands of the British. The French supplied arms and money to the rebels. French officers and soldiers also served in Washington's army. In February 1778, following a British defeat, the French granted diplomatic recognition to the new United States. When Spain and the Dutch Republic entered the war, the British faced war with the Europeans as well as the Americans.

When General Cornwallis was forced to surrender to the American and French forces under Washington at Yorktown in 1781, the British decided to end the war. In 1783 the Treaty of Paris recognized the independence of the American colonies. The treaty also granted the Americans control of the western territory from the Appalachians to the Mississippi River.

✓ **READING PROGRESS CHECK**

Explaining Why did some American colonists seek independence from Great Britain?

The Birth of a New Nation

GUIDING QUESTIONS ***What were the effects of the American Revolution? Why did intellectuals believe the formation of the United States carried out Enlightenment thought?***

After overthrowing British rule, the former colonies feared the power of a strong central government. The states' first constitution, the Articles of

▲ The Constitutional Convention of 1787 resulted in the creation of the United States Constitution and a new government for the young country.

Confederation (1781), created a weak central government that lacked the power to deal with the nation's problems. In 1787 delegates met in Philadelphia at the Constitutional Convention to revise the Articles of Confederation. The delegates decided to plan for an entirely new government.

The Constitution and Bill of Rights

The proposed Constitution created a **federal system** in which the national government and the state governments shared power. Based on Montesquieu's ideas, the national, or federal, government was separated into three branches: executive, legislative, and judicial. Each branch had power to check, or restrain, acts of the other branches. This system enshrines the political idea of the separation of powers in the United States Constitution, and serves to ensure that no single aspect of government could overpower another and create a tyranny.

federal system a form of government in which power is shared between the national and state governments

A president served as the head of the executive branch, which is why it may be referred to as a presidential democracy. The legislative branch consisted of elected representatives in two houses—the Senate and the House of Representatives. The Supreme Court and other courts formed the judicial branch. After ratification by 9 of the 13 states, the Constitution took effect.

As promised during negotiations over ratification, the new Congress proposed 12 **amendments** to the Constitution. The states approved 10 of

amendment an alteration proposed or effected by parliamentary or constitutional procedure

▲ On July 26, 1788, New Yorkers celebrated the ratification of the Constitution.

the amendments. Together, these amendments became known as the Bill of Rights. As we have seen, the Glorious Revolution of 1688 in England had also resulted in a Bill of Rights.

These 10 amendments serve as a legal **guaranteed** for freedom of religion, speech, press, petition, and assembly. They gave Americans the right to bear arms and to be protected against unreasonable searches and arrests. They guaranteed trial by jury, due process of law, and the protection of property rights.

guarantee to assure fulfillment of a condition

Many of the rights in the Bill of Rights were derived from the natural rights proposed by the eighteenth-century philosophes and John Locke. European intellectuals saw the American Revolution as the confirmation of the premises of the Enlightenment. A new age and a better world could be achieved.

✓ **READING PROGRESS CHECK**

Analyzing What was the purpose of separating the federal government into three separate branches?

LESSON 4 REVIEW TEKS

Reviewing Vocabulary

1. ***Explaining*** Describe the federal system of government.

Using Your Notes

2. ***Summarizing*** Use your graphic organizer to write a paragraph identifying important elements of the government created by the American colonists.

Answering the Guiding Questions

3. ***Identifying Cause and Effect*** What were the causes of and influences on the American Revolution?

4. ***Making Connections*** Why did intellectuals believe the formation of the United States carried out Enlightenment thought?

5. ***Drawing Conclusions*** What were the effects of the American Revolution?

Writing Activity

6. **INFORMATIVE/EXPLANATORY** Write an essay discussing the influence of Enlightenment philosophy on the American Revolution, the Declaration of Independence, and the Constitution.

CHAPTER 21 Assessment

TEKS

Directions: On a separate sheet of paper, answer the questions below. Make sure you read carefully and answer all parts of the questions.

Lesson Review

Lesson 1

1. ***Identify and Describe*** What changes in thought brought about the Scientific Revolution? **1E, 27D**

2. ***Describing*** What were the contributions of Copernicus and Galileo to the science of astronomy? **27E**

3. ***Explaining*** What was the significance of Isaac Newton's ideas? **27E**

4. ***Drawing Inferences*** Who was one of the first scientists to conduct controlled experiments in chemistry? **27E**

Lesson 2

5. ***Identifying Influences*** What was the goal of the philosophes? How did their movement influence political developments and revolutions? **1E, 9D, 25C**

6. ***Stating*** In Adam Smith's The Wealth of Nations, what were the three roles he suggested government should have?

7. ***Identifying*** What are the origins and characteristics of the free enterprise system? **18A**

8. ***Identifying*** How was William Wilberforce successful in shifting political thought? **21C**

Lesson 3

9. ***Specifying*** Create a chart demonstrating the alliances formed during the Seven Years' War. Considering the relationship between geography and the development of a nation, why did countries create their particular alliances? **15A**

10. ***Differentiating*** Identify the characteristics of an absolute monarchy. Then answer the question: Was Catherine the Great an enlightened ruler? Why or why not? **19B**

11. ***Summarizing*** Britain and France continued the Seven Years' War on North American soil. What key areas in North America did both countries desire, and why would these areas have benefited either country? What was the end result of the conflict?

Lesson 4

12. ***Summarizing*** How did the American Revolution draw on international resources, thus making it an international affair in which Britain had to face more than just revolting colonists?

13. ***Identifying Causes*** What role did the Enlightenment play in inspiring the American Revolution? **9A**

14. ***Identifying Effects*** What were the outcomes of the American Revolution? **9A**

Need Extra Help?

If You've Missed Question	1	2	3	4	5	6	7	8	9	10	11	12	13	14
Go to page	472	473	474	475	478	480	480	481	486	485	488	491	491	492

Exploring the Essential Question

15 ***Identifying Perspectives*** Work with a partner to create a word web showing how the Enlightenment changed ways of thinking. Start with a circle labeled "Enlightenment." Draw three circles beyond it labeled "politics," "religion," and "the arts." Add circles to these three describing changes in attitudes and behaviors. To the side, place a circle labeled "Scientific Revolution." Draw circles beyond it labeled "natural laws," "rational criticism," and "rights for all." Add lines connecting circles where the values of the Scientific Revolution overlap those of the Enlightenment. You may include artwork, maps, and primary sources in your web.

16 ***Explaining and Describing*** What were the effects of the Scientific Revolution? Explain the Scientific Revolution's impact on scientific thinking worldwide.

17 ***Draw Conclusions*** Francis Bacon's ideas about opinions, reasons, facts, and observations resulted in the new practice of following a scientific method. What does this new innovation of thought processes and knowledge collecting lead you to conclude about the way information was previously brought into the collective knowledge?

18 ***Synthesizing*** During the Enlightenment, how did book publishing open up reading to different groups in society, and simultaneously, how did topics and types of printed material begin to shift?

19 ***Explaining Relationships*** What is secularism? How is this concept evident in Enlightenment thought? What were the political consequences of the growth of secularism during the Enlightenment? **25C**

20 ***Explaining and Identifying Perspectives*** Describe Jean-Jacques Rousseau's political philosophy explained in his work The Social Contract. **5A, 7F, 18F**

21 ***Identifying and Analyzing*** Choose an example of art, architecture, and music from the Enlightenment period. Discuss the characteristics of each and how it reflects the culture in which it was produced. Make a claim arguing what it is about these pieces that make them remain popular today. **26A, 26B, 26C**

Social Studies Skills

22 ***Identifying Continuity and Change*** How did the discoveries of Copernicus, Kepler, Galileo, and Newton validate each other? **29D**

23 ***Evaluating*** Compare the works of two Enlightenment authors, Rousseau and the baron de Montesquieu, and evaluate the validity of the works as texts of the Enlightenment. How does Rousseau's *The Social Contract* link to Montesquieu's *The Spirit of the Laws*? Identify the intention of each work that places each in the Enlightenment. **29D**

24 ***Explaining*** Explain the political philosophies of Montesquieu. How did this Enlightenment thinker contribute to the development of democratic-republican government? **20A, 20C**

25 ***Describing*** How did Mary Wollstonecraft contribute to the changing roles of women during the Enlightenment? **24A**

26 ***Identifying Perspectives*** What did Voltaire believe in respect to politics and religion, and what type of view did he hold regarding the world and its order? **20C**

27 ***Compare and Contrast*** What was the significance of the legal and political ideas contained in the U.S. Declaration of Independence? What did it have in common with documents and ideas from other countries? **20B**

28 ***Identifying*** What was the impact of the legal and political ideas contained in the U.S. Constitution? How are these ideas a result of Enlightenment thought? **1E, 20B**

29 ***Identifying Significance*** Explain the impact of the political ideas in the Declaration of Independence. **20B**

Need Extra Help?

If You've Missed Question	15	16	17	18	19	20	21	22	23	24	25	26	27	28	29
Go to page	478	472	476	481	481	481	482	473	479	479	481	479	490	492	491

DBQ Analyzing Primary Sources

Read the document to answer the following questions.

4. To understand political Power right ,and derive it from its Original, we must consider, what State all Men are naturally in, and that is, a *State of perfect Freedom* to order their Actions, and dispose of their Possessions, and Persons as they think fit, within the Bounds of the Law of Nature, without asking Leave, or depending upon the Will of any other Man. A *State* also of *Equality* wherein all the Power and Jurisdiction is Reciprocal, no one having more than another; there being nothing more evident, than that the Creatures of the same Species and Rank, promiscuously born to all the same advantages of Nature, and the use of the same Faculties, should also be equal one amongst another without Subordination or Subjection, unless the Lord and Master of them all should by any Manifest Declaration of his Will set one above another, and confer on him, by an evident and clear Appointment, an undoubted Right to Dominion and Sovereignty.

6. But though this be a *State of Liberty* yet it is not a *State of License;* though Man in that State have an uncontroulable Liberty, to dispose of his Person or Possessions.

30. ***Analyzing*** What does Locke believe true freedom is? **20C**

31. ***Evaluating*** What is Locke's opinion of the kings making laws? Where did he acquire his distrust of rulers with absolute power? **20C**

32. ***Theorizing*** What reaction do you think Locke's treatise received from those who first read it, and why? **20C**

33. ***Identifying Significance*** Identify the political philosophies of Thomas Jefferson and explain their significance in the development of the Declaration of Independence, as well as how the ideas inspired revolutions. **20C, 9D**

Analyzing Visuals

Use the image to answer the following questions.

34. ***Interpreting*** How does this painting reflect the themes of the rococo movement? **26C**

35. ***Analyzing Visuals*** Describe the artistic style and visual principles used by the painter. What style does the painter use?

36. ***Analyzing Viewpoints*** Consider the viewpoints of leaders of women's rights during the Enlightenment period, such as Mary Wollstonecraft. How might Wollstonecraft respond to the depiction of the women in the painting? What scenes might she suggest an artist depict?

Extended Response Question

37. ***Expository*** Trace the belief in natural rights from its origins to 1776.

PHOTO: SuperStock

Need Extra Help?

If You've Missed Question	30	31	32	33	34	35	36	37
Go to page	490	492	491	490	496	496	496	484

The French Revolution and Napoleon

1789–1815

ESSENTIAL QUESTIONS • *What causes revolution?*
• *How does revolution change society?*

networks

There's More Online! about the French Revolution and Napoleon.

CHAPTER 22

The Story Matters...

The French Revolution was a major turning point in Western history. At its most essential, it was a struggle for representational government, equality of opportunity, and a response to the near collapse of the French economy. As a child of the revolution, Napoleon Bonaparte created a legal code for France that realized some of the dreams of the revolutionaries: economic freedom, legal equality, and religious toleration, at least in part.

◀ This detail from *Portrait of Napoleon Bonaparte in the Garb of the King of Italy,* by Andrea Appiani, shows Napoleon wearing a laurel wreath, a classical symbol of triumph.

CHAPTER 22

Place and Time: France 1785–1815

The political, economic, and social conflicts that led to the French Revolution changed the role of citizens and the structure of political systems in France. However, it was not the only conflict of the latter eighteenth century. Countries around the world engaged in conflict over territories, resources, or independence. This resulted in sweeping social and cultural change.

Step Into the Place

Read the quotes and look at the information presented on the map.

DBQ **Analyzing Historical Documents** How do the concerns addressed in the quotes correspond to the styles of governments in Europe on the eve of the revolution?

PRIMARY SOURCE

“[A country] where certain areas are totally freed from burdens of which others bear the full weight, where the richest class contributes least, where privileges destroy all balance, where it is impossible to have either a constant rule or a common will, is necessarily a very imperfect kingdom, brimming with abuses, and one that is impossible to govern well.”

— Charles Alexandre de Calonne, France's finance minister, from a memorandum on reform to Louis XVI, 1786

PRIMARY SOURCE

“I conceive that there are two kinds of inequality among the human species; one, which I call natural or physical, because it is established by nature, and consists in a difference of age, health, bodily strength, and the qualities of the mind or of the soul: and another, which may be called moral or political inequality, because it depends on a kind of convention, and is established, or at least authorized by the consent of men. This latter consists of the different privileges, which some men enjoy to the prejudice of others; such as that of being more rich, more honoured, more powerful or even in a position to exact obedience.”

— Jean-Jacques Rousseau, from *A Dissertation on the Origin and Foundation of the Inequality of Mankind*, 1755

Step Into the Time

Integrating Information

Choose an event from the France portion of the time line and write a paragraph predic ting the general social, political, or economic consequence that event might have on the world.

FRANCE

- **July 14, 1789** The Storming of the Bastille
- **August 26, 1789** The Declaration of the Rights of Man and the Citizen is approved
- **January 21, 1793** Louis XVI, King of France, is executed
- **September 1793** Reign of Terror begins
- **November 1795** The Directory heads French government

1785 — 1790 — 1795

THE WORLD

- **1789** George Washington inaugurated as first U.S. president
- **1792** English writer Mary Wollstonecraft writes *A Vindication of the Rights of Woman*
- **1794** American inventor Eli Whitney patents the cotton gin
- **1794** Persia's Qājār dynasty begins
- **1796** English physician Edward Jenner vaccinates first child against smallpox

networks
There's More Online!

- **MAP** Explore the interactive version of this map on Networks.
- **TIME LINE** Explore the interactive version of the time line on Networks.

Europe 1789

November 9, 1799 Napoleon overthrows the French government

December 2, 1804 Napoleon crowns himself emperor

June–December 1812 Napoleon Bonaparte invades Russia and retreats in defeat

April 6, 1814 Napoleon abdicates as emperor

June 18, 1815 Allies defeat Napoleon at the Battle of Waterloo

1800 **1805** **1810** **1815**

1803 United States purchases Louisiana Territory from France

1804 Francois-Dominique Toussaint-Louverture's leadership leads to Haitian independence

1806 Abdication of Emperor Francis II ends the Holy Roman Empire

1810 Miguel Hidalgo leads Mexican independence movement

1814 Congress of Vienna in Austria

networks

There's More Online!

- BIOGRAPHY Louis XVI
- IMAGE Bread Riot in Paris
- IMAGE Declaration of the Rights of Man and of the Citizen
- IMAGE Storming the Bastille
- IMAGE The Three Estates
- INTERACTIVE SELF-CHECK QUIZ
- TIME LINE The French Revolution
- VIDEO The French Revolution

LESSON 1

The French Revolution Begins

ESSENTIAL QUESTIONS • *What causes revolution?* • *How does revolution change society?*

Reading **HELP**DESK

Academic Vocabulary

- **consumer**
- **exclusion**

Content Vocabulary

- **estate**
- **taille**
- **bourgeoisie**
- **sans-culottes**

TAKING NOTES:

Key Ideas and Details

Differentiating Use a graphic organizer like the one below to identify long-range and immediate causes of the French Revolution.

The French Revolution	
Long-Range	Immediate

TEKS Texas Essential Knowledge and Skills

1E identify major causes and describe the major effects of the following important turning points in world history from 1750 to 1914: the Scientific Revolution, the Industrial Revolution and its impact on the development of modern economic systems, European imperialism, and the Enlightenment's impact on political revolutions

continued on the next page

It Matters Because

Two far-reaching events occurred in 1789: the beginning of a new United States of America and the beginning of the French Revolution. Compared with the American Revolution, the French Revolution was more complex and radical. It established a new political and social order.

Causes of the French Revolution

GUIDING QUESTIONS *How did the structure of social classes in France lead to discontent? How did the economic crises in France lead to the meeting of the Estates-General?*

The French Revolution has often been seen as a major turning point in European history. The institutions of the Old Regime were destroyed. A new order emerged, based on individual rights, representative institutions, and a concept of loyalty to the nation rather than the monarch.

The long-range causes of the French Revolution are to be found in the condition of French society. Before the Revolution, French society was based on inequality. Since the Middle Ages, France's population was divided into three orders, or **estates**.

The First Estate, or clergy, numbered about 130,000 (out of a total population of 27 million) and owned about 10 percent of the land. The clergy were radically divided. The higher clergy—cardinals, bishops, and heads of monasteries—were from noble families and shared their outlook and interests. The parish priests were often poor and from the class of commoners.

The Second Estate, or nobility, numbered about 350,000 and owned about 25 to 30 percent of the land. They played a crucial role in society in the 1700s. They held leading positions in the government, in the military, in the law courts, and in the Roman Catholic Church. Despite controlling most of the wealth, neither the clergy nor the nobles had to pay the **taille** (TAH • yuh), France's chief tax.

Unlike the First and Second Estates, the Third Estate was divided by vast differences in occupation, level of education, and wealth. Peasants made up 75 to 80 percent of the Third Estate and owned about 35 to 40 percent of the land. Middle-class members of the Third Estate owned the rest. At least half the peasants had little or no land to live on.

Peasants owed certain duties to the nobles, which were a holdover from medieval times when serfdom was widespread. For example, a peasant had to pay a fee to grind his flour or press his grapes because the local lord controlled the flour mill and wine press. When the harvest time came, the peasant had to work a certain number of days harvesting the noble's crop. Peasants fiercely resented these duties.

Another part of the Third Estate consisted of urban craftspeople, shopkeepers, and workers. These people too were struggling to survive. In the 1700s, the price of **consumer** goods increased much faster than wages, which left these urban groups with decreased buying power.

The **bourgeoisie** (burzh • wah • ZEE), or middle class, was another part of the Third Estate. This group included about 8 percent of the population, or more than 2 million people. They owned about 20 to 25 percent of the land. The bourgeoisie included merchants, bankers, and industrialists, as well as professional people—lawyers, holders of public offices, doctors, and writers.

The middle class was unhappy with the privileges held by nobles. They did not want to abolish the nobility, however, but to better their own position. Some bourgeoisie had managed to become nobles by being appointed to public offices that conferred noble status. About 6,500 new nobles had been created by appointment during the 1700s.

The bourgeoisie also shared certain goals with the nobles. Both groups were increasingly upset with a monarchical system resting on privileges and on an old and rigid social order. Both were also drawn to the new political ideas of the Enlightenment.

Increased criticism of the old order of society had been part of the eighteenth-century Enlightenment. The philosophes did not advocate revolution. Their ideas, however, were widely spread among the

estate one of the three classes into which French society was divided before the revolution: the clergy (First Estate), the nobles (Second Estate), and the townspeople (Third Estate)

taille an annual direct tax, usually on land or property, that provided a regular source of income for the French monarchy

consumer one who consumes or uses economic goods

bourgeoisie the middle class, including merchants, industrialists, and professional people

(continued from p. 500)

TEKS **Texas Essential Knowledge and Skills**

9A compare the causes, characteristics, and consequences of the American and French revolutions, emphasizing the role of the Enlightenment, the Glorious Revolution, and religion

9D identify the influence of ideas such as separation of powers, checks and balances, liberty, equality, democracy, popular sovereignty, human rights, constitutionalism, and nationalism on political revolutions

continued on the next page

THE THREE ESTATES

POLITICAL CARTOON

This French political cartoon depicts the Three Estates. The circular object that pushes down on the middle figure represents the monarchy, who is burdening the people with taxes. The armored figure on the left side of the cartoon represents the nobility, the Second Estate. The robed figure on the right side of the cartoon represents the clergy, the First Estate. The crouched figure in the middle of the cartoon represents the commoners in France, the Third Estate.

▸ CRITICAL THINKING

Analyzing Information How are each of the three estates depicted? What is the commentary being made?

(continued from p. 501)

TEKS **Texas Essential Knowledge and Skills**
20B identify the impact of political and legal ideas contained in the following documents: Hammurabi's Code, the Jewish Ten Commandments, Justinian's Code of Laws, Magna Carta, the English Bill of Rights, the Declaration of Independence, the U.S. Constitution, and the Declaration of the Rights of Man and of the Citizen

literate middle class and noble elites of France. Works by Enlightenment writers, especially Rousseau, had a major impact on the French Revolution.

Social conditions and Enlightenment ideas, then, were underlying causes of the French Revolution. The immediate cause of the revolution was the near collapse of the French budget. Although the economy had been expanding for 50 years, there were periodic crises. Bad harvests in 1787 and 1788 and a slowdown in manufacturing led to food shortages, rising prices for food, and unemployment.

On the eve of the revolution, the French economy was in crisis. Despite these problems, the French king and his ministers continued to spend enormous sums of money on wars and court luxuries. The queen, Marie Antoinette, was especially known for her extravagance and this too caused popular resentment. When the government decided to spend huge sums to help the American colonists against Britain, the budget went into total crisis.

With France on the verge of financial collapse, Louis XVI was forced to call a meeting of the Estates-General. This was the French parliament, and it had not met since 1614.

✓ READING PROGRESS CHECK

Identifying Cause and Effect How were economic problems a contributing cause of the French Revolution?

The National Assembly

GUIDING QUESTIONS *Why did the Third Estate declare itself to be the National Assembly? What were the French peasants reacting to in their rebellions of 1789?*

Louis XVI called a meeting of the Estates-General at Versailles on May 5, 1789. In the Estates-General, the First and Second Estates each had about 300 representatives. The Third Estate had almost 600 representatives. Most of the Third Estate wanted to set up a constitutional government that would make the clergy and nobility pay taxes, too.

From the start, there were arguments about voting. Traditionally, each estate had one vote—the First and Second Estates could outvote the Third Estate two to one. The Third Estate demanded instead that each deputy have one vote. Under this new system, with the help of a few nobles and clerics, the Third Estate would then have a majority vote. The king, however, stated that he favored the current system.

▶ CRITICAL THINKING

Drawing Conclusions David was a member of the Third Estate. How might his painting convey a biased view of the oath?

▼ *The Oath of the Tennis Court June 20th 1789,* by Jacques-Louis David

PHOTO: AKG-Images

On June 17, 1789, the Third Estate boldly declared that it was the National Assembly and would draft a constitution. Three days later, on June 20, its deputies arrived at their meeting place, only to find the doors had been locked. They then moved to a nearby indoor tennis court and swore that they would continue meeting until they had a new constitution. The oath they swore is known as the Tennis Court Oath.

Louis XVI prepared to use force against the Third Estate. On July 14, 1789, about 900 Parisians gathered in the courtyard of the Bastille (ba • STEEL)—an old fortress used as a prison and armory. They stormed the Bastille, and after four hours of fighting, the prison warden surrendered. The rebels cut off the warden's head and demolished the Bastille brick by brick. Paris was abandoned to the rebels.

When King Louis XVI returned to his palace at Versailles after a day of hunting, the duc de la Rochefoucauld-Liancourt told him about the fall of the Bastille. Louis is said to have exclaimed, "Why, this is a revolt." "No, Sire," replied the duke. "It is a revolution."

Louis XVI was informed that he could no longer trust royal troops to shoot at the mob. The king's authority had collapsed in Paris. Meanwhile, all over France, revolts were breaking out. Popular hatred of the entire landholding system, with its fees and obligations, had finally spilled over into action.

Peasant rebellions became part of the vast panic known as the Great Fear. Rumors spread from village to village that foreign troops were on the way to put down the revolution. The peasants reacted by breaking into the houses of the lords to destroy the records of their obligations.

✓ READING PROGRESS CHECK

Making Connections What was the connection between the actions of the representatives of the Third Estate and the Estates-General and those of the peasants during the Great Fear?

Analyzing
PRIMARY SOURCES

Declaration of the Rights of Man and the Citizen

"**1.** Men are born and remain free and equal in rights; social distinctions can be established only for the common benefit.

7. No man can be accused, arrested, or detained except in cases determined by the law, and according to the forms which it has prescribed . . .

10. No one may be disturbed because of his opinions, even religious, provided that their public demonstration does not disturb the public order established by law."

—from the Declaration of the Rights of Man and the Citizen, 1789

DBQ ***IDENTIFYING*** How does this document reflect Enlightenment thought?

End of the Old Regime

GUIDING QUESTION *How did the French Revolution enter a new phase after the storming of the Bastille?*

The National Assembly reacted to news of peasant rebellions and rumors of a possible foreign invasion. On August 4, 1789, the National Assembly voted to abolish all legal privileges of the nobles and clergy.

Declaration of the Rights of Man and of the Citizen

On August 26, the National Assembly adopted the Declaration of the Rights of Man and the Citizen. Inspired by the English Bill of Rights of 1689 and by the American Declaration of Independence and Constitution, this charter of basic liberties began with "the natural and imprescriptible rights of man" to "liberty, property, security, and resistance to oppression."

The declaration was an effect of Enlightenment thought and the declaration proclaimed that all men were free and equal before the law, that appointment to public office should be based on talent, and that no group should be exempt from taxation. Freedom of speech and of the press were affirmed. The political and legal ideas in the declaration had a major impact on France and raised an important issue. Should equal rights include women? Many deputies agreed, provided that, as one man said, "women do not [hope] to exercise political rights and functions." One writer, Olympe de Gouges, refused to accept this **exclusion** of women. Echoing the words of the official declaration, she wrote:

exclusion the act of excluding

PRIMARY SOURCE

"Believing that ignorance, omission, or scorn for the rights of woman are the only causes of public misfortunes and of the corruption of governments, the women have resolved to set forth in a solemn declaration the natural, inalienable, and sacred rights of woman in order that this declaration, constantly exposed before all the members of the society, will ceaselessly remind them of their rights and duties."

—from Declaration of the Rights of Woman and the Female Citizen, 1791

The King Concedes

In the meantime, Louis XVI remained quiet at Versailles. He refused to accept the National Assembly's decrees. On October 5, thousands of Parisian women armed with broomsticks, pitchforks, pistols, and other weapons marched to Versailles. Some of the women then met with the king. They told him that their children were starving because there was no bread. These women forced Louis to accept the new decrees.

The crowd insisted that the royal family return to Paris. On October 6, they did so. As a goodwill gesture, they carried wagonloads of flour from the palace storehouse. They were escorted by women who chanted: "We are bringing back the baker, the baker's wife, and the baker's boy." The king, the queen, and their son were now virtual prisoners in Paris.

Church Reforms

Under the old regime, the Catholic Church had been an important pillar of the old order. The revolutionaries believed they had to reform it, too. The new revolutionary government had another serious motivation, however: the need for money. By seizing and selling off Church lands, the National Assembly was able to increase the state's revenues.

Finally, the Church was formally brought under the control of the state. A new Civil Constitution of the Clergy said that bishops and priests were to be elected by the people, not appointed by the pope and the Church hierarchy. The state would also pay the salaries of the bishops and priests. Because of these changes, many Catholics became enemies of the revolution.

▶ **CRITICAL THINKING**

Identifying Central Ideas Why did the royal family attempt to leave France?

New Constitution and New Fears

The new Constitution of 1791 set up a limited monarchy. There was still a king, but a Legislative Assembly would make the laws. The Legislative Assembly was to consist of 745 representatives chosen in such a way that only the more affluent members of society would be elected.

By 1791, the old order had been destroyed, but the new government did not have universal support. Political radicals wanted more reform. The king detested the new order and his loss of absolute power. In June 1791, the royal family attempted to flee France in disguise. They almost succeeded but were recognized, captured, and brought back to Paris. In this unsettled situation, the new Legislative Assembly first met in October 1791. France's relations with the rest of Europe soon led to the king's downfall.

▼ The arrest of Louis XVI and his family at Varennes, July 1791

War With Austria

Over time, some European leaders began to fear that revolution would spread to their countries. The kings of Austria and Prussia even threatened to use force to restore Louis XVI to full power. Insulted by this threat and fearing attack, the Legislative

Assembly decided to strike first, declaring war on Austria in the spring of 1792. The French fared badly in the initial fighting. A frantic search for scapegoats began. One observer in France noted:

PRIMARY SOURCE

"Everywhere you hear the cry that the king is betraying us, the generals are betraying us, that nobody is to be trusted; . . . that Paris will be taken in six weeks by the Austrians. . . . We are on a volcano ready to spout flames."

— quoted in *The Oxford History of the French Revolution*

Rise of the Paris Commune

In the spring of 1792, angry citizens demonstrated to protest food shortages and defeats in the war. In August, Paris radicals again decided the fate of the revolution. They declared themselves a commune—a popularly run city council—and attacked the royal palace and Legislative Assembly.

The French Revolution was entering a more radical and violent stage. Members of the new Paris Commune took the king captive. They forced the Legislative Assembly to suspend the monarchy and to call for a National Convention. The members of the Commune were influenced by the idea of democracy, and this time they wanted a more radical change. Representatives would be elected through universal male suffrage, in which all adult males had the right to vote. This would broaden the group of voters to include men who did not meet the initial standards for citizenship established by the Assembly.

Many members of the Paris Commune proudly called themselves **sans-culottes**, meaning "without breeches." Wearing long trousers, not the knee-length breeches of the nobles, they identified themselves as ordinary patriots. Often, sans-culottes are depicted as poor workers, but many were merchants or artisans—the elite of their neighborhoods.

sans-culottes "without breeches"; members of the Paris Commune who considered themselves ordinary patriots (in other words, they wore long trousers instead of the fine knee-length breeches of the nobles)

READING PROGRESS CHECK

Analyzing In what ways did the end of the old order move the revolution toward a more radical phase?

LESSON 1 REVIEW TEKS

Reviewing Vocabulary

1. ***Describing*** Write a paragraph describing all the types of people who made up the French bourgeoisie. Be sure to explain how people within this class might have different points of view about the French government.

Using Your Notes

2. ***Comparing and Contrasting*** Use your notes on the long-range and immediate causes of the French Revolution to compare and contrast one long-range and one immediate cause of the French Revolution.

Answering the Guiding Questions

3. ***Evaluating*** How did the structure of social classes in France lead to discontent?
4. ***Identifying Central Issues*** How did the economic crises in France lead to the meeting of the Estates-General?
5. ***Drawing Conclusions*** Why did the Third Estate declare itself to be the National Assembly?
6. ***Making Connections*** What were the French peasants reacting to in their rebellions of 1789?
7. ***Theorizing*** How did the French Revolution enter a new phase after the storming of the Bastille? 1E, 20B

Writing Activity

8. **INFORMATIVE/EXPLANATORY** Write an essay exploring the influences on the Declaration of the Rights of Man and the Citizen. Be sure to include a discussion of influential documents from other countries. Also discuss influences specific to France, identifying cultural, political, and economic concerns the authors wanted to address.

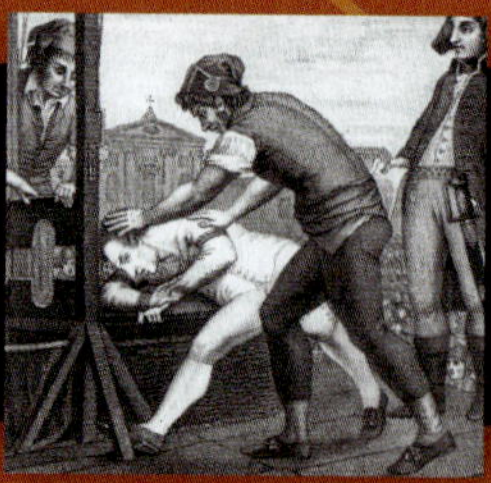

networks

There's More Online!

- ☑ BIOGRAPHY Georges Danton
- ☑ BIOGRAPHY Jean Paul Marat
- ☑ BIOGRAPHY Marie Antoinette
- ☑ CHART/GRAPH Government Bodies of Revolutionary France
- ☑ CHART/GRAPH Political Groups of the French Revolution
- ☑ INTERACTIVE SELF-CHECK QUIZ
- ☑ MAP The Counterrevolution
- ☑ TIME LINE The Reign of Terror
- ☑ VIDEO Marie Antoinette

LESSON 2
Radical Revolution and Reaction

ESSENTIAL QUESTIONS • *What causes revolution?* • *How does revolution change society?*

Reading HELPDESK

Academic Vocabulary
- **domestic**
- **percent**

Content Vocabulary
- **electors**
- **coup d'état**

TAKING NOTES:
Key Ideas and Details

Differentiating Use a graphic organizer like the one below to list actions taken by the National Convention.

Actions Taken by the National Convention
1.
2.
3.
4.

TEKS Texas Essential Knowledge and Skills

9A compare the causes, characteristics, and consequences of the American and French revolutions, emphasizing the role of the Enlightenment, the Glorious Revolution, and religion

IT MATTERS BECAUSE

The French Revolution could be chaotic. The government repeatedly changed hands, foreign powers threatened to intervene, and economic conditions in France showed little improvement. This instability led to calls for new measures to be taken to secure the future of the revolution and to improve the living conditions of the people in France.

The Move to Radicalism

GUIDING QUESTION *Why did the French Revolution become more radical?*

In September 1792, the newly elected National Convention began meeting. The Convention had been called to draft a new constitution, but it also served as the ruling body of France. It was dominated by lawyers, professionals, and property owners. Two-thirds of its deputies were under the age of 45, but most had some political experience as a result of the revolution. Almost all distrusted the king. It was therefore no surprise that the National Convention's first major step on September 21 was to abolish the monarchy and to establish a republic.

After 1789, citizens had formed political clubs of varying social and political views. Many deputies belonged to these clubs. The Girondins (juh • RAHN • duhns) tended to represent areas outside Paris. They feared the radical mobs of Paris. The Mountain represented the interests of radicals in Paris, and many belonged to the Jacobin (JA • kuh • buhn) club. Increasingly, they believed the king needed to be executed to ensure he was not a rallying point for opponents of the republic.

In early 1793, the Mountain convinced the Convention to pass a decree condemning Louis XVI to death. On January 21, the king was beheaded on the guillotine. Revolutionaries had adopted this machine because it killed quickly and, they thought, humanely. The king's execution created new enemies for the revolution, both at home and abroad. A new crisis was at hand.

The execution of King Louis XVI reinforced the trend toward a new radical phase. The local government in Paris—the Commune—had a number of working-class leaders who wanted radical change. Led by Georges Danton, it put constant pressure on the National Convention to adopt more radical measures. Moreover, the National Convention itself still did not rule all France. Peasants in western France, as well as many people in France's major cities, refused to accept the authority of the Convention.

A foreign crisis also loomed large. After Louis XVI was executed, a coalition of Austria, Prussia, Spain, Portugal, Britain, and the Dutch Republic took up arms against France. The French armies began to fall back. By late spring 1793, the coalition was poised to invade. It seemed possible that the revolution would be destroyed and the old regime reestablished.

✓ READING PROGRESS CHECK

Identifying What radical steps did the National Convention take?

▲ This print by Faucher-Gudin depicts Louis XVI's execution on January 21, 1793.

▶ CRITICAL THINKING

Drawing Inferences Why might the method of the king's execution be significant?

The Reign of Terror

GUIDING QUESTION *How did the new French government deal with crises?*

To meet these crises, the National Convention gave broad powers to a special committee of 12 known as the Committee of Public Safety. It came to be dominated by the radical Jacobin Maximilien Robespierre. For approximately a year during 1793 and 1794, the Committee of Public Safety took control of the government. To defend France from **domestic** threats, the Committee adopted policies that became known as the Reign of Terror.

domestic relating to or originating within one's country

As a temporary measure, revolutionary courts were set up to prosecute counterrevolutionaries and traitors. Almost 40,000 people were killed during the French Reign of Terror. Of those, 16,000 people, including Marie Antoinette and Olympe de Gouges, died by the guillotine. Most executions occurred in towns that had openly rebelled against the Convention.

Revolutionary armies were set up to bring rebellious cities under the control of the Convention. The Committee of Public Safety decided to make an example of Lyon, a city that rebelled during a time when the Republic was in peril, and 1,880 citizens of Lyon were executed. When guillotining proved too slow, the condemned were shot with grapeshot (a cluster of small iron balls) into open graves. A foreign witness wrote:

PRIMARY SOURCE

"Whole ranges of houses, always the most handsome, burnt. The churches, convents, and all the dwellings of the former patricians were in ruins. When I came to the guillotine, the blood of those who had been executed a few hours beforehand was still running in the street . . . I said to a group of sans-culottes. . . that it would be decent to clear away all this human blood.— Why should it be cleared? one of them said to me. It's the blood of aristocrats and rebels. The dogs should lick it up."

—quoted in *The Oxford History of the French Revolution*

In western France, too, revolutionary armies were brutal and merciless in defeating rebels. Perhaps the most notorious violence occurred in the city of Nantes, where victims were executed by being loaded onto and then sunk in barges in the Loire River.

percent a part of a whole divided into 100 parts

People from all classes were killed during the Terror. Clergy and nobles made up about 15 **percent** of the victims, while the rest were from the Third Estate. The Committee of Public Safety held that all this bloodletting was only temporary. When the war and domestic crisis were over, the true "Republic of Virtue" would follow, and the Declaration of the Rights of Man and the Citizen would be realized.

In addition to the Terror, the Committee of Public Safety took other steps to control and shape a French society. Robespierre called this new order the Republic of Virtue—a democratic republic composed of good citizens. As outward signs of support for the republic, the titles "citizen" and "citizeness" were to replace "mister" and "madame." Women wore long dresses inspired by the clothing worn in the ancient Roman Republic.

Good citizens would be formed by good education. A law aimed at primary education for all was passed but not widely implemented. Another law abolished slavery in French colonies.

Because people were alarmed about high inflation, the Committee tried to control the prices of essential goods such as food, fuel, and clothing. The controls did not work well because the government had no way to enforce them.

From the beginning, women had been active participants in the revolution, although they had no official power. During the radical stage of the revolution, women observed sessions of the National Convention and were not shy about making their demands.

In 1793, two women founded the Society for Revolutionary Republican Women in Paris. Most members were working-class women who asserted that they were ready to defend the republic. Most men, however, believed that women should not participate in either politics or the military.

The Convention also pursued a policy of de-Christianization. Its members believed that the religion encouraged superstition, rather than the use of reason. The word *saint* was removed from street names, churches were looted and closed by revolutionary armies, and priests were encouraged to marry. In Paris, the cathedral of Notre Dame, the center of the Catholic religion in France, was designated a "temple of reason." In November 1793, a public ceremony dedicated to the worship of reason was held in the former cathedral. Patriotic young girls dressed in white dresses paraded before a temple of reason where the high altar had once stood.

▶ **CRITICAL THINKING**

Interpreting Significance Why, by 1793, would some Parisians hold a parade mocking the Church?

▼ **Parade in Paris ridiculing Christianity and the Church, 1793**

Another example of de-Christianization was the adoption of a new calendar. Years would no longer be numbered from the birth of Jesus but from September 22, 1792—the first day of the French Republic. The calendar contained 12 months. Each month consisted of three 10-day weeks, with the tenth day of each week a day of rest.

These changes in the calendar had a significant effect on religion in France, eliminating Sundays, Sunday worship services, and church holidays. Robespierre came to realize, however, that most French people would not accept these efforts at de-Christianization. France was still overwhelmingly Catholic.

▲ The Battle of Valmy was a victory for the French over the Austrians.

▶ **CRITICAL THINKING**

Identifying Central Ideas What was the cause of the foreign crisis in the spring of 1793?

✓ **READING PROGRESS CHECK**

Questioning Why did the French government use force against its own people?

A Nation in Arms

GUIDING QUESTION *How did the new French government deal with crises?*

As foreign troops gathered on its borders, the revolution seemed to be in danger. To save the republic, the Committee of Public Safety issued a decree to raise an army:

PRIMARY SOURCE

"Young men will fight, young men are called to conquer. Married men will forge arms, transport military baggage and guns and will prepare food supplies. Women, who at long last are to take their rightful place in the revolution and follow their true destiny, will forget their futile tasks: their delicate hands will work at making clothes for soldiers; they will make tents and they will extend their tender care to shelters where the defenders of the *Patrie* [homeland] will receive the help that their wounds require. Children will make lint of old cloth. It is for them that we are fighting: children, those beings destined to gather all the fruits of the revolution, will raise their pure hands toward the skies. And old men, performing their missions again, as of yore, will be guided to the public squares of the cities where they will kindle the courage of young warriors and preach the doctrines of hate for kings and the unity of the Republic."

—from the mobilization decree, August 23, 1793

In less than a year, the new French government had raised a huge army—by September 1794, it had more than a million soldiers. It was the largest army ever seen in Europe, and it pushed the invaders back across the Rhine. It even conquered the Austrian Netherlands. In earlier times, wars were the business of rulers who fought rivals with professional soldiers. The new French army was created by a people's government. Its wars were now people's wars.

By the summer of 1794, the French had largely defeated their foreign foes. There was less need for the Reign of Terror, but it continued nonetheless. Robespierre was obsessed with ridding France of all the corrupt elements. Many in the National Convention who feared Robespierre decided to act, lest they be the next victims. They gathered enough votes to condemn him, and Robespierre was guillotined on July 28, 1794.

✓ **READING PROGRESS CHECK**

Summarizing How did the French army become the people's army?

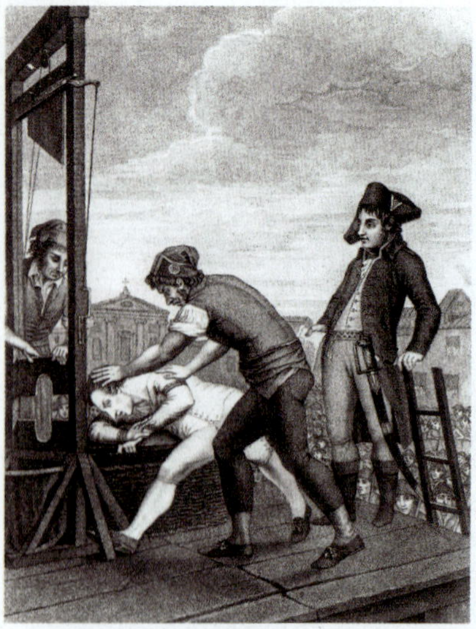

▲ Execution of Robespierre on July 28, 1794

The Directory

GUIDING QUESTION *How did the constant transition within the French government influence its effectiveness?*

After the death of Robespierre, a reaction set in as more moderate middle-class leaders took control. The Reign of Terror came to a halt. The National Convention reduced the power of the Committee of Public Safety. Churches were allowed to reopen. Finally, a new constitution was created.

The Constitution of 1795 set up two legislative houses. A lower house, the Council of 500, drafted laws. An upper house of 250, the Council of Elders, accepted or rejected proposed laws. Members of both houses were chosen by **electors,** or qualified voters. Only those who owned or rented property worth a certain amount could be electors—only 30,000 people in the whole nation qualified. This was a significant change from the universal male suffrage the Paris Commune had demanded.

Under the new constitution, the executive was a committee of five called the Directory, chosen by the Council of Elders. The Directory, which lasted from 1795 to 1799, became known mainly for corruption. People reacted against the sufferings and sacrifices that had been demanded in the Reign of Terror. Some people made fortunes from government contracts or by loaning the government money at very high interest rates. They took advantage of the government's severe money problems during these difficult times.

At the same time, the government of the Directory faced political enemies from both conservatives and radicals. Some people wanted to bring back the monarchy, while others plotted to create a more radical regime like Robespierre's. Likewise, economic problems continued with no solution in sight. Finally, France was still conducting expensive wars against foreign enemies.

To stay in power, the Directory began to rely on the military, but one military leader turned on the government. In 1799 the successful and popular general Napoleon Bonaparte toppled the Directory in a **coup d'état** (KOO day • TAH), a sudden overthrow of the government. Napoleon then seized power.

electör an individual qualified to vote in an election

coup d'état a sudden overthrow of the government

SKILLS PRACTICE

In your own words, write a summary of the shift to radicalism in the French Revolution. Be sure to explain the sources of the shift and how it affected life in France.

✓ **READING PROGRESS CHECK**

Evaluating Did the transition from the Committee of Public Safety to the Directory help respond to the French people's needs?

PHOTO: ©A.H.C./Age Fotostock America

LESSON 2 REVIEW TEKS

Reviewing Vocabulary

1. ***Examining*** Explain how the coup d'état in which Napoleon took part differed from other transitions in the revolutionary French government.

Using Your Notes

2. ***Applying*** Use your notes to write a paragraph describing the actions taken by the National Convention and some of the consequences of these actions.

Answering the Guiding Questions

3. ***Theorizing*** Why did the French Revolution become more radical?

4. ***Identifying*** How did the new French government deal with crises?

5. ***Analyzing*** How did the constant transition within the French government influence its effectiveness?

Writing Activity

6. **INFORMATIVE/EXPLANATORY** Write an essay tracing the changes in the French government between the Constitution of 1791 and the Constitution of 1795. Include defining characteristics of each new form of government and how it led to the next change in leadership.

networks
There's More Online!

- ☑ CHART/GRAPH Napoleon's Civil Law Code and Louisiana Civil Law
- ☑ CHART/GRAPH Napoleon's Domestic Policies
- ☑ IMAGE Napoleon's Civil Code
- ☑ INTERACTIVE SELF-CHECK QUIZ
- ☑ MAP Napoleonic Europe
- ☑ PRIMARY SOURCE The Concordat of 1801
- ☑ VIDEO Napoleon

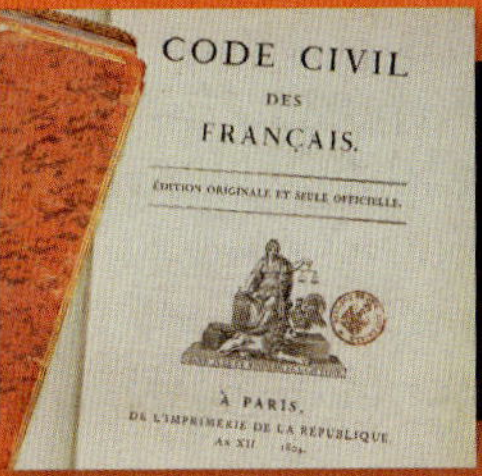

LESSON 3
The Rise of Napoleon and the Napoleonic Wars

ESSENTIAL QUESTIONS • *What causes revolution?* • *How does revolution change society?*

Reading HELPDESK

Academic Vocabulary
- **capable**
- **liberal**

Content Vocabulary
- **consulate**
- **nationalism**

TAKING NOTES:
Key Ideas and Details

Differentiating As you read, create a diagram like the one below to list achievements of Napoleon's rule.

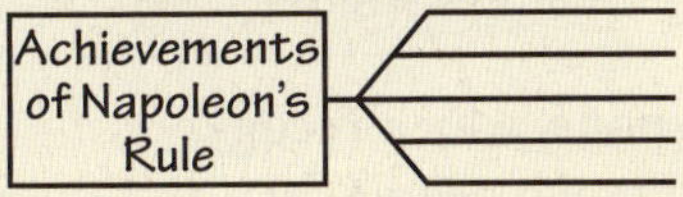

TEKS Texas Essential Knowledge and Skills

9B explain the impact of Napoleon Bonaparte and the Napoleonic Wars on Europe and Latin America

9D identify the influence of ideas such as separation of powers, checks and balances, liberty, equality, democracy, popular sovereignty, human rights, constitutionalism, and nationalism on political revolutions

It Matters Because

Napoleon Bonaparte dominated French and European history from 1799 to 1815. During his reign, Napoleon built and lost an empire and also spread ideas about nationalism throughout much of Europe.

The Rise of Napoleon

GUIDING QUESTION *How did instability in the French government create an opportunity for Napoleon to take power?*

Napoleon Bonaparte's role in the French Revolution is complex. In one sense, he brought it to an end when he came to power in 1799. Yet he was a child of the revolution as well. Without it, he would never have risen to power, and he himself never failed to remind the French that he had preserved the best parts of the revolution during his reign as emperor.

Early Life

Napoleon was born in 1769 in Corsica, an island in the Mediterranean, only a few months after France had annexed the island. His father came from minor nobility in Italy, but the family was not rich. Napoleon was talented, however, and won a scholarship to a famous military school.

When he completed his studies, Napoleon was commissioned as a lieutenant in the French army. Although he became one of the world's greatest generals and a man beloved by his soldiers, there were few signs of his future success at this stage. He spoke with an Italian accent and was not popular with his fellow officers.

Napoleon devoted himself to his goals. He read what French philosophers had to say about reason, and he studied famous military campaigns. When revolution and war with Europe came about, there were many opportunities for Napoleon to use his knowledge and skills.

▲ *The Coronation of the Emperor Napoleon I* by Jacques-Louis David

▶ **CRITICAL THINKING**

Making Generalizations How does David portray Napoleon in this painting?

Military Successes

Napoleon rose quickly through the ranks. In 1792 he became a captain. Two years later, at age 24, the Committee of Public Safety made him a brigadier general. In 1796 he became commander of the French armies in Italy. There Napoleon won a series of battles with speed, surprise, and decisive action. He also defeated the armies of the Papal States and their Austrian allies. These victories gave France control of northern Italy. Throughout the Italian campaigns, Napoleon's energy and initiative earned him the devotion of his troops. His personal qualities allowed him to win the support of those around him. In 1797 he returned to France as a hero. He was given command of an army in training to invade Britain, but he knew the French could not carry out that invasion. Instead, Napoleon suggested striking indirectly at Britain by taking Egypt.

Egypt lay on the route to India, one of Britain's most important colonies and a major source of its wealth. The British were a great sea power and controlled the Mediterranean. By 1799, the British had defeated the French naval forces supporting Napoleon's army in Egypt. Seeing certain defeat, Napoleon abandoned his army and returned to Paris.

Consul and Emperor

consulate government established in France after the overthrow of the Directory in 1799, with Napoleon as first consul in control of the entire government

In Paris, Napoleon took part in the coup d'état of 1799 that overthrew the Directory and set up a new government, the **consulate**. In theory, it was a republic, but, in fact, Napoleon held absolute power. Napoleon was called first consul, a title borrowed from ancient Rome. He appointed officials, controlled the army, conducted foreign affairs, and influenced the legislature. In 1802 Napoleon was made consul for life. Two years later, he crowned himself Emperor Napoleon I.

Peace with the Church

One of Napoleon's first moves at home was to establish peace with the Catholic Church. In matters of religion, Napoleon was a man of the Enlightenment. He believed in reason and felt that religion was at most a social convenience. However, since most of France was Catholic, it was a good idea to mend relations with the Church.

In 1801 Napoleon came to an agreement with the pope, which recognized Catholicism as the religion of a majority of the French people. In return, the pope would not ask for the return of the Church lands seized in the revolution.

With this agreement, the Catholic Church was no longer an enemy of the French government. It also meant that people who had acquired Church lands in the revolution became avid supporters of Napoleon.

Codification of the Laws

Napoleon's most famous domestic achievement was to codify the laws. Before the revolution, France had almost 300 different legal systems. During the revolution, efforts were made to prepare a single law code for the nation. However, the work was not completed until Napoleon's reign.

Seven law codes were created, but the most important was the Civil Code, or Napoleonic Code, introduced in 1804. It preserved many of the principles that the revolutionaries had fought for: equality of all citizens before the law; the right of the individual to choose a profession; religious toleration; and the abolition of serfdom and all feudal obligations.

For women and children, the Civil Code was a step back. During the radical stage of the revolution, new laws had made divorce easier and allowed children, even daughters, to inherit property on an equal basis. The Civil Code undid these laws. Women were now "less equal than men." When they married, they lost control over any property they had. They could not testify in court, and it became more difficult for them to begin divorce proceedings. In general, the code treated women like children, who needed protection and who did not have a public role.

A New Bureaucracy

Napoleon also developed a powerful, centralized administrative machine. He focused on developing a bureaucracy of **capable** officials. Early on, the regime showed that it did not care about rank or birth. Public officials and military officers alike were promoted based on their ability. Opening careers to men of talent was a reform that the middle class had clamored for before the revolution.

capable having or showing ability

Napoleon also created a new aristocracy based on meritorious service to the nation. Between 1808 and 1814, Napoleon created about 3,200 nobles. Nearly 60 percent were military officers, while the rest were civil service or state and local officials. Socially, only 22 percent of this new aristocracy were from noble families of the old regime; about 60 percent were middle class in origin.

Preserver of the Revolution?

In his domestic policies, then, Napoleon did keep some major reforms of the French Revolution. Under the Civil Code, all citizens were equal before the law. The concept of opening government careers to more people was another gain of the revolution that he retained.

On the other hand, Napoleon destroyed some revolutionary ideals. Liberty was replaced by a despotism that grew increasingly arbitrary, in spite of protests by such citizens as the prominent writer Anne-Louise-Germaine de Staël. Napoleon shut down 60 of France's 73 newspapers and banned books, including de Staël's. He insisted that all manuscripts be subjected to government scrutiny before they were published. Even the mail was opened by government police.

✓ READING PROGRESS CHECK

Synthesizing How did Napoleon's Civil Code address the problems with the French legal system that were present before the revolution?

Napoleon's Empire

GUIDING QUESTIONS *Why would changes in France cause concern in other European countries? How did Napoleon's military background shape his perspective?*

Napoleon is, of course, known less for his domestic policies than for his military leadership. His conquests began soon after he rose to power.

Building the Empire

When Napoleon became consul in 1799, France was at war with a European coalition of Russia, Great Britain, and Austria. Napoleon realized the need for a pause in the war. "The French Revolution is not finished," he said, "so long as the scourge of war lasts .... I want peace, as much to settle the present French government, as to save the world from chaos." In 1802 a peace treaty was signed, but it did not last long. War with Britain broke out again in 1803. Gradually, Britain was joined by Austria, Russia, Sweden, and Prussia. In a

GEOGRAPHY CONNECTION

Napoleon's Grand Empire spread over much of Europe.

1. **HUMAN SYSTEMS** *Why might Napoleon have chosen to ally with states instead of taking them over?*
2. **ENVIRONMENT AND SOCIETY** *What do the countries allied against France have in common?*

series of battles at Ulm, Austerlitz, Jena, and Eylau from 1805 to 1807, Napoleon's Grand Army defeated the Austrian, Prussian, and Russian armies.

From 1807 to 1812, Napoleon was the master of Europe. His Grand Empire was composed of three major parts: the French Empire, dependent states, and allied states. The French Empire was the inner core of the Grand Empire. It consisted of an enlarged France extending to the Rhine in the east and including the western half of Italy north of Rome.

Dependent states were kingdoms ruled by relatives of Napoleon. Eventually these included Spain, Holland, the kingdom of Italy, the Swiss Republic, the Grand Duchy of Warsaw, and the Confederation of the Rhine—a union of all German states except Austria and Prussia.

Allied states were countries defeated by Napoleon and then forced to join his struggle against Britain. These states included Prussia, Austria, Russia, and Sweden.

Spreading the Principles of the Revolution

Within his empire, Napoleon sought to spread some of the principles of the French Revolution, including legal equality, religious toleration, and economic freedom. In the inner core and dependent states of his Grand Empire, Napoleon tried to destroy the old order. The nobility and the clergy everywhere in these states lost their special privileges. Napoleon decreed equality of opportunity with offices open to those with ability, equality before the law, and religious toleration. The spread of French revolutionary principles was an important factor in the development of **liberal** traditions in these countries.

liberal broad-minded; associated with ideals of the individual, especially economic freedom and greater participation in government

Like Hitler 130 years later, Napoleon hoped that his Grand Empire would last for centuries, but his empire collapsed almost as rapidly as it was formed. Two major reasons help explain this collapse: Britain's ability to resist Napoleon and the rise of nationalism.

British Resistance

Napoleon was never able to conquer Great Britain because of its sea power, which made it almost invulnerable. Napoleon hoped to invade Britain, but the British defeated the combined French-Spanish fleet at Trafalgar in 1805. This battle ended Napoleon's plans for invasion.

Napoleon then turned to his Continental System to defeat Britain. The aim of the Continental System was to stop British goods from reaching the European continent to be sold there. By weakening Britain economically, Napoleon would destroy its ability to wage war.

The Continental System also failed. Allied states resented being told by Napoleon that they could not trade with the British. Some began to cheat. Others resisted. Furthermore, new markets in the Middle East and in Latin America gave Britain new outlets for its goods. Indeed, by 1810, British overseas exports were at near-record highs.

Nationalism

A second significant factor in the defeat of Napoleon was **nationalism**. One of the most important forces of the nineteenth century, nationalism is the sense of unique identity of a people based on common language, religion, and national symbols. A new era was born when the French people decided that they were the nation.

Napoleon marched his armies through the Germanies, Spain, Italy, and Poland, arousing new ideas of nationalism in two ways. First, the conquered peoples became united in their hatred of the invaders. Second, the conquered peoples saw the power and strength of national feeling. It was a lesson not lost on them or their rulers. Nationalism continued to influence political movements and revolutions to the present day.

✓ READING PROGRESS CHECK

Evaluating What were the consequences for a country conquered by Napoleon's Grand Army?

Analyzing PRIMARY SOURCES

Napoleon's Reign

"What is the throne?—a bit of wood gilded and covered with velvet—I am the state—I alone am here the representative of the people. Even if I had done wrong you should not have reproached me in public—people wash their dirty linen at home. France has more need of me than I of France."

—Napoleon, quoted in *The History of Napoleon Buonaparte*

DBQ ***DRAWING CONCLUSIONS*** How did Napoleon understand his role as leader of the French people?

nationalism the unique cultural identity of a people based on common language, religion, and national symbols

LESSON 3 REVIEW TEKS

Reviewing Vocabulary

1. ***Identifying Central Issues*** What is nationalism, and what role did it play in Napoleon's fall from power? **9B, 9D**
2. ***Interpreting*** Why do you think Napoleon used the ancient Roman term *first consul* to define his new role in the government?

Using Your Notes

3. ***Comparing*** Use your notes on the achievements of Napoleon to compare Napoleon's achievements to those of the French government during the Reign of Terror.

Answering the Guiding Questions

4. ***Identifying*** How did instability in the French government create an opportunity for Napoleon to take power?
5. ***Drawing Conclusions*** Why would changes in France cause concern in other European countries?
6. ***Making Inferences*** How did Napoleon's military background shape his perspective?

Writing Activity

7. **ARGUMENT** Write an essay analyzing whether Napoleon did or did not preserve the ideals of the French Revolution through his domestic and foreign policies. Demonstrate your knowledge of both sides of the argument, but ultimately choose one side using support from the text.

networks

There's More Online!

- BIOGRAPHY Duke of Wellington
- BIOGRAPHY Klemens von Metternich
- IMAGE The Congress of Vienna
- INTERACTIVE SELF-CHECK QUIZ
- MAP Europe after the Congress of Vienna, 1815
- PRIMARY SOURCE Napoleon's Retreat from Russia
- SLIDE SHOW Napoleon's Final Days
- VIDEO Napoleon in Exile

Reading HELPDESK

Academic Vocabulary

- **civil**
- **constitution**

Content Vocabulary

- **conservatism**
- **principle of intervention**
- **liberalism**

TAKING NOTES:

Key Ideas and Details

Differentiating As you read, use a diagram like the one below to summarize what led to Napoleon's downfall and how leaders in Europe attempted to restore order.

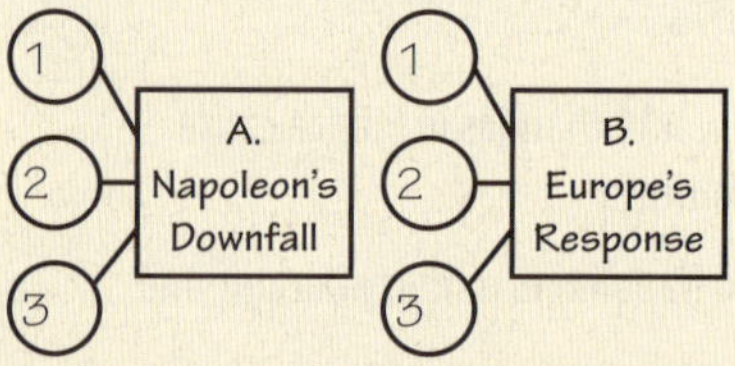

TEKS Texas Essential Knowledge and Skills

1E identify major causes and describe the major effects of the following important turning points in world history from 1750 to 1914: the Scientific Revolution, the Industrial Revolution and its impact on the development of modern economic systems, European imperialism, and the Enlightenment's impact on political revolutions

continued on the next page

LESSON 4

The Fall of Napoleon and the European Reaction

ESSENTIAL QUESTIONS • *What causes revolution?* • *How does revolution change society?*

It Matters Because

After the turmoil of the French revolutionary years and the eventual fall of Napoleon, European rulers wanted to return to a conservative order, keeping a balance of power among nations. Liberals and nationalists, however, struggled to achieve more liberal governments and new nations.

The Fall of Napoleon

GUIDING QUESTION *How did Napoleon lose his empire?*

Napoleon's downfall began in 1812 when he decided to invade Russia. Within only a few years, his fall was complete.

The Russians had refused to remain in the Continental System, leaving Napoleon with little choice but to invade. He knew the risks in invading such a large country, but he also knew that if he did not punish the Russians for ignoring the Continental System, other nations would follow suit.

In June 1812, a Grand Army of more than 600,000 men entered Russia. Napoleon's hopes depended on a quick victory over the Russians, but they refused to do battle. Instead they retreated for hundreds of miles. As they retreated, they burned their own villages and countryside to keep Napoleon's army from finding food. When the Russians did fight at Borodino, Napoleon's forces won an indecisive victory, which cost many lives.

Finally reaching Moscow, the Grand Army found the city ablaze. With no food or supplies for his army, Napoleon abandoned the Russian capital in late October. As the winter snows began, Napoleon led the "Great Retreat" west across Russia. Thousands of soldiers starved and froze along the way. Fewer than 40,000 of the original 600,000 soldiers arrived back in Poland in January 1813.

This military disaster led other European states to rise up and attack the crippled French army. Paris was captured in March 1814. Napoleon was soon sent into exile on the island of Elba, off the northwest coast of Italy. The victorious powers restored monarchy to France in the person of Louis XVIII, brother of the executed king, Louis XVI.

The new king had little support, and the French people were not ready to surrender the glory of empire. Nor was Napoleon ready to give up. Restless in exile, he left the island of Elba and slipped back into France. The new king sent troops to capture Napoleon, who opened his coat and addressed them: "Soldiers of the 5th regiment, I am your Emperor. . . . If there is a man among you [who] would kill his Emperor, here I am!"

No one fired a shot. Shouting "Long live the Emperor!" the troops went over to his side. On March 20, 1815, Napoleon entered Paris in triumph.

Russia, Great Britain, Austria, and Prussia again pledged to defeat the man they called the "Enemy and Disturber of the Tranquility of the World." Meanwhile, Napoleon raised another French army of devoted veterans who rallied from all over France. He then readied an attack on the allied troops stationed across the border in Belgium.

At Waterloo in Belgium on June 18, 1815, Napoleon met a combined British and Prussian army under the Duke of Wellington and suffered a bloody defeat. This time, the victorious allies exiled him to St. Helena, a small island in the south Atlantic. Napoleon remained in exile until his death in 1821, but his memory haunted French political life for many decades.

✓ READING PROGRESS CHECK

Analyzing How did Napoleon's disaster in Russia affect both his Grand Army and the French nation?

(continued from p. 516)

TEKS **Texas Essential Knowledge and Skills**

9B explain the impact of Napoleon Bonaparte and the Napoleonic Wars on Europe and Latin America

9D identify the influence of ideas such as separation of powers, checks and balances, liberty, equality, democracy, popular sovereignty, human rights, constitutionalism, and nationalism on political revolutions

▲ The burning of Moscow in October of 1812

European Reaction

GUIDING QUESTION ***Why did the turmoil of the French revolutionary years result in a conservative European reaction?***

After the defeat of Napoleon, European rulers moved to restore the old order. Napoleon Bonaparte had reshaped governments across Europe. In addition, he had dismantled many of the privileges of the nobility and clergy. The goal of the victors—Great Britain, Austria, Prussia, and Russia—was to undo these changes when they met at the Congress of Vienna in September 1814 to arrange a final peace settlement that ended the Napoleonic Wars.

The haughty Austrian foreign minister, Prince Klemens von Metternich (MEH • tuhr • nihk), was the most influential leader at that meeting in Vienna. Metternich claimed that the principle of legitimacy guided him. He meant that lawful monarchs from the royal families who had ruled before Napoleon would be restored to their positions of power. This, they believed, would ensure peace and stability in Europe.

Practical considerations of power were addressed at the Congress of Vienna. The powers at Vienna wanted to keep any one country from dominating Europe. This meant balancing political and military forces that guaranteed the independence of the great powers. To balance Russian territorial gains, for example, new territories were given to Prussia and Austria.

The arrangements worked out at the Congress of Vienna were a victory for rulers, who wanted to reverse the impact of the Napoleonic Wars. The agreement returned deposed governments to power. The former rulers such as Metternich, believed in the political philosophy known as **conservatism**.

conservatism a political philosophy based on tradition and social stability, favoring obedience to political authority and organized religion

GEOGRAPHY CONNECTION

The Congress of Vienna rearranged territories to maintain a balance of power.

1. **THE WORLD IN SPATIAL TERMS** *In what political boundaries is Vienna located?*
2. **HUMAN SYSTEMS** *Compare this map to the map of Napoleonic Europe in Lesson 3. What countries gained territory from France after the Congress of Vienna?*

principle of intervention idea that great powers have the right to send armies into countries where there are revolutions to restore legitimate governments

liberalism a political philosophy originally based largely on Enlightenment principles, holding that people should be as free as possible from government restraint and that civil liberties—the basic rights of all people—should be protected

Most conservatives at that time favored obedience to political authority. They also believed that religion was crucial to keep order in society. Con-servatives hated revolutions and were unwilling to accept demands from people who wanted either individual rights or representative governments.

To maintain the new balance of power, Great Britain, Russia, Prussia, and Austria (and later France) agreed to meet in conferences to discuss their common interests and to maintain peace in Europe. These meetings came to be called the Concert of Europe.

The great powers adopted a **principle of intervention**. According to this principle, they had the right to send armies into countries in order to restore legitimate monarchs to their thrones. Britain argued that they should not interfere in the internal affairs of other states. However, the other great powers used military force to end revolutions in Spain and Italy.

✓ **READING PROGRESS CHECK**

Identifying Central Issues Why did European leaders think it was important to apply conservatism at the Congress of Vienna?

Forces of Change

GUIDING QUESTION *What happened to revolutionary ideas after the French Revolution was over?*

Between 1815 and 1830, conservative governments throughout Europe worked to maintain the old order. However, powerful forces for change—known as liberalism and nationalism—were also at work.

Liberalism is a political philosophy that grew out of Enlightenment ideas. **Liberalism** held that people should be as free as possible from government restraint. Liberal beliefs included the protection of **civil** liberties, the basic rights of all people. Civil liberties included equality before the law and freedom of assembly, speech, and the press. Liberals believed that these human rights should be guaranteed by a document such as the American Bill of Rights. The idea of human rights influenced both the American and French Revolutions.

civil involving the general public or civic affairs

constitution the basic principles and laws of a nation, state, or social group that determine the powers and duties of the government and guarantee certain rights to the people in it

Many liberals favored a government ruled by a **constitution**—a concept called constitutionalism. For example, in a constitutional monarchy, a king must follow the laws of the constitution. Liberals believed that written documents would help guarantee people's rights.

Most liberals wanted religious toleration for all, as well as separation of church and state. Liberals also demanded the right of peaceful opposition to the government. They believed that a representative assembly (legislature) elected by qualified voters should make laws. These liberal ideals were similar to republicanism, the belief that a government's power comes from the rule of law and the citizens who are allowed to vote.

Liberals did not believe everyone had a right to vote. They thought the right to vote and hold office should be open only to men of property. Liberalism was tied to middle-class men who wanted voting rights for themselves so they could share power with the landowning classes. The liberals feared mob rule and had little desire to let the lower classes share power.

Nationalism arose when people began to identify themselves as part of a community, a nation, defined by a distinctive language, common institutions, and customs. In earlier centuries, people's loyalty belonged to a king or to their town or region. In the nineteenth century, people began to believe that their chief loyalty was to the nation.

Nationalism did not become a popular force for change until the French Revolution. From then on, nationalists came to believe that each nationality should have its own government. Thus, the Germans, who were separated into many principalities, wanted national unity under one central government in a German nation-state. Subject peoples, such as the Hungarians, wanted the right to establish their own governments.

Nationalism was a threat to the existing order. A united Germany would upset the balance of power set up at the Congress of Vienna in 1815. An independent Hungarian state would mean the breakup of the Austrian Empire. Conservatives feared such change and tried to repress nationalism.

Nationalism found a strong ally in liberalism. Most liberals believed that freedom could only be possible in people who ruled themselves. Each group of people should have its own state.

✓ **READING PROGRESS CHECK**

Identifying Why did nationalism become popular after the French Revolution?

Comparing the American and French Revolutions

GUIDING QUESTION *How did the American and French Revolutions differ?*

The American Revolution and the French Revolution had much in common, including many of their causes. Many of the impulses for both revolutions grew out of Enlightenment ideas about personal freedom and the power of the state. In the American colonies, these ideas appeared in the writings of Thomas Paine and Thomas Jefferson. In France, they appeared in the works of Jean-Jacques Rousseau.

Religion played its role in both revolutions as well. In the American colonies, a series of religious revivals known as the Great Awakening began in the 1700s. The Great Awakening stressed individual religious piety and encouraged challenges to traditional religious authority. This contributed to a willingness to challenge political authority as well, given how closely political and religious authority was connected in Britain. In France, resentment of the excesses of certain Church officials and their influence over the state fueled revolutionary sentiment. In practice, however, many French people remained faithful Catholics.

The Glorious Revolution also influenced the American and French Revolutions. This event in England firmly established the ideas that monarchies could be limited, changed when desired by the people, and that the people should have a direct hand in government. These ideas later took shape in America's Continental Congress and in France's National Assembly.

In both revolutions, public opinion swayed strongly against monarchical rule, and common people were drawn to fight in the cause. Their outcomes, however, were quite different. In America, the colonists formed armies and fought a long war against the British monarchy. While the colonists gained independence, the monarchy remained intact in Great Britain. In France, however, revolutionaries overthrew the monarchy quickly and violently, executing the king and many members of his family. Participants in both revolutions were quick to organize new governments based on democratic-republican principles.

▲ Though their outcomes differed, the United States and France have their separate revolutions in common. This bond is often represented with the Statue of Liberty, a gift to the United States from France.

It is in their consequences that these two revolutions share their greatest differences. The American Revolution resulted in a national government ruled first in a loose confederation and later by a constitution. This government was formed through heated debate and several compromises, but its development was not marred by much violence. The French Revolution ended quite differently. In France, the monarchy was ended, but the new democratic government soon gave way to dominant despotic figures like Robespierre and Napoleon. The horrific violence of the Terror, too, darkened the outcome of the French Revolution. Despite these bleak periods, the French people remained committed to democratic-republican ideas and the spirit of "Liberty, Equality, and Fraternity" continues to inspire French government and social life.

✓ **READING PROGRESS CHECK**

Describing How did the Enlightenment inspire the American and French Revolutions?

LESSON 4 REVIEW TEKS

Reviewing Vocabulary

1. ***Explaining*** Write a paragraph explaining how the principle of intervention is an idea based on conservatism. 9B

Using Your Notes

2. ***Summarizing*** Use your notes on Napoleon's downfall and Europe's response to list the various European responses to Napoleon's downfall. 9B

Answering the Guiding Questions

3. ***Drawing Conclusions*** How did Napoleon lose his empire?

4. ***Evaluating*** Why did the turmoil of the French revolutionary years result in a conservative European reaction? 9B

5. ***Identifying the Main Idea*** What happened to revolutionary ideas after the French Revolution was over? 9B

Writing Activity

6. INFORMATIVE/EXPLANATORY Using outside research, write an essay describing Napoleon's invasion of Russia. Be sure to cover his motivations for invasion, the logistical difficulties in carrying out the invasion, Russia's response, and the economic, political, and human toll of Napoleon's retreat.

SKILLBUILDER

TEKS 16C

Interpreting Charts: Human Geography

Why Learn This Skill?

In addition to maps, historians use other visual representations to display and interpret information. Charts make large amounts of information easier to read and understand.

Learning the Skill

Charts organize data into boxes, bubbles, or grids. While many kinds of charts exist, they all have the same purpose: to arrange related pieces of information in an organized manner. The ability to interpret a chart allows you to make connections in information that might be more difficult to see if the information were presented in text form.

Sometimes charts have boxes connected by arrows. These are often called "flowcharts." Facts in a flowchart are usually connected by a chronological sequence or a cause-and-effect relationship. Grid-like charts organize information into rows and columns. To find key information, look for intersections of columns and rows.

To explore the topic of geography in a chart, look for place names and geographic terms. Remember that geography includes both physical and human factors. Physical geography describes land features and physical processes. Human geography describes human behaviors and events and their impact on Earth.

Practicing the Skill

The eighteenth century was a period of power struggles and change in Europe. France experienced the greatest tumult in the region, but Prussia, Austria, and Russia saw changes, as well. Monarchies persisted in these places, though internal and external factors reshaped their countries.

Study this chart. When juggling information about three countries, six rulers, and many decades, a chart can help make sense of the information. In short, a chart can present patterns that can be hard to find in plain text.

Skills Assessment

Look at this chart to find the important connections between facts. Pay particular attention to geographic factors, including both place names and terms of human geography. Answer the following questions:

1. How did geography influence the lives of people in these countries in the eighteenth century?
2. How did geography influence events in these countries in the eighteenth century?

Name	Location	Years of Rule	Major Accomplishments
Frederick William II (Frederick the Great)	Prussia	1740–1786	made enlightened reforms; increased Prussia's territories; made Prussia the foremost military power in Europe
Joseph II	Austria	1765–1780 (while still a minor, was coruler with his mother, Maria Theresa) 1780–1790 (sole ruler)	abolished serfdom; granted freedom of the press; enacted religious reforms
Peter III	Russia	January 5, 1762–July 9, 1762	formed an alliance with Prussia; withdrew from the Sevens' Year War

Applying the Skill

Interpreting Charts Think of ways that geography influences people and events in your community. Be sure to consider both physical and human geographic factors. List at least five influences, including at least one human and one physical geographic factor. Make a chart that presents your information in a clear, visual manner. Trade charts with a partner and interpret each other's chart. Discuss how the charts succeed or fail to communicate the geographic information.

CHAPTER 22 Assessment

TEKS

Directions: On a separate sheet of paper, answer the questions below. Make sure you read carefully and answer all parts of the questions.

Lesson Review

Lesson 1

1. ***Describing*** Describe the variation of position and financial status within the First Estate. Why do you think the parish priests and other clergy came from different classes?

2. ***Evaluating*** Describe the variation of position and financial status among the Third Estate. How did this variation likely help the lowest group?

3. ***Describing*** What was the Great Fear, and how did peasant actions reflect the system of Estates they had lived under?

4. ***Identifying Cause and Effect*** What changes did the new order bring to Catholic clergy's methods of election and compensation?

5. ***Identifying*** How did the Enlightenment impact the French Revolution? **1E**

6. ***Identifying*** How did the idea of direct democracy influence the leaders of the Paris Commune and the French Revolution? **9D**

7. ***Identifying*** How did political and legal ideas contained in Rousseau's *Declaration of the Rights of Man and of the Citizen* impact the French Revolution? **20B**

Lesson 2

8. ***Summarizing*** What was the Reign of Terror and how did it end?

9. ***Describing*** Under the National Convention, what efforts were made to de-Christianize France?

10. ***Assessing*** What effect did the Constitution of 1795 have?

11. ***Explaining*** Following the Reign of Terror, as the Directory, why was the French government potentially vulnerable to takeover?

Lesson 3

12. ***Summarizing*** In what ways was the Civil Code, or the Napoleonic code, a regression of women's rights?

13. ***Listing*** What powers did Napoleon exercise as First Consul in France?

14. ***Evaluating*** Why would writers, newspapers, or book publishers have believed that their professions were in jeopardy during Napoleon's reign?

15. ***Identifying*** How did the idea of nationalism rise from the Napoleonic Wars? What effect do you think this idea came to have in European politics? **9B, 9D**

Lesson 4

16. ***Explaining*** How did the Napoleonic Wars change Europe? **9B**

17. ***Identifying*** What are the characteristics of a limited or constitutional monarchy? **19B**

18. ***Describing*** How was the French Revolution influenced by liberalism and the concept of "human rights"? **9D**

Need Extra Help?

If You've Missed Question	1	2	3	4	5	6	7	8	9	10	11	12	13	14	15	16	17	18
Go to page	500	501	503	504	502	505	503	507	508	510	510	510	512	513	515	517	519	518

19 ***Identifying*** Which nations met at the Congress of Vienna in 1814 after Napoleon had been exiled for a second time?

20 ***Comparing*** How are the causes and effects of the French and American Revolutions similar in terms of Enlightenment ideas, the Glorious Revolution, religion, other characteristics, and ultimately, the consequences? **9A**

Exploring the Essential Question

21 ***Synthesizing*** Work with a partner to create an illustrated time line showing five pivotal events that occurred in France between 1789 and 1815. Include visuals such as photographs, sketched images, and maps, along with primary sources. Be prepared to explain how the events you select led to the exchange of new ideas.

Critical Thinking

22 ***Analyzing*** What was the significance of the meeting of the Estates-General in 1789?

23 ***Identifying Central Issues*** What were the four major principles that were reflected in the Napoleonic Code?

24 ***Making Connections*** How did the political philosophies of nationalism and liberalism connect with one another?

25 ***Exploring Issues*** How did the great powers maintain the balance of power in Europe and what was the motivation behind this strategy?

26 ***Comparing and Contrasting*** Compare and contrast the methods of demise, and ultimately death, for a series of French rulers: Louis XVI and Marie Antoinette, Jacobin Maximilien Robespierre, and Napoleon Bonaparte.

Social Studies Skills

27 ***Categorizing*** Which of the following ideologies belong within the category of liberalism and which belong within the category of conservatism: adherence to tradition; freedom for government restraint; obedience to political authority; equality before the law; freedom of assembly, speech, and the press; and organized religion? **29F**

28 ***Identifying Cause and Effect*** How did the Committee of Public Safety deal with opposition? What were the effects of its policies?

29 ***Economics*** What was the Continental System, and was it effective? Explain.

30 ***Creating Presentations*** Research more about storming the Bastille on July 14, 1789 and the national holiday in France that commemorates this date and the events of July 14, 1790. Visually share information that explains customs tied to the holiday. **30C**

31 ***Creating Graphs*** Use the data you learned about the percentages of land ownership by the First Estate (clergy), Second Estate (nobles), and Third Estate (peasants and middle class) along with average population figures to create a visual graph that will convey the balance or imbalance of land ownership. Conduct additional research about population statistics, if necessary. **15A**

If You've Missed Question	19	20	21	22	23	24	25	26	27	28	29	30	31
Go to page	517	517	498	502	512	515	518	506	518	507	515	503	500

Analyzing Primary Sources

Use the document to answer the following questions.

While emperor, Napoleon attempted to spread revolutionary ideals to other nations. He shares these ideas with his brother Jerome, the new king of Westphalia, in 1807:

PRIMARY SOURCE

"What the peoples of Germany desire most impatiently is that talented commoners should have the same right to your esteem and to public employments as the nobles, that any trace of serfdom and of an intermediate hierarchy between the sovereign and the lowest class of the people should be completely abolished. The benefits of the Code Napoléon, the publicity of judicial procedure, the creation of juries must be so many distinguishing marks of your monarchy."

—Napoleon in a letter to the king of Westphalia, 1807

32. ***Explaining*** How would historians interpret Napoleon's ideas regarding the promotion of civil and military workers in the context of the French Revolution? **29B**

33. ***Examining*** In the excerpt, Napoleon describes "the peoples of Germany." Based on the historical context, how would the nobles of various German states be likely to respond to Napoleon's ideas and why? **29C**

34. ***Specifying*** In this text, how does Napoleon encourage the King of Westphalia to improve his justice system?

Analyzing Visuals

Use the image to answer the following questions.

35. ***Identifying Bias in Visual Material*** Which elements suggest the parade participants' bias against Christianity and the Church? **29E**

36. ***Evaluating Visual Material*** The parade participants favored reason over a religion that they believed encouraged superstition. Does the image support the idea of reason? Explain your thinking.

Extended Response Question

37. ***Expository*** How did the ideas of the Enlightenment help cause the French Revolution? How closely did the various factions of revolutionaries follow Enlightenment beliefs? How closely did Napoleon follow Enlightenment beliefs when he ruled France? **1E, 9B, 9D, 20B**

Need Extra Help?

If You've Missed Question	32	33	34	35	36	37
Go to page	513	519	524	508	524	501

Industrialization and Nationalism

1800–1870

ESSENTIAL QUESTIONS • *How can innovation affect ways of life?* • *How does revolution bring about political and economic change?*

networks

There's More Online! about industrialization and nationalism.

CHAPTER 23

The Story Matters...

The ideals of the American and French Revolutions encouraged independence movements in other parts of the world. Napoleon's invasion of Spain weakened Spanish control of its Latin American colonies, resulting in nationalist uprisings there. These revolts were led by members of a Latin American-born elite of Spanish descent, such as Simón Bolívar, who vowed to bring freedom and independence to Latin America.

◄ Painted in about 1829 by Antonio Salas, this portrait of Bolívar, showing him as a dramatic figure posed against a dark background, presents the nationalist as a triumphant military leader.

CHAPTER 23

Place and Time: Europe 1800–1880

The people of the nineteenth century witnessed the dramatic rise and fall of governments, the explosion of war and changing borders, and the rise of liberal economics and nationalist politics. The British government's support for free trade and its willingness to make political compromises to the middle classes helped it avoid the fate of many European nations where citizens took up arms for national identity in 1848. There were many causes of the Revolutions of 1848, including nationalism, the repressive nature of governments, and famines. The men and women of the middle classes and the urban working classes were discontented with their leaders.

Step Into the Place

Read the quotes and look at the information presented on the map.

DBQ Compare the lines from Shelley's poem to the excerpt from Macaulay's speech, focusing on their views of revolution. Use the map to draw a conclusion about which viewpoint dominated British politics in the nineteenth century.

PRIMARY SOURCE

"Men of England, wherefore plough
For the lords who lay ye low?
Wherefore weave with toil and care
The rich robes your tyrants wear? . . .

Sow seed,—but let no tyrant reap:
Find wealth,—let no imposter heap;
Weave robes,—let not the idle wear;
Forge arms,—in your defence to bear . . ."

—Percy Bysshe Shelley, from "A Song: 'Men of England,'" 1819

PRIMARY SOURCE

"For the sake, therefore, of the whole society, for the sake of the labouring classes themselves, I hold it to be clearly expedient that, in a country like this, the right of suffrage should depend on a pecuniary [monetary] qualification . . . I am opposed to Universal Suffrage, because I think that it would produce a destructive revolution. I support this plan [electoral reform], because I am sure that it is our best security against a revolution."

—Thomas Babington Macaulay, from a speech in Parliament, March 2, 1831

Step Into the Time

Choose an event from the time line and explain how it shows a consequence of political unrest in Europe or a consequence of the Industrial Revolution.

EUROPE

- **1804** Richard Trevithick's steam locomotive runs on an industrial rail line in Britain
- **1807** Britain abolishes the slave trade
- **1814** Congress of Vienna meets
- **1830** French Revolution of 1830–Charles X flees the country to be replaced by the new constitutional monarchy of Louis-Philippe

1800 **1820**

THE WORLD

- **1789–1807** Selim III reigns as sultan of the Ottoman Empire and attempts reform efforts
- **1804** Haitians defeat French invasion and declare independence
- **1810–1825** Wars of independence in Latin America
- **1820** Mexico declares independence from Spain

networks
There's More Online!

- **MAP** Explore the interactive version of this map on Networks.
- **TIME LINE** Explore the interactive version of the time line on Networks.

Revolutionary Outbursts and Political Revolutions 1830–1848

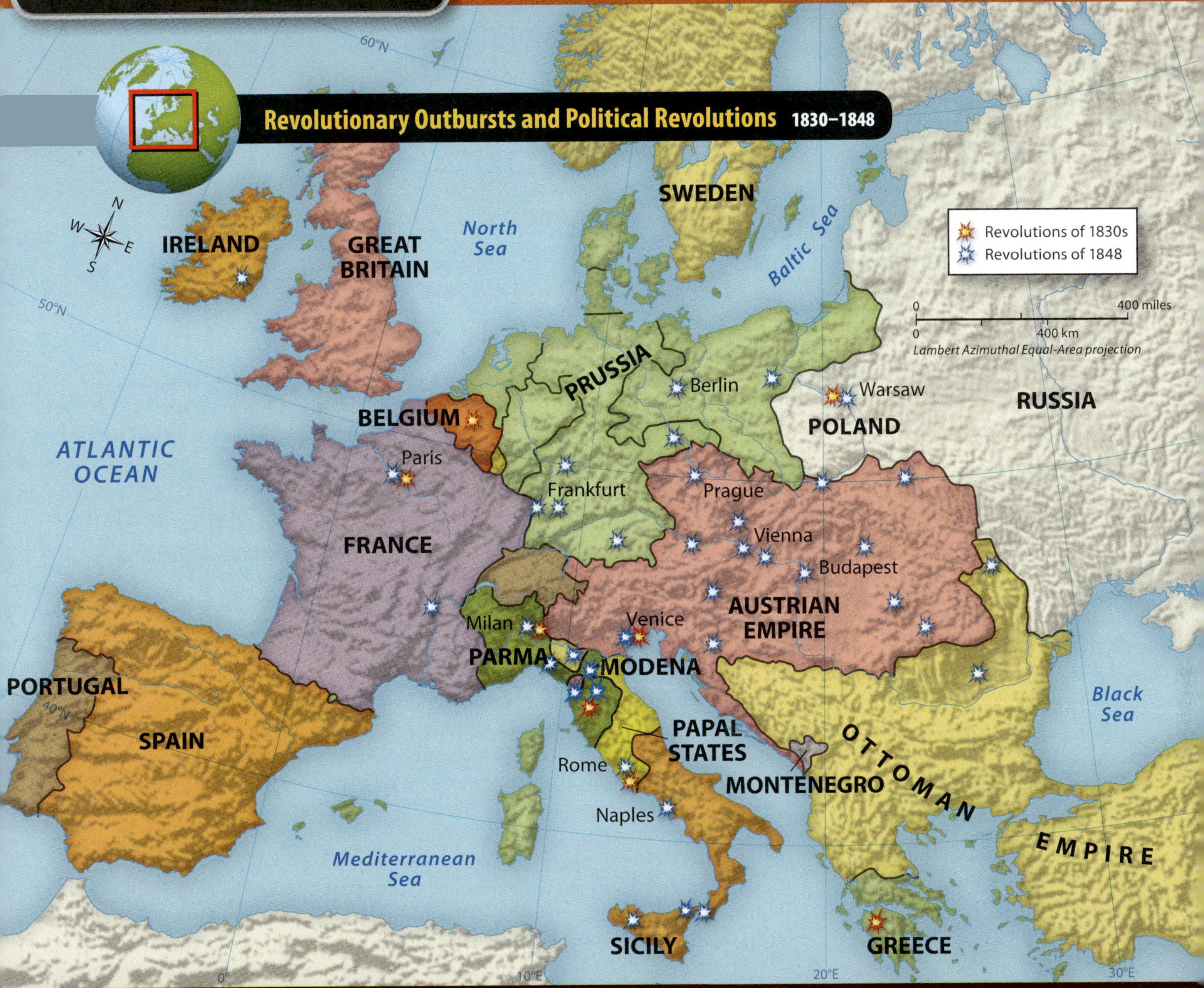

1833 British Factory Act begins age of government regulations over factories

1839 Opium War begins in China

1842 Treaty of Nanjing grants Hong Kong Island to Britain in perpetuity

1848 Revolutions erupt in Europe, beginning with the overthrow of Louis-Philippe in France

1850 Taiping Rebellion begins in China

1852 A year after a coup d'état overthrows the French Republic, Second Empire is proclaimed in France

1853–1856 Crimean War

1865 Confederate forces surrender, ending the American Civil War

1867 French troops withdraw from Mexico

1867 Dual monarchy of Austria-Hungary is created

1868 Meiji Restoration in Japan

1869 Opening of the Suez Canal, ending overland route and reducing shipping costs

1871 German unification achieved under William I

1840 — 1860 — 1880

networks

There's More Online!

- ☑ BIOGRAPHY James Watt
- ☑ BIOGRAPHY Robert Fulton
- ☑ IMAGE The Rocket Steam Engine
- ☑ IMAGE Women Working in an English Cotton Mill
- ☑ INTERACTIVE SELF-CHECK QUIZ
- ☑ MAP Industry in Great Britain, 1850
- ☑ PRIMARY SOURCE A Miner's Story, 1842
- ☑ PRIMARY SOURCE Condition of the Working Class in England, 1844
- ☑ VIDEO The Industrial Revolution

LESSON 1
The Industrial Revolution

ESSENTIAL QUESTIONS • *How can innovation affect ways of life?* • *How does revolution bring about political and economic change?*

Reading HELPDESK

Academic Vocabulary

- **labor**
- **derived**

Content Vocabulary

- **capital**
- **entrepreneur**
- **cottage industry**
- **factory system**
- **puddling**
- **industrial capitalism**
- **socialism**

TAKING NOTES:
Key Ideas and Details

Categorizing As you read, use a table like the one below to name important inventors mentioned in this section and their inventions.

Inventors	Inventions

It Matters Because

During the late eighteenth century, the Industrial Revolution began in Great Britain. This resulted in a shift from an economy based on farming and handicrafts to one based on machine manufacturing.

The Industrial Revolution Begins

GUIDING QUESTIONS *What was the significance of the Agricultural Revolution in Great Britain? Why did the Industrial Revolution start in Great Britain?*

The Industrial Revolution began in Great Britain in the 1780s. However, it took decades to spread to other Western nations. Several factors contributed to make Great Britain the starting place.

First, an Agricultural Revolution beginning in the eighteenth century changed agricultural practices. Expansion of farmland, good weather, improved transportation, and new crops such as the potato dramatically increased the food supply. More people could be fed at lower prices with less **labor**. Now even ordinary British families could use some of their income to buy manufactured goods.

Second, with the increased food supply, the population grew. When Parliament passed enclosure movement laws in the eighteenth century, landowners fenced off common lands. This forced many peasants to move to towns, creating a labor supply for factories.

Third, Britain had a ready supply of money, or **capital**, to invest in new machines and factories. **Entrepreneurs** found new business opportunities and new ways to make profits.

Fourth, natural resources were plentiful in Britain. The country's rivers provided water power for the new factories and a means for transporting raw materials and finished products. Britain also had abundant supplies of coal and iron ore.

Finally, a supply of markets gave British manufacturers a ready outlet for their goods. Britain had a vast colonial empire, and British ships could transport goods anywhere in the world. Also, because of population growth and cheaper food at home, domestic markets increased. A growing demand for cotton cloth led British manufacturers to look for ways to increase production.

Textile Manufacturing and the Industrial Revolution

In the eighteenth century, Great Britain had surged far ahead in the production of inexpensive cotton goods. The manufacture of cotton cloth was a two-step process. First, spinners made cotton thread from raw cotton. Then, weavers wove the cotton thread into cloth on looms. In the eighteenth century, individuals did these tasks in their rural cottages. This production method was thus called a **cottage industry**.

A series of technological and scientific advances during this time made the cottage industry inefficient. Many of these developments were related to textile manufacturing, and they spurred the development of the Industrial Revolution. In 1764 James Hargreaves invented a machine called the spinning jenny, which made the spinning process much faster. In fact, spinners produced thread faster than weavers could use it.

The invention of a water-powered loom by Edmund Cartwright in 1787 made it possible for the weaving of cloth to catch up with the spinning of thread. It was now more efficient to bring workers to the new machines and have them work in factories near streams and rivers, which were used to power many of these early machines.

The cotton industry became even more productive when James Watt, a Scottish engineer and inventor, improved the steam engine in the 1760s. In 1782 Watt made changes that enabled the engine to drive machinery. Steam power could now be used to spin and weave cotton. Since coal fueled steam engines, mills no longer need to be located by rivers. Before long, cotton mills using steam engines could be found throughout Britain.

British cotton cloth production increased dramatically. In 1760 Britain had imported 2.5 million pounds (1.14 million kg) of raw cotton, which was used to produce cloth in cottage industries. By 1840, 366 million pounds (166 million kg) of cotton were imported each year. By this time, cotton cloth was Britain's most valuable product. Sold around the world, British cotton goods were produced mainly in factories.

The factory was another important element in the Industrial Revolution. From its beginning, the factory created a new labor system. Factory owners wanted to use their new machines constantly. So, workers were forced to work in shifts to keep the machines producing at a steady rate.

The Factory System and Free Enterprise

The **factory system** was another important element in the Industrial Revolution. The factory system is the use of machines, powered by water, steam, or electricity, to manufacture goods. The factory system also featured the use of unskilled labor, the centralization of machinery under one roof, and the standardization of parts used to operate machinery and manufacture goods. From its beginning, the factory had an impact on systems of labor, human life, and economics.

Early factory workers came from rural areas where they were used to periods of hectic work, such as the harvest, followed by periods of inactivity. Early factory owners therefore were required to discipline their workers to a system of regular hours and repetitive tasks. Factory owners wanted to use their new machines constantly. So, multiple daily work shifts were instituted to keep the machines producing at a steady rate. This system of shift work persists in manufacturing today.

The factory system advanced the onset of the Industrial Revolution. Goods produced in the factory system were made quickly and in large numbers. As a result, factories soon came to replace cottage industries. The efficiency of the

labor work performed by people that provides the goods or services in an economy

capital money available for investment

entrepreneur a person who finds new business opportunities and new ways to make profits

cottage industry a method of production in which tasks are done by individuals in their rural homes

factory system a system of production where goods are manufactured by machines under one roof, with unskilled labor, using standardized parts

TEKS Texas Essential Knowledge and Skills

1E identify major causes and describe the major effects of the following important turning points in world history from 1750 to 1914: the Scientific Revolution, the Industrial Revolution and its impact on the development of modern economic systems, European imperialism, and the Enlightenment's impact on political revolutions

8A explain how 17th and 18th century European scientific advancements led to the Industrial Revolution

8B explain how the Industrial Revolution led to political, economic, and social changes in Europe

continued on the next page

▼ Titled *Carding, Drawing, and Roving*, this print shows girls and women working in an English cotton mill.

▶ **CRITICAL THINKING**

Analyzing Information In what way does this image depict factory work?

(continued from p. 529)

TEKS **Texas Essential Knowledge and Skills**

8E explain the effects of free enterprise in the Industrial Revolution

17A identify important changes in human life caused by the Neolithic Revolution and the Industrial Revolution

18A identify the historical origins and characteristics of the free enterprise system, including the contributions of Adam Smith, especially the influence of his ideas found in The Wealth of Nations

18C identify the historical origins and characteristics of socialism

continued on the next page

factory system meant other industries outside the textile industry began to adopt it. By the mid-1800s the mills and smokestacks of new factories dotted Great Britain's landscape.

As the Industrial Revolution progressed, many European governments adopted free enterprise ideas. Free enterprise is an economic system where governments place few restrictions on business ownership or decisions. Under a free enterprise system, factory owners could make decisions based solely on the needs of their business. This freedom allowed factory owners to maximize production and make large profits. In turn, these profits would often be used to expand industries. Free enterprise allowed for the rapid growth of industrialism.

Coal, Iron, and Railroads

The steam engine was crucial to Britain's Industrial Revolution. For fuel, the engine depended on coal, which seemed then to be unlimited in quantity. The success of the steam engine increased the need for coal and led to an expansion in coal production. New processes using coal aided the transformation of another industry—the iron industry.

puddling the process in which coke derived from coal is used to burn away impurities in crude iron to produce high quality iron

derived obtained from; came from

Britain's natural resources included large supplies of crude iron called pig iron. In the 1780s Henry Cort developed a process called **puddling**. In this process, coke, which was **derived** from coal, was used to burn away impurities in crude iron, pig iron, leaving iron of a much higher quality. This scientific advancement changed the way iron was produced and was important to the Industrial Revolution.

The British iron industry boomed. In 1740 Britain had produced 17,000 tons (15,419 metric tons or t) of iron. After Cort's process came into use in the 1780s, production jumped to nearly 70,000 tons (63,490 t). In 1852 Britain produced almost 3 million tons (2.7 million t)—more iron than was produced by the rest of the world combined. High-quality iron was used to build new machines, especially trains.

In the eighteenth century, more efficient means of moving resources and goods developed. Railroads were particularly important to the success of the Industrial Revolution. Richard Trevithick, an English engineer, built the first steam locomotive. In 1804 Trevithick's locomotive ran on an industrial rail line in Britain. It pulled 10 tons (9 t) of ore and 70 people at 5 miles (8.05 km) per hour. Better locomotives soon followed. One called the *Rocket* was used on the first public railway line, which opened in 1830 and extended 32 miles (51.5 km) from the cotton-manufacturing town of Manchester to the thriving port of Liverpool.

The *Rocket* sped along at 16 miles (25.7 km) per hour while pulling a 40-ton (36-t) train. Within 20 years, locomotives were able to reach 50 miles (80.5 km) per hour, an incredible speed. In 1840 Britain had almost 2,000 miles (3,218 km) of railroads. In 1850 more than 6,000 miles (9,654 km) of railroad track crisscrossed much of the country.

Building railroads created new jobs for farm laborers and peasants. Less expensive transportation led to lower-priced goods, thus creating larger markets. More sales meant more demand and the need for more factories and more machinery. Business owners could reinvest their profits in new equipment, adding to the growth of the economy. This type of regular, ongoing economic growth became a basic feature of the new industrial economy.

✓ READING PROGRESS CHECK

Making Inferences Why might it be important to have fast, reliable transportation between Manchester and Liverpool?

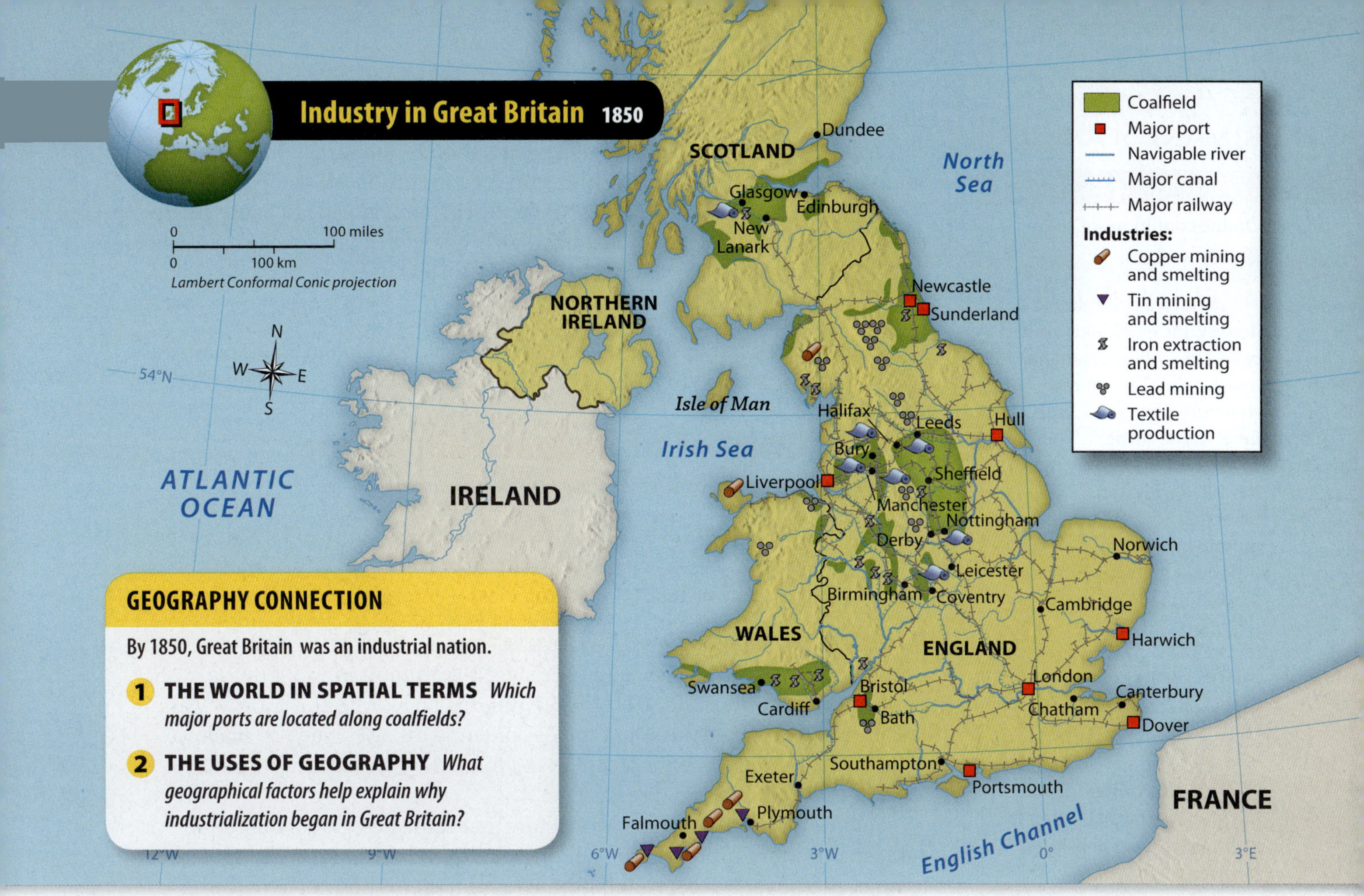

GEOGRAPHY CONNECTION

By 1850, Great Britain was an industrial nation.

1. **THE WORLD IN SPATIAL TERMS** *Which major ports are located along coalfields?*
2. **THE USES OF GEOGRAPHY** *What geographical factors help explain why industrialization began in Great Britain?*

The Spread of Industrialization

GUIDING QUESTION *What factors fed the spread of industrialization in Europe and North America?*

By the mid-nineteenth century, Great Britain had become the world's first industrial nation. It had also become the world's richest nation. Great Britain produced one-half of the world's coal and manufactured goods. Its cotton industry alone in 1850 was equal in size to the industries of all other European countries combined.

The Industrial Revolution spread to the rest of Europe at different times and at different speeds. Belgium, France, and the German states were the first to be industrialized in continental Europe, and their governments actively encouraged such development. For example, governments provided funds to build roads, canals, and railroads. By 1850, a network of iron rails spread across Europe.

An Industrial Revolution also occurred in the United States during the first half of the nineteenth century. In 1800 more than 5 million people lived in the United States, and nearly 6 out of every 7 American workers were farmers. No city had more than 100,000 people. In contrast, the U.S. population had grown to more than 30 million people by 1860. Many of these people moved into the cities. Eight cities had populations over 100,000, and only about 50 percent of American workers were farmers.

A large country, the United States needed a good transportation system to move goods across the nation. Thousands of miles of roads and canals were built to link east and west. Robert Fulton built the first paddle-wheel steamboat, the *Clermont*, in 1807. Steamboats made transportation easier on the waterways of the United States.

(continued from p. 530)

TEKS **Texas Essential Knowledge and Skills**

18F formulate generalizations on how economic freedom improved the human condition, based on students' knowledge of the benefits of free enterprise in Europe's Commercial Revolution, the Industrial Revolution, and 20th-century free market economies, compared to communist command communities

28A explain the role of textile manufacturing and steam technology in initiating the Industrial Revolution and the role of the factory system and transportation technology in advancing the Industrial Revolution

28E identify the contributions of significant scientists and inventors such as Marie Curie, Thomas Edison, Albert Einstein, Louis Pasteur, and James Watt

Analyzing PRIMARY SOURCES

Children in Factories

On the conditions of child factory workers:

"Provided a child should be drowsy, the overlooker walks round the room . . . and he touches the child on the shoulder, and says, 'Come here.' In the corner of the room there is an iron cistern; it is filled with water . . . he takes this boy, and holding him up by the legs, dips him over head in the cistern, and sends him to work for the remainder of the day. . . ."

—from a British Parliament report, quoted in *The History of the Factory Movement, Vol I*, 1857

DBQ ***MAKING INFERENCES*** Why might the British Parliament have examined the conditions of child factory workers?

Most important in the development of an American transportation system was the railroad. By 1860, about 30,000 miles (48,270 km) of railroad track covered the continental United States. The railroad soon turned the country into a single massive market for the manufactured goods produced in the Northeast.

Labor for the growing number of factories in the Northeast came chiefly from the farm population. Women and girls made up a large majority of the workers in large textile (cotton and wool) factories.

✓ **READING PROGRESS CHECK**

Comparing How did the effects of industrialization in the United States compare with those in Great Britain?

Social Impact of Industrialization

GUIDING QUESTION *What was the social impact of industrialization in Europe?*

The Industrial Revolution drastically changed society. In the first half of the nineteenth century, cities grew and two new social classes—the industrial middle class and the industrial working class—emerged.

Population Growth and Urbanization

European population stood at an estimated 140 million in 1750. By 1850, the population had almost doubled to 266 million. The key to this growth was a decline in death rates, wars, and major epidemic diseases, such as smallpox and plague. Because of an increase in the food supply, people were better fed and more resistant to disease.

Famine and poverty were two factors that impacted global migration and urbanization. More than 1 million people died during the Irish potato famine, and poverty led a million more to migrate to the Americas. Industrialization also spurred urbanization, as large numbers of people migrated from the countryside to cities to work in factories.

In 1800 Great Britain had one major city, London, with a population of about 1 million. Six cities had populations between 50,000 and 100,000. By 1850, London's population had swelled to about 2.5 million. Nine cities had populations over 100,000. Also, more than 50 percent of the population lived in towns and cities.

The rapid growth of cities in the first half of the nineteenth century led to pitiful living conditions for many, leading urban reformers to call on local governments to clean up their cities. Reform would be undertaken in the second half of the nineteenth century.

New Social Classes

industrial capitalism an economic system based on industrial production or manufacturing

The Middle Ages saw the rise of commercial capitalism, an economic system based on trade. **Industrial capitalism**, an economic system based on industrial production, developed during the Industrial Revolution. This system produced a new middle-class group—the industrial middle class.

In the Middle Ages, the bourgeoisie, or middle-class person, was the burgher or town dweller. The bourgeoisie were merchants, officials, artisans, lawyers, or intellectuals. Later, the term *bourgeois* came to include people involved in industry and banking, as well as lawyers, teachers, or doctors. The new industrial middle class that emerged during the Industrial Revolution was made up of the people who built the factories, bought the machines, and developed the markets. They had initiative, vision, ambition, and often greed. One said, "Getting of money... is the main business of the life of Man. . . ."

each day, 6 days per week. There was no security of employment, and there was no minimum wage.

Conditions in the coal mines were harsh. Steam-powered engines lifted the coal from the mines to the top, but the men inside the mines dug out the coal. Dangerous conditions, including cave-ins, explosions, and gas fumes, were a way of life. The cramped conditions in the mines and their constant dampness led to workers' deformed bodies and ruined lungs.

The worst conditions were in the cotton mills, which were also dirty, dusty, dangerous, and unhealthy. In Britain, women and children made up two-thirds of the cotton industry's workforce by 1830. However, the number of child laborers declined after the Factory Act of 1833. This act set nine as the minimum age for employment and limited hours for older children. After this, women came to make up 50 percent of the British labor force in textile factories. They were paid half or less than half of what men received. When the work hours of children and women were limited, a new pattern of work emerged. Men now earned most of the family income by working outside the home. Women took over daily care of the family and performed low-paying jobs that could be done at home.

▲ Children and women working in an English coal mine

PHOTO: The Stapleton Collection/Bridgeman Art Library

Early Socialism

In the first half of the nineteenth century, the pitiful conditions created by the Industrial Revolution gave rise to a movement and economic system known as **socialism**. The central characteristic of socialism is that society—usually in the form of the government—owns and controls some means of production, such as factories and utilities.

socialism a system in which society, usually in the form of the government, owns and controls the means of production

Early socialism was largely the idea of intellectuals. To later socialists, especially the followers of Karl Marx, such ideas were impractical dreams. They contemptuously labeled the earlier reformers utopian socialists, a term that has lasted to this day. Robert Owen, a British cotton manufacturer, was one utopian socialist. He believed that humans would show their natural goodness if they lived in a cooperative environment. Owen transformed the squalid factory town of New Lanark, Scotland, into a flourishing community. He created a similar community at New Harmony, Indiana, in the United States in the 1820s, which failed.

✓ **READING PROGRESS CHECK**

Drawing Conclusions Why do you think the working conditions during the Industrial Revolution led some to argue for socialism?

LESSON 1 REVIEW TEKS

Reviewing Vocabulary

1. ***Summarizing*** Write a paragraph describing the importance of urbanization to the growth of industrial capitalism in Great Britain.

Using Your Notes

2. ***Organizing*** Use your graphic organizer to discuss the major inventors and inventions covered in this lesson.

Answering the Guiding Questions

3. ***Evaluating*** What was the significance of the Agricultural Revolution in Great Britain?
4. ***Identifying*** Why did the Industrial Revolution start in Great Britain?
5. ***Making Connections*** What factors fed the spread of industrialization in Europe and North America?
6. ***Drawing Conclusions*** What was the social impact of industrialization in Europe?

Writing Activity

7. **INFORMATIVE/EXPLANATORY** Using the information you collected in your graphic organizer, write a paragraph describing the impact the various inventions had on the Industrial Revolution.

SKILLBUILDER

TEKS 15A

Interpreting Charts: Development

Why Learn This Skill?

A key skill in social studies is establishing connections between facts. Charts provide a great way to compare facts and see how they relate to each other. Being able to create and interpret charts gives you a clearer picture of history.

Learning the Skill

Facts can sometimes feel buried in a large block of text, but charts can help cut through the clutter. A visual representation of data—including maps, charts, graphs, and so on—arranges pieces of information in an organized manner. In a grid-like chart, find key information by looking for intersections of columns and rows.

Practicing the Skill

The nineteenth century was a period of great change in western Europe. The Industrial Revolution changed how people lived and worked, while reform movements reshaped human rights and political structures. The historical developments that occurred during this period fundamentally altered the social, economic, and political landscape of Europe.

Study this chart. While most people lived through major changes during this century, each country experienced the historical developments in a different way. This chart organizes information about reform movements according to geography. The ability to create and interpret charts such as this one helps you to see patterns in historical data.

	Goals	Results	Those Desiring Reform
Great Britain	Increasing Voting Rights	The Reform Act of 1832 and 1867 expanded voting rights to many more adult males.	Radicals, the lower classes
France	Paris modernization; democratic reform	Paris was rebuilt in a new style The legislature was given more power.	Lower class Parisians, Napoleon III
Austrian Empire	Greater rights for ethnic minorities.	The Compromise of 1867 created the dual monarchy of Austria-Hungary.	Magyars, Romanians, Czechs, Croats
Russia	Freedom for serfs and judicial reforms.	The emancipation edict freed the serfs but landownders kept best land. Alexander II reformed the judiciary along western models.	Serfs, Alexander II

Skills Assessment

Look at this chart and pay particular attention to geographic factors. Answer the following question:

1. Interpret the chart and describe the relationship between geography and the historical development of the region.
2. Create a chart of your own that demonstrates the relationship between geography and the historical development of a region or nation. The chart can be a simple graphic organizer that contains data from the textbook. Remember, historical development refers to how something changes over time.

Applying the Skill

Interpreting Charts One of the most useful charts is the cause-and-effect chart. The most simple of these includes only two boxes and an arrow connecting them. Since geography is a major cause of historical change, a cause-and-effect chart is a good way to demonstrate that relationship. Create three simple cause-and-effect charts showing the relationship between geography and the historical development of a region or nation.

SKILLBUILDER

TEKS 29F

Identifying an Argument

Why Learn This Skill?

In everyday conversation, the word argument refers to a conflict involving two or more opinions. However, in writing and in formal debate, an argument is the full presentation of a single opinion. An argument uses facts to support a particular opinion. After hearing these facts, it is then up to you to determine whether the argument is valid or not.

Learning the Skill

There are three basic elements to consider in an argument.

What is the main idea? The main idea of an argument is its thesis, or the writer's basic position or viewpoint on the subject. In some arguments the main idea is stated explicitly. In others, you must read carefully to find the main idea, or identify the argument.

What are the supporting reasons, examples, and facts? The writer supports the main idea with reasons and supports the reasons with examples or facts.

What are its strengths and weaknesses? Before accepting or rejecting an argument, evaluate its strengths and weaknesses. How well is each reason supported by facts and examples? Does the author's bias invalidate the argument?

Practicing the Skill

Read the following quotation from a speech in Parliament by Thomas Babington Macaulay on March 2, 1831.

"For the sake, therefore, of the whole society, for the sake of the labouring classes themselves, I hold it to be clearly expedient that, in a country like this, the right of suffrage should depend on a pecuniary [monetary] qualification . . . . I am opposed to Universal Suffrage, because I think that it would produce a destructive revolution. I support this plan [electoral reform], because I am sure that it is our best security against a revolution."

Study this quotation closely and look for supporting reasons, examples, and facts.

Skills Assessment

1. What is the writer's main idea? In other words, what is the writer's argument?
2. What reasons does the writer give to support this argument?
3. Do any facts support the statement that Universal Suffrage would produce a revolution?
4. What is your reaction to the author's argument?

Applying the Skill

Finding the Main Idea Find a recent article that states an argument about a political or historical issue. Find the main idea of the argument and the major reasons and evidence supporting it. Decide whether you accept or reject this argument and explain why.

networks

There's More Online!

- BIOGRAPHY Charles Louis Napoleon Bonaparte
- CHART/GRAPH Revolutions of 1830
- IMAGE Overthrow of King Louis Philippe
- IMAGE Revolt in the Austrian Empire
- INTERACTIVE SELF-CHECK QUIZ
- MAP Nationalities in Austria-Hungary, Mid-1800s
- VIDEO Potato Famine

Reading HELPDESK

Academic Vocabulary

- **radical**
- **temporary**

Content Vocabulary

- **universal male suffrage**
- **multinational empire**

TAKING NOTES:

Key Ideas and Details

Comparing and Contrasting Use your graphic organizer to compare and contrast the revolutions of 1830 and 1848.

	1830	1848
Governments/ countries in power		
Groups revolting		
Outcomes		

TEKS Texas Essential Knowledge and Skills

9D identify the influence of ideas such as separation of powers, checks and balances, liberty, equality, democracy, popular sovereignty, human rights, constitutionalism, and nationalism on political revolutions

continued on the next page

LESSON 2

Nationalism and Political Revolutions

ESSENTIAL QUESTIONS • *How can innovation affect ways of life?* • *How does revolution bring about political and economic change?*

IT MATTERS BECAUSE

After the Napoleonic wars, European rulers sought to restore stability by reestablishing much of the old order. They also wanted to keep a balance of power among nations. New forces for change, however, especially liberalism and nationalism, had become too powerful to be contained. Revolts and revolutions soon shook Europe.

The Revolutions of the 1830s

GUIDING QUESTION *How did liberalism and nationalism present a challenge to conservatism in Europe during the 1830s and 1840s?*

Governments in Europe attempted to maintain the old order during the nineteenth century. Beginning in 1830, however, the forces of change—liberalism and nationalism—began to break through the conservative domination of Europe.

In France the Bourbon monarch Charles X, a reactionary, attempted to censor the press and take away voting rights from much of the middle class. In response, liberals overthrew Charles X in 1830 and established a constitutional monarchy. Louis-Philippe, a cousin of Charles X, took the throne. Political support for the new monarch came from the upper-middle class.

In the same year, three more revolutions occurred in Europe. Nationalism was the chief force in all three of them. Belgium, which had been annexed to the former Dutch Republic in 1815, rebelled and created an independent state. Both Poland and Italy, which were ruled by foreign powers, made efforts to break free. These efforts, however, were less successful. Russian troops crushed the Polish attempt to establish an independent Polish nation. Meanwhile, Austrian troops marched south and put down revolts in a number of Italian states.

READING PROGRESS CHECK

Evaluating In what ways were liberalism and nationalism causes for the revolutions of the 1830s in Europe?

PHOTO: (l to r) The People Burning the Throne at the Place de la Bastille, 1848 (colour litho), French School, (19th century)/Bibliotheque Nationale, Paris, France/Archives Charmet/Bridgeman Images, Imagno/Hulton Archive/Getty Images, ©The Print Collector/Age Fotostock, America.

The Revolutions of 1848

GUIDING QUESTIONS *How did liberalism and nationalism present a challenge to conservatism in Europe during the 1830s and 1840s? What were the results of the revolutionary uprisings that occurred throughout Europe in 1848?*

(continued from p. 536)

TEKS **Texas Essential Knowledge and Skills**

21A describe how people have participated in supporting or changing their governments

21B describe the rights and responsibilities of citizens and noncitizens in civic participation throughout history

28A explain the role of textile manufacturing and steam technology in initiating the Industrial Revolution and the role of the factory system and transportation technology in advancing the Industrial Revolution

Despite liberal and nationalist successes in France and Belgium, the conservative order still dominated much of Europe as the midpoint of the nineteenth century approached. However, the forces of liberalism and nationalism continued to grow. These forces of change erupted once more in the revolutions of 1848.

Another French Revolution

Revolution in France was again the spark for revolution in other countries. Severe economic problems beginning in 1846 brought untold hardship in France to the lower middle class, workers, and peasants. At the same time, members of the middle class clamored for the right to vote. The government of Louis-Philippe refused to make changes, and opposition grew.

The monarchy was finally overthrown in 1848. A group of moderate and **radical** republicans set up a provisional, or **temporary**, government. The republicans were people who wanted France to be a republic—a government in which leaders are elected.

radical relating to a political group associated with views, practices, and policies of extreme change

temporary lasting for a limited time; not permanent

The provisional government called for the election of representatives to a Constituent Assembly that would draw up a new constitution. Election would be determined by **universal male suffrage**, or the right of all adult men to vote. The provisional government also set up national workshops to provide work for the unemployed. From March to June, the number of unemployed enrolled in the national workshops rose from about 66,000 to almost 120,000. This emptied the treasury and frightened the moderates, who reacted by closing the workshops on June 21, 1848.

universal male suffrage the right of all males to vote in elections

The workers refused to accept this decision to close down the workshops. They poured into the streets in protest. In four days of bitter and bloody fighting, government forces crushed the working-class revolt. Thousands were killed and thousands more were sent to the French prison colony of Algeria in northern Africa.

▲ Burning the French throne at the Place de la Bastille, 1848

▶ **CRITICAL THINKING**

Drawing Inferences Describe the symbolic meaning of this painting.

The new French constitution, ratified on November 4, 1848, set up a republic called the Second Republic. The Second Republic had a single legislature elected by universal male suffrage. A president, also chosen by universal male suffrage, served for four years. In the elections for the presidency held in December 1848, Charles Louis Napoleon Bonaparte (called Louis-Napoleon), the nephew of the famous French ruler, won a resounding victory.

▲ The National Guard breaks up a labor uprising in Vienna, 1848.

▶ **CRITICAL THINKING**

Drawing Conclusions How does this image illustrate the chaos and level of participation in the 1848 revolts?

Revolt in the German States

News of the 1848 revolution in France led to upheaval in other parts of Europe. The Congress of Vienna, which lasted from 1814 to 1815, had recognized the existence of 38 independent German states (called the German Confederation). Of these, Austria and Prussia were the two great powers. The other states varied in size.

In 1848 cries for change led many German rulers to promise constitutions, a free press, jury trials, and other liberal reforms. In May 1848, an all-German parliament, called the Frankfurt Assembly, was held to fulfill a liberal and nationalist dream—the preparation of a constitution for a new united Germany. The Frankfurt Assembly's proposed constitution provided for a German state with a parliamentary government and a hereditary emperor ruling under a limited monarchy. The constitution also allowed for direct election of deputies to the parliament by universal male suffrage.

Ultimately, however, the Frankfurt Assembly failed to gain the support needed to achieve its goal. Frederick William IV of Prussia, to whom the throne was offered, refused to accept the crown from a popularly elected assembly. Thus, the assembly members had no real means of forcing the German rulers to accept their drafted constitution. German unification was not achieved.

Revolutions in Central Europe

multinational empire an empire in which people of many nationalities live

The Austrian Empire also had its problems. It was a **multinational empire**—a collection of different peoples, including Germans, Czechs, Magyars (Hungarians), Slovaks, Romanians, Slovenes, Poles, Croats, Serbs, Ruthenians (Ukrainians), and Italians. Only the German-speaking Hapsburg dynasty held the empire together. The Germans, though only a quarter of the population, played a leading role in governing the Austrian Empire.

In March 1848, demonstrations erupted in the major cities. To calm the demonstrators, the Hapsburg court dismissed Metternich, the Austrian foreign minister, who fled to England. In Vienna, revolutionary forces took control of the capital and demanded a liberal constitution. To appease the revolutionaries, the government gave Hungary its own legislature. In Bohemia, the Czechs clamored for their own government.

Austrian officials had made concessions to appease the revolutionaries but were determined to reestablish their control over the empire. In June 1848, Austrian military forces crushed the Czech rebels in Prague. By the end of October, the rebels in Vienna had been defeated as well. With the help of a Russian army of 140,000 men, the Hungarian revolutionaries were finally subdued in 1849. The revolutions in the Austrian Empire had failed.

Revolts in the Italian States

The Congress of Vienna had set up nine states in Italy, which were divided among the European powers. These states included the Kingdom of Piedmont in the north; the Two Sicilies (Naples and Sicily); the Papal States; a handful of small states; and the northern provinces of Lombardy and Venetia, which were now part of the Austrian Empire.

In 1848 a revolt broke out against the Austrians in Lombardy and Venetia. Revolutionaries in other Italian states also took up arms and sought to create liberal constitutions and a unified Italy. By 1849, however, the Austrians had reestablished complete control over Lombardy and Venetia. The old order also prevailed in the rest of Italy.

The Failures of 1848

Throughout Europe in 1848, popular revolts started upheavals that led to liberal constitutions and liberal governments. But how could so many successes in 1848 soon be followed by so many failures? Two particular reasons stand out.

The unity of the revolutionaries had made the revolutions possible. However, moderate liberals and more radical revolutionaries were soon divided over their goals; therefore, conservative rule was reestablished.

In 1848 nationalities everywhere had also revolted in pursuit of self-government. However, little was achieved as divisions among nationalities proved disastrous. The Hungarians, for example, sought their freedom from the Austrians. At the same time, they refused the same to their minorities—the Slovenes, Croats, and Serbs. Instead of joining together to fight the old empire, minorities fought each other. The old order prevailed. Even with the reestablishment of conservative governments, however, the forces of nationalism and liberalism continued to influence political events.

✓ **READING PROGRESS CHECK**

Drawing Conclusions Why did the revolutions of 1848 fail?

Analyzing PRIMARY SOURCES

Giuseppe Mazzini on Young Italy

"Young Italy is a brotherhood of Italians who believe in a law of *Progress* and *Duty*, and are convinced that Italy is destined to become one nation. . .

Young Italy is *Unitarian*.

Because, without unity, there is no true nation.

Because without unity, there is no real strength; and Italy, surrounded as she is by powerful, united, and jealous nations, has need of strength before all things. . . ."

—Giuseppe Mazzini, from *General Instructions for the Members of Young Italy*, 1832

DBQ ***MAKING INFERENCES*** Why would Italy's history have convinced Mazzini of the need for national unity?

LESSON 2 REVIEW TEKS

Reviewing Vocabulary

1. ***Describing*** Define the term *universal male suffrage* and give examples of when it affected the revolutions of 1848.

Using Your Notes

2. ***Comparing and Contrasting*** Use your graphic organizer to discuss the similarities and differences between the revolutions of the 1830s and 1848.

Answering the Guiding Questions

3. ***Determining Cause and Effect*** How did liberalism and nationalism present a challenge to conservatism in Europe during the 1830s and 1840s?
4. ***Making Observations*** What were the results of the revolutionary uprisings that occurred throughout Europe in 1848?

Writing Activity

5. **ARGUMENT** Write a paragraph that argues for or against the following statement: The revolutions of the 1830s ultimately failed.

networks

There's More Online!

- BIOGRAPHY Czar Alexander II
- BIOGRAPHY Queen Victoria
- CHART/GRAPH Emancipation Edict of 1861
- IMAGE Paris Reconstruction
- PRIMARY SOURCE Garibaldi's Speech to His Soldiers
- PRIMARY SOURCE Newspaper Account of the Crimean War
- TIME LINE Unification of Germany
- TIME LINE Unification of Italy
- VIDEO Alexander II

LESSON 3

Nationalism, Unification, and Reform

ESSENTIAL QUESTIONS • *How can innovation affect ways of life?* • *How does revolution bring about political and economic change?*

Reading HELPDESK

Academic Vocabulary

- **unification** • **regime**

Content Vocabulary

- **militarism**
- **kaiser**
- **plebiscite**
- **emancipation**
- **abolitionism**

TAKING NOTES:

Key Ideas and Details

Summarizing Information As you read, use a table like the one below to list the changes that took place in the indicated countries during the nineteenth century.

Great Britain	France	Austrian Empire	Russia

TEKS Texas Essential Knowledge and Skills

24B describe the major influences of women such as Elizabeth I, Queen Victoria, Mother Teresa, Indira Gandhi, Margaret Thatcher, and Golda Meir during major eras of world history

IT MATTERS BECAUSE

Although the revolutions of 1848 were unsuccessful, the forces of nationalism and liberalism remained powerful for the rest of the nineteenth century. Italy and Germany were eventually unified, and Great Britain and France became more liberal.

Toward National Unification

GUIDING QUESTION *What led to the unification of Italy and Germany after the revolution of 1848?*

The revolutions of 1848 had failed. By 1871, however, both Germany and Italy would be unified. The changes that made this possible began with the Crimean War.

Breakdown of the Concert of Europe

The Crimean War was the result of a long-term struggle between Russia and the Ottoman Empire. The Ottoman Empire had long controlled most of the Balkans in southeastern Europe. By 1800, however, the Ottoman Empire was in decline.

Russia was especially interested in expanding its power into Ottoman lands in the Balkans. This expansion would allow Russian ships to sail through the Dardanelles, the straits between the Black Sea and the Mediterranean Sea. If Russia could achieve this goal, it would become the major power in eastern Europe and challenge British naval control of the eastern Mediterranean. Other European nations feared Russian ambition and had their own interest in the decline of the Ottoman Empire.

In 1853 the Russians invaded the Turkish Balkan provinces of Moldavia and Walachia. In response, the Ottoman Turks declared war on Russia. Great Britain and France, fearful of Russian gains in this war, declared war on Russia the following year. This conflict came to be called the Crimean War. The Crimean War was poorly planned and poorly fought. Eventually, heavy losses caused the Russians to seek peace. By the Treaty of Paris, signed in March 1856,

Russia agreed to allow Moldavia and Walachia to be placed under the protection of all the great powers.

The effect of the Crimean War was to destroy the Concert of Europe. Austria and Russia, the chief powers maintaining the status quo before the 1850s, were now enemies. Austria, with its own interests in the Balkans, had refused to support Russia in the Crimean War. A defeated and humiliated Russia withdrew from European affairs for the next 20 years. Austria was now without friends among the great powers. This situation opened the door to the **unification** of Italy and Germany.

unification the act, process, or result of making into a coherent or coordinated whole; the state of being unified

Italian Unification

In 1850 Austria was still the dominant power on the Italian Peninsula. After the failure of the revolution of 1848, people began to look to the northern Italian state of Piedmont for leadership in achieving the unification of Italy. The royal house of Savoy ruled the Kingdom of Piedmont. Included in the kingdom were Piedmont, the island of Sardinia, Nice, and Savoy. The ruler of the kingdom, beginning in 1849, was King Victor Emmanuel II.

The king named Camillo di Cavour his prime minister in 1852. As prime minister, Cavour pursued a policy of economic growth in order to equip a large army. Cavour, however, knew that Piedmont's army was not strong enough to defeat the Austrians. So he made an alliance with the French emperor Louis-Napoleon. Cavour then provoked the Austrians into declaring war in 1859.

GEOGRAPHY CONNECTION

By 1871 Italy and Germany had unified.

1. **PLACES AND REGIONS** *Describe the sequence of events in Italian unification.*
2. **HUMAN SYSTEMS** *What provinces did Germany win in the Franco-Prussian War?*

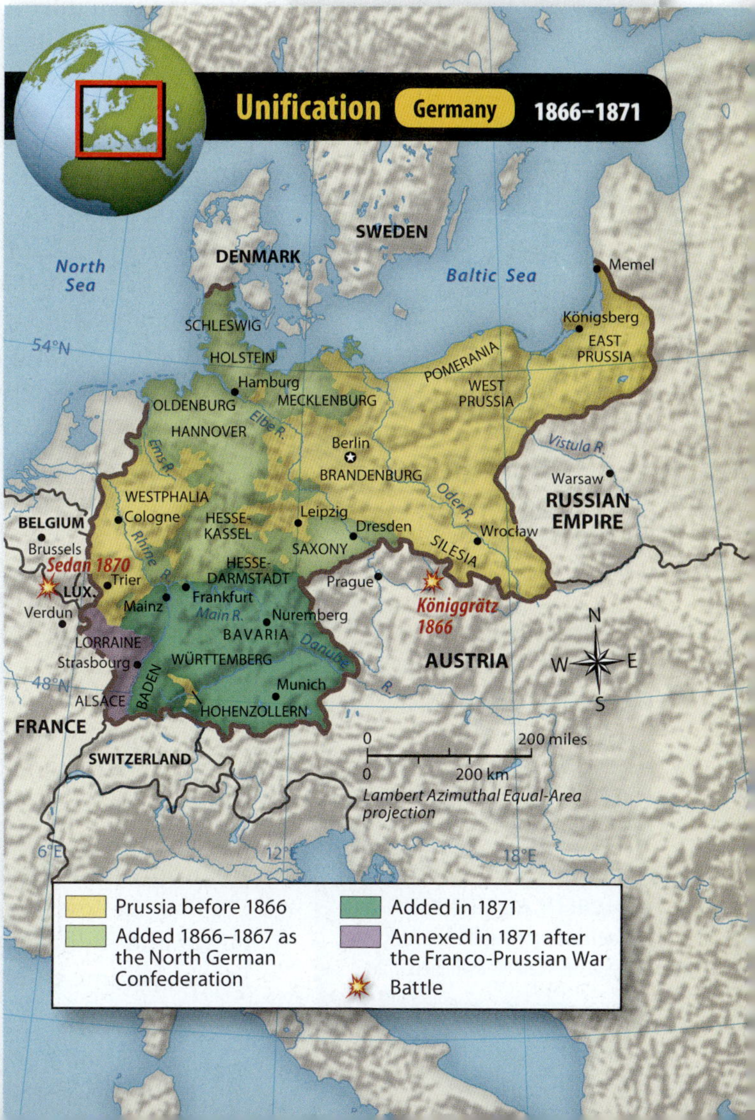

BIOGRAPHIES

Giuseppe Garibaldi (1807–1882)

Giuseppe Garibaldi, an Italian patriot and soldier, was instrumental in the unification of Italy. He raised an army of men called Red Shirts and seized Sicily and Naples. He handed over control of southern Italy to Victor Emmanuel II, whom he declared the first king of a united Italy. Garibaldi retired to the small island of Caprera but was soon called back into military service and continued fighting until Italy was completely free.

Otto von Bismarck (1815–1898)

Otto von Bismarck came from the class of aristocratic Prussian landowners known as *Junkers*. Under his leadership, Prussia won a series of European wars that united the German states under Prussian rule. Bismarck became a national hero. In 1871, when King William I of Prussia was proclaimed the German kaiser, Bismarck became chancellor of this new German empire.

▶ CRITICAL THINKING

Contrasting How did Bismarck's and Garibaldi's careers as unifiers differ?

Following that conflict, a peace settlement gave Nice and Savoy to the French. Lombardy, which had been under Austrian control, was given to Piedmont. Austria retained control of Venetia. Cavour's success caused nationalists in other Italian states (Parma, Modena, and Tuscany) to overthrow their governments and join their states to Piedmont.

Meanwhile, in southern Italy, a new Italian leader had arisen. Giuseppe Garibaldi, a dedicated patriot, raised an army of a thousand volunteers. A branch of the Bourbon dynasty ruled the Two Sicilies (Sicily and Naples), and a revolt had broken out in Sicily against the king. Garibaldi's forces landed in Sicily and, by the end of July 1860, controlled most of the island. In August, Garibaldi's forces crossed over to the mainland and began a victorious march up the Italian Peninsula. The entire Kingdom of the Two Sicilies fell in early September.

Garibaldi chose to turn over his conquests to Piedmont. On March 17, 1861, a new state of Italy was proclaimed under King Victor Emmanuel II. The task of unification was not yet complete, however. Austria still held Venetia in the north; and Rome was under the control of the pope, supported by French troops.

The Italians gained control of Venetia as a result of supporting Prussia in a war between Austria and Prussia. In 1870, during the Franco-Prussian War, French troops withdrew from Rome. Their withdrawal enabled the Italian army to annex Rome on September 20, 1870. Rome became the capital of the new European state.

German Unification

After the Frankfurt Assembly failed to achieve German unification in 1848 and 1849, Germans looked to Prussia for leadership in the cause of German unification. In the course of the nineteenth century, Prussia had become a strong, prosperous, and authoritarian state. The Prussian king had firm control over the government and the army. Prussia was also known for its **militarism**, or reliance on military strength.

In the 1860s, King William I tried to enlarge the Prussian army. When the Prussian legislature refused to levy new taxes for the proposed changes, William I appointed a new prime minister, Count Otto von Bismarck.

Bismarck has often been seen as the foremost nineteenth-century practitioner of realpolitik—the "politics of reality," a politics based on practical matters rather than on ethics. Bismarck openly voiced his strong dislike for anyone who opposed him. After his appointment, Bismarck ignored the legislative opposition to the military reforms. He proceeded to collect taxes and strengthen the army. From 1862 to 1866, Bismarck governed Prussia without approval of the parliament. In the meantime, he followed an active foreign policy, which soon led to war.

After defeating Denmark with Austrian help in 1864, Prussia gained control of the duchies of Schleswig and Holstein. Bismarck then goaded the Austrians into a war on June 14, 1866. The Austrians, no match for the well-disciplined Prussian army, were defeated on July 3.

Prussia now organized the German states north of the Main River into the North German Confederation. The southern German states, which were largely Catholic, feared Protestant Prussia. However, they also feared France, their western neighbor. As a result, they agreed to sign military alliances with Prussia for protection against France.

Prussia now dominated all of northern Germany, and the growing power and military might of Prussia worried France. In 1870 Prussia and France became embroiled in a dispute over the candidacy of a relative of the Prussian king for the throne of Spain. Taking advantage of the situation, Bismarck pushed the French into declaring war on Prussia on July 19, 1870—a conflict called the Franco-Prussian War.

Prussian armies advanced into France. At Sedan, on September 2, 1870, an entire French army and the French ruler, Napoleon III, were captured. Paris finally surrendered on January 28, 1871. An official peace treaty was signed in May. France had to pay 5 billion francs (about $1 billion) and give up the provinces of Alsace and Lorraine to the new German state. The loss of these territories left the French burning for revenge.

Even before the war had ended, the southern German states had agreed to enter the North German Confederation. On January 18, 1871, Bismarck and 600 German princes, nobles, and generals filled the Hall of Mirrors in the palace of Versailles, 12 miles (19.3 km) outside Paris. William I of Prussia was proclaimed **kaiser**, or emperor, of the Second German Empire (the first was the medieval Holy Roman Empire).

The Prussian monarchy and the Prussian army had achieved German unity. The authoritarian and militaristic values of Prussia were triumphant in the new German state. With its industrial resources and military might, Germany had become the strongest power in Europe.

militarism the reliance on military strength

kaiser German for "caesar"; the title of the emperors of the Second German Empire

plebiscite a popular vote

READING PROGRESS CHECK

Explaining How did the Crimean War destroy the Concert of Europe?

Nationalism and Reform in Europe

GUIDING QUESTION *What were the political climates in Great Britain, France, Austria, and Russia?*

While Italy and Germany were being unified, other states in Europe were also experiencing changes.

Great Britain

Great Britain managed to avoid the revolutionary upheavals of the first half of the nineteenth century. In 1815 aristocratic landowning classes, which dominated both houses of Parliament, governed Great Britain. In 1832 Parliament passed a bill that increased the number of male voters. The new voters were chiefly members of the industrial middle class. By giving the industrial middle class an interest in ruling, Britain avoided revolution in 1848. In the 1850s and 1860s, Parliament made social and political reforms that helped the country remain stable. Another reason for Britain's stability was its continuing economic growth. By 1850, industrialization had brought prosperity to the British middle class. After 1850, real wages of workers also rose significantly.

Queen Victoria, whose reign from 1837 to 1901 was the longest in English history, reflected perfectly the national pride of the British. Her sense of duty and moral respectability greatly influenced the values and attitudes of her age, which was later called the Victorian Age.

France

In France, events after the revolution of 1848 moved toward the restoration of the monarchy. Four years after his election as president in 1848, Louis-Napoleon returned to the people to ask for the restoration of the empire. In this **plebiscite**, or popular vote, 97 percent responded with a yes vote. On December 2, 1852, Louis-Napoleon assumed the title of Emperor Napoleon III (Napoleon II was the son of Napoleon Bonaparte, but he never ruled France). The Second Empire had begun.

SKILLS PRACTICE

Before reading a new section, look for boldface words. Find their definitions in the selection or the glossary. Then use a thesaurus to find other meanings for the words.

▲ Great Britain's Queen Victoria in her coronation robes, 1838

PHOTO: Popperfoto/Getty Images

The government of Napoleon III was clearly authoritarian. As chief of state, Napoleon III controlled the armed forces, police, and civil service. Only he could introduce legislation and declare war. The Legislative Corps gave an appearance of representative government, because the members of the group were elected by universal male suffrage for six-year terms. However, they could neither initiate legislation nor affect the budget.

Napoleon III completely controlled the government and limited civil liberties. To distract the public from their loss of political freedom, he focused on expanding the economy. Government subsidies helped foster the rapid construction of railroads, harbors, roads, and canals.

In the midst of this economic expansion, Napoleon III also carried out a vast rebuilding of the city of Paris. The old Paris of narrow streets and walls was replaced by a modern Paris of broad boulevards, spacious buildings, public squares, an underground sewage system, a new public water supply system, and gaslights.

regime the government in power

In the 1860s, opposition to some of Napoleon's economic and governmental policies arose. In response, Napoleon III began to liberalize his **regime**. For example, he gave the legislature more power. After the French were defeated in the Franco-Prussian War in 1870, however, the Second Empire fell.

The Austrian Empire

Nationalism was a major force in nineteenth-century Europe. However, one of Europe's most powerful states—the Austrian Empire—was a multinational empire that had been able to frustrate the desire of its ethnic groups for independence.

After the Hapsburg rulers crushed the revolutions of 1848 and 1849, they restored centralized, autocratic government to the empire. Austria's defeat at the hands of the Prussians in 1866, however, forced the Austrians to make concessions to the fiercely nationalistic Hungarians. The result was the Compromise of 1867, which created the dual monarchy of Austria-Hungary. Each of these two components of the empire now had its own constitution, its own legislature, its own government bureaucracy, and its own capital (Vienna for Austria and Budapest for Hungary). Holding the two states together were a single monarch—Francis Joseph was emperor of Austria and king of Hungary—and a common army, foreign policy, and system of finances.

emancipation the act of setting free

Russia

At the beginning of the nineteenth century, Russia was still rural, agricultural, and autocratic. The Russian czar was regarded as a divine-right monarch with unlimited power. In 1856, however, the Russians suffered a humiliating defeat in the Crimean War. Even conservatives realized that Russia was falling hopelessly behind the western European states. Czar Alexander II decided to make some reforms.

Serfdom was the largest problem in czarist Russia. On March 3, 1861, Alexander issued an **emancipation** edict, which freed the serfs. Peasants could now own property. The government provided land for the peasants by buying it from the landlords. The new land system, however, was not very helpful to the peasants. The landowners often kept the best lands for themselves. The Russian peasants had little good land to support themselves. Emancipation, then, led not to a free, landowning peasantry but to an unhappy, land-starved peasantry that followed old ways of farming.

▼ Russian peasants in the late nineteenth century

▶ CRITICAL THINKING
Making Generalizations How does this image convey the possible living conditions of Russian peasants?

PHOTO: The Stapleton Collection/Bridgeman Art Library

Alexander II attempted other reforms as well, but he could please no one. Reformers wanted more changes, but conservatives thought that the czar was destroying Russia's basic institutions. When radicals assassinated Alexander II in 1881, his son, Alexander III, turned against reform and returned to the old methods of repression.

✓ **READING PROGRESS CHECK**

Examining What concessions did the Hungarians gain from the Compromise of 1867?

Nationalism in the United States

GUIDING QUESTION ***How did nationalism influence events in the United States during the 1800s?***

The U.S. Constitution committed the nation to liberalism and nationalism. Yet unity did not come easily. Two factions fought bitterly about the division of power in the new government. The Federalists favored a strong central government. The Republicans wanted the federal government to be subordinate to the state governments.

By the mid-nineteenth century, slavery had become a threat to American unity. Four million enslaved African Americans were in the South by 1860, compared with one million in 1800.

The South's economy was based on growing cotton on plantations, chiefly by slave labor. The South was determined to maintain the cotton economy and plantation-based slavery. **Abolitionism**, a movement to end slavery, arose in the North and challenged the Southern way of life. As opinions over slavery grew more divided, compromise became less possible. Abraham Lincoln said in a speech in 1858 that "this government cannot endure, permanently half slave and half free." When Lincoln was elected president in November 1860, war became certain. In April, fighting erupted between North and South—the Union and the Confederacy.

abolitionism a movement to end slavery

The American Civil War (1861–1865) was a bloody struggle. Lincoln's Emancipation Proclamation declared most of the nation's enslaved people "forever free." The Confederate forces surrendered on April 9, 1865. The United States remained united, "one nation, indivisible."

✓ **READING PROGRESS CHECK**

Identifying What issues divided Americans in the 1800s?

LESSON 3 REVIEW TEKS

Reviewing Vocabulary

1. ***Making Connections*** Write a paragraph about the Civil War in which you define the terms *emancipation* and *abolitionism*. Indicate relationships between these terms.

Using Your Notes

2. ***Describing*** Use your graphic organizer to write a paragraph describing the changes and conflicts that took place in Great Britain, France, the Austrian Empire, and Russia during the nineteenth century.

Answering the Guiding Questions

3. ***Identifying Cause and Effect*** What led to the unification of Italy and Germany after the revolution of 1848?
4. ***Describing*** What were the political climates in Great Britain, France, Austria, and Russia?
5. ***Identifying Central Issues*** How did nationalism influence events in the United States during the 1800s?

Writing Activity

6. **INFORMATIVE/EXPLANATORY** Write an essay evaluating the nineteenth-century social reforms that took place in Great Britain, Russia, and the United States. Were the reforms successful? Did they contribute to the stability of these nations?

networks
There's More Online!

- BIOGRAPHY Antonio López de Santa Anna
- BIOGRAPHY José de San Martín
- BIOGRAPHY Simón Bolívar
- IMAGE Monopoly in Latin America
- IMAGE San Martín Crossing the Andes in 1817
- INTERACTIVE SELF-CHECK QUIZ
- MAP European Colonies in Latin America
- VIDEO Railways and the Mexican Revolution

LESSON 4
Nation Building in Latin America

ESSENTIAL QUESTIONS • *How can innovation affect ways of life?* • *How does revolution bring about political and economic change?*

Reading **HELP**DESK

Academic Vocabulary
- **intervention**
- **erupt**

Content Vocabulary
- **creole**
- **peninsulare**
- **mestizo**
- **caudillo**
- **cash crop**

TAKING NOTES:
Key Ideas and Details

Categorizing Use a graphic organizer like this one to record places where revolts occurred and the leaders and the outcomes of these revolts. Add rows as needed.

Revolts in Latin America

Place	Leader	Outcome

TEKS Texas Essential Knowledge and Skills

9B explain the impact of Napoleon Bonaparte and the Napoleonic Wars on Europe and Latin America

9C trace the influence of the American and French revolutions on Latin America, including the role of Simón Bolivar

It Matters Because

The success of the American Revolution and the ideals of the French Revolution spread throughout Latin America. One by one, the Portuguese and Spanish colonies rebelled and won their independence. Political independence, however, was achieved more easily in the new republics than political stability.

Nationalist Revolts

GUIDING QUESTION *How were nationalist revolts in Latin America influenced by the French and American Revolutions?*

By the end of the eighteenth century, the new political ideals stemming from the successful American Revolution were beginning to influence the creole elites. **Creoles** were the descendants of Europeans who had permanently settled in Latin America. They controlled land and business and were attracted to the principles of equality of all people in the eyes of the law, free trade, and a free press. The creoles especially disliked the domination of their trade by Spain and Portugal.

The creole elites soon began to use their new ideas to denounce the rule of the Spanish and Portuguese monarchs and their ***peninsulares*** (Spanish and Portuguese officials who resided temporarily in Latin America for political and economic gain and then returned to their homeland). The creole elites resented the *peninsulares,* who dominated Latin America and drained the region of its wealth.

At the beginning of the nineteenth century, Napoleon's wars provided the creoles with an opportunity for change. When Napoleon overthrew the monarchies of Spain and Portugal, the authority of the Spaniards and Portuguese in their colonial empires was weakened. Then, between 1807 and 1825, a series of revolts enabled most of Latin America to become independent.

Revolt in Haiti

An unusual revolution occurred before the main independence movements. Saint Domingue—on the island of Hispaniola—was a French sugar colony. François-Dominique Toussaint-Louverture (too • SAN • loo • VUHR • TYUR) led more than 100,000 enslaved people in revolt. They seized control of all of Hispaniola. On January 1, 1804, the western part of Hispaniola, now called Haiti, became the first independent state in Latin America.

creole a person of European descent born in Latin America and living there permanently

peninsulare a person born on the Iberian Peninsula; typically, a Spanish or Portuguese official who resided temporarily in Latin America for political and economic gain and then returned to Europe

Revolt in Mexico

Beginning in 1810, Mexico also experienced a revolt. The first real hero of Mexican independence was Miguel Hidalgo. A parish priest, Hidalgo lived in a village about 100 miles (160 km) from Mexico City.

Hidalgo had studied the French Revolution. He roused the local Native Americans and **mestizos**, people of mixed European and Native American descent, to free themselves from the Spanish: "Will you be free? Will you make the effort to recover from the hated Spaniards the lands stolen from your forefathers, three hundred years ago?"

mestizo a person of mixed European and Native American descent

On September 16, 1810, Hidalgo led this ill-equipped army of thousands of Native Americans and mestizos in an attack against the Spaniards. His forces were soon crushed, and a military court later sentenced Hidalgo to death. However, his memory lives on even today. In fact, September 16, the first day of the uprising, is Mexico's Independence Day.

The role of Native Americans and mestizos in Mexico's revolt against Spanish control frightened the creoles and the *peninsulares*. Afraid of the masses, they cooperated in defeating the revolutionary forces. Creoles and *peninsulares* then decided to overthrow Spanish rule. These conservative elites wanted an independent nation ruled by a monarch. They selected a creole military leader, Agustín de Iturbide (ee • tur • BEE • thay), to set up a new government. In 1821 Mexico declared its independence from Spain. Iturbide named himself emperor in 1822 but was deposed in 1823. Mexico then became a republic.

Revolts in South America

José de San Martín of Argentina and Simón Bolívar of Venezuela, both members of the creole elite, were hailed as the "Liberators of South America." Bolívar began the struggle for Venezuelan independence in 1810, inspired by the French and American revolutions. He also led revolts in New Granada (Colombia) and Ecuador. By 1819, these countries had formed Gran Colombia.

By 1810, the forces of San Martín had liberated Argentina from Spanish authority. In January 1817, San Martín led his forces over the Andes Mountains to attack the Spanish in Chile. The journey was an amazing feat. Soldiers suffered from lack of oxygen and severe cold while crossing mountain passes more than two miles (3.2 km) above sea level.

The arrival of San Martín's forces in Chile completely surprised the Spanish forces there. As a result, they were badly defeated at the Battle of Chacabuco on February 12, 1817. Chile declared its independence in 1818. In 1821 San Martín advanced on Lima, Peru, the center of Spanish authority.

San Martín was convinced that he could not complete the liberation of Peru alone. He welcomed Simón Bolívar and his forces. Bolívar, the "Liberator of Venezuela," took on the task of crushing the last significant Spanish army at Ayacucho on December 9, 1824.

▼ General San Martín after crossing the Andes in 1817

By the end of 1824, Peru, Uruguay, Paraguay, Colombia, Venezuela, Argentina, Bolivia, and Chile had become free of Spain. Earlier, in 1822, the prince regent of Brazil had declared Brazil's independence from Portugal. The Central American states had become independent in 1823. In 1838 and 1839, they divided into five republics: Guatemala, El Salvador, Honduras, Costa Rica, and Nicaragua.

Threats to Independence

In the early 1820s, one major threat remained to the newly won independence of the Latin American states. Members of the Concert of Europe favored using troops to restore Spanish control in Latin America. The British, who wished to trade with Latin America, disagreed. They proposed joint action with the United States against any European moves against Latin America.

Distrustful of British motives, James Monroe, the president of the United States, acted alone in 1823. In the Monroe Doctrine, he declared that the Americas were off limits for any colonizational efforts, and strongly warned against any European **intervention** in the Americas.

intervention the involvement in a situation to alter the outcome

More important to Latin American independence than American words, however, was the British navy. Other European powers feared the power of the British navy, which stood between Latin America and any planned European invasion force.

✓ **READING PROGRESS CHECK**

Comparing What do Hidalgo, José de San Martín, and Simón Bolívar have in common?

Nation Building

GUIDING QUESTIONS ***What difficulties did newly independent Latin American countries face? How did economic dependence on foreign investment influence Latin America through the mid-1800s?***

The new Latin American nations faced a number of serious problems between 1830 and 1870. The wars for independence had resulted in a staggering loss of people, property, and livestock. During the course of the nineteenth century, the new Latin American nations would become economically dependent on Western nations once again.

Rule of the Caudillos and Inequality

Most of the new nations of Latin America began with republican governments, but they had no experience in self-rule. Soon after independence, strong leaders known as **caudillos** gained power.

caudillo in post-revolutionary Latin America, a strong leader who ruled chiefly by military force, usually with the support of the landed elite

Caudillos ruled chiefly by military force and were usually supported by the landed elites. Many kept the new national states together. Some were also modernizers who built roads and canals, ports, and schools. Others were destructive.

Mexican General Antonio López de Santa Anna, for example, ruled Mexico from 1833 to 1855. He misused state funds, halted reforms, and created chaos. In 1835 American settlers in the Mexican state of Texas revolted against Santa Anna's rule. Texas gained its independence in 1836 and U.S. statehood in 1845. War between Mexico and the United States soon followed (1846–1848). Mexico was defeated and lost almost one-half of its territory to the United States.

Fortunately for Mexico, Santa Anna's disastrous rule was followed by a period of reform from 1855 to 1876. This era was dominated by Benito Juárez, a Mexican national hero. The son of Native American peasants, President Juárez brought liberal reforms to Mexico, including separation of church and state, land distribution to the poor, and an educational system for all of Mexico.

Other caudillos, such as Juan Manuel de Rosas in Argentina, were supported by the masses. These caudillos became extremely popular and brought about radical change. Unfortunately, the caudillo's authority depended on his personal power. When he died or lost power, civil wars for control of the country often **erupted**.

A fundamental problem for all the new Latin American nations was the domination of society by the landed elites. Large estates remained a way of life in Latin America. By 1848, for example, the Sánchez Navarro family in Mexico possessed 17 estates made up of 16 million acres (6,480,000 ha).

Land remained the basis of wealth, social prestige, and political power throughout the nineteenth century. Landed elites ran governments, controlled courts, and kept a system of inexpensive labor. These landowners made enormous profits by growing single **cash crops**, such as coffee, for export. Most of the population had no land to grow basic food crops. As a result, the masses experienced dire poverty.

▲ Mexican General Antonio López de Santa Anna

erupt to suddenly become active or violent

cash crop a crop that is grown for sale rather than for personal use

Imperialism and Economic Dependence

Political independence brought economic independence, but old patterns were quickly reestablished. Instead of Spain and Portugal, Great Britain now dominated the Latin American economy. British merchants moved into Latin America, and British investors poured in funds. Old trade relationships soon reemerged.

Latin America continued to serve as a source of raw materials and foodstuffs for the industrial nations of Europe and the United States. Exports included wheat, tobacco, wool, sugar, coffee, and hides. At the same time, Latin American countries imported finished consumer goods, especially textiles, and had limited industry.

The emphasis on exporting raw materials and importing finished products ensured the ongoing domination of the Latin American economy by foreigners. Latin American countries remained economically dependent on Western nations, even though they were no longer colonies.

✓ **READING PROGRESS CHECK**

Identifying Central Issues Why did Latin American countries continue to experience economic dependence after achieving political independence?

LESSON 4 REVIEW TEKS

Reviewing Vocabulary

1. ***Explaining*** Give examples of three cash crops that were grown in Latin America and explain why they were cash crops.

Using Your Notes

2. ***Generalizing*** Use your graphic organizer on the revolts in Latin America to write a paragraph that makes a generalization about the successes or failures of the revolutions.

Answering the Guiding Questions

3. ***Drawing Conclusions*** How were nationalist revolts in Latin America influenced by the French and American Revolutions?

4. ***Gathering Information*** What difficulties did newly independent Latin American countries face?

5. ***Identifying Cause and Effect*** How did economic dependence on foreign investment influence Latin America through the mid-1800s?

Writing About History

6. **NARRATIVE** Imagine you are a creole leader in Mexico at the time when Miguel Hidalgo is rousing the Native Americans and mestizos or leading them into battle. Write a diary entry that shows your feelings about the events you witness.

networks

There's More Online!

- ☑ BIOGRAPHY Charles Darwin
- ☑ BIOGRAPHY Charles Dickens
- ☑ BIOGRAPHY Louis Pasteur
- ☑ BIOGRAPHY Ludwig van Beethoven
- ☑ IMAGE Battle of Poitiers by Eugene Delacroix
- ☑ IMAGE Paris Opera House
- ☑ IMAGE The Old Mill by John Constable
- ☑ INTERACTIVE SELF-CHECK QUIZ
- ☑ VIDEO William Blake

LESSON 5

Romanticism and Realism

ESSENTIAL QUESTIONS • *How can innovation affect ways of life?* • *How does revolution bring about political and economic change?*

Reading HELPDESK

Academic Vocabulary
- **individuality**
- **approach**

Content Vocabulary
- **romanticism**
- **secularization**
- **natural selection**
- **realism**

TAKING NOTES:
Key Ideas and Details

Listing Examples Use a table like this one to list examples of literature from the romantic and realist movements.

Romanticism	Realism

TEKS Texas Essential Knowledge and Skills

26A identify significant examples of art and architecture that demonstrate an artistic ideal or visual principle from selected cultures

continued on p. 552

It Matters Because

Romanticism was a response to the Enlightenment and the Industrial Revolution. Romantics believed that emotions, rather than reason, should guide them. By the mid-nineteenth century, romanticism had given way to a new movement called realism. Realists focused on the everyday world and ordinary people.

Romanticism

GUIDING QUESTION *How did the idea of romanticism differ from those of the Enlightenment?*

At the end of the 1700s, a new intellectual movement, known as **romanticism**, emerged as a reaction to the ideas of the Enlightenment. The Enlightenment had stressed reason as the chief means for discovering truth. The romantics emphasized feelings, emotion, and imagination as sources of knowing.

Romantics valued individualism, or the belief in the uniqueness of each person. Many romantics rebelled against middle-class conventions. Male romantics grew long hair and beards, and men and women often wore outrageous clothes in order to express their **individuality**.

Many romantics had a passionate interest in past ages, especially the Middle Ages. Romantic architects revived medieval styles and built castles, cathedrals, city halls, parliamentary buildings, and railway stations in a style called neo-Gothic. The British Houses of Parliament in London are a prime example of this architectural style.

Romanticism in Art and Music

Romantic artists shared at least two features. First, to them, all art was a reflection of the artist's inner feelings. A painting should mirror the artist's vision of the world and be the instrument of the artist's imagination. Second, romantic artists abandoned classical reason for warmth and emotion.

Eugène Delacroix (DEH • luh • KWAH) was one of the most famous romantic painters from France. His paintings showed two chief characteristics: a fascination with the exotic and a passion for color. His works, such as the *Battle of Poitiers*, demonstrated that artistic ideal that "a painting is to be a fest to the eye."

In music, too, romantic trends dominated the first half of the nineteenth century. One of the most famous composers of this era whose works reflect the spirit of romanticism was Ludwig van Beethoven. Beethoven's early work fell largely within the classical form of the eighteenth century. However, his *Third Symphony* embodied the elements of romanticism with powerful melodies that created dramatic intensity. For Beethoven, music had to reflect his deepest feelings: "I *must* write—for what weighs on my heart I *must* express." Beethoven's music is still commonly played by musicians and enjoyed by many people across the globe today.

▲ *Battle of Poitiers* by Eugène Delacroix, 1830

▶ **CRITICAL THINKING**

Interpreting Significance Why might Delacroix have chosen to depict a scene from a French battle from 1356?

Romanticism in Literature

The literary arts were deeply affected by the romantic interest in the past. Sir Walter Scott's *Ivanhoe*, for example, a best seller in the early nineteenth century, told of clashes between knights in medieval England. Many romantic writers chose medieval subjects and created stories that expressed their strong nationalism, reflecting the passions of their time.

An attraction to the exotic and unfamiliar gave rise to Gothic literature. Chilling examples are Mary Shelley's novel *Frankenstein* in Britain and Edgar Allan Poe's short stories of horror in the United States, both of which have transcended the cultures in which they were created and remain popular today. Some romantics even sought the unusual in their own lives, exploring their dreams and nightmares.

The romantics viewed poetry as the direct expression of the soul. Romantic poetry gave expression to one of the most important characteristics of romanticism—its love of nature. Romantics believed that nature served as a mirror into which humans could look to learn about themselves. This is especially evident in the poetry of William Wordsworth, the foremost English romantic poet of nature. His experience of nature was almost mystical:

PRIMARY SOURCE

> "One impulse from a vernal wood
> May teach you more of man,
> Of moral evil and of good,
> Than all the sages can."
>
> —**William Wordsworth, from *The Tables Turned***

The worship of nature also caused Wordsworth and other romantic poets to be critical of eighteenth-century science, which, they believed, had reduced nature to a cold object of study. To Wordsworth, the scientists' dry, mathematical **approach** left no room for the imagination or for the human soul. Many romantics were convinced that industrialization would cause people to become alienated, both from their inner selves and from the natural world.

✔ **READING PROGRESS CHECK**

Drawing Conclusions How did science and industrialization contribute to the development of romanticism's celebration of nature?

romanticism an intellectual movement that emerged at the end of the eighteenth century in reaction to the ideas of the Enlightenment; it stressed feelings, emotion, and imagination as sources of knowing

individuality a total character that distinguishes an individual from others

approach the way or method in which one examines or studies an issue or a concept

Connections to TODAY

From Mendeleyev to Particle Physics

Dmitry Mendeleyev's discovery of recurring patterns in the properties of chemical elements is one of the foundations of modern chemistry. In 1869 when he proposed his periodic law, 70 elements were known. Before his death in 1907, Mendeleyev saw his predictions of the existence of several previously unknown elements confirmed. Since that time, many more elements have been discovered, bringing the total up to well over 100 today. Although electrons were discovered before Mendeleyev died, he had no idea of the complexity of the subatomic world, in which scientists have discovered more than 200 types of subatomic particles.

secularization indifference to or rejection of religion or religious consideration

natural selection the principle that some organisms are more adaptable to the environment than others

New Age of Science

GUIDING QUESTION *How did advances in science influence life during the Industrial Revolution?*

The Scientific Revolution had created a modern, rational approach to the study of the natural world. For a long time, only the educated elite understood its importance. With the Industrial Revolution, however, came a heightened interest in scientific research. By the 1830s, new discoveries in science had led to benefits that affected all Europeans. Science came to have a greater and greater impact on people.

In biology, the Frenchman Louis Pasteur, a prominent scientist, proposed the germ theory of disease, which was crucial to the development of modern scientific medical practices. In chemistry, the Russian Dmitry Mendeleyev in the 1860s classified all the material elements then known on the basis of their atomic weights. In physics, British scientist and inventor Michael Faraday put together a primitive generator that laid the foundation for the use of electric current.

Dramatic material benefits such as these led Europeans to have a growing faith in science. This faith, in turn, undermined the religious faith of many people. It is no accident that the nineteenth century was an age of increasing **secularization**, indifference to or rejection of religion in the affairs of the world. For many people, truth was now to be found in science and the concrete material existence of humans.

More than anyone else, it was Charles Darwin who promoted the idea that humans are material beings who are part of the natural world. In 1859 Darwin published *On the Origin of Species by Means of Natural Selection*. The basic idea of this book was that each species, or kind, of plant and animal had evolved over a long period of time from earlier, simpler forms of life. Darwin called this principle organic evolution.

How did this natural process work? According to Darwin, in every species, "many more individuals of each species are born than can possibly survive," which results in a "struggle for existence." Darwin believed that some organisms are born with variations, or differences, that make them more adaptable to their environment than other organisms, a process that Darwin called **natural selection**.

Those organisms that are naturally selected for survival reproduce and thrive. This is known as "survival of the fittest." In this process, the unfit do not survive. The fit that survive pass on the variations that enabled them to survive until, according to Darwin, a new, separate species emerges. In *The Descent of Man,* published in 1871, Darwin argued that human beings had animal origins and were not an exception to the rule governing the development of other species.

Darwin's ideas raised a storm of controversy. Some people did not take his ideas seriously. Other people objected that Darwin's theory made human beings ordinary products of nature rather than unique creations of God. Others were bothered by his idea of life as a mere struggle for survival. Some believers felt Darwin had not acknowledged God's role in creation. Some detractors scorned Darwin and depicted him unfavorably in cartoons. Gradually, however, many scientists and other intellectuals came to accept Darwin's theory. His theory changed thinking in countless fields from biology to anthropology.

✓ **READING PROGRESS CHECK**

Predicting Consequences Why might the scientific developments described in this lesson lead to increased secularization?

(continued from p. 550)

TEKS **Texas Essential Knowledge and Skills**

26B analyze examples of how art, architecture, literature, music, and drama reflect the history of the cultures in which they are produced

26C identify examples of art, music, and literature that transcend the cultures in which they were created and convey universal themes

28E identify the contributions of significant scientists and inventors such as Marie Curie, Thomas Edison, Albert Einstein, Louis Pasteur, and James Watt

Realism

GUIDING QUESTION *What factors contributed to the movement known as realism?*

The belief that the world should be viewed realistically, a view often expressed after 1850, was closely related to the scientific outlook of the time. In politics, Bismarck practiced the "politics of reality." In the literary and visual arts, **realism** also became a movement.

The literary realists of the mid-nineteenth century rejected romanticism. They wanted to write about ordinary characters from life, not romantic heroes in exotic settings. They also tried to avoid emotional language by using precise description. They preferred novels to poems. Many literary realists combined their interest in everyday life with an examination of social issues. These artists expressed their social views through the characters in their novels.

The French author Gustave Flaubert, who was a leading novelist of the 1850s and 1860s, perfected the realist novel. His work *Madame Bovary* presents a critical description of small-town life in France. In Great Britain, Charles Dickens became a huge success with novels that showed the realities of life for the lower and middle classes in the early Industrial Age. Novels such as *Oliver Twist* and *David Copperfield* created a vivid picture of the brutal life of London's poor.

In art, too, realism became dominant after 1850. Realist artists sought to show the everyday life of ordinary people and the world of nature with photographic realism. The French became leaders in realist painting.

The French painter Gustave Courbet was the most famous artist of the realist school. He loved to portray scenes from everyday life. His subjects were factory workers and peasants. "I have never seen either angels or goddesses, so I am not interested in painting them," Courbet once commented. To Courbet, no subject was too ordinary.

▲ *Girl with Seagulls* by Gustave Courbet, 1865

▶ **CRITICAL THINKING**

Comparing and Contrasting In what ways does this painting illustrate Courbet's rejection of romanticism?

realism a mid-nineteenth century movement that rejected romanticism and sought to portray lower- and middle-class life as it actually was

✓ **READING PROGRESS CHECK**

Predicting Consequences Why might the work of realists, like Charles Dickens, have inspired social reform?

LESSON 5 REVIEW TEKS

Reviewing Vocabulary

1. ***Describing*** How did the concepts of natural selection and secularization demonstrate a changing worldview?

Using Your Notes

2. ***Contrasting*** Using examples from your graphic organizer of literary works, write a paragraph contrasting the characteristics of romanticism and realism in literature.

Answering the Guiding Questions

3. ***Contrasting*** How did the ideas of romanticism differ from those of the Enlightenment?
4. ***Identifying Cause and Effect*** How did advances in science influence life during the Industrial Revolution?
5. ***Identifying Cause and Effect*** What factors contributed to the movement known as realism?

Writing About History

6. **NARRATIVE** Write a paragraph describing some key event in your life using the style of the romantics or the realists.

CHAPTER 23 Assessment

TEKS

Directions: On a separate sheet of paper, answer the questions below. Make sure you read carefully and answer all parts of the questions.

Lesson Review

Lesson 1

1. ***Describing*** Describe how the British Agricultural Revolution in the 1780s, along with other aspects of British government and life at that time, impacted British labor and production.

2. ***Explaining*** How did Britain's supply of iron ore and Henry Cort's invention impact the British iron industry?

3. ***Explaining*** Explain the shift in the British textile manufacturing from the 18th century to the 19th century helping to initiate the Industrial Revolution. What key inventions and inventors led the way? **28A, 28E**

4. ***Specifying*** How did the factory impact the lives of the new factory workers, many of whom came from rural areas and agricultural work? **17A**

Lesson 2

5. ***Identifying Ideas*** Why might a multinational empire like the Austrian Empire be difficult to govern? What idea was most likely behind the revolutions in this empire in 1848? **9D**

6. ***Identifying Influences*** How did the ideas of liberalism influence political revolutions? **9D**

7. ***Drawing Inferences*** What might you infer about the economic hardships in France beginning in 1846 and the cry for the universal male right to vote and ultimately the overthrow of the French government?

8. ***Identifying Central Issues*** In 1848, even though European nationalities sought independence, why weren't groups successful in their objectives?

Lesson 3

9. ***Defining*** Who was involved in the Crimean War, and what took place?

10. ***Sequencing*** By 1870, the Italian peninsula had been annexed into the Italian kingdom of Piedmont, creating a unified Italy. Which countries had control of the portions of the peninsula previously, and what actions allowed for the unified state?

11. ***Identifying Cause and Effect*** How did Britain's economic condition affect its political stability?

12. ***Explaining*** How did Napoleon III distract French citizens during his authoritarian regime where the Legislative Corps had little power?

13. ***Describing*** What was the influence of Queen Victoria in Britain? **24B**

14. ***Describing*** Describe the troubles in Russian at the beginning of the nineteenth century. How did leadership infringe upon progress for the people?

Lesson 4

15. ***Interpreting*** What were the influences of Central and South American revolutionaries, including Simón Bolívar?

16. ***Explaining*** What was the impact of the Napoleonic Wars on Latin America? **9B**

17. ***Identifying Cause and Effect*** How did the domination of large estates that produced cash crops affect a majority of the Latin American population—the non-landowning population?

Need Extra Help?

If You've Missed Question	1	2	3	4	5	6	7	8	9	10	11	12	13	14	15	16	17
Go to page	528	530	529	530	538	537	537	539	540	541	543	544	543	544	547	546	549

Lesson 5

18 ***Identifying*** In what ways was the individualism prized by the romantic artists, writers, and musicians a reflection of the historical response to the Industrial Revolution? **26B**

19 ***Identifying*** What themes of realist literature apply to all cultural circumstances? **26B**

20 ***Identifying*** Identify the importance of Louis Pasteur's germ theory, and explain why the Industrial Revolution spurred new scientific theories and concepts. **26E**

Exploring the Essential Questions

21 ***Synthesizing*** With a partner, create a multimedia display of nineteenth-century changes and their causes in Europe, the United States, and Latin America. Include an example of technological, social, political, and economic change from each area that resulted from civic participation. Provide a photo, drawing, or artifact that symbolizes each change and an audio or written explanation of how people supported the change and the forces that led to it. You may also include primary sources. **21A, 21B, 22F**

Critical Thinking

22 ***Synthesizing*** Explain how inventions of seventeenth- and eighteenth-century Europe and the roles of steam technology, transportation, and the factory system led to and advanced the Industrial Revolution. **8A, 28A**

23 ***Speculating*** Identify the historical origins of socialism as tied to the working conditions of the industrial working class. **17A, 17B, 18C**

24 ***Identifying Cause and Effect*** Around 1860, how did the new network of 30,000 miles (48, 270 km) of railroads in the United States affect the production of manufactured goods in the Northeast?

25 ***Synthesizing*** After Latin American countries gained their independence, why did they enter into an era of reliance upon Western nations even though they had earn independence?

26 ***Identify and Compare*** Give an example of a musician from the Romantic Movement and describe the characteristics of his compositions. Explain why audiences of the period and audiences of today continue to listen to and appreciate this music. **26C**

27 ***Explaining and Sequencing*** Trace how American and French Revolutions influenced Latin American countries' quests for independence, and explain Simón Bolívar's role in Latin American independence in the early 1800s. **9C**

Social Studies Skills

28 ***Interpreting Charts*** Refer to the Skillbuilder to interpret the relationship between geography and the development of industry in 1850. What connections can you make between geography and industrial development? **15A**

29 ***Identifying*** Which were the first European countries to enter the Industrial Revolution after Great Britain and why?

30 ***Evaluating*** What benefits did foreign investors provide to newly independent Latin American countries? What were the drawbacks of foreign investment?

31 ***Geography Skills*** Create a map that shows the expanse of the Austrian Empire in the 1840s. Label the nations of people it encompassed. Include an inset of modern Europe today that shows a comparison of the past to present-day national borders.

Need Extra Help?

If You've Missed Question	18	19	20	21	22	23	24	25	26	27	28	29	30	31
Go to page	550	553	552	528	529	533	532	548	550	546	534	531	548	527

DBQ Analyzing Primary Sources

Use the document to answer the following questions.

The British Parliament debated a bill that would ban factory owners from hiring children under the age of nine or working those children under sixteen longer than sixteen hours in a day.

PRIMARY SOURCE

"[Lord Kenyon] proceeded to enter into some detail of the evidence given before the committee, for the purpose of showing the injury that resulted to the health of the children, from being employed for 14, 15, or 16 hours a day in places heated to 80, 85 and nearly 90 degrees. . . .

The Earl of Rosslyn said, . . . [it was] as an incontestible fact, that parents were the natural guardians of the health and prosperity of their own children, and that the legislature ought to be slow to interfere with free labour . . ."

—from the record of the House of Lords debate on the Cotton Factories Regulation Bill, June 14, 1819

32 ***Analyzing*** What reason does the Earl of Rosslyn give for arguing against legislation that would protect child workers? What can be inferred about his reasons? **29F**

33 ***Evaluating*** Is Lord Kenyon's evidence of children's working conditions in cotton mills believable?

34 ***Making Inferences*** What can you infer about the opportunities for children to attend school at this time?

Analyzing Visuals

Use the image to answer the following questions.

This painting by John Constable entitled "The Old Mill" shows an idyllic rural scene. Painted in the early nineteenth century, it is an example of a romanticist landscape painting.

35 ***Analyzing Visuals*** How does this painting reflect the visual principles of realism as well as the ideals of romanticism?

36 ***Interpreting*** Notice the rustic countryside setting as well as the "snapshot" scene of rural life. Considering the historical context of this painting, what commentary might the artist be making?

Extended Response Question

37 ***Informative/Explanatory*** How did free market principles advance the Industrial Revolution? How did these developments improve the human condition? **1E, 8E, 17A, 18F**

Need Extra Help?

If You've Missed Question	32	33	34	35	36	37
Go to page	556	556	556	523	556	529

Mass Society and Democracy

1870–1914

ESSENTIAL QUESTIONS • *How can industrialization affect a country's economy?* • *How are political and social structures influenced by economic changes?*

networks

There's More Online! about mass society and democracy.

CHAPTER 24

The Story Matters...

The industrialization that began transforming Europe in the late 1700s had largely matured by a century later. Starting around 1850, the Second Industrial Revolution produced goods on a much larger scale. It created largely urban societies and a growing working class. This phase of industrialization also saw new advances in communications technology. A key figure was physicist and inventor Guglielmo Marconi.

◄ By applying research in electromagnetic waves, Marconi invented the wireless telegraph. Marconi is shown here with his invention, which became the basis of modern radio.

CHAPTER 24

Place and Time: Europe 1870–1914

In the late 1800s, the European population increased in industrial areas. Workers migrated from the countryside to find employment in coal mines, factories, domestic service, and offices. Working-class families crowded into urban areas, where they struggled with insufficient housing and services. Urbanization often caused poverty, unemployment, the spread of disease, and political unrest. Between 1870 and1914, Great Britain, France, and Germany gradually responded to the needs of their growing populace.

Step Into the Place

Read the quotes and look at the information presented on the map.

DBQ What challenges did population growth and urbanization cause in Europe at the turn of the twentieth century?

PRIMARY SOURCE

"For the next three months I was nearer to starvation than any time since. I learned the bitterness of a hopeless search for work. . . .The best plan was to visit the wholesale firms in the City and get information about vacancies from the commercial travellers, and then journey as fast as the old horse buses allowed—perhaps right across London—only to find a queue of 150 to 200 applicants already there."

—Margaret Bondfield, from *A Life's Work*, on her unemployment before becoming one of the first female members of Parliament in Britain

PRIMARY SOURCE

"It is like this in working-class families. The man, the one who after all has to work (*sic*), consumes the largest share of the available food. The children too have as much as possible. In most cases the mother is left out—she has to be satisfied with one or two mouthfuls if there is not enough to go round, and lives on bread, coffee, and potatoes. A working man's wife makes daily sacrifices for her family. She is happy if nobody shouts for more, even is [sic] she is still hungry herself."

—from Union of Construction Workers, Hamburg, Germany, 1908

Step Into the Time

Choose an event from the time line and explain how it shows a consequence of the rise of mass society and democratic reforms.

EUROPE

- **1870** Women in Great Britain win the right to own some property
- **1875** German Social Democratic Party emerges
- **1876** Alexander Graham Bell invents telephone
- **1884** British Reform Act increases the number of adult male voters

1870 1875 1880 1885

THE WORLD

- **1876** Ottoman Empire's first Constitution
- **1884** Berlin West Africa conference opens
- **1885** Indian National Congress forms

networks
There's More Online!

- **MAP** Explore the interactive version of this map on Networks.
- **TIME LINE** Explore the interactive version of the time line on Networks.

Population Density in Europe 1900

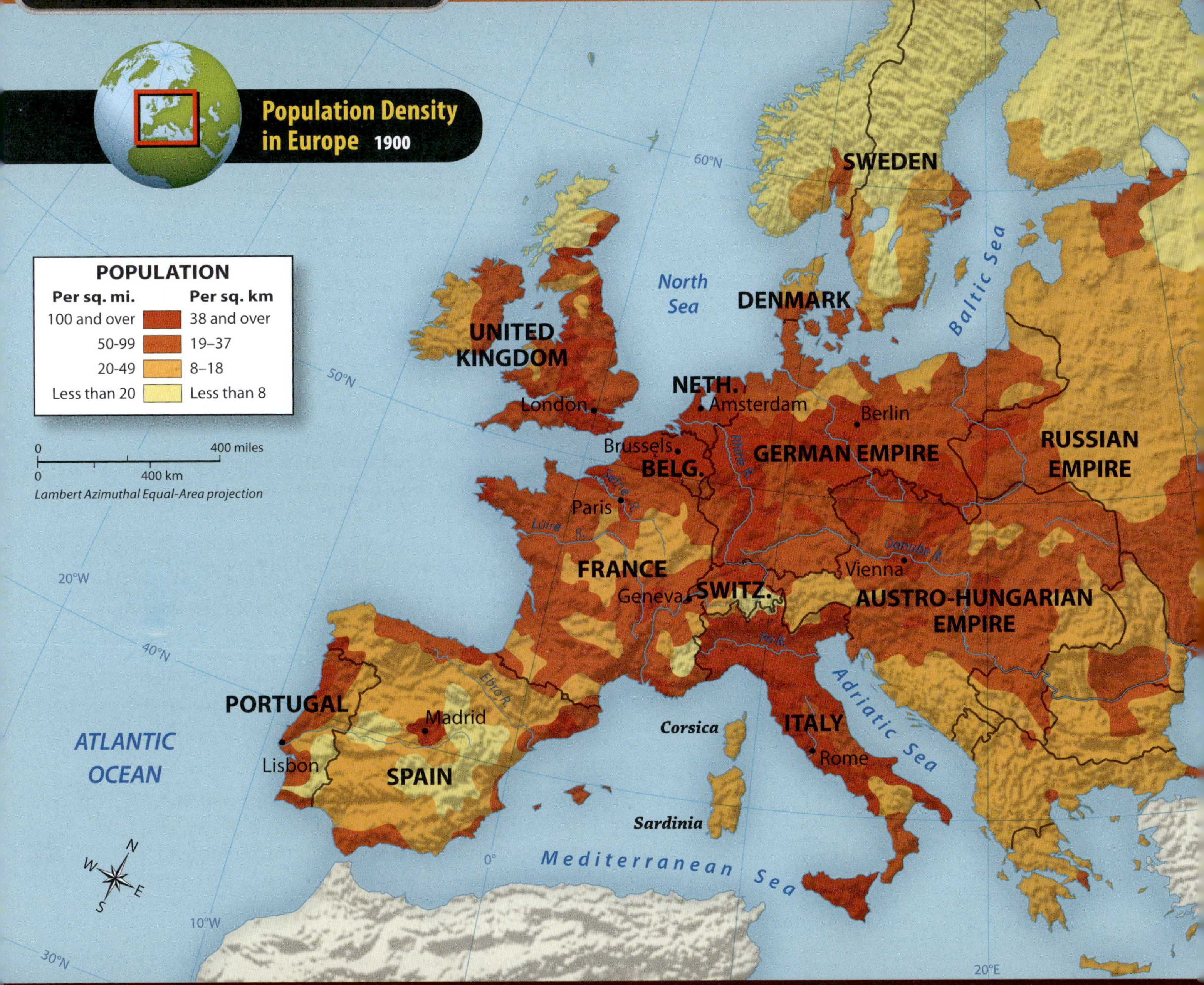

- **1888** Abolition of slavery in Brazil
- **1890** Emperor William II fires Otto von Bismarck
- **1894** Czar Nicholas II begins reign over Russian Empire
- **1894** China and Japan go to war over Korea
- **1899** South African War (Boer War) begins
- **1900** Labour Party forms in Great Britain
- **1900** Boxer Rebellion in China
- **1903** Emmeline Pankhurst and her daughters found the Women's Social and Political Union
- **1908** Congo annexed by Belgium
- **1910** Mexican revolution begins
- **1912** Universal male suffrage begins in Italy
- **1912** African National Congress forms
- **1914** Panama Canal opens

1890 1895 1900 1905 1910 1914

networks

There's More Online!

- BIOGRAPHY Thomas Edison
- BIOGRAPHY The Wright Brothers
- IMAGE Ford Assembly Line
- IMAGE German Social Democratic Party Poster
- INTERACTIVE SELF-CHECK QUIZ
- MAP Industrialization in Europe by 1914
- PRIMARY SOURCE The Communist Manifesto
- SLIDE SHOW Inventions of the Second Industrial Revolution
- VIDEO Nikola Tesla

LESSON 1

The Growth of Industrial Prosperity

ESSENTIAL QUESTIONS

- *How can industrialization affect a country's economy?*
- *How are political and social structures influenced by economic changes?*

Reading HELPDESK

Academic Vocabulary

- **transition**

Content Vocabulary

- **assembly line**
- **mass production**
- **communism**
- **bourgeoisie**
- **proletariat**
- **revisionists**

TAKING NOTES:

Key Ideas and Details

Identifying Cause and Effect As you read, use the organizer to show the effects of each innovation.

Steel	»	
Electricity	»	
Internal-combustion engine	»	

TEKS Texas Essential Knowledge and Skills

1E identify major causes and describe the major effects of the following important turning points in world history from 1750 to 1914: the Scientific Revolution, the Industrial Revolution and its impact on the development of modern economic systems, European imperialism, and the Enlightenment's impact on political revolutions

continued on the next page

It Matters Because

By the late 1800s, the Second Industrial Revolution transformed most of Europe into industrialized societies. However, the transition was not easy for workers. Many sought reform to improve their lives.

The Second Industrial Revolution

GUIDING QUESTION *What were the causes and effects of the Second Industrial Revolution in western Europe?*

The first Industrial Revolution had given rise to textiles, railroads, iron, and coal. In the Second Industrial Revolution, steel, chemicals, electricity, and petroleum led the way to new industrial frontiers.

New Products and Patterns

In 1855 Sir Henry Bessemer patented a new process for making high-quality steel efficiently and cheaply known as the Bessemer process. Steel soon replaced iron and was used in the building of lighter, smaller, and faster machines and engines. It was also used in railways, ships, and weapons. In 1860 Great Britain, France, Germany, and Belgium produced 125,000 tons (112,500 t) of steel. By 1913, the total was an astounding 32 million tons (29 million t).

Electricity was a valuable new form of energy. It was easily converted into other energy forms, such as heat, light, and motion, and moved easily through wires. In the 1870s, the first practical generators of electrical current were developed. By 1910, hydroelectric power stations and coal-fired steam-generating plants connected homes and factories to a common source of power.

Electricity gave birth to a series of inventions. Homes and cities began to have electric lights when Thomas Edison in the United States and Joseph Swan in Great Britain created the lightbulb. A revolution in communications also began. Alexander Graham Bell invented the telephone in 1876. Guglielmo Marconi sent the first radio waves across the Atlantic Ocean in 1901.

By the 1880s, streetcars and subways powered by electricity had appeared in major European cities. Electricity transformed the factory as well. Conveyor belts, cranes, and machines could all be powered by electricity. With electric lights, factories could remain open 24 hours a day.

The development of the internal-combustion engine, fired by oil and gasoline, provided a new source of power in transportation. This engine gave rise to ocean liners with oil-fired engines, as well as to the airplane and the automobile. In 1903 Orville and Wilbur Wright made the first flight in a fixed-wing plane at Kitty Hawk, North Carolina. In 1919 the first regular passenger air service was established.

One of the major effects of the Industrial Revolution was a boom in industrial productivity. Manufacturing efficiency increased in part because of the **assembly line**, a new manufacturing method pioneered by Henry Ford in 1913. The assembly line allowed a much more efficient **mass production** of goods. There was also an economic impact. Prices for manufactured goods were lower because of reduced transportation costs. Greatly increased sales of these goods followed. Europeans could now afford to buy more consumer products. Employment and wages for workers increased after 1870.

In the cities, the first department stores began to sell a new range of consumer goods. These goods—clocks, bicycles, electric lights, and typewriters, for example—were made possible by the steel and electrical industries.

Not everyone benefited from the Second Industrial Revolution. By 1900, Europe was divided into two economic zones. Great Britain, Belgium, France, the Netherlands, Germany, the western part of the

(continued from p. 560)

TEKS Texas Essential Knowledge and Skills

8B explain how the Industrial Revolution led to political, economic, and social changes in Europe

18B identify the historical origins and characteristics of communism, including the influences of Karl Marx

18C identify the historical origins and characteristics of socialism

continued on p. 563

assembly line pioneered by Henry Ford in 1913, a manufacturing method that allowed much more efficient mass production of goods

mass production production of goods in quantity usually by machinery

GEOGRAPHY CONNECTION

1. **HUMAN SYSTEMS** *What parts of Europe were the least industrialized?*

2. **ENVIRONMENT AND SOCIETY** *How do you think the environment was affected in areas of industrial concentration?*

▲ Workers build Model T automobiles at a Ford assembly plant.

▶ **CRITICAL THINKING**

Making Connections How did the assembly line transform the car industry?

Austro-Hungarian Empire, and northern Italy made up an advanced industrialized core. These nations had a high standard of living and adequate systems of transportation.

Another part of Europe to the south and east was still largely agricultural. It consisted of southern Italy, most of Austria-Hungary, Spain, Portugal, the Balkan kingdoms, and Russia. These countries provided food and raw materials for the industrial countries and had a much lower standard of living than the rest of Europe.

Toward a World Economy

The Second Industrial Revolution, combined with the growth of transportation by steamship and railroad, fostered a true world economy. By 1900, Europeans were receiving beef and wool from Argentina and Australia, coffee from Brazil, iron ore from Algeria, and sugar from Java.

European capital was also invested abroad to develop railways, mines, electrical power plants, and banks. Of course, foreign countries also provided markets for Europe's manufactured goods. With its capital, industries, and military might, Europe dominated the world economy by 1900.

READING PROGRESS CHECK

Stating How were the effects of industrialization uneven across Europe?

Connections to TODAY

Dependence on Raw Materials

Both the First and Second Industrial Revolution depended on vast imports of raw materials such as cotton (for textile manufacturing) and copper wire (for electricity). One legacy of the invention of the internal combustion engine during the Second Industrial Revolution is today's dependence on a global trade in oil.

Organizing the Working Classes

GUIDING QUESTION *How was socialism a response to industrialization?*

The **transition** to an industrialized society was very hard on workers. Despite improved wages, many workers suffered from poor working and living conditions. The desire to improve these conditions led to political changes in Europe. Many industrial workers formed socialist political parties and socialist trade unions. These parties sought to represent the interests of workers in government and to organize workers' votes. The theory on which these parties were based had been developed by the economic philosopher Karl Marx. One form of Marxist socialism that changed the shape of Western politics was called communism. **Communism** is a political and economic system in which the government owns the means of production. The characteristics of communism include the ideas of a classless society and the end of private property.

Marx's Theory

In 1848 *The Communist Manifesto* was published. It was written by two Germans, Karl Marx and Friedrich Engels, who were appalled at the horrible conditions in the industrial factories. They blamed the system of industrial capitalism for these conditions. Their ideas formed the core concepts of socialism and communism.

Marx believed that all of world history was a "history of class struggles." According to Marx, oppressor and oppressed have always "stood in constant opposition to one another." One group—the oppressors—owned the means of production, such as land, raw materials, and money. They

transition changeover; the move from one form, stage, or style to another

communism a system of socialism developed by the German writer Karl Marx who believed that the class struggle would end with the collapse of capitalism and new society without classes

bourgeoisie the middle class, including merchants, industrialists, and professional people

proletariat the working class

controlled government and society. The other group—the oppressed—owned nothing and depended on the owners of the means of production.

Marx believed he saw a society that was "more and more splitting up into two great hostile camps, into two great classes directly facing each other: Bourgeoisie and Proletariat." The **bourgeoisie**—the middle class—were the oppressors. The **proletariat** (PROH • luh • TEHR • ee • uht)—the working class—were the oppressed.

Marx predicted that the struggle between the two groups would finally lead to a revolution. The proletariat would violently overthrow the bourgeoisie. After their victory, the proletariat would form a dictatorship to organize the means of production. However, because the proletariat victory would essentially abolish the economic differences that create separate social classes, Marx believed that the final revolution would ultimately produce a classless society. The state itself, which had been a tool of the bourgeoisie, would wither away.

Socialist Parties

Socialist political parties emerged in European states. Some, like the German Social Democratic Party in Germany, met with electoral success. In 1889 leaders of the various socialist parties joined together and formed the Second International. This was an association of national socialist groups that would fight against capitalism worldwide.

Marxist parties were divided over their goals. Pure Marxists thought that capitalism could be defeated only by a violent revolution. Other Marxists, called **revisionists**, rejected the revolutionary approach. They argued that workers must continue to organize in mass political parties and even work with other parties to gain reforms. As workers received the vote, they could achieve their aims by working within democratic systems.

Trade Unions

Another force working for evolutionary, rather than revolutionary, socialism was the trade union, or labor union. To improve their conditions, workers organized in a union. The right to strike was an important part of the trade union movement. In a strike, a union calls on its members to stop work in order to pressure employers to meet their demands for higher wages or improved factory safety. At first, laws were passed that made strikes illegal under any circumstances. In Great Britain, unions won the right to strike in the 1870s. By 1914, there were almost 4 million workers in British trade unions. In the rest of Europe, trade unions had varying degrees of success in helping workers achieve a better life.

✓ **READING PROGRESS CHECK**

Identifying What issue divided pure Marxist socialists from revisionists?

▲ This German Social Democratic Party poster from 1904 proclaims "Proletarians of the World, Unite!"

▶ **CRITICAL THINKING**

Analyzing Visuals What does the poster convey about Marx's ideas?

revisionist a Marxist who rejected the revolutionary approach, believing instead in evolution by democratic means to achieve the goal of socialism

(continued from p. 561)

TEKS **Texas Essential Knowledge and Skills**

18F formulate generalizations on how economic freedom improved the human condition, based on students' knowledge of the benefits of free enterprise in Europe's Commercial Revolution, the Industrial Revolution, and 20th-century free market economies, compared to communist command communities

28E identify the contributions of significant scientists and inventors such as Marie Curie, Thomas Edison, Albert Einstein, Louis Pasteur, and James Watt

LESSON 1 REVIEW TEKS

Reviewing Vocabulary

1. ***Speculating*** What social and economic effects did mass production and the assembly line have on the bourgeoisie? 1E, 8B, 8E, 18F

Using Your Notes

2. ***Making Connections*** Use your notes to write two paragraphs discussing the effects of technological breakthroughs on daily life and on world trade during the Second Industrial Revolution. 8B

Answering the Guiding Questions

3. ***Identifying Causes and Effects*** What were the causes and effects of the Second Industrial Revolution in western Europe? 1E, 8B

4. ***Inferring*** How was socialism a response to industrialization? 8B, 17B

Writing Activity

5. **INFORMATIVE/EXPLANATORY** Write a paragraph describing the obstacles that trade unions faced in their effort to improve labor conditions.

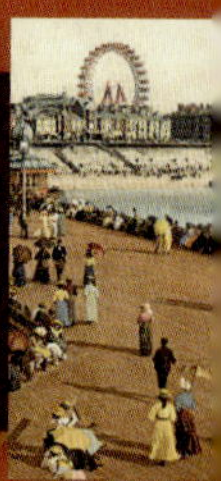

networks

There's More Online!

- IMAGE Amusement Park in England, 1900
- IMAGE Emmeline Pankhurst
- IMAGE Domestic Servants, 1886
- INTERACTIVE SELF-CHECK QUIZ
- VIDEO Women's Suffrage

LESSON 2
The Emergence of Mass Society

ESSENTIAL QUESTIONS
- *How can industrialization affect a country's economy?*
- *How are political and social structures influenced by economic changes?*

It Matters Because

By the end of the nineteenth century, the new industrial world had led to the emergence of a mass society in which the lower classes were demanding some governmental attention. Governments worked to improve public health and sanitation services in the cities. Women began to advocate for their rights, and many Western governments financed public education.

Reading HELPDESK

Academic Vocabulary
- **advocate**

Content Vocabulary
- **feminism**
- **suffrage**

TAKING NOTES:
Key Ideas and Details

Summarizing Use the graphic organizer to track the changes in each social class discussed in the lesson.

New Elite	Middle Class	Working Class

TEKS Texas Essential Knowledge and Skills
8B explain how the Industrial Revolution led to political, economic, and social changes in Europe
24A describe the changing roles of women, children, and families during major eras of world history

The New Urban Environment

GUIDING QUESTION *Why did European cities grow so quickly in the nineteenth century?*

The First and Second Industrial Revolutions led to great changes in society. Governments now had to consider how to appeal to mass society. No longer could they cater only to the wealthier citizens. Housing and public sanitation in the cities were two areas of great concern.

With few jobs available in the countryside, people from rural areas migrated to cities to find work in the factories. As a result, more and more people lived in cities. In the 1850s, urban dwellers made up about 40 percent of the English population, 15 percent in France, and 10 percent in Prussia (Prussia was the largest German state). By 1890, urban dwellers had increased to about 60 percent in England, 25 percent in France, and 30 percent in Prussia. In industrialized nations, cities grew tremendously. Between 1800 and 1900, the population in London grew from 960,000 to 6,500,000.

Cities also grew faster in the second half of the nineteenth century because of improvements in public health and sanitation. Improvements came in the 1840s after a number of urban reformers urged local governments to do something about the filthy living conditions that caused deadly epidemic diseases in the cities. Cholera (KAH • luh • ruh), for example, had ravaged Europe in the early 1830s and 1840s.

On the advice of reformers, city governments created boards of health to improve housing quality. City medical officers and building inspectors were authorized to inspect dwellings for public health hazards. Regulations required running water and internal drainage systems for new buildings.

Clean water and an effective sewage system were critical to public health. The need for freshwater was met by a system of dams and reservoirs that stored the water. Aqueducts and tunnels then carried water from the countryside to the city and into homes. Gas and electric heaters made regular hot baths possible. The treatment of sewage was improved by building underground pipes that carried raw sewage far from the city for disposal. A public campaign in Frankfurt, Germany, featured the slogan "from the toilet to the river in half an hour."

SKILLS PRACTICE

As you learn about the growth of urban areas and changes to society, raise your hand for help when somebody says a word you do not know. Then use the word often when you speak until you are comfortable with its meaning.

✓ **READING PROGRESS CHECK**

Theorizing Present three reasons for the growth of European cities in order of importance. Explain your answer.

Social Structure of Mass Society

GUIDING QUESTION *How did class divisions in Europe change during the nineteenth century?*

After 1871, most people enjoyed a higher standard of living. Still, great poverty remained in Western society. Between the few who were rich and the many who were poor existed several middle-class groups.

The New Elite

At the top of European society stood a wealthy elite. This group made up only 5 percent of the population but controlled from 30 to 40 percent of the wealth. During the 1800s, the most successful industrialists, bankers, and merchants—the wealthy upper-middle class—had joined with the landed aristocracy—the upper class—to form this new elite. Whether aristocratic or upper-middle class in background, members of the elite became leaders in the government and military.

The Diverse Middle Classes

While some members of the upper-middle class became part of the new elite, the rest of the middle class consisted of several groups at varying economic and social levels. Below the upper-middle class was a middle group that included lawyers, doctors, members of the civil service, business managers, engineers, architects, accountants, and chemists. Beneath this solid and comfortable middle group was a lower-middle class of small shopkeepers, traders, and prosperous farmers.

The Second Industrial Revolution produced a new group of white-collar workers between the lower-middle class and the lower classes. This group included traveling salespeople, bookkeepers, telephone operators, department store salespeople, and secretaries. Although not highly paid, these white-collar workers were often committed to middle-class ideals.

The middle classes shared a certain lifestyle with values that dominated much of nineteenth-century society. The European middle classes believed in hard work, which was open to everyone and guaranteed positive results. Outward appearances were also very important to the middle classes. The etiquette book *The Habits of Good Society* was a best seller.

▲ These women and girls were domestic servants in a British home in 1886.

▶ **CRITICAL THINKING**

Drawing Conclusions To which social class did these women belong? What was the social class of their employer?

PHOTO: Popperfoto/Getty Images

The Working Classes

Below the middle classes on the social scale were the working classes—also referred to as the lower classes—which made up almost 80 percent of the

European population. These classes included landholding peasants, farm laborers, and sharecroppers.

The urban working class consisted of many different groups. They might be skilled artisans or semiskilled laborers, but many were unskilled day laborers or domestic servants. In Britain in 1900, one out of every seven employed persons was a domestic servant. Most servants were women.

After 1870, urban workers began to live more comfortably. Reforms created better living conditions in cities. In addition, a rise in wages, along with a decline in many consumer costs, made it possible for workers to buy extra clothes or pay to entertain themselves in their few leisure hours. In organizing and conducting strikes, workers had won the 10-hour workday with a Saturday afternoon off.

✓ **READING PROGRESS CHECK**

Categorizing Discuss the major social changes that occurred during the Second Industrial Revolution.

Women's Experiences

GUIDING QUESTION *How did the Second Industrial Revolution influence women's roles in society?*

In 1800 women were mainly defined by their families and household roles. In the nineteenth century, women struggled to change their status.

New Job Opportunities

During much of the nineteenth century, working-class groups maintained the belief that women should remain at home to bear and nurture children and should not be allowed in the industrial workforce.

The Second Industrial Revolution opened the door to new jobs for women. There were not enough men to fill the relatively low-paid, white-collar jobs being created. Both industrial plants and retail shops hired women as clerks, typists, secretaries, and salesclerks.

The expansion of government services also created job opportunities for women. Women took jobs in education, health, and social services. Middle-class women held these jobs, but they were mainly filled by the working class.

Marriage and the Family

As the chief family wage earners, men worked outside the home. Women were left to care for the family. Throughout the 1800s, marriage remained almost the only honorable and available career for most women. The number of children born to the average woman began to decline—the most significant development in the modern family. This decline was tied to improved economic conditions and increased use of birth control.

The family was the central institution of middle-class life. With fewer children in the family, mothers could devote more time to child care and domestic leisure. The middle-class family fostered an ideal of togetherness. The Victorians in Britain created the family Christmas with its Yule log, tree, songs, and exchange of gifts.

The lives of working-class women were different from those of their middle-class counterparts, but these women saw changing roles, as well. Most working-class women had to earn money to help support their families. For the children of the working classes, childhood was over by the age of 9 or 10. As the Industrial Revolution developed, children often worked in factories to supplement family income. Children not working in factories were often obligated to stay at home to care for family members, since both parents had moved into the workforce.

Analyzing PRIMARY SOURCES

Emmeline Pankhurst on Militancy

"Be militant in your own way. Those of you who can express your militancy by going to the House of Commons and refusing to leave without satisfaction, as we did in the early days—do so. . . . Those of you who can express your militancy by joining us in our anti-Government by-election policy—do so. Those of you who can break windows—do so (great applause) . . . "

—Emmeline Pankhurst, from a speech on October 17, 1912

DBQ ***DRAWING CONCLUSIONS***

What do the different types of militancy outlined by Pankhurst show about her approach to the struggle for women's rights?

Between 1890 and 1914, family patterns among the working class began to change. Higher-paying jobs in heavy industry made it possible for working-class families to depend on the income of husbands alone. By the early twentieth century, some working-class mothers could afford to stay at home, following the pattern of middle-class women. The lives of children slowly improved, as well, as new laws outlawed child labor.

Women's Rights

Modern **feminism**, or the movement for women's rights, had its beginnings during the Enlightenment. At this time, some women **advocated** equality for women based on the doctrine of natural rights.

feminism the movement for women's rights

advocate to support; to speak in favor of

In the 1830s, a number of women in the United States and Europe argued for the right of women to own property. By law, a husband had almost total control over his wife's property. These early efforts were not very successful, however. Married women did not win the right to own some property until 1870 in Great Britain, 1900 in Germany, and 1907 in France.

The fight for property rights was only the beginning of the women's movement. Some middle- and upper-middle-class women fought for and gained access to universities. Others sought entry into occupations dominated by men. Although training to become doctors was largely closed to women, some entered the medical field by becoming nurses. The efforts of the British nurse Florence Nightingale, combined with those of Clara Barton in the U.S. Civil War, transformed nursing into a profession of trained, middle-class "women in white."

By the 1840s and 1850s, the movement for women's rights expanded as women called for equal political rights. They believed that **suffrage**, the right to vote, was the key to improving their overall position. Members of the women's movement, called suffragists, had one basic aim: the right of women to full citizenship in the nation-state.

suffrage the right to vote

The British women's movement was the most active in Europe. The Women's Social and Political Union, founded in 1903 by Emmeline Pankhurst and her daughters, used unusual publicity stunts to call attention to its demands. Its members pelted government officials with eggs, chained themselves to lampposts, and smashed department store windows. British police answered with arrests and brutal treatment of leading activists.

◀ Emmeline Pankhurst and her daughters try to enter Buckingham Palace to present a petition for women's rights to the King of England.

▶ **CRITICAL THINKING**

Drawing Conclusions Why did British police prevent the Pankhursts from entering Buckingham Palace?

Before 1914, women had the right to vote in only a few nations, such as Norway and Finland, along with some American states. It took the upheaval of World War I to make governments give in on this basic issue.

✓ READING PROGRESS CHECK

Distinguishing How did the working-class family change in the late 1800s?

Education and Leisure

GUIDING QUESTION ***How did society change as a result of urbanization and industrialization?***

Universal education was a product of the mass society of the late ineteenth and early twentieth centuries. Before that time, education was reserved mostly for the elite and the wealthier middle class. Between 1870 and 1914, most Western governments began to finance a system of primary education. Boys and girls between the ages of 6 and 12 were required to attend these schools.

Why did Western nations make this commitment to public education? One reason was industrialization. In the First Industrial Revolution, workers without training or experience were able to meet factory needs. The new firms of the Second Industrial Revolution needed trained, skilled workers.

The chief motive for public education was political. Giving more people the right to vote created a need for better-educated voters. Even more importantly, primary schools instilled patriotism.

Compulsory elementary education created a demand for teachers, and most of them were women. Many men saw teaching as a part of women's "natural role" as nurturers of children. Women were also paid lower salaries than men, which in itself was a strong incentive for states to set up teacher-training schools for women.

The Second Industrial Revolution allowed people to pursue new forms of leisure. Popular mass leisure both entertained large crowds and distracted them from the realities of work lives. Leisure came to be viewed as what people do for fun after work. The industrial system gave people new times—evening hours, weekends, and a week or two in the summer—to indulge in leisure activities. Amusement parks, dance halls, and organized team sports became enjoyable ways for people to spend their leisure hours.

▼ At the turn of the twentieth century, Europeans enjoyed beaches and amusment parks such as this one at Blackpool on the Irish Sea in Lancashire, England.

▶ CRITICAL THINKING

Comparing and Contrasting Compare and contrast the amusement park at Blackpool with those of today.

PHOTO: The Granger Collection, NYC

✓ READING PROGRESS CHECK

Explaining What were some reasons governments promoted public education?

LESSON 2 REVIEW TEKS

Reviewing Vocabulary

1. ***Determining Importance*** Why did members of the women's rights movement believe that suffrage was the key to improving the position of women in society? 24A

Using Your Notes

2. ***Comparing*** Use your notes to write a paragraph detailing the changes in social structure that happened during the emergence of mass society.

Answering the Guiding Questions

3. ***Identifying Cause and Effect*** Why did European cities grow so quickly in the nineteenth century?
4. ***Identifying*** How did class divisions in Europe change during the nineteenth century?
5. ***Making Generalizations*** How did the Second Industrial Revolution influence women's roles in society? 24A
6. ***Drawing Conclusions*** How did society change as a result of industrialization?

Writing Activity

7. **NARRATIVE** Assume the identity of a male member of the European middle class living in a big city in the year 1900. Write a diary entry in which you describe your day at work and what you looked forward to at home at the end of the day.

SKILLBUILDER

TEKS 15B

Analyzing Maps

Why Learn This Skill?

Maps can present many kinds of information. They can be loaded with layers of information depicted in symbols, shading, and countless other visual markers. Without the ability to analyze a map, you might miss its information entirely.

Learning the Skill

Follow these steps to analyze a map:

- Read the map title to identify its purpose.
- Read the map's key, labels, and captions to determine what is being illustrated. These features are the user's guide to understanding the map.
- If the map has shading, determine which colors represent which data sets. This information is usually found in the key. Often, darker colors represent higher numbers. Also, colors usually represent a range of numbers, rather than specific numbers.
- Note placement of any symbols on the map.
- Look for patterns in the data. Ask yourself what geographical features are shared by areas that stand out in the map.
- Analyze the map to draw conclusions about the data presented.

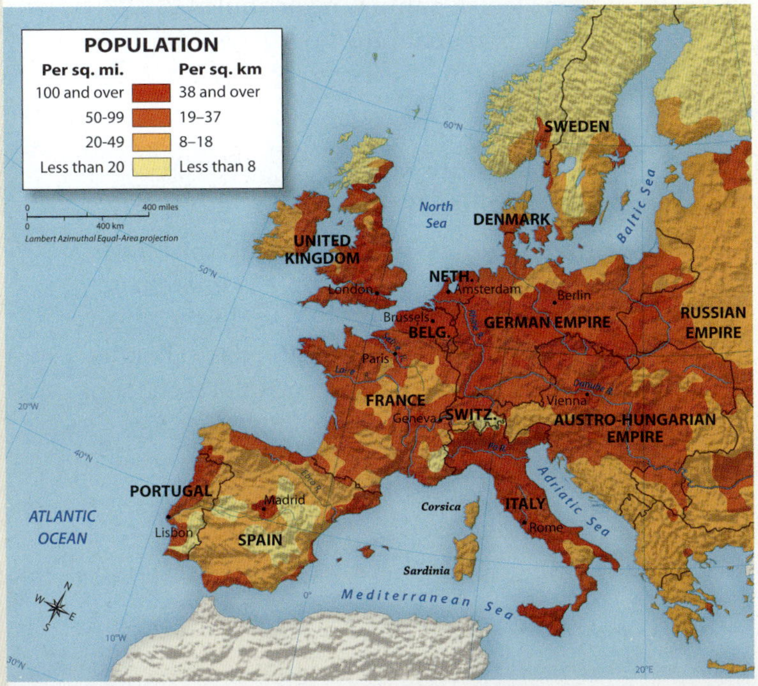

Practicing the Skill

Study the map on this page. This is a population density map that presents the crucial information as shading. The darker colors represent higher population densities. Note where areas of darker and lighter shading appear. Look for geographic features in those areas that might explain the higher or lower population densities.

Recall what you have learned about these countries in the past to help you understand the map. Perhaps you know facts about a country's history or climate that might lead to a higher or lower population density. Consider the role that urbanization has played in shaping population density across the region.

Skills Assessment

After studying the map closely, answer the following questions.

1. Explain the geographic distribution of people in the German Empire. How do you explain this pattern of population density?
2. Compare two distributions of population shown on the map. What would account for the varying population densities?
3. Besides population density, what other information is presented on this map?

Applying the Skill

Analyzing Maps Spend a few minutes finding a map that interests you in the textbook and analyzing it. Write down as many facts from your map as possible. Are there geographic distributions on the map? Divide into pairs and trade maps. (First, make sure you haven't chosen the same map!) Analyze your partner's map, noting geographic distributions in particular. Then, with your partner, discuss your findings on each other's maps. Who identified the most facts? Compare geographic distributions on the maps. What conclusions can you draw from your findings?

SKILLBUILDER

TEKS 29E

Identifying Bias in Written Material

Why Learn This Skill?

Suppose you see an ad showing two happy customers shaking hands with a used-car salesman. The ad says, "Visit Honest Harry for the best deal on wheels." That evening you see a television program that investigates used-car sales businesses. The report says that many of these businesses cheat their customers.

Each message expresses a bias—an inclination or prejudice that inhibits impartiality. Harry wants to sell cars; the television station wants to attract viewers. Most people have preconceived feelings, opinions, and attitudes that affect their judgment on many topics. Ideas stated as facts may be opinions. Detecting bias enables us to evaluate the accuracy of information.

Learning the Skill

In detecting bias in written material:

- Identify the writer's purpose.
- Watch for emotionally charged language such as *exploit, terrorize,* and *cheat.*
- Look for visual images that provoke a strong emotional response.
- Look for overgeneralizations, such as *unique, honest,* and *everybody.*
- Notice italics, underlining, and punctuation that highlight particular ideas.
- Examine the material to determine whether it presents equal coverage of differing views.

Practicing the Skill

Read the following excerpt from *The Communist Manifesto,* written by Karl Marx and Friedrich Engels in 1848.

"The bourgeoisie . . . has put an end to all feudal, patriarchal, idyllic relations. It has pitilessly torn asunder the motley feudal ties that bound man to his 'natural superiors,' and has left remaining no other nexus [link] between man and man than naked self-interest, than callous 'cash payment.' It has drowned the most heavenly of ecstasies of religious fervor, of chivalrous enthusiasm . . . in the icy water of egotistical calculation. . . . In one word, for exploitation, veiled by religious and political illusions, it has substituted naked, shameless, direct, brutal exploitation."

Follow the steps under "Learning the Skill" to identify the bias in this text. Note the emotionally charged language and the strong visual images.

Skills Assessment

After reading the excerpt closely, answer the following questions.

1. What is the purpose of this quote?
2. What are three examples of emotionally charged language?
3. According to Marx and Engels, why is the bourgeoisie inhumane or abusive?
4. What bias about the bourgeoisie is expressed in this excerpt?

Applying the Skill

Identifying Bias in Written Material Find written material about a topic of interest in your community. Possible sources include editorials, letters to the editor, and pamphlets from political candidates and interest groups. Write a short report analyzing the text for evidence of bias. Be sure to include specific examples to support your analysis.

networks

There's More Online!

- BIOGRAPHY Czar Nicholas II
- IMAGE New York City, 1873
- IMAGE William II Fires Bismarck
- INTERACTIVE SELF-CHECK QUIZ
- MAP Europe, 1871
- PRIMARY SOURCE Labour Party Speech Before the House of Commons
- PRIMARY SOURCE Liberal Party Speech Before the House of Commons
- VIDEO Queen Victoria

LESSON 3
The National State and Democracy

ESSENTIAL QUESTION
How are political and social structures influenced by economic changes?

IT MATTERS BECAUSE

During the late 1800s and early 1900s, democracy expanded in western Europe, while the old order preserved authoritarianism in central and eastern Europe. During this time, the United States recovered from the Civil War and became the world's richest nation. Meanwhile, international rivalries began to set the stage for World War I.

Reading HELPDESK

Academic Vocabulary
- **insecure**
- **controversy**

Content Vocabulary
- **ministerial responsibility**
- **Duma**

TAKING NOTES:
Key Ideas and Details

Identifying As you read, use a table like the one below to list the different forms of European governments.

Nation	Form of Government
Great Britain	
France	
Germany	
Austria-Hungary	
Russia	

TEKS Texas Essential Knowledge and Skills

19B identify the characteristics of the following political systems: theocracy, absolute monarchy, democracy, republic, oligarchy, limited monarchy, and totalitarianism

Western Europe: Political Democracy

GUIDING QUESTION *What happened with democracy in western Europe in the late nineteenth century?*

By the late nineteenth century, the modern shape of that political democracy was taking form in western Europe. First, universal male suffrage laws were passed. Second, the prime minister was responsible to the popularly elected legislative body, not to a king or president. This principle is called **ministerial responsibility** and is crucial for democracy. The third characteristic of democracy was the formation of mass political parties.

Great Britain had long had a working two-party parliamentary system. In a parliamentary system, the party with the greatest representation in parliament forms the government, the leader of which is the prime minister. The two parties—the Liberals and Conservatives—competed to pass laws that expanded the right to vote. Reform acts in 1867 and 1884 increased the number of adult male voters. By 1918, males over 21 and women over 30 could vote.

At the beginning of the twentieth century, then, political democracy was becoming well established in Britain. Social reforms for the working class soon followed. In 1900, a new Labour Party emerged and dedicated itself to the interests of workers. To retain the workers' support, the Liberals voted for social reforms, such as unemployment benefits and old-age pensions.

In France, the collapse of Louis-Napoleon's Second Empire left the country in confusion. Finally, in 1875, the Third Republic gained a republican constitution. The new government had a president and a

GEOGRAPHY CONNECTION

In 1871 Europe was mostly controlled by large empires.

1. **HUMAN SYSTEMS** *What do the country names tell you about democracy in Europe in 1871?*
2. **REGION** *Based on what you know of world geography, which European empire of 1871 do you think lasted the longest?*
3. **LOCATION** *Which country appears to be most vulnerable to future invasions?*

two-house legislature. The upper house, or Senate, was elected by high-ranking officials. All adult males voted for members of the lower house, the Chamber of Deputies. A premier (or prime minister), who led the government, was responsible to the Chamber of Deputies.

France failed to develop a strong parliamentary system. The existence of a dozen political parties forced the premier to depend on a coalition of parties to stay in power. Nevertheless, by 1914, the Third Republic had the loyalty of most voters.

Italy had emerged by 1870 as a united state. However, there was little national unity because of the gulf between the poverty-stricken south and the industrialized north. Turmoil between labor and industry weakened the social fabric of the nation. Even universal male suffrage, granted in 1912, did little to halt the widespread government corruption and weakness.

✓ **READING PROGRESS CHECK**

Comparing How did Italy's government in the 1870s compare to Great Britain's?

ministerial responsibility the idea that the prime minister is responsible to the popularly elected legislative body and not to the king or president

Central and Eastern Europe: The Old Order

GUIDING QUESTION *What political developments did central and eastern Europe experience in the late nineteenth century?*

Central and eastern Europe had more conservative governments than did western Europe. In Germany, the Austro-Hungarian Empire, and Russia the old ruling groups continued to dominate politics.

The constitution of the new imperial Germany that Otto von Bismarck began in 1871 set up a two-house legislature. The lower house, the Reichstag, was elected on the basis of universal male suffrage. Ministers of government, however, were responsible not to the parliament but to the emperor, who controlled the armed forces, foreign policy, and the bureaucracy. As chancellor (prime minister), Bismarck worked to keep Germany from becoming a democracy.

By the reign of William II, kaiser from 1888 to 1918, Germany had become the strongest military and industrial power in Europe. With the expansion of industry and cities came demands for democracy.

Conservative forces—especially the nobility and big industrialists—tried to thwart the movement for democracy by supporting a strong foreign policy. They believed that expansion abroad would increase their profits and would also divert people from pursuing democratic reforms.

After the creation of the dual monarchy of Austria-Hungary in 1867, Austria adopted a constitution that, in theory, set up a parliamentary system with ministerial responsibility. In reality, the emperor, Francis Joseph, largely ignored this system. He appointed and dismissed his own ministers and issued decrees when the parliament was not in session.

The empire remained troubled by conflicts among its ethnic groups. A German minority governed Austria but felt increasingly threatened by Czechs, Poles, and other Slavic groups within the empire. Representatives of these groups in the parliament agitated for their freedom, which encouraged the emperor to ignore the parliament and govern by imperial decrees.

Unlike Austria, Hungary had a parliament that worked. It was controlled by landowners who dominated the peasants and ethnic groups.

In Russia, Nicholas II began his rule in 1894 believing that the absolute power of the czars should be preserved. Conditions were changing, however. By 1900, Russia had become the fourth-largest producer of steel. With industrialization came factories, an industrial working class, and pitiful working≈and living conditions. Socialist parties developed, but government repression forced them underground.

Growing discontent and opposition to the czarist regime finally exploded. On January 22, 1905, a massive procession of workers went to the Winter Palace in St. Petersburg to present a petition of grievances to the czar. Troops opened fire on the peaceful demonstration, killing hundreds. This "Bloody Sunday" caused workers throughout Russia to strike.

Nicholas II was eventually forced to grant civil liberties and to create a legislative assembly, the **Duma**. By 1907, the czar curtailed the power of the Duma and again used the army and bureaucracy to rule Russia.

Duma the Russian legislative assembly

✓ **READING PROGRESS CHECK**

Identifying Central Issues Did the government of Germany, Austria-Hungary, or Russia adhere to the principle of ministerial responsibility?

The United States

GUIDING QUESTION *How did the Second Industrial Revolution affect the United States?*

Four years of civil war had preserved the American nation, but the old South had been destroyed. In 1865 the Thirteenth Amendment to the Constitution was passed, abolishing slavery. Later, the Fourteenth and Fifteenth Amendments gave citizenship to African Americans and the right to vote to African American males. New state laws in the South, however, soon stripped African Americans of the right to vote. By 1880, supporters of white supremacy were back in power everywhere in the South.

Between 1860 and 1914, the United States shifted from a farm-based economy to an industrial economy. American steel and iron

▼ At the beginning of his rule, Czar Nicholas II said, "I shall maintain the principle of autocracy just as firmly and unflinchingly as did my unforgettable father."

▶ **CRITICAL THINKING**

Drawing Conclusions What changes in Russia challenged the autocracy of the czar?

production was the best in the world in 1900. Industrialization led to urbanization. By 1900, the United States had three cities with populations of more than 1 million, with New York reaching 4 million.

In 1900 the United States was the world's richest nation, but the richest 9 percent of Americans owned 71 percent of the wealth. Many workers labored in unsafe factories, and devastating cycles of unemployment made them **insecure**. Many tried to organize unions, but the American Federation of Labor represented only 8.4 percent of the labor force.

insecure uncertain, shaky; not adequately covered or sustained

In the late 1800s, the United States began to expand abroad. The Samoan Islands in the Pacific were the first important U.S. colony. By 1887, Americans controlled the sugar industry on the Hawaiian Islands. As more Americans settled in Hawaii, they wanted political power. When Queen Liliuokalani (lih • LEE • uh • woh • kuh • LAH • nee) tried to strengthen the monarchy to keep the islands under her people's control, the United States sent military forces to the islands. The queen was deposed and the United States annexed Hawaii in 1898. In 1898 the United States defeated Spain in the Spanish-American War. As a result, the United States acquired the former Spanish possessions of Puerto Rico, Guam, and the Philippines.

✓ READING PROGRESS CHECK

Analyzing How did the U.S. Civil War affect African Americans?

International Rivalries

GUIDING QUESTION *How did international rivalries push Europe close to war?*

Otto von Bismarck realized that Germany's emergence in 1871 as the most powerful state in continental Europe had upset the balance of power established at Vienna in 1815. Fearing that France intended to create an anti-German alliance, Bismarck made a defensive alliance with Austria-Hungary in 1879. In 1882 Italy joined this alliance.

This Triple Alliance thus united the powers of Germany, Austria-Hungary, and Italy in a defensive alliance against France. At the same time, Bismarck maintained a separate treaty with Russia.

New Directions: William II

In 1890 Kaiser William II fired Bismarck and took control of Germany's foreign policy. The kaiser embarked on an activist policy dedicated to enhancing German power. He wanted, as he put it, to find Germany's rightful "place in the sun."

One of the changes William made in foreign policy was to drop the treaty with Russia. Almost immediately, in 1894, France formed an alliance with Russia. Germany thus had a hostile power on her western border and on her eastern border—exactly the situation Bismarck had feared!

Over the next decade, German policies caused the British to draw closer to

POLITICAL CARTOON

WILLIAM II FIRES BISMARCK

In this political cartoon, Emperor William II (seated) dismisses Otto von Bismarck (standing), while Germany, represented by the figure in the background, looks on.

▸ CRITICAL THINKING

1. ***Analyzing Visuals*** Of what is Wiilliam II's throne constructed?
2. ***Determining Cause and Effect*** According to the cartoonist, what consequences might result from the firing of Bismarck?

France. By 1907, an alliance of Great Britain, France, and Russia—the Triple Entente—stood opposed to the Triple Alliance. Europe was now dangerously divided into two opposing camps unwilling to compromise.

Crises in the Balkans

In the 1800s, the Ottoman Empire began to fall apart. Most of its Balkan provinces gained their freedom. As this was happening, two Great Powers saw their chance to gain influence in the Balkans: Austria-Hungary and Russia. Their rivalry over the Balkans was one of the causes of World War I.

By 1878, Greece, Serbia, Romania, and Montenegro had become independent. Bulgaria was not independent but was allowed to operate autonomously under Russian protection. The Balkan territories of Bosnia and Herzegovina were placed under the protection of Austria-Hungary.

In 1908 Austria-Hungary took the drastic step of annexing Bosnia and Herzegovina. Serbia was outraged. The annexation of Bosnia and Herzegovina, two Slavic-speaking territories, led to an international **controversy** and dashed the Serbians' hopes of creating a large Serbian kingdom that would include most of the southern Slavs.

The Russians, self-appointed protectors of their fellow Slavs, supported the Serbs and opposed the annexation. Backed by the Russians, the Serbs prepared for war against Austria-Hungary. At this point, Emperor William II of Germany demanded that the Russians accept Austria-Hungary's annexation of Bosnia and Herzegovina or face war with Germany.

Weakened from their defeat in the Russo-Japanese War in 1905, the Russians backed down but vowed revenge. Two wars between Balkan states in 1912 and 1913 further embittered the inhabitants and created more tensions among the Great Powers.

The Serbs blamed Austria-Hungary for their failure to create a large Serbian kingdom. Austria-Hungary was convinced that Serbia and Serbian nationalism were mortal threats to its empire and must be crushed.

As Serbia's chief supporters, the Russians were angry and determined not to back down again in the event of another confrontation with Austria-Hungary or Germany in the Balkans. Finally, the allies of Austria-Hungary and Russia were determined to support their respective allies more strongly in another crisis. By the beginning of 1914, these countries viewed each other with suspicion. Europe was on the verge of war.

✓ READING PROGRESS CHECK

Sequencing Describe the events in the Balkans up through 1914.

Triple Alliance, 1882
• Germany
• Austria-Hungary
• Italy
Triple Entente, 1907
• Great Britain
• France
• Russia

▸ CRITICAL THINKING

1 ***Transferring Knowledge*** Create a political map that shows the Triple Alliance and the Triple Entente.

2 ***Interpreting Significance*** How did these alliances help create a crisis in the Balkans?

controversy a dispute or quarrel

LESSON 3 REVIEW TEKS

Reviewing Vocabulary

1. ***Identifying*** What is ministerial responsibility, and why is it important? 19B

Using Your Notes

2. ***Summarizing*** Using the information in your notes, list the forms of government in Great Britain, France, Germany, Austria-Hungary, and Russia.

Answering the Guiding Questions

3. ***Making Generalizations*** What happened with democracy in western Europe in the late nineteenth century?
4. ***Drawing Conclusions*** What political developments did central and eastern Europe experience in the late nineteenth century?
5. ***Explaining*** How did the Second Industrial Revolution affect the United States?
6. ***Making Connections*** How did international rivalries push Europe close to war?

Writing Activity

7. **INFORMATIVE/EXPLANATORY** Write a short paragraph about the impact of labor issues in Great Britain and Russia.

LESSON 4
Modern Ideas and Uncertainty

networks
There's More Online!

- BIOGRAPHY Marie Curie
- BIOGRAPHY Albert Einstein
- BIOGRAPHY Sigmund Freud
- IMAGE Id, Ego, and Superego
- INFOGRAPHIC Advancements in Chemistry and Physics
- INTERACTIVE SELF-CHECK QUIZ
- PRIMARY SOURCE J'accuse
- SLIDE SHOW Modern Painting and Architecture
- VIDEO Marie Curie

ESSENTIAL QUESTION *How are political and social structures influenced by economic changes?*

IT MATTERS BECAUSE

During the late nineteenth and early twentieth centuries, people moved toward a modern consciousness. Their changing worldview was expressed in new art movements, while developments in the sciences also changed how people saw themselves and their world.

Reading HELPDESK

Academic Vocabulary
- **abstract**
- **intensity**

Content Vocabulary
- **modernism**
- **psychoanalysis**
- **Social Darwinism**
- **pogroms**
- **Zionism**

TAKING NOTES:
Key Ideas and Details

Organizing Use the following graphic organizer to name an artist and a characteristic of the art movement indicated.

Movement	Artist	Characteristic
Impressionist		
Post-impressionist		
Cubist		
Abstract		

TEKS Texas Essential Knowledge and Skills

26A identify significant examples of art and architecture that demonstrate an artistic ideal or visual principle from selected cultures

continued on the next page

The Culture of Modernity

GUIDING QUESTION *How did innovation change literature, the visual arts, and music in the late 1800s and early 1900s?*

Between 1870 and 1914, many writers and artists rebelled against the traditional literary and artistic styles that had dominated European cultural life since the Renaissance. The changes they produced have since been called **modernism**.

Literature

Western novelists and poets who followed the naturalist style wrote modernist works that reflected common social concerns. Henrik Ibsen and Émile Zola, for example, explored the role of women in society, as well as alcoholism, and urban slums, in their work.

The symbolist writers had a different idea about what was real. They believed the external world, including art, was only a collection of symbols reflecting the true reality—the human mind. Art, the symbolists believed, should function for its own sake, not criticize or seek to understand society.

Painting and Architecture

Since the Renaissance, Western artists had tried to represent reality as accurately as possible. By the late 1800s, artists were seeking new forms of expression to reflect their changing worldviews. Impressionism was a movement that began in France in the 1870s, when a group of artists rejected indoor studios and went to the countryside to paint nature directly. One important impressionist was Claude Monet (moh • NAY), whose paintings captured the interplay of light, water, and sky and demonstrated the artistic ideals of the time.

In the 1880s, a new movement, known as postimpressionism, arose in France and soon spread. For Vincent van Gogh, art was a spiritual experience. He was especially interested in color and believed that it could act as its own form of language. Van Gogh's idea that artists should paint what they feel reflected the history of increasing individual freedoms in Europe.

By the early 1900s, artists were no longer convinced that their main goal was to represent reality. This was especially true in the visual arts. One reason for the decline of realism in painting was photography, which became popular after George Eastman created the Kodak camera in 1888.

Artists tended to focus less on mirroring reality, which the camera could do, and more on creating reality. Painters and sculptors, like the symbolist writers of the time, looked for meaning in individual consciousness. Between 1905 and 1914, this search for expression created modern art.

By 1905, Pablo Picasso, an important figure in modern art, was beginning his career. Picasso created a new artistic style—cubism. Cubism used geometric designs to re-create reality in the viewer's mind.

Abstract painting emerged around 1910. Wassily Kandinsky, a Russian, was one of the first to use an abstract style. Kandinsky sought to avoid visual reality altogether. He believed that art should speak directly to the soul. To do so, it must use only line and color.

Modernism in the arts revolutionized architecture and gave rise to functionalism. Functionalism was the idea that buildings, like the products of machines, should be functional, or useful. Functionalism's focus on removing a building's ornamentation demonstrated the artistic ideal of the time and the growing passion to be "modern." Architects, led by Louis H. Sullivan, used reinforced concrete, steel frames, and electric elevators to build skyscrapers virtually free of ornamentation.

modernism a movement in which writers and artists between 1870 and 1914 rebelled against the traditional literary and artistic styles that had dominated European cultural life since the Renaissance

(continued from p. 576)

TEKS **Texas Essential Knowledge and Skills**

26B analyze examples of how art, architecture, literature, music, and drama reflect the history of the cultures in which they are produced

28E identify the contributions of significant scientists and inventors such as Marie Curie, Thomas Edison, Albert Einstein, Louis Pasteur, and James Watt

abstract a style of art, emerging around 1910, that spoke directly to the soul and avoided visual reality by using only lines and color

ANALYZING PRIMARY SOURCES

▲ Claude Monet, *Haystacks*, 1891

▲ Pablo Picasso, *Houses on the Hill*, 1909

Impressionism and Cubism: Monet and Picasso

Contrast these two landscape paintings by impressionist Claude Monet (left) and cubist Pablo Picasso (right). Impressionists presented their impression of a scene at a specific moment in time. In Haystacks, *Monet captures the constantly shifting light and color of the natural world. Cubist painters built on the abstraction of impressionist art and took it considerably further. In* Houses on the Hill, *Picasso distills a landscape scene into its underlying geometric shapes.*

DBQ Analyzing Historical Documents

1. ***Examining*** What techniques does Monet use to convey this rural landscape? Consider features of the painting such as Monet's brushstrokes as well as his choices of color, shape, and composition.
2. ***Comparing and Contrasting*** In what ways are Impressionism and Cubism similar? In what ways are they different? Refer to these two paintings to defend your claims.

Music

At the beginning of the twentieth century, developments in music paralleled those in painting. The music of the Russian composer Igor Stravinsky exploited expressive sounds and bold rhythms.

Stravinsky's ballet *The Rite of Spring* revolutionized music. When it was performed in Paris in 1913, the sounds and rhythms of the music and dance caused a near riot by an outraged audience.

✓ READING PROGRESS CHECK

Explaining Why did modern artists turn away from realism?

Uncertainty Grows

GUIDING QUESTION *How did scientific discoveries in the late 1800s impact the way people saw themselves and their world?*

Science was one of the chief pillars supporting the worldview of many Westerners in the nineteenth century. Many believed that by applying scientific laws, humans could understand the physical world and reality.

▲ **Marie Curie was the first woman to win a Nobel Prize. With her husband, she was awarded half the Nobel Prize for Physics in 1903 for their study in radiation.**

▶ **CRITICAL THINKING**

Contrasting How was the practice of science different at the turn of the twentieth century than it is today?

Curie and the Atom

Throughout much of the 1800s, Westerners believed in a mechanical conception of the universe that was based on the ideas of Isaac Newton. The universe was viewed as a giant machine. Time, space, and matter were objective realities existing independently of those observing them. Matter was thought to be made of solid material bodies called atoms.

These views were seriously questioned at the end of the nineteenth century. The French scientist Marie Curie discovered that an element called radium gave off energy, or radiation, that apparently came from within the atom itself. Atoms were not just material bodies but small, active worlds.

Einstein and Relativity

In the early twentieth century, Albert Einstein, a German-born scientist provided a new view of the universe. His special theory of relativity stated that space and time are not absolute but are relative to the observer.

According to this theory, neither space nor time has an existence independent of human experience. Moreover, matter and energy reflect the relativity of time and space. Einstein concluded that matter is just another form of energy. The vast energies contained within the atom were explained. To some, however, a relative universe was one without certainty.

Freud and Psychoanalysis

Sigmund Freud (FROYD), a doctor from Vienna, proposed theories regarding the nature of the human mind. His major theories were published in 1900 in *The Interpretation of Dreams*.

According to Freud, human behavior was strongly determined by past experiences and internal forces of which people were largely unaware. Repression of such experiences began in childhood, so he devised a method—known as **psychoanalysis**—by which a therapist could probe deeply into the patient's memory. In this way, they could retrace the repressed thoughts all the way back to their childhood origins. If the patient's conscious mind could be made aware of the unconscious and its repressed contents, the patient could be healed.

psychoanalysis a method by which a therapist and patient probe deeply into the patient's memory; by making the patient's conscious mind aware of repressed thoughts, healing can take place

✓ READING PROGRESS CHECK

Explaining According to Freud, what determines much of human behavior?

Extreme Nationalism

GUIDING QUESTION *What role did nationalism play in the late 1800s?*

Nationalism became more intense in many countries in the late 1800s. **Social Darwinism** was the radical belief that Darwin's theory of natural selection could be applied to modern human societies. A British philosopher, Herbert Spencer, argued that social progress came from "the survival of the fittest"—that is, the strong advanced while the weak declined. This kind of thinking allowed some people to reject the idea that they should take care of the less fortunate.

Extreme nationalists also used Social Darwinism. They said that nations, too, were engaged in a "struggle for existence" in which only the fittest nations would survive. This idea was also used to justify racism, or the belief that some peoples were superior to others.

The growth of extreme nationalism and racism also led to the growth of anti-Semitism, or hostility toward and discrimination against Jews. The **intensity** of anti-Semitism was evident from the Dreyfus affair in France. In 1894, a military court found Alfred Dreyfus, a Jewish captain in the French general staff, guilty of selling army secrets. After the trial, evidence emerged that proved Dreyfus innocent. A wave of public outcry finally forced the government to pardon Dreyfus in 1899.

The worst treatment of Jews at the turn of the century occurred in Russia. Persecutions and **pogroms**, or organized massacres, were widespread. Hundreds of thousands of Jews decided to emigrate to escape the persecution. Some Jews, probably about 25,000, immigrated to Palestine, in the Ottoman Empire, which became home for a Jewish nationalist movement called **Zionism**.

For many Jews, the land of ancient Israel, had long been the land of their dreams. A key figure in the growth of political Zionism was Theodor Herzl, who stated in his book *The Jewish State* (1896), "The Jews who wish it will have their state." Settlement in the Palestine region was difficult, however, because it was then part of the Ottoman Empire, which was opposed to Jewish immigration. Although 3,000 Jews went annually to Palestine between 1904 and 1914, the Zionist desire for a homeland remained only a dream on the eve of World War I.

Social Darwinism theory used by Western nations in the late nineteenth century to justify their dominance; it was based on Charles Darwin's theory of natural selection, "the survival of the fittest," and applied to modern human activities

intensity extreme degree of strength, force, energy, or feeling

pogrom the organized massacre of a minority group, especially Jews

Zionism an international movement originally for the establishment of a Jewish national homeland in Palestine, where ancient Israel was located, and later for the support of modern Israel

✓ **READING PROGRESS CHECK**

Analyzing How did the Dreyfus affair illustrate anti-Semitism in France?

LESSON 4 REVIEW TEKS

Reviewing Vocabulary

1. ***Synthesizing*** Write a paragraph on European nationalism and persecution in the late nineteenth and early twentieth centuries in which you define the terms *pogrom* and *Zionism*.

Using Your Notes

2. ***Identifying*** Use your notes to name four artists and identify characteristics of the art movements in which they participated. 26A

Answering the Guiding Questions

3. ***Evaluating*** How did innovation change literature, the visual arts, and music in the late 1800s? 26A, 26B

4. ***Identifying Central Issues*** How did scientific discoveries in the late 1800s impact the way people saw themselves and their world? 28E

5. ***Drawing Conclusions*** What role did nationalism play in the late 1800s?

Writing Activity

6. **INFORMATIVE/EXPLANATORY** Write a paragraph in which you explore how modern artistic and scientific ideas could lead to an understanding of the world as less certain than was previously believed but also, perhaps, as more exciting. Discuss at least one example of an artist and one example of a scientist. 26A, 28E

CHAPTER 24 Assessment

TEKS

Directions: On a separate sheet of paper, answer the questions below. Make sure you read carefully and answer all parts of the questions.

Lesson Review

Lesson 1

1. ***Identifying*** Which contributions of this era made day-to-day living easier? **28E**

2. ***Specifying*** Which "firsts" of this era would come to influence communication and travel?

3. ***Identifying*** What led to the start of the Second Industrial Revolution? **1E, 8E**

4. ***Explaining*** How did consumers' ability to make purchases, including what and where they purchased, shift?

5. ***Explaining*** How did the Second Industrial Revolution cause political and economic changes in Europe? **8B, 17B**

6. ***Identifying*** What were the characteristics of communism and socialism? Explain the influence of Karl Marx on these ideas. **18B, 18C**

Lesson 2

7. ***Describing*** Describe the new white-collar workers and the variety of middle-class occupations.

8. ***Explaining*** What reforms and advancements led to improved living conditions for the new urban majority? **8B**

9. ***Identifying Cause and Effect*** How did higher-paying jobs for the working class shift the structure and roles for working-class families?

10. ***Describing*** Briefly, explain the progression of the women's rights movement during this period. **24A**

Lesson 3

11. ***Identifying*** What characteristics of democracy were apparent in western Europe by the late nineteenth century? **19B**

12. ***Comparing*** Compare the governing systems in the dual Austro-Hungarian Empire?

13. ***Explaining*** What led to the event in St. Petersburg known as "Bloody Sunday"?

14. ***Identifying Central Issues*** How was wealth distributed among U.S. citizens?

Lesson 4

15. ***Identifying*** What significant examples of art demonstrate artistic ideals or visual principles from the period? **26A**

16. ***Identifying*** What significant examples of architecture demonstrate artistic ideals or visual principles from the period? **26A**

17. ***Analyzing*** What examples of literature from the period reflect and transcend the culture in which they were produced and convey universal themes? **26B, 26C**

18. ***Identifying*** What were the *pogroms*, and how did they lead to a new settlement in Palestine?

Need Extra Help?

If You've Missed Question	1	2	3	4	5	6	7	8	9	10	11	12	13	14	15	16	17	18
Go to page	560	560	560	561	562	562	565	566	567	567	571	573	573	574	576	577	576	579

Exploring the Essential Question

19 ***Synthesizing*** Create a word web with the word *Industrialization* in the center circle. Draw arrows to two radiating circles, labeled *Strong Economy* and *Weak Economy*. Draw another layer of radiating circles from each of these circles to show which political and social structures were influenced by economic changes in 1870–1914. Explain each of the connections. **8B, 17B, 24A**

Critical Thinking

20 ***Comparing and Contrasting*** What did the First and Second Industrial Revolutions have in common? In what ways did they differ?

21 ***Comparing and Contrasting*** Compare and contrast pure Marxism with revisionist Marxism.

22 ***Constructing Arguments*** Argue for or against Marx's description of European society in the mid-1800s as two distinct groups, the bourgeoisie and the proletariat.

23 ***Drawing Conclusions*** What conclusions can you draw about the quality of life and lifestyle of urban workers in the 1870s, the period that followed labor reforms, such as 10-hour workdays, six-day work week, and increased wages?

24 ***Making Inferences*** When did public education become widespread and why had it not happened earlier?

25 ***Speculating*** How might extreme nationalists' perceptions of themselves have led them to believe in Social Darwinism?

26 ***Drawing Conclusions*** What conclusion can you draw about Igor Stravinsky's composition *The Rite of Spring* based on the extreme reaction of the audience?

Social Studies Skills

27 ***Economics*** Compare the two main zones of European economic development in the early twentieth century.

28 ***Economics*** How did industrial investments and activities, as well as the global marketplace, lead Europe to becoming dominant in the world economy by 1900?

29 ***Understanding Relationships Among Events*** What were some reasons that democracy was expanding in the late nineteenth century?

30 ***Research Skills*** Choose one of the figures that impacted scientific thinking in the late 1800s, such as Marie Curie, Albert Einstein, and Sigmund Freud, and summarize the shift in thinking that came as a result of his or her work. **28E**

DBQ Analyzing Primary Sources

Use the document to answer the following questions.

Emmeline Pankhurst explained in a 1913 speech why it was so important for women to have a voice in their government:

PRIMARY SOURCE

"I wonder that women have the courage to take upon themselves the responsibilities of marriage and motherhood when I see how little protection the law of my country affords them. I wonder that a woman will face the ordeal of childbirth with the knowledge that after she has risked her life to bring a child into the world she has absolutely no parental rights over the future of that child."

—quoted in *Sources of the Western Tradition, Volume II: From the Renaissance to the Present*

31 ***Identifying Bias in Written Material*** How does Pankhurst show bias in this excerpt? **29E**

32 ***Drawing Conclusions*** How does Pankhurst's description reflect the changing roles of women discussed in this lesson? **24A**

Need Extra Help?

If You've Missed Question	19	20	21	22	23	24	25	26	27	28	29	30	31	32
Go to page	560	560	563	563	566	568	579	578	561	562	571	578	581	566

33 ***Interpreting*** How do Pankhurst's words introduce doubts about the accepted tradition of women's roles, and how might people have reacted to her instigation that former ideas should shift?

Analyzing Visuals

Use the image to answer the following questions.

The map shows the population density in Europe in 1900.

34 ***Analyzing Geographic Distributions*** What can you conclude about the yellow areas of the map surrounding the orange and red areas? **15B**

35 ***Comparing Geographic Distributions*** How do the German and Austro-Hungarian Empires compare with the Russian Empire? **15B**

Extended Response Question

36 ***Expository*** How do the living conditions of the masses affect how a nation is governed? How does a move toward democracy affect these living conditions?

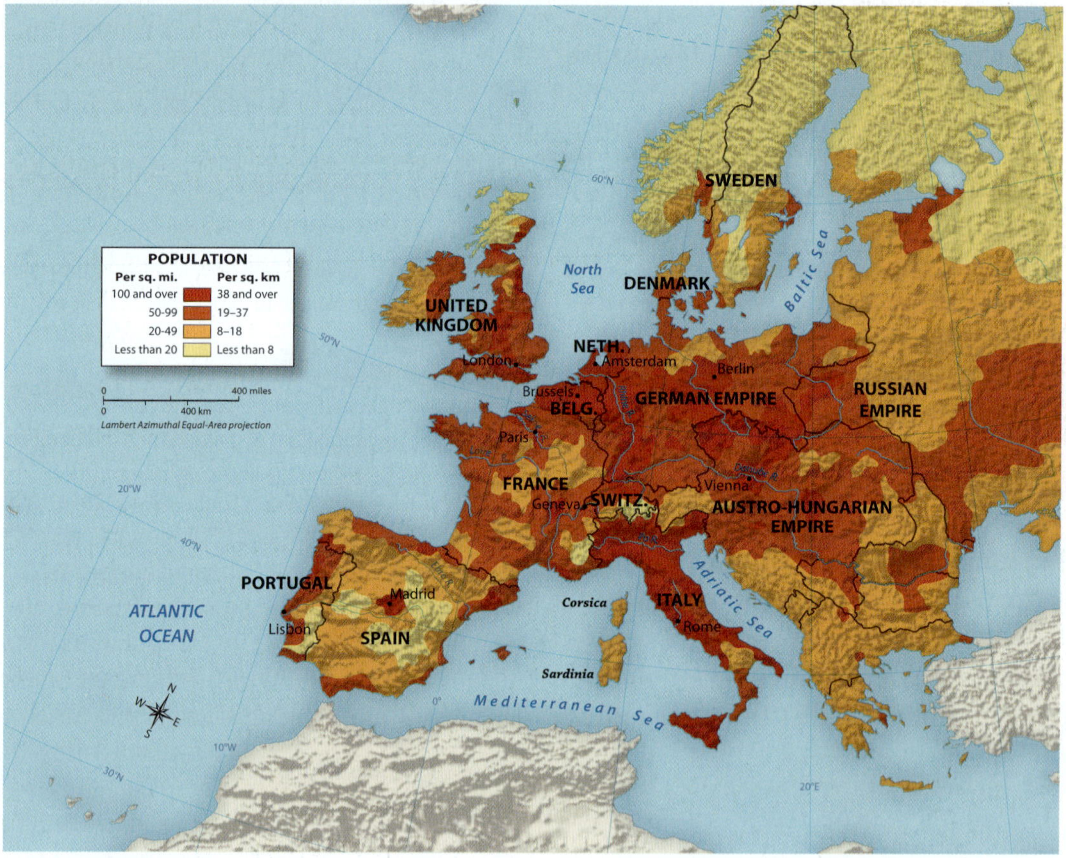

Need Extra Help?

If You've Missed Question	33	34	35	36
Go to page	581	569	569	564

The Reach of Imperialism

1800–1914

ESSENTIAL QUESTIONS • *What are the causes and effects of imperialism?* • *How do some groups resist control by others?*

networks

There's More Online! about the reach of imperialism.

CHAPTER 25

The Story Matters...

After 1870 the industrialized nations of Europe engaged in an unprecedented competition to acquire overseas colonies. A struggle for economic and military power largely motivated this intense rivalry, which historians refer to as the "new imperialism." The "Jewel in the Crown" of the vast British Empire was India. The British attempted to dominate every aspect of Indian life, including the culture. One Indian who resisted this cultural imperialism was the Bengali writer Rabindranath Tagore.

◀ This photograph shows Tagore in 1929, when he was nearly 70. Although a passionate nationalist, he nevertheless strove for a balance between modern Western influence and ancient Indian traditions. One expression of this effort was his habit of writing his poetry first in Bengali and then translating it into English.

CHAPTER 25

Place and Time: Asia and Africa 1800–1914

The nineteenth century was known for a new wave of imperialism as European powers, Japan, and the United States seized control of new territories and conquered peoples in Asia and Africa. The race for new colonies was fueled by competition among the European powers, nationalism, demand for raw materials, superior technology, and a belief in racial hierarchies. In Latin America, independence movements struggling to throw off Spanish authority succeeded by the mid-nineteenth century.

Step Into the Place

Read the quotes and look at the information presented on the map.

DBQ **Analyzing Historical Documents** In 1893 Frederick Lugard was arguing for more funding for African colonies, while journalists like Edmund Morel argued against the practice. What were the central motivations for imperialism, and what were the perceived costs to conquered peoples?

PRIMARY SOURCE

"We owe to the instincts of colonial expansion of our ancestors, those vast and noble dependencies which are our pride and the outlets of our trade to-day; and we are accountable to posterity that opportunities which now present themselves of extending the sphere of our industrial enterprise are not neglected, for the opportunities now offered will never recur again."

—Frederick Lugard, British colonial administrator, from *The Rise of Our East African Empire,* 1893

PRIMARY SOURCE

"What the partial occupation of his soil by the white man has failed to do; what the mapping out of European political 'spheres of influence' has failed to do; what the maxim and the rifle, the slave gang, labour in the bowels of the earth and the lash, have failed to do; what imported [diseases] have failed to do; what even the oversea slave trade failed to do, the power of modern capitalistic exploitation, assisted by modern engines of destruction, may yet succeed in accomplishing. For from the evils of the latter, scientifically applied and enforced, there is no escape for the African."

—Edmund D. Morel, British author, from *The Black Man's Burden,* 1920

PHOTO: (l)Library of Congress, Prints & Photographs Division, (r)©Pictoral Press Ltd/Alamy

Step Into the Time

Choose an event from the time line and explain how it shows resistance to European imperialism.

AFRICA, ASIA, AND LATIN AMERICA

- **1819** Great Britain sends Sir Thomas Raffles to Singapore.
- **1830** French take over Algeria
- **1830** Belgium creates an independent state
- **1841** Explorer David Livingstone arrives in Africa

1800 — 1815 — 1830

THE WORLD

- **1807** Slave trade to British colonies outlawed
- **1812** Napoleon invades Russia

networks *There's More Online!*

- **MAP** Explore the interactive version of this map on Networks.
- **TIME LINE** Explore the interactive version of the time line on Networks.

The Spread of European Colonialism by 1914

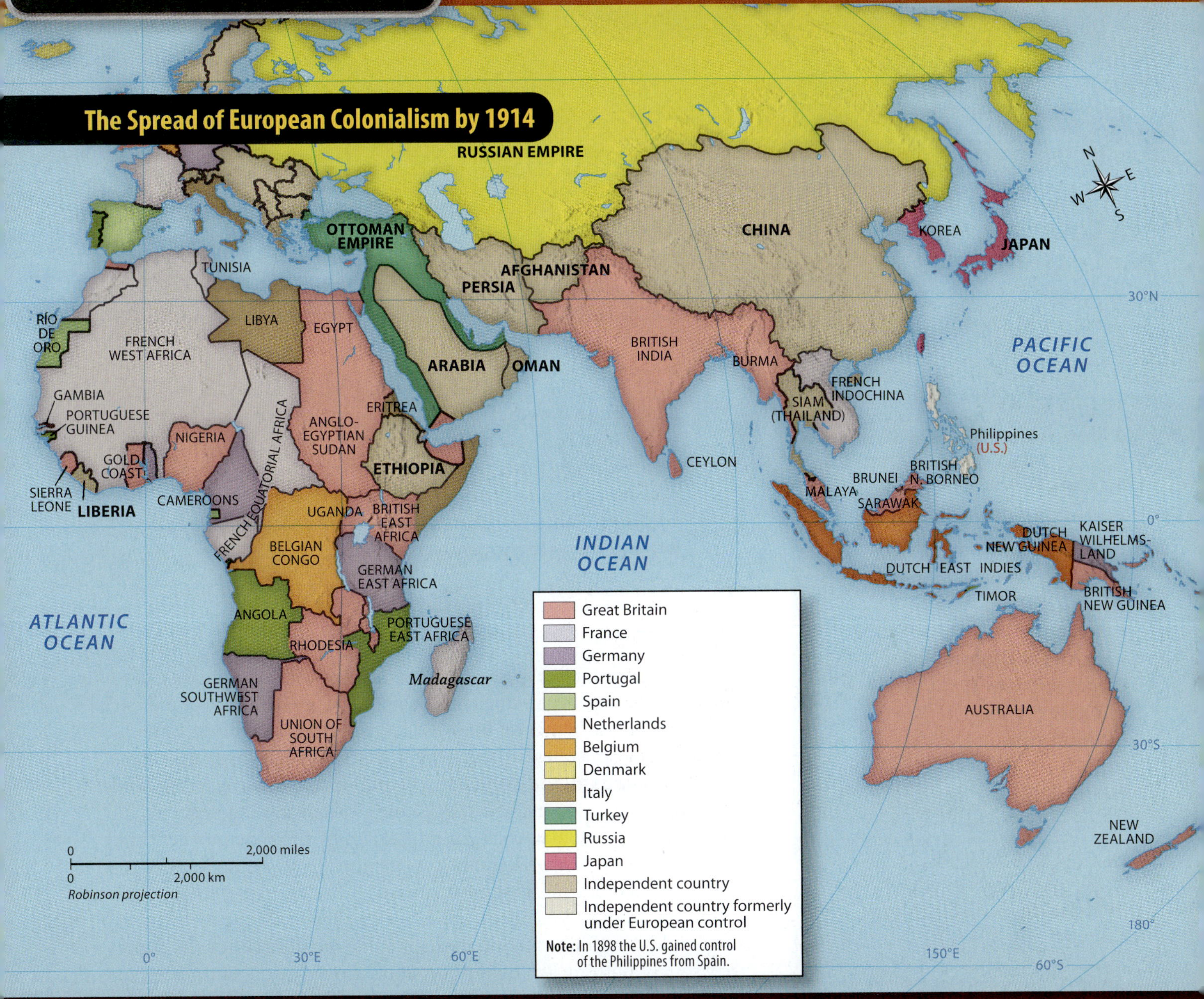

1845 – 1914

- **1848** Demonstrations erupt in the Austrian Empire
- **1857** Great Rebellion begins in India
- **1861** Jefferson Davis leads Confederacy as U.S. Civil War begins
- **1874** Great Britain annexes west coastal states of Africa
- **1877** "Jim Crow" laws enforce segregation in southern United States
- **1893** Union of French Indochina formed
- **1896** Ethiopians defeat Italian army at Adowa
- **1900** Most of Southeast Asia under Western rule
- **1907** France, Great Britain, and Russia create Triple Entente
- **1914** Panama Canal opens
- **1914** Assassination of Archduke Francis Ferdinand

networks

There's More Online!

- ☑ CHART/GRAPH Major Regions of European Control
- ☑ IMAGE Government Palace at Saigon
- ☑ IMAGE Infrastructure in Cambodia, 1900
- ☑ IMAGE Revolt Against Colonialism in the Philippines, 1899
- ☑ INTERACTIVE SELF-CHECK QUIZ
- ☑ MAP Imperialism in Southeast Asia, 1900
- ☑ VIDEO Colonial Trade

Reading HELPDESK

Academic Vocabulary

- **exploit**
- **export**

Content Vocabulary

- **imperialism**
- **racism**
- **gunboat diplomacy**
- **protectorate**
- **indirect rule**
- **direct rule**

TAKING NOTES:

Key Ideas and Details

Identifying Use a graphic organizer like this one to identify the political status of various regions of Southeast Asia.

Region	Political Status
Burma	
Singapore	
Vietnam	
Thailand	
Philippines	

imperialism the extension of a nation's power over other lands

LESSON 1
Colonial Rule in Southeast Asia

ESSENTIAL QUESTIONS

- *What are the causes and effects of imperialism?*
- *How do some groups resist control by others?*

It Matters Because

During the nineteenth century, many Western powers scrambled for new territories in Southeast Asia and Africa. Governing by either indirect or direct rule, the Western powers controlled the governments and economies of their colonies. Some territories resisted colonial rule, but most early resistance movements failed.

The New Imperialism

GUIDING QUESTION *What were the motivations for the new imperialism?*

In the nineteenth century, a new phase of Western expansion began. European nations began to view Asia and Africa as a source of industrial raw materials and a market for Western manufactured goods. In the 1880s, European states began an intense scramble for overseas territory. **Imperialism**, the extension of a nation's power over other lands, was not new. Europeans had set up colonies and trading posts in North America, South America, and Africa by the sixteenth century.

However, the imperialism of the late nineteenth century, called the "new imperialism" by some historians, was different. Earlier, European states had been content to set up a few trading posts where they could carry on trade and perhaps some missionary activity. Now they sought nothing less than direct control over vast territories.

Why did Westerners begin to increase their search for colonies after 1880? Economic and political motivations were central. Capitalist states in the West were looking for both markets and raw materials such as rubber, oil, and tin for their industries. European nation-states also wanted to acquire colonies to gain advantages over their political rivals. Colonies were a source of prestige. To some people, in fact, a nation could not be great without colonies.

In addition, imperialism had major social motivations and was tied to Social Darwinism and racism. Social Darwinists believed that in the struggle between nations, the fit are victorious. **Racism** is the belief that race determines traits and capabilities. Racists erroneously believe that particular races are superior or inferior.

Racist beliefs led to the use of military force against other nations. Some Europeans had more religious and humanitarian social motivations. They believed Europeans had a moral responsibility to civilize primitive people. They called this responsibility the "white man's burden." To some, this meant bringing the Christian message to the "heathen masses." To others, it meant bringing the benefits of Western democracy and capitalism to these societies.

The Role of Technology in Imperialism

Nineteenth-century technological developments were also important in the development and growth of imperialism. New military weapons, such as the machine gun, gave Europeans a superior military force, enabling them in pitched battles to massacre natives who resisted a takeover of their lands. Military superiority also gave European nations a huge advantage over these new territories. European nations could often get what they wanted from Asian and African societies with only the presence of a powerful navy, a process referred to as **gunboat diplomacy**.

New forms of transportation, a direct result of the Industrial Revolution in Europe, helped advance imperialism as well. Technological developments in railroad and steam power allowed Europeans to travel more easily. These new forms of transportation also helped Europeans remove resources from colonies more easily. Moreover, new forms of communication played a role in advancing imperialism. The telegraph, for example, allowed colonial regimes to communicate with Europe faster than ever before, giving European nations a high degree of control over their colonies.

Medical advancements also served to further imperialist adventures. Long journeys and tropical climates took a heavy toll on European conquerors. New medicines, such as the use of quinine to combat malaria, made it possible for

racism the belief that race determines a person's traits and capabilities

gunboat diplomacy The practice of one state threatening another state with a nearby navy to force a treaty or unfair privileges.

SKILLS PRACTICE

As you read about colonial rule in Southeast Asia, think about the new words you see. Do you already know something about these words?

TEKS Texas Essential Knowledge and Skills

1E identify major causes and describe the major effects of the following important turning points in world history from 1750 to 1914: the Scientific Revolution, the Industrial Revolution and its impact on the development of modern economic systems, European imperialism, and the Enlightenment's impact on political revolutions

8C identify the major political, economic, and social motivations that influenced European imperialism

continued on the next page

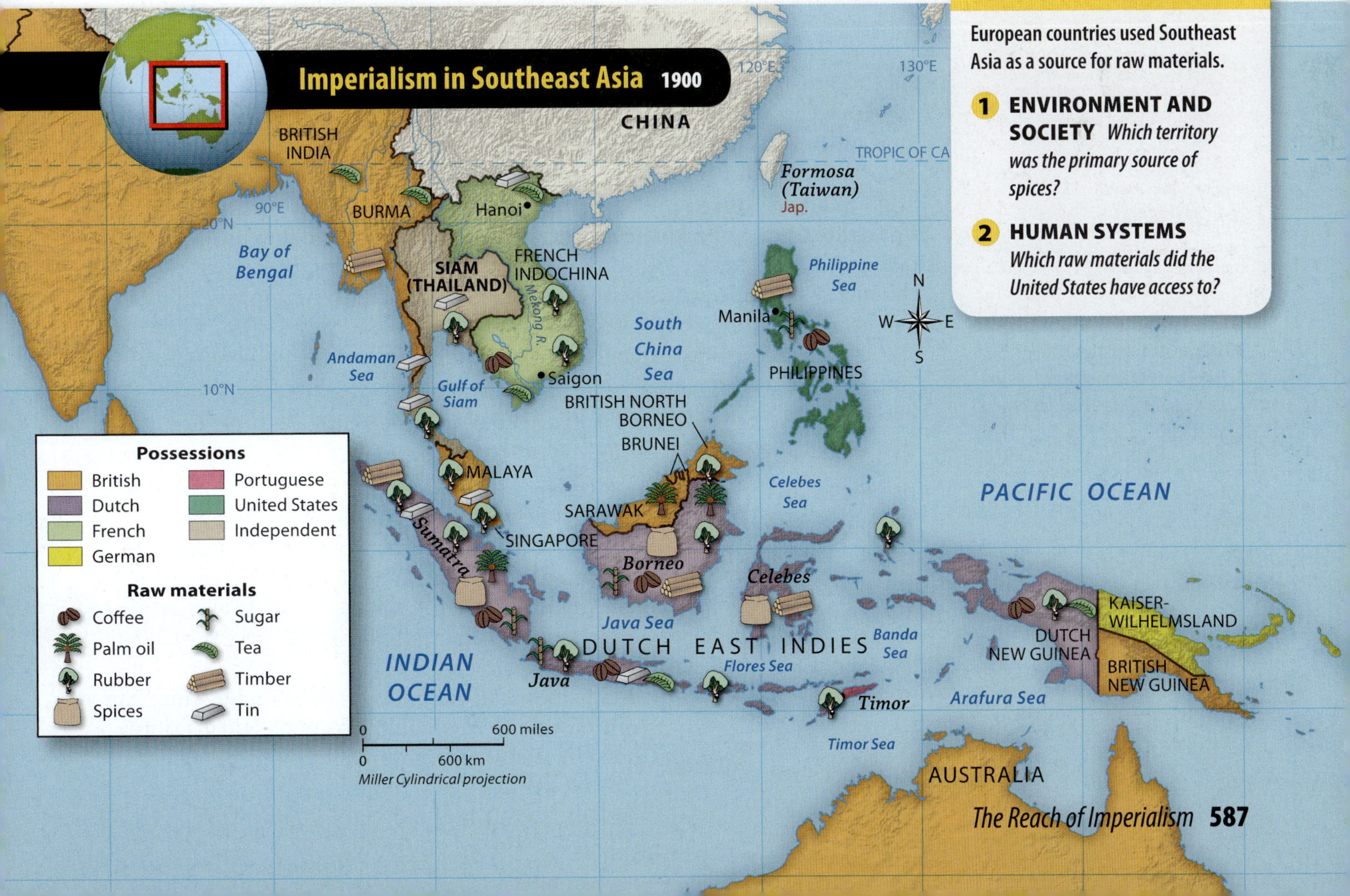

GEOGRAPHY CONNECTION

European countries used Southeast Asia as a source for raw materials.

1. **ENVIRONMENT AND SOCIETY** *Which territory was the primary source of spices?*
2. **HUMAN SYSTEMS** *Which raw materials did the United States have access to?*

Analyzing PRIMARY SOURCES

American Imperialism

"Mr. President, the times call for candor. The Philippines are ours forever. And just beyond the Philippines are China's illimitable markets. We will not retreat from either. We will not abandon an opportunity in [Asia]. We will not renounce our part in the mission of our race, trustee, under God, of the civilization of the world."

—Senator Albert Beveridge, from a speech before the U.S. Senate, January 9, 1900

DBQ ***ANALYZING*** How does Beveridge's statement reflect a mixture of moral idealism and a desire for profit?

protectorate a political unit that depends on another government for its protection

(continued from p. 587)

TEKS **Texas Essential Knowledge and Skills**

8D explain the major characteristics and impact of European imperialism

28B explain the roles of military technology, transportation technology, communication technology, and medical advancements in initiating and advancing 19th century imperialism

Europeans to live in difficult climates. Thus, larger numbers of Europeans could now survive in Africa and Asia.

✓ READING PROGRESS CHECK

Explaining How did Europeans justify imperialism?

Colonial Takeover

GUIDING QUESTION ***What led to Western dominance in Southeast Asia?***

The new imperialism was evident in Southeast Asia. In 1800 the Europeans ruled only two societies in this area: the Spanish Philippines and the Dutch East Indies. By 1900 virtually the entire area was under Western rule.

Great Britain

The process began with Great Britain. In 1819 Great Britain sent Sir Thomas Stamford Raffles to found a new colony on a small island at the tip of the Malay Peninsula. Called Singapore ("city of the lion"), in the new age of steamships, it soon became a major stopping point for traffic traveling to or from China.

During the next few decades, the British advance into Southeast Asia continued. Next to fall was the kingdom of Burma (modern Myanmar). Britain wanted control of Burma in order to protect its possessions in India. It also sought a land route through Burma into southern China. Although the difficult terrain along the frontier between Burma and China caused this effort to fail, British activities in Burma led to the collapse of the Burmese monarchy. Britain soon established control over the entire country.

France

France, which had some missionaries operating in Vietnam, nervously watched the British advance into Burma. The local Vietnamese authorities, who viewed Christianity as a threat to Confucian doctrine, persecuted the French missionaries. However, Vietnam failed to stop the Christian missionaries. Vietnamese internal rivalries divided the country into two separate governments—the north and the south.

France was especially alarmed by British attempts to monopolize trade. To stop any British movement into Vietnam, the French government decided in 1857 to force the Vietnamese to accept French protection.

The French eventually succeeded in making the Vietnamese ruler give up territories in the Mekong River delta. The French occupied the city of Saigon and, during the next 30 years, extended their control over the rest of the country. In 1883 France seized the city of Hanoi and later made the Vietnamese empire a French **protectorate**.

In the 1880s, France extended its control over neighboring Cambodia, Annam, Tonkin, and Laos. By 1887 France included all its new possessions in a new Union of French Indochina.

The United States

In 1898 during the Spanish-American War, U.S. naval forces under Commodore George Dewey defeated the Spanish fleet in Manila Bay in the Philippines. Believing it was his moral obligation to "civilize" other parts of the world, President William McKinley decided to turn the Philippines, which had been under Spanish control, into an American colony. This action would also prevent the area from falling into the hands of the Japanese. The islands gave the United States convenient access to trade with China.

Many Filipinos did not wish to be under American control. Emilio Aguinaldo (AH • gee • NAHL • doh) was the leader of a movement for independence in

▼ This photograph shows King Norodom of Cambodia and his son being transported in a Western-style carriage in 1900.

▶ CRITICAL THINKING

Drawing Conclusions How did the French influence life in Cambodia?

the Philippines. He began his revolt against the Spanish and went into exile in 1898. When the United States acquired the Philippines, Aguinaldo continued the revolt and set himself up as the president of the Republic of the Philippines. Led by Aguinaldo, the guerrilla forces fought bitterly against the U.S. troops to establish their independence.

The fight for Philippine independence resulted in three years of bloody warfare. However, the United States eventually defeated the guerrilla forces, and President McKinley had his stepping-stone to the rich markets of China.

✓ READING PROGRESS CHECK

Identifying What prompted Britain to colonize Singapore and Burma?

▲ Filipinos mount an insurrection against the Americans in Manila in February 1899.

▶ CRITICAL THINKING

Analyzing Visuals Contrast the depiction of the Filipinos with that of the American soldiers.

Impact of Imperialism in Southeast Asia

GUIDING QUESTION *How did colonial powers govern their colonies?*

Western powers governed their new colonial empires by either indirect or direct rule. Their chief goals were to **exploit** the natural resources of the lands and to open up markets for their own manufactured goods.

exploit to make use of meanly or unfairly for one's own advantage

Indirect and Direct Rule

Sometimes a colonial power could realize its goals by cooperating with local political elites. For example, the Dutch East India Company used **indirect rule** in the Dutch East Indies. Under indirect rule, local rulers were allowed to keep their authority and status in a new colonial setting. This made access to the region's natural resources easier. Indirect rule was cheaper because fewer officials had to be trained. It also affected local culture less.

indirect rule a colonial government in which local rulers are allowed to maintain their positions of authority and status

However, indirect rule was not always possible. Some local elites resisted foreign conquest. In these cases, the local elites were replaced with Western officials. This system was called **direct rule**. Great Britain administered Burma directly through its colonial government in India. In Indochina, France used both systems. It imposed direct rule in southern Vietnam but ruled indirectly through the emperor in northern Vietnam.

direct rule colonial government in which local elites were removed from power and replaced by a new set of officials brought from the colonizing country

To justify their conquests, Western powers spoke of bringing the blessings of Western civilization to their colonial subjects, including representative government. However, many Westerners came to fear the idea of native peoples (especially educated ones) being allowed political rights.

Colonial Economies

The colonial powers did not want their colonists to develop their own industries. Thus, colonial policy stressed the **export** of raw materials. This policy often led to the development of plantation agriculture. In this system, peasants worked as wage laborers on the foreign-owned plantations. Plantation owners kept wages at poverty levels to increase profits. Conditions on plantations were often so unhealthful that thousands died. Also, peasants bore the burden of high taxes.

export to send a product or service for sale to another country

Nevertheless, colonial rule did bring some benefits to Southeast Asia. A modern economic system began there. Colonial governments built railroads, highways, and other structures that benefited native peoples as well as colonials. The development of an export market helped create an entrepreneurial class in rural areas. In the Dutch East Indies, for example, small growers of rubber, palm oil, coffee, tea, and spices began to share in the profits of the colonial enterprise. Most of the profits, however, were taken back to the colonizing country.

✓ READING PROGRESS CHECK

Describing What kind of economic system did colonial rulers establish?

Resistance to Colonial Rule

GUIDING QUESTION *How did indigenous people in Southeast Asia respond to colonial rule?*

Many subject peoples in Southeast Asia resented colonization. At first, resistance came from the existing ruling class. In Burma, for example, the monarch himself fought Western domination. By contrast, in Vietnam, after the emperor had agreed to French control of his country, a number of government officials set up an organization called Can Vuong ("Save the King"). They fought against the French without the emperor's help.

Sometimes resistance to Western control took the form of peasant revolts. Peasants were often driven off the land to make way for plantation agriculture. Angry peasants then vented their anger at the foreign invaders. For example, in Burma, in 1930 the Buddhist monk Saya San led a peasant uprising against the British colonial regime.

Early resistance movements failed. They were overcome by Western powers. In the early 1900s, however, a new kind of resistance emerged that was based on nationalism. The leaders were often from a new class that the colonial rule had created: Westernized intellectuals in the cities. They were the first generation of Asians to embrace the institutions and values of the West. Many were educated in the West, spoke Western languages, and worked in jobs connected with the colonial regimes.

At first, many of the leaders of these movements did not focus clearly on the idea of nationhood. Instead, they simply tried to defend the economic interests or religious beliefs of the native peoples. In Burma, for example, students at the University of Rangoon formed an organization to protest against official persecution of the Buddhist religion and British lack of respect for local religious traditions. They protested against British arrogance and failure to observe local customs in Buddhist temples. Not until the 1930s, however, did these resistance movements, such as those begun in Burma, begin to demand national independence.

▼ This 1874 engraving depicts the government palace at Saigon, which the French constructed to administer Indochina.

PHOTO: The new government palace at Saigon, from L'Illustration, 1874 (engraving), French School, (19th century)/Private Collection/Archives Charmet/The Bridgeman Art Library

READING PROGRESS CHECK

Analyzing Why were resistance movements often led by Southeast Asian people who had been educated in the West?

LESSON 1 REVIEW TEKS

Reviewing Vocabulary

1. ***Describing*** Write a paragraph describing different forms of colonial rule. Be sure to define *protectorate, direct rule,* and *indirect rule* and to discuss specific examples.

Using Your Notes

2. ***Summarizing*** Use your notes to write a paragraph summarizing the political situation of the regions of Southeast Asia by 1900.

Answering the Guiding Questions

3. ***Analyzing*** What were the motivations for the new imperialism?
4. ***Identifying Cause and Effect*** What led to Western dominance in Southeast Asia?
5. ***Explaining*** How did colonial powers govern their colonies?
6. ***Analyzing*** How did indigenous people in Southeast Asia respond to colonial rule?

Writing Activity

7. **INFORMATIVE/EXPLANATORY** Write an essay discussing the effects of colonial rule on the countries that were colonized. Be sure to discuss at least two specific examples.

networks

There's More Online!

- IMAGE Diamond Mine in South Africa
- IMAGE Henry Stanley and David Livingstone
- IMAGE Surrender of Zulu Chief Cetewayo, 1879
- INTERACTIVE SELF-CHECK QUIZ
- MAP Imperialism in Africa, 1914
- PRIMARY SOURCE Stanley Finds Livingstone
- TIME LINE Colonialism in South Africa
- VIDEO The Zulu War

LESSON 2
Empire Building in Africa

ESSENTIAL QUESTIONS

- *What are the causes and effects of imperialism?*
- *How do some groups resist control by others?*

Reading **HELP**DESK

Academic Vocabulary

- **uncharted** • **traditions**

Content Vocabulary

- **annex** • **indigenous**

TAKING NOTES:

Key Ideas and Details

Categorizing Use the graphic organizer to show which countries controlled different parts of Africa.

Western Power	Area of Africa
Belgium	
Britain	
France	
Germany	

TEKS Texas Essential Knowledge and Skills

1E identify major causes and describe the major effects of the following important turning points in world history from 1750 to 1914: the Scientific Revolution, the Industrial Revolution and its impact on the development of modern economic systems, European imperialism, and the Enlightenment's impact on political revolutions

8D explain the major characteristics and impact of European imperialism

continued on the next page

IT MATTERS BECAUSE

During the late nineteenth century, the major European powers scrambled to colonize Africa. Virtually all of Africa was under European rule by 1900. Maintaining that rule was not easy, however. African nationalism emerged during the early part of the twentieth century.

West Africa and North Africa

GUIDING QUESTION *Why were European countries interested in West Africa and North Africa?*

Before 1880, Europeans controlled little of the African continent directly. They were content to let African rulers and merchants represent European interests. Between 1880 and 1900, however, Great Britain, France, Germany, Belgium, Italy, Spain, and Portugal, spurred by intense rivalries among themselves, placed virtually all of Africa under European rule.

West Africa

Europeans had a keen interest in Africa's raw materials, especially those of West Africa—peanuts, timber, hides, and palm oil. Earlier in the nineteenth century, Europeans had profited from the slave trade in this region of Africa. By the late 1800s, however, trade in enslaved people had virtually ended. As the slave trade declined, Europe's interest in other forms of trade increased. The growing European presence in West Africa led to increasing tensions with African governments in the region.

For a long time, most African states were able to maintain their independence. However, in 1874 Great Britain **annexed** (incorporated a country within another country) the west coastal states as the first British colony of Gold Coast. At about the same time, Britain established a protectorate in Nigeria. By 1900, France had added the huge area of French West Africa to its colonial empire. This left France in control of the largest part of West Africa. In addition, Germany controlled Togo, Cameroon, German Southwest Africa, and German East Africa.

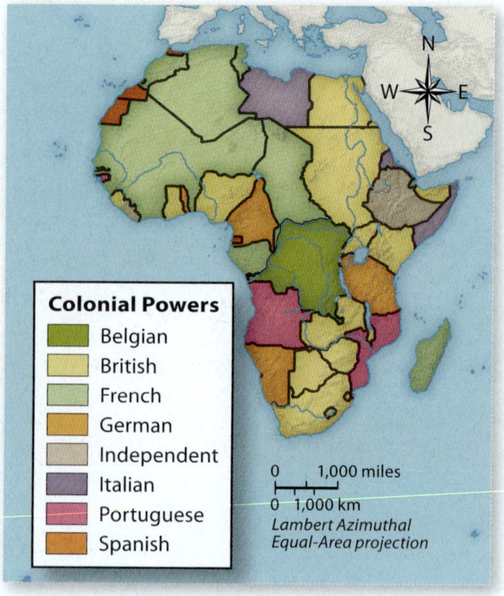

▶ **CRITICAL THINKING**

Drawing Conclusions Which colonial power controlled most of West Africa?

North Africa

Egypt had been part of the Ottoman Empire, but as Ottoman rule declined, the Egyptians sought their independence. In 1805 an officer of the Ottoman army named Muhammad Ali seized power and established a separate Egyptian state.

During the next 30 years, Muhammad Ali introduced a series of reforms to bring Egypt into the modern world. He modernized the army, set up a public school system, and helped create small industries that refined sugar, produced textiles and munitions, and built ships.

The growing economic importance of the Nile Valley in Egypt, along with the development of steamships, gave Europeans the desire to build a canal east of Cairo to connect the Mediterranean and Red Seas. Suez, located in Egypt on a thin strip of land between these seas, was an ideal location for a canal. Such a canal would allow transport between Europe and Asia, without traveling around Africa.These factors of human and physical geography were sufficient justification for French entrepreneur, Ferdinand de Lesseps, to sign a contract in 1854 to begin building the Suez Canal. The canal was completed in 1869.

The British took an active interest in Egypt after the Suez Canal was opened. Believing that the canal was its "lifeline to India," Great Britain tried to gain as much control as possible over the canal area.

In 1875 Britain bought Egypt's share in the Suez Canal. When an Egyptian army revolt against foreign influence broke out in 1881, Britain suppressed the revolt. Egypt became a British protectorate in 1914.

The British believed that they should also control Sudan, south of Egypt, to protect their interests in Egypt and the Suez Canal. In 1881 Muslim cleric Muhammad Ahmad, known as the Mahdi (in Arabic, "the rightly guided one"), launched a revolt that brought much of Sudan under his control.

annex to incorporate into an existing political unit, such as a city or country

Britain sent a military force under General Charles Gordon to restore Egyptian authority over Sudan. However, Muhammad Ahmad's troops wiped out Gordon's army at Khartoum in 1885. General Gordon himself died in the battle. Not until 1898 were British troops able to seize Sudan.

The French also had colonies in North Africa. In 1879 after about 150,000 French people had settled in the region of Algeria, the French government established control there. Two years later, France imposed a protectorate on neighboring Tunisia. In 1912 France established a protectorate over much of Morocco.

Italy joined the competition for colonies in North Africa by attempting to take over Ethiopia. In 1896, however, the Italian invading forces were defeated. Italy now was the only European state defeated by an African state. This humiliating loss led Italy to try again in 1911. Italy invaded and seized Turkish Tripoli, which it renamed Libya.

✓ **READING PROGRESS CHECK**

Summarizing What motivated the British to compete for control of Egypt?

(continued from p. 591)

TEKS **Texas Essential Knowledge and Skills**

16B analyze the influence of human and physical geographic factors on major events in world history, including the development of river valley civilizations, trade in the Indian Ocean, and the opening of the Panama and Suez canals

21B describe the rights and responsibilities of citizens and noncitizens in civic participation throughout history

Central and East Africa

GUIDING QUESTION ***Why did European countries compete for colonies in Central Africa and East Africa?***

Central Africa

Central African territories were soon added to the list of European colonies. European explorers aroused popular interest in the dense tropical jungles of Central Africa.

David Livingstone was one such explorer. He arrived in Africa in 1841 as a 27-year-old medical missionary. During the 30 years he spent in Africa, Livingstone trekked through **uncharted** regions. He sometimes traveled by canoe, but mostly Livingstone walked and spent much of his time exploring the interior of the continent.

uncharted not mapped; unknown

During his travels through Africa, Livingstone made detailed notes of his discoveries. He sent this information back to London whenever he could. The maps of Africa were often redrawn based on Livingstone's eyewitness accounts and reports. A major goal of Livingstone's explorations was to find a navigable river that would open Central Africa to European commerce and to Christianity.

When Livingstone disappeared for a while, an American newspaper, the *New York Herald,* hired a young journalist, Henry Stanley, to find the explorer. Stanley did find him, on the eastern shore of Lake Tanganyika. Overwhelmed by finding Livingstone alive if not well, Stanley greeted the explorer with these now-famous words, "Dr. Livingstone, I presume?"

After Livingstone's death in 1873, Stanley decided to carry on the great explorer's work. Unlike Livingstone, however, Henry Stanley had a strong dislike of Africa. He once said, "I detest the land most heartily."

In the 1870s, Stanley explored the Congo River in Central Africa and sailed down it to the Atlantic Ocean. Soon, he was encouraging the British to send settlers to the Congo River basin. When Britain refused, Stanley turned to King Leopold II of Belgium.

King Leopold II was the real driving force behind the colonization of Central Africa. He rushed enthusiastically into the pursuit of an empire in Africa. "To open to civilization," he said, "the only part of our globe where it has yet to penetrate, to pierce the darkness which envelops whole populations, it is, I dare to say, a crusade worthy of this century of progress." Profit, however, was equally important to Leopold. In 1877 he hired Henry Stanley to set up Belgian settlements in the Congo.

Leopold's claim to the vast territories of the Congo aroused widespread concern among other European states. France, in particular, rushed to plant its flag in the heart of Africa. Leopold ended up with the territories around the Congo River. France occupied the areas farther north.

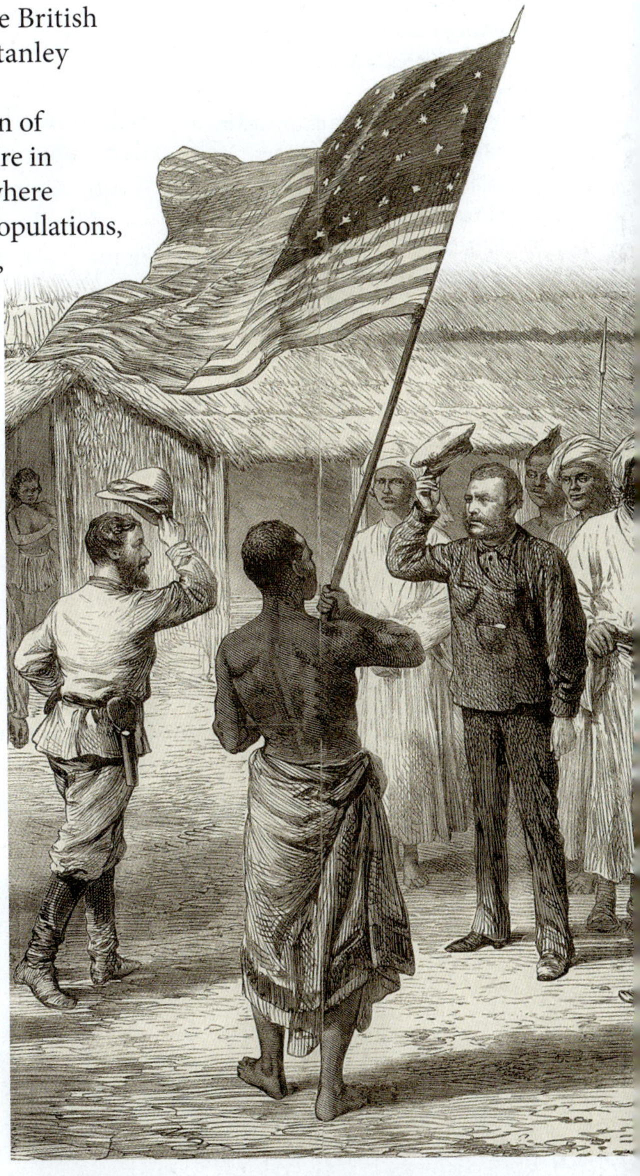

▼ This 1872 British illustration depicts the meeting between Stanley and Livingstone on November 19, 1872.

▶ **CRITICAL THINKING**

Analyzing Why did the phrase "Dr. Livingstone, I presume?" become so famous?

East Africa

By 1885 Britain and Germany had become the chief rivals in East Africa. Germany came late to the ranks of the imperialist powers. At first, the German chancellor Otto von Bismarck had downplayed the importance of colonies. As more and more Germans called for a German empire, however, Bismarck became a convert to colonialism. As he expressed it, "All this colonial business is a sham, but we need it for the elections."

In addition to its West Africa holdings, Germany tried to develop colonies in East Africa. Most of East Africa had not yet been claimed by any other power. However, the British were also interested in the area because control of East Africa would connect the British Empire in Africa from South Africa to Egypt. Portugal and Belgium also claimed parts of East Africa.

To settle conflicting claims, European countries met at the Berlin Conference in 1884 and 1885. The conference officially recognized both British and German claims for territory in East Africa. Portugal received a clear claim on Mozambique. No African delegates, however, were present at this conference.

READING PROGRESS CHECK

Explaining How did Leopold's aggression promote Western imperialism in Africa?

South Africa

GUIDING QUESTION ***How was European dominance different in South Africa?***

indigenous native to a region

Nowhere in Africa did the European presence grow more rapidly than in the south. By 1865 the total white population of South Africa had risen to nearly 200,000 people. The Boers, or Afrikaners—as the descendants of the original Dutch settlers were called—had occupied Cape Town and surrounding areas in South Africa since the seventeenth century. During the Napoleonic Wars, however, the British seized these lands from the Dutch. Afterward, the British encouraged settlers to come to what they called Cape Colony.

The Boer Republics

In the 1830s, disgusted with British rule, the Boers moved from the coastal lands and headed northward on the Great Trek. Altogether one out of every five Dutch-speaking South Africans joined the trek. Their parties eventually settled in the region between the Orange and Vaal (VAHL) Rivers and in the region north of the Vaal River. In these areas, the Boers formed two independent republics—the Orange Free State and the Transvaal (later called the South African Republic).

The Boers believed that white superiority was ordained by God. They denied non-Europeans any place in their society, other than as laborers or servants. As they settled the lands, the Boers put many of the **indigenous** peoples, those native to a region, in these areas on reservations.

The Boers had frequently battled the indigenous Zulu people. In the early nineteenth century, the Zulu, under a talented ruler named Shaka, had carved out their own empire. Even after Shaka's death, the Zulu remained powerful. In the late 1800s, the Zulu were defeated when the British military joined the conflict.

▶ **CRITICAL THINKING**

Analyzing Visuals What conditions did men endure in South African diamond mines?

▼ **After diamonds were discovered in 1867, thousands of Europeans came to Africa to make their fortunes. In 1881 Cecil Rhodes formed the De Beers Mining Company, which still dominates the world diamond market.**

Cecil Rhodes

In the 1880s, British policy in South Africa was influenced by Cecil Rhodes. Rhodes had founded diamond and gold mining companies that had made him a fortune. Rhodes was a great champion of British expansion. He said once, "I think what [God] would like me to do is to paint as much of Africa British red as possible." One of Rhodes's goals was to create a series of British colonies "from the Cape to Cairo"—all linked by a railroad.

When gold and diamonds were discovered in the Transvaal, British settlers swarmed in looking to make their fortunes. The Boer residents resented the settlers and they were sometimes mistreated.

Rhodes then secretly backed a raid that was meant to spark an uprising among British settlers against the Transvaal government. The raid failed, and the British government forced Rhodes to resign as head of the Cape Colony. This action was too late, however, to prevent a war between the British and the Boers.

The Boer War

This war, called the Boer War, dragged on from 1899 to 1902. Fierce guerrilla resistance by the Boers angered the British. They responded by burning crops and forcing about 120,000 Boer women and children into detention camps, where lack of food caused some 20,000 deaths. Eventually, the vastly larger British army won. A peace treaty was signed in 1902.

In 1910 the British created an independent Union of South Africa, which combined the old Cape Colony and the Boer republics. The new state would be a self-governing nation within the British Empire. To appease the Boers, the British agreed that only whites, with a few propertied Africans, would vote.

✓ READING PROGRESS CHECK

Identifying Central Issues What role did Cecil Rhodes play in promoting British imperialism in the south of Africa?

▲ The Zulu chief Cetewayo surrendered to the British after they captured the city of Ulundi in July 1879.

▶ CRITICAL THINKING

Drawing Conclusions Why was Zulu chief Cetewayo unable to maintain power?

Impact of Imperialism in Africa

GUIDING QUESTION *How did European governance lead to African nationalism?*

By 1914 Great Britain, France, Germany, Belgium, Italy, Spain, and Portugal had divided up Africa. Only Liberia, which had been created as a homeland for the formerly enslaved persons of the United States, and Ethiopia remained free states. Native peoples who dared to resist were devastated by the Europeans' superior military force.

Colonial Rule in Africa

As was true in Southeast Asia, most European governments ruled their new territories in Africa with the least effort and expense possible. Indirect rule meant relying on existing political elites and institutions. The British especially followed this approach. At first, in some areas, the British simply asked a local ruler to accept British authority and to fly the British flag over official buildings.

The concept of indirect rule was introduced in the Islamic state of Sokoto, in northern Nigeria, beginning in 1903. This system of indirect rule in Sokoto had one good feature: It did not disrupt local customs and institutions. However, it did have some unfortunate consequences.

The system of indirect rule was basically a fraud because British administrators made all major decisions. The native authorities served chiefly to enforce those decisions.

Another problem was that the policy of indirect rule kept the old African elite in power. Such a policy provided few opportunities for ambitious and talented young Africans from outside the old elite. In this way, British indirect rule sowed the seeds for class and ethnic tensions, which erupted after independence came in the twentieth century.

Most other European nations governed their African possessions through a form of direct rule. This was true in the French colonies. At the top was a French official, usually known as a governor-general. He was appointed from Paris and governed with the aid of a bureaucracy in the capital city of the colony.

The French ideal was to assimilate African subjects into French culture rather than preserve native **traditions**. Africans were eligible to run for office and even serve in the French National Assembly in Paris. A few were also appointed to high-powered positions in the colonial administration.

traditions the established customs of a people

Analyzing PRIMARY SOURCES

Imperialism in Africa

"Some time ago a party of men came to my country, the principal one appearing to be a man called Rudd. They asked me for a place to dig for gold, and said they would give me certain things for the right to do so. I told them to bring what they could give and I would show them what I would give. A document was written and presented to me for signature. I asked what it contained, and was told that in it were my words and the words of those men. I put my hand to it. About three months afterwards I heard from other sources that I had given by the document the right to all the minerals of my country."

—Lobengula, a southern African king, in a letter to Queen Victoria, quoted in *The Imperialism Reader*

DBQ ***IDENTIFYING*** How did the Europeans take advantage of Lobengula?

Rise of African Nationalism

A new class of leaders emerged in Africa by the beginning of the twentieth century. Educated in colonial schools or in Western nations, they were the first generation of Africans to know a great deal about the West.

The members of this new class admired Western culture and sometimes disliked the ways of their own countries. They were eager to introduce Western ideas and institutions into their own societies. Still, many of these new leaders came to resent the foreigners and their arrogant contempt for African peoples. These intellectuals recognized the gap between theory and practice in colonial policy. Westerners had exalted democracy, equality, and political freedom but did not apply these values in the colonies.

There were few democratic institutions. Native peoples could have only low-paying jobs in the colonial bureaucracy. To many Africans, colonialism had meant losing their farmlands or working on plantations or in factories run by foreigners. Some African leaders lost even more, such as the rights to mine the natural resources in their country.

Middle-class Africans did not suffer as much as poor African peasants. However, members of the middle class also had complaints. They usually qualified only for menial jobs in the government or business. Even then, their salaries were lower than those of Europeans in similar jobs.

Europeans expressed their assumed superiority over Africans in other ways. Segregated clubs, schools, and churches were set up as more European officials brought their wives and began to raise families. Europeans were also condescending in their relationships with Africans. For instance, Europeans had a habit of addressing Africans by their first names.

Such conditions led many members of the new urban educated class to feel great confusion toward their colonial rulers and the civilization the colonists represented. The educated Africans found many aspects of Western culture to be superior to their own. However, these intellectuals fiercely hated colonial rule and were determined to assert their own nationality and cultural destiny. Out of this mixture of hopes and resentments emerged the first stirrings of modern nationalism in Africa.

During the first quarter of the twentieth century, resentment turned to action. Across Africa, native peoples began to organize political parties and movements seeking the end of foreign rule. They wanted to be independent and self-governing.

✓ **READING PROGRESS CHECK**

Drawing Conclusions In what ways were Western nations hypocritical in their treatment of their colonies?

LESSON 2 REVIEW

TEKS

Reviewing Vocabulary

1. ***Identifying*** While defining the terms, explain how the traditions of indigenous Africans influenced their relations with Europeans.

Using Your Notes

2. ***Summarizing*** Use your notes to indicate the predominant areas of Africa controlled by various European nations.

Answering the Guiding Questions

3. ***Determining Cause and Effect*** Why were European countries interested in West Africa and North Africa?
4. ***Analyzing Information*** Why did European countries compete for colonies in Central Africa and East Africa?
5. ***Identifying Central Issues*** How was European dominance different in South Africa?
6. ***Drawing Conclusions*** How did European governance lead to African nationalism?

Writing Activity

7. **INFORMATIVE/EXPLANATORY** In one or two paragraphs, explain the effects of the Berlin conference of 1884–1885 on the scramble for Africa.

networks

There's More Online!

- ☑ BIOGRAPHY Mohandas Gandhi
- ☑ IMAGE Life Under the British Raj
- ☑ IMAGE The Great Rebellion
- ☑ INTERACTIVE SELF-CHECK QUIZ
- ☑ MAP British Possessions in India, 1858–1914
- ☑ PRIMARY SOURCE Poem by Rabindranath Tagore
- ☑ VIDEO British India

LESSON 3
British Rule in India

ESSENTIAL QUESTIONS
- *What are the causes and effects of imperialism?*
- *How do some groups resist control by others?*

Reading HELPDESK

Academic Vocabulary
- **civil**
- **estate**

Content Vocabulary
- **sepoys**
- **viceroys**

TAKING NOTES:
Key Ideas and Details

Determining Cause and Effect
Use a chart like this one to identify some causes and effects of British influence on India.

Causes	Effect
British manufactured goods	
Cotton crops	
School system	
Railroad, telegraph, telephone services	

It Matters Because

The British brought order and stability to India, but India paid a high price for British rule. The mistrust and cultural differences between the British and Indians sparked an independence movement and renewed interest among Indians in their culture and history.

The Great Rebellion

GUIDING QUESTION *What was the source of conflict between the British and the Indian people?*

Over the course of the eighteenth century, British power in India had increased while the power of the Mogul rulers had declined. The British government gave a trading company, the British East India Company, power to become actively involved in India's political and military affairs. To rule India, the British East India Company had its own soldiers and forts. It also hired Indian soldiers, known as **sepoys**, to protect the company's interests in the region.

Events Leading to Rebellion

In 1857 a growing Indian distrust of the British led to a revolt. The British call the revolt the Sepoy Mutiny. Indians call it the First War of Independence. Neutral observers label it the Great Rebellion.

The major immediate cause of the revolt was a rumor that the troops' new rifle cartridges were greased with cow and pig fat. The cow was sacred to Hindus. The pig was taboo to Muslims. To load a rifle at that time, soldiers had to bite off the end of the cartridge. To the sepoys, touching these greased cartridges to their lips would mean that they were polluted.

A group of sepoys at an army post in Meerut, near Delhi, refused to load their rifles with the cartridges. The British charged them with mutiny, publicly humiliated them, and put them in prison. This treatment of their comrades enraged the sepoy troops in Meerut. They went on a rampage, killing 50 European men, women, and children. Soon other Indians joined the revolt, including princes whose land the British had taken.

▲ This engraving of the Battle of Kanpur (Cawnpore) shows sepoys on horseback fighting British soldiers.

▶ **CRITICAL THINKING**

Analyzing Visuals Which side had the military advantage in this battle? Why?

sepoy an Indian soldier hired by the British East India Company to protect the company's interests in the region

SKILLS PRACTICE

Before you read about British colonial rule, use a graphic organizer to record what you know about the topic. In another column, write what you would like to learn. Use the third column to record what you learn as you read.

TEKS Texas Essential Knowledge and Skills

1E identify major causes and describe the major effects of the following important turning points in world history from 1750 to 1914: the Scientific Revolution, the Industrial Revolution and its impact on the development of modern economic systems, European imperialism, and the Enlightenment's impact on political revolutions

8D explain the major characteristics and impact of European imperialism

Within a year, however, Indian troops loyal to the British and fresh British troops had crushed the rebellion. Although Indian troops fought bravely and outnumbered the British by about 230,000 to 45,000, they were not well organized. Rivalries between Hindus and Muslims kept the Indians from working together.

Atrocities were terrible on both sides. At Kanpur (Cawnpore), Indians massacred 200 defenseless women and children in a building known as the House of the Ladies. Recapturing Kanpur, the British took their revenge before executing the Indians.

Effects of the Rebellion

As a result of the uprising, the British Parliament transferred the powers of the East India Company directly to the British government. In 1876 Britain's Queen Victoria took the title Empress of India. The people of India were now her colonial subjects, and India then became her "Jewel in the Crown."

Although the rebellion failed, it helped fuel Indian nationalism. The rebellion marked the first significant attempt by the people of South Asia to throw off British Raj (rule). Later, a new generation of Indian leaders would take up the cause.

✔ **READING PROGRESS CHECK**

Determining Cause and Effect What were the effects of the Great Rebellion in India?

British Colonial Rule

GUIDING QUESTION *What were the consequences of British rule in India?*

After the Sepoy Mutiny, the British government began to rule India directly. They appointed a British official known as a **viceroy** (a governor who ruled as a representative of a monarch). A British **civil** service staff assisted the viceroy. This staff of about 3,500 officials ruled almost 300 million people, the largest colonial population in the world. British rule involved both benefits and costs for Indians.

British rule in India had several benefits for colonial subjects. It brought order and stability to a society badly divided into many states with different, and sometimes opposing, political systems. It also led to a fairly honest, efficient government.

Through the efforts of the British administrator and historian Lord Thomas Macaulay, a new school system was set up. The new system used the English language, as Macaulay explained:

PRIMARY SOURCE

"What then shall [the language of education] be? [Some] maintain that it should be the English. The other half strongly recommend the Arabic and Sanskrit. The whole question seems to me to be, which language is the best worth knowing? . . . It is, I believe, no exaggeration to say that all the historical information which has been collected from all the books written in the Sanskrit language is less valuable [than] what may be found in [short textbooks] used at preparatory schools in England."

—Lord Macaulay, from speech to Parliament, February 2, 1835

The goal of the new school system was to train Indian children to serve in the government and army. The new system served only elite, upper-class Indians, however. Ninety percent of the population remained uneducated and illiterate.

The British hired Indians and built roads, canals, universities, and medical centers. A postal service was introduced shortly after it appeared in Great Britain. India's first rail network, beginning in Bombay, opened in 1853. By 1900, 25,000 miles (40,225 km) of railroads crisscrossed India. Health and sanitation conditions were also improved.

But the Indian people paid a high price for the peace and stability brought by British rule. Perhaps the greatest cost was economic. British entrepreneurs and a small number of Indians reaped financial benefits from British rule, but it brought hardship to millions of others in both the cities and the countryside. British manufactured goods destroyed local industries. British textiles put thousands of women out of work and severely damaged the Indian textile industry.

In rural areas, the British sent the zamindars to collect taxes. The British believed that using these local officials would make it easier to collect taxes from the peasants. However, the zamindars in India took advantage of their new authority. They increased taxes and forced the less fortunate peasants to become tenants or lose their land entirely. Peasant unrest grew.

The British also encouraged many Indian farmers to switch from growing food to growing cotton. As a consequence, food supplies could not keep up with the growing population. Between 1800 and 1900, 30 million Indians died of starvation.

Finally, British rule was degrading, even for the newly educated upper classes who benefited the most from it. The best jobs and the best housing were reserved for Britons. Although many British colonial officials sincerely tried to improve the lot of the people in India, British arrogance and racial attitudes cut deeply into the pride of many Indians and led to the rise of an Indian nationalist movement.

✓ READING PROGRESS CHECK

Analyzing Information What was the price Indians had to pay for the increased stability of British rule?

Analyzing PRIMARY SOURCES

Rabindranath Tagore on India

"The conditions which have prevailed in India from a remote antiquity have guided its history along a particular channel, which does not and cannot coincide with the lines of evolution taken by other countries under different sets of influences. It would be a sad misreading of the lessons of the past to tread too closely in the footsteps of any other nation, however successful in its own career.

I feel strongly that our country has been entrusted with a message which is not a mere echo of the living voices that resound from western shores . . ."

—Rabindranath Tagore
from a letter, January 4, 1909

DBQ ***DRAWING CONCLUSIONS***
What attitude would Tagore have had toward the opinion expressed by Macaulay about the use of English to educate Indians?

viceroy a governor who ruled as a representative of a monarch

civil involving the general public or civic affairs

Indian Nationalists

GUIDING QUESTION *What led to an Indian independence movement?*

The first Indian nationalists were upper-class and English-educated. Many of them were from urban areas, such as Bombay (Mumbai), Madras (Chennai), and Calcutta (Kolkata). Some were trained in British law and were members of the civil service.

At first, many Indian nationalists preferred reform to revolution. However, the slow pace of reform convinced many that relying on British goodwill was futile. In 1885 a small group of Indians met in Bombay to form the Indian National Congress (INC). The INC did not demand immediate independence. Instead, the group called for a share in the governing process.

The INC had difficulties because of religious differences. The INC sought independence for all Indians, regardless of class or religious background. However, many of its leaders were Hindu and reflected Hindu concerns. Later, Muslims called for the creation of a separate Muslim League. Such a league would represent the interests of the millions of Muslims in Indian society.

In 1914 the return of a young Hindu from South Africa brought new life to India's struggle for independence. Mohandas Gandhi was born in 1869 in Gujarat, in western India. He studied in London and became a lawyer. In 1893 Gandhi went to South Africa to work in a law firm serving Indian workers there. He soon learned of the racial exploitation of Indians living in South Africa.

On his return to India, Gandhi became active in the independence movement. Using his experience in South Africa, he began a movement based on nonviolent resistance. Its aim was to force the British to improve the lot of the poor and to grant independence to India. Ultimately, Gandhi's movement led to Indian independence.

✓ **READING PROGRESS CHECK**

Identifying Central Issues What difficulties did the Indian National Congress face?

Colonial Indian Culture

GUIDING QUESTION *How did British rule influence Indian culture?*

From the beginning of their rule, the British often showed disrespect for India's cultural heritage. The Taj Mahal, for example, was built as a tomb for the beloved wife of an Indian ruler. The British used it as a favorite site for weddings and parties. Many partygoers even brought hammers to chip off pieces as souvenirs.

The love-hate tension in India that arose from British domination led to a cultural awakening as well. The cultural revival began in the early nineteenth century with the creation of a British college in Calcutta. A local publishing house was opened. It issued textbooks on a variety of subjects, including the sciences, Sanskrit, and Western literature. The publisher also printed grammars and dictionaries in various Indian languages.

This revival soon spread to other regions of India. It led to a search for a new national identity and a modern literary expression. Indian novelists and poets began writing historical romances and epics. Some wrote in English, but most were uncomfortable with a borrowed colonial language. They preferred to use their own regional tongues.

Connections to TODAY

Commonwealth Games

One legacy of imperialism is evident in the Commonwealth Games. Participation in the games is limited to amateur athletes who come from one of the countries of the British Commonwealth, the free association of states that includes many former parts of the British Empire. A more recent addition to the games is cricket, which the British brought to their colonies. Cricket is especially popular in India.

Printed in the various regional Indian languages, newspapers were a common medium used to arouse mass support for nationalist causes. These newspapers reached the lower-middle-class populations—tens of thousands of Indians who had never learned a word of English. In his newspaper *Kesari* ("The Lion"), journalist Balwantrao Gangadhar Tilak used innuendo (suggestion) to convey the negative feelings about the British without ever writing anything disloyal.

The most famous Indian author was Rabindranath Tagore, winner of the Nobel Prize in Literature in 1913. A great writer and poet, Tagore had many talents. He was also a social reformer, spiritual leader, educator, philosopher, singer, painter, and international spokesperson for the moral concerns of his age. Tagore liked to invite the great thinkers of the time to his expansive country home, or **estate**. There he set up a school that became an international university.

estate a landed property usually with a large house

Tagore's life mission was to promote pride in a national Indian consciousness in the face of British domination. He wrote a widely read novel in which he portrayed the love-hate relationship of India toward its colonial mentor. The novel reflected an Indian people who admired and imitated the British but who agonized over how to establish their own national identity.

Rabindranath Tagore, however, was more than an Indian nationalist. His life's work was one long prayer for human dignity, world peace, and the mutual understanding and union of East and West. As Tagore once said,

PRIMARY SOURCE

"It is my conviction that my countrymen will truly gain their India by fighting against the education that teaches them that a country is greater than the ideals of humanity."

—Rabindranath Tagore, from *Nationalism*

READING PROGRESS CHECK

Drawing Conclusions How did newspapers and literature help shape the nationalist movement?

▼ Many Indians worked as domestic servants in the homes of British colonialists.

▶ CRITICAL THINKING

Making Connections Why might Indian domestic servants have become resentful of British rule?

LESSON 3 REVIEW TEKS

Reviewing Vocabulary

1. ***Identifying*** What were the roles of viceroys and civil servants in India and whom did they represent?

Using Your Notes

2. ***Summarizing*** Use your notes on the causes and effects of British rule in India to write a paragraph summarizing its effects.

Answering the Guiding Questions

3. ***Identifying*** What was the source of conflict between the British and the Indian people?

4. ***Evaluating*** What were the consequences of British rule in India?

5. ***Identifying Cause and Effect*** What led to an Indian independence movement?

6. ***Explaining*** How did British rule influence Indian culture?

Writing Activity

7. **INFORMATIVE/EXPLANATORY** Write a short paragraph outlining the general British attitude toward the people of India and the consequences of that attitude.

networks

There's More Online!

- IMAGE Construction of the Panama Canal
- IMAGE Leaders of the Mexican Revolution
- IMAGE The Roosevelt Corollary
- INTERACTIVE SELF-CHECK QUIZ
- MAP Sea Routes Before and After the Panama Canal
- PRIMARY SOURCE Mexican Constitution of 1917
- VIDEO Latin American Imperialism

LESSON 4

Imperialism in Latin America

ESSENTIAL QUESTIONS

- *What are the causes and effects of imperialism?*
- *How do some groups resist control by others?*

Reading HELPDESK

Academic Vocabulary

- **whereas**
- **sector**

Content Vocabulary

- **dollar diplomacy**

TAKING NOTES:

Key Ideas and Details

Listing Use a graphic organizer like this one to list problems faced by Mexico after 1870 and reforms enacted in the constitution of 1917.

Problems
Reforms

TEKS Texas Essential Knowledge and Skills

16B analyze the influence of human and physical geographic factors on major events in world history, including the development of river valley civilizations, trade in the Indian Ocean, and the opening of the Panama and Suez canals

It Matters Because

In the course of the nineteenth century, the new nations of Latin America found themselves dependent on the West. The United States was especially prominent in the economic and political affairs of its southern neighbors. Social and political inequalities also continued to characterize many Latin American nations.

The U.S. in Latin America

GUIDING QUESTION *What was the impact of U.S. involvement in Latin America in the early 1900s?*

In the late 1800s, the United States began to intervene in the affairs of its southern neighbors. In 1895 exile José Martí returned to Cuba to lead a revolt against Spanish rule. The brutality with which the Spanish crushed the rebellion shocked Americans and began a series of events that led the United States to declare war against Spain in 1898. As a result of the Spanish-American War, Cuba effectively became a protectorate of the United States. By the treaty that ended the war, Puerto Rico was also annexed to the United States.

In 1903 President Theodore Roosevelt supported a rebellion that allowed Panama to separate from Colombia and establish a new nation. In return, the United States was granted control of a 10-mile strip of land through the country. There the United States built the Panama Canal, which opened in 1914. These human geographic factors that led to the canal were similar to other political manipulations common in most imperialistic interventions. Physical geographic factors, on the other hand, influenced the location and construction of the canal. Panama was an ideal location for the canal because in no other place were the Atlantic and Pacific Oceans so close together. The roughness of the terrain, however, meant that construction was difficult. Indeed, the canal was one of the world's greatest engineering feats of its time.

In 1904 President Roosevelt expanded American involvement in Latin America. At the time, European powers threatened to send warships to Santo Domingo in the Dominican Republic to collect debts owed to them. In a statement that became known as the Roosevelt Corollary to the Monroe Doctrine, Roosevelt claimed that the United States could intervene in any Latin American nation guilty of "chronic misconduct" (such as the inability to repay debts). The United States then took control of debt collection in the Dominican Republic.

American investments in Latin America soon expanded. In the early 1900s, the United States began to pursue "**dollar diplomacy**," extending its influence by investing in Latin American development. The United States soon replaced Europe as the source of loans and investments. Direct U.S. investments reached $3.5 billion, out of a world total of $7.5 billion.

dollar diplomacy
diplomacy that seeks to strengthen the power of a country or effect its purposes in foreign relations by the use of its financial resources

As American investments grew, so too did the resolve to protect those investments. U.S. military forces were sent to Cuba, Mexico, Guatemala, Honduras, Nicaragua, Panama, Colombia, Haiti, and the Dominican Republic to protect American interests. Some expeditions stayed for years.

✓ **READING PROGRESS CHECK**

Analyzing Ethical Issues In what ways were U.S. actions in Latin America during the early 1900s imperialist?

Revolution in Mexico

GUIDING QUESTION *What were the causes and effects of the Mexican Revolution?*

After 1870, large landowners in Latin American began to take a more direct interest in national politics and even in governing. In Argentina and Chile, for example, landholding elites controlled the governments. They adopted constitutions similar to those of the United States and European democracies. The ruling elites, however, limited voting rights.

In some countries, large landowners supported dictators who looked out for the interests of the ruling elite. Porfirio Díaz, who ruled Mexico between 1877 and 1911, created a conservative, centralized government. The army, foreign capitalists, large landowners, and the Catholic Church supported Díaz. All these groups benefited from their alliance with Díaz. However, growing forces for change in Mexico led to a revolution.

▼ Workers wait along the railroad tracks during the construction of the Panama Canal at Gatun, Panama. The canal changed commercial shipping patterns in the Western Hemisphere.

▶ **CRITICAL THINKING**
Making Connections How did ships travel before the opening of the Panama Canal?

whereas although

During Díaz's dictatorial reign, the wages of workers had declined. Ninety-five percent of the rural population owned no land, **whereas** about 1,000 families owned almost all of Mexico. A liberal landowner, Francisco Madero, forced Díaz from power in 1911. The door to a wider revolution then opened.

Madero made a valiant effort to handle the revolutionary forces. He put some of the best officials in his administration, and he sought a balance in dealing with foreign interests. However, his efforts proved ineffective.

▲ Revolutionary leaders, such as Pancho Villa (seated left) and Emiliano Zapata (seated right), raised armies from the masses of discontented poor to fight for land reform in Mexico.

▶ **CRITICAL THINKING**

Analyzing Visuals What is the significance of this 1915 photograph of Mexican revolutionaries?

The northern states were in near anarchy as Pancho Villa's armed masses of bandits swept the countryside. The federal army was full of hard-minded generals who itched to assert their power. Even the liberal politicians and idealists found fault with Madero for not solving all of the country's problems at once.

Francisco Madero's ineffectiveness created a demand for agrarian reform. This new call for reform was led by Emiliano Zapata. Zapata aroused the masses of landless peasants and began to seize and redistribute the estates of wealthy landholders. Although Madero tried to reach an agreement with him for land reforms, Zapata refused to disarm his followers.

Between 1910 and 1920, the Mexican Revolution caused great damage to the Mexican economy. Finally, a new constitution was enacted in 1917. This constitution set down many goals of the revolution. For revolutionary leaders, the goal was political reform. For peasants, it was about land reform. The constitution set up a government led by a president and elected by universal male suffrage. It also created land-reform policies, established limits on foreign investors, and set an agenda to help the workers. This agenda included the rights of workers to form unions, set a minimum wage, and limit working hours. Eventually, the revolution helped bring about a more democratic and politically stable Mexico.

The revolution also led to an outpouring of patriotism throughout Mexico. National pride was evident as intellectuals and artists sought to capture what was unique about Mexico with special emphasis on its past.

✓ **READING PROGRESS CHECK**

Identifying Central Issues How did Díaz, Madero, Villa, and Zapata help incite or prolong the Mexican Revolution?

Prosperity and Social Change

GUIDING QUESTION *How did prosperity change Latin America after 1870?*

After 1870, Latin America began an age of prosperity based to a large extent on the export of a few basic items. These included wheat and beef from Argentina, coffee from Brazil, coffee and bananas from Central America, and sugar and silver from Peru. These foodstuffs and raw materials were largely exchanged for finished goods—textiles, machines, and luxury items—from Europe and the United States.

After 1900, Latin Americans also increased their own industrialization. They built factories to produce textiles, foods, and construction materials. But because the growth of the Latin American economy came mostly from the export of raw materials, Latin America remained economically dependent on Western nations and their foreign investment.

Despite its economic growth, Latin America was still an underdeveloped region of the world. Old patterns still largely prevailed in Latin American societies. Rural elites dominated their estates and their workers. Slavery had been abolished by 1888, but former enslaved people and their descendants were at the bottom of society. The indigenous peoples were still poverty stricken.

One result of the prosperity of increased exports was growth in the middle **sectors** of Latin American society. Lawyers, merchants, shopkeepers, businesspeople, schoolteachers, professors, bureaucrats, and military officers increased in numbers.

sector a sociological, economic, or political subdivision of society

Regardless of the country in which they lived, middle-class Latin Americans shared some common characteristics. They lived in cities and sought education and decent incomes. They also saw the United States as a model, especially in regard to industrialization. The middle class sought liberal reform, not revolution. After they had the right to vote, they generally sided with the landholding elites.

As Latin American export economies boomed, the working class grew. So too did the labor unions, especially after 1914. Radical unions often advocated the use of the general strike as an instrument for change. By and large, the governing elites were able to stifle the political influence of the working class by limiting their right to vote.

The need for industrial workers also led Latin American countries to seek immigrants from Europe. For example, between 1880 and 1914, 3 million Europeans, primarily Italians and Spaniards, settled in Argentina.

As in Europe and the United States, in Latin America, industrialization led to urbanization. Buenos Aires (called "the Paris of South America") had 750,000 inhabitants by 1900 and 2 million by 1914. By that time, 53 percent of Argentina's population lived in cities.

Thinking Like a HISTORIAN

Determining Cause and Effect

Historians look for patterns to determine causes and effects of important historical phenomena and events, such as industrialization. As it had earlier in western Europe and the United States, industrialization caused changes in Latin American societies. Did the process of industrialization have the same effects on Latin American societies as it did on European societies? Use historical analysis skills to answer this question.

✓ READING PROGRESS CHECK

Explaining How did an increase in exports change Latin America after 1870?

LESSON 4 REVIEW TEKS

Reviewing Vocabulary

1. ***Explaining*** Write a paragraph explaining why the term *dollar diplomacy* appears in quotation marks in the text.

Using Your Notes

2. ***Differentiating*** Use your notes listing problems in Mexico after 1870 to write a paragraph that outlines how the new constitution tried to address these problems.

Answering the Guiding Questions

3. ***Identifying Cause and Effect*** What was the impact of U.S. involvement in Latin America in the early 1900s?
4. ***Identifying Cause and Effect*** What were the causes and effects of the Mexican Revolution?
5. ***Assessing*** How did prosperity change Latin America after 1870?

Writing Activity

6. **ARGUMENT** Write a paragraph that supports or argues against this point of view: The United States was right to do whatever was necessary to build the Panama Canal because it is such an important and strategic waterway.

Assessment

Directions: On a separate sheet of paper, answer the questions below. Make sure you read carefully and answer all parts of the questions.

Lesson Review

Lesson 1

1. ***Identifying Central Issues*** What are the characteristics of imperialism? Describe two types of imperial rule. What was the impact of European imperialism in the late nineteenth century? **1E, 8D**

2. ***Examining*** What was the impact of European imperialism in the late nineteenth century? **8D**

3. ***Describing*** Describe the various philosophies tied to nineteenth-century imperialism. **8C**

4. ***Making Inferences*** What new class did colonial rule create? How did this eventually lead to the end of colonialism? **1E**

5. ***Summarizing*** Summarize France's presence in Vietnam and other Southeast Asia countries during the mid-to-late 1800s.

6. ***Identifying Cause and Effect*** What political concerns prompted President McKinley to turn his attention to the Philippines?

Lesson 2

7. ***Summarizing*** What economic motivations led Europeans to seize control in West Africa? Describe which European nations gained control in West Africa. **1E, 8C**

8. ***Identifying*** What was the social motivation that influenced European missionaries as they traveled to the rain forests of Central Africa?

9. ***Making Connections*** Describe the connections among Dr. Livingstone, Henry Stanley, and King Leopold II?

Lesson 3

10. ***Speculating*** Why didn't the British set up universal public education in India?

11. ***Identifying Cause and Effect*** What was the reason for and effect of Indian farmers growing cotton instead of food?

12. ***Specifying*** Why did nationalist newspapers print articles in regional Indian languages instead of English?

13. ***Finding the Main Idea*** What was the spark for India's cultural revival? What are some examples of it?

Lesson 4

14. ***Sequencing*** What events led to Puerto Rico's annexation into the United States?

15. ***Interpreting*** For what economic reason would the United States have wanted to build the Panama Canal?

16. ***Specifying*** What provisions did the Mexican Constitution of 1917 include?

17. ***Making Connections*** What caused the increase in the number of Latin Americans in the middle class in the late nineteenth century?

18. ***Identifying Cause and Effect*** Even after 1900, why were Latin American countries dependent on Western nations and foreign investments?

Exploring the Essential Question

19. ***Identifying Cause and Effect*** Work with a partner to create a time line showing at least three causes and three effects of imperialism, as well as three examples of resistance to imperialism (successful or unsuccessful) between 1800 and 1914. Include visuals such as photos, sketches, and maps. You may also include primary sources. Be prepared to explain any connections you find.

Need Extra Help?

If You've Missed Question	1	2	3	4	5	6	7	8	9	10	11	12	13	14	15	16	17	18	19
Go to page	586	588	586	590	588	588	591	593	593	599	599	601	600	602	602	604	605	605	584

Critical Thinking

20 ***Identifying Cause and Effect*** For what reason did colonial powers mandate export of raw materials in colonies and what labor structure did this establish?

21 ***Sequencing*** Within resistance movements in India, what area of focus came first, and what shifted in their focus and purpose beginning in the 1930s?

22 ***Comparing and Contrasting*** Compare and contrast the system of indirect colonial rule and direct colonial rule. What were the pros and cons for the people being ruled in each system?

23 ***Explaining and Evaluating*** Explain the roles of military, transportation, communication, and medical technology in advancing imperialism in the nineteenth century. Make a claim as to which advancement had the greatest impact, using reasons and evidence to support your argument. **28B**

24 ***Identifying and Arguing*** Of the economic, political, or social motivations that led the wave of European imperialism in the nineteenth century, which do you consider to be a the primary motivation? Describe each motivating factor and make your argument for which was the most powerful. **1E, 8C**

Social Studies Skills

25 ***Geography Skills*** Create a map that shows the Suez Canal and the neighboring African and Mediterranean countries, key cities, and bodies of water. Include a key that reflects the accurate length of the canal. **15A**

26 ***Understanding Relationships Among Ideas*** Who were the Boers? How did they influence the European presence in South Africa?

27 ***Identifying Perspectives*** What can you deduce from the three different names for the rebellion of 1857 in India and the perspectives of the groups that use them?

28 ***Analyzing*** Analyze the influence of human and physical geography on the opening of the Suez Canal. How are these factors similar to or different from the opening of the Panama Canal? **16B**

29 ***Research Skills*** Choose one of the colonial regimes described in this chapter, such as French Indochina or British India, and research how today's independent nations of Vietnam and India, for example, have cultural traditions that are rooted in their colonial history. Or, conversely, research how the countries European nations colonized impacted cultural practices at home. Areas of research could include food, art, music, games and sports, or other aspects of culture. Communicate your findings through writing and images using computer software to publish your work.

30 ***Analyzing Information*** Gather information about the activities and events tied to a leader who fought for reform under colonial or oppressive rule, or prevented colonial rule, such as Mohandas Gandi, Emiliano Zapata, or King Mongkut. Create a time line of key events that show how the sequence of activities led to a final outcome. **29F**

Need Extra Help?

If You've Missed Question	20	21	22	23	24	25	26	27	28	29	30
Go to page	589	597	589	587	583	592	594	597	592	583	583

DBQ Analyzing Primary Sources

Use the document to answer the following questions.

In 1893 Captain F. D. Lugard presented a justification for Great Britain's indirect rule of East Africa.

PRIMARY SOURCE

> "There are some who say we have no *right* in Africa at all, that 'it belongs to the natives.' I hold that our right is the necessity that is upon us to provide for our ever-growing population—either by opening new fields for emigration, or by providing work. . . . In Africa, moreover, there is among the people a natural inclination to submit to a higher authority. That intense detestation of control which animates our Teutonic races does not exist among the tribes of Africa, and if there is any authority that we replace, it is the authority of the Slavers and Arabs, or the intolerable tyranny of the 'dominant tribe'."
>
> —quoted *in Civilization Past & Present*

31 ***Identifying*** What three reasons does Captain Lugard give to justify Great Britain's takeover of African nations?

32 ***Evaluating*** How convincing do Captain Lugard's arguments seem today? Give details.

Analyzing Visuals

Use the image to answer the following questions.

This photograph, taken in Cambodia in 1900, is titled "King Norodom and Son in Carriage."

33 ***Analyzing Visuals*** What evidence of Western influence can you identify in this photograph?

34 ***Interpreting*** Were there benefits to European imperialism in Cambodia? Use the photograph to make your argument.

Extended Response Question

35 ***Argument*** Compare and contrast the native peoples' resistance to colonization in Southeast Asia, Africa, India, and Latin America. Discuss who resisted, the tactics they used, and their successes or failures.

Need Extra Help?

If You've Missed Question	31	32	33	34	35
Go to page	608	608	608	608	583

Challenge and Transition in East Asia

1800–1914

ESSENTIAL QUESTIONS

- *How can new ideas accelerate economic and political change?*
- *How do cultures influence each other?*

Sun Yat-sen was a patriot and visionary dedicated to bringing China and its ancient traditions into the modern world. His political program was founded on principles of national self-determination, democracy, and equality. This photograph, taken around 1910, features Sun in European-influenced clothing. His knowledge of the Western world helped make him a symbol of modernization.

PHOTO: Stringer/Fotosearch/Getty Images

networks

There's More Online! about challenge and transition in East Asia.

CHAPTER 26

The Story Matters...

In the nineteenth century, the Qing dynasty's growing weakness led to civil war, rebellion, and Western intervention. Followers of reformer Sun Yat-sen began an uprising in 1911 that ended the Qing dynasty and more than two thousand years of imperial rule. However, the new Chinese republic was not strong enough to maintain control, and China slipped into civil disorder and the rule of warlords. Throughout this period, Western economic and cultural influence on China continued to grow.

CHAPTER 26

Place and Time: East Asia 1800–1914

The centuries-old Qing dynasty, China's last , finally fell as a result of many factors, including foreign pressures, social unrest, and the resistance of the autocratic government to the introduction of reforms. By contrast, Japan's empire expanded as its leaders embraced industrial development and commerce, undertook educational and governmental reform, and used Western ideas, institutions, and technology to create a new national order. Important victories over China and Russia secured Japanese military leadership in East Asia.

Step Into the Place

Read the quotes and look at the information presented on the map.

DBQ **Analyzing Historical Documents** How might attitudes toward change in China and Japan have affected the two countries' histories during this period?

PRIMARY SOURCE

"Those who insist that there is no need for reform still say, 'Let us follow the ancients, follow the ancients.' They coldly sit and watch everything being laid to waste by following tradition, and there is no concern in their hearts. . . . Now there is a big mansion which has lasted a thousand years. The tiles and bricks are decayed and the beams and rafters are broken up, its fall is foredoomed. Yet the people in the house are still happily playing or soundly sleeping. Even some who have noted the danger know only how to weep bitterly, folding their arms and waiting for death without thinking of any remedy. . . . A nation is also like this."

—Liang Qichao, comment made in 1896 after China's defeat by Japan, quoted in *East Asia: A New History*

PRIMARY SOURCE

"I am willing to admit my pride in Japan's accomplishments [in rapid modernization]. The facts are these: It was not until the sixth year of Kaei (1853) that a steamship was seen for the first time. . . . by 1860, the science was sufficiently understood to enable us to sail a ship across the Pacific. . . . I think we can without undue pride boast before the world of this courage and skill. . . . I feel convinced that there is no other nation which has the ability or the courage to navigate a steamship across the Pacific after a period of five years of experience in navigation and engineering."

—Fukuzawa Yukichi, from his autobiography, 1898

PHOTO: Fierce Fighting between Japanese and Chinese Troops in a Chinese City, an episode from the Sino-Japanese War, late 19th century (colour woodblock print), Japanese School, (19th century) / Private Collection / Archives Charmet / The Bridgeman Art Library

Step Into the Time

Synthesizing Information

Research an event from the time line and explain how it shows either the disintegration of the Qing dynasty in China or the expansion of Japan's imperialist power.

EAST ASIA

- **1800** Qing dynasty at the height of its power
- **1800** China prohibits trade in opium
- **1804** Russian ambassador arrives in Nagasaki
- **1839** Opium War begins in China

1800 1820 1840

THE WORLD

- **1804** Napoleon Bonaparte is crowned Emperor
- **1821** José de San Martín advances on Lima, Peru
- **1823** Monroe Doctrine is announced

networks
There's More Online!

- **MAP** Explore the interactive version of this map on Networks.
- **TIME LINE** Explore the interactive version of the time line on Networks.

1850 Tai Ping Rebellion begins in China

1853 U.S. asks Japan to open foreign relations

1856 Second Opium War begins

1868 Japanese emperor Mutsuhito begins Meiji rule

1899 U.S. establishes Open Door Policy with China

1905 Russia grants Liaodong Peninsula to Japan

1910 Japan annexes Korea

1911 Followers of Sun Yat-sen launch Chinese rebellion

1860 **1880** **1900** **1914**

1848 Nationalist and liberal revolutions erupt in Europe

1865 American Civil War ends

1879 Thomas Edison develops the electric light bulb

1894 José Martí leads revolt against Spanish rule in Cuba

1902 Afrikaners are defeated in the Boer War

1914 World War I begins

networks

There's More Online!

- BIOGRAPHY Empress Ci Xi
- CHART/GRAPH Opium Imported into China
- IMAGE Naval Battle During the Opium War
- IMAGE Prisoners from the Boxer Rebellion
- INTERACTIVE SELF-CHECK QUIZ
- MAP Spheres of Influence in China, 1900
- VIDEO The Opium Wars

LESSON 1

The Decline of the Qing Dynasty

ESSENTIAL QUESTIONS

- *How can new ideas accelerate economic and political change?*
- *How do cultures influence each other?*

Reading HELPDESK

Academic Vocabulary

- **highlighted**
- **exclusive**

Content Vocabulary

- **extraterritoriality**
- **self-strengthening**
- **spheres of influence**
- **Open Door policy**
- **indemnity**

TAKING NOTES:

Key Ideas and Details

Comparing and Contrasting As you read, create a chart like the one below to compare and contrast the Tai Ping and Boxer Rebellions.

	Tai Ping	Boxer
Reforms Demanded		
Method Used		
Outcomes		

TEKS Texas Essential Knowledge and Skills

8D explain the major characteristics and impact of European imperialism

IT MATTERS BECAUSE

China preferred to keep its culture free of Western influences. However, as the Qing government grew more unstable, foreign powers created spheres of influence and pursued a policy to secure trading rights. The Chinese resisted but were eventually overcome, weakening the imperial government even more.

Causes of Decline

GUIDING QUESTION *What factors influenced the decline of the Qing Empire?*

In 1800, after a long period of peace and prosperity, the Qing dynasty of the Manchus was at the height of its power. A little more than a century later, however, humiliated and harassed by the Western powers, the Qing dynasty collapsed.

One important reason for the abrupt decline and fall of the Qing dynasty was the intense external pressure that the modern West applied to Chinese society. However, internal problems also played a role.

After an extended period of growth, the Qing dynasty began to suffer from corruption, peasant unrest, and incompetence. These weaknesses were made worse by rapid growth in the country's population. By 1900, there were 400 million people in China. Population growth created a serious food shortage. In the 1850s, one observer wrote, "Not a year passes in which a terrific number of persons do not perish of famine in some part or other of China."

The ships, guns, and ideas of foreigners **highlighted** the growing weakness of the Qing dynasty and probably hastened its end. By 1800, Europeans had been in contact with China for more than 200 years. Wanting to limit contact with outsiders, the Qing dynasty had restricted European merchants to a small trading outlet at Guangzhou (GWAHNG • JOH), or Canton. The merchants could deal with only a few Chinese firms. The British did not like this arrangement.

Britain had a trade deficit, or an unfavorable trade balance, with China. That is, it imported more goods from China than it exported to China. Britain had to pay China with silver for the difference between its imports—tea, silk, and porcelain—from China and its exports—Indian cotton—to China. At first, the British tried to negotiate with the Chinese to improve the trade imbalance. When negotiations failed, the British turned to trading opium.

highlighted centered attention on

The Opium War

Opium was grown in northern India under the sponsorship of the British East India Company and then shipped directly to Chinese markets. Demand for opium—a highly addictive drug—in South China jumped dramatically. Soon, silver was flowing out of China and into the pockets of the officials of the British East India Company.

The Chinese reacted strongly. They appealed to the British government on moral grounds to stop the traffic in opium. Lin Zexu, a Chinese government official, wrote to Queen Victoria:

PRIMARY SOURCE

"Suppose there were people from another country who carried opium for sale to England and seduced your people into buying and smoking it; certainly your honorable ruler would deeply hate it and be bitterly aroused."

—quoted in *The British Imperial Century, 1815–1914*

The British refused to halt their activity, however. As a result, the Chinese blockaded the foreign area in Guangzhou to force traders to surrender their opium. The British responded with force, starting the Opium War (1839–1842).

The Chinese were no match for the British. British warships destroyed Chinese coastal and river forts. When a British fleet sailed almost unopposed up the Chang Jiang (Yangtze River) to Nanjing, the Qing dynasty made peace.

In the Treaty of Nanjing in 1842, the Chinese agreed to open five coastal ports to British trade, limit taxes on imported British goods, and pay for the costs of the war. China also agreed to give the British ownership of the island of Hong Kong. Nothing was said in the treaty about the opium trade.

◀ This illustration by E. Duncan shows the British steamship *Nemesis* destroying Chinese war junks in Anson's Bay, 1841.

▶ **CRITICAL THINKING**

Transferring Use the information in the table to create a bar graph of the amount of opium imported into China.

Opium Imported into China*

Year	Number of Chests
1729	200
1767	1,000
1830	10,000
1838	40,000

*(1 chest = approximately 135 pounds)

extraterritoriality living in a section of a country set aside for foreigners but not subject to the host country's laws

Moreover, in the five ports, Europeans lived in their own sections and were subject not to Chinese laws but to their own laws—a practice known as **extraterritoriality**.

The Opium War marked the beginning of the establishment of Western influence in China. For the time being, the Chinese dealt with the problem by pitting foreign countries against one another. Concessions granted to the British were offered to other Western nations, including the United States. Soon, thriving foreign areas were operating in the five treaty ports along the southern Chinese coast.

The Tai Ping Rebellion

In the meantime, the failure of the Chinese government to deal with pressing internal economic problems led to a peasant revolt, known as the Tai Ping (TIE PING) Rebellion (1850–1864). It was led by Hong Xiuquan, a Christian convert who viewed himself as a younger brother of Jesus.

Hong was convinced that God had given him the mission of destroying the Qing dynasty. Joined by great crowds of peasants, Hong captured the town of Yongan and proclaimed a new dynasty, the Heavenly Kingdom of Great Peace (*Tai Ping Tianguo* in Chinese—hence the name of the rebellion).

In March 1853, the rebels seized Nanjing, the second largest city of the empire, and massacred 25,000 men, women, and children. The revolt continued for 10 more years but gradually began to fall apart. Europeans came to the aid of the Qing dynasty when they realized the destructive nature of the Tai Ping forces. One British observer noted there was "no hope of any good ever coming of the rebel movement. They do nothing but burn, murder, and destroy."

GEOGRAPHY CONNECTION

By 1900, parts of China were divided into separate spheres of influence.

1. **HUMAN SYSTEMS** *After Russia, which country had the largest sphere of influence?*
2. **THE USES OF GEOGRAPHY** *Why were countries able to maintain ports in other countries' spheres of influence?*

In 1864, Chinese forces, with European aid, recaptured Nanjing and destroyed the remaining rebel force. The Tai Ping Rebellion was one of the most devastating civil wars in history. As many as 20 million people died during the 14-year struggle.

China's ongoing struggle with the West prevented the Qing dynasty from dealing effectively with the internal unrest. Beginning in 1856, the British and the French applied force to gain greater trade privileges. As a result of the Treaty of Tianjin in 1858, the Chinese agreed to legalize the opium trade and to open new ports to foreign trade. They also surrendered the Kowloon Peninsula to Great Britain.

Efforts at Reform

By the late 1870s, the Qing dynasty was in decline. Unable to restore order themselves, government troops had relied on forces recruited by regional warlords to help fight the Tai Ping Rebellion. To finance their armies, the warlords had collected taxes from local people. After the revolt, many of these warlords kept their armies.

In its weakened state, the Qing court finally began to listen to the appeals of reform-minded officials. The reformers called for a new policy they called "**self-strengthening**." That is, China should adopt Western technology but keep its Confucian values and institutions.

self-strengthening a policy promoted by reformers toward the end of the Qing dynasty under which China would adopt Western technology while keeping its Confucian values and institutions

Some reformers wanted to change China's traditional political institutions by introducing democracy. However, such ideas were too radical for most reformers. During the last quarter of the nineteenth century, the Chinese government tried to modernize China's military forces and build up industry without touching the basic elements of Chinese civilization. Railroads, weapons factories, and shipyards were built. However, the Chinese value system remained unchanged.

✓ **READING PROGRESS CHECK**

Analyzing Information Why do you think the Qing dynasty wanted to limit contact with foreign nations?

The Impact of European Imperialism

GUIDING QUESTION *Why were spheres of influence established in China?*

In the end, however, the changes did not help the Qing stay in power. The European advance into China continued during the last two decades of the nineteenth century. Internal conditions also continued to deteriorate.

Mounting Pressures

In the north and northeast, Russia took advantage of the Qing dynasty's weakness to force China to give up territories north of the Amur River in Siberia. In Tibet, a struggle between Russia and Great Britain kept both powers from seizing the territory outright. This allowed Tibet to become free from Chinese influence.

Even more ominous changes were taking place in the Chinese heartland. European states began to create **spheres of influence**, areas in which the imperial powers had **exclusive** trading rights. After the Tai Ping Rebellion, warlords in the provinces began to negotiate directly with foreign nations. In return for money, the warlords granted these nations exclusive trading rights or railroad-building and mining privileges. In this way, Britain, France, Germany, Russia, and Japan all established spheres of influence in China.

spheres of influence areas in which foreign powers have been granted exclusive rights and privileges, such as trading rights and mining privileges

exclusive limited to a single individual or group

BIOGRAPHY

Ci Xi (1835–1908)

Though never the official ruler of China, Ci Xi was the power behind the throne for 47 years. Ci Xi was appointed regent when her son, the emperor's only heir, became emperor at age six. After her son died, she ruled for her three-year-old nephew, Guang Xu. Ci Xi officially retired when Guang Xu came of age. Later, however, when he tried to institute reforms, Ci Xi had him imprisoned and resumed the regency. In 1899 she supported the Boxer Rebellion, which ultimately failed, and fled Beijing after China's defeat. She did not return to Beijing until 1902.

▶ **CRITICAL THINKING**

Drawing Conclusions How did Ci Xi acquire and maintain power in a political system dominated by men?

In 1894, another blow furthered the disintegration of the Qing dynasty. The Chinese went to war with Japan over Japanese inroads into Korea, a land that the Chinese had controlled for a long time. The Chinese were soundly defeated. Japan demanded and received the island of Taiwan and the Liaodong (LYOW • DOONG) Peninsula. Fearing Japan's growing power, however, the European powers forced Japan to give the Liaodong Peninsula back to China.

New pressures for Chinese territory soon arose. In 1897, Chinese rioters murdered two German missionaries. Germany used this as a pretext to demand territories in the Shandong (SHON • DOONG) Peninsula. When the Chinese government approved the demand, other European nations made new claims on Chinese territory.

Internal Crisis

This latest scramble for territory took place at a time of internal crisis in China. In June 1898, the young emperor Guang Xu (GWANG SHYOO) launched a massive reform program based on changes in Japan. During the following weeks, known as the One Hundred Days of Reform, the emperor issued edicts calling for major political, administrative, and education reforms. With these reforms, Guang Xu intended to modernize government bureaucracy by following Western models; to adopt a new education system that would replace the traditional civil service examinations; and to adopt Western-style schools, banks, and a free press. Guang Xu also intended to train the military to use modern weapons and Western fighting techniques.

Many conservatives at court, however, opposed these reforms. They saw little advantage in copying the West. As one said, "An examination of the causes of success and failure in government reveals that . . . the adoption of foreignism leads to disorder." According to this conservative, traditional Chinese rules needed to be reformed and not rejected in favor of Western changes.

Most important, Empress Dowager Ci Xi (TSUH • SEE), the emperor's aunt, opposed the new reform program. Ci Xi became a dominant force at court and opposed the emperor's reforms. With the aid of the imperial army, she eventually imprisoned the emperor. Other supporters of the reforms were imprisoned, exiled, or prosecuted. These actions ended Guang Xu's reforms. Although Guang Xu's efforts aroused popular sympathy, they had limited support within Chinese society overall.

✓ **READING PROGRESS CHECK**

Drawing Conclusions Why did Guang Xu's reforms fail to achieve the modernization of the government and military?

Responses to Imperialism

GUIDING QUESTION *What were the responses to imperialism in China?*

As foreign pressure on the Qing dynasty grew stronger, both Great Britain and the United States feared that other nations would overrun the country should the Chinese government collapse.

Opening the Door to China

In 1899, U.S. secretary of state John Hay wrote a note to Britain, Russia, Germany, France, Italy, and Japan. Hay presented a proposal that ensured equal access to the Chinese market for all nations and preserved the unity of the Chinese empire. When none of the other imperialist governments

PHOTO: Hu Weibiao/Panorama/The Image Works

expressed opposition to the idea, Hay proclaimed that all major states with economic interests in China had agreed that the country should have an Open Door policy.

In part, the **Open Door policy** reflected American concern for the survival of China. However, it also reflected the interests of some U.S. trading companies. These companies wanted to operate in open markets and disliked the existing division of China into separate spheres of influence dominated by individual countries.

The Open Door policy did not end the system of spheres of influence. However, it did reduce restrictions on foreign imports imposed by the dominating power within each sphere. The Open Door policy also helped reduce imperialist hysteria over access to the China market. The policy lessened fears in Britain, France, Germany, and Russia that other powers would take advantage of China's weakness and attempt to dominate the China market for themselves.

Open Door policy a policy, proposed by U.S. secretary of state John Hay in 1899, that stated all powers with spheres of influence in China would respect equal trading opportunities with China and not set tariffs giving an unfair advantage to the citizens of their own country

indemnity the payment for damages

The Boxer Rebellion

The Open Door policy came too late to stop the Boxer Rebellion. Boxer was the popular name given to members of a secret organization called the Society of Harmonious Fists. Members practiced a system of exercise—a form of shadowboxing, or boxing with an imaginary opponent—that they thought would protect them from bullets.

The Boxers were upset by economic distress and the foreign takeover of Chinese lands. They wanted to push foreigners out of China. Their slogan was "destroy the foreigner." They especially disliked Christian missionaries and Chinese converts to Christianity who seemed to threaten Chinese traditions. At the beginning of 1900, Boxer bands roamed the countryside and slaughtered foreign missionaries and Chinese Christians. Foreign businesspeople and the German envoy to Beijing were also victims.

Response to the killings was immediate and overwhelming. An allied army consisting of 20,000 British, French, German, Russian, American, and Japanese troops attacked Beijing in August 1900. The army restored order and demanded more concessions from the Chinese government. The Chinese government was forced to pay a heavy **indemnity** to the powers that had crushed the uprising. The imperial government was now weaker than ever.

▶CRITICAL THINKING

Making Inferences Why do you think the foreign response to the Boxer Rebellion was "immediate and overwhelming"?

▼ This photograph, from around 1901, shows Chinese men who took part in the Boxer Rebellion. They were captured and imprisoned by the American forces at Tientsin, China.

PHOTO: Library of Congress

✓ READING PROGRESS CHECK

Drawing Conclusions Did the Boxer Rebellion do anything to reduce the foreign presence in China? Explain your answer.

LESSON 1 REVIEW TEKS

Reviewing Vocabulary

1. ***Identifying Cause and Effect*** Write a short paragraph describing the Open Door policy and its effect on the existing spheres of influence in China.

Using Your Notes

2. ***Comparing and Contrasting*** Use your notes to answer the following questions. How were the Tai Ping and Boxer Rebellions different? How were they similar?

Answering the Guiding Questions

3. ***Identifying*** What factors influenced the decline of the Qing Empire?
4. ***Theorizing*** Why were spheres of influence established in China?
5. ***Synthesizing*** What were the responses to imperialism in China?

Writing Activity

6. **INFORMATIVE/EXPLANATORY** Write a short paragraph describing the major events in China related to imperialism during the nineteenth and early twentieth centuries.

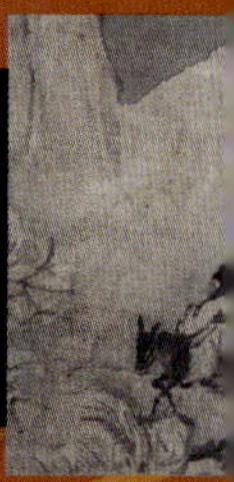

networks

There's More Online!

- IMAGE Chinese Emperor Henry Pu Yi at Age Three
- IMAGE Chinese Men Voluntarily Cut Their Pigtails
- IMAGE New Market in Hong Kong
- IMAGE The Revolution of 1911
- INTERACTIVE SELF-CHECK QUIZ
- PRIMARY SOURCE Sun Yat-sen
- PRIMARY SOURCE Yuan Shigai
- VIDEO The Chinese Revolution

LESSON 2
Revolution in China

ESSENTIAL QUESTIONS

- *How can new ideas accelerate economic and political change?*
- *How do cultures influence each other?*

Reading HELPDESK

Academic Vocabulary

- **phase**
- **motive**

Content Vocabulary

- **provincial**
- **commodities**

TAKING NOTES:

Key Ideas and Details

Comparing and Contrasting Use the graphic organizer to compare and contrast the reforms of Empress Dowager Ci Xi with those proposed by Sun Yat-sen.

Empress Dowager Ci Xi	Sun Yat-sen

IT MATTERS BECAUSE

After the Boxer Rebellion failed, China made desperate reform efforts. However, when Empress Dowager Ci Xi died in 1908, the Qing dynasty was near collapse. China slipped into revolution and civil war.

The Fall of the Qing

GUIDING QUESTION *What led to the fall of the Qing dynasty?*

After the Boxer Rebellion, the Qing dynasty in China tried desperately to reform itself. Ci Xi, who had long resisted suggestions from her advisers for change, now embraced a number of reforms.

A new education system based on the Western model was adopted, and the civil service examination system was dropped. In 1909 legislative assemblies were formed at the **provincial**, or local, level. Elections for a national assembly were held in 1910.

The emerging new elite, composed of merchants, professionals, and reform-minded gentry, soon became impatient with the slow pace of political change. They were angry when they discovered that the new assemblies were not allowed to pass laws but could only give advice to the ruler. Moreover, the recent reforms had done nothing for the peasants, artisans, and miners, whose living conditions were getting worse as taxes increased. Unrest grew in the countryside as the dynasty continued to ignore deep-seated resentments.

The Rise of Sun Yat-sen

The first signs of revolution appeared during the 1890s when the young radical Sun Yat-sen formed the Revive China Society.

Sun Yat-sen believed that the Qing dynasty was in a state of decay and could no longer govern the country. Unless the Chinese were united under a strong government, they would remain at the mercy of other countries. Although Sun believed that China should follow the pattern of Western countries, he also knew that the Chinese people were hardly ready for democracy.

Sun instead developed a three-stage reform process. The first stage would be a military takeover. In the second stage, a transitional **phase**, Sun's own revolutionary party would prepare the people for democratic rule. The final stage called for establishment of a constitutional democracy.

At a convention in Tokyo in 1905, Sun united members of radical groups from across China and formed the Revolutionary Alliance, which eventually became the Nationalist Party. In presenting his program, Sun Yat-sen called for the following changes:

provincial local; of or relating to a province

phase a part in the development cycle

PRIMARY SOURCE

"Establish the Republic: Now our revolution is based on equality, in order to establish a republican government. All our people are equal and all enjoy political rights. . . . Equalize land ownership: The good fortune of civilization is to be shared equally by all the people of the nation. . . . Its [the land's] present price shall be received by the owner . . . after the revolution [it] shall belong to the state."

—quoted in *Sources of Chinese Tradition*, 1960

Sun's new organization advocated his Three People's Principles, which promoted nationalism, democracy, and the right for people to pursue their own livelihoods. Although the new organization was small, it benefited from the rising discontent generated by the Qing dynasty's failure to improve conditions in China.

The Revolution of 1911

The Qing dynasty was near its end. In 1908, Empress Dowager Ci Xi died. Her nephew Guang Xu, a prisoner in the palace, died one day before his aunt. The throne was now occupied by China's "last emperor," the infant Henry Pu Yi.

ANALYZING PRIMARY SOURCES

The End of the Qing Dynasty

As the Qing Dynasty was coming to an end, Sun Yat-sen and Yuan Shigai communicated via telegrams about who would assume the presidency of a new China. Even though he was a general in the Qing dynasty, Yuan Shigai became president of the new Chinese republic in 1911.

"I beg to call the attention of Premier Yüan in Peking to the fact that when I reached Shanghai two days ago my comrades entrusted me with the responsibility of organizing a provisional government. . . . Although I have accepted this position for the time being, it is actually waiting for you, and my offer will eventually be made clear to the world. I hope that you will decide to accept this offer."

—telegram from Sun Yat-sen to Yuan Shigai, January 1, 1911, quoted in *The Political History of China, 1840–1928*

"I have received your telegram of the first. The choice between monarchism and republicanism in the political system is to be decided by public opinion and there is no way to predict what the decision will be. I dare not participate in the provisional government. You have been kind to offer me such great honor, but I am sorry to say that I dare not accept it; I hope I shall be excused from doing so."

—telegram from Yuan Shigai to Sun Yat-sen, January 2, 1911, quoted in *The Political History of China, 1840–1928*

DBQ Analyzing Historical Documents

1. ***Paraphrasing*** Summarize the excerpt from Sun Yat-sen's telegram to Yuan Shigai in your own words.
2. ***Making Inferences*** Why do you think Yuan Shigai initially declined Sun Yat-sen's offer?

Thinking Like a HISTORIAN

Classification and Revolutions

Historians look for general characteristics and particular patterns to classify events. Political revolutions are important phenomena that historians analyze. For example, a historian might classify one event as a revolution while another as an uprising. The author of this textbook notes that "the events of 1911 were less a revolution than a collapse of the old order." In other words, the revolution of 1911 was not really a revolution. Think about other revolutions you have learned about in your textbook and why this might be so.

In October 1911, followers of Sun Yat-sen launched an uprising in central China. At the time, Sun was traveling in the United States. Thus, the revolt had no leader, but the government was too weak to react. The Qing dynasty collapsed, opening the way for new political forces.

Sun's party had neither the military nor the political strength to form a new government. The party was forced to turn to a member of the old order, General Yuan Shigai (YOO • AHN SHUR • GIE), who controlled the army.

Yuan was a prominent figure in military circles. He had been placed in charge of the imperial army sent to suppress the rebellion. However, he abandoned the government and negotiated with members of Sun Yat-sen's party. General Yuan agreed to serve as president of a new Chinese republic and to allow the election of a legislature. Sun arrived in China in January 1912, after reading about the revolution in a Denver, Colorado, newspaper.

In the eyes of Sun Yat-sen's party, the events of 1911 were a glorious revolution that ended 2,000 years of imperial rule. However, the 1911 uprising was hardly a revolution. It produced no new political or social order. Sun Yat-sen and his followers still had much to accomplish.

The Revolutionary Alliance was supported mainly by an emerging urban middle class, and its program was based largely on Western liberal democratic principles. However, the urban middle class in China was too small to support a new political order. Most of the Chinese people still lived on the land, and few peasants supported Sun Yat-sen's party. In effect, then, the events of 1911 were less a revolution than a collapse of the old order.

An Era of Civil War

After the collapse of the Qing dynasty, the military took over. Sun Yat-sen and his colleagues had accepted General Yuan Shigai as president of the new Chinese republic in 1911 because they lacked the military force to compete with his control over the army. Many feared that if the revolt lapsed into chaos, the Western powers would intervene. If that happened, the last shreds of Chinese independence would be lost. However, even the general's new allies distrusted his **motives**.

motive a reason to take action

Yuan understood little of the new ideas sweeping into China from the West. He ruled in a traditional manner and even tried to set up a new imperial dynasty. The reformers hated Yuan for using murder and terror to destroy the new democratic institutions. The traditionalists hated Yuan for being disloyal to the dynasty he had served.

Yuan's dictatorial efforts rapidly led to clashes with Sun's party, now renamed the *Guomindang*, or Nationalist Party. When Yuan dissolved the new parliament, the Nationalists launched a rebellion. The rebellion failed, and Sun Yat-sen fled to Japan.

Yuan was strong enough to brush off the challenge from the revolutionary forces, but he could not turn back history. He died in 1916 and was succeeded by one of his officers. Over the next several years, China slipped into civil war as the power of the central government disintegrated and military warlords seized power in the provinces. Their soldiers caused massive destruction throughout China.

✓ **READING PROGRESS CHECK**

Explaining Why did rebellions occur in China after Yuan Shigai became president of the new republic in 1911?

Cultural Changes

GUIDING QUESTION *How did Western influences change Chinese society and culture?*

Western influences forced the Chinese to adapt to new ways of thinking and living. Early twentieth-century Chinese culture reflected the struggle between Confucian social ideas and those of the West.

▲ As part of the changes to the Chinese economy, trade increased between China and the West, as shown in this circa 1900 photograph of the New Market in Hong Kong.

▶ **CRITICAL THINKING**

Analyzing Visuals How does this image show the mixture of Chinese and Western influence in Chinese society?

commodities agricultural, mined, and mass-produced marketable goods

Society in Transition

When European traders began to move into China in greater numbers in the mid-1800s, Chinese society was in a state of transition. The growth of industry and trade was especially noticeable in the cities, where a national market for **commodities** such as oil, copper, salt, and tea had appeared.

The Chinese economy had never been more productive. Faster and more reliable transportation and a better system of money and banking had begun to create the foundation for a money economy. Foreign investments in China grew rapidly, and the money went into modernizing the Chinese economy. New crops brought in from abroad increased food production and encouraged population growth.

The coming of Westerners to China affected the Chinese economy in three ways. Westerners introduced modern means of transportation and communications, created an export market, and integrated the Chinese market into the nineteenth-century world economy.

To some, these changes were beneficial. Shaking China out of its old ways quickened a process of change that had already begun. Western influences forced the Chinese to adopt new ways of thinking and acting, and Western ideas stimulated the desire to modernize. Westerners also provided something else to the Chinese. They gave them a model, funds, and the technical knowledge to modernize.

At the same time, China paid a heavy price for the new ways. Imperialism imposed a state of dependence on China, and many Chinese were exploited. Imperialism condemned the country to a condition of underdevelopment. Its local industry was largely destroyed. Also, many of the profits in the new economy went to foreign countries rather than back into the Chinese economy.

During the first quarter of the twentieth century, the pace of change in China quickened even more. After World War I, which temporarily drew foreign investment out of the country, Chinese businesspeople began to develop new ventures. Shanghai became the bastion of the new bourgeoisie. People lived in Shanghai at the same rhythm they lived in other modern cities. Wuhan, Tianjin, and Guangzhou also became major industrial and commercial centers with a growing middle class and an industrial working class.

In 1800 daily life in China was the same as it had been for centuries. Most Chinese were farmers, living in millions of villages near rice fields and on hillsides throughout the countryside. A farmer's life was governed by the harvest cycle, village custom, and family ritual. A few men were educated in the Confucian classics. Women stayed at home or in the fields.

Analyzing PRIMARY SOURCES

Ba Jin on writing

Ba Jin once described his compulsion to express himself:

"Before my eyes are many miserable scenes, the suffering of others and myself forces my hands to move. I become a machine for writing."

—Ba Jin, *China Daily*

DBQ ***DRAWING CONCLUSIONS***
What do you think motivated Ba Jin to write?

All children were expected to obey their parents, and wives were expected to submit to the wishes of their husbands.

A visitor to China 125 years later would have seen a different society, although it would still have been recognizably Chinese. The changes were most striking in the cities, among the urban middle class. Here the educated and wealthy had been visibly affected by the growing Western cultural presence. Confucian social ideas were declining rapidly in influence.

Culture in Transition

Nowhere in China was the struggle between old and new more visible than in the culture. Radical reformers wanted to eliminate traditional culture, condemning it as an instrument of oppression. They were interested in creating a new China that would be respected by the modern world.

The first changes in traditional culture came in the late nineteenth century. Intellectuals began to introduce Western books, art, and ideas to China. Soon, China was flooded by Western culture as intellectuals called for a new culture based on that of the modern West.

Western literature and art became popular in China, especially among the urban middle class. Traditional culture, however, remained popular, especially in rural areas. Most creative artists followed foreign trends, while traditionalists held on to Chinese culture.

Literature in particular was influenced by foreign ideas. Western novels and short stories began to attract a larger audience. Although most Chinese novels written after World War I dealt with Chinese subjects, they reflected the Western tendency toward a realistic portrayal of society. Often, they dealt with the new Westernized middle class. Most of China's modern authors showed a clear contempt for the past.

Mao Dun became known as one of China's best modern novelists. *Midnight*, Dun's most popular work, was also published in French and English. A naturalistic novel, *Midnight* described the changing customs of Shanghai's urban elites.

Ba Jin, the author of numerous novels and short stories, was one of China's foremost writers of the twentieth century. Born in 1904, Ba Jin was well attuned to the rigors and expected obedience of Chinese family life. In his trilogy, *Family, Spring*, and *Autumn*, he describes the disintegration of traditional Confucian ways as the younger members of a large family attempt to break away from their elders.

✓ **READING PROGRESS CHECK**

Identifying How did education reforms during the late Qing dynasty contribute to intellectual and cultural innovations following the revolution?

LESSON 2 REVIEW TEKS

Reviewing Vocabulary

1. ***Making Generalizations*** Write a paragraph in which you define the term *commodities* and discuss the impact of domestic and international trade on China in the late nineteenth and early twentieth century.

Using Your Notes

2. ***Comparing and Contrasting*** Use your notes to write a paragraph comparing the reforms undertaken by Ci Xi toward the end of her reign with those proposed by Sun Yat-sen.

Answering the Guiding Questions

3. ***Identifying Cause and Effect*** What led to the fall of the Qing dynasty?

4. ***Making Connections*** How did Western influences change Chinese society and culture?

Writing Activity

5. **INFORMATIVE/EXPLANATORY** In what ways did Sun Yat-sen and the intellectuals and writers who succeeded him embrace Western ideas? How did they adapt these ideas to the Chinese context?

networks

There's More Online!

- CHART/GRAPH Japan's Foreign Trade, 1878–1917
- IMAGE Japanese Garden and Tea House
- IMAGE Tokyo-Yokohama Railway
- IMAGE Western Style Houses in Tokyo
- INTERACTIVE SELF-CHECK QUIZ
- MAP Japanese Expansion, 1870–1918
- TIME LINE Japanese Expansion, 1868–1910
- VIDEO The Rise of Modern Japan

LESSON 3

The Rise of Modern Japan

ESSENTIAL QUESTIONS

- *How can new ideas accelerate economic and political change?*
- *How do cultures influence each other?*

Reading HELPDESK

Academic Vocabulary

- **subsidy**
- **context**

Content Vocabulary

- **concessions**
- **prefecture**

TAKING NOTES:

Key Ideas and Details

Organizing As you read, create a table like the one below listing the political, economic, and social reforms of the Meiji Restoration.

Political	Economic	Social

It Matters Because

In the mid-nineteenth century, the United States forced Japan to open its doors to trade with Western nations. After the Sat-Cho alliance overthrew the shogun, the Meiji Restoration began. Japan emerged as a modern industrial society.

Japan Responds to Foreign Pressure

GUIDING QUESTION *How did Japan respond to foreign pressure to end its isolationist policies?*

By the end of the nineteenth century, Japan was emerging as a modern imperialist power. The Japanese followed the example of Western nations, while trying to preserve Japanese values.

By 1800, the Tokugawa shogunate had ruled Japan for 200 years. It had kept an isolationist policy, allowing only Dutch and Chinese merchants at its port at Nagasaki. Western nations wanted to end Japan's isolation, believing that the expansion of trade on a global basis would benefit all nations.

The first foreign power to succeed with Japan was the United States. In the summer of 1853, Commodore Matthew Perry arrived in Edo Bay (now Tokyo Bay) with an American fleet of four warships. Perry brought a letter from President Millard Fillmore, asking the Japanese for better treatment of sailors shipwrecked on the Japanese islands. (Foreign sailors shipwrecked in Japan were treated as criminals and exhibited in public cages.) He also asked to open foreign relations between the United States and Japan. Perry returned about six months later for an answer, this time with a larger fleet. Some shogunate officials recommended **concessions**, or political compromises. The guns of Perry's ships ultimately made Japan's decision.

Under military pressure, Japan agreed to the Treaty of Kanagawa with the United States. The treaty provided for the return of shipwrecked American sailors, the opening of two Japanese ports to Western traders, and the establishment of a U.S. consulate in Japan.

concession a political compromise

In 1858 a more detailed treaty called for the opening of several new ports to U.S. trade and residence. Japan soon signed similar treaties with several European nations.

Resistance to opening foreign relations was especially strong among the samurai warriors in two southern territories, Satsuma and Choshu. In 1863 the Sat-Cho alliance (from Satsuma-Choshu) forced the shogun to promise to end relations with the West. In 1868, when the shogun refused, the Sat-Cho leaders attacked the shogun's palace in Kyōto. His forces collapsed, ending the shogunate system and beginning the Meiji Restoration.

SKILLS PRACTICE

As you read about changes in Japanese politics, create a list of the words you do not know well. Find and write down the definitions for each word. Then, have a partner quiz you on the definitions of the words until you know them by sight.

✓ **READING PROGRESS CHECK**

Applying What led to the collapse of the shogunate system in Japan?

The Meiji Restoration

GUIDING QUESTION *How did the Meiji Restoration change Japan?*

The Sat-Cho leaders had genuinely mistrusted the West, but they soon realized that Japan must change to survive. The new leaders embarked on a policy of reform that transformed Japan into a modern industrial nation. The symbol of the new era was the young emperor Mutsuhito. He called his reign the Meiji (MAY • jee), or "Enlightened Rule." This period has thus become known as the Meiji Restoration.

Of course, the Sat-Cho leaders controlled the Meiji ruler, just as the shogunate had controlled earlier emperors. In recognition of the real source of political power, the capital was moved from Kyōto to Edo (now named Tokyo), the location of the new leaders.

▲ Japanese artist Hiroshige III created this woodblock print of the Tokyo-Yokohama railway just years after the Meiji Restoration opened the door to Western trade and ideas.

▶ **CRITICAL THINKING**

Identifying Bias Do you think the artist was biased in his depiction of the railway? Why or why not?

Transformation of Japanese Politics

When in power, the new leaders moved to abolish the old order and to strengthen power in their hands. To undercut the power of the daimyo (the local nobles) the new leaders stripped them of their lands in 1871. In turn, the lords were named governors of the territories formerly under their control. The territories were now called **prefectures**.

The Meiji reformers set out to create a modern political system based on the Western model. During the next 20 years, the Meiji government carefully studied Western political systems. As the process evolved, two main factions appeared, the Liberals and the Progressives. The Liberals wanted political reform based on the Western liberal democratic model, which vested supreme authority in a parliament. The Progressives wanted power to be shared between the legislative and executive branches, with the executive branch having more control.

During the 1870s and 1880s, these factions fought for control. The Progressives won. The Meiji constitution, adopted in 1889, was modeled after that of Imperial Germany. It gave most authority to the executive branch.

In theory, the emperor exercised all executive authority, but in practice he was a figurehead. Real executive authority rested in the prime minister and his cabinet of ministers chosen by the Meiji leaders. The upper house included royal appointees and elected nobles, while the lower house was elected. The two houses were to have equal legislative powers.

The final result was a political system that was democratic in form but authoritarian in practice. Although modern in external appearance, it was still traditional because power remained in the hands of a ruling oligarchy (the Sat-Cho leaders). The system allowed the traditional ruling class to keep its influence and economic power.

prefecture in the Japanese Meiji Restoration, a territory governed by its former daimyo lord

Meiji Economics

The Meiji leaders also set up a land reform program, which made the traditional lands of the daimyo the private property of the peasants. The daimyo were compensated with government bonds. The Meiji leaders then levied a new land tax, which was set at an annual rate of 3 percent of the estimated value of the land. The new tax was a great source of revenue for the government but a burden for farmers.

Under the old system, farmers had paid a fixed percentage of their harvest to the landowners. In bad harvest years, they had owed little or nothing. Under the new system, the farmers had to pay the land tax every year, regardless of the quality of the harvest. As a result, in bad years, many peasants were unable to pay their taxes. This forced them to sell their lands to wealthy neighbors and become tenant farmers who paid rent to the new owners. By the end of the nineteenth century, about 40 percent of all farmers were tenants.

With its budget needs met by the land tax, the government turned to the promotion of industry. The Meiji government gave **subsidies** to needy industries, provided training and foreign advisers, and improved transportation and communications. By 1900, Japan's industrial sector was beginning to grow. Besides tea and silk, other key industries were weapons and shipbuilding.

From the start, a unique feature of the Meiji model of industrial development was the close relationship between government and private business. The government encouraged new industries by giving businesspeople money and privileges. After an industry was on its feet, it was turned over entirely to private ownership.

▲ These woodblock prints are part of a series called "Famous Places on the Tokaido: A Record of the Process of Reform" (1875).

▶ **CRITICAL THINKING**

Analyzing Visuals How do these prints show the effects of reform on Japanese society?

Modern Institutions and Social Structures

The Meiji reformers also transformed other institutions. A new imperial army based on compulsory military service was formed in 1871. All Japanese men now served for three years. The new army was well equipped with modern weapons.

Education also changed. The Meiji leaders realized the need for universal education. In 1871 a new ministry of education adopted the American model of elementary schools, secondary schools, and universities. It brought foreign specialists to Japan to teach, and it sent students to study abroad.

Before the Meiji reforms, the lives of all Japanese people were determined by their membership in families, villages, and social classes. Japanese society was highly hierarchical. Belonging to a particular social class determined a person's occupation and social relationships. Women were especially limited by the "three obediences": child to father, wife to husband, and widow to son. Husbands could obtain a divorce; wives could not. Marriages were arranged, and the average marital age of females was 16 years. Females did not share inheritance rights with males. Few received any education outside the family.

The Meiji Restoration had a marked effect on the traditional social system in Japan. Special privileges for the aristocracy were abolished. For the first time, women were allowed to seek an education. As the economy shifted from an agricultural to an industrial base, many Japanese began to get new jobs and establish new social relationships.

Western fashions and culture became the rage. A new generation began to imitate the clothing styles, eating habits, and social practices of Westerners. The game of baseball was imported from the United States.

subsidy government payment to encourage or protect a certain economic activity

PHOTO: Asian Art & Archaeology / CORBIS

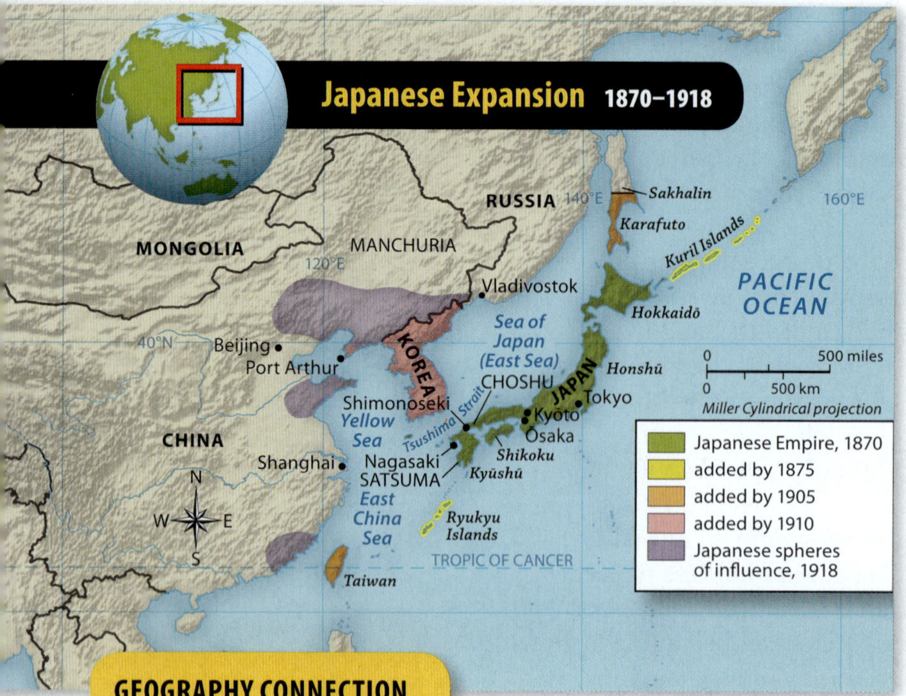

GEOGRAPHY CONNECTION

From 1870 to 1918 Japan expanded into Korea and China.

1. **THE WORLD IN SPATIAL TERMS** *What lands did Japan take by 1905?*
2. **HUMAN SYSTEMS** *What countries did Japan come into conflict with as it expanded?*

context the circumstances surrounding a situation or event

The social changes brought about by the Meiji Restoration also had a less attractive side. Many commoners were ruthlessly exploited in the coal mines and textile mills. Workers labored up to 20 hours a day. Coal miners in some areas worked in temperatures up to 130 degrees Fahrenheit (54 degrees C). When they tried to escape, they were shot.

The transformation of Japan into a "modern society" did not detach the country entirely from its old values, however. Traditional values based on loyalty to the family and community were still taught in schools. Traditional Japanese values were also given a firm legal basis in the 1889 constitution, which limited the right to vote to men. The Civil Code of 1898 played down individual rights and placed women within the **context** of their family role.

READING PROGRESS CHECK

Examining How did Meiji reforms reflect a mix of Western and traditional values?

Japanese Expansion

GUIDING QUESTION *Why did Japan turn itself into an imperialist power?*

The Japanese soon copied Western imperialism. The Japanese knew that Western nations had amassed some of their wealth and power because of their colonies. Those colonies had provided sources of raw materials, inexpensive labor, and markets for manufactured products. To compete, Japan would also have to expand.

The Japanese began their program of territorial expansion close to home. In 1874 Japan claimed control of the Ryukyu (ree • YOO • kyoo) Islands, which belonged to the Chinese Empire. Two years later, Japan's navy forced the Koreans to open their ports to Japanese trade. The Chinese grew concerned by Japan's growing influence there.

In the 1880s, Chinese-Japanese rivalry over Korea intensified. In 1894, the two nations went to war, and Japan won. In the treaty ending the war, China recognized Korea's independence.

China also ceded Taiwan and the Liaodong Peninsula, with its strategic naval base at Port Arthur, to Japan. In time, the Japanese gave the Liaodong Peninsula back to China.

Rivalry with Russia over influence in Korea led to increasingly strained relations. The Russo-Japanese War began in 1904. Japan launched a surprise attack on the Russian naval base at Port Arthur, which Russia had taken from China in 1898. In the meantime, Russia had sent its Baltic fleet halfway around the world to East Asia, only to be defeated by the new Japanese navy off the coast of Japan. After their defeat, the Russians agreed to a humiliating peace in 1905. They gave the Liaodong Peninsula back to Japan, as well as the southern part of Sakhalin (SA • kuh • LEEN), an island north of Japan. The Japanese victory stunned the world. Japan had become one of the great powers.

When Japan established a sphere of influence in Korea, the United States recognized Japan's role there. In return, Japan recognized American authority in the Philippines. In 1910 Japan annexed Korea outright.

Some Americans began to fear Japan's power in East Asia. In 1907 President Theodore Roosevelt made a "gentlemen's agreement" with Japan that essentially stopped Japanese immigration to the United States.

✓ READING PROGRESS CHECK

Identifying How did Japan benefit from its imperialist strategy?

Culture in an Era of Transition

GUIDING QUESTION ***How did contact between Japan and the West influence culture?***

The wave of Western technology and ideas that entered Japan after 1850 greatly altered traditional Japanese culture. Dazzled by European literature, Japanese authors began imitating the imported models. They began to write novels that were patterned after the French tradition of realism. Japanese authors presented social conditions and the realities of war as objectively as possible.

Other aspects of Japanese culture were also changed. The Japanese invited engineers, architects, and artists from Europe and the United States to teach their "modern" skills to Japanese students. The Japanese copied Western architectural styles. Huge buildings of steel and reinforced concrete, adorned with Greek columns, appeared in many Japanese cities.

A national reaction had begun by the end of the 1800s, and many Japanese artists began to return to older techniques. In 1889 the Tokyo School of Fine Arts was established to promote traditional Japanese art.

Cultural exchange also went the other way. Japanese arts and crafts, porcelains, textiles, fans, folding screens, and woodblock prints became fashionable in Europe and North America. Japanese gardens, with their close attention to the positioning of rocks and falling water, became especially popular in the United States.

✓ READING PROGRESS CHECK

Drawing Conclusions What inspired Japanese artists to return to traditional forms?

▶ CRITICAL THINKING

Making Inferences Why did aspects of Japanese culture become fashionable in the United States?

▼ This Japanese garden and tea house was showcased at the World's Fair in St. Louis, Missouri, in 1904.

LESSON 3 REVIEW TEKS

Reviewing Vocabulary

1. ***Explaining*** Explain how the prefecture system affected the daimyo.

Using Your Notes

2. ***Identifying*** Use the information from your notes to help explain the results of the Meiji Restoration.

Answering the Guiding Questions

3. ***Drawing Conclusions*** How did Japan respond to foreign pressure to end its isolationist policies?
4. ***Analyzing*** How did the Meiji Restoration change Japan?
5. ***Identifying Cause and Effect*** Why did Japan turn itself into an imperialist power?
6. ***Making Connections*** How did contact between Japan and the West influence culture?

Writing Activity

7. **INFORMATIVE/EXPLANATORY** Write two descriptive paragraphs about the woodblock prints in this lesson. In your answer, cite the artist's use of color, texture, line, shape, space, and perspective.

CHAPTER 26 Assessment

TEKS

Directions: On a separate sheet of paper, answer the questions below. Make sure you read carefully and answer all parts of the questions.

Lesson Review

Lesson 1

1. ***Theorizing*** What were the goals of the Tai Ping Rebellion? Why do you think Western nations fought against the rebels?

2. ***Explaining*** What were spheres of influence? How did Western nations and Japan acquire spheres of influence in China?

3. ***Specifying*** How did Russia acquire territory in Siberia, and how did Tibet manage to be free from either Chinese or Russian rule?

4. ***Explaining*** Explain the relationship among China, Japan, and Korea.

Lesson 2

5. ***Summarizing*** Why were the Qing reforms after the Boxer Rebellion unsuccessful?

6. ***Making Inferences*** Make inferences about the manner in which the 1911 Qing Dynasty collapse took place and about Sun Yat-sen's role and reaction, as well as General Yuan Shigai's acceptance of a presidency.

7. ***Summarizing*** In what ways did Westerners impact the Chinese economy?

8. ***Describing*** How did Western ideas influence Chinese authors?

9. ***Formulating Questions*** Ask and answer questions about the literature written during this time.

Lesson 3

10. ***Explaining*** Why did Western nations want to end Japan's long-held isolationist policy?

11. ***Making Inferences*** Make an inference about why the samurai warriors were especially resistant to Western or foreign negotiations.

12. ***Describing*** Why did the traditional ruling class of Japan continue to keep its influence even after the Meiji constitution?

13. ***Specifying*** What was the Treaty of Kanagawa? Why did Japan sign it?

14. ***Exploring Issues*** Which Western values inspired Meiji reforms? Which did the Meiji not copy?

Exploring the Essential Question

15. ***Analyzing*** Work with a partner to create two maps, one of China and one of Japan, showing places where new ideas accelerated economic or political change. Include labels explaining the ideas and the changes involved. Add visuals of people and places that represented change. Draw conclusions about why cultures change.

Need Extra Help?

If You've Missed Question	1	2	3	4	5	6	7	8	9	10	11	12	13	14	15
Go to page	614	615	615	616	618	619	621	622	622	623	624	624	623	625	609

Critical Thinking

16 ***Explaining Relationships*** How did European imperialism impact China? 8D

17 ***Economics*** Why did Britain begin selling opium to China? What was the intended effect, and what were some major unintended effects?

18 ***Comparing and Contrasting*** Using what you learned and additional research, compare the life of a Chinese farmer in 1800 with the life of a middle-class person 125 years later. How might their beliefs, work, income, and politics differ?

19 ***Explaining*** What did the Meiji claim their land reforms would give the peasants? How did those reforms actually work out?

20 ***Identifying Cause and Effect*** How did the Meiji reformers increase Japan's industrial sector?

21 ***Speculating*** Speculate about the family dynamic under the practice of "three obediences," especially for wives and daughters.

22 ***Theorizing*** What does the exchange of cultural ideas and traditional craft between Japan and North American and European countries tell you about the impact of Japanese culture on these groups?

Social Studies Skills

23 ***Synthesizing*** What role did Ci Xi play in the reform movements of China over time?

24 ***Identifying Cause and Effect*** What impact did the Open Door policy have on spheres of influence in China?

25 ***Understanding Relationships Among Events*** What was the relationship between the Meiji Restoration's industrial efforts and Japanese commoners who carried out the labor?

26 ***Interpreting*** What was Sun Yat-sen's vision for reform in China?

27 ***Identifying Continuity and Change*** What turn of events solidified Japan as one of the great powers and reduced Russia's domination?

28 ***Evaluating*** What was the significance of Japan's takeover of Chinese and Russian territories?

29 ***Creating Presentations*** Conduct research on Confucianism, and create a presentation that explains some of its key principles and expressions. Explain how Westernized thinking began to change Confucianism.

Need Extra Help?

If You've Missed Question	16	17	18	19	20	21	22	23	24	25	26	27	28	29
Go to page	616	613	609	625	625	625	627	616	617	625	618	626	626	609

DBQ Analyzing Primary Sources

Use the document to answer the following questions.

In 1868, after ending the shogunate, the Sat-Cho reformers insisted that the new emperor sign the Charter Oath below.

PRIMARY SOURCE

> "Article 1. Deliberative assemblies shall be widely established and all matters decided by public discussion.
> Article 2. All classes, high and low, shall unite in vigorously carrying out the administration of the affairs of state.
> Article 3. The common people, no less than the civil and military officials, shall each be allowed to pursue his own calling so that there may be no discontent.
> Article 4. Evil customs of the past shall be broken off and everything based upon the just laws of Nature.
> Article 5. Knowledge shall be sought throughout the world so as to strengthen the foundation of imperial rule."
>
> —quoted in *East Asia: A New History*

30. ***Analyzing Primary Sources*** Does the Charter Oath fit the mood of Japan in 1868? Explain.

31. ***Comparing and Contrasting*** What are the similarities and differences between the Meiji Charter Oath and Sun Yat-sen's Three People's Principles in China?

Analyzing Visuals

Use the image to answer the following questions.

32. ***Interpreting*** How does this print reflect the changes in Japanese society during the Meiji Restoration?

33. ***Analyzing*** How does this print show a blend of Japanese traditional culture with Western culture, and how does it show variation of economic status among people?

Extended Response Question

34. ***Expository*** How did Western culture affect China and Japan? How did Chinese and Japanese culture affect Western nations?

Need Extra Help?

If You've Missed Question	30	31	32	33	34
Go to page	630	619	630	630	609

World War I and the Russian Revolution

1914–1919

ESSENTIAL QUESTIONS • *Why do politics often lead to war?*
• *How can technology impact war?*

networks

There's More Online! about World War I and the Russian Revolution.

CHAPTER 27

The Story Matters...

On June 28, 1914, an assassination in the Balkans created an international crisis, igniting a European powder keg created by nationalism, massive military buildups, complex alliances, and imperial rivalries. By August, Europe was at war. The widespread use of trench warfare on the Western Front in France created a destructive stalemate that lasted four years. The introduction of new weapons, including heavy artillery, tanks, machine guns, and poison gas, produced casualty levels that dwarfed those of previous wars.

◄ A young French infantryman pauses for a photograph during World War I. In France, the troops of the enemy armies lived in trenches in the ground and faced each other across the barbed wire marking the limits of the narrow, deadly strip known as "no-man's land."

PHOTO: Rue des Archives/The Granger Collection, NYC

CHAPTER 27

Place and Time: Europe and Russia 1914–1919

In the years before World War I, European powers made use of the industrial innovations of the late nineteenth century to create new weapons. Most European nations also enlarged their armies. In 1882 Germany, Italy, and Austria-Hungary came together in the Triple Alliance, while in 1907 Great Britain, France, and Russia formed the Triple Entente. Retaliation against the 1914 assassination of Francis Ferdinand, Archduke of Austria-Hungary, tested those alliances and eventually drew Europe into World War I.

Step Into the Place

Read the quote and look at the information presented on the map.

DBQ Why did the assassination of Archduke Francis Ferdinand spark World War I?

PRIMARY SOURCE

“A note of genuine regret is that, deprived of the Archduke's strong personality, Austria inevitably will be more subject to German influence. Several journalists express the fear that the consequences will be sufficiently serious again to plunge the Balkans, if not Europe, into a conflict.

Apprehension lest the Sarajevo crime prove a dire blow to the stability of Europe almost overshadows the feeling of horror and reprobation over the assassination and deep sympathy for the aged Emperor in the comments of the morning papers.”

—from a special cable from Paris to *The New York Times*, June 29, 1914

PHOTO: Henry Guttmann/Hulton Archive/Getty Images

Step Into the Time

Choose a European event from the time line and write a paragraph predicting how it might influence the events of World War I.

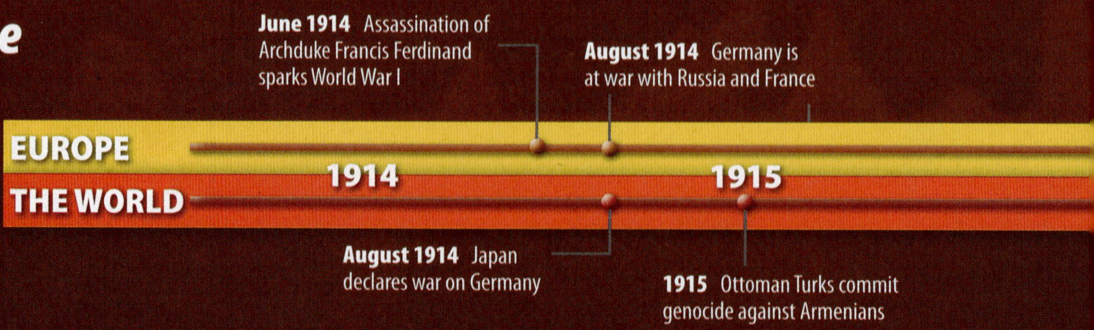

networks
There's More Online!

- ☑ ***Map*** Explore the interactive version of this map on Networks.
- ☑ ***Time Line*** Explore the interactive version of the time line on Networks.

1916 Germany engages in unrestricted submarine warfare

1916 Germans flee Cameroon for Spanish Guinea

February-December 1916
German offensive at the Battle of Verdun

1917 Russian Revolution begins

1917 U.S. enters World War I

October, 1917 Brazil declares war on Germany

December 1917
The peace conference at Brest-Litovsk opens

1918 Germany agrees to truce

1918 Worldwide influenza epidemic begins

November 11, 1918 Germany and Allies sign an armistice

June 1919 Treaty of Versailles signed

1919 U.S. president Woodrow Wilson helps form the League of Nations

1919 Togo becomes a French mandate

1916 **1917** **1918** **1919**

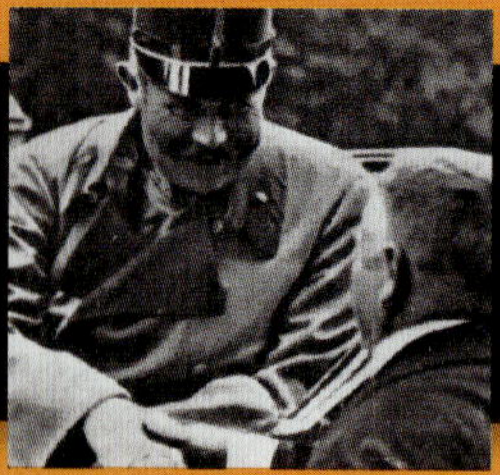

networks

There's More Online!

- BIOGRAPHY Archduke Francis Ferdinand
- CHART/GRAPH Estimated Army Size, 1914
- IMAGE German Mobilization
- INTERACTIVE SELF-CHECK QUIZ
- MAP Alliances in Europe, 1914
- MAP The Schlieffen Plan
- PRIMARY SOURCE The Assassination of Francis Ferdinand
- TIME LINE The Outbreak of World War I
- VIDEO World War I

LESSON 1
World War I Begins

ESSENTIAL QUESTIONS • *Why do politics often lead to war?* • *How can technology impact war?*

Reading HELPDESK

Academic Vocabulary
- **military**
- **complex**

Content Vocabulary
- **conscription**
- **mobilization**

TAKING NOTES:
Key Ideas and Details

Sequencing Use a sequence chain like the one below to list the events leading up to World War I.

June 28, 1914:
↓
July 28, 1914:
↓
August 1, 1914:
↓
August 3, 1914:
↓
August 4, 1914:

TEKS Texas Essential Knowledge and Skills

1F identify major causes and describe the major effects of the following important turning points in world history from 1914 to the present: the world wars and their impact on political, economic, and social systems; communist revolutions and their impact on the Cold War; independence movements; and globalization

continued on the next page

It Matters Because

As European countries formed alliances and increased the sizes of their armed forces, they set the stage for a global war. All they needed was a good reason to mobilize troops. When a Serbian terrorist assassinated Archduke Francis Ferdinand and his wife, World War I soon followed.

Causes of the War

GUIDING QUESTION *What factors contributed to the start of World War I?*

Nineteenth-century liberals believed that if European states were organized along national lines, these states would work together and create a peaceful Europe. They were very wrong.

Nationalism, Imperialism, Militarism, and Alliances

The system of nation-states that emerged in Europe in the last half of the nineteenth century led not to cooperation but rather to competition. Each European nation-state regarded itself as subject to no higher interest or authority. Each state was guided by its own self-interests and success. Furthermore, most leaders thought that war was an acceptable way to preserve the power of their national states. These attitudes made war an ever-present possibility.

The imperialist expansion of the last half of the nineteenth century also played a role in the coming of war. The competition for lands abroad, especially in Africa, led to conflict and heightened the existing rivalries among European states.

Nationalism, along with imperialism, had another serious result. Not all ethnic groups had become nations in Europe. Slavic minorities in the Balkans and the Austro-Hungarian Empire still dreamed of their own national states. The Irish in the British Empire and the Poles in the Russian Empire had similar dreams.

Industrialization offered new methods of shipbuilding and the use of iron, steel, and chemicals for new weapons. The growth of mass armies and navies after 1900 heightened tensions in Europe. It was obvious that if war did come, it would be highly destructive.

Most Western countries had established **conscription**, a **military** draft, as a regular practice before 1914. European armies doubled in size between 1890 and 1914. With its 1.3 million men, the Russian army had grown to be the largest. The French and German armies were not far behind, with 900,000 soldiers each. The British, Italian, and Austro-Hungarian armies numbered between 250,000 and 500,000 soldiers each.

Militarism—the aggressive preparation for war—was growing. As armies grew, so did the influence of military leaders. They drew up vast and **complex** plans for quickly mobilizing millions of soldiers and enormous quantities of supplies in the event of war.

Fearing that any changes would cause chaos in the armed forces, military leaders insisted that their plans could not be altered. This left European political leaders with little leeway. In 1914 they had to make decisions for military instead of political reasons.

At the same time, a system of alliances intensified the dangers of militarism. Europe's great powers had been divided into two loose political alliances. Germany, Austria-Hungary, and Italy formed the Triple Alliance in 1882. France, Great Britain, and Russia created the Triple Entente in 1907.

In the early years of the twentieth century, a series of crises tested these alliances. Especially troublesome were the crises in the Balkans between 1908 and 1913. These events left European states angry at each other and eager for revenge. By 1914 the major European states had come to believe that their allies were important. They were willing to use war to preserve their power and the power of their allies.

conscription military draft

military relating to the armed forces or to soldiers, arms, or war

complex having many intricate parts

(continued from p. 634)

TEKS **Texas Essential Knowledge and Skills**
10A identify the importance of imperialism, nationalism, militarism, and the alliance system in causing World War I

GEOGRAPHY CONNECTION

In 1914 Europe was divided into the Triple Alliance and Triple Entente.

1. **THE WORLD IN SPATIAL TERMS** *Which alliance controlled the most territory?*
2. **HUMAN SYSTEMS** *Which alliance had the most soldiers in 1914?*

ESTIMATED ARMY SIZE, 1914

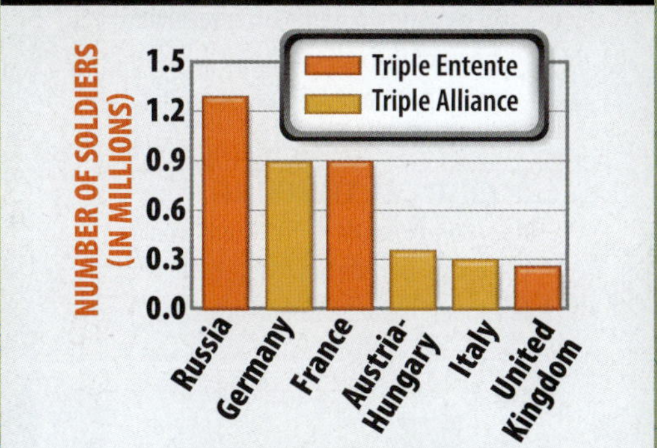

Source: *Encyclopedia of the First World War*

Internal Dissent

National desires were not the only source of internal strife at the beginning of the twentieth century. Socialist labor movements also had grown more powerful. The Socialists were increasingly inclined to use strikes, even violent ones, to achieve their goals.

Some conservative leaders, alarmed at the increase in labor strife and class division, feared that European nations were on the verge of revolution. This desire to suppress internal disorder might have encouraged various leaders to take the plunge into war in 1914.

✓ **READING PROGRESS CHECK**

Analyzing How might internal dissent in European states have led to World War I?

The Outbreak of War

GUIDING QUESTION ***How did the assassination of Archduke Francis Ferdinand spark the outbreak of war?***

Nationalism and imperialism, militarism and alliances, and the desire to stifle internal dissent might all have played a role in starting World War I. However, it was the decisions that European leaders made in response to a crisis in the Balkans that led directly to the conflict.

Assassination in Sarajevo and Responses

By 1914 Serbia, supported by Russia, was determined to create a large, independent Slavic state in the Balkans. Austria-Hungary, which had its own Slavic minorities to contend with, was equally determined to prevent that from happening.

On June 28, 1914, Archduke Francis Ferdinand, the heir to the Hapsburg throne of Austria-Hungary, and his wife Sophia visited the city of Sarajevo (SAR • uh • YAY • voh) in Bosnia. A group of conspirators waited there in the streets.

In that group was Gavrilo Princip, a 19-year-old Bosnian Serb. Princip was a member of the Black Hand, a Serbian terrorist organization that wanted Bosnia to be free of Austria-Hungary and to become part of a large Serbian kingdom. An assassination attempt earlier that morning by one of the conspirators had failed. Later that day, however, Princip succeeded in fatally shooting the archduke and his wife.

The Austro-Hungarian government did not know if the Serbian government was directly involved in the archduke's assassination, but it did not care. It saw an opportunity to "render Serbia innocuous once and for all by a display of force," as the Austrian foreign minister put it. Austrian leaders wanted to attack Serbia but feared that Russia would intervene on Serbia's behalf. So, they asked for—and received—the backing of their German allies.

▼ **Men marched through the streets of downtown Berlin after receiving news of the call for the mobilization of German troops in World War I.**

▶ **CRITICAL THINKING**

Analyzing Visuals What words would you use to describe how these Berliners felt about the mobilization for war?

Emperor William II of Germany gave Austria-Hungary a "blank check," promising Germany's full support if war broke out between Russia and Austria-Hungary. On July 28, Austria-Hungary declared war on Serbia.

Russia was determined to support Serbia's cause. On July 28, Czar Nicholas II ordered partial mobilization of the Russian army against Austria-Hungary. **Mobilization** is the process of assembling troops and supplies for war. In 1914 mobilization was considered an act of war.

Leaders of the Russian army informed the czar that they could not partially mobilize. Their mobilization plans were based on a war against both Germany and Austria-Hungary. Mobilizing against only the one front of Austria-Hungary, they claimed, would create chaos in the army. Based on this claim, the czar ordered full mobilization of the Russian army on July 29, knowing that Germany would consider this order an act of war.

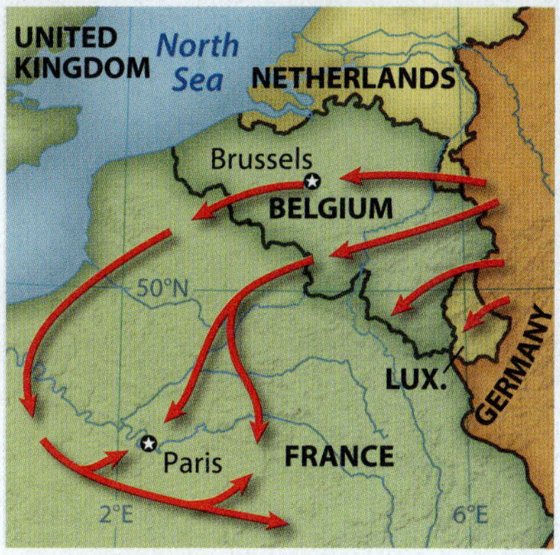

▲ The Schlieffen Plan had German troops attack France by quickly moving through Belgium.

▶ **CRITICAL THINKING**

Analyzing How did the implementation of the Schlieffen Plan broaden the conflict in Europe?

mobilization the process of assembling troops and supplies and making them ready for war

The Conflict Broadens

Indeed, Germany reacted quickly. The German government warned Russia that it must halt its mobilization within 12 hours. When Russia ignored this warning, Germany declared war on Russia on August 1.

Like the Russians, the Germans had a military plan. General Alfred von Schlieffen (SHLEE • fuhn) had helped draw up the plan, which was known as the Schlieffen Plan. It called for a two-front war with France and Russia because the two had formed a military alliance in 1894.

According to the Schlieffen Plan, Germany would conduct a small holding action against Russia while most of the German army would carry out a rapid invasion of France. This meant invading France by moving quickly along the level coastal area through Belgium. After France was defeated, the German invaders would move to the east against Russia.

Under the Schlieffen Plan, Germany could not mobilize its troops solely against Russia. Therefore, it declared war on France on August 3. At about the same time, it issued an ultimatum to Belgium demanding that German troops be allowed to pass through Belgian territory. Belgium, however, was a neutral nation.

On August 4, Great Britain declared war on Germany, officially for violating Belgian neutrality. In fact, Britain, which was allied with France and Russia, was concerned about maintaining its own world power. As one British diplomat put it, if Germany and Austria-Hungary won the war, "what would be the position of a friendless England?" By August 4, all the great powers of Europe were at war.

✓ **READING PROGRESS CHECK**

Interpreting What roles did the assassination of Francis Ferdinand and the existence of prior military plans play in leading quickly to the outbreak of World War I?

LESSON 1 REVIEW TEKS

Reviewing Vocabulary

1. **Making Connections** How is mobilization related to militarism?

Using Your Notes

2. ***Constructing Arguments*** Use your notes to discuss how alliances helped lead to the start of World War I. 1F, 10A

Answering the Guiding Questions

3. ***Identifying Causes*** What factors contributed to the start of World War I? 1F, 10A
4. ***Interpreting*** How did the assassination of Archduke Francis Ferdinand spark the outbreak of war?

Writing Activity

5. **NARRATIVE** Imagine you are an ordinary citizen of Germany. You have been reading the newspapers daily since the assassination of Francis Ferdinand, archduke of Austria. Write two or more journal entries on different days between the assassination on June 28, 1914, and August 4, 1914, reflecting on the events.

networks

There's More Online!

- BIOGRAPHY Woodrow Wilson
- IMAGE Armored Tank
- IMAGE British Propaganda Poster
- IMAGE German Fighter Pilot Manfred von Richthofen
- IMAGE World War I Machine Gunners
- INFOGRAPHIC The Technology of Trench Warfare
- INTERACTIVE SELF-CHECK QUIZ
- PRIMARY SOURCE The Zimmermann Telegram
- VIDEO America Enters the War

LESSON 2
World War I

ESSENTIAL QUESTIONS • *Why do politics often lead to war?* • *How can technology impact war?*

Reading HELPDESK

Academic Vocabulary

- **target**
- **unrestricted**

Content Vocabulary

- **propaganda**
- **trench warfare**
- **war of attrition**
- **total war**
- **planned economies**

TAKING NOTES:

Key Ideas and Details

Identifying Use a graphic organizer like the one below to identify how alliances shifted during World War I.

World War I Alliances

	Allied Powers	Central Powers
Pre-war name		
Original members		
Later additions		

TEKS Texas Essential Knowledge and Skills

1F identify major causes and describe the major effects of the following important turning points in world history from 1914 to the present: the world wars and their impact on political, economic, and social systems; communist revolutions and their impact on the Cold War; independence movements; and globalization

continued on the next page

It Matters Because

The war that many thought would be over in a few weeks lasted far longer, resulting in many casualties on both sides. The war widened, and the United States entered the fray in 1917. As World War I escalated, governments took control of their economies, rationing food and supplies and calling on civilians to work and make sacrifices for the war effort.

1914 to 1915: Illusions and Stalemate

GUIDING QUESTION *How did the war on the Eastern Front differ from war on the Western Front?*

Before 1914 many political leaders believed war to be impractical because it involved so many political and economic risks. Others believed that diplomats could easily prevent war. In August 1914 both ideas were shattered. However, the new illusions that replaced them soon proved to be equally foolish.

Government **propaganda**—ideas that are spread to influence public opinion for or against a cause—had stirred national hatreds before the war. Now, in August 1914, the urgent pleas of European governments for defense against aggressors fell on receptive ears in every nation that was at war. Most people seemed genuinely convinced that their nation's cause was just.

A new set of illusions also fed the enthusiasm for war. In August 1914 almost everyone believed that the war would be over in a few weeks. After all, almost all European wars since 1815 had, in fact, ended in a matter of weeks. The soldiers who boarded the trains for the war front in August 1914 and the jubilant citizens who saw them off believed that the warriors would be home by Christmas.

The Western Front

German hopes for a quick end to the war rested on a military gamble. The Schlieffen Plan called for the German army to make a vast encircling movement through Belgium into northern France. According to the plan, the German forces would sweep around Paris. This would enable them to surround most of the French army.

However, the German advance was halted a short distance from Paris at the First Battle of the Marne (September 6–10). To stop the Germans, French military leaders loaded 2,000 Parisian taxicabs with fresh troops and sent them to the front line.

The war quickly turned into a stalemate as neither the Germans nor the French could dislodge each other from the trenches they had dug for shelter. Two lines of trenches soon reached from the English Channel to the frontiers of Switzerland. The Western Front had become bogged down in **trench warfare**. Both sides were kept in virtually the same positions for four years.

propaganda ideas spread to influence public opinion for or against a cause

trench warfare fighting from ditches protected by barbed wire, as in World War I

(continued from p. 636)

TEKS **Texas Essential Knowledge and Skills**

10B identify major characteristics of World War I, including total war, trench warfare, modern military technology, and high casualty rates

24A describe the changing roles of women, children, and families during major eras of world history

28C explain the effects of major new military technologies on World War I, World War II, and the Cold War

The Eastern Front

Unlike the Western Front, the war on the Eastern Front was marked by mobility. The cost in lives, however, was equally enormous. At the beginning of the war, the Russian army moved into eastern Germany but was decisively defeated at the Battle of Tannenberg on August 30 and the Battle of Masurian Lakes on September 15. After these defeats, the Russians were no longer a threat to Germany.

Austria-Hungary, Germany's ally, fared less well at first. The Austrians had been defeated by the Russians in Galicia and thrown out of Serbia as well. To make matters worse, the Italians betrayed their German and Austrian allies in the Triple Alliance by attacking Austria in May 1915. Italy thus joined France, Great Britain, and Russia, who had previously been known as the Triple Entente, but now were called the Allied Powers, or Allies.

GEOGRAPHY CONNECTION

World War I took place along two main fronts.

1. **HUMAN SYSTEMS** *What generalizations can you make about the war based on the dates of important victories for the Allied and Central Powers?*
2. **THE USES OF GEOGRAPHY** *Why does the farthest advance of the Allied and Central Powers change more on the Eastern Front than the Western Front?*

▲ A boy delivers a newspaper to men living in the trenches during World War I.

▶ **CRITICAL THINKING**
Explaining What was unique about trench warfare?

By this time, the Germans had come to the aid of the Austrians. A German-Austrian army defeated the Russian army in Galicia and pushed the Russians far back into their own territory. Russian casualties stood at 2.5 million killed, captured, or wounded. The Russians were almost knocked out of the war.

Encouraged by their success against Russia, Germany and Austria-Hungary, joined by Bulgaria in September 1915, attacked and eliminated Serbia from the war. Their successes in the east would enable the German troops to move back to the offensive in the west.

✓ **READING PROGRESS CHECK**

Inferring Why did trench warfare develop on the Western Front but not on the Eastern Front?

Trench and Air Warfare

GUIDING QUESTION *What made World War I more devastating than any previous wars?*

On the Western Front, the trenches dug in 1914 had by 1916 become elaborate systems of defense. The Germans and the French each had hundreds of miles of trenches, which were protected by barbed-wire entanglements up to 5 feet (about 1.5 m) high and 30 yards (about 27 m) wide. Concrete machine-gun nests and other gun batteries, supported further back by heavy artillery, protected the trenches. Troops lived in holes in the ground, separated from each other by a strip of territory known as no-man's-land.

Trench warfare baffled military leaders who had been trained to fight wars of movement and maneuver. At times, the high command on either side would order an offensive that would begin with an artillery barrage to flatten the enemy's barbed wire and leave them in a state of shock. After "softening up" the enemy in this fashion, a mass of soldiers would climb out of their trenches with fixed bayonets and hope to work their way toward the enemy trenches.

The attacks rarely worked because men advancing unprotected across open fields could be fired at by the enemy's machine guns. In 1916 and 1917, millions of young men died in the search for the elusive breakthrough. In just 10 months at Verdun, France, 700,000 men lost their lives over a few miles of land. World War I had turned into a **war of attrition**, a war based on wearing down the other side with constant attacks and heavy losses.

war of attrition a war based on wearing down the other side with constant attacks and heavy losses, such as World War I

By the end of 1915, modern military technology such as airplanes appeared on the battlefront for the first time in history. Planes were first used to spot the enemy's position. Soon, planes also began to attack ground **targets**, especially enemy communications. Fights for control of the air space occurred, and then increased over time. At first, pilots fired at each other with handheld pistols. Later, machine guns were mounted on the noses of planes, which made the skies considerably more dangerous.

target something or someone marked for attack

The Germans also used their giant airships—the zeppelins—to bomb London and eastern England. This caused little damage but frightened many people. Germany's enemies, however, soon found that zeppelins, which were filled with hydrogen gas, quickly became raging infernos when hit by antiaircraft guns.

✓ **READING PROGRESS CHECK**

Drawing Conclusions Why did technology make it difficult for armies on the Western Front to mount a successful offensive attack?

A World War

GUIDING QUESTION *Why did the war widen to become a world conflict?*

Because of the stalemate on the Western Front, both sides sought to gain new allies. Each side hoped new allies would provide a winning advantage, as well as a new source of money and war goods.

Widening of the War

Bulgaria entered the war on the side of the Central Powers, as Germany, Austria-Hungary, and the Ottoman Empire were called. Russia, Great Britain, and France—the Allied Powers—declared war on the Ottoman Empire. The Allies tried to open a Balkan front by landing forces at Gallipoli (guh • LIH • puh • lee), southwest of Constantinople, in April 1915. However, the campaign was disastrous and the Allies withdrew.

By 1917 the war had truly become a world conflict. That year, while stationed in the Middle East, a British officer known as Lawrence of Arabia urged Arab princes to revolt against their Ottoman overlords. In 1918 British forces from Egypt mobilized troops from India, Australia, and New Zealand and worked to destroy the Ottoman Empire in the Middle East.

The Allies also took advantage of Germany's preoccupations in Europe and lack of naval strength to seize German colonies in the rest of the world. Japan, a British ally beginning in 1902, seized a number of German-held islands in the Pacific. Australia seized German New Guinea.

THE NEW YORK HERALD.

THE LUSITANIA IS SUNK; 1,000 PROBABLY ARE LOST

GERMANS TORPEDO THE GIANT STEAMSHIP AND SHE FOUNDERS EIGHT MILES FROM IRISH COAST

RESCUE VESSELS SPEED TO THE SCENE TO PICK UP SURVIVORS; ONLY 500 ARE ACCOUNTED FOR

George A. Kessler One of Those Saved, Cable Message to Cunard Office Says

▲ The sinking of the *Lusitania* made the front page of *The New York Herald.* Germany claimed that the British passenger ship was a fair target because it carried 173 tons of ammunitions as cargo.

▶ **CRITICAL THINKING**

Inferring Why did this event help lead to the U.S. entry in the war?

Entry of the United States

At first, the United States tried to remain neutral. As World War I dragged on, however, it became more difficult to do so. The immediate cause of the United States's involvement grew out of the naval war between Germany and Great Britain.

Britain had used its superior navy to set up a blockade of Germany. The blockade kept war materials and other goods from reaching Germany by sea. Germany, in turn, set up its own blockade of Britain and enforced it with the use of **unrestricted** submarine warfare, including the sinking of passenger liners.

On May 7, 1915, German forces sank the British ship *Lusitania*. About 1,100 civilians, including more than 100 Americans, died. After strong protests from the United States, the German government suspended unrestricted submarine warfare in September 1915 to avoid antagonizing the United States further. Only once did the Germans and British engage in direct naval battle—at the Battle of Jutland on May 31, 1916; neither side won a conclusive victory.

By January 1917, however, the Germans were eager to break the deadlock in the war. German naval officers convinced Emperor William II that resuming the use of unrestricted submarine warfare could starve the British into submission within six months. When the emperor expressed concern

unrestricted having no restrictions or bounds

Connections to TODAY

Influenza Pandemic of 2009

The pandemic of 1918 was caused by a type of the H1N1 influenza virus. A previously unknown strain of this virus appeared in 2009. First occurring in Mexico in February 2009, the disease spread rapidly worldwide, presumably due to high levels of air travel. In June, the World Health Organization (WHO) declared that H1N1 had become a pandemic, or an outbreak affecting a high proportion of the population over a wide geographic area. Unlike the 1918 outbreak, the H1N1 flu did not mutate into a more deadly form, and the death toll remained relatively low. In August 2010, the WHO announced that the H1N1 flu had moved into a post-pandemic stage.

about the United States, German Admiral Holtzendorf assured him: "I give your Majesty my word as an officer that not one American will land on the continent."

The German naval officers were quite wrong. The British were not forced to surrender, and the return to unrestricted submarine warfare brought the United States into the war in April 1917. U.S. troops did not arrive in large numbers in Europe until 1918. However, the entry of the United States into the war gave the Allied Powers a psychological boost and a major new source of money and war goods.

✓ **READING PROGRESS CHECK**

Analyzing How did imperialism contribute to the widening of World War I?

The Impact of Total War

GUIDING QUESTION ***What was the impact of total war?***

As World War I dragged on, it became a **total war** involving a complete mobilization of resources and people. It affected the lives of all citizens in the warring countries, however far from the battlefields. The home front was rapidly becoming a cause for as much effort as the war front.

Increased Government Powers

Most people had expected the war to be short. Little thought had been given to long-term wartime needs. Governments had to respond quickly, however, when the new war machines failed to achieve their goals. Many more men and supplies were needed to continue the war effort. To meet these needs, governments expanded their powers. Countries drafted tens of millions of young men, hoping for that elusive breakthrough to victory.

Wartime governments throughout Europe also expanded their power over their economies. Free-market capitalistic systems were temporarily put aside. Governments set up price, wage, and rent controls. They also rationed food supplies and materials; regulated imports and exports; and took over transportation systems and industries. In effect, in order to mobilize all the resources of their nations for the war effort, European nations set up **planned economies**.

As a result of total war mobilization, the differences between soldiers at war and civilians at home were narrowed. In the view of political leaders, all citizens were part of a national army that was dedicated to victory. Woodrow Wilson, president of the United States, said that the men and women "who remain to till the soil and man the factories are no less a part of the army than the men beneath the battle flags."

Manipulation of Public Opinion

As the war continued and casualties worsened, the patriotic enthusiasm that marked the early stages of the war began to wane. By 1916 signs indicated that civilian morale was beginning to crack. War governments, however, fought back against growing opposition to the war.

Authoritarian regimes, such as those of Germany, Russia, and Austria-Hungary, relied on force to subdue their populations. With the pressures of the war, however, even democratic states expanded their police powers to stop internal dissent. The British Parliament, for example, passed the Defence of the Realm Act (DORA). It allowed the government to arrest protesters as traitors. Newspapers were censored, and sometimes publication was suspended.

total war a war that involved the complete mobilization of resources and people, affecting the lives of all citizens in the warring countries, even those remote from the battlefield

planned economy an economic system directed by government agencies

Wartime governments made active use of propaganda to increase enthusiasm for the war. As the war progressed and morale sagged, governments were forced to devise new techniques for motivating citizens.

Total War and Society

In the fall of 1918, a deadly influenza struck, adding to the horrors of World War I. Probably spread by soldiers returning from the front, influenza becamethe deadliest epidemic in history. An estimated total of 50 million people died worldwide.

Total war also had a significant impact on European society. World War I created new roles for women. Because so many men left to fight at the front, women were asked to take over jobs that were not available to them before. Women found themselves employed in jobs that once were considered beyond their capacity. These jobs included civilian occupations such as chimney sweeps, truck drivers, farm laborers, and factory workers in heavy industry. For example, 38 percent of the workers in the Krupp Armaments works in Germany in 1918 were women.

The place of women in the workforce was far from secure, however. Both men and women seemed to expect that many of the new jobs for women were only temporary.

At the end of the war, as men returned to the job market, governments quickly removed women from the jobs they were encouraged to take earlier. By 1919, 650,000 women in Great Britain were unemployed. Wages for the women who were still employed were lowered.

Nevertheless, in some countries the role women played in wartime economies had a positive impact on the women's movement for social and political emancipation. The most obvious gain was the right to vote, which was given to women in Germany, Austria, and the United States immediately after the war. British women over the age of 30 gained the right to vote, together with the right to stand for Parliament, in 1918.

Many upper- and middle-class women also gained new freedoms. In ever-increasing numbers, young women from these groups took jobs, lived in their own apartments, and relished their new independence.

✓ READING PROGRESS CHECK

Explaining Why did women in some countries receive the right to vote after the war?

▶ CRITICAL THINKING

Drawing Conclusions How might this poster have increased British support for the war?

▼ This British recruiting poster is an example of wartime propaganda.

LESSON 2 REVIEW TEKS

Reviewing Vocabulary

1. ***Applying*** Describe the steps that resulted in the development of trench warfare. 10B

Using Your Notes

2. ***Identifying*** Use your notes to describe the ways in which alliances shifted during World War I.

Answering the Guiding Questions

3. ***Contrasting*** How did the war differ on the Western and Eastern Fronts? 10B
4. ***Drawing Conclusions*** What made World War I more devastating than any previous wars? 10B, 28C
5. ***Identifying*** Why did the war widen to become a world conflict?
6. ***Determining Cause and Effect*** What was the impact of total war? 1F, 10B, 24A, 28C

Writing Activity

7. **INFORMATIVE/EXPLANATORY** Write a paragraph discussing the role that women played in World War I. 1F, 24A

networks

There's More Online!

- BIOGRAPHY V.I. Lenin
- IMAGE Bolshevik Attack on the Winter Palace
- IMAGE The Red Army
- IMAGE The Romanov Family
- INTERACTIVE SELF-CHECK QUIZ
- MAP Russian Revolution and Civil War, 1917–1922
- PRIMARY SOURCE An Ambassador's Memoirs
- TIME LINE Russia and Europe, 1914–1918
- VIDEO The Russian Revolution

Reading **HELP**DESK

Academic Vocabulary

- **revolution** • **aid**

Content Vocabulary

- **soviet**
- **war communism**
- **abdicate**

TAKING NOTES:

Key Ideas and Details

Categorizing Information As you read, use a chart like the one below to identify the factors and events that led to Lenin's rise to power in 1917.

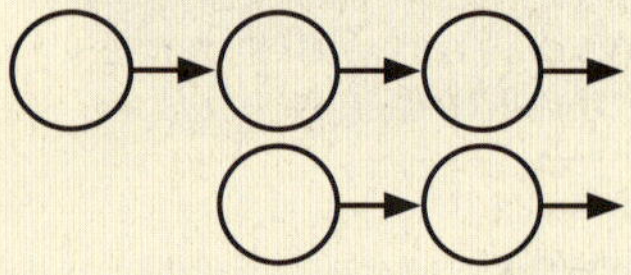

TEKS Texas Essential Knowledge and Skills

1F identify major causes and describe the major effects of the following important turning points in world history from 1914 to the present: the world wars and their impact on political, economic, and social systems; communist revolutions and their impact on the Cold War; independence movements; and globalization

continued on the next page

LESSON 3

The Russian Revolution

ESSENTIAL QUESTIONS • *Why do politics often lead to war?* • *How can technology impact war?*

It Matters Because

As the war dragged on, Russia stirred with unrest. The Romanov dynasty of Russia ended when Czar Nicholas II stepped down and a provisional government was put in power. Then the Bolsheviks under V. I. Lenin overthrew the government and by 1921 were in total command of Russia.

Background to Revolution

GUIDING QUESTION *What factors and events led to the Russian Revolution?*

After its defeat by Japan in 1905 and the Revolution of 1905, Russia was unprepared militarily and technologically for the total war of World War I. Russia had no competent military leaders. Even worse, Czar Nicholas II insisted on taking personal charge of the armed forces despite his lack of ability and training.

In addition, Russian industry was unable to produce the weapons needed for the army. Many soldiers trained using broomsticks. Others were sent to the front without rifles and told to pick one up from a dead comrade. Thus, it is not surprising that the Russian army suffered incredible losses. Two million soldiers were killed between 1914 and 1916, and another 4 to 6 million were wounded or captured. By 1917 the Russian will to fight had vanished.

An autocratic ruler, Czar Nicholas II relied on the army and bureaucracy to hold up his regime. He was further cut off from events when a man named Grigory Rasputin (ra • SPYOO • tuhn), known to be a mystic, began to influence the czar's wife, Alexandra. With the czar at the battlefront, it was rumored that Alexandra made all of the important decisions after consulting Rasputin. Rasputin's influence made him an important power behind the throne.

As the leadership stumbled its way through a series of military and economic disasters, the Russian people grew more upset with the czarist regime. Even conservative aristocrats who supported the monarchy felt the need to do something. They assassinated Rasputin in December 1916, but it was too late to save the monarchy.

At the beginning of March 1917, working-class women took an active role in changing their government as well as the course of Russian history by leading a series of strikes in the capital city of Petrograd (formerly St. Petersburg). A few weeks earlier, the Russian government had started bread rationing in Petrograd after the price of bread skyrocketed. Many of the women who stood in the lines waiting for bread were also factory workers who worked 12-hour days. Exhausted from standing in line, and distraught over their half-starving and sick children, the women finally revolted.

On March 8, about 10,000 women marched through the city of Petrograd demanding "Peace and Bread" and "Down with Autocracy." Soon other workers joined the women and called for a general strike. The strike shut down all the factories in the city on March 10 and became known as the February (March) Revolution of 1917.

Alexandra wrote to her husband Nicholas II at the battlefront: "This is a hooligan movement. If the weather were very cold they would all probably stay at home." Nicholas ordered troops to break up the crowds by shooting them if necessary. Soon, however, large numbers of the soldiers joined the demonstrators and refused to fire on the crowds.

The Duma, or legislative body, which the czar had tried to dissolve, met anyway. On March 12, it established the provisional government, which mainly consisted of middle-class representatives. It urged the czar to step down. Because he no longer had the support of the army or even the aristocrats, Nicholas II reluctantly agreed and stepped down on March 15, ending the 300-year-old Romanov dynasty.

The provisional government, headed by Aleksandr Kerensky (keh • REHN • skee), decided to carry on the war to preserve Russia's honor. This decision to remain in World War I was a major blunder. It satisfied neither the workers nor the peasants, who were tired and angry from years of suffering and wanted an end to the war.

The government also faced a challenge to its authority—the **soviets**. The soviets were councils comprised of representatives from the workers and soldiers. The soviet of Petrograd was formed in March 1917. At the same time, soviets sprang up in army units, factory towns, and rural areas. The soviets, largely made up of Socialists, represented the more radical interests of the lower classes. One group—the Bolsheviks—came to play a crucial role.

✓ **READING PROGRESS CHECK**

Drawing Conclusions What grievances did the Russian people have with the provisional government?

Lenin and the Bolsheviks

GUIDING QUESTION *How did Russia move from a czarist regime to a Communist regime?*

The Bolsheviks began as a small faction of a Marxist party called the Russian Social Democrats. The Bolsheviks came under the leadership of Vladimir Ilyich Ulyanov (ool • YAH • nuhf), known to the world as V. I. Lenin. Under Lenin's direction, the Bolsheviks became a party dedicated to violent **revolution**. Lenin believed that only violent revolution could destroy the capitalist system. A "vanguard" (forefront) of activists, he said, must form a small party of well-disciplined, professional revolutionaries to accomplish the task.

Between the years 1900 and 1917, Lenin spent most of his time abroad. When the Russian provisional government was formed in March 1917, he saw an opportunity for the Bolsheviks to seize power. In April 1917,

Thinking Like a HISTORIAN

How Important Was Rasputin?

In the introduction to his best-selling book *Nicholas and Alexandra*, historian Robert Massie quotes Aleksandr Kerensky's observation, "If there had been no Rasputin, there would have been no Lenin." The role of Rasputin in the history of Russia is one debated by historians. Was he such an important figure or was his influence merely the stuff of legends? How much influence can one man have to effect historical change? Use the Internet to find reliable sources about how much Rasputin contributed to the fall of the Russian monarchy.

soviets Russian councils composed of representatives from the workers and soldiers

(continued from p. 642)

TEKS **Texas Essential Knowledge and Skills**

10D identify the causes of the February (March) and October revolutions of 1917 in Russia, their effects on the outcome of World War I, and the Bolshevik establishment of the Union of Soviet Socialist Republics

18B identify the historical origins and characteristics of communism, including the influences of Karl Marx

21A describe how people have participated in supporting or changing their governments

revolution a overthrow of government

SKILLS PRACTICE

After reading about Lenin and the Bolsheviks, write five questions about what you have read. Exchange papers with a partner and answer each other's questions.

German military leaders, hoping to create disorder in Russia, shipped Lenin back to Russia. Lenin and his associates were sent in a sealed train to prevent their ideas from infecting Germany.

Lenin's arrival in Russia began a new phase of the Russian Revolution. Lenin maintained that the soviets of soldiers, workers, and peasants were ready-made instruments of power. He believed that the Bolsheviks should work toward gaining control of these groups and then use them to overthrow the provisional government.

At the same time, the Bolsheviks reflected the discontent of the people. They promised an end to the war. They also promised to redistribute all land to the peasants, to transfer factories and industries from capitalists to committees of workers, and to transfer government power from the provisional government to the soviets. Three simple slogans summed up the Bolshevik program: "Peace, Land, Bread," "Worker Control of Production," and "All Power to the Soviets."

✓ READING PROGRESS CHECK

Inferring Why did German military leaders return Lenin to Russia?

The Bolsheviks Seize Power

GUIDING QUESTION *How did Russia move from a czarist regime to a Communist regime?*

By the end of October 1917, Bolsheviks made up a slight majority in the Petrograd and Moscow soviets. The number of party members had grown from 50,000 to 240,000. With Leon Trotsky as head of the Petrograd soviet, the Bolsheviks were in a position to claim power in the name of the soviets. During the night of November 6, Bolshevik forces seized the Winter Palace, the seat of the provisional government. The government quickly collapsed with little bloodshed. This overthrow, today called the October Revolution, coincided with a meeting of the all-Russian Congress of Soviets, which represented local soviets countrywide. Outwardly, Lenin turned over the power of the provisional government to the Congress of Soviets. The real power, however, passed to a council headed by Lenin.

The Bolsheviks, who soon renamed themselves the Communists, still had a long way to go. Lenin had promised peace, yet he realized delivering that would not be easy. It would mean the humiliating loss of much Russian territory, but there was no real choice.

▼ **This painting depicts the Bolshevik attack on the Winter Palace during the October Revolution.**

▶ **CRITICAL THINKING**

Analyzing Why did the Bolsheviks choose the Winter Palace as the place to attack?

On March 3, 1918, Lenin signed the Treaty of Brest-Litovsk with Germany and gave up eastern Poland, Ukraine, Finland, and the Baltic provinces. To his critics, Lenin argued that it made no difference. The spread of the socialist revolution throughout Europe would make the treaty largely irrelevant. In any case, he had promised peace to the Russian people. Real peace did not come, however, because the country soon sank into civil war.

✓ READING PROGRESS CHECK

Making Generalizations Why might the promises of the Bolsheviks have been appealing to the Russian people?

Russian Revolution and Civil War 1917–1922

GEOGRAPHY CONNECTION

The events of the Russian Revolution led to a civil war.

1. **THE WORLD IN SPATIAL TERMS** *Measure the distance from Russia's westernmost border in 1914 to the western border under Bolshevik control in October 1919.*
2. **HUMAN SYSTEMS** *Why were many of the White Russian or Allied attacks from outside of Russia?*

Civil War in Russia

GUIDING QUESTION *What forces opposed the Communist government?*

Many people were opposed to the new Bolshevik, or Communist, government. These people included not only groups that were loyal to the czar but also liberal and anti-Leninist socialists. They were joined by the Allies, who were concerned about the Communist takeover. The Allies sent troops to Russia in the hope of bringing Russia back into the war. The Allies rarely fought on Russian soil, but they gave material **aid** to anti-Communists.

Between 1918 and 1921, the Communist, or Red, Army fought on many fronts. The first serious threat to the Communists came from Siberia. An anti-Communist, or White, force attacked and advanced almost to the Volga River before being stopped. Attacks also came from the Ukrainians and from the Baltic regions. In mid-1919, White forces swept through Ukraine and advanced almost to Moscow before being pushed back.

By 1920, however, the major White forces had been defeated and Ukraine retaken. The next year, the Communist regime regained control over the independent nationalist governments in Georgia, Russian Armenia, and Azerbaijan.

The royal family was another victim of the civil war. After the czar **abdicated**, he, his wife, and their five children had been held as prisoners. In April 1918, they were moved to Yekaterinburg, a mining town in the Urals. On the night of July 16, members of the local soviet murdered the czar and his family and burned their bodies in a nearby mine shaft.

aid assistance such as money or supplies

abdicate to formally give up control of a country or state

✓ **READING PROGRESS CHECK**

Contrasting How were the White forces and the anti-Leninist socialists different?

Triumph of the Communists

GUIDING QUESTION *What factors helped the Communists win the Russian civil war?*

How did Lenin and the Communists triumph in the civil war over such overwhelming forces? One reason was that the Red Army was a well-disciplined fighting force. This was largely due to the organizational genius of Leon Trotsky. As commissar of war, Trotsky reinstated the draft and insisted on rigid discipline. Soldiers who deserted or refused to obey orders were executed on the spot.

Furthermore, the disunity of the anti-Communist forces weakened their efforts. Political differences created distrust among the Whites. Some Whites insisted on restoring the czarist regime. Others wanted a more liberal and democratic program. The Whites, then, had no common goal.

The Communists, in contrast, had a single-minded sense of purpose and were recognized by their distinct characteristics. Inspired by their vision of a new socialist order, they had revolutionary zeal and strong convictions. They also were able to translate their revolutionary faith into practical instruments of power. A policy of **war communism**, for example, was used to ensure regular supplies for the Red Army. This meant the government controlled the banks and most industries, seized grain from peasants, and centralized state administration under Communist control.

war communism in World War I Russia, government control of banks and most industries, the seizing of grain from peasants, vand the centralization of state administration under Communist control

Another instrument was Communist revolutionary terror. A new Red secret police—known as the Cheka—began a Red Terror. Aimed at destroying all those who opposed the new regime, the Red Terror added an element of fear to the Communist regime.

Finally, foreign armies on Russian soil enabled the Communists to appeal to the powerful force of Russian patriotism. At one point, more than 100,000 foreign troops—mostly Japanese, British, American, and French—were stationed in Russia in support of anti-Communist forces. Their presence made it easy for the Communist government to call on patriotic Russians to fight foreign attempts to control the country.

By 1921 the Communists were in total command of Russia. The Communist regime had transformed Russia into a centralized state dominated by a single party. The state was also largely hostile to the Allied Powers, because the Allies had tried to help the Communists' enemies in the civil war.

✓ **READING PROGRESS CHECK**

Identifying Central Issues What was war communism, and why was it important?

LESSON 3 REVIEW TEKS

Reviewing Vocabulary

1. ***Making Generalizations*** During the civil war that followed the revolution, why did the Allies give aid to the anti-Communist forces? **1F**

Using Your Notes

2. ***Determining Cause and Effect*** Using your notes, list the factors and events that brought Lenin to power in 1917. **10D**

Answering the Guiding Questions

3. ***Identifying Central Issues*** What factors and events led to the Russian Revolution? **10D**
4. ***Determining Cause and Effect*** How did Russia move from a czarist regime to a Communist regime? **10D**
5. ***Analyzing Information*** What forces opposed the Communist government?
6. ***Drawing Conclusions*** What factors helped the Communists win the Russian civil war? **1F**

Writing Activity

7. **PERSUASIVE** Write a short paragraph arguing that the Russian Revolution was a result of World War I.

SKILLBUILDER

TEKS 15B

Understanding Geographic Distributions and Patterns: Graphs

Why Learn This Skill?

Graphs are visual representations of statistical data. Graphs can condense large amounts of data into an easy-to-read format. Not only do graphs allow you to see relationships between facts more clearly than in plain text, you can do it more quickly.

Geographic information benefits enormously from being presented in graphs. There are nearly two hundred countries in the world, and a graph is a good way to present information about multiple countries in an efficient manner. Learning how to decipher geographic distributions and patterns in graphs is a great skill for understanding history.

Learning the Skill

To understand geographic distributions and patterns in graphs, follow these steps:

- Read the graph title to identify the subject.
- Study the labels to understand the geographical information presented. Geographical information includes data about things such as natural resources, population, languages, and religions.
- Study the information presented. Make a note of place names and geographic terms. This will help you understand the geographic distributions and patterns.
- Compare the lines, bars, or segments in the graph and look for relationships in order to draw conclusions.
- An example of a geographic distribution might be the size of the population in different regions or countries. An example of a geographic pattern might be how population is clustered around cities rather than mountains or how one climate has more successful agriculture than another.

Practicing the Skill

Study the graph on this page. The x-axis lists names of countries or empires involved in World War I. The y-axis measures the number of soldiers sent by each country. A key indicates yet another layer of data: which alliance each country belonged to. The graph makes it easy to see geographic distributions and patterns.

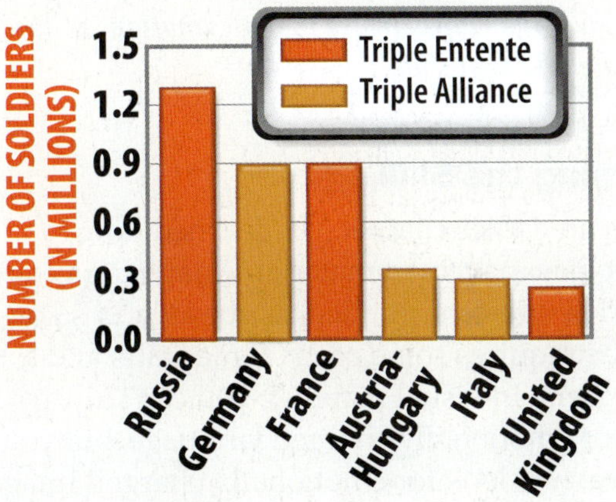

Source: *Encyclopedia of the First World War*

Skills Assessment

After studying the graph closely, think about how the information would look in text form. Next, try writing a short paragraph with this information. Now, write a few sentences describing which presentation you think is more effective—the graph or the text. Be sure to address the geographic distributions—how many soldiers were from each country—you see in the graph and how the countries compare with each other.

Applying the Skill

Analyze the graph and the map that accompanies it for geographic patterns. Compare the sizes of the countries with the number of soldiers from each. What other patterns can you see from analyzing the graph? Using a graph combined with a map or chart can give you more information and help you analyze and compare geographic patterns in world history.

SKILLBUILDER

TEKS 29E

Identifying Bias in Visual Material

Why Learn This Skill?

We live in a world saturated with information and opinions. Finding information about a topic is no longer much of a challenge. But how can we know which information is useful and accurate? As more information moves to the Internet, it is increasingly important that we learn to identify bias in visual material. This helps ensure the information we find is accurate and truthful.

Learning the Skill

In an earlier chapter, you learned how to detect bias in written material. Analyzing visual material—posters, political cartoons, and so on—for bias requires some of the same skills and a few others. In visual material, you can't always look for emotionally charged language, but you will learn to look for emotionally charged images.

The first step in identifying bias is the same: Identify the artist's purpose. What is the artist trying to accomplish with the image? Next, look for elements that provoke a strong emotional response. For example, many wartime propaganda posters contain monstrous figures that represent the enemy.

In general, be on the lookout for one-sided messages. When language and images are manipulative and meant to convey a single message, it is very possible that bias is present in the material.

Practicing the Skill

Study this image created by the British government during World War I. This is a propaganda poster that focuses on the domestic front rather than the enemy. The poster contains a written message that helps you determine the artist's purpose. Note any visual elements that stand out to you. Important questions include: Why does the father look distracted and sad? What does it mean that the boy is joyfully playing with toy soldiers? How is the message written to emphasize certain words?

Skills Assessment

After studying the poster closely, write a paragraph explaining what you think the artist's purpose was and how he or she attempted to achieve this goal. When identifying bias in visual material, be sure to include specific details from the image.

Applying the Skill

Conduct research to find several examples of propaganda posters. Good resources include the websites of the Library of Congress and the National Archives. Use the steps above to identify bias in each example. Write a short description of each poster and the bias found in it and prepare a short presentation for the class. If possible, display the posters during your presentation.

PHOTO: Library of Congress

networks

There's More Online!

- IMAGE The Treaty of Versailles
- INTERACTIVE SELF-CHECK QUIZ
- MAP Europe and the Middle East After WWI
- PRIMARY SOURCE Charter of the League of Nations
- PRIMARY SOURCE The Treaty of Versailles
- PRIMARY SOURCE Wilson's Fourteen Points
- VIDEO Peace After World War I

LESSON 4

World War I Ends

ESSENTIAL QUESTIONS • *Why do politics often lead to war?* • *How can technology impact war?*

Reading HELPDESK

Academic Vocabulary

- **psychological**
- **cooperation**

Content Vocabulary

- **armistice**
- **mandate**
- **reparation**

TAKING NOTES:

Key Ideas and Details

Organizing Information As you read, use a chart like the one below to identify the national interests of each country as it approached the Paris Peace Conference.

France	Great Britain	United States

TEKS Texas Essential Knowledge and Skills

1F identify major causes and describe the major effects of the following important turning points in world history from 1914 to the present: the world wars and their impact on political, economic, and social systems; communist revolutions and their impact on the Cold War; independence movements; and globalization

10B identify major characteristics of World War I, including total war, trench warfare, modern military technology, and high casualty rates

continued on the next page

It Matters Because

Governments, troops, and civilians were weary as World War I continued through 1917. Shortly after the United States entered the war, Germany made its final military gamble on the Western Front and lost. The war finally ended on November 11, 1918. New nations were formed, and a League of Nations was created to resolve future international disputes.

The Last Year of the War

GUIDING QUESTION *How did World War I come to an end?*

The year 1917 was not a good one for the Allies. Allied offensives on the Western Front had been badly defeated. In Russia, the February (March) Revolution weakened an already demoralized and undersupplied Russian army, contributing to the success of the October Revolution and further instability in Russia. The October Revolution led to Russia's withdrawal from the war a few months later. On the positive side, however, the entry of the United States into the war in 1917 gave the Allies a much-needed **psychological** boost. The United States also provided fresh troops and supplies.

For Germany, the withdrawal of the Russians offered new hope for a successful end to the war. Germany was then free to concentrate entirely on the Western Front. Erich Ludendorff, who guided German military operations, decided to make one final military gamble—a grand offensive in the west.

The German attack was launched in March 1918. By April, German troops were within about 50 miles (80 km) of Paris. However, the German advance was stopped at the Second Battle of the Marne on July 18. French, Moroccan, and American troops (140,000 fresh American troops had just arrived), supported by hundreds of tanks, pushed the Germans back over the Marne. Ludendorff's gamble had failed.

With more than a million American troops pouring into France, Allied forces began an advance toward Germany. On September 29,

1918, General Ludendorff told German leaders that the war was lost. He demanded that the government ask for peace at once.

psychological mental; directed toward the will or mind

Collapse and Armistice

German officials soon found that the Allies were unwilling to make peace with the autocratic imperial government of Germany. Reforms for a liberal government came too late for the tired, angry German people.

On November 3, 1918, sailors in the northern German town of Kiel mutinied. Within days, councils of workers and soldiers formed throughout northern Germany and took over civilian and military offices. Emperor William II gave in to public pressure and left the country on November 9. After his departure, the Social Democrats under Friedrich Ebert announced the creation of a democratic republic. Two days later, on November 11, 1918, the new German government signed an **armistice** to end the fighting.

armistice a truce or an agreement to end fighting

(continued from p. 649)

TEKS **Texas Essential Knowledge and Skills**

10C explain the political impact of Woodrow Wilson's Fourteen Points and the political and economic impact of the Treaty of Versailles, including changes in boundaries and the mandate system

10D identify the causes of the February (March) and October revolutions of 1917 in Russia, their effects on the outcome of World War I, and the Bolshevik establishment of the Union of Soviet Socialist Republics

20D explain the significance of the League of Nations and the United Nations

Revolutionary Forces

The war was over, but the revolutionary forces that had been set in motion in Germany were not yet exhausted. A group of radical socialists, unhappy with the Social Democrats' moderate policies, formed the German Communist Party in December 1918. A month later, the Communists tried to seize power in Berlin.

The new Social Democratic government, backed by regular army troops, crushed the rebels and murdered Rosa Luxemburg and Karl Liebknecht (LEEP • KNEHKT), leaders of the German Communists. A similar attempt at Communist revolution in the city of Munich, in southern Germany, was also crushed. The new German republic had been saved. The attempt at revolution, however, left the German middle class with a deep fear of communism.

Austria-Hungary also experienced disintegration and revolution. As the empire grew war weary, ethnic groups increasingly sought to achieve their independence. By the time World War I ended, the Austro-Hungarian Empire had ceased to exist. The empire was replaced by the independent republics of Austria, Hungary, and Czechoslovakia, along with the large monarchical state called Yugoslavia.

✓ READING PROGRESS CHECK

Describing What happened in Germany after its military defeat?

▼ British cavalry pass the ruins of the Albert Cathedral. It was destroyed in the Second Battle of the Somme in France.

▶ CRITICAL THINKING

Explaining What does this photograph tell you about the changing nature of warfare in World War I?

The Peace Settlements

GUIDING QUESTION *How was a final settlement of World War I established?*

In January 1919, representatives of 27 victorious Allied nations met in Paris to make a final settlement of World War I. Over a period of years, the reasons for fighting World War I had changed dramatically. When European nations went to war in 1914, they sought territorial gains. By the beginning of 1918, however, they also were expressing more idealistic reasons for the war.

Wilson's Proposals

No one expressed these idealistic reasons for war better than the president of the United States, Woodrow Wilson. Even before the end of the war, Wilson outlined "Fourteen Points" to the U. S. Congress—his basis for a peace settlement that he believed justified the enormous military struggle being waged.

Wilson's proposals for a truly just and lasting peace included reaching the peace agreements openly rather than through secret diplomacy. His proposals also included reducing armaments (military forces or weapons) and ensuring self-determination (the right of each people to have their own nation).

Wilson portrayed World War I as a people's war against "absolutism and militarism." These two enemies of liberty, he argued, could be eliminated only by creating democratic governments and a "general association of nations." This association would guarantee "political independence and territorial integrity" to all states.

Wilson became the spokesperson for a new world order based on democracy and international **cooperation**. When he arrived in Europe for the peace conference, Wilson was cheered enthusiastically by many Europeans. President Wilson soon found, however, that more practical motives guided other states.

cooperation a common effort

reparation a payment made to the victor by the vanquished to cover the costs of war

The Paris Peace Conference

Delegates met in Paris in early 1919 to determine the peace settlement. Complications soon arose at the Paris Peace Conference. For one thing, secret agreements that had been made before the war had raised the hopes of European nations for territorial gains. These hopes, however, conflicted with the principle of self-determination put forth by Wilson.

National interests also complicated the deliberations of the Paris Peace Conference. David Lloyd George, prime minister of Great Britain, had won a decisive victory in elections in December 1918. His platform was simple: To make the Germans pay for this dreadful war.

France's approach to peace was chiefly guided by its desire for national security. To Georges Clemenceau (KLEH • muhn • SOH), the premier of France, the French people had suffered the most from German aggression. The French desired security against future German attacks. Clemenceau wanted Germany stripped of all weapons, vast German payments—**reparations**—to cover the costs of the war, and a separate Rhineland as a buffer state between France and Germany.

The most important decisions at the Paris Peace Conference were made by Wilson, Clemenceau, and Lloyd George, acting on behalf of the United States, France, and Great Britain (who were called the Big Three). Germany was not invited to attend, and Russia could not be present because of its civil war.

In view of the conflicting demands that arose at the Paris Peace Conference, it was no surprise that the Big Three quarreled. Wilson wanted to

▲ *The Signing of Peace in the Hall of Mirrors, Versailles, 28th June 1919* **by Sir William Orpen depicts the major powers at Versailles. Wilson, Clemenceau, and Lloyd George (left to right) are seated at the table across from the German delegate.**

▶ CRITICAL THINKING

Analyzing Visuals What is significant about the placement of the delegates around the table?

PHOTO: Imperial War Museum/akg-images

Europe and the Middle East After WWI 1922

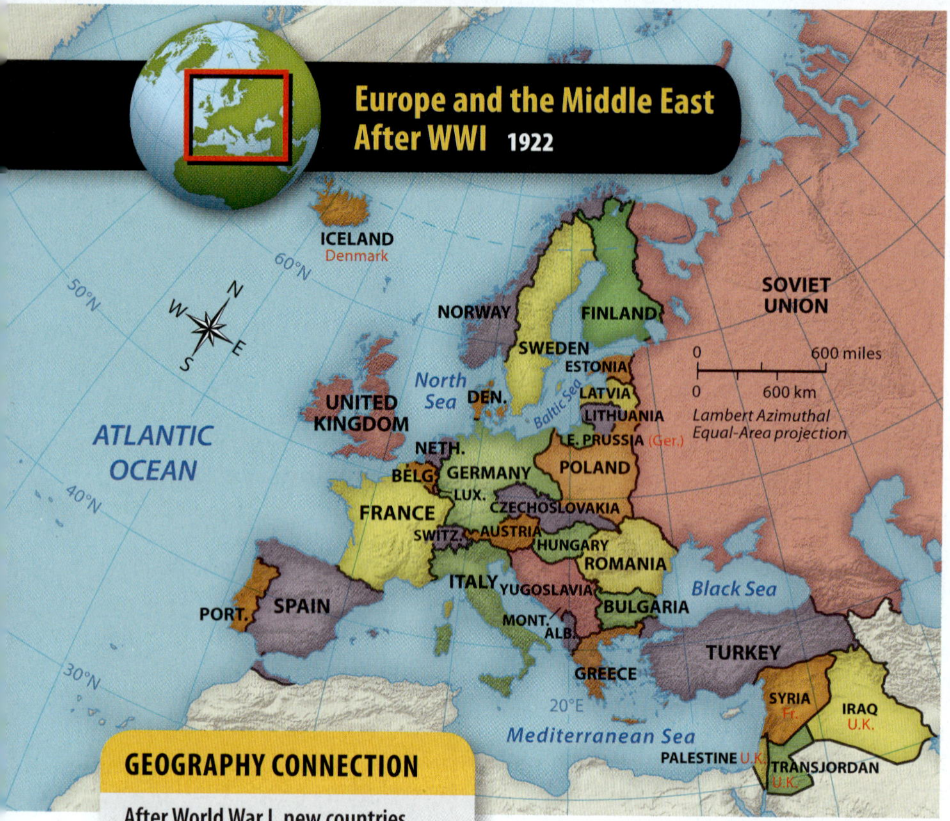

GEOGRAPHY CONNECTION

After World War I, new countries and mandates were formed in Europe and the Middle East.

1. **HUMAN SYSTEMS** *Compare this map with the map on the Place and Time feature in this chapter. Which countries no longer existed after World War I?*
2. **ENVIRONMENT AND SOCIETY** *Why do you think East Prussia was separated from the rest of Germany?*

create a world organization, the League of Nations, to prevent future wars. Clemenceau and Lloyd George wanted to punish Germany. In the end, only compromise made it possible to achieve a peace settlement.

Wilson's wish for the creation of an international peacekeeping organization was granted. On January 25, 1919, the conference accepted the idea of a League of Nations, a unique concept wherein a body of states would arbitrate disputes and prevent wars. In return, Wilson agreed to make compromises on territorial arrangements among the countries, believing the League of Nations could later fix unfair settlements.

Clemenceau also compromised to obtain some guarantees for French security. He gave up France's wish for a separate Rhineland and instead accepted a defensive alliance with Great Britain and the United States. However, the U.S. Senate refused to ratify this agreement, which weakened the Versailles peace settlement.

The Treaty of Versailles

The final peace settlement of Paris consisted of five separate treaties with the defeated nations of Germany, Austria, Hungary, Bulgaria, and Turkey. The Treaty of Versailles with Germany was by far the most important.

The Germans considered it a harsh peace. They were unhappy with Article 231, the so-called War Guilt Clause, which declared that Germany (and Austria) were responsible for starting the war. The treaty ordered Germany to pay reparations (financial compensation) for all damages that the Allied governments and their people had sustained as a result of the war. The military and territorial provisions of the Treaty of Versailles also angered the Germans. Germany had to reduce its army to 100,000 men, cut back its navy, and eliminate its air force. Alsace and Lorraine, taken by the Germans from France in 1871, were returned. Sections of eastern Germany were awarded to the new Polish and Czechoslovakian states. In total, Germany lost over one-tenth of its territory and its population, reductions that would have economic consequences.

German land along the Rhine River became a demilitarized zone, stripped of all weapons and fortifications. This, it was hoped, would serve as a barrier to any future German moves against France. Although outraged by the "dictated peace," Germany accepted the treaty.

The Legacies of the War

The war, the Treaty of Versailles, and the separate peace treaties made with the other Central Powers redrew the map of eastern Europe. Many of these changes had already taken place at the end of the war. The German and Russian empires lost considerable territory in eastern Europe. The Austro-Hungarian Empire disappeared.

The political impact of the Fourteen Points can be seen in the emergence of new nation-states emerged from the lands of these three empires: Finland,

Latvia, Estonia, Lithuania, Poland, Czechoslovakia, Austria, and Hungary. New territorial arrangements were also made in the Balkans. Romania acquired additional lands. Serbia formed the nucleus of a new state, called Yugoslavia, which combined Serbs, Croats, and Slovenes.

The principle of self-determination supposedly guided the Paris Peace Conference. However, the mixtures of peoples in eastern Europe made it impossible to draw boundaries along strict ethnic lines. As a result of compromises, almost every eastern European state was left with ethnic minorities, leading to later conflicts: Germans in Poland; Hungarians, Poles, and Germans in Czechoslovakia; Hungarians in Romania; and Serbs, Croats, Slovenes, Macedonians, and Albanians in Yugoslavia.

Yet another centuries-old empire—the Ottoman Empire—was broken up by the peace settlement. To gain Arab support against the Ottoman Turks during the war, the Western Allies had promised to recognize the independence of Arab states in the Ottoman Empire. Once World War I was over, however, the Western nations changed their minds. France controlled the territory of Syria, and Britain controlled the territories of Iraq and Palestine.

These acquisitions were officially called **mandates**. Woodrow Wilson opposed the outright annexation of colonial territories by the Allies. By including certain territories as mandates, rather than including them as direct annexations, victorious nations would not have to include their value as possessions against reparations required by the treaty. As a result, in the mandate system, a nation officially governed a territory on a temporary basis as a mandate on behalf of the League of Nations, but did not own the territory.

World War I shattered the liberal, rational society of pre-war Europe. A high casualty rate and a death toll of nearly 10 million people, as well as the incredible destruction caused by the war, undermined the whole idea of progress. Entire populations had participated in a devastating slaughter.

World War I was a total war—one that involved a complete mobilization of resources and people. As a result, the power of governments over the lives of their citizens increased. Freedom of the press and speech were limited in the name of national security. World War I made the practice of strong central authority a way of life.

The turmoil created by the war also seemed to open the door to even greater insecurity. Revolutions broke up old empires and created new states, which led to new problems. The hope that Europe and the rest of the world would return to normalcy was soon dashed.

✓ READING PROGRESS CHECK

Explaining What did Wilson hope to accomplish by creating the League of Nations?

Analyzing PRIMARY SOURCES

Treaty of Versailles

"The Allied and Associated Governments affirm and Germany accepts the responsibility of Germany and her allies for causing all the loss and damage to which the Allied and Associated Governments and their nationals have been subjected as a consequence of the war imposed upon them by the aggression of Germany and her allies."

Article 231 of the Treaty of Versailles, 1919

DBQ ***ANALYZING*** Why do you think the Germans found Article 231 of the Treaty of Versailles so objectionable?

mandate a territory temporarily governed by another country on behalf of the League of Nations

LESSON 4 REVIEW TEKS

Reviewing Vocabulary

1. ***Defining*** Write a short paragraph defining the terms *armistice* and *reparations* and discussing their significance for Germany at the end of World War I.

Using Your Notes

2. ***Identifying*** Use your notes to write a paragraph identifying the national interests of Great Britain, France, and the United States as they entered the Paris Peace Conference. **20D**

Answering the Guiding Questions

3. ***Identifying Cause and Effect*** How did World War I come to an end?
4. ***Identifying Central Issues*** How was a final settlement of World War I established?

Writing Activity

5. **INFORMATIVE/EXPLANATORY** Write an essay discussing the elements of the World War I peace settlement that seemed likely to lead to future conflict. **10C**

CHAPTER 27 Assessment

TEKS

Directions: On a separate sheet of paper, answer the questions below. Make sure you read carefully and answer all parts of the questions.

Lesson Review

Lesson 1

1. ***Describing*** Describe the system of nation-states, and why were nation-state leaders open to war? **1F, 10A**

2. ***Naming*** Which ethnic groups desired independence at this time but had still not acquired nation-state status?

3. ***Explaining*** How did imperialism generate competition among European nations? **10A**

4. ***Making Inferences*** How were other countries pulled into the conflict between Serbia and Austria-Hungary? What effect did their alliances have on prospects for war? **10A**

Lesson 2

5. ***Defining*** What is the meaning of "total war" and how did this status impact Americans and Europeans on the home front in the short term and long term? **1F**

6. ***Identifying*** How did government actions during World War I affect Europe economically? **1F**

7. ***Identifying*** How did traditional social roles change on the home front during World War I? **1F, 24A**

8. ***Identifying*** How did trench warfare change military strategy during World War I? What was the impact of new technologies on warfare during this period? **10B, 28C**

Lesson 3

9. ***Identifying*** What role did Grigory Rasputin play in the czarist regime and how did Russian people eventually respond?

10. ***Identifying*** How did the decision to remain in World War I contribute to the March and October Revolutions in Russia? **10D, 21A**

11. ***Specifying*** What was the effect of the March Revolution in Russia on the outcome of World War I?

12. ***Describing*** Describe war communism and how the Bolsheviks carried it out. **18B**

Lesson 4

13. ***Identifying*** What were the major causes of the independence movements that followed World War I? **1F**

14. ***Summarizing*** Summarize the political philosophy behind Wilson's peace treaty proposal—the Fourteen Points. **10C**

15. ***Explaining*** How did Wilson's principle of self-determination impact European boundary changes reflected in the Treaty of Versailles? **10C**

16. ***Explaining*** What were the political and economic impacts of the mandate system as established in the Treaty of Versailles? **10C**

17. ***Identifying*** How did Russian withdrawal from the war as a result of the October Revolution affect World War I? **10D**

18. ***Explaining*** What was the significance of the League of Nations? **20D**

Need Extra Help?

If You've Missed Question	1	2	3	4	5	6	7	8	9	10	11	12	13	14	15	16	17	18
Go to page	634	634	634	636	642	643	643	640	644	645	645	648	652	653	653	655	646	654

Exploring the Essential Questions

19 ***Synthesizing*** Work with a partner to create a multimedia display of political motives and technological advances that contributed to the destructiveness of World War I. Provide a photograph, a drawing, or an artifact that symbolizes each contributing factor and an audio or a written explanation of the factor. You may also include primary sources. **1F, 10B, 28C**

Critical Thinking

20 ***Synthesizing*** How did militarism and alliances contribute to the start of World War I? **1F, 10A**

21 ***Analyzing*** Why did the countries fighting the war seek new allies? Which countries joined the conflict on which side?

22 ***Identifying*** What characteristic of World War I was the result of the use of machine guns and trench warfare? **10B**

23 ***Sequencing*** What events after Russia left the war led to Germany's signing an armistice on November 11, 1918?

24 ***Making Predictions*** Summarize the requirements of the Treaty of Versailles for Germany. What might you expect a defeated nation to do in the years following such demands?

25 ***Analyzing*** Why did the major powers and authors of the Treaty of Versailles require so much of Germany, and what can you conclude about Germany's vulnerability for economic success in the years following?

Social Studies Skills

Use the image to answer the following questions.

26 ***Identifying Bias in Visual Material*** Does this poster show bias in favor of or against the war? How do you know? **29E**

27 ***Identifying Bias in Visual Material*** How does the creator of the poster persuade viewers to agree with his or her bias? **29E**

28 ***Identifying Bias in Visual Material*** What visual elements in the illustration extend the emotional response initiated by the text?

29 ***Time, Chronology, and Sequencing*** Create a pair of maps that show the historical and political boundaries in Europe before the Treaty of Versailles and after the treaty. Use hand-drawn illustrations or computer software to clearly show the changes. Explore the best method of presentation, perhaps through overlays or use of color. Provide data about the changes, such as number of independent states or population distribution. **15A**

PHOTO: Library of Congress

Need Extra Help?

If You've Missed Question	19	20	21	22	23	24	25	26	27	28	29
Go to page	638	635	635	636	651	654	654	650	650	650	633

DBQ Analyzing Primary Sources

Use the document to answer the following questions.

Many soldiers were exposed to chemical weapons during the war. Doctors could do nothing to help them. One nurse described the situation in a hospital near the Western Front.

PRIMARY SOURCE

"I wish those people who write so glibly about this being a holy war and the orators who talk so much about going on no matter how long the war lasts and what it may mean could see a case—to say nothing of ten cases—of mustard gas in its early stages—could see the poor things burnt and blistered all over with great mustard-coloured suppurating [oozing] blisters, with blind eyes . . . all sticky and stuck together, and always fighting for breath, with voices a mere whisper, saying that their throats are closing and they know they will choke."

—quoted in Eye-Deep in Hell: Trench Warfare in World War I

30 ***Identifying Bias in Written Material*** What does the nurse believe is making those who are in favor of the war ignore its human costs? **29E**

31 ***Analyzing*** What words or phrases used by the nurse tell the reader how she feels about the war?

32 ***Drawing Inferences*** What inference can you make about the use of mustard gas as a weapon in the context of medical expertise and history?

Analyzing Visuals

Use the graph to answer the following questions.

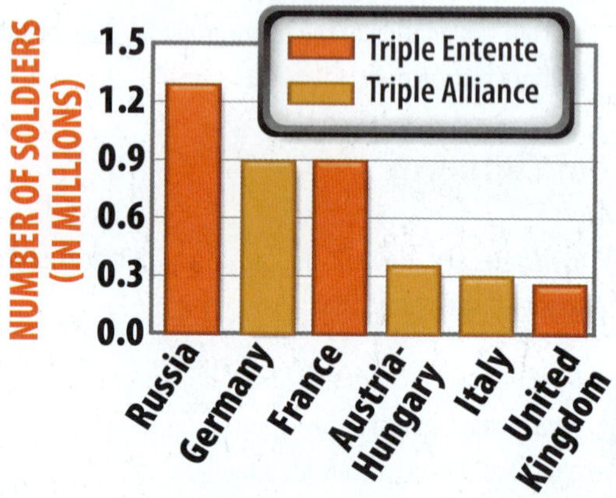

Source: *Encyclopedia of the First World War*

In 1914, Europe was divided into the Triple Alliance and the Triple Entente. This graph shows the estimated army size of each country in each alliance in 1914. As you examine the distributions or patterns on this graph, you may wish to consult a relevant map of Europe.

33 ***Analyzing and Interpreting Geographic Distributions Shown on Graphs*** Which alliance had the greatest number of soldiers? How might Russia's early departure from World War I have affected the Triple Entente? **15A, 15B, 16C**

34 ***Analyzing Geographic Patterns Shown on Graphs*** What geographical pattern do you find between the alliances and what might be the significance of this pattern? **15B**

Extended Response Question

35 ***Expository*** In what ways was World War I a bigger and more destructive conflict than any previous conflicts? **10A, 10B, 28C**

Need Extra Help?

If You've Missed Question	30	31	32	33	34	35
Go to page	658	658	658	635	635	638

The West Between the Wars

1919–1939

ESSENTIAL QUESTIONS • *What can cause economic instability?* • *How might political change impact society?*

networks

There's More Online! about the West between the wars.

CHAPTER 28

The Story Matters...

Bitterness over the Treaty of Versailles and severe economic problems helped the rise of Adolf Hitler's Nazi movement in Germany. The Hitler Youth (*Hitlerjugend*) organization was created in 1926 to win young people over to the Nazi cause. When Hitler took power in 1933, the Hitler Youth had about 100,000 members. Boys and girls in the Hitler Youth were indoctrinated to be race-conscious, obedient, and put the needs of the nation above their own. By the early years of World War II, about 90 percent of the country's young people belonged to the Hitler Youth.

◀ Boys in the Hitler Youth participated in Nazi rallies and activities where they spent time with other children with minimal parental guidance. This photograph was taken circa 1939.

CHAPTER 28

Place and Time: Europe 1919–1939

At the end of the First World War, world leaders attempted to craft a lasting peace. However, the 1920s and 1930s witnessed severe economic crises that led to political instability. Authoritarian political leaders used widespread fear of disorder to gain power. Once in power, they violently suppressed all opposition.

Step Into the Place

Read the quotes and look at the information presented on the map.

DBQ Discuss the differences between Adolf Hitler's and Joseph Stalin's ideas about the goal of government. Look at the map and draw conclusions about the success of both leaders' policies.

PRIMARY SOURCE

"[T]he Soviet power is a *new form* of state organization, different in principle from the old bourgeois-democratic and parliamentary form, a *new type* of state, adapted not to the task of exploiting and oppressing the labouring masses, but to the task of completely emancipating them from all oppression and exploitation, to the task facing the dictatorship of the proletariat."

—Stalin, from *Foundations of Leninism,* 1939

PRIMARY SOURCE

"The state is a means to an end. Its end lies in the preservation and advancement of a community of physically and psychically homogeneous creatures. This preservation itself comprises first of all existence as a race and thereby permits the free development of all the forces dormant in this race. Of them a part will always primarily serve the preservation of physical life, and only the remaining part the promotion of a further spiritual development."

—Hitler, from *Mein Kampf*

Step Into the Time

Determining Cause and Effect

Research an event on the time line, and explain how it was a direct or an indirect result of the Treaty of Versailles.

EUROPE

- **1919** Treaty of Versailles
- **1922** Vladimir Lenin and the Communists create the USSR
- **1923** French and Belgian troops occupy the Ruhr Valley
- **1924** Joseph Stalin leads Soviet Union after Lenin's death
- **1926** Benito Mussolini establishes a Fascist dictatorship in Italy

1919 **1925**

THE WORLD

- **1920** First meeting of the League of Nations
- **1922** League of Nations confirms British Mandate for Palestine
- **1923** Mustafa Kemal, Atatürk, proclaims Republic of Turkey
- **1923** Nationalists and Communists are allies in China
- **1926** Fidel Castro, future president of Cuba, is born

networks
There's More Online!

- **MAP** Explore the interactive version of this map on Networks.
- **TIME LINE** Explore the interactive version of the time line on Networks.

1929 U.S. stock market crashes; Great Depression begins

1930 Gandhi's civil disobedience movement begins in India

1932 Ibn Sa'ūd establishes the kingdom of Saudi Arabia

1933 Paul von Hindenburg appoints Adolf Hitler as Chancellor

1934 Beginning of the Long March by Chinese Communists

1935 Nuremberg laws in Germany strip Jews of their citizenship

1938 Japan passes military draft law

April 1, 1939 Francisco Franco overthrows the Spanish Republic

1930 — 1935 — 1939

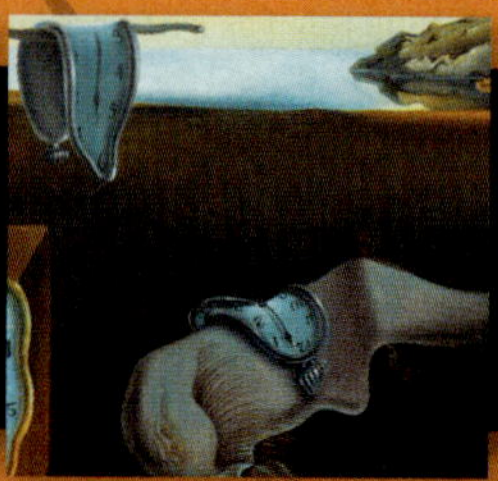

networks

There's More Online!

- BIOGRAPHY Albert Einstein
- CHART/GRAPH Unemployment, 1928–1938
- IMAGE Hyperinflation in Germany
- IMAGE The Persistence of Memory
- INTERACTIVE SELF-CHECK QUIZ
- MAP The Ruhr Valley
- PRIMARY SOURCE Locarno Gives Hope of an Era of Peace
- SLIDE SHOW Photomontage, Dadaism, and Surrealism
- VIDEO The Great Depression

LESSON 1
Instability After World War I

ESSENTIAL QUESTIONS • *What can cause economic instability?* • *How might political change impact society?*

Reading HELPDESK

Academic Vocabulary

- **annual**
- **appropriate**

Content Vocabulary

- **depression**
- **collective bargaining**
- **deficit spending**
- **surrealism**
- **uncertainty principle**

TAKING NOTES:

Key Ideas and Details

Organizing As you read, use a table like the one below to compare France's Popular Front with the New Deal in the United States.

Popular Front	New Deal

TEKS Texas Essential Knowledge and Skills

1F identify major causes and describe the major effects of the following important turning points in world history from 1914 to the present: the world wars and their impact on political, economic, and social systems; communist revolutions and their impact on the Cold War; independence movements; and globalization

continued on the next page

IT MATTERS BECAUSE

The peace settlement of World War I left many nations unhappy. The economic collapse of the Great Depression, beginning in 1929, shook people's confidence in democracy.

Uneasy Peace, Uncertain Security

GUIDING QUESTION *What led to new problems in the years after World War I?*

From the beginning, the peace settlement at the end of World War I left nations unhappy. President Woodrow Wilson had realized that the peace settlement included provisions that could serve as new causes for conflict. He had placed many of his hopes for the future in the League of Nations. This organization, however, was not very effective in maintaining the peace.

One problem was the failure of the United States to join the League. Most Americans wanted to avoid involvement in European affairs. The U.S. Senate, in spite of President Wilson's wishes, refused to ratify, or approve, the Treaty of Versailles. That meant the United States could not join the League of Nations. Without the United States, the League of Nations' effectiveness was weakened.

Between 1919 and 1924, desire for security led the French government to demand strict enforcement of the Treaty of Versailles. This tough policy began with the issue of reparations (payments) that the Germans were supposed to make for the damage they had done in the war. In April 1921, the Allied Reparations Commission determined that Germany owed 132 billion German marks (33 billion U.S. dollars) for reparations, payable in **annual** installments of 2.5 billion marks.

The new German republic made its first payment in 1921. One year later, the German government faced a financial crisis and announced that it could not pay any more reparations. Outraged, France sent troops to occupy the Ruhr Valley, Germany's chief industrial and mining center. France planned to collect reparations by using the Ruhr mines and factories.

Inflation in Germany

The German government adopted a policy of passive resistance to this French occupation. German workers went on strike. The German government mainly paid their salaries by printing more paper money. This only added to the inflation (rise in prices) that had already begun in Germany by the end of the war. The German mark soon became worthless. In 1914, 4.2 marks equaled 1 U.S. dollar. By the end of November 1923, the ratio had reached an incredible 4.2 trillion marks to equal 1 dollar.

Both France and Germany began to seek a way out of the disaster. In August 1924, an international commission adopted a new plan for reparations. The Dawes Plan, named after the American banker who chaired the commission, first reduced reparations. It then coordinated Germany's annual payments with its ability to pay.

The Dawes Plan also granted an initial $200 million loan for German recovery. This loan soon opened the door to heavy American investment in Europe. A brief period of European prosperity followed.

▶ CRITICAL THINKING

Analyzing Why was the Ruhr Valley important to Germany?

annual yearly

The Treaty of Locarno

With prosperity came a new European diplomacy. The foreign ministers of Germany and France, Gustav Stresemann and Aristide Briand, fostered a spirit of cooperation. In 1925, they signed the Treaty of Locarno, which guaranteed Germany's new western borders with France and Belgium. Many viewed the Locarno pact as the beginning of a new era of European peace.

Three years later, the Kellogg-Briand Pact brought even more hope. Sixty-five nations signed this accord and pledged to "renounce [war] as an instrument of national policy." Nothing was said, however, about what would be done if anyone violated the pact.

✓ READING PROGRESS CHECK

Explaining What contributed to the German mark becoming worthless?

The Great Depression

GUIDING QUESTION *What triggered the Great Depression?*

The brief period of prosperity that began in Europe in 1924 ended in an economic collapse that came to be known as the Great Depression. A **depression** is a period of low economic activity and rising unemployment.

Two factors played a major role in the start of the Great Depression. First was a series of downturns in the economies of individual nations in the second half of the 1920s. For example, prices for farm products, especially wheat, fell rapidly due to overproduction. An increase in the use of oil and hydroelectricity led to a slump in the coal industry.

The second trigger was an international financial crisis involving the U.S. stock market. Much of the European prosperity between 1924 and 1929 was built on U.S. bank loans to Germany. During the 1920s, the U.S. stock market boomed. By 1928, American investors pulled money out of Germany to invest it in stocks. Then, in October 1929, the U.S. stock market crashed. Stock prices plunged.

In a panic, U.S. investors withdrew more funds from Germany and other European markets. By 1931 trade was slowing, industrial production was declining, and unemployment was rising.

✓ READING PROGRESS CHECK

Applying Why were farmers hit hard at the onset of the Great Depression?

(continued from p. 662)

TEKS **Texas Essential Knowledge and Skills**

11A summarize the international, political, and economic causes of the global depression

11B explain the responses of governments in the United States, Germany, and the Soviet Union to the global depression

continued on the next page

▲ **This woman uses German marks to light her stove during the Great Depression.**

▶ CRITICAL THINKING

Explaining Why would this woman burn money during the Great Depression?

depression a period of low economic activity and rising unemployment

CHARTS/GRAPHS

UNEMPLOYMENT 1928–1938

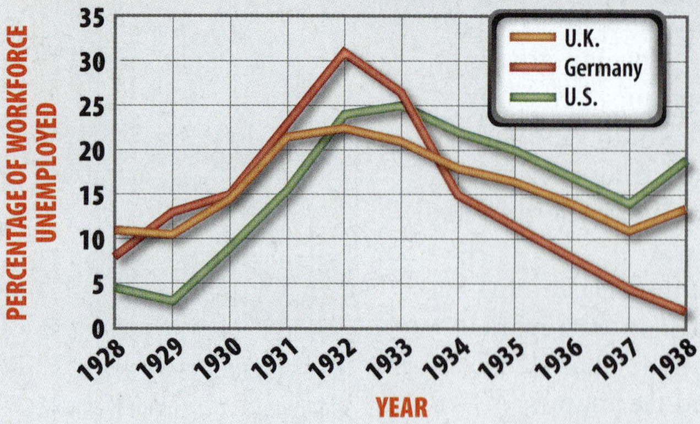

Sources: *European Historical Statistics, 1750–1970; Historical Statistics of the United States.*

▲ Long lines of unemployed workers sought food and jobs.

▶ CRITICAL THINKING

1 ***Drawing Conclusions*** When was the height of the Great Depression?

2 ***Transferring*** Which country experienced the largest rise in unemployment?

Responses to the Depression

GUIDING QUESTION ***How did the Great Depression affect people's confidence in democracy?***

Economic depression was not new to Europe. However, the extent of the economic downturn after 1929 truly made this the Great Depression. During 1932, the worst year of the Depression, nearly 1 in every 4 British workers was unemployed. About 5.5 million Germans, or roughly 30 percent of the German labor force, had no jobs. The unemployed and homeless filled the streets.

Governments were unsure of how to react, and their actions helped turn the crisis into a global depression. They raised tariffs to exclude foreign goods from home markets. Some governments also attempted to slow investments prior to the crash, then did nothing after the crash occurred. These actions worsened the crisis and had serious political effects.

The Great Depression also led masses of people to follow political leaders who offered simple solutions in return for dictatorial power. Everywhere, democracy seemed on the defensive.

In 1919, most European states, both major and minor, had democratic governments. In a number of states, women could now vote. Male political leaders had rewarded women for their contributions to the war effort by granting them voting rights. (However, women could not vote until 1944 in France, 1945 in Italy, and 1971 in Switzerland.) In the 1920s, maintaining these democratic governments was not easy.

Germany

Imperial Germany ended in 1918 with Germany's defeat in the war. A German democratic state known as the Weimar (VY • mahr) Republic was then created. The Weimar Republic was plagued by serious economic problems. Germany experienced runaway inflation in 1922 and 1923. With it came serious social problems. Families on fixed incomes watched their life savings disappear.

To make matters worse, after a period of relative prosperity from 1924 to 1929, Germany was struck by the Great Depression. In 1930, unemployment had grown to 3 million people by March and to 4.38 million by December. The Depression paved the way for fear and the rise of extremist parties.

SKILLS PRACTICE

Work with a partner to compare the graphs in this lesson with the information in the paragraphs. Take turns reading the paragraphs aloud while your partner identifies the corresponding information in the visuals.

(continued from p. 663)

TEKS **Texas Essential Knowledge and Skills**

20D explain the significance of the League of Nations and the United Nations

26A identify significant examples of art and architecture that demonstrate an artistic ideal or visual principle from selected cultures

28E identify the contributions of significant scientists and inventors such as Marie Curie, Thomas Edison, Albert Einstein, Louis Pasteur, and James Watt

France

France, too, suffered from financial problems after the war. Because it had a more balanced economy, France did not begin to feel the full effects of the Great Depression until 1932. The economic instability it then suffered soon had political effects. During a 19-month period in 1932 and 1933, six different cabinets were formed as France faced political chaos. Finally, in June 1936, a coalition of leftist parties—Communists, Socialists, and Radicals—formed the Popular Front government.

The Popular Front started a program for workers that some have called the French New Deal. This program was named after the New Deal in the United States. The French New Deal gave workers the right to **collective bargaining**, a 40-hour workweek in industry, and a minimum wage.

Great Britain

Although Britain experienced limited prosperity from 1925 to 1929, by 1929 it too faced the growing effects of the Great Depression. The Labour Party failed to solve the nation's economic problems and fell from power in 1931. A new government, led by the Conservatives, claimed credit for bringing Britain out of the worst stages of the Depression by using the traditional policies of balanced budgets and protective tariffs.

Political leaders in Britain largely ignored the new ideas of a British economist, John Maynard Keynes. Keynes argued that unemployment came from a decline in demand, not from overproduction. He believed governments could increase demand by creating jobs through **deficit spending**, or going into debt if necessary. Keynes's ideas differed from those who believed that depressions should be left to resolve themselves without government interference.

The United States

After Germany, no Western nation was more affected by the Great Depression than the United States. All segments of society suffered. By 1932, U.S. industrial production fell by almost 50 percent from its 1929 level. By 1933, there were more than 12 million unemployed. Under these conditions, Democrat Franklin D. Roosevelt won the presidential election in 1932 by a landslide. Believing in free enterprise, Roosevelt felt that capitalism must be reformed to save it. He pursued a policy of active governmental economic intervention known as the New Deal.

The New Deal included an increased program of public works. The Works Progress Administration (WPA), established in 1935, was a government organization employing about 3 million people at its peak. Workers built bridges, roads, post offices, and airports.

The Roosevelt administration instituted new social legislation that began the U.S. welfare system. In 1935, the Social Security Act created a system of old-age pensions and unemployment insurance. These reforms may have prevented a social revolution in the United States, but they did not solve the unemployment problems. In 1938, U.S. unemployment was more than 10 million. Only World War II and the growth of weapons industries brought U.S. workers back to full employment.

✓ **READING PROGRESS CHECK**

Defining How might collective bargaining have helped French workers?

Connections to TODAY

Depression vs. Recession

When the United States experienced a recession in 2008, people worried unemployment would reach Great Depression levels. But in studying unemployment numbers, economists discovered that, while the economic downturn was the worst since World War II, it was nowhere near as bad as the Great Depression. In 1933, unemployment had reached 29.4 percent. In December 2010, 9.4 percent of the U.S. population was unemployed.

collective bargaining the right of unions to negotiate with employers over wages and hours

deficit spending when a government pays out more money than it takes in through taxation and other revenues, thus going into debt

appropriate suitable or compatible; fitting

surrealism an artistic movement that seeks to depict the world of the unconscious

uncertainty principle the idea put forth by Werner Heisenberg in 1927 that the behavior of subatomic particles is uncertain, suggesting that all of the physical laws governing the universe are based on uncertainty

Arts and Sciences

GUIDING QUESTION *How were the arts and sciences influenced by World War I?*

With political, economic, and social uncertainties came intellectual uncertainties. These were evident in the artistic and scientific achievements of the years following World War I. After 1918, the prewar fascination with the absurd and the unconscious content of the mind seemed even more **appropriate** in light of the nightmare landscapes of the World War I battlefronts. "The world does not make sense, so why should art?" was a common remark. This sentiment gave rise to Dadaism and surrealism.

The dadaists were artists who were obsessed with the idea that life has no purpose. They tried to express the insanity of life in their art. A more important artistic movement than Dadaism was **surrealism**. By portraying the unconscious—fantasies, dreams, and even nightmares—the surrealists sought to show the greater reality that exists beyond the world of physical appearances. One of the world's foremost surrealist painters, the Spaniard Salvador Dalí, placed recognizable objects in unrecognizable relationships, thus making the irrational visible.

▲ *The Persistence of Memory* (1931), a surrealist painting by Salvador Dalí

The prewar physics revolution begun by Albert Einstein continued in the 1920s and 1930s. In fact, some have called the 1920s the "heroic age of physics." Newtonian physics had made people believe that all phenomena could be completely defined and predicted. In 1927, German physicist Werner Heisenberg's **uncertainty principle** shook this belief. Physicists knew that atoms were made of smaller parts (subatomic particles). The uncertainty principle is based on the unpredictable behavior of these subatomic particles. Heisenberg's theory essentially suggests that all physical laws are based on uncertainty. This theory challenged Newtonian physics and represented a new worldview. The principle of uncertainty fit in well with the other uncertainties of the interwar years.

✓ READING PROGRESS CHECK

Assessing Why was nonrealistic art popular after World War I?

LESSON 1 REVIEW TEKS

Reviewing Vocabulary

1. ***Applying*** Explain why John Maynard Keynes argued for the concept of deficit spending.

Using Your Notes

2. ***Identifying*** Use your notes to write a summary of the key points of the Popular Front and the New Deal.

Answering the Guiding Questions

3. ***Exploring Issues*** What led to new problems in the years after World War I?
4. ***Discussing*** What triggered the Great Depression?
5. ***Evaluating*** How did the Great Depression affect people's confidence in democracy?
6. ***Identifying*** How were the arts and sciences influenced by World War I?

Writing Activity

7. **INFORMATIVE/EXPLANATORY** Write an essay that explains how President Roosevelt's New Deal had immediate and far-reaching effects on the U.S. economy.

networks

There's More Online!

- BIOGRAPHY Benito Mussolini
- BIOGRAPHY Francisco Franco
- BIOGRAPHY Joseph Stalin
- CHART/GRAPH Soviet Industry, 1927–1938
- IMAGE Guernica
- INTERACTIVE SELF-CHECK QUIZ
- MAP Politics in Europe, 1930s
- MAP Soviet Union, 1939
- VIDEO Joseph Stalin

Reading HELPDESK

Academic Vocabulary

- **media**
- **attitudes**

Content Vocabulary

- **totalitarian state**
- **fascism**
- **collectivization**

TAKING NOTES:

Key Ideas and Details

Sequencing As you read, use a sequence chain like the one below to record the events leading up to Franco's authoritarian rule of Spain.

TEKS Texas Essential Knowledge and Skills

10D identify the causes of the February (March) and October revolutions of 1917 in Russia, their effects on the outcome of World War I, and the Bolshevik establishment of the Union of Soviet Socialist Republics

11B explain the responses of governments in the United States, Germany, and the Soviet Union to the global depression

continued on p. 669

LESSON 2

The Rise of Dictatorial Regimes

ESSENTIAL QUESTIONS • *What can cause economic instability?* • *How might political change impact society?*

IT MATTERS BECAUSE

After World War I, European democracy was under threat. A new kind of dictatorship emerged with Mussolini's fascist state in Italy and Stalin's totalitarian rule in the Soviet Union. Other Western states such as Spain maintained authoritarian regimes.

The Rise of Dictators

GUIDING QUESTION *How did Mussolini create a dictatorial state in Italy?*

By 1939, only two major European states—France and Great Britain—remained democratic. The world war significantly impacted the political systems of Italy, the Soviet Union, and Germany, who were left prey to totalitarian political systems due to losses real and perceived.

A new form of dictatorship was the modern totalitarian state. A **totalitarian state** is characterized by the government's aims to control the political, economic, social, intellectual, and cultural lives of its citizens. Totalitarianism pushed the central state's power far beyond what it had been in the past. These regimes wanted more than passive obedience; they wanted to conquer the minds and hearts of their subjects. They achieved this goal through mass propaganda techniques and modern communications.

The totalitarian states were further characterized by the leadership of a single leader and a single party. They rejected the ideal of limited government power and the guarantee of individual freedoms. Instead, individual freedom was subordinated to the collective will of the masses as determined by the leader.

Fascism in Italy

In the 1920s, Benito Mussolini (MOO • suh • LEE • nee) set up the first European fascist movement in Italy. Mussolini began his political career as a Socialist. In 1919, he created a new political group, the *Fascio di Combattimento*, or League of Combat. *Fascism* comes from that name.

GEOGRAPHY CONNECTION

1. **THE WORLD IN SPATIAL TERMS** *Where were authoritarian governments located?*
2. **HUMAN SYSTEMS** *Which countries transitioned from democratic to nondemocratic in the 1930s?*

totalitarian state a government that aims to control the political, economic, social, intellectual, and cultural lives of its citizens

fascism a political philosophy that glorifies the state above the individual by emphasizing the need for a strong central government led by a dictatorial ruler

As a political philosophy, **fascism** (FA • SHIH • zuhm) glorifies the state above the individual by emphasizing the need for a strong central government led by a dictatorial ruler. In a fascist state, the government controls the people and stifles any opposition.

By 1922, Mussolini's movement was growing quickly. The middle-class fear of socialism, communism, and disorder made the Fascists increasingly attractive to many people. Mussolini knew that many Italians were still angry over the failure to receive more land from the peace treaty. He knew nationalism was a powerful force and demanded more land for Italy. Mussolini converted thousands to the Fascist Party with his nationalistic appeals.

In 1922, Mussolini and the Fascists threatened to march on Rome if they were not given power. Victor Emmanuel III, the king of Italy, gave in and made Mussolini prime minister. Mussolini used his position as prime minister to create a Fascist dictatorship. He was made head of the government with the power to make laws by decree. The police were given unrestricted authority to arrest and jail anyone for either political or nonpolitical crimes. In 1926, the Fascists outlawed all other political parties in Italy and set up a secret police, known as the OVRA. By the end of the year, Mussolini ruled Italy as *Il Duce* (eel DOO • chay), "The Leader."

The Fascist State

Believing that the Fascist state should be totalitarian, Mussolini used various means to establish complete control over the Italian people. The OVRA watched citizens' political activities and enforced government policies. The Italian Fascists also tried to exercise control over the mass **media**, including newspapers, radio, and film. The media was used to spread propaganda. Simple slogans like "Mussolini Is Always Right" were used to mold Italians into a single-minded Fascist community.

The Fascists also used organizations to promote the ideals of fascism. For example, by 1939, about 66 percent of the population between the ages of 8 and 18 were members of Fascist youth groups. These youth groups particularly focused on military activities and values.

With these organizations, the Fascists hoped to create a nation of new Italians who were fit, disciplined, and war-loving. In practice, however, the Fascists largely maintained traditional social **attitudes**. This was especially evident in their policies on women. The Fascists portrayed the family as the pillar of the state. Seen as the foundation of the family, women were to be homemakers and mothers. According to Mussolini, these roles were "their natural and fundamental mission in life."

In spite of his attempts, Mussolini never achieved the degree of totalitarian control seen in Hitler's Germany or Stalin's Soviet Union. The Italian Fascist Party did not completely destroy the country's old power structure. Mussolini's compromise with the traditional institutions of Italy was evident in his dealings with the Catholic Church. In the Lateran Accords of February 1929, Mussolini's regime recognized the sovereign independence of a small area of 109 acres (about 44 hectares) within Rome known as Vatican City. The Church had claimed this area since Italian unification in 1870. Mussolini's regime also recognized Catholicism as the "sole religion of the State." In return, the Catholic Church urged Italians to support the Fascist regime.

▲ Mussolini addressing a crowd of over 500,000 people

media channels or systems of communication

attitude a mental position regarding a fact or state

✓ **READING PROGRESS CHECK**

Analyzing Why did many Italian people find fascism acceptable?

From Russia to the USSR

GUIDING QUESTION *How did Stalin gain and maintain power in the USSR?*

During the civil war in Russia, Lenin had followed a policy of war communism. The government controlled most industries and seized grain from peasants to ensure supplies for the army. When the war was over, peasants began to sabotage the Communist program by hoarding food. Moreover, drought caused a terrible famine between 1920 and 1922. As many as 5 million died. With agricultural disaster came industrial collapse. By 1921, industrial output was only 20 percent of its 1913 level. Russia was exhausted. A peasant banner proclaimed, "Down with Lenin and horseflesh. Bring back the czar and pork." As Leon Trotsky said, "The country, and the government with it, were at the very edge of the abyss."

Lenin's New Economic Policy

In March 1921, Lenin pulled Russia back from the abyss. He abandoned war communism in favor of his New Economic Policy (NEP). The NEP was a modified version of the old capitalist system. Peasants were allowed to sell their produce openly. Retail stores, as well as small industries that employed fewer than 20 workers, could be privately owned and operated. Heavy industry, banking, and mines, however, remained in the hands of the government.

(continued from p. 667)

TEKS **Texas Essential Knowledge and Skills**

12A describe the emergence and characteristics of totalitarianism

18D identify the historical origins and characteristics of fascism

19B identify the characteristics of the following political systems: theocracy, absolute monarchy, democracy, republic, oligarchy, limited monarchy, and totalitarianism

22C identify examples of politically motivated mass murders in Cambodia, China, Latin America, the Soviet Union, and Armenia

GEOGRAPHY CONNECTION

By 1939, the Soviet Union was increasingly industrialized and collectivized.

1. **THE WORLD IN SPATIAL TERMS** *What resource was plentiful near the Caspian Sea?*
2. **HUMAN SYSTEMS** *Why do you think the forced labor region was located in the far east of Russia?*

The Soviet Union

In 1922, Lenin and the Bolsheviks, who ultimately became the Communist Party, formally created a new state called the Union of Soviet Socialist Republics (USSR), or the Soviet Union (its shortened form). By that time, a revived market and a good harvest had ended the famine. Soviet agricultural production climbed to 75 percent of its prewar level.

Overall, the NEP saved the Soviet Union from complete economic disaster. Lenin, however, intended the NEP to be only a temporary retreat from the goals of communism.

Lenin died in 1924. A struggle for power began at once among the seven members of the Politburo (PAH • luht • BYUR • OH)—the Communist Party's main policy-making body. The Politburo was severely divided over the future direction of the Soviet Union.

One group, led by Leon Trotsky, wanted to end the NEP and to launch Russia on a path of rapid industrialization, chiefly at the expense of the peasants. This group also wanted to spread communism abroad. It believed that the revolution in Russia would survive only with new communist states.

Another group in the Politburo rejected the idea of worldwide communist revolution. Instead, it wanted to focus on building a socialist state in Russia and to continue Lenin's NEP. This group believed that rapid industrialization would harm the living standards of the peasants.

Stalin and His Five-Year Plans

These divisions were further strained by an intense personal rivalry between Leon Trotsky and another Politburo member, Joseph Stalin. In 1924, Trotsky held the post of commissar of war. Stalin held the bureaucratic job of party general secretary. Stalin used his post as general secretary to gain complete control of the Communist Party. By 1926, Stalin had removed the Bolsheviks of the revolutionary era from the Politburo and had established a powerful dictatorship. Trotsky, pushed out of the party in 1927, eventually made his way to Mexico. There he was murdered in 1940, probably on Stalin's orders.

Politically isolated from the world and not involved in trade, the Soviet Union was largely unaffected by the global depression. However, Stalin did make broad changes to Soviet economic policy. In 1928 Stalin ended the NEP and launched his First Five-Year Plan. The Five-Year Plans set economic goals for five-year periods. Their purpose was to transform Russia virtually overnight from an agricultural into an industrial country.

The First Five-Year Plan focused on production of military and capital goods (goods devoted to the production of other goods such as heavy machines). The plan quadrupled the production of heavy machinery and doubled oil production. Between 1928 and 1937, during the first two Five-Year Plans, steel production in Russia increased from 4 million to 18 million tons (3.6 to 16.3 million t) per year.

Costs of Stalin's Programs

The social and political costs of industrialization were enormous. The number of workers increased by millions between 1932 and 1940, but investment in housing actually declined after 1929. The result was that millions of workers and their families lived in miserable conditions. Real wages of industrial workers declined by 43 percent between 1928 and 1940.

With rapid industrialization came an equally rapid **collectivization** of agriculture—a system in which private farms were eliminated. Instead, the government owned all the land, and the peasants worked it. The peasants resisted by hoarding crops and killing livestock. In response, Stalin stepped up the program. By 1934, 26 million family farms had been collectivized into 250,000 units.

Collectivization had political motivations, but its outcomes were deadly. Hoarding food and slaughtering livestock led to widespread famine. Stalin is supposed to have said that 10 million died in the famine of 1932 to 1933. Each collective farm worker was given only one concession: one tiny, privately owned garden plot.

To achieve his goals, Stalin strengthened his control over the party. Those who resisted were sent into forced labor camps in Siberia. During the time known as the Great Purge, Stalin expelled army officers, diplomats, union officials, intellectuals, and ordinary citizens. About 8 million were arrested and sent to labor camps; they never returned. Others were executed. It was little else than political mass murder.

The Stalin era also overturned permissive social legislation enacted in the early 1920s. To promote equal rights for women, the Communists had made the divorce process easier. After Stalin came to power, the family was praised as a small collective. Parents were responsible for teaching the values of hard work, duty, and discipline to their children.

✓ READING PROGRESS CHECK

Stating Explain how Joseph Stalin used his position in the Communist Party and other means to gain control over the USSR.

Authoritarian States in the West

GUIDING QUESTION *What was the goal of authoritarian governments in the West?*

A number of governments in the Western world were not totalitarian but were authoritarian. These states adopted some of the features of totalitarian states, in particular, their use of police powers. However, these authoritarian governments did not want to create a new kind of mass society. Instead, they wanted to preserve the existing social order.

Analyzing PRIMARY SOURCES

Stalin's Purge

Poet Anna Andreyevna Gorenko, who wrote under the pseudonym Anna Akhmatova, was silenced during the Great Purge and watched as loved ones and fellow writers were imprisoned and disappeared. In 1942, her poem "Courage" appeared:

"We know that our fate in the balance is cast
And we are the history makers.
The hour for courage has sounded at last
And courage has never forsaken us.
We do not fear death where the wild bullets screech,
Nor weep over homes that are gutted,
For we shall preserve you our own Russian speech,
The glorious language of Russia!
Your free and pure utterance we shall convey
To new generations, unshackled you'll stay
Forever!"

—quoted in *Anna Akhmatova and Her Circle*

DBQ *DRAWING CONCLUSIONS*
According to this poem, what may be lost in the Great Purge that "we" must save?

collectivization a system in which private farms are eliminated and peasants work land owned by the government

Eastern Europe

At first, it seemed that political democracy would become well established in eastern Europe after World War I. Austria, Poland, Czechoslovakia, Yugoslavia (known as the kingdom of the Serbs, Croats, and Slovenes until 1929), Romania, Bulgaria, and Hungary all adopted parliamentary systems. However, authoritarian regimes soon replaced most of these systems.

Parliamentary systems failed in most eastern European states for several reasons. These states had little tradition of political democracy. In addition, they were mostly rural and agrarian. Large landowners still dominated most of the land. Powerful landowners, the churches, and even some members of the small middle class feared land reform. They also feared communist upheaval and ethnic conflict. These groups looked to authoritarian governments to maintain the old system. Only Czechoslovakia, which had a large middle class, a liberal tradition, and a strong industrial base, maintained its political democracy.

Spain

In Spain, too, political democracy failed to survive. Led by General Francisco Franco, Spanish military forces revolted against the democratic government in 1936. A brutal and bloody civil war began.

Foreign intervention complicated the Spanish Civil War. The fascist regimes of Italy and Germany aided Franco's forces with arms, money, and soldiers. Hitler used the Spanish Civil War as an opportunity to test the new weapons of his revived air force. German bombers destroyed the city of Guernica in April 1937. The Spanish republican government was aided by 40,000 foreign volunteers. The Soviet Union sent in trucks, planes, tanks, and military advisers.

The Spanish Civil War came to an end when Franco's forces captured Madrid in 1939. Franco established a dictatorship that lasted until his death in 1975. Because Franco's dictatorship favored traditional groups and did not try to control every aspect of people's lives, it is an example of an authoritarian rather than a totalitarian regime. Nevertheless, his rule was harsh. He relied on special police forces, and opponents to the regime who had not fled into exile were imprisoned.

▼ In his mural *Guernica* Spanish artist Pablo Picasso immortalized the horrible destruction of the city of Guernica in April 1937.

▶ **CRITICAL THINKING**

Analyzing Visuals What one word best describes your response to *Guernica*? Use details from the painting to explain how the artist creates this feeling.

PHOTO: Art Archive/Reina Sofia Museum, Madrid

✔ **READING PROGRESS CHECK**

Describing In what ways did Franco's government preserve the existing social order?

LESSON 2 REVIEW TEKS

Reviewing Vocabulary

1. ***Describing*** Describe the restriction of individual rights and the use of mass terror in Italy and the Soviet Union.

Using Your Notes

2. ***Sequencing*** Use your notes and details from the text to explain how Franco established an authoritarian government in Spain.

Answering the Guiding Questions

3. ***Organizing*** How did Mussolini create a dictatorial state in Italy?
4. ***Identifying Cause and Effect*** How did Stalin gain and maintain power in the USSR?
5. ***Interpreting*** What was the goal of authoritarian governments in the West?

Writing Activity

6. **ARGUMENT** Imagine you are a middle-class Italian in the 1920s. Write a letter to the editor of the local newspaper supporting Mussolini's new government.

networks

There's More Online!

- IMAGE Filming of *Triumph of the Will*
- IMAGE Nazi Propaganda Poster
- IMAGE SS Marching in Berlin
- INTERACTIVE SELF-CHECK QUIZ
- PRIMARY SOURCE Kristallnacht Directive from Reinhard Heydrich
- SLIDE SHOW The Hitler Youth
- VIDEO The Rise of Hitler

LESSON 3

Hitler and Nazi Germany

ESSENTIAL QUESTIONS • *What can cause economic instability?* • *How might political change impact society?*

It Matters Because

Recovering from the loss of World War I and from the Great Depression, Germans found extremist parties more attractive. Adolf Hitler's Nazi Party promised to build a new Germany, and his party's propaganda appealed to the German sense of national honor.

Reading HELPDESK

Academic Vocabulary

- **require**
- **prohibit**

Content Vocabulary

- **Nazi**
- **concentration camp**
- **Aryan**

TAKING NOTES:

Key Ideas and Details

Categorizing As you read, use a chart like the one below to list anti-Semitic policies enforced by the Nazi Party.

Anti-Semitic Policies

TEKS Texas Essential Knowledge and Skills

11B explain the responses of governments in the United States, Germany, and the Soviet Union to the global depression

26B analyze examples of how art, architecture, literature, music, and drama reflect the history of the cultures in which they are produced

Hitler and Nazism

GUIDING QUESTION *What was the basis of Adolf Hitler's ideas?*

Adolf Hitler was born in Austria in 1889. A failure in school, he traveled to Vienna to become an artist but was rejected by the academy. Here he developed his basic political ideas. At the core of Hitler's ideas was racism, especially anti-Semitism (hostility toward Jews). Hitler was also an extreme nationalist who knew how political parties could effectively use propaganda and terror.

After serving four years on the Western Front during World War I, Hitler remained in Germany and entered politics. In 1919, he joined the little-known German Workers' Party, one of several right-wing extreme nationalist parties in Munich.

By the summer of 1921, Hitler had taken total control of the party. By then, the party had been renamed the National Socialist German Workers' Party (NSDAP, an abbreviation of the German name), or **Nazi**, for short. Within two years, party membership had grown to 55,000 people, with 15,000 in the party militia. The militia was variously known as the SA, the Storm Troops, or the Brownshirts, after the color of their uniforms.

An overconfident Hitler staged an armed uprising against the government in Munich in November 1923. This uprising, called the Beer Hall Putsch, was quickly crushed, and Hitler was sentenced to prison, where he wrote *Mein Kampf*, or *My Struggle*, an account of his movement and its basic ideas.

In *Mein Kampf*, Hitler links extreme German nationalism, strong anti-Semitism, and anticommunism together by a Social Darwinian theory of struggle. This theory emphasizes the right of "superior"

Nazi shortened form of the German *Nazional,* or the National Socialist German Workers' Party; a member of such party

nations to *Lebensraum* (LAY • buhnz • ROWM)—"living space"—through expansion. It also upholds the right of "superior" individuals to gain authoritarian leadership over the masses.

Rise of Nazism

In prison, Hitler realized that the Nazis would have to attain power legally, not by a violent overthrow of the Weimar Republic. This meant that the Nazi Party would have to be a mass party that could compete for votes.

When out of prison, Hitler expanded the Nazi Party in Germany. By 1929, it had a national party organization. Three years later, it had 800,000 members and had become the largest party in the Reichstag—the German parliament.

No doubt, Germany's economic difficulties were a crucial factor in the Nazi rise to power. Unemployment had risen dramatically, growing from 4.35 million in 1931 to about 5.5 million by the winter of 1932. Hitler also promised a new Germany that appealed to nationalism and militarism.

The Nazis Take Control

After 1930, the German government ruled by decree with the support of President Hindenburg. The Reichstag had little power. Increasingly, the right-wing elites of Germany—the industrial leaders, landed aristocrats, military officers, and higher bureaucrats—looked to Hitler for leadership. Under pressure, Hindenburg agreed to allow Hitler to become chancellor in 1933 and to create a new government.

Within two months, Hitler had laid the foundation for the Nazi Party's complete control over Germany. Hitler's "legal seizure" of power came on March 23, 1933, when a two-thirds' vote of the Reichstag passed the Enabling Act. This law gave the government the power to ignore the constitution for four years while it issued laws to deal with the country's problems. It also gave Hitler's later actions a legal basis. He no longer needed the Reichstag or President Hindenburg. In effect, Hitler became a dictator appointed by the parliamentary body itself.

With their new power, the Nazis quickly brought all institutions under their control. They purged the civil service of democratic elements and of Jews—whom they blamed for Europe's economic woes. They set up prison camps called **concentration camps** for people who opposed them. All political parties except the Nazis were abolished.

concentration camp a camp where prisoners of war, political prisoners, or members of minority groups are confined, typically under harsh conditions

By the end of the summer of 1933, only seven months after being appointed chancellor, Hitler had established the basis for a totalitarian state. When Hindenburg died in 1934, the office of president was abolished. Hitler became sole ruler of Germany. People took oaths of loyalty to their *Führer* (FYUR • uhr), or "Leader."

✓ **READING PROGRESS CHECK**

Identifying Central Issues How did the Enabling Act contribute to Hitler's rise to power?

Aryan a term used to identify people speaking Indo-European languages; Nazis misused the term, treating it as a racial designation and identifying the Aryans with the ancient Greeks and Romans and twentieth-century Germans and Scandinavians

The Nazi State, 1933–1939

GUIDING QUESTION ***How did Hitler build a Nazi state?***

Hitler wanted to develop a totalitarian state. He had not simply sought power for power's sake. He had a larger goal—the development of an **Aryan** racial state that would dominate Europe and possibly the world for generations to come. (*Aryan* is a term used to identify people speaking Indo-European languages. The Nazis misused the term by treating it as a racial designation and identifying the Aryans with the ancient Greeks and Romans and twentieth-century Germans and Scandinavians.) The Nazis thought the Germans were the true descendants and leaders of the Aryans and would create an empire.

To achieve his goal, Hitler needed the active involvement of the German people. Hitler stated:

PRIMARY SOURCE

"We must develop organizations in which an individual's entire life can take place. Then every activity and every need of every individual will be regulated by the collectivity represented by the party. There is no longer any arbitrary will, there are no longer any free realms in which the individual belongs to himself. . . . The time of personal happiness is over."

—quoted in *Hitler,* 2002

The Nazis pursued the creation of the totalitarian state in several ways. For one thing, they used mass demonstrations and spectacles to make the German people an instrument of Hitler's policies. These meetings, especially the Nuremberg party rallies that were held every September, usually evoked mass enthusiasm and excitement.

The State and Terror

As sole ruler of Nazi Germany, Hitler relied on instruments of terror to maintain control. The *Schutzstaffeln* ("Guard Squadrons"), known as the SS, were an important force for maintaining order. The SS was originally created as Hitler's personal bodyguard. Under the direction of Heinrich Himmler, the SS came to control not only the secret police forces that Himmler had set up but also the regular police forces.

The SS was based on two principles: terror and ideology. Terror included the instruments of repression and murder—secret police, criminal police, concentration camps, and later, execution squads and death camps (concentration camps in which prisoners are killed). For Himmler, the chief goal of the SS was to further the "Aryan master race".

▲ SS troops march through the streets of Berlin on Hitler's birthday in 1939.

▶ CRITICAL THINKING

Analyzing How did marches such as this one help create allegiance to the Nazi state?

Economics

In the economic sphere, Hitler used public works projects and grants to private construction firms to put people back to work and end the depression. A massive rearmament program, however, was the key to solving the unemployment problem. Unemployment, which had reached more than 5 million in 1932, dropped to less than 500,000 in 1937. The regime claimed full credit for solving Germany's economic woes. Its part in ending the depression was an important factor in leading many Germans to accept Hitler and the Nazis.

▲ This Nazi propaganda poster features a mother with her children. It says, "Now we again have a happy future. For that, we thank the Führer on December 4."

require to demand as being necessary

prohibit to prevent or to forbid

Women and Nazism

Women played a crucial role in the Aryan state as bearers of the children who, the Nazis believed, would bring about the triumph of the "Aryan race". The Nazis believed men were destined to be warriors and political leaders, while women were meant to be wives and mothers. In this way, each could best serve to maintain the entire community.

Nazi ideas determined employment opportunities for women. Jobs in heavy industry, the Nazis thought, might hinder women from bearing healthy children. Professions such as university teaching, medicine, and law were also considered unsuitable for women, especially married women. The Nazis instead encouraged women to pursue occupations such as social work and nursing. The Nazi regime pushed its campaign against working women with poster slogans such as "Get hold of pots and pans and broom and you'll sooner find a groom!"

Anti-Semitic Policies

From its beginning, the Nazi Party reflected the strong anti-Semitic beliefs of Adolf Hitler. When in power, the Nazis translated anti-Semitic ideas into anti-Semitic policies.

In September 1935, the Nazis announced new anti-Semitic laws at the annual party rally in Nuremberg. These Nuremberg laws defined who was considered a Jew—anyone with even one Jewish grandparent. They also stripped Jews of their German citizenship and civil rights and forbade marriages between Jews and German citizens. Eventually, German Jews were also **required** to wear yellow Stars of David and to carry identification cards saying they were Jewish.

A more violent phase of anti-Jewish activity began on the night of November 9, 1938—*Kristallnacht,* or the "night of shattered glass." In a destructive rampage, Nazis burned synagogues and destroyed some 7,000 Jewish businesses in Germany, Austria, and in the Sudetenland in Czechoslovakia.. Thirty thousand Jewish males were arrested and sent to concentration camps. Jews were now barred from all public transportation and all public buildings, including schools and hospitals. They were **prohibited** from owning, managing, or working in any retail store. Finally, under the direction of the SS, Jews were encouraged to emigrate from Germany. The fortunate Jews were the ones who managed to escape from the country.

Culture and Leisure

A series of inventions in the late 1800s had led the way for a revolution in mass communications. Especially important was Marconi's discovery of wireless radio waves. By the end of the 1930s, there were 9 million radios in Great Britain. Full-length motion pictures appeared shortly before World War I. By 1939, about 40 percent of adults in the more developed countries were attending a movie once a week.

Of course, radio and the movies could be used for political purposes. Radio offered great opportunities for reaching the masses. The Nazi regime encouraged radio listening by urging manufacturers to produce inexpensive radios that could be bought on an installment plan.

Film also had propaganda potential, a fact not lost on Joseph Goebbels (GUHR • buhlz), the German propaganda minister. Believing that film was one of the "most modern and scientific means of influencing the masses," Goebbels created a special film division in his Propaganda Ministry, which supported the making of both dramatic feature films and documentaries. Reflective of the propaganda culture in which they were created, these films carried the Nazi message.

The Nazis also made use of the new mass leisure activities that had emerged by 1900. Mass leisure offered new ways for totalitarian states to control the people. The Nazi regime adopted a program called *Kraft durch Freude* ("Strength through Joy"). The program offered a variety of leisure activities to amuse the working class. These activities included concerts, operas, films, guided tours, and sporting events. Hitler used sporting events like the Olympic Games, which were held in Berlin in 1936, to show the world Germany's physical strength and prestige.

✓ READING PROGRESS CHECK

Predicting Consequences How do you think the Nazi control of media such as radio and film helped keep the regime in power?

Thinking Like a HISTORIAN

Detecting Bias

In 1934 Adolf Hitler commissioned Leni Riefenstahl to film the 1934 Nazi party rally in Nuremberg. The resulting film, *Triumph of the Will*, is considered an important documentary—and a chilling piece of Nazi propaganda.

Ultimately, Riefenstahl was cleared of complicity in Nazi war crimes, but she was blacklisted as a director. Riefenstahl later said of the film, "It reflects the truth that was then, in 1934, history. It is therefore a documentary, not a propaganda film." As a record of an actual event that happened at a specific time, it is a documentary. However, Riefenstahl's powerful and positive images of Hitler as a kind of savior attempt to influence the audience's attitude toward the Nazis—which is the goal of propaganda.

◄ **Director Leni Riefenstahl filming *Triumph of the Will* at the Luitpoldhain Arena in Nuremberg, 1934**

LESSON 3 REVIEW TEKS

Reviewing Vocabulary

1. ***Identifying Central Issues*** What does the term *Aryan* mean and how did the Nazis misuse the term?

Using Your Notes

2. ***Categorizing Information*** Use your notes to identify the anti-Semitic policies enforced by the Nazi Party.

Answering the Guiding Questions

3. ***Analyzing Information*** What was the basis of Adolf Hitler's ideas?

4. ***Drawing Conclusions*** How did Hitler build a Nazi state?

Writing Activity

5. **INFORMATIVE/EXPLANATORY** Write a paragraph discussing how Hitler used the existing German political structure and the economic situation in Germany to rise to power.

CHAPTER 28 Assessment

TEKS

Directions: On a separate sheet of paper, answer the questions below. Make sure you read carefully and answer all parts of the questions.

Lesson Review

Lesson 1

1. ***Naming*** What was the intended purpose of the League of Nations, and why was it only minimally effective? **20D**
2. ***Explaining*** Explain the outcomes of the Treaty of Versailles, including the economic impact. **10C**
3. ***Describing*** How did France respond when Germany was unable to pay more reparations?
4. ***Identifying Cause and Effect*** What factors incited the Great Depression?
5. ***Identifying*** What artistic principles began in the 1920s? What was a root cause for this outlook? **26A**

Lesson 2

6. ***Identifying*** What were the main characteristics of the totalitarian states? **12A, 19B**
7. ***Explaining*** How did totalitarian leaders rise to power during the 1920s and 1930s? **12A**
8. ***Identifying*** What are the characteristics of fascism? Describe Benito Mussolini's role in its emergence before World War II. **12B, 18D**
9. ***Interpreting*** Why was Mussolini's movement appealing to many Italians, and through what means did Mussolini and the Fascists establish control over the Italian people?
10. ***Making Connections*** Once in power in Italy, how did Fascists treat other political groups? **18D**

Lesson 3

11. ***Explaining*** What was Adolf Hitler's role in creating a totalitarian state prior to World War II? **12B**
12. ***Economics*** How did the Hitler's government respond to the depression? **11B**
13. ***Identifying Perspectives*** What perspective was rooted in Hitler's vision of a totalitarian state that would dominate Europe and possibly the world?
14. ***Sequencing*** In what order did Hitler's actions against Jews happen? What does this chronology show about the effects of escalating hate speech and behavior?
15. ***Hypothesizing*** Hitler insisted that women should concentrate on keeping house and raising children, yet he chose a woman, Leni Riefenstahl, to direct the famous Nazi propaganda film *Triumph of the Will*. Why do you think Hitler chose to contradict his beliefs?

Exploring the Essential Question

16. ***Gathering Information*** Work with a small group to research first-person accounts of life in the 1920s and 1930s, with special attention to economic difficulties and the effects of political change on individuals and families. You may find accounts in books, online, or by interviewing people directly. Take turns reading accounts to your class.

Need Extra Help?

If You've Missed Question	1	2	3	4	5	6	7	8	9	10	11	12	13	14	15	16
Go to page	662	662	662	663	666	667	668	668	668	668	674	675	674	676	676	662

Critical Thinking

17 ***Evaluating*** Explain the economic philosophy of John Maynard Keynes, and evaluate the logic and potential for application using what you know about the Great Depression.

18 ***Creating and analyzing arguments*** Explain the responses of Germany, the United States, and the Soviet Union to the global depression. Evaluate each nation's method of facing this challenge and support your claims with reasons and evidence. **11B**

19 ***Identifying Cause and Effect*** How did agricultural collectivization impact the Russian peasants?

20 ***Comparing and Contrasting*** Compare and contrast the styles of government in Italy and Spain under the leadership of Mussolini and Franco.

21 ***Identifying Cause and Effect*** Describe the political environment in Italy and Germany after World War I. How were these environments a consequence of World War I? Include examples from several countries in your response, and make generalizations based upon the similarities you identify. **1F**

22 ***Analyzing*** Consider the types of propaganda used by totalitarian governments, such as radio programs, rallies, posters, and documentaries, and analyze why drama films were an effective form of persuasion. Make a claim and use reasons and evidence to support your argument. **26B**

23 ***Making Connections*** How were Joseph Stalin and Leon Trotsky connected?

24 ***Explaining*** How did the Nazis use leisure activities to create bonds and loyalty for the Nazi regime, and how was this method of control an obvious contradiction to the termination of Jewish people?

Social Studies Skills

25 ***Economics*** What led to inflation in Germany and how and when did Germany enter a period of reprieve?

26 ***Identifying and Explaining*** Describe the events that occurred in Russia after World War I. Address the Bolshevik establishment of the USSR and the characteristics of Joseph Stalin's dictatorship, including politically motivated mass murders. Describe the consequences of these events. **10D, 22C**

27 ***Summarizing*** Summarize the international causes of the global depression. **11A**

28 ***Summarizing*** What political and economic causes led to the global depression? **11A**

29 ***Time, Chronology, and Sequencing*** How did Lenin's policies shift from wartime control to peasant resistance in the early 1920s with the formation of the Union of Soviet Socialist Republics?

Need Extra Help?

If You've Missed Question	17	18	19	20	21	22	23	24	25	26	27	28	29
Go to page	665	664	671	667	664	676	670	677	663	669	663	663	669

DBQ Analyzing Primary Sources

Use the cartoon to answer the following questions.

This political cartoon by John Baer was published in 1932, shortly after Franklin Roosevelt first used the term New Deal.

30 ***Naming*** Who are the card players demanding a new deal? Who is happy with the old deal?

31 ***Making Inferences*** What details in the cartoon provide insight into Baer's views on the distribution of wealth in the United States?

Analyzing Visuals

Use the image to answer the following questions.

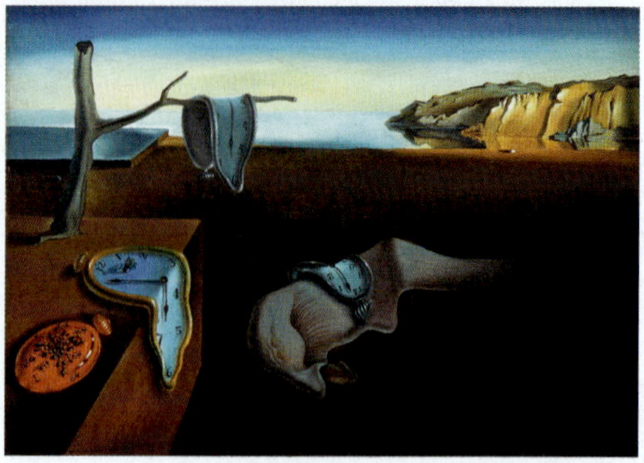

This painting, *The Persistence of Memory*, was painted by Salvador Dalí in 1931.

32 ***Analyzing Visuals*** What style of art is this painting? Support your answer with details from the painting.

33 ***Interpreting*** Why might some have suggested that Dalí was playing on Einstein's theory of relativity? How does this reflect the mood in Europe after World War I?

34 ***Making Inferences*** How does the title of the piece connect with the imagery, and what can you infer about the intended meaning of the title?

Extended Response Question

35 ***Informative/Explanatory*** Use the actions of Mussolini, Stalin, and Hitler to identify five things to avoid in order to protect the United States from a dictator. Add a sentence or two of explanation to each list item.

Need Extra Help?

If You've Missed Question	30	31	32	33	34	35
Go to page	680	680	666	666	666	668

Nationalism Around the World

1919–1939

ESSENTIAL QUESTIONS • *How can political control lead to nationalist movements?* • *How does economic exploitation lead to nationalist movements?*

networks

There's More Online! about nationalism around the world.

CHAPTER 29

The Story Matters...

World War I slowed the push toward independence among colonies in many parts of the world, but the end of the war gave a new strength to these efforts. Mohandas Gandhi was the charismatic leader of the Indian nationalist movement against British rule. He was committed to nonviolent action as a method for political and social change. Using peaceful methods, he eventually led India to independence. His actions inspired people to seek the end of colonialism, racism, and violence.

◀ This photograph shows Gandhi in his characteristic white garb woven of homespun cloth that he wore as a sign of solidarity with India's poor and as a rejection of foreign-made goods.

CHAPTER 29

Place and Time: Africa and Asia 1919–1939

In the 1920s and 1930s, independence movements, already present before World War I, strengthened in many parts of the world. The collapse of the Ottoman Empire led to the creation of Turkey, Iraq, and Saudi Arabia. In Africa, a new generation educated abroad and African veterans of World War I often led protests to colonial governments, but independence would not be achieved until after World War II. Asian nationalists, including Mohandas Gandhi in British India and Ho Chi Minh in French Indochina, struggled against colonial rule. In China, an alliance against imperialists between Nationalists and Communists broke down, leading to civil war.

Step Into the Place

Read the quotes and look at the information presented on the map.

DBQ **Analyzing Historical Documents** What did nationalist leaders hope to achieve? How did they differ in their approach to achieving their goals?

PRIMARY SOURCE

"A revolution is not a dinner party, or writing an essay, or painting a picture, or doing embroidery; it cannot be so refined, so leisurely and gentle, so temperate, kind, courteous, restrained and magnanimous. A revolution is an insurrection, an act of violence by which one class overthrows another."

—Mao Zedong, from *Report on an Investigation of the Peasant Movement in Hunan*, 1927

PRIMARY SOURCE

"Passive resistance is a method of securing rights by personal suffering; it is the reverse of resistance by arms. When I refuse to do a thing that is repugnant to my conscience, I use soul-force . . . If I do not obey the law and accept the penalty for its breach, I use soul-force. . . Everybody admits that sacrifice of self is infinitely superior to sacrifice of others."

—Mohandas Gandhi, from *Indian Home Rule*, 1909

Step Into the Time

Research an event from the time line and explain how it shows either the decline of an empire or the rise of nationalism.

AFRICA AND ASIA

- **1919** British massacre of unarmed Indian protesters at Amritsar
- **1920–1922** Mohandas Gandhi's Non-Cooperation Movement
- **1921** Young Kikuyu Association protests British taxes in Africa
- **1922** Independence of Egypt

THE WORLD

- **1919** League of Nations formed; League of Nations Mandates established

1919 — 1924

networks
There's More Online!

- **MAP** Explore the interactive version of this map on Networks.
- **TIME LINE** Explore the interactive version of the time line on Networks.

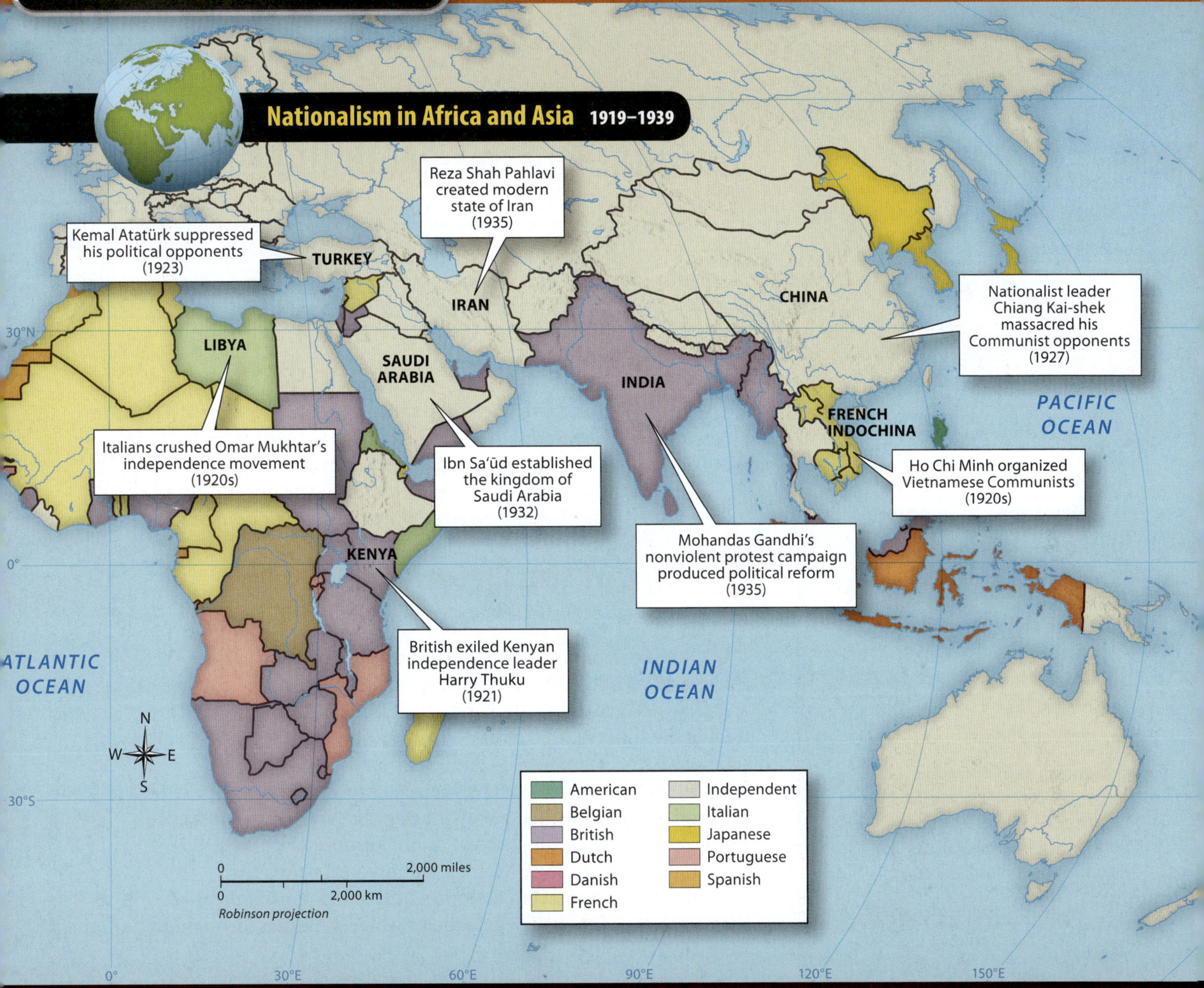

1928 Chiang Kai-shek becomes head of the Nationalists in China

1928 Jomo Kenyatta leads Kikuyu (Bantus) political association

1929 Jawaharlal Nehru elected President of Indian National Congress

1931 Japanese troops invade Manchuria following Mukden Incident

1934–36 Mao Zedong leads Long March of Chinese Communists

1929 — **1934** — **1939**

1929 Great Depression begins

1932 Independence for Iraq

1933 FDR announces the Good Neighbor policy

1938 Getúlio Vargas founds authoritarian state in Brazil

1938 Lázaro Cárdenas seizes control of Mexican oil industry

1939 World War II begins

1939 British limit number of Jewish immigrants to Palestine

- CHART/GRAPH Goals of the Young Turks
- CHART/GRAPH Oil Discovery in the Middle East
- IMAGE Atatürk
- IMAGE T. E. Lawrence
- IMAGE Young Turks
- INTERACTIVE SELF-CHECK QUIZ
- MAP Middle East, 1919–1935
- VIDEO The Armenian Genocide

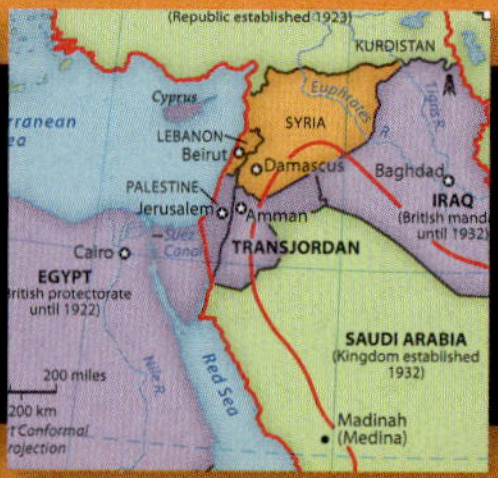

LESSON 1

Nationalism in the Middle East

ESSENTIAL QUESTIONS

- *How can political control lead to nationalist movements?*
- *How does economic exploitation lead to nationalist movements?*

Reading HELPDESK

Academic Vocabulary

- **legislature**
- **element**

Content Vocabulary

- **genocide**
- **ethnic cleansing**
- **caliphate**

TAKING NOTES:

Key Ideas and Details

Comparing and Contrasting As you read, make a graphic organizer like the one below comparing and contrasting the national policies of Atatürk and Reza Shah Pahlavi.

Atatürk Both Pahlavi

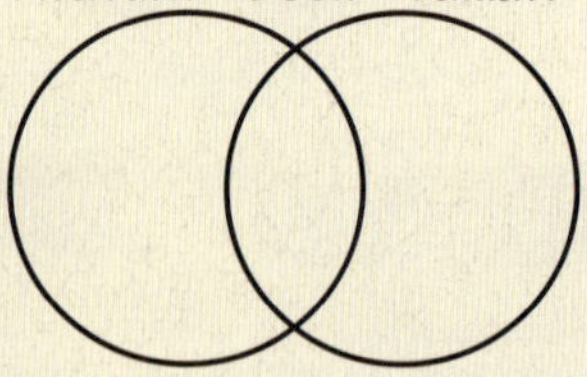

TEKS Texas Essential Knowledge and Skills

1F identify major causes and describe the major effects of the following important turning points in world history from 1914 to the present: the world wars and their impact on political, economic, and social systems; communist revolutions and their impact on the Cold War; independence movements; and globalization

continued on the next page

IT MATTERS BECAUSE

The Ottoman Empire ended shortly after World War I. While the new Turkish Republic modernized, Persia evolved into the modern state of Iran, and the kingdom of Saudi Arabia was established. In the Palestine Mandate, tensions mounted as both Arabs and Jews viewed the area as their homeland.

Decline of the Ottoman Empire

GUIDING QUESTION *What led to the final decline and fall of the Ottoman Empire?*

The Ottoman Empire—which once included parts of eastern Europe, the Middle East, and North Africa—had been growing steadily weaker. The empire's size had decreased dramatically during the nineteenth century when it lost much of its European territory. Ottoman rule also ended in North Africa.

In 1876 Ottoman reformers seized control of the empire's government and adopted a constitution that set up a **legislature**. However, the sultan they placed on the throne, Abdülhamīd II, suspended the new constitution. Abdülhamīd paid a high price for his authoritarian actions—he lived in constant fear of assassination. He kept 1,000 loaded revolvers hidden throughout his guarded estate.

The suspended constitution became a symbol of change to a group of reformers named the Young Turks. This group forced the restoration of the constitution in 1908 and deposed the sultan the following year. However, the Young Turks lacked strong support for their government.

Impact of World War I

The final blow to the old empire came from World War I. After the Ottoman government allied with Germany, the British sought to undermine Ottoman rule in the Arabian Peninsula by supporting Arab nationalist activities there. The nationalists were aided by the dashing British adventurer T.E. Lawrence, popularly known as Lawrence of Arabia.

In 1916 Arabia declared its independence from Ottoman rule. British troops advanced from Egypt and seized the region of Palestine. After suffering more than 300,000 deaths during the war, the Ottoman Empire made peace with the Allies in October 1918.

legislature an organized body that makes laws

The Armenian Genocide

During the war the Ottoman Turks alienated the Allies with their policies toward minority subjects, especially the Armenians. The Christian Armenian minority had been pressing the Ottoman government for its independence for years. In 1915 the Ottoman government accused the Armenians of supporting the Russians and used those allegations to kill or exile all Armenians.

Within seven months, 600,000 Armenians were killed, and 500,000 were deported. Of those, 400,000 died while marching through the deserts and swamps of Syria and Mesopotamia. By September 1915, an estimated 1 million Armenians were dead. They were victims of **genocide**, the deliberate mass murder of a particular racial, political, or cultural group. (A similar practice would be called **ethnic cleansing** in the Bosnian War of 1993–1996.) One eyewitness to the 1915 Armenian deportation said:

genocide the deliberate mass murder or physical extinction of a particular racial, religious, political, or cultural group

ethnic cleansing a policy of killing or forcibly removing an ethnic group from its lands; used by the Serbs against the Muslim minority in Bosnia

PRIMARY SOURCE

"[She] saw vultures hovering over children who had fallen dead by the roadside. She saw beings crawling along, maimed, starving and begging for bread. . . . [S]he passed soldiers driving before them . . . whole families, men, women and children, shrieking, pleading, wailing . . . setting out for exile into the desert from which there was no return."

—from *The Nili Spies*, by Anita Engle

By 1918, another 400,000 Armenians were massacred. Russia, France, and Britain denounced the Turkish actions as being "crimes against humanity and civilization." Because of the war, however, the killings continued.

READING PROGRESS CHECK

Summarizing In what ways did the war effort affect the Ottoman government?

(continued from p. 684)

TEKS **Texas Essential Knowledge and Skills**

13E summarize the rise of independence movements in Africa, the Middle East, and South Asia and reasons for ongoing conflicts

22C identify examples of politically motivated mass murders in Cambodia, China, Latin America, the Soviet Union, and Armenia

Middle East Changes

GUIDING QUESTION *How did the Middle East change after the fall of the Ottoman Empire?*

While Turkey, Iran, and Saudi Arabia emerged as modern states, tensions mounted between the Jewish and Muslim inhabitants in the Palestine Mandate.

The Modernization of Turkey

At the end of World War I, the tottering Ottoman Empire collapsed. Great Britain and France made plans to divide Ottoman territories in the Middle East. Only the area of present-day Turkey remained under Ottoman control. Then, Greece invaded Turkey and seized the western parts of the Anatolian Peninsula.

The invasion alarmed key **elements** in Turkey, who were organized under the leadership of the war hero Colonel Mustafa Kemal. Kemal summoned a national congress calling for the creation of an elected government and a new Republic of Turkey. His forces drove the Greeks from the Anatolian Peninsula. In 1923 the last of the Ottoman sultans fled the country, which was then declared to be the Turkish Republic. The Ottoman Empire had finally come to an end.

element a distinct group within a larger group

President Kemal was now popularly known as Atatürk (AT • uh • TUHRK), or "father Turk." Over the next several years, he tried to transform Turkey into a modern state. A democratic system was put in place, but Atatürk did not tolerate opposition and harshly suppressed his critics.

caliphate the office of the caliph

Atatürk's changes went beyond politics. Many Arabic elements were eliminated from the Turkish language, which was now written in the Roman alphabet. Popular education was introduced, and all Turkish citizens were forced to adopt family (last) names, in the European style.

Atatürk also took steps to modernize Turkey's economy. Factories were established, and a five-year plan provided for state direction over the economy. Atatürk also tried to modernize farming, although he had little effect on the nation's peasants.

Perhaps the most significant aspect of Atatürk's reform program was his attempt to break the power of the Islamic religion. He wanted to transform Turkey into a secular state—a state that rejects religious influence on its policies. Atatürk said, "Religion is like a heavy blanket that keeps the people of Turkey asleep."

▲ The Young Turks rode through the streets of Turkey waving flags in 1908.

▶ **CRITICAL THINKING**

Analyzing Visuals What about this photograph suggests it is from before Atatürk's rule?

The **caliphate** was formally abolished in 1924. Men were forbidden to wear the fez, the brimless cap worn by Turkish Muslims. When Atatürk began wearing a Western panama hat, one of his critics remarked, "You cannot make a Turk into a Westerner by giving him a hat."

Women were strongly discouraged from wearing the veil, a traditional Islamic custom. New laws gave women marriage and inheritance rights equal to men's. In 1934 women received the right to vote. All citizens were also given the right to convert to other religions.

The legacy of Kemal Atatürk was enormous. In practice, not all of his reforms were widely accepted, especially by devout Muslims. However, most of the changes that he introduced were kept after his death in 1938. By and large, the Turkish Republic was the product of Atatürk's determined efforts.

The Beginnings of Modern Iran

A similar process of modernization was underway in Persia. Under the Qājār dynasty (1794–1925), the country had not been very successful in resolving its domestic problems. Increasingly, the dynasty turned to Russia and Great Britain to protect itself from its own people, which led to a growing foreign presence in Persia. The discovery of oil in the southern part of the country in 1908 attracted more foreign interest. Oil exports increased, and most of the profits went to British investors.

The growing foreign presence led to the rise of a native Persian nationalist movement. In 1921 Reza Khan, an officer in the Persian army, led a military mutiny that seized control of Tehran, the capital city. In 1925 Reza Khan established himself as shah, or king, and was called Reza Shah Pahlavi. The name of the new dynasty he created, Pahlavi, was the name of the ancient Persian language.

During the next few years, Reza Shah Pahlavi tried to follow the example of Kemal Atatürk in Turkey. He introduced a number of reforms to strengthen and modernize the government, the military, and the economic system. Persia became the modern state of Iran in 1935.

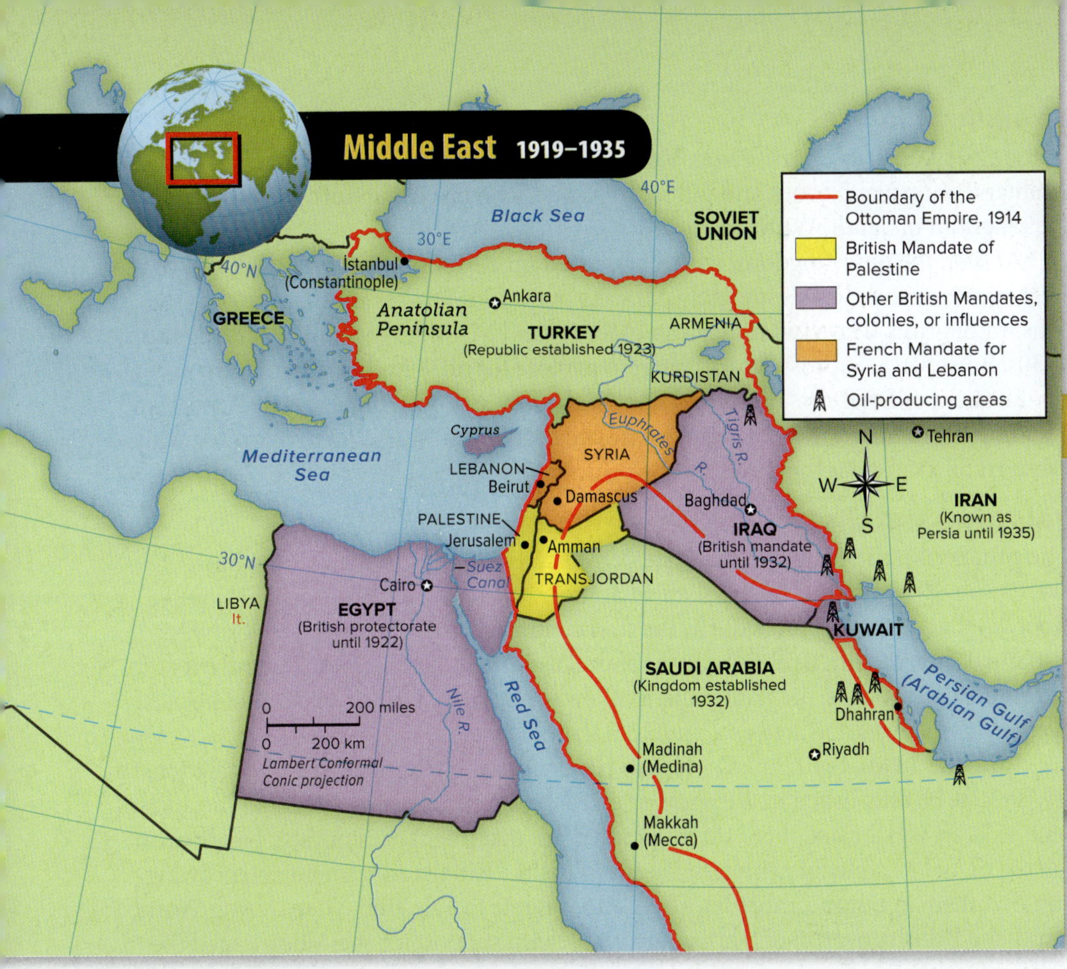

GEOGRAPHY CONNECTION

After the fall of the Ottoman Empire, mandates were established in the Middle East.

1. **PLACES AND REGIONS** *What happened to the Ottoman Empire after World War I?*
2. **THE WORLD IN SPATIAL TERMS** *Which mandates had access to oil reserves?*

Unlike Atatürk, Reza Shah Pahlavi did not try to destroy the power of Islamic beliefs. However, he did encourage the creation of a Western-style educational system and forbade women to wear the veil in public.

Foreign powers continued to harass Iran. To free himself from Great Britain and the Soviet Union, Reza Shah Pahlavi drew closer to Nazi Germany. During World War II, the shah rejected the demands of Great Britain and the Soviet Union to expel a large number of Germans from Iran. In response, Great Britain and the Soviet Union sent troops into the country. Reza Shah Pahlavi resigned and was replaced by his son, Mohammad Reza Pahlavi.

Arab Nationalism

World War I offered the Arabs an excellent opportunity to escape from Ottoman rule. However, what would replace that rule? The Arabs did not have nation-state, but they were united by their language and by the Islamic cultural and religious heritage that nearly all of them shared. However, efforts by generations of political leaders to create a single Arab nation have not succeeded.

Because Britain supported the efforts of Arab nationalists in 1916, the nationalists hoped this support would continue after the war. Instead, Britain agreed with France to create mandates in the area. These were former Ottoman territories that the new League of Nations now supervised. The League, in turn, granted its members the right to govern particular mandates. The Iraq and Palestine Mandates (which included Transjordan) were assigned to Great Britain; the Syria and Lebanon Mandates were assigned to France.

For the most part, Europeans created the modern map of the Middle East. The Europeans determined the future borders and divided the peoples. In general, the people in these states had no strong identification with their designated country. However, a sense of Arab nationalism remained.

Connections to TODAY

World Oil Reserves

Saudi Arabia has the largest oil reserves in the world, possessing one-fifth of Earth's known supplies. The Saudi reserves are estimated to be more than 260 billion barrels. Saudi Arabia is also the location of the world's largest oil field, Al-Ghawār, which was discovered in 1948 and still holds 70 billion barrels after 60 years of production. Following Saudi Arabia in estimated oil reserves are Canada, Iran, Iraq, and Kuwait. The United States, with estimated reserves of 19 billion barrels, ranks only 14th, just behind China.

Analyzing PRIMARY SOURCES

The Balfour Declaration

"His Majesty's Government view with favour the establishment in Palestine of a national home for the Jewish people, and will use their best endeavors to facilitate the achievement of this object, it being clearly understood that nothing shall be done which may prejudice the civil and religious rights of existing non-Jewish communities in Palestine, or the rights and political status enjoyed by Jews in any other country."

—from the Balfour Declaration

DBQ ***DRAWING CONCLUSIONS***

How does the Balfour Declaration simultaneously acknowledge the Zionist desire for a Jewish state and the challenges in the region?

Saudi Arabia

In the early 1920s, a reform leader, Ibn Sa'ūd, united Arabs in the northern part of the Arabian Peninsula. Devout and gifted, Ibn Sa'ūd won broad support. He established the kingdom of Saudi Arabia in 1932.

At first, the new kingdom, which consisted mostly of the vast central desert of the Arabian Peninsula, was desperately poor. Its main source of income came from the Muslim pilgrims who visited Makkah (Mecca) and Madinah (Medina). During the 1930s, however, U.S. prospectors began to explore for oil. Standard Oil made a successful strike at Dhahran, on the Persian Gulf, in 1938. Soon, the Arabian-American oil company Aramco was created. The isolated kingdom was suddenly flooded with Western oil industries that brought the promise of wealth.

Palestine and the Balfour Declaration

The situation in the Palestine Mandate complicated matters in the Middle East even more. Although the land of Israel had been the home of the Jews in antiquity, some Jews were forced into exile in the first century A.D. A Jewish presence always remained, but Muslim Arabs made up about 80 percent of the region's population. In the Palestine Mandate, the nationalism of Jews and Arabs came into conflict because both groups viewed the area as a potential national state.

Since the 1890s, the Zionists—Jewish nationalists—movement had advocated that a Jewish state be established in the ancient Jewish homeland. Jews recalled that the ancient state of Israel was located there. Arabs pointed out that their ancestors also had lived in the region of Palestine for centuries. As a result of the Zionist movement and growing anti-Semitism in Europe, more Jews began to migrate to Palestine. Then during World War I, the British government, hoping to win Jewish support for the Allies, issued the Balfour Declaration. It expressed support for a national home for the Jews in Palestine, but it also added that this goal should not undermine the rights of the non-Jewish peoples living there or the rights of Jews living in other countries. The League of Nations' British Mandate for Palestine (1922) incorporated the Balfour Declaration.

The Balfour Declaration drew even more Jews to the Palestine Mandate. In 1933 the Nazi regime in Germany began policies that later led to the Holocaust and the murder of 6 million Jews. During the 1930s, many Jews fled to the Palestine Mandate. Violence flared between Arab and Jewish inhabitants.

In 1936, Arabs in the Palestine Mandate revolted, demanding both independence from Britain and an end to Jewish immigration to the mandate. Trying to end the revolt, the British declared in 1939, on the eve of the Holocaust, that only 75,000 Jewish people would be allowed to immigrate to Palestine over the next five years; after that, no more Jews could do so. This decision, which closed one of the only escape routes for Jews in Nazi-occupied Europe, only intensified the tension and increased the bloodshed.

✓ **READING PROGRESS CHECK**

Contrasting Contrast the emergence of modern Turkey and Iran.

LESSON 1 REVIEW TEKS

Reviewing Vocabulary

1. ***Analyzing*** What role does the legislature or parliament fulfill in a constitutional monarchy?

Using Your Notes

2. ***Making Connections*** Why did the occupation of Kemal Atatürk and Reza Shah Pahlavi give them a shared outlook?

Answering the Guiding Questions

3. ***Determining Cause and Effect*** What led to the final decline and fall of the Ottoman Empire?
4. ***Drawing Conclusions*** How did the Middle East change after the fall of the Ottoman Empire?

Writing Activity

5. **INFORMATIVE/EXPLANATORY** Write a short paragraph that compares the original context of the Balfour Declaration with its role in subsequent decades.

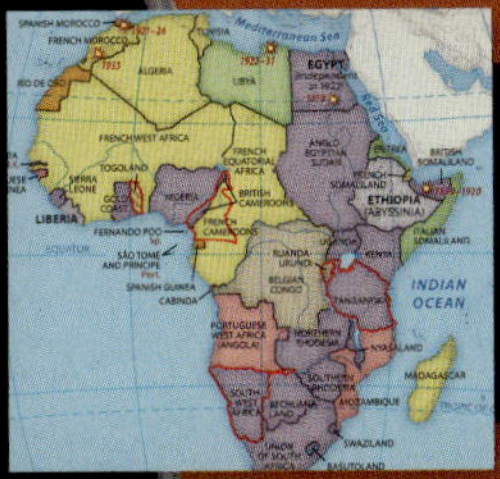

networks

There's More Online!

- BIOGRAPHY Jawaharlal Nehru
- BIOGRAPHY Mohandas Gandhi
- IMAGE Japanese Silk Factory
- IMAGE Women Protesting in Bombay
- INTERACTIVE SELF-CHECK QUIZ
- MAP Imperialism in Africa, 1914
- PRIMARY SOURCE Garveyism in Africa
- PRIMARY SOURCE Government of India Act of 1935
- VIDEO Gandhi

Reading HELPDESK

Academic Vocabulary

- **volunteer**
- **compensation**

Content Vocabulary

- **Pan-Africanism**
- **civil disobedience**
- ***zaibatsu***

TAKING NOTES:

Key Ideas and Details

Contrasting Use a table like the one below to contrast the backgrounds and values of Gandhi and Nehru.

Mohandas Gandhi	Jawaharlal Nehru

TEKS Texas Essential Knowledge and Skills

1F identify major causes and describe the major effects of the following important turning points in world history from 1914 to the present: the world wars and their impact on political, economic, and social systems; communist revolutions and their impact on the Cold War; independence movements; and globalization

continued on the next page

LESSON 2
Nationalism in Africa and Asia

ESSENTIAL QUESTIONS

- *How can political control lead to nationalist movements?*
- *How does economic exploitation lead to nationalist movements?*

It Matters Because

Nationalism spread throughout Africa and Asia in the early twentieth century. In Africa, calls for independence came from a new generation of Western-educated African leaders. As communism spread in Asia, Mohandas Gandhi and Jawaharlal Nehru worked for the independence of India. Militarists gained control of the Japanese government.

African Independence Movements

GUIDING QUESTION *What motivated African independence movements after World War I?*

Black Africans fought in World War I in British and French armies. Many Africans hoped that independence after the war would be their reward. As one newspaper in the Gold Coast argued, if African **volunteers** who fought on European battlefields were "good enough to fight and die in the Empire's cause, they were good enough to have a share in the government of their countries." Most European leaders were not ready to give up their colonies.

The peace settlement after World War I was a huge disappointment. Germany was stripped of its African colonies, but these colonies were awarded to Great Britain and France to be administered as mandates for the League of Nations. Britain and France now governed a vast portion of Africa.

African Protests

After World War I, Africans became more active politically. The foreign powers that conquered and exploited Africa also introduced Western education. In educating Africans, the colonial system gave them visions of a world based on the ideals of liberty and equality. In Africa, the missionary schools taught these ideals to their pupils. The African students who studied abroad, especially in Britain and the United States, and the African soldiers who served in World War I learned new ideas about freedom and nationalism in the West. As more Africans became aware of the enormous gulf between Western ideals and practices, they decided to seek reform.

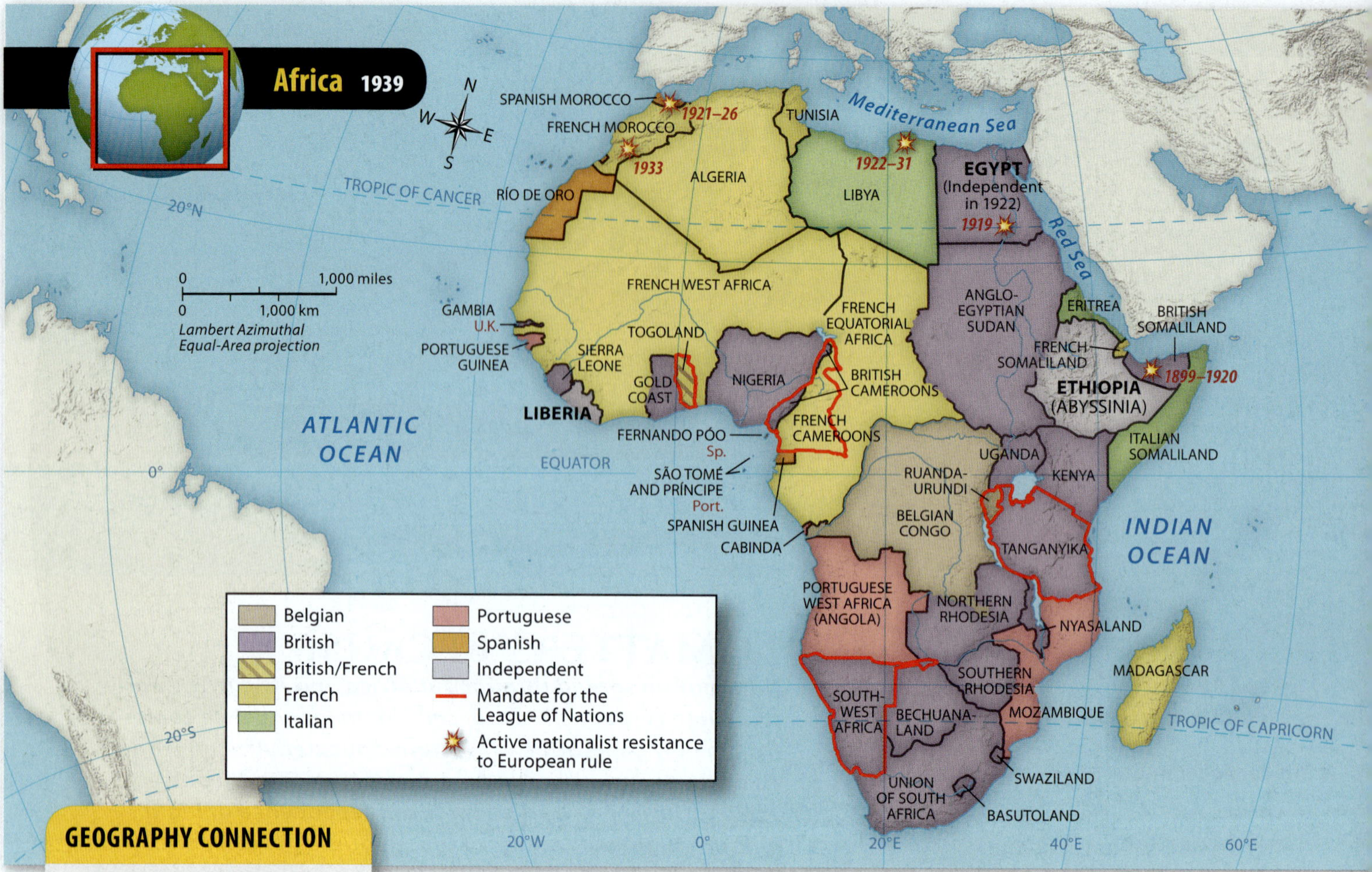

GEOGRAPHY CONNECTION

In 1939 nationalist resistance to European rule spread across Africa.

1. **PLACES AND REGIONS** *Which countries had active nationalist resistance movements by 1939?*
2. **HUMAN SYSTEMS** *Where did the first nationalist resistance movement shown on this map occur?*

volunteer one who enters the military voluntarily

compensation payment

(continued from p. 689)

TEKS **Texas Essential Knowledge and Skills**

12B explain the roles of various world leaders, including Benito Mussolini, Adolf Hitler, Hideki Tojo, Joseph Stalin, Franklin D. Roosevelt, and Winston Churchill, prior to and during World War II

13E summarize the rise of independence movements in Africa, the Middle East, and South Asia and reasons for ongoing conflicts

continued on the next page

Reform movements took different forms. One of the most important issues in Kenya concerned land redistribution. Large tracts of land were given to white settlers. Black Africans received little if any **compensation** for this land and became squatters on the land they believed was their own.

During the 1920s, moderate protest organizations, mostly founded by the Kikuyu, emerged in Kenya. The Kikuyu Association, founded in 1920 by farmers, was intent on blocking further land confiscation. This association was willing to work for reform within the existing colonial structure.

Some of the Kenyan protesters were more radical, however. The Young Kikuyu Association, organized by Harry Thuku in 1921, challenged European authority. Thuku, a telephone operator, protested against the high taxes levied by the British rulers. His message was simple:

PRIMARY SOURCE

> “Hearken, every day you pay . . . tax to the Europeans of Government. Where is it sent? It is their task to steal the property of the Kikuyu people.”
>
> —quoted in *Africa: History of a Continent*

Thuku was arrested. When an angry crowd stormed the jail and demanded his release, government authorities fired into the crowd and killed at least 20 people. Thuku was sent into exile.

Libya also struggled against foreign rule in the 1920s. Forces led by Omar Mukhtar used guerrilla warfare against the Italians and defeated them a number of times. The Italians reacted ferociously. They established concentration camps and used all available modern weapons to crush the revolt. Mukhtar's death ended the movement.

Although colonial powers typically responded to such movements with force, they also began to make some reforms. They made these reforms in an effort to satisfy African peoples. Reforms, however, were too few and too late. By the 1930s, an increasing number of African leaders were calling for independence, not reform.

New Leaders

Calls for independence came from a new generation of young African leaders. Many had been educated abroad, in Europe and the United States. Those who studied in the United States were especially influenced by the ideas of W.E.B. Du Bois and Marcus Garvey.

Du Bois, an African American who was educated at Harvard University, was the leader of a movement that tried to make all Africans aware of their own cultural heritage. Garvey, a Jamaican who lived in Harlem in New York City, stressed the need for the unity of all Africans, a movement known as **Pan-Africanism**. His *Declaration of the Rights of the Negro Peoples of the World*, issued in 1920, had a strong impact on later African leaders.

Leaders and movements in individual African nations also appeared. Educated in Great Britain, Jomo Kenyatta of Kenya argued in his book *Facing Mount Kenya* that British rule was destroying the traditional culture of the peoples of Africa.

Léopold Senghor, who studied in France and wrote poetry about African culture, organized an independence movement in Senegal. Nnamdi Azikiwe of Nigeria began a newspaper, *The West African Pilot*, in 1937 and urged nonviolence as a method of gaining independence. These are just a few of the leaders who worked to end colonial rule in Africa. Success, however, would not come until after World War II.

✓ READING PROGRESS CHECK

Listing Name four African leaders and discuss their motivations for African independence.

Analyzing PRIMARY SOURCES

Colonialism in Africa

"By driving [the African] off his ancestral lands, the Europeans have … reduced him to a state of serfdom incompatible with human happiness. The African is conditioned, by the cultural and social institutions of centuries, to a freedom of which Europe has little conception, and it is not in his nature to accept serfdom for ever. He realizes that he must fight unceasingly for his own complete emancipation [freedom]."

—Jomo Kenyatta, from *Facing Mount Kenya*

DBQ ***DRAWING CONCLUSIONS***
Why does Kenyatta equate colonialism with serfdom?

Pan-Africanism
the unity of all black Africans, regardless of national boundaries

Revolution in Southeast Asia

GUIDING QUESTION *Why was communism more accepted in Asia after World War I?*

Before World War I, the Marxist doctrine of social revolution had no appeal for Asian intellectuals. After all, most Asian societies were still agricultural and hardly ready for revolution. That situation changed after the revolution in Russia in 1917. Lenin and the Bolsheviks showed that a revolutionary Marxist party could overturn an outdated system—even one that was not fully industrialized—and begin a new one.

In 1920 Lenin adopted a new revolutionary strategy aimed at societies outside the Western world. He spread the word of Karl Marx through the Communist International, or Comintern, a worldwide organization of Communist parties formed in 1919 to advance world revolution. Agents were trained in Moscow and then returned to their countries to form Marxist parties. By the end of the 1920s, almost every colonial society in Asia had a Communist party.

How successful were these new parties? In some countries, the local Communists established a cooperative relationship with nationalist parties to struggle against Western imperialism. This was true in French Indochina. Moscow-trained Ho Chi Minh organized the Vietnamese Communists in

(continued from p. 690)

TEKS **Texas Essential Knowledge and Skills**
22E identify examples of individuals who led resistance to political oppression such as Nelson Mandela, Mohandas Gandhi, Oscar Romero, Natan Sharansky, Las Madres de la Plaza de Mayo, and Chinese student protestors in Tiananmen Square

the 1920s. The strongest Communist-nationalist alliance was formed in China. In most colonial societies, though, Communist parties of the 1930s failed to gain support among the majority of the population.

✓ **READING PROGRESS CHECK**

Summarizing How did communism spread to Asia after World War I?

SKILLS PRACTICE

During the class discussion, write down any questions you have about the concept of civil disobedience. Ask for an explanation during or after the lesson.

Indian Independence

GUIDING QUESTION ***Who and what shaped India's independence movement?***

Mohandas Gandhi was active in the Indian National Congress and a leader of resistance to British political oppression before World War I. The Indian people began to refer to him as India's "Great Soul," or Mahatma. After the war, Gandhi remained an important figure, and new leaders also arose.

Protest and Reform

Gandhi left South Africa in 1914. When he returned to India, he organized mass protests against British laws. A believer in nonviolence, Gandhi used the methods of **civil disobedience** to push for Indian independence.

civil disobedience refusal to obey laws that are considered to be unjust

In 1919 British troops killed hundreds of unarmed protesters in Amritsar, in northwestern India. Horrified at the violence, Gandhi briefly retreated from active politics but was later arrested and imprisoned for his role in protests.

In 1935 Britain passed the Government of India Act, which expanded the role of Indians in governing. Before, the Legislative Council could give advice only to the British governor. Now, it became a two-house parliament, and two-thirds of its Indian members were to be elected. Five million Indians (still a small percentage of the total population) were given the right to vote.

A Push for Independence

The Indian National Congress (INC), founded in 1885, sought reforms in Britain's government of India. Reforms, however, were no longer enough. Under its new leader, Motilal Nehru, the INC wanted to push for full independence from Britain.

Gandhi, now released from prison, returned to his earlier policy of civil disobedience. He worked hard to inform ordinary Indians of his beliefs and methods. It was wrong, he said, to harm any living being. He believed that hate could be overcome only by love, and love, rather than force, could win people over to one's position.

Nonviolence was central to Gandhi's campaign of noncooperation and civil disobedience. To protest unjust British laws, Gandhi told his people: "Don't pay your taxes or send your children to an English-supported school .... Make your own cotton cloth by spinning the thread at home, and don't buy English-made goods. Provide yourselves with home-made salt, and do not buy government-made salt."

Britain had increased the salt tax and prohibited Indians from manufacturing or harvesting their own salt. In 1930 Gandhi led a protest. He walked to the sea with his supporters in what was called the Salt March. On reaching the coast, Gandhi picked up a pinch of salt. Thousands of Indians followed his act of civil disobedience. Gandhi and many other members of the INC were arrested.

New Leaders and Problems

In the 1930s, Jawaharlal Nehru entered the movement. The son of Motilal Nehru, Jawaharlal studied law in Great Britain. He was a new kind of Indian politician—upper class and intellectual.

The independence movement in India split into two paths. The one identified with Gandhi was religious, anti-Western, and traditional. The other, identified with Nehru, was secular, pro-Western, and modern. The two approaches created uncertainty about India's future path.

In the meantime, another problem arose in the independence movement. Hostility between Hindus and Muslims had existed for centuries. Muslims were dissatisfied with the Hindu dominance of the INC and raised the cry "Islam is in danger."

By the 1930s, the Muslim League was under the leadership of Mohammed Ali Jinnah. The league believed in the creation of a separate Muslim state of Pakistan ("the land of the pure") in the northwest.

✓ READING PROGRESS CHECK

Identifying What was Gandhi's role in the Indian independence movement?

A Militarist Japan

GUIDING QUESTION *What triggered the rise of militarism in Japan?*

Japanese society developed along a Western model. Meiji Era reforms led to increasing prosperity and a modern industrial and commercial sector.

zaibatsu in the Japanese economy, a large financial and industrial corporation

A *Zaibatsu* Economy

In the Japanese economy, various manufacturing processes were concentrated within a single enterprise called the **zaibatsu**, a large financial and industrial corporation. These vast companies controlled major segments of the Japanese industrial sector. By 1937, the four largest *zaibatsu* (Mitsui, Mitsubishi, Sumitomo, and Yasuda) controlled 21 percent of the banking, 26 percent of the mining, 35 percent of the shipbuilding, and more than 60 percent of the paper manufacturing and insurance industries.

The concentration of wealth led to growing economic inequalities. City workers were poorly paid and housed. Economic crises added to this problem. After World War I, inflation in food prices led to food riots. A rapid increase in population led to food shortages. (The populationof the Japanese islands increased from 43 million in 1900 to 73 million in 1940.) Later, when the Great Depression struck, workers and farmers suffered the most.

With hardships came calls for a return to traditional Japanese values. Traditionalists especially objected to the growing influence of Western ideas and values on Japanese educational and political systems. At the same time, many citizens denounced Japan's attempt to find security through cooperation with the Western powers. Instead, they demanded that Japan use its strength to dominate Asia.

▼ Japanese women at a silk factory in 1913 check the unreeling of raw silk.

▶ **CRITICAL THINKING**

Contrasting Contrast the Japanese economy before and after World War I.

Japan and the West

In the early twentieth century, Japan had difficulty finding sources of raw materials and foreign markets for its manufactured goods. Until World War I, Japan fulfilled these needs by seizing territories, such as Taiwan (Formosa), Korea, and southern Manchuria. This policy succeeded but aroused the concern of the Western nations, especially the United States.

In 1922 the United States held a conference of nations with interests in the Pacific. This conference created a nine-power treaty that recognized the territorial integrity of China and the maintenance of the Open Door policy. Japan agreed, in return for recognition of its control of southern Manchuria. However, this agreement did not prove popular. Heavy industry, mining, and manufacture of appliances and automobiles require resources that are not found in abundance in Japan. The Japanese government came under pressure to find new sources for raw materials abroad.

The Rise of Militarism

During the early 1900s, Japan had moved toward a more democratic government. The parliament and political parties grew stronger. The influence of the old ruling oligarchy, however, remained strong.

At the end of the 1920s, a militant group within the ruling party gained control of the political system. Some militants were civilians who were convinced that Western ideas had corrupted the parliamentary system. Others were military members who were angered by the cuts in military spending and the government's pacifist policies of the early 1920s.

During the early 1930s, civilians and members of the armed forces formed extremist patriotic organizations such as the Black Dragon Society. One group of middle-level army officers invaded and conquered Manchuria without government approval in 1931, including up-and-coming officer, Hideki Tōjō. The Japanese government opposed the conquest, but the Japanese people supported it. Military leaders, such as Tōjō, soon dominated the government, which was unable to stop them.

Japanese society was put on wartime status. A military draft law was passed in 1938. Economic resources were placed under strict government control. All political parties were merged into the Imperial Rule Assistance Association, which called for Japanese expansion abroad. Labor unions were disbanded, and education and culture were purged of most Western ideas.

✓ **READING PROGRESS CHECK**

Making Connections Explain the relationship between the *zaibatsu* and militarism.

LESSON 2 REVIEW TEKS

Reviewing Vocabulary

1. ***Naming*** Name the different forms that civil disobedience took under Gandhi's leadership.

Using Your Notes

2. ***Differentiating*** Use your notes to write a paragraph explaining how Gandhi and Jawaharlal Nehru waged the same yet different battles for their nation.

Answering the Guiding Questions

3. ***Exploring Issues*** What motivated African independence movements after World War I?
4. ***Identifying Causes and Effects*** Why was communism more accepted in Asia after World War I?
5. ***Gathering Information*** Who and what shaped India's independence movement?
6. ***Analyzing*** What triggered the rise of militarism in Japan?

Writing Activity

7. **NARRATIVE** Imagine you were a participant in the Salt March in India. Write several paragraphs expressing the feelings you had as you and others reached the sea and picked up salt.

LESSON 3
Revolutionary Chaos in China

networks

There's More Online!

- ☑ BIOGRAPHY Mao Zedong
- ☑ CHART/GRAPH The Urban/Rural Divide in 1930s China
- ☑ IMAGE Chinese Refugees from the Northern Expedition
- ☑ IMAGE Rural Life in China
- ☑ INTERACTIVE SELF-CHECK QUIZ
- ☑ MAP China, 1926–1937
- ☑ PRIMARY SOURCE China's Destiny
- ☑ VIDEO The Rise of Communist China

ESSENTIAL QUESTIONS
- *How can political control lead to nationalist movements?*
- *How does economic exploitation lead to nationalist movements?*

Reading HELPDESK

Academic Vocabulary
- **cease**
- **eventually**

Content Vocabulary
- **guerrilla tactics**
- **redistribution of wealth**

TAKING NOTES:
Key Ideas and Details

Summarizing As you read, make a cluster diagram like the one below showing the Confucian values that Chiang Kai-shek used to bring modern Western ideas into a culturally conservative population.

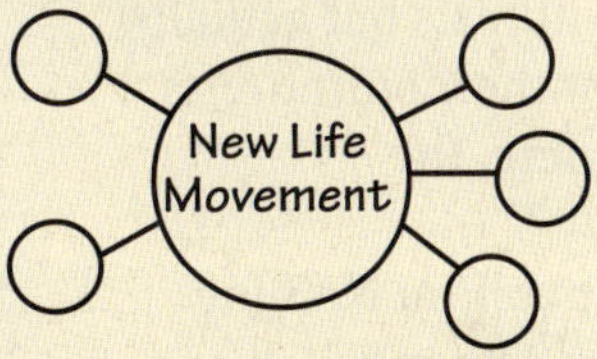

TEKS Texas Essential Knowledge and Skills
13B summarize the factors that contributed to communism in China, including Mao Zedong's role in its rise, and how it differed from Soviet communism

IT MATTERS BECAUSE

In 1923 the Nationalist and Communist parties formed an alliance to drive the imperialists out of China. Tensions between the two parties grew, however. Sun Yat-sen's successor, Chiang Kai-shek, struck against the Communists. Many Communists went into hiding or fled to the mountainous north, where Mao Zedong set up a Communist base.

Nationalists and Communists

GUIDING QUESTION *What was the relationship between the Nationalists and the Communists?*

Revolutionary Marxism had its greatest impact in China. By 1920 central authority had almost **ceased** to exist in China. Two different political forces began to emerge as competitors for the right to rule China: Sun Yat-sen's Nationalist Party, which had been driven from the political arena several years earlier, and the Chinese Communist Party.

The Nationalist-Communist Alliance

In 1921 a group of young radicals, including several faculty and staff members from Beijing University, founded the Chinese Communist Party (CCP) in the commercial and industrial city of Shanghai. Comintern agents soon advised the new party to join with the more experienced Nationalist Party.

Sun Yat-sen, leader of the Nationalists, welcomed the cooperation. He needed the expertise and the diplomatic support that the Soviet Union could provide. His anti-imperialist words alienated many Western powers. One English-language newspaper in Shanghai wrote: "All his life, all his influence, all his energies are devoted to ideas that keep China in turmoil, and it is utterly undesirable and improper that he should be allowed to prosecute those aims here." In 1923 the Nationalists and Communists formed an alliance to oppose the warlords and drive the imperialist powers out of China.

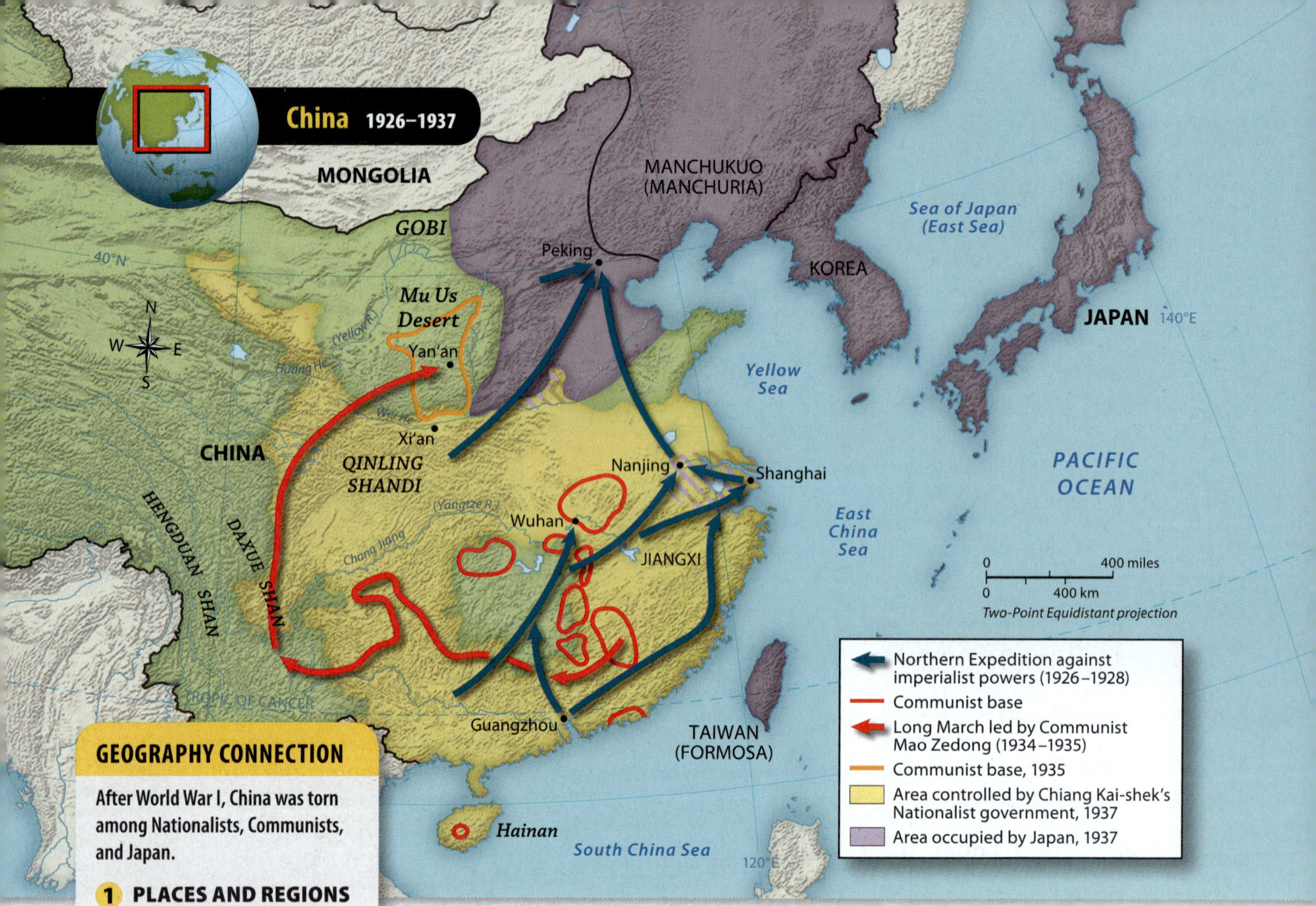

GEOGRAPHY CONNECTION

After World War I, China was torn among Nationalists, Communists, and Japan.

1. **PLACES AND REGIONS** *Why would the occupation of Nanjing be significant for the Nationalists?*
2. **THE USES OF GEOGRAPHY** *What geographic features likely helped the Communists defend their 1935 base?*

cease to come to an end

eventually in the end

For more than three years, the two parties overlooked their mutual suspicions and worked together. They formed a revolutionary army to march north and seize control over China. The so-called Northern Expedition began in the summer of 1926. By the following spring, revolutionary forces had taken control of all of China south of the Chang Jiang (Yangtze River), including the major river ports of Wuhan and Shanghai.

Tensions between the parties **eventually** rose to the surface. Sun Yat-sen died in 1925, and General Chiang Kai-shek (JYAHNG KY • SHEHK), his military subordinate, succeeded him as head of the Nationalist Party. Chiang pretended to support the alliance with the Communists but actually planned to destroy them. In April 1927, he struck against the Communists in Shanghai, killing thousands. After the Shanghai Massacre, the Nationalist-Communist alliance ceased to exist.

In 1928 Chiang Kai-shek founded a new Chinese republic at Nanjing. During the next three years, he worked to reunify China. Although Chiang saw Japan as a serious threat, he believed that the Communists were more dangerous. He once remarked that "the Japanese are like a disease of the skin, but the Communists are like a disease of the heart."

The Communists in Hiding

After the Shanghai Massacre of April 1927, most of the Communist leaders went into hiding in the city. There, they tried to revive the Communist movement in its traditional urban base among the working class. Shanghai was a rich recruiting ground for the party. People were discontented and looking for leadership.

Some party members, however, fled to the mountainous Jiangxi (JYAHNG • SHEE) Province south of the Chang Jiang. They were led by the young Communist organizer Mao Zedong (MOW DZUH • DUNG). Unlike most other leading members of the Communist Party, Mao was convinced that a Chinese revolution would be driven by the poverty-stricken peasants in the countryside rather than by the urban working class. Mao, the son of a prosperous peasant, had helped organize a peasant movement in southern China during the early 1920s.

Chiang Kai-shek now tried to root the Communists out of their urban base in Shanghai and their rural base in Jiangxi Province. He succeeded in the first task in 1931. Most party leaders in Shanghai were forced to flee to Mao's base in southern China.

Chiang Kai-shek then turned his forces against Mao's stronghold in Jiangxi Province. Chiang's forces far outnumbered Mao's, but Mao made effective use of **guerrilla tactics**, using unexpected methods like sabotage and deception to fight the enemy. Four slogans by Mao describe his methods:

PRIMARY SOURCE

"When the enemy advances, we retreat! When the enemy halts and camps, we trouble them! When the enemy tries to avoid battle, we attack! When the enemy retreats, we pursue!"

—quoted in *Red Star Over China*

The Long March

In 1934 Chiang's troops, with their superior military strength, surrounded the Communist base in Jiangxi and set up a blockade of the stronghold. With the villages behind Chiang's troops, no food or supplies could pass to the Communist base. Chiang even built small forts to prevent Communist raids. However, Mao's army, the People's Liberation Army (PLA), broke through the Nationalist lines and began its famous Long March.

Both Mao and Chiang knew that unless Mao's army could cross the Chang Jiang, it would be wiped out. Mao's army began a desperate race. Moving on foot through mountains, marshes, rivers, and deserts, the army traveled almost 6,000 miles (9,600 km), averaging 24 miles (38 km) each day, to reach the last surviving Communist base in northwest China. All along those miles, Mao's troops had to fight Chiang's army. Many of Mao's troops froze or starved. One survivor of the Long March remembered:

PRIMARY SOURCE

"As the days went by, there was less and less to eat. After our grain was finished, we ate the horses and then we lived on wild vegetables. When even the wild vegetables were finished, we ate our leather belts. After that we had to march on empty stomachs."

—quoted in *A Short History of China*

One year later, Mao's troops reached safety in the dusty hills of northern China. Of the 90,000 troops who had embarked on the journey, only 9,000 remained. In the course of the Long March, Mao Zedong had become the sole leader of the Chinese Communist Party. To people who lived at the time, it must have seemed that the Communist threat to the Nanjing regime was over. To the Communists, however, there remained hope for the future.

READING PROGRESS CHECK

Identifying Central Issues Why did the Nationalists and Communists form an alliance?

BIOGRAPHY

Mao Zedong (1893–1976)

Mao Zedong was the founding chairman of the Peoples' Republic of China. As a young communist revolutionary, he went to his home in the countryside of Hunan, where he saw political unrest growing among the peasants. He realized that the Soviet-style communism that he and others were pursuing—focusing on factory workers in cities—was not a perfect fit for China. Instead, he decided to organize a revolution of rural peasants. Mao sought to adapt communism to fit the conditions, culture, and traditions of China. Mao was largely responsible for laying the groundwork for a modern, self-sufficient China, but at an extreme cost. Many of his later policies, such as the Great Leap Forward and the Cultural Revolution, brought enormous suffering and political repression.

▶ CRITICAL THINKING

Predicting Consequences Why was it important that Mao focused on the revolutionary potential among the peasants in rural China rather than the factory workers in the cities?

guerrilla tactics the use of unexpected maneuvers like sabotage and subterfuge to fight an enemy

The New China

GUIDING QUESTION *What characterized the new China?*

Even while trying to root out Mao's Communist forces, Chiang was trying to build a new Chinese nation. He publicly declared his commitment to Sun Yat-sen's plans for a republican government. But first, a transitional period would occur. In Sun's words:

PRIMARY SOURCE

"China . . . needs a republican government just as a boy needs school. As a schoolboy must have good teachers and helpful friends, so the Chinese people, being for the first time under republican rule, must have a farsighted revolutionary government for their training. This calls for the period of political tutelage, which is a necessary transitional stage from monarchy to republicanism. Without this, disorder will be unavoidable."

—quoted in *Sources of Chinese Tradition*

In keeping with Sun's program, Chiang announced a period of political tutelage (training) to prepare the Chinese people for a final stage of

▼ Rural peasants toil in the fields in 1930s China.

▶ **CRITICAL THINKING**
Contrasting How was life different in urban and rural China in the 1930s?

constitutional government. Even the humblest peasant would be given time to understand the country's problems and the new government. In the meantime, the Nationalists used their dictatorial power to carry out a land-reform program and the modernization of the urban industrial sector.

A Class Divide

It would take more than plans on paper to create a new China, however. Years of neglect and civil war had severely weakened the political, economic, and social fabric of the nation. Faint signs of an impending industrial revolution were appearing in the major urban centers. However, most of the people who lived in the countryside were drained by warfare and civil strife. Rural peasants—up to 80 percent of China's population—were still poor and overwhelmingly illiterate.

Meanwhile, a Westernized middle class began to form in the cities. It was here that the new Nanjing government found much of its support. However, the new Westernized elite were concerned with the middle-class Western values of individual advancement and material accumulation. They had few links with the peasants in the countryside or with the rickshaw (a small, two-wheeled cart that usually carried one passenger and was pulled by a person) driver, "running in this world of suffering," in the words of a Chinese poet. In the cities, observers would have believed that Chiang Kai-shek had lifted China into the modern world. Young people in cities wore European clothes; they went to the movies and listened to the radio.

Innovations and Traditions

Chiang Kai-shek was aware of the problem of introducing foreign ideas into a population that was still culturally conservative. Thus, while attempting to build a modern industrial state, he tried to bring together modern Western innovations with traditional Confucian values of hard work and obedience. With his U.S.-educated wife Soong Mei-ling, Chiang set up a "New Life Movement." Its goal was to promote traditional Confucian social ethics, such as integrity, propriety, and righteousness. Four ancient Confucian virtues would serve as guides for living: Li (courtesy), I (duty), Lien (honesty), and Chih (honor). At the same time, it rejected what was viewed as the excessive individualism and material greed of Western capitalist values.

Unfortunately for Chiang Kai-Shek, Confucian ideas had been widely discredited when the traditional system failed to provide answers to China's decline. Moreover, Chiang Kai-shek faced a host of other problems. The Nanjing government had total control over only a handful of provinces in the Chang Jiang valley. Also, the Japanese threatened to gain control of northern China. The Great Depression also was having an ill effect on China's economy. All of these problems created difficulties for Chiang.

Limited Progress

In spite of these problems, Chiang did have some success. He undertook a massive road-building project and repaired and extended much of the country's railroad system as well. More than 50,000 miles (80,467 km) of highways were built around and through the coastal areas. New factories, mostof which the Chinese owned, were opened. Through a series of agreements,the foreign powers ended many of their leases, gave up extra-territorial rights, and returned the customs service to Chinese control. Chiang established a national bank and improved the education system.

Analyzing PRIMARY SOURCES

The New Life Movement

"The new life movement is based upon the preservation of these four virtues [courtesy, duty, honesty, and honor], and it aims to apply them to actual, existing conditions, in order that the moral character of the nation shall attain the highest possible standard."

—Madame Chiang Kai-shek, quoted in *War Messages and Other Selections*

DBQ ***DRAWING CONCLUSIONS***
What were the goals of the New Life Movement?

redistribution of wealth the shifting of wealth from a rich minority to a poor majority

The government was also repressive. Fearing Communist influence, Chiang suppressed all opposition and censored free expression. In so doing, he alienated many intellectuals and political moderates. Because Chiang's support came from the rural landed gentry as well as the urban middle class, he did not push for programs that would lead to a **redistribution of wealth,** the shifting of wealth from a rich minority to a poor majority. A land-reform program was enacted in 1930, but it had little effect on the country. For the peasants and poor townspeople, no real improvement occurred under the Nanjing government.

Sun Fo, Sun Yat-sen's son, expressed disapproval of the Nanjing government:

PRIMARY SOURCE

"We must frankly admit the fact that in these twenty years the machinery and practice of the Kuomintang [Chinese Nationalist Party] have turned in a wrong direction, inconsistent with the party constitution drafted by Dr. Sun Yat-sen in 1923 and contrary to the spirit of democracy. The practice of the revolutionary party has subsequently become the same as that of a bureaucratic regime."

—quoted in *China,* 1946

Chiang Kai-shek's government had a little more success in promoting industrial development. Between 1927 and 1937, industrial growth in China averaged only about one percent per year. Much of the national wealth was in the hands of the so-called "four families," a group of senior officials and close subordinates of the ruling elite. Military expenses took up approximately half of the budget. Little money was left for social and economic development.

The new government, then, had little success in dealing with the deep-seated economic and social problems that affected China during the interwar years. This was especially true when internal disintegration and foreign pressure were occurring during the virtual collapse of the global economic order during the Great Depression. In addition, militant political forces in Tokyo were determined to extend Japanese influence and power in an unstable China.

✓ **READING PROGRESS CHECK**

Drawing Conclusions Why did Chiang Kai-shek believe a period of political tutelage was necessary for China?

LESSON 3 REVIEW TEKS

Reviewing Vocabulary

1. ***Paraphrasing*** Describe Mao Zedong's guerrilla tactics.

Using Your Notes

2. ***Synthesizing*** Using your notes, list the Confucian values that Chiang Kai-shek used to bring modern Western ideas into a culturally conservative population. Why do you think Chiang Kai-shek used those particular values to introduce Western culture to China?

Answering the Guiding Questions

3. ***Identifying Central Issues*** What was the relationship between the Nationalists and the Communists?

4. ***Analyzing Information*** What characterized the new China?

Writing Activity

5. **NARRATIVE** Imagine that you are a young person living in China. Choose a year covered in this lesson and then choose where in China you live. Write a diary entry describing the events that are happening in your hometown. Be sure to use specific details and events as you write.

networks

There's More Online!

- ☑ CHART/GRAPH Great Depression in Latin America
- ☑ CHART/GRAPH Goods Exported from Latin America, 1937–1938
- ☑ IMAGE Good Neighbor Policy
- ☑ IMAGE United Fruit Company Workers
- ☑ INTERACTIVE SELF-CHECK QUIZ
- ☑ SLIDE SHOW Modern Art of Latin America
- ☑ VIDEO Diego Rivera

Reading HELPDESK

Academic Vocabulary

- **investor**
- **establish**

Content Vocabulary

- **oligarchy**

TAKING NOTES:

Key Ideas and Details

Summarizing Use the following graphic organizer to identify countries and regions in Latin America and their primary exports.

Country or Region	Export
Argentina	
Brazil	
Chile	
Central America	
Caribbean	

TEKS Texas Essential Knowledge and Skills

19B identify the characteristics of the following political systems: theocracy, absolute monarchy, democracy, republic, oligarchy, limited monarchy, and totalitarianism

PHOTO: (l to r)©Jacob J. Gayer/National Geographic Society/Corbis, Library of Congress Prints & Photographs Division, Library of Congress, ©Christie's Images/SuperStock, Library of Congress Prints & Photographs Division.

LESSON 4

Nationalism in Latin America

ESSENTIAL QUESTIONS

- *How can political control lead to nationalist movements?*
- *How does economic exploitation lead to nationalist movements?*

It Matters Because

During the 1920s, investors in the United States poured funds directly into Latin American businesses. The Great Depression devastated Latin America's economy and created instability. This turmoil led to the creation of military dictatorships and authoritarian states in Latin America in the 1930s.

The Latin American Economy

GUIDING QUESTION *What factors influenced the Latin American economy during the 1920s and 1930s?*

In the early twentieth century, the Latin American economy was based largely on the export of foodstuffs and raw materials. Some countries relied on only one or two products for sale abroad. Argentina, for example, exported beef and wheat; Chile, nitrates and copper; Brazil, coffee and cotton; Caribbean nations, such as Cuba, sugar; and Central America, bananas. A few reaped large profits from these exports. For most of the people, however, the returns were small.

Role of the United States

Beginning in the 1920s, the United States began to replace Great Britain as the major **investor** in Latin America. British investors had put money into stocks and other forms of investment that did not give them direct control of the companies. U.S. investors, however, put their funds directly into production facilities and ran companies themselves. In this way, large segments of Latin America's export industries fell into U.S. hands. A number of smaller Central American countries became independent republics, but their economies often depended on wealthy nations. The U.S.-owned United Fruit Company, for example, owned land, packing plants, and railroads in Central America. American firms also gained control of the copper-mining industry in Chile and Peru, as well as of the oil industry in Mexico, Peru, and Bolivia.

investor a person or entity that commits money to earn a financial return

Many Latin Americans resented U.S. control of Latin American industries. A growing nationalist awareness led many of them to view the United States as an imperialist power. It was not difficult for Latin American nationalists to show that profits from U.S. businesses were sometimes used to keep ruthless dictators in power. In Venezuela, for example, U.S. oil companies had close ties to the dictator Juan Vicente Gómez.

The United States had always cast a large shadow over Latin America. It had intervened militarily in Latin American affairs for years. This was especially true in Central America and the Caribbean. Many Americans considered both regions vital to U.S. security.

The United States made some attempts to change its relationship with Latin America in the 1930s. In 1933 President Franklin D. Roosevelt announced the Good Neighbor policy, rejecting the use of U.S. military force in Latin America. The president then withdrew the last U.S. Marines from Haiti in 1934. For the first time in 30 years, no U.S. troops were stationed in Latin American countries.

Impact of the Great Depression

The Great Depression was a disaster for Latin America's economy. Weak U.S. and European economies meant less demand for Latin American exports, especially coffee, sugar, metals, and meat. The total value of Latin American exports in 1930 was almost 50 percent below the figures for the years 1925 through 1929. The countries that depended on the export of only one product were especially hurt.

The Great Depression, however, had one positive effect on the Latin American economy. When exports declined, Latin American countries could no longer buy manufactured goods from abroad. Thus their governments began to encourage the development of new industries to produce manufactured goods. The hope was that industrial development would bring greater economic independence.

Often, however, individuals could not start new industries because capital was scarce in the private sector. Governments then invested in the new industries. This led to government-run steel industries in Chile and Brazil and government-run oil industries in Argentina and Mexico.

✓ **READING PROGRESS CHECK**

Contrasting How did the U.S. method of investing differ from that of Great Britain?

▼ Workers load bananas at a United Fruit Company farm in Central America.

▶ **CRITICAL THINKING**

Evaluating Who reaped most of the profits from the export of bananas?

Authoritarian Rule

GUIDING QUESTION ***Who controlled politics in Latin America?***

Most Latin American countries had republican forms of government. In reality, however, a relatively small group of church officials, military leaders, and large landowners ruled each country. This elite group controlled the masses of people, who were mostly poor peasants. Military forces were crucial in keeping these special-interest groups in power. Indeed, military leaders often took control of the government.

This trend toward authoritarianism increased during the 1930s, largely because of the impact of the Great Depression. Domestic instability caused by economic crises led to the creation of many military dictatorships in the early 1930s. This trend was especially evident in Argentina, Brazil, and Mexico. Together, these nations possessed more than half of the land and wealth of Latin America.

Argentina

Argentina was controlled by an **oligarchy**, a government in which a select group of people exercises control. This oligarchy of large landowners who had grown wealthy from the export of beef and wheat failed to realize the growing importance of industry and cities in their country. This group also ignored the growing middle class, which reacted by forming the Radical Party in 1890.

oligarchy "the rule of the few;" a form of government in which a select group of people exercises control

In 1916 Hipólito Irigoyen (ee • PAW • lee • TOH IHR • ih • GOH • YEHN), leader of the Radical Party, was elected president of Argentina. The Radical Party, however, feared the industrial workers, who were using strikes to improve their conditions. The party thus drew closer to the large landowners and became more corrupt.

The military also was concerned with the rising power of the industrial workers. In 1930 the Argentine army overthrew President Irigoyen and reestablished the power of the large landowners. Through this action, the military hoped to continue the old export economy and thus stop the growth of working-class power that would come with more industrialization.

During World War II, restless military officers formed a new organization, the Group of United Officers (GOU). They were unhappy with the Argentinian government and overthrew it in June 1943.

Brazil

In 1889 the army overthrew the Brazilian monarchy and **established** a republic. It was controlled chiefly by the landed elites, who had become wealthy from large coffee plantations.

establish to set up permanently; to found

By 1900, three-fourths of the world's coffee was grown in Brazil. As long as coffee prices remained high, the ruling oligarchy was able to maintain its power. The oligarchy largely ignored the growth of urban industry and the working class that came with it.

The Great Depression devastated the coffee industry. By the end of 1929, coffee prices had hit a record low. In 1930 a military coup made Getúlio Vargas, a wealthy rancher, president of Brazil. Vargas ruled Brazil from 1930 to 1945. Early in his rule, he appealed to workers by establishing an eight-hour day and a minimum wage.

Faced with strong opposition in 1937, Vargas made himself dictator. Beginning in 1938 he established his New State. It was basically an authoritarian state with some fascist-like features. Political parties were outlawed, and civil rights were restricted. Secret police silenced Vargas's opponents.

Analyzing PRIMARY SOURCES

President Cárdenas on Oil and the United States

Cárdenas in his first report to Congress in 1935:

"The exploitation of oil in Mexico has, for many years, taken place in a way characteristic of foreign companies; that is to say, our country, though independent and enjoying advanced social ideas, permits the extraction of its wealth and natural resources by the foreigner without preserving for itself any permanent benefit."

—quoted in *Oil and Politics in Latin America: Nationalist Movements and State Companies*

DBQ ***ANALYZING INFORMATION*** How did Cárdenas attempt to address the injustice that he perceived in this relationship?

Vargas also pursued a policy of stimulating new industries. The government established the Brazilian steel industry and set up a company to explore for oil. By the end of World War II, Brazil had become Latin America's chief industrial power. In 1945 the army, fearing that Vargas might prolong his power illegally after calling for new elections, forced him to resign.

Mexico

Mexico was not an authoritarian state, but neither was it truly democratic. The Mexican Revolution of the early twentieth century was the first significant effort in Latin America to overturn the system of large landed estates and raise the living standards of the masses. Out of the revolution emerged a relatively stable political order.

The government was democratic in form. However, the official political party of the Mexican Revolution, known as the Institutional Revolutionary Party, or PRI, controlled the major groups within Mexican society. Every six years, party bosses of the PRI chose the party's presidential candidate. That candidate was then dutifully elected by the people.

A new wave of change began with Lázaro Cárdenas (KAHR • duhn • AHS), president of Mexico from 1934 to 1940. He moved to fulfill some of the original goals of the revolution. His major step was to distribute 44 million acres (17.8 million ha) of land to landless Mexican peasants. This action made him enormously popular with the peasants.

President Cárdenas also took a strong stand with the United States over oil. By 1900, Mexico was known to have enormous oil reserves, especially in the Gulf of Mexico. Over the next 30 years, oil companies from Britain and, in particular, the United States made large investments in the Mexican oil industry. After a dispute with the foreign-owned oil companies over workers' wages, the Cárdenas government seized control of the oil fields and the property of the foreign-owned oil companies.

The U.S. oil companies were furious and asked President Franklin D. Roosevelt to intervene. He refused, reminding them of his promise in the Good Neighbor policy not to send U.S. troops into Latin America. Mexicans cheered Cárdenas as the president who stood up to the United States.

Eventually, the Mexican government did pay the oil companies for their property. It then set up PEMEX, a national oil company, to run the oil industry. PEMEX did not do well at first, however, because exports fell. Still, for many, PEMEX was a symbol of Mexican independence.

✓ **READING PROGRESS CHECK**

Specifying How was the Mexican government democratic in form but not in practice?

Culture in Latin America

GUIDING QUESTION ***How was Latin American culture influenced by European art?***

During the early twentieth century, European artistic and literary movements began to penetrate Latin America. In major cities, such as Buenos Aires, Argentina, and São Paulo, Brazil, wealthy elites expressed interest in the work of modern artists.

Latin American artists went abroad to Europe and brought back modern techniques, which they often adapted to their native roots. Many artists and writers used their work to promote the emergence of a new national spirit. An example was the Mexican artist Diego Rivera. Rivera had studied in Europe, where he was especially influenced by fresco painting in Italy. After his return to Mexico, he developed a monumental style that filled wall after wall with murals. Rivera's wall paintings can be found in such diverse places as the Ministry of Education and the Social Security Hospital. His works were aimed at the masses of people, many of whom could not read.

Rivera sought to create a national art that would portray Mexico's past, especially its Aztec legends, as well as Mexican festivals and folk customs. His work also carried a political and social message. Rivera did not want people to forget the Mexican Revolution, which had overthrown the large landowners and the foreign interests that supported them.

✓ **READING PROGRESS CHECK**

Explaining To which subjects did Diego Rivera turn to create a national art of Mexico?

◄ This detail from Diego Rivera's *The Conquest or Arrival of Hernán Cortés in Veracruz* is part of a series of frescoes on pre-Hispanic and colonial Mexico painted on the inner courtyard walls of the National Palace in Mexico City.

► **CRITICAL THINKING**

Identifying How does Rivera portray Cortés and his men?

LESSON 4 REVIEW TEKS

Reviewing Vocabulary

1. ***Explaining*** Write a paragraph in which you explain the role of U.S. investors in Latin American economies and the role of the oligarchy in Argentina and Brazil.

Using Your Notes

2. ***Summarizing*** Use your notes to write a paragraph identifying five countries or regions in Latin America and their primary exports as well as what those exports have in common.

Answering the Guiding Questions

3. ***Identifying Central Issues*** What factors influenced the Latin American economy during the 1920s and 1930s?
4. ***Evaluating*** Who controlled politics in Latin America?
5. ***Making Connections*** How was Latin American culture influenced by European art?

Writing Activity

6. **INFORMATIVE/EXPLANATORY** How did U.S. and British companies influence the development of nationalism in Latin American countries?

Assessment

Directions: On a separate sheet of paper, answer the questions below. Make sure you read carefully and answer all parts of the questions.

Lesson Review

Lesson 1

1. ***Summarizing*** What factors led to the decline of the Ottoman Empire after World War I? 1F

2. ***Describing*** In what ways did President Kemal reform Turkish society at the end of the Ottoman Empire ?

3. ***Explaining*** In what way did the Ottoman government's killing of Armenians in 1915 constitute genocide? 22C

4. ***Explaining*** How and why was Great Britain involved with Palestine in the late 1930s?

Lesson 2

5. ***Naming*** Which African states did France occupy and which did Italy occupy?

6. ***Analyzing*** Why did communism spread to some Asian countries after World War I? 1F

7. ***Specifying*** What are examples of acts of noncooperation and civil disobedience that Gandhi encouraged?

8. ***Explaining*** What role did Hideki Tōjō play in the rise of Japanese militarism prior to World War II? 12B

Lesson 3

9. ***Identifying Central Issues*** Why did the Nationalist Party and the Communist Party in China form an alliance, and what events occurred as a result?

10. ***Evaluating*** What role did Mao Zedong play in the rise of communism in China? 13B

11. ***Explaining*** What tactics did General Chiang Kai-shek use to reduce the presence of Communists in China between 1927 and 1934?

12. ***Identifying Cause and Effect*** After one year, what was the outcome of the Long March?

13. ***Describing*** Describe the class divide in the 1930s under Chiang Kai-shek's rule.

Lesson 4

14. ***Identifying*** What characteristics did oligarchies in Argentina and Brazil display? 19B

15. ***Making Connections*** What effect did the economic crises of the 1930s have on many Latin American countries?

16. ***Identifying Cause and Effect*** Why did many Latin Americans resent the United States' presence and control of industry?

17. ***Sequencing*** Describe the course of events that led to Getúlio Vargas as the Brazilian president, and what type of government did he run?

18. ***Summarizing*** How did President Franklin D. Roosevelt attempt to improve U.S.-Latin American relations?

Exploring the Essential Questions

19. ***Analyzing*** Work with a partner to create a cause-and-effect chart on poster board that lists one nationalist movement from each lesson and some specific political causes of the movement. Include visuals such as maps, sketches, and photos or art. 1F

Need Extra Help?

If You've Missed Question	1	2	3	4	5	6	7	8	9	10	11	12	13	14	15	16	17	18	19
Go to page	684	686	685	688	690	691	692	694	695	697	696	697	699	703	702	702	703	702	684

20 ***Describing*** Assume the role of a native resident in one of the following locations in 1921: Persia, Kenya, China, or Mexico. Describe how economic oppression led this person to support a nationalist movement. **1F**

Critical Thinking

21 ***Speculating*** Write a paragraph in which you identify the results of the Arab independence movement and speculate about what might have happened differently had Arabs been able to unite as one nation after World War I. **1F**

22 ***Constructing Arguments*** Write an argument in which you defend or denounce Chiang Kai-shek's policies and their effectiveness in China.

23 ***Assessing*** Write a paragraph that explains the impact Gandhi and his policy of civil disobedience as a means of resisting political oppression had on India and the world at large. **22E**

24 ***Theorizing*** Compare the efforts of independence movements from this era to modern independence movements. How might today's technology impact independent movements in comparison to older movements?

25 ***Comparing and Contrasting*** Compare and contrast two or more the governments and their leaders of two or more Latin American countries during the 1930s and early 1940s. Analyze any connections between the countries and outside powers, such as the United States or Europe.

Social Studies Skills

26 ***Understanding Relationships Among Events*** In what ways did World War I and European actions in its aftermath lead to the rise of nationalist movements in Africa? **1F**

27 ***Identifying Cause and Effect*** What impact did World War I have on political systems in the Middle East and Southeast Asia? **1F**

28 ***Comparing and Contrasting*** In what ways were Mohandras Gandhi's and Jawaharlal Nehru's goals similar but approaches different, and how did their differences affect the Indian independence movement? **1F**

29 ***Economics*** Describe the economic structure of the Japanese *zaibatsu*.

30 ***Research Skills*** Research one of the leaders of the African independence movement and explain his contributions, including any significant writing. Consider individuals such as Jomo Kenyatta and Léopold Senghor.

Need Extra Help?

If You've Missed Question	20	21	22	23	24	25	26	27	28	29	30
Go to page	686	687	696	692	684	703	689	691	692	693	689

PHOTO: Bettmann/CORBIS

DBQ Document-Based Questions

Use the document to answer the following questions.

In this cartoon the man (left), John Bull (middle), and the woman represent the Ottoman Turks, England, and Armenians respectively.

JOHN BULL HATED TO DROP HIS BUNDLE.
That's why the Turk always laughed at the idea of Christian retribution

31 ***Identifying Purpose*** What message is the cartoonist trying to convey?

32 ***Making Inferences*** How is Armenia conveyed in the cartoon? Do you think the cartoonist supports the Armenians?

Analyzing Visuals

Use the image to answer the following questions.

This image shows a detail from Diego Rivera's *The Conquest or Arrival of Hernán Cortéz in Veracruz,* part of a series of frescoes painted on the walls of the National Palace in Mexico City.

33 ***Describing*** How does Rivera portray Cortéz and his men?

34 ***Analyzing Visuals*** In what way is this painting a typical Diego Rivera work in terms of its subject matter and themes?

Extended Response Question

35 ***Expository*** Write an essay that compares and contrasts the ways in which two nationalist movements arose and developed in the years following World War I. What caused each movement to take hold? What events took place as a result? The essay should include an introduction, at least three paragraphs and a conclusion that supports your main idea. Use information gathered from primary and secondary sources to support your answer. **1F**

Need Extra Help?

If You've Missed Question	31	32	33	34	35
Go to page	707	707	708	704	681

World War II and the Holocaust

1939–1945

ESSENTIAL QUESTIONS • *Why do political actions often lead to war?* • *How does war impact society and the environment?*

networks

There's More Online! about World War II and the Holocaust.

CHAPTER 30

The Story Matters...

From 1933 to 1945, the Nazis fought two wars: one against the Allies and another for "racial purity." At first, the Nazis sent European Jews to concentration camps. Later, they developed horribly efficient killing centers such as Auschwitz and Treblinka. By the time Allied forces liberated the death camps in 1945, the Nazis had murdered nearly two out of every three European Jews during the Holocaust.

◀ These prisoners at Auschwitz were liberated by the Soviets in January 1945. Victims of the Holocaust suffered cruelty at the hands of their Nazi captors. Those who survived were ill or dying of starvation and maltreatment.

CHAPTER 30

Place and Time: Europe 1939–1945

World War II was the most devastating war in history. Germany and Japan achieved stunning territorial victories between 1939 and 1942. In 1941 the United States and the Soviet Union entered the war, turning the tide against fascist expansion. New military technology, such as aerial photography, informed the military strategies of both the Axis and Allied powers and changed the way the war was fought.

Step Into the Place

Read the quotes and look at the information presented on the map.

DBQ **Analyzing Historical Documents** How did the Allies use aerial photographs for strategic purposes during the war in Europe?

PRIMARY SOURCE

"Aerial photos were the only solid, irrefutable evidence of where an enemy was, what he was doing and what he had with which to do it. Intelligence was a 'force multiplier,' permitting our side to put resources or air strikes on the most critical ground, and aerial photographic intelligence was the most reliable source."

—Colonel Roy M. Stanley, United States Air Force, *Asia from Above*

PRIMARY SOURCE

"These [36-inch cameras mounted on the belly of the aircraft] produced 3-D views of the areas being photographed, which were then examined by our intelligence people. Details as small as a golf ball were detectable. We also carried a smaller camera in the port side of the aircraft, and with this we could take oblique pictures. Some of the trips involved low-level photographs, and this required flying at tree-top level. On 15 May [1943] we were jumped by six Bf 109s [German fighter planes] while flying photo runs over Oslo. . . We were able to do ever decreasing turns and avoid their gunfire. We were also able to inch our way over to Sweden. The Swedes will never know how grateful we were to them as they opened up with every flak [anti-aircraft] battery on their coast."

—Flight Lieutenant Bill White, Royal Air Force, recalling a reconnaissance mission to find a German battleship harbored in Norway, quoted in *Mosquito Photo-Reconnaissance Units of World War 2*

Step Into the Time

Determining Importance

Choose an event from the time line and explain why it was an important development in the Second World War.

EUROPEAN AND NORTH AFRICAN THEATER

- **September 1, 1939** German invasion of Poland
- **September 3, 1939** Britain and France declare war on Germany
- **June 1940** France falls to Germany
- **1941** Germany invades the Soviet Union

PACIFIC THEATER

- **1939** Japan shocked by signing of Nazi-Soviet Nonaggression Pact
- **1940** Japan demands rights to resources in French Indochina
- **1941** Japan acquires Chinese territory in Second Sino-Japanese War

networks
There's More Online!

- ☑ **MAP** Explore the interactive version of this map on Networks.
- ☑ **TIME LINE** Explore the interactive version of the time line on Networks.

World War II in Europe and North Africa 1941–1945

1942–1943 Allies and Germany battle for control over North Africa

June 6, 1944 Allies under U.S. General Dwight D. Eisenhower launch D-Day invasion

March 1945 Allies cross the Rhine after the Battle of the Bulge

May 7, 1945 Germany surrenders

1942 **1943** **1944** **1945**

December 7, 1941 Japanese attack Pearl Harbor

1942 Japanese conquer Thailand, Philippines, Malaya

1942 United States Navy defeats Japanese at Battle of Midway Island

May 1943 Japanese launch offensive in central China

December 8, 1944 U.S. Air Force begins bombardment of Iwo Jima

August 1945 United States drops atomic bombs on Japan

August 14, 1945 Japan surrenders

networks

There's More Online!

- BIOGRAPHY Winston Churchill
- IMAGE Bombing of Shanghai
- IMAGE The Munich Conference
- IMAGE The Nazi-Soviet Nonaggression Pact
- INTERACTIVE SELF-CHECK QUIZ
- MAP German and Italian Expansion, 1935–1939
- MAP Japanese Expansion, 1933–1941
- PRIMARY SOURCE Germany's Invasion of the Rhineland
- VIDEO Soviet Invasion of Poland

LESSON 1

World War II Begins

ESSENTIAL QUESTIONS • *Why do political actions often lead to war?* • *How does war impact society and the environment?*

Reading HELPDESK

Academic Vocabulary

- **dominate** • **violation**

Content Vocabulary

- **demilitarized**
- **appeasement**
- **sanctions**

TAKING NOTES:

Key Ideas and Details

Categorizing As you read, create a chart like the one below listing examples of Japanese and German aggression prior to the outbreak of World War II.

Japanese Aggression	German Aggression

TEKS Texas Essential Knowledge and Skills

1F identify major causes and describe the major effects of the following important turning points in world history from 1914 to the present: the world wars and their impact on political, economic, and social systems; communist revolutions and their impact on the Cold War; independence movements; and globalization

continued on the next page

It Matters Because

In the 1930s, Germany and Japan invaded neighboring countries to gain resources and land. Hitler allied with Italy, annexed Austria, and occupied the Sudetenland. Japan made a quick conquest of Manchuria. At first, other world powers allowed these acts of aggression. They wanted to avoid war—yet the path to war was already paved.

The German Path to War

GUIDING QUESTIONS *What was Hitler's motivation for German expansion? What alliances and events contributed to the outbreak of World War II?*

World War II in Europe had its beginnings in the ideas of Adolf Hitler. He believed that Germans belonged to a so-called Aryan race that was superior to all other races and nationalities. Consequently, Hitler believed that Germany was capable of building a great civilization. To be a great power, however, he thought that Germany needed more land to support a larger population.

Already in the 1920s, Hitler had indicated that a Nazi regime would find this land to the east—in the Soviet Union. Germany therefore must prepare for war with the Soviet Union. After the Soviet Union had been conquered, according to Hitler, its land would be resettled by German peasants. The Slavic peoples could be used as slave labor to build an Aryan racial state that Hitler thought would **dominate** Europe for a thousand years.

Hitler Violates Treaty

After World War I, the Treaty of Versailles had limited Germany's military power. As chancellor, Hitler, posing as a man of peace, stressed that Germany wished to revise the unfair provisions of the treaty by peaceful means. Germany, he said, only wanted its rightful place among the European states.

On March 9, 1935, however, Hitler announced the creation of a new air force. One week later, he began a military draft that would expand Germany's army from 100,000 to 550,000 troops. These steps were in direct **violation** of the Treaty of Versailles. France, Great Britain, and Italy condemned Germany's actions and warned against future aggressive steps. In the midst of the Great Depression, however, these nations were distracted by their own internal problems and did nothing further.

Hitler was convinced that the Western states had no intention of using force to maintain the Treaty of Versailles. Hence, on March 7, 1936, he sent German troops into the Rhineland. The Rhineland was part of Germany, but, according to the Treaty of Versailles, it was a **demilitarized** area. That is, Germany was not allowed to have weapons or fortifications there. France had the right to use force against any violation of this provision but would not act without British support.

Great Britain did not support the use of force against Germany. The British government viewed the occupation of German territory by German troops as a reasonable action by a dissatisfied power. *The London Times* noted that the Germans were "only going into their own back garden." Great Britain thus began to practice a policy of **appeasement**. This policy was based on the belief that if European states satisfied the reasonable demands of dissatisfied powers, the dissatisfied powers would be content, and stability and peace would be achieved in Europe.

New Alliances

Meanwhile, Hitler gained new allies. Benito Mussolini of Italy had long dreamed of creating a new Roman Empire. In October 1935, Mussolini's forces invaded Ethiopia. Angered by French and British opposition to his invasion, Mussolini welcomed his role as Hitler's ally, drawing closer to the German dictator.

In 1936 both Germany and Italy sent troops to Spain to help General Francisco Franco in the Spanish Civil War. In October 1936, Mussolini and Hitler made an agreement recognizing their common interests. One month later, Mussolini spoke of the new alliance between Italy and Germany, called the Rome-Berlin Axis. Also in November, Germany and Japan signed the Anti-Comintern Pact, promising a common front against communism.

Union With Austria

By 1937, Germany was once more a "world power," as Hitler proclaimed. He was convinced that neither France nor Great Britain would provide much opposition to his plans. In 1938 he decided to pursue one of his goals: *Anschluss* (AHN • shloos), or union, with Austria, his native land.

dominate to influence or control

violation a disregard of rules or agreements

demilitarized elimination or prohibition of weapons, fortifications, and other military installations

appeasement satisfying reasonable demands of dissatisfied powers in an effort to maintain peace and stability

(continued from p. 712)

TEKS Texas Essential Knowledge and Skills
12B explain the roles of various world leaders, including Benito Mussolini, Adolf Hitler, Hideki Tojo, Joseph Stalin, Franklin D. Roosevelt, and Winston Churchill, prior to and during World War II

continued on the next page

GEOGRAPHY CONNECTION

Germany expanded its borders from 1935–1939.

1. **THE WORLD IN SPATIAL TERMS** *Which countries did Germany take land from during this time period?*
2. **HUMAN SYSTEMS** *What was Germany's rationale for expansion?*

(continued from p. 713)

TEKS Texas Essential Knowledge and Skills

12C explain the major causes and events of World War II, including the German invasions of Poland and the Soviet Union, the Holocaust, Japanese imperialism, the attack on Pearl Harbor, the Normandy landings, and the dropping of the atomic bombs

By threatening Austria with invasion, Hitler forced the Austrian chancellor to put Austrian Nazis in charge of the government. The new government promptly invited German troops to enter Austria and "help" in maintaining law and order. One day later, on March 13, 1938, after his triumphal return to his native land, Hitler annexed Austria to Germany.

Demands and Appeasement

Hitler's next objective was the destruction of Czechoslovakia. On September 15, 1938, he demanded that Germany be given the Sudetenland, an area in northwestern Czechoslovakia that was inhabited largely by Germans. He was willing to risk "world war" to achieve his objective.

At a hastily arranged conference in Munich, British, French, German, and Italian representatives did not object to Hitler's plans but instead reached an agreement that met virtually all Hitler's demands. German troops were allowed to occupy the Sudetenland. The Czechs, abandoned by their Western allies, stood by helplessly.

The Munich Conference was the high point of Western appeasement of Hitler. When Neville Chamberlain, the British prime minister, returned to England from Munich, he boasted that the agreement meant "peace for our time." However, British statesman Winston Churchill rejected the agreement, which he saw as appeasement, warning that the settlement at Munich was "a disaster of the first magnitude." Hitler, however, had promised Chamberlain that he would make no more demands. Like many others, Chamberlain believed Hitler's promises.

▲ **After the Munich Conference, Adolf Hitler, Nevile Henderson, Neville Chamberlain, and Joachim von Ribbentrop (left to right) at the Munich airport on September 29, 1938.**

▶ **CRITICAL THINKING**

Evaluating Why is the Munich Conference an oft-used example of the failure of appeasement?

In fact, Hitler was more convinced than ever that the Western democracies would not fight. Increasingly, he was sure that he could not make a mistake, and he had by no means been satisfied at Munich.

In March 1939, Hitler invaded and took control of Bohemia and Moravia in western Czechoslovakia. In the eastern part of the country, Slovakia became a puppet state controlled by Nazi Germany. On the evening of March 15, 1939, Hitler triumphantly declared in Prague that he would be known as the greatest German of them all.

At last, the Western states reacted to the Nazi threat. Hitler's aggression had made clear that his promises were worthless. When Hitler began to demand the Polish port of Danzig, Great Britain saw the danger and offered to protect Poland in the event of war. At the same time, both France and Britain realized that only the Soviet Union was powerful enough to help contain Nazi aggression. They began political and military negotiations with Joseph Stalin, the Soviet dictator.

Hitler and the Soviets

Meanwhile, Hitler continued to believe that the West would not fight over Poland. He now feared, however, that the West and the Soviet Union might make an alliance. Such an alliance could mean a two-front war for Germany. To prevent this, Hitler made his own agreement with Stalin.

On August 23, 1939, Germany and the Soviet Union signed the Nazi-Soviet Nonaggression Pact, in which they promised not to attack each other. Stalin accepted the offer of control over eastern Poland and the Baltic states in exchange for signing the nonaggression pact. Because he expected to fight the Soviet Union anyway, it did not matter to Hitler what he promised—he was accustomed to breaking promises.

▲ **This political cartoon depicts Adolf Hitler and Joseph Stalin as a newlywed couple after the signing of the Nazi-Soviet Nonaggression Pact.**

Hitler shocked the world when he announced the treaty. Hitler was now free to attack Poland. He told his generals, "Now Poland is in the position in which I wanted her . . . . I am only afraid that at the last moment some swine will yet submit to me a plan for mediation."

Hitler need not have worried. On September 1, German forces invaded western Poland. Two days later, Britain and France declared war on Germany. World War II had begun in Europe.

✓ **READING PROGRESS CHECK**

Determining Cause and Effect How did World War I affect European leaders' attitudes toward international aggression?

The Japanese Path to War

GUIDING QUESTION ***Why did Japan want to seize other countries?***

On the night of September 18, 1931, Japanese soldiers, disguised as Chinese soldiers, blew up a small section of the Manchurian Railway near the city of Mukden. Japan owned this area, and the Japanese soldiers wanted to blame the"Mukden incident" on the Chinese. The Japanese army used this incident to justify its taking all of Manchuria in a series of rapid military advances.

After conquest of Manchuria, the Japanese army became committed to an expansionist policy—meant to enlarge the Japanese Empire through further conquest. This imperialist policy would eventually lead Japan into World War II.

By September 1932, the Japanese army had formed Manchuria into a separate state and renamed it Manchukuo. They placed a puppet ruler, Henry Pu Yi, on the throne. As an infant, Henry Pu Yi had been China's "last emperor." He had abdicated that throne, however, following the revolution of 1911 in China.

Worldwide protests against the Japanese seizure of Manchuria led the League of Nations to send in investigators. When the investigators issued a report condemning the seizure, Japan withdrew from the League. The United States refused to recognize the Japanese takeover of Manchuria but was unwilling to threaten force.

Over the next several years, Japan continued its expansion and established control over the eastern part of Inner Mongolia and areas in north China around Beijing. Neither Emperor Hirohito nor government leaders could control the army. In fact, it was the army that established Japanese foreign policy. The military held the upper hand. By the mid-1930s, militants connected to the government and the armed forces had gained control of Japanese politics.

▲ **During the Sino-Japanese War, the Japanese air force bombed Shanghai.**

▶ **CRITICAL THINKING**

Making Inferences What role did the Sino-Japanese War play in the Chinese civil war?

War With China

Chiang Kai-shek tried to avoid a conflict with Japan so that he could deal with what he considered the greater threat, the Chinese Communists. When clashes between Chinese and Japanese troops broke out, he sought to appease Japan by allowing it to govern areas in north China.

As Japan moved steadily southward, protests against Japanese aggression grew stronger in Chinese cities. In December 1936, Chiang ended his military efforts against the Communists and formed a new united front against the Japanese. In July 1937, Chinese and Japanese forces clashed south of Beijing and hostilities spread.

Although Japan had not planned to declare war on China, the 1937 incident turned into a major conflict, led by newly appointed Chief-of-Staff Hideki Tōjō. Japan seized the Chinese capital of Nanjing in December. The Japanese Army destroyed the city and massacred more than 100,000 civilians and prisoners of war. The event was so brutal it became known as the "Rape of Nanjing." Chiang Kai-shek refused to surrender and moved his government upriver, first to Hankou, then to Chongqing.

The New Asian Order

Japanese military leaders had hoped to force Chiang to agree to join a New Order in east Asia, comprising Japan, Manchuria, and China. Japan would attempt to establish a new system of control in Asia with Japan guiding its Asian neighbors to prosperity.

Part of Japan's plan was to seize Soviet Siberia, with its rich resources. During the late 1930s, Japan began to cooperate with Nazi Germany. Japan assumed that the two countries would ultimately launch a joint attack on theSoviet Union and divide Soviet resources between them.

When Germany signed the nonaggression pact with the Soviets in August 1939, Japanese leaders had to rethink their goals. Because Japan lacked the resources to defeat the Soviet Union, it looked to south Asia for raw materials for its military machine.

Japan Launches Attack

sanctions restrictions intended to enforce international law

A move southward would risk war with the European powers and the United States. Japan's attack on China had already aroused strong criticism, especially in the United States. Still, in the summer of 1940, Japan demanded the right to exploit economic resources in French Indochina.

The United States objected. It warned Japan that it would apply economic **sanctions** unless Japan withdrew from the area and returned to its borders of 1931. Japan badly needed the oil and scrap iron it was getting from the United States. Should these resources be cut off, Japan would have to find them elsewhere. This would threaten Japan's long-term objectives.

Japan was now caught in a dilemma. To guarantee access to raw materials in Southeast Asia, Japan had to risk losing them from the United States. After much debate, Japan decided to launch a surprise attack on U.S. and European colonies in Southeast Asia.

SKILLS PRACTICE

As you read about the German and Japanese paths to war, make a list of the academic and content vocabulary words and their meanings as you encounter them in the text. Once you have finished reading the lesson, work with a partner and take turns summarizing the lesson using the words on your list.

✓ **READING PROGRESS CHECK**

Summarizing What regions did Japan consider in its search for natural resources?

LESSON 1 REVIEW TEKS

Reviewing Vocabulary

1. ***Explaining*** What is the connection between national sovereignty and demilitarization?

Using Your Notes

2. ***Comparing*** Use your graphic organizer to compare how German and Japanese aggression affected the United States.

Answering the Guiding Questions

3. ***Summarizing*** What was Hitler's motivation for German expansion?

4. ***Distinguishing*** What alliances and events contributed to the outbreak of World War II?

5. ***Analyzing*** Why did Japan want to seize other countries?

Writing Activity

6. **ARGUMENT** Write a paragraph that argues for or against the following statement: The British policy of appeasement was the main cause for Germany's aggressive actions.

networks

There's More Online!

- BIOGRAPHY Franklin D. Roosevelt
- BIOGRAPHY Hideki Tōjō
- CHART/GRAPH The Axis and the Allies, 1939–1945
- IMAGE Battle of Midway Island
- INFOGRAPHIC Pearl Harbor
- INTERACTIVE SELF-CHECK QUIZ
- MAP WWII in Asia and the Pacific, 1941–1942
- MAP WWII in Europe and North Africa, 1939–1942
- VIDEO Hitler vs. Stalin

LESSON 2
World War II

ESSENTIAL QUESTIONS • *Why do political actions often lead to war?* • *How does war impact society and the environment?*

Reading **HELP**DESK

Academic Vocabulary

- **resolve**
- **involvement**

Content Vocabulary

- **blitzkrieg**
- **isolationism**
- **neutrality**

TAKING NOTES:

Key Ideas and Details

Determining Cause and Effect As you read, use a chart like the one below to list key events during World War II and their effect on the course of the war.

Event	Effect

TEKS Texas Essential Knowledge and Skills

12B explain the roles of various world leaders, including Benito Mussolini, Adolf Hitler, Hideki Tojo, Joseph Stalin, Franklin D. Roosevelt, and Winston Churchill, prior to and during World War II

12C explain the major causes and events of World War II, including the German invasions of Poland and the Soviet Union, the Holocaust, Japanese imperialism, the attack on Pearl Harbor, the Normandy landings, and the dropping of the atomic bombs

continued on p. 719

It Matters Because

In the first years of World War II, Hitler, with his blitzkrieg, had gained control of much of western and central Europe. Victories over Britain and Russia remained elusive, however. When the United States entered the war, the Allies agreed to fight until the Axis Powers surrendered unconditionally.

Europe at War

GUIDING QUESTION *What were Germany's gains and losses during the early years of the war?*

Hitler stunned Europe with the speed and efficiency of the German attack on Poland. His **blitzkrieg**, or "lightning war," used fast armored columns, called panzer divisions, made possible by technological developments of military weapons like tanks and airplanes. Each panzer division was a strike force of about 300 tanks with accompanying forces and supplies.

The forces of the blitzkrieg broke quickly through Polish lines and encircled the bewildered Polish troops. Regular infantry units then moved in to hold the newly conquered territory. Within four weeks, Poland had surrendered. On September 28, 1939, Germany and the Soviet Union divided Poland.

Hitler's Early Victories

After a winter of waiting, Hitler resumed the attack on April 9, 1940, with another blitzkrieg against Denmark and Norway. One month later, Germany launched an attack on the Netherlands, Belgium, and France. The main assault was through Luxembourg and the Ardennes Forest. German panzer divisions broke through weak French defensive positions there and raced across northern France.

French and British forces were taken by surprise. Anticipating a German attack, France had built a defense system, called the Maginot (MA • zhuh • NOH) Line, along its border with Germany. The line was a series of concrete and steel fortifications armed with heavy artillery. The Germans, however, decided not to cross the Maginot Line. Instead, they went around it and attacked France from its border with Belgium.

BIOGRAPHY

Franklin D. Roosevelt (1882–1945)

President Franklin D. Roosevelt was the only U.S. president elected to serve four terms in office. He led the United States during two major crises—the Great Depression and World War II. Before Pearl Harbor, President Roosevelt convinced the U.S. Congress to send "all aid short of war" to Britain and the Soviet Union to help fight the Nazis. The United States sent ships and guns in exchange for military bases in Britain. After the attack on Pearl Harbor, the United States entered the war in earnest. Roosevelt led the war effort until his death in office in 1945.

▶ **CRITICAL THINKING**
Making Inferences How did the Great Depression prepare Roosevelt for the war effort?

By going around the Maginot Line, the Germans split the Allied armies, trapping French troops and the entire British army on the beaches of Dunkirk. Only by the heroic efforts of the Royal Navy and civilians in private boats did the British manage to evacuate 338,000 Allied (mostly British) troops. An English skipper described the scene:

PRIMARY SOURCE

"The soldiers were coming off the beach clinging to bits of wood and wreckage and anything that would float. As we got close enough we began . . . picking up as many as we could . . . [and taking] them off to one of the ships lying off in the deep water."

—quoted in *Blood, Tears and Folly,* 1993

The French signed an armistice on June 22, 1940. German armies now occupied about three-fifths of France. An authoritarian regime under German control was set up over the remainder of the country. It was known as Vichy France and was led by an aged French hero of World War I, Marshal Henri Pétain. Germany was now in control of western and central Europe, but Britain had still not been defeated. In fact, after Dunkirk, the British **resolve** heightened. Especially helpful in rallying the British people were the stirring speeches of Winston Churchill, who had become prime minister in May 1940.

President Franklin D. Roosevelt denounced the aggressors, but the United States followed a strict policy of **isolationism**. A series of **neutrality** acts, passed in the 1930s, prevented the United States from taking sides or becoming involved in any European wars. Many Americans felt that the United States had been drawn into World War I due to economic **involvement** in Europe, and they wanted to prevent a recurrence. Roosevelt was convinced that the neutrality acts actually encouraged Axis aggression and were gradually relaxed as the United States supplied food, ships, planes, and weapons to Britain.

The Battle of Britain

Hitler realized that an amphibious (land-sea) invasion of Britain could succeed only if Germany gained control of the air. At the beginning of August 1940, the Luftwaffe (LOOFT • vah • fuh)—the German air force—launched a major offensive. German planes bombed British air and naval bases, harbors, communication centers, and war industries.

The British fought back with determination with Winston Churchill, now Prime Minister, boosting morale at home. British air defenses were supported byan effective new technology called the radar system that gave them early warning of German attacks. Nevertheless, the British air force suffered critical losses.

In September, in retaliation for a British attack on Berlin, Hitler ordered a shift in strategy. Instead of bombing military targets, the Luftwaffe began massive bombing of British cities. Hitler hoped in this way to break British morale. Instead, because military targets were not being hit, the British were able to rebuild their air strength quickly. Soon, the British air force was inflicting major losses on Luftwaffe bombers. Hitler postponed the invasion of Britain indefinitely.

Attack on the Soviet Union

Although he had no desire for a two-front war, Hitler became convinced that Britain was remaining in the war only because it expected Soviet support. If the Soviet Union were smashed, Britain's last hope would be eliminated. Moreover, Hitler had convinced himself that the Soviet Union had a pitiful army and could be defeated quickly.

blitzkrieg German for "lightning war"; a swift and sudden military attack; used by the Germans during World War II

resolve determination; a fixed purpose

isolationism a policy of national isolation by abstention from alliances and other international political and economic relations

neutrality refusal to take sides or become involved in wars between other nations

GEOGRAPHY CONNECTION

By 1941, Germany had conquered most of continental Europe.

1 PLACES AND REGIONS *What offensive did the Axis powers carry out in Africa?*

2 THE USES OF GEOGRAPHY *Why was it significant that Germany failed to control Moscow by 1941?*

Hitler's invasion of the Soviet Union was scheduled for the spring of 1941, but the attack was delayed because of problems in the Balkans. Hitler had already gained the political cooperation of Hungary, Bulgaria, and Romania. However, the failure of Mussolini's invasion of Greece, part of his design for reviving the Roman Empire, in 1940 had exposed Hitler's southern flank to British air bases in Greece. Mussolini's plan also distracted from the overall Axis war effort. To secure his Balkan flank, Hitler seized both Greece and Yugoslavia in April.

Reassured, Hitler invaded the Soviet Union on June 22, 1941. He believed that the Russians could still be decisively defeated before the brutal winter weather set in. The massive attack stretched out along a front some 1,800 miles (about 2,900 km) long. German troops advanced rapidly. By November, one German army group had swept through the Ukraine. A second army was besieging the city of Leningrad, while a third approached within 25 miles of Moscow, the Soviet capital.

An early winter and fierce Soviet resistance, however, halted the German advance. Certain of quick victory, the Germans had not planned for winter uniforms. For the first time in the war, German armies had been stopped. A counterattack in December 1941 by a Soviet army came as an ominous ending to the year for the Germans.

✓ READING PROGRESS CHECK

Predicting Consequences What assumptions did Hitler make about invading the Soviet Union? Do you think the invasion would have gone differently if he had not made those assumptions?

(continued from p. 717)

TEKS Texas Essential Knowledge and Skills
28C explain the effects of major new military technologies on World War I, World War II, and the Cold War

Japan at War

GUIDING QUESTION ***What brought the United States into the war?***

On December 7, 1941, Japanese aircraft attacked the U.S. naval base at Pearl Harbor in Hawaii. The surprise attack damaged or destroyed more than 350 aircraft, damaged or sunk 18 ships, and killed or wounded more than 3,500 Americans. The same day, the Japanese attacked the Philippines and advanced on Malaya. Later, they invaded the Dutch East Indies and occupied several islands in the Pacific Ocean. By the spring of 1942, almost all of Southeast Asia and much of the western Pacific had fallen to the Japanese.

A triumphant Japan now declared the creation of a "community" of nations: the Greater East Asia Co-Prosperity Sphere. The entire region would now be under Japanese direction. Japan also announced its intention to liberate areas of Southeast Asia from Western colonial rule. For the moment, however, Japan needed the resources of the region for its war machine and treated the countries under its rule as conquered lands.

Japanese policy was now largely dictated by Prime Minister Hideki Tōjō—formerly a general—who in the course of the war became a virtual military dictator. Tōjō had hoped that Japan's lightning strike at American bases would destroy the U.S. fleet in the Pacific. The Roosevelt administration, he thought, would now accept Japanese domination of the Pacific.

But Tōjō miscalculated. The attack on Pearl Harbor unified American opinion about becoming involved in the war. The United States, under the leadership of Roosevelt, joined with European nations and Nationalist China in a combined effort to defeat Japan. Believing American **involvement** in the Pacific would make the United States ineffective in the European theater of war, Hitler declared war on the United States four days after Pearl Harbor. As in World War I, another European conflict had turned into a global war.

involvement a commitment or a connection to

✓ **READING PROGRESS CHECK**

Identifying Why did the United States stay out of World War II until the Pearl Harbor attack?

The Allies Advance

GUIDING QUESTION ***How did the involvement of the United States change the war?***

The entry of the United States into the war created a new coalition, the Grand Alliance. To overcome mutual suspicions, the three major Allies—Great Britain, the United States, and the Soviet Union—agreed to stress military operations and to ignore political differences. At the beginning of 1943, the Allies agreed to fight until the Axis Powers—Germany, Italy, and Japan—surrendered unconditionally, which required the Axis nations to surrender without any favorable condition. This cemented the Grand Alliance by making it nearly impossible for Hitler to divide his foes.

The European Theater

Defeat was far from Hitler's mind at the beginning of 1942. As Japanese forces advanced into Southeast Asia and the Pacific, Hitler and his allies continued fighting the war in Europe against Britain and the Soviet Union.

Until late 1942, it seemed that the Germans might still prevail. In North Africa, German forces broke through the British defenses in Egypt and advanced toward Alexandria. A renewed German offensive in the Soviet Union led to the capture of the entire Crimea in the spring of 1942. However, by the fall of 1942, the war had turned against the Germans.

Analyzing PRIMARY SOURCES

Hitler in August 1942

"As the next step, we are going to advance south of the Caucasus and then help the rebels in Iran and Iraq against the English. Another thrust will be directed along the Caspian Sea toward Afghanistan and India. Then the English will run out of oil. In two years we'll be on the borders of India. Twenty to thirty elite German divisions will do. Then the British Empire will collapse."

—quoted in *Spandau*, 1976

DBQ ***ANALYZING*** Why was Hitler so optimistic after he captured the Crimea?

The Tide Turns

In North Africa, British forces had stopped General Erwin Rommel's troops at El Alamein in the summer of 1942. The Germans then retreated back across the desert. In November 1942, British and American forces invaded French North Africa. They forced the German and Italian troops there to surrender in May 1943.

On the Eastern Front, after the capture of the Crimea, Hitler's generals wanted him to concentrate on the Caucasus and its oil fields. Hitler, however, decided that Stalingrad, a major industrial center on the Volga River, should be taken first. In perhaps the most terrible battle of the war, between November 1942 and February 2, 1943, the Soviets launched a counterattack. German troops were stopped and then encircled, and supply lines were cut off, all in frigid winter conditions. The Germans were forced to surrender at Stalingrad. The entire German Sixth Army, considered the best of the German troops, was lost.

By February 1943, German forces in Russia were back to their positions of June 1942. By the spring, even Hitler knew that the Germans would not defeat the Soviet Union.

▲ A group of U.S. fighter planes fly over the reefs at Midway Island, November 14, 1942.

▶ **CRITICAL THINKING**

Assessing What Allied strategies helped change the tide of battle in the East?

The Asian Theater

In 1942 the tide of battle in the East also changed dramatically. In the Battle of the Coral Sea on May 7 and 8, 1942, American naval forces stopped the Japanese advance and saved Australia from being invaded.

The turning point of the war in Asia came on June 4, at the Battle of Midway Island. U.S. planes destroyed four attacking Japanese aircraft carriers. The United States defeated the Japanese navy and established naval superiority in the Pacific.

By the fall of 1942, Allied forces in Asia were gathering for two operations. One, commanded by U.S. general Douglas MacArthur, would move into the Philippines through New Guinea and the South Pacific Islands. The other would move across the Pacific with a combination of U.S. Army, Marine, and Navy attacks on Japanese-held islands. The policy, called "island hopping," was to capture some Japanese-held islands and to bypass others to reach Japan. After engagements near the Solomon Islands from August to November 1942, Japanese fortunes began to fade.

✓ **READING PROGRESS CHECK**

Summarizing Why was the German assault on Stalingrad a crushing defeat for the Germans?

LESSON 2 REVIEW TEKS

Reviewing Vocabulary

1. ***Explaining*** What is a blitzkrieg, and what supplies and equipment did it require?

Using Your Notes

2. ***Determining Cause and Effect*** Use your notes to explain the effects of key events in World War II.

Answering the Guiding Questions

3. ***Analyzing Information*** What were Germany's gains and losses during the early years of the war?
4. ***Determining Cause and Effect*** What brought the United States into the war?
5. ***Making Generalizations*** How did the involvement of the United States change the war?

Writing Activity

6. **NARRATIVE** Research one of the battles described in this lesson. Then write a descriptive account of the battle from the perspective of a soldier fighting in that battle.

networks

There's More Online!

- IMAGE American Propaganda Poster
- IMAGE B-29 Superfortresses
- IMAGE Coventry Cathedral After a German Bombing Raid
- IMAGE Soviet Propaganda Poster
- IMAGE Woman at Work in a Munitions Factory
- INTERACTIVE SELF-CHECK QUIZ
- VIDEO U-Boats

LESSON 3

The Home Front and Civilians

ESSENTIAL QUESTION

- *How does war impact society and the environment?*

It Matters Because

During World War II, nations mobilized their people and geared their economies to war. While the troops fought, the citizens on the home front made personal sacrifices to produce the materials and supplies needed to fuel the war. Hundreds of thousands lost their lives in bombing raids.

Reading **HELP**DESK

Academic Vocabulary

- **widespread**
- **circumstance**

Content Vocabulary

- **mobilization**
- **kamikaze**
- **blitz**

TAKING NOTES:

Key Ideas and Details

Organizing As you read, complete a chart like this one to show the impact of World War II on the lives of civilians.

Country	Impact on Civilian Lives
Soviet Union	
United States	
Japan	
Germany	

The Mobilization of Four Nations

GUIDING QUESTION *How did countries mobilize for war?*

Even more than World War I, World War II was a total war. Fighting was much more **widespread** and covered most of the world. The war also had a heavy economic impact, as resources, industries, and even women were **mobilized** for the war effort. The number of civilians killed—almost 20 million—was far higher than those killed in World War I. Many of these victims were children.

World War II had an enormous impact on civilian life in the Soviet Union, the United States, Germany, and Japan. We consider thehome fronts of those four nations next.

The Soviet Union

Known to the Soviets as the Great Patriotic War, the German-Soviet war witnessed the greatest land battles in history, as well as incredible ruthlessness. The initial military defeats suffered by the Soviet Union led to drastic emergency measures that affected the lives of the civilian population. The city of Leningrad (now St. Petersburg), for example, experienced 900 days of siege. Its inhabitants became so desperate for food that they even ate dogs, cats, and mice. Probably 1.5 million people died in the city.

As the German army made its rapid advance into Soviet territory, Soviet workers dismantled and shipped the factories in the western part of the Soviet Union to the interior—to the Urals, western Siberia, and the Volga regions. Machines were placed on the bare ground. As laborers began their work, walls went up around them.

PHOTO: (l to r)Stringer/Hulton Archive/Getty Images, ©akg-images / The Image Works, Corbis, Laski Diffusion/Getty Images News/Getty Images, Library of Congress.

Stalin called the widespread military and industrial mobilization of the nation a "battle of machines." The Soviets won, producing 78,000 tanks and 98,000 artillery pieces. In 1943, 55 percent of the Soviet national income went for war materials, compared with 15 percent in 1940. As a result of the emphasis on military goods, Soviet citizens experienced severe shortages of both food and housing.

Soviet women played a major role in the war effort. Women and girls worked in industries, mines, and railroads. Overall, the number of women working in industry increased almost 60 percent. Soviet women were also expected to dig antitank ditches and to work as air-raid wardens. Also, the Soviet Union was the only country in World War II to use women in battle. Soviet women served as snipers and in aircrews of bomber squadrons.

widespread widely extended or spread out

mobilization the process of assembling troops and supplies and making them ready for war

TEKS Texas Essential Knowledge and Skills

1F identify major causes and describe the major effects of the following important turning points in world history from 1914 to the present: the world wars and their impact on political, economic, and social systems; communist revolutions and their impact on the Cold War; independence movements; and globalization

12B explain the roles of various world leaders, including Benito Mussolini, Adolf Hitler, Hideki Tojo, Joseph Stalin, Franklin D. Roosevelt, and Winston Churchill, prior to and during World War II

continued on the next page

The United States

The home front in the United States was quite different from that of the other major powers. The United States was not fighting on its own territory. Eventually, the United States became the arsenal of the Allied Powers; it produced much of the military equipment the Allies needed. The height of war production came in November 1943. At that point, the country was building 6 ships a day and 96,000 planes per year.

The mobilization of the American economy and workforce resulted in some social turmoil, however. The construction of new factories created boomtowns. Thousands came there to work but then faced a shortage of houses and schools. Sixteen million men and women were enrolled in the military and moved frequently. Millions of women entered the workforce, taking on jobs left by men who had enrolled in the military.

More than a million African Americans moved from the rural South to the cities of the North and West looking for jobs in industry. The presence of African Americans in areas in which they had not lived before led to racial tensions and sometimes even racial riots. In Detroit in June 1943, for example, white mobs roamed the streets attacking African Americans. One million African Americans joined the military, where they served in segregated units. For some, this treatment later led to a fight for their civil rights.

▲ An African-American woman works in a U.S. munitions factory during World War II

▶ **CRITICAL THINKING**

Making Inferences How did munitions factories like the one shown above impact U.S. communities?

Japanese Americans faced even more serious issues. On the West Coast, 110,000 Japanese Americans, 65 percent of whom had been born in the United States, were removed to camps surrounded by barbed wire and required to take loyalty oaths. Public officials claimed this policy was necessary for security reasons. California governor Culbert Olson expressed the racism in this policy:

PRIMARY SOURCE

"When I look out at a group of Americans of German or Italian descent, I can tell whether they're loyal or not. I can tell how they think and even perhaps what they are thinking. But it is impossible for me to do this with inscrutable Orientals, and particularly the Japanese."

—quoted in Spickard, *Japanese Americans: The Formation and Transformation of an Ethnic Group*

Connections to TODAY

Women in the U.S. Military

During World War II, women participated in organizations such as the Women's Army Corps (WACs), where they served in administrative, noncombat positions. In 1948 President Harry S. Truman signed the Women's Armed Services Integration Act, which enabled women to become active members of all branches of the U.S. military. At that time, women made up 2 percent of the armed forces. Today, women make up 15 percent of the military, though they are often excluded from direct combat missions. In 2009 only 6 percent of the Marine Corps was made up of women, while women accounted for 20 percent of the Air Force, 14 percent of the Army, and 15 percent of the Navy.

(continued from p. 723)

TEKS **Texas Essential Knowledge and Skills**

21A describe how people have participated in supporting or changing their governments

24A describe the changing roles of women, children, and families during major eras of world history

28C explain the effects of major new military technologies on World War I, World War II, and the Cold War

kamikaze Japanese for "divine wind"; a suicide mission in which young Japanese pilots intentionally flew their airplanes into U.S. fighting ships at sea

Germany

In August 1914, Germans had enthusiastically cheered their soldiers marching off to war. In September 1939, the streets were quiet. Many Germans did not care. Even worse for the Nazi regime, many feared disaster.

Hitler was well aware of the importance of the home front. He believed that the collapse of the home front in World War I had caused Germany's defeat. To avoid a repetition of that experience, he adopted economic policies that may have cost Germany the war.

To maintain the morale of the home front during the first two years of the war, Hitler refused to cut consumer goods production or to increase the production of armaments. Blitzkrieg gave the Germans quick victories and enabled them to plunder the food and raw materials of conquered countries. In this way, they could avoid taking away resources from the civilian economy. After German defeats on the Russian front and the American entry into the war, however, the economic situation in Germany changed.

Early in 1942, Hitler finally ordered a massive increase in armaments production and in the size of the army. Hitler's architect, Albert Speer, was made minister for armaments and munitions in 1942. Speer was able to triple the production of armaments between 1942 and 1943, in spite of Allied air raids.

A total mobilization of the economy was put into effect in July 1944. Schools, theaters, and cafés were closed. By that time, though, total war mobilization was too late to save Germany from defeat.

Nazi attitudes toward women changed over the course of the war. Before the war, the Nazis had worked to keep women out of the job market. As the war progressed and more and more men were called up for military service, this position no longer made sense. In spite of this change, the number of women working in industry, agriculture, commerce, and domestic service increased only slightly. The total number of employed women in September 1944 was 14.9 million, compared with 14.6 million in May 1939. Many women, especially those of the middle class, did not want jobs, particularly in factories.

Japan

Wartime Japan was a highly mobilized society. To guarantee its control over all national resources, the government created a planning board to control prices, wages, labor, and resources. Traditional habits of obedience and hierarchy were used to encourage citizens to sacrifice their resources, and sometimes their lives, for the national cause.

The calls for sacrifice reached a high point in the final years of the war. Young Japanese were encouraged to volunteer to serve as pilots in suicide missions against U.S. fighting ships at sea. These pilots were known as **kamikaze**, or "divine wind."

Japan was reluctant to mobilize women on behalf of Japan's war effort. General Hideki Tōjō, prime minister from 1941 to 1944, opposed female employment. He argued in October 1943:

PRIMARY SOURCE

"The weakening of the family system would be the weakening of the nation. . . . We are able to do our duties . . . only because we have wives and mothers at home."

—quoted in *Valley of Darkness: The Japanese People and World War Two,* 1978

Female employment increased during the war but only in areas such as the textile industry and farming, in which women had traditionally worked. Instead of using women to meet labor shortages, the Japanese government brought in Korean and Chinese laborers.

✓ **READING PROGRESS CHECK**

Contrasting How were war preparations in Germany different from war preparations in the United States?

The Bombing of Cities

GUIDING QUESTION ***How did the bombing of cities impact the home front?***

Bombing was used in World War II against military targets, enemy troops, and civilian populations. Bombing made the home front a dangerous place.

Although a few bombing raids had been conducted in the last year of World War I, the aircraft of the time were limited by how far they could fly and by how much they could carry. The bombing of civilians had led to a public outcry, leading many leaders to believe that bombing civilian populations would force governments to make peace. As a result, European air forces began to develop long-range bombers that carried enormous payloads in the 1930s.

blitz the British term for the German air raids on British cities and towns during World War II

Britain

The first sustained use of civilian bombing began in early September 1940. Londoners took the first heavy blows. For months, the German air force bombed London nightly. Thousands of civilians were killed or injured, and enormous damage was done to the buildings of London. In spite of the extensive damage done to lives and property, Londoners' morale remained high.

The **blitz**, as the British called the German air raids, soon became a national experience. The blitz was carried to many other British cities and towns. The ability of Londoners to maintain their morale set the standard for the rest of the British population. The theory that the bombing of civilians would force peace was proved wrong.

Many children were evacuated from cities during the war to avoid the bombing. The British moved about 6 million children and their mothers in 1939. Some British parents even sent their children to Canada and the United States. This, too, could be dangerous. When the ocean liner *Arandora Star* was hit by a German torpedo, it had 77 British children on board. They never made it to Canada.

▲ **The blitz leveled buildings in England. A man stands amid the rubble of what was the Coventry Cathedral in November 1940.**

▶ **CRITICAL THINKING**

Drawing Conclusions What effects did the blitz have on England?

Germany

The British failed to learn from their own experience, however. Churchill and his advisers believed that destroying German communities would break civilian morale and bring victory. Major bombing raids on German cities began in 1942. On May 31, 1942, Cologne became the first German city to be attacked by 1,000 bombers.

Bombing raids added an element of terror to the dire **circumstances** caused by growing shortages of food, clothing, and fuel. The Germans, too, sought to protect their children from the bombings by evacuating them from the cities.

circumstance state of affairs

They had a program that created about 9,000 camps for children in the countryside. Especially fearful to the Germans were the incendiary bombs, which created firestorms that swept through cities. The ferocious bombing of Dresden from February 13 to 15, 1945, created a firestorm that may have killed as many as 35,000 inhabitants and refugees.

Germany suffered enormously from the Allied bombing raids. Millions of buildings were destroyed; half a million civilians died. Nevertheless, it is highly unlikely that Allied bombing sapped the German morale. Instead, Germans, whether pro-Nazi or anti-Nazi, fought on stubbornly, often driven simply by a desire to live. At times, even young people were expected to fight in the war. In the last years of the war, Hitler Youth members, often only 14 or 15 years old, served in the front lines.

Nor did the bombing destroy Germany's industrial capacity. Production of war materials actually increased between 1942 and 1944, in spite of the bombing. However, the widespread destruction of transportation systems and fuel supplies made it extremely difficult for the new materials to reach the German military.

▲ B-29 Superfortresses fly over Mount Fuji en route to Tokyo.

PHOTO: © Bettman/CORBIS

Japan

Japan was open to air raids toward the end of the war because its air force had almost been destroyed. Moreover, its crowded cities were built of flimsy materials that were especially vulnerable to fire.

Attacks on Japanese cities by the new U.S. B-29 Superfortresses, the biggest bombers of the war, had begun on November 24, 1944. By the summer of 1945, many of Japan's industries had been destroyed, along with one-fourth of its dwellings. To add to the strength of its regular army, the Japanese government decreed the mobilization of all people between the ages of 13 and 60 into a People's Volunteer Corps.

In Japan, the bombing of civilians reached a new level with the use of the first atomic bomb. Fearing high U.S. casualties in a land invasion of Japan, President Truman and his advisers decided to drop atomic bombs in August 1945. The result was the deaths of thousands of Japanese civilians.

✓ **READING PROGRESS CHECK**

Drawing Conclusions How did the development of airplanes change the way militaries fought?

LESSON 3 REVIEW TEKS

Reviewing Vocabulary

1. ***Describing*** Describe the social effects of U.S. mobilization for World War II.

Using Your Notes

2. ***Comparing and Contrasting*** Use your notes to write a paragraph comparing and contrasting the effects of World War II on civilians in the Soviet Union, the United States, Germany, and Japan.

Answering the Guiding Questions

3. ***Gathering Information*** How did countries mobilize for war?
4. ***Identifying Cause and Effects*** How did the bombing of cities impact the home front?

Writing Activity

5. **INFORMATIVE/EXPLANATORY** Do research to find out more about the blitz in London or another city in Great Britain. In paragraph form, present a detailed sequence of steps or events that would typically occur for average citizens in their homes from the time planes were sighted until the "all clear" signal. Use transitional words and phrases, and list your source or sources.

networks

There's More Online!

- CHART/GRAPH Jewish Population in Europe Before and After World War II
- IMAGE German Prison Camp
- IMAGE Heinrich Himmler
- IMAGE Japanese Troops Arriving at Haiphong Port
- INTERACTIVE SELF-CHECK QUIZ
- MAP Major Nazi Death Camps
- PRIMARY SOURCE An Eyewitness to the Holocaust
- VIDEO Auschwitz

LESSON 4

The New Order and the Holocaust

ESSENTIAL QUESTIONS • *Why do political actions often lead to war?* • *How does war impact society and the environment?*

Reading HELPDESK

Academic Vocabulary

- **ethnic**
- **occupation**

Content Vocabulary

- **genocide**
- **collaborator**

TAKING NOTES:

Key Ideas and Details

Comparing and Contrasting As you read, use a Venn diagram like the one below to compare and contrast the New Order of Germany with the New Order of Japan.

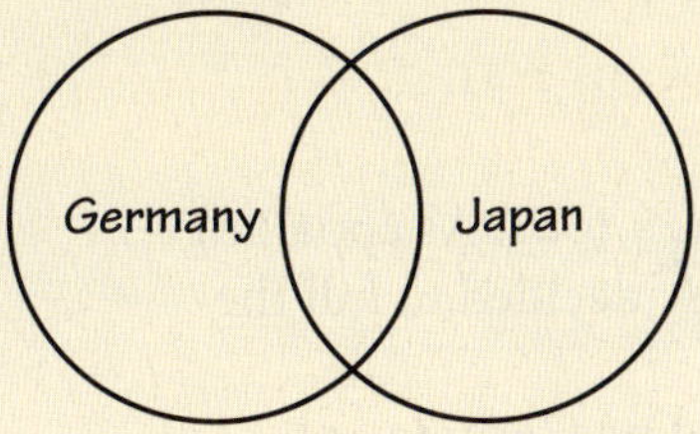

TEKS Texas Essential Knowledge and Skills

1F identify major causes and describe the major effects of the following important turning points in world history from 1914 to the present: the world wars and their impact on political, economic, and social systems; communist revolutions and their impact on the Cold War; independence movements; and globalization

continued on the next page

It Matters Because

Japan exploited the resources of the nations it conquered. In Germany, the Nazis began a terrifying genocide, carried out by death squads and death camps. Nearly two out of every three European Jews died in the Holocaust.

The New Order in Europe

GUIDING QUESTION *How did Germany establish a New Order in Europe?*

In 1942 the Nazi regime stretched across continental Europe from the English Channel in the west to the outskirts of Moscow in the east. Nazi-occupied Europe was largely organized in one of two ways. Nazi Germany directly annexed some areas, such as western Poland, and made them into German provinces. Most of occupied Europe, however, was run by German military or civilian officials with help from local people who collaborated with the Nazis.

Nazi administration in the conquered lands to the east was especially ruthless. Seen as the "living space" for German expansion, these lands were populated, Nazis thought, by racially inferior Slavic peoples. Hitler's plans for an Aryan racial empire were so important to him that the Nazis began to put their racial program into effect soon after the conquest of Poland.

Heinrich Himmler, the leader of the SS, was in charge of German resettlement plans in the east. Himmler's task was to move the Slavic peoples out and to replace them with Germans. Slavic peoples included Czech, Polish, Serbo-Croatian, Slovene, and Ukrainian people. One million Poles were uprooted and moved to southern Poland. Hundreds of thousands of **ethnic** Germans were brought in to colonize the German provinces in Poland.

The invasion of the Soviet Union made the Nazis even more excited about German colonization. Hitler planned a colossal project of social engineering after the war. Poles, Ukrainians, and Russians would be removed and become slave labor. German peasants would settle on the abandoned lands and "Germanize" them.

By the summer of 1944, more than 7 million European workers labored in Germany. They made up approximately 20 percent of Germany's labor force. Another 7 million workers were forced to labor for the Nazis in their own countries on farms, in industries, and in military camps.

The use of forced labor caused many problems for Germany. Sending so many workers to Germany disrupted industrial production in the occupied countries. Then, too, the brutal way in which Germany recruited foreign workers led more and more people to resist the Nazi **occupation** forces.

✓ READING PROGRESS CHECK

Analyzing How did resettlement contribute to the goals of Hitler's New Order?

The Holocaust

GUIDING QUESTION ***How did Adolf Hitler's views on race influence the New Order?***

No aspect of the Nazi New Order was more terrifying than the deliberate attempt to exterminate the Jews. Racial struggle was a key element in Hitler's world of ideas. He saw it as a clearly defined conflict of opposites. On one side were the Aryans, who were the creators of human cultural development, according to Hitler. On the other side were the Jews, whom Hitler blamed for Germany's defeat in World War I and the Depression.

Himmler and the SS closely shared Hitler's racial ideas. The SS was given responsibility for what the Nazis called their Final Solution to the Jewish problem. The Final Solution was **genocide** of the Jewish people.

The *Einsatzgruppen*

Reinhard Heydrich, head of the SS's Security Service, had the task of administering the Final Solution. Heydrich created special strike forces, called *Einsatzgruppen*, to carry out Nazi plans. After the defeat of Poland, these forces rounded up all Polish Jews and put them in ghettos set up in many Polish cities. Conditions in the ghettos were horrible. Families were crowded together in unsanitary housing. The Nazis tried to starve residents by allowing only minimal amounts of food. In spite of their suffering, residents carried on, and some organized resistance against the Nazis.

In June 1941, the *Einsatzgruppen* were given the new job acting as mobile killing units. These SS death squads followed the regular army's advance into the Soviet Union. Their job was to round up Jews in their villages to execute them, and to bury them in mass graves.

The Death Camps

The *Einsatzgruppen* probably killed more than 1 million Jews. As appalling as that sounds, it was too slow by Nazi standards. They decided to kill the European Jews in specially built death camps.

Beginning in 1942, Jews from countries occupied by Germany or sympathetic to Germany were rounded up, packed like cattle into freight trains, and shipped to Poland. Six extermination centers were built in Poland for this purpose. The largest was Auschwitz (OWSH • VIHTS).

About 30 percent of the new arrivals at Auschwitz were sent to a labor camp, where many were starved or worked to death. The remainder of the people went to the gas chambers. Some inmates were subjected to cruel and painful "medical" experiments.

By the spring of 1942, the death camps were in full operation. First priority was given to the elimination of the Polish ghettos. By the summer of 1942, Jews were also being shipped from France, Belgium, and Holland.

Analyzing PRIMARY SOURCES

Nazi Death Squads

"The unit selected for this task would enter a village or city and order the prominent Jewish citizens to call together all Jews for the purpose of resettlement. They were requested to hand over their valuables to the leaders of the unit, and shortly before the execution to surrender their outer clothing. The men, women, and children were led to a place of execution which in most cases was located next to a more deeply excavated anti-tank ditch. Then they were shot, kneeling or standing, and the corpses thrown into the ditch."

—from *Nazi Conspiracy and Aggression*, vol. 5, 1946

DBQ ***CLASSIFYING*** How do the actions described above exemplify genocide?

(continued from p. 727)

TEKS **Texas Essential Knowledge and Skills**

12B explain the roles of various world leaders, including Benito Mussolini, Adolf Hitler, Hideki Tojo, Joseph Stalin, Franklin D. Roosevelt, and Winston Churchill, prior to and during World War II

continued on the next page

ethnic relating to people who have common racial, religious, or cultural origins

occupation the military force occupying a country or the policies carried out by it

genocide the deliberate mass murder or physical extinction of a particular racial, political, or cultural group

Major Nazi Death Camps

GEOGRAPHY CONNECTION

1. **THE WORLD IN SPATIAL TERMS** *Where were the death camps located?*
2. **HUMAN SYSTEMS** *Why do you think the* Einsatzgruppen *operated in Eastern Europe and the Soviet Union?*

Even as the Allies were winning the war in 1944, Jews were shipped from Greece and Hungary. In spite of Germany's desperate military needs, even late in the war when Germany was facing utter defeat, the Final Solution often had priority in using railroad cars to ship Jews to the death camps.

The Death Toll

The Germans killed approximately 6 million Jews, more than 3 million of them in the death camps. Even in concentration camps that were not designed specifically for mass murder, large numbers of inmates were worked to death or subjected to deadly medical experiments. Virtually 90 percent of the Jewish populations of Poland, the Baltic countries, and Germany were killed. Overall, the Holocaust was responsible for the death of nearly two out of every three European Jews.

The Nazis were also responsible for the deliberate death by shooting, starvation, or overwork of as many as another 9 to 10 million non-Jewish people. The Nazis considered the Roma, who are sometimes known as Gypsies, to be an alien race. About 40 percent of Europe's Roma were killed in the death camps.

The leading citizens of the Slavic peoples were arrested and killed. Probably an additional 4 million Poles, Ukrainians, and Belorussians lost their lives as slave laborers. Finally, at least 3 to 4 million Soviet prisoners of war were killed.

This mass slaughter of European Jews is known as *Shoah*—a Hebrew word meaning "total destruction." Many Jews attempted to resist the Nazis. Friends and strangers aided some Jews, hiding them or smuggling them to safe areas. A few foreign diplomats saved Jews by issuing exit visas. The nation of Denmark saved almost its entire Jewish population.

Some people did not believe the accounts of death camps because, during World War I, allies had greatly exaggerated German atrocities to arouse enthusiasm for the war. Most often, people pretended not to notice what was happening. Even worse, **collaborators** helped the Nazis hunt down Jews. Although the Allies were aware of the concentration camps and death

(continued from p. 728)

TEKS **Texas Essential Knowledge and Skills**

12C explain the major causes and events of World War II, including the German invasions of Poland and the Soviet Union, the Holocaust, Japanese imperialism, the attack on Pearl Harbor, the Normandy landings, and the dropping of the atomic bombs

22D identify examples of genocide, including the Holocaust and genocide in the Balkans, Rwanda, and Darfur

collaborator a person who assists the enemy

camps, they chose to concentrate on ending the war. Not until after the war did the full extent of the horror and inhumanity of the Holocaust impress itself upon people's consciousness.

READING PROGRESS CHECK

Explaining What was the role of the *Einsatzgruppen*?

The New Order in Asia

GUIDING QUESTION ***What characterized the New Order in Asia?***

▲ Japanese troops arrive at Haiphong Port in Indochina

Japan needed its new possessions in Asia to meet its growing need for raw materials, such as tin and oil, and as markets for its manufactured goods. To organize these possessions, Japanese leaders included them in the Greater East Asia Co-Prosperity Sphere. This economic community supposedly would provide mutual benefits to the occupied areas and to Japan.

The Japanese had conquered Southeast Asia under the slogan "Asia for the Asiatics." Japanese officials in occupied territories promised that local governments would be established under Japanese control. In fact, real power rested with Japanese military authorities in each territory. In turn, the Army General Staff in Tokyo controlled the local Japanese military command. Japan used the economic resources of its colonies for its war machine and recruited the native peoples to serve in local military units or in public works projects. In some cases, these policies brought severe hardships to the native peoples. In Vietnam more than a million people starved in 1944 and 1945 when Japan forcibly took their rice to sell abroad.

At first, many Southeast Asian nationalists took Japanese promises at face value and agreed to cooperate. Eventually, the nature of Japanese occupation policies became clear, and sentiment turned against Japan. Japanese officials provoked such attitudes by their contempt for local customs. Like the Germans, Japanese military forces often had little respect for the lives of their subject peoples. To help their war effort, the Japanese used labor forces composed of both prisoners of war and local peoples.

This behavior created a dilemma for many nationalists. They had no desire to see the return of the colonial powers, but they did not like what the Japanese were doing. Some turned against the Japanese. Others simply did nothing. Some nationalists tried to have it both ways. Indonesian patriots pretended to support Japan while actually sabotaging them.

READING PROGRESS CHECK

Assessing As part of its New Order, how did Japan treat the peoples it conquered?

LESSON 4 REVIEW TEKS

Reviewing Vocabulary

1. ***Expressing*** Explain how some collaborators helped make genocide possible.

Using Your Notes

2. ***Contrasting*** Use your notes to write a paragraph contrasting the New Order of Germany with the New Order of Japan.

Answering the Guiding Questions

3. ***Analyzing*** How did Germany establish a New Order in Europe?
4. ***Identifying Cause and Effect*** How did Adolf Hitler's views on race influence the New Order?
5. ***Summarizing*** What characterized the New Order in Japan?

Writing Activity

6. **INFORMATIVE/EXPLANATORY** Using a variety of sources, research and analyze the causes and consequences of the Holocaust. Be careful to use only reputable sources. Be sure to include information on the role of anti-Semitism.

networks

There's More Online!

- IMAGE Bombing of Hiroshima
- IMAGE Invasion at Omaha Beach
- IMAGE Prison Camp Liberation
- INTERACTIVE SELF-CHECK QUIZ
- MAP World War II in Asia and the Pacific, 1943–1945
- PRIMARY SOURCE Churchill's Iron Curtain Speech
- TIME LINE The Final Months of World War II
- VIDEO The Atomic Bomb

LESSON 5

World War II Ends

ESSENTIAL QUESTIONS • *Why do political actions often lead to war?* • *How does war impact society and the environment?*

Reading HELPDESK

Academic Vocabulary

- **ideological**
- **assure**

Content Vocabulary

- **partisan**
- **Cold War**

TAKING NOTES:

Key Ideas and Details

Listing As you read, use a table like the one below to list three of the major military events that brought an end to World War II and where they took place.

Event	Location

TEKS Texas Essential Knowledge and Skills

1F identify major causes and describe the major effects of the following important turning points in world history from 1914 to the present: the world wars and their impact on political, economic, and social systems; communist revolutions and their impact on the Cold War; independence movements; and globalization

12B explain the roles of various world leaders, including Benito Mussolini, Adolf Hitler, Hideki Tojo, Joseph Stalin, Franklin D. Roosevelt, and Winston Churchill, prior to and during World War II

continued on the next page

It Matters Because

By 1943, the Allies had strengthened their strategies and stopped the advances of both the Germans and the Japanese. Germany surrendered on May 7, 1945, and Japan surrendered on August 14. When the war ended, political tensions, suspicions, and conflicts of ideas led to a new struggle—the Cold War.

Last Years of the War

GUIDING QUESTION *How did the tide of battle turn against Germany, Italy, and Japan?*

By the beginning of 1943, the tide of battle had turned against Germany, Italy, and Japan. Axis forces in Tunisia surrendered on May 13, 1943. The Allies then crossed the Mediterranean and carried the war to Italy, an area that Winston Churchill, prime minister of Great Britain, called the "soft underbelly" of Europe. After taking Sicily, the Allies began an invasion of mainland Italy in September.

The European Theater

After Sicily fell, King Victor Emmanuel III of Italy arrested Mussolini, but in a daring raid the Germans liberated him. He was then made the head of a German puppet state in northern Italy as German troops moved in and occupied much of Italy.

The Germans set up defense lines in the hills south of Rome. The Allies advanced up the peninsula with heavy casualties, but they took Rome on June 4, 1944. By then, the Italian war was secondary as the Allied forces opened their long-awaited "second front" in western Europe.

Since the autumn of 1943, the Allies had planned an invasion of France from Great Britain, across the English Channel. Finally, on June 6, 1944 (D-Day), Allied forces under U.S. general Dwight D. Eisenhower landed on the Normandy beaches in history's greatest naval invasion. The Allies fought their way past hidden underwater mines, treacherous barbed wire, and horrible machine

▲ **On D-Day, June 6, 1944, Allied troops departed landing craft and moved inland. This map of Omaha Beach was created on April 21, 1944, in preparation for the Normandy invasion.**

▶ CRITICAL THINKING

Determining Cause and Effect Why is the Normandy invasion considered a turning point in the war?

gun fire. Believing the battle was a diversion and the real invasion would occur elsewhere, the Germans responded slowly. This gave the Allied forces time to set up a beachhead. Within three months, the Allies had landed 2 million men and 500,000 vehicles. Allied forces then began pushing inland and broke through German defensive lines.

Allied troops liberated Paris by the end of August 1944. In December, with Allied aircraft grounded, the Germans launched a counteroffensive to regain the seaport of Antwerp in Belgium. The Battle of the Bulge was named for the "bulge" the German attack caused in Allied lines. By January 1945, both sides had suffered heavy losses, but the Allied lines held. In March 1945, the Allied forces crossed the Rhine River and advanced into Germany. At the end of April 1945, Allied armies in northern Germany moved toward the Elbe River, where they linked up with the Soviets.

The Soviets had come a long way since the Battle of Stalingrad in 1943. The Soviets had soundly defeated the German forces at the Battle of Kursk (July 5 to 12), the greatest tank battle of World War II. Soviet forces now began a steady advance westward. Reoccupying the Ukraine by the end of 1943, they moved into the Baltic states by early 1944. Advancing along a northern front, Soviet troops occupied Warsaw in January 1945 and entered Berlin in April. Meanwhile, Soviet troops along a southern front swept through Hungary, Romania, and Bulgaria.

As the Allied forces advanced into Nazi-occupied Europe, they also liberated the concentration camps and death camps. Although the Nazis tried to destroy some of the evidence, the Allies were able to see for themselves the crimes against humanity carried out by the Nazis.

By January 1945, Adolf Hitler had moved into a bunker 55 feet (almost 17 m) under the city of Berlin. In his final political testament, Hitler, consistent to the end in his anti-Semitism, blamed the Jews for the war. He wrote:

PRIMARY SOURCE

"Above all I charge the leaders of the nation and those under them to scrupulous observance of the laws of race and to merciless opposition to the universal poisoner of all peoples, international Jewry."

—from Hitler's Final Will and Testament, April 29, 1945

Hitler committed suicide on April 30, two days after Italian **partisans**, or resistance fighters, shot Mussolini. On May 7, 1945, Germany surrendered. The war in Europe was finally over.

(continued from p. 731)

TEKS **Texas Essential Knowledge and Skills**

12C explain the major causes and events of World War II, including the German invasions of Poland and the Soviet Union, the Holocaust, Japanese imperialism, the attack on Pearl Harbor, the Normandy landings, and the dropping of the atomic bombs

continued on the next page

partisan a resistance fighter in World War II

The Asian Theater

The war in Asia continued. Beginning in 1943, U.S. forces went on the offensive and advanced across the Pacific. Along with their allies, the U.S. forces continued their island-hopping campaign. At the beginning of 1945, the acquisition of Iwo Jima and Okinawa helped the Allied military power draw even closer to the main Japanese islands. The islands of Iwo Jima and Okinawa were of great strategic importance. Iwo Jima was essential to the air war on Japan. This small volcanic island had two airfields used by the Japanese to attack Allied aircraft and to support their naval forces. The Allies felt capturing Iwo Jima would lessen the Japanese threat and could aid in the invasion of the Japanese mainland. The Allies hoped that controlling Okinawa would also provide them with a base near the mainland.

The Allies were victorious in both battles, but the victories came at a great cost. Casualties were great on both sides, and many began to fear even more losses if the war in the Pacific continued. This left Harry S. Truman, who had become president after Roosevelt died in April, with a difficult decision to make. Scientists, including Enrico Fermi, worked on a top-secret project called the Manhattan Project. Their efforts led to the development of the atomic bomb. Should he use newly developed atomic weapons to bring the war to an end? If the United States invaded Japan, Truman and his advisers were convinced that American troops would suffer heavy casualties. There were only two bombs; no one knew how effective they would be.

(continued from p. 732)

TEKS **Texas Essential Knowledge and Skills**

13A summarize how the outcome of World War II contributed to the development of the Cold War

20D explain the significance of the League of Nations and the United Nations

24A describe the changing roles of women, children, and families during major eras of world history

28C explain the effects of major new military technologies on World War I, World War II, and the Cold War

GEOGRAPHY CONNECTION

1. **THE WORLD IN SPATIAL TERMS** *From which islands did Allied air operations begin?*
2. **HUMAN SYSTEMS** *What strategy did Allied forces use to advance on Japan?*

▲ Of Hiroshima's 350,000 inhabitants, 190,000 died—some immediately and others after suffering the effects of radiation.

▶ **CRITICAL THINKING**

Determining Cause and Effect What effects did the bombings of Hiroshima and Nagasaki have on Japan?

Truman decided to use the bombs. The first bomb was dropped on the Japanese city of Hiroshima on August 6. Of the city's 350,000 inhabitants, 190,000 died—some immediately and others after suffering the effects of radiation. Three days later, a second bomb was dropped on Nagasaki. Both cities were leveled. Thousands of people died immediately after the bombs were dropped. Thousands more died in later months from radiation. The devastation led Emperor Hirohito to accept the Allied forces' demands for unconditional surrender on August 14, 1945.

World War II was finally over. Seventeen million had died in battle. Perhaps 20 million civilians had perished as well. Some estimates place total losses at 60 million.

The dropping of the atomic bombs in Japan also marked the beginning of the Nuclear Age. After the world had witnessed the deadly potential of nuclear energy, other countries raced to build their own nuclear weapons. In August 1949, the Soviet Union set off its first atomic bomb, starting an arms race with the United States that lasted for 40 years.

✓ **READING PROGRESS CHECK**

Identifying What was the strategic importance of the "second front" that the Allies opened in western Europe?

Peace and a New War

GUIDING QUESTION *What led to the Cold War?*

Cold War the period of political tension following World War II and ending with the fall of Communism in the Soviet Union at the end of the 1980s

ideological based on a set of beliefs

assure to make certain of something; to guarantee

No real peace but a period of political tensions, known as the **Cold War**, followed the total victory of the Allies in World War II. An **ideological** conflict between the United States and the Soviet Union, the Cold War dominated world affairs until the end of the 1980s.

Stalin, Roosevelt, and Churchill were the leaders of the Big Three (the Soviet Union, the United States, and Great Britain) of the Grand Alliance. They met at Tehran in November 1943 to discuss strategy. Their major tactical decision had concerned the final assault on Germany—an American-British invasion through France scheduled for the spring of 1944.

The acceptance of this plan had important consequences. It meant that Soviet and British-American forces would meet in defeated Germany along a north-south dividing line. Most likely, Soviet forces would liberate Eastern Europe. The Allies also agreed to a partition of postwar Germany.

The Big Three powers met again at Yalta in southern Russia in February 1945. By then, the defeat of Germany was **assured.** The Western powers, having once believed that the Soviets were in a weak position, now faced the reality of 11 million Soviet soldiers taking possession of Eastern Europe and much of central Europe.

Stalin was deeply suspicious of the Western powers. He wanted a buffer to protect the Soviet Union from possible future Western aggression. This meant establishing pro-Soviet governments along the Soviet Union's borders. Roosevelt favored the idea of self-determination for Europe. This involved a pledge to help liberated Europe create "democratic institutions of their own choice" through free elections. Roosevelt also agreed to Stalin's price for military aid against Japan: Sakhalin and the Kuril Islands, ruled by Japan, as well as two warm-water ports and railroad rights in Manchuria.

The creation of the United Nations was a major American concern. Both Churchill and Stalin accepted Roosevelt's plans for the establishment of the United Nations and set the first meeting for San Francisco in April 1945.

The issues of Germany and Eastern Europe were treated less decisively. After Germany surrendered, the Big Three agreed to divide Germany into four zones, one each for the United States, Great Britain, France, and the Soviet Union to occupy and to govern. Stalin compromised and agreed to free elections in Poland. However, it was clear that Stalin might not honor this provision for other Eastern European countries. The issue of free elections caused a serious split between the Soviets and Americans. This split became more evident when the Big Three next met at Potsdam, Germany.

The Potsdam Conference of July 1945 began in a cloud of mistrust. President Harry S. Truman, having succeeded Roosevelt, demanded free elections in Eastern Europe. Stalin responded, "A freely elected government in any of these East European countries would be anti-Soviet, and that we cannot allow." Stalin sought absolute security for the Soviets. Free elections would threaten his goal of controlling Eastern Europe. Short of an invasion by Western forces, nothing would undo developments in Eastern Europe. After the war's most destructive conflict had just ended, very few supported a policy of invasion.

The Allies agreed that trials should be held of leaders who had committed crimes against humanity during the war. In 1945 and 1946, Nazi leaders were tried and condemned at war crimes trials in Nuremberg, Germany. War crimes trials were also held in Japan and Italy.

As the war slowly receded into the past, a new struggle was already beginning. Many in the West thought Soviet policy was part of a worldwide Communist conspiracy. The Soviets viewed Western, and especially American, policy as nothing less than global capitalist expansionism.

In March 1946, in a speech to an American audience, the former British prime minister Winston Churchill declared that "an iron curtain" had "descended across the continent," dividing Europe into two hostile camps. Stalin branded Churchill's speech "a call to war on the USSR." Only months after the world's most devastating conflict had ended, the world seemed to be bitterly divided once again.

▲ Austrian SS chief Ernst Kaltenbrunner addresses the court during his trial for war crimes at Nuremberg.

▶ **CRITICAL THINKING**

Analyzing Why is it important that war crimes trials were held?

✓ **READING PROGRESS CHECK**

Identifying Central Issues What was the major disagreement between the United States and the Soviet Union at the conclusion of World War II?

LESSON 5 REVIEW TEKS

Reviewing Vocabulary

1. ***Defining*** Write a paragraph in which you answer the question: *What was the central ideological conflict of the Cold War?* Be sure to define the terms *ideological* and *Cold War* in your discussion.

Using Your Notes

2. ***Identifying*** Use your notes to identify three of the major military events that brought an end to World War II and where they took place. Briefly explain the significance of each event.

Answering the Guiding Questions

3. ***Analyzing*** How did the tide of battle turn against Germany, Italy, and Japan?

4. ***Explaining*** What led to the Cold War?

Writing Activity

5. **ARGUMENT** Imagine that you are an adviser to President Truman. You must persuade him to use or not to use the atomic bomb against Japan. Which position do you take? How do you make your case?

CHAPTER 30 Assessment

Directions: On a separate sheet of paper, answer the questions below. Make sure you read carefully and answer all parts of the questions.

Lesson Review

Lesson 1

1. ***Explaining*** How did Germany first violate the Treaty of Versailles in 1935 and 1936?

2. ***Summarizing*** How did Great Britain and France differ in their reactions to Germany's treaty violations?

3. ***Explaining*** What actions did Hitler take as leader of Germany that led the world into war? What were Hitler's motivations for his actions? **12B**

4. ***Explaining*** What demand of Hitler's led to open warfare between Germany and Poland? **12C**

5. ***Explaining*** What role did Franklin Roosevelt and Winston Churchill play prior to the war? What were their roles during the war? **12B**

Lesson 2

6. ***Naming*** What Southeast Asian countries did Japan take under its control creating what they termed the Greater East Asia Co-Prosperity Sphere?

7. ***Describing*** When and where did Soviet military decisions combined with weather work to defeat Hitler's army?

8. ***Explaining*** What new technology and strategy of war made Hitler's invasion of Poland so successful? **28C**

9. ***Locating*** What was the turning point for the Allies in the Asian theater of operations? How did they turn the tide? **16A**

10. ***Describing*** Describe the U.S. military "island hopping" strategy against Japan in 1942.

Lesson 3

11. ***Identifying Cause and Effect*** How and why did World War II impact economic and social systems for citizens on the home fronts in the Soviet Union, the United States, Germany, and Japan? **1F**

12. ***Explaining*** What was the effect of new airplane technology on World War II strategies? Was this strategy successful? **28C**

13. ***Explaining*** Why did the British mobilize the relocation of approximately 6 million children and their mothers during the war?

Lesson 4

14. ***Identify and Explain*** What was the Holocaust? What methods did the Nazis use to carry out the Holocaust? **12C, 22D**

15. ***Explaining*** What was Hideki Tōjō's role prior to and in World War II? How did his slogan "Asia for the Asiatics" differ from the reality of Japanese imperialism? **12B, 12C**

Lesson 5

16. ***Hypothesizing and Explaining*** Why was opening up a "second front" in Europe so important to the Allies? Explain the significance of the Normandy landings. **12C, 16A**

17. ***Explaining*** At the end of the war, why was Eastern Europe vulnerable to Soviet controlled governments?

18. ***Summarizing*** How did the outcome of World War II contribute to the development of the Cold War? **1F, 13A**

Exploring the Essential Question

19. ***Identifying Political Impacts*** Working with a small group, find a map of the world showing borders before and after World War II. Mark four borders that changed because of the war, and write labels explaining how political decisions contributed to those changes. **1F**

Need Extra Help?

If You've Missed Question	1	2	3	4	5	6	7	8	9	10	11	12	13	14	15	16	17	18	19
Go to page	710	711	711	712	712	718	717	715	719	719	720	723	723	726	728	729	733	732	729

Critical Thinking

20 ***Identifying Perspectives*** After the Munich Conference, how did Winston Churchill's perspective on Hitler's demands differ from British Prime Minister Neville Chamberlain's perspective? **12B**

21 ***Explaining*** Explain Stalin's role prior to and during World War II. In your response, explain Stalin's relationship with Hitler before the war, why their relationship changed, and Stalin's response. **12B, 12C**

22 ***Identifying Cause and Effect*** What caused Great Britain and France to begin negotiations with Stalin, and how did Hitler react?

23 ***Understanding Relationships among Events*** Define and describe the effects of the Nazis' Final Solution.

24 ***Comparing*** Compare Nazi Germany efforts for expansion and control with those of Japan, such as Japan's Manchuria invasion.

25 ***Use a Decision-making Process*** Choose one of the leaders during World War II, such as Roosevelt, Truman, or Churchill. Use what you've learned to speculate about the process of making a key wartime decision, such as dropping the atomic bomb. Identify the information the leader would have gathered, options, possible consequences, and ultimately the action he implemented. **12B, 31B**

Social Studies Skills

26 ***Economics*** What resources was Hideki Tōjō looking for when Japan attacked Southeast Asia? What dilemma did Tōjō face, and how did the bombing of Pearl Harbor seem like a solution? Describe the roles of Tōjō and U.S. President Roosevelt during this period of World War II. **12B, 12C**

27 ***Explaining*** What was Mussolini's role prior to and during World War II? **12B**

28 ***Explaining*** How did Churchill perform as Prime Minister during World War II? **12B**

29 ***Creating Thematic Charts*** Create a chart that records the countries Nazi Germany invaded and controlled while World War II raged. Following World War II, many of the same countries fell under Soviet control. Maintain and update this chart as you learn more about the years following the end of the war. **15A**

DBQ Analyzing Primary Sources

Use the document to answer the following questions.

After the United States dropped the first atomic bomb, the White House released a statement announcing the bombing of Hiroshima.

PRIMARY SOURCE

"Sixteen hours ago an American airplane dropped one bomb on Hiroshima and destroyed its usefulness to the enemy. That bomb had more power than 20,000 tons of TNT. It had more than two thousand times the blast power of the British 'Grand Slam' which is the largest bomb ever yet used in the history of warfare. The Japanese began the war from the air at Pearl Harbor. They have been repaid many fold. And the end is not yet."

—from a White House press release, August 6, 1945

30 ***Interpreting*** Provide access to the recording of Roosevelt's statement after the Japanese bombing, as written above. Listen and analyze bias and the validity of the text based on its language and source, the United States White House. How does Truman refer to Japan and does the use of the term support his claim and America's actions? Discuss with a partner to interpret this social studies information. **29D, 29E, 30C**

Need Extra Help?

If You've Missed Question	20	21	22	23	24	25	26	27	28	29	30
Go to page	712	712	712	726	710	710	718	711	716	711	735

31 ***Evaluating and Explaining*** Based on what you learned in Lesson 5 about the dropping of the atomic bombs, is the press release from the White House accurate? Explain your answer. **12C**

32 ***Interpreting*** Why did the author of this press release include that Japan "began the war from the air at Pearl Harbor"?

Analyzing Visuals

Use the image to answer the following questions.

This poster from 1942 encouraged American women to participate in the war effort.

33 ***Analyzing Visuals*** What message is this propaganda poster sending?

34 ***Interpreting*** What does this poster tell you about the changing roles of women during World War II? **24A**

35 ***Interpreting*** How can the poster text be interpreted in more than one way?

Extended Response Question

36 ***Argument*** Write a paragraph comparing and contrasting Hitler's and Tōjō's goals when they expanded. How was their treatment of people in occupied regions similar? Why do you think their methods were similar? **12B**

Need Extra Help?

If You've Missed Question	31	32	33	34	35	36
Go to page	736	736	736	736	736	710

The Cold War

1945–1989

ESSENTIAL QUESTION
How does conflict influence political relationships?

networks
There's More Online! about the Cold War.

CHAPTER 31

The Story Matters ...

In 1957 when the Soviets launched the first satellite into space, both the USSR and the United States possessed nuclear missiles. By the time Vice President Richard Nixon visited the Soviet Union in 1959, relations between the two countries were already extremely tense. During Nixon's trip, he and Soviet Premier Nikita Khrushchev participated in a heated debate about capitalism and communism. Their argument illustrates the nature of the growing rivalry between the two nations.

◀ During an impromptu "kitchen debate," Soviet Premier Nikita Khrushchev and U.S. Vice President Richard Nixon argued about politics at the American National Exhibit in Moscow, 1959. They are pictured here, quarrelling in the kitchen of a model suburban American home.

PHOTO: Howard Sochurek/Time & Life Pictures/Getty Images

CHAPTER 31

Place and Time: U.S. and USSR 1945–1975

The United States and the Soviet Union were allies during World War II, but enemies after 1945 until 1989, a period known as the Cold War. The world came to be divided into United States-aligned, Soviet Union-aligned, and non-aligned camps. While the United States and the Soviet Union avoided direct military confrontation, they intervened in proxy wars and influenced foreign policy in other nations. Especially in the early years of the Cold War, both sides saw the struggle between them as one between communism and capitalism.

Step Into the Place

Read the quotes and look at the information presented on the map.

DBQ **Analyzing Historical Documents** How did Soviet and American views of the spread of the Soviet system differ?

PRIMARY SOURCE

"When we say that the socialist system will win in the competition between the two systems—the capitalist and the socialist—this by no means signifies that its victory will be achieved through armed interference by the socialist countries in the internal affairs of the capitalist countries. Our certainty of the victory of communism is based on the fact that the socialist mode of production possesses decisive advantages over the capitalist mode of production. Precisely because of this, the ideas of Marxism-Leninism are more and more capturing the minds of the broad masses of the working people in the capitalist countries, just as they have captured the minds of millions of men and women in our country and the People's Democracies."

—Premier Nikita Khrushchev, from the Report to the Twentieth Party Congress, February, 1956

PRIMARY SOURCE

"International Communism, of course, seeks to mask its purposes of domination by expressions of good will and by superficially attractive offers of political, economic and military aid. But any free nation, which is the subject of Soviet enticement, ought, in elementary wisdom, to look behind the mask.

Remember Estonia, Latvia and Lithuania! . . .

Soviet control of the satellite nations of Eastern Europe has been forcibly maintained in spite of solemn promises of a contrary intent, made during World War II. . . ."

—President Dwight D. Eisenhower, Special Message to the Congress on the Situation in the Middle East, January 5, 1957

PHOTO: (l)Library of Congress, (r)©Bettmann/CORBIS.

Step Into the Time

Making Connections Choose an event from the time line and explain how it shows an important development in the Cold War.

THE USSR & THE U.S.

- **1945** World War II ends
- **1947** U.S. president Truman establishes Truman Doctrine
- **1949** NATO forms
- **1955** Warsaw Pact forms

1945 — 1955

THE WORLD

- **September 1949** Mao Zedong takes control of China
- **June 1950** Korean War begins
- **July 1954** Geneva Accords divide Vietnam

networks
There's More Online!

- ☑ **MAP** Explore the interactive version of this map on Networks.
- ☑ **TIME LINE** Explore the interactive version of the time line on Networks.

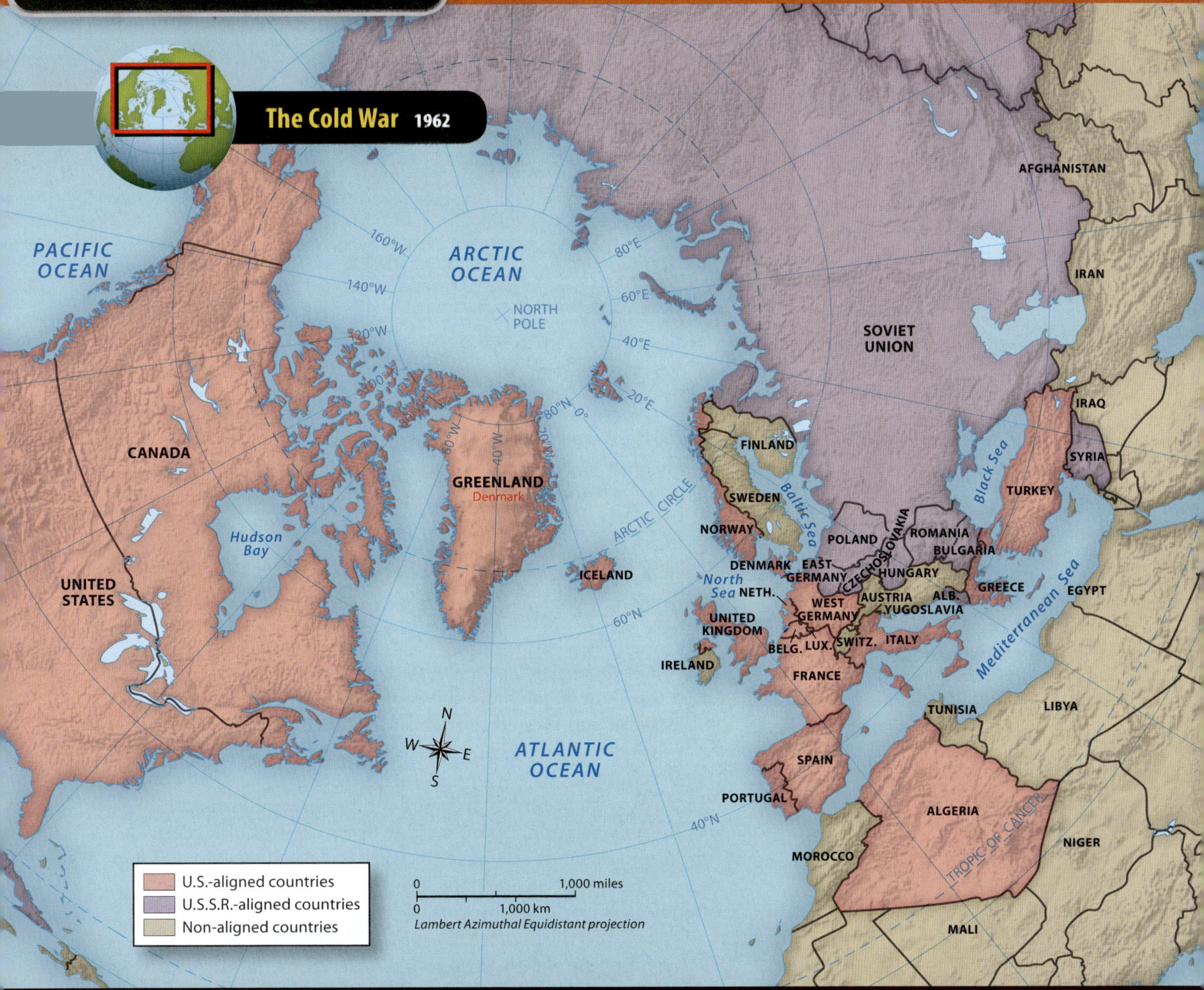

- **1957** Soviets launch Sputnik I
- **1958** Mao Zedong begins the Great Leap Forward
- **1961** Berlin Wall is constructed
- **1962** Cuban missile crisis
- **1965**
- **1966** Mao Zedong launches Great Proletarian Cultural Revolution in China
- **1972** U.S. President Nixon makes a state visit to China
- **1973** Nixon announces Paris Peace Accords
- **1975**
- **April 17, 1975** North Vietnam defeats South Vietnam; war ends

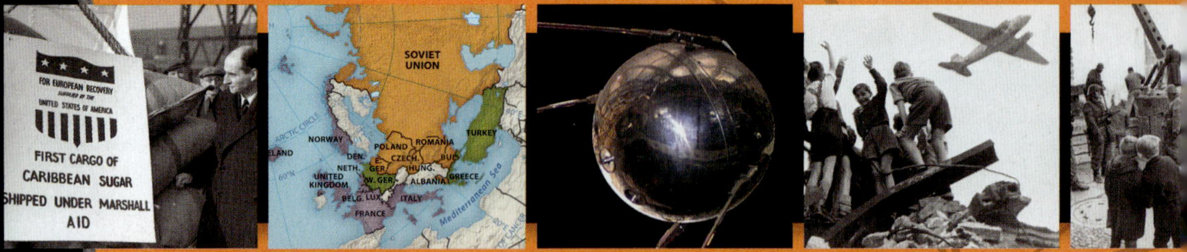

networks

There's More Online!

- BIOGRAPHY Harry S. Truman
- BIOGRAPHY Nikita Khrushchev
- CHART/GRAPH Postwar Economic Plans
- CHART/GRAPH The Nuclear Arms Race
- IMAGE Building the Berlin Wall
- IMAGE Sputnik I
- IMAGE The Marshall Plan
- INTERACTIVE SELF-CHECK QUIZ
- MAP NATO and Warsaw Pact Members, 1949–1955
- VIDEO The Berlin Wall

LESSON 1

The Cold War Begins

ESSENTIAL QUESTION

How does conflict influence political relationships?

Reading **HELP**DESK

Academic Vocabulary

- **liberate**
- **nuclear**

Content Vocabulary

- **satellite state**
- **policy of containment**
- **arms race**
- **deterrence**

TAKING NOTES:

Key Ideas and Details

Determining Cause and Effect As you read, create a chart like the one below listing U.S. actions and the Soviet response to them.

U.S. Action	Soviet Response

TEKS Texas Essential Knowledge and Skills

1F identify major causes and describe the major effects of the following important turning points in world history from 1914 to the present: the world wars and their impact on political, economic, and social systems; communist revolutions and their impact on the Cold War; independence movements; and globalization

continued on the next page

It Matters Because

At the end of World War II, a new conflict erupted in the Western world as the two new superpowers, the United States and the Soviet Union, competed for political domination of the world. Europeans were forced to become supporters of one side or the other.

Balance of Power After World War II

GUIDING QUESTION *Why did the United States and the Soviet Union become political rivals after World War II?*

The defeat of the Axis Powers revealed a growing political divide between the United States and the Soviet Union. Stalin still feared the capitalist West, and Western leaders still had a great fear of communism. It should not surprise us that two such different systems would come into conflict.

Because of its need to feel secure on its western border, the Soviet Union was not prepared to give up its control of Eastern Europe after Germany's defeat. Nor were American leaders willing to give up the power and prestige the United States had gained throughout the world. Suspicious of each other's motives, the United States and the Soviet Union soon became rivals.

Eastern Europe was the first area of disagreement. The United States and Great Britain believed that the **liberated** nations of Eastern Europe should freely determine their own governments. Stalin, however, fearful that these nations would be anti-Soviet if they were permitted to have free elections, opposed the West's plans. Having freed Eastern Europe from the Nazis, the Soviet army stayed in the conquered areas and set up pro-Soviet regimes in Poland, Romania, Bulgaria, and Hungary.

A civil war in Greece created another area of conflict between the superpowers. The Communist People's Liberation Army and anticommunist forces supported by Great Britain fought for control of reece in 1946. However, Britain had its own economic problems, which caused it to withdraw its aid from Greece.

The Truman Doctrine and the Marshall Plan

President Harry S. Truman of the United States, alarmed by British weakness and the possibility of Soviet expansion into the eastern Mediterranean, responded with the Truman Doctrine. This doctrine, created in 1947, said that the United States would provide money to countries (in this case, Greece and Turkey) that were threatened by communist expansion. If the Soviet Union was not stopped in Greece and Turkey, the Truman argument ran, then the United States would have to face the spread of communism throughout the free world. As Dean Acheson, U.S. undersecretary of state, explained on February 29, 1947:

(continued from p. 742)

TEKS **Texas Essential Knowledge and Skills**

13C identify the following major events of the Cold War, including the Korean War, the Vietnam War, and the arms race

28C explain the effects of major new military technologies on World War I, World War II, and the Cold War

liberate to free

PRIMARY SOURCE

> "Like apples in a barrel infected by one rotten one, the corruption of Greece would infect Iran and all to the east. It would also carry infection to Africa through Asia Minor and Egypt, and to Europe . . ."
>
> — from *Present at the Creation: My Years in the State Department*

satellite state a country that is economically and politically dependent on another country

The European Recovery Program soon followed the Truman Doctrine. Proposed in June 1947 by General George C. Marshall, U.S. secretary of state, it is better known as the Marshall Plan. Marshall believed that communism was successful only in countries that had economic problems. To prevent the spread of communism and boost economic systems significantly impacted by World War II, the Marshall Plan provided close to $13 billion to rebuild wartorn Europe.

The Marshall Plan did not intend to exclude the Soviet Union or its economically and politically dependent Eastern European **satellite states**. Those states refused to participate, however. According to the Soviet view, the Marshall Plan guaranteed "American loans in return for the relinquishing by the European states of their economic and later also their political independence." The Soviets saw the Marshall Plan as an attempt to buy the support of the smaller European countries.

In 1949 the Soviet Union responded to the Marshall Plan by founding the Council for Mutual Economic Assistance (COMECON) for the economic cooperation of the Eastern European states. COMECON largely failed, however, because the Soviet Union was unable to provide much financial aid.

▲ Goods sent as part of the Marshall Plan arrive at Royal Victoria Dock in London, England, on February 3, 1949.

▶ **CRITICAL THINKING**

Analyzing What was the goal of the Marshall Plan?

By 1947, the split in Europe between the United States and the Soviet Union had become a fact of life. In July 1947, George Kennan, a well-known U.S. diplomat with much knowledge of Soviet affairs, argued for a **policy of containment** to keep communism within its existing boundaries and to prevent further Soviet aggressive moves. Containment of the Soviet Union became formal U.S. policy.

The Division of Germany and the Berlin Airlift

The fate of Germany also became a source of heated contention between the Soviets and the West. At the end of World War II, the Allied Powers had divided Germany into four zones, each occupied by one of the Allies—the United States, the Soviet Union, Great Britain, and France. The city of Berlin, located deep inside the Soviet zone, was also divided into four zones.

policy of containment a plan to keep something, such as communism, within its existing geographical boundaries and prevent further aggressive moves

PHOTO: Edward Miller/Hulton Archive/Getty Images

The foreign ministers of the four occupying powers met repeatedly in an attempt to arrive at a final peace treaty with Germany but had little success. At the same time, Great Britain, France, and the United States gradually began to merge their zones economically. By February 1948, Great Britain, France, and the United States were making plans to unify the three Western sections of Germany (and Berlin) and create a West German government.

The Soviets reacted with a blockade of West Berlin, which allowed neither trucks, nor trains, nor barges to enter the city's three Western zones. Food and supplies could no longer get through to the 2.5 million people in these zones. The Russians hoped to secure economic control of all Berlin and force the Western powers to halt the creation of a separate West German state.

The Western powers faced a dilemma. No one wanted to risk World War III. Therefore, an attempt to break through the Soviet blockade with tanks and trucks was ruled out. However, how could the people in the Western zones of Berlin be kept alive when the whole city was blockaded inside the Soviet zone? The solution was the Berlin Airlift—supplies would be flown in by American and British airplanes. For more than 10 months, more than 200,000 flights carried 2.3 million tons (1.4 million t) of supplies. At the height of the Berlin Airlift, 13,000 tons (11,800 t) of supplies were flown daily to Berlin. The Soviets, also not wanting war, finally gave in and lifted the blockade in May 1949.

The blockade of Berlin increased tensions between the United States and the Soviet Union. It also brought the separation of Germany into two states. In September 1949, the Federal Republic of Germany, or West Germany, was formally created. Its capital was Bonn. Less than a month later, a separate East German state, the German Democratic Republic, was set up by the Soviets. East Berlin became its capital. Berlin was now divided into two parts, a reminder of the division between West and East.

SKILLS PRACTICE

Work with a group. As you study the beginning of the Cold War, look at the pictures and boldfaced words in your text. Ask group members to tell you what they know about a topic, and tell them what you know.

✓ READING PROGRESS CHECK

Comparing What did the Marshall Plan and COMECON have in common?

The Spread of the Cold War

GUIDING QUESTION ***What was the result of increased tensions between the superpowers?***

In 1949 the Cold War spread from Europe to the rest of the world. The victory of the Chinese Communists in the Chinese civil war created a new Communist regime and strengthened fears in the United States about the spread of communism.

▼ German children cheer an American cargo plane airlifting supplies to Berlin in 1948.

▶ CRITICAL THINKING

Sequencing What were the effects of the Berlin airlift?

PHOTO: Bettmann/CORBIS

GEOGRAPHY CONNECTION

1. **THE WORLD IN SPATIAL TERMS** *How could geographic factors have determined which alliance a country joined?*
2. **PLACES AND REGIONS** *Create a chart listing all the NATO and Warsaw Pact countries as of 1955.*

New Military Alliances

The search for security during the Cold War led to the formation of new military alliances. The North Atlantic Treaty Organization (NATO) was formed in April 1949 when Belgium, Luxembourg, France, the Netherlands, Great Britain, Italy, Denmark, Norway, Portugal, and Iceland signed a treaty with the United States and Canada. These powers agreed to provide mutual help if any one of them was attacked. A few years later, Greece and Turkey joined, followed by West Germany.

The Eastern European states soon followed suit with a military alliance. In 1955 the Soviet Union joined with Albania, Bulgaria, Czechoslovakia, East Germany, Hungary, Poland, and Romania in a formal military alliance known as the Warsaw Pact. Europe was once again divided into hostile alliance systems, just as it had been before World War I.

New military alliances spread to the rest of the world after the United States became involved in the Korean War. The war began in 1950 as an attempt by the Communist government of North Korea, which was allied with the Soviet Union, to take over South Korea. The Korean War confirmed American fears of communist expansion. More determined than ever to contain Soviet power, the United States extended its military alliances around the world. By the mid-1950s, the United States was in military alliances with 42 states around the world.

The Arms Race Begins

By the mid-1950s, the United States and the Soviet Union had become involved in a growing **arms race**, in which both countries built up their armies and increased the sizes of their weapons arsenals. New military technologies, such as **nuclear** weapons, added an increasingly frightening element to the Cold War as each superpower raced to build deadlier bombs and farther-reaching delivery systems.

arms race building up armies and stores of weapons to keep up with an enemy

nuclear being a weapon whose destructive power comes from a nuclear reaction

▲ The Soviet Union launched *Sputnik I*, the first artificial satellite, on October 4, 1957.

▶ **CRITICAL THINKING**

Explaining What was the significance of the *Sputnik I* launch?

deterrence during the Cold War, the U.S. and Soviet policies of holding huge arsenals of nuclear weapons to prevent war; each nation believed that neither would launch a nuclear attack since both knew that the other side could strike back with devastating power

Also by the mid-1950s, the United States feared that the Soviet Union was gaining ground in the arms race. The Soviet Union had set off its first atomic bomb in 1949. In the early 1950s, the Soviet Union and the United States developed the deadlier hydrogen bomb. By the late-1950s, both had intercontinental ballistic missiles (ICBMs), which made them capable of sending bombs anywhere.

The United States and the Soviet Union now worked to build up stockpiles of nuclear weapons. The search for security soon took the form of **deterrence**. This policy held that huge arsenals of nuclear weapons on both sides prevented war. The belief was that neither side would launch a nuclear attack, because both knew that the other side would be able to strike back with devastating power.

In 1957 the Soviets sent *Sputnik I,* the first human-made space satellite, to orbit Earth. New fears seized the American public. Was there a "missile gap" between the United States and the Soviet Union? Could the Soviet Union build a military base in outer space from which itcould dominate the world? One American senator said, "It was time... for Americans to be prepared to shed blood, sweat and tears if this country and the free world are to survive."

A Wall in Berlin

Nikita Khrushchev (kroosh • CHAWF), who emerged as the new leader of the Soviet Union in 1955, tried to take advantage of the American concern over missiles to solve the problem of West Berlin. West Berlin remained a "Western island" of prosperity in the midst of the relatively poverty-stricken East Germany. Many East Germans, tired of Communist repression, managed to escape East Germany by fleeing through West Berlin.

Khrushchev realized the need to stop the flow of refugees from East Germany through West Berlin. In August 1961, the East German government began to build a wall separating West Berlin from East Berlin. Eventually it became a massive concrete block wall 15 feet (4.5 m) high topped with barbed wire. Hundreds of machine-gun watchtowers lined the wall, which stretched 28 miles (45km) through the city. Another 75-mile-(120.7-km) long section of wall separated West Berlin from the surrounding East German countryside. The Berlin Wall became a striking symbol of the division between the two superpowers.

✓ **READING PROGRESS CHECK**

Making Connections How were the theory of deterrence and the arms race related?

PHOTO: NASA

LESSON 1 REVIEW TEKS

Reviewing Vocabulary

1. ***Applying*** Explain how the United States and the Soviet Union used nuclear weapons as a form of deterrence.

Using Your Notes

2. ***Identifying*** Use your notes to write a paragraph explaining how the Soviets responded to U.S. actions.

Answering the Guiding Questions

3. ***Analyzing*** Why did the United States and the Soviet Union become political rivals after World War II?
4. ***Drawing Conclusions*** What was the result of increased tensions between the superpowers?

Writing Activity

5. **ARGUMENT** Write an essay arguing whether using nuclear weapons as a form of deterrence was an effective strategy for preventing conflict between the West and the Soviet Union.

networks

There's More Online!

- CHART/GRAPH Grain Production in China, 1950–1970
- IMAGE Cultural Revolution Propaganda
- IMAGE The Little Red Book
- IMAGE The Red Guard
- INTERACTIVE SELF-CHECK QUIZ
- MAP China Since 1945
- PRIMARY SOURCE Life During China's Cultural Revolution
- PRIMARY SOURCE The Little Red Book
- VIDEO Mao

LESSON 2

China After World War II

ESSENTIAL QUESTION

How does conflict influence political relationships?

Reading HELPDESK

Academic Vocabulary

- **final**
- **source**

Content Vocabulary

- **commune**
- **permanent revolution**

TAKING NOTES:

Key Ideas and Details

Categorizing As you read, use a chart like the one below to list communism's effects on China's international affairs.

Communism → [ ] / → [ ] / → [ ]

TEKS Texas Essential Knowledge and Skills

1F identify major causes and describe the major effects of the following important turning points in world history from 1914 to the present: the world wars and their impact on political, economic, and social systems; communist revolutions and their impact on the Cold War; independence movements; and globalization

continued on the next page

IT MATTERS BECAUSE

In 1949 Chiang Kai-shek finally lost control of China, and the Communist Mao Zedong announced the formation of the People's Republic of China. Mao's victory strengthened U.S. fears about the spread of communism. To build his socialist society in China, Mao Zedong launched the Great Leap Forward and the Great Proletarian Cultural Revolution. Neither program was especially successful at achieving its goals.

Civil War in China

GUIDING QUESTIONS *How did Mao use economic policies to try to establish a classless society? Why did Mao believe permanent revolution was necessary?*

At the end of World War II, two Chinese governments existed side by side. The Nationalist government of Chiang Kai-shek, based in southern and central China, was supported by the United States. The Communists, led by Mao Zedong, had built a strong base in northern China. By the end of World War II, 20 to 30 million Chinese were living under Communist rule. The People's Liberation Army of the Communists included nearly 1 million troops.

When efforts to form a coalition government in 1946 failed, a full-scale civil war broke out between the Nationalists and the Communists. In the countryside, promises of land attracted millions of peasants to the Communist Party. Many joined Mao's People's Liberation Army. In the cities, middle-class Chinese, who were alienated by Chiang's repressive policies, supported the Communists. Chiang's troops began to defect to the Communists. Sometimes whole divisions—officers and ordinary soldiers—changed sides.

By 1948, the People's Liberation Army had surrounded Beijing. The following spring it crossed the Chang Jiang (Yangtze River) and occupied Shanghai. During the next few months, Chiang Kai-shek and 2 million followers fled to the island of Taiwan. Many loyal to the

(continued from p. 747)

TEKS Texas Essential Knowledge and Skills

13B summarize the factors that contributed to communism in China, including Mao Zedong's role in its rise, and how it differed from Soviet communism

22C identify examples of politically motivated mass murders in Cambodia, China, Latin America, the Soviet Union, and Armenia

24A describe the changing roles of women, children, and families during major eras of world history

Nationalist government who were left behind, however, were killed in acts of political mass murder. On October 1, 1949, Mao Zedong mounted the rostrum of the Gate of Heavenly Peace in Beijing and made a victory statement to the thousands gathered in the square before him. "The Chinese people have stood up," he said, "nobody will insult us again."

The Great Leap Forward

The Communist Party, under the leadership of its chairman, Mao Zedong, now ruled China. In 1955 the Chinese government launched a new program to build a socialist society. Virtually all private farmland was collectivized. Peasant families were allowed to keep small plots for their private use, but they worked chiefly in large collective farms. In addition, most industry and commerce were nationalized.

Chinese leaders hoped that collective farms would increase food production, allowing more people to work in industry. Food production, however, did not grow. Meanwhile, China's vast population continued to expand. By 1957, China had approximately 657 million people living within its borders.

In 1958 Mao began a more radical program known as the Great Leap Forward. Under this program, more than 700,000 existing collective farms, normally the size of a village, were combined into 26,000 vast **communes**. Each commune contained more than 30,000 people who lived and worked together. Since they had communal child care, more than 500,000 Chinese mothers worked beside their husbands in the fields by mid-1958.

Mao Zedong hoped his Great Leap Forward program would mobilize the people for a massive effort to speed up economic growth and reach the **final** stage of communism—the classless society—before the end of the twentieth century. The Communist Party's official slogan promised the following to the Chinese people: "Hard work for a few years, happiness for a thousand."

commune in China during the 1950s, a group of collective farms, which contained more than 30,000 people who lived and worked together

final the last in a series, process, or progress

Despite such slogans, the Great Leap Forward was an economic disaster. Bad weather, which resulted in droughts and floods, and the peasants' hatred of the new system, drove food production down. Nearly 15 million people died in the resulting famine. Some groups in Chinese society were killed at this time in acts of political mass murder. Members of what Mao considered "black elements" of society, like political enemies and religious or wealthy citizens were given the lowest priority for food distribution. In 1960 the government made some changes. It began to break up the communes and return to collective farms and some private plots.

▼ A Chinese woman and child hold up Mao's *Little Red Book* during the Cultural Revolution.

▶ **CRITICAL THINKING**

Describing What one word would you use to describe the *Little Red Book* during the Cultural Revolution? Why?

The Cultural Revolution

Despite opposition within the Communist Party and the commune failure, Mao still dreamed of a classless society. In Mao's eyes, only **permanent revolution**, an atmosphere of constant revolutionary fervor, could enable the Chinese to overcome the past and achieve the final stage of communism.

In 1966 Mao launched the Great Proletarian Cultural Revolution. The Chinese name literally meant "great revolution to create a proletarian (working class) culture." A collection of Mao's thoughts, called the *Little Red Book*, became a sort of bible for the Chinese Communists. It was hailed as the most important **source** of knowledge in all areas. The book was in every hotel, in every school, and in factories, communes, and universities. Few people conversed without first referring to the *Little Red Book*.

To further the Cultural Revolution, the Red Guards were formed. These were revolutionary groups composed of unhappy party members and discontented young people. They were urged to take to the streets to cleanse Chinese society of impure elements guilty of taking the capitalist road. In June 1966, all schools and universities in China were closed for six months to prepare for a new system of education based on Mao's ideas. Mao had launched China on a new forced march toward communism.

The Red Guards set out across the nation to eliminate the "Four Olds"—old ideas, old culture, old customs, and old habits. The Red Guards destroyed temples, books written by foreigners, and foreign music. They tore down street signs and replaced them with ones carrying revolutionary names. The city of Shanghai even ordered that red (the revolutionary color) traffic lights would indicate that traffic could move, not stop.

Destruction of property was matched by vicious attacks on individuals who had supposedly deviated from Mao's thought. Those so accused were humiliated at public meetings, where they were forced to admit their "crimes." Many were brutally beaten, often fatally. Intellectuals and artists accused of being pro-Western were especially open to attack. Red Guards broke the fingers of one pianist for the "crime" of playing the works of Frederic Chopin, the nineteenth-century European composer. Nien Cheng, who worked for the British-owned Shell Oil Company in Shanghai, was imprisoned for seven years. She told of her experience in *Life and Death in Shanghai.*

From the start of its socialist revolution, the Communist Party had wanted to create a new kind of citizen, one who would give the utmost for the good of all China. In Mao's words, the people "should be resolute, fear no sacrifice, and surmount every difficulty to win victory."

During the 1950s and 1960s, the Chinese government made some basic changes in the roles of women, children, and families. Women could now take part in politics and had equal marital rights—a dramatic shift. Mao feared that loyalty to the family would interfere with loyalty to the state. During the Cultural Revolution, for example, children were encouraged to report negative comments their parents made about the government.

Mao found during the Cultural Revolution, however, that it is not easy to maintain a permanent revolution, or constant mood of revolutionary enthusiasm. Key groups, including Communist Party members and many military officers, did not share Mao's desire for permanent revolution. Many people, disgusted by the actions of the Red Guards, began to turn against the movement. In September 1976, Mao Zedong died at the age of 82. A group of practical-minded reformers, led by Deng Xiaoping (DUHNG SHYOW • PIHNG), seized power and soon brought the Cultural Revolution to an end.

✓ READING PROGRESS CHECK

Drawing Conclusions Why did the Red Guards specifically target intellectuals and artists?

▲ This poster urges the Chinese people to give energetic support to agriculture.

▶ CRITICAL THINKING

Making Inferences Why was agricultural reform particularly important to the Chinese Communists?

permanent revolution an atmosphere of constant revolutionary fervor favored by Mao Zedong to enable China to overcome the past and achieve the final stage of communism

source a document or primary reference book that gives information

China and the Cold War

GUIDING QUESTION *How was China affected by the Cold War?*

In 1949 the Cold War spread from Europe to Asia when the Chinese Communists won the Chinese civil war and set up a new Communist regime. American fears about the spread of communism intensified, especially when the new Chinese Communist leaders made it clear that they supported "national wars of liberation"—or movements for revolution—in Africa, Asia, and Latin America. When Communist China signed a pact of friendship and cooperation with the Soviet Union in 1950, some Americans began to speak of a Communist desire for world domination. When war broke out in Korea, the Cold War had arrived in Asia.

China's involvement in the Korean War led to renewed Western fears of China. In turn, China became even more isolated from the major Western powers. The country was forced to rely almost entirely on the Soviet Union for technological and economic aid.

▲ During Nixon's visit to China, the United States and China competed in ping pong.

▶ **CRITICAL THINKING**

Evaluating What was the significance of Nixon's "ping pong diplomacy"?

PHOTO: John Dominis/Time & Life Pictures/Getty Images

However, several issues divided China and the Soviet Union. For one thing, the Chinese followed a specific version of Communism called Maoism, which valued rural farmers over urban factory workers. Maoists believed that farming peasants, as opposed to the industrial working class, were central to communist revolutions worldwide. A more important issue, however, was their disagreement over the Cold War. Mao did not favor friendly relations with noncommunist states. The Chinese wanted the Soviets to go on the offensive to promote world revolution and help them in retaking Taiwan. The Soviets, however, were trying to improve relations with the West and refused.

In the 1960s, the dispute between China and the Soviet Union broke into the open. Military units on both sides of the frontier clashed on a number of occasions. Faced with internal problems and a serious security threat from the Soviets on its northern frontier, some Chinese leaders decided to improve relations with the United States. In 1972 President Richard Nixon made a state visit to China. The two sides agreed to improve relations. China's long isolation from the West was coming to an end.

The end of the Cultural Revolution also affected Chinese foreign policy. In the late 1970s, under Deng Xiaoping, China sought to improve relations with the Western states. Diplomatic ties were established with the United States in 1979. In the 1980s, Chinese relations with the Soviet Union also gradually improved. By the 1990s, China emerged as an independent power and began to play an increasingly active role in Asian affairs.

✓ **READING PROGRESS CHECK**

Analyzing Why did Chinese-Soviet relations change after the Korean War?

LESSON 2 REVIEW TEKS

Reviewing Vocabulary

1. ***Making Connections*** How did the *Little Red Book* help sustain Mao's Cultural Revolution? 26B

Using Your Notes

2. ***Drawing Conclusions*** Use your notes to describe how communism affected China's foreign policy.

Answering the Guiding Questions

3. ***Summarizing*** How did Mao use economic policies to try and establish a classless society?
4. ***Identifying*** Why did Mao believe permanent revolution was necessary?
5. ***Analyzing*** How was China affected by the Cold War?

Writing Activity

6. **NARRATIVE** Imagine you are a Chinese peasant who was sent to a commune during the Great Leap Forward. Write an essay describing how this event has affected your life.

SKILLBUILDER

TEKS 29E

Identifying Bias in Oral Material

Why Learn This Skill?

Radio talk shows are full of strong opinions. But how do you know what is biased and what isn't? Most shows on commercial radio are loud and boisterous—that's how they get an audience—but does that mean the shows are biased? There is a way to identify bias in oral material, and it is an important skill for the media-savvy citizen.

Learning the Skill

Oral material includes speeches, radio programs, podcasts, and other such material. To detect bias in oral material, follow these steps:

- Identify the speaker's purpose.
- Be on the lookout for loud, dramatic proclamations. The manner in which someone speaks is often an indication of the speaker's purpose. Loud speech often signifies a point the speaker wants you to believe, while quiet speech often signifies a point the speaker wants you to think about.
- As in written material, emotionally charged language is often a sign of bias.
- A speaker's use of oversimplifications sometimes indicates bias and the presence of opinion rather than fact.
- Make sure the speaker is not only presenting a single view.

Practicing the Skill

Read the following excerpt from an address by Nikita Khrushchev in 1956.

"When we say that the socialist system will win in the competition between the two systems—the capitalist and the socialist—this by no means signifies that its victory will be achieved through armed interference by the socialist countries in the internal affairs of the capitalist countries. Our certainty of the victory of communism is based on the fact that the socialist mode of production possesses decisive advantages over the capitalist mode of production. Precisely because of this, the ideas of Marxism-Leninism are more and more capturing the minds of the broad masses of the working people in the capitalist countries, just as they have captured the minds of millions of men and women in our country and the People's Democracies."

Follow the steps above to identify the bias in this material. Note the aggressive language, the speaker's certainty, and the one-sided nature of the argument.

Skills Assessment

After reading the excerpt closely, answer the following questions.

1. What is the purpose of this quote?
2. What are two examples of emotionally charged language?
3. According to Khrushchev, why are the ideas of Marxism-Leninism going to triumph over capitalism?
4. What bias is expressed in this excerpt?

Applying the Skill

Write a speech that you could deliver to your fellow students in an assembly. The speech should be on the topic of a well-known school issue, such as cafeteria food or an upcoming student council election. But here's the twist: Write your speech to be as biased as possible! Do everything you can to make your speech biased, including underlining any passages that should be spoken in a loud or dramatic fashion. Speeches should be 100–200 words. Then present your speech to your class.

SKILLBUILDER

TEKS 15A

Reading a Thematic Map

Why Learn This Skill?

In your study of world history, you will often encounter thematic maps. Knowing how to read a thematic map will help you get more out of it.

Learning the Skill

Military maps use colors, symbols, and arrows to show major battles, troop movements, and defensive positions during a particular battle or over a period of time. When reading a military map, follow these steps:

- **Read the map title.** This will indicate the location and time period covered on the map.
- **Read the map key.** This tells what the symbols on the map represent. For example, battle sites may be indicated by crossed swords or burst shells.
- **Study the map itself.** This will reveal the actual event or sequence of events that took place. Notice the geography of the area and try to determine how it could have affected the events.

Practicing the Skill

The map on this page shows the major battles and troop movements of the Vietnam War. Analyze the information on the map, then answer the following questions.

1. Which countries are shown on this map?
2. What suggests that the war widened in the early 1970s?
3. What neutral countries were bombed by the United States?

Skills Assessment

Create a thematic map that is similar to this map but about the Franco-Prussian War of 1870. Conduct research to find facts about the war using this textbook or a reputable website. Include as many facts as possible and focus on geographic details, such as locations. Use small text boxes to explain how borders changed as a result of the war. When you are finished, trade maps with a partner and spend five minutes studying your partner's map. Afterward, each of you should summarize how the thematic map demonstrates the relationship between geography and the historical development of the region.

Applying the Skill

Write a quiz containing five new questions interpreting the map on this page. Two of the questions should be "identify" questions—dealing with specific details of the geography. Three of the questions must be "critical thinking" questions—addressing the historical development of the region.

networks

There's More Online!

- IMAGE 38th Parallel
- IMAGE Khrushchev and Castro
- INTERACTIVE SELF-CHECK QUIZ
- MAP Cuban Missile Crisis, October 1962
- MAP Korean War, 1950–1953
- MAP Vietnam War, 1968–1975
- VIDEO The Korean War

LESSON 3

Cold War Conflicts

ESSENTIAL QUESTION

How does conflict influence political relationships?

IT MATTERS BECAUSE

In the decades after World War II, the Cold War between the United States and the Soviet Union spread, creating military alliances and defining the postwar era. The competition between the superpowers also affected "hot" wars, especially in Korea and Vietnam.

Reading HELPDESK

Academic Vocabulary

- **temporary**
- **emerge**

Content Vocabulary

- **proxy war**
- **domino theory**

TAKING NOTES:

Key Ideas and Details

Categorizing As you read, use a chart like the one below to list the different proxy wars fought by the United States and the Soviet Union.

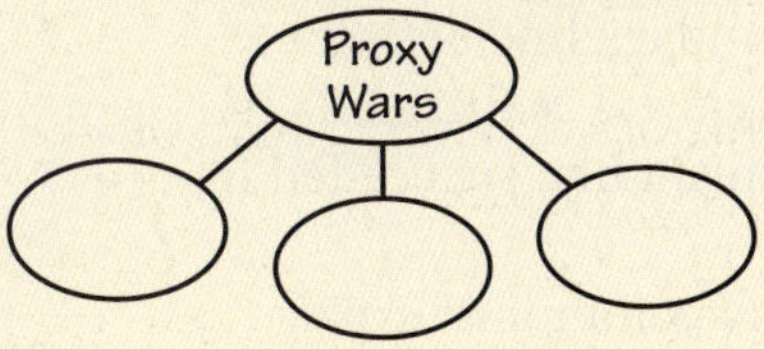

TEKS Texas Essential Knowledge and Skills

1F identify major causes and describe the major effects of the following important turning points in world history from 1914 to the present: the world wars and their impact on political, economic, and social systems; communist revolutions and their impact on the Cold War; independence movements; and globalization

continued on the next page

PHOTO: (l to r)©Bettmann/CORBIS, Library of Congress, Prints & Photographs Division, drawing by Edmund S. Valtman, LC-USZ62-130423, ©US National Archives/Roger-Viollet/The Image Works.

The United States and the Soviet Union

GUIDING QUESTIONS *What common factor triggered the "hot" wars in Asia during the Cold War? How did nuclear weapons influence political relationships during the Cold War?*

World War II destroyed European supremacy in world affairs, and Europe did not recover from this. As the Cold War conflict between the world's two superpowers—the United States and the Soviet Union—grew stronger, the European nations were divided into two armed camps dependent upon one or the other of these two major powers. This division, however, also spread to the rest of the world. The United States and the Soviet Union, whose rivalry brought the world to the brink of nuclear war, seemed to hold the survival of the world in their hands.

Neither power, however, ever went to war directly with the other. Instead, the United States and the Soviet Union fought a series of **proxy wars**. A proxy war occurs when two powers in conflict use substitutes instead of fighting each other directly. Proxy wars were common during the Cold War. Armed with devastating nuclear arsenals, neither the United States nor the Soviet Union wanted to fight each other directly. However, both nations were willing to support opposing sides in local wars in the ongoing struggle between their two worldviews.

Each superpower used military and economic aid to win the support of other nations. In addition to NATO in Europe, the United States also built alliances in other parts of the world. To stem Communist aggression in the East, the United States, Great Britain, France, Pakistan, the Philippines, Australia, and New Zealand

proxy war a war in which the powers in conflict use third parties as substitutes instead of fighting each other directly

formed the Southeast Asia Treaty Organization (SEATO). The Central Treaty Organization (CENTO), which included Turkey, Iraq, Iran, Pakistan, Great Britain, and the United States, was meant to prevent Soviet expansion into the Middle East. The Soviet Union also created a series of alliances.

Two major conflicts of the Cold War were the wars that broke out in Korea and Vietnam. The Soviet Union and the United States each sent military support to prevent the other side from expanding its influence. In addition, a Cold War proxy conflict almost turned into a major nuclear war over the small island of Cuba.

(continued from p. 753)

TEKS Texas Essential Knowledge and Skills
13C identify the following major events of the Cold War, including the Korean War, the Vietnam War, and the arms race

✓ **READING PROGRESS CHECK**

Comparing What did NATO, SEATO, and CENTO have in common?

The Korean War

GUIDING QUESTION ***What common factor triggered the "hot" wars in Asia during the Cold War?***

Japan controlled Korea until 1945. In August 1945, the Soviet Union and the United States agreed to divide Korea into two zones at the 38th parallel. The plan was to hold elections after World War II to reunify Korea. As American-Soviet relations grew worse, however, two separate governments emerged in Korea—Communist in the north and anti-Communist in the south.

▲ **United Nations forces withdraw from P'yŏngyang, North Korea, recrossing the 38th parallel, the dividing line between North and South Korea.**

Tension between the two governments increased. With the apparent approval of Joseph Stalin, Communist North Korean troops invaded South Korea on June 25, 1950. President Harry S. Truman of the United States, seeing this as yet another example of Communist aggression and expansion, gained the approval of the United Nations (UN) and sent U.S. troops to repel the invaders. Several other countries sent troops as well. In October, UN forces—mostly American—marched across the 38th parallel with the aim of unifying Korea. Greatly alarmed, the Chinese sent hundreds of thousands of troops into North Korea and pushed UN forces back across the 38th parallel.

Three more years of fighting led to no final victory. An armistice was finally signed in 1953. The 38th parallel remained, and remains today, the boundary line between North Korea and South Korea. The division of Korea was reaffirmed. To many Americans, the policy of containing communism had succeeded in Asia, just as it had earlier in Europe.

The Korean War also confirmed American fears of communist expansion. The United States was now more determined than ever to contain Soviet power. In the mid-1950s, the administration of President Dwight D. Eisenhower adopted a policy of massive retaliation. Any Soviet advance, even a ground attack in Europe, would be met with the full use of American nuclear bombs. Moreover, it was after the Korean War that American military alliances were extended around the world. As President Eisenhower explained, "The freedom we cherish and defend in Europe and in the Americas is no different from the freedom that is imperiled in Asia."

✓ **READING PROGRESS CHECK**

Determining Cause and Effect What effects did the Korean War have on U.S. foreign policy in the mid-1950s?

The Cuban Missile Crisis

GUIDING QUESTION *How did nuclear weapons influence political relationships during the Cold War?*

During the administration of John F. Kennedy, the Cold War confrontation between the United States and the Soviet Union reached frightening levels. In 1959 a left-wing revolutionary named Fidel Castro overthrew the Cuban dictator Fulgencio Batista and set up a Soviet-supported totalitarian regime in Cuba. Having a socialist regime with Communist contacts so close to the mainland was considered to be a threat to the security of the United States.

President Kennedy feared that if he moved openly against Castro, then the Soviets might retaliate by moving against Berlin. As a result, the stage might be set for the two superpowers to engage in a nuclear war.

For months, Kennedy considered alternatives. He finally approved a plan that the CIA had proposed. Exiled Cuban fighters would invade Cuba at the Bay of Pigs. The purpose of the invasion was to cause a revolt against Castro. The invasion, which began on Sunday, April 16, 1961, was a disaster. By Wednesday, the exiled fighters began surrendering. One hundred fourteen died; the rest were captured by Castro's troops.

After the Bay of Pigs, the Soviet Union sent advisers to Cuba. In 1962 Khrushchev began to place nuclear missiles in Cuba, which were meant to counteract U.S. nuclear weapons placed in Turkey. Khrushchev said: "Your rockets are stationed in Turkey. You are worried over Cuba . . . because it lies at a distance of 90 miles across the sea from the shores of the United States. However, Turkey lies next to us."

SKILLS PRACTICE

Look at titles, notifications, warnings, and other labels to find words that appear in this lesson. Think about what the words mean and how they relate to the use of these same words in this lesson.

ANALYZING PRIMARY SOURCES

▲ This American political cartoon was published on October 30, 1962. Khrushchev is depicted as a dentist removing Castro's teeth, which appear as missiles.

The Cuban Missile Crisis

The Cuban missile crisis brought the United States and the Soviet Union to the brink of nuclear war. It was, perhaps, the most frightening moment of the Cold War. These sources focus on Khrushchev's agreement to remove Soviet missiles from Cuba.

"I appreciate your assurance that the United States will not invade Cuba. Hence, we have ordered our officers to stop building bases, dismantle the equipment, and send it back home.

We must not allow the situation to deteriorate, (but) eliminate hotbeds of tension, and we must see to it that no other conflicts occur which might lead to a world nuclear war."

—Letter from Nikita Khrushchev to President John F. Kennedy, October 28, 1962

DBQ Analyzing Historical Documents

1. ***Analyzing Primary Sources*** What does the letter to President Kennedy suggest about Khrushchev's reaction to the crisis?

2. ***Drawing Conclusions*** Look at the caption of the cartoon on the left. What point is the cartoonist making about the Cuban missile crisis?

PHOTO: Library of Congress, Prints & Photographs Division, drawing by Edmund S. Valtman, LC-USZ62-130423

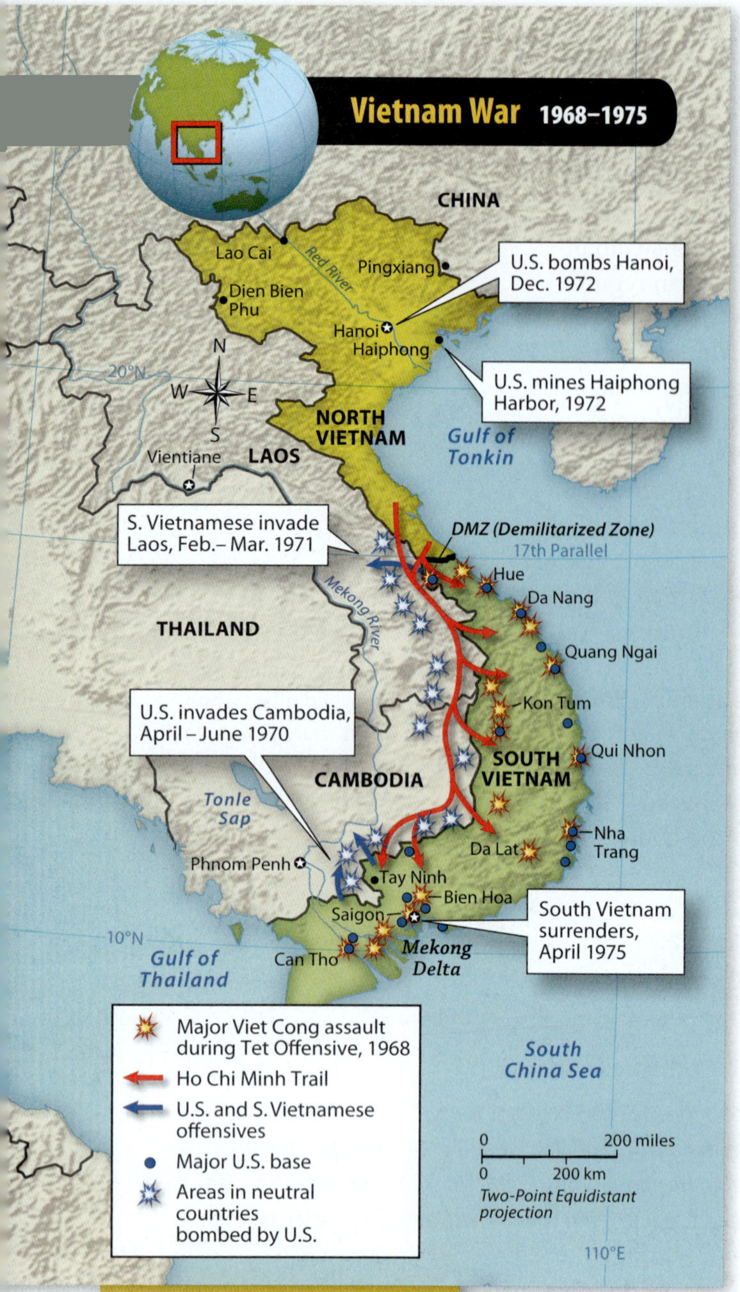

GEOGRAPHY CONNECTION

1. **THE USES OF GEOGRAPHY** *What suggests that the war widened in the early 1970s?*
2. **THE WORLD IN SPATIAL TERMS** *What neutral countries were bombed by the United States?*

temporary lasting for a limited time; not permanent

The United States was not willing to allow nuclear weapons within such close striking distance of its mainland. In October 1962, Kennedy found out that Soviet ships carrying missiles were heading to Cuba. He decided to blockade Cuba to prevent the fleet from reaching its destination. This approach gave each side time to find a peaceful solution. Khrushchev agreed to turn back the fleet and remove Soviet missiles from Cuba if Kennedy pledged not to invade Cuba.

The Cuban missile crisis seemed to bring the world frighteningly close to nuclear war. Indeed, in 1992 a high-ranking Soviet officer revealed that short-range rockets armed with nuclear devices would have been used against U.S. troops if the United States had invaded Cuba, an option that Kennedy fortunately had rejected. The realization that the world might have been destroyed in a few days had a profound influence on both sides. A hotline communications system between Moscow and Washington, D.C., was installed in 1963. The two superpowers could now communicate quickly in times of crisis.

✓ **READING PROGRESS CHECK**

Summarizing How was the Cuban missile crisis resolved?

The Vietnam War

GUIDING QUESTION *What common factor triggered the "hot" wars in Asia during the Cold War?*

By 1963, the United States had been drawn into a new struggle that had an important impact on the Cold War—the Vietnam War. After World War II, most states in Southeast Asia gained independence from their colonial rulers. The Philippines became independent of the United States in 1946. Great Britain also ended its colonial rule in Southeast Asia. France refused, however, to let go of Indochina. This led to a long war in Vietnam.

Leading the struggle against French colonial rule was the local Communist Party, headed by Ho Chi Minh. In August 1945, the Vietminh, an alliance of forces under Communist leadership, seized power throughout most of Vietnam. Ho Chi Minh was elected president of a new republic in Hanoi. Refusing to accept the new government, France seized the southern part of the country. For years, France fought Ho Chi Minh's Vietminh for control of Vietnam without success. In 1954, after a huge defeat at Dien Bien Phu, France agreed to sign the Geneva Peace Accords. Because of the Korean War, China and the Soviet Union wanted to avoid another conflict with the United States. They pressured Vietnam to agree to a **temporary** partition of Vietnam. This was meant to save French pride and satisfy the Americans. Vietnam was divided into two parts. In the north were the Communists, based in Hanoi; in the south, the non-Communists, based in Saigon.

Both sides agreed to hold elections in two years to create a single government. Instead, the conflict continued, and Vietnam soon became part of the Cold War. The United States, opposed to the spread of communism, aided South Vietnam under nationalist leader Ngo Dinh Diem. In spite of this aid, the Viet Cong, South Vietnamese Communist guerrillas supported by North Vietnam, were on the verge of seizing control of the entire country by early 1965. Their forces also received military aid from China.

In March 1965, President Johnson sent troops to South Vietnam to keep the Communist regime of North Vietnam from gaining control of South Vietnam. U.S. policy makers saw the conflict in terms of a **domino theory** concerning the spread of communism. If the Communists succeeded in South Vietnam, the argument went, all the other countries in Asia that were freeing themselves from colonial domination would likewise fall (like dominoes) to communism.

domino theory idea that if one country falls to communism, neighboring countries will also fall

North Vietnam responded to the American troops by sending more forces into the south. Despite the massive superiority in equipment and firepower of the American forces, the United States failed to defeat the North Vietnamese. The growing number of American troops in Vietnam soon produced an antiwar movement in the United States, especially among college students of draft age. The mounting destruction of the conflict, seen on television, also turned public opinion against the war.

President Johnson, condemned for his handling of the costly and indecisive war, decided not to run for reelection. Former vice president Richard M. Nixon won the election with his pledge to stop the war and bring the American people together. Finally, in 1973, President Nixon reached an agreement with North Vietnam in the Paris Peace Accords that allowed the United States to withdraw its forces. Within two years after the American withdrawal, Communist armies from the North had forcibly reunited Vietnam.

Despite the success of the North Vietnamese Communists, the domino theory proved to be unfounded. A noisy split between Communist China and the Soviet Union put an end to the Western idea that there was a single form of communism directed by Moscow. Under President Nixon, American relations with China were resumed. New nations in Southeast Asia also managed to avoid Communist governments. Above all, Vietnam helped show the limitations of American power. By the end of the Vietnam War, a new era in American-Soviet relations had begun to **emerge**.

emerge to come into being through evolution

✓ READING PROGRESS CHECK

Applying Why is the Vietnam War sometimes understood as a proxy war?

LESSON 3 REVIEW TEKS

Reviewing Vocabulary

1. ***Identifying*** Why did the domino theory cause the United States to become involved in Vietnam?

Using Your Notes

2. ***Classifying*** Use your notes to identify the proxy wars the United States was involved in during the Cold War.

Answering the Guiding Questions

3. ***Making Generalizations*** What common factor triggered the "hot" wars in Asia during the Cold War?
4. ***Analyzing*** How did nuclear weapons influence political relationships during the Cold War?

Writing Activity

5. **INFORMATIVE/EXPLANATORY** Pick one of the proxy wars discussed in the lesson and write a short paragraph explaining why the United States decided it was important to fight the war.

CHAPTER 31 Assessment

TEKS

Directions: On a separate sheet of paper, answer the questions below. Make sure you read carefully and answer all parts of the questions.

Lesson Review

Lesson 1

1. ***Explaining*** Explain the thinking behind the Marshall Plan. What was the Soviet plan that attempted to rival it?

2. ***Identifying Cause and Effect*** What was the North Atlantic Treaty Organization? Why was it formed?

3. ***Explaining*** Why did Khrushchev support the building of the Berlin Wall? Describe the military enforcement at the wall.

4. ***Summarizing*** What events led to the Berlin Airlift? How did the Soviets react?

5. ***Explaining*** What effect did nuclear reaction technology have on the Cold War? **28C**

Lesson 2

6. ***Exploring Issues*** What steps did Mao Zedong take to increase food production? What were their effects? Why could the outcome be considered politically motivated mass murder? **22C**

7. ***Describing*** Who were the Red Guards? What did the Red Guards do to enforce the Cultural Revolution?

8. ***Explaining*** Why were artists and musicians often targets of the Red Guard?

9. ***Identifying Perspectives*** What was Mao's perspectives on family loyalty, and how did he encourage children to put the state first?

10. ***Describing Relationships*** Describe the dynamic between China and the Soviet Union in the late 1950s. On what issues did the two nations disagree?

Lesson 3

11. ***Explaining*** What is a proxy war? What two proxy wars were the Soviet Union and the United States involved in during the Cold War?

12. ***Drawing Conclusions*** How did the Cuban missile crisis ultimately create common ground between the Soviet Union and the United States?

13. ***Identifying*** Explain the role of communication technology once the U.S. and Soviet Union resolved the Cuban missile crisis, and how might have the technology been innovative at that time?

14. ***Sequencing*** What sequence of events followed after the division of Korea into two zones?

Exploring the Essential Question

15. ***Identifying Causes and Effects*** Write a five-paragraph essay explaining how conflict affected the political relationship between the Soviet Union and the United States during the Cold War. Make sure you write about several events throughout the chapter that caused conflict, such as the impact of World War II on political and economic systems, or the communist revolutions. Describe how each event positively or negatively influenced the relationship. Create a graphic organizer showing the events cited. **1F**

Need Extra Help?

If You've Missed Question	1	2	3	4	5	6	7	8	9	10	11	12	13	14	15
Go to page	741	743	744	741	743	746	747	747	747	748	751	753	754	752	751

Critical Thinking

16 ***Describing and Evaluating*** Describe the arms race between the United States in the 1950s. Evaluate whether each group was reactionary, strategic, or both.

17 ***Making Inferences*** What can you infer about the widespread publication and reference of the *Little Red Book?*

18 ***Sequencing*** How long did the Great Proletarian Cultural Revolution last? How did it come to an end?

19 ***Understanding Relationships*** When and how did the Cold War spread from Europe to Asia?

20 ***Analyzing*** How did Cold War fears help lead to the partition of Vietnam? Did the partition have the intended effect? Explain how the United States responded.

21 ***Analyzing Information*** Create a chart to analyze the Cold War proxy wars and combat wars of Vietnam and Korea. Include sections for each type of war and then specific examples for each type. Offer a summary based on the sets of notes. Analyze the ways one type of war is different from the other and similar to one another.

22 ***Analyzing Arguments*** Some U.S. policy makers believed in the domino theory—if the Communists conquered South Vietnam, then other countries in that region would eventually be conquered as well. Did the theory turn out to be valid? Explain.

23 ***Constructing Arguments*** Construct an argument that supports or refutes the viewpoint of the domino theory. Offer reasons to support your argument.

Social Studies Skills

24 ***Identifying Cause and Effect*** What caused the independence movement in Vietnam? What were the effects? **1F**

25 ***Creating Thematic Maps*** Create a map that shows the relationship between geography and the historical development of the "Iron Curtain" between 1949 and 1955. Write a caption that explains your map. **15A**

26 ***Summarizing*** How did communism in China differ from Soviet communism? **13B**

27 ***Synthesizing*** How did the roles of women, children, and families change in Communist China? **24A**

28 ***Research Skills*** Research the construction of the Berlin Wall and share your findings in a visual and written presentation. If possible, conduct interviews with people who were affected by the wall's construction. Display or post presentations across classrooms, in a school media center, or on a school Web site or blog. **30C**

29 ***Creating Time Lines*** Create a time line showing government and military activity in China beginning in 1948 with the People's Liberation Army entering Beijing and concluding with Mao Zedong's death in 1976. Provide a brief description for each point on the time line.

Need Extra Help?

If You've Missed Question	16	17	18	19	20	21	22	23	24	25	26	27	28	29
Go to page	743	746	746	743	754	751	755	755	754	742	741	747	744	745

DBQ Analyzing Historical Documents

Use the document to answer the following questions.

After World War II, Berlin was divided into four sectors, one each for the British, the French, the Americans, and the Soviets.

30 ***Interpreting Thematic Maps*** What does this map tell you about the relationship between geography and the historical development of postwar Berlin? **15A**

31 ***Predicting Consequences*** How might the separation of East and West Berlin by the wall have affected the economic life of the city?

Analyzing Visuals

Use the image to answer the following questions.

In 1948, the Soviet Union completely blocked all routes into West Berlin. This photograph shows German children in West Berlin waving to an American cargo plane airlifting supplies into the city.

32 ***Interpreting*** How do the children in the photograph feel about the arrival of the American cargo plane? How can you tell? Why do you think they feel this way?

33 ***Making Inferences*** How might this photograph influence international opinion of communism?

34 ***Theorizing*** How might have the activity shown in the photograph have impacted international relations in the years following, and why?

Extended Response Question

35 ***Informative/Explanatory*** Compare and contrast U.S. foreign policy that conflicted with the Soviet Union and China throughout the Cold War.

Need Extra Help?

If You've Missed Question	30	31	32	33	34	35
Go to page	758	758	758	758	758	743

Independence and Nationalism in the Developing World

1945–1993

ESSENTIAL QUESTIONS • *How can political change cause conflict?* • *How can political relationships affect economic relationships?*

networks

There's More Online! about independence and nationalism in the developing world.

CHAPTER 32

The Story Matters…

In 1950 the South African government passed laws segregating black Africans from white Africans. This system of legalized racism is known as apartheid. Opposition and resistance to apartheid came from leaders within South Africa, such as Nelson Mandela. Mandela, head of the African National Congress, was imprisoned for 27 years because of his protests. Following his release, Mandela led negotiations to transform the South African government into one based on equality. In 1994 he became South Africa's first democratically elected black president.

◄ In 1993 Mandela received the Nobel Peace Prize. He is shown here just after his release from prison in 1990.

PHOTO: © Louise Gubb/Corbis SABA

Place and Time: Africa and Asia 1945–1993

After World War II, the map of the world was dramatically transformed as colonies in Africa and Asia won their independence from European powers. But even after these nations gained their independence, they struggled to maintain balanced economies and political stability.

Step Into the Place

Read the quote and look at the information presented on the map.

DBQ What were the goals of nationalist leaders?

PRIMARY SOURCE

“For centuries, Europeans dominated the African continent. The white man arrogated to himself the right to rule and to be obeyed by the non-white; his mission, he claimed, was to 'civilise' Africa. Under this cloak, the Europeans robbed the continent of vast riches and inflicted unimaginable suffering on the African people. All this makes a sad story . . . All we ask of the former colonial powers is their goodwill and co-operation to remedy past mistakes and injustices and to grant independence to the colonies in Africa.”

—Kwame Nkrumah, from *I Speak of Freedom*, 1961

Step Into the Time

Choose an event from the time line and explain how it illustrates the struggle for independence or the growth of nationalism in the developing world.

AFRICA AND ASIA

- **1947** India and Pakistan gain independence
- **1948** State of Israel established
- **1949** Indonesia gains independence
- **1957** Ghana becomes first British colony to gain independence

1945 — 1955

THE WORLD

- **1946** Juan Perón is elected president of Argentina
- **1959** Fidel Castro seizes power in Cuba

networks
There's More Online!

- **MAP** Explore the interactive version of this map on Networks.
- **TIME LINE** Explore the interactive version of the time line on Networks.

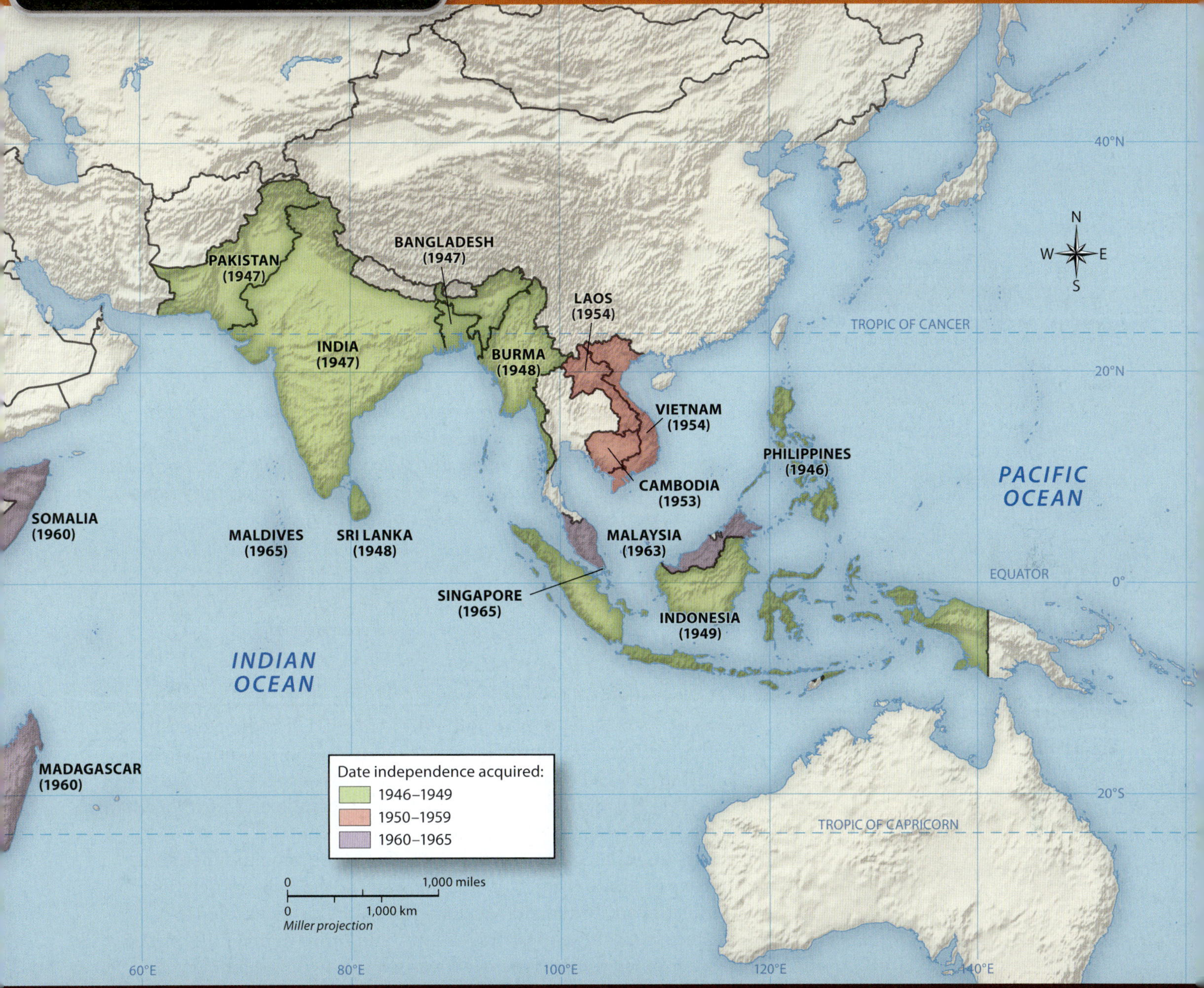

1963 Dr. Martin Luther King, Jr., delivers "I Have a Dream" speech

1965

1966 Indira Gandhi becomes Prime Minister of India

1968 Student uprising in France

1973 U.S. president Richard Nixon signs cease-fire agreement with North Vietnam

1973 Israeli Prime Minister Golda Meir responds to attacks by Egypt and Syria

1975

1979 Egypt-Israel Peace Treaty signed

1979 Reza Shah Pahlavi is overthrown in Iranian revolution

1980 Poland's Solidarity union is founded

1985

1990 Nelson Mandela is released from prison

1991 Aung San Suu Kyi wins Nobel Peace Prize for pro-democracy efforts in Myanmar

1992 Peace settlement ends war in El Salvador

1993 Oslo Accords gives PLO control of semi-independent area

1993

networks

There's More Online!

- BIOGRAPHY Indira Gandhi
- BIOGRAPHY Jawaharlal Nehru
- BIOGRAPHY Mother Teresa
- CHART/GRAPH Religion in India
- IMAGE Aung San Suu Kyi
- IMAGE Refugees Migrate Between India and Pakistan
- IMAGE Student Activists in the Philippines
- INTERACTIVE SELF-CHECK QUIZ
- MAP The Partition of India, 1947
- VIDEO The Assassination of Indira Gandhi

LESSON 1
South and Southeast Asia

ESSENTIAL QUESTIONS • *How can political change cause conflict?* • *How can political relationships affect economic relationships?*

Reading HELPDESK

Academic Vocabulary

- **transfer**
- **role**

Content Vocabulary

- **principle of nonalignment**
- **discrimination**

TAKING NOTES:
Key Ideas and Details

Categorizing As you read, use a web diagram like the one below to identify challenges India faced after gaining independence.

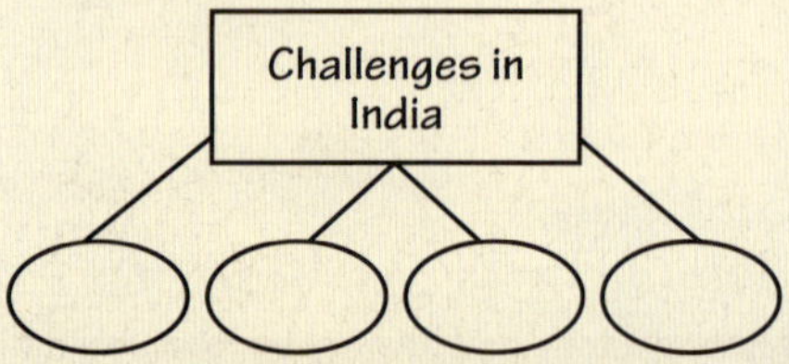

TEKS Texas Essential Knowledge and Skills

1F identify major causes and describe the major effects of the following important turning points in world history from 1914 to the present: the world wars and their impact on political, economic, and social systems; communist revolutions and their impact on the Cold War; independence movements; and globalization

continued on the next page

It Matters Because

Following World War II, many South and Southeast Asian states gained their independence. British India was split into two nations—India and Pakistan. While some Southeast Asian countries have moved toward democracy, they have faced some serious obstacles along that path.

India Divided

GUIDING QUESTION *How did India emerge as an independent country?*

World War II led to the end of British dominion in India. British India's Muslims and Hindus were divided in their independence movements. The leaders in India decided British India would have to be divided into two countries, one Hindu (India) and one Muslim (Pakistan). Pakistan consisted of two regions separated by India. One part, West Pakistan, was to the northwest of India and East Pakistan was to the northeast.

On August 15, 1947, India and Pakistan became independent. Millions of Hindus and Muslims fled across the new borders, Hindus toward India and Muslims toward Pakistan. Violence resulted from these mass migrations, and more than a million people were killed. One of the dead was well known. On January 30, 1948, a Hindu militant assassinated Mohandas Gandhi as he was going to morning prayer. India's new beginning had not been easy.

The New India

Having worked closely with Mohandas Gandhi for Indian independence, Jawaharlal Nehru (juh • WAH • huhr • LAHL NEHR • oo) led the Congress Party, formerly the Indian National Congress. Nehru admired the socialist ideals of the British Labour Party. His goal was a parliamentary government led by a prime minister and a moderate socialist economy. Under Nehru's leadership, the state took ownership of major industries, utilities, and transportation. Private enterprise was allowed at the local level, and farmland was left in private hands. The Indian government also sought to avoid dependence on foreign investment. India developed a large industrial sector, and industrial production almost tripled between 1950 and 1965.

Nehru also guided India's foreign policy according to a **principle of nonalignment**. Concerned about military conflict between the United States and the Soviet Union and about the influence of former colonial powers, Nehru refused to align India with either bloc. Rather, he joined other developing countries in the idea that they should not take sides in the growing Cold War.

After Nehru's death, the Congress Party selected his daughter, Indira Gandhi (not related to Mohandas Gandhi), as prime minister. She held office for most of the time between 1966 and 1984. During her period in office, India grew to be a South Asian regional power. However, India faced many problems during this period. In the 1950s and 1960s, India's population grew by 2 percent a year, contributing to widespread poverty. Millions lived in vast city slums. It was in the slums of Kolkata (formerly Calcutta) that Mother Teresa, a Catholic nun, brought to light the plight of the urban poor in India and became a byword for compassionate care.

Growing ethnic and religious strife presented another major problem. One conflict involved the Sikhs. Some Sikhs wanted autonomy for Punjab, a state in northern India with a Sikh majority. They organized nonviolent protests from the Golden Temple, the most prominent Sikh house of worship. As news of a planned government attack on the Golden Temple leaked, Sikh activists fortified it with arms. Over a thousand Sikhs were killed when the Golden Temple was attacked in June 1984. Soon after, two of Gandhi's Sikh bodyguards assassinated her. In pogroms that followed, thousands more Sikhs were killed.

Conflict between Hindus and Muslims also continued. Religious differences fueled a long-term dispute between India and Pakistan over Kashmir, a territory between the two nations.

Gandhi's son Rajiv replaced his mother as prime minister and began to move the government in new directions. Private enterprise was encouraged, as well as foreign investment. His successors continued to **transfer** state-run industries into private hands and to rely on the free market. This led to a noticeable growth in the middle class.

Rajiv Gandhi was prime minister from 1984 to 1989. While campaigning for reelection in 1991, he was assassinated. In the following years, the Congress Party lost its leadership position and had to compete with new political parties.

principle of nonalignment Jawaharlal Nehru's refusal to align India with any bloc or alliance

transfer to take over the control of

(continued from p. 762)

TEKS **Texas Essential Knowledge and Skills**

13E summarize the rise of independence movements in Africa, the Middle East, and South Asia and reasons for ongoing conflicts

22C identify examples of politically motivated mass murders in Cambodia, China, Latin America, the Soviet Union, and Armenia

23B identify examples of religious influence on various events referenced in the major eras of world history

24B describe the major influences of women such as Elizabeth I, Queen Victoria, Mother Teresa, Indira Gandhi, Margaret Thatcher, and Golda Meir during major eras of world history

▼ **During partition, nearly 2 million refugees fled to either India or Pakistan.**

▶ **CRITICAL THINKING**

Making Inferences Why are the people in the photograph sitting on top of train cars?

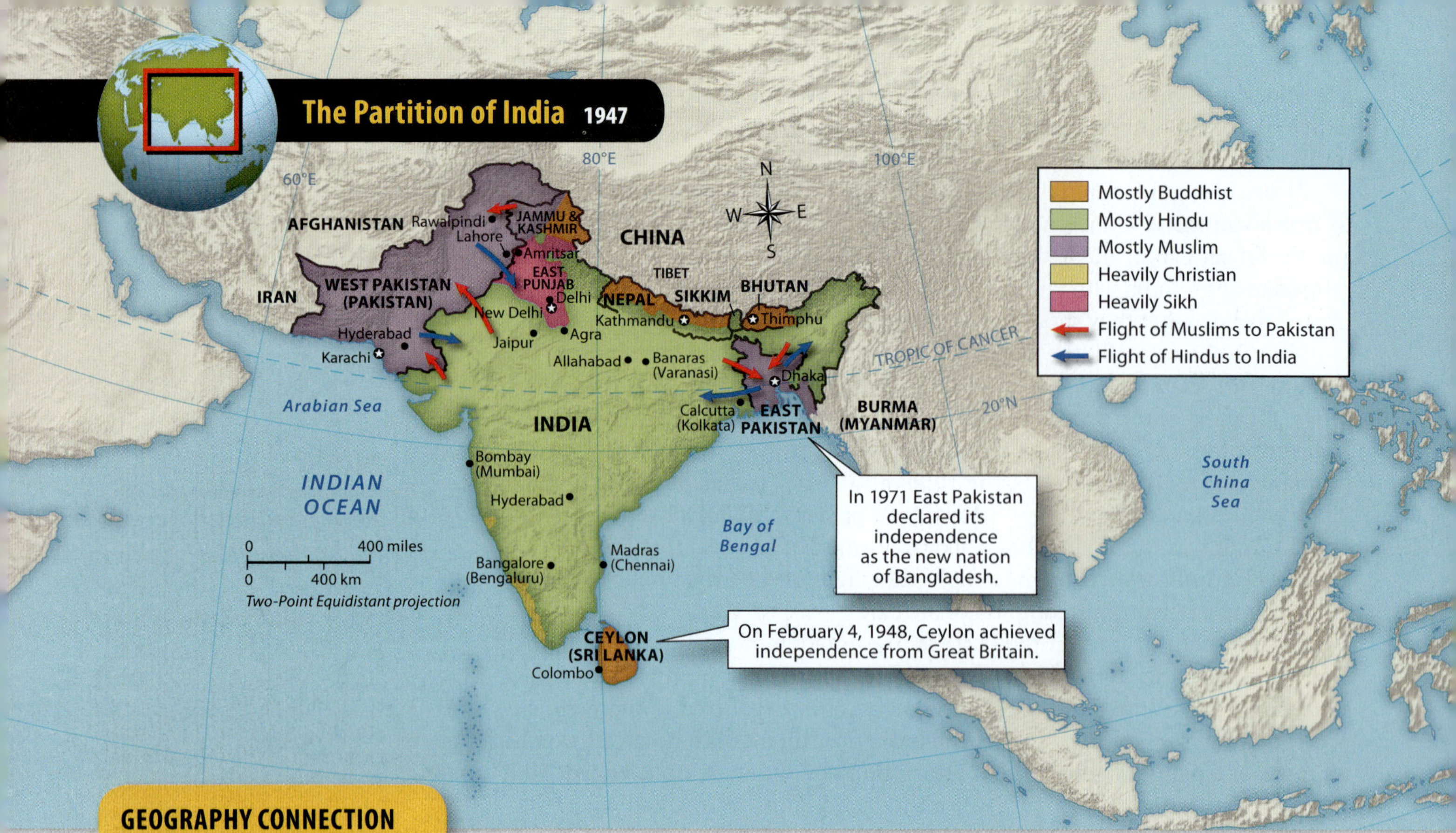

GEOGRAPHY CONNECTION

1. **HUMAN SYSTEMS** *To what areas did India's Muslims flee? Why?*
2. **PLACES AND REGIONS** *The Kashmir region has experienced conflict until the present day. Why do you think this is?*

Pakistan and Bangladesh

Unlike its neighbor India, Pakistan was a completely new nation when it attained independence in 1947. The growing division between East and West Pakistan, separate regions with different geographical features, caused internal conflicts. Many in East Pakistan felt that the government, based in West Pakistan, ignored their needs. In 1971 East Pakistan declared its independence from Pakistan. After a brief civil war, it became the new nation of Bangladesh.

Both Bangladesh and Pakistan (formerly West Pakistan) have remained very poor. They also have had difficulty establishing stable governments. Military officials have often seized control of the civilian government.

✓ READING PROGRESS CHECK

Identifying Cause and Effect What were the immediate effects of the partition of British India?

Southeast Asia

GUIDING QUESTION *What experiences did independence bring to new Southeast Asian countries?*

After World War II, most states in Southeast Asia gained independence from their colonial rulers. The process varied considerably across the region, however. In July 1946, the United States granted total independence to the Philippines. Great Britain was also willing to end its colonial rule in Southeast Asia. In 1948 Burma became independent from Great Britain.

Political changes ignited by World War II spawned independence movements in Southeast Asia. These movements were inspired by Gandhi's actions in India, fueled by colonial participation in the world wars, and made inevitable by the exhaustion post-war Europe. Admiring Western political and economic practices, many Southeast Asia leaders hoped to form democratic, capitalist states. By the end of the 1950s, however, internal disputes weakened the new democratic governments, opening the door to both military and one-party autocratic regimes.

Indonesia and Myanmar

The Netherlands was less willing than Great Britain to abandon its colonial empire in Southeast Asia. The Netherlands tried to suppress a new Indonesian republic proclaimed by Achmed Sukarno. When the Indonesian Communist Party attempted to seize power, however, the United States pressured the Netherlands to grant independence to Sukarno and his non-Communist Nationalist Party. In 1949 the Netherlands recognized the new Republic of Indonesia.

In 1950 the new leaders created a parliamentary system and Sukarno was elected the first president. In the late 1950s, however, he dissolved the constitution and tried to rule on his own through what he called "guided democracy." Sukarno also nationalized foreign-owned enterprises and sought economic aid from China and the Soviet Union. Military officers overthrew Sukarno and established a military government under General Suharto. Democracy had failed.

In Burma, which is now the nation of Myanmar, the military has been in complete control since the early 1960s. The people of Myanmar have continued to fight for democracy, however. Leading the struggle is Aung San Suu Kyi, the daughter of Aung San, who led the Burma Independence Army in 1947. Educated abroad, Suu Kyi returned to Myanmar in 1988 and became involved in the movement for democracy. Her party won a landslide victory in 1990, but the military rulers refused to hand over power. Instead, Suu Kyi was placed under house arrest for many years. In 1991 Suu Kyi won the Nobel Peace Prize for her pro-democracy efforts.

▲ Aung San Suu Kyi, Myanmar's pro-democracy opposition leader.

Vietnam and Cambodia

By 1975, North Vietnamese Communist armies had forcibly reunited Vietnam and begun the process of rebuilding that shattered land. The reunification of Vietnam under Communist rule had an immediate impact on the region. By the end of 1975, both Laos and Cambodia had Communist governments. In Cambodia, Pol Pot, leader of the Khmer Rouge, massacred more than 1 million Cambodians. Pol Pot wanted to eradicate anyone connected with the former government, as well as ethnic minorities and Buddhist monks. It was not until 1993 that Cambodians held free UN-sponsored elections. Meanwhile, the government in Vietnam remained suspicious of Western-style democracy and repressed any opposition to the Communist Party's guiding **role** over the state.

role a socially-expected behavior pattern

The Philippines

In more recent years, some Southeast Asian societies have shown signs of moving again toward more democratic governments. One example is the Philippines. There, President Ferdinand Marcos came to power in 1965. Fraud and corruption became widespread in the Marcos regime. In the early 1980s, Marcos was accused of involvement in the killing of a popular opposition leader, Benigno Aquino. Corazon Aquino, wife of the murdered leader, became president in 1986 and worked for democratic reforms. Nevertheless, she soon proved unable to resolve many of the country's chronic economic and social problems.

▲ Filipino students hold a political rally during the funeral procession of Benigno Aquino.

▶ **CRITICAL THINKING**

Speculating Why are these men featured on the poster?

discrimination prejudicial treatment usually based on race, religion, class, sex, or age

Women in South and Southeast Asia

Across South and Southeast Asia, the rights and roles of women have changed. In India, women's rights expanded after independence. Its constitution of 1950 forbade **discrimination** based on gender and called for equal pay for equal work. Child marriage was also outlawed. Women were encouraged to attend school and to enter the labor market. In Southeast Asia, virtually all the newly independent states granted women full legal and political rights. Women have become more active in politics and occasionally hold senior political or corporate positions.

✓ **READING PROGRESS CHECK**

Comparing What challenges did Indonesia and Myanmar confront following independence?

LESSON 1 REVIEW TEKS

Reviewing Vocabulary

1. ***Applying*** How did the Cold War influence India's principle of nonalignment?

Using Your Notes

2. ***Identifying*** Use your notes to identify some of the problems India faced after its independence.

Answering the Guiding Questions

3. ***Analyzing*** How did India emerge as an independent country?

4. ***Drawing Conclusions*** What experiences did independence bring to new Southeast Asian countries?

Writing Activity

5. **NARRATIVE** Pretend you are a citizen of a South or Southeast Asian country that gained its independence. Write an essay about your experiences.

networks

There's More Online!

- ☑ BIOGRAPHY Gamal Abdel Nasser
- ☑ BIOGRAPHY Golda Meir
- ☑ IMAGE Protest During the Iranian Revolution
- ☑ IMAGE Women in Dubai
- ☑ INTERACTIVE SELF-CHECK QUIZ
- ☑ MAP Arab-Israeli Disputes, 1947–1993
- ☑ PRIMARY SOURCE Cairo Trilogy
- ☑ TIME LINE Arab-Israeli Relations
- ☑ VIDEO The Ayatollah Khomeni

LESSON 2
The Middle East

ESSENTIAL QUESTIONS • *How can political change cause conflict?* • *How can political relationships affect economic relationships?*

Reading HELPDESK

Academic Vocabulary

- **issue**
- **revenue**
- **parallel**

Content Vocabulary

- **Pan-Arabism**
- **intifada**

TAKING NOTES:

Key Ideas and Details

Sequencing As you read, create a table like the one below and list events in the history of Arab-Israeli conflicts.

Year	Event

TEKS **Texas Essential Knowledge and Skills**

1F identify major causes and describe the major effects of the following important turning points in world history from 1914 to the present: the world wars and their impact on political, economic, and social systems; communist revolutions and their impact on the Cold War; independence movements; and globalization

continued on p. 770

IT MATTERS BECAUSE

Since 1948, there have been a number of Arab-Israeli wars in the Middle East. In Iran a revolution established an Islamic Republic while war broke out in Afghanistan. Iraq's conquest of Kuwait led to war in the Middle East.

The Mideast Crisis

GUIDING QUESTION *What key issues underlie the Arab-Israeli conflicts?*

In the Middle East, as in Asia and Africa, a number of independence movements emerged during and after World War II. Syria and Lebanon gained their independence just before the end of the war. Jordan achieved complete self-rule soon afterward.

The Palestine Mandate

In the years between the two world wars, many Jews had immigrated to the Palestine Mandate, which is their historic homeland and religious center. Arab immigration to the mandate also increased. Tensions between Jews and Arabs had intensified during the 1930s. After a massive Arab revolt, that lasted from 1936-1939, Great Britain, which governed the region under a the League of Nations' mandate, decided to limit Jewish immigration into the area and rejected proposals for an independent Jewish state.

The Zionist movement wanted the land of ancient Israel to be a home for the Jewish people and had begun building the institutions necessary for statehood in the late 1900s. Many people had been shocked at the end of World War II when they learned about the deliberate killing of 6 million European Jews in Nazi death camps. As a result, sympathy for the Jewish cause grew. In 1947, the United Nations (UN) voted in favor of a partition plan that divided the Palestine Mandate into a Jewish state and an Arab state. The Arabs rejected the plan, while the Jews accepted it. In accordance with the partition plan, the State of Israel was established on May 14, 1948.

The Arab states saw the creation of the State of Israel as a betrayal of the Palestinian Arabs and rejected the existence of a Jewish state. In

GEOGRAPHY CONNECTION

1. **THE USES OF GEOGRAPHY** *What is the strategic importance of the Sinai Peninsula?*
2. **PLACES AND REGIONS** *What was a result of the 1993 Oslo Peace Accords?*

response five Arab countries invaded Israel. The invasion failed, but the Arab states continued to refuse to recognize the State of Israel, leading to ongoing conflict. As a result of these events, hundreds of thousands of Palestinian Arabs fled to neighboring Arab countries, including the Jordanian-ruled West Bank and Egyptian ruled Gaza Strip. Many fled at the urging of the Arab states who told them they could return once Israel was destroyed.

After the invasion failed, the Arab states refused to assimilate the Palestinian Arabs who had arrived as refugees. The Palestinians were forced to remain in refugee camps near Israel's borders because the Arab states insisted they had a right to return to land within Israel, and could use the status of the refugees to put political pressure on Israel. Only Jordan granted the Palestinians citizenship. Those Palestinians that did not flee became citizens of Israel. Another result of the conflict was that hundreds of thousands of Jews in Muslim countries in the Middle East and North Africa were expelled, or forced to flee due to persecution. Most of these Jewish refugees sought refuge in Israel where they received citizenship.

Nasser and Pan-Arabism

In Egypt, a new leader arose who played an important role in the Arab world. Colonel Gamal Abdel Nasser took control of the Egyptian government in the early 1950s. Nasser strongly supported Arab nationalism and also opposed the existence of Israel. He ordered a blockade of the Straits of Tiran to stop ships heading to Israel's southern port of Eilat and supported terrorist attacks on Israel. On July 26, 1956, he seized the Suez Canal Company, which had been under British and French administration since the 1800s.

Great Britain and France were upset by this threat to their world positions. The Suez Canal was an important waterway linking the Mediterranean Sea to Asia. Great Britain and France decided to strike back against Egypt, and Israel quickly joined them. The three nations launched a joint attack on Egypt, starting the Suez War of 1956.

The United States and the Soviet Union joined in supporting Nasser. Both countries opposed French and British influence in the Middle East. They forced Britain, France, and Israel to withdraw from Egypt.

Nasser emerged from the conflict as a powerful leader. He began to promote **Pan-Arabism**, or Arab unity. In February 1958, Egypt formally united with Syria in the United Arab Republic (UAR). Nasser was named the first president of the new state. Egypt and Syria hoped that the union would eventually include all Arab states.

Many other Arab leaders were suspicious of Pan-Arabism. Oil-rich Arab states were concerned they would have to share **revenues** with poorer states in the Middle East. In Nasser's view, Arab unity meant that wealth derived

issue a vital or unsettled matter

Pan-Arabism Arab unity, regardless of national boundaries

revenue the yield of sources of income that a nation or state collects and deposits into its treasury for public use from oil, which currently flowed into a few Arab states or to foreign interests, could be used to improve the standard of living throughout the Middle East.

In 1961 Syrian military leaders took over Syria and withdrew the country from its union with Egypt. Nasser continued to work on behalf of Arab interests.

The Arab-Israeli Dispute

Between 1956 and 1967, tensions between the Arab states and Israel increased. In 1967, Nasser again imposed a blockade against Israeli shipping and made speeches publicly threatening Israel. He declared "We are now ready to confront Israel ... We are [now] ready to deal with the entire Palestine question." and in another speech stated that Egypt was "ready to enter a general war with Israel . . . and our basic objective will be to destroy Israel." Even as he gave these speeches in the spring of 1967, Arab armies began massing in Syria, Jordan, and Egypt near Israel's borders.

Fearing attack by Egypt and other Arab states, on June 5, 1967, Israel launched air strikes against Egypt and destroyed most of Egypt's air force. When Jordan joined the war, Israeli responded with air strikes. In just six days, the Israeli army broke the blockade, defeated the Arab forces, and took control of Gaza and the Sinai Peninsula from Egypt, the West Bank and East Jerusalem from Jordan, and the Golan Heights from Syria. As a result, a million Palestinians now lived in areas under Israeli control, most on the West Bank. Following the war, Israel proposed to return the Sinai and Golan Heights and begin negotiations on the status of Gaza and the West Bank in exchange for Arab recognition of Israel and its right to exist in peace. However, the Arab states responded with the Khartoum Resolution: "no peace with Israel, no recognition of Israel, no negotiations with it.

Over the next few years, Arab states continued to demand the return of the West Bank and Gaza. Nasser died in 1970, and Anwar el-Sadat succeeded him. On October 6, 1973 (on Yom Kippur, Judaism's holiest day of the year), Egypt and Syria launched a coordinated surprise attack against Israel. Golda Meir, Israel's first female prime minister, had little time to mobilize troops. Soon, however, Israeli forces went on the offensive and pushed into Egypt. A UN-negotiated cease-fire on October 22 stopped the fighting. An agreement in 1974 officially ended the conflict, but tensions remained.

Meanwhile, however, the war was having indirect results in Western nations. In 1960 several oil-producing states had formed OPEC, the Organization of the Petroleum Exporting Countries, to control the price of oil. During the Yom Kippur War, some OPEC nations announced large increases in the price of oil to foreign countries. The price hikes, coupled with cuts in oil production, led to oil shortages and serious economic problems in the West.

In 1977 U.S. President Jimmy Carter began to press for a compromise peace between Arabs and Israelis. In September 1978, President Carter met with President Sadat of Egypt and Israeli prime minister Menachem Begin (BAY • gihn) at Camp David in the United States. The result was the Camp David Accords, an agreement to sign an Israeli-Egyptian peace treaty. The treaty, signed by Sadat and Begin in March 1979, led to a complete Israeli withdrawal from the Sinai Peninsula and ended the state of war between Egypt and Israel. Many Arab countries, however, continued to refuse to recognize Israel.

In 1964 the Egyptians took the lead in forming the Palestine Liberation Organization (PLO) to represent Palestinian interests. The PLO believed that only the Palestinian Arabs should have a state in the Palestine regionand called for the destruction of Israel. At the same time, a guerrilla movement called al-Fatah, headed by the PLO political leader Yasir Arafat, began to launch terrorist attacks on Israel that lasted for decades.

BIOGRAPHY

David Ben-Gurion (1886-1973)

David Ben-Gurion was born David Grün in Plonsk, Poland, in what was at the time part of the Russian Empire. In 1906 he immigrated to the city of Jaffa, then in the Ottoman Empire. Here he became active in politics and in the Zionist movement. In 1912 he moved to Constantinople, the capital of the empire, to study law. While in Constantinople he changed his surname to the Hebrew name "Ben-Gurion." In the 1920s and 1930s Ben-Gurion became a key leader in the Zionist movemnet. His policy of "Havlagah", or restraint, lead many Jewish civilians to not retailate for attacks against them and to only concentrate on self-defense. On May 14, 1948, in the Museum Hall in Tel Aviv he announced the independence of the state of Israel. He would be the state's first Prime Minister serving (with one small break from 1954-1955) until 1963. As Prime Minister he helped establish the state and build its early government institutions.

DBQ ***DESCRIBING*** Ben-Gurion arrived in the region prior to the release of which document important to the establishment of the state of Israel?

(continued from p. 767)

TEKS **Texas Essential Knowledge and Skills**

13E summarize the rise of independence movements in Africa, the Middle East, and South Asia and reasons for ongoing conflicts

13F explain how Arab rejection of the State of Israel has led to ongoing conflict

14A summarize the development and impact of radical Islamic fundamentalism on events in the second half of the 20th century, including Palestinian terrorism and the growth of al Qaeda

24B describe the major influences of women such as Elizabeth I, Queen Victoria, Mother Teresa, Indira Gandhi, Margaret Thatcher, and Golda Meir during major eras of world history

25D explain how Islam influences law and government in the Muslim world

intifada "uprising"; a militant movement that arose during the 1980s among supporters of the Palestine Liberation Organization living in Israel

During the 1980s, Palestinian Arabs, frustrated by their failure to achieve self-rule, launched an increasing number of terrorist attacks, some of which were motivated not only by national grievances but also by radical Islamic fundamentalism. This militancy led to a movement called an **intifada**, or uprising, concentrated in the territories controlled by Israel since the 1967 Arab-Israeli war. Eventually, in the Oslo Peace Accords of 1993, Israel and the PLO agreed that the PLO would control a semi-independent area known as the Palestinian Authority. In return, the PLO recognized the Israeli state.

In 1993, the Oslo accords made possible the establishment of a Palestinian Authority that was granted considerable autonomy in parts of the West Bank and in Gaza. Nevertheless, serious clashes erupted after efforts to achieve a permanent peace failed. Israel withdrew from Gaza in 2005. An extremist organization called Hamas, whose stated objective is the destruction of Israel, took control of Gaza in 2006 and has regularly fired rockets into Israel, leading to repeated conflicts. Despite many efforts at peace, tensions in the region continue to this day.

✓ **READING PROGRESS CHECK**

Sequencing Place the events of the Six-Day War in order.

Iran, Iraq, and Afghanistan

GUIDING QUESTION ***How has the move for self-rule led to turmoil among the countries of the Middle East?***

The conflict between Israel and the Palestinians is one of many challenges in the Middle East. As in other parts of the world, a few people are rich while many are poor. Some countries prosper because of oil, but others remain in poverty. A response to these problems is the growth of movements based on Islam. Many of these groups believe that Muslims must return to a pure Islamic culture and values to build prosperous societies. Some are willing to use violence to bring about an Islamic revolution. Such a revolution took place in Iran.

The Iranian Revolution

The leadership of Reza Shah Pahlavi and revenue from oil helped make Iran a rich country. Iran was also an ally of the United States in the Middle East in the 1950s and 1960s.

However, there was much opposition to the shah in Iran. Many Muslims looked with distaste at the new Iranian society. In their eyes, it was based on greed and materialism, which they identified with American influence. Leading the opposition to the shah was the Ayatollah Ruhollah Khomeini (ko • MAY • nee), a

▼ A pro-Khomeini demonstration during the Iranian Revolution, December 1978.

▶ **CRITICAL THINKING**

Analyzing Visuals How would you describe the participants in this demonstration?

member of the Muslim clergy. By the late 1970s, many Iranians had begun to respond to Khomeini's words. In 1979 the shah's government collapsed and was replaced by an Islamic republic.

The new government, led by the Ayatollah Khomeini, moved to restore Islamic law. Supporters of the shah were executed or fled Iran. Anti-American feelings erupted when militants seized 52 Americans in the United States embassy in Tehran and held them hostage for more than a year.

After Khomeini's death in 1989, a more moderate government allowed some civil liberties. Some Iranians were dissatisfied with the government's economic performance. Others, especially young people, pressed for more freedoms and an end to the rule of conservative Muslim clerics.

The Iran-Iraq War

To the west of Iran was a militant and hostile Iraq, led by Saddam Hussein since 1979. Iran and Iraq have long had an uneasy relationship. Religious differences have fueled their disputes. Although both are Muslim nations, the Iranians are mostly Shia Muslims. The Iraqi leaders under Saddam Hussein, on the other hand, were mostly Sunni Muslims. Iran and Iraq have fought over territory, too, especially over the Strait of Hormuz. Strategically very important, the strait connects the Persian Gulf and the Gulf of Oman.

In 1980 Saddam Hussein launched a brutal war against Iran. During the Iran-Iraq War children were used to clear dangerous minefields. Saddam Hussein used poison gas against soldiers and civilians, especially the Kurds, an ethnic minority in the north who wanted their own state. In 1988, Iran and Iraq signed a cease-fire without resolving the war's basic issues.

The Persian Gulf War

In August 1990, Saddam Hussein sent his troops across the border to seize Kuwait, an oil-rich country on the Persian Gulf. The invasion began the Gulf War. The United States led the international forces that freed Kuwait. Hoping an internal revolt would overthrow Hussein, the allies imposed harsh economic sanctions on Iraq. The overthrow of Saddam Hussein, however, did not happen.

Afghanistan and the Taliban

After World War II, the king of Afghanistan, in search of economic assistance for his country, developed close ties with the Soviet Union. Internal fighting was followed in 1979 by a full-scale invasion of Afghanistan by the Soviets, who occupied the country for 10 years. Anti-Communist Islamic forces (known collectively as the mujahideen), supported by the United States and Pakistan, eventually ousted them. When the Soviets left, the Islamic groups began to fight for control of Afghanistan. One of these, the Taliban, seized the capital city of Kabul in 1996. By the fall of 1998, the Taliban controlled more than two-thirds of the country.

Backed by conservative religious forces in Pakistan, the Taliban provided a base of operations for Osama bin Laden. Bin Laden came from a wealthy family in Saudi Arabia and used his wealth to support the Afghan resistance. In 1988 bin Laden founded al-Qaeda, or "the base," which appealed to fundamentalist elements within Islam and recruited Muslims to drive Westerners out of nations with a largely Muslim population. After the Taliban seized control of much of Afghanistan, bin Laden used bases there to train al-Qaeda recruits.

✓ **READING PROGRESS CHECK**

Identifying Central Issues What role did religious differences play in the Iranian revolution and the Iran-Iraq War?

BIOGRAPHY

Golda Meir (1898–1978)

Golda Meir was born in Kiev, Russia, but immigrated with her family to Milwaukee, Wisconsin, at the age of eight. In her early 20s, she moved to the Palestine Mandate, where she was active in politics and the Zionist movement. Meir signed Israel's declaration of independence in 1948. She was subsequently elected to parliament and later served as both labor and foreign minister. In 1969 Meir became the prime minister of Israel and led her country during the Yom Kippur War. During her career, she attempted to establish peace with neighboring Arab states and fostered diplomacy with foreign powers.

DBQ ***DRAWING CONCLUSIONS*** How do you think Meir's upbringing affected her foreign policy decisions?

▲ Women ride an escalator at an upscale shopping center in Dubai.

▶ **CRITICAL THINKING**

Describing How does this photograph show the contrast between tradition and modernity in the contemporary Middle East?

Society and Culture

GUIDING QUESTION *How has Islam influenced society and culture in the Middle East?*

In recent years, conservative religious forces in the Middle East have tried to replace foreign culture and values with Islamic forms of belief and behavior. This movement is called Islamic fundamentalism or Islamic activism. For some Islamic leaders, Western values and culture are based on materialism, greed, and immorality. Extremists want to remove all Western influence in Muslim countries. These extremists give many Westerners an unfavorable impression of Islam.

Islamic fundamentalism began in Iran under the Ayatollah Khomeini. There the return to traditional Muslim beliefs reached into clothing styles, social practices, and the legal system. These ideas and practices spread to other Muslim countries. In Egypt, for example, militant Muslims assassinated President Sadat in 1981.

At the beginning of the twentieth century, women's place in Middle Eastern society had changed little for hundreds of years. Early Muslim women had participated in the political life of society and had extensive legal, political, and social rights. Cultural practices in many countries had overshadowed those rights, however.

In the nineteenth and twentieth centuries, Muslim scholars debated issues surrounding women's roles in society. Many argued for the need to rethink outdated interpretations and cultural practices that prevented women from realizing their potential. Until the 1970s, the general trend in urban areas was toward a greater role for women. Beginning in the 1970s, however, there was a shift toward more traditional roles for women. This trend was especially noticeable in Iran.

The literature of the Middle East since 1945 has reflected a rise in national awareness, and this in turn encouraged interest in historical traditions. Writers also began to deal more with secular themes for broader audiences, not just the elite. For example, *Cairo Trilogy* by Egyptian writer Naguib Mahfouz tells about a merchant family in Egypt in the 1920s. The changes in the family **parallel** the changes in Egypt. Mahfouz was the first writer in Arabic to win the Nobel Prize in Literature (in 1988). Another Middle Eastern writer, Shmuel Yosef Agnon, was the first writer in Hebrew to win a Nobel Prize in Literature (in 1966). The central themes of Agnon's writing explore the relationships between traditional Jewish life, the Hebrew language, and the modern world.

parallel having the same direction or course; similar

✓ **READING PROGRESS CHECK**

Making Connections Why was there a turn toward more traditional roles for Iranian women beginning in the 1970s?

LESSON 2 REVIEW TEKS

Reviewing Vocabulary

1. ***Identifying*** How did concern over revenue help lead to suspicion of Pan-Arabism?

Using Your Notes

2. ***Sequencing*** Use your notes to list specific events in the Arab-Israeli conflict.

Answering the Guiding Questions

3. ***Analyzing*** What events led to the dispute between Israel and its Arab neighbors?
4. ***Drawing Conclusions*** How has the move for self-rule led to turmoil among the countries of the Middle East?
5. ***Making Generalizations*** How has Islam influenced society and culture in the Middle East?

Writing Activity

6. **INFORMATIVE/EXPLANATORY** Research Golda Meir and find out how she became a leader of Israel. What did a woman rising to this position of power say about the State of Israel at that time?

networks

There's More Online!

- ☑ BIOGRAPHY Jomo Kenyatta
- ☑ BIOGRAPHY Nelson Mandela
- ☑ CHART/GRAPH Trends in Africa: Population, Poverty, and Water
- ☑ IMAGE African Art
- ☑ IMAGE Africa's First Democratic Election
- ☑ IMAGE Slums Outside of Nairobi
- ☑ INTERACTIVE SELF-CHECK QUIZ
- ☑ MAP Independent Africa
- ☑ VIDEO Apartheid

Reading HELPDESK

Academic Vocabulary

- **goal**
- **diverse**
- **theme**

Content Vocabulary

- **apartheid**
- **HIV/AIDS**
- **Pan-Africanism**

TAKING NOTES:

Key Ideas and Details

Categorizing As you read, complete a chart like the one below identifying the different economic views held by African leaders after independence.

African Leader	Country	Economic Views

TEKS Texas Essential Knowledge and Skills

1F identify major causes and describe the major effects of the following important turning points in world history from 1914 to the present: the world wars and their impact on political, economic, and social systems; communist revolutions and their impact on the Cold War; independence movements; and globalization

continued on the next page

LESSON 3
Africa

ESSENTIAL QUESTIONS • *How can political change cause conflict?* • *How can political relationships affect economic relationships?*

IT MATTERS BECAUSE

Africa's road to independence has not been an easy one. Free from colonial rule, many African nations faced serious political, economic, social, and health challenges.

Independence and New Nations

GUIDING QUESTION *What challenges did newly independent African countries face? What challenges have been overcome by African countries?*

The absolute exhaustion of Europe after World War II resulted in the end of the political system of colonialism. The Charter of the United Nations, established to support international cooperation, supported all colonial peoples' right to self-determination. In the late 1950s and 1960s, most African nations achieved independence.

In 1957 the Gold Coast, renamed Ghana and under the guidance of Kwame Nkrumah, was the first British colony to gain independence. In 1960 the Belgian Congo (renamed Zaire, now Democratic Republic of the Congo) and Nigeria gained their independence from the Belgians and the British, respectively. Many other nations followed, including Uganda, Kenya, and Botswana. Portugal finally surrendered Mozambique and Angola in 1975.

In North Africa, the French granted full independence to Morocco and Tunisia in 1956. Because Algeria was home to a million French settlers, France chose to keep control there. However, Algerian nationalists began a guerrilla war to liberate their homeland. The French leader, Charles de Gaulle, granted Algeria its independence in 1962.

South Africa and Apartheid

In South Africa, where whites dominated the political system, the process was more complicated. Blacks began organizing against white rule and formed the African National Congress in 1912. Its **goal** of economic and political reform met with little success.

At the same time, by the 1950s, South African whites (descendants of the Dutch, known as Afrikaners) had strengthened the laws separating whites and blacks. The result was a system of racial segregation known as **apartheid** ("apartncss").

Blacks demonstrated against these laws, but the white government brutally repressed the demonstrators. In 1960 police opened fire on people who were leading a peaceful march in Sharpeville, killing 69 people, two-thirds of whom were shot in the back. After the arrest of African National Congress (ANC) leader Nelson Mandela in 1962, members of the ANC called for armed resistance to the white government.

New Nations and New Leaders

The African states that achieved independence in the 1950s, 1960s, and 1970s still faced many problems. The leaders of these states, as well as their citizens, dreamed of stable governments and economic prosperity. Many of these dreams have yet to be realized.

Most leaders of the newly independent states came from the urban middle class. They had studied in Europe or the U.S. and knew European languages. They believed in using the Western democratic model in Africa.

The views of these African leaders on economics were somewhat more **diverse**. Some, such as Jomo Kenyatta of Kenya and General Mobutu Sese Seko of the present-day Democratic Republic of the Congo, believed in Western-style capitalism. Leaders in Angola and Mozambique followed Soviet-style communism. Other leaders, such as Julius Nyerere of Tanzania, Kwame Nkrumah of Ghana, Sékou Touré of Guinea, and Patrice Lumumba of the Republic of Congo, preferred an "African form of socialism."

The African form of socialism was not like that practiced in the Soviet Union or Eastern Europe. Instead, it was based on African traditions of community in which ownership of the country's wealth would be put into the hands of the people. As Nyerere declared in 1967, "The basis of socialism is a belief in the oneness of man and the common historical destiny of mankind. Its basis … is human equality."

Some African leaders believed in the dream of **Pan-Africanism**—the unity of all black Africans, regardless of national boundaries. In the view of Pan-Africanists, all black African peoples shared a common identity. Several of the new African leaders, including Léopold Senghor of Senegal, Kwame Nkrumah, and Jomo Kenyatta, supported Pan-Africanism.

Nkrumah in particular hoped that a Pan-African union would join all the new countries of the continent in a broader community. His dream never became reality. However, the Organization of African Unity (OAU), founded by the leaders of 32 African states in 1963, was a concrete result of the belief in Pan-Africanism. The OAU gave support to African groups fighting against colonialism. The group also presented a united front against the influence of the United States and the Soviet Union during the Cold War. Some African countries were part of the nonaligned movement and did not take sides in the Cold War.

Economic and Political Challenges

Independence did not bring economic prosperity to the new African nations. Most still relied on the export of a single crop or natural resource. Liberia, for example, depended on the export of rubber; Nigeria, on oil. When prices dropped, their economies suffered. To make matters worse, Africa depended on foreign investment. Most African states imported technology and manufactured goods from the West and depended on foreign financial aid to develop their countries.

goal an aim or a purpose

apartheid "apartness"; the system of racial segregation in South Africa from the 1950s until 1991

(continued from p. 773)

TEKS **Texas Essential Knowledge and Skills**

13E summarize the rise of independence movements in Africa, the Middle East, and South Asia and reasons for ongoing conflicts

20D explain the significance of the League of Nations and the United Nations

22E identify examples of individuals who led resistance to political oppression such as Nelson Mandela, Mohandas Gandhi, Oscar Romero, Natan Sharansky, Las Madres de la Plaza de Mayo, and Chinese student protestors in Tiananmen Square

diverse varied and not alike

Pan-Africanism the unity of all black Africans, regardless of national boundaries

Analyzing PRIMARY SOURCES

Nelson Mandela on Democracy

"During my lifetime I have dedicated myself to this struggle of the African people. I have fought against white domination, and I have fought against black domination. I have cherished the ideal of a democratic and free society in which all persons live together in harmony and with equal opportunities. It is an ideal which I hope to live for and to achieve. But if needs be, it is an ideal for which I am prepared to die."

—Nelson Mandela, statement at the Rivonia Trial, April 20, 1964, from *In His Own Words*

DBQ ***IDENTIFYING POINTS OF VIEW*** How did Mandela's words challenge the idea of apartheid?

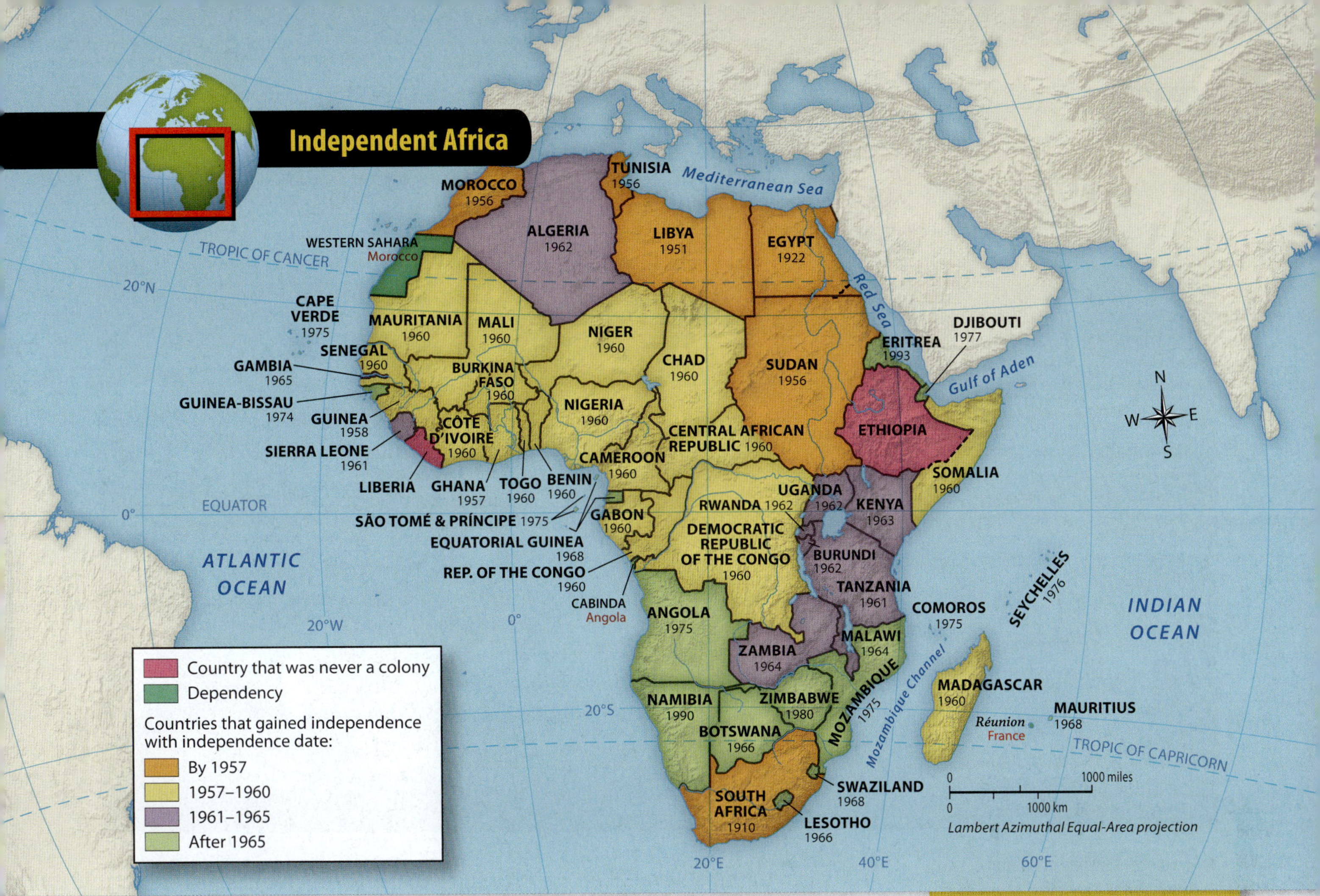

GEOGRAPHY CONNECTION

1. **PLACES AND REGIONS**
   Which African nations became independent after 1965?
2. **HUMAN SYSTEMS**
   Create a table of select African countries that includes the name of the European country that previously controlled it.

The new states also sometimes created their own problems. Scarce national resources were spent on military equipment or expensive consumer goods rather than on building the foundations for an industrial economy. Corruption was common.

Droughts and rapid population growth have also slowed economic growth and taxed resources. Since the 1980s, recurring droughts in many African countries, including Djibouti, Eritrea, Ethiopia, Kenya, Somalia, and Uganda have caused starvation and migration.

As a result of these problems, poverty was widespread among both rural and urban dwellers. As cities grew, massive slums populated by displaced rural people surrounded cities, overwhelming sanitation and transportation systems. Pollution and perpetual traffic jams were the result. Millions lived without access to electricity or even clean water. Meanwhile, the fortunate few enjoyed lavish lifestyles. The rich in many East African countries are known as the *wabenzi*, or Mercedes-Benz people.

Diseases, such as **HIV/AIDS**, also presented major challenges to African progress. AIDS is a worldwide epidemic, but Africa is hardest hit. HIV/AIDS has had a serious impact on children and families in Africa. Many children have lost one or both parents to AIDS. Often, relatives are too poor to care for these children. Many orphans thus become heads of households filled with younger siblings. Extended families have been the source of support in difficult times, especially in rural Africa. The HIV/AIDS epidemic, however, has overwhelmed this support system.

HIV/AIDS human immunodeficiency virus/acquired immunodeficiency syndrome; any of the strains of HIV-1 and HIV-2 that infect and destroy the immune system's helper T cells causing a large drop in their numbers, and becomes AIDS when a person has 20 percent or less than the normal level of helper T cells

▲ **The modern skyline of Nairobi, Kenya, forms a backdrop to one of the slums that surround the city.**

▶ CRITICAL THINKING
Contrasting How do the lives of rich and poor African urban dwellers differ?

African nations have taken steps to fight the epidemic. It has proved a tremendous burden, however, because many of these countries do not have the money or health facilities to educate their citizens about the disease and how to protect against it. Nor can they purchase the drugs that would extend the lives of those with HIV.

Africans also faced political challenges. Many people hoped that independence would lead to democracies. They were soon disappointed as democratic governments failed. Between 1957 and 1982, more than 70 leaders were violently overthrown. In the 1980s, either the military or a single party ruled many major African states. In the 1990s, multiparty elections increased, but single-party rule still predominated.

Despite the OAU's push for non-alignment in the Cold War, some African nations were drawn into proxy wars as the U.S. and the Soviet Union took opposing sides in political struggles in the newly independent countries, notably in Angola, Somalia, and Zaire. This caused prolonged conflict in some parts of Africa that undermined political development.

Within many African nations, warring ethnic groups undermined the concept of nationhood. This is not surprising, because the colonial powers had drawn the boundaries of African nations arbitrarily, leading to internal chaos and conflict. Virtually all these states included widely diverse ethnic, linguistic, and territorial groups.

For example, during the late 1960s, civil war tore Nigeria apart. Conflicts also broke out among ethnic groups in Zimbabwe. Farther north, in central Africa, fighting between the Hutu and Tutsi created unstable governments in Rwanda and Burundi. During the colonial period, Hutu and Tutsi peoples lived together under European control. After independence in 1962, two new countries were created: Rwanda and

Burundi. The population in both countries was mixed, but in Rwanda, the Hutu majority ran the government. They resented the position of the Tutsis, who had gotten the best education and jobs under the Belgians. In 1994 a Hutu rampage left some 500,000 Tutsi dead in Rwanda.

Not all the news in Africa has been bad. Popular demonstrations led to the collapse of one-party regimes and the emergence of democracies in several countries. One case was that of Idi Amin of Uganda. After ruling by terror and brutal repression throughout the 1970s, Amin was deposed in 1979. Dictatorship also came to an end in Ethiopia, Liberia, and Somalia. In these cases, however, the fall of the regime was later followed by bloody civil war. Apartheid also ended in South Africa.

The End of Apartheid

One of the most remarkable events of recent African history was the 1994 election of Nelson Mandela to the presidency of the Republic of South Africa. Imprisoned in 1962 for his activities with the African National Congress in resisting political oppression, Mandela spent almost 26 years in maximum-security prisons in South Africa. Mandela never wavered from his resolve to secure the freedom of his country.

Mandela was offered freedom in 1985, with conditions. Yet he refused to accept a conditional freedom: "Only free men can negotiate. Prisoners cannot enter into contracts.... Your freedom and mine cannot be separated."

Nobel Peace Prize winner (1984) Bishop Desmond Tutu and others worked to free Mandela and to end apartheid. Eventually, worldwide pressure forced the South African government to dismantle apartheid laws. In 1990 Mandela was released from prison. In 1993 the government of F. W. de Klerk agreed to hold democratic national elections—the first in South Africa's history. In 1994 Nelson Mandela became South Africa's first black president. In his presidential inaugural address, he expressed his hopes:

▲ After his release from prison in 1990, Nelson Mandela visits Bishop Desmond Tutu.

PRIMARY SOURCE

"We shall build the society in which all South Africans, both black and white, will be able to walk tall, without any fear in their hearts, assured of their inalienable right to human dignity—a rainbow nation at peace with itself and the world."

—from *In His Own Words*

✔ **READING PROGRESS CHECK**

Evaluating To what extent were the goals of Pan-Africanism realized in Africa in the years following independence?

Society and Culture

GUIDING QUESTION *What factors have affected African society and culture?*

Africa is a study in contrasts. Old and new, indigenous and foreign, live side by side. One result is a constant tension between traditional ways and Western culture in most African countries.

In general, the impact of the West has been greatest in the cities. After all, the colonial presence was first and most firmly established in the cities. Many cities, including Lagos, Nigeria; Cape Town, South Africa; Brazzaville, Republic of the Congo; and Nairobi, Kenya, are direct products of colonial rule. Most African cities today look like cities elsewhere in the world.

Outside the major cities, where about three-fourths of the inhabitants of Africa live, modern influence has had less of an impact. Millions of people

▲ South Africans wait in line to vote in the nation's first democratic election.

throughout Africa live much as their ancestors did—in thatched dwellings without modern plumbing and electricity. They farm, hunt, or raise livestock by traditional methods, wear traditional clothing, and practice traditional beliefs. Conditions such as drought or flooding affect the ability of rural Africans to grow crops or to tend herds. Migration to the cities for work is one solution. This can be very disruptive to families and villages. Many urban people view rural people as backward. Rural dwellers view the cities as corrupting and destructive to traditional African values.

After independence, women's roles in African society changed. Almost without exception, women were allowed to vote and run for political office. Some became leaders of their countries. Women still hold few political offices, however. Although women dominate some professions, such as teaching, child care, and clerical work, they do not share in all career opportunities. Most African women are employed in low-paid positions, such as farm laborers, factory workers, and servants. Furthermore, in many rural areas, traditional attitudes toward women, including arranged marriages, prevail.

The tension between traditional and modern and between indigenous and foreign also affects African culture. Africans have kept their local artistic traditions and have adapted them to foreign influences. A dilemma for many contemporary African artists is finding a balance between Western techniques and training on the one hand and the rich heritage of traditional African art forms on the other. In some countries, governments make the artists' decisions. Artists are told to depict scenes of traditional African life. These works are designed to serve the tourist industry.

theme a subject or topic of artistic work

African writers have often addressed the tensions and dilemmas that modern Africans face. The conflicting demands of town versus country and indigenous versus foreign were the **themes** of most of the best-known works of the 1960s and 1970s. Chinua Achebe, a Nigerian novelist and winner of the Nobel Prize for literature in 1989, writes about the problems of Africans caught up in the conflict between traditional and Western values. In his most famous novel *Things Fall Apart*, Achebe portrays the simple dignity of traditional African village life.

PHOTO: ©Peter Turnley/Corbis

✓ READING PROGRESS CHECK

Differentiating How are women's roles different in rural and urban areas in Africa?

LESSON 3 REVIEW TEKS

Reviewing Vocabulary

1. ***Assessing*** How successful was the African National Congress in its goal of reforming the South African government and ending apartheid?

Using Your Notes

2. ***Making Connections*** Use your notes to identify post-independence African leaders and their economic views.

Answering the Guiding Questions

3. ***Identifying*** What challenges did newly independent African countries face?
4. ***Drawing Conclusions*** What challenges have been overcome by African countries?
5. ***Making Generalizations*** What factors have affected African society and culture?

Writing Activity

6. **INFORMATIVE/EXPLANATORY** Research independence movements in two African nations. Evaluate their success and compare how political ideology, ethnicity, and religion shaped their future governments.

networks

There's More Online!

- BIOGRAPHY Fidel Castro
- BIOGRAPHY François Duvalier
- BIOGRAPHY Oscar Romero
- CHART/GRAPH GDP Per Capita in Selected Latin American Countries
- IMAGE Mothers of the Plaza de Mayo
- INTERACTIVE SELF-CHECK QUIZ
- MAP Struggles for Democracy, 1945–1993
- PRIMARY SOURCE One Hundred Years of Solitude
- VIDEO The Cuban Revolution

LESSON 4

Latin America

ESSENTIAL QUESTIONS • *How can political change cause conflict?* • *How can political relationships affect economic relationships?*

Reading HELPDESK

Academic Vocabulary

- **consent**
- **target**

Content Vocabulary

- **privatization**
- **trade embargo**
- **cartels**
- **magic realism**
- **megacity**

TAKING NOTES:

Key Ideas and Details

Categorizing As you read, use a table like the one below to list significant events that happened in each country during the Cold War.

Country	Significant Events
Haiti	
El Salvador	
Nicaragua	
Chile	
Colombia	

TEKS Texas Essential Knowledge and Skills

22C identify examples of politically motivated mass murders in Cambodia, China, Latin America, the Soviet Union, and Armenia

continued on the next page

It Matters Because

After World War II, Latin American countries faced many economic, social, and political challenges. These challenges arose from a rise in population, a large foreign debt, and ongoing foreign military involvement.

General Trends in Latin America

GUIDING QUESTIONS *How did the involvement of the United States and the Soviet Union increase instability in Latin American countries? What economic and political challenges did Latin American countries face during the Cold War?*

Since the 1800s, Latin Americans have exported raw materials and bought manufactured goods from industrialized countries. The Great Depression caused exports to fall, and revenues to buy manufactured goods declined. In response, Latin Americans developed industries to produce their own goods.

By the 1960s, however, Latin American countries were still experiencing economic problems. They depended on the United States, Europe, and Japan, especially for the advanced technology needed for modern industries. Also, many Latin American countries had failed to find markets abroad to sell their manufactured products.

These economic failures led to political instability. In the 1960s, repressive military regimes in Chile, Brazil, and Argentina abolished political parties and returned to export-import economies financed by foreigners. These regimes also encouraged multinational corporations (companies with divisions in more than two countries) to come to Latin America. This made these Latin American countries even more dependent on industrialized nations. In the 1970s, Latin American countries tried to maintain their weak economies by borrowing money. Between 1970 and 1982, debt to foreigners grew from $27 billion to $315.3 billion. A number of Latin American economies began to crumble. Wages fell, and unemployment and inflation skyrocketed. As the economy declined, people continued to move from the countryside into the cities.

GEOGRAPHY CONNECTION

Latin American countries have moved toward democracy.

1. **PLACES AND REGIONS** *Of the countries shown on the map, which has experienced the longest period of electoral democracy?*
2. **THE USES OF GEOGRAPHY** *What problems did countries with little experience with electoral democracy face?*

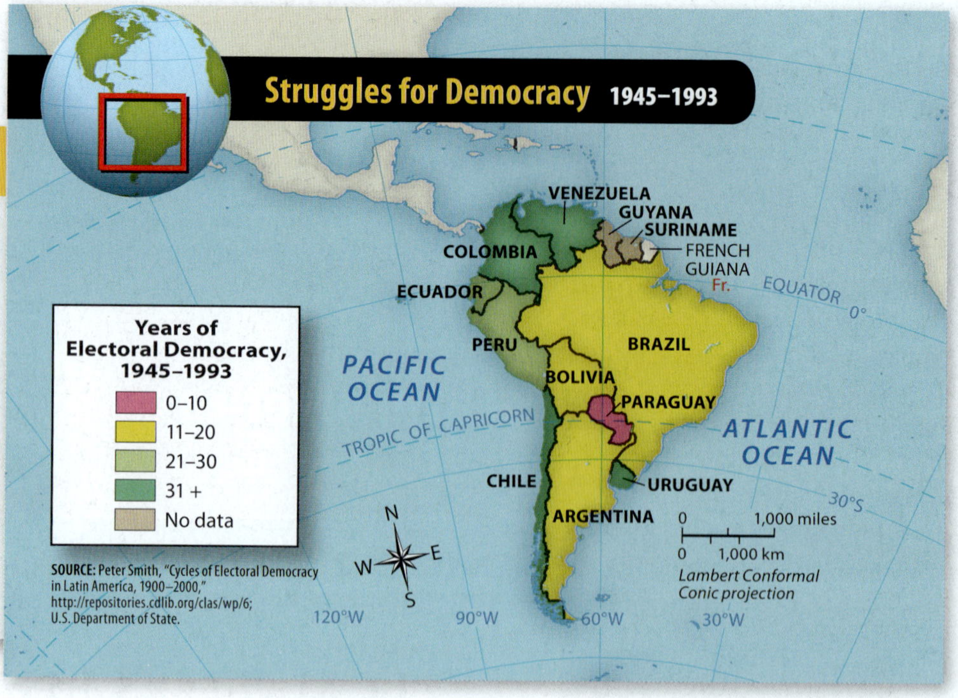

A Move Toward Democracy

With the debt crisis in the 1980s came a movement toward democracy. Some military leaders could not deal with their nations' debt problems. At the same time, many realized that military power without popular **consent** could not maintain a strong state. As a result, a movement toward democracy was the most noticeable trend of the 1980s and the early 1990s in Latin America.

consent approval

The United States has always played a large role in Latin America. In 1948 the states of the Western Hemisphere formed the Organization of American States (OAS), which called for an end to military action by one state in the affairs of any other state.

The formation of the OAS, however, did not end the interference of the United States in Latin American affairs. As the Cold War developed, so too did the anxiety of U.S. policy makers about the possibility of communist regimes in Central America and the Caribbean. As a result, the United States returned to a policy of taking action when it believed that Soviet agents were trying to set up governments hostile to U.S. interests.

After Fidel Castro's communist revolution in Cuba, the desire of the United States to prevent "another Cuba" largely determined U.S. policy toward Latin America during the Cold War. In the 1960s, President John F. Kennedy's Alliance for Progress encouraged social reform and economic development in Latin America. It was hoped that economic growth would keep people happy and less inclined to follow radical leaders, but it failed. Much of the money intended for economic development ended up in the pockets of the rich.

When Cuba began to start guerrilla wars in other Latin American countries, the United States reacted by sending massive military aid to anti-Communist regimes, regardless of their nature. In the 1980s and 1990s, the United States returned to a policy of direct intervention in Latin American affairs.

(continued from p. 779)

TEKS **Texas Essential Knowledge and Skills**
22E identify examples of individuals who led resistance to political oppression such as Nelson Mandela, Mohandas Gandhi, Oscar Romero, Natan Sharansky, Las Madres de la Plaza de Mayo, and Chinese student protestors in Tiananmen Square

SKILLS PRACTICE

Use a graphic organizer to take notes about the economic and political development in Latin America. Use your notes to write a summary of everything you learned.

✓ READING PROGRESS CHECK

Explaining What was the Alliance for Progress, and why did it fail?

Mexico and the Caribbean

GUIDING QUESTION *What economic and political challenges did Latin American countries face during the Cold War?*

Throughout the twentieth century, Mexico and the Caribbean have experienced political turmoil and economic crises.

Mexico

The Mexican Revolution in the early 1900s created a political order that remained stable for many years. The official political party of the Mexican Revolution—the Institutional Revolutionary Party, or PRI—came to dominate Mexico. Every six years, leaders of the PRI chose the party's presidential candidate, who was then elected by the people. During the 1950s and 1960s, steady economic growth led to real gains in wages in Mexico.

At the end of the 1960s, student protests against Mexico's one-party government system led to change. Two presidents, Luis Echeverría and José López Portillo, made political reforms, and new political parties emerged. Greater freedom of debate in the press and universities was allowed.

In the late 1970s, vast new reserves of oil were discovered in Mexico. The government became more dependent on revenues from foreign oil sales. Then, when world oil prices dropped in the mid-1980s, Mexico was no longer able to make payments on its foreign debt. The government adopted new economic policies. One was **privatization**, the sale of government-owned companies to private firms.

privatization the sale of government-owned companies to private firms

President Carlos Salinas de Gortari sped up privatization to relieve the debt crisis. In 1992 de Gortari began working with the U.S. president and the Canadian prime minister to form the North American Free Trade Agreement (NAFTA). It went into effect in 1994.

▲ Fidel Castro and two guerillas at their mountain hideout during the insurgency against Cuban dictator Fulgencio Batista.

The Cuban Revolution

In the 1950s, an opposition movement arose in Cuba. It aimed to overthrow the government of the dictator Fulgencio Batista, who had controlled Cuba since 1933. The leader of the movement was a man named Fidel Castro. In 1954 Fidel and his brother Raúl teamed up with a small band of revolutionaries. As the rebels gained more support, the Batista regime collapsed. Castro's revolutionaries seized Havana on January 3, 1959. Many Cubans who disagreed with Castro fled to the United States.

Relations between Cuba and the United States quickly deteriorated when Castro's regime began to receive aid from the Soviet Union. In October 1960, the United States declared a **trade embargo** with Cuba. Just three months later, all diplomatic relations with Cuba were broken.

trade embargo a policy prohibiting trade with a particular country

After the failure of the Bay of Pigs invasion and the Cuban Missile Crisis, Cuba became less dependent on the Soviet Union and pursued a new strategy of fomenting revolution in the rest of Latin America. Although Cuba's strategy failed, Castro's Marxist regime continued but with mixed results. The Cuban people did secure some social gains, such as free medical services for all citizens. With improvements in education, illiteracy was nearly eliminated.

Haiti

After American troops left Haiti in 1934, the Haitians made several efforts to move toward democracy. In 1957, however, in elections controlled by the military, François Duvalier became president. He created a private militia,

BIOGRAPHY

Oscar Romero (1917–1980)
Oscar Romero was appointed Archbishop of San Salvador in part because of his moderate political views. But in his weekly radio broadcasts, he soon began to attack the Salvadoran government's violent practices. Romero quickly became, in the words of his personal aide, "the most loved person and the most hated person" in the country. On March 24, 1980, Romero was murdered while he celebrated mass in a private chapel in San Salvador. His death was the most notable in a 12-year-long civil war in which more than 70,000 Salvadorans died.

▶ **CRITICAL THINKING**
Specifying How did Oscar Romero's political views change?

established dictatorial rule, and terrorized the country, killing tens of thousands. After his death in 1971, his son continued to rule Haiti with an iron fist. Growing opposition to his rule led to the collapse of his regime in 1986, followed five years later by a return to democracy with the election of Jean-Bertrand Aristide.

✓ **READING PROGRESS CHECK**

Determining Cause and Effect What immediate effects did the Cuban revolution have on Cuba's relationship with the United States?

Central America

GUIDING QUESTION ***What economic and political challenges did Latin American countries face during the Cold War?***

Central America includes seven countries: Costa Rica, Nicaragua, Honduras, El Salvador, Panama, Belize, and Guatemala. Economically, Central America has historically depended on the export of bananas, coffee, and cotton. Prices for these products have varied over time, however, creating economic crises. In addition, a huge gulf between a wealthy elite and poor peasants has created a climate of instability in the region. The U.S. fear of the spread of communism often led to U.S. support for repressive regimes in Central America. The involvement of the United States was especially evident in the nations of Guatemala, El Salvador, and Nicaragua.

Guatemala

In 1954, with support from the United States, Jacobo Arbenz of Guatemala was overthrown. A series of military or military-dominated dictators then ruled the country for years. Guerrilla forces began forming to oppose the government, which responded in the early 1980s by using military action and economic reforms to defeat the guerrillas. As in El Salvador, right-wing death squads began attacking anyone they believed belonged to the opposition, especially the indigenous people of Guatemala, the descendants of the ancient Maya. The government killed as many as 200,000 people, mostly unarmed Maya.

El Salvador

After World War II, the wealthy elite and the military controlled the government in El Salvador. The rise of an urban middle class led to hope for a more democratic government. The army, however, refused to accept the results of free elections that were held in 1972.

World attention focused on El Salvador in the late 1970s and the 1980s when the country was rocked by a bitter civil war. Marxist-led, leftist guerrillas and right-wing groups battled one another. The Catholic Church became a main **target**, and a number of priests were killed or tortured, among them Archbishop Oscar Romero. The United States began to provide weapons and training to the Salvadoran army to defeat the guerrillas. The hope was to bring stability to the country, but the killings continued until a 1992 peace settlement ended the war.

target something or someone marked for attack

Nicaragua

In Nicaragua, the Somoza family seized control of the government in 1937 and maintained control for the next 43 years. Over most of this period, the Somoza regime had the support of the United States. The Somozas enriched themselves at the expense of the Nicaraguan people and used murder and torture to silence opposition.

By 1979, the United States, under President Jimmy Carter, had grown unwilling to support the corrupt regime. In that same year, Marxist guerrilla forces known as the Sandinista National Liberation Front won a number of military victories against government forces and gained control of the country. Soon, a group opposed to the Sandinistas' policies, called the contras, began to try to overthrow the new government. Worried by the Sandinistas' alignment with the Soviet Union, the United States supported the contras.

▲ This Nicaraguan mural depicts the killing of four students at an anti-Somoza protest on July 23, 1959.

The war waged by the contras undermined support for the Sandinistas. In 1990 the Sandinistas, led by Daniel Ortega, agreed to free elections and lost to a coalition headed by Violeta Barrios de Chamorro, who became Nicaragua's first female president.

✓ **READING PROGRESS CHECK**

Comparing What experiences did Guatemala, El Salvador, and Nicaragua have in common in the post-World War II period?

South America

GUIDING QUESTION ***What economic and political challenges did Latin American countries face during the Cold War?***

Throughout the twentieth century, most South American countries experienced political unrest and had economic and social problems.

Chile

The history of Chile has mirrored the experience of other Latin American countries. However, it took a dramatic step in 1970 when Salvador Allende (ah • YEHN • day), a Marxist, became president.

Allende tried to create a socialist society through constitutional means. His first steps were to increase wages and to nationalize the largest corporations. Allende's policies were not popular with everyone. Nationalization of the copper industry angered the companies' owners in the United States, as well as the U.S. government. However, Allende gained support in the Chilean congress. Afraid of Allende's growing strength, General Augusto Pinochet (PEE • noh • CHEHT) moved to overthrow the government. In September 1973 military forces killed Allende and set up a dictatorship.

The Pinochet regime was one of the most brutal in Chile's history. Thousands of opponents were imprisoned, tortured, or murdered. The regime also outlawed all political parties and did away with the congress. These horrible abuses of human rights led to growing unrest in the mid-1980s. Thousands of Pinochet opponents and other civilians were arrested and were never seen again. Pinochet finally lost in 1989 in free presidential elections.

Argentina

Argentina, Latin America's second-largest country, was once ruled by a powerful oligarchy who needed the army's support to remain in power. In 1943, during World War II, a group of army officers overthrew the oligarchy. Unsure how to deal with the working classes, Juan Perón devised a new strategy. Using

PHOTO: Paul Kennedy/Alamy

his position as labor secretary in the military government, Perón sought to win over the workers, known as the *descamisados* (the shirtless ones). He encouraged them to join labor unions and increased job benefits. With the support of the laborers and urban middle class, Juan Perón was elected president of Argentina. His wife, Eva Perón, was equally adored, and together they brought social reforms to Argentina.

To please his supporters, Perón followed a policy of increased industrialization. He sought to free Argentina from foreign investors. The government bought the railways and took over the banking, insurance, shipping, and communications industries. Perón's regime, however, was also authoritarian. He created Fascist gangs that used violent means to terrify his opponents.

▲ The Mothers of the Plaza de Mayo, mothers and grandmothers of the *desaparecidos* (the disappeared) of Argentina's "dirty war," demonstrate outside La Casa Rosada in Buenos Aires.

The military overthrew the Argentinean leader in September 1955. Perón went into exile in Spain for nearly 20 years. He was reelected as president in 1973 but died a year later. In 1976 the military once again took over power. The new regime tolerated no opposition. It is believed that 36,000 people were killed. The Mothers of the Plaza de Mayo, an association of Argentine mothers whose children "disappeared" during the military dictatorship, began to march in 1977 at the Plaza de Mayo in Buenos Aires, in front of the Casa Rosada presidential palace. They did so in public defiance of the government's state terrorism intended to silence all opposition.

In April 1982, the military regime invaded the Falkland Islands off the coast of Argentina. Great Britain, which had controlled the islands since the 1800s, sent ships and troops and took the islands back. The loss discredited the military and opened the door to civilian rule in Argentina. When Raúl Alfonsín was elected president in 1983, he restored democracy and prosecuted the former military leaders.

Colombia

Colombia has long had a democratic political system, but a conservative elite led by the owners of coffee plantations has dominated the government. Coffee is an important crop for Colombia, making up about half of the country's legal exports. Yet because the economy relies heavily upon the coffee trade, price fluctuations in either direction can have a negative effect on the overall economy.

In addition to economic problems, political problems troubled Colombia in the twentieth century. After World War II, Marxist guerrilla groups began to organize Colombian peasants. The government responded violently. More than 200,000 peasants had been killed by the mid-1960s. Violence continued in the 1980s and 1990s.

cartels groups of drug businesses

Peasants who lived in poverty turned to a new cash crop—coca leaves, which are used to make cocaine. As the lucrative drug trade grew, two major **cartels** formed in Colombia.

The drug cartels used bribes and violence to force government cooperation in the drug traffic and to dominate the market. Colombia became the major cocaine supplier of the international drug market. Violence increased as rebel guerrillas made deals with the cartels to oppose the government. The government used an aerial eradication program to try to wipe out cocaine fields, but the program did not have much success. Despite the money earned from drug and coffee exports, the Colombian economy remained weak because of high unemployment and the disruption of civil war.

✓ **READING PROGRESS CHECK**

Explaining How did the invasion of the Falkland Islands affect Argentina?

Latin American Society and Culture

GUIDING QUESTION *How did Latin American society and culture change after World War II?*

Latin America's economic problems have been made worse by its dramatic growth in population. Both Latin America and North America (the United States and Canada) had the same populations in 1950—about 165 million people. By the mid-1980s, however, Latin America's population had exploded to 400 million. That of North America was about 270 million. With the increase in population came a rapid rise in the size of cities. By 1990, there were 29 cities with more than a million people, including Mexico City and Buenos Aires. Analysts refer to such cities as megacities. **Megacities** in Latin America have often grown so fast that regular urban services cannot be provided.

megacity a very large city

Latin American women's roles have changed. Although the traditional role of homemaker continues, women have also moved into new jobs. In addition to farm labor, women have found jobs in industry and as teachers, professors, doctors, and lawyers.

Twentieth-century Latin American writers and artists have played important roles in their society. Their work is seen as expressing the hopes of the people. Because of this, artists and writers hold high status in Latin American society.

In the 1940s, Latin American writers developed a unique form of expression called magic realism. **Magic realism** brings together realistic events with dreamlike or fantasy backgrounds. The rules of ordinary life are suspended in order to comment on a national or social situation. Perhaps the foremost example of magic realism is *One Hundred Years of Solitude*, a novel by Gabriel García Márquez, a Colombian writer, who won the Nobel Prize in literature in 1982. In this story of the fictional town of Macondo, the point of view slips back and forth between fact and fantasy. According to Márquez, fantasy and fact depend on one's point of view.

magic realism a form of expression unique to Latin American literature; it combines realistic events with dreamlike or fantasy backgrounds

Latin American art and architecture were strongly influenced by international styles after World War II. Perhaps the most notable example of modern architecture can be seen in Brasília, the capital of Brazil, which was built in the 1950s and 1960s. Brazilian architect Oscar Niemeyer was appointed chief architect for the new capital.

✓ **READING PROGRESS CHECK**

Defining What problems do megacities cause in Latin America?

LESSON 4 REVIEW TEKS

Reviewing Vocabulary

1. ***Analyzing*** How did the drug cartels in Colombia maintain their control over the cocaine trade?

Using Your Notes

2. ***Comparing*** Use your notes to describe the similarities among major events in Latin American countries during the Cold War.

Answering the Guiding Questions

3. ***Identifying Central Issues*** How did the involvement of the United States and the Soviet Union increase instability in Latin American countries?
4. ***Making Generalizations*** What economic and political challenges did Latin American countries face during the Cold War?
5. ***Identifying*** How did Latin American society and culture change after World War II?

Writing Activity

6. **ARGUMENT** The United States has increasingly tried to use economic tools rather than military force to resolve conflicts in Latin America. Research the trade embargo imposed on Cuba. Write a persuasive argument for or against the embargo.

CHAPTER 32 Assessment

TEKS

Directions: On a separate sheet of paper, answer the questions below. Make sure you read carefully and answer all parts of the questions.

Lesson Review

Lesson 1

1. ***Explaining*** After World War II, what decision did Indian Prime Minister Jawaharlal Nehru make in following the principle of nonalignment?

2. ***Summarizing*** How did women's roles change across South and Southeast Asia after the war?

3. ***Identifying*** What were Pol Pot's political motivations for mass murder in Cambodia? **22C**

4. ***Describing*** How did Indira Gandhi, Mother Teresa, and Golda Meir influence world history? **24B**

Lesson 2

5. ***Identifying Cause and Effect*** What led to the Six-Day War, and what were some outcomes?

6. ***Summarizing*** What led to the rise of independence movements in the Middle East? What were the reasons for the Middle East's ongoing conflicts? **13E, 25D**

7. ***Explaining*** How has radical Islamic fundamentalism contributed to the development of Palestinian terrorism? **14A**

8. ***Summarizing*** Why did the United States and the Soviet Union join forces to assist in a conflict over the Suez Canal, and what was the result?

9. ***Explaining*** What event led to the Gulf War?

Lesson 3

10. ***Summarizing*** What led to the rise of independence movements in Africa, including the significance of the United Nations? **13E, 20D**

11. ***Explaining*** What were reasons for Africa's ongoing conflicts? **13E**

12. ***Making Inferences*** In South Africa in 1960, two-thirds of the 69 people killed during a peaceful antiapartheid march were shot in the back. What does this suggest happened?

Lesson 4

13. ***Identifying*** What political changes occurred in the late 1960s in Mexico?

14. ***Identifying*** What characteristic of democracy did military leaders in Latin American come to realize was essential to a strong state? **19B**

15. ***Identifying*** What were the causes and effects of the communist Cuban Revolution, including the impact on the Cold War? **1F**

16. ***Identifying*** What were the government's political motivations for mass murder in Guatemala? **22C**

Exploring the Essential Question

17. ***Analyzing Cause and Effect*** Create a cause-and-effect diagram with a partner showing the conflicts two or more African states of your choice have encountered as they struggled to gain independence and how their political relationships have affected economic relationships with other countries or states. Illustrate your diagram using other forms of media, such as photographs, maps, or graphs. For example, you might include a photograph depicting a demonstration in South Africa and a map showing Rwanda and Uganda. **13E**

Need Extra Help?

If You've Missed Question	1	2	3	4	5	6	7	8	9	10	11	12	13	14	15	16	17
Go to page	765	768	767	765	771	769	771	788	773	775	778	776	783	782	783	784	775

Critical Thinking

18. ***Making Connections*** What caused changes to the political systems of many European colonial territories in the mid to late-1900s? What were the effects of these changes? **1F**

19. ***Identifying Central Issues*** What main issue did Indian leadership experience after India became independent in 1947?

20. ***Synthesizing*** What events led to the rise of independence movements in South Asia? Why did independence movements and new regimes in South Asia experience conflicts and instability? **13E**

21. ***Drawing Conclusions*** What conclusion can you draw about Burma's Aung San Suu Kyi's election results and her house arrest?

22. ***Summarizing*** What is al-Qaeda? How did radical Islamic fundamentalism contribute to the growth of al-Qaeda? **14A**

23. ***Analyzing*** Why has it been difficult to resolve conflict in the Middle East? Give specific examples. **13E, 13F**

24. ***Speculating*** What might have happened if Pan-Arabism had been more widely accepted among Arab states?

25. ***Identifying*** How did Oscar Romero and Las Madres de la Plaza de Mayo lead resistance to political oppression in Latin America? **26E**

26. ***Analyzing*** How does Gabriel García Márquez's *One Hundred Years of Solitude* reflect and transcend the culture in which it was produced? **26B, 26C**

Social Studies Skills

27. ***Economics*** How were Western countries affected by the formation of OPEC?

28. ***Identifying Continuity and Change*** What changed for the Philippines after World War II? What were the experiences of this country as a result of this change?

29. ***Geography Skills*** Explain the impact of a rapid rise in population on Latin American cities.

DBQ Analyzing Historical Documents

Use the document to answer the following questions.

In the Rivonia Trial, named for a suburb in Johannesburg where a group of African National Congress militants hid, Nelson Mandela and other opponents of South African apartheid were charged with sabotage and conspiracy. Mandela spoke these words at the Palace of Justice in Pretoria:

PRIMARY SOURCE

> "During my lifetime I have dedicated myself to the struggle of the African people. I have fought against domination, and I have fought against black domination. I have cherished the ideal of a democratic and free society in which all persons live together in harmony and with equal opportunities, It is an ideal which I hope to live for and to achieve. But if needs be, it is an ideal for which I am prepared to die."
>
> —Nelson Mandela, statement at the Rivonia Trial, April 20, 1964, from *In His Own Words*

30. ***Analyzing Content*** What two extremes in the fight against apartheid does Mandela stand against? **22E**

Need Extra Help?

If You've Missed Question	18	19	20	21	22	23	24	25	26	27	28	29	30
Go to page	775	764	764	767	773	769	770	784	787	771	766	787	789

(31) ***Analyzing Style*** How does Mandela use parallelism and opposition to make his final appeal? Is this final appeal effective? Explain. **22E**

(32) ***Analyzing Style*** Mandela spoke these words while standing trial for the accusation of conspiracy. Yet, how does Mandela's statement differ from a not-guilty plea, and why might he have communicated in this manner? **22E**

DBQ Analyzing Visuals

In 1992, Mexican President Carlos Salinas de Gortari began working with the U.S. president and the Canadian prime minister to form the North American Free Trade Agreement (NAFTA). It went into effect in 1994.

U.S. AGRICULTURAL TRADE WITH NAFTA PARTNERS, 1989–2002

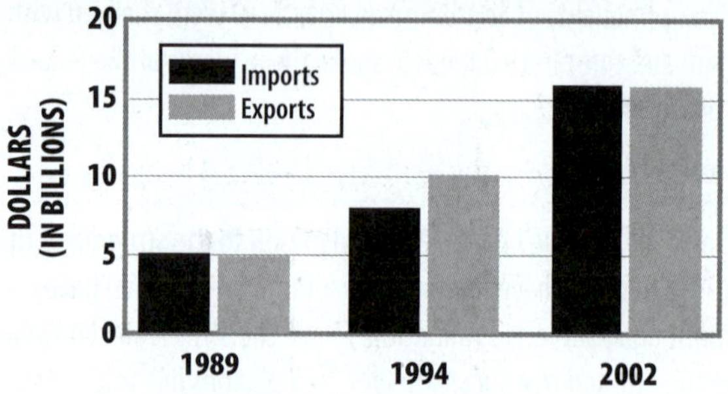

Source: U.S. Department of Agriculture

Use the document to answer the following questions.

(33) ***Using Graphs*** How did NAFTA affect agricultural trade among the United States, Mexico, and Canada?

(34) ***Comparing and Contrasting*** Compare and contrast what has happened to the imports and exports between the United States and its NAFTA partners.

Extended Response Question

(35) ***Expository*** Write a multiparagraph essay explaining how religious, political, economic, and ethnic reasons have fueled conflicts in South and Southeast Asia, the Middle East, Africa, and Latin America since World War II. Give one or more examples from each of the four lessons in the chapter to illustrate each reason. **13E**

Need Extra Help?

If You've Missed Question	31	32	33	34	35
Go to page	789	789	790	790	764

Life During the Cold War

1945–1989

ESSENTIAL QUESTIONS • *How does war result in change?* • *What challenges may countries face as a result of war?*

networks

There's More Online! about life during the Cold War.

CHAPTER 33

The Story Matters...

During the Cold War, the United States and the Soviet Union had stockpiles of nuclear weapons. When the arms race led to increased hostility between the two nations, the world prepared for the threat of nuclear war. The Soviet Union and United States organized civil defense programs designed to train the civilian population how to react in the event of a nuclear attack. The programs involved "duck and cover" and evacuation drills, as well as widely circulated public safety announcements.

◀ "Duck and cover" drills taught school children how to protect themselves from a nuclear attack. However, these drills would have provided no real protection from the destruction of a bomb or the resulting nuclear radiation.

PHOTO: ©Bettmann/Corbis

CHAPTER 33

Place and Time: Europe and the U.S. 1945–1989

During the decades of the Cold War, the tension between the United States and the Soviet Union not only colored foreign affairs but also influenced the nature of daily life. Citizens grew increasingly anxious under the threat of nuclear war. In the United States and Western Europe, students protested political and economic conditions. In the Eastern bloc countries, popular discontent increased when the state did not provide political freedoms or economic security. While the methods of political protest were similar, their goals were different. Furthermore, the level of political freedom in the East and West helped determine the fate of these protest movements.

Step Into the Place

Read the quotes and look at the information presented on the map.

DBQ **Analyzing Historical Documents** What were the goals of political protests? Which movements do you think were successful?

PRIMARY SOURCE

"We consider socialist democracy to be a system in which the working man has his own standing and value, his security, his right, and his future. It is based upon human participation, coherence, and cooperation. We wish to meet people's longing for a society in which they can feel to be human among humans. This active, humane, integrating part of socialism, a society without antagonism, that is what we want to realize systematically and gradually, serving the people."

—First Secretary Alexander Dubček, from a speech to the Central Committee of the Communist Party of Czechoslovakia, April 1, 1968

PRIMARY SOURCE

"We are occupying the faculties, you are occupying the factories. Aren't we fighting for the same thing? Higher education only contains 10 percent workers' children. Are we fighting so that there will be more of them, for a democratic university reform? That would a good thing, but it's not the most important. These workers' children would become just like other students. We are not aiming for a worker's son to be a manager. We want to wipe out segregation between workers and management."

—The March 22 Movement, "Your Struggle Is Ours," May 21, 1968

Step Into the Time

Predicting Consequences

Choose an event from the time line and explain how it might have affected everyday life in the United States or Europe during the Cold War.

EUROPE AND THE UNITED STATES

1945 World War II ends

1946 Great Britain passes the National Insurance Act and National Health Service Act

1956 Hungarians revolt against Soviets

1960 France explodes its first nuclear bomb

1963 U.S. passes the Equal Pay Act

1945

1955

THE WORLD

1948 UN adopts Universal Declaration of Human Rights

1956 Gamal Abdel Nasser takes over Egyptian government

1962 Nikita Khrushchev allows publication of *One Day in the Life of Ivan Denisovich*

1963 Nelson Mandela delivers speech during Rivonia trial

networks
There's More Online!

- ☑ **MAP** Explore the interactive version of this map on Networks.
- ☑ **TIME LINE** Explore the interactive version of the time line on Networks.

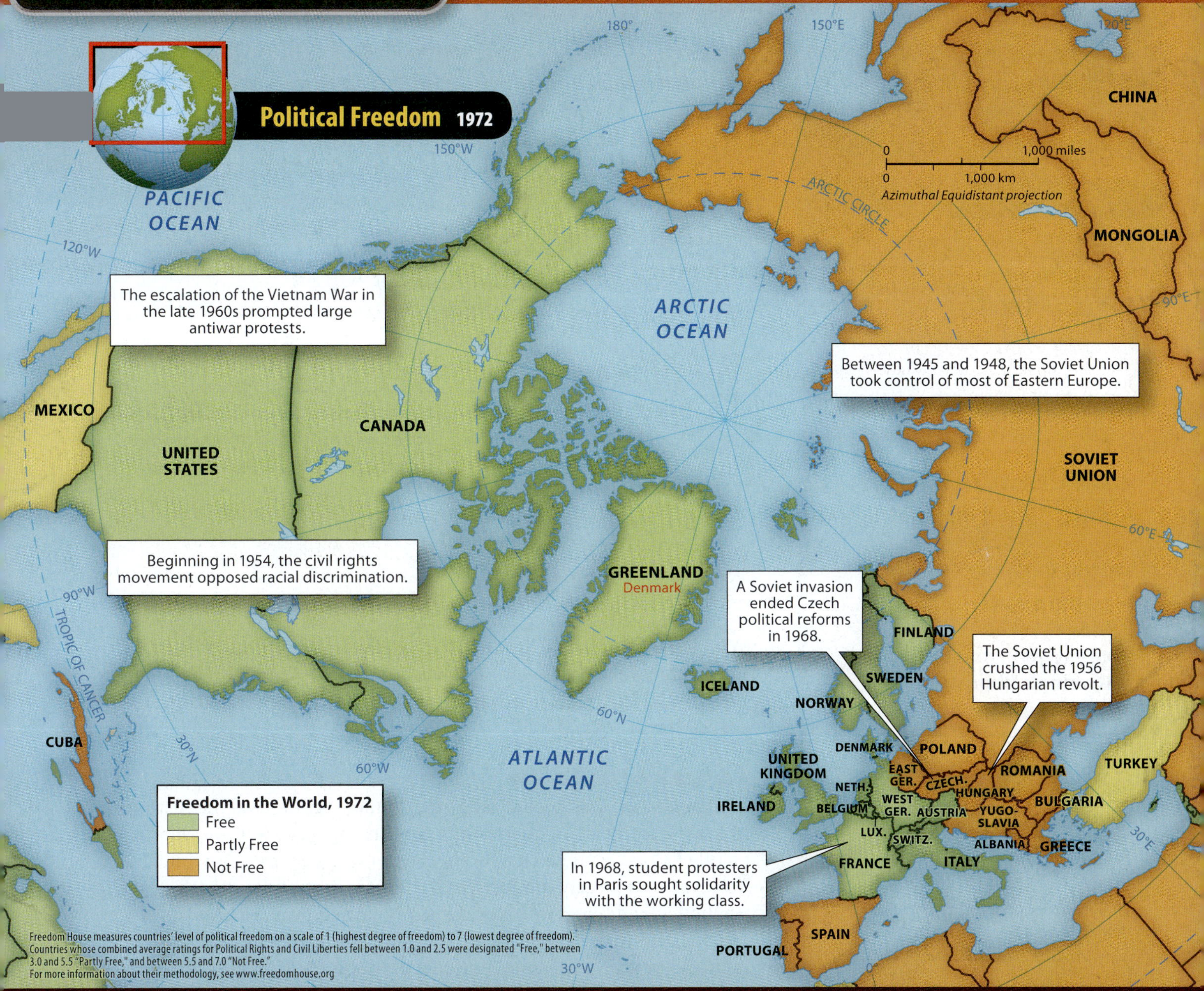

1964 U.S. president Lyndon B. Johnson signs the Civil Rights Act of 1964

1968 "Prague Spring" in Czechoslovakia

1974 Gerald Ford becomes U.S. president after Nixon resigns

1984 USSR, East Germany, and Cuba boycott Los Angeles Olympics

1965 **1975** **1985** **1989**

1964 Creation of the Palestinian Liberation Organization (PLO)

1966 Mao Zedong launches Cultural Revolution

1978 Camp David Accords negotiate peace between Egypt and Israel

1979 Soviet Union invades Afghanistan

networks

There's More Online!

- ☑ CHART/GRAPH The Pay Gap
- ☑ CHART/GRAPH Women's Suffrage by Country and Year
- ☑ IMAGE Equal Rights Amendment Rally in Pittsburgh, 1976
- ☑ IMAGE Family Life in the 1950s
- ☑ IMAGE Integration of Little Rock Central High School
- ☑ INTERACTIVE SELF-CHECK QUIZ
- ☑ MAP European Economic Community, 1989
- ☑ VIDEO Vinyl Records

LESSON 1
Western Europe and North America

ESSENTIAL QUESTIONS • *How does war result in change?* • *What challenges may countries face as a result of war?*

Reading HELPDESK

Academic Vocabulary

- **shift**
- **minimal**

Content Vocabulary

- **welfare state**
- **bloc**
- **consumer society**
- **women's liberation movement**
- **real wages**

TAKING NOTES:
Key Ideas and Details

Identifying As you read, use a chart like the one below to identify the economic policies of Western countries during the Cold War.

Country	Policies
France	
West Germany	
Great Britain	
United States	
Canada	

IT MATTERS BECAUSE

Most Western European countries recovered rapidly from World War II. The United States experienced an economic boom after World War II but was troubled by social and political issues.

Western Europe

GUIDING QUESTION *How did Western Europe recover from World War II?*

With the economic aid of the Marshall Plan, the countries of Western Europe recovered relatively rapidly from the devastation of World War II. By 1950, industrial output in Europe was 30 percent above prewar levels.

France and de Gaulle

One man—the war hero Charles de Gaulle—dominated the history of France for nearly a quarter of a century after the war. In 1946 de Gaulle helped establish a new government, the Fourth Republic. It, however, was largely ineffective. In 1958 leaders of the Fourth Republic, frightened by bitter divisions caused by a crisis in the French colony of Algeria, asked de Gaulle to form a new government. That year, de Gaulle drafted a new constitution for the Fifth Republic that enhanced the power of the president. The French president would now have the right to choose the prime minister, dissolve parliament, and supervise defense and foreign policy. French voters approved the constitution, and de Gaulle became the first president of the Fifth Republic.

As president, de Gaulle wanted France to be a world power once again. To achieve this, de Gaulle invested heavily in nuclear arms. France exploded its first nuclear bomb in 1960.

During de Gaulle's presidency, the French economy grew at an annual rate of 5.5 percent, faster than the rate of growth in the United States. France became a major industrial producer and exporter, especially of automobiles and weapons. Nevertheless, problems remained. Large government deficits and a rise in the cost of living led to unrest. In May 1968, a series of student protests was followed by a general labor strike. Discouraged, de Gaulle resigned from office in April 1969 and died within a year.

In the 1970s, a deteriorating economic situation caused a political **shift** to the left. By 1981, the Socialists gained power in the National Assembly. Socialist François Mitterrand was elected president. He initiated a number of measures to aid workers—an increased minimum wage, a 39-hour work week, and higher taxes for the rich. The Socialist government also nationalized, or took over, major banks, the steel industry, the space and electronics industries, and insurance firms.

Socialist policies, however, largely failed to work, and France's economic decline continued. In the elections in March of 1993, the Socialists won only 28 percent of the vote. A coalition of conservative parties gained 80 percent of the seats in the National Assembly.

West Germany: The Economic Miracle

The three Western zones of Germany were unified as the Federal Republic of Germany in 1949. From 1949 to 1963, Konrad Adenauer (AHD • uh • NAU • uhr), the leader of the Christian Democratic Union (CDU), served as chancellor (head of state). Adenauer sought respect for West Germany. He cooperated with the United States and other Western European nations, especially France—Germany's longtime enemy.

Under Adenauer, West Germany experienced an "economic miracle." This revival of the West German economy was largely guided by the minister of finance, Ludwig Erhard. Unemployment fell from 8 percent in 1950 to 0.4 percent in 1965. After Adenauer resigned in 1963, Erhard succeeded him as chancellor and largely continued his policies.

An economic downturn in the mid-1960s brought the Social Democratic Party into power in 1969. The Social Democrats, a moderate socialist party, were led by Willy Brandt, mayor of West Berlin. In December 1972, Brandt signed a treaty that led to greater contact between East Germany and West Germany. Economic, cultural, and personal ties between the countries were stronger as a result. For his efforts, Brandt received the Nobel Peace Prize for 1971.

Great Britain

The end of World War II left Great Britain with massive economic problems. In elections held immediately after the war, the Labour Party overwhelmingly defeated Churchill's Conservative Party.

Under Clement Attlee, the new prime minister, the Labour government set out to create a modern **welfare state**, a state in which the government takes responsibility for providing citizens with services and a **minimal** standard of living. In 1946 the new government passed the National Insurance Act and the National Health Service Act. The insurance act provided government funds to help the unemployed, the sick, and the aged. The health act created a system of socialized medicine that ensured medical care for everyone. The British welfare state became the norm for most European states after the war.

Continuing economic problems brought the Conservatives back into power from 1951 to 1964. Although they favored private enterprise, the Conservatives accepted the welfare state and extended it by financing an ambitious building program to improve British housing.

Between 1964 and 1979, power alternated between Great Britain's Conservative Party and Labour Party. In 1979 the Conservatives came to

TEKS Texas Essential Knowledge and Skills

1F identify major causes and describe the major effects of the following important turning points in world history from 1914 to the present: the world wars and their impact on political, economic, and social systems; communist revolutions and their impact on the Cold War; independence movements; and globalization

22E identify examples of individuals who led resistance to political oppression such as Nelson Mandela, Mohandas Gandhi, Oscar Romero, Natan Sharansky, Las Madres de la Plaza de Mayo, and Chinese student protestors in Tiananmen Square

24A describe the changing roles of women, children, and families during major eras of world history

24B describe the major influences of women such as Elizabeth I, Queen Victoria, Mother Teresa, Indira Gandhi, Margaret Thatcher, and Golda Meir during major eras of world history

shift a change in direction

welfare state a state in which the government takes responsibility for providing citizens with services such as health care

minimal barely adequate

▲ West German chancellor Willy Brandt

GEOGRAPHY CONNECTION

1. **HUMAN SYSTEMS** *Create a map of Europe in 1989 of non-EEC members. How do EEC and non-EEC countries differ?*
2. **PLACES AND REGIONS** *Create a graph or chart of the expansion of EEC membership.*

power under Margaret Thatcher, Britain's first female prime minister. Thatcher pledged to limit social welfare, to restrict union power, and to end inflation. She was also successful in promoting privatization. Although she did not eliminate the basic social welfare system, Thatcher broke the power of the labor unions and controlled inflation.

Thatcherism, as her economic policy was termed, improved the British economic situation, but at a price. Business investment and the number of small businesses increased substantially. The south of England, for example, prospered. Old industrial areas elsewhere, however, were beset by high unemployment, poverty, and violence. Thatcher dominated British politics in the 1980s, but in 1990 her popularity fell, and she resigned as prime minister.

The European Economic Community

The destructiveness of two world wars caused many thoughtful Europeans to consider the need for some form of European unity. National feeling was still too powerful, however, for European nations to give up their political sovereignty. As a result, the desire for unity focused chiefly on the economic arena, not the political one.

In 1957 France, West Germany, the Benelux countries (Belgium, the Netherlands, and Luxembourg), and Italy signed the Rome Treaty. This treaty created the European Economic Community (EEC), also known as the Common Market.

The EEC was a free-trade area made up of the six member nations. These six nations would impose no tariffs, or import charges, on each other's goods. However, as a group, they would be protected by a tariff imposed on goods from non-EEC nations. In this way, the EEC encouraged cooperation among the member nations' economies.

bloc a group of nations with a common purpose

By the 1960s, the EEC had become an important trading **bloc** (a group of nations with a common purpose.) In 1973 Britain, Denmark, and Ireland joined the EEC. With a total population of 165 million, the EEC was the world's largest exporter and purchaser of raw materials. By 1986, Spain, Portugal, and Greece had become members. By 1992, the European Economic Community comprised 344 million people and was the world's largest single trading bloc.

✓ **READING PROGRESS CHECK**

Describing How was the Fifth Republic in France different from the Fourth Republic?

The U.S. After the War

GUIDING QUESTION *What social and political issues challenged the United States during the Cold War?*

Between 1945 and 1970, the ideals of Franklin Delano Roosevelt's New Deal largely determined the patterns of American domestic politics. The New

Deal brought basic changes to American society. These changes included a dramatic increase in the role and power of the federal government, the rise of organized labor, the beginning of a welfare state, and a realization of the need to deal fairly with the concerns of minorities, especially African Americans.

The New Deal tradition in American politics was reinforced by the election of Democratic presidents—Harry S. Truman in 1948, John F. Kennedy in 1960, and Lyndon B. Johnson in 1964. Even the election of a Republican president, Dwight D. Eisenhower, in 1952 and 1956, did not change the basic direction of the New Deal.

An economic boom followed World War II. A shortage of consumer goods during the war left Americans with extra income and the desire to buy goods after the war. In addition, the growth of labor unions brought higher wages and gave more workers the ability to buy consumer goods. Between 1945 and 1973, **real wages** grew an average of 3 percent per year, the most prolonged advance ever in American history.

real wages the actual purchasing power of income

Prosperity was not the only characteristic of the early 1950s. Communist revolutions elsewhere in the world caused a widespread fear that Communists had infiltrated the United States. Senator Joseph R. McCarthy of Wisconsin publicly charged that hundreds of supposed Communists were in high government positions, the effect of which was to help create a massive "Red Scare"—fear of Communist subversion. When McCarthy attacked "Communist conspirators" in the U.S. Army, he was condemned by the Senate in 1954. Very quickly, his anti-Communist crusade came to an end.

The 1960s and Civil Rights

In August 1963, the Reverend Martin Luther King, Jr., leader of a movement for racial equality, led a march on Washington, D.C., to dramatize the African American desire for equality. King's march and his impassioned plea for racial equality had an electrifying effect on the American people. By the end of 1963, a majority of the American people called civil rights the most significant national issue.

After the assassination of John Kennedy, Lyndon B. Johnson became president. Following his landslide victory in 1964, he pursued the cause of equal rights for African Americans. The Civil Rights Act of 1964 created the machinery to end segregation and discrimination in the workplace and all public places. The Voting Rights Act made it easier for African Americans to vote in Southern states.

Laws alone, however, could not guarantee the Great Society that Johnson talked about creating. He soon faced bitter social unrest. In 1968 Martin Luther King, Jr., was assassinated. Riots hit more than 100 cities, including Washington, D.C. The riots led to a "white backlash" (whites became less sympathetic to the cause of racial equality) and continued the racial division of the United States. Antiwar protests also divided the United States as some Americans turned against the Vietnam War.

The combination of antiwar demonstrations and riots in the cities caused many people to call for law and order. This was the appeal used by Richard Nixon, the Republican presidential candidate in 1968. With Nixon's election, a shift to the political right in American politics began.

▼ **The Reverend Martin Luther King, Jr., at the March on Washington, August 28, 1963.**

▶ **CRITICAL THINKING**

Determining Cause and Effect What do you think was the effect of the March on Washington?

Analyzing PRIMARY SOURCES

The Voting Rights Act of 1965

"This act flows from a clear and simple wrong. Its only purpose is to right that wrong. Millions of Americans are denied the right to vote because of their color. This law will ensure them the right to vote. . . . I pledge you that we will not delay, or we will not hesitate, or we will not turn aside until Americans of every race and color and origin in this country have the same right as all others to share in the process of democracy."

—President Lyndon B. Johnson, "Remarks in the Capitol Rotunda at the Signing of the Voting Rights Act," August 6, 1965

DBQ ***DRAWING CONCLUSIONS*** What is the significance of the Voting Rights Act of 1965?

The 1970s and 1980s

As president, Nixon used illegal methods to gain information about his opponents. This led to the Watergate scandal. After lying to the American public about his involvement in the affair, secret tapes of his conversations in the White House revealed the truth. On August 9, 1974, Nixon resigned rather than face possible impeachment.

In the 1976 election, the former governor of Georgia, Jimmy Carter, became president. A crisis abroad erupted when the Iranian government of the Ayatollah Khomeini (koh • MAY • nee) held 52 Americans hostage. Carter's inability to gain the release of the American hostages contributed to his loss to Ronald Reagan in the 1980 election.

Canada

After the war, Canada began developing electronic, aircraft, nuclear, and chemical engineering industries on a large scale. Under Lester Pearson, the Liberal government laid the groundwork for Canada's welfare state. A national social security system and health insurance program were enacted.

When Pierre Trudeau (TROO • DOH) became prime minister in 1968, he supported a vigorous program of industrialization. He was also dedicated to preserving a united Canada. At the same time, he acknowledged the rights of French-speaking Canadians. His government passed the Official Languages Act, which allowed English and French to be used in the federal civil service.

✓ READING PROGRESS CHECK

Drawing Conclusions In the United States, how was the decade of the 1970s a reaction to the 1960s?

Western Society

GUIDING QUESTION ***How did Western society change during the Cold War?***

After World War II, Western society witnessed rapid change. New inventions such as computers, televisions, and jet planes altered the pace and nature of human life.

A New Social Structure

Postwar Western society was marked by a changing social structure. Especially noticeable were changes in the middle class. Traditional middle-class groups were made up of businesspeople, lawyers, doctors, and teachers. A new group of managers and technicians, hired by large companies and government agencies, now joined the middle class.

Changes also occurred among the lower classes. The shift of people from rural to urban areas continued. The number of people in farming declined drastically. By the 1950s, the number of farmers in most parts of Europe dropped by 50 percent. The number of industrial workers declined as white-collar workers increased.

At the same time, a noticeable increase in the real wages of workers made it possible for them to imitate the buying patterns of the middle class. This led to what some observers have called the **consumer society**. Buying on credit became widespread in the 1950s. Workers could now buy such products as televisions, washing machines, refrigerators, and stereos.

consumer society a society preoccupied with buying goods

Women in the Postwar World

Women's participation in the world wars had led to changing roles. They had achieved one of the major aims of the nineteenth-century feminist movement—the right to vote.

During World War II, women had entered the workforce in huge numbers. At the war's end, however, they were removed to provide jobs for soldiers returning home. For a time, women fell back into traditional roles. Birthrates rose, creating a "baby boom" in the late 1940s and the 1950s.

By the end of the 1950s, however, the birthrate began to fall, and family roles began to change again. More married women opted to enter the workplace in the United States and Europe. These women, especially working-class women, faced an old problem. They still earned less than men for equal work. In addition, women still tended to enter traditionally female jobs. Many faced the double burden of earning income and raising a family. Such inequalities led increasing numbers of women to rebel. In the late 1960s came renewed interest in feminism, or the **women's liberation movement**.

In the 1960s and 1970s, the women's movement emerged in the United States and quickly spread to Western Europe. Supporters of the movement wanted to change the basic conditions of women's lives. The United States passed the Equal Pay Act in 1963. It required women to be paid the same as men for performing the same work.

A controversial issue was abortion. In 1973 the U.S. Supreme Court legalized abortion in *Roe* v. *Wade*. Although national health insurance covered abortion in most of Europe, the procedure was debated in the United States.

▲ Men and women march together at an Equal Rights Amendment (ERA) rally in Pittsburgh, Pennsylvania, in 1976.

▶ **CRITICAL THINKING**

Analyzing Visuals Interpret the meaning of the signs carried at the rally.

women's liberation movement the renewed feminist movement of the late 1960s, which demanded political and economic equality with men

Student Revolts

Growing discontent among university students led to an outburst of student revolts in the late 1960s. Many protests were an extension of the revolts against the Vietnam War. Other students believed they were becoming small cogs in the large bureaucratic wheels of the modern world. The roles of children and teens were changing during this period, as well, as they became consumers of popular culture.

PHOTO: Barbara Freeman/Hulton Archive/Getty Images

✓ **READING PROGRESS CHECK**

Summarizing What was a goal of the women's liberation movement?

LESSON 1 REVIEW TEKS

Reviewing Vocabulary

1. ***Making Connections*** How does the rise of the modern welfare state represent a shift to the left in European nations?

Using Your Notes

2. ***Identifying*** Use your notes to identify economic policies that Western countries implemented after World War II.

Answering the Guiding Questions

3. ***Describing*** How did Western Europe recover from World War II?

4. ***Analyzing Information*** Which social and political issues challenged the United States during the Cold War?

5. ***Evaluating*** How did Western society change during the Cold War?

Writing Activity

6. **INFORMATIVE/EXPLANATORY** Pick one of the countries discussed in the lesson and, using information from the lesson and outside research, write a short essay about the postwar reforms implemented in the country and discuss whether they were successful.

networks

There's More Online!

- IMAGE Factory in Poland
- IMAGE Hungarian Revolt of 1956
- IMAGE Siberian Labor Camp
- IMAGE Soviet Tanks in Budapest
- INTERACTIVE SELF-CHECK QUIZ
- PRIMARY SOURCE Soviet Control Over the Arts
- VIDEO The Soviet Invasion of Czechoslovakia

LESSON 2

Eastern Europe and the Soviet Union

ESSENTIAL QUESTIONS • *How does war result in change?* • *What challenges may countries face as a result of war?*

Reading HELPDESK

Academic Vocabulary

- **enhanced**
- **participation**
- **sole**

Content Vocabulary

- **heavy industry**
- **de-Stalinization**
- **détente**
- **dissidents**

TAKING NOTES:

Key Ideas and Details

Comparing As you read, use a table like the one below to compare the policies of Khrushchev and Brezhnev.

Policies	Khrushchev	Brezhnev

TEKS Texas Essential Knowledge and Skills

22E identify examples of individuals who led resistance to political oppression such as Nelson Mandela, Mohandas Gandhi, Oscar Romero, Natan Sharansky, Las Madres de la Plaza de Mayo, and Chinese student protestors in Tiananmen Square

continued on the next page

It Matters Because

Stalin was a repressive leader who wanted to bring Eastern Europe under Soviet control. Many Communist countries came under Soviet control during this era, including Poland, Hungary, and Czechoslovakia. After Stalin's death, Nikita Khrushchev denounced the most brutal policies of the Stalin regime.

Postwar Soviet Union

GUIDING QUESTION *What political, economic, and social shifts occurred in the Soviet Union during the Cold War?*

World War II devastated the Soviet Union. To create a new industrial base, Stalin returned to the method that he had used in the 1930s. Soviet workers were expected to produce goods for export with little in return for themselves. The incoming capital from abroad could then be used to buy machinery and Western technology.

Economic recovery in the Soviet Union was spectacular in some respects. By 1950, Russian industrial production surpassed prewar levels by 40 percent. New power plants, canals, and giant factories were built. **Heavy industry** increased, chiefly for military benefit. The hydrogen bomb in 1953 and the first space satellite, *Sputnik I*, in 1957 **enhanced** the Soviet Union's reputation as a world power.

Yet the Soviet people were shortchanged. The production of consumer goods did not increase as much as heavy industry, and there was a housing shortage. As a British official in Moscow reported, "Every room is both a living room by day and a bedroom by night."

The Rule of Stalin

Stalin was the undisputed master of the Soviet Union. He distrusted competitors, exercised **sole** power, and had little respect for other Communist Party leaders. He is reported to have said to members of his inner circle in 1952, "You are as blind as kittens. What would you do without me?"

PHOTO: (l to r)Neil Beer/Photodisc/Getty Images, ©Tramonto/Age Fotostock America, ©akg-images/RIA Nowosti/The Image Works, Keystone/France/Gamma-Keystone/Getty Images, ©Michel Philippot/Sygma/Corbis.

Stalin's suspicions added to the regime's increasing repression. In 1946 the government ordered all literary and scientific work to conform to the state's political needs. Along with this anti-intellectual campaign came political terror. The threat of more purges in 1953 disappeared when Stalin died on March 5, 1953.

heavy industry the manufacture of machines and equipment for factories and mines

enhanced improved

sole being the only one

The Khrushchev Era

A group of leaders succeeded Stalin, but the new general secretary of the Communist Party, Nikita Khrushchev, soon emerged as the chief Soviet policy maker. After he was in power, Khrushchev took steps to undo some of the worst features of Stalin's regime.

(continued from p. 800)

TEKS **Texas Essential Knowledge and Skills**
16C TK

At the Twentieth Congress of the Communist Party in 1956, Khrushchev condemned Stalin for his "administrative violence, mass repression, and terror." The process of eliminating the more ruthless policies of Stalin became known as **de-Stalinization**.

de-Stalinization the process of eliminating Stalin's more ruthless policies

Khrushchev loosened government controls on literary and artistic works. In 1962, for example, he allowed the publication of *One Day in the Life of Ivan Denisovich.* This novel, written by Aleksandr Solzhenitsyn (SOHL • zhuh • NEET • suhn), is a grim portrayal of life in a Siberian labor camp and reflects the history of the Soviet government's oppression of its own people. Many Soviets identified with Ivan as a symbol of the suffering endured under Stalin.

Khrushchev also tried to place more emphasis on producing consumer goods. He attempted to increase agricultural output by growing corn and cultivating vast lands east of the Ural Mountains. The attempt was unsuccessful. This failure, combined with increased military spending, hurt the

PHOTO: Neil Beer/Photodisc/Getty Images

ANALYZING PRIMARY SOURCES

Contrasting these depictions of Soviet society

Soviet control over the arts was rigid. Artists had to work within the confines of socialist realist art, which was meant to portray the ideals of Soviet society. Common themes included portraits of Soviet political leaders, people performing manual labor, and industrial progress, such as the sculpture Worker and Kolkhoz [collective farm] Woman *by Vera Mukhina (right). Not everyone worked within these confines, however. Aleksandr Solzhenitsyn was exiled for writing* The Gulag Archipelago, *which revealed life in the forced labor camps to which many political opponents were sent in the 1950s. "Archipelago" was his metaphor for forced labor camps and "Gulag" is an acronym for the agency that supervised the camps.*

"But the whole central meaning of their existence was identical for serfdom and the Archipelago; they were forms of social organization for the forced and pitiless exploitation of the unpaid labor of millions of slaves."

— Aleksandr Solzhenitsyn, from *The Gulag Archipelago*

DBQ Analyzing Historical Documents

1. ***Differentiating*** How do the text and the sculpture demonstrate differing views of life under the Soviet regime?
2. ***Making Inferences*** Serfdom was abolished in Russia in 1861. What do you think Solzhenitsyn means when he writes that the "meaning of their existence was identical for serfdom and the Archipelago"?

BIOGRAPHY

Natan Sharansky (1948-)

During the 1970s, the Soviet government continued to crack down on internal protestors. One was Natan Sharansky, a Soviet Jew who wanted to emigrate to Israel in 1973 but was denied the right. The government's refusal led Sharansky to help found the Refusenik movement, a group of activists speaking out about Soviet political oppression. Sharansky worked as a human rights activist and spoke to Western journalists to spread the word about life in the Soviet Union.

In 1977 Sharansky was arrested, charged with treason and spying, convicted in a secret trial, and sent to a labor camp in Siberia. Sharansky spent almost ten years in prison. During his imprisonment, his wife and leaders in the West called for his release. These pressures helped lead to his release in a prisoner exchange in 1986. He soon moved to Israel where he entered politics, rising to the level of Deputy Prime Minister.

Soviet economy. The industrial growth rate, which had soared in the early 1950s, now declined sharply from 13 percent in 1953 to 7.5 percent in 1964.

Foreign policy failures also damaged Khrushchev's reputation among his colleagues. His rash plan to place missiles in Cuba was the final straw. While he was away on vacation in 1964, a special meeting of the Soviet leaders voted him out of office (because of "deteriorating health") and forced him into retirement.

The Brezhnev Era

When Nikita Khrushchev was removed from office in 1964, two men, Alexei Kosygin and Leonid Brezhnev (BREHZH • nehf) replaced him. Brezhnev emerged as the dominant leader in the 1970s. He was determined to keep Eastern Europe in Communist hands and was not interested in reform. Brezhnev insisted on the Soviet Union's right to intervene if communism was threatened in another Communist state (known as the Brezhnev Doctrine).

At the same time, Brezhnev benefited from **détente**, a relaxation of tensions and improved relations between the United States and the Soviet Union. In the 1970s, the two superpowers signed SALT I and SALT II (Strategic Arms Limitation Treaties) and the Anti-Ballistic Missile (ABM) Treaty to limit nuclear arms. Because they felt more secure, Soviet leaders relaxed their authoritarian rule and allowed more access to Western music, dress, and art. Of course, **dissidents**—those who spoke out against the regime—were still suppressed. For example, Andrei Sakharov, father of the Soviet hydrogen bomb, was punished for defending human rights.

In his economic policies, Brezhnev continued to emphasize heavy industry. Two problems, however, weakened the Soviet economy. First, the government's central planning led to a huge, complex bureaucracy that discouraged efficiency and led to indifference. Second, collective farmers had no incentive to work hard. Many preferred working their own small private plots to laboring in the collective work brigades.

By the 1970s, the Communist ruling class in the Soviet Union had become complacent and corrupt. Party and state leaders, as well as army leaders and secret police (KGB), enjoyed a high standard of living. Brezhnev was unwilling to tamper with the party leadership and state bureaucracy regardless of the inefficiency and corruption that the system encouraged.

By the 1970s, détente had allowed U.S. grain and consumer goods to be sold to the Soviet Union. However, détente collapsed in 1979 when the Soviet Union invaded Afghanistan. A new period of East-West confrontation began. The Soviet Union wanted to restore a pro-Soviet regime in Afghanistan. The United States viewed this as an act of expansion. To show his disapproval, President Jimmy Carter canceled U.S. **participation** in the 1980 Olympic Games to be held in Moscow. He also placed an embargo on the shipment of U.S. grain to the Soviets.

Relations became even chillier when Ronald Reagan became president of the United States. Calling the Soviet Union an "evil empire," he began a military buildup and a new arms race. Reagan also gave military aid to the Afghan rebels to maintain a war in Afghanistan that the Soviet Union could not win.

✓ READING PROGRESS CHECK

Contrasting How were U.S.-Soviet relations different during the Khrushchev and Brezhnev regimes?

détente a phase of relaxed tensions and improved relations between two adversaries

dissident a person who speaks out against the regime in power

participation having a part in or sharing in something

SKILLS PRACTICE

Write the vocabulary words from this lesson on cards. Read the cards often until you can read and understand the words quickly on sight.

Eastern Europe

GUIDING QUESTION *How was Eastern Europe affected by communism after World War II?*

At the end of World War II, Soviet military forces occupied all of Eastern Europe and the Balkans (except for Greece, Albania, and Yugoslavia). All the occupied states came under Soviet control.

Communist Patterns of Control

The timetable of the Soviet takeover varied from country to country. Between 1945 and 1947, Soviet-controlled Communist governments became firmly entrenched in East Germany, Bulgaria, Romania, Poland, and Hungary. In Czechoslovakia, where there was a tradition of democracy and a multi-party system, the Soviets did not seize control of the government until 1948. At that time they dissolved all but the Communist Party.

Albania and Yugoslavia were exceptions to this pattern of Soviet dominance. During the war, both countries had strong Communist movements that resisted the Nazis. After the war, local Communist parties took control. Communists in Albania set up a Stalinist-type regime that grew more and more independent of the Soviet Union.

In Yugoslavia, Josip Broz, known as Tito, had been the leader of the Communist resistance movement. After the war, he created an independent Communist state in Yugoslavia. Stalin hoped to take control of Yugoslavia, just as he had done in other Eastern European countries. Tito, however, refused to give in to Stalin's demands. He gained the support of the people by portraying the struggle as one of Yugoslav national freedom. Tito ruled Yugoslavia until his death in 1980. Although Yugoslavia had a Communist government, it was not a Soviet satellite state.

▲ The head of a destroyed statue of Stalin in the middle of a Budapest street during the Hungarian revolt of 1956.

▶ **CRITICAL THINKING**

Analyzing Visuals What is the symbolic importance of the fallen statue?

Between 1948 and Stalin's death in 1953, the Eastern European satellite states, directed by the Soviet Union, followed Stalin's example. They instituted Soviet-type five-year plans with emphasis on heavy industry rather than consumer goods. They collectivized agriculture, eliminated all noncommunist parties, and set up the institutions of repression—secret police and military forces.

Revolts Against Communism

Communism did not develop deep roots among the peoples of Eastern Europe. Moreover, the Soviets exploited Eastern Europe economically for their own benefit and made living conditions harsh for most people. These factors became causes of independence movements within the Soviet bloc.

After Stalin's death, many Eastern European states began to pursue a new course. In the late 1950s and 1960s, however, the Soviet Union made it clear—especially in Poland, Hungary, and Czechoslovakia—that it would not allow its Eastern European satellites to become independent of Soviet control.

In 1956 protests erupted in Poland. In response, the Polish Communist Party adopted a series of reforms in October and elected Władysław Gomułka as first secretary. Gomułka declared that Poland had the right to follow its own socialist path. Fearful of Soviet armed response, however, the Poles compromised. Poland pledged to remain loyal to the Warsaw Pact.

Developments in Poland in 1956 led Hungarian Communists to seek the same kinds of reforms. Unrest in Hungary, combined with economic difficulties, led to calls for revolt. To quell the rising rebellion Imre Nagy, the Hungarian leader, declared Hungary a free nation on November 1, 1956, and promised free elections. It soon became clear that this could mean the end of Communist rule in Hungary.

▲ Soviet tanks left Hungary on October 30, 1956, but the Soviets soon returned, crushing the revolt and reestablishing control.

Khrushchev was in no position at home to allow a member of the Communist group of nations to leave, however. Three days after Nagy's declaration, the Soviet Army attacked Budapest. The Soviets reestablished control over the country. Nagy was seized by the Soviet military and executed two years later.

The situation in Czechoslovakia in the 1950s was different. There, Stalin had placed Antonín Novotný, the "Litte Stalin," in power in 1953. By the late 1960s, however, he had alienated many members of his own party. He was especially disliked by Czechoslovakia's writers. A writers' rebellion, which encouraged the people to take control of their own lives, led to Novotný's resignation in 1968.

In January 1968, Alexander Dubček (DOOB • chehk) was elected first secretary of the Communist Party. He introduced a number of reforms, including freedom of speech and press and freedom to travel abroad. He relaxed censorship, began to pursue an independent foreign policy, and promised a democratization of the Czechoslovakian political system. Dubček hoped to create "socialism with a human face." A period of euphoria broke out that came to be known as the "Prague Spring."

The euphoria proved to be short-lived. To forestall the spreading of this "spring fever," the Soviet Army invaded Czechoslovakia in August 1968 and crushed the reform movement. Gustav Husák replaced Dubček, revoked his reforms, and reestablished the old order. Yet again, the effects of Eastern European independence movements were violent crackdowns. These crackdowns, however, showed the outside world the brutality of Soviet power.

✓ **READING PROGRESS CHECK**

Drawing Conclusions Why was Yugoslavia different from other Eastern European countries during the Cold War?

LESSON 2 REVIEW TEKS

Reviewing Vocabulary

1. ***Making Connections*** How did the period of détente between the United States and the Soviet Union lead to a relaxation of authoritarian rule?

Using Your Notes

2. ***Comparing and Contrasting*** Use your notes to compare and contrast the rule of Khrushchev and Brezhnev.

Answering the Guiding Questions

3. ***Drawing Conclusions*** What political, economic, and social shifts occurred in the Soviet Union during the Cold War?

4. ***Analyzing Information*** How were Eastern Europeans affected by communism after World War II?

Writing Activity

5. **INFORMATIVE/EXPLANATORY** Research and write an essay about the "Prague Spring." What did it hope to achieve, and why was it unsuccessful? Be sure to include a bibliography of the sources you consulted.

SKILLBUILDER

TEKS 16C

Interpreting Graphs

Why Learn This Skill?

Graphs are a good method of illustrating dates, facts, and figures. With a graph, you can compare change or differences easily. For example, imagine your parents say you spend too much money on clothes. You disagree, but then they show you a bar graph of your weekly expenses. The bar for each week shows how the money you spend on clothes is twice as high as what you spend on anything else. With a quick glance, you immediately see that they are right.

Learning the Skill

There are basically three types of graphs:

- **Circle graphs** They look like a pizza that has been divided into different sized slices. They are useful for showing comparisons and percentages.
- **Bar graphs** Individual bars are drawn for each item being graphed. The lengths of the bars easily illustrate differences or changes over time.
- **Line graphs** Each item is indicated by a point on the graph. The points are then connected by a line. You can tell how values have changed by whether the line goes up or down.

Most graphs also have titles and labels that include extra information. If the title is called "Maria's Weekly Clothing Expenses," then it will plot how much Maria spends on clothes every week. Labels would indicate when Maria spent money on clothes and how much. The viewer can determine relationships between different numbers in the graph with a simple look. If it is a bar graph, the bars representing different numbers will be different sizes.

Percentage of World Population

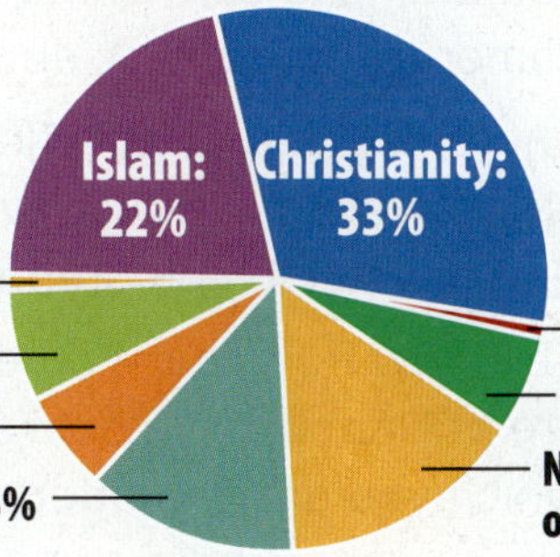

Note: Total exceeds 100% because numbers were rounded.
Sources: www.cia.gov, The World Factbook 2006; www.adherents.com.

Practicing the Skill

Look closely at the circle graph on this page. The graph visually compares the percentages of the world's population who practice different religions.

Some graphs need a key to indicate what different colors represent. This graph does not need that kind of key because each segment of the circle is labeled. Still, the fact that each segment has a different color helps them stand apart from each other. This separation helps the viewer compare the sizes of the different segments.

Skills Assessment

Study the circle graph and the world map and answer the following questions:

1. Which religion is practiced by the most people?
2. What percentage of people worldwide practices Buddhism?
3. How did spreading religions affect the people of North Africa?
4. How do the red arrows in the map and the largest section of the circle graph have a cause-and-effect relationship?

Applying the Skill

Study the circle graph on this page closely and write a paragraph summarizing how geography has influenced people and events in the past. Remember, a graph does not just present individual facts—it also presents relationships between those facts.

PRIMARY SOURCES

In 1962 John J. Glenn, Jr., took a trip that no other American had ever taken. Glenn piloted the Mercury spacecraft around the earth, circling the earth three times in under five hours. During the trip, he reached speeds of over 17,000 miles per hour. Six days after his return from orbit, Glenn addressed a joint meeting of Congress about the significance of the trip.

Progress Never Stops

What did we learn from the flight? . . . The Mercury spacecraft and systems design concepts are sound and have now been verified during **manned** flight. We also proved that man can operate intelligently in space and can adapt rapidly to this new environment.

Zero G or weightlessness appears to be no problem. As a matter of fact, lack of gravity is a rather fascinating thing. Objects within the cockpit can be parked in midair. For example, at one time during the flight, I was using a hand-held camera. Another system needed attention; so it seemed quite natural to let go of the camera, take care of the other chore, then reach out, grasp the camera, and go back about my business.

There seemed to be little **sensation** of speed although the craft was traveling at about five miles per second—a speed that I too find difficult to comprehend.

The view from that altitude defies description. The horizon colors are brilliant and sunsets are spectacular. It is hard to beat a day in which you are permitted the luxury of seeing four sunsets. . . .

Our efforts today and what we have done so far are but small building blocks in a huge pyramid to come.

But questions are sometimes raised regarding the immediate payoffs from our efforts. Explorations and the pursuit of knowledge have always paid dividends in the long run—usually far greater than anything expected at the **outset.** Experimenters with common, green mold, little dreamed what effect their discovery of penicillin would have.

We are just probing the surface of the greatest advancements in man's knowledge of his surroundings that has ever been made.

. . . Knowledge **begets** knowledge. Progress never stops.

VOCABULARY

manned
supplying people for a service or a ship

sensation
a bodily feeling caused by the senses or excitement

outset
the beginning

begets
causes

DBQ Analyzing Historical Documents

1. **Listing** According to Glenn, what knowledge was gained by the mission?
2. **Identifying Points of View** Why did Glenn choose to explain that the ship moved at "a speed that I too find difficult to comprehend"?
3. **Identifying Central Ideas** What are the immediate and long-term "payoffs" of John Glenn's 1962 space mission, according to his report to Congress?

networks

There's More Online!

- ☑ IMAGE Hiroshima Peace Memorial
- ☑ IMAGE Hong Kong
- ☑ IMAGE Port of Singapore
- ☑ IMAGE Reporters Trying to See Douglas MacArthur in Japan
- ☑ INTERACTIVE SELF-CHECK QUIZ
- ☑ MAP The Economy of Modern Japan
- ☑ PRIMARY SOURCE A Wild Sheep Chase
- ☑ VIDEO The Rise of Communist China

LESSON 3
The Asian Rim

ESSENTIAL QUESTIONS • *How does war result in change?* • *What challenges may countries face as a result of war?*

Reading HELPDESK

Academic Vocabulary
- **maintain**
- **stable**

Content Vocabulary
- **occupied**
- **state capitalism**

TAKING NOTES:
Key Ideas and Details

Organizing As you read, use a table like the one below to list the key areas of economic development in South Korea, Taiwan, and Singapore.

South Korea	Taiwan	Singapore

IT MATTERS BECAUSE

Japan made a dramatic recovery, transforming itself from the ruins of war to an industrial power. The "Asian tigers" imitated Japan's success and became industrial powerhouses.

The Transformation of Japan

GUIDING QUESTION *How was Japan transformed after World War II?*

In August 1945, Japan was in ruins, and a foreign army occupied its land. A mere 50 years later, Japan emerged as the second-greatest industrial power in the world.

From 1945 to 1952, Japan was **occupied** by Allied military forces under the command of U.S. General Douglas MacArthur. Under his firm direction, Japanese society was remodeled along Western lines. A new constitution renounced war as a national policy. Japan agreed to **maintain** armed forces sufficient only for self-defense. The constitution established a parliamentary system and reduced the power of the emperor (who was forced to announce that he was not a god). It guaranteed basic rights and gave women the right to vote.

On September 8, 1951, a peace treaty restored Japanese independence. Since then, Japan has emerged as an economic giant. The country's dramatic recovery from the war has been described as the "Japanese miracle." How did the miracle occur?

Modeled on the U.S. Constitution, Japan's new constitution guaranteed basic civil and political rights, and it called for universal suffrage and a balance of power among the executive, legislative, and judicial branches of government. However, it retained some of Japan's nineteenth-century political system under the Meiji. An example involves the distribution of political power. Japan has a multiparty system with two major parties—the Liberal Democrats and the Socialists. In practice, however, the Liberal Democrats have dominated the government. A few party leaders decided key issues such as who should be the prime minister.

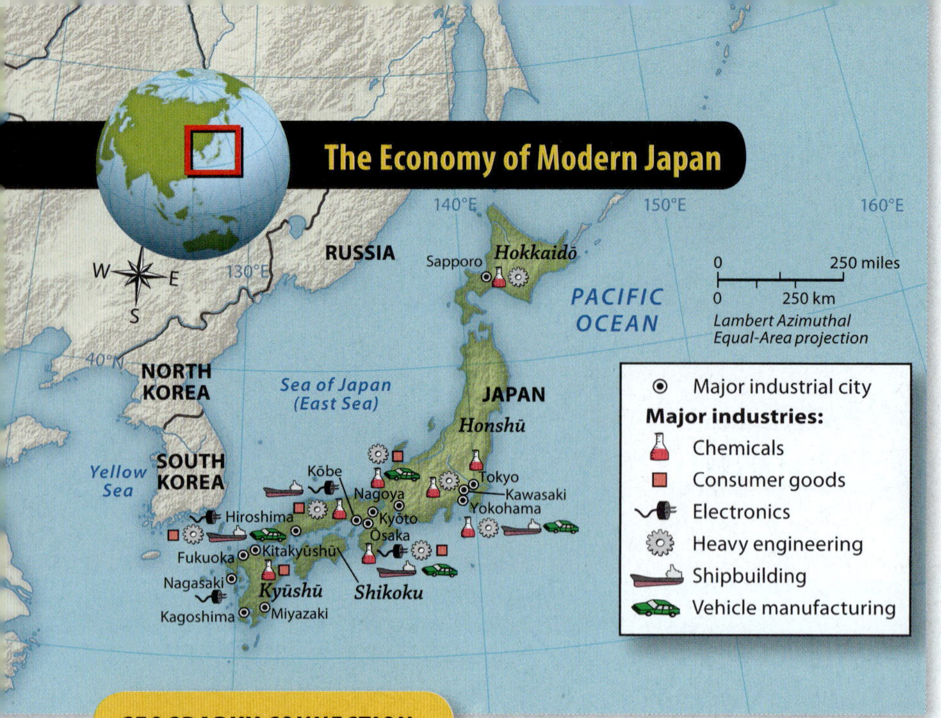

GEOGRAPHY CONNECTION

Japan has one of the world's largest economies.

1. **ENVIRONMENT AND SOCIETY** *How has Japan's geography influenced its economy?*
2. **HUMAN SYSTEMS** *What do you think are Japan's major exports and imports?*

occupied held by a foreign power

maintain to keep in an existing state of repair or efficiency

state capitalism an economic system in which the central government plays an active role in the economy, establishing price and wage policies and subsidizing vital industries

The central government plays an active role in the economy. It establishes price and wage policies and subsidizes vital industries. This government role is widely accepted in Japan. Indeed, it is often cited as a key reason for the efficiency of Japanese industry and the emergence of Japan as an industrial giant. Japan's economic system has been described as **state capitalism**.

During their occupation of Japan, Allied officials had planned to dismantle the business conglomerations known as the *zaibatsu*. But with the Cold War, the policy was scaled back. Only the 19 largest companies were affected. Also, the policy did not keep companies from forming ties with each other, which basically gave rise to another *zaibatsu* system.

The occupation administration had more success with its land-reform program. Half of the population lived on farms, and half of all farmers were tenants of large landowners. Under the reform program, lands were sold on easy credit terms to the tenants. The reform program created a strong class of independent farmers.

At the end of the Allied occupation in 1952, the Japanese gross national product was one-third that of Great Britain or France. By the 1980s, it was larger than both combined. After several decades of impressive growth, Japan was considered a model of economic success.

During the occupation, Allied planners tried to eliminate the aggressiveness that had been part of Japanese behavior. A new education system stressed individualism and removed references to patriotism and loyalty to the emperor. Efforts to remake Japanese behavior through laws were only partly successful, however. Many characteristics of traditional society have persisted. Emphasis on the work ethic, for example, remained strong. The tradition of hard work is stressed in the education system.

Women's roles are another example of the difficulty of social change. After the war, women gained the vote and were encouraged to enter politics. However, the subordinate role of women has not been eliminated. Women are legally protected against discrimination in employment, yet very few have reached senior levels in business, education, or politics. Most women are employed in retail or service occupations. Also, their average salary is only about 60 percent that of men.

✓ **READING PROGRESS CHECK**

Hypothesizing How did the Japanese "miracle" occur?

The "Asian Tigers"

GUIDING QUESTION *What changes did the Asian Rim countries experience after World War II?*

Sometimes called the "Asian tigers," South Korea, Taiwan, Singapore, and Hong Kong have imitated Japan in creating successful industrial societies. Australia and New Zealand, to the south and east of Asia, now have closer trade relations with their Asian neighbors.

In 1953 the Republic of Korea (South Korea), was under the dictatorial president Syngman Rhee. Rhee ruled harshly. In the spring of 1960, demonstrations broke out in Seoul. Rhee was forced to retire. A coup d'état in 1961 put General Park Chung Hee in power. Two years later, Park was elected president and began to strengthen the South Korean economy. South Korea gradually emerged as a major industrial power in East Asia. The key areas for industrial development were chemicals, textiles, shipbuilding, and automobile production.

Like many other countries in the region, South Korea was slow to develop democratic principles. Park ruled by autocratic means and suppressed protest. However, after his assassination, democratic elections were restored by the early 1990s.

Defeated by the Communists, Chiang Kai-shek and his followers established their capital at Taipei on Taiwan. Chiang Kai-shek said that the Republic of China was the legitimate government of all Chinese people. Of course, the Communist government on the mainland claimed to rule all of China, including Taiwan. With the protection of American military forces, Chiang Kai-shek's regime focused on economic growth with no worries about a Communist invasion.

▲ The busy port of Singapore, full of containers and container ships, is an international trading hub.

Making good use of foreign aid and the efforts of its people, the Republic of China built a modern industrialized society. A land-reform program, which put farmland in the hands of peasants, doubled food production. Local manufacturing and commerce also expanded. Prosperity did not at first lead to democracy. Chiang Kai-shek ruled by decree and did not allow new political parties to form. After his death in 1975, the Republic of China slowly moved toward a more representative form of government.

Singapore, once a British colony and briefly a part of the state of Malaysia, is now an independent state. Under the leadership of Prime Minister Lee Hsien Loong, Singapore developed a free-market economy based on banking, shipbuilding, oil refineries, and electronics. The authoritarian political system created a **stable** environment for economic growth. Its citizens, however, began to demand more political freedoms.

stable not changing or fluctuating; steady

Like Singapore, Hong Kong became an industrial powerhouse with high standards of living. Having ruled Hong Kong for more than 150 years, Great Britain returned control of Hong Kong to mainland China in 1997. China, in turn, promised that, for the next 50 years, Hong Kong would enjoy a high degree of economic freedom under a capitalist system.

✓ **READING PROGRESS CHECK**

Comparing During the initial post-World War II period, in what ways were the "Asian tigers" similar?

LESSON 3 REVIEW TEKS

Reviewing Vocabulary

1. ***Gathering Information*** Why was Japan allowed to maintain their armed forces?

Using Your Notes

2. ***Making Connections*** Use your notes to identify how South Korea, Taiwan, and Singapore grew their economies after the war.

Answering the Guiding Questions

3. ***Identifying*** How was Japan transformed after World War II?

4. ***Making Generalizations*** What changes did the Asian Rim countries experience after World War II?

Writing Activity

5. **INFORMATIVE/EXPLANATORY** Do additional research on Japan and the "Asian tigers" and explain in an essay why these countries have been so successful.

CHAPTER 33 Assessment

TEKS

Directions: On a separate sheet of paper, answer the questions below. Make sure you read carefully and answer all parts of the questions.

Lesson Review

Lesson 1

1. ***Explaining*** Explain the two different government structures in France, including the period under Charles de Gaulle and the period in the 1970s and 1980s.

2. ***Specifying*** What did German Social Democratic Party leader Willy Brandt accomplish during his role?

3. ***Sequencing*** Explain the formation and purpose of the European Economic Community (EEC) and how it changed from the time of its inception until 1986.

4. ***Explaining*** How did the role of young people change during the Cold War years? **24A**

Lesson 2

5. ***Describing*** Describe the imbalance of industry in the Soviet Union after World War II. **1F**

6. ***Identifying*** What caused independence movements to arise in the Soviet satellite states of Poland, Hungary, and Czechoslovakia, and what were the results of these movements?

7. ***Analyzing*** How did Natan Sharansky lead resistance to political oppression in the Soviet Union during the 1970s? **22E**

8. ***Explaining*** How did complex bureaucracy and collective farming harm the Soviet economy under Brezhnev?

Lesson 3

9. ***Summarizing*** After World War II, what changes and reforms did the Allied occupation administration lead Japan to make and how successful were they?

10. ***Defining*** Explain state capitalism, and why it is cited as a reason Japan became an industrial giant.

11. ***Comparing and Contrasting*** How were South Korea, Taiwan, the Republic of China, and Singapore the same as and different from Japan in the years after World War II?

12. ***Specifying*** What special consideration did Hong Kong receive after Britain handed control over to China in 1997, and why might this concession have been made between the two governments?

Exploring the Essential Questions

13. ***Identifying*** Work with a partner to choose one of the regions discussed in this chapter and create a chart on poster board that identifies and categorizes changes created by World War II in countries of that region. **1F**

14. ***Comparing and Contrasting*** Write an essay that compares and contrasts the ways in which two different nations in the world dealt with major political, economic, social, and cultural challenges that arose after World War II and during the Cold War. How and why were these nations successful or not successful in the long term at addressing these challenges? **1F**

Critical Thinking

15. ***Making Connections*** Write a paragraph in which you analyze how Aleksandr Solzhenitsyn's *The Gulag Archipelago* and *One Day in the Life of Ivan Denisovich* reflect the culture of the Soviet Union during Stalin's regime. **26B**

16. ***Describing*** What were the goals of Margaret Thatcher? What was the outcome of her economic policies in Great Britain? **24B**

17. ***Identifying Central Issues*** Describe the central issues behind the development of the consumer society.

Need Extra Help?

If You've Missed Question	1	2	3	4	5	6	7	8	9	10	11	12	13	14	15	16	17
Go to page	792	793	794	796	798	801	800	800	805	806	806	807	792	792	799	794	796

18 ***Identifying Cause and Effect*** What changes in the post-World War II era caused a wave of births known as the "baby boom"?

19 ***Identifying Perspectives*** Based on Khrushchev's approval for books published about years under Stalin's regime, what perspective of his predecessor did Khrushchev have?

20 ***Making Generalizations*** What economic and political structure did Soviet satellite nations follow based on Stalin's template in the Soviet Union, and what can you generalize about the satellite nations' plans?

21 ***Drawing Conclusions*** What conclusions can you draw about Tito based on his success in keeping Yugoslavia a country free of Stalin's demands?

Social Studies Skills

22 ***Defining and Drawing Conclusions*** What is a "welfare state," and why did Great Britain set a trend for most other European states after the war?

23 ***Understanding Relationships Among Events*** Which events was Richard Nixon taking advantage of when he appealed to "law and order" during his presidential campaign in 1968?

24 ***Identifying Cause and Effect*** What impact did communist movements and struggles elsewhere in the world have on the United States during the Cold War? **1F**

25 ***Identifying Cause and Effect*** How did the role of women change in the decades following World War II and how did families change as a result? **24A**

26 ***Creating and Interpreting Graphs*** Research the reduction in farming after World War II as tied to population shifts from rural to urban areas. Create a graph showing the shift designating a starting date and an end date for representation. Identify country or countries researched. Have a peer review the graph and discuss how the data can be interpreted. **16C**

27 ***Creating Maps*** Prime Minister Pierre Trudeau passed the Official Languages Act in 1968 making both English and French national languages. Create a map of Canada showing the provinces and indicate the percentage of French-speaking citizens in each province. Analyze any patterns between geography and language. **15A**

28 ***Creating Presentations*** Choose one or more of the Eastern European national revolts between the mid-1950s and late 1960s and share the sequence of events from citizen outcry to the Soviet re-establishment of control. Share impressions of the value of the reform efforts even though they ended unsuccessfully. Presentations can combine writing and visual elements. **30C**

DBQ Analyzing Historical Documents

Use the document to answer the following questions.

Bob Dylan expressed the feeling of the younger generation with his song "The Times they Are a-Changin'," released in 1964. Read the excerpt from the song and answer the questions that follow.

PRIMARY SOURCE

> "***The Times They Are a-Changin'***
> *Come gather 'round people*
> *Wherever you roam*
> *And admit that the waters*
> *Around you have grown*
> *And accept it that soon*
> *You'll be drenched to the bone*
> *If your time to you*
> *Is worth savin'*
> *Then you better start swimmin'*
> *Or you'll sink like a stone*
> *For the times they are a-changin'* . . . "

29 ***Theorizing*** To whom was Bob Dylan directing "come gather 'round people"?

30 ***Making inferences*** What did Dylan mean when he wrote "admit that the waters around you have grown"?

Need Extra Help?

If You've Missed Question	18	19	20	21	22	23	24	25	26	27	28	29	30
Go to page	801	801	801	801	793	795	794	796	796	796	801	809	809

31. ***Analyzing Style*** How does the style of Dylan's lyrics impact the delivery of his message, and why might his style choices have been intentional?

Analyzing Visuals

Use the image to answer the following questions.

This photograph shows the Reverend Martin Luther King, Jr., delivering his famous "I Have a Dream" speech at the Lincoln Memorial during the March on Washington on August 28, 1963.

32. ***Analyzing Visuals*** What information does this photograph provide about the March on Washington and role King played in it?

33. ***Making Connections*** What impact did King's "I Have a Dream" speech have on the civil rights movement and on literary history?

34. ***Comparing and Contrasting*** What might be different between the crowd at the Lincoln Memorial in 1964 and a crowd at a political or social rally today in terms of the individuals' in the crowd ability to communicate with those not present? How might communication affect the impact of such an event?

Extended Response Question

35. ***Expository*** Write an essay that compares and contrasts the civil rights movement and the women's liberation movement in the United States. What issues caused each movement to arise at about the same time in history? What events took place as part of these movements? Which leaders were significant and why? What political and social changes occurred as a result? The essay should include an introduction, at least three paragraphs, and a conclusion that supports your main idea. Use information gathered from primary and secondary sources to support your answer. **24A**

Need Extra Help?

If You've Missed Question	31	32	33	34	35
Go to page	810	810	795	810	795

A New Era Begins

1989–Present

ESSENTIAL QUESTIONS • *What motivates political change?*
• *How can economic and social changes affect a country?*

networks

There's More Online! about the beginning of a new era.

CHAPTER 34

The Story Matters...

The Berlin Wall stood as a potent symbol of the division of the world into two hostile camps during the Cold War. From 1961 to 1989, the Berlin Wall separated West and East Berlin, dividing families and limiting travel across the border. In a major Cold War speech in 1987, U.S. president Ronald Reagan stood in front of the Brandenburg Gate of the Berlin Wall as he challenged the Soviet leader: "Mr. Gorbachev, tear down this wall!" In 1989 the East German government finally ended the political division between West and East.

◄ A child peers through a hole in the Berlin Wall after its destruction in 1989. The fall of the Berlin Wall reunited Germany and marked the beginning of a new era of diplomacy between the Soviet Union and the West.

CHAPTER 34

Place and Time: Eastern Europe 1989–Present

In July 1989, the Soviet premier Mikhail Gorbachev announced that countries in the Warsaw Pact were free to determine their own futures. In November the Berlin Wall fell, symbolizing the end of the Cold War era. Revolutions both peaceful and violent erupted in the following months as Central and Eastern European countries declared their independence. By the end of 1991, the Soviet Union had virtually dissolved, resulting in the formation of 15 newly independent states.

Step Into the Place

Read the quotes and look at the information presented on the map.

DBQ What details in these primary sources tell us that perestroika and glasnost led to independence movements in the USSR and Soviet satellite states? How does Gorbachev's statement compare to the letter?

PRIMARY SOURCE

"Our perestroika led us to the conclusion that the revolutionary course would not receive the support of the working class if [its] living standards were not improving. But it turned out that the problem of sausage and bread is not the only one. The people demand a new social atmosphere, more oxygen in the society, especially because we are talking about the socialist regime. . .

It is important not to miss our chance here. The party should have its own position on these issues, its own clear policy in this respect also. Life itself will punish us if we are late."

—Mikhail Gorbachev, statement on October 7, 1989

PRIMARY SOURCE

"Thanks to glasnost, the mass media have told us a great deal about the past. We learned about the persecution of talented people, who either were victims of repressions or were forced to emigrate abroad, but still remained patriots of their country. We found out a lot about the genocide carried out by the 'Father of All Peoples [Stalin],' about the significant mistakes made before and during the Great Patriotic War, and the truth about the Afghanistan war. We learned about environmental problems, although sometimes too late (the Chernobyl tragedy, for example). . . . How could the mood of the people be good after all that?"

—Letter to the editor of *Ogonyok* Magazine (Moscow), May 15, 1989

Step Into the Time

Choose an event from the time line and explain the role it played in bringing the Cold War to an end.

EASTERN EUROPE AND CENTRAL ASIA

1989 Fall of the Berlin Wall

1990 Nobel Peace Prize recipient Lech Walesa elected president of Poland

1991 Soviet Union dissolves

1992 Yugoslavia disintegrates; Bosnian crisis follows

1990

THE WORLD

1989 Tiananmen Square protests

1990 Iraq invades Kuwait

1990 Sandinistas defeated in elections in Nicaragua

1991 Persian Gulf War

1994 North Atlantic Free Trade Agreement goes into effect

networks
There's More Online!

- ☑ **MAP** Explore the interactive version of this map on Networks.
- ☑ **TIME LINE** Explore the interactive version of the time line on Networks.

The Fall of Communism 1989–1991

1995 — 2000 — 2005 — 2010

- **1995** Terrorists release deadly chemicals in Tokyo subway
- **1995** Fourth World Conference on Women, Beijing
- **2000** Vladimir Putin is elected president of Russia
- **2001** China joins the World Trade Organization
- **2001** Al-Qaeda-led terrorist attacks in the United States on September 11
- **2004** Chechen rebels seize Russian school; many children die
- **2006** Slobodan Milosevic dies while on trial for war crimes
- **2008** Kosovo declares its independence
- **2011** Popular uprisings erupt in Tunisia, Egypt, Bahrain, and Libya
- **2012** Barack Obama is reelected president of the United States.

networks

There's More Online!

- BIOGRAPHY Boris Yeltsin
- BIOGRAPHY Mikhail Gorbachev
- BIOGRAPHY Natan Sharansky
- IMAGE NATO Air Strikes on Serbia
- IMAGE Russians Protest Social Conditions at the Winter Palace
- IMAGE Solidarity Demonstration
- INTERACTIVE SELF-CHECK QUIZ
- MAP Breakup of Yugoslavia
- PRIMARY SOURCE End of the Soviet Union
- TIME LINE Breakup of Yugoslavia
- VIDEO Gorbachev

LESSON 1
End of the Cold War

ESSENTIAL QUESTIONS • *What motivates political change?* • *How can economic and social changes affect a country?*

Reading HELPDESK

Academic Vocabulary

- **demonstration**
- **collapse**

Content Vocabulary

- **perestroika**
- **glasnost**
- **ethnic cleansing**
- **autonomous**

TAKING NOTES:

Key Ideas and Details

Categorizing As you read, use a table like the one below to identify events that happened after the fall of communism in Poland, Czechoslovakia, and Romania.

Poland	Czechoslovakia	Romania

TEKS Texas Essential Knowledge and Skills

1F identify major causes and describe the major effects of the following important turning points in world history from 1914 to the present: the world wars and their impact on political, economic, and social systems; communist revolutions and their impact on the Cold War; independence movements; and globalization

continued on the next page

IT MATTERS BECAUSE

After 40 years of the Cold War, the new division of Europe between West and East seemed to be permanent. Then a revolutionary upheaval in the Soviet Union and Eastern Europe brought an end to the Cold War and to this division.

Gorbachev and Perestroika

GUIDING QUESTION *How did Mikhail Gorbachev's reforms change the Soviet Union?*

By 1980, the Soviet Union was ailing. It had a declining economy, a rise in infant mortality rates, a dramatic surge in alcoholism, and poor working conditions. Within the Communist Party, a small group of reformers emerged. One was Mikhail Gorbachev. When the party chose him as leader in March 1985, a new era began.

From the start, Gorbachev preached the need for radical reforms based on **perestroika** (PEHR • uh • STRAWIH • kuh), or restructuring. At first, this meant restructuring economic policy. Gorbachev envisioned a market economy more responsive to consumers. It was to have limited free enterprise so that some businesses would be privately owned and operated. He realized, however, that reforming the economy would not work without political reform. He hoped to achieve this through **glasnost**, or openness, a policy that encouraged Soviet citizens and officials to discuss openly the strengths and weaknesses of the Soviet Union.

At the 1988 Communist Party conference, Gorbachev set up a new Soviet parliament of elected members, the Congress of People's Deputies. It met in 1989. He then created a new state presidency, removing many powers from the Communist Party. Gorbachev's willingness to rethink Soviet domestic and foreign policy led to stunning changes and the eventual end to the Cold War.

PHOTO: (l to r)©Peter Turnley/Corbis, ©Mike Stewart/Sygma/Corbis, ©SuperStock/Age Fotostock America, ©Steve Raymer/Corbis, ©Shepard Sherbell/Corbis.

Gorbachev and U.S. president Ronald Reagan made an agreement in 1987, the Intermediate-Range INF Treaty, to eliminate intermediate-range nuclear weapons. Gorbachev hoped to focus national resources on social and economic change. The United States wanted to cut its national debt, which had tripled during the Reagan presidency.

President Reagan hoped to end the Cold War through several means. He resolved to take a firm line against communism, giving a speech in 1987 in which he referred to the Berlin Wall, saying "Mr. Gorbachev, tear down this wall!" He also funded new military technology, such as the Strategic Defense Initiative (SDI), which was meant to defend the West against missile attacks. He was also willing to meet with compromise with the Soviets, as evidenced through nuclear arms treaties. Through Reagan's resolve and his willingness to compromise, he played a significant role in bringing an end to the Cold War.

When Gorbachev stopped giving Soviet military support to Communist governments in Eastern Europe, it opened the door to the overthrow of Communist regimes. A mostly peaceful revolutionary movement swept through Eastern Europe in 1989. The reunification of Germany on October 3, 1990, was a powerful symbol of the end of the Cold War. In 1991 the Soviet Union itself was dissolved.

READING PROGRESS CHECK

Describing How did Gorbachev's reforms affect Soviet foreign relations?

Revolutions in Eastern Europe

GUIDING QUESTIONS ***How did popular revolutions help end Communist regimes in Eastern Europe?***

When Gorbachev decided the Soviets would no longer send troops to support the governments of the satellite countries, revolutions broke out throughout Eastern Europe. A look at three Eastern European states shows how these independence movements formed.

Workers' protests led to demands for change in Poland. In 1980, a worker named Lech Wałesa (lehk vah • LEHN • suh) organized a powerful national trade union known as Solidarity. Solidarity also gained the support of the Roman Catholic Church and its leader, Pope John Paul II, the first Polish pope. The pope's vocal support for Solidarity and freedom in Eastern Europe helped the independence movement, even after Walesa was arrested. Finally, in 1988, the Polish regime agreed to free parliamentary elections—the first free elections in Eastern Europe in 40 years. A new government was elected, ending 45 years of Communist rule.

In December 1990, Wałesa was chosen as president. Poland's new path, however, was not easy. Rapid free-market reforms led to severe unemployment. Aleksander Kwasniewski, who succeeded Wałesa, continued Poland's move toward an increasingly prosperous free-market economy and democracy. Recent presidents have emphasized the need to combine modernization with tradition.

The Soviets crushed and then repressed the Czechoslovakian reform movement of 1968. Writers and other intellectuals continued to oppose the government, but they at first had little success. Then in 1988 and 1989, mass **demonstrations** took place throughout Czechoslovakia. By November 1989, the independence movement was generating crowds as large as 500,000 in Prague.

PHOTO: Chris Niedenthal/Time & Life Pictures/Getty Images

BIOGRAPHY

Lech Wałesa (1943–)

In 1980 during protests at the shipyards in Gdansk, Poland, Lech Wałesa, a former electrician turned labor activist, was elected leader of a strike committee. As a result of his successful negotiations with Poland's Communist government, workers won the right to form the national labor organization known as Solidarity. Although Solidarity was soon outlawed and its leadership arrested, Wałesa won the 1983 Nobel Peace Prize for his efforts. Deteriorating economic conditions later forced the government to accept Solidarity; and in 1990 voters elected Wałesa president.

CRITICAL THINKING

Drawing Conclusions What different factors contributed to Wałesa's success?

(continued from p. 816)

TEKS **Texas Essential Knowledge and Skills**

13D explain the roles of modern world leaders, including Ronald Reagan, Mikhail Gorbachev, Lech Walesa, and Pope John Paul II, in the collapse of communism in Eastern Europe and the Soviet Union

18E explain why communist command economies collapsed in competition with free market economies at the end of the 20th century

continued on the next page

perestroika fundamental restructuring of the Soviet economy; a policy introduced by Gorbachev

glasnost a Soviet policy permitting open discussion of political and social issues

demonstration a public display of group feeling toward a person or cause

collapse to break down completely; to suddenly lose force or effectiveness

Thinking Like a HISTORIAN

What Caused the Collapse of the Soviet Union?

International affairs expert Zbigniew Brzezinski attributed the collapse of communism to its failure to "deliver on the material level while its political practices compromised—indeed, discredited—its moral claims." What did Brzezinski mean? What other causes (such as nationalism, for example) do you think might have contributed? Use the Internet to find reliable sources about the various factors that contributed to the fall of the Soviet Union.

In December 1989, the Communist government **collapsed**. At the end of, that month, Václav Havel (VAHT • SLAHF HAH • vehl), a writer who had played an important role in bringing down the Communist government, became the new president. Havel was an eloquent spokesperson for Czech democracy and a new order in Europe.

The new government soon faced old ethnic conflicts. The Czechs and Slovaks agreed to a peaceful division of Czechoslovakia, which split into the Czech Republic and Slovakia. Havel became the first president of the Czech Republic, and Michal Kovác became the first president of Slovakia.

Under its second president, Václav Klaus, the Czech Republic has one of the most stable and prosperous economies of the post-Communist Eastern European states. Slovakia has managed to make the transition from a centrally planned economy to a market economy.

Communist leader Nicolae Ceauşescu (nee • kaw • LY chau • SHEHS • koo) ruled Romania with an iron grip, using secret police to crush all dissent. Nonetheless, opposition grew. His economic policies led to a sharp drop in living standards. Food shortages caused rationing. In December 1989, the secret police murdered thousands of people who were peacefully demonstrating. Finally, the army refused to support any more repression. Ceauşescu and his wife were captured and executed. A new government was quickly formed.

Former Communists dominated the government until 1996. The current president, Traian Basescu, leads a country that is just beginning to show economic growth and the rise of a middle class.

✓ **READING PROGRESS CHECK**

Identifying What role did protestors play in the new governments that formed after the fall of Communism in Eastern Europe?

End of the Soviet Union

GUIDING QUESTION *How did Mikhail Gorbachev's reforms change the Soviet Union?*

The Soviet Union was made of 15 separate republics that included 92 ethnic groups and 112 different languages. As Gorbachev released the iron grip of the Communist Party, centered in Moscow, old ethnic tensions came to the fore. Nationalist movements began. In 1989 and 1990, calls for independence came first in Soviet Georgia and then in the Baltic States (Latvia, Lithuania, and Estonia), Moldova, Uzbekistan, and Azerbaijan.

The conservative leaders of the traditional Soviet institutions—the army, government, KGB, and military industries—were worried that the breakup of the Soviet Union would end their privileges. On August 19, 1991, a group of these conservative leaders arrested Gorbachev and tried to seize power. The attempt failed, however, when Boris Yeltsin, president of the Russian Republic, and thousands of Russians bravely resisted the rebel forces in Moscow.

The Soviet republics now moved for complete independence. Ukraine voted for independence on December 1, 1991. A week later, the leaders of Russia, Ukraine, and Belarus announced that the Soviet Union had "ceased to exist."

✓ **READING PROGRESS CHECK**

Analyzing Why was President Gorbachev arrested on August 19, 1991?

(continued from p. 815)

TEKS **Texas Essential Knowledge and Skills**

18F formulate generalizations on how economic freedom improved the human condition, based on students' knowledge of the benefits of free enterprise in Europe's Commercial Revolution, the Industrial Revolution, and 20th-century free market economies, compared to communist command communities

21A describe how people have participated in supporting or changing their governments

22D identify examples of genocide, including the Holocaust and genocide in the Balkans, Rwanda, and Darfur

28C explain the effects of major new military technologies on World War I, World War II, and the Cold War

GEOGRAPHY CONNECTION

1. **PLACES AND REGIONS** *Create a table of the newly independent states.*
2. **HUMAN SYSTEMS** *Why might regional trade be more difficult after the breakup?*

The New Russia

GUIDING QUESTION *What are political, economic, and social challenges faced by the new Russia?*

Gorbachev resigned on December 25, 1991. He turned over his responsibilities as commander-in-chief to Boris Yeltsin, the new president of Russia. By the end of 1991, one of the largest empires in world history had ended.

Boris Yeltsin was committed to introducing a free market economy as quickly as possible, but the transition was not easy. Economic hardships and social disarray were made worse by a dramatic rise in organized crime.

Another problem Yeltsin faced was in Chechnya, a province in the south that wanted to secede from Russia and become independent. Yeltsin used brutal force against the Chechens (CHEH • chuhnz) to keep the province as part of Russia.

At the end of 1999, Yeltsin resigned and was replaced by Vladimir Putin, who was elected president in 2000. Putin, a former KGB officer, was widely seen as someone who wanted to keep a tight rein on government power. In July 2001, Putin launched reforms to boost growth and budget revenues. The reforms included the free sale and purchase of land and tax cuts. In spite of these changes, the business climate remained uncertain, which stifled foreign investment.

Since Putin's reforms, Russia has experienced a budget surplus and a growing economy. Russia can attribute much of its economic growth to its oil and gas exports. The country has an estimated 6 percent of the world's oil deposits and about 30 percent of the world's natural gas deposits.

The new president also vowed to return the breakaway state of Chechnya to Russian authority and to adopt a more assertive role in international affairs. Fighting in Chechnya continued throughout 2000, nearly reducing the republic's capital city of Grozny to ruins.

Despite economic gains, Russia still faces challenges. Rising alcoholism, criminal activities, and the decline of the traditional family system give Russians concern.

In 2008 Dmitry Medvedev became president of Russia. Putin could not run for reelection because of limits in Russia's constitution, but he became prime minister. However, since Russia's contitution limits only consecutive terms, Putin won the presidency again in 2012. Putin will be eligible to run for reelection in 2018.

✓ **READING PROGRESS CHECK**

Describing What were the effects of Russia's transition to a market economy?

The Disintegration of Yugoslavia

GUIDING QUESTION ***How did the fall of the Soviet Union impact Eastern Europe?***

ethnic cleansing a policy of killing or forcibly removing an ethnic group from its lands; used by the Serbs against the Muslim minority in Bosnia

autonomous self-governing

Yugoslavia had a Communist government but was never a Soviet satellite state. After World War II, its dictatorial leader, Josip Broz Tito, worked to keep together the six republics and two provinces that made up Yugoslavia. By 1990, however, the Communist Party collapsed.

The Yugoslav political scene was complex. Slobodan Miloševic (slaw • BAW • dahn muh • LOH • suh • VIHCH), leader of Serbia, rejected efforts toward independence. In Miloševic's view, the republics' borders first needed to be redrawn to form a new Greater Serbian state. When negotiations failed, Slovenia and Croatia declared their independence in June 1991. In September 1991, the Yugoslav army attacked Croatia. Increasingly, Serbia dominated the Yugoslav army. Serbian forces captured one-third of Croatia's territory before the conflict ended.

The Serbs next attacked Bosnia-Herzegovina and acquired 70 percent of Bosnian territory in the Balkans. Many Bosnians were Muslims. The Serbs followed a policy called **ethnic cleansing** toward Bosnians—killing or forcibly emoving them from their lands. Ethnic cleansing is a form of genocide that revived memories of Nazi atrocities in World War II. In 1995, with support from NATO air attacks, Bosnian and Croatian forces regained considerable territory lost to Serbian forces. The Serbs signed a formal peace treaty that split Bosnia into a Serb republic and a Muslim-Croat federation.

A new war erupted in 1998 over Kosovo, an **autonomous**, or self-governing province within Yugoslavia. After Slobodan Miloševic stripped Kosovo of its autonomy in 1989, groups of ethnic Albanians founded the Kosovo Liberation Army (KLA) and began a campaign against Serbian rule. To crush the KLA, Serb forces massacred ethnic Albanians. The United States and NATO allies worked on a settlement that would end the killing. The Albanians in Kosovo regained their autonomy in 1999. Miloševic's rule ended in 2000. While on trial for his role in the massacre of Kosovo civilians, Miloševic died in 2006.

The last political vestiges of Yugoslavia ceased to exist in 2004 when the government officially renamed the country Serbia and Montenegro. The people of Montenegro voted for independence in 2006; and in 2008, Kosovo declared its independence. Thus, all six republics that formed Yugoslavia in 1918 were again independent nations, and a new one (Kosovo) was born.

▼ **A police building destroyed during NATO air strikes in Pristina**

✓ **READING PROGRESS CHECK**

Describing What role did NATO play in the conflicts in the former Yugoslavia?

Command Economies vs. Free Market Economies

GUIDING QUESTION *What characteristics of a communist command economy led to its collapse at the end of the twentieth century?*

The end of the twentieth century provided a vivid comparison between free market economies and command economies. Between World War II and 1989, free market economies found in the United States, Western Europe, Japan, and elsewhere thrived and grew wealthy. During the same period, command economies found in communist countries, such as the Soviet Union and North Korea, struggled to provide necessary goods and services to their citizens. The quality of free market economies that allows competition between businesses helped industries to improve and grow. This competition was lacking in command economies. While free market economies grew, command economies stagnated.

Change was another constant feature in free market economies. Products were ever changing, as businesses strove to invent new goods and new ways to make money. Command economies lacked this feature and experienced less innovation as a result. Free market economies' experience with change made the societies living in them more open to cultural change, as well. Popular music, television, and movies were constantly evolving and bringing new sights, sounds, and messages to their audiences. A society open to change stands a better chance of adapting to a shifting world.

The benefits of free enterprise in twentieth-century free market economies could be measured in several ways when compared to communist command economies. The standard of living in free market economies excelled, as people enjoyed higher incomes and a wider array of consumer goods. Free market economies also produced greater advances in medicine, transportation, and technology that were accessible to many people. Competition, openness, and innovation helped free market economies improve the human condition in many tangible ways.

In the second half of the twentieth century, command economies were unable to deliver many of these benefits. An overreliance on centralized decision making and a lack of innovation made these economies and their workers content to do things as they had always been done. As a result, these economies slowly slipped behind their free market counterparts. While West Germany sparkled with new cars and architecture, East Germany remained gray and depressing, decade after decade. The same differences occurred between South Korea and North Korea.

✓ **READING PROGRESS CHECK**

Describing Explain why communist command economies collapsed in competition with free market economies at the end of the twentieth century.

LESSON 1 REVIEW TEKS

Reviewing Vocabulary

1. ***Making Inferences*** How did the policies of perestroika and glasnost lead to the end of the Soviet Union?

Using Your Notes

2. ***Comparing*** Use your notes to identify similarities among the countries of Eastern Europe after the fall of communist regimes.

Answering the Guiding Questions

3. ***Making Generalizations*** How did Mikhail Gorbachev's reforms change the Soviet Union?
4. ***Drawing Conclusions*** How did popular revolutions help end Communist regimes in Eastern Europe?
5. ***Assessing*** What are the political, economic, and social challenges faced by the new Russia?
6. ***Analyzing*** How did the fall of the Soviet Union impact eastern Europe?

Writing Activity

7. **INFORMATIVE/EXPLANATORY** Research and write an essay about how life has changed in Russia since the fall of the Soviet Union.

SKILLBUILDER

TEKS 16A

Locating World Regions

Why Learn This Skill?

When asking the vital questions *Who, What, When, Where*, and *Why*, this is the *Where*. Being able to locate regions that have historical significance is a crucial step in studying history and understanding current events.

Learning the Skill

Locating world regions begins with a map. The map needs to be big or you might never find the region you're looking for; for example, if you're looking for Russia, you won't find it on a map of Mexico City.

Next, ask yourself a few questions about location to help narrow your search:

1. In which continent is the region located?
2. Does the region have any neighboring countries that you can recall?
3. Does the region have any landforms or bodies of water that played a role in its history?

Answering these questions will guide you in locating regions of historical significance. Remember, your region might not conform to the lines you see on your map. For example, most of the borders around Russia changed in 1991. If you see a discrepancy, it merely means the map you are using represents a different era. In this case, you can still locate and label your historical region.

Some regions played a significant role in major eras of world history—think about the role of Latin America during the colonial era or the role of the Middle East during the Cold War. Meanwhile, some regions played a major role in turning points of world history—think about the role of Normandy and northern France in World War II or the role of the Iron Curtain region during the Cold War. Some regions have played such a pivotal role in shaping world history that they can be called turning points.

Practicing the Skill

Using the Internet, find a copy of a world map that has country borders without labels or names. Locate three regions of historical significance that are related to major eras in world history. Recall that major eras include the periods such as the eras of exploration, industrialization, colonization, and so on. Next, locate three regions related to turning points in world history. If necessary, flip through your textbook to remind yourself of eras and turning points.

Skills Assessment

Using the map you found above, locate the following regions directly related to major eras. Draw a light circle around each region and write its name in its center.

"New World" and "Old World"; Eastern bloc (Warsaw pact) and Western bloc (NATO); North America, Latin America, Western Europe, Eastern Europe, Russia, Middle East, Africa south of the Sahara, South Asia, Southeast Asia, Central Asia, East Asia, Australia, and Oceania

Next, use the map to locate regions directly related to turning points: Normandy, the Vietnam/Cambodia/Laos border, Iron Curtain, former Soviet Union.

Applying the Skill

Locating World Regions Create a board game in which players locate regions on a world map. Follow these steps. 1) Make a game board that includes an unlabeled world map with border lines drawn on it. 2) Make or find objects to serve as game pieces. 3) Make cards to draw that include the names of regions. Use the list of regions in the Skills Assessment. 4) Write instructions for the game. 5) Give your game a fun title. Once you're finished with your game, play it with a family member.

networks

There's More Online!

- IMAGE Destruction of the Berlin Wall
- IMAGE Fans of an American Musician in Japan
- IMAGE Fest Noz
- IMAGE Modern Art Installation
- IMAGE Tony Blair and George W. Bush
- INTERACTIVE SELF-CHECK QUIZ
- VIDEO The World's Only Superpower

Reading HELPDESK

Academic Vocabulary

- **currency**
- **symbol**

Content Vocabulary

- **budget deficit**
- **postmodernism**
- **popular culture**
- **cultural imperialism**

TAKING NOTES:

Key Ideas and Details

Organizing As you read, use a flow chart like the one below to identify events that led to the reunification of Germany.

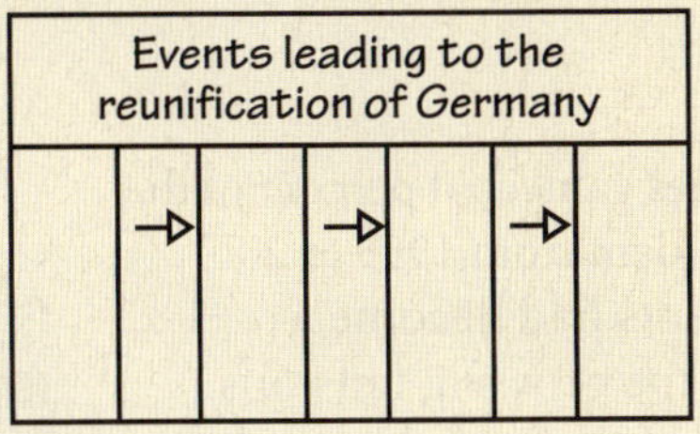

TEKS Texas Essential Knowledge and Skills

24A describe the changing roles of women, children, and families during major eras of world history

26B analyze examples of how art, architecture, literature, music, and drama reflect the history of the cultures in which they are produced

continued on the next page

LESSON 2
Western Europe and North America

ESSENTIAL QUESTIONS • *What motivates political change?* • *How can economic and social changes affect a country?*

IT MATTERS BECAUSE

During the last decade of the twentieth century and the first decade of the twenty-first century, the leaders of Western European and North American countries faced many economic challenges. Western culture has continued to influence many parts of the world.

Winds of Change in Western Europe

GUIDING QUESTION *What were the political, social, and cultural trends in Western Europe and North America since the end of the Cold War?*

In the course of the 1980s, Western European economies recovered, but problems remained. Unemployment was still high. Despite their economic woes, however, the Western European states seemed quite capable of prospering.

Especially important in that respect was the European Community (EC), which was chiefly an economic union. The Treaty on European Union, which went into effect on November 1, 1993, turned the EC into the European Union (EU). One of the EU's first goals was to establish a common **currency**, the euro. By January 2010, the euro had officially replaced 17 national currencies and served approximately 327 million people. A major crisis for the euro emerged in the same year, when the public debts of Greece and Ireland threatened bankruptcy for those countries and financial disaster for the euro.

Between 2004 and 2007, the EU expanded, by adding 12 new members, mostly from Eastern Europe. These included nations that became independent after the collapse of the Soviet Union. The end of the Soviet Union also had a major impact on the fate of Germany.

Reunification of Germany

In 1982 the Christian Democratic Union of Helmut Kohl formed a new, more conservative government in West Germany. Kohl was a smart politician who benefited greatly from an economic boom in the mid-1980s. Then events in East Germany led to the unexpected reunification of the two Germanies in 1990.

currency coins, for example, that are in circulation and used as a medium of exchange

symbol something that stands for something else by way of association; a visible sign of something invisible

Erich Honecker, head of the Communist Party in East Germany, ruled harshly. While many East Germans fled their country, others led mass demonstrations against the regime in 1989. When the Communist government opened its entire border with the West, thousands of East Germans swarmed across the border to reunite with their families and friends. The Berlin Wall, long a **symbol** of the Cold War, was torn down. The reunification of Germany took place on October 3, 1990. What had seemed almost impossible became a reality—the countries of West and East Germany had formed one Germany.

With a population of 79 million people, the new Germany became the leading power in Europe. The joy over reunification soon faded as new problems arose. It became clear that the rebuilding of eastern Germany would take far more money than had been thought.

▲ East Germans take sledgehammers to the Berlin Wall, dismantling it piece by piece.

▶ **CRITICAL THINKING**

Analyzing Why was the Berlin Wall such a potent symbol of the Cold War?

Kohl's government was soon forced to raise taxes. In addition, the virtual collapse of the economy in eastern Germany had led to extremely high unemployment and severe discontent. One result was a return to power for the Social Democrats, who were victorious in the 1998 elections. However, the Social Democrats had little success in solving Germany's economic woes. In 2005 Angela Merkel, leader of the Christian Democrats, became the first female chancellor in German history.

The collapse of the German economy also led to increasing attacks on foreigners. For years, illegal immigrants and foreigners seeking refuge had found haven in Germany because of its very liberal immigration laws. Increased unemployment and economic problems caused tensions between some Germans and immigrant groups.

Great Britain

After Margaret Thatcher resigned as prime minister in 1990, the Conservative Party, now led by John Major, failed to capture the imagination of most Britons. In new elections in 1997, the Labour Party won a landslide victory. Moderate Tony Blair became prime minister. However, his ongoing support of the U.S. war in Iraq, when most Britons opposed it, caused his popularity to plummet. Another member of the Labour Party, Gordon Brown, became prime minister in June 2007. New elections in May 2010 led to Conservative David Cameron's becoming prime minister.

France

In the elections of 1993, a coalition of conservative parties gained 80 percent of the seats in the National Assembly. Jacques Chirac was president from 1995 to 2007.

By 1995, resentment against foreign-born residents had become a growing political reality. Especially noticeable were the growing tensions between the Muslim community and the remainder of the French population. These tensions helped elect Nicolas Sarkozy president in 2007.

France did not escape the financial woes of the euro crisis. Amid the failing economy and low approval ratings, Sarkozy lost his reelection bid in a run-off election in May 2012. He was defeated by François Hollandé of France's Socialist Party.

✓ **READING PROGRESS CHECK**

Determining Cause and Effect What happened after the Berlin Wall was dismantled?

(continued from p. 823)

TEKS **Texas Essential Knowledge and Skills**

26C identify examples of art, music, and literature that transcend the cultures in which they were created and convey universal themes

The United States and Canada

GUIDING QUESTION *What were the political, social, and cultural trends in Western Europe and North America since the end of the Cold War?*

As the Cold War was coming to a close, U.S. politics oscillated between the right and left as economic issues became a focus. Canadians were also concerned about economic problems and the status of Quebec.

▲ U.S. president Barack Obama faced economic challenges in the United States and around the globe during his two terms in the White House.

The United States

The Reagan Revolution, as it has been called, sent U.S. policy in new directions. Reagan reduced welfare policies by cutting spending on food stamps, school lunch programs, and job programs. At the same time, Reagan oversaw the largest peacetime military buildup in U.S. history.

Total federal spending rose from $631 billion in 1981 to over a trillion dollars by 1987. The spending policies of the Reagan administration produced record government **budget deficits**. A budget deficit exists when the government spends more than it collects in revenues. In the 1970s, the total deficit was $420 billion. Between 1981 and 1987, budget deficits were three times that amount.

George Bush, Reagan's vice president, succeeded him as president. Bush's inability to deal with the federal deficit and an economic downturn, however, allowed Democrat Bill Clinton to be elected president in 1992. Clinton claimed to be a new kind of Democrat, one who favored several Republican policies of the 1980s. A lengthy economic revival won Clinton popular support, but his second term was overshadowed by charges of presidential misconduct. Clinton's problems helped Republican George W. Bush, son of the first President Bush, to win the presidency in 2000.

budget deficit the state that exists when a government spends more than it collects in revenues

The Bush administration was largely occupied with the war on terrorism and the U.S.-led war on Iraq. Bush and Congress passed tax cuts to boost the economy but also helped to produce record deficits. From 2004 to 2008, Bush's popularity fell due to growing discontent over the Iraq War and a significant downturn in the economy caused in part by problems in the home mortgage industry. These key issues in the 2008 presidential race led to a change in American politics with the election of Barack Obama, the first African American president. In 2009 Obama moved to deal with the worst economic recession since the Great Depression, the passage of national healthcare legislation, and the war in Afghanistan. He was reelected in 2012.

Canada

In 1993 Canada approved the North American Free Trade Agreement (NAFTA), along with the United States and Mexico, to make trade easier and more profitable. Many Canadians thought the agreement was too favorable to the United States.

The status of the French-speaking Quebec province has been an issue for decades. In 1995 Quebec voters only narrowly rejected secession. The debate still divides Canadians.

✓ **READING PROGRESS CHECK**

Describing What role did the economy play in U.S. presidential administrations in the first two decades of the 2000s?

Society and Culture in the West

GUIDING QUESTION *What were the political, social, and cultural trends in Western Europe and North America since the end of the Cold War?*

Among the effects of globalization is the spread of culture, and Western culture has expanded to and influenced most parts of the world.

▲ *Cold Dark Matter: An Exploded View* (1991) by the English sculptor Cornelia Parker is a postmodern art installation.

The Women's Movement

In the 1990s, there was a backlash against the women's movement. Some women urged a return to traditional gender roles. Other women rejected these ideas and continued to find ways to balance career and family. While there have been gains in the women's movement in the 2000s, women continue to do most of the child rearing and domestic work in most homes. Worldwide, roles for women continue to slowly change as women's liberation becomes more accepted. The roles of families continue to change, as well, as family sizes continue to shrink, creating more attention and opportunity for each child.

Art and Popular Culture

The United States dominated the art world after World War II. Abstractionism dominated modern art after 1945 and reflected Western culture's search for meaning during a period of rapid social and technological change. Abstract artists tried to convey emotion and feeling through simple forms. By the 1980s, **postmodernism** emerged, blending elements of film, performance, popular culture, and sculpture. Both of these art movements conveyed universal themes, such as purity or self-awareness. Music and drama evolved after the war, as well, reflecting culture's attempt to make sense of change. Today's artists and performers often assemble works using pieces of other works.

postmodernism an artistic movement that emerged in the 1980s; its artists do not expect rationality in the world and are comfortable with many "truths"

Music, movies, television, sports—all are part of our **popular culture**. Known throughout the world, American performers, musicians, and filmmakers create works with universal themes that transcend American culture. This universal appeal has made American popular culture widely popular. From early rock 'n' roll songs to famous Hollywood movies, the world participates in America's pop culture. Children and teenagers play a major role in spreading popular culture. As the Internet has connected people all over the world, this role has had an even greater impact.

popular culture entertainment created for a profit and for a mass audience

Television and sports have created a sense that Americans and Europeans share a culture. As cultural exports, these have become big business. Some nations' peoples worry that American entertainment weakens their own language and culture. Critics refer to this as **cultural imperialism**. Although Western music and movies may still dominate, trends in the opposite direction are developing. For example, the reggae music native to Jamaica has an enormous following, and Latin pop has become so popular that there have been Latin Grammy awards since 1999.

cultural imperialism referring to Western nations' control of other world cultures similar to how they had controlled colonial governments

✓ **READING PROGRESS CHECK**

Drawing Conclusions Why has the spread of American popular culture led some critics to be concerned about U.S. cultural imperialism?

LESSON 2 REVIEW TEKS

Reviewing Vocabulary

1. ***Identifying*** What happened to budget deficits in the United States from the 1970s to the 1980s?
2. ***Making Connections*** How is American popular culture related to the idea of cultural imperialism?

Using Your Notes

3. ***Sequencing*** Use your notes to list the events that led to the reunification of Germany.

Answering the Guiding Questions

4. ***Making Generalizations*** What were the political, social, and cultural trends in Western Europe and North America since the end of the Cold War?

Writing Activity

5. **NARRATIVE** Write an essay describing how popular culture has affected your life. Be sure to include examples of music, film, television, and art and how it impacted you.

SKILLBUILDER

TEKS 30C

Developing Multimedia Presentations

Why Learn This Skill?

Imagine you have been assigned a research project about Brazil's rain forest. To vividly present the important issues to your classmates, you want to show them slides of the endangered animals and plants in the rain forest, along with videos of the region and recordings of native music. This type of presentation is called a multimedia presentation because it uses a variety of media, such as photographs, music, and video, to convey information to others.

Learning the Skill

At its most basic, a multimedia presentation can be as simple as using equipment such as a DVD player and a portable stereo. However, you can create a great digital presentation on a computer. A digital multimedia presentation can combine text, graphics, audio, animation, and video. To create this kind of multimedia presentation, you might use traditional graphic tools and draw programs or animation programs that make still images move. You can also record digital video and audio and insert them into a presentation. Presentation software assembles all of the pieces together. A good presentation has a well-organized structure, just like an essay, including having a title, introduction, and conclusion.

Practicing the Skill

In creating your digital multimedia presentation about the Brazilian rain forest, you start to list elements you want to include. You want to record a narration—called a voice-over—that will play over the visual material you choose. Ask yourself the following questions to develop an effective multimedia presentation.

- Which forms of media do I want to include besides the voice-over? Photographs? Video? Music? Graphics? Animation? Anything else?
- If I want to make a digital presentation, which of these media forms are best suited?
- What equipment would I need to capture or record the media I want to use?
- How would I store and transfer the media?
- What kind of software or apps (software for mobile devices) do I need to collect and assemble the pieces?

Skills Assessment

Think of a topic in this chapter that would be suitable for a multimedia presentation. Following the guidelines above, plan your presentation by taking notes about the individual elements you want to include, including both oral and visual material. Write and edit your narration before you record it, in order to make it polished. Collect your multimedia elements and assemble them into a five-minute presentation. Deliver your presentation to the class. Afterward, give your written narration to your teacher.

Applying the Skill

Developing Multimedia Presentations To improve your preparation skills, plan an entire multimedia presentation on paper. The presentation should be ten minutes long and discuss the topic of pop culture in the United States during the time period of this chapter. Assume that you will have an audio-visual expert to help you with any technical needs; in other words, be ambitious about including different forms of media. Create a flowchart that includes all of the elements of your presentation.

SKILLBUILDER

TEKS 30D

Interpreting Presentations

Why Learn This Skill?

A key skill in social studies is interpreting information in a variety of formats, including written, oral, and visual material. The ability to interpret these presentations gives you the ability to extract meaning, identify bias, and establish connections between facts.

Learning the Skill

Interpreting written, oral, and visual presentations calls upon a variety of skills. Study the following steps:

- **Extract meaning** In order to uncover the most meaningful information in any presentation, one must filter out any unnecessary content. Look for facts, which are often denoted by the presence of names, dates, and places.
- **Identify bias** To look for bias, identify the writer's, speaker's, or artist's purpose and look for emotionally charged languages or images that provoke an emotional response. Remember, sometimes there will be no bias present.
- **Establish connections** To look for connections between facts, look for topics connected by chronology, geography, or subject area.

Practicing the Skill

Locate a sample of a written, an oral, and a visual presentation of a social studies topic. Examples of a written presentation include a piece of text or a historical Web site. An oral presentation might include a podcast or radio program. A visual presentation might include a map, graph, or historical video such as a documentary. Spend five minutes applying your skills of interpretation to each one—extract meaning, identify bias, and establish connections. Take notes on each one. Some presentations of information are clearer and more organized than others, so it is wise to be patient and methodical in your work.

Skills Assessment

Search the textbook to locate an example of a written, an oral, and a visual presentation. (The oral presentation can be an excerpt of a speech.) Create a three-page document titled "Interpreting Presentations." In this document, write a page formally interpreting each kind of presentation. Use the steps above to concentrate on each kind of presentation. Write your critiques in paragraph form. Conclude each interpretation with a summary of the presentation. At the end of the document, attach copies of the original presentations you interpreted.

Applying the Skill

Interpreting Presentations Play "Interpretation Roulette" with two of your classmates. First, each of you should locate a sample of a written, oral (such as a speech), or visual presentation of a social studies topic; choose among yourselves who will find each one. Use research resources such as your textbook, print material from the library, or the Internet. Print a folded-up copy of each sample and place them all in a hat. Take turns reaching into the hat and pulling out a presentation to interpret. Once you have finished the round, discuss the similarities and differences of interpretation among the three acts.

networks

There's More Online!

- CHART/GRAPH North Korean Conflicts
- CHART/GRAPH Oil Production and Consumption in China
- CHART/GRAPH Population Distribution in Japan
- IMAGE Border Between North Korea and South Korea
- IMAGE Chinese Household in the 1990s
- IMAGE Deng Xiaoping
- INTERACTIVE SELF-CHECK QUIZ
- VIDEO Tiananmen Square

LESSON 3
China, Japan, and the Koreas

ESSENTIAL QUESTIONS • *What motivates political change?* • *How can economic and social changes affect a country?*

Reading HELPDESK

Academic Vocabulary
- **unify**
- **sector**

Content Vocabulary
- **per capita**
- **one-child policy**
- **deflation**

TAKING NOTES:
Key Ideas and Details

Organizing As you read, use a chart to list the actions Deng Xiaoping took to help modernize China's industry and agriculture.

Industry	Agriculture

TEKS Texas Essential Knowledge and Skills

22E identify examples of individuals who led resistance to political oppression such as Nelson Mandela, Mohandas Gandhi, Oscar Romero, Natan Sharansky, Las Madres de la Plaza de Mayo, and Chinese student protestors in Tiananmen Square

It Matters Because

Although the Chinese Communist Party has managed to retain power, China has taken giant steps toward becoming an economic world power. Meanwhile, Japan's economy has suffered in recent decades. There is an uneasy peace between North Korea and South Korea, which are vastly different countries.

China After Mao

GUIDING QUESTION *What political and social changes has China undergone in the late twentieth and early twenty-first centuries?*

Under the leadership of Deng Xiaoping (DUHNG SHYOW • PIHNG), the new Chinese government after the death of Mao Zedong called for Four Modernizations—new policies in industry, agriculture, technology, and national defense. For more than 20 years, China had been isolated from the technological advances taking place elsewhere in the world. To make up for lost time, the government invited foreign investors to China. The government also sent thousands of students abroad to study science, technology, and modern business techniques.

A new agricultural policy began. Collective farms could now lease land to peasants who paid rent to the collective. Anything produced above the value of the rent could be sold for profit. Peasants were also allowed to make goods to sell.

By adopting this practical approach, China began to make great strides in ending its problems of poverty and underdevelopment. **Per capita** (per person) income, including farm income, doubled during the 1980s. Housing, education, and sanitation improved. Both agriculture and industrial output skyrocketed. Clearly, China had begun to enter the Industrial Age.

Despite such achievements, many complained that Deng Xiaoping's program had not achieved a fifth modernization—democracy.

▲ A demonstrator stands in front of the tanks at Tiananmen Square.

▶ CRITICAL THINKING

Reasoning Why do you think the Chinese government responded with such overwhelming force?

per capita per person

unify to make into a unit or whole; unite

People could not directly criticize the Communist Party. Those who called for democracy were often sentenced to long terms in prison.

The problem intensified in the late 1980s. More Chinese studied abroad and learned about the West. As the economy prospered, students and other groups wanted better living conditions and greater freedom. Rising inflation led to growing discontent among salaried workers. Corruption and special treatment for officials and party members led to increasing criticism as well. In May 1989, student protesters called for an end to the corruption and demanded the resignation of China's aging Communist Party leaders. The students' calls for resistance to political oppression received widespread support from people in the cities. Discontent led to massive demonstrations in Tiananmen Square in Beijing.

Deng Xiaoping believed the protesters were calling for an end to Communist rule. He ordered tanks and troops into the square to crush the demonstrators. Between 500 and 2,000 were killed and many more injured. Democracy was a dream.

Throughout the 1990s and into the 2000s, China's human rights violations, its determination to **unify** with Taiwan, and its increasing military power created international concern. China's neighbors, especially Japan, India, and Russia, fear the increasingly active role China is playing in its area of the world. To Chinese leaders, however, such actions represent China's rightful role in the region.

For now, a strong patriotism seems to be on the rise. This is encouraged by the government as a means of holding the country together. When China was selected to host the 2008 Olympic Games, the Chinese celebrated enthusiastically. The event seemed to symbolize China's emergence as a major national power on the world stage.

Problems remain, however. For example, unrest is growing among China's national minorities. This is especially true in Tibet, where the Chinese government has violently suppressed Tibetan culture.

✓ **READING PROGRESS CHECK**

Identifying What is the "fifth modernization," and how has China failed to achieve it?

Chinese Society and Economy

GUIDING QUESTIONS *What political and social changes has China undergone in the late twentieth and early twenty-first centuries? How has modern China become a world economic power?*

From the start, the Communist Party wanted to create a new kind of citizen, one who would give the utmost for the good of all China. In Mao's words, the people should "be resolute, fear no sacrifice, and surmount every difficulty to win victory."

During the 1950s and 1960s, the Chinese government began to allow women to take part in politics and gave them equal marital rights—a dramatic shift. After Mao's death, family traditions returned. People now had more freedom in everyday matters and had better living conditions. Married couples who had been given patriotic names chose more elegant names for their own children. Clothing choices were no longer restricted to a baggy "Mao suit." Today, young Chinese people wear jeans and athletic shoes.

Mao's successors have followed one of his goals to the present day—the effort to control population growth. In 1979 the state began advocating a **one-child policy**. Incentives such as education benefits, child care, and housing were offered to couples who limited their families to one child. Although criticized as oppressive, the policy has continued, with a few exceptions for rural areas and some minorities. One effect is that China's population growth rate has declined from 2.2 percent in 1970–1975 to an estimated 0.6 percent in 2005–2010. Another effect has been an aging population. Life expectancy is increasing, but the birth rate remains low.

one-child policy China's effort, beginning in 1979, to control population growth; incentives such as education benefits, child care, and housing are offered to couples who limit their families to one child

After the Tiananmen Square demonstrations, the Chinese government adopted a policy of promoting rapid economic growth while cracking down harshly on political dissenters. Especially noticeable was the attempt to win middle-class support in the cities by guaranteeing more consumer goods.

sector a sociological, economic, or political subdivision of society

During the 1990s, growth rates in industry remained high, leading to predictions that China would become one of the economic superpowers of the twenty-first century. Domestic capital in China became available to compete with the growing presence of foreign enterprises. The government also shut down inefficient state enterprises. By the early 2000s, the private **sector** accounted for more than 10 percent of the nation's gross domestic product. A stock market opened. At the same time, China was strengthening international trade relations. China joined the World Trade Organization in 2001 and normalized trade relations with the United States in 2002.

Rapid economic change, however, never comes without cost. Workers in Chinese factories complain about poor working conditions and low salaries, leading to labor unrest. Many farmers are also unhappy. They earn only about half the salary of urban workers. In desperation, millions flee to the big cities, where they are forced to live in pitiful conditions in tenements.

▲ China joined the WTO in 2001 after 15 years of negotiations, becoming the 143rd member.

✓ **READING PROGRESS CHECK**

Summarizing What negative effects has rapid economic change had on China?

Japan

GUIDING QUESTION ***What changes have occurred in Japan from the 1990s to the present?***

Between 1950 and 1990, Japan became the greatest exporting nation in the world. It also developed the world's largest economy after that of the United States. Some economists even predicted that Japan would pass the United States as the world's largest economy by 2010. At the end of the 1980s, however, a collapse of the Japanese real estate market sent the economy into a tailspin.

By the 1990s, the Japanese economy had slipped into a recession that has largely continued until the present day. Job security declined as large numbers of workers were laid off. Many older Japanese saw their savings decline. Retirement programs were increasingly strained by the demands of a rapidly aging population. Japan today has the highest proportion of people more than age 65 of any industrialized country in the world—17 percent of the country's total population of about 130 million.

deflation a contraction in the volume of available money or credit that results in a general decline in prices

For more than 20 years, Japan has witnessed slow economic growth and a decline in prices, known as **deflation**. A crisis of confidence has led to deep pessimism about the future and a decline in spending, especially among young Japanese who have now known nothing other than economic decline.

In recent years, Japanese consumers have also complained about a decline in the quality of some domestic products. One government official accused Japanese firms of "sloppiness." Even the Japanese automaker Toyota was faced with quality problems in its best-selling fleet of cars.

▲ The 2011 tsunami devastated towns like Natori, Japan. The tsunami also led to rising radiation levels from the damaged Fukushima Daiichi nuclear plant.

▶ **CRITICAL THINKING**
Theorizing Do you think the damage at the Fukushima Daiichi nuclear plant will limit the development of new nuclear power plants in the United States? Why or why not?

The country's economic decline was evident when China passed Japan in the second quarter of 2010 as the world's second-largest economy behind the United States. Despite government attempts to stimulate the economy in 2010, Japan faced a growing government debt and increasing rates of poverty.

On March 11, 2011, Japan received another crushing economic blow as a result of a devastating natural catastrophe. An offshore earthquake produced a gigantic tsunami, or tidal wave, that destroyed cities and farmland on the northeast coast. Recorded at 9.0 on the Richter scale, it was the most powerful quake to hit a country that was accustomed to periodic earthquakes. Thousands of people were killed, and hundreds of thousands were left homeless. Authorities began a massive rescue and recovery effort. A month after the disaster, the official death toll was over 12,000, and nearly 15,000 people remained missing.

The tsunami also damaged the nuclear power plant at Fukushima Daiichi and created the worst nuclear disaster since the accident at Chernobyl in Ukraine in 1986. Leaks of radioactive gas into the atmosphere not only endangered the lives of many Japanese but also brought threats of radioactive contamination to Japan's food supplies. Japanese officials worked overtime to contain the damage.

✓ **READING PROGRESS CHECK**

Making Connections What factors have affected Japan's economy since the 1990s?

The Koreas

GUIDING QUESTION *What are the major differences between North Korea and South Korea?*

Although the Korean War ended in 1953, political tensions between North Korea and South Korea continue to threaten the peace between the two countries, primarily due to North Korea's nuclear weapons program. At the same time, South Korea has become one of the strongest economies in Asia.

North Korea

North Korea remained an isolated country under a military dictatorship led by Kim Jong Il. Only the second leader since the formation of North Korea in 1953,

Kim Jong Il attempted to secure his country by creating a nuclear program. Multinational negotiations to persuade the regime to suspend its nuclear program reached a fragile agreement in 2008.

Internal problems continue to plague North Korea. Droughts and famines during the 1990s led North Korea to seek help from the United Nations and the United States. Economic problems forced the North Korean government to devalue its currency in 2009. The World Food Program estimates that one in five North Korean children is underweight.

After Kim Jong Il died in December 2011, his son Kim Jong Un became North Korea's leader. At 29, he is the youngest head of state in the world. He continues his father's legacy in his role as leader of North Korea.

▲ North Korean and South Korean soldiers guard the demilitarized zone, which is a constant reminder of tensions between the two countries.

PHOTO: ©Stefania Mizara/Corbis

South Korea

Since 1990, South Korea has experienced a growing democracy. National elections held since 1989 removed former military leaders from power, replacing them with civilian leaders.

North Korea's nuclear program continues to cause tension between the two countries. President Lee Myung-bak, elected in 2007, pushed for North Korea to abandon its nuclear program. Tensions have risen between North and South Korea following the 2010 sinking of a military ship killing 46 soldiers. South Korea has blamed North Korea for the attack. Conflict continued in late 2010 between the two countries following the live-artillery firing on an island off the coast of South Korea.

South Korea has also faced economic problems as a result of the Asian financial crises of 1997 following the collapse of Taiwan's banking industry. But South Korea's strong education institutions and economic policies enabled South Korea to weather the 2008 global economic crisis with an unemployment rate of 3.8 percent in 2009.

Culturally, South Korea is changing rapidly as almost every household has high-speed Internet and cell phones. South Korean television and movies have great popularity throughout Asia, and education remains the number-one priority. The third-largest group of foreign students in the United States comes from South Korea.

✓ **READING PROGRESS CHECK**

Identifying What has led to increased tensions between North Korea and South Korea in recent decades?

LESSON 3 REVIEW TEKS

Reviewing Vocabulary

1. ***Making Connections*** What is deflation, and how did it hurt the Japanese economy?

Using Your Notes

2. ***Identifying*** Use your notes to identify the policies of Deng Xiaoping that were intended to help modernize China.

Answering the Guiding Questions

3. ***Making Generalizations*** What political and social changes has China undergone in the late twentieth and early twenty-first centuries?
4. ***Drawing Conclusions*** How has modern China become a world economic power?
5. ***Analyzing Information*** What changes have occurred in Japan from the 1990s to the present?
6. ***Contrasting*** What are the major differences between North Korea and South Korea?

Writing Activity

7. **NARRATIVE** Imagine you are a foreign exchange student attending a Beijing university in 1989. You witness the demonstration at Tiananmen Square. Write a letter to a friend describing what you saw.

networks

There's More Online!

- BIOGRAPHY Manmohan Singh
- BIOGRAPHY Michelle Bachelet
- CHART/GRAPH Challenges and Changes in Latin America
- CHART/GRAPH India's Political Parties
- IMAGE Protests in Tahrir Square
- INTERACTIVE SELF-CHECK QUIZ
- MAP World Population Cartogram
- TIME LINE U.S. Involvement in the Middle East
- VIDEO Regions After the Cold War

LESSON 4

Regions After the Cold War

ESSENTIAL QUESTION • *What motivates political change?* • *How can economic and social changes affect a country?*

Reading HELPDESK

Academic Vocabulary

- **evolve**
- **evident**

Content Vocabulary

- **jurisdiction**
- **corruption**

TAKING NOTES:

Key Ideas and Details

Summarizing As you read, use a chart to list the major events in these regions since the end of the Cold War.

Middle East & North Africa	Africa South of the Sahara
South & Southeast Asia	**Latin America**

TEKS Texas Essential Knowledge and Skills

13E summarize the rise of independence movements in Africa, the Middle East, and South Asia and reasons for ongoing conflicts

continued on the next page

IT MATTERS BECAUSE

After the end of the Cold War, significant developments were occurring throughout the Middle East, Africa, Asia, and Latin America. A movement toward democracy and a desire for a better life led to increasing political participation.

Middle East and North Africa

GUIDING QUESTION *What changes have occurred in the Middle East and North Africa since the 1990s?*

Many countries in these regions have been plagued with political instability, ethnic tensions, high unemployment, growing poverty rates, poor education, and limited civil liberties.

Region Overview

Efforts to reach a peace agreement between the Israelis and the Palestinians, represented by the PLO (Palestinian Liberation Organization), have failed due to unresolved disputes regarding final borders, including the status of Jerusalem, Jewish settlements in the West Bank, Palestinian recognition of Israel as a Jewish State, the return of Arab refugees and their descendants to Israel, and more. Continued Palestinian terrorist attacks, often carried out by groups like Hamas that are inspired to a significant degree by radical Islamic fundamentalism, further complicate the quest for peace.

Iran, an oil-rich country, remains under the control of Muslim clerics, who enforce strict adherence to Islamic law. They limit the rights of women, and the right to free assembly and a free press. In 2009, hundreds of thousands of Iranians protested the reelection of Mahmoud Ahmadinejad and declared the election a fraud.

After the terrorist attacks on the World Trade Center on September 11, 2001, the United States invaded Afghanistan in 2001 and Iraq in 2003. Under the control of the Taliban, Afghanistan was harboring Osama bin Laden, the head of al-Qaeda, who claimed responsibility for the attacks. After the invasion of Iraq, the country fell into civil war between the Shia Muslims, who controlled southern Iraq, and the Sunni Muslims, who controlled central Iraq. Elections held in 2010 led to the election of Prime Minister Nuri Kamal al-Maliki eight months later.

PHOTO: John Moore/Staff/Getty Images News/Getty Images, Stephane De Sakutin/Staff/AFP/Getty Images, © Jane Hahn/Corbis, Adeel Halim/Bloomberg/Getty Images, Marcelo Hernandez/LatinContent/Getty Images.

Revolutionary Upheaval

North Africa and the Middle East were rocked by an immense uprising that led to a regime change in Tunisia and Egypt. Most countries in the region have a high percentage of young people; more than half of Egypt's 80 million people are under the age of 25. Most of these young people are unemployed. After 23 years of oppressive government, Tunisian president Zine el-Abidine Ben Ali fled the country following mass protests that began in December 2010. Other protests in the region soon followed.

In Egypt, an oppressive regime used torture and brutality to suppress any political opposition. In January 2011, hundreds of thousands of Egyptians, including women, from all walks of life flooded Tahrir (Liberation) Square in downtown Cairo. Protesters used social networking to organize protests. After 18 days of sometimes violent retaliation by police forces, the Egyptian army sided with the protesters, forcing the president to leave the country. Since the uprising, Egypt has sentenced its former president to life in prison. A new constitution was written, and elections were held in 2012. However, the new government and its president soon became unpopular and were thrown out by the military with public support. Differences between Egypt's political factions are a source of ongoing conflict.

In Libya, protesters rebelled against the authoritarian regime of Colonel Muammar al-Qaddafi. After Colonel Qaddafi's troops began to use force against the protesters, the UN Security Council voted to authorize military action. In March 2011, American and European forces began air strikes against the Qaddafi regime. Libyan rebel forces took control of Tripoli in August, ousting Qaddafi from power. It was not until Qaddafi was killed in October, however, that the creation of a new Libya could begin in earnest.

On July 7, 2012, Libya held its first free election since 1952. Libya's new Prime Minister Mustafa Abushagur faces ongoing political unrest as parties struggle for control of the country and anti-America protests make headlines around the world.

Protests spread throughout the entire region to Algeria, Yemen, Jordan, Bahrain, Oman, Morocco, Saudi Arabia, and Syria. Despite the successes in Tunisia and Egypt, the protests in these other nations have been met with force. Nevertheless, after decades of conflict, political oppression, and exploitation, the revolutionary upheaval led by young people has brought a new beginning to the Middle East and North Africa.

✓ **READING PROGRESS CHECK**

Comparing and Contrasting How are the uprisings in Egypt and Libya similar? How are they different?

Africa South of the Sahara

GUIDING QUESTION ***What challenges have confronted countries in Africa south of the Sahara since the end of the Cold War?***

African societies have not yet begun to overcome the challenges they have faced since independence. Most African states are still poor, and African concerns continue to carry little weight in the international community. There are signs of progress toward political stability in some countries. Other nations, however, are still racked by civil war or ruled by brutal dictatorships.

(continued from p. 834)

TEKS **Texas Essential Knowledge and Skills**

14A summarize the development and impact of radical Islamic fundamentalism on events in the second half of the 20th century, including Palestinian terrorism and the growth of al Qaeda

▲ **Antigovernment demonstrators In Tahrir Square in Cairo demand the resignation of Egyptian president Hosni Mubarak.**

▶ **CRITICAL THINKING**

Analyzing Visuals What words would you use to describe the demonstrators?

SKILLS PRACTICE

As your class discusses challenges faced by African societies, pay attention to gestures people make as they speak. If your instructor teaches words before the lesson, listen for them in the lesson.

evolve develop; work out

▲ A health counselor teaches South African students about HIV/AIDS prevention.

jurisdiction the limits or territory within which authority may be exercised

Region Overview

Africans have found ways to address their political problems, to cooperate with one another, and to protect and promote their own interests. In 1991 the Organization of African Unity (OAU) agreed to establish the African Economic Community (AEC). This group is intended to provide greater political and economic integration throughout Africa on the pattern of the EU. In 2001 the African Union (AU) replaced the OAU. The new organization has already sought to mediate several of the conflicts in the region. The AU also promotes democracy and economic growth in Africa.

As Africa **evolves**, it is important to remember that economic and political change is often a slow and painful process. Introduced to industrialization and ideas of Western democracy only a century ago, African societies are still looking for ways to graft Western political institutions and economic practices onto indigenous structures still influenced by traditional values and attitudes.

African countries face many social and economic problems. Rapid population growth has slowed economic growth. In the first decade of the 2000s, Africa's population growth rate was 2.3 percent compared to 1.24 percent in the rest of the world. As a result, poverty remains widespread. Cities have grown tremendously. By 2007, approximately 39 percent of Africans lived in urban areas where there are massive slums and high levels of pollution.

Moreover, AIDS remains a serious concern in Africa. More than two-thirds (22.9 million) of all persons infected with HIV are living in Africa south of the Sahara. In this area during 2010, 1.9 million people became infected with HIV and more than 1.2 million died of AIDS.

Some African nations have mounted an impressive effort to fight AIDS. In Uganda President Yoweri Museveni involved a wide range of natural leaders in Ugandan society as well as international health and social service agencies. Uganda has made significant progress in its fight against AIDS. The numbers of cases of HIV in Uganda stabilized in the early 2000s.

Politically, Africa has witnessed a number of women as leaders of their countries. For example, Luisa Diogo became prime minister of Mozambique in 2004. There has also been a trend toward multiparty elections. In Senegal, for example, national elections held in the summer of 2000 brought an end to four decades of rule by the once-dominant Socialist Party.

Religion has contributed to ongoing conflicts in parts of Africa. An Islamic resurgence was evident in a number of African countries. It surfaced in Ethiopia where Muslim tribespeople rebelled against a Marxist regime and eventually established an independent Eritrea.

More recently, in Nigeria and other nations of West Africa, divisions between Muslims and Christians have erupted into violence. In the early 2000s, riots between Christians and Muslims broke out in several northern cities as a result of the decision by Muslim local officials to apply Islamic law throughout their **jurisdictions**. The violence has lessened as local officials managed to craft compromise policies that limit some of the harsher aspects of Muslim law. Nevertheless, the dispute continues to threaten the fragile unity of Nigeria, Africa's most populous country.

Côte d'Ivoire

The religious tensions that erupted in Nigeria have spilled over into neighboring states. Under its first president, Felix Houphouet-Boigny, Côte d'Ivoire (Ivory Coast) was often seen as a model of religious and ethnic harmony. But his death in 1993 led to an outbreak of long-simmering resentment between

PHOTO: Stephane De Sakutin/Staff/AFP/Getty Images

Christians in the south and Muslim immigrants in the north. Elections held in 2000 resulted in the election of a Christian president. The elections were marked by violence and widespread charges of voting irregularities.

In 2002, an armed uprising split the nation into a Muslim, rebel-dominated north and a Christian, government-controlled south. A power-sharing deal brought temporary peace in 2007. It was also believed that a presidential election in November 2010 might bring a new unity. Laurent Gbagbo, who had been president since 2000, lost to Alassane Ouattara, who was declared the winner by the United Nations. Gbagbo used the army in an attempt to stay in power, while UN peacekeeping forces guarded Ouattara. Gbagbo's forces terrorized civilians in order to remain in power. A peaceful march of unarmed women, for example, was stopped by machine gun fire from Gbagbo's armed followers. In November 2011, Gbagbo was arrested and sentenced to prison for crimes against humanity.

As in other African countries, civil war has devastated the economy of Côte d'Ivoire. The city of Abidjan once had a shining downtown. Now it is a jungle of darkened high-rise windows. Jobs have disappeared; 4 million men are out of work in a country of 21 million. Banks and businesses have closed, and food shortages are widespread.

▲ A suburb of Abidjan shows the aftermath of the fighting that followed the 2010 election in Côte d'Ivoire.

▶ **CRITICAL THINKING**

Describing Write a sentence or two that describes the scene in this photograph.

✓ **READING PROGRESS CHECK**

Analyzing What role has religion played in recent African conflicts?

South and Southeast Asia

GUIDING QUESTION *What different economic and political issues have affected the countries of South and Southeast Asia since the 1990s?*

South Asia comprises the states of India, Pakistan, Bangladesh, Nepal, Bhutan, Sri Lanka, and the Maldives. Important developments in South Asia since the 1990s are the growing economic power of India, the continuing rivalry between India and Pakistan, and the instability in Pakistan.

Region Overview

During the early 1990s, the Congress Party remained the leading party in India. Its powerful hold, however, began to decline. New parties, such as the militantly Hindu Bharata Janata Party (BJP), competed with the Congress Party for control of the central and state governments. Growing political instability was accompanied by rising tensions between Hindus and Muslims. After a series of coalition governments headed by the BJP leader A. B. Vajpayee between 1996 and 2004, the Congress Party returned to power at the head of a coalition government based on a commitment to maintain economic growth and carry out reforms in rural areas. These reforms included public works projects and hot lunch programs for all primary school children. Manmohan Singh, who had carried out economic reforms in India in 1991 as finance minister, became prime minister. He was reelected in 2009 and has become highly regarded by other world leaders.

India's economy has emerged as one of the world's largest and fastest growing. Economic reforms in 1991 fostered foreign investment and began to move India toward a market-based economy. Although agriculture is still the occupation of many Indians, the service and industrial sectors now account for much of India's GDP. Many economists believe that India is a rising economic superpower and may have the world's third-largest economy by 2035.

▲ A General Motors plant in India

▶ **CRITICAL THINKING**

Hypothesizing Why do you think jobs in the automotive industry have moved to India?

Religious differences between Hindus and Muslims have fueled ongoing conflicts, especially the dispute between India and Pakistan over Kashmir, a territory between the two countries. The danger escalated in 1998 when both countries tested nuclear warheads. Border conflicts in 2002 led to threats of war, but in 2003 the countries agreed to a cease-fire and restored diplomatic relations.

Since 1990, most countries in Southeast Asia have experienced strong economic growth. Especially strong economies are **evident** in the Philippines, Indonesia, Malaysia, Singapore, Thailand, and Vietnam. Myanmar, Cambodia, and Laos have not kept pace.

evident apparent

In recent years, some Southeast Asian societies have once again moved toward democracy. However, serious troubles remain. The financial crisis of the 1990s aroused political unrest in Indonesia. Myanmar remains isolated and mired in brutal military rule. Although the Philippines is democratic, terrorism remains a challenge. Muslim rebels on the island of Mindanao, for example, have used terror to promote their demands for independence. Regional cooperation, however, has continued through the Association of Southeast Asia Nations (ASEAN), which fosters trade among Asian states.

Pakistan

After her dismissal by the military on charges of corruption, Benazir Bhutto was reelected as president in 1993. She attempted to crack down on opposition forces but was removed once again in 1997 amid renewed charges of corruption. Her successor, too, was ousted in 1999 by a military coup led by General Pervez Musharraf, who promised to restore honest government.

In September 2001, Pakistan became the focus of international attention when a coalition of forces arrived in Afghanistan to overthrow the Taliban regime. Despite considerable support for the Taliban among the local population, President Musharraf pledged his help in bringing terrorists to justice.

By 2003, problems had escalated. As Musharraf sought to fend off challenges from radical Muslim groups, secular opposition figures criticized his regime's authoritarian nature. Exiled, Bhutto planned her return.

PRIMARY SOURCE

“God willing, I will return to my homeland and once again lead the forces of democracy in electoral battle against the entrenched power of dictators, generals, and extremists. This is my destiny.”

—from *Daughter of Destiny: An Autobiography,* April 2007

She did return to Pakistan early in 2008 to run for president, but she was assassinated. This led to widespread suspicions of official involvement. In September 2008, amid growing political turmoil, Bhutto's widower, Asif Ali Zardari, was elected president of Pakistan. He remains in power, despite accusations of **corruption** and misuse of public funds.

corruption impairment of integrity, virtue, or moral principle

✓ **READING PROGRESS CHECK**

Describing What political changes have India and Pakistan experienced in recent decades?

Latin America

GUIDING QUESTION ***How have economic issues affected Latin American countries since the end of the Cold War?***

For much of Latin America's history, Latin Americans have struggled to free themselves from oppressive rule, civil war, poverty, and economic dependence on foreign countries. Since 1990, many countries have created democratic governments and reformed their social and economic structures.

PHOTO: Adeel Halim/Bloomberg/Getty Images

Region Overview

Programs for increased public education and greater economic growth have helped to alleviate Latin America's greatest challenge, income inequality, or the large gap between rich and poor. However, countries in South America have fared better than in Central America, where many countries remain poverty stricken and are often involved in deadly drug wars.

At the end of the 1900s and beginning of the 2000s, a noticeable political trend in Latin America has been the election of left-wing governments. This is evident in the election of Hugo Chavez in Venezuela in 1998; Luiz Inácio Lula da Silva in Brazil in 2002 and his successor, Dilma Rousseff, in 2010; Michelle Bachelet in Chile in 2006; and Daniel Ortega in Nicaragua in 2007 and 2011.

Most, but not all, of these countries have pushed for democratic freedoms, social reforms, and economic growth. While Nicaragua remains poverty stricken, Brazil and Chile have seen unprecedented economic growth. In Brazil Lula da Silva pursued a policy of increased trade and education reform. He expanded the middle class and created new consumers while continuing to increase exports. In Chile Bachelet used revenue from copper resources to fund social programs for women and children.

Drug Wars in Mexico

High poverty rates, illiteracy, high unemployment, and political corruption have led to a violent drug war in Mexico. More than 35,000 people have been killed since President Felipe Calderón, elected in 2006, ordered a military response against the country's drug gangs.

Colombia is the world's biggest producer of cocaine. Mexico serves as the gateway into the United States, which is the largest market for the drug. Mexican drug cartels, or criminal organizations whose chief purpose is to promote and control drug trafficking operations, began to transport drugs for the Colombians. More recently, however, they have taken over the distribution of drugs in the United States. This has led to considerable violence on the border of Mexico and the United States.

Mexican drug cartels recruit their members from a pool of soldiers who had served in the armies of several countries, including Guatemala and El Salvador. Increasingly, Mexican drug cartels also rely upon young people of Central America, who are poor and unemployed. These teenagers are willing to transport drugs, watch kidnap victims, and perform other low-level tasks.

READING PROGRESS CHECK

Describing How do Mexican drug cartels traffic in drugs?

BIOGRAPHY

PHOTO: Marcelo Hernandez/LatinContent/Getty Images

Michelle Bachelet (1951–)

Michelle Bachelet was born into a political family. Her father was a member of President Salvador Allende's government and was imprisoned and tortured by the regime of Augusto Pinochet. He died in jail. In 1975 she was kidnapped and tortured, and then went into exile. She later returned to Chile, completed her studies in medicine, and became a pediatrician. She became involved in government service after becoming active with the Socialist Party. From 2006–2010, Michelle Bachelet was president of Chile. She was the first female to be elected president of the country. Bachelet focused on improving the social and health conditions of Chileans. After leaving office, she became the head of UN Women.

CRITICAL THINKING

Making Connections How do you think Bachelet's young adulthood affected her political involvement?

LESSON 4 REVIEW TEKS

Reviewing Vocabulary

1. ***Making Generalizations*** Why are leaders who are charged with corruption sometimes forced out of office?

Using Your Notes

2. ***Contrasting*** Use your notes to find differences among major events in the regions in this lesson since the end of the Cold War.

Answering the Guiding Questions

3. ***Identifying Central Issues*** What changes have occurred in the Middle East and North Africa since the 1990s?
4. ***Analyzing*** What challenges have confronted countries in Africa south of the Sahara since the end of the Cold War?
5. ***Identifying*** What different economic and political issues have affected the countries of South and Southeast Asia since the 1990s?
6. ***Determining Causes and Effects*** How have economic issues affected Latin American countries since the end of the Cold War?

Writing About History

7. **ARGUMENT** Do you think the uprisings in North Africa in 2009 and 2010 would have been as effective without the use of social networking sites? Why or why not?

CHAPTER 34 Assessment

TEKS

Directions: On a separate sheet of paper, answer the questions below. Make sure you read carefully and answer all parts of the questions.

Lesson Review

Lesson 1

1. ***Explaining and Making Inferences*** Explain Gorbachev's role in the fall of communism. Why do you think Gorbachev believed that in order for his economic reforms to be successful, there would also need to be a policy of glasnost? **13D**

2. ***Identifying*** What has greatly helped Russia's economic growth?

3. ***Explaining*** What role did Lech Walesa and Pope John Paul II play in the fall of communism in Eastern Europe? **13D**

Lesson 2

4. ***Identifying Cause and Effect*** What events led to the reunification of the two Germanies in the 1990s? What makes this region a historically significant part of this era? **16A**

5. ***Identifying Cause and Effect*** Why did German reunification lead to some economic problems?

6. ***Summarizing*** Summarize the attitudes among and actions of Chinese students and other groups in 1989? **22E**

7. ***Describing*** How have the roles of women and children changed at the end of the twentieth and beginning of the twenty-first centuries? **24A**

Lesson 3

8. ***Evaluating*** Do you think the one-child policy in China is oppressive? Why or why not?

9. ***Describing*** Describe the new agricultural policy that helped China move into the Industrial Age and improve its economy.

10. ***Making Connections*** How have nuclear weapons affected North Korea and South Korea?

Lesson 4

11. ***Identifying Cause and Effect*** What happened in Libya in 2011, and how did the international community respond?

12. ***Describing*** How has India transformed its economy to become a rising economic superpower?

13. ***Sequencing*** Describe the leadership changes in Pakistan from the years 1993 through 2008. What accounted for these changes in leadership?

14. ***Specifying*** How do Mexican drug cartels exploit young people?

Exploring the Essential Question

15. ***Synthesizing*** With a partner or in a small group select a country or region discussed in the chapter, and create a chronological multimedia presentation showing political, economic, and social changes that have occurred in that

Need Extra Help?

If You've Missed Question	1	2	3	4	5	6	7	8	9	10	11	12	13	14	15
Go to page	816	819	817	823	824	830	825	831	829	832	835	837	838	839	816

country or region over the past 30 or so years. Be sure to include how the country or region was affected.

Critical Thinking

16 ***Comparing and Contrasting*** Compare the aims of Gorbachev and Reagan in the mid-to-late 1980s. How did their goals impact the Cold War and end to communism in Eastern Europe?

17 ***Making Predictions*** Make a prediction about Chinese society in the future based on the current one-child policy.

18 ***Analyzing Arguments*** What are some possible reasons for the decline in the Japanese economy?

19 ***Analyzing*** Research the HIV/AIDS epidemic in Africa. Create a graph that illustrates the social impact of the disease.

20 ***Explaining and Generalizing*** Why did communist command economies collapse in competition with free market economies at the end of the twentieth century? How did the human condition improve for those living in free enterprise economies as compared to command economies? **18E, 18F**

21 ***Analyzing*** How do American music, art, and film reflect the culture of the times? How have they transcended America to impact other cultures? Identify examples and explain how universal themes in American art and music appeal to people of all cultures, and consider the changing role that children play in spreading American popular culture. **24A, 26B, 26C**

22 ***Summarizing*** Summarize the reasons for ongoing conflicts in Africa, such as religion, politics, and territorial disputes. **13E, 14A**

23 ***Comparing*** Compare the reasons for ongoing conflicts in the Middle East and South Asia. Examine issues of religion, politics, and territorial disputes. **13E, 14A**

24 ***Making Inferences*** After the collapse of Communist governments in Czechoslovakia and Yugoslavia, both nations underwent civil conflicts that concluded with new divisions and new nations within the former national borders. What can be inferred from these parallel events and outcomes?

25 ***Making Inferences*** Make an inference about the high percentage of young people in countries such as Tunisia and Egypt and the protests that began in December of 2010.

26 ***Use a Problem-solving Process*** Choose an area of conflict from the chapter and use a problem-solving process to generate a possible solution that satisfies both sides. Be sure to gather information, consider more than one option, and weigh pros and cons. Explain how you would implement the solution and explain why you think it would be effective. **31A**

Social Studies Skills

27 ***Identifying Causes and Effects*** What led to the breakup of Yugoslavia? In your answer, describe the event that caused NATO to support Bosnian and Croatian forces. **1F, 22D**

28 ***Economics*** Why did the euro go through a major crisis in 2010?

Need Extra Help?

If You've Missed Question	16	17	18	19	20	21	22	23	24	25	26	27	28
Go to page	817	831	831	836	821	826	835	834	817	835	816	820	823

29 ***Explaining*** What role did Ronald Reagan play in the collapse of communism? How did his support of new military technologies factor into his role? **13D, 28C**

30 ***Identifying*** How did students spark resistance to political oppression in China? What was the outcome? **22E**

31 ***Research Skills*** Research the current status of Quebec and its call for independence from Canada. Investigate the culture of the province and how it exudes its own unique qualities, as well as qualities reflective of national Canadian identity. Share research through a written or oral presentation.

32 ***Geography Skills*** Create an illustrated or digital map showing Germany before and after its reunification in 1990. Include former and current capitals and a map key with any population data available.

DBQ Analyzing Primary Sources

Read the excerpt of Yeltsin's resignation speech in which he addresses the many challenges he faced during his presidency, and answer the questions that follow.

PRIMARY SOURCE

"I want to ask for your forgiveness for the fact that many of the dreams we shared did not come true. And for the fact that what seemed simple to us turned out to be tormentingly difficult. I ask forgiveness for not justifying some hopes of those people who believed that at one stroke, in one spurt, we could leap from the gray, stagnant, totalitarian past in to the light, rich, civilized future."

—Boris Yeltsin, December 31, 1999

33 ***Analyzing*** Did Yeltsin believe he succeeded in transforming post-Soviet Russia? Cite evidence to support your answer.

34 ***Evaluating*** Why might moving from a totalitarian government to a successful and prosperous country "in one spurt" not have been a reasonable hope? Explain.

Analyzing Visuals

Use the image to answer the following questions.

This photograph was taken at a Polish protest against the communist regime in 1987.

35 ***Making Connections*** Analyze the photograph and use details in this image to explain the fall of communism in Poland.

Extended Response Question

36 ***Expository*** Compare and contrast the movements to free their country of communism that occurred in Poland, Czechoslovakia, and Romania. Discuss their causes, outcomes, and long-term effects. **1F**

Need Extra Help?

If You've Missed Question	29	30	31	32	33	34	35	36
Go to page	817	829	825	823	842	842	842	817

Contemporary Global Issues

1989–Present

ESSENTIAL QUESTIONS • *What influences global political and economic relationships?* • *How do social and environmental issues affect countries differently?*

networks

There's More Online! about contemporary global issues.

CHAPTER 35

The Story Matters...

The world faces a daunting array of challenges in the twenty-first century. Some of these, such as nuclear proliferation and cyberterrorism, are relatively new. Other problems, such as war, poverty, hunger, and disease, have a long history. Creative solutions are needed to address these problems. Microcredit loans are one example. Microcredit banks make small loans to individual entrepreneurs, the majority of them women, enabling them to start small businesses and to escape from poverty.

◀ Photographed in 2001, this woman is a Rwandan refugee now living in Nairobi, Kenya. She was able to set up her business as a seamstress with a loan from a microcredit bank.

CHAPTER 35

Place and Time: The World 1989–Present

One of the most significant parts of the human story has been the growth of cities. Civilization began with the first cities 5,000 years ago. Urbanization greatly accelerated with the Industrial Revolution. If current trends in population growth and economic development continue, the human future will be a story of megacities. A megacity is an urban area with more than 10 million inhabitants. In 1950 there were only two megacities—New York City and Tokyo. Today, the United Nations estimates that there are 26 megacities.

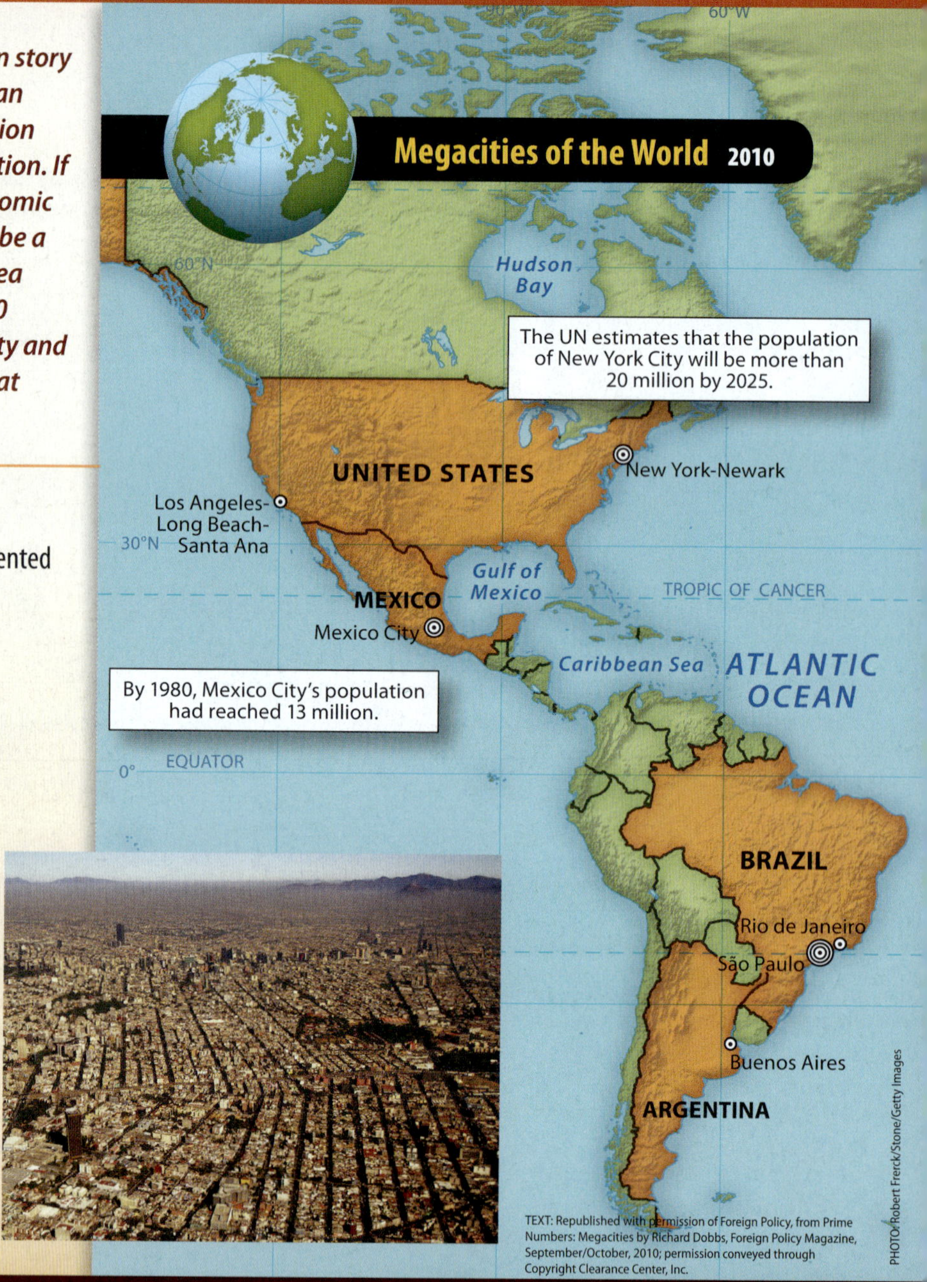

Step Into the Place

Read the quotation and look at the information presented on the map.

DBQ What will be the biggest challenge facing megacities?

PRIMARY SOURCE

"Over the next two decades, the world will see a burst of urban expansion at a speed and on a scale never before witnessed in human history. But not all the world will take part. When you hear about the coming urban age, it's really a story about rising Asia and the two countries that will define this new era of the megacity: China and India. Half of Asia will become urbanized, and nearly a billion people will shift from countryside to cityscape. Trillions of dollars will need to be spent on roads, trains, power plants, water systems, and social services. And it's going to happen in less than half the time that it took the West."

—Richard Dobbs, from "Megacities," *Foreign Policy*, Sept./Oct. 2010

Step Into the Time

Select several events from the time line and use them as evidence for a generalization about world population patterns.

MEGACITIES

1990 The number of megacities in the world reaches 10

1995 India has three megacities—Mumbai, Delhi, and Kolkata

THE WORLD

1989

1990 World Wide Web created

1995 World Trade Organization (WTO) begins operations

networks
There's More Online!

- **MAP** Explore the interactive version of this map on Networks.
- **TIME LINE** Explore the interactive version of the time line on Networks.

- **2000** Shanghai becomes China's first megacity
- **2000** Number of international NGOs reaches nearly 37,000
- **2001** Terrorists attack U.S. World Trade Center and Pentagon
- **2002** The Euro is launched as a common currency in many Western European nations
- **2003** U.S.-led army invades Iraq
- **2005** The number of megacities in the world reaches 19
- **2007** UN estimates world population at 6.7 billion
- **2008** Worldwide recession
- **2009** H1N1 flu pandemic outbreak
- **2010** Nine percent of the world's population lives in megacities
- **2010** More than 1 billion Internet users exist worldwide
- **2011** Protests break out in Tunisia, Egypt, Libya, and Bahrain
- **2012** The number of megacities in the world reaches 26.
- **2015** China's economy projected to be nearly the world's largest

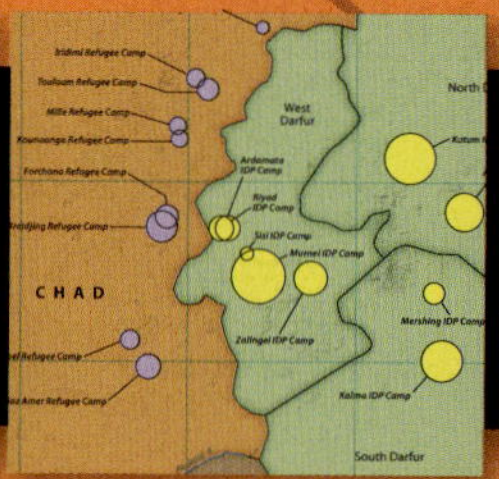

networks

There's More Online!

- CHART/GRAPH Countries with Nuclear Weapons Capability
- IMAGE Elections in East Timor
- IMAGE Ground Zero, New York City
- IMAGE UN General Assembly
- IMAGE UN Peacekeeping Forces in Sudan
- INTERACTIVE SELF-CHECK QUIZ
- MAP Darfur Refugee and Displaced Persons Camps
- PRIMARY SOURCE United Nations Charter
- VIDEO September 11th

Reading HELPDESK

Academic Vocabulary

- **chemical**
- **drama**
- **arbitrarily**

Content Vocabulary

- **peacekeeping forces**
- **nuclear proliferation**
- **bioterrorism**

TAKING NOTES:

Key Ideas and Details

Summarizing As you read, use a table like the one below to identify important political events that have occurred in modern Africa, Asia, and Latin America.

Africa	Asia	Latin America

TEKS **Texas Essential Knowledge and Skills**

13E summarize the rise of independence movements in Africa, the Middle East, and South Asia and reasons for ongoing conflicts

continued on p. 848

LESSON 1

Political Challenges in the Modern World

ESSENTIAL QUESTION

What influences global political and economic relationships?

It Matters Because

In today's world, problems in one part of the world can affect people all over the globe. Terrorism, civil war, and ethnic conflict are some of the most difficult political challenges of the modern world.

The United Nations

GUIDING QUESTION *What are the structure and goals of the United Nations?*

During the twentieth century, many nations became convinced that there are significant problems that can be solved only by working with other nations. After World War I, world leaders created the League of Nations. While limited in its accomplishments, the organization was significant for testing the concept of an international organization working for world peace. The United Nations (UN) proved more effective than the League of Nations. Founded in 1945 at the end of World War II, the UN is one of the most visible symbols of the new globalism. Two of the UN's goals are peace and human dignity. Its members pledged:

PRIMARY SOURCE

"to save succeeding generations from the scourge of war. . . to reaffirm faith in fundamental human rights. . . and to promote social progress and better standards of life in larger freedom."

—from the Preamble to the United Nations Charter, June 26, 1945

The General Assembly of the United Nations is made of representatives from all member nations. It has the power to discuss any important question and to recommend action. The Security Council advises the General Assembly and passes resolutions that require the organization to act. Five nations have permanent seats on the Security Council: the United States, Russia, Great Britain, France, and China. Ten other members are chosen by the General Assembly

PHOTO: (l to r)BETH A. KEISER/AFP/Getty Images, ©Justin Lane/epa/Corbis, GUILLAUME LAVALLEE/AFP/Getty Images, JEWEL SAMAD/AFP/Getty Images.

and serve for limited terms. Because each permanent member can veto a decision, the UN's accomplishments are often limited.

UN programs and specialized agencies do significant work to address economic and social problems. Often, the UN is the only organization that can arbitrate an international dispute. UN **peacekeeping forces** settle conflicts and supervise truces in "hot spots" around the globe.

✓ **READING PROGRESS CHECK**

Contrasting How do the UN General Assembly and the UN Security Council differ?

International Security

GUIDING QUESTION ***What international security issues confront the post-Cold War world?***

Despite the efforts of the United Nations, numerous challenges remain in the effort to provide security in today's world.

Weapons of Mass Destruction

Modern technology has led to frightening methods of mass destruction: nuclear, biological, and **chemical** weapons. The end of the Cold War reduced the risk of nuclear conflict between the United States and the Soviet Union. However, nuclear weapons still exist and nuclear conflicts remain possible.

The UN established the International Atomic Energy Agency (IAEA) in 1957. This agency is a safeguard system against **nuclear proliferation**—the spread of nuclear weapons production technology and knowledge to nations without that capability. The following countries have not joined the Nuclear Nonproliferation Treaty (NPT)—India, Pakistan, Israel, and North Korea. In 1998 India and Pakistan exploded nuclear devices underground. North Korea performed its first nuclear test in October 2006. Although Israel is widely believed to have developed nuclear weapons, it has never publicly confirmed that belief, nor has it conducted a nuclear test. Iran has violated the NPT and is believed to be developing a nuclear weapon. Despite international sanctions, Iran has refused to shelve its nuclear enrichment program.

Since 2000, there has also been an increased awareness of the threat from biological and chemical weapons. Biowarfare, the use of disease and poison against civilians and soldiers in wartime, is not new. For example, chemical weapons were used extensively in World War I and during the Iran-Iraq war in the 1980s. Governments have agreed to limit the research, production, and use of weapons of mass destruction, but these agreements are difficult to enforce. Furthermore, these measures have not prevented terrorists from practicing **bioterrorism**, the use of biological and chemical weapons in terrorist attacks.

The Challenge of Terrorism

Acts of terrorism have become a regular feature of modern society. Terrorists' reasons for killing civilians or taking hostages include the attempt to achieve political goals. Radical Islamic fundamentalism has had an impact on many terrorists, including inspiring al-Qaeda and Palestinian terrorists to attack the West or Israel. Terrorists often kill civilians and take hostages to achieve their political goals. Beginning in the late 1970s and 1980s, many countries placed their concern about terrorism at the top of foreign policy agendas. Terrorist acts have received considerable media attention. When Palestinian terrorists kidnapped and killed 11 Israeli athletes at the Munich Olympic Games in 1972, hundreds of millions of people watched the **drama** unfold on television.

Analyzing **PRIMARY SOURCES**

Nuclear Proliferation

"The threat of nuclear terrorism is real and current… the existence of a nuclear threat anywhere is a threat everywhere, and as a global community, we will win or lose this battle together."

—Dr. Mohamed ElBaradei, Director General, IAEA, November 8, 2004

DBQ ***DRAWING CONCLUSIONS*** Why does the Director General argue that stopping nuclear terrorism requires a global effort?

peacekeeping forces military forces drawn from neutral members of the United Nations to settle conflicts and supervise truces

chemical used in or produced by chemistry

nuclear proliferation the spread of nuclear weapons production technology and knowledge to nations without that capability

bioterrorism the use of biological and chemical weapons in terrorist attacks

drama state of intense conflict

▲ Fire and rescue workers search for surviviors amid the rubble of the World Trade Center two days after the September 11, 2001, attacks.

▶ **CRITICAL THINKING**
Describing What was the immediate response to the attacks of September 11, 2001?

Some terrorists are militant nationalists who want separatist states. The Irish Republican Army (IRA), for example, wants to unite Northern Ireland with the Irish Republic. IRA leaders now seem more willing to open normal relations with the police of Northern Ireland after decades of violence. The group Basque Fatherland and Liberty (ETA) employs violence as a tool to free the Basque region in the western Pyrenees from Spanish control.

A radical Communist guerrilla group in Peru, known as Shining Path, also used terrorist violence. Aiming to create a classless society, Shining Path killed mayors, missionaries, priests, and peasants across Peru.

One of the most destructive acts of terrorism occurred on September 11, 2001. Al-Qaeda terrorists carefully planned the devastating attack. Radical Islamic fundamentalism and opposition to the West fueled the growth of al-Qaeda during the1990s. Directed by Osama bin Laden, al-Qaeda hijacked four commercial jets in Boston, Newark, and Washington, D.C., flying two into the World Trade Center and one into the Pentagon. Almost 3,000 people were killed. President George W. Bush vowed to wage war on terrorism. The U.S. response began with military action by the United States and its allies against Afghanistan in October 2001. President Barack Obama announced a major U.S. victory against al-Qaeda in 2011, when U.S. forces killed bin Laden at his hideout in Pakistan.

Worldwide, another response to the attacks of September 11, 2001, has been increased security at airports. Many European and Asian governments have also begun working more closely together in their intelligence and police activities to track down terrorists.

Challenges in the Middle East

The war on terrorism spread to the Middle East when the United States attacked Iraq in March 2003. President Bush claimed that Iraq's leader, Saddam Hussein, had chemical and biological weapons of mass destruction and that Saddam had close ties to al-Qaeda. Both claims turned out to be mistaken and the United States soon became bogged down in a war in which Hussein's supporters, foreign terrorists, and Islamic militants all battled the American-led forces.

(continued from p. 846)

TEKS **Texas Essential Knowledge and Skills**

14A summarize the development and impact of radical Islamic fundamentalism on events in the second half of the 20th century, including Palestinian terrorism and the growth of al Qaeda

14B explain the U.S. response to terrorism from September 11, 2001, to the present

20D explain the significance of the League of Nations and the United Nations

22D identify examples of genocide, including the Holocaust and genocide in the Balkans, Rwanda, and Darfur

22F assess the degree to which American ideals have advanced human rights and democratic ideas throughout the world

By 2006, Iraq seemed to be descending into a widespread civil war, especially between the Shia, who controlled southern Iraq, and the Sunnis, who controlled central Iraq. An American troop surge in 2007 helped stabilize conditions within a year. The U.S. and Iraqi governments then agreed to a complete withdrawal of American troops by 2011. President Obama fulfilled this promise. After more than nine years in Iraq, all remaining American troops left the country on December 18, 2011.

Much of the ongoing conflict in the Middle East includes terrorism that is aimed against the West. One reason Middle Eastern terrorists have targeted Westerners can be traced to Western investment in the Middle East oil industry, which began in the 1920s. This industry brought wealth to ruling families in some Middle Eastern kingdoms, but most citizens remained very poor. They often blamed the West, especially the United States, for supporting the ruling families.

The oil business increased Middle Eastern contact with the West. Some Muslims feared that this contact would weaken their religion and their way of life. Some Muslims began organizing to overthrow their pro-Western governments. Muslims who support these movements are called fundamentalist militants. They promote their own vision of what a pure Islamic society should be. Most Muslims around the world do not share this vision, and do not support terrorism, and some are terror victims themselves.

✓ **READING PROGRESS CHECK**

Determining Cause and Effect How have governments responded to terrorism since September 11, 2001?

Civil War, Ethnic Conflict, and New Democracies

GUIDING QUESTIONS ***How have civil war, ethnic conflict, and genocide affected some nations in the post-Cold War period, and how have governments and nongovernmental organizations responded to them? Where have new democracies emerged in the late twentieth and early twenty-first centuries?***

Ethnic and religious conflicts, which often lead to civil war, have plagued many developing nations and some developed nations in Europe. In Northern Ireland, Protestants and Catholics have frequently clashed. The Serbs used ethnic cleansing in the 1990s to kill Bosnian Muslims during the war in Bosnia. After Cyprus achieved independence, fighting between Greek and Turkish Cypriots led to a division of the island.

Some conflicts that stem from regional, ethnic, and religious differences in the 1990s and 2000s have led to the creation of new countries with fledgling democracies. Several states of the former Yugoslavia and East Timor became independent democratic states in recent years.

Africa

Within many African nations, warring ethnic groups undermined the concept of nationhood. This is not surprising because the colonial powers had **arbitrarily** drawn the boundaries of African nations. Virtually all of these states included widely different ethnic, linguistic, and territorial groups. In central Africa, fighting between the Hutu and the Tutsi created unstable governments. In Rwanda, brutal civil war broke out in 1994 as Hutu militias began a campaign of genocide against Tutsis, killing at least 500,000. As thousands of Rwandan refugees died in camps, the United States began a relief operation in conjunction with the UN. In 1997 a UN-sponsored war crimes tribunal began in Tanzania. In 1998 the tribunal

arbitrarily at one's discretion; randomly

▲ Independence for South Sudan was a cause for celebration for many in the new country.

▼ A poll worker counts ballots for the 2007 election in East Timor.

sentenced the former Rwandan prime minister to life imprisonment for genocide.

Ethnic violence and acts of genocide also plagued Sudan, Africa's largest nation. In the western province of Darfur, Arab militias attacked African ethnic groups with the support of the Arab-led government. Entire villages were burned, more than 200,000 people died, and more than 2 million fled their homes. The UN took over a struggling peacekeeping operation from the African Union at the end of 2007. In 2008 the International Criminal Court issued an arrest warrant for the sitting Sudanese president, Omar Hassan al-Bashir, for genocide, war crimes, and crimes against humanity. In a 2011 referendum, southern Sudan voted to become independent from the north.

Desire for more democratic government led to a series of protests in Egypt and surrounding countries in 2011. Working to end nearly 30 years of autocratic rule, protesters demanded that Egyptian president Hosni Mubarak step down. After days of continued unrest, Mubarak resigned.

Asia

Several areas in Asia and Southeast Asia experienced ethnic and religious conflict, including Tibet, East Timor, and Sri Lanka. Tibet seeks independence from the Chinese government that has suppressed dissent among ethnic minorities. The Dalai Lama led the government of Tibet in exile from India since 1959 but stepped down in 2011.

In 1999 the people of East Timor voted to become free of Indonesian rule, which was followed by violence between Christians and Muslims on the island. Nearly 10,000 died from the conflict. In 2002 East Timor (Timor-Leste) was internationally recognized as an independent country. In 2007, with the help of the UN, East Timor held mostly peaceful democratic elections.

In Sri Lanka, ongoing conflicts since 1983 can be traced to ethnic and religious causes. Tensions between the majority Sinhalese (who are mostly Buddhist) who lead the government and the minority Tamils (who are mostly Hindu) are the reason for years of violence. A 2002 ceasefire halted the violence temporarily, but it ended with renewed violence in 2008. The military conflict ended in 2010.

Latin America

In recent years, democracy has also begun to flourish in Latin America. With the debt crisis in Latin America in the 1980s came a movement toward democracy as people realized that military power without popular consent could not maintain a strong state.

PHOTO: (t) Roberto Schmidt/AFP/Getty Images, (bl) JEWEL SAMAD/AFP/Getty Images

In Brazil the military leadership opened the door to a return to democracy in 1985. In the 1990s, democratic presidents restored some stability to the economy, but the gap between rich and poor remained wide. This led to the election of Luiz Inacio Lula da Silva in 2002, Brazil's first left-wing president in four decades. He was successful in promoting rapid economic growth.

A series of military dictators ruled Venezuela during the first half of the twentieth century. Hugo Chavez became a folk hero to the Venezuelan people when he opposed the military government. As a result, he was elected as president in 1998 in a landslide victory and reelected in 2006. In 2007 Chavez began to nationalize energy and communications firms, reducing foreign influence in its economy. Critics charge that he has taken away the freedom of the press.

✓ **READING PROGRESS CHECK**

Explaining How did governments and international organizations respond to the conflicts in Rwanda and Darfur?

The Role of the United States

GUIDING QUESTION ***How have American ideals advanced the ideas of human rights and democracy throughout the world?***

American ideals have advanced democratic ideas and human rights throughout the world since the colonial period. The Declaration of Independence laid out fundamental democratic-republican ideas and led the colonies into the American Revolution. Those democratic ideas did not stay confined to American borders, however; over time, the declaration and its ideas spread throughout the world and continues to inspire leaders and reformers to this day. The U.S. Constitution was the next American document to aid the development of democracy elsewhere. The Constitution enshrined the democratic principles of individual rights and limited government and provided a template for other new democracies, such as Mexico.

American ideals also advanced human rights. The most basic American statement of human rights was the Bill of Rights, the first ten amendments to the U.S. Constitution. This list established fundamental human rights that the government could not infringe upon.

PHOTO: Staff Sgt. Brendan Stephens/US Army/DoD

◀ The United States frequently donates humanitarian aid to international communities in crisis.

As the United States matured and became an active power on the world stage, it continued to advance democratic ideas and human rights. Often this happened as a side effect of the United States pursuing its own self-interests. The American policy that came to be known as the Monroe Doctrine was an attempt to warn European powers against interfering in the western hemisphere. While this policy served U.S. interests, it also had the effect of freeing the countries of the western hemisphere from a degree of European power. U.S. involvement in the Spanish-American War is another example of a policy serving American interests while spreading democracy to certain parts of the world.

Like most countries, the United States has at times taken actions that limit democracy and deny certain groups their human rights. The decades-long U.S. policy of slavery is an obvious example of denying human rights. The United States has at times worked against democracy, as well, such as its fight against Philippine independence.

U.S. involvement in Latin America in the 1900s demonstrated the varying degrees to which the United States has advanced democracy and human rights throughout the world. While the United States took part in antidemocratic government takeovers, such as the coup in Guatemala in 1953, it also has a record of removing dictators, such as Manuel Noriega in Panama.

America's history in the world wars of the twentieth century demonstrates the U.S. advancement of democratic ideas and human rights. The most obvious example is the U.S. success in helping to stop the spread of Nazism in World War II. American efforts in the Korean and Vietnam Wars, likewise, were efforts to stop the spread of Communism and Soviet control over Asia.

In addition to advancing democratic ideas and human rights, the United States is known worldwide for its significant charitable donations. The American flag is a well known symbol in part because of its appearance on food aid and medicine distributed across the world. The United States is a famous destination for immigrants, as well. For centuries, America has been a harbor for immigrants seeking freedom, opportunity, human rights, and democracy.

✓ **READING PROGRESS CHECK**

Analyzing Assess the degree to which American ideals have advanced democratic ideas and human rights throughout the world.

LESSON 1 REVIEW TEKS

Reviewing Vocabulary

1. ***Making Inferences*** Why have countries sought to stop nuclear proliferation and the use of chemical and biological weapons?

Using Your Notes

2. ***Comparing*** Use your notes to compare the political challenges faced in Africa, Asia, and Latin America.

Answering the Guiding Questions

3. ***Identifying*** What are the structure and goals of the United Nations?
4. ***Drawing Conclusions*** What international security issues confront the post-Cold War world?
5. ***Assessing*** How have civil war, ethnic conflict, and genocide affected some nations in the post-Cold War period, and how have governments and nongovernmental organizations responded to them?
6. ***Stating*** Where have new democracies emerged in the late twentieth and early twenty-first centuries?

Writing Activity

7. **ARGUMENT** Research a place where the United Nations has deployed peacekeeping forces, and write an essay on whether or not those forces have been effective at promoting the UN's goals.

On September 11, 2001, terrorists crashed airliners into buildings in New York City and Washington, D.C., and into a field in Pennsylvania killing over 3,000 people. Nine days later, President George W. Bush addressed a joint session of Congress about his plans to fight terrorism.

President Bush's Address to Joint Session of Congress, September 20, 2001

". . . On September the eleventh, enemies of freedom committed an act of war against our country. . . . Americans have known surprise attacks—but never before on thousands of civilians. All of this was brought upon us in a single day—and night fell on a different world, a world where freedom itself is under attack. . . .

The evidence we have gathered all points to a collection of loosely **affiliated** terrorist organizations known as al-Qaeda. . . . Our war on terror begins with al-Qaeda, but it does not end there. It will not end until every terrorist group of global reach has been found, stopped and defeated.

Americans are asking: Why do they hate us? They hate what we see right here in this chamber—a democratically elected government.

Their leaders are self-appointed. They hate our freedoms. . . . By sacrificing human life to serve their radical visions—by abandoning every value except the will to power—they follow in the path of **fascism**, and Nazism, and totalitarianism. And they will follow that path all the way, to where it ends: in history's unmarked grave of discarded lives.

. . . We will direct every resource at our command—every means of diplomacy, every tool of intelligence, every instrument of law enforcement, every financial influence, and every necessary weapon of war—to the disruption and defeat of the global terror network.

I know there are struggles ahead, and dangers to face. But this country will define our times, not be defined by them. . . . Great harm had been done to us. We have suffered great loss. And in our grief and anger we have found our mission and our moment. . . . Our Nation—this generation—will lift a dark threat of violence from our people and our future. We will rally the world to this cause, by our efforts and by our courage. We will not tire, we will not **falter**, and we will not fail."

VOCABULARY

affiliated
closely connected with as a member or associate

fascism
a government led by a dictator that controls business and labor and opposition is not permitted

falter
to hesitate in action or purpose

DBQ Analyzing Historical Documents

1. **Explaining** According to President Bush, why does al-Qaeda hate Americans?
2. **Interpreting** What did President Bush mean when he said "night fell on a different world"?
3. **Making Connections** President Bush's speech was delivered on September 20, 2001. In your opinion, has the passage of time affected the political stance described here or the public's opinion of this tragic event? Write a paragraph explaining your thoughts.

SKILLBUILDER

TEKS 15A

Making Connections

Why Learn This Skill?

Making connections between facts is a vital social studies skill. Creating graphs is a great way to illustrate these connections, since facts and figures can be placed next to each other visually. Reading graphs helps you find connections, too, and often more easily than in texts.

Learning the Skill

Visual representations of data, such as graphs, arrange information in a thematic way that helps you quickly understand the data. In a previous Skillbuilder, you learned that there are three main kinds of graphs—bar, line, and circle. All of these graphs accomplish the same goal of removing unnecessary information and illustrating what is most important.

In order to make connections in history, look for relationships between facts based on chronology, geography, or subject area. For example, if you noticed that two events happened in 1831 or in a remote location, you might wonder if they were connected in some way. Perhaps something happened in 1831 or in that location that caused both events.

Practicing the Skill

Quickly create a bar graph that illustrates how many countries on each continent have 60–80 percent of their population living on less than $1.25/day. The x-axis of the bar graph should list each continent, while the y-axis should list numbers. Label the y-axis "number of countries with 60–80% of its population living on less than $1.25/day." Now, look closely at your graph and answer the following questions:

1. At a quick glance, which continent appears to have the most people living in poverty?
2. What do the different heights of the bars represent on the graph?

Skills Assessment

Study the map and answer the following:

1. Describe the relationship between geography and the historical development of continents as it is seen in this map.
2. Look again at your graph. How does the graph communicate information about patterns more quickly than the map?
3. Look again at the map and your graph. If you changed the y-axis to measure the number of countries with 10–30 percent of its population living on less than $1.25/day, which continent would have the tallest bar?

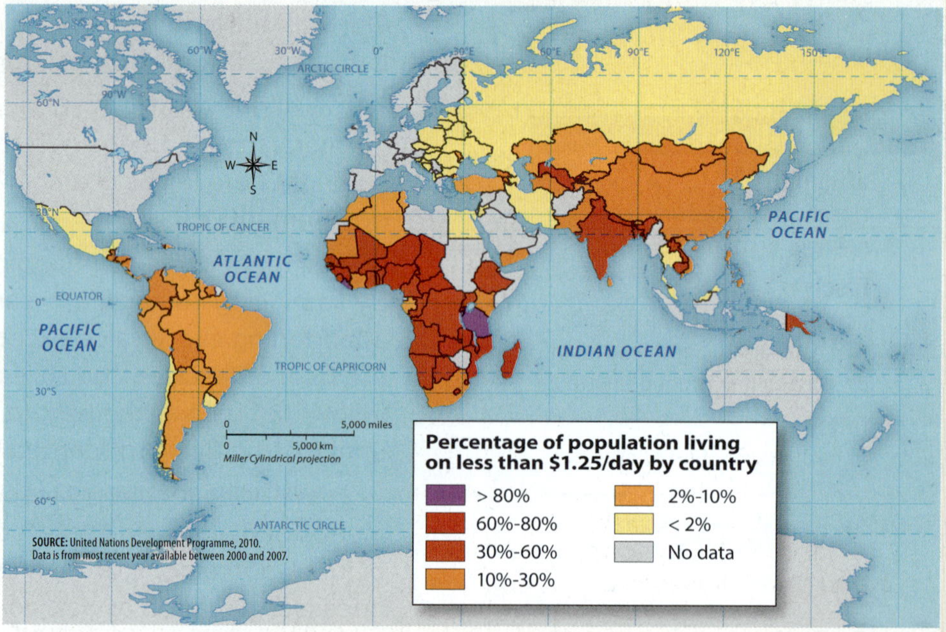

Applying the Skill

Looking for relationships between facts based on chronology, geography, or subject area is a great way to make connections. Write a sentence or two speculating how the following facts might be connected:

1. Multiple countries suffer increasing unemployment in 1929.
2. Airplane manufacturers develop new jets around the time coast-to-coast travel begins to increase.

networks

There's More Online!

- IMAGE Applying for a Microloan in Bangladesh
- IMAGE Global Health Scares
- IMAGE NGO Provides Safe Drinking Water in Zimbabwe
- INFOGRAPHIC Microloans
- INTERACTIVE SELF-CHECK QUIZ
- MAP Percentage of Population Living on Less Than $1.25/Day
- MAP World Population Density
- VIDEO Population Growth

LESSON 2

Social Challenges in the Modern World

ESSENTIAL QUESTIONS • *What influences global political and economic relationships?* • *How do social and environmental issues affect countries differently?*

Reading HELPDESK

Academic Vocabulary

- **projection**
- **migration**

Content Vocabulary

- **pandemic**
- **nongovernmental organization**

TAKING NOTES:

Key Ideas and Details

Organizing As you read, use a chart like the one below to identify factors that can cause world hunger.

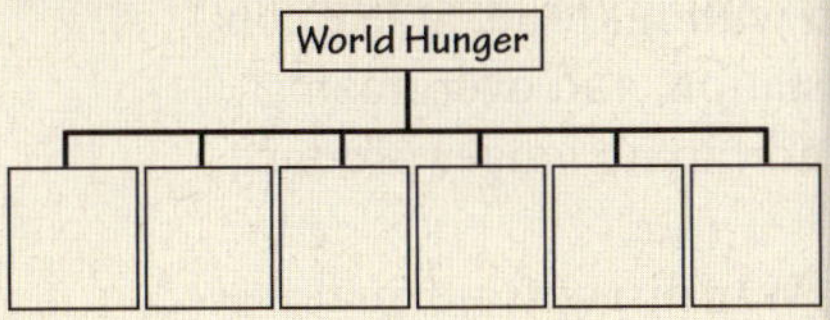

TEKS Texas Essential Knowledge and Skills

21B describe the rights and responsibilities of citizens and noncitizens in civic participation throughout history

22A describe how people have participated in supporting or changing their governments

24A describe the changing roles of women, children, and families during major eras of world history

continued on p. 857

IT MATTERS BECAUSE

More and more people are becoming aware of the global nature of our contemporary problems. Those problems include world hunger, global health pandemics, human rights and equality for women, and population and migration trends. At the same time, new transnational grassroots social movements have arisen to address these problems.

Global Poverty

GUIDING QUESTION *What is the social impact of poverty, hunger, and health pandemics in developing nations?*

Developing nations confront many serious problems, not the least of which is extreme poverty. About 1 billion people in developing nations live on less than 1 dollar a day, which can cause poor health, illness, and even death. About 18 million people a year worldwide die from poverty-related causes. Poverty is a complex problem that creates many other challenges for developing nations. It can keep children from attending school, limit access to clean water and sanitation, and cause people to live in unsafe housing and is a primary cause of worldwide hunger.

World Hunger

Growing or purchasing enough food for more and more people creates a severe problem in many developing countries. An estimated 1 billion people worldwide suffer from hunger. About 75 percent of the hungry live in rural areas of developing countries, and 25 percent of them are children.

The effects of hunger and malnutrition are devastating. Every year, more than 10 million people die of hunger and hunger-related diseases. The long-term health problems caused by malnutrition are severe. Undernourished infants and children suffer from blindness, mental retardation, and increased susceptibility to disease.

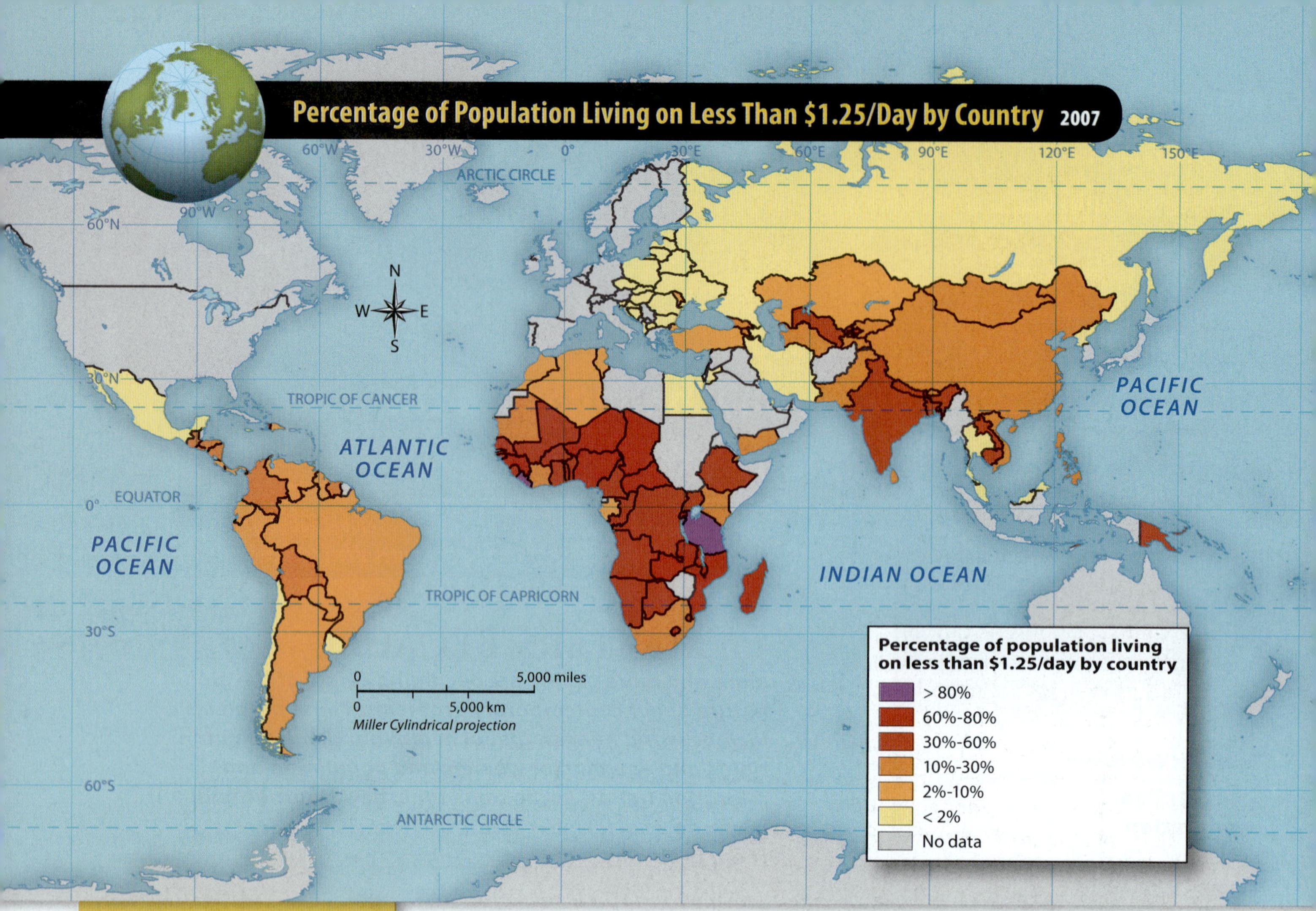

GEOGRAPHY CONNECTION

Much of the world population lives below the global poverty line of $1.25 per day.

1. **PLACES AND REGIONS** *Which continent has the most countries with 60–80% of the population living on less than $1.25 a day?*

2. **HUMAN SYSTEMS** *Choose a continent and create a graph or chart that shows the percentage of people living below the global poverty line by country.*

Among the many causes of worldwide hunger, poverty and economic factors are by far the major ones. The poor do not have enough money to produce or buy an adequate amount of food. For those living in poverty, food is costly. Food prices increased 45 percent from the end of 2006 to 2008. Prices for corn, wheat, and rice reached record highs, due in part to increasing demand from developing economies, rising biofuel production, drought conditions, and higher costs to produce these foods.

Natural disasters can also bring about hunger. Droughts, earthquakes, hurricanes, floods, and tsunamis cause many to go without food, at least on a short-term basis. Poor farming practices, deforestation, and overgrazing can also lead to hunger if land becomes depleted and can no longer produce as much food.

Food shortages can also result from civil war. War disrupts normal farming, and warring groups often try to limit their enemies' access to food. For example, in Sudan, 1.3 million people starved when combatants of a civil war in the 1980s interrupted the food supply.

Global Health Pandemics

pandemic a widespread outbreak of a disease

The fear of a global swine flu **pandemic** in 2009 made people aware that in a global age, infectious diseases can easily spread as a result of international interactions. Global infectious diseases, such as HIV and AIDS, have raised concerns in recent decades. In 2010 nearly 1.8 million people died of AIDS and 2.7 million were newly infected with HIV. Africa has been especially devastated. According to the UN, more than two-thirds of the 34 million people living with HIV are in Africa south of the Sahara. AIDS has had a serious impact on children and families in Africa. Many children have lost one or both parents to AIDS. Often, relatives are too poor to care for these children. Many orphans thus become heads of households filled with younger siblings.

Still, there has been some good news: Global AIDS deaths have declined and the percentage of the world's population living with HIV has stabilized. Organizations, such as UNAIDS, continue to sponsor initiatives to educate the public, to prevent HIV infection, to provide AIDS treatment, and to search for a cure.

✓ **READING PROGRESS CHECK**

Making Connections How are problems of poverty and world hunger related?

Human Rights and Equality for Women

GUIDING QUESTION ***How have problems involving human rights and gender inequality been addressed in the late twentieth and early twenty-first centuries?***

The United Nations took the lead in affirming the basic human rights of all people. On December 10, 1948, the UN General Assembly adopted the Universal Declaration of Human Rights (UDHR). This declaration is a set of basic human rights and standards for government that has been agreed to by almost every country in the world. It affirms everyone's right to life, liberty, and security of person as well as the right to freedom of movement and the freedom of opinion and expression.

Since the adoption of the UDHR, the human rights movement has achieved much success in freeing political prisoners and bringing economic and political change around the world. Nevertheless, human rights violations still occur worldwide.

Governments themselves often carry on the violence. Dictators and military regimes punish people who disagree with their views. In Cuba, Chile, Myanmar, Iraq, Iran, and other countries, people have been persecuted for opposing repressive governments. In other countries, such as Bosnia and Rwanda, ethnic, religious, and racial hatreds have led to the mass murder of hundreds of thousands of people.

The Rule of Law

Central to the development of human rights is the concept of the rule of law. The rule of law is an important component of good government and a principle of democracy. The rule of law holds that all citizens must follow the same laws, including government officials. The rule of law as it is known today has developed over thousands of years.

The Ten Commandments in the Judeo-Christian legal tradition, for instance, hold that all people should follow the same law. And in ancient Greece, the philosopher Aristotle held that laws, rather than men, should govern. Further on in the Medieval era, the English document called the Magna Carta established protections for individual rights against the power of government. Later, Enlightenment ideas about personal freedom and the limits of government began to further question the absolute rule of monarchies. These developments inspired conflicts like the English Civil War and the American and French Revolutions. These developments helped shape the creation of the documents central to the rule of law such as the English Bill of Rights and the United States Constitution.

Analyzing PRIMARY SOURCES

Universal Declaration of Human Rights, 1948

"All human beings are born free and equal in dignity and rights. . . . Everyone is entitled to all the rights and freedoms set forth in this Declaration, without distinction of any kind, such as race, colour, sex, language, religion, political or other opinion, national or social origin, property, birth or other status. . . . Everyone has the right to life, liberty and security of person. . . . Everyone has the right to freedom of movement. . . Everyone has the right to freedom of opinion and expression."

—from the Universal Declaration of Human Rights, adopted by the UN General Assembly on December 10, 1948

DBQ ***PARAPHRASING*** Describe the human rights listed above in your own words.

(continued from p. 855)

TEKS **Texas Essential Knowledge and Skills**

29F analyze information by sequencing, categorizing, identifying cause-and-effect relationships, comparing, contrasting, finding the main idea, summarizing, making generalizations and predictions, drawing inferences and conclusions, and developing connections between historical events over time

▲ A central concept of the rule of law is the idea that the law applies to all people equally.

The development of the rule of law has brought about more stable and free societies. Democratic governments have replaced many monarchies and dictatorships throughout the world. However, the rule of law is not necessarily absolute. In places where the rule of law disappears in modern times, tyranny or chaos can emerge. In these places, terrorists, criminals, or warlords can acquire power and resources, and human rights in general are often ignored.

Equality for Women

▼ For many women and girls in the developing world there is limited access to education.

In the social and economic spheres of the Western world, the gap that once separated men and women steadily narrowed in the twentieth century. Changing roles for women took them into the workplace in large numbers, and now women make up half the university graduates in Western countries. Many countries have laws that require equal pay for women and men doing the same work. Nevertheless, women in many Western countries still do not hold many top positions in business or government.

Bound to their homes and families and subordinate to men, women in developing nations face considerable difficulties and have seen fewer role changes than in Western countries. They are often unable to obtain education, property rights, or decent jobs. Indeed, one of the UN Millennium Development Goals is to "promote gender equality and empower women." Still, some women in developing nations have become leaders of their countries, such as Ellen Johnson Sirleaf, who became president of Liberia in 2006, and Joyce Hilda Banda, who became Malawi's first female vice president in 2009.

✓ **READING PROGRESS CHECK**

Evaluating What is the danger in losing the rule of law?

PRIMARY SOURCES

The role of science in government and society was the topic of Manmohan Singh's address to the Indian Science Congress in 2012. Singh described the promises of science and technology to meet India's social and economic challenges.

Manmohan Singh Addresses the Indian Science Congress

"I have often spoken about the commitment of our Government to give a boost to the science and technology sector in the country. We have taken several steps towards this end.

- We have greatly expanded the higher education **infrastructure** for Science and Technology by establishing new institutions. . . .
- We have introduced a large number of scholarships; most notably, the Innovation in Science Pursuit for Inspired Research or INSPIRE scheme which gives awards to one million science students.

. . . The university research system is also showing signs of rejuvenation. In 2008, I gave away incentive awards to 14 universities under the Promotion of University Research and Scientific Excellence (PURSE) scheme. In 2010, 30 more universities have qualified under the same criteria. . . .

. . . Things are changing but we cannot be satisfied with what has been achieved. We need to do much more to change the face of Indian science. . . . While it is true that science and engineering continue to attract some of our best students, many of them later opt for other careers because of relatively poorer prospects in science.

. . . An occasion like the present one should be used to revisit a fundamental question: what is the role of science in a country like India? There is no simple answer. But for a country grappling with the challenges of poverty and development, the **over-riding** objective of a comprehensive and well-considered policy for science, technology and innovation should be to support the national objective of faster, sustainable and inclusive development.

There is much that the scientific community can do to achieve these objectives. Research should be directed to providing **'frugal'** solutions to our chronic problems of providing food, energy and water security to our people. Science should help us understand how to give practical meaning to the concept of sustainable development and green growth. Science should help us shift our mindsets from the allocation of resources to their more efficient use. Technology and process engineering should help us reach the benefits of development to those who need it most. . . .

In the final analysis, the pursuit of science is a process of unlocking the human mind. It is an exploration of the mystery, beauty and method in the universe by stretching the frontiers of our imagination. We need to invoke the power of science in every sphere of our economy and way of life.

VOCABULARY

nfrastructure
an organization's structure or plan for forward progress

over-riding
chief, most important; the main focus

frugal
sparing; using resources carefully and economically

DBQ Analyzing Historical Documents

1. **Analyzing** Why, according to the prime minister, is a focus on the development of science education and increasing the number of trained scientists a necessary goal?
2. **Identifying** What specific examples are cited that indicate that India has been targeting ways to improve the development of scientists within the nation?

Population and Migration Trends

GUIDING QUESTION *How have population trends affected developed and developing nations?*

projection an estimate or a calculation

Estimates by the Population Reference Bureau put the 2010 world population at about 6.9 billion. Their **projections** estimate that the global population could reach 9.4 billion by 2050. The world population is expected to increase approximately one-third over the next four decades.

Almost all population growth is from the developing nations. The most populous have taken steps to decrease growth. China has a one-child policy, and India promotes a national family welfare program but has had limited success. By 2050, India will have surpassed China in population and will likely remain the most populous country in the world thereafter.

Meanwhile, many wealthy regions, such as Western Europe, are declining in population. In fact, by 2050, the United States is expected to be the only wealthy nation with a growing population. The developed nations are also "graying"—a larger percentage of the population is reaching retirement age. In the more developed regions, more than one-fifth of the population is aged 60 or over. By 2050, it is expected to reach one-third. The global age distribution is shifting toward older people because of increases in life expectancies, lower birthrates, and lower death rates. The number of people aged 80 and over and those who live beyond 100 is rising, placing increased demands on the economies of developed nations.

Developing countries face different problems. Between 2010 and 2050, the population in developing countries is expected to grow from 6.8 billion to 8.1 billion. Also, the trend of increased urbanization is expected to continue. Because many cities lack the infrastructure to support larger populations, concerns are rising about future international health and environmental problems, especially in developing nations.

migration the movement of people from one country, place, or locality to another

Connected to population growth is the problem of global **migrations**. In 2010 there were about 214 million international migrants. Although about 60 percent of migrants live in more developed countries, the remainder relocated from one developing country to another.

There are several reasons people migrate. Persecution for political reasons and brutal civil wars in Asia, Africa, the Middle East, and Europe have led millions of refugees to seek safety in neighboring countries. Many have migrated for economic reasons. For example, guest workers from Turkey, India, Pakistan, and North Africa entered more prosperous European countries.

CHARTS/GRAPHS

The world population is projected to reach over 9 billion by 2050.

1. ***Problem-Solving*** By what percent is the world population expected to increase from 1980 to 2020?
2. ***Interpreting*** In which decade is there projected to be the smallest population increase?

WORLD POPULATION GROWTH, 1950–2050

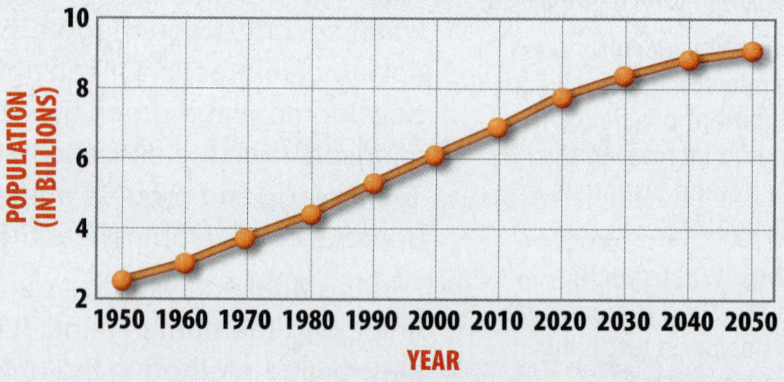

Source: United Nations Population Division, 2010

But foreign workers often become scapegoats when countries face economic problems. Political parties in France and Norway in the 1990s, for example, called for the removal of blacks and Arabs to protect the ethnic purity of their nations.

✓ READING PROGRESS CHECK

Contrasting How do population issues affect developed and developing countries differently?

▲ An international NGO builds a well to provide safe drinking water for a village in Zimbabwe.

Transnational Organizations

GUIDING QUESTION *What role do transnational and non-governmental organizations play in the international arena?*

Global awareness has led to new social movements that focus on problems that nations share. These problems include areas such as the environment, gender inequality, child labor, the appropriate use of technology, and the promotion of peace. Groups such as the International Red Cross and Red Crescent Movement draw their membership from different countries. Other groups have members in one country. Many individuals act at the grassroots level, that is, in their own community. A favorite slogan of grassroots groups is "Think globally, act locally."

Another movement that addresses world problems is the growth of **nongovernmental organizations** (NGOs). NGOs are often represented at the United Nations. They include professional, business, and cooperative organizations, as well as foundations. Also included are religious, peace, and disarmament groups that work to limit the size of military forces and weapons stocks. Other NGOs protect the welfare of women and children and include environmental and human rights groups.

nongovernmental organization an organization that has no government ties and works to address world problems

American educator Elise Boulding promoted NGOs. She believed they can educate people to consider problems globally. She said that all NGOs are expected "to define problems in global terms, to take account of human interests and needs as they are found in all parts of the planet." The number of international NGOs increased from 176 in 1910 to nearly 37,000 in 2000.

✓ READING PROGRESS CHECK

Describing How are grassroots organizations related to NGOs?

LESSON 2 REVIEW TEKS

Reviewing Vocabulary

1. ***Drawing Conclusions*** Why are pandemics a concern in an increasingly globalized world?

Using Your Notes

2. ***Identifying*** Use your notes to identify the causes of worldwide hunger.

Answering the Guiding Questions

3. ***Making Generalizations*** What is the social impact of poverty, hunger, and health pandemics in developing nations?
4. ***Evaluating*** How have problems involving human rights and gender inequality been addressed in the late twentieth and early twenty-first centuries?
5. ***Differentiating*** How have population and migration trends affected developed and developing nations?
6. ***Analyzing*** What role do transnational and nongovernmental organizations play in the international arena?

Writing Activity

7. **INFORMATIVE/EXPLANATORY** Choose one nongovernmental organization to research. Write an essay about the organization's mission, goals, accomplishments, and challenges it faces.

networks

There's More Online!

- ☑ CHART/GRAPH U.S. Housing Prices
- ☑ CHART/GRAPH World's Largest Economies
- ☑ CHART/GRAPH WTO Members
- ☑ IMAGE Ghanaian Migrant Worker
- ☑ IMAGE Globalization Protests
- ☑ IMAGE Stock Market Trouble, 2008
- ☑ INTERACTIVE SELF-CHECK QUIZ
- ☑ MAP The European Union, 2010
- ☑ MAP World GDP
- ☑ VIDEO The Arab Spring

LESSON 3
Global Economies

ESSENTIAL QUESTIONS
- *What influences global political and economic relationships?*
- *How do social and environmental issues affect countries differently?*

Reading HELPDESK

Academic Vocabulary
- **currency**
- **dynamic**

Content Vocabulary
- **multinational corporation**
- **globalization**
- **collateralized debt obligation**
- **subprime investments**

TAKING NOTES:
Key Ideas and Details

Organizing As you read, use a table like the one below to identify global economic organizations and regional trade organizations.

Global Economic Organizations	Regional Trade Organizations

It Matters Because

The technology revolution has tied people and nations closely together and contributed to globalization. Economically, globalization has taken the form of a global economy.

Global Economic Organizations

GUIDING QUESTION *What are the roles of global economic organizations in the world economy?*

The global economy began to develop after World War II and gained momentum in the 1980s and 1990s. After World War II, the United States and other nations set up the World Bank and the International Monetary Fund (IMF) as a means of expanding global markets and avoiding economic crises. The World Bank is largely controlled by developed countries and provides grants, loans, and advice for economic development in developing countries. The IMF, founded in 1945, oversees the global financial system by watching exchange rates and offering financial and technical assistance to developing nations. Meanwhile, advances in technology, communication, transportation, and computing all led to a "smaller" world where people could meet and interact more easily than ever before. These causes of **globalization**, or the process by which people and nations have become more interdependent, became major influences on the second half of the twentieth century.

Multinational corporations are a major outcome of globalization. Examples of multinational corporations that have a significant impact on twentieth-century globalization include Siemens, General Motors, Exxon Mobil, Mitsubishi, and the Sony Corporation. These companies are among the 200 largest multinational corporations, which are responsible for more than half the world's industrial production. A recent comparison of corporate sales and national gross domestic product revealed that only 49 of the world's 100 largest economic entities are nations. The remaining 51 are corporations. For this reason, some people believe that economic globalization might best be called "corporate globalization."

As multinational corporations increasingly tie one country to another as a part of globalization, another economic effect is that a downturn in one country is often felt as a negative economic impact in others. When countries become economically interdependent, they rise and fall together.

Global trade is another important component of the global economy. Over the years, many nations joined in talks to make trade between countries free and easy. These talks led to the General Agreement on Trade and Tariffs (GATT). In 1995 the nations that had signed the GATT treaties agreed to create the World Trade Organization (WTO). Made of more than 150 member nations, the WTO arranges trade agreements and settles trade disputes. These trade organizations were the direct effects of globalization and had significant impacts on the twentieth-century economy.

multinational corporation a company with divisions in more than two countries

✓ READING PROGRESS CHECK

Contrasting How are the World Bank and International Monetary Fund different?

WORLD'S LARGEST MULTINATIONAL CORPORATIONS, 2010

CHARTS/GRAPHS

Rank/Company	Country of Origin	Industry	Sales ($bil)	Profits ($bil)
1. JPMorgan Chase	United States	Banking	115.63	11.65
2. General Electric	United States	Conglomerates	156.78	11.03
3. Bank of America	United States	Banking	150.45	6.28
4. ExxonMobil	United States	Oil & Gas Operations	275.56	19.28
5. ICBC	China	Banking	71.86	16.27
6. Banco Santander	Spain	Banking	109.57	12.34
7. Wells Fargo	United States	Banking	98.64	12.28
8. HSBC Holdings	United Kingdom	Banking	103.74	5.83
9. Royal Dutch Shell	Netherlands	Oil & Gas Operations	278.19	12.52
10. BP	United Kingdom	Oil & Gas Operations	239.27	16.58
11. BNP Paribas	France	Banking	101.06	8.37
12. PetroChina	China	Oil & Gas Operations	157.22	16.8

Source: www.forbes.com

In 2010 many of the largest multinational corporations were in the banking and the oil and gas operations industries and had their headquarters in the United States.

▶ CRITICAL THINKING

1. ***Transferring Knowledge*** Create a bar graph that displays the multinational corporations with profits over $12 billion.
2. ***Interpreting*** Create a circle graph that summarizes the country of origin of the 12 largest multinational corporations.

Regional Trade Organizations

GUIDING QUESTION ***What are the effects of regional trade organizations on national and regional economies?***

Groups of nations have also joined together to form trading blocs to foster regional prosperity. Mercosur, for example, is an economic union of Argentina, Brazil, Paraguay, and Uruguay. Trading blocs resulting from globalization created significant economic impacts in the twentieth century.

NAFTA

In 1992 the Mexican president Carlos Salinas de Gortari began to work with U.S. president George H. W. Bush and the Canadian prime minister Brian Mulroney to form the North American Free Trade Agreement (NAFTA). It was ratified and put into effect in the beginning of 1994. It created a free trade area for Canada, the United States, and Mexico. Some economists have argued that it has been beneficial to business owners but harmful to

TEKS **Texas Essential Knowledge and Skills**

1F identify major causes and describe the major effects of the following important turning points in world history from 1914 to the present: the world wars and their impact on political, economic, and social systems; communist revolutions and their impact on the Cold War; independence movements; and globalization

17C summarize the economic and social impact of 20th century globalization

GEOGRAPHY CONNECTION

1. **PLACES AND REGIONS** *What percent of EU members are using the euro?*
2. **THE WORLD IN SPATIAL TERMS** *Which countries of the former Yugoslavia are candidates for EU membership?*

others. Farmers in Mexico, for example, saw prices for their food products drop as cheap American foodstuffs were imported. Industrial workers in the United States lost jobs as American companies outsourced jobs to Mexico in order to use cheap labor. However, the economic impact of the trading bloc is undeniable—every year, the United States has over one and a half trillion dollars in trade with NAFTA countries.

European Union

The European Community (EC) was chiefly an economic union. By 1992, it comprised 344 million people and was the world's largest single trading bloc. The Treaty on European Union was an attempt to create a true economic and monetary union of all EC members. On January 1, 1994, the EC renamed itself the European Union (EU). One of the EU's first goals was to establish a common **currency**, called the euro, adopted by 12 EU nations early in 1999. On June 1, 1999, a European Central Bank was created, and by January 2010, the euro had officially replaced 16 national currencies. The euro serves approximately 327 million people and has become the world's second-largest reserve currency after the U.S. dollar.

currency coins, for example, that are in circulation and used as a medium of exchange

In addition to having a single internal market for its members and a common currency, the European Union also established a common agricultural policy. It provides subsidies to farmers to enable them to sell their goods competitively on the world market. The policy also provides aid to the EU's poorest countries and subsidies for job training, education, and modernization programs.

The EU has been less successful in setting common foreign policy goals. Individual nations still see foreign policy as a national right and are reluctant to give it up. Although EU foreign ministers meet periodically, they usually do not draw up a uniform policy. Nevertheless, the EU did create a military force of 60,000 to be used chiefly for peacekeeping purposes.

In 2009 the European Union ratified the Lisbon Treaty, which created a full-time presidential post and a new voting system that reflected each country's population size. It also provided more power for the European Parliament in an effort to promote the EU's foreign policy goals.

✔ **READING PROGRESS CHECK**

Classifying Would you describe the European Union as solely an economic entity?

Aspects of Globalization

GUIDING QUESTION ***What are the costs and benefits of globalization?***

Politically and socially, globalization has led to the emergence of citizen groups and other transnational organizations that work across national boundaries to bring solutions to common problems. Not everyone, however, is happy with the globalization of the economy.

Protests

Global economic organizations have come under attack. Both the World Bank and the IMF have been criticized for forcing inappropriate Western economic practices on non-Western nations. Critics also argue that World Bank and IMF policies aggravate the poverty and debt of developing nations. The WTO has been criticized for ignoring environmental and health concerns and for leaving out small and developing countries.

There have also been direct protests against globalization. Critics of globalization have accused multinational corporations of maximizing profits by supporting pitiful workers' wages and working conditions and ignoring environmental concerns. Antiglobalization protesters have clashed with police when trying to disrupt meetings of the IMF and World Bank in cities around the world.

Another challenge to globalization stems from the wide gap between rich and poor nations. Rich nations, or developed nations, are located mainly in the Northern Hemisphere. They include countries such as the United States, Canada, Germany, and Japan, which have well-organized industrial and agricultural systems, advanced technologies, and effective education systems. The poor nations, or developing nations, include many nations in Africa, Asia, and Latin America. They are often primarily agricultural nations with little technology and income inequality.

Global Financial Crisis

The global economy experienced worldwide financial troubles beginning in 2007 following the collapse of the U.S. housing market. Spurred by low interest rates in the early 2000s, easily available mortgages drove up housing values. In response, investors began selling financial investments called **collateralized debt obligations** (CDOs), or investments based upon bundled mortgages. Banks in New York sold CDOs to banks in Europe and elsewhere, spreading the wealth and the risk of investment. Many of these mortgages had been to borrowers with a low credit rating and high rate of default. As the initial rates on the mortgages ended, default rates increased and securities began to lose their value. By September 2008, a number of insurance and mortgage companies, investment firms, and banks fell into bankruptcy. Stock values fell by almost $8 trillion from mid-September to November.

In effect, the crash of the United States housing market in 2008 led to a worldwide recession. As the American economy slowed, trade decreased

Thinking Like a HISTORIAN

Interpreting Secondary Sources

Widespread use of the term *globalization* to refer to the movement toward a more integrated and interdependent world economy is relatively recent. How old do you think globalization is as a historical phenomenon? For example, do you think it dates back to the rise of global trading empires that began during the Age of Exploration? Historians differ on whether the concept of globalization should be applied only to the modern era. Use your school library to locate secondary sources from two different historians with conflicting interpretations of this concept.

globalization the movement toward a more integrated and interdependent world economy

collateralized debt obligation a security guaranteed by a pool of, bonds, loans, and other types of debt

▼ Anti-globalization activists protest outside World Bank headquarters in Washington, D.C.

PHOTO: ©YURI GRIPAS/Reuters/Corbis

SKILLS PRACTICE

As you read about growing economies, make a list of words you do not know. Look up the definitions of these words in the glossary or a dictionary. Then, think of things from your own life that remind you of these words. Write sentences or draw pictures of your experiences beneath the words to help you remember their meanings.

subprime investments
investments based on loans that have an interest rate that is higher than a prime rate and is extended especially to low-income borrowers

dynamic an activity or change that is continuous and productive

worldwide because the American consumer, who had been consuming because of higher home values, could no longer do so. Production in Asia decreased and commodity prices fell, especially that of oil, making an impact on both Middle Eastern countries and Russia.

The United States responded to the financial crisis with an emergency program to recapitalize financial institutions and a stimulus package to support growth and to curb unemployment. Europe faced less severe problems than the United States, although European banks with exposure to **subprime investments** required government assistance to recapitalize. In Eastern Europe, recent free market economies experienced a drastic devaluation of their currencies as investors fled to the stronger dollar and euro. Governmental measures prevented a total failure of the world financial system. However, high unemployment and weak consumption will probably plague Western nations for years to come.

Emerging Economic Powers

China and India are experiencing economic growth on a scale rarely seen before. For the past 20 years, China's growth rate has been 9.5 percent a year; India's, 6 percent. Both have the potential for such growth rates to continue for decades. Some economists predict that China's economy will overtake that of the United States by 2050.

The economies of China and India are not the same. China is supreme in mass manufacturing. India is a growing power in design services and software. Globalization has allowed multinational corporations to have their products built in China with software designed in India. One major economic impact of globalization is the outsourcing of jobs from the United States to both India and China, much to the concern of U.S. political leaders who seem helpless to stop the trend.

But both countries have serious problems. Poverty is still prevalent for hundreds of millions of people in India and China. Moreover, environmental problems are growing. Fertile land is in increasingly short supply while the rate of air pollution, especially in China, is 10 times the level in the United States, contributing to growing health concerns. Smog smothers the air in both Shanghai, China, and Mumbai, India. Finally, no one is sure that both countries can continue on their **dynamic** rate of economic growth. Per capita income in the United States is six times as high as in China. In India, an estimated 350 million Indians earn less than one U.S. dollar a day.

✓ READING PROGRESS CHECK

Analyzing Why have some individuals protested the practices of global economic organizations?

LESSON 3 REVIEW TEKS

Reviewing Vocabulary

1. ***Drawing Conclusions*** How does the large number of multinational corporations reflect increasing globalization?

Using Your Notes

2. ***Identifying*** Use your notes to identify different global and regional trade and economic organizations.

Answering the Guiding Questions

3. ***Making Generalizations*** What are the roles of global economic organizations in the world economy?
4. ***Evaluating*** What are the effects of regional trade organizations on national and regional economies?
5. ***Differentiating*** What are the costs and benefits of globalization?

Writing Activity

6. **ARGUMENT** Write an essay arguing whether free trade agreements are a good idea or a bad idea. Be sure to focus on the costs and benefits to both developed and developing countries.

networks

There's More Online!

- ☑ CHART/GRAPH Mobile Phone and Internet Use, 2009
- ☑ IMAGE Destruction of Rainforests in South America
- ☑ IMAGE International Space Station
- ☑ IMAGE Technology in the Classroom
- ☑ INTERACTIVE SELF-CHECK QUIZ
- ☑ MAP Desertification in Africa
- ☑ PRIMARY SOURCE Newspaper Article About the Kyoto Protocol
- ☑ VIDEO Climate Change

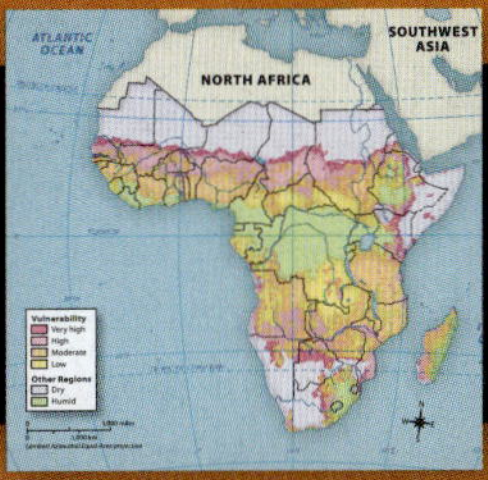

LESSON 4
Science, Technology, and the Environment

ESSENTIAL QUESTION
How do social and environmental issues affect countries differently?

Reading HELPDESK

Academic Vocabulary
- **intense**
- **manipulation**

Content Vocabulary
- **microchip**
- **ecology**
- **deforestation**
- **desertification**
- **greenhouse effect**
- **sustainable development**

TAKING NOTES:
Key Ideas and Details

Summarizing As you read, use a table like the one below to identify important technological advances discussed in this lesson.

Communication, Transportation, and Space	Health Care	Agriculture

TEKS Texas Essential Knowledge and Skills
17C summarize the economic and social impact of 20th century globalization
continued on the next page

IT MATTERS BECAUSE
In the twenty-first century, science and technology continue to build a global community connected by the Internet. Scientific advances have brought benefits in communications, transportation, space exploration, health care, and agriculture. Unfortunately, they have also produced environmental challenges.

Technological Revolution

GUIDING QUESTION *How have scientific discoveries and technological innovations transformed society?*

Since World War II, but especially since the 1970s, a stunning array of changes has created a technological revolution. Like the first and second Industrial Revolutions, this revolution is also having a profound effect on people's daily lives and on entire societies. This technological revolution is also closely interrelated with new scientific discoveries.

Communication, Transportation, and Space

Global transportation and communication technologies are developing our modern global society. People are connected and "online" throughout the world as they have never been before. Space exploration and orbiting satellites have increased our understanding of our world and of solar systems beyond our world.

Advances in transportation technology have brought people closer together and helped drive the global economy. Since the 1970s, jumbo jet airliners have moved millions of people around the world and created an air-freight industry worth billions of dollars. The container ship has made sea transportation much more efficient and has allowed manufacturers to locate their factories all around the globe. Satellites, cellular telephones, and computers enable people to communicate with one another practically everywhere in the world. Communication and transportation systems have made the world a global economy and a global village.

(continued from p. 867)

TEKS Texas Essential Knowledge and Skills

28D explain the role of telecommunication technology, computer technology, transportation technology, and medical advancements in developing the modern global economy and society

The computer may be the most revolutionary of all technological inventions of the twentieth century. The first computer was really a product of World War II. British mathematician Alan Turing designed the first electronic computer to crack enemy codes. Turing's machine did calculations faster than any human. IBM of the United States made the first computer with stored memory in 1948. The development of the transistor and the silicon chip made computers much faster.

Then, in 1971, the microprocessor was invented and paved the way for the personal computer. Both small and powerful, the personal computer became a regular fixture in businesses, schools, and homes by the 1990s. The computer made many routine tasks easier and played a major role in developing the global economy. Computers revolutionized accounting, banking, and manufacturing by making these activities cheaper and faster. With new computer technology came new communication technology, which further drove the new global economy. Once computers were linked all over the world, a company could have its headquarters in one country, its research division in another, and its factories in yet another. Today, when offices in Texas close for the day, office coworkers on the other side of the world can keep working, creating a 24-hour workday.

Through their personal computers, people can access the Internet, a huge web of linked computer networks. The Internet was introduced to the public for the first time in 1972, and computer technology began to contribute to our modern global society. That same year, electronic mail, or e-mail, was introduced. The system expanded dramatically in the 1990s, the same period that saw rapid globalization. The social impacts of globalization grew as people connected with each other like never before. The invention of Web browsers made it easier for people to use the Internet. By 2010, there were more than 1 billion Internet users worldwide. These advances in technology and communication drove globalization and reshaped how people interact.

As Web capabilities increased, Web sites such as Myspace, Facebook, Twitter, and YouTube contributed to globalization by revolutionizing communication. Soon, these Web sites, some of which are called "social networking" sites, gave people all over the world an easy way to share their ideas, art, and stories. The social impacts of globalization grew as people began to communicate more effectively. Significant recent social impacts include successful charity drives and the organization of democratic movements in the Middle East.

Advances in telecommunications led to cellular, or mobile, phones. Though cellular phones existed in the 1970s and the 1980s, it was not until

microchip also called an integrated circuit; a tiny assembly of electronic components and their connections that is produced in or on a tiny bit of material, usually silicon

intense marked by great zeal, energy, determination, or concentration

CHARTS/GRAPHS

MOBILE PHONE AND INTERNET USE, 2009

▶ CRITICAL THINKING

1. ***Drawing Conclusions*** How do developed and developing countries differ in their access to technology?
2. ***Contrasting*** Which country has the most mobile phone and Internet users? Which has the least?

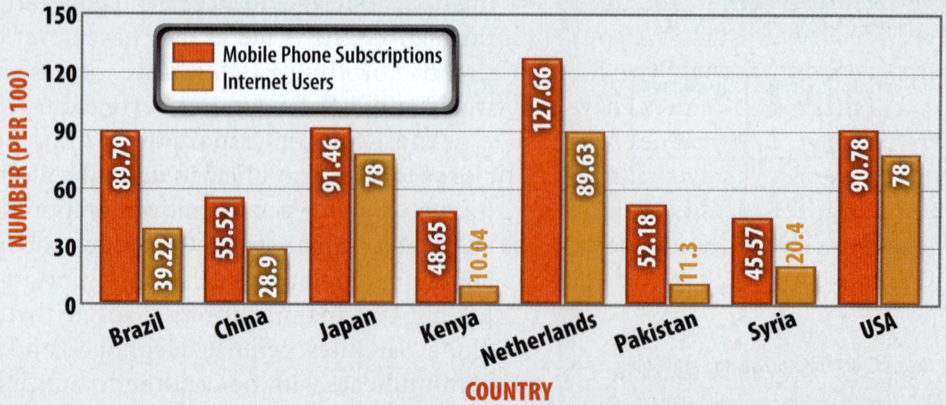

Source: International Telecommunications Union, 2010

the invention of the **microchip**, a small semiconductor used to relay information, that cell phones became truly portable. Today, cell phones are everywhere, and their ability to transfer data electronically has made text messaging and mobile "apps," or programs, hugely popular. These technologies have helped develop our modern global society.

▲ From 2000 to 2010, 196 individuals from eight different countries have visited the International Space Station.

▶ **CRITICAL THINKING**

Speculating There have been over 100 launches to the space station. Which two countries do you think have sent the most vehicles? Why?

Technological developments have also improved our ability to explore space. Ever since Neil Armstrong and Buzz Aldrin landed on the moon in 1969, the exploration of space has continued. Space probes have increased our understanding of distant planets.

Today hundreds of satellites orbit Earth. Some are used to predict the weather, and others help navigate ships, aircraft, and cars. Communications satellites are used to relay radio, television, and telephone signals.

Launched in 1990, the Hubble Space Telescope (HST), a large astronomical observatory, orbits about 375 miles (603 km) above Earth's surface. Thus, the HST avoids the distorting effects of Earth's atmosphere and provides clear views of our solar system and distant galaxies.

The National Aeronautics and Space Administration (NASA) sent two rovers, called *Spirit* and *Opportunity*, to the planet Mars in 2004. Based on the minerals that the rovers found in Mars's rocks, NASA scientists determined that the now-barren planet once had abundant supplies of water. NASA continues its Mars Exploration Program, analyzing data transmissions from rovers to Earth via the *Odyssey* orbiter, which was launched in 2001. Such data includes radiation risks for potential future human exploration of Mars.

Health Care

New technologies in health care have helped develop modern global society and allowed people to live longer and more productive lives. For example, doctors use mechanical valves and pumps for the heart and transplant organs. New medicines can treat both physical and mental illness. From 1990 to 2003, the Human Genome Project unlocked the secrets of DNA, leading to new ways to diagnose and treat genetic diseases. The discovery of DNA itself—the molecule that carries genetic information from one generation to another—was the work of James Watson, Francis Crick, and Maurice Wilkins, who received a joint Nobel Prize for Medicine in 1962.

Medical advancements have contributed to the global economy, as well. Pharmaceutical companies have poured billions of dollars into research, and the widespread use of new medicines has made the pharmaceutical industry big business. Likewise, the invention of new technologies, such as the MRI (magnetic resonance imaging) machine, has created jobs for researchers, manufacturers, trainers, and technicians.

Agriculture

In agriculture, the development of new strains of rice, corn, and other grains, known as genetically engineered (GE) foods, has resulted in greater yields. Scientists and world leaders disagree over the use of GE foods, which are

Connections to TODAY

Medical Advancements

Many medical advancements that have had a major impact on our lives today were developed during World War II. For example, Charles R. Drew, an African American physician, started the American Red Cross blood banking program to assist soldiers. Today, nearly 3 percent of the U.S. population donates blood, which is used to save military and civilian lives across the country. Likewise, Dr. Jonas Salk developed vaccines for the flu and polio. Today, mass vaccinations prevent many childhood illnesses each year, and polio is close to being eradicated globally.

▲ A farmer clears an area of the Amazon rain forest.

▶ **CRITICAL THINKING**

Determining Cause and Effect
What may be the global effects of deforestation on the environment?

created by the **manipulation** of the DNA of plants to improve crops. Some experts see GE foods as a way to solve hunger crises in developing countries, although others worry about the effects GE foods have on the health of individuals and the ecosystem. Huge quantities of chemical fertilizers, which many farmers cannot afford, are needed to grow these new strains of foods.

The growing concern with chemical pesticides has led to an increase in organic farming in industrialized countries and the profitable export of organically grown crops by developing nations. Organic farming rejects the use of chemical fertilizers and pesticides, growth hormones, and livestock feed additives. Its goal is to maintain a healthy and sustainable environment.

✓ **READING PROGRESS CHECK**

Identifying Points of View What are the arguments for and against the use of GE foods?

manipulation skillful or artful management

ecology the study of the relationships between living things and their environment

deforestation the clearing of forests

desertification formation of degraded soil, turning semi-arid lands into nonproductive deserts

Environmental Challenges

GUIDING QUESTION *What are the environmental challenges of the twenty-first century and how have governments and citizens responded to them?*

In *Silent Spring,* published in 1962, Rachel Carson, an American scientist, argued that the buildup of pesticides—chemicals sprayed on crops to kill insects—was having unforeseen results. Insects were dying, but so too were birds, fish, and other wild animals. Also, the pesticide residue on food harmed humans.

Carson's warnings alarmed many scientists and gave rise to the new science of **ecology**, the study of the relationship between living things and their environment. Since then, scientific research studies have shown that dangers to the environment have many sources.

Impact of Population Growth

Some fear that population is growing too fast for Earth's resources to support it. **Deforestation** is one by-product of a growing population. Forests and jungles have been cut down to provide more farmland, firewood, and timber.

Especially worrisome is the rapid destruction of tropical rain forests near Earth's equator. Although tropical rain forests cover only 6 percent of Earth's surface, they support 50 percent of the world's species of plants and animals. The tropical rain forests are also crucial to human survival because they remove carbon dioxide from the air and return oxygen to it.

Desertification is another by-product of population growth. Overgrazing, poor cultivation practices, and destruction of vegetation in semiarid lands are human-caused factors that destroy the soil's productivity. More than 250 million people are directly affected by desertification.

Chemical Wastes and Disasters

Chemical wastes pose another danger to the environment. The release of chlorofluorocarbons—gases used in aerosol cans, refrigerators, and air conditioners—destroys the ozone layer. This thin layer in the upper atmosphere shields Earth from the sun's ultraviolet rays. Acid rain results when sulfur from factories mixes with moisture in the air. Acid rain is responsible for killing forests and damaging buildings.

Ecological disasters also leave long-lasting consequences. Toxic fumes from a chemical plant at Bhopal, India, in 1984; a nuclear accident at Chernobyl, Ukraine, in 1986; an oil spill from the *Exxon Valdez* in Alaska in 1989;

and an oil platform explosion in the Gulf of Mexico in 2010 caused ecological and health problems that can still be seen today.

Yet another threat to the environment is global climate change, which has the potential to create a worldwide crisis. Many of the world's scientists agree that the **greenhouse effect**, the warming of Earth due to the buildup of carbon dioxide in the atmosphere, is contributing to devastating droughts and storms, the melting of the polar ice caps, and rising sea levels that could flood coastal regions in the second half of the twenty-first century. Also alarming is the potential loss of biodiversity. Seven out of ten biologists believe the planet is now experiencing a surprising extinction of both plant and animal species.

In an attempt to reduce carbon emissions, more than 150 nations have signed the Kyoto Protocol, which calls on countries to cut air pollution. The United States did not ratify the treaty, saying that the required changes would be too costly.

A number of nations, however, have already begun to reduce their dependence on fossil fuels by introducing geothermal and hydroelectric power plants. Another clean source of energy is wind. Scientists estimate that one-third of the world's electricity could be supplied by wind generators by 2050. That would be enough to prevent 113 billion metric tons of carbon dioxide from entering the atmosphere each year. Wind farms have sprouted around the world—including in the United States.

greenhouse effect global warming caused by the buildup of carbon dioxide in the atmosphere

sustainable development economic development that does not limit the ability of future generations to meet their basic needs

Sustainable Development

Economic development that does not limit the ability of future generations to meet their basic needs is known as **sustainable development**. In promoting sustainable development, the United Nations urges countries to work to conserve all natural resources. Many countries have already enacted recycling and water conservation programs, along with curbing the dumping of toxic materials. A limited water supply affects 4 out of every 10 people globally. People without access to a source of clean water often get sick with cholera, typhoid, and diarrhea. More than 5 million people die every year from the lack of water or from drinking untreated water.

▼ Rooftop gardens, like the one below, help the environment by insulating the roof which helps save energy.

PHOTO: ©Amy Sussman/Corbis

✓ READING PROGRESS CHECK

Summarizing How have nations responded to global environmental challenges?

LESSON 4 REVIEW

TEKS

Reviewing Vocabulary

1. ***Drawing Conclusions*** How can sustainable development prevent deforestation and desertification?

Using Your Notes

2. ***Identifying*** Use your notes to identify the technological breakthroughs discussed in this lesson.

Answering the Guiding Questions

3. ***Evaluating*** How have scientific discoveries and technological innovations transformed society?

4. ***Identifying Central Issues*** What are the environmental challenges of the twenty-first century, and how have governments and citizens responded to them?

Writing Activity

5. **NARRATIVE** Identify a technology discussed in the lesson and write an essay about how this technology has affected your life. The essay should also include thoughts on how your life would be different without this technology.

CHAPTER 35 Assessment

TEKS

Directions: On a separate sheet of paper, answer the questions below. Make sure you read carefully and answer all parts of the questions.

Lesson Review

Lesson 1

1. ***Summarizing*** What are the reasons for ongoing conflicts in Africa, the Middle East, and South Asia? **13E**

2. ***Summarizing*** In the second half of the twentieth century, what has been the impact of radical Islamic fundamentalism on the growth of Palestinian terrorism and groups like al-Qaeda? **14A**

3. ***Explaining*** Since September 11, 2001, how has the U.S. responded to terrorism? **14B**

4. ***Explaining*** How are the League of Nations and United Nations similar? Explain the effectiveness of both bodies. Explain the structure and system of membership in the United Nations. **20D**

5. ***Identifying*** Describe the events of genocide in Rwanda and Darfur. **22D**

Lesson 2

6. ***Summarizing*** Summarize the development of the rule of law from ancient to modern times. **22A**

7. ***Analyzing*** Analyze the connections over time between ideas presented in the Magna Carta and the ideas of the Enlightenment, and the creation of the English Bill of Rights and United States Constitution. **29F**

8. ***Summarizing*** Summarize the various population trends across the world and include 2050 projections.

Lesson 3

9. ***Describing*** What led to the development of globalization? How has this development changed the world? **1F, 17C**

10. ***Identifying Perspectives*** What are the viewpoints of critics of global economic organizations and globalization?

Lesson 4

11. ***Explaining*** What is the role of transportation technology in developing the modern global economy and society? **28D**

12. ***Summarizing*** How have computer technology and telecommunication advancements played a role in the global economy and global society? Consider advancements, such as the introduction of the Internet and the invention of the microchip. **28D**

13. ***Specifying*** What was the Kyoto Protocol, and what are examples tied to its specifications?

Exploring the Essential Question

14. ***Synthesizing*** Write a multiparagraph essay describing at least four events that have influenced global political and economic relationships since World War II. Cite at least two examples for each event to show how it has influenced countries worldwide.

Need Extra Help?

If You've Missed Question	1	2	3	4	5	6	7	8	9	10	11	12	13	14
Go to page	848	847	848	846	849	857	857	858	862	865	867	868	871	846

Critical Thinking

15. ***Interpreting*** How have medical advancements played a role in the global economy and global society? **28D**

16. ***Analyzing*** How can globalization contribute to infectious disease pandemics?

17. ***Identifying Cause and Effect*** What is the effect of global awareness on the development of new social movements, and why?

18. ***Identifying Cause and Effect*** What was the reason for protests in Egypt in 2011, and what was the outcome?

19. ***Finding the Main Ideas*** Beginning in the 1980s, what was the shift in Latin American countries' style of government that resulted in greater popular approval and often improved economies?

20. ***Analyzing*** How has NAFTA impacted farmers in Mexico and industrial workers in the United States?

21. ***Analyzing Causes and Effects*** How did the collapse of the United States housing market in 2008 contribute to a worldwide recession?

22. ***Defending*** What arguments might you use to convince others that genetically engineered foods are a good idea?

23. ***Analyzing*** How have American ideals advanced human rights and democratic ideas throughout the world? **22F**

Social Studies Skills

24. ***Creating Graphs*** Use information in the text and additional research if needed to create a graph that demonstrates the relationship between geography and the historical development of a region or a nation. Refer to the Skillbuilder about population and poverty for information and ideas. Then, exchange graphs with a partner and interpret and discuss the data. **15A**

25. ***Decision Making*** Do you think that the huge media attention terrorist acts have received has helped reduce or increase these acts? Explain your answer.

26. ***Research Skills*** Using what you learn about the United Nations' efforts as peacekeeping forces, as well as from additional research about the United Nations, write a summary about the work the United Nations does around the world during times of conflict and unrest. Cite specific examples of their efforts.

27. ***Creating Charts*** Create a chart that lists countries from Asia and Southeast Asia that went through ethnic and religious conflicts and notes the final resolution. Charts can have a column for country name, conflict, and resolution. Include key dates.

Need Extra Help?

If You've Missed Question	15	16	17	18	19	20	21	22	23	24	25	26	27
Go to page	869	856	860	850	850	863	865	869	851	854	847	846	850

DBQ Analyzing Primary Sources

Use the document to answer the following questions.

At the United Nations Millennium Summit in 2000, world leaders agreed to work together to achieve eight development goals by 2015. These goals include eradicating extreme poverty and hunger, achieving universal primary education, promoting gender equality, reducing child mortality, and combating diseases.

PRIMARY SOURCE

"We will have time to reach the Millennium Development Goals . . . but only if we break with business as usual . . . . Success will require sustained action . . . . It takes time to train the teachers, nurses and engineers; to build the roads, schools and hospitals; to grow the small and large businesses able to create the jobs and income needed. So we must start now. And we must more than double global development assistance over the next few years. Nothing less will help to achieve the Goals."

—Kofi Annan, former UN Secretary-General, June 7, 2005

28. ***Summarizing*** According to Kofi Annan, how can the goals be achieved?

29. ***Assessing*** What role does the UN play in achieving these goals, and why is this role significant?

30. ***Making Inferences*** What do these goals tell you about the world economies of many governments?

Analyzing Visuals

Use the graph to answer the following questions.

This graph shows the growth of five of the world's largest economies over twenty years.

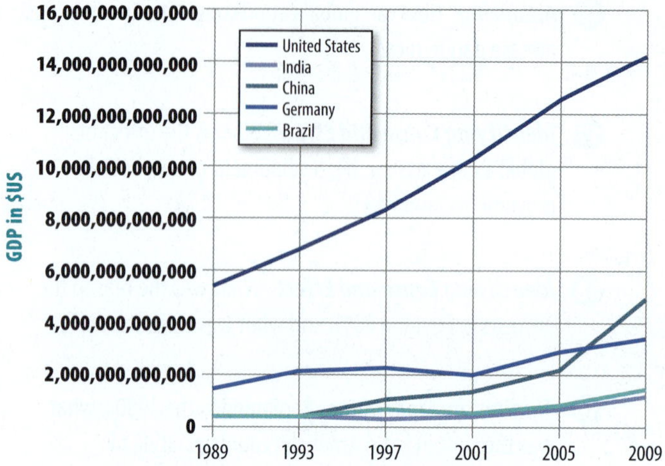

31. ***Analyzing*** What do the geographic distributions and patterns on this graph suggest about development in these nations? **15B**

32. ***Comparing*** How do the economies of Brazil, India, and Germany compare or contrast with the economies of the U.S. and China? **15B**

Extended Response Question

33. ***Expository*** Find two or more primary sources on the conflict between Tutsis and Hutus. Write an analysis of the causes and effects of the conflict.

Need Extra Help?

If You've Missed Question	28	29	30	31	32	33
Go to page	874	846	862	874	874	849

CONTENTS

What Role Did Hobbes and Locke Play in Government?

Who played a major role in England's power struggle during the 1600s? During the struggle for power that dominated English life in the 1600s, the differing political views of Thomas Hobbes and John Locke played significant roles in reinforcing, as well as inflaming, the attitudes of the two sides of the conflict: the monarchy and Parliament.

What happened in England as a result of this political discourse? At the heart of the issue was the ongoing dispute over what kind of monarchy would rule England. Simply put, Hobbes supported an absolute monarchy, in which the king had complete and sole power. Locke believed in a limited monarchy, in which the king and parliament shared power. These different views of government and the political conflicts that resulted from them were very complicated, but the eventual outcome of the dispute was clear and uncomplicated. With the ascension of William and Mary to the throne in 1689, supporters of a limited monarchy had won a permanent victory.

PRIMARY SOURCE

This excerpt from Hobbes's *Leviathan* was published in 1651.

> There is a sixth doctrine, plainly, and directly against the essence of a commonwealth, and 'tis this, that the **sovereign**[1] power may be divided. For what is it to divide the power of a commonwealth, but to dissolve it? for powers divided mutually destroy each other. And for these doctrines, men are chiefly **beholding**[2] to some of those, that making profession of the laws, endeavour to make them depend upon their own learning, and not upon the legislative power.
>
> Lastly, when in a warre (forraign, or intestine,) the enemies got a final Victory; so as (the forces of the Common-wealth keeping the field no longer) there is no farther protection of Subjects in their loyalty; then is the Common-wealth DISSOLVED, and every man at liberty to protect himself by such courses as his own discretion shall suggest unto him. For the Soveraign, is the publique Soule, giving Life and Motion to the Common-wealth; which expiring, the Members are governed by it no more, than the Carcasse of a man, by his departed (though Immortal) Soule.

1 **sovereign:** politically independent

2 **beholding:** looking upon

PRIMARY SOURCE

This passage is from Locke's *Two Treatises of Government,* which was published in 1690.

> People have not appointed so to do, they make Laws, whom the People have not appointed so to do, they make Laws without Authority, which the People are not therefore bound to obey; by which means they come again to be out of **subjection**[3], and may constitute to themselves a new Legislative, as they think best, being in full liberty to resist the force of those, who without Authority would impose any thing upon them. Everyone is at the disposure of his own Will, when those who had by the delegation of the Society, the declaring of the publick [sic] Will, are excluded from it, and others **usurp**[4] the place who have no such Authority or Delegation. . . . When such a single Person or Prince sets up his own Arbitrary Will in place of the Laws, which are the Will of the Society, declared by the Legislative, then the Legislative is changed.

3 **subjection:** to force under one's control

4 **usurp:** to seize and hold by force or without the right to do so

▲ *The John Trumbull painting,* Declaration of Independence, *depicts the presentation of the Declaration of Independence to John Hancock (seated right), president of the Continental Congress.*

PRIMARY SOURCE

This excerpt from the Declaration of Independence, which was written in 1776, draws on the conventions of Locke's theories of government.

We hold these truths to be self-evident, that all men are created equal, that they are endowed by their Creator with certain unalienable Rights, that among these are Life, Liberty and the pursuit of Happiness. —That to secure these rights, Governments are instituted among Men, deriving their just powers from the consent of the governed, —That whenever any Form of Government becomes destructive of these ends, it is the Right of the People to alter or to abolish it, and to institute new Government, laying its foundation on such principles and organizing its powers in such form, as to them shall seem most likely to effect their Safety and Happiness.

5 **impel:** to urge into action

DBQ Document Based Questions

1. ***Comparing and Contrasting*** When Hobbes uses the term *legislative power*, to whom is he referring? To whom is Locke referring when he uses the term *Legislative*? Who is the "single Person or Prince" Locke mentions?
2. ***Analyzing Central Ideas*** Why does Hobbes believe that power in a commonwealth should not be divided?
3. ***Drawing Conclusions*** According to Hobbes, what do people mistakenly assume when they advocate that a division of powers is good for a commonwealth?
4. ***Making Inferences*** When Locke says that people are not obligated to obey laws that are made without their authority and have a right to install a new government under such circumstances, what is he implying about their rule in a commonwealth?
5. ***Making Connections*** Locke's views on government influenced some of the ideas in the U.S. Declaration of Independence and the U.S. Constitution. What ideas in the excerpt from *Two Treatises* can you find in the Declaration of Independence to support this statement?
6. ***Interpreting*** According to the Declaration of Independence, what duty does mankind have to fulfill when faced with a tyrannical government?

Who Should be a Citizen?

What is a citizen? One definition of a citizen is a free person who owes loyalty to a nation and who receives protection, rights, and privileges in return. In the 1700s the meaning of this definition was challenged by both men and women for different reasons.

Who should be a citizen? At the time of the American Revolution only free, white adult males who owned property or paid taxes could vote.

In France, the *Declaration of the Rights of Man and the Citizen* addressed social distinctions, but opinions differed on how to interpret the document. Read the excerpts from Robespierre and d'Aelders and study Fragonard's painting to see how they viewed citizenship and the continuing struggle for rights.

PRIMARY SOURCE

In this speech from October 1789, Maximilien Robespierre stated his view on property requirements for holding office and voting.

All citizens, whoever they are, have the right to aspire to all levels of office-holding. Nothing is more in line with your declaration of rights, according to which all privileges, all distinctions, all exceptions must disappear. The Constitution establishes that **sovereignty**[1] resides in the people, in all the individuals of the people. Each individual therefore has the right to participate in making the law which governs him and in the administration of the public good which is his own. If not, it is not true that all men are equal in rights, that every man is a citizen. If he who only pays a tax **equivalent**[2] to a day of work has fewer rights than he who pays the equivalent to three days of work, and he who pays at the level of ten days has more rights than he whose tax only equals that value of three, then he who enjoys 100,000 livres [French pounds] of **revenue**[3] has 100 times as many rights as he who only has 1,000 livres of revenue. It follows from all your **decrees**[4] that every citizen has the right to participate in making the law and consequently that of being an elector or eligible for office without the distinction of wealth.

PRIMARY SOURCE

Etta Palm d'Aelders was a woman active in a reform group called the Cercle Social (Social Circle). D'Aelders expressed her opinions in "The Injustices of the Laws and Favor of Men at the Expense of Women" (December, 1790).

Do not be just by halves, Gentlemen; . . . justice must be the first virtue of free men, and justice demands that the laws be the same for all beings, like the air and the sun. And yet everywhere, the laws favor men at the expense of women, because everywhere power is in your hands. What! Will free men, an **enlightened**[5] people living in a century of enlightenment and philosophy, will they **consecrate**[6] what has been the abuse of power in a century of ignorance? . . .

The prejudices with which our sex has been surrounded—supported by unjust laws which only accord us a secondary existence in society and which often force us into the humiliating necessity of winning over the **cantankerous**[7] and **ferocious**[8] character of a man, who, by the greed of those close to us has become our master—those prejudices have changed what was for us the sweetest and most saintly of duties, those of wife and mother, into a painful and terrible slavery. . . .

Oh! Gentlemen, if you wish us to be enthusiastic about the happy constitution that gives back men their rights, then begin by being just toward us. From now on we should be your voluntary companions and not your slaves. Let us merit your attachment!

1 **sovereignty:** power; authority

2 **equivalent:** same, of equal force

3 **revenue:** income

4 **decrees:** authoritative decisions; declarations

▲ *Boissy d'Anglas salutes the head of the deputy Feraud, May 20, 1795, by Alexandre Fragonard.*

PRIMARY SOURCE

On May 20, 1795, an angry mob in the Convention hacked the head off deputy Feraud and presented it to the chairman, Boissy d'Anglas, who saluted the head. After this incident, d'Anglas presented measures to prevent the return of the Reign of Terror and to take precautions against anarchy.

Usually the crowds in the balcony were merely rowdy, insulting and threatening the deputies. At times like the one in the painting, they became a mob, invading the chamber and killing deputies with whom they disagreed. Some leaders thought the poor and the uneducated would take over the government, leading to violence and disorder. They feared "mob rule."

5 **enlightened:** knowledgeable, comprehending

6 **consecrate:** make sacred

7 **cantankerous:** having a bad disposition; quarrelsome

8 **ferocious:** brutal, fierce

DBQ Analyzing Historical Documents

1. ***Analyzing*** What does Robespierre think about basing citizenship on whether a person has property or pays taxes?
2. ***Explaining*** What does d'Aelders mean by women's "secondary existence in society"?
3. ***Making Inferences*** What do you think Fragonard's opinion might have been of universal suffrage—the right of all citizens to vote?
4. ***Comparing*** Although Robespierre was not a supporter of equal rights for women, list some similarities between his and d'Aelders's arguments.
5. ***Contrasting*** How does d'Aelders's portrayal of women contrast with Fragonard's?
6. ***Defending*** How would you answer the question "Who should be a citizen?" Which source has a position most like your own? Write a letter to the editor that explains your position on universal suffrage and identifies the source with which you most agree.

Describing the Lives of Workers in the Early 1800s

What hardships did industrialization create for workers? Though it transformed the British economy with the addition of jobs, industrialization had a drastic social impact on the working people of England.

How did industrialization affect living conditions in cities? The Industrial Revolution not only brought waves of new factories, it caused masses of workers to move to the cities to find jobs at these factories. Both developments had a profound impact on the lives of England's workers.

The Industrial Revolution altered both the working and living conditions of Britain's working class. Read the excerpts and study the illustration to learn more about how industrialization impacted the people of England during the first half of the nineteenth century.

PRIMARY SOURCE

Miner Betty Harris, 37, gave testimony to an 1842 Royal Commission investigating conditions in British mines.

I was married at 23, and went into a **colliery** when I was married. I . . . can neither read nor write. . . . I am a **drawer**[2], and work from 6 in the morning to 6 at night. Stop about an hour at noon to eat my dinner; have bread and butter for dinner; I get no drink. . . .

I have a belt round my waist, and a chain passing between my legs, and I go on my hands and feet. The road is very steep, and we have to hold by a rope; and when there is no rope, by anything we can catch hold of. There are six women and about six boys and girls in the pit I work in; it is very hard work for a woman. The pit is very wet where I work, and the water comes over our clog-tops always, and I have seen it up to my thighs; it rains in at the roof terribly. My clothes are wet through almost all day long. . . .

My cousin looks after my children in the day time. I am very tired when I get home at night; I fall asleep sometimes before I get washed. . . . the belt and chain is worse when we are **in the family way**[3]. My feller (husband) has beaten me many a times for not being ready.

PRIMARY SOURCE

German socialist Friedrich Engels, co-founder of Marxism, described industrial Manchester in his book, *The Condition of the Working-Class in England in 1844.*

The first court below Ducie Bridge . . . was in such a state at the time of the cholera that the sanitary police ordered it evacuated, swept, and disinfected with **chloride of lime**[4]. . . . At the bottom flows, or rather stagnates, the Irk, a narrow, coal-black, foul-smelling stream, full of debris and refuse, which it deposits on the shallower right bank. . . .

Above the bridge are **tanneries**[5], **bone mills**[6], and gasworks, from which all drains and refuse find their way into the Irk, which receives further the contents of all the neighboring sewers and **privies**[7]. . . . Below the bridge you look upon the piles of debris, the refuse, the filth, and offal from the courts on the steep left bank; here each house is packed close behind its neighbor and a piece of each is visible, all black, smoky, crumbling, ancient, with broken panes and window frames. . . .

Such is the Old Town of Manchester . . . [in] defiance of all considerations of cleanliness, ventilation, and health which characterize the construction of this single district, containing at least twenty to thirty thousand inhabitants.

1 **colliery:** coal mine and its connected buildings

2 **drawer:** worker who pulled coal tubs in a mine; tubs were attached to the drawer's belt with a chain

3 **in the family way:** pregnant

4 **chloride of lime:** bleaching powder

▲ *This illustration shows a female drawer—as portrayed by Betty Harris in Parliamentary Papers of 1842—in a coal pit in Little Bolton, England in 1842.*

PRIMARY SOURCE

England's Industrial Revolution increased the need for coal. By 1841, more than 200,000 men, women and children were working in the mines. Women and young boys were used to remove the coal from the mines.

The above print of a woman drawer in a coal pit was created to accompany Betty Harris's testimony to the Royal Commission in 1842. The image shows the belt around her waist and the chain between her legs. In Betty's testimony, she claimed that she worked in these conditions with other women and small children.

The Mines Act passed in August 1842, prohibiting femal labor and boys under the age of 10 from working in the mines.

5 **tanneries:** buildings where skins and hides are tanned

6 **bone mills:** mills that convert animal bones into fertilizer

7 **privies:** outhouses

Hulton Archive/Getty Images

DBQ Document Based Questions

1. ***Calculating*** How many hours did Betty Harris work each day?
2. ***Recognizing Bias*** How could Engels's background have affected his assessment of Manchester? How might a description of the city written by a factory owner contrast from that written by Engels?
3. ***Integrating Visual Information*** How does the above illustration support Harris's testimony about the work experience for women in mines?
4. ***Contrasting*** How have working conditions changed in the United States since Industrialization? What laws protect the rights of workers?
5. ***Synthesizing*** How could Engels have used Harris's testimony to support his main point about industrialization?
6. ***Problem-Solving*** Consider the lives of England's workers in the early 1800s. Suppose you are an adviser to the British government. Write a letter to government leaders recommending changes for work conditions.

What Were the Causes of World War II?

How did the international community try to prevent war? The League of Nations, disarmament conferences, and mutual defense treaties were efforts used in the 1920s and 1930s by the international community to maintain world peace.

Why did these efforts fail to prevent World War II? Japan, Italy, and Germany each used its military to occupy foreign territories in the 1930s. Their aggressive moves led to the outbreak of a global conflict by the end of the decade.

After World War I ended in 1918, global leaders resolved to prevent future wars. Nonetheless, only two decades later, the most destructive conflict in human history broke out. Read the excerpts and study the cartoon to learn more about the causes of World War II.

PRIMARY SOURCE

British historian Dr. G.P. Gooch addressed the threat of war in his 1938 article, "The Breakdown of the System of Collective Security."

"Since the Allies declined to scale down their armaments to the German level, Germany was certain to climb towards theirs as soon as she felt strong enough to do so with **impunity**[1].

The Disarmament Conference which opened at Geneva in February 1932 had taken years to prepare, and it met too late. Even the chance of a limited agreement was lost owing to the lack of a strong lead at the outset by a Great Power . . . Each country was **virtuously**[2] ready for reductions in categories which were not of vital importance to itself, but stood out for those which it needed most. Thus Great Britain longed for the abolition of the submarine, which nearly starved us in 1917, while she clung to the **capital ship**[3]. . . . When the Conference adjourned for the summer holidays in 1932, it was clear that it had failed. In the autumn Germany retired, but was brought back by a promise of equality of status. . . . Such a system proved unattainable, and a year later Hitler's Germany withdrew not only from the Conference but from the League [of Nations] itself. . . . Since that moment Germany has been re-arming at feverish speed, and Europe is back again in its pre-War mood when everyone was afraid of Berlin. Our own colossal re-armament programme is the measure of our alarm."

PRIMARY SOURCE

The following passages are from 1938 diary entries of Victor Klemperer, a Jewish professor who lived in Nazi Germany.

The immense act of violence on the [German] **annexation**[4] of Austria, the immense increase in [Germany's] power both internally and externally, the defenseless trembling fear of England, France, etc. We shall not live to see the end of the Third Reich. . . .

The Third Reich will win again—whether by bluff or by force. . . . Chamberlain flies to Hitler for the second time tomorrow. England and France remain calm, in Dresden the **Sudeten German "Freikorps**[5]**"** is almost ready to invade [Czechoslovakia]. And the populace here is convinced that the Czechs alone are to blame and that Hitler loves peace. . . .

Four-power meeting[6] today [September 29] at three in Munich. Czechoslovakia continues to exist, Germany gets the Sudetenland, probably a colony as well. . . . For the populace on the front pages of the German press it is of course the absolute success of Hitler, the prince of peace and brilliant diplomat. . . . No shot is fired, and the [German] troops have been marching in since yesterday. Wishes for peace and friendship have been exchanged with England and France, Russia is cowering and silent, a zero. Hitler is being acclaimed even more extravagantly than in the Austria business.

1 **impunity:** freedom from punishment

2 **virtuously:** morally

3 **capital ship:** large class warship, such as a battleship

4 **annexation:** the act of incorporating new territory

The weakness of the League of Nations is illustrated in this 1931 cartoon, "Let Sam Do It," by Winsor McCay.

PRIMARY SOURCE

At the end of World War I, United States president Woodrow Wilson lobbied for the creation of an international organization to help prevent future conflicts. The League of Nations formed in 1919. Many Americans, however, feared that joining the League would drag the country into foreign wars. As a result, the U.S. Senate refused to allow the nation to become a member of the League.

In 1931, the League of Nations faced a major challenge to its ability to maintain world peace when Japan invaded China. Artist Winsor McCay published the above cartoon after Japanese soldiers captured Manchuria from the Chinese. The man standing on the right side of the cartoon, Uncle Sam, represents the United States.

5 **Sudeten German "Freikorps":** German guerrilla force that sought to add the Sudetenland region to Germany

6 **Four-power meeting:** meeting of Germany, Italy, France, and Britain to discuss Germany's claims to the Sudetenland

DBQ Document Based Questions

1. ***Explaining*** According to Gooch, why did the Disarmament Conference in Geneva fail?
2. ***Recognizing Bias*** What does Klemperer suggest about how most Germans felt about Hitler in 1938? Why do you think the German populace felt that way about Hitler?
3. ***Interpreting*** What does McCay believe about the likelihood of stopping the conflict between Japan and China?
4. ***Analyzing*** Do Gooch and Klemperer primarily agree or disagree in their assessments of the threat to world peace in 1938?
5. ***Comparing*** What common point does each of the three sources make about the international efforts to prevent war in the 1930s?
6. ***Drawing Conclusions*** What were the causes of World War II? Do you think the Western powers could have prevented the war? Why or why not?

What Challenges Did Apartheid Create for South Africans?

How did apartheid affect South Africa? For much of the twentieth century, South Africa's white-run government denied political and economic equality to the country's black majority.

What progress have South Africans made in overcoming the effects of apartheid? Despite facing harsh government repression, South Africans carried on a decades-long campaign against apartheid. The nation finally held free elections in 1994, marking the end of apartheid and the beginning of democracy with the election of Nelson Mandela.

Apartheid in South Africa attracted international attention. Read the excerpts and study the cartoon to learn more about how South Africa faced this challenge.

PRIMARY SOURCE

The following passage is from a speech by Desmond Tutu, a black Anglican Archbishop, to the United Nations Security Council on October 23, 1984.

For my beloved country is wracked by division, by alienation, by **animosity**[1], by separation, by injustice, by unavoidable pain and suffering. It is a deeply **fragmented**[2] society, ridden by fear and anxiety . . . and a sense of desperation, split up into hostile, warring factions. . . .

There is little freedom to disagree with the determinations of the authorities. There is large scale unemployment here because of the drought and the recession that has hit most of the world's economy. And it is such a time that the authorities have increased the prices of various foodstuffs and also of rents in black townships—measures designed to hit hardest those least able to afford the additional costs. . . .

The authorities have not stopped stripping blacks of their South African citizenship. . . . The South African government is turning us into aliens in the land of our birth.

White South Africans are . . . scared human beings, many of them; who would not be, if they were outnumbered five to one? Through this lofty body I wish to appeal to my white fellow South Africans to share in building a new society, for blacks are not intent on driving whites into the sea but on claiming only their rightful place in the sun in the land of their birth.

1 **animosity:** resentment

2 **fragmented:** broken into pieces

PRIMARY SOURCE

African National Congress leader Nelson Mandela discussed South Africa's past and future in a speech he gave after his release from prison in 1990.

Today, the majority of South Africans, black and white, recognize that **apartheid**[3] has no future. It has to be ended by our own decisive mass action in order to build peace and security. The mass campaigns of defiance and other actions of our organizations and people can only **culminate**[4] in the establishment of democracy. The apartheid's destruction on our subcontinent is incalculable. The fabric of family life of millions of my people has been shattered. Millions are homeless and unemployed. Our economy lies in ruins and our people are embroiled in political strife. . . .

We call on our people to seize this moment, so that the process toward democracy is rapid and uninterrupted. . . . We must not allow fear to stand in our way. Universal suffrage on a common voters roll in a united, democratic and non-racial South Africa is the only way to peace and racial harmony. . . .

I have fought against white domination, and I have fought against black domination. I have cherished the ideal of a democratic and free society in which all persons live together in harmony and with equal opportunity. It is an ideal which I hope to live for and to achieve. But, if need be, it is an ideal for which I am prepared to die.

3 **apartheid:** policy of racial segregation

4 **culminate:** conclude

▲ *Nelson Mondela was sworn in as South Africa's first democratically elected president in 1994.*

PRIMARY SOURCE

In the 1940s the African National Congress (ANC) formed a Youth League to lead a nonviolent campaign against the apartheid policies of South Africa. In 1960 South African police fired on unarmed demonstrators at Sharpeville, killing 67. A year later the ANC formed an armed wing, Umkhonto we Sizwe, headed by Nelson Mandela to carry out sabotage against government installations.

In 1963 the South African government arrested Mandela and, a year later, sentenced him to life imprisonment. In 1990, amidst growing international and domestic pressure, the government released Mandela. Four years later, he was elected president by voters in South Africa. His **inauguration** marked the end of apartheid.

5 **inauguration:** ceremonial induction into office

DBQ Document Based Questions

1. ***Explaining*** According to Bishop Tutu, what problems did South Africa face in 1984?
2. ***Drawing Conclusions*** What do you think Mandela hoped to accomplish with his speech?
3. ***Assessing*** What does the cartoon reveal about the state of the South African nation after Mandela gained his freedom?
4. ***Identifying Points of View*** How do you think Mandela's experiences influenced the opinions he expressed in his speech?
5. ***Synthesizing*** What similarities exist between the messages conveyed by all three sources?
6. ***Defending*** What challenges did apartheid create for South Africans? Write a paragraph explaining whether you believe that Mandela and Tutu offered effective ideas to deal with these challenges.

What was Social Media's Role in the Arab Spring?

What was the Arab Spring? In 2011, a wave of democratic popular protests swept across dictatorships in the Muslim nations of North Africa. This movement was called the Arab Spring by journalists covering the events.

How did the use of social media lead to the overthrow of Muslim nations? Protesters used Facebook, Twitter, and YouTube to connect and organize supporters for their cause and build international support in such a way that could not be accomplished through state-run media outlets.

Read the excerpts to learn more about the role of social media in the movement known as the Arab Spring.

PRIMARY SOURCE

This excerpt from New York Times journalist Anthony Shadid describes the Syrian regime's attempts to regain control of Homs amidst a revolution fueled by the use of social media. The article "In Assad's Syria, There is No Imagination", was published on November 8, 2011. Shadid died of an asthma attack in February 2012 while on assignment in Syria.

Bashar seemed to think he was different. . . .

For a time, his seeming humility brought a measure of support his father never enjoyed . . . But Bashar believed his own **aura**[2]. In those days, he declared his state immune from the upheavals of Egypt and Tunisia. He insisted that his foreign policy, built rhetorically on **enmity**[3] with Israel, opposition to American **hegemony**[4] and support for the kind of resistance preached by Lebanon's Hezbollah, reflected the sentiments of an Arab world long humiliated by its impotence.

Even today, eight months after an uprising and a ferocious crackdown that, by the United Nations' count, has killed more than 3,000 people and, by the Arab League's estimate, put more than 70,000 in jail, people who have seen Bashar contend that he still doesn't recognize the severity of the challenge.

As in Iraq, Syria's neighbor to the east, the clichés of superficial analysis that preceded tumult now threaten to come true: Us or chaos. The regime posed as the guardian of Syria's diversity, even as the House of Assad and its lieutenants relentlessly stirred that diversity so as to divide and rule. Pitting community against community, never in a more pronounced way than now, it may finally bring forth the civil war that it long claimed it was the **bulwark**[5] against.

In their ambition at least, the Arab revolts and revolutions were about a positive sort of legitimacy: democracy, freedom, social justice and individual rights. They remain an unfulfilled promise, but no one in Egypt, Tunisia or Libya is really afraid to speak anymore. The **cacophony**[6] that has ensued is the most liberating feature of rejuvenated societies. It already echoes in parts of Syria. When I was in Hama this summer, a city still scarred by memory and for a brief moment freed from security forces, youths embraced their new space by protesting every couple of hours in streets made kinetic by the allure of self-determination. They demonstrated simply because they could. In Homs, a city whose uprising could prove Syria's demise or salvation, youths drawn from an eclectic array of leftists, liberals, nationalists, Islamists and the simply pissed-off articulated the essence of courage: They had come too far to go back.

"In the end, I'm a person now," a young activist named Iyad told me in Homs. "I can say what I want. I love you if I want to love you, I hate you if I want to hate you. I can denounce your beliefs or I can support them. I can agree with your position or disagree with it. But I'm a person now." He dragged on his cigarette, and we shared more tea. "We're not waiting to live our lives until after the fall of the regime," he went on. "We started living them the first day of the protests."

1 **rue:** to feel regret

2 **aura:** a distinct atmosphere or quality surrounding a person, place, or thing

3 **enmity:** an extremely unfriendly or hostile feeling toward something

4 **hegemony:** dominance by one country or social group

▲ During the Arab Spring protest movement, many in the Middle East used social network sites on the Internet to spread organization plans. These sites also kept the world informed of their actions.

PRIMARY SOURCE

This is an excerpt from an article entitled "The Arab Spring's Cascading Effects."

Over the last few months, social unrest has cascaded across the major urban centers of North Africa and the Middle East. Journalists and communications media are often part of such moments of upheaval. Yet this recent wave of unrest is unlike other discrete periods of rapid political change. Through digital media, the stories of success in Tunisia and Egypt have spread over social networks to many other authoritarian regimes. Digital media has not only caused a cascade of civil disobedience to spread among populations living under the most **unflappable**[7] dictators, it has made for unique new means of civic organizing.

During the heady days of protests in Cairo, one activist **succinctly**[8] tweeted about why digital media was so important to the organization of political unrest. "We use Facebook to schedule the protests, Twitter to coordinate, and YouTube to tell the world," she said. The protesters openly acknowledge the role of digital media as a fundamental **infrastructure**[9] for their work. Moammar Gadhafi's former aides have advised him to submit his resignation through Twitter.

Yet digital media didn't oust Hosni Mubarak. The committed Egyptians occupying the streets of Cairo did that. As Barack Obama put it, mobile phones and the Internet were the media by which soulful calls for freedom have cascaded across North Africa and the Middle East. Just as the fall of Suharto in Indonesia is a story that involves the creative use of mobile phones by student activists, the falls of Zine El Abidine Ben Ali in Tunisia and Mubarak in Egypt will be recorded as a process of Internet-enabled social **mobilization**[10].

DBQ Document Based Questions

1. ***Contrasting*** Based on the context clues provided, what do you think Howard meant when he referred to "discrete periods" of political change? How was this different from the Arab Spring?
2. ***Identifying*** According to Shadid, what was the primary ambition of the Arab revolts?
3. ***Analyzing*** What reasoning does Shadid use as evidence to the protestors' "essence of courage" in the face of opposition? What event in American History could be related to such a statement?
4. ***Identifying*** What evidence did Bashar ignore that signified the challenges in his country might be insurmountable?
5. ***Comparing*** What ideal is expressed in both accounts?
6. ***Drawing Conclusions*** Based on the photographs of the protestors, what conclusions can you make about the participants in the Arab Spring and the connection to social media? How is this form of communication different from traditional media?

5 **bulwark:** support or protection

6 **cacophony:** harsh unpleasant noise

7 **unflappable:** not easily upset or bothered

8 **succinctly:** concisely

9 **infrastructure:** underlying foundation or basic framework

10 **mobilization:** to make ready for action

▲ *This rendition of an Egyptian father teaching his son is on the wall of the Tomb of Sennedjem.*

VOCABULARY

fraud
to deceive with dishonest methods

inclines
"leans toward" or persuades

astray
off the correct path

An Egyptian Father's Advice to His Son

Upper-class Egyptians enjoyed compiling collections of wise sayings to provide guidance for leading an upright and successful life. This excerpt from The Instruction of the Vizier Ptah-hotep *dates from around 2450* B.C.

Then he said to his son:

If you are a leader commanding the affairs of the many, seek out for yourself every good deed, until it may be that your own affairs are without wrong. Justice is great, and it is lasting; it has been disturbed since the time of him who made it, whereas there is punishment for him who passes over its laws. Wrongdoing has never brought its undertaking into port. It may be that it is **fraud** that gains riches, but the strength of justice is that it lasts . . . .

If you are a man of standing who is pleasing to god, if he is correct and **inclines** toward your ways and listens to your instruction, while his manners in your house are fitting, and if he takes care of your property as it should be, seek out for him every useful action. He is your son, . . . you should not cut your heart off from him.

If he [the son] goes **astray** and does not carry out your instruction, so that his manners in your household are wretched, and he rebels against all that you say, while his mouth runs on in the most wretched talk, quite apart from his experience, while he possesses nothing, you should cast him off: he is not your son at all. He was not really born to you . . . He is one whom god has condemned in the very womb.

DBQ Analyzing Historical Documents

1. ***Identifying*** According to the Egyptian father, which is more important—riches or justice?

2. ***Determining Word Meanings*** Use the context clues from the excerpt to determine whether the word "wretched" has a positive or negative connotation.

3. ***Evaluating*** Does any part of the Egyptian father's advice have value today for sons or daughters? Be specific and support your answer.

▲ *China's emperor's used book burnings to destroy all history and potential influence from previous dynasties.*

The Burning of Books

Li Su was a chief minister of the First Qin Emperor. A follower of Legalism, he hoped to eliminate all rival theories of government.

Your servant suggests that all books in the **imperial archives**, save the memoirs of Qin, be burned. All persons in the empire, except members of the Academy of Learned Scholars, in possession of the Book of Odes, the Book of History, and **discourses** of the hundred philosophers [including Confucius] should take them to the local governors and have them burned. Those who dare to talk to each other about the Book of Odes and the Book of History should be executed and their bodies exposed in the market place. Anyone referring to the past to criticize the present should, together with all members of his family, be put to death. Officials who fail to report cases that have come under their attention are equally guilty. After thirty days from the time of issuing the **decree**, those who have not destroyed their books are to be branded and sent to build the Great Wall. Books not to be destroyed will be those on medicine and pharmacy, agriculture and arboriculture [the cultivation of trees and shrubs]. People wishing to pursue learning should take the officials as their teachers.

VOCABULARY

imperial
relating to the empire or the emperor

archives
official documents that are preserved for historical or public use

discourse
discussion

decree
an order that has the force of law

DBQ Analyzing Historical Documents

1. ***Drawing Conclusions*** Why did Li Su think that burning books would eliminate all rival theories of government?
2. ***Identifying*** Which books were saved? Why were these books not burned?
3. ***Argument*** Do you agree or disagree with burning or banning books with what some consider objectionable content? Why or why not? What amendment protects this right? Write a paragraph defending your position.

▲ *The plague affected all classes of men. Athenian statesman Pericles died in 429 B.C. after becoming infected by the plague that killed nearly one-third of all Athenians.*

VOCABULARY

livid
bruised and disolored

calamity
an event that brings great harm

profane
to treat something that is sacred with disrespect

Plague in Athens

Thucydides (471–c. 400 B.C.) is regarded as the first scientific historian. In his account of the plague that broke out in Athens in 430 B.C., Thucydides simply presents the facts, describing the disease's symptoms and impact on the city itself.

. . . Externally, the body was not so very warm to the touch; it was not pale, but reddish, **livid**, and breaking out in small blisters and ulcers. But internally it was consumed by such a heat that the patients could not bear to have on them the lightest coverings or linen sheets. . . .

The Athenians suffered further hardships owing to the crowding into the city of the people from the country districts; and this affected the new arrivals especially. For since no houses were available for them and they had to live in huts that were stifling in the hot season, they perished in wild disorder. Bodies of dying men lay one upon another, and half-dead people rolled about in the streets and, in their longing for water, near all the fountains. . . . The **calamity** which weighed upon them was so overpowering that men became careless of all law, sacred as well as **profane**. And the customs which they had hitherto observed regarding burial were all thrown into confusion, and they buried their dead each one as he could. . . .

DBQ Analyzing Historical Documents

1. ***Identifying Points of View*** How does Thucydides' perspective as a scientific historian affect his account of the plague?
2. ***Analyzing*** Why were the sick—and the dead—gathered around the fountains? How could this have potentially made things worse?
3. ***Identifying*** What hardships did newcomers to Athens face during the time of the plague?

The Justinian Code

The Justinian Code stands as a monumental document in all of Western culture because it recorded the common understanding of law within the Roman Empire for the previous 1000 years, as well as of current law. The recording of all Roman laws had never been attempted before. The Justinian Code clarified the accepted laws of the Roman Empire. The Justinian Code is made up of four parts: the Codex, the Digest, the Institutes, and the Novels which set the standard for Roman law until the empire ceased to exist in 1453.

Civil law is thus distinguished from the law of nations. Every community governed by laws and customs uses partly its own law, partly laws common to all mankind. The law which a people makes for its own government belongs exclusively to that state and is called the civil law, as being the law of the particular state. But the law which natural reason appoints for all mankind obtains equally among all nations, because all nations make use of it. The people of Rome, then, are governed partly by their own laws, and partly by the laws which are common to all mankind. We will take notice of this **distinction** as occasion may arise.

—From Book II, Natural, Common and Civil Law, 527–565

A person who takes a thing belonging to another by force is liable to an action of theft, for who can be said to take the property of another more against his will than he who takes it by force? And he is therefore rightly said to be an *improbus fur*. The **praetor**, however, has introduced a peculiar action in this case, called *vi bonorum raptorum*; by which, if brought within a year after the robbery, quadruple the value of the thing taken may be recovered; but if brought after the expiration of a year, then the single value only may be brought even against a person who has only taken by force a single thing, and one of the most trifling value. But this quadruple of the value is not altogether a penalty, as in the action *furtum manifestum*; for the thing itself is included, so that, strictly, the penalty is only three times the value. And it is the same, whether the robber was or was not taken in the actual commission of the crime. For it would be ridiculous that a person who uses force should be in a better condition than he who secretly commits a theft.

—From Book IV, Goods Taken by Force, 527–565

VOCABULARY

distinction
setting some things apart from one another

praetor
high ranking Roman official

DBQ Analyzing Historical Documents

1. ***Analyzing*** How is civil law different from the law of nations?
2. ***Identifying*** Why does the code mention both civil law and the law of nations?
3. ***Identifying Continuity and Change*** Is the position of the Justinian Code on the law of nations and civil law similar to or different from the modern law in the United States? Explain your answer.

The Magna Carta

The Magna Carta, sealed by King John of England in 1215, marked a decisive step forward in the development of English constitutional government. Later, it served as a model for the colonists, who carried the Magna Carta's guarantees of political rights to America.

"John, by the grace of God, king of England, lord of Ireland, duke of Normandy and Aquitaine, and count of Anjou; to the archbishops, bishops, abbots, earls, barons, justiciaries, foresters, sheriffs, reeves, ministers, and all bailiffs, and others his faithful subjects, greeting. . . .

1. We have, in the first place, granted to God, and by this our present charter, confirmed for us and our heirs forever that the English church shall be free. . . .
9. Neither we nor our bailiffs shall seize any land or rent for any debt so long as the debtor's chattels are sufficient to discharge the same. . . .
12. No scutage [tax] or aid shall be imposed in our kingdoms unless by the common counsel thereof. . . .
14. For obtaining the common counsel of the kingdom concerning the assessment of aids . . . or of scutage, we will cause to be summoned, severally by our letters, the archbishops, bishops, abbots, earls, and great barons; we will also cause to be summoned generally, by our sheriffs and bailiffs, all those who hold lands directly of us, to meet on a fixed day . . . and at a fixed place. . . .
20. A free man shall be amerced [punished] for a small fault only according to the measure thereof, and for a great crime according to its magnitude. . . . None of these achievements shall be imposed except by the oath of honest men of the neighborhood.
21. Earls and barons shall be amerced only by their peers and only in proportion to the measure of the offense. . . .
38. In the future no bailiff shall upon his own unsupported accusation put any man to trial without producing credible witnesses to the truth of the accusation.
39. No free man shall be taken, imprisoned, disseised [seized], outlawed, banished, or in any way destroyed, nor will we proceed against or prosecute him, except by the lawful judgment of his peers and by the law of the land.
40. To no one will we sell, to none will we deny or delay, right or justice. . . .
42. In the future it shall be lawful . . . for anyone to leave and return to our kingdom safely and securely by land and water, saving his fealty to us. Excepted are those who have been imprisoned or outlawed according to the law of the land. . . .
61. Whereas we, for the honor of God, and the amendment of our realm, and in order the better to allay the discord arisen between us and our barons, have granted all these things aforesaid. . . .
63. Wherefore we will, and firmly charge that all men in our kingdom shall have and hold all the aforesaid liberties, rights, and concessions . . . fully, and wholly to them and their heirs . . . in all places ever. . . . It is moreover sworn, as well on our part as on the part of the barons, that all these matters aforesaid will be kept in good faith and without deceit. Witness the above named and many others. Given by our hand in the meadow which is called Runnymeade. . . ."

DBQ Analyzing Historical Documents

1. ***Identifying*** Which paragraph discusses the idea of a punishment "fitting" a crime?
2. ***Citing Text Evidence*** What are the similarities between the Magna Carta and the Bill of Rights? Provide at least one specific example from the text of the Magna Carta to support your comparison.
3. ***Assessing*** Which paragraphs address an individual's right to a trial by jury?

▲ *Christine de Pizan writes at her desk.*

A Woman May Need to Have the Heart of a Man

Christine de Pizan was widowed at age 25. She supported her three children by copying manuscripts, compiling a manual of instructions for knights, and writing books. The following is from her 1405 work, The Treasure of the City of Ladies.

It is the responsibility of every baron to spend the least possible time at his manors and his own estate, for his duties are to bear arms, to attend the court of his prince and to travel. Now, his lady stays behind and must take his place. . . . Her men should be able to rely on her for all kinds of protection in the **absence** of their lord. . . . She ought to know how to use weapons and be familiar with everything that pertains to them, so that she may be ready to command her men if the need arises. She should know how to launch an attack or to defend against one.

In addition she will do well to be a very good manager of the estate. . . . She will busy herself around the house; she will find plenty of orders to give. She will have the animals brought in at the right time [and] take care how the shepherd looks after them. . . .

In the winter-time, she will have her men cut her willow groves and make vine props to sell in the season. She will never let them be idle. . . . She will employ her women . . . to attend to the livestock, . . . [and] to weed the courtyards. . . . There is a great need to run an estate well, and the one who is most diligent and careful about it is more than wise and ought to be highly praised.

VOCABULARY

absence
not being present

DBQ Analyzing Historical Documents

1. ***Identifying*** What are some of the duties and responsibilities of the medieval gentlewoman, according to Christine de Pizan's account?
2. ***Describing*** Based on the excerpt, how would you describe Pizan's opinion of barons and their responsibilities?
3. ***Narrative*** Suppose you are a widow in the 1400s? How would you support your family? Write a journal entry detailing your plans.

▲ *Silk in China has been woven on hand looms for many years.*

VOCABULARY

lowly
low rank or position in society

hemp
a fiber from the mulberry bush

loom
a frame or machine for weaving yarns or threads in order to make cloth

The Silk Industry in China

.During the 1600s Sung Ying-Hsing wrote a book on Chinese industry called T'ien-kung K'ai-wu (Chinese Technology in the Seventeenth Century), *which included sections on the production of silk.*

. . . Members of the aristocracy are clothed in flowing robes decorated with patterns of magnificent mountain dragons, and they are rulers of the country. Those of **lowly** stations would be dressed in **hempen** jackets and cotton garments to protect themselves from the cold winter and cover their nakedness in summer, in order to distinguish themselves from the birds and beasts. Therefore nature has provided the materials for clothing. Of these, the vegetable [plant] ones are cotton, hemp, meng hemp, and creeper hemp; those derived from birds, animals, and insects are furs, woolens, silk, and spun silk. . . .

But, although silk **looms** are to be found in all parts of the country, how many persons have actually seen the remarkable functioning of the draw-loom: Such words as "orderly government" [chih, i.e., the word used in silk reeling], "chaos" [luan, i.e., when the fibers are entangled], "knowledge or good policy" [ching-lun, i.e., the warp thread and the woven pattern] are known by every schoolboy, but is it not regrettable that he should never see the actual things that gave rise to these words?

DBQ Analyzing Historical Documents

1. ***Differentiating*** How was clothing used to establish class in Chinese society?
2. ***Identifying Points of View*** Which class of Chinese society do you suppose the narrator belongs to? Provide evidence from the excerpt to support your conclusion.
3. ***Listing*** According to Sung Ying-Hsing, from what sources was all clothing made?
4. ***Narrative*** Is class division apparent in the clothing of modern American society? Write a journal entry that describes your impression of clothing and class in your school. Are the two related?

PHOTO: Glow Images

from The Wealth of Nations

Adam Smith's most influential work was The Wealth of Nations. *In this excerpt, Smith argues that even though business leaders and investors are motivated to build businesses to make money for themselves, their work helps society as well. The "invisible hand" is an image Smith made famous as an explanation of why this happens.*

It is only for the sake of profit that any man employs a **capital** in the support of industry; and he will always, therefore, endeavor to employ it in the support of that industry of which the produce is likely to be of the greatest value, or to exchange for the greatest quantity either of money or of other goods.

But the annual revenue of every society is always precisely equal to the exchangeable value of the whole annual produce of its industry, or rather is precisely the same thing with that exchangeable value. As every individual, therefore, **endeavors** as much as he can both to employ his capital in the support of domestic industry, and so to direct that industry that its produce may be of the greatest value; every individual necessarily labors to render the annual revenue of the society as great as he can. He generally, indeed, neither intends to promote the public interest, nor knows how much he is promoting it. By preferring the support of domestic to that of foreign industry, he intends only his own security; and by directing that industry in such a manner as its produce may be of the greatest value, he intends only his own gain, and he is in this, as in many other cases, led by an invisible hand to promote an end which was no part of his intention. Nor is it always the worse for the society that it was no part of it. By pursuing his own interest he frequently promotes that of the society more effectually than when he really intends to promote it.

VOCABULARY

capital
In this context, Smith refers to money used for investment.

endeavors
to attempt to achieve

DBQ Analyzing Historical Documents

1. ***Analyzing*** How does Smith portray the nature of businessmen or investors?
2. ***Identifying*** What is the difference, according to Smith, between domestic and foreign industry?

▲ *Madame Aubry, Olympe de Gouges*

VOCABULARY

utility
something useful or designed for use

imprescriptible
cannot be taken away by law

rigorous
extremely strict

Declaration of the Rights of Woman and the Female Citizen

Olympe de Gouges composed her own Declaration of the Rights of Woman and the Female Citizen *in 1791. Following are excerpts.*

1. Woman is born free and lives as equal to man in her rights. Social distinctions can be based only on the common **utility**.
2. The purpose of any political association is the conservation of the natural and **imprescriptible** rights of woman and man; these rights are liberty, property, security, and especially resistance to oppression. . . .
3. Liberty and justice consist of restoring all that belongs to others; thus, the only limits on the exercise of the natural rights of woman are perpetual male tyranny; these limits are to be reformed by the laws of nature and reason. . . .
4. The law must be . . . the same for all: male and female citizens. . . .
5. No woman is an exception; she is accused, arrested, and detained in cases determined by law. Women, like men, obey this **rigorous** law. . . .
6. The free communication of thoughts and opinions is one of the most precious rights of woman, since that liberty assured the recognition of children by their fathers. . . .

DBQ Analyzing Historical Documents

❶ ***Listing*** According to Gouges, what are the four "imprescriptible rights" of men and women?

❷ ***Analyzing*** What does Gouges blame for the limits on the rights of women?

❸ ***Defending*** Olympe de Gouges states that free communication of thoughts is one of the most precious rights of women. Do you agree or disagree? Write a paragraph defending your position.

▲ 19th century portrait of Russian Czar Alexander II

▲ On March 1, 1881 Alexander II was assassinated. This magazine Illustration shows the Russian Chief of the Police escorting the czar's body to the Winter Palace.

Imperial Decree to Free the Serfs

In 1861 the Russian czar Alexander II issued the Emancipation Manifesto, *an imperial decree to free his country's serfs.*

By the grace of God, we, Alexander II, Emperor and **Autocrat** of all the Russias, King of Poland, Grand Duke of Finland, etc., to all our faithful subjects, make known: Examining the condition of classes and professions comprising the state, we became convinced that the present state legislation favors the upper and middle classes, . . . but does not equally favor the serfs. . . . These facts had already attracted the attention of our **predecessors**, and they had adopted measures aimed at improving the conditions of the peasants. But decrees on free farmers and serfs have been carried out on a limited scale only.

We thus came to the conviction that the work of a serious improvement of the condition of the peasants was a sacred inheritance **bequeathed** to us by our ancestors, a mission which, in the course of events Divine Providence called upon us to fulfill. . . .

In virtue of the new dispositions above mentioned, the peasants attached to the soil will be invested within a term fixed by the law with all the rights of free cultivators. . . .

At the same time, they are granted the right of purchasing their **close**, and, with the consent of the proprietors, they may acquire in full property the arable lands and other appurtenances [rights of way] which are allotted to them as a permanent holding. By the acquisition in full property of the quantity of land fixed, the peasants are free from their obligations towards the proprietors for land thus purchased, and they enter definitely into the condition of free peasants-landholders

VOCABULARY

autocrat
a monarch who rules with unlimited authority

predecessors
a person who has held a certain position or office before another

bequeathed
to leave property or possessions to someone in a will

close
an enclosed area of land

DBQ Analyzing Historical Documents

1. ***Identifying*** What new right did the decree give to serfs?
2. ***Predicting Consequences*** What affect do you think the decree had on the relationship between the classes?
3. ***Explaining*** Why does Czar Alexander II free the serfs?

▲ *Women worked long hours around heavy equipment for very little pay. This illustration shows a woman examining a power loom in a textile factory.*

VOCABULARY

abject
existing in a low state or condition

repose
to rest

league
a measure of distance between approximately 2.4 and 4.6 miles

The Unfortunate Situation of Working Women

This article was published in L'Atelier, *a Parisian workingman's newspaper, in 1842.*

Although women's work is less productive for society than that of men, it does, nevertheless, have a certain value, and, moreover, there are professions that only women can practice. For these, women are indispensable. . . . It is these very workers in all these necessary trades who earn the least and who are subject to the longest layoffs. Since for so much work they earn only barely enough to live from day to day, it happens that during times of unemployment they sink into **abject** poverty.

Who has not heard of the women silkworkers' dirty, unhealthy, and badly paid work; of the women in the spinning and weaving factories working fourteen to sixteen hours (except for one hour for both meals); always standing, without a single minute for **repose**, putting forth an enormous amount of effort. And many of them have to walk a **league** or more, morning and evening, to get home. Nor should we neglect to mention the danger that exists merely from working in these large factories, surrounded by wheels, gears, enormous leather belts that always threaten to seize you and pound you to pieces.

The existence of women who work as day laborers, and are obliged to abandon . . . the care of their children to indifferent neighbors is no better. . . . We believe that the condition of women will never really improve until workingmen can earn enough to support their families, which is only fair. Woman is so closely linked to man that the position of the one cannot be improved without reference to the position of the other.

DBQ Analyzing Historical Documents

1. ***Paraphrasing*** Using your own words, explain the author meant by "indifferent neighbors." How does this word choice convey the author's opinion about working women?

2. ***Describing*** How would you describe working conditions for women?

3. ***Identifying Points of View*** What is the attitude of the *L'Atelier* writer toward women and women's work? Is the author of the article likely to be a woman or a man? What makes you think so?

Dadabhai Naoroji was an outspoken Indian nationalist and a critic of Britain's economic policies in India. In his speech Poverty and Un-British Rule in India, he argued that Britain was overtaxing India.

The Impact of British Rule in India

In 1871 Dadabhai Naoroji commented on the benefits and the problems of British rule in India.

Benefits of British Rule:

In the Cause of Humanity: Abolition of suttee and **infanticide**. Civilization: Education, both male and female. . . . **Resuscitation** of India's own noble literature. Politically: Peace and order. Freedom of speech and liberty of the press. . . . Improvement of government in the native states. Security of life and property. Freedom from oppression. . . . Materially: Loans for railways and irrigation. Development of a few valuable products, such as indigo, tea, coffee, silk, etc. Increase of exports. Telegraphs.

The Detriments of British Rule:

In the Cause of Humanity: Nothing. Civilization: [T]here has been a failure to do as much as might have been done. Politically: Repeated breach of pledges to give the natives a fair and reasonable share in the higher administration of their own country, . . . an utter disregard of the feelings and views of the natives. Financially: [N]ew modes of taxation, without any adequate effort to increase the means of the people to pay.

Summary:

British rule has been: morally, a great blessing; politically, peace and order on one hand, **blunders** on the other; materially, **impoverishment**. . . . Our great misfortune is that you do not know our wants. When you will know our real wishes, I have not the least doubt that you would do justice. The genius and spirit of the British people is fair play and justice.

VOCABULARY

infanticide
killing an infant

resuscitation
restoration or renewal

blunders
mistakes

impoverishment
to make poor or to take riches from someone

DBQ Analyzing Historical Documents

1. ***Explaining*** According to Naoroji, did British rule improve certain ways of life for Indian men, women, or both? Explain your answer.
2. ***Listing*** What natural resources of India were developed under British rule? How could the development of natural resources cause problems for the two countries?
3. ***Defending*** Were the benefits of British rule in India worth the disadvantages? Write a paragraph explaining your position. Use evidence from the excerpt to defend your position.

▲ *Allied soldiers went "Over the Top" in the 1916 Battle of the Somme to battle German forces.*

An American Soldier Remembers World War I

Arthur Guy Empey reflects upon his experiences during World War I in the trenches in France. This is an excerpt from his book Over the Top.

Suddenly, the earth seemed to shake and a thunderclap burst in my ears. I opened my eyes,—I was splashed all over with sticky mud, and men were picking themselves up from the bottom of the trench. The **parapet** on my left had toppled into the trench, completely blocking it with a wall of tossed-up earth. The man on my left lay still. . . . A German "Minnie" (trench mortar) had exploded in the [trench].

. . . Stretcher-bearers came up the trench on the double. After a few minutes of digging, three still, muddy forms on stretchers were carried down the communication trench to the rear. Soon they would be resting "somewhere in France," with a little wooden cross over their heads. They had done their bit for King and Country, had died without firing a shot. . . . I was dazed and motionless. Suddenly a shovel was pushed into my hands, and a rough but kindly voice said: "Here, my lad, lend a hand clearing the trench, but keep your head down, and look out for **snipers**. . . ."

Lying on my belly on the bottom of the trench, I filled sandbags with the sticky mud.

. . . The harder I worked, the better I felt.

Occasionally a bullet would crack overhead, and a machine gun would kick up the mud on the bashed-in parapet. At each crack I would duck and shield my face with my arm. One of the older men noticed this action of mine, and whispered: "Don't duck at the crack of a bullet, Yank; the danger has passed,—you never hear the one that wings you. Always remember that if you are going to get it, you'll get it, so never worry." . . . [Days later] we received the cheerful news that at four in the morning we were to go over the top and take the German frontline trench. My heart turned to lead.

VOCABULARY

parapet
wall of earth piled on top of a trench

snipers
people who shoot at exposed individuals from a concealed location

DBQ Analyzing Historical Documents

1. ***Using Context Clues*** The title of the excerpt tells the reader that the narrator is American. What clue from the excerpt also reveals this fact?

2. ***Integrating Visual Information*** Study the photograph. Does it convey the mood of the excerpt? How?

3. ***Expressing*** How does Arthur Guy Empey uses sarcasm in the final paragraph?

▲ *Mohandas Gandhi led a campaign of nonviolent resistance against British rule in India until his assassination in 1948.*

Gandhi Takes the Path of Civil Disobedience

Mohandas Gandhi explains why British rule in India must end.

Before embarking on **civil disobedience** and taking the risk I have dreaded to take all these years, I would fain approach you and find a way out.

My personal faith is absolutely clear. I cannot intentionally hurt anything that lives, much less fellow human beings, even though they may do the greatest wrong to me and mine. Whilst, therefore, I hold the British rule to be a curse, I do not intend harm to a single Englishman or to any legitimate interest he may have in India.

. . . Though I hold the British rule in India to be a curse, I do not, therefore, consider Englishmen in general to be worse than any other people on earth. I have the privilege of claiming many Englishmen as dearest friends. Indeed much that I have learned of the evil of British rule is due to the writings of frank and courageous Englishmen who have not hesitated to tell the truth about that rule.

And why do I regard British rule as a curse? It has impoverished the ignorant millions by a system of progressive **exploitation** and by a ruinously expensive military and civil administration which the country can never afford.

It has reduced us politically to serfdom. It has sapped the foundations of our culture. And, by the policy of cruel **disarmament**, it has degraded us spiritually. Lacking the inward strength, we have been reduced . . . to a state bordering on cowardly helplessness. . . .

VOCABULARY

civil disobedience
refusal to obey government demands

exploitation
unfair use for one's own advantage

disarmament
reducing or eliminating weapons

DBQ Analyzing Historical Documents

1. ***Making Inferences*** Using what you know about the relationship between Britain and India and the concept of serfdom, explain what Gandhi meant when he stated that India had been "reduced . . . to serfdom."
2. ***Determining Word Meanings*** Based on the context clues provided in the text, how would you define the word "frank?"
3. ***Analyzing*** Why do you think Gandhi believed that nonviolent civil disobedience would encourage the British to free India? Write a short "letter to the editor" of a British newspaper in support of the policies of either Britain or Ghandi. Provide examples to defend your position.

▲ Children gather behind a barbed-wire fence while imprisoned at Auschwitz concentration camp in Poland in 1945.

▲ These railroad tracks brought thousands of Jews to Auschwitz Millions of Jewish men, women, and children were killed at this camp during World War II.

The Holocaust—The Camp Victims

A French doctor describes the victims of one of the gas chambers at Auschwitz-Birkenau during the Holocaust.

It is mid-day, when a long line of women, children, and old people enter the yard. The senior official in charge . . . climbs on a bench to tell them that they are going to have a bath and that afterwards they will get a drink of hot coffee. They all undress in the yard. . . . The doors are opened and an **indescribable jostling** begins. The first people to enter the gas chamber begin to draw back. They sense the death which awaits them. The SS men put and end to the pushing and shoving with blows from their rifle butts beating the heads of the horrified women who are desperately hugging their children. The massive oak double doors are shut. For two endless minutes one can hear banging on the walls and screams which are no longer human. And then—not a sound. Five minutes later the doors are opened. The corpses, **squashed** together and **distorted**, fall out like a waterfall. The bodies which are still warm pass through the hands of the hairdresser who cuts their hair and the dentist who pulls out their gold teeth. . .

VOCABULARY

indescribable
impossible to explain or describe

jostling
pushing around

squashed
to end or stop something by using force

distorted
to unnaturally twist

DBQ Analyzing Historical Documents

1. ***Identifying Points of View*** What is the French doctor's point of view about the events he describes at the Auschwitz-Birkenau death camp?
2. ***Using Context Clues*** Which words or phrases from the excerpt provide evidence that the doctor was horrified by the event?
3. ***Analyzing Visual Information*** Study the photographs from the concentration camp. How do the photographs convey the mood of the excerpt?

▲ *Nelson Mandela visits the jail cell where he served a twenty-seven year sentence for opposition to apartheid. He became the first democratically elected president of South Africa in 1994.*

An Ideal for Which I am Prepared to Die

Nelson Mandela delivered his speech "I am the First Accused" during the Rivonia Trial in Pretoria, South Africa on April 20, 1964. Following the trial, he was sentenced to life in prison. The following is an excerpt from his speech.

. . . The whites enjoy what may well be the highest standard of living in the world, whilst Africans live in poverty and misery. Forty percent of the Africans live in hopelessly overcrowded and, in some cases, drought-stricken **reserves**, where soil erosion and the overworking of the soil make it impossible for them to live properly off the land. Thirty percent are labourers, labour tenants, and **squatters** on white farms . . . The other thirty percent live in towns where they have developed economic and social habits which bring them closer, in many respects, to white standards. Forty-six percent of all African families in Johannesburg do not earn enough to keep them going. . . .

. . . The complaint of Africans, however, is not only that they are poor and whites are rich, but that the laws which are made by the whites are designed to preserve this situation. . . .

. . . During my lifetime I have dedicated my life to this struggle of the African people. I have fought against white **domination**, and I have fought against black domination. I have cherished the ideal of a democratic and free society in which all persons live together in harmony with equal opportunities. It is an ideal which I hope to live for, and to see realized. It is an ideal which I hope to live for and to achieve. But if needs be, it is an ideal for which I am prepared to die.

VOCABULARY

reserves
a reservation; land set aside for use by a particular group

squatters
those who settle on public land without rights or permission

domination
to hold a commanding position or controlling power over something or someone

DBQ Analyzing Historical Documents

1. ***Analyzing*** According to Mandela, what role does soil play in South Africa's divided society?
2. ***Identifying*** What argument do poor South Africans make regarding the country's laws?
3. ***Explaining*** What ideal does Nelson Mandela discuss?

from "A new chapter in China's reform and opening"

World Trade Organization Director-General Pascal Lamy, in a speech at a forum in Beijing on 11 December 2011 commemorating the 10th anniversary of China's inclusion in the WTO.

Ten years is a long minute in China's **millenary** history. And yet these ten years have witnessed an unprecedented transformation of China's economy and society.

My first trip to China was in the 1980s, accompanying the then President of the European Commission on his first visit to Deng Xiaoping. Bicycles in ChangAn Street were the rule. . . . Ten years later, the streets of Beijing are crowded with family cars, not bicycles. . . . Millions of Chinese farmers have moved to the cities, employed by a rapidly expanding industrial sector, including multinational corporations which have come into China at unprecedented speed since 2001 and played a key part in creating a network of global value chains. . . .

China's accession to the WTO proved decisive in several respects.

The goal to become a WTO member acted as a lever for the process of domestic modernization. . . .

WTO membership also underpinned Chinese export-led growth with a strong insurance policy against **protectionism**.

. . . And yet the lesson learnt from the recent global economic crisis is that the WTO has a significant role to play as a bulwark against protectionism. This is particularly true of China which would have been much more severely affected by protectionist measures, given its prominence in world trade. The WTO has so far protected China against high intensity protectionism during the crisis.

Looking into the future, as a key member of the WTO family, China's role and influence will be vital in our collective endeavour to advance trade opening and global trade regulation. . . .

Today, the Chinese economy and its influence are greater and stronger than ten years ago. As a global power, it is only natural that the expectations of other countries on China have also grown. China's participation and support are vital in any collective action to address global challenges. With today's economic difficulties across the world, resolve and leadership are in desperate need. We all need a **proactive** China. . . .

On this tenth anniversary, and as we look forward for the next decade, I have two wishes that I would like to express.

The first is that China's involvement in the WTO helps us all in keeping this organization on the move towards more open and fairer trade.

The second is that the WTO's relevance for China keeps growing and helps this country to address its reform challenges.

VOCABULARY

millenary
relating to 1,000 years

protectionism
an economic system that aims to encourage growth of domestic business and industry by placing restrictions on foreign imports

proactive
to anticipate and devise plans to solve future problems

DBQ Analyzing Historical Documents

1. ***Analyzing*** How does Pascal Lamy view the global role of China now and going forward?

2. ***Identifying*** What has changed in China's economy since it was granted admission into the World Trade Organization?

from Tawakkol Karman's Nobel Peace Prize Speech

In 2011, Tawakkol Kaman gave her acceptance speech in receipt of the Nobel Peace Prize. She spoke about the democratic movement, known as the Arab Spring, that was affecting her home country of Yemen.

"Your Majesties, Highnesses, Excellencies, Distinguished Committee of the Nobel Peace Prize, Arab spring and revolution youth in the arena of freedom and change, and all free people of the world,

Peace upon you from the Nobel Peace **rostrum**.

. . . Alfred Nobel's dream of a world, where peace prevails and wars disappear, has not been achieved yet, but the hope to make it come true has grown large, and the effort to achieve it has doubled. The Nobel Peace Prize still offers this hope spiritual and conscientious momentum. For more than a hundred years, this award has stood as proof of the values of peaceful struggle for rights, justice and freedom, and also as proof of how wrong violence and wars are with all their backfiring and devastating results.

I have always believed that resistance against repression and violence is possible without relying on similar represson and violence. I have always believed that human civilization is the fruit of the effort of both women and men. So, when women are treated unjustly and are deprived of their natural right in this process, all social deficiencies and cultural illnesses will be unfolded, and in the end the whole community, men and women, will suffer. The solution to women's issues can only be achieved in a free and democratic society in which human energy is liberated, the energy of both women and men together. Our civilization is called human civilization and is not attributed only to men or women.

. . . At this moment, as I speak to you here, young Arab people, both women and men, march in peaceful demonstrations demanding freedom and dignity from their rulers. They go forward on this noble path armed not with weapons, but with faith in their right to freedom and dignity. They march in a dramatic scene which embodies the most beautiful of the human spirit of sacrifice and the **aspiration** to freedom and life, against the ugliest forms of selfishness, injustice, and the desire to hold on to power and wealth.

. . . The democratic world, which has told us a lot about the virtues of democracy and good governance, should not be indifferent to what is happening in Yemen and Syria, and happened before that in Tunisia, Egypt, and Libya, and happens in every Arab and non-Arab country aspiring for freedom. All of that is just hard labour during the birth of democracy which requires support and assistance, not fear and caution.

Allow me, ladies and gentlemen, to share my belief that peace will remain the hope of mankind forever, and that the best hope for a better future for mankind will always drive us to speak noble words and do noble deeds. Together, we will push the horizons, one after another, towards a world of true human perfection. . . .

VOCABULARY

rostrum
a stage or platform for public speaking

aspiration
the desire to achieve a goal

DBQ Analyzing Historical Documents

1. ***Analyzing*** What is Kaman's view about the equality of men and women?

2. ***Identifying*** How does Kaman believe democracies in the West should react to the protests that made up the Arab Spring movement?

from the "World Economic Outlook"

Olivier Blanchard was the Economic Counsellor of the International Monetary Fund, a group of 188 countries whose aim is to encourage stable global economic activity and global economic growth. In this segment of the World Economic Outlook report, Blanchard discusses the economic crisis that hit the European Union economies in the first decade of the twenty-first century.

Soon after the September 2011 *World Economic Outlook* went to press, the euro area went through another **acute** crisis. . . . With the value of some of [Spain and Italy's] banks' assets now in doubt, questions arose as to whether those banks would be able to convince investors to roll over their loans. Worried about funding, banks froze credit. Confidence decreased, and activity slumped.

Strong policy responses turned things around. Elections in Spain and the appointment of a new prime minister in Italy gave some reassurance to investors. The adoption of a fiscal compact showed the commitment of EU members to dealing with their deficits and debt. . . .

With the passing of the crisis, and some good news about the U.S. economy, some optimism has returned. It should remain **tempered**. Even absent another European crisis, most advanced economies still face major brakes on growth. . . .

[There are] two main brakes on growth: fiscal consolidation and **bank deleveraging**. Both reflect needed adjustments, but both decrease growth in the short term. . . .

Emerging economies are not immune to these developments. Low advanced economy growth has meant lower export growth. And financial uncertainty, together with sharp shifts in risk appetite, has led to volatile capital flows. For the most part, however, emerging economies have enough policy room to maintain solid growth. . . .

Turning to policies aimed at reducing risks, the focus is clearly on Europe. . . . Measures should be taken to decrease the links between sovereigns and banks, from the creation of euro level deposit insurance and bank resolution to the introduction of limited forms of Eurobonds, such as the creation of a common euro bill market. These measures are urgently needed and can make a difference were another crisis to take place soon.

Taking one step back, perhaps the highest priority, but also the most difficult to achieve, is to durably increase growth in advanced economies, and especially in Europe. . . . For the moment, the focus should be on measures that increase demand. Looking forward, however, the focus should also be on measures that increase potential growth. The Holy Grail would be measures that do both. There are probably few of those. More realistically, the search must be for reforms that help in the long term but do not depress demand in the short term. Identifying these reforms, and addressing their potentially adverse short-term effects, should be very high on the policy agenda.

VOCABULARY

acute
characterized by severity or size of problem

tempered
qualifying or adjusting a point of view, not jumping to a conclusion

bank deleveraging
the action of a bank reducing its amount of debt, in proportion to its amount of fiscal assets

DBQ Analyzing Historical Documents

1. ***Analyzing*** How can bank deleveraging help in the context of the fiscal crisis that was being battled in Europe?

2. ***Identifying*** What is meant by the recommendation to "decrease the links between sovereigns and banks"?

CONTENTS

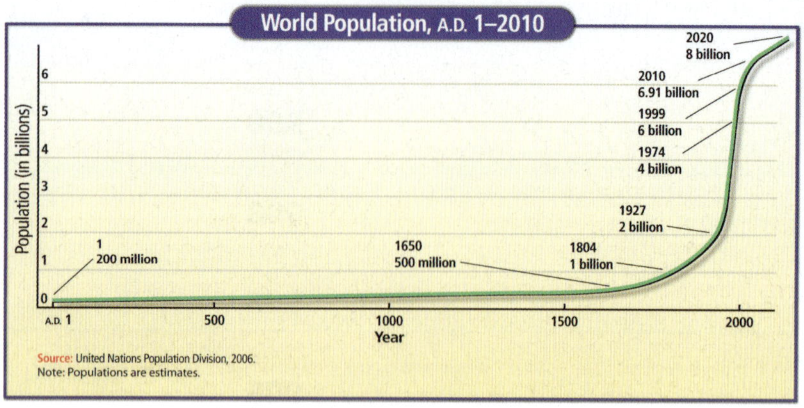

Population by Continent, 2012

Continent	Population, 2010	Projected Population 2050
Asia	4.133 billion	5.167 billion
Africa	1.015 billion	2.138 billion
Europe	734 million	671 million
North America	539 million	739 million
South America	396 million	520 million
Australia/Oceania	35 million	49 million

Source: www.census.gov

Life Expectancy

Country	Years
Japan	83.91
Andorra	82.50
France	81.46
Israel	81.07
New Zealand	80.71
United Kingdom	80.17
United States	78.49
Chile	78.10
China	74.84
Egypt	72.93
Brazil	72.79
India	67.14
Russia	66.46
Mozambique	52.02
South Africa	49.41

Source: *The World Factbook*, 2012, CIA

Infant Mortality

Country	Infant Deaths per 1,000 Live Births
South Africa	43
India	46
Egypt	24
Brazil	21
China	16
Russia	10
Chile	8
United States	6
South Korea	4
United Kindgom	5
Canada	5
Germany	4
France	3
Japan	2

Source: *The World Factbook*, 2012, CIA

Most Populous Countries

Country	Population
China	1,340,000,000
India	1,200,000,000
United States	314,000,000
Indonesia	249,000,000
Brazil	200,000,000
Pakistan	190,000,000
Nigeria	170,000,000
Bangladesh	161,000,000
Russia	143,000,000
Japan	127,000,000

Source: *The World Factbook*, 2012, CIA

World's Richest Countries

Country	Gross National Income per Capita (in U.S. dollars)
Liechtenstein	141,000
Qatar	104,300
Luxembourg	81,100
Bermuda	69,900
Singapore	60,500
Jersey	57,000
Falkland Islands	55,400
Norway	54,200
Brunei	50,000
Hong Kong	49,800

Source: *The World Factbook*, 2012, CIA

World's Poorest Countries

Country	Gross National Income per Capita (in U.S. dollars)
The Democratic Republic of Congo	400
Liberia	500
Zimbabwe	500
Burundi	600
Somalia	600
Eritrea	700
Niger	800
Central African Republic	800
Madagascar	900
Malawi	900

Source: *The World Factbook*, 2012, CIA

Highest Inflation Rates

Country	Rate of Inflation (percent)
Belarus	52.40
Ethiopia	33.20
Venezuela	26.10
Iran	22.50
Argentina	22.00
Yemen	20.00
Eritrea	20.00
Suriname	19.50
Uganda	18.70
Vietnam	18.70

Source: *The World Factbook*, 2012, CIA

Lowest Inflation Rates

Country	Rate of Inflation (percent)
Bahrain	-0.40
Japan	-0.30
Kiribati	0.20
Switzerland	0.20
Liechtenstein	0.30
Saint Maarten	0.70
United Arab Emirates	0.90
Vanuatu	0.90
French Polynesia	1.10

Source: *The World Factbook*, 2012, CIA

World's Ten Largest Economies

Economy	GDP (Purchasing Power Parity in U.S. Dollars)
European Union	15.7 trillion
United States	15.3 trillion
China	11.4 trillion
India	4.5 trillion
Japan	4.5 trillion
Germany	3.1 trillion
Russia	2.4 trillion
Brazil	2.3 trillion
United Kingdom	2.3 trillion
France	2.2 trillion

Source: *The World Factbook*, 2012, CIA

Regional Water and Sanitation

Region	Access to Improved Water	Access to Improved Sanitation
World	87	61
Middle East and North Africa	87	84
Latin America and Caribbean	93	79
Europe and Central Asia	95	89
East Asia and Pacific	88	59
South Asia	87	36
Sub-Saharan Africa	60	31

Source: *The World Factbook*, 2012, CIA

Highest Adult Literacy Rates

Country	Rate of Literacy (percent)
Andorra	100
Finland	100
Greenland	100
Liechtenstein	100
Norway	100
Cuba	99.8
Estonia	99.8
Azerbaijan	99.8
Georgia	99.7

Source: *The World Factbook*, 2012, CIA

Lowest Adult Literacy Rates

Country	Rate of Literacy (percent)
Burkina Faso	21.8
South Sudan	27
Afghanistan	28.1
Niger	28.7
Chad	34.5
Sierra Leone	35.1
Somalia	37.8
Senegal	39.3
Guinea	41

Source: *The World Factbook*, 2012, CIA

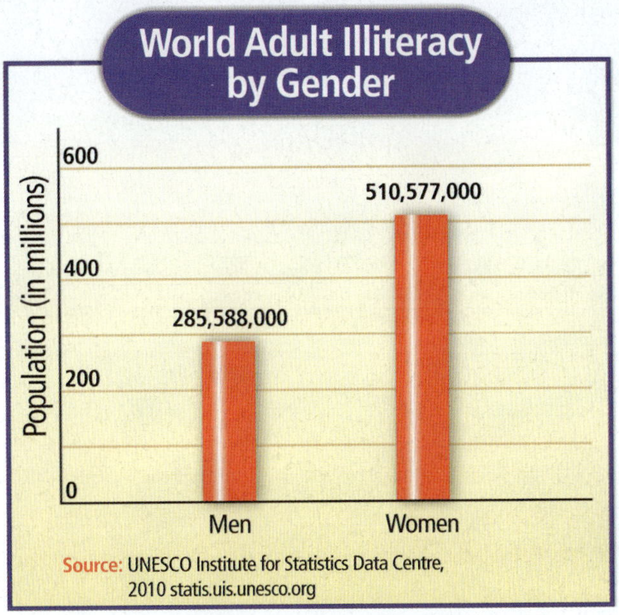

Years, by Country, in Which Women Gained the Right to Vote

Year	Country	Year	Country
1893	New Zealand	1945	Italy
1902	Australia	1945	Japan
1913	Norway	1947	Argentina
1918	United Kingdom	1947	Mexico
1918	Canada	1950	India
1919	Germany	1952	Greece
1920	United States	1956	Egypt
1930	South Africa	1963	Kenya
1934	Brazil	1971	Switzerland
1944	France	1980	Iraq

Source: *The World Factbook*, 2012, CIA

Highest Military Expenditures

Country	GDP	Billions of U.S. Dollars per Year	Percentage of Gross Domestic Product (GDP)
United States	15.29	626.89	4.1
China	11.44	491.92	4.3
France	2.246	58.36	2.6
Japan	4.497	3.5976	0.8
United Kingdom	2.29	61.83	2.7
Germany	3.139	47.085	1.5
Italy	1.871	33.678	1.8
South Korea	1.574	42.498	2.7
India	4.515	112.87	2.5
Saudi Arabia	691.5	691.5	10.0

Source: *The World Factbook*, 2012, CIA

Nuclear Weapons Capability

Country	Date of First Test
United States	1945
Russia (Soviet Union)	1949
United Kingdom	1952
France	1960
China	1964
India	1974
Pakistan	1998
North Korea	2006

Source: U.S. Department of State and *TIME* magazine

Reference Atlas

ATLAS KEY

SYMBOL KEY

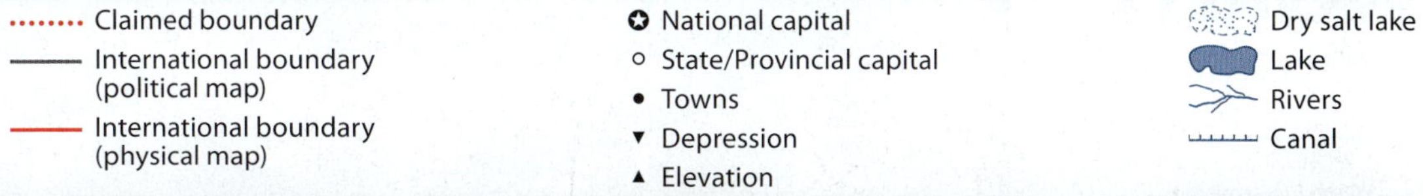

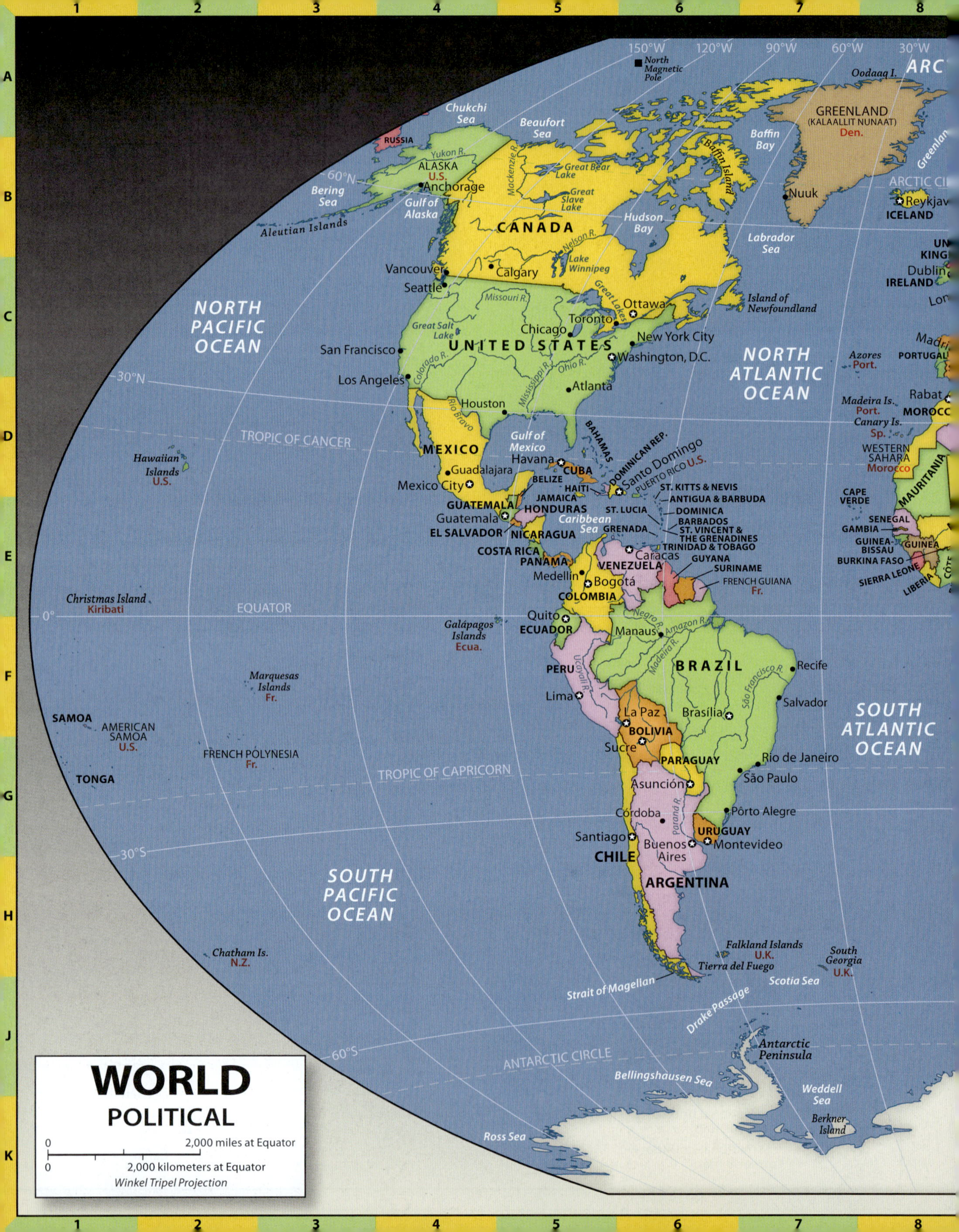
WORLD
POLITICAL
0
2,000 miles at Equator
0
2,000 kilometers at Equator
Winkel Tripel Projection
150°W
120°W
90°W
60°W
30°W
North Magnetic Pole
Oodaaq I.
ARC
Chukchi Sea
Beaufort Sea
RUSSIA
Yukon R.
ALASKA
U.S.
Anchorage
60°N
Bering Sea
Gulf of Alaska
Aleutian Islands
Mackenzie R.
Great Bear Lake
Great Slave Lake
Baffin Island
Baffin Bay
GREENLAND
(KALAALLIT NUNAAT)
Den.
Nuuk
ARCTIC CI
Reykjav
ICELAND
CANADA
Hudson Bay
Nelson R.
Lake Winnipeg
Labrador Sea
Vancouver
Calgary
Seattle
Great Lakes
Ottawa
Island of Newfoundland
UN
KING
Dublin
IRELAND
Lon
NORTH PACIFIC OCEAN
Missouri R.
Great Salt Lake
Toronto
Chicago
New York City
San Francisco
UNITED STATES
Washington, D.C.
Colorado R.
Ohio R.
Mississippi R.
Los Angeles
30°N
Atlanta
NORTH ATLANTIC OCEAN
Azores
Port.
Madri
PORTUGAL
Houston
Rio Bravo
Madeira Is.
Port.
Rabat
MOROCC
Canary Is.
Sp.
TROPIC OF CANCER
Gulf of Mexico
BAHAMAS
WESTERN SAHARA
Morocco
MAURITANIA
Hawaiian Islands
U.S.
MEXICO
Havana
CUBA
DOMINICAN REP.
Santo Domingo
PUERTO RICO U.S.
Guadalajara
BELIZE
HAITI
Mexico City
JAMAICA
ST. KITTS & NEVIS
ANTIGUA & BARBUDA
CAPE VERDE
GUATEMALA
HONDURAS
ST. LUCIA
DOMINICA
Guatemala
Caribbean Sea
BARBADOS
SENEGAL
GAMBIA
EL SALVADOR
NICARAGUA
GRENADA
ST. VINCENT & THE GRENADINES
GUINEA-BISSAU
GUINEA
COSTA RICA
TRINIDAD & TOBAGO
Caracas
GUYANA
BURKINA FASO
PANAMA
VENEZUELA
SURINAME
SIERRA LEONE
Medellín
Bogotá
FRENCH GUIANA
Fr.
LIBERIA
Côte
Christmas Island
Kiribati
COLOMBIA
EQUATOR
0°
Quito
Negro R.
Amazon R.
Galápagos Islands
Ecua.
ECUADOR
Manaus
Madeira R.
PERU
BRAZIL
Recife
Ucayali R.
São Francisco R.
Marquesas Islands
Fr.
Lima
Salvador
SOUTH ATLANTIC OCEAN
SAMOA
AMERICAN SAMOA
U.S.
La Paz
Brasília
BOLIVIA
Sucre
FRENCH POLYNESIA
Fr.
PARAGUAY
Rio de Janeiro
TONGA
TROPIC OF CAPRICORN
São Paulo
Asunción
Paraná R.
Pôrto Alegre
Córdoba
URUGUAY
Santiago
Buenos Aires
Montevideo
30°S
CHILE
ARGENTINA
SOUTH PACIFIC OCEAN
Falkland Islands
U.K.
South Georgia
U.K.
Chatham Is.
N.Z.
Tierra del Fuego
Strait of Magellan
Scotia Sea
Drake Passage
Antarctic Peninsula
60°S
ANTARCTIC CIRCLE
Bellingshausen Sea
Weddell Sea
Berkner Island
Ross Sea
1
2
3
4
5
6
7
8
A
B
C
D
E
F
G
H
J
K

9
10
11
12
13
14
15
16
A
B
C
D
E
F
G
H
J
K
30°E
60°E
90°E
120°E
150°E
OCEAN
N
Svalbard
Nor.
Franz Josef Land
Barents Sea
Novaya Zemlya
Severnaya Zemlya
Kara Sea
New Siberian Islands
Laptev Sea
East Siberian Sea
Norwegian Sea
Lena R.
Yenisey R.
60°N
Bering Sea
Kamchatka Peninsula
Sea of Okhotsk
Sakhalin
Yakutsk
RUSSIA
Ob' R.
Angara R.
Irtysh R.
Volga R.
Amur R.
Lake Baikal
NORWAY
SWEDEN
FINLAND
Oslo
St. Petersburg
Yekaterinburg
Omsk
Novosibirsk
Baltic Sea
EST.
LATVIA
LITH.
DENMARK
NETH.
Moscow
Samara
POLAND
BELARUS
GERMANY
BELG.
CZECH REP.
Kyiv (Kiev)
UKRAINE
MOLD.
Paris
SWITZ.
AUST.
SLOV.
HUNG.
SLOVAKIA
ROMANIA
CROAT.
SERB.
FRANCE
ITALY
BULGARIA
Black Sea
Rome
MACED.
ALB.
KOS.
GREECE
Astana
KAZAKHSTAN
Aral Sea
Ural R.
Caspian Sea
AZERBAIJAN
GEORGIA
ARMENIA
Ankara
TURKEY
Almaty
Bishkek
Tashkent
UZBEKISTAN
KYRGYZSTAN
TAJIKISTAN
TURKMENISTAN
Dushanbe
Ashkhabad
Kabul
AFGHANISTAN
Islamabad
Lahore
Tehran
IRAN
Ulaanbaatar
MONGOLIA
Harbin
NORTH KOREA
Sea of Japan (East Sea)
Hokkaidō
Sapporo
Honshū
Shenyang
Beijing
Tianjin
P'yŏngyang
Seoul
SOUTH KOREA
JAPAN
Tokyo
Osaka
Kyūshū
Huang He (Yellow R.)
CHINA
Chang Jiang (Yangtze R.)
Shanghai
Chengdu
Wuhan
East China Sea
The People's Republic of China claims Taiwan as its 23rd province.
Taipei
TAIWAN
Guangzhou
Hong Kong
NORTH PACIFIC OCEAN
30°N
Philippine Sea
Mediterranean Sea
Algiers
TUNISIA
Tripoli
CYPRUS
LEBANON
ISRAEL
SYRIA
IRAQ
Baghdad
JORDAN
KUWAIT
ALGERIA
LIBYA
Cairo
EGYPT
Nile R.
BAHRAIN
QATAR
Riyadh
SAUDI ARABIA
U.A.E.
OMAN
Red Sea
PAKISTAN
Indus R.
Karachi
Masqat
New Delhi
Delhi
NEPAL
BHUTAN
Brahmaputra R.
Ganges R.
BANGLADESH
Dhaka
Kolkata (Calcutta)
MYANMAR (BURMA)
Nay Pyi Taw
LAOS
Hanoi
VIETNAM
Hainan
South China Sea
Luzon
Manila
PHILIPPINES
NORTHERN MARIANA ISLANDS
U.S.
NIGER
CHAD
ERITREA
Khartoum
SUDAN
Sanaa
YEMEN
DJIBOUTI
Socotra
Yemen
Arabian Sea
Mumbai (Bombay)
INDIA
Hyderabad
Bay of Bengal
Bengaluru (Bangalore)
Chennai (Madras)
THAILAND
Bangkok
CAMBODIA
Phnom Penh
Ho Chi Minh City
Niamey
N'Djamena
NIGERIA
GHANA
BENIN
Lagos
CAMEROON
CENTRAL AFRICAN REPUBLIC
Addis Ababa
SOUTH SUDAN
ETHIOPIA
SOMALIA
Juba
Bangui
EQ. GUINEA
GABON
DEM. REP. OF THE CONGO
CONGO
UGANDA
KENYA
Mogadishu
Nairobi
SÃO TOMÉ & PRÍNCIPE
CABINDA
Ang.
Brazzaville
Kinshasa
RWANDA
BURUNDI
SEYCHELLES
Dodoma
Dar es Salaam
TANZANIA
Luanda
ANGOLA
ZAMBIA
MALAWI
COMOROS
Lusaka
SRI LANKA
Colombo
MALDIVES
EQUATOR
BRUNEI
MALAYSIA
Kuala Lumpur
Borneo
SINGAPORE
Sumatra
Celebes
Mindanao
PALAU
MARSHALL ISLANDS
FEDERATED STATES OF MICRONESIA
KIRIBATI
NAURU
INDONESIA
Java
Jakarta
Surabaya
New Guinea
PAPUA NEW GUINEA
Port Moresby
SOLOMON ISLANDS
TUVALU
INDIAN OCEAN
EAST TIMOR (TIMOR-LESTE)
Arafura Sea
Darwin
Coral Sea
VANUATU
FIJI ISLANDS
New Caledonia
Fr.
Antananarivo
MADAGASCAR
MAURITIUS
Réunion
Fr.
NAMIBIA
Harare
ZIMBABWE
MOZAMBIQUE
BOTSWANA
Windhoek
Gaborone
Tshwane (Pretoria)
Maputo
SWAZILAND
Bloemfontein
LESOTHO
SOUTH AFRICA
Cape Town
AUSTRALIA
Brisbane
Perth
Darling R.
Murray R.
Sydney
Canberra
Melbourne
SOUTH PACIFIC OCEAN
30°S
North Island
Tasman Sea
Auckland
NEW ZEALAND
Wellington
South Island
Tasmania
PRIME MERIDIAN (MERIDIAN OF GREENWICH)
Kerguelen Islands
Fr.
The Atlantic, Indian, and Pacific Oceans merge around Antarctica. Some define this as an ocean, calling it the Antarctic Ocean, Austral Ocean, or Southern Ocean. While most accept four oceans (including the Arctic Ocean), there is little international agreement on the name and extent of a fifth ocean.
SOUTHERN OCEAN
South Magnetic Pole
60°S
Ross Sea
ANTARCTICA
ABBREVIATIONS
ALB. .... ALBANIA
AUST. .... AUSTRIA
B.&H. .... BOSNIA & HERZEGOVINA
BELG. .... BELGIUM
CROAT. .... CROATIA
CZECH REP. .... CZECH REPUBLIC
DEM. REP. OF THE CONGO .... DEMOCRATIC REPUBLIC OF THE CONGO
EQ. GUINEA .... EQUATORIAL GUINEA
EST. .... ESTONIA
HUNG. .... HUNGARY
KOS. .... KOSOVO
LITH. .... LITHUANIA
MACED. .... MACEDONIA
MOLD. .... MOLDOVA
NETH. .... NETHERLANDS
SERB. .... SERBIA
MONT. .... MONTENEGRO
SLOV. .... SLOVENIA
SWITZ. .... SWITZERLAND
U.A.E. .... UNITED ARAB EMIRATES

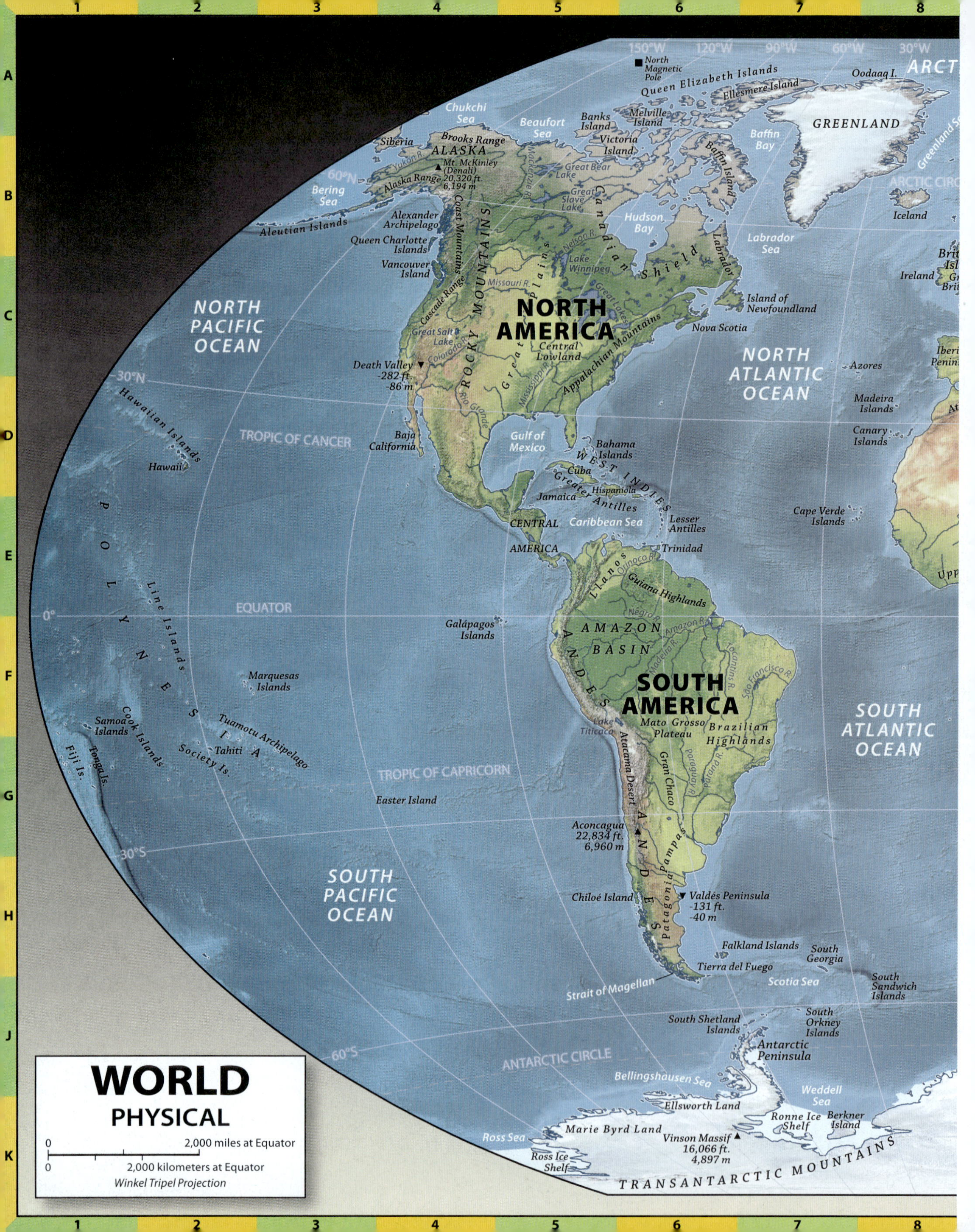
WORLD
PHYSICAL
0 2,000 miles at Equator
0 2,000 kilometers at Equator
Winkel Tripel Projection
150°W
120°W
90°W
60°W
30°W
60°N
30°N
0°
30°S
60°S
North Magnetic Pole
Queen Elizabeth Islands
Ellesmere Island
Oodaaq I.
GREENLAND
Chukchi Sea
Beaufort Sea
Banks Island
Melville Island
Victoria Island
Baffin Bay
Baffin Island
Siberia
Brooks Range
ALASKA
Mt. McKinley (Denali) 20,320 ft. 6,194 m
Alaska Range
Yukon R.
Mackenzie R.
Great Bear Lake
Great Slave Lake
Bering Sea
Aleutian Islands
Alexander Archipelago
Queen Charlotte Islands
Vancouver Island
Coast Mountains
Cascade Range
ROCKY MOUNTAINS
Hudson Bay
Canadian Shield
Labrador
Labrador Sea
Iceland
Ireland
ARCTIC CIRCLE
Nelson R.
Lake Winnipeg
Missouri R.
Great Plains
Great Lakes
NORTH AMERICA
Central Lowland
Appalachian Mountains
Island of Newfoundland
Nova Scotia
NORTH PACIFIC OCEAN
NORTH ATLANTIC OCEAN
Great Salt Lake
Colorado R.
Death Valley -282 ft. -86 m
Mississippi R.
Rio Grande
Azores
Madeira Islands
Canary Islands
Hawaiian Islands
Hawaii
TROPIC OF CANCER
Baja California
Gulf of Mexico
Bahama Islands
WEST INDIES
Cuba
Greater Antilles
Hispaniola
Jamaica
Lesser Antilles
CENTRAL AMERICA
Caribbean Sea
Trinidad
Cape Verde Islands
POLYNESIA
Line Islands
Llanos
Orinoco R.
Guiana Highlands
EQUATOR
Galápagos Islands
AMAZON BASIN
Negro R.
Amazon R.
Madeira R.
Tocantins R.
São Francisco R.
ANDES
SOUTH AMERICA
Marquesas Islands
SOUTH ATLANTIC OCEAN
Lake Titicaca
Mato Grosso Plateau
Brazilian Highlands
Samoa Islands
Cook Islands
Fiji Is.
Tonga Is.
Tuamotu Archipelago
Tahiti
Society Is.
Atacama Desert
Gran Chaco
Paraguay R.
Paraná R.
TROPIC OF CAPRICORN
Easter Island
Aconcagua 22,834 ft. 6,960 m
Pampas
SOUTH PACIFIC OCEAN
Chiloé Island
Valdés Peninsula -131 ft. -40 m
Patagonia
Falkland Islands
South Georgia
Tierra del Fuego
Scotia Sea
South Sandwich Islands
Strait of Magellan
South Shetland Islands
South Orkney Islands
Antarctic Peninsula
ANTARCTIC CIRCLE
Bellingshausen Sea
Weddell Sea
Ellsworth Land
Ronne Ice Shelf
Berkner Island
Ross Sea
Marie Byrd Land
Vinson Massif 16,066 ft. 4,897 m
Ross Ice Shelf
TRANSANTARCTIC MOUNTAINS

9
10
11
12
13
14
15
16
30°E
60°E
90°E
120°E
150°E
OCEAN
N
Svalbard
Barents Sea
Kara Sea
Severnaya Zemlya
New Siberian Islands
Laptev Sea
East Siberian Sea
Novaya Zemlya
Norwegian Sea
Scandinavia
North Sea
Baltic Sea
Northern European Plain
EUROPE
Ural Mountains
Yenisey R.
Central Siberian Plateau
S I B E R I A
West Siberian Plain
Ob R.
Irtysh R.
Lena R.
Angara R.
Sea of Okhotsk
Bering Sea
Kamchatka Peninsula
Aleutian Is.
60°N
Lake Baikal
Amur R.
Volga R.
Elbrus
18,510 ft.
5,642 m
Caucasus Mts.
The Steppes
Aral Sea
Caspian Sea
Altay Shan
ASIA
GOBI
Kuril Islands
Hokkaidō
Alps
Danube R.
Black Sea
Corsica
Sardinia
Sicily
Mediterranean Sea
Cyprus
Tian Shan
Taklimakan Desert
Kunlun Shan
Plateau of Tibet
Huang He (Yellow R.)
North China Plain
Sea of Japan (East Sea)
Korea
Yellow Sea
Japan
Honshu
NORTH PACIFIC OCEAN
30°N
Zagros Mountains
Dead Sea
-1,312 ft.
-400 m
Mountains
Nile R.
Libyan Desert
S A H A R A
ARABIAN PENINSULA
Red Sea
H I M A L A Y A
Indus R.
Brahmaputra R.
Ganges R.
Mt. Everest
29,028 ft.
8,848 m
Chang Jiang (Yangtze R.)
East China Sea
Ryukyu Islands
Nampo Shoto
Taiwan
Philippine Sea
INDIA
Deccan Plateau
Arabian Sea
Bay of Bengal
Hainan
Luzon
Mekong R.
Salween R.
S A H E L
Niger R.
AFRICA
Blue Nile R.
White Nile R.
Gulf of Aden
Ethiopian Highlands
Somali Peninsula
Andaman Islands
Andaman Sea
Indochina Peninsula
South China Sea
Philippine Islands
Mariana Islands
M I C R O N E S I A
Guinea
Sri Lanka
Nicobar Is.
Malay Peninsula
Marshall Islands
Gulf of Guinea
Congo R.
Lake Victoria
Maldive Islands
EQUATOR
Borneo
Moluccas
Gilbert Islands
Kilimanjaro
19,341 ft.
5,895 m
Congo Basin
Lower Guinea
Sumatra
Indonesia
Celebes
M E L A N E S I A
Greater Sunda Islands
Lake Tanganyika
Seychelles
New Guinea
Bismarck Archipelago
Java
Solomon Islands
Arafura Sea
INDIAN OCEAN
Madagascar
Zambezi R.
Mascarene Islands
Coral Sea
Vanuatu
Fiji Islands
Namib Desert
Kalahari Desert
Drakensberg
Great Sandy Desert
Great Dividing Range
New Caledonia
AUSTRALIA
Lake Eyre
-52 ft.
-16 m
Great Victoria Desert
Darling R.
SOUTH PACIFIC OCEAN
30°S
Murray R.
Mt. Kosciusko
7,310 ft.
2,228 m
Tasman Sea
North Island
NEW ZEALAND
Tasmania
South Island
Kerguelen Islands
PRIME MERIDIAN (MERIDIAN OF GREENWICH)
The Atlantic, Indian, and Pacific Oceans merge around Antarctica. Some define this as an ocean, calling it the Antarctic Ocean, Austral Ocean, or Southern Ocean. While most accept four oceans (including the Arctic Ocean), there is little international agreement on the name and extent of a fifth ocean.
Auckland Islands
SOUTHERN OCEAN
South Magnetic Pole
60°S
Queen Maud Land
Transantarctic Mountains
Victoria Land
Ross Sea
Ross Ice Shelf
ANTARCTICA
A
B
C
D
E
F
G
H
J
K

NORTH AMERICA
POLITICAL
ASIA
ARCTIC OCEAN
North Magnetic Pole
N
Chukchi Sea
Bering Sea
Bering Strait
Point Barrow
Beaufort Sea
Greenland Sea
GREENLAND (KALAALLIT NUNAAT)
Den.
Ellesmere Island
Queen Elizabeth Islands
Parry Islands
Banks Island
Victoria Island
Boothia Peninsula
Baffin Bay
Baffin Island
Qeqertarsuaq
Davis Strait
Nuuk (Godthab)
Labrador Sea
Nunavut
ARCTIC CIRCLE
Southampton Island
Hudson Bay
Alaska
Yukon R.
Gulf of Alaska
Yukon Territory
Northwest Territories
Great Bear Lake
Mackenzie R.
Great Slave Lake
British Columbia
Alberta
Saskatchewan
Manitoba
Lake Winnipeg
Severn R.
Ontario
Quebec
Newfoundland and Labrador
St. Pierre and Miquelon Fr.
Gulf of St. Lawrence
P.E.I.
N.B.
Nova Scotia
CANADA
ROCKY MOUNTAINS
Vancouver Island
Lake Superior
Ottawa
ATLANTIC OCEAN
PACIFIC OCEAN
Washington
Oregon
Idaho
Montana
Wyoming
North Dakota
South Dakota
Nebraska
Minn.
Wis.
Michigan
Lake Michigan
Lake Huron
Lake Ontario
L. Erie
Iowa
Ill.
Ind.
Ohio
Pa.
New York
Vt.
Maine
New Hampshire
Massachusetts
Rhode Island
Connecticut
New Jersey
Delaware
Maryland
Washington, D.C.
W. Va.
Virginia
Kentucky
North Carolina
Tennessee
South Carolina
Georgia
Ala.
Miss.
Ark.
La.
Florida
Missouri
Missouri R.
Mississippi R.
Kansas
Oklahoma
Texas
Rio Grande
New Mexico
Colorado
Utah
Arizona
Nevada
California
Great Salt Lake
UNITED STATES
Bermuda U.K.
Guadalupe I. Mex.
TROPIC OF CANCER
Gulf of Mexico
MEXICO
Mexico City
see inset below
BAHAMAS
Nassau
Havana
CUBA
Turks and Caicos Islands U.K.
Puerto Rico U.S.
San Juan
Hispaniola
Port-au-Prince
HAITI
Santo Domingo
DOMINICAN REPUBLIC
see inset above
Cayman Is. U.K.
JAMAICA
Kingston
Aruba Neth.
Caribbean Sea
BELIZE
Belmopan
HONDURAS
Tegucigalpa
Guatemala
GUATEMALA
San Salvador
EL SALVADOR
NICARAGUA
Managua
San José
COSTA RICA
Panama Canal
Panama
PANAMA
SOUTH AMERICA
EQUATOR
Virgin Islands U.S.
British Virgin Islands U.K.
Anguilla U.K.
St. Martin Fr.
St. Maarten Neth.
St. Barthélemy Fr.
ANTIGUA AND BARBUDA
Saba Neth.
St. Eustatius Neth.
Montserrat U.K.
Guadeloupe Fr.
ST. KITTS AND NEVIS
DOMINICA
Martinique Fr.
Caribbean Sea
ST. LUCIA
ST. VINCENT AND THE GRENADINES
BARBADOS
GRENADA
TRINIDAD AND TOBAGO
0 200 mi.
0 200 km
1. BAJA CALIFORNIA
2. BAJA CALIFORNIA SUR
3. SONORA
4. CHIHUAHUA
5. SINALOA
6. DURANGO
7. COAHUILA
8. NUEVO LEÓN
9. ZACATECAS
10. TAMAULIPAS
11. NAYARIT
12. AGUASCALIENTES
13. SAN LUIS POTOSÍ
14. JALISCO
15. GUANAJUATO
16. QUERÉTARO
17. HIDALGO
18. COLIMA
19. MICHOACÁN
20. MÉXICO
21. DISTRITO FEDERAL
22. TLAXCALA
23. MORELOS
24. PUEBLA
25. VERACRUZ
26. GUERRERO
27. OAXACA
28. TABASCO
29. CHIAPAS
30. CAMPECHE
31. QUINTANA ROO
32. YUCATÁN
0 1,000 miles
0 1,000 kilometers
Lambert Azimuthal Equal-Area Projection

NORTH AMERICA
PHYSICAL
ASIA
EUROPE
SOUTH AMERICA
CANADA
UNITED STATES
MEXICO
GREENLAND
ALASKA
ARCTIC OCEAN
ATLANTIC OCEAN
PACIFIC OCEAN
North Magnetic Pole
N
Chukchi Sea
Bering Sea
St. Lawrence Island
Bering Strait
Seward Peninsula
Point Barrow
Beaufort Sea
Brooks Range
North Slope
Yukon R.
Kuskokwim R.
Mt. McKinley (Denali) 20,320 ft. 6,194 m
Alaska Range
Bristol Bay
Aleutian Range
Kenai Peninsula
Kodiak I.
Gulf of Alaska
Yukon Plateau
Mt. Logan 19,551 ft. 5,959 m
Mackenzie Mts.
Mackenzie R.
Great Bear Lake
Great Slave Lake
ARCTIC CIRCLE
Lincoln Sea
Ellesmere Island
Queen Elizabeth Islands
Hayes Peninsula
Gunnbjorn 12,139 ft. 3,700 m
Greenland Sea
Baffin Bay
Devon I.
Melville Island
Banks Island
Prince of Wales I.
Somerset I.
Victoria Island
Boothia Peninsula
Melville Peninsula
Baffin Island
Qeqertarsuaq
Davis Strait
Nuuk (Godthab)
Cape Farewell
Labrador Sea
Foxe Basin
Southampton Island
Hudson Strait
Ungava Bay
Hudson Bay
Belcher Islands
James Bay
LABRADOR
Island of Newfoundland
Avalon Peninsula
CANADIAN SHIELD
Lake Athabasca
Athabasca R.
Peace R.
Slave R.
Churchill R.
Nelson R.
Severn R.
Saskatchewan R.
Lake Winnipeg
Lake Superior
Ottawa
Laurentian Mts.
St. Lawrence R.
Gaspé Pen.
Gulf of St. Lawrence
Cape Breton Island
Prince Edward Island
Nova Scotia
Bay of Fundy
Gulf of Maine
Cape Cod
Alexander Archipelago
Queen Charlotte Islands
Coast Mts.
Fraser Plateau
Columbia Mts.
ROCKY MOUNTAINS
GREAT PLAINS
Vancouver Island
Olympic Peninsula
Cascade Range
Columbia Plateau
Snake R.
Coast Ranges
Sierra Nevada
Cape Mendocino
Great Basin
Great Salt Lake
Colorado Plateau
Grand Canyon
Colorado R.
Mt. Whitney 14,495 ft. 4,418 m
Death Valley -282 ft. -86 m
Channel Islands
Sonoran Desert
Baja California
Gulf of California
High Plains
Platte R.
Missouri R.
Arkansas R.
Red R.
Ozark Plateau
Mississippi R.
Ohio R.
CENTRAL LOWLAND
Lake Michigan
Lake Huron
Lake Erie
Lake Ontario
Appalachian Mts.
Long Island
Washington, D.C.
Chesapeake Bay
Cape Hatteras
Bermuda Islands
COASTAL PLAIN
Florida
Rio Grande
Sierra Madre Occidental
Sierra Madre Oriental
Gulf of Mexico
Florida Keys
BAHAMAS
WEST INDIES
Havana
CUBA
Hispaniola
HAITI
DOMINICAN REPUBLIC
Puerto Rico
Virgin Is.
Guadeloupe
Martinique
Trinidad
Greater Antilles
Lesser Antilles
Cayman Is.
JAMAICA
Caribbean Sea
Mexico City
Orizaba 18,700 ft. 5,700 m
Sierra Madre Sur
Yucatán Peninsula
BELIZE
Belmopan
Isthmus of Tehuantepec
HONDURAS
Tegucigalpa
Guatemala
GUATEMALA
Gulf of Tehuantepec
San Salvador
EL SALVADOR
NICARAGUA
Managua
Lake Nicaragua
San José
COSTA RICA
Isthmus of Panama
Panama
PANAMA
Panama Canal
Gulf of Panama
CENTRAL AMERICA
TROPIC OF CANCER
EQUATOR
180°
160°W
140°W
120°W
100°W
80°W
60°W
40°W
20°W
80°N
60°N
40°N
20°N
20°S
0 1,000 miles
0 1,000 kilometers
Lambert Azimuthal Equal-Area Projection
1 2 3 4 5 6 7 8
A B C D E F G H J K

SOUTH AMERICA
POLITICAL
Lambert Azimuthal Equal-Area Projection
0 1,000 miles
0 1,000 kilometers
N
Caribbean Sea
PACIFIC OCEAN
ATLANTIC OCEAN
EQUATOR
TROPIC OF CAPRICORN
80°W
60°W
40°W
100°W
20°W
0°
20°S
40°S
VENEZUELA
GUYANA
SURINAME
FRENCH GUIANA
Fr.
COLOMBIA
ECUADOR
PERU
BRAZIL
BOLIVIA
PARAGUAY
CHILE
ARGENTINA
URUGUAY
A M A Z O N
B A S I N
A N D E S
A N D E S
Santa Marta
Barranquilla
Cartagena
Maracaibo
Caracas
Valencia
Lake Maracaibo
Ciudad Guayana
Bucaramanga
San Cristóbal
Orinoco R.
Georgetown
Paramaribo
Cayenne
Medellín
Bogotá
Malpelo I.
Col.
Cali
Boa Vista
Boundary claimed by Suriname
Marajó Island
Esmeraldas
Quito
Rio Negro
Amazon R.
Belém
São Luís
Guayaquil
Manaus
Santarém
Iquitos
Marañón R.
Amazon R.
Tapajós R.
Fortaleza
Teresina
Purus R.
Madeira R.
Xingu R.
Natal
Ucayali R.
Araguaia R.
Tocantins R.
Campina Grande
Recife
São Francisco R.
Rio Branco
Pôrto Velho
Callao
Lima
Machu Picchu
Cuzco
Ayacucho
Lake Titicaca
Trinidad
Salvador
La Paz
Brasília
Arequipa
Goiânia
Oruro
Santa Cruz
Sucre
Paraguay R.
Campo Grande
Uberlândia
Uberaba
Arica
Belo Horizonte
Iquique
Tarija
Paraná R.
Londrina
Campinas
Nova Iguaçu
Antofagasta
São Paulo
Rio de Janeiro
Santos
Salta
Asunción
Curitiba
San Félix I.
San Ambrosio I.
Chile
San Miguel de Tucumán
Uruguaiana
Paraná R.
Uruguay R.
La Serena
Coquimbo
Santa Maria
Pôrto Alegre
Córdoba
Rosario
Valparaíso
Santiago
Mendoza
Juan Fernández Is.
Chile
Buenos Aires
Montevideo
La Plata
Río de la Plata
Concepción
Colorado R.
Mar del Plata
Negro R.
Bahía Blanca
Puerto Montt
Comodoro Rivadavia
Falkland Islands (Islas Malvinas)
Stanley
Administered by United Kingdom
Claimed by Arg.
Río Gallegos
Punta Arenas
Ushuaia
Strait of Magellan
Cape Horn
South Georgia Island
U.K.
1 2 3 4 5 6 7 8
A B C D E F G H J K

SOUTH AMERICA
PHYSICAL
Caribbean Sea
Lambert Azimuthal Equal-Area Projection
0
1,000 miles
0
1,000 kilometers
N
Caracas
VENEZUELA
Lake Maracaibo
Orinoco R.
L L A N O S
Angel Falls
Total drop 3,212 ft. 979 m
GUYANA
Georgetown
SURINAME
Paramaribo
Cayenne
FRENCH GUIANA
Bogotá
Malpelo I.
GUIANA HIGHLANDS
Boundary claimed by Suriname
COLOMBIA
Marajó Island
Rio Negro
Quito
ECUADOR
EQUATOR
A M A Z O N
B A S I N
S e l v a s
Amazon R.
Marañón R.
Purus R.
Madeira R.
Tapajós R.
Xingu R.
Araguaia R.
Tocantins R.
São Francisco R.
Ucayali R.
PERU
A N D E S
BRAZIL
Lima
Machu Picchu
MATO GROSSO PLATEAU
B R A Z I L I A N
H I G H L A N D S
Brasília
Lake Titicaca
La Paz
BOLIVIA
Altiplano
Sucre
Salar de Uyuni
CHACO
Paraguay R.
Paraná R.
PARAGUAY
TROPIC OF CAPRICORN
Iguazú Falls
Asunción
GRAN CHACO
San Ambrosio I.
San Félix I.
ATLANTIC OCEAN
CHILE
P A M P A S
Uruguay R.
Aconcagua 22,834 ft. 6,960 m
Juan Fernández Is.
Santiago
Buenos Aires
URUGUAY
Montevideo
ARGENTINA
Río de la Plata
Colorado R.
Negro R.
Valdés Peninsula -131 ft. -40 m
Chiloé Island
P A T A G O N I A
Gulf of San Jorge
PACIFIC OCEAN
Taitao Peninsula
Falkland Islands (Islas Malvinas)
Wellington I.
Stanley
Tierra del Fuego
Strait of Magellan
Cape Horn
South Georgia Island
80°W
60°W
40°W
100°W
20°W
0°
20°S
40°S

EUROPE
POLITICAL
ICELAND
Reykjavík
Akureyri
ARCTIC CIRCLE
PRIME MERIDIAN
Norwegian Sea
Faeroe Islands
Denmark
Tórshavn
Shetland Islands
Lerwick
Isle of Lewis
Orkney Islands
NORWAY
Trondheim
Ålesund
Bergen
Stavanger
Oslo
SWEDEN
Åre
Sundsvall
Uppsala
Stockholm
Göteborg
Malmö
Skagerrak
Inverness
SCOTLAND
Aberdeen
Glasgow
Edinburgh
NORTHERN IRELAND
Belfast
UNITED KINGDOM
IRELAND
Dublin
Cork
Irish Sea
Manchester
Liverpool
WALES
ENGLAND
Birmingham
Cardiff
London
Thames R.
Southampton
Land's End
Celtic Sea
North Sea
DENMARK
Århus
Copenhagen
Kiel
Hamburg
Elbe R.
NETHERLANDS
Amsterdam
The Hague
Brussels
BELGIUM
English Channel
ATLANTIC OCEAN
GERMANY
Berlin
Bonn
Frankfurt
Rhine R.
Munich
Danube R.
POLAND
Gdańsk
Bydgoszcz
Wrocław
Oder R.
Prague
CZECH REPUBLIC
Bratislava
LIECHTENSTEIN
Vaduz
Vienna
AUSTRIA
Budapest
HUNGARY
SLOVENIA
Ljubljana
Zagreb
CROATIA
BOSNIA & HERZEGOVINA
Sarajevo
MONTENEGRO
Podgorica
ALBANIA
Tirana
Le Havre
Brest
Rennes
Paris
Seine R.
LUXEMBOURG
Luxembourg
Strasbourg
Nantes
Loire R.
La Rochelle
FRANCE
Limoges
Bay of Biscay
Bordeaux
Geneva
Lyon
Rhone R.
Zürich
Bern
SWITZERLAND
ALPS
Milan
Turin
Po R.
Venice
Genoa
Donostia-San Sebastián
Toulouse
Andorra la Vella
Marseille
Nice
MONACO
SAN MARINO
Adriatic Sea
ITALY
Rome
VATICAN CITY (within Rome)
Naples
Corsica
France
Sardinia
Italy
Cagliari
Tyrrhenian Sea
Palermo
Sicily
Italy
Messina
Catania
Ionian Sea
MALTA
Valletta
La Coruña
Vigo
Porto
Coimbra
PORTUGAL
Lisbon
Cape St. Vincent
Bilbao
Valladolid
Ebro R.
Pyrenees
ANDORRA
Madrid
Zaragoza
Barcelona
Tagus R.
SPAIN
Valencia
Córdoba
Seville
Murcia
Cádiz
Málaga
Cartagena
Palma
Balearic Islands
Spain
Strait of Gibraltar
GIBRALTAR
U.K.
Mediterranean
AFRICA
70°N
60°N
50°N
40°N
30°N
30°W
20°W
10°W
0°
10°E
N

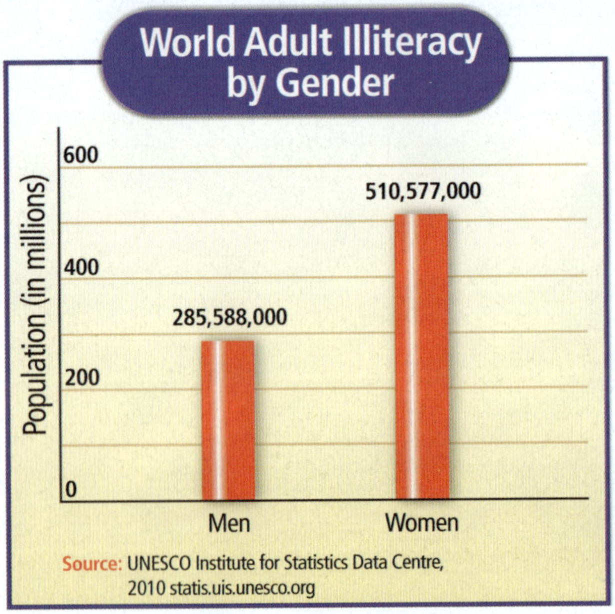

Years, by Country, in Which Women Gained the Right to Vote

Year	Country	Year	Country
1893	New Zealand	1945	Italy
1902	Australia	1945	Japan
1913	Norway	1947	Argentina
1918	United Kingdom	1947	Mexico
1918	Canada	1950	India
1919	Germany	1952	Greece
1920	United States	1956	Egypt
1930	South Africa	1963	Kenya
1934	Brazil	1971	Switzerland
1944	France	1980	Iraq

Source: *The World Factbook*, 2012, CIA

Highest Military Expenditures

Country	GDP	Billions of U.S. Dollars per Year	Percentage of Gross Domestic Product (GDP)
United States	15.29	626.89	4.1
China	11.44	491.92	4.3
France	2.246	58.36	2.6
Japan	4.497	3.5976	0.8
United Kingdom	2.29	61.83	2.7
Germany	3.139	47.085	1.5
Italy	1.871	33.678	1.8
South Korea	1.574	42.498	2.7
India	4.515	112.87	2.5
Saudi Arabia	691.5	691.5	10.0

Source: *The World Factbook*, 2012, CIA

Nuclear Weapons Capability

Country	Date of First Test
United States	1945
Russia (Soviet Union)	1949
United Kingdom	1952
France	1960
China	1964
India	1974
Pakistan	1998
North Korea	2006

Source: U.S. Department of State and *TIME* magazine

A commonly accepted division between Asia and Europe—here marked by a gray line—is formed by the Ural Mountains, Ural River, Caspian Sea, Caucasus Mountains, and the Black Sea with its outlets, the Bosporus and the Dardanelles.
Europe/Asia boundary
RUSSIA
ASIA
URAL MOUNTAINS
Barents Sea
White Sea
Kola Peninsula
LAPLAND
FINLAND
ESTONIA
LATVIA
LITHUANIA
BELARUS
UKRAINE
MOLDOVA
ROMANIA
SERBIA
KOSOVO
MACEDONIA
BULGARIA
GREECE
TURKEY
GEORGIA
AZERBAIJAN
KAZAKHSTAN
CYPRUS
Caspian Sea
Black Sea
Sea of Azov
Sea of Marmara
Aegean Sea
Bosporus
Dardanelles
Crimea
Caucasus Mountains
Carpathian Mts.
Balkan Mts.
Peloponnese
Rhodes
Crete
Greece
Bothnia
Sea
Lake Onega
Lake Ladoga
Northern Dvina R.
Volga R.
Don R.
Dnieper R.
Dniester R.
Vistula R.
Ural R.
Tobseda
Murmansk
Kirovsk
Umba
Ivalo
Kiruna
Kemi
Luleå
Umeå
Oulu
Kem'
Arkhangel'sk
Severodvinsk
Pechora
Syktyvkar
Vaasa
Kuopio
Pori
Tampere
Turku
Helsinki
St. Petersburg
Tallinn
Perm'
Kirov
Ufa
Kazan'
Novgorod
Yaroslavl'
Nizhniy Novgorod
Tver'
Moscow
Samara
Orenburg
Riga
Daugavpils
Vitsyebsk
Smolensk
Ryazan'
Penza
Vilnius
Kaunas
Kaliningrad
Minsk
Oral
Saratov
Bryansk
Homyel'
Kursk
Chernihiv
Sumy
Warsaw
Kyiv (Kiev)
Kharkiv
Poltava
Volgograd
L'viv
Vinnytsya
Donets'k
Dnipropetrovs'k
Astrakhan'
Rostov
Chișinău
Stavropol'
Odessa
Kerch
Grozny
Simferopol'
Sevastopol'
Yalta
Belgrade
Bucharest
Constanța
Baku
Varna
Priština
Sofia
İstanbul
Skopje
Thessaloniki
Athens
Nicosia
Iraklion
30°E
40°E
50°E
60°E
70°E
80°E
60°N
50°N
40°N
30°N
0
400 miles
400 kilometers
Lambert Azimuthal Equal-Area Projection
9
10
11
12
13
14
15
16
A
B
C
D
E
F
G
H
J
K

EUROPE
PHYSICAL
1
2
3
4
5
6
7
8
A
B
C
D
E
F
G
H
J
K
N
30°W
20°W
10°W
70°N
0°
10°E
60°N
50°N
40°N
30°N
20°W
10°W
ARCTIC CIRCLE
PRIME MERIDIAN
Reykjavík
ICELAND
Norwegian Sea
Faeroe Islands
Shetland Islands
Orkney Islands
Outer Hebrides
British Isles
Highlands
Edinburgh
Belfast
UNITED KINGDOM
IRELAND
Dublin
Irish Sea
North Sea
Great Britain
Celtic Sea
Cardiff
Thames R.
London
Land's End
ATLANTIC OCEAN
English Channel
NORWAY
SCANDI
Oslo
SWEDEN
Stockholm
Gotl
Skagerrak
Kattegat
Jutland
Zealand
DENMARK
Copenhagen
Bal
NETHERLANDS
Amsterdam
Elbe R.
Berlin
Brussels
BELGIUM
Rhine R.
NORT
GERMANY
POLAN
Oder
Brittany
Seine R.
Paris
Luxembourg
LUXEMBOURG
Prague
CZECH REPUBLIC
Bratislava
Loire R.
Danube R.
FRANCE
LIECHTENSTEIN
Vienna
SLOV
Bern
Vaduz
Budapest
Bay of Biscay
SWITZERLAND
AUSTRIA
HUNGA
Mont Blanc 15,771 ft. 4,807 m
ALPS
Drava R.
SLOVENIA
Massif Central
Rhone R.
Ljubljana
Zagreb
Cantabrian Mountains
CROATIA
Pyrenees
Po R.
Andorra la Vella
MONACO
Adriatic Sea
BOSNIA HERZEGOV
Douro R.
Ebro R.
IBERIAN
SAN MARINO
Sarajevo
Riviera
Apennines
Madrid
ANDORRA
Corsica
ITALY
MONTENEG
Lisbon
Tagus R.
Podgoric
PORTUGAL
SPAIN
Rome
PENINSULA
Tira
Cape St. Vincent
Sardinia
VATICAN CITY (within Rome)
ALBAN
Balearic Islands
Baetic Mountains
Strait of Gibraltar
GIBRALTAR
Tyrrhenian Sea
Mediterranean
Ion Se
Sicily
Etna 10,902 ft. 3,323 m
MALTA
Valletta
AFRICA
10°W
30°N
0°
10°E

North Cape
Barents Sea
Kola Peninsula
White Sea
LAPLAND
AVIA
Bothnia
FINLAND
Lake Region
Helsinki
Gulf of Finland
Tallinn
ESTONIA
Sea
LATVIA
Riga
LITHUANIA
Vilnius
RUSSIA
Minsk
BELARUS
Warsaw
Vistula R.
Lake Onega
Lake Ladoga
Pechora R.
Northern Dvina R.
URAL MOUNTAINS
Europe/Asia boundary
ASIA
RUSSIA
NORTHERN EUROPEAN PLAIN
Moscow
CENTRAL RUSSIAN UPLAND
Don R.
Volga R.
Ural R.
KAZAKHSTAN
Caspian Depression
(Kyiv) Kiev
Dnieper R.
Dniester R.
UKRAINE
Carpathian Mts.
Tisza R.
MOLDOVA
Chişinău
ROMANIA
Belgrade
Bucharest
Danube R.
SERBIA
BALKAN PENINSULA
KOSOVO
Priština
Sofia
Balkan Mts.
BULGARIA
Skopje
MACEDONIA
GREECE
Dardanelles
Aegean Sea
Athens
Peloponnese
Crete
Rhodes
Nicosia
CYPRUS
Sea of Azov
Crimea
Black Sea
Bosporus
Sea of Marmara
TURKEY
Mt. Elbrus 18,510 ft. 5,642 m
Caucasus Mountains
GEORGIA
AZERBAIJAN
Baku
Caspian Sea
ASIA
0
400 miles
0
400 kilometers
Lambert Azimuthal Equal-Area Projection
30°E
40°E
50°E
60°E
70°E
80°E
60°N
50°N
40°N
30°N

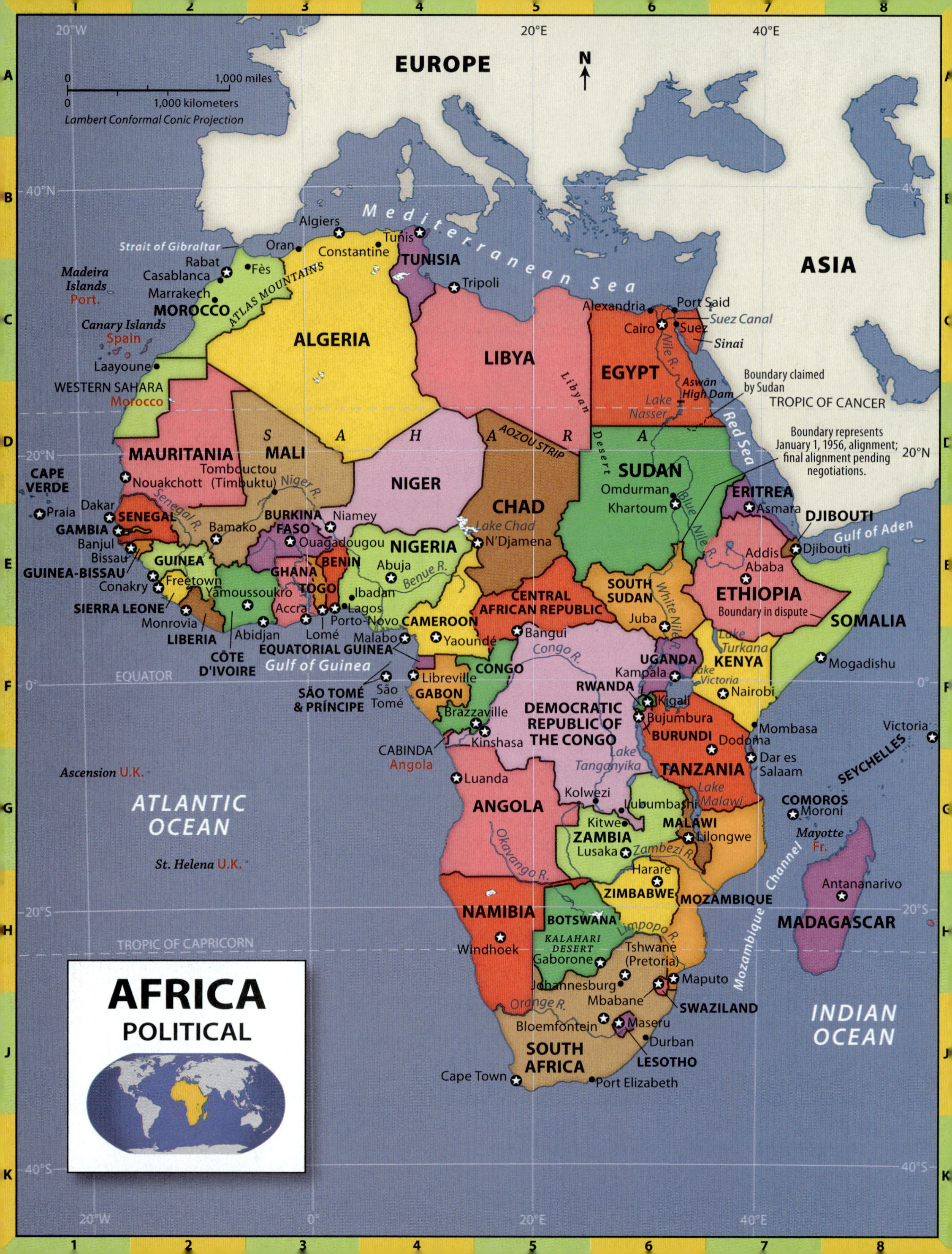
AFRICA
POLITICAL
0 1,000 miles
0 1,000 kilometers
Lambert Conformal Conic Projection
EUROPE
ASIA
N
20°W
0°
20°E
40°E
40°N
20°N
0°
20°S
40°S
EQUATOR
TROPIC OF CANCER
TROPIC OF CAPRICORN
1
2
3
4
5
6
7
8
A
B
C
D
E
F
G
H
J
K
Mediterranean Sea
Strait of Gibraltar
Madeira Islands
Port.
Canary Islands
Spain
ATLAS MOUNTAINS
Algiers
Oran
Constantine
Tunis
TUNISIA
Tripoli
Rabat
Fès
Casablanca
Marrakech
MOROCCO
ALGERIA
LIBYA
Libyan Desert
EGYPT
Alexandria
Port Said
Cairo
Suez
Suez Canal
Sinai
Nile R.
Aswân High Dam
Lake Nasser
Boundary claimed by Sudan
Red Sea
Laayoune
WESTERN SAHARA
Morocco
S A H A R A
AOZOU STRIP
MAURITANIA
Nouakchott
MALI
Tombouctou (Timbuktu)
Niger R.
NIGER
CHAD
SUDAN
Omdurman
Khartoum
Blue Nile R.
Boundary represents January 1, 1956, alignment; final alignment pending negotiations.
20°N
ERITREA
Asmara
DJIBOUTI
Djibouti
Gulf of Aden
CAPE VERDE
Praia
Dakar
SENEGAL
Senegal R.
GAMBIA
Banjul
Bissau
GUINEA-BISSAU
GUINEA
Conakry
Freetown
SIERRA LEONE
Monrovia
LIBERIA
Bamako
BURKINA FASO
Ouagadougou
Niamey
NIGERIA
Abuja
Benue R.
Ibadan
Lagos
Porto-Novo
BENIN
TOGO
Lomé
GHANA
Accra
Yamoussoukro
Abidjan
CÔTE D'IVOIRE
Lake Chad
N'Djamena
CENTRAL AFRICAN REPUBLIC
Bangui
SOUTH SUDAN
Juba
White Nile R.
ETHIOPIA
Addis Ababa
Boundary in dispute
SOMALIA
Mogadishu
CAMEROON
Yaoundé
Malabo
EQUATORIAL GUINEA
Gulf of Guinea
SÃO TOMÉ & PRÍNCIPE
São Tomé
Libreville
GABON
CONGO
Brazzaville
Kinshasa
Congo R.
DEMOCRATIC REPUBLIC OF THE CONGO
UGANDA
Kampala
Lake Victoria
Lake Turkana
KENYA
Nairobi
Mombasa
RWANDA
Kigali
Bujumbura
BURUNDI
Lake Tanganyika
TANZANIA
Dodoma
Dar es Salaam
Victoria
SEYCHELLES
COMOROS
Moroni
Mayotte
Fr.
CABINDA
Angola
Luanda
ANGOLA
Kolwezi
Lubumbashi
Kitwe
ZAMBIA
Lusaka
Zambezi R.
Lake Malawi
MALAWI
Lilongwe
Okavango R.
Harare
ZIMBABWE
MOZAMBIQUE
Mozambique Channel
MADAGASCAR
Antananarivo
NAMIBIA
Windhoek
BOTSWANA
KALAHARI DESERT
Gaborone
Limpopo R.
Tshwane (Pretoria)
Johannesburg
Maputo
Mbabane
SWAZILAND
Orange R.
Bloemfontein
Maseru
LESOTHO
Durban
SOUTH AFRICA
Cape Town
Port Elizabeth
Ascension U.K.
ATLANTIC OCEAN
St. Helena U.K.
INDIAN OCEAN

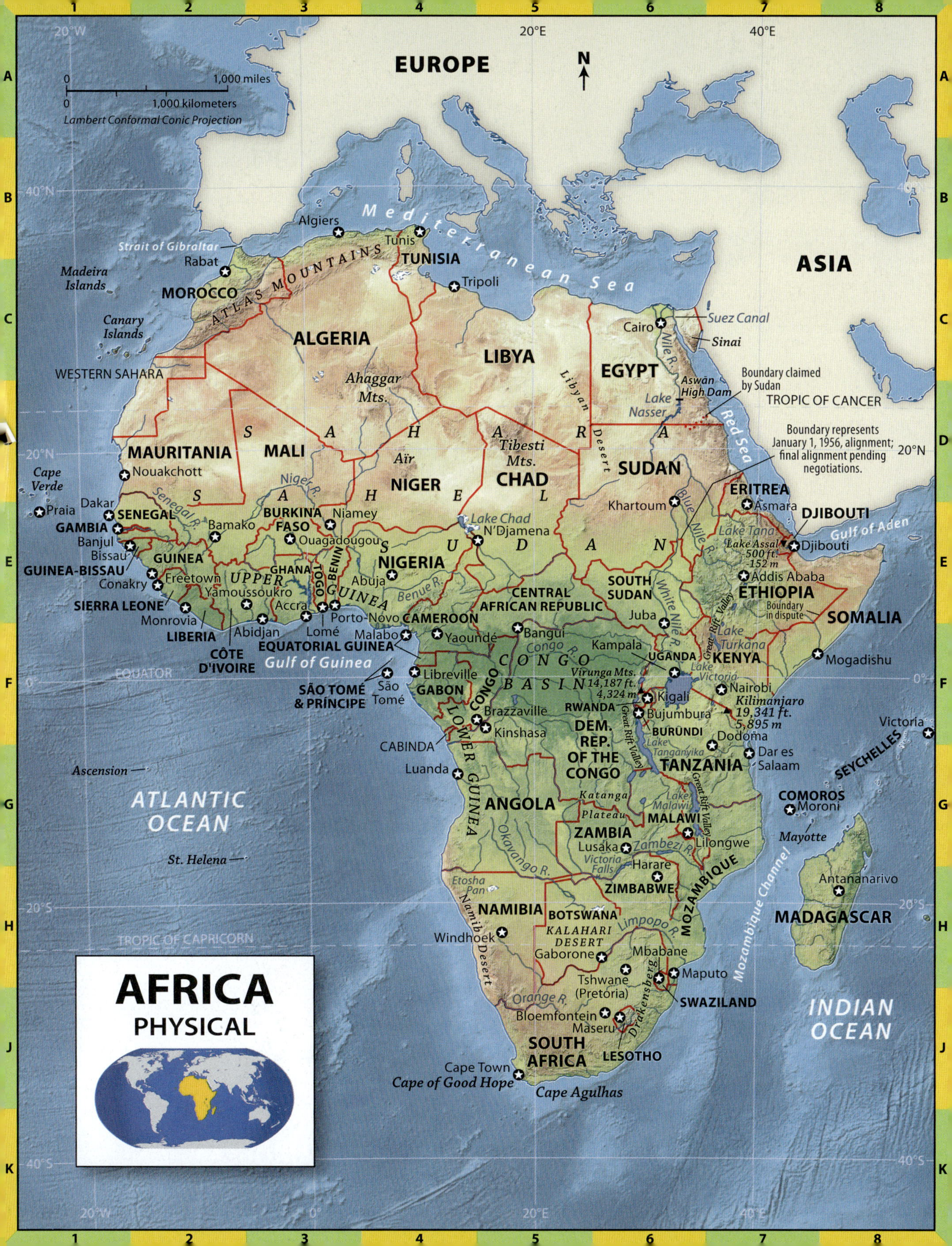

AFRICA
PHYSICAL
EUROPE
ASIA
N
0 1,000 miles
0 1,000 kilometers
Lambert Conformal Conic Projection
20°E
40°E
20°W
40°N
20°N
0°
20°S
40°S
Mediterranean Sea
Strait of Gibraltar
Madeira Islands
Canary Islands
Algiers
Tunis
TUNISIA
Rabat
MOROCCO
ATLAS MOUNTAINS
Tripoli
ALGERIA
LIBYA
EGYPT
Cairo
Suez Canal
Sinai
Nile R.
Aswân High Dam
Lake Nasser
Boundary claimed by Sudan
TROPIC OF CANCER
Libyan Desert
WESTERN SAHARA
Ahaggar Mts.
Tibesti Mts.
S A H A R A
S A H E L
MAURITANIA
Nouakchott
MALI
NIGER
Aïr
CHAD
SUDAN
Red Sea
Boundary represents January 1, 1956, alignment; final alignment pending negotiations.
Cape Verde
Praia
Dakar
SENEGAL
Senegal R.
GAMBIA
Banjul
Bissau
GUINEA-BISSAU
GUINEA
Conakry
Freetown
SIERRA LEONE
Monrovia
LIBERIA
Bamako
Niger R.
BURKINA FASO
Ouagadougou
Niamey
Yamoussoukro
CÔTE D'IVOIRE
Abidjan
GHANA
Accra
TOGO
Lomé
BENIN
Porto-Novo
UPPER GUINEA
NIGERIA
Abuja
Benue R.
Lake Chad
N'Djamena
Khartoum
Blue Nile R.
ERITREA
Asmara
DJIBOUTI
Djibouti
Gulf of Aden
Lake Tana
Lake Assal 500 ft. -152 m
Addis Ababa
ETHIOPIA
Boundary in dispute
SOMALIA
SOUTH SUDAN
White Nile R.
Juba
Great Rift Valley
Lake Turkana
CENTRAL AFRICAN REPUBLIC
CAMEROON
Malabo
Yaoundé
Bangui
EQUATORIAL GUINEA
Gulf of Guinea
EQUATOR
SÃO TOMÉ & PRÍNCIPE
São Tomé
Libreville
GABON
CONGO
Congo R.
CONGO BASIN
Virunga Mts. 14,187 ft. 4,324 m
Kampala
UGANDA
KENYA
Mogadishu
Lake Victoria
Nairobi
Kilimanjaro 19,341 ft. 5,895 m
Kigali
RWANDA
Bujumbura
BURUNDI
Brazzaville
Kinshasa
DEM. REP. OF THE CONGO
CABINDA
Luanda
LOWER GUINEA
Lake Tanganyika
Dodoma
TANZANIA
Dar es Salaam
Victoria
SEYCHELLES
Ascension
ATLANTIC OCEAN
ANGOLA
Katanga Plateau
Lake Malawi
MALAWI
Lilongwe
COMOROS
Moroni
Mayotte
St. Helena
ZAMBIA
Lusaka
Zambezi R.
Victoria Falls
Harare
ZIMBABWE
MOZAMBIQUE
Mozambique Channel
Antananarivo
MADAGASCAR
Okavango R.
Etosha Pan
Namib Desert
NAMIBIA
Windhoek
BOTSWANA
KALAHARI DESERT
Gaborone
Limpopo R.
TROPIC OF CAPRICORN
Mbabane
Maputo
Tshwane (Pretoria)
SWAZILAND
Drakensberg
Orange R.
Bloemfontein
Maseru
LESOTHO
SOUTH AFRICA
Cape Town
Cape of Good Hope
Cape Agulhas
INDIAN OCEAN

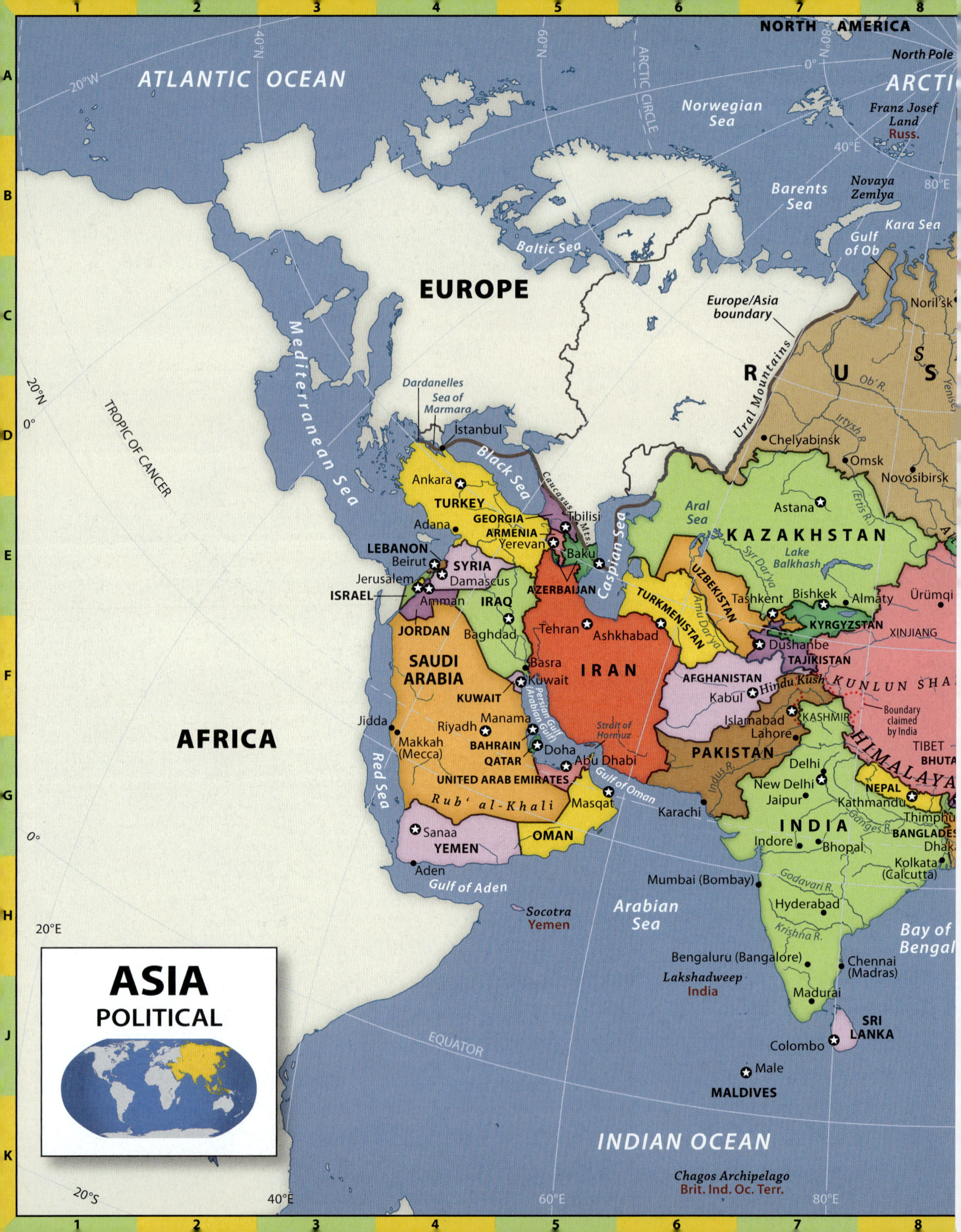
ASIA
POLITICAL
NORTH AMERICA
North Pole
ATLANTIC OCEAN
ARCTIC
Norwegian Sea
Franz Josef Land
Russ.
ARCTIC CIRCLE
Barents Sea
Novaya Zemlya
Kara Sea
Gulf of Ob
Baltic Sea
EUROPE
Europe/Asia boundary
Noril'sk
Mediterranean Sea
TROPIC OF CANCER
Dardanelles
Sea of Marmara
Istanbul
Black Sea
Ural Mountains
R U S S
Ob' R.
Irtysh R.
Yenisei
Chelyabinsk
Omsk
Novosibirsk
Ankara
TURKEY
Adana
GEORGIA
Tbilisi
ARMENIA
Yerevan
Caucasus Mts.
Baku
Caspian Sea
Aral Sea
Astana
Irtysh R.
KAZAKHSTAN
Syr Darya
Lake Balkhash
LEBANON
Beirut
SYRIA
Damascus
Jerusalem
ISRAEL
Amman
IRAQ
AZERBAIJAN
UZBEKISTAN
TURKMENISTAN
Amu Darya
Tashkent
Bishkek
Almaty
Ürümqi
KYRGYZSTAN
XINJIANG
JORDAN
Baghdad
Tehran
Ashkhabad
Dushanbe
TAJIKISTAN
SAUDI ARABIA
Basra
IRAN
Kuwait
KUWAIT
AFGHANISTAN
Kabul
Hindu Kush
KUNLUN SHA
Persian Gulf (Arabian Gulf)
Jidda
Riyadh
Manama
Strait of Hormuz
Islamabad
KASHMIR
Boundary claimed by India
Lahore
Makkah (Mecca)
BAHRAIN
Doha
QATAR
Abu Dhabi
PAKISTAN
Indus R.
TIBET
HIMALAYA
BHUTA
Red Sea
UNITED ARAB EMIRATES
Gulf of Oman
Delhi
New Delhi
Jaipur
NEPAL
Kathmandu
Thimphu
Masqat
Karachi
Rub' al-Khali
INDIA
Ganges R.
BANGLADES
Sanaa
OMAN
Indore
Bhopal
Dhak
YEMEN
Kolkata (Calcutta)
Aden
Gulf of Aden
Mumbai (Bombay)
Godavari R.
Hyderabad
Socotra
Yemen
Arabian Sea
AFRICA
Krishna R.
Bay of Bengal
Bengaluru (Bangalore)
Chennai (Madras)
Lakshadweep
India
Madurai
SRI LANKA
Colombo
EQUATOR
Male
MALDIVES
INDIAN OCEAN
Chagos Archipelago
Brit. Ind. Oc. Terr.
20°W
40°N
60°N
80°N
0°
40°E
80°E
20°N
20°E
20°S
60°E
1 2 3 4 5 6 7 8
A B C D E F G H J K

NORTH AMERICA
Bering Strait
Chukchi Sea
Gulf of Anadyr
Bering Sea
OCEAN
Wrangel I.
New Siberian Islands
East Siberian Sea
Severnaya Zemlya
Laptev Sea
Taymyr Peninsula
Cherski Range
Kolyma Mts.
Verkhoyanski Mts.
Lena R.
Commander Is.
Kamchatka Peninsula
Sea of Okhotsk
Yakutsk
B E R I A
S I A
Sakhalin
Kuril Islands
Hokkaidō
Sapporo
Irkutsk
Lake Baikal
MANCHURIA
Vladivostok
Honshū
Sea of Japan (East Sea)
JAPAN
Tokyo
Ulaanbaatar
MONGOLIA
Shan
GOBI
Shenyang
NORTH KOREA
P'yŏngyang
Kyōto
Ōsaka
Seoul
Beijing
Yellow Sea
SOUTH KOREA
Hiroshima
Shikoku
Kyūshū
Shijiazhuang
Qingdao
Huang He (Yellow R.)
Lanzhou
Xuzhou
Xi'an
Nanjing
Shanghai
East China Sea
Ryukyu Islands
Okinawa
C H I N A
Boundary claimed by China
Chengdu
Chang Jiang (Yangtze R.)
Nanchang
Changsha
Fuzhou
Taipei
Guiyang
TAIWAN
Kunming
Xi R.
Guangzhou
Macau
Hong Kong
Hanoi
Haiphong
Hainan
MYANMAR (BURMA)
LAOS
Nay Pyi Taw
Yangon (Rangoon)
Vientiane
Da Nang
THAILAND
Bangkok
VIETNAM
CAMBODIA
Phnom Penh
Ho Chi Minh City
Andaman Islands
India
Andaman Sea
Nicobar Islands
India
Gulf of Thailand
Luzon
PHILIPPINES
Quezon City
Manila
South China Sea
Samar
Mindoro
Panay
Leyte
Negros
Palawan
Mindanao
Bandar Seri Begawan
BRUNEI
SABAH
M A L A Y S I A
SARAWAK
Medan
Kuala Lumpur
SINGAPORE
Borneo
Sumatra
Mentawai Islands
I N D O N E S I A
Greater Sunda Islands
Java Sea
Jakarta
Java
Morotai
Halmahera
Moluccas
Sulawesi (Celebes)
Buru
Ceram
Biak
Jayapura
New Guinea
Aru Is.
Dolak
Tanimbar Is.
Arafura Sea
Dili
EAST TIMOR (TIMOR-LESTE)
Timor
Kupang
Timor Sea
AUSTRALIA
Marcus I.
Japan
Bonin Is.
Japan
Volcano Is.
Japan
PACIFIC OCEAN
Parece Vela
Japan
Philippine Sea
0
1,000 miles
0
1,000 kilometers
Two-Point Equidistant Projection
TROPIC OF CANCER
EQUATOR
160°W
180°
160°E
120°E
100°E
140°E
80°N
60°N
40°N
20°N
0°
20°S
9 10 11 12 13 14 15 16
A B C D E F G H J K

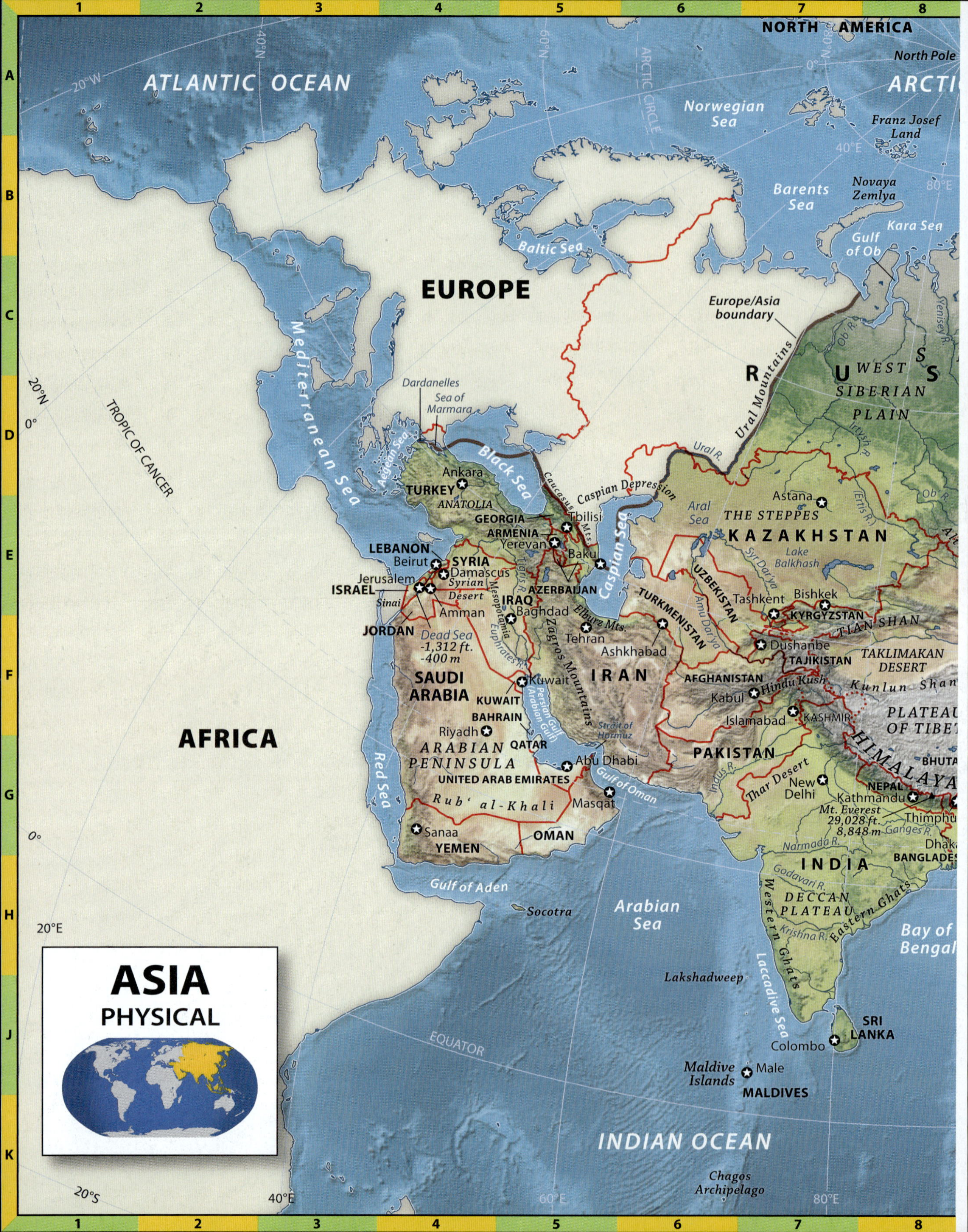
ASIA
PHYSICAL
NORTH AMERICA
North Pole
ATLANTIC OCEAN
ARCTIC
Norwegian Sea
Franz Josef Land
Barents Sea
Novaya Zemlya
Kara Sea
Gulf of Ob
Baltic Sea
ARCTIC CIRCLE
EUROPE
Europe/Asia boundary
Mediterranean Sea
Dardanelles
Sea of Marmara
Aegean Sea
Black Sea
Ural Mountains
Ural R.
WEST SIBERIAN PLAIN
Ob R.
Irtysh R.
Yenisey R.
Caucasus Mts.
Caspian Depression
Caspian Sea
Aral Sea
Astana
THE STEPPES
KAZAKHSTAN
Lake Balkhash
Syr Darya
Amu Darya
Ankara
TURKEY
ANATOLIA
GEORGIA
Tbilisi
ARMENIA
Yerevan
Baku
AZERBAIJAN
LEBANON
Beirut
SYRIA
Damascus
Syrian Desert
Jerusalem
ISRAEL
Sinai
Amman
JORDAN
Dead Sea
-1,312 ft.
-400 m
IRAQ
Baghdad
Mesopotamia
Tigris R.
Euphrates R.
Elburz Mts.
Tehran
Zagros Mountains
IRAN
TURKMENISTAN
Ashkhabad
UZBEKISTAN
Tashkent
Bishkek
KYRGYZSTAN
TIAN SHAN
Dushanbe
TAJIKISTAN
TAKLIMAKAN DESERT
Kunlun Shan
AFGHANISTAN
Hindu Kush
Kabul
Islamabad
KASHMIR
PLATEAU OF TIBET
HIMALAYA
PAKISTAN
Indus R.
Thar Desert
New Delhi
NEPAL
Kathmandu
Mt. Everest
29,028 ft.
8,848 m
Thimphu
BHUTAN
Ganges R.
Dhaka
BANGLADESH
SAUDI ARABIA
Kuwait
KUWAIT
BAHRAIN
Persian Gulf
Arabian Gulf
Strait of Hormuz
Riyadh
QATAR
ARABIAN PENINSULA
Abu Dhabi
UNITED ARAB EMIRATES
Gulf of Oman
Masqat
Rub' al-Khali
OMAN
Sanaa
YEMEN
Red Sea
Gulf of Aden
Socotra
AFRICA
Arabian Sea
INDIA
Narmada R.
Godavari R.
DECCAN PLATEAU
Krishna R.
Western Ghats
Eastern Ghats
Bay of Bengal
Lakshadweep
Laccadive Sea
SRI LANKA
Colombo
Maldive Islands
Male
MALDIVES
INDIAN OCEAN
Chagos Archipelago
TROPIC OF CANCER
EQUATOR
20°N
0°
20°S
20°W
20°E
40°E
60°E
80°E
40°N
60°N
80°N
1
2
3
4
5
6
7
8
A
B
C
D
E
F
G
H
J
K

9 10 11 12 13 14 15 16
A B C D E F G H J K
NORTH AMERICA
Bering Strait
Chukchi Sea
Chukchi Peninsula
Gulf of Anadyr
OCEAN
Wrangel I.
Bering Sea
New Siberian Islands
East Siberian Sea
160°E
160°W
40°N
Aleutian Islands
Severnaya Zemlya
120°E
Laptev Sea
Taymyr Peninsula
Kolyma R.
Kolyma Mts.
0
1,000 miles
1,000 kilometers
Two-Point Equidistant Projection
Cherski Range
Commander Is.
Kamchatka Peninsula
Verkhoyanski Mts.
Lena R.
CENTRAL SIBERIAN PLATEAU
Sea of Okhotsk
20°N
SIBERIA
ASIA
Aldan R.
Kuril Islands
Sakhalin
Lena R.
Angara R.
Sikhote-Alin' Range
Amur R.
Lake Baikal
Yablonovyy Range
Hokkaidō
180°
TROPIC OF CANCER
Greater Khingan Range
Manchurian Plain
Honshū
Ulaanbaatar
NORTH KOREA
Sea of Japan (East Sea)
JAPAN
Tokyo
Shan
MONGOLIA
GOBI
P'yŏngyang
Nampo Shoto
Beijing
Seoul
SOUTH KOREA
Shikoku
Yellow Sea
Kyūshū
Huang He (Yellow R.)
North China Plain
Qilian Shan
Qaidam Basin
CHINA
East China Sea
PACIFIC OCEAN
Mariana Islands
Mekong R.
Chang Jiang (Yangtze R.)
Okinawa
Salween R.
Sichuan Basin
Ryukyu Islands
Gongga Shan 24,790 ft. 7,556 m
Taipei
TAIWAN
Xi R.
Caroline Islands
Brahmaputra
Irrawaddy R.
Philippine Sea
0°
MYANMAR (BURMA)
Hanoi
PHILIPPINE ISLANDS
LAOS
Hainan
Luzon
Nay Pyi Taw
Salween R.
Vientiane
Mekong R.
South China Sea
Manila
Samar
EQUATOR
THAILAND
Mindoro
Bangkok
VIETNAM
PHILIPPINES
Andaman Islands
CAMBODIA
Phnom Penh
Palawan
Mindanao
Andaman Sea
Gulf of Thailand
Sulu Sea
Nicobar Islands
Bandar Seri Begawan
Celebes Sea
BRUNEI
Moluccas
Malay Peninsula
MALAYSIA
New Guinea
Kuala Lumpur
Ceram
Aru Is.
SINGAPORE
Borneo
Sulawesi (Celebes)
Buru
Dolak
INDONESIA
Tanimbar Is.
Mentawai Islands
Sumatra
Greater Sunda Islands
Arafura Sea
Java Sea
Dili
EAST TIMOR (TIMOR-LESTE)
AUSTRALIA
120°E
Timor
Timor Sea
100°E
Jakarta
Java
140°E
20°S
160°E

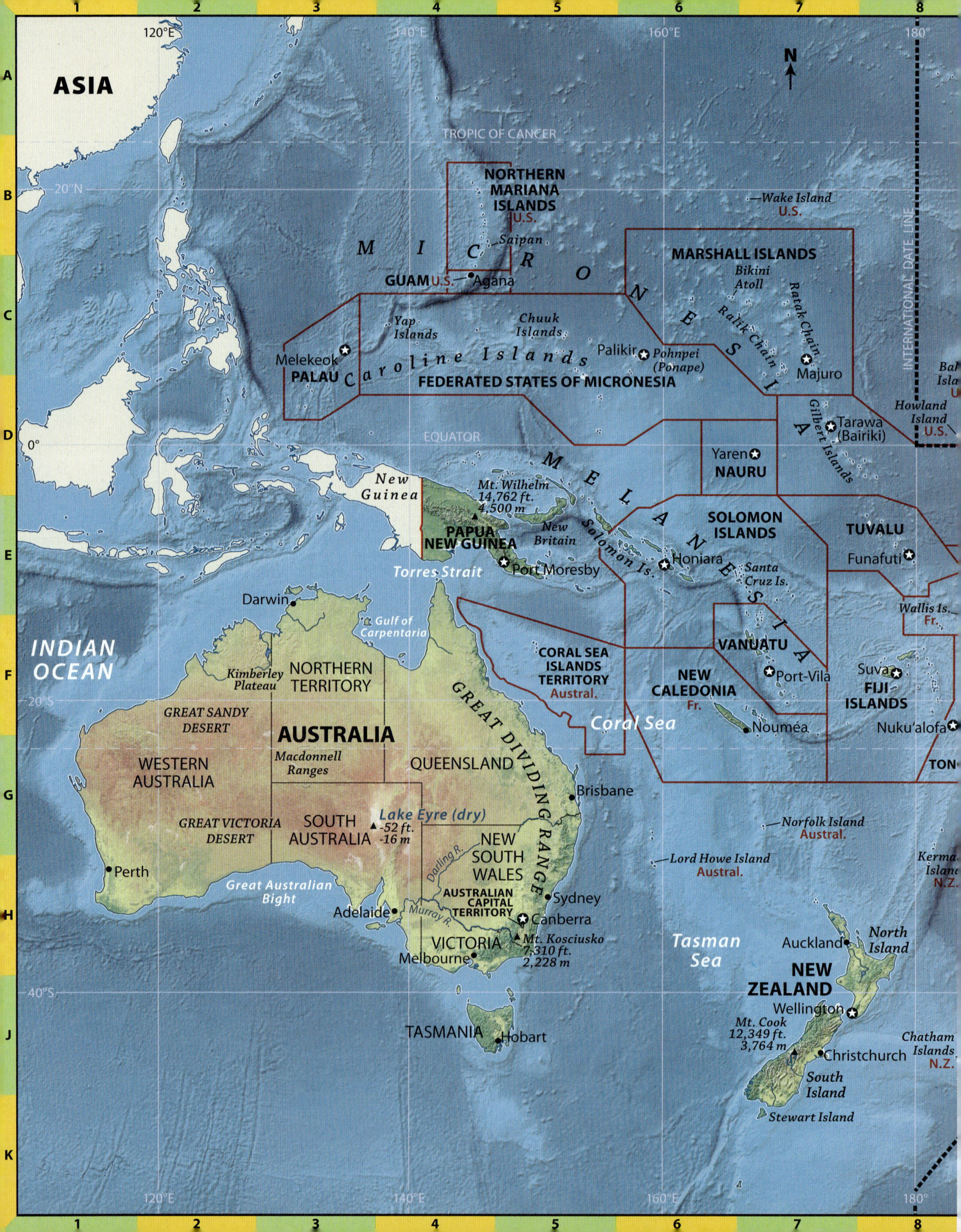

ASIA
INDIAN OCEAN
TROPIC OF CANCER
EQUATOR
INTERNATIONAL DATE LINE
NORTHERN MARIANA ISLANDS U.S.
Saipan
GUAM U.S.
Agana
M I C R O N E S I A
Wake Island U.S.
MARSHALL ISLANDS
Bikini Atoll
Ralik Chain
Ratak Chain
Majuro
Yap Islands
Chuuk Islands
Caroline Islands
Palikir
Pohnpei (Ponape)
Melekeok
PALAU
FEDERATED STATES OF MICRONESIA
Gilbert Islands
Tarawa (Bairiki)
Howland Island U.S.
Yaren
NAURU
M E L A N E S I A
New Guinea
Mt. Wilhelm 14,762 ft. 4,500 m
PAPUA NEW GUINEA
New Britain
Solomon Is.
Port Moresby
Torres Strait
SOLOMON ISLANDS
Honiara
Santa Cruz Is.
TUVALU
Funafuti
Wallis Is. Fr.
Darwin
Gulf of Carpentaria
CORAL SEA ISLANDS TERRITORY Austral.
VANUATU
Port-Vila
NEW CALEDONIA Fr.
Nouméa
Coral Sea
Suva
FIJI ISLANDS
Nuku'alofa
TON
Kimberley Plateau
NORTHERN TERRITORY
GREAT SANDY DESERT
AUSTRALIA
Macdonnell Ranges
WESTERN AUSTRALIA
QUEENSLAND
GREAT DIVIDING RANGE
Brisbane
GREAT VICTORIA DESERT
SOUTH AUSTRALIA
Lake Eyre (dry) -52 ft. -16 m
NEW SOUTH WALES
Darling R.
Murray R.
Perth
Great Australian Bight
Adelaide
AUSTRALIAN CAPITAL TERRITORY
Sydney
Canberra
Norfolk Island Austral.
Lord Howe Island Austral.
Mt. Kosciusko 7,310 ft. 2,228 m
VICTORIA
Melbourne
Tasman Sea
TASMANIA
Hobart
Auckland
North Island
NEW ZEALAND
Wellington
Mt. Cook 12,349 ft. 3,764 m
Christchurch
South Island
Stewart Island
Chatham Islands N.Z.
120°E
140°E
160°E
180°
20°N
0°
20°S
40°S

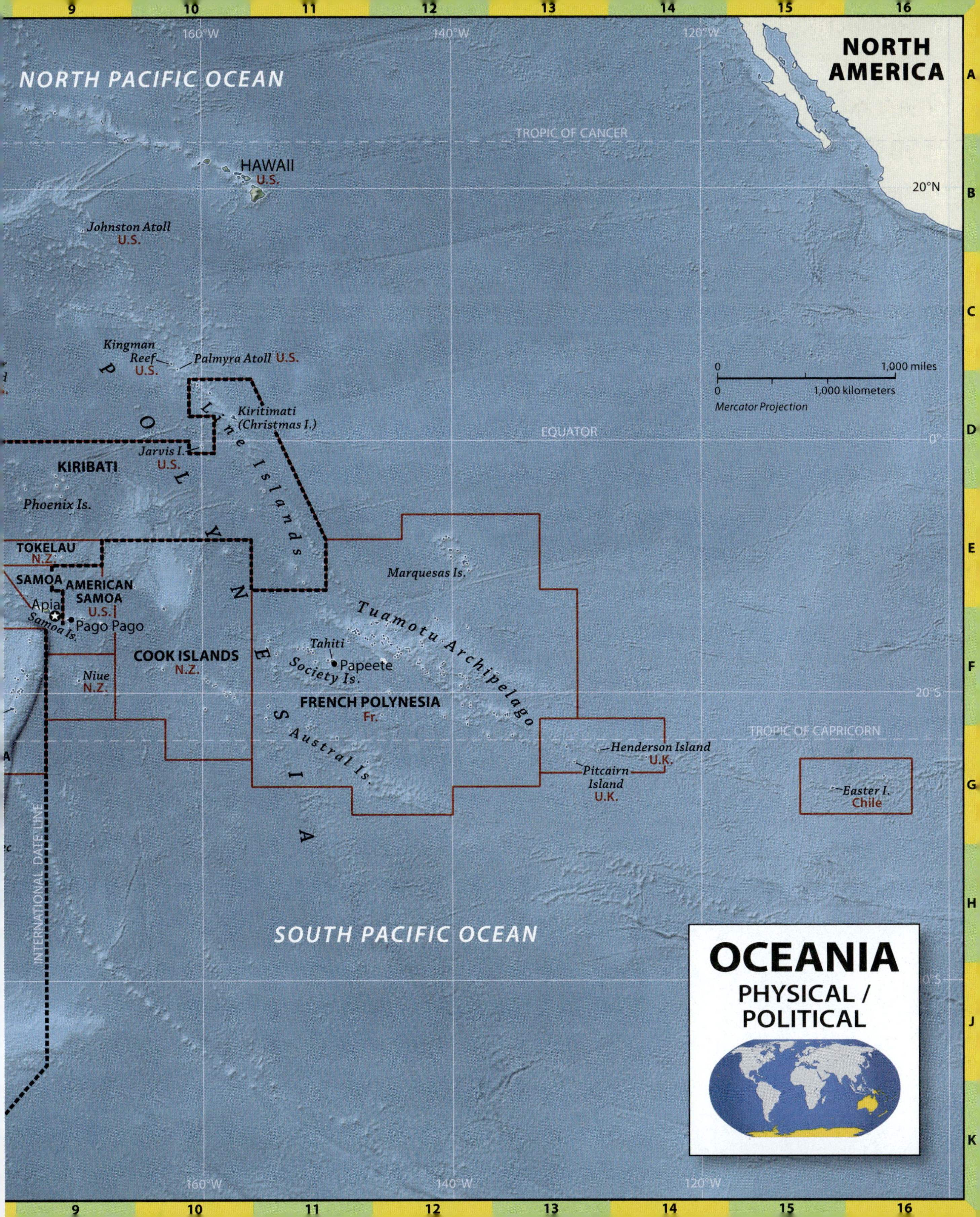
NORTH PACIFIC OCEAN
NORTH AMERICA
TROPIC OF CANCER
HAWAII
U.S.
Johnston Atoll
U.S.
Kingman Reef
U.S.
Palmyra Atoll U.S.
Kiritimati (Christmas I.)
Line Islands
0 1,000 miles
0 1,000 kilometers
Mercator Projection
EQUATOR
Jarvis I.
U.S.
KIRIBATI
Phoenix Is.
POLYNESIA
TOKELAU
N.Z.
SAMOA
AMERICAN SAMOA
U.S.
Apia
Samoa Is.
Pago Pago
Marquesas Is.
Tuamotu Archipelago
Tahiti
Papeete
Society Is.
COOK ISLANDS
N.Z.
Niue
N.Z.
FRENCH POLYNESIA
Fr.
Austral Is.
TROPIC OF CAPRICORN
Henderson Island
U.K.
Pitcairn Island
U.K.
Easter I.
Chile
INTERNATIONAL DATE LINE
SOUTH PACIFIC OCEAN
160°W
140°W
120°W
20°N
0°
20°S
OCEANIA
PHYSICAL / POLITICAL

RUSSIA
Lake Baikal
Yablonovyy Range
Bering Sea
ALEUTIAN ISLANDS
KAMCHATKA PENINSULA
Sea of Okhotsk
Sakhalin
Kuril Islands
Ulaanbaatar
MONGOLIA
ALTAY SHAN
GOBI
Greater Khingan Range
Manchurian Plain
Amur R.
Sikhote-Alin' Range
Hokkaido
NORTH PACIFI
Beijing
CHINA
P'yongyang
NORTH KOREA
Seoul
SOUTH KOREA
Sea of Japan (East Sea)
Honshu
JAPAN
Tokyo
Huang He (Yellow R.)
Yellow Sea
Kyushu
Shikoku
Nampo Shoto
INTERNATIONAL DATE LINE
Chang Jiang (Yangtze R.)
East China Sea
Ryukyu Islands
Hawaii
INDIA
Taipei
TAIWAN
MYANMAR (BURMA)
Hanoi
LAOS
Nay Pyi Taw
Vientiane
VIETNAM
THAILAND
Hainan
South China Sea
Luzon
PHILIPPINE ISLANDS
Philippine Sea
NORTHERN MARIANA ISLANDS U.S.
MICRONESIA
MARSHALL ISLANDS
Ratak Chain
Ralik Chain
Bangkok
Mekong
CAMBODIA
Phnom Penh
Manila
PHILIPPINES
GUAM U.S.
Andaman Sea
Bandar Seri Begawan
BRUNEI
Sulu Sea
Melekeok
PALAU
Caroline Islands
Palikir
Majuro
Mindanao
FEDERATED STATES OF MICRONESIA
Kuala Lumpur
MALAYSIA
SINGAPORE
Celebes Sea
Borneo
Sumatra
INDONESIA
GREATER SUNDA ISLANDS
Sulawesi (Celebes)
Moluccas
Tarawa (Bairiki)
Gilbert Islands
KIRIBATI
Phoenix Is.
Yaren NAURU
MELANESIA
New Guinea
SOLOMON ISLANDS
Jakarta
Java
Java Sea
Dili
EAST TIMOR (TIMOR-LESTE)
Arafura Sea
PAPUA NEW GUINEA
Port Moresby
Solomon Is.
Honiara
TUVALU
Funafuti
Tokelau N.Z.
Lesser Sunda Islands
Santa Cruz Islands
WALLIS AND FUTUNA IS. Fr.
SAMOA
Apia
AMERICAN SAMOA U.S.
CORAL SEA ISLANDS TERRITORY Austral.
VANUATU
Port-Vila
NEW CALEDONIA Fr.
Suva
FIJI ISLANDS
TONGA
Nuku'alofa
Niue N.Z.
Coral Sea
AUSTRALIA
Norfolk Island Austral.
Kermadec Islands N.Z.
Lord Howe Island Austral.
Darling R.
Great Australian Bight
INDIAN OCEAN
Canberra
Tasman Sea
NEW ZEALAND
Wellington
Tasmania
Chatham Island N.Z.
0 1,000 miles
0 1,000 kilometers
Mercator Projection
100°E
120°E
140°E
160°E
180°
40°N
20°N
0°
20°S
40°S
1 2 3 4 5 6 7 8
A B C D E F G H J K

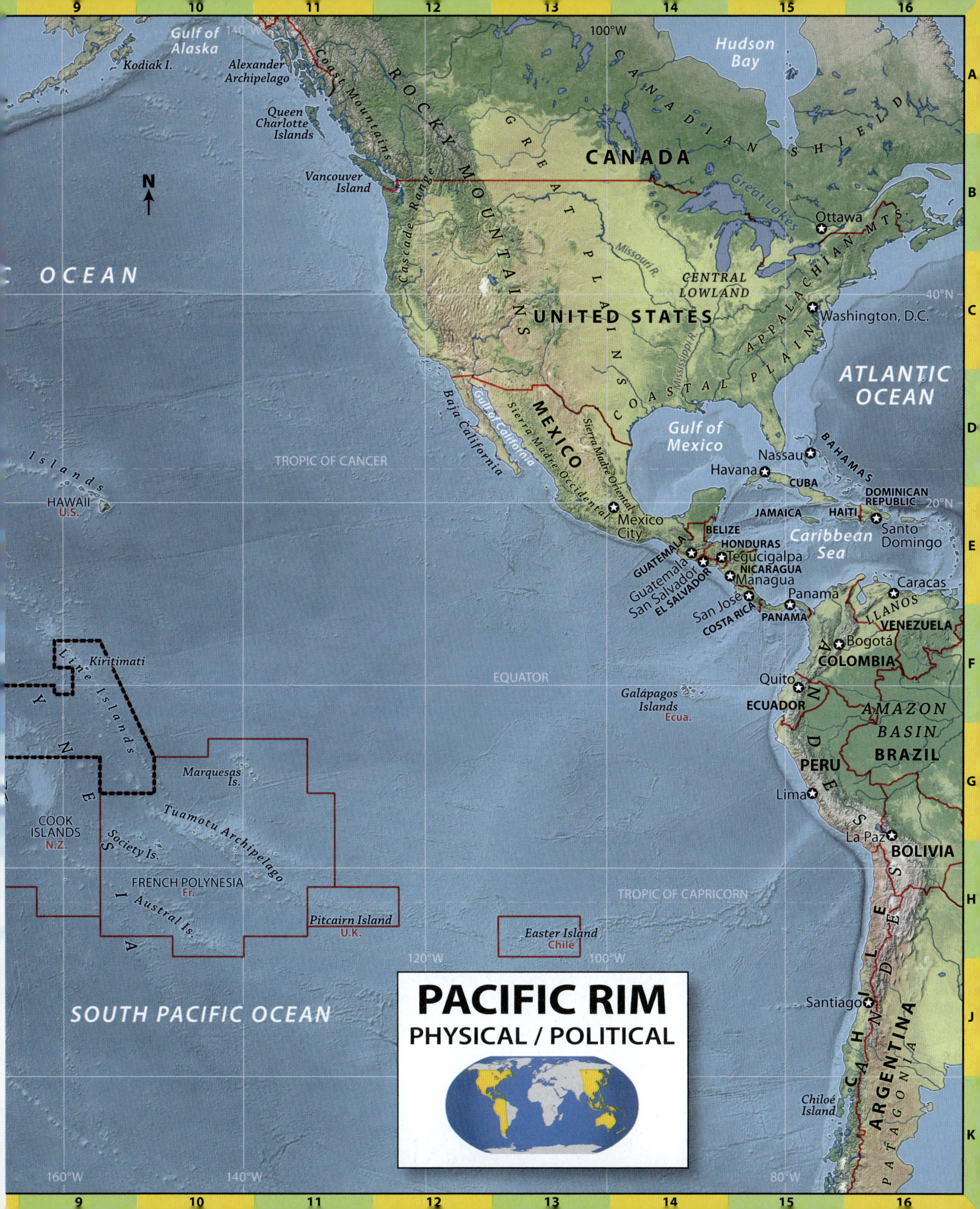

PACIFIC RIM
PHYSICAL / POLITICAL
Gulf of Alaska
Kodiak I.
Alexander Archipelago
Queen Charlotte Islands
Vancouver Island
Coast Mountains
ROCKY MOUNTAINS
Cascade Range
Hudson Bay
CANADIAN SHIELD
CANADA
GREAT PLAINS
Great Lakes
Ottawa
Missouri R.
CENTRAL LOWLAND
APPALACHIAN MTS.
UNITED STATES
Washington, D.C.
Mississippi R.
COASTAL PLAIN
ATLANTIC OCEAN
OCEAN
Baja California
Gulf of California
Sierra Madre Occidental
Sierra Madre Oriental
MEXICO
Gulf of Mexico
Mexico City
Nassau
BAHAMAS
Havana
CUBA
DOMINICAN REPUBLIC
HAITI
JAMAICA
Santo Domingo
BELIZE
HONDURAS
Caribbean Sea
GUATEMALA
Guatemala
San Salvador
EL SALVADOR
Tegucigalpa
NICARAGUA
Managua
San José
COSTA RICA
Panama
PANAMA
Caracas
LLANOS
VENEZUELA
Bogotá
COLOMBIA
Quito
ECUADOR
Galápagos Islands
Ecua.
AMAZON BASIN
BRAZIL
PERU
Lima
ANDES
La Paz
BOLIVIA
Santiago
ARGENTINA
PATAGONIA
Chiloé Island
CHILE
Islands
HAWAII
U.S.
TROPIC OF CANCER
EQUATOR
TROPIC OF CAPRICORN
Kiritimati
Line Islands
POLYNESIA
Marquesas Is.
Tuamotu Archipelago
Society Is.
COOK ISLANDS
N.Z.
FRENCH POLYNESIA
Fr.
Austral Is.
Pitcairn Island
U.K.
Easter Island
Chile
SOUTH PACIFIC OCEAN
140°W
100°W
40°N
20°N
120°W
160°W
80°W

World Religions

World Economy

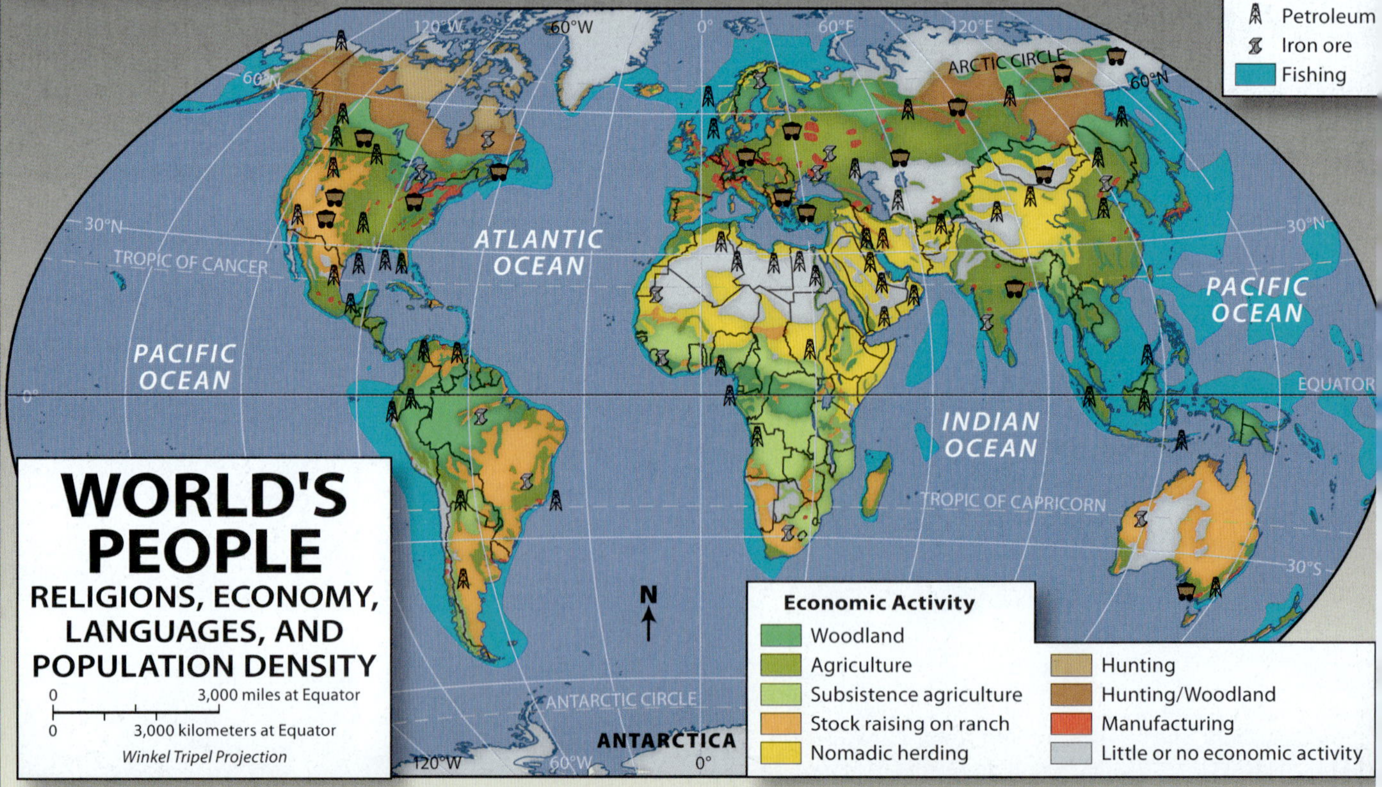

WORLD'S PEOPLE

RELIGIONS, ECONOMY, LANGUAGES, AND POPULATION DENSITY

0 — 3,000 miles at Equator

0 — 3,000 kilometers at Equator

Winkel Tripel Projection

World Language Families

World Population Density

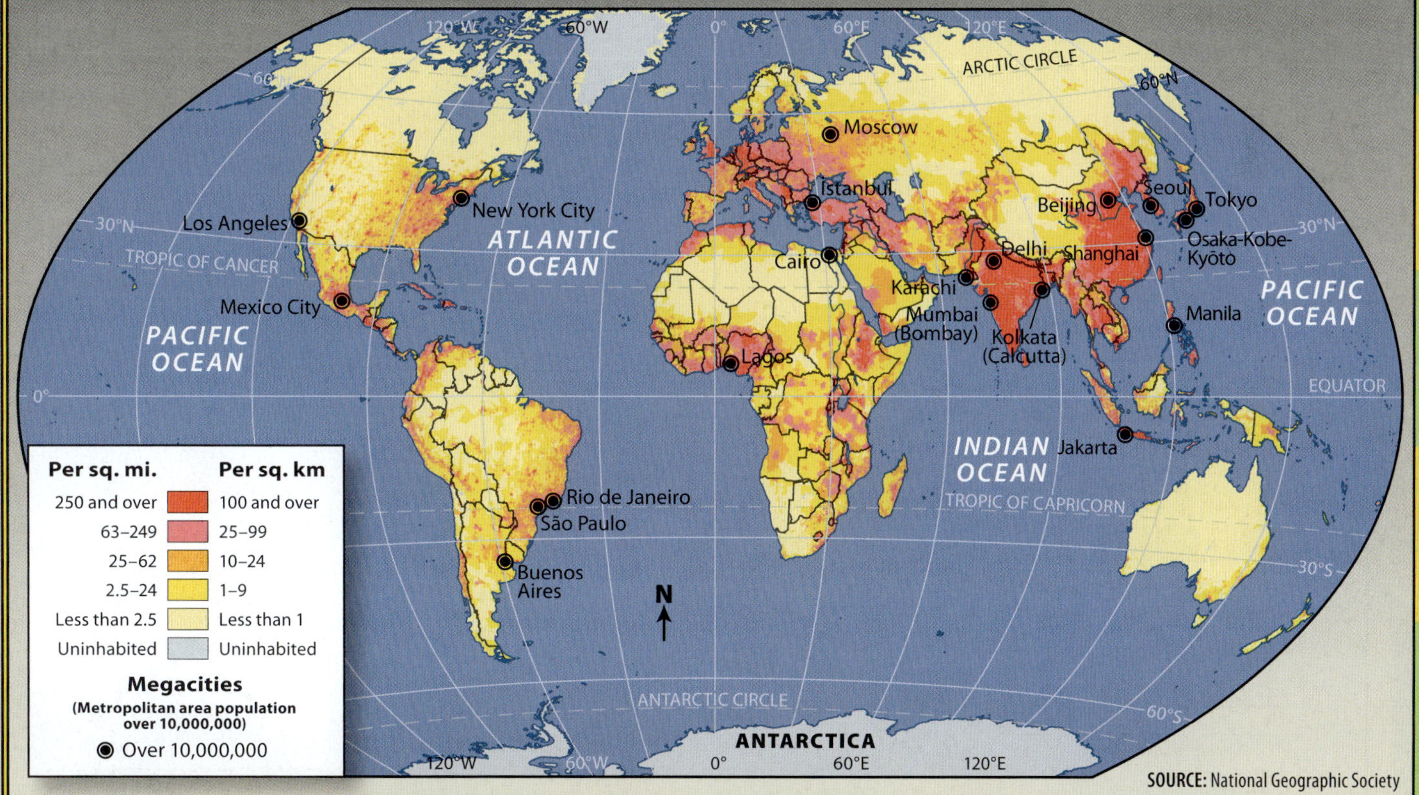

SOURCE: National Geographic Society

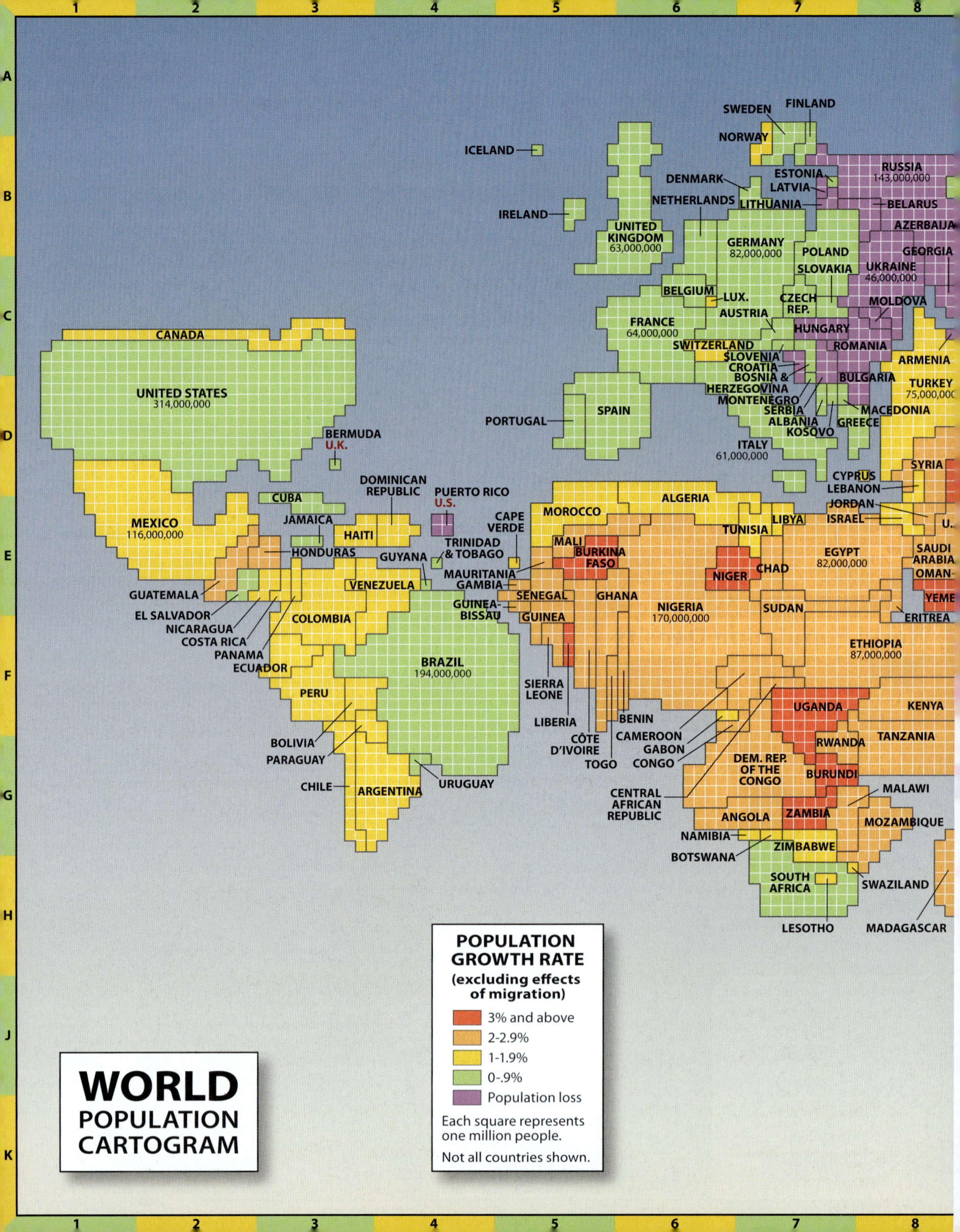
WORLD POPULATION CARTOGRAM
POPULATION GROWTH RATE (excluding effects of migration)
3% and above
2-2.9%
1-1.9%
0-.9%
Population loss
Each square represents one million people.
Not all countries shown.
1 2 3 4 5 6 7 8
A B C D E F G H J K
CANADA
UNITED STATES 314,000,000
MEXICO 116,000,000
BERMUDA U.K.
CUBA
JAMAICA
HAITI
DOMINICAN REPUBLIC
PUERTO RICO U.S.
HONDURAS
GUATEMALA
EL SALVADOR
NICARAGUA
COSTA RICA
PANAMA
ECUADOR
COLOMBIA
VENEZUELA
GUYANA
TRINIDAD & TOBAGO
BRAZIL 194,000,000
PERU
BOLIVIA
PARAGUAY
CHILE
ARGENTINA
URUGUAY
ICELAND
IRELAND
UNITED KINGDOM 63,000,000
SWEDEN
FINLAND
NORWAY
DENMARK
NETHERLANDS
ESTONIA
LATVIA
LITHUANIA
RUSSIA 143,000,000
BELARUS
GEORGIA
UKRAINE 46,000,000
GERMANY 82,000,000
POLAND
SLOVAKIA
BELGIUM
LUX.
CZECH REP.
AUSTRIA
MOLDOVA
FRANCE 64,000,000
HUNGARY
SWITZERLAND
ROMANIA
SLOVENIA
CROATIA
BOSNIA & HERZEGOVINA
BULGARIA
ARMENIA
MONTENEGRO
SERBIA
ALBANIA
KOSOVO
MACEDONIA
GREECE
PORTUGAL
SPAIN
ITALY 61,000,000
CYPRUS
LEBANON
JORDAN
ISRAEL
SYRIA
MOROCCO
ALGERIA
TUNISIA
LIBYA
CAPE VERDE
MALI
BURKINA FASO
NIGER
CHAD
EGYPT 82,000,000
SAUDI ARABIA
MAURITANIA
GAMBIA
SENEGAL
GHANA
GUINEA-BISSAU
GUINEA
NIGERIA 170,000,000
SUDAN
ERITREA
ETHIOPIA 87,000,000
SIERRA LEONE
LIBERIA
CÔTE D'IVOIRE
TOGO
BENIN
CAMEROON
GABON
CONGO
CENTRAL AFRICAN REPUBLIC
UGANDA
KENYA
RWANDA
TANZANIA
DEM. REP. OF THE CONGO
BURUNDI
MALAWI
ANGOLA
ZAMBIA
MOZAMBIQUE
NAMIBIA
BOTSWANA
ZIMBABWE
SOUTH AFRICA
SWAZILAND
LESOTHO
MADAGASCAR

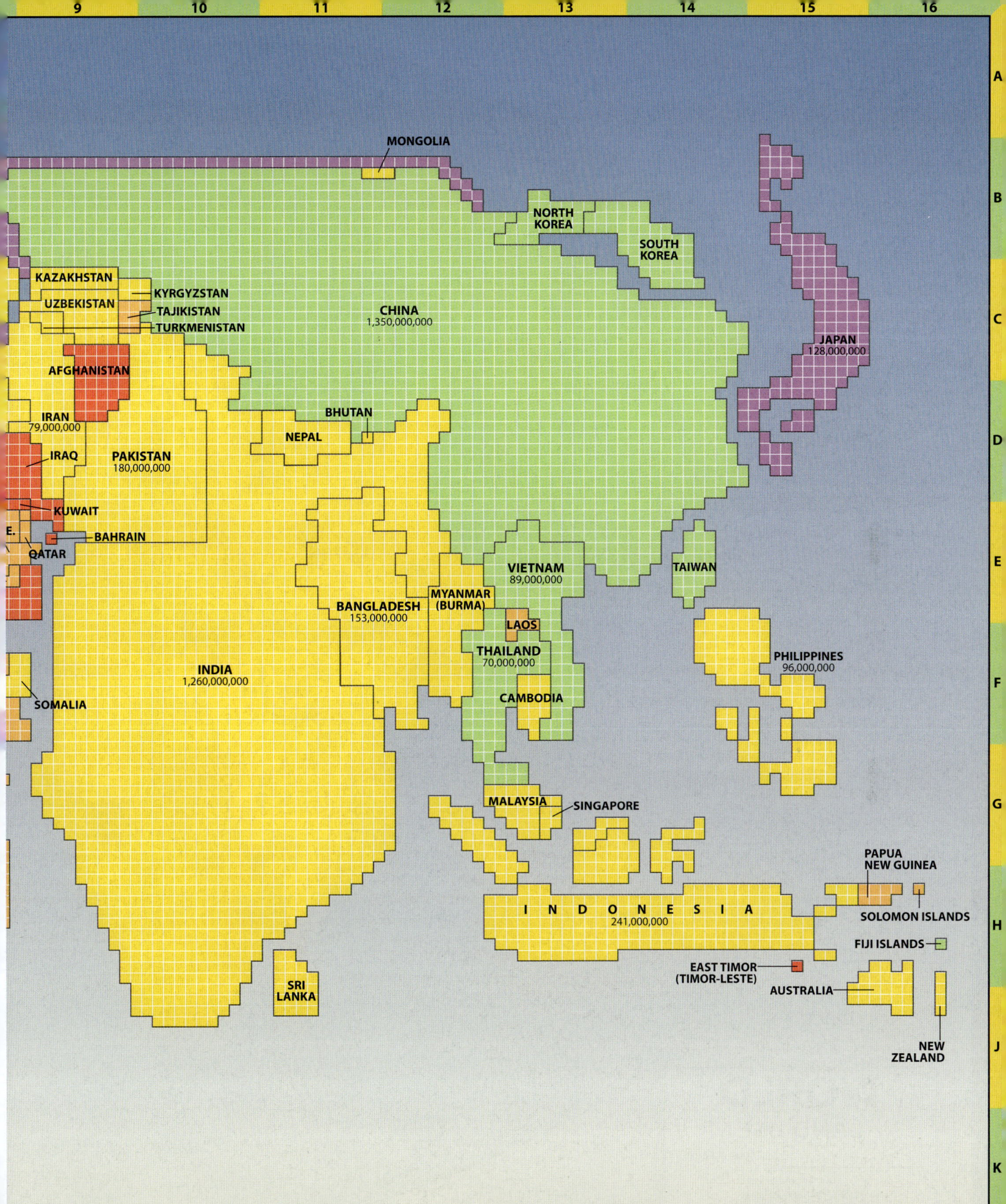

SOURCE: Population Reference Bureau, Population and Economic Development 2012 Data Sheet

WORLD
LAND USE
0
2,000 miles at Equator
0
2,000 kilometers at Equator
Winkel Tripel Projection
Woodland
Agriculture
Subsistence agriculture
Stock raising on ranch
Nomadic herding
Hunting
Hunting/Woodland
Manufacturing
Fishing
Little or no economic activity
Largest urban areas
(selected urban areas are named)
NORTH AMERICA
SOUTH AMERICA
NORTH PACIFIC OCEAN
NORTH ATLANTIC OCEAN
SOUTH PACIFIC OCEAN
SOUTH ATLANTIC OCEAN
Chukchi Sea
Beaufort Sea
Bering Sea
Great Bear Lake
Great Slave Lake
Hudson Bay
Baffin Bay
Labrador Sea
Greenland Sea
Lake Winnipeg
Great Lakes
Great Salt Lake
Gulf of Mexico
Caribbean Sea
Scotia Sea
Bellingshausen Sea
Weddell Sea
Ross Sea
Los Angeles
New York City
Mexico City
Rio de Janeiro
São Paulo
Buenos Aires
Lond
ARCT
ARCTIC CIRC
TROPIC OF CANCER
TROPIC OF CAPRICORN
ANTARCTIC CIRCLE
60°N
30°N
0°
30°S
60°S
150°W
120°W
90°W
60°W
30°W
1
2
3
4
5
6
7
8
A
B
C
D
E
F
G
H
J
K

9
10
11
12
13
14
15
16
A
B
C
D
E
F
G
H
J
K
30°E
60°E
90°E
120°E
150°E
OCEAN
N
Barents Sea
Kara Sea
Laptev Sea
East Siberian Sea
Norwegian Sea
60°N
Bering Sea
Sea of Okhotsk
North Sea
Baltic Sea
Moscow
Lake Baikal
ASIA
Paris
EUROPE
Aral Sea
Sea of Japan (East Sea)
NORTH PACIFIC OCEAN
Black Sea
Caspian Sea
Seoul
Yellow Sea
Tokyo
Mediterranean Sea
30°N
Shanghai
East China Sea
TROPIC OF CANCER
Cairo
Red Sea
Philippine Sea
Kolkata (Calcutta)
Mumbai (Bombay)
Bay of Bengal
South China Sea
Gulf of Aden
AFRICA
Arabian Sea
Andaman Sea
Lagos
Gulf of Guinea
EQUATOR
0°
Lake Victoria
Kinshasa
Lake Tanganyika
Arafura Sea
INDIAN OCEAN
Coral Sea
TROPIC OF CAPRICORN
AUSTRALIA
SOUTH PACIFIC OCEAN
30°S
Sydney
Tasman Sea
PRIME MERIDIAN (MERIDIAN OF GREENWICH)
The Atlantic, Indian, and Pacific Oceans merge around Antarctica. Some define this as an ocean, calling it the Antarctic Ocean, Austral Ocean, or Southern Ocean. While most accept four oceans (including the Arctic Ocean), there is little international agreement on the name and extent of a fifth ocean.
SOUTHERN OCEAN
60°S
Ross Sea
ANTARCTICA

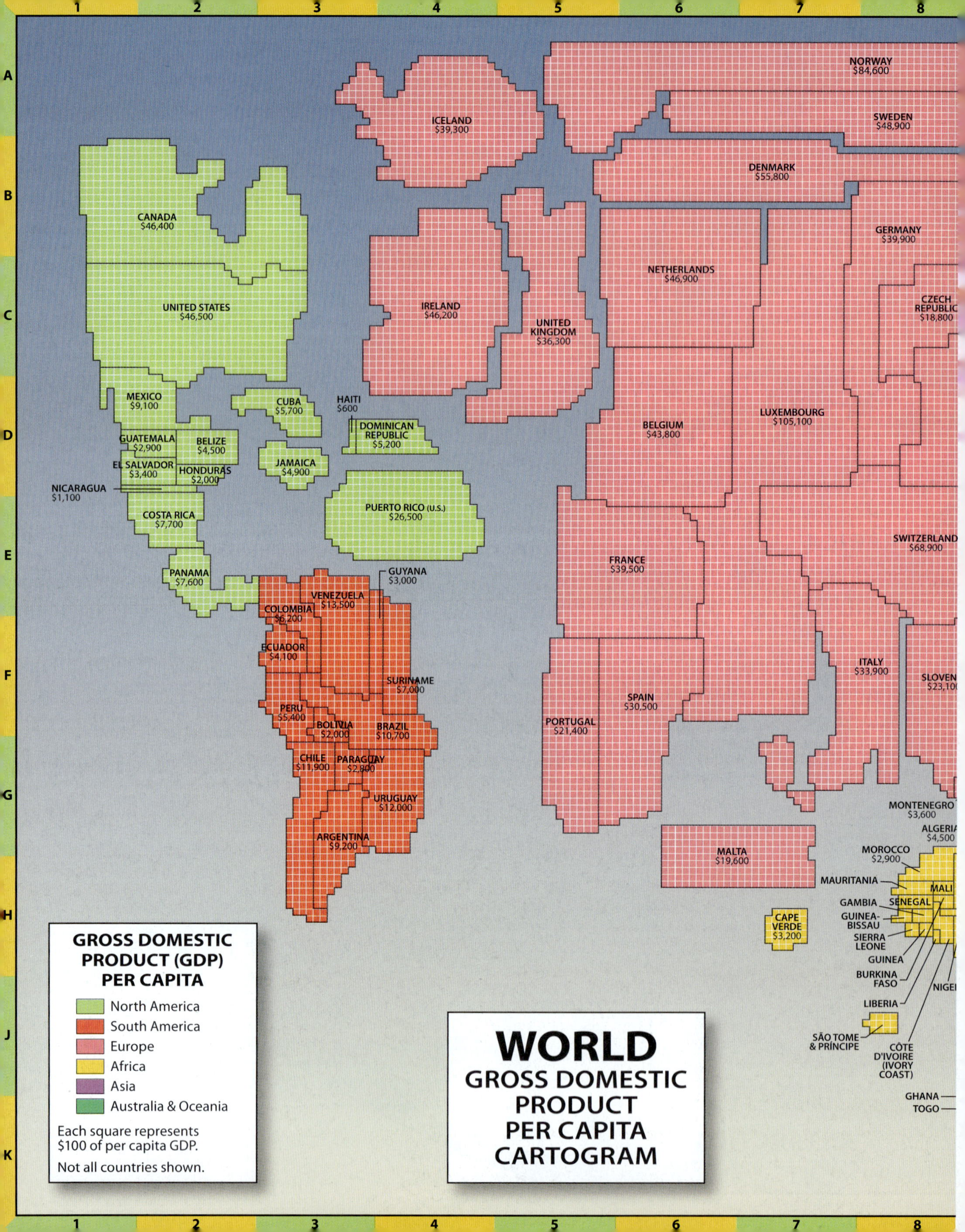
WORLD
GROSS DOMESTIC PRODUCT PER CAPITA CARTOGRAM
GROSS DOMESTIC PRODUCT (GDP) PER CAPITA
North America
South America
Europe
Africa
Asia
Australia & Oceania
Each square represents $100 of per capita GDP.
Not all countries shown.
CANADA $46,400
UNITED STATES $46,500
MEXICO $9,100
GUATEMALA $2,900
BELIZE $4,500
EL SALVADOR $3,400
HONDURAS $2,000
NICARAGUA $1,100
COSTA RICA $7,700
PANAMA $7,600
CUBA $5,700
HAITI $600
DOMINICAN REPUBLIC $5,200
JAMAICA $4,900
PUERTO RICO (U.S.) $26,500
GUYANA $3,000
VENEZUELA $13,500
COLOMBIA $6,200
ECUADOR $4,100
SURINAME $7,000
PERU $5,400
BOLIVIA $2,000
BRAZIL $10,700
CHILE $11,900
PARAGUAY $2,800
URUGUAY $12,000
ARGENTINA $9,200
ICELAND $39,300
NORWAY $84,600
SWEDEN $48,900
DENMARK $55,800
IRELAND $46,200
UNITED KINGDOM $36,300
NETHERLANDS $46,900
GERMANY $39,900
CZECH REPUBLIC $18,800
BELGIUM $43,800
LUXEMBOURG $105,100
FRANCE $39,500
SWITZERLAND $68,900
ITALY $33,900
PORTUGAL $21,400
SPAIN $30,500
MALTA $19,600
MONTENEGRO $3,600
MOROCCO $2,900
MAURITANIA
MALI
SENEGAL
GAMBIA
GUINEA-BISSAU
SIERRA LEONE
GUINEA
BURKINA FASO
LIBERIA
CAPE VERDE $3,200
SÃO TOME & PRÍNCIPE
CÔTE D'IVOIRE (IVORY COAST)
GHANA
TOGO

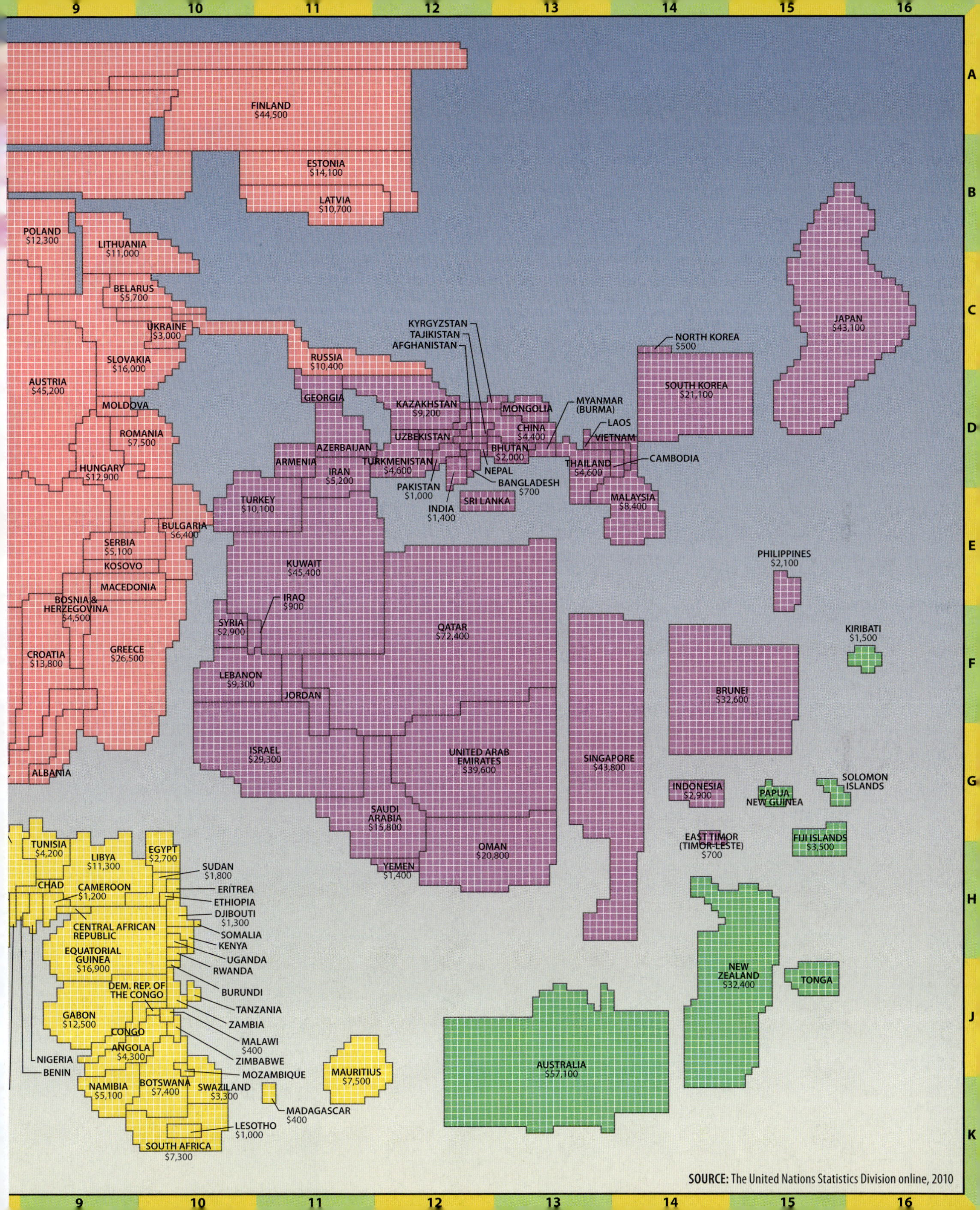

SOURCE: The United Nations Statistics Division online, 2010

TEXAS
PHYSICAL / POLITICAL
COLORADO
KANSAS
MISSOURI
OKLAHOMA
ARKANSAS
NEW MEXICO
LA.
MEXICO
HIGH PLAINS
Canadian R.
Amarillo
LLANO ESTACADO
Lubbock
Caprock Escarpment
Red R.
Lake Texoma
Wright Patman Lake
Plano
Garland
Irving
L. Tawakoni
Caddo Lake
Fort Worth
Dallas
Arlington
Sabine R.
Abilene
El Paso
Guadalupe Peak 8,749 ft. 2,667 m
Guadalupe Mts.
Pecos R.
(Rio Bravo del Norte)
Rio Grande
Davis Mts.
Glass Mts.
Stockton Plateau
Chisos Mts.
TEXAS
EDWARDS PLATEAU
Leon R.
Waco
Brazos R.
Trinity R.
Neches R.
Toledo Bend Res.
Sam Rayburn Reservoir
Lake Livingston
Austin
Colorado R.
Guadalupe R.
Beaumont
Houston
Pasadena
Balcones Escarpment
San Antonio
Amistad Reservoir
Nueces
Choke Canyon Reservoir
COASTAL PLAINS
Galveston Bay
Galveston Island
Matagorda Bay
Matagorda Island
Corpus Christi
Corpus Christi Bay
Laredo
Falcon Lake
Padre Island
Brownsville
Gulf of Mexico
0 100 miles
0 100 kilometers
Lambert Azimuthal Equal-Area Projection
40°N
35°N
30°N
25°N
105°W
100°W
95°W
N

TEXAS
LAND USE
COLORADO
KANSAS
MISSOURI
OKLAHOMA
ARKANSAS
NEW MEXICO
LA.
MEXICO
TEXAS
N
40°N
35°N
30°N
25°N
105°W
100°W
95°W
Amarillo
Lubbock
Midland
Odessa
El Paso
Guadalupe Peak
8,749 ft.
2,667 m
San Angelo
Abilene
Wichita Falls
Sherman
Denton
Lewisville
Plano
Garland
Irving
Mesquite
Dallas
Fort Worth
Arlington
Texarkana
Longview
Tyler
Waco
Killeen
Temple
Bryan
College Station
Austin
San Antonio
Victoria
Houston
Pasadena
Texas City
Galveston
Beaumont
Port Arthur
Corpus Christi
Laredo
McAllen
Harlingen
Brownsville
Canadian R.
Red R.
Lake Texoma
Wright Patman Lake
Caddo Lake
Sabine R.
Toledo Bend Res.
Sam Rayburn Reservoir
Lake Livingston
Neches R.
Trinity R.
Brazos R.
Leon R.
Colorado R.
Guadalupe R.
Pecos R.
Rio Grande
(Rio Bravo del Norte)
Nueces R.
Amistad Reservoir
Choke Canyon Reservoir
Falcon Lake
Galveston Bay
Galveston Island
Matagorda Bay
Matagorda Island
Corpus Christi Bay
Padre Island
Gulf of Mexico
Agriculture
Stock raising on ranch
Manufacturing
Fishing
0
100 miles
0
100 kilometers
Lambert Azimuthal Equal-Area Projection

How do I study **Geography?**

Geographers have tried to understand the best way to teach and learn about geography. In order to do this, geographers created the *Five Themes of Geography*. The themes acted as a guide for teaching the basic ideas about geography to students like yourself.

People who teach and study geography, though, thought that the Five Themes were too broad. In 1994, geographers created 18 national geography standards. These standards were more detailed about what should be taught and learned. The Six Essential Elements act as a bridge connecting the Five Themes with the standards.

These pages show you how the Five Themes are related to the Six Essential Elements and the 18 standards.

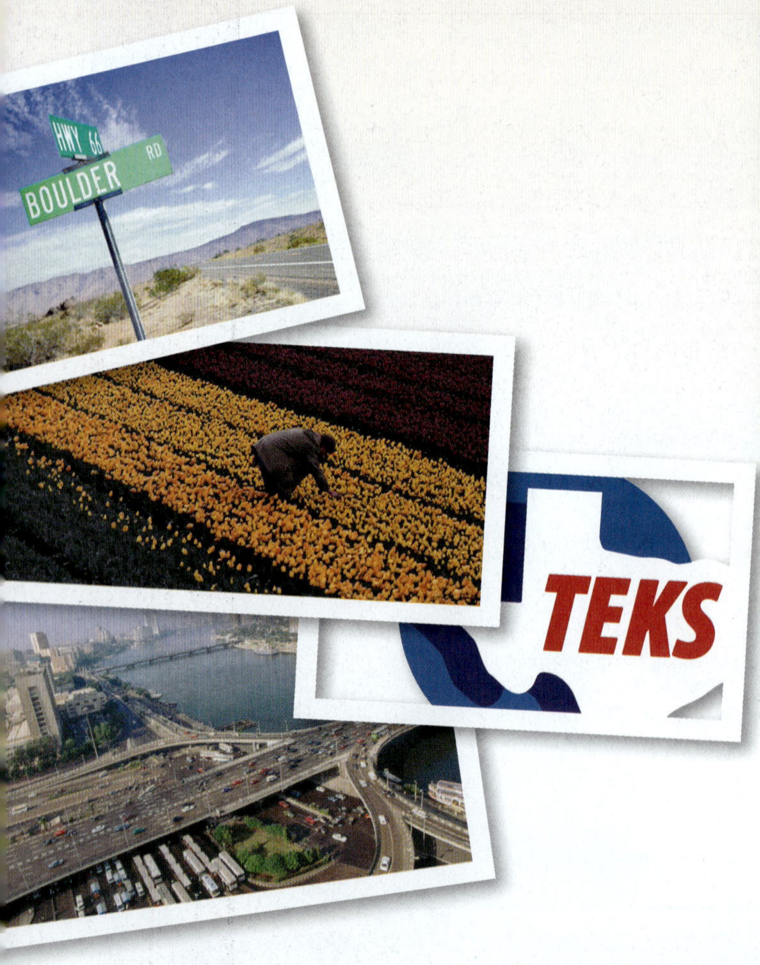

5 Themes of Geography

1 Location

Location describes where something is. Absolute location describes a place's exact position on the Earth's surface. Relative location expresses where a place is in relation to another place.

2 Place

Place describes the physical and human characteristics that make a location unique.

3 Regions

Regions are areas that share common characteristics.

4 Movement

Movement explains how and why people and things move and are connected.

5 Human-Environment Interaction

Human-Environment Interaction describes the relationship between people and their environment.

6 Essential Elements

18 Geography Standards

I. The World in Spatial Terms

Geographers look to see where a place is located. Location acts as a starting point to answer "Where is it?" The location of a place helps you orient yourself as to where you are.

1 How to use maps and other tools.

2 How to use mental maps to organize information.

3 How to analyze the spatial organization of people, places, and environments.

II Places and Regions

Place describes physical characteristics such as landforms, climate, and plant or animal life. It might also describe human characteristics, including language and way of life. Places can also be organized into regions. **Regions** are places united by one or more characteristics.

4 The physical and human characteristics of places.

5 How people create regions to interpret Earth's complexity.

6 How culture and experience influence people's perceptions of places and regions.

III. Physical Systems

Geographers study how physical systems, such as hurricanes, volcanoes, and glaciers, shape the surface of the Earth. They also look at how plants and animals depend upon one another and their surroundings for their survival.

7 The physical processes that shape Earth's surface.

8 The distribution of ecosystems on Earth's surface.

IV. Human Systems

People shape the world in which they live. They settle in certain places, but not in others. An ongoing theme in geography is the movement of people, ideas, and goods.

9 The characteristics, distribution, and migration of human populations.

10 The complexity of Earth's cultural mosaics.

11 The patterns and networks of economic interdependence.

12 The patterns of human settlements.

13 The forces of cooperation and conflict.

V. Environment and Society

How does the relationship between people and their natural surroundings influence the way people live? Geographers study how people use the environment and how their actions affect the environment.

14 How human actions modify the physical environment.

15 How physical systems affect human systems.

16 The meaning, use, and distribution of resources.

VI. The Uses of Geography

Knowledge of geography helps us understand the relationships among people, places, and environments over time. Applying geographic skills helps you understand the past and prepare for the future.

17 How to apply geography to interpret the past.

18 How to apply geography to interpret the present and plan for the future.

GEOGRAPHY SKILLS HANDBOOK

CONTENTS

Geography Skills Handbook

Throughout this text, you will discover how geography has shaped the course of events in history. Landforms, waterways, climate, and natural resources all have helped or hindered human activities. Usually people have learned either to adapt to their environments or to transform it to meet their needs. The resources in this Geography Skills Handbook will help you get the most out of your textbook—and provide you with skills you will use for the rest of your life.

Geographers use a wide array of tools to collect and analyze information to help them understand the Earth. The study of geography is more than knowing a lot of facts about places. Rather, it has more to do with asking questions about the Earth, pursuing their answers, and solving problems. Thus, one of the most important geographic tools is inside your head: the ability to think geographically.

Globes and Maps

A **globe** is a scale model of the Earth. Because Earth is round, a globe presents the most accurate depiction of geographic information such as area, distance, and direction. However, globes show little close-up detail. A printed **map** is a symbolic representation of all or part of the planet. Unlike globes, maps can show small areas in great detail.

From 3-D to 2-D

Think about the surface of the Earth as the peel of an orange. To flatten the peel, you have to cut it into segments that are still connected as one piece. To create maps that are not interrupted, mapmakers, or **cartographers**, use mathematical formulas to transfer information from the three-dimensional globe to the two-dimensional map. However, when the curves of a globe become straight lines on a map, distortion of size, shape, distance, or area occurs.

Great Circle Routes

A straight line of true direction—one that runs directly from west to east, for example—is not always the shortest distance between two points. This is due to the curvature of the Earth. To find the shortest distance, stretch a piece of string around the globe from one point to the other. The string will form part of a *great circle*, an imaginary line that follows the curve of the Earth. Ship captains and airline pilots use these **great circle routes** to reduce travel time and conserve fuel.

The idea of a great circle route in an important difference between globes and maps. A round globe accurately shows a great circle route, as indicated on the top right map. However, the flat map below it shows the great circle distance (dotted line) between Tokyo and Los Angeles to be far longer than the true direction distance (solid line). In fact, the great circle distance is 315 miles (506 km) shorter.

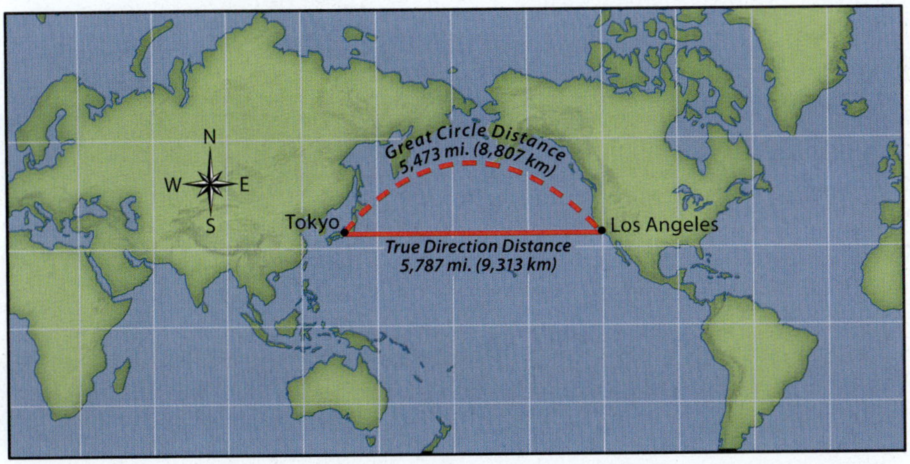

VOCABULARY

globe
a scale model of the Earth

maps
a symbolic representation of all or part of the planet

cartographers
mapmakers

great circle route
a straight line of true direction on a globe

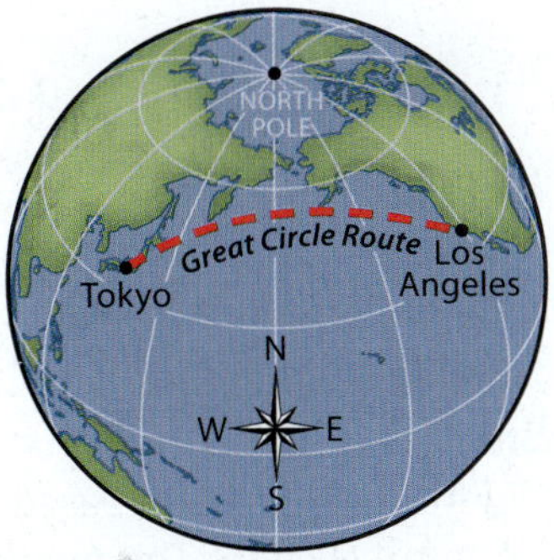

GEOGRAPHY CONNECTION

1. ***Explain*** the significance of: globe, map, cartographer, great circle route.
2. ***Describe*** the problems that arise when the curves of a globe become straight lines on a map.
3. ***Use*** a Venn diagram like the one below to identify the similarities and differences between globes and maps.

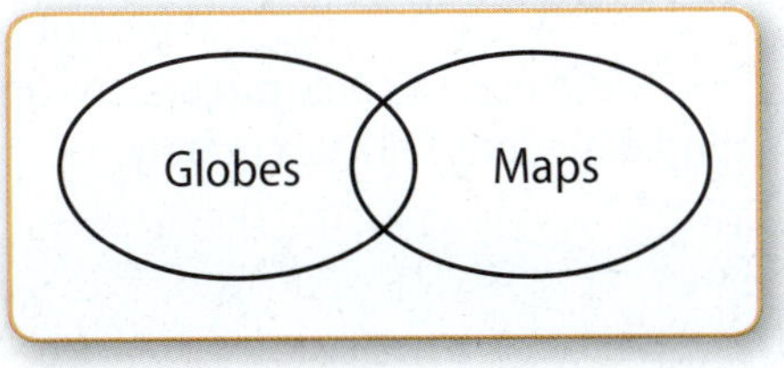

Projections

To create maps, cartographers project the round Earth onto a flat surface—making a **map projection.** Distance, shape, direction, or size may be distorted by a projection. As a result, the purpose of the map usually dictates which projection is used. There are many kinds of map projections, some with general names and some named for the cartographers who developed them. Three basic categories of map projections are shown here: **planar, cylindrical,** and **conic**.

Planar Projection

A planar projection shows the Earth centered in such a way that a straight line coming from the center to any point represents the shortest distance. Also known as an azimuthal projection, it is most accurate at its center. As a result, it is often used for maps of the Poles.

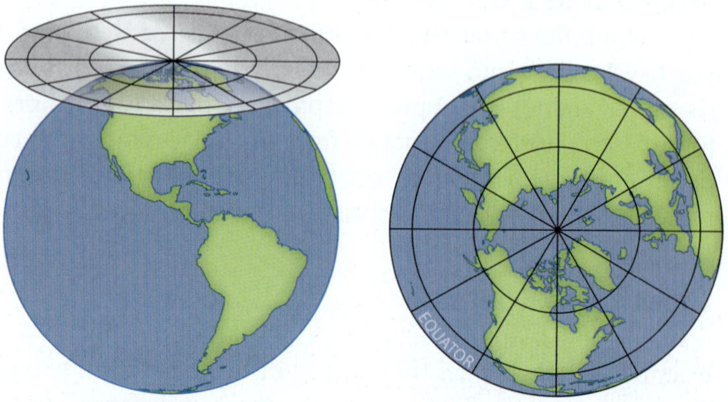

Cylindrical Projection

A cylindrical projection is based on the projection of the globe onto a cylinder. This projection is most accurate near the Equator, but shapes and distances are distorted near the Poles.

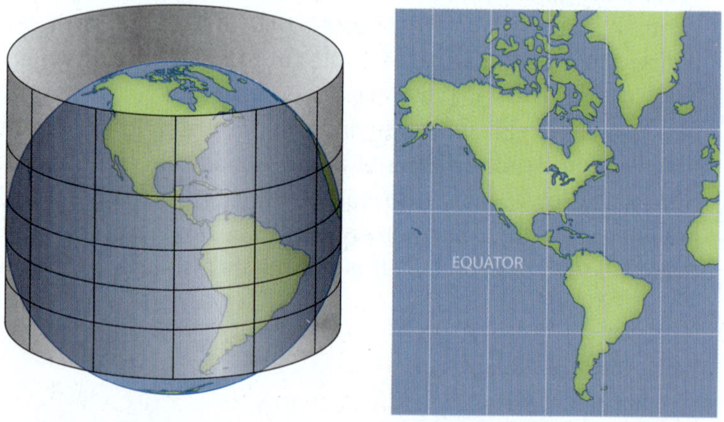

Conic Projection

A conic projection comes from placing a cone over part of the globe. Conic projections are best suited for showing limited east-west areas that are not far from the Equator. For these uses, a conic projection can indicate distances and directions fairly accurately.

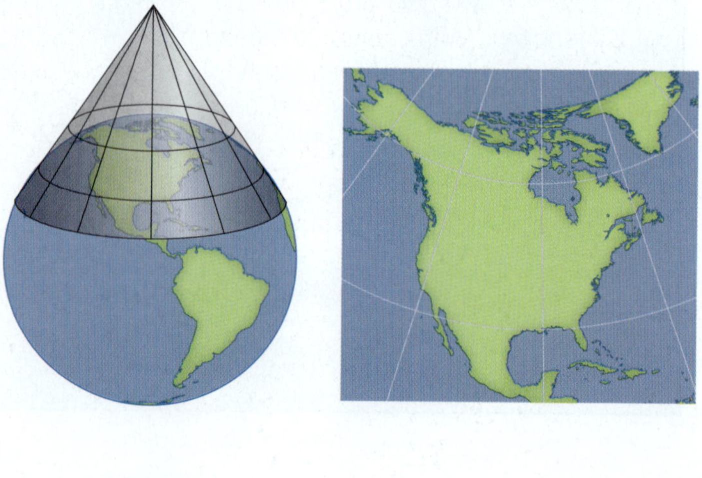

Common Map Projections

Each type of map projection has advantages and some degree of inaccuracy. Four of the most common projections are shown here.

Winkel Tripel Projection

Most general reference world maps are the Winkel Tripel projection. It provides a good balance between the size and shape of land areas as they are shown on the map. Even the polar areas are depicted with little distortion of size and shape.

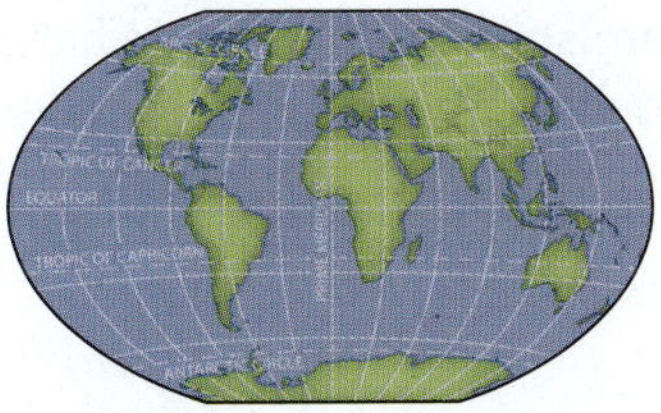

Robinson Projection

The Robinson projection has minor distortions. The sizes and shapes near the eastern and western edges of the map are accurate, and outlines of the continents appear much as they do on the globe. However, the polar areas are flattened.

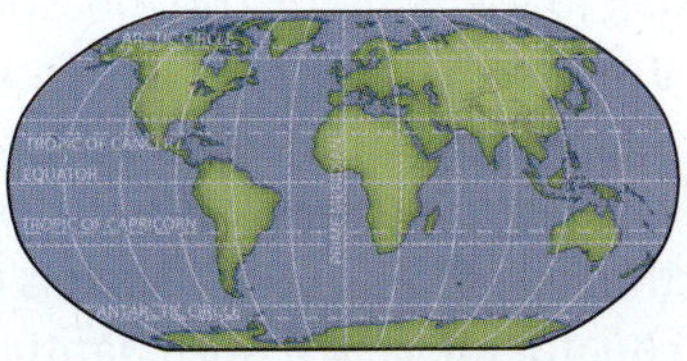

Goode's Interrupted Equal-Area Projection

An interrupted projection looks something like a globe that has been cut apart and laid flat. Goode's Interrupted Equal-Area projection shows the true size and shape of Earth's landmasses, but distances are generally distorted.

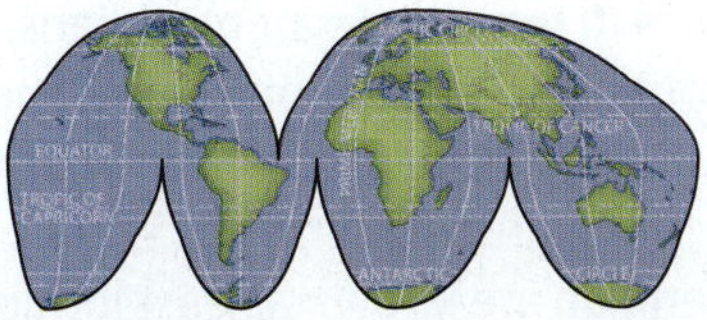

Mercator Projection

The Mercator projection increasingly distorts size and distance as it moves away from the Equator. However, Mercator projections do accurately show true directions and the shapes of landmasses, making these maps useful for sea travel.

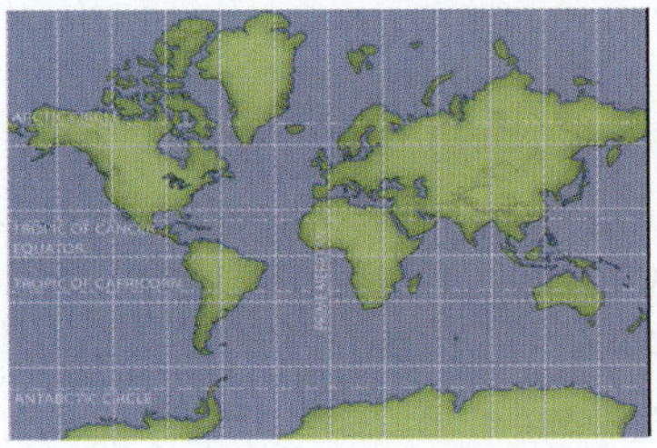

VOCABULARY

map projection
the image of a round Earth onto a flat surface

planar
a map projection that is most accurate at the center

cylindrical
a map projection that is most accurate near the Equator

conic
a map projection that accurately shows east-west areas near the Equator.

GEOGRAPHY CONNECTION

1. ***Explain*** the significance of: map projection, planar, cylindrical, conic.
2. ***How*** does a cartographer determine which map projection to use?
3. ***How*** is Goode's Interrupted Equal-Area projection different from the Mercator projection?
4. ***Which*** of the four common projections described above is the best one to use when showing the entire world? Why?
5. ***Use*** a Venn diagram like the one below to identify the similarities and differences between the Winkel Tripel and Mercator projections.

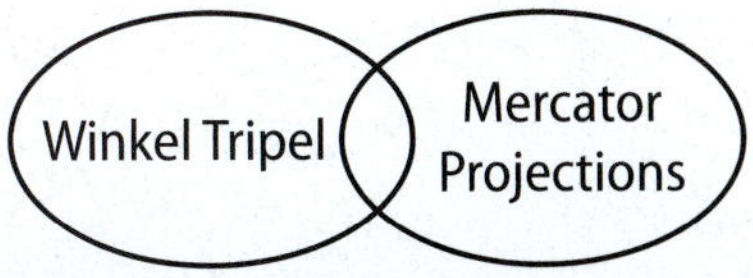

VOCABULARY

grid system
a pattern of lines on a map or globe that determine exact locations on Earths' surface

hemisphere
one of the halves that geographers divide the Earth into

latitude
lines that circle the Earth parallel to the Equator

longitude
lines that circle the Earth from Pole to Pole

Prime Meridian
the line of longitude set at 0°

absolute location
a global address determined by the intersection of longitude and latitude lines

Determining Location

Geography is often said to begin with the question: *Where?* The basic tool for answering the question is *location*. Lines on globes and maps provide information that can help you locate places. These lines cross one another forming a pattern called a **grid system**, which helps you find exact places on the Earth's surface.

A **hemisphere** is one of the halves into which the Earth is divided. Geographers divide the Earth into hemispheres to help them classify and describe places on Earth. Most places are located in two of the four hemispheres.

Latitude

Lines of **latitude**, or parallels, circle the Earth parallel to the Equator and measure the distance north or south of the Equator in degrees. The Equator is measured at 0° latitude, while the Poles lie at latitudes 90°N (north) and 90°S (south). Parallels north of the Equator are called north latitude. Parallels south of the Equator are called south latitude.

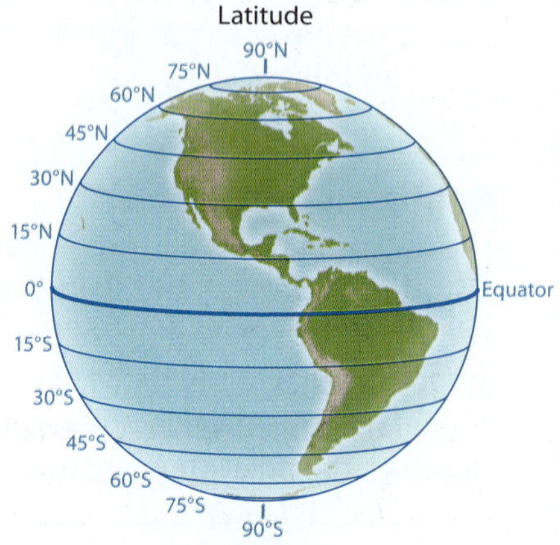

Longitude

Lines of **longitude**, or meridians, circle the Earth from Pole to Pole. These lines measure distance east or west of the **Prime Meridian** at 0° longitude. Meridians east of the Prime Meridian are known as east longitude. Meridian west of the Prime Meridian are known as west longitude. The 180° meridian on the opposite side of the Earth is called the International Date Line.

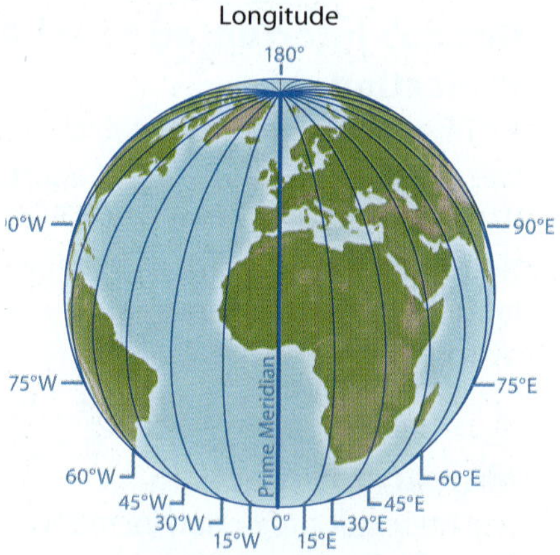

The Global Grid

Every place has a global address, or **absolute location**. You can identify the absolute location of a place by naming the latitude and longitude lines that cross exactly at that place. For example, Tokyo, Japan is located at 36°N latitude and 140°E longitude. For more precise readings, each degree is further divided into 60 units called minutes.

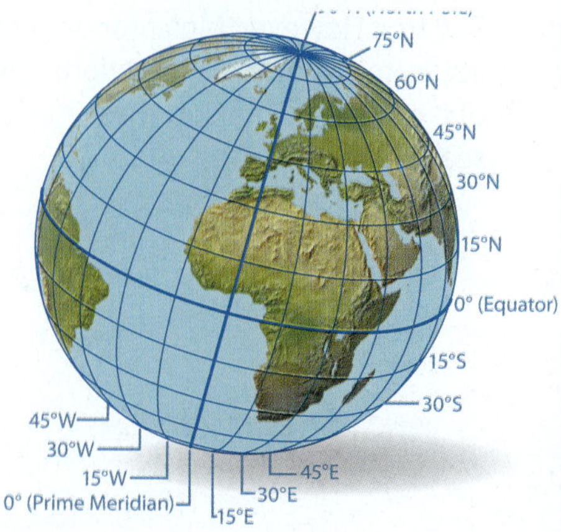

Northern and Southern Hemispheres

The diagram below shows that the Equator divides the Earth into the Northern and Southern Hemispheres. Everything north of the Equator is in the **Northern Hemisphere**. Everything south of the Equator is in the **Southern Hemisphere**.

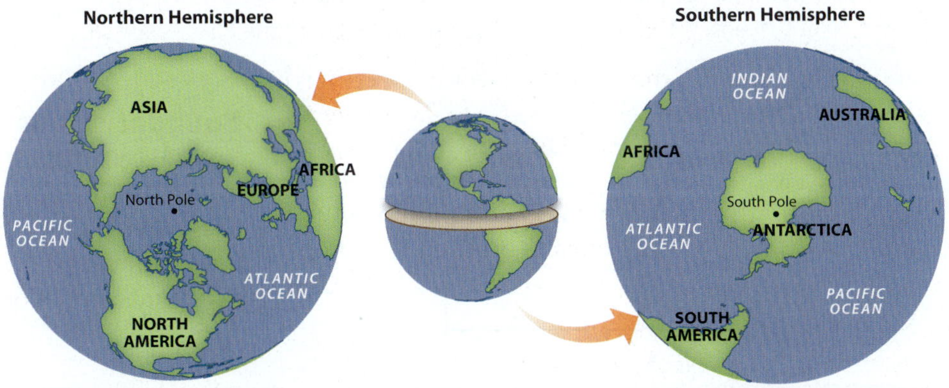

Eastern and Western Hemispheres

The Prime Meridian and the International Date Line divide the Earth into the Eastern and Western Hemispheres. Everything east of the Prime Meridian for 180° is in the **Eastern Hemisphere**. Everything west of the Prime Meridian for 180° is in the **Western Hemisphere**.

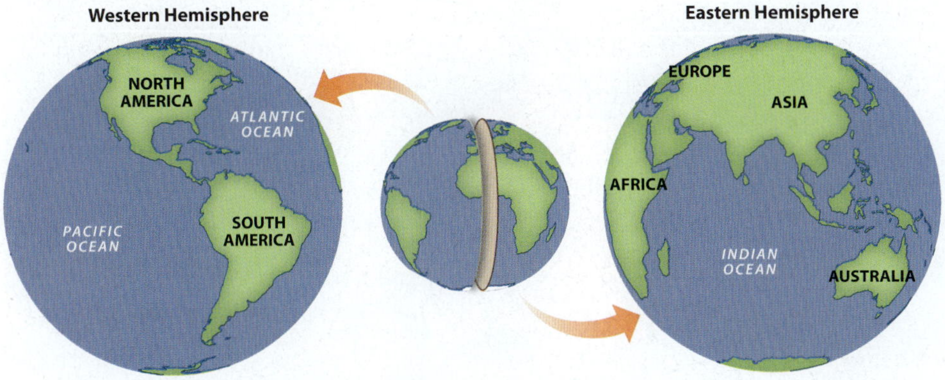

VOCABULARY

Northern Hemisphere
the half of the globe north of the Equator

Southern Hemisphere
the half of the globe south of the Equator

Eastern Hemisphere
the half of the globe east of the Prime Meridian for 180°

Western Hemisphere
the half of the globe west of the Prime Meridian for 180°

GEOGRAPHY CONNECTION

1. ***Explain*** the significance of: location, grid system, hemisphere, Northern Hemisphere, Southern Hemisphere, Eastern Hemisphere, Western Hemisphere, latitude, longitude, Prime Meridian, absolute location.
2. ***Why*** do all maps label the Equator 0° latitude and the Prime Meridian 0° longitude?
3. ***Which*** lines of latitude and longitude divide the Earth into hemispheres?
4. ***Using*** the Reference Atlas maps, fill in a chart by writing the latitude and longitude of three world cities. Have a partner try to identify the cities listed in your chart.
5. ***Use*** a chart like the one below to identify the continents in each hemisphere. Some may be in more than one hemisphere.

Hemisphere	***Continents***
Northern	
Southern	
Eastern	
Western	

Reading a Map

In addition to latitude and longitude, maps feature other important tools to help you interpret the information they contain. Learning to use these map tools will help you read the symbolic language of maps more easily.

Key
The key lists and explains the symbols, colors, and lines used on the map. The key is sometimes called a legend.

Title
The title tells you what kind of information the map is showing.

Boundary Lines
On political maps of large areas, boundary lines highlight the borders between different countries or states.

Compass Rose
The compass rose indicates directions. The four cardinal directions—north, south, east, and west—are usually indicated with arrows or the points of a star. The intermediate directions—northeast, northwest, southeast, and southwest—may also be shown.

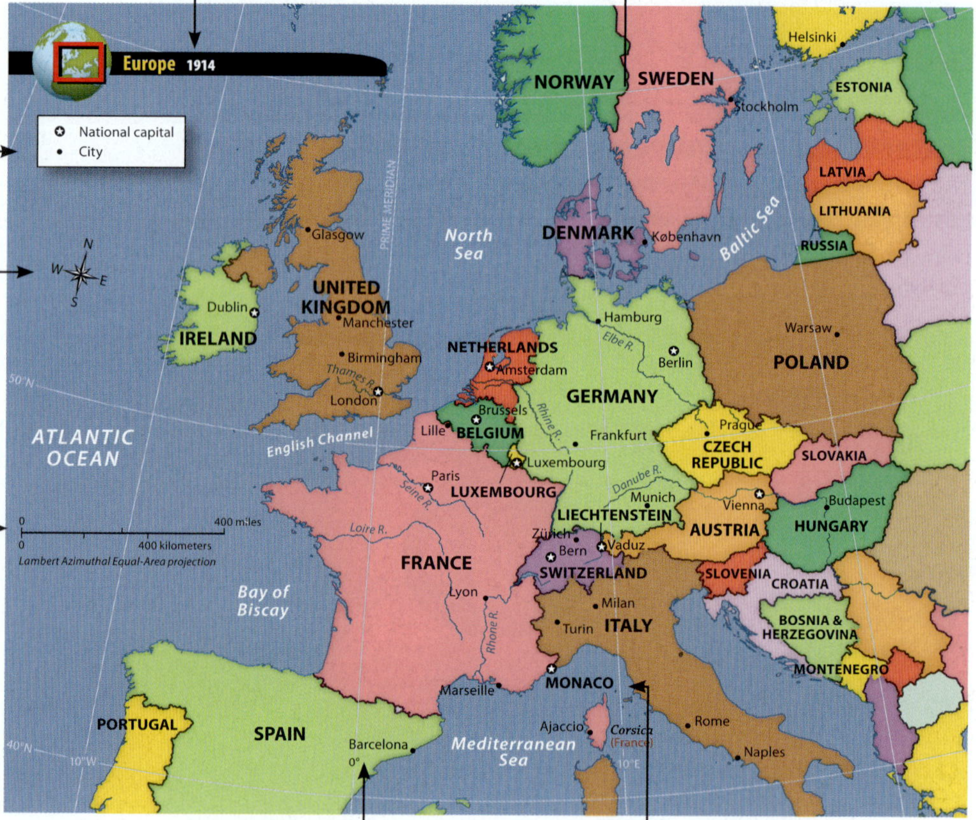

Scale Bar
The scale bar shows the relationship between map measurements and actual distances on the Earth. By laying a ruler along the scale bar, you can calculate how many miles or kilometers are represented per inch or centimeter. The map projection used to create the map is often listed near the scale bar.

Cities
Cities are represented by a dot. Sometimes the relative sizes of cities are shown using dots of different sizes.

Capitals
National capitals are often represented by a star within a circle.

Using Scale

All maps are drawn to a certain scale. **Scale** is a consistent, proportional relationship between the measurements shown on the map and the measurement of the Earth's surface.

Small-Scale Maps A small-scale map, like this political map of France, can show a large area but little detail. Note that the scale bar on this map indicates that about 1 inch is equal to 200 miles.

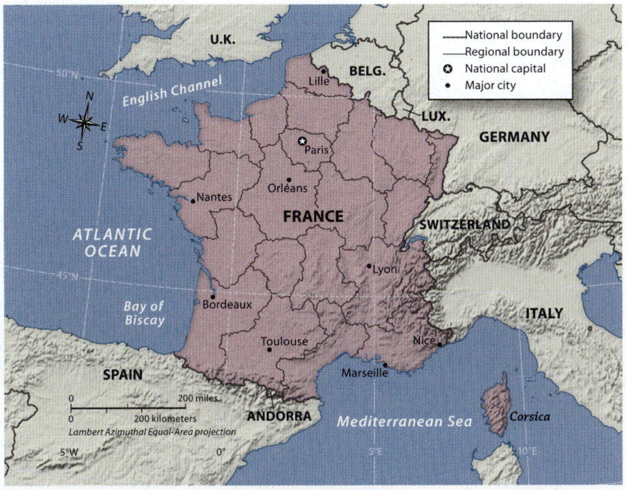

Large-Scale Maps A large-scale map, like this map of Paris, can show a small area with a great amount of detail. Study the scale bar. Note that the map measurements correspond to much smaller distances than on the map of France.

Absolute and Relative Location

Absolute location is the exact point where a line of latitude crosses a line of longitude. Another way to indicate location is by **relative location**, or the location of one place in relation to another. To find relative location, find a reference point—a location you already know—on a map. Then look in the appropriate direction for the new location. For example, locate Paris (your reference point) on the map of France above. The relative location of Lyon can be described as southeast of Paris.

VOCABULARY

Scale
a consistant, proportional relationship between measurements shown on a map and measurements of the Earth's surface

relative location
the location of one place in relation to another

GEOGRAPHY CONNECTION

1. ***Explain*** the significance of: key, compass rose, cardinal directions, intermediate directions, scale bar, scale, relative location.
2. ***Describe*** the elements of a map that help you interpret the information displayed on the map.
3. ***How*** does the scale bar help you determine distances on the Earth's surface?
4. ***Describe*** the relative location of your school in two different ways.
5. ***Use*** a Venn diagram to identify the similarities and differences of small-scale maps and large-scale maps.

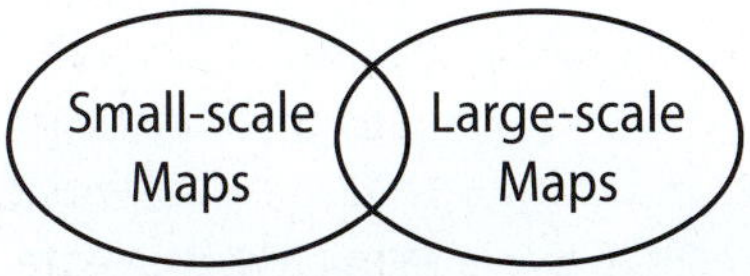

VOCABULARY

physical map
a map that shows the location and shape of the Earth's physical features

political map
a map that shows the boundaries and locations of political units such as countries, states, and cities

Physical and Political Maps

Physical and political are the two main types of maps in this book. A **physical map** shows the location and the topography, or shape of the Earth's physical features. A study of an area's physical features often helps explain its historical development. A **political map** shows the boundaries and locations of political units such as countries, states, and cities. Non subject area is usually shown in a different color to set it apart from the main area of the map. This nonsubject area gives you a context for the region you are studying.

Physical Maps

Physical maps use shading and texture to show general relief—the differences in elevation or height, of landforms. Landforms are physical features such as plains, mountains, plateaus, and valleys. Physical maps show rivers, streams, lakes, and other water features.

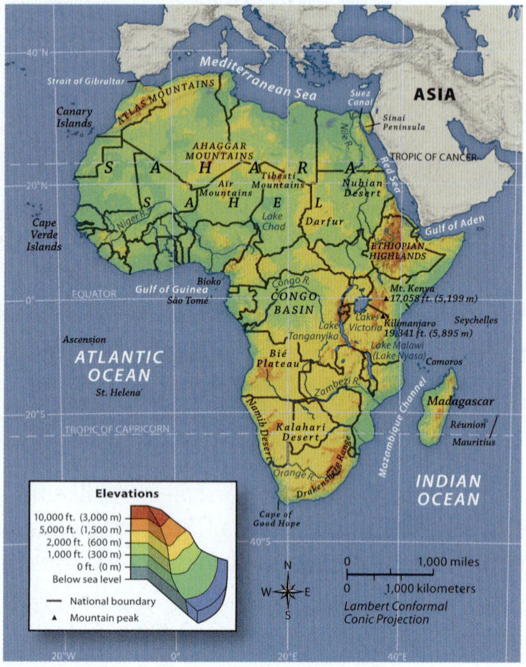

Political Maps

Many features on a political map are human-made, or determined by humans rather than by nature. Some human-made features are boundaries, capital cities, and roads. Political maps may also show physical features such as mountains and rivers.

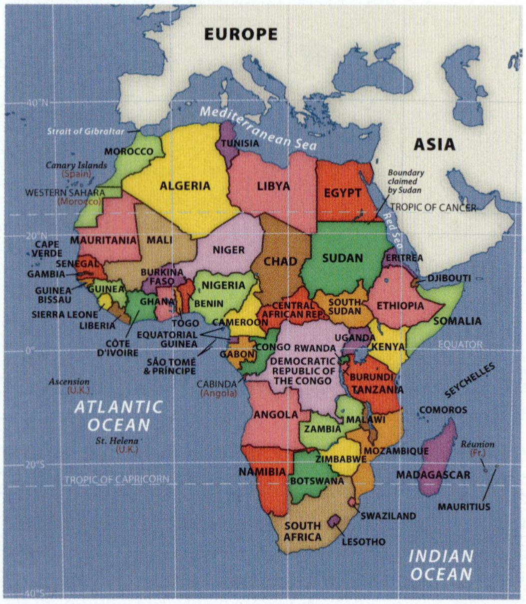

Thematic Maps

Maps that emphasize a particular kind of information or a single idea are called **thematic maps**. This textbook includes thematic maps that show civilizations, migrations, natural resources, war, trade, and exploration.

VOCABULARY

thematic maps
maps focused on a kind of information or a single idea

Qualitative Maps

Maps that use colors, symbols, lines, or dots to show information related to a specific idea are called qualitative maps.

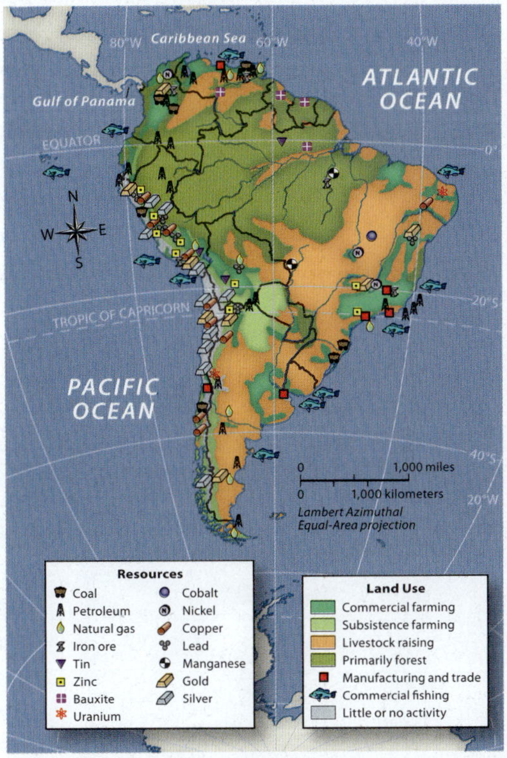

Flow-Line Maps

Maps that use arrows to show the movement of people, ideas, or physical systems are called flow-line maps.

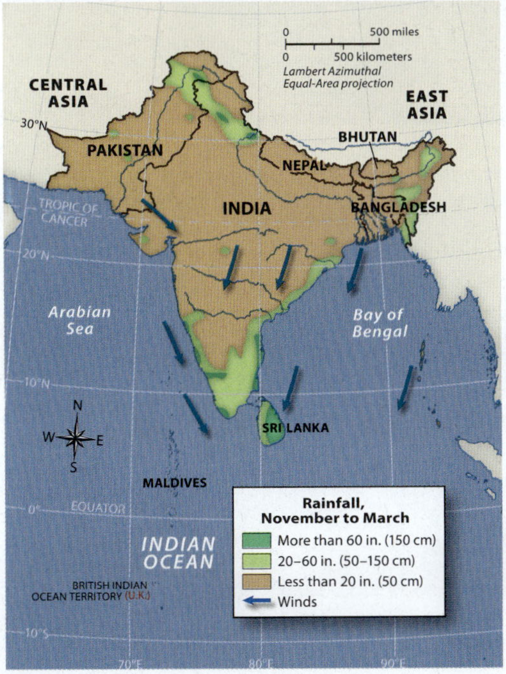

GEOGRAPHY CONNECTION

1. ***Explain*** the significance of: physical map, political map, thematic map, qualitative map, flow-line map.

2. ***Complete*** a Venn diagram like the one below to compare physical and political maps.

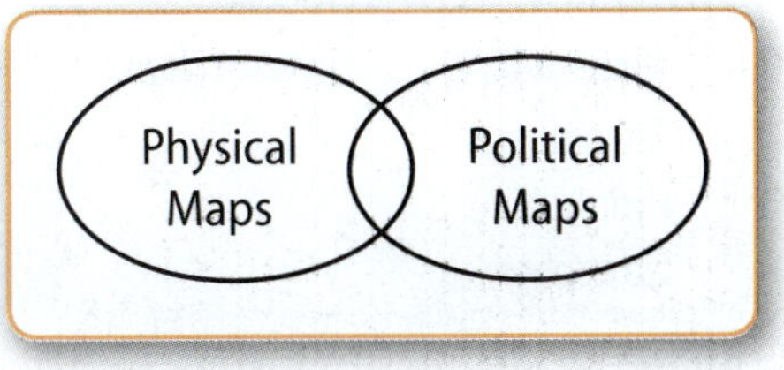

VOCABULARY

ecosystem
a community of plants and animals that depend upon one another and their surroundings for survival

Biodiversity
the variation of lifeforms within an ecosystem

Ecosystems and Biodiversity

An **ecosystem** is a community of plants and animals that depend upon one another and their surroundings for survival. There are many different ecosystems on Earth. Plants, animals, and micro-organisms interact within an ecosystem. **Biodiversity** is the variation of life forms within an ecosystem.

Rain forests are one type of ecosystem. Nowhere is biodiversity more apparent than in tropical rain forests, which harbor at least half of all animal and plant species on Earth. Although the world's largest remaining tropical rain forests are in Brazil, there are temperate rain forests from North America to Australia, as seen in the photograph.

Desert climates occur in just under one-third of the Earth's total land area. The natural vegetation of a desert ecosystem consists of scrub and cactus, plants that tolerate low and unreliable precipitation, low humidity, and wise temperate ranges. This arid landscape is in Arizona.

Biodiversity at Risk As the human communities expand, they threaten natural ecosystems. Because the Earth's land, air, and water are interrelated, what effects one part of the system affects all the other parts—including humans and other living things. The photograph shows deforestation, in this case clear-cutting of the Brazilian rain forest.

GEOGRAPHY CONNECTION

1. ***Explain*** the significance of: ecosystem, biodiversity.

2. ***Complete*** a table like the one below to list some of the types of interactions in the physical systems.

Hemisphere	*Interactions*
Atmosphere	
Hydrosphere	
Lithosphere	

Geographic Information Systems

Modern technology has changed the way maps are made. Most cartographers use computers with software programs called **geographic information systems** (GIS). A GIS is designed to accept data from different sources—maps, satellite images, printed text, and statistics. The GIS converts the data into a digital code, which arranges it in a database. Cartographers then program the GIS to process the data and produce maps. With GIS, each kind of information on a map is saved as a separate electronic layer.

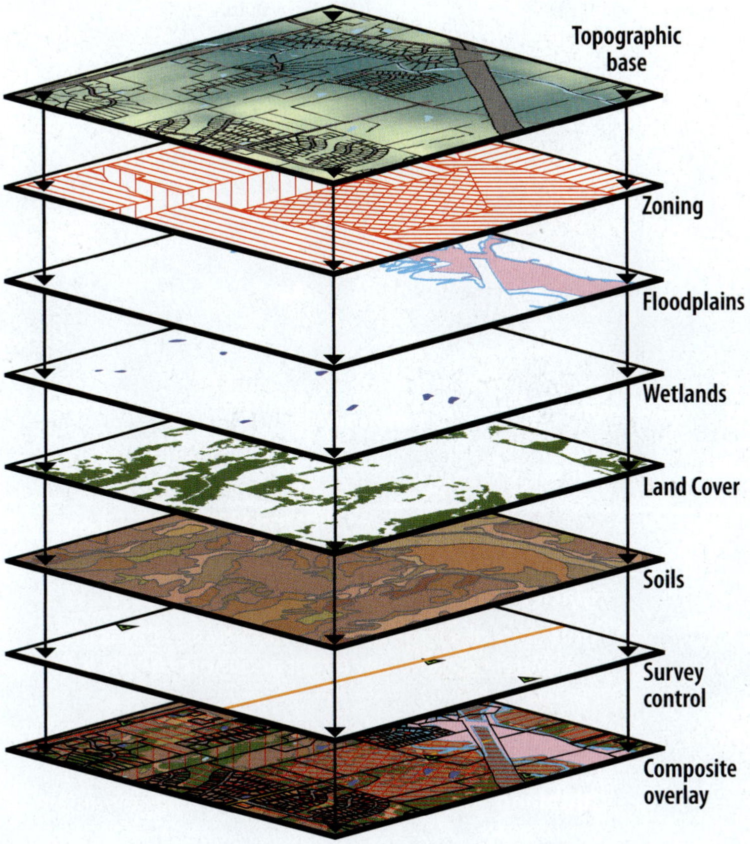

VOCABULARY

geographic information systems
a software program used by cartographers that arranges a variety of data in a database and uses those data layers to produce maps

GEOGRAPHY CONNECTION

1. ***How*** does GIS allow cartographers to create maps and make changes to maps quickly and easily?

2. ***Complete*** a chart like the one below by identifying the different types of layers available in a GIS to make more ***informative maps.***

Layers

GEOGRAPHIC DICTIONARY

archipelago a group of islands

basin area of land drained by a given river and its branches; area of land surrounded by lands of higher elevations

bay part of a large body of water that extends into a shoreline, generally smaller than a gulf

canyon deep and narrow valley with steep walls

cape point of land that extends into a river, lake, or ocean

channel wide strait or waterway between two landmasses that lie close to each other; deep part of a river or other waterway

cliff steep, high wall of rock, earth, or ice

continent one of the seven large landmasses on the Earth

delta flat, low-lying land built up from soil carried downstream by a river and deposited at its mouth

divide stretch of high land that separates river systems

downstream direction in which a river or stream flows from its source to its mouth

escarpment steep cliff or slope between a higher and lower land surface

glacier large, thick body of slowly moving ice

gulf part of a large body of water that extends into a shoreline, generally larger and more deeply indented than a bay

harbor a sheltered place along a shoreline where ships can anchor safely

highland elevated land area such as a hill, mountain, or plateau

hill elevated land with sloping sides and rounded summit; generally smaller than a mountain

island land area, smaller than a continent, completely surrounded by water

isthmus narrow stretch of land connecting two larger land areas

lake a sizable inland body of water

lowland land, usually level, at a low elevation

mesa broad, flat-topped landform with steep sides; smaller than a plateau

mountain land with steep sides that rises sharply (1,000 feet or more) from surrounding land; generally larger and more rugged than a hill

mountain peak pointed top of a mountain

mountain range a series of connected mountains

mouth (of a river) place where a stream or river flows into a larger body of water

oasis small area in a desert where water and vegetation are found

ocean one of the four major bodies of salt water that surround the continents

ocean current stream of either cold or warm water that moves in a definite direction through an ocean

peninsula body of land jutting into a lake or ocean, surrounded on three sides by water

physical feature characteristic of a place occurring naturally, such as a landform, body of water, climate pattern, or resource

plain area of level land, usually at low elevation and often covered with grasses

plateau area of flat or rolling land at a high elevation, about 300 to 3,000 feet (90 to 900 m) high

reef a chain of rocks, coral or sand at or near the surface

river large natural stream of water that runs through the land

sea large body of water completely or partly surrounded by land

seacoast land lying next to a sea or an ocean

sound broad inland body of water, often between a coastline and one or more islands off the coast

source (of a river) place where a river or stream begins, often in highlands

strait narrow stretch of water joining two larger bodies of water

tributary small river or stream that flows into a large river or stream; a branch of the river

upstream direction opposite the flow of a river; toward the source of a river or stream

valley area of low land usually between hills or mountains

volcano mountain or hill created as liquid rock and ash erupt from inside the Earth

GLOSSARY/GLOSARIO

- Content vocabulary are words that relate to world history content.
- Words that have an asterisk (*) are academic vocabulary. They help you understand your school subjects.
- All vocabulary words are **boldfaced or highlighted in yellow** in your textbook.

ENGLISH	ESPAÑOL
	A
abbess the head of a convent (p. 191)	**abadesa** directora de un convento (pág. 191)
abdicate to formally give up control of a country or state (p. 647)	**abdicar** renunciar formalmente al control de un país o Estado (pág. 647)
abolitionism a movement to end slavery (p. 545)	**abolicionismo** movimiento para acabar con la esclavitud (pág. 545)
absolute monarchy form of monarchy where the power of the monarch is not limited by laws or by a constitution (p. 484)	**monarquía absoluta** forma de monarquía en que los poderes del monarca no se limitan por la ley ni la constitución (pág. 484)
absolutism a political system in which a ruler holds total power (p. 415)	**absolutismo** sistema político en el que el gobernante mantiene un poder total (pág. 415)
***abstract** a style of art, emerging around 1910, that spoke directly to the soul and avoided visual reality by using only lines and color (p. 577)	***abstracto** estilo artístico que surgió alrededor de 1910; hablaba directamente al alma y evitaba la realidad visual usando sólo líneas y colores (pág. 577)
***acquired** came into possession or control of (p. 258)	***adquirido** bajo posesión o control (pág. 258)
acropolis in early Greek city-states, a fortified gathering place at the top of a hill that was sometimes the site of temples and public buildings (p. 80)	**acrópolis** en las primeras ciudades-Estado griegas, plaza fortificada en la cima de una montaña en la que a veces se ubicaban los templos y edificios públicos (pág. 80)
administrative relating to the execution of public affairs, as distinguished from policy making (p. 311)	**administrativo** relativo a la ejecución de los asuntos públicos, a diferencia de la creación de las políticas (pág. 311)
***administrator** one who manages the affairs of a government or a business (p. 436)	***administrador** persona que maneja los asuntos de un gobierno o un negocio (pág. 436)
***advocate** support; speak in favor of (p. 567)	***defender** apoyar; hablar en favor de (pág. 567)
***Age of Pericles** the period between 461 B.C. and 429 B.C. when Pericles dominated Athenian politics and Athens reached the height of its power (p. 89)	***era de Pericles** periodo comprendido entre 461 A. C. y 429 A. C. cuando Pericles dominó la política ateniense y Atenas alcanzó la cumbre de su poder (pág. 89)
***agora** in early Greek city-states, an open area that served as a gathering place and as a market (p. 80)	***ágora** en las primeras ciudades-Estado griegas, espacio abierto que servía como sitio de reunión y mercado (pág. 80)
***aid** assistance such as money or supplies (p. 647)	***ayuda** asistencia económica o en especie (pág. 647)
Allah Arabic for *God;* the supreme god of Islam (p. 207)	**Alá** en árabe, *Dios*; deidad suprema del islam (pág. 207)
***amendment** an alteration proposed or effected by parliamentary or constitutional procedure (p. 492)	***enmienda** alteración propuesta o realizda por el parlamento o un procedimiento constitucional (pág. 492)
anarchy political disorder; lawlessness (p. 436)	**anarquía** desorden político; situación al margen de la ley (pág. 436)
annex to incorporate into an existing political unit, such as a city or country (p. 591)	**anexar** incorporar a una unidad política existente, como una ciudad o un país (pág. 591)

***annual** yearly (p. 662)	**anual** que sucede una vez al año (pág. 662)
annul declare invalid (p. 370)	**anular** declarar no válido (pág. 370)
anthropology the study of human life and culture based on artifacts and human fossils (p. 4)	**antropología** estudio de la vida y la cultura humanas con base en artefactos y fósiles humanos (pág. 4)
anti-Semitism hostility toward or discrimination against Jews (p. 291)	**antisemitismo** hostilidad hacia los judíos o discriminación en su contra (pág. 291)
apartheid "apartness"; the system of racial segregation in South Africa from the 1950s until 1991 (p. 776)	**apartheid** "separación"; sistema de segregación racial que se dio en Suráfrica desde la década de 1950 hasta 1991 (pág. 776)
appeasement satisfying reasonable demands of dissatisfied powers in an effort to maintain peace and stability (p. 713)	**apaciguamiento** satisfacer demandas razonables de potencias insatisfechas en un esfuerzo por mantener la paz y la estabilidad (pág. 713)
***approach** the way or method in which one examines or studies an issue or a concept (p. 551)	***enfoque** forma o método para examinar o estudiar un aspecto o un concepto (pág. 551)
***appropriate** suitable or compatible; fitting (p. 666)	***apropiado** adecuado o compatible; que encaja (pág. 666)
arabesques geometric patterns repeated over and over to completely cover a surface with decoration (p. 221)	**arabescos** patrones geométricos que se repiten una y otra vez y decoran completamente una superficie (pág. 221)
***arbitrarily** (adverb form of *arbitrary*) at one's discretion; randomly (p. 849)	***arbitrariamente** (adverbio de arbitrario) a discreción propia; al azar (pág. 849)
***arbitrary** at one's discretion; random (p. 481)	***arbitrario** a discreción personal; al azar (pág. 481)
***archaeology** the study of past societies through an analysis of the items people left behind them (p. 4)	***arqueología** estudio de las sociedades antiguas mediante un análisis de los objetos que los pueblos dejaron tras de sí (pág. 4)
archipelago a chain of islands (pp. 260, 462)	**archipiélago** cadena de islas (págs. 260, 462)
area a geographic region (p. 324)	**área** región geográfica (pág. 324)
arête in early Greece, the qualities of excellence that a hero strives to win in a struggle or contest (p. 79)	**areté** en la antigua Grecia, cualidades de excelencia que un héroe se esforzaba por ganar en una lucha o competencia (pág. 79)
aristocracy an upper class whose wealth is based on land and whose power is passed on from one generation to another (p. 43)	**aristocracia** clase alta cuya riqueza se basa en la tierra y cuyo poder se transmite de generación en generación (pág. 43)
armada a fleet of warships (p. 406)	**armada** flota de barcos de guerra (pág. 406)
armistice a truce or an agreement to end fighting (p. 652)	**armisticio** tregua o acuerdo para poner fin a un combate (pág. 652)
arms race building up armies and stores of weapons to keep up with an enemy (p. 745)	**carrera armamentista** acumulación de ejércitos y reservas de armas para hacer frente al enemigo (pág. 745)
artisan a skilled worker who makes products such as weapons and jewelry (p. 13)	**artesano** trabajador hábil que elabora productos como armas y joyas (pág. 13)
Aryan a term used to identify people speaking Indo-European languages; Nazis misused the term, treating it as a racial designation and identifying the Aryans with the ancient Greeks and Romans and twentieth-century Germans and Scandinavians (p. 674)	**ario** término usado para identificar a los hablantes de alguna lengua indoeuropea. Los nazis tergiversaron el uso del término empleándolo como una designación racial e identificaron a los arios con los antiguos griegos y romanos, y con los germanos y escandinavos del siglo XX (pág. 674)
***assemble** to gather; to meet together (p. 80)	***congregar** juntar; reunirse (pág. 80)

Glossary/Glosario

ENGLISH	ESPAÑOL
assembly line pioneered by Henry Ford in 1913, a manufacturing method that allowed much more efficient mass production of goods (p. 561)	**cadena de montaje** método de producción instaurado por Henry Ford en 1913, que permitía una producción masiva de bienes más eficiente (pág. 561)
***assume** to take up or in; to take control of (p. 60)	***asumir** hacerse cargo, asimilar; tomar el control (pág. 60)
***assure** to make certain of something; to guarantee (p. 734)	***asegurar** cerciorarse de algo; garantizar (pág. 734)
astrolabe an instrument used by sailors to determine their location by observing the positions of stars (p. 220)	**astrolabio** instrumento que los navegantes usaban para determinar su localización al observar la posición de las estrellas (pág. 220)
***attain** to gain or achieve (p. 349)	***obtener** ganar o alcanzar (pág. 349)
***attitude** a mental position regarding a fact or state (p. 669)	***actitud** posición mental con respecto a un hecho o un estado (pág. 669)
***authority** power; person in command (pp. 415, 439)	***autoridad** poder; persona a cargo (págs. 415, 439)
autonomous self-governing (p. 820)	**autónomo** que se gobierna a sí mismo (pág. 820)
***available** ready for immediate use; accessible (p. 259)	***disponible** listo para uso inmediato; accesible (pág. 259)

B

ENGLISH	ESPAÑOL
baroque an artistic style of the seventeenth century characterized by complex forms, bold ornamentation, and contrasting elements (p. 421)	**Barroco** estilo artístico del siglo XVII caracterizado por formas complejas, una decoración recargada y elementos que contrastan (pág. 421)
bazaar a covered market in Islamic cities (p. 217)	**bazar** mercado cubierto en ciudades islámicas (pág. 217)
bedouin a nomadic Arab who lives in the Arabian, Syrian, or North African deserts (p. 208)	**beduino** árabe nómada que habita en los desiertos de Arabia, Siria y el norte de África (pág. 208)
bioterrorism the use of biological and chemical weapons in terrorist attacks (p. 847)	**bioterrorismo** uso de armas biológicas y químicas en ataques terroristas (pág. 847)
bishopric a group of Christian communities, or parishes, under the authority of a bishop (p. 189)	**diócesis** grupo de comunidades cristianas, o parroquias, que se hallan bajo la autoridad de un obispo (pág. 189)
blitz the British term for the German air raids on British cities and towns during World War II (p. 725)	**bombardeo aéreo** término con que los británicos designaron los ataques aéreos alemanes sobre las ciudades y los pueblos británicos durante la Segunda Guerra Mundial (pág. 725)
blitzkrieg German for "lightning war"; a swift and sudden military attack; used by the Germans during World War II (p. 717)	***blitzkriegk*** en alemán, "guerra relámpago"; ataque militar rápido y sorpresivo; usado por los alemanes durante la Segunda Guerra Mundial (pág. 717)
bloc a group of nations with a common purpose (p. 796)	**bloque** grupo de naciones con un propósito común (pág. 796)
bourgeoisie the middle class, including merchants, industrialists, and professional people (pp. 235, 501, 563)	**burguesía** la clase media, que incluye comerciantes, industriales y profesionales (págs. 235, 501, 563)
boyar a Russian noble (p. 418)	**boyar** noble ruso (pág. 418)
Buddhism a religious doctrine introduced in northern India in the sixth century B.C. by Siddhārtha Gautama, known as the Buddha, or "Enlightened One" (p. 112)	**budismo** doctrina religiosa introducida en el norte de la India durante el siglo VI A. C. por Siddhārtha Gautama, conocido como el Buda, o "el Iluminado" (pág. 112)

budget deficit the state that exists when a government spends more than it collects in revenues (p. 825)

déficit presupuestario estado que tiene lugar cuando los gastos de un gobierno superan los ingresos que recauda (pág. 825)

bureaucracy an administrative organization that relies on nonelective officials and regular procedures (pp. 27, 462)

burocracia organización administrativa que se basa en funcionarios que no son elegidos y en procedimientos habituales (págs. 27, 462)

burgher a member of the middle class who lived in a city or town (p. 346)

burgués miembro de la clase media que vivía en una ciudad o un pueblo (pág. 346)

Bushido "the way of the warrior"; the strict code by which Japanese samurai were supposed to live (p. 261)

bushido "el camino del guerrero"; estricto código que regía las vidas de los samuráis japoneses (pág. 261)

C

caliph a successor of Muhammad as spiritual and temporal leader of the Muslims (p. 210)

califa sucesor de Mahoma como líder espiritual y temporal de los musulmanes (pág. 210)

***caliphate** the office of the caliph (pp. 210, 212, 686)

***Califato** jurisdicción del califa (págs. 210, 212, 686)

***capable** having or showing ability (p. 513)

***capaz** que tiene o demuestra habilidad (pág. 513)

capital money available for investment (p. 528)

capital dinero disponible para invertir (pág. 528)

caravel a small, fast, maneuverable ship that had a large cargo hold and usually three masts with lateen sails (p. 381)

carabela embarcación pequeña, rápida y maniobrable con una gran capacidad de carga y que por lo general tenía tres mástiles con velas latinas (pág. 381)

carruca a heavy, wheeled plow with an iron plowshare (p. 232)

carruca arado pesado y con ruedas, con una reja de hierro (pág. 232)

cartel a group of drug businesses (p. 786)

cartel grupo dedicado al narcotráfico (pág. 786)

cash crop a crop that is grown for sale rather than for personal use (p. 549)

cultivo comercial cultivo destinado a la venta, no para el uso personal (pág. 549)

caste system a set of rigid categories in ancient India that determined a person's occupation and economic potential, as well as his or her position in society, based partly on skin color (p. 109)

sistema de castas grupo de categorías rígidas de la antigua India que determinaban la ocupación y el potencial económico de una persona, así como su posición en la sociedad, en parte por el color de la piel (pág. 109)

caudillo in post-revolutionary Latin America, a strong leader who ruled chiefly by military force, usually with the support of the landed elite (p. 548)

caudillo en la América Latina posrevolucionaria, líder fuerte que gobernaba principalmente mediante la fuerza militar, por lo general con el apoyo de la élite latifundista (pág. 548)

Cavaliers supporters of King Charles I in the English Civil War (p. 410)

caballeros partidarios del rey Carlos I durante la Guerra Civil Inglesa (pág. 410)

***cease** to come to an end (p. 695)

***cesar** terminar (pág. 695)

***censorate** part of the Chinese bureaucracy that made sure government officials were doing their jobs (p. 139)

***buró de censura** parte de la burocracia china que se aseguraba de que los funcionarios del gobierno estuvieran haciendo su trabajo (pág. 139)

***challenge** a summons that is often stimulating, inciting, or threatening (p. 238)

***desafío** citación estimulante, incitadora o amenazante (pág. 238)

chanson de geste a type of vernacular literature, this heroic epic was popular in medieval Europe and described battles and political contests (p. 289)

cantar de gesta tipo de literatura vernácula. Esta épica heroica fue popular en la Europa medieval y describía batallas y contiendas políticas (pág. 289)

chariot a two-wheeled horse-drawn battle cart, also used in processions and races (p. 59)

carruaje carro de batalla de dos ruedas tirado por caballos; también se usaba en procesiones y carreras (pág. 59)

***chemical** used in or produced by chemistry (p. 847)

***producto químico** que se usa o es producido por productas químicos (pág. 847)

chivalry in the Middle Ages, the ideal of civilized behavior that developed among the nobility; it was a code of ethics that knights were supposed to uphold (p. 231)

caballería en la Edad Media, el ideal de comportamiento civilizado desarrollado entre la nobleza; era un código de ética que los caballeros debían mantener (pág. 231)

Christian humanism a movement that developed in northern Europe during the Renaissance combining classical learning (humanism) with the goal of reforming the Catholic Church (p. 236)

humanismo cristiano movimiento desarrollado en el norte de Europa durante el Renacimiento, que combina el aprendizaje clásico (humanismo) con el objetivo de reformar la Iglesia católica (pág. 236)

***circumstance** a determining condition (p. 352); a state of affairs (p. 621)

***circunstancia** condición determinante (pág. 352);estado de un asunto (pág. 621)

city-state a state with political and economic control over the surrounding countryside (p. 17)

ciudad-Estado Estado con control político y económico sobre el territorio que lo rodea (pág. 17)

***civil** involving the general public or civic affairs (pp. 519, 598)

***civil** que implica asuntos relacionados con el público o los asuntos cívicos (págs. 519, 598)

civil disobedience refusal to obey laws that are considered to be unjust (p. 692)

desobediencia civil negativa a obedecer leyes que se consideran injustas (pág. 692)

civilization a complex culture in which large numbers of people share a number of common elements such as social structure, religion, and art (p. 14)

civilización cultura compleja en la cual un gran número de personas comparten elementos comunes como la estructura social, la religión y el arte (pág. 14)

civil service the administrative service of a government, not including the armed forces, in which appointments are determined by competitive examination (p. 140)

servicio civil servicio administrativo de un gobierno, que no incluye las fuerzas armadas, en el cual los nombramientos se determinan mediante pruebas de competitividad (pág. 140)

clan a group of related families (pp. 323, 454)

clan grupo de familias relacionadas (págs. 323, 454)

***classical** authoritative, traditional; relating to the literature, art, architecture, and ideals of the ancient Greek and Roman world (p. 76)

***clásico** fidedigno, tradicional; relativo a la literatura, el arte, la arquitectura y los ideales del antiguo mundo grecorromano (pág. 76)

clergy church leaders (p. 181)

clero líderes de la iglesia (pág. 181)

***code** a system of principles or rules (p. 261)

***código** sistema de principios o reglas (pág. 261)

Cold War the period of political tension following World War II and ending with the fall of Communism in the Soviet Union at the end of the 1980s (p. 734)

Guerra Fría periodo de tensión política posterior a la Segunda Guerra Mundial, que terminó con la caída del comunismo en la Unión Soviética, a finales de la década de 1980 (pág. 734)

collaborator a person who assists the enemy (p. 725)

colaborador persona que ayuda al enemigo (pág. 725)

***collapse** to break down completely; to suddenly lose force or effectiveness (pp. 185, 818)

***colapsar** desplomarse por completo; perder fuerza o efectividad de manera repentina (págs. 185, 818)

collateralized debt obligation a debt security collateralized by a variety of debt obligations including bonds and loans of different maturities and credit quality (p. 865)

obligaciones de deuda colateralizada "valor garantizado por un conjunto de bonos, prestamos y otros tipos de deuda" (pág. 865)

collective bargaining the right of unions to negotiate with employers over wages and hours (p. 665)

negociación colectiva derecho de los sindicatos a negociar con los empleadores los salarios y horarios de trabajo (pág. 665)

Glossary/Glosario

collectivization a system in which private farms are eliminated and peasants work land owned by the government (p. 671)	**colectivización** sistema en el cual se eliminan las granjas privadas y los campesinos trabajan la tierra que pertenece al gobierno (pág. 671)
colony a settlement of people living in a new territory, linked with the parent country by trade and direct government control (p. 386)	**colonia** asentamiento de personas que viven en un nuevo territorio y que guardan un vínculo con su país de origen por el comercio y el control directo del gobierno (pág. 386)
***commentary** an explanatory treatise (p. 220)	***comentario** tratado de tipo explicativo (pág. 220)
commodities agricultural, mined, and mass-produced marketable goods (p. 621)	**bienes de consumo** bienes comercializables agrícolas, mineros y de producción masiva (pág. 621)
common law a uniform system of law that developed in England based on court decisions and on customs and usage rather than on written law codes; replaced law codes that varied from place to place (p. 238)	**derecho consuetudinario** sistema legal uniforme desarrollado en Inglaterra que se basaba en las decisiones de los tribunales y en los usos y las costumbres, más que en códigos escritos; reemplazó a los códigos legales que variaban de un lugar a otro (pág. 238)
***commonwealth** a republic (p. 410)	***mancomunidad** república (pág. 410)
commune in China during the 1950s, a group of collective farms which contained more than 30,000 people who lived and worked together (p. 748)	**comuna** en la China de la década de 1950, grupo de granjas colectivas donde vivían y trabajaban juntas más de 30,000 personas (pág. 748)
***communicate** to make known or share information about (p. 44)	***comunicar** dar a conocer o compartir información (pág. 44)
Communism a system of socialism developed by the German writer Karl Marx who believed that the class struggle would end with the collapse of capitalism and new society without classes (p. 562)	**comunismo** un sistema de socialismo desarrollado por el escritor alemán Karl Marx quien creyó que la pelea entre clases terminaría en el colapso de capitalismo con el resultado de una sociedad nueva sin clases (pág. 562)
***community** a group of people with common interests and characteristics living together within a larger society (pp. 371, 457)	***comunidad** grupo de personas con intereses y características comunes que viven juntos dentro de una sociedad (págs. 371, 457)
***compensation** payment (p. 690)	***compensación** pago (pág. 690)
***complex** having many intricate parts (pp. 213, 635)	***complejo** que tiene muchas partes intrincadas (págs. 213, 635)
***complexity** the state of being complex or of having many intricate parts (p. 253)	***complejidad** que es complejo o que tiene muchas partes intricadas (pág. 253)
concentration camp a camp where prisoners of war, political prisoners, or members of minority groups are confined, typically under harsh conditions (p. 674)	**campo de concentración** campo donde se confinaba a los prisioneros de guerra, prisioneros políticos o miembros de grupos minoritarios, por lo general en condiciones inhumanas (pág. 674)
concession a political compromise (p. 623)	**concesión** compromiso político (pág. 623)
***conflict** opposition; a fight, battle, or war (p. 405)	***conflicto** oposición; lucha, batalla o guerra (pág. 405)
***conform** to adhere to rules or standards; to fit in (p. 436)	***cumplir** ceñirse a las normas o estándares; encajar (pág. 436)
Confucianism the system of political and ethical ideas formulated by the Chinese philosopher Confucius toward the end of the Zhou dynasty; it was intended to help restore order to a society that was in a state of confusion (p. 130)	**confucianismo** sistema de ideas políticas y éticas formulado por el filósofo chino Confucio hacia el final de la dinastía Zhou; su propósito era restaurar el orden en una sociedad que se hallaba en un estado de confusión (pág. 130)
conquistador a leader in the Spanish conquest of the Americas (p. 385)	**conquistador** líder en la conquista española de América (pág. 385)
conscription military draft (p. 634)	**conscripción** reclutamiento military (pág. 634)

***consent** approval (p. 782)

***consentimiento** aprobación (pág. 782)

***consequence** the effect or result of an action (p. 291)

***consecuencia** efecto o resultado de una acción (pág. 291)

conservatism a political philosophy based on tradition and social stability, favoring obedience to political authority and organized religion (p. 517)

conservadurismo filosofía política basada en la tradición y la estabilidad social, que apoya la obediencia a la autoridad política y la religión organizada (pág. 517)

consist to be composed of or made up of (p. 323)

constar estar compuesto o formado por determinadas partes (pág. 323)

***constitution** the basic principles and laws of a nation, state, or social group that determine the powers and duties of the government and guarantee certain rights to the people in it (p. 579)

***constitución** principios y leyes básicos de una nación, Estado o grupo social, que determinan los poderes y deberes del gobierno y garantizan algunos derechos a sus habitantes (pág. 579)

consul a chief executive officer of the Roman Republic; two were elected each year to run the government and to lead the army into battle (p. 153)

cónsul máximo magistrado de la república romana; cada año se elegían dos para gobernar y dirigir el ejército a la batalla (pág. 153)

consulate the government established in France after the overthrow of the Directory in 1799, with Napoleon as first consul in control of the entire government (p. 512)

Consulado el gobierno establecido en Francia después del derrocamiento del Directorio en 1799, con Napoleón como el primer cónsul a cargo de todo el gobierno (pág. 512)

***consumer** one who consumes or uses economic goods (p. 501)

***consumidor** quien consume o usa bienes económicos (pág. 501)

consumer society a society preoccupied with buying goods (p. 798)

sociedad de consumo sociedad que se preocupa por comprar bienes (pág. 798)

***context** the circumstances surrounding a situation or event (p. 626)

***contexto** circunstancias que rodean una situación o evento (pág. 626)

***contract** a binding agreement between two or more people or parties (p. 224)

***contrato** acuerdo vinculante entre dos o más personas o partes (pág. 224)

***controversy** a dispute or quarrel (p. 575)

***controversia** disputa o discrepancia (pág. 575)

***conversion** the change from one belief or form to another (p. 117)

***conversión** cambio de una creencia o forma a otra (pág.117)

***convert** to change from one belief to another (p. 411)

***convertirse** cambiar de una creencia a otra (pág. 411)

***cooperation** a common effort (p. 653)

***cooperación** esfuerzo común (pág. 653)

***core** the basic or essential part (p. 350)

***núcleo** parte básica o esencial (pág. 350)

***corporation** a form of business organization that has a separate legal entity with all the rights and responsibilites of an individual, including the right to buy and sell property, enter into legal contracts, and sue and be sued (p. 288)

sociedad anónima forma de organización empresarial con personalidad jurídica independiente que tiene los mismos derechos y responsabilidades que una persona natural, como el derecho de comprar y vender propiedades, participar en contratos legales, y demandar y ser demandada (pág. 288)

***corruption** impairment of integrity, virtue, or moral principle (p. 838)

ruta de la seda corrupción falta de integridad, virtud o principios morales (pág. 838)

cosmopolitan a place or area that contains several different cultures and groups (p. 213)

cosmopolita un lugar o área que contiene varios grupos y culturas (pág. 213)

cottage industry a method of production in which tasks are done by individuals in their rural homes (p. 529)

industria artesanal método de producción en el cual los individuos realizan el trabajo en sus hogares rurales (pág. 529)

coup d'état a sudden overthrow of the government (p. 510)

golpe de Estado derrocamiento repentino de un gobierno (pág. 510)

***created** made or brought something new into existence (p. 41)

***creado** hecho, o algo nuevo a lo que se le ha dado existencia (pág. 41)

***creative** imaginative (p. 423)

***creativo** imaginativo (pág. 423)

creole a person of European descent born in Latin America and living there permanently (pp. 394, 546)

criollo persona de ascendencia europea nacida en América Latina y que vive allí permanentemente (págs. 394, 546)

***crucial** essential; important (p. 232)

***crucial** esencial; importante (pág. 232)

Crusades military expeditions carried out by European Christians in the Middle Ages to regain the Holy Land from the Muslims (p. 283)

cruzadas expediciones militares llevadas a cabo por los cristianos europeos durante la Edad Media con el fin de recuperar la Tierra Santa que estaba en manos de los musulmanes (pág. 283)

cultural imperialism referring to Western nations' control of other world cultures similar to how they had controlled colonial governments (p. 826)

imperialismo cultural relativo al control que ejercen las naciones occidentales sobre otras culturas, semejante a la manera en que estas naciones controlaban los gobiernos de las colonias (pág. 826)

***culture** the customary beliefs, social forms, and material traits of a racial, religious, or social group (p. 14)

***cultura** creencias, formas sociales y rasgos materiales tradicionales de un grupo racial, religioso o social (pág. 14)

***cuneiform** "wedge-shaped"; a system of writing developed by the Sumerians using a reed stylus to create wedge-shaped impressions on a clay tablet (p. 19)

***cuneiforme** "en forma de cuña"; sistema de escritura desarrollado por los sumerios, quienes usaban un estilete de caña para crear impresiones en forma de cuña sobre una tableta de arcilla (pág. 19)

***currency** coins, for example, that are in circulation and used as a medium of exchange (pp. 823, 864)

***moneda** billetes y monedas, por ejemplo, que están en circulación y se usan como medio de intercambio (págs. 823, 864)

***cycle** a series of events that recur regularly and usually lead back to the starting point (p. 45)

***ciclo** serie de eventos que se repiten con regularidad y que por lo general llevan de nuevo al punto de partida (pág. 45)

czar Russian for *caesar;* the title used by Russian emperors (p. 418)

zar "césar" en ruso; título adoptado por los emperadores rusos (pág. 418)

D

daimyo "great names"; the head of noble families in Japan who controlled vast landed estates and relied on samurai for protection (pp. 262, 456)

daimio "gran nombre"; jefe de una familia noble japonesa que controlaba grandes propiedades de tierra y dependía de la protección de los samuráis (págs. 262, 456)

Dao "Way"; the correct or divine way (p. 45)

tao "camino"; la forma correcta o divina (pág. 45)

Daoism a system of ideas based on the teachings of Laozi; teaches that the will of Heaven is best followed through inaction so that nature is allowed to take its course (p. 132)

taoísmo sistema de ideas basadas en las enseñanzas de Lao Tse; enseña que la voluntad del Cielo se sigue mejor mediante la inacción, en consecuencia se deja que la naturaleza siga su curso (pág. 132)

***debated** discussed by considering opposing viewpoints (p. 78)

***debatido** que se analizó considerando puntos de vista opuestos (pág. 78)

***decline** a change to a lower state or level (pp. 344, 420)

***descenso** cambio a un estado o nivel inferior (págs. 344, 420)

deflation a contraction in the volume of available money or credit that results in a general decline in prices (p. 832)

deflación reducción en el volumen de dinero o crédito disponible que lleva a una caída general en los precios (pág. 832)

deficit spending when a government pays out more money than it takes in through taxation and other revenues, thus going into debt (p. 665)

gasto deficitario cuando un gobierno paga más dinero del que recibe por concepto de impuestos y otros ingresos, y por lo tanto se endeuda (pág. 665)

deforestation the clearing of forests (p. 870)

deforestación devastación de los bosques (pág. 870)

deism an eighteenth-century religious philosophy based on reason and natural law (p. 479)

deísmo filosofía religiosa del siglo XVIII basada en la razón y la ley natural (pág. 479)

demilitarized elimination or prohibition of weapons, fortifications, and other military installations (p. 713)

desmilitarización eliminación o prohibición de usar armas, fortalezas u otras instalaciones militares (pág. 713)

democracy "the rule of many"; government by the people, either directly or through their elected representatives (p. 82)

democracia "gobierno de muchos"; gobierno del pueblo, ya sea directamente o por intermedio de sus representantes elegidos (pág. 82)

***demonstration** a public display of group feeling toward a person or cause (p. 817)

***manifestación** expresión pública de los sentimientos de un grupo hacia una persona o causa (pág. 817)

depression a period of low economic activity and rising unemployment (p. 663)

depresión periodo de baja actividad económica y aumento del desempleo (pág. 663)

***derived** obtained from; came from (p. 530)

***derivación** obtenido de; vino de (p. 530)

desertification formation of degraded soil, turning semi-arid lands into nonproductive deserts (p. 870)

desertificación formación de suelo degradado que transforma tierras semiáridas en desiertos improductivos (pág. 870)

de-Stalinization the process of eliminating Stalin's more ruthless policies (p. 801)

desestalinización proceso de eliminación de las políticas más despiadadas de Stalin (pág. 801)

détente a phase of relaxed tensions and improved relations between two adversaries (p. 802)

détente fase de alivio de las tensiones y mejoramiento de las relaciones entre dos adversarios (pág. 802)

deterrence during the Cold War, the U.S. and Soviet policies of holding huge arsenals of nuclear weapons to prevent war; each nation believed that neither would launch a nuclear attack since both knew that the other side could strike back with devastating power (p. 746)

disuasión durante la Guerra Fría, política de Estados Unidos y la Unión Soviética que consistía en poseer enormes arsenales de armas nucleares para evitar la guerra; cada nación creía que ninguna de ellas lanzaría un ataque nuclear porque ambas sabían que la contraparte podría responder con una fuerza devastadora (pág. 746)

***devote** to commit by solemn act (p. 111)

***consagrarse** comprometerse mediante un acto solemne (pág. 111)

dharma in Hinduism, the divine law that rules karma; it requires all people to do their duty based on their status in society (p. 111)

dharma en el hinduismo, ley divina que regula el karma; exige que todas las persona cumplan con su deber de acuerdo con su estatus social (pág. 111)

dictator an absolute ruler (p. 160)

dictador gobernante absoluto (pág. 160)

direct democracy a system of government in which the people participate directly in government decision making through mass meetings (p. 89)

democracia directa sistema de gobierno en el cual las personas participan directamente en la toma de decisiones del gobierno mediante encuentros masivos (pág. 89)

direct rule colonial government in which local elites are removed from power and replaced by a new set of officials brought from the colonizing country (p. 589)

gobierno directo gobierno colonial en el cual se retira del poder a las élites locales y las reemplaza un nuevo grupo de funcionarios del país colonizador (pág. 589)

discrimination prejudicial treatment usually based on race, religion, class, sex, or age (p. 768)

discriminación tratamiento que va en detrimento de las personas por razones de raza, religión, clase social, sexo o edad (pág. 768)

dissident a person who speaks out against the regime in power (p. 802)

disidente persona que habla en contra del régimen en el poder (pág. 802)

***diverse** varied and not alike (p. 776)

***diverso** variado, diferente (pág. 776)

diviner a person who is believed to have the power to foretell events (p. 305)

adivino persona que se cree que tiene la facultad de predecir sucesos (pág. 305)

divine right of kings the belief that the kings receive their power from God and are responsible only to God (p. 409)

derecho divino de los reyes creencia de que los reyes reciben su poder de Dios y son responsables solo ante Él (pág. 409)

***document** an original or official paper that gives proof of or support to (p. 238)

***documento** escrito original u oficial que sirve de prueba o respaldo (pág. 238)

dollar diplomacy the diplomacy that seeks to strengthen the power of a country or effect its purposes in foreign relations by the use of its financial resources (p. 603)

diplomacia del dólar diplomacia que busca fortalecer el poder de un país o alcanzar sus propósitos en las relaciones internacionales mediante el uso de sus recursos financieros (pág. 603)

***domain** a territory over which control is exercised (p. 432)

***dominio** territorio sobre el cual se ejerce control (pág. 432)

***domestic** relating to or originating within one's country (p. 507)

***interno** relativo al país de una persona o que se origina allí (pág. 507)

***domesticated** adapted to life with and to the advantage of humans (p. 31)

***domesticado** adaptado a la vida con los seres humanos y para el aprovechamiento de estos (pág. 31)

***dominate** to influence or control (pp. 342, 712)

***dominar** influir o controlar (págs. 342, 712)

domino theory the idea that if one country falls to communism, neighboring countries will also fall (p. 649)

teoría del efecto dominó idea según la cual si un país cede al comunismo, los países vecinos también lo harán (pág. 649)

dowry a gift of money or property paid at the time of marriage, either by the bride's parents to her husband or, in Islamic societies, by a husband to his wife (pp. 219, 254)

dote dinero o propiedad que los padres de la novia pagan al novio o, en las sociedades islámicas, el esposo a su esposa, cuando se casan (págs. 219, 254)

draft to select for some purpose; to conscript (p. 396)

reclutar elegir para algún propósito; conscribir (pág. 396)

***drama** a composition that tells a story usually involving conflicts and emotions through action and dialogue and typically designed for the theater (p. 422); state of intense conflict (p. 823)

***drama** composición que cuenta una historia que usualmente implica conflictos y emociones mediante la acción y el uso de diálogos; por lo general se crea para el teatro (pág. 422); estado de conflicto intenso (pág. 823)

Duma the Russian legislative assembly (p. 573)

duma Asamblea Legislativa de Rusia (pág. 573)

***dynamic** an activity or change that is continuous and productive (p. 866)

***dinámica** actividad o cambio que es continuo y productivo (pág. 866)

dynasty a family of rulers whose right to rule is passed on within the family (p. 27)

dinastía familia de gobernantes cuyo derecho a gobernar se transmite dentro de la familia (pág. 27)

E

ecology the study of the relationships between living things and their environment (p. 870)

ecología estudio de las relaciones entre los seres vivos y su medioambiente (pág. 870)

elector individual qualified to vote in an election (p. 510)

elector una persona calificada para votar en una elección (pág. 510)

***element** a distinct group within a larger group (p. 685)

***elemento** un grupo distinto dentro de un grupo más grande (pág. 685)

emancipation the act of setting free (p. 544)

emancipación acción de poner en libertad (pág. 544)

***emerge** to become manifest; to become known (p. 108); to come into being through evolution; to develop (p. 417)

***emerger** hacerse manifiesto; darse a conocer (pág. 108); surgir por evolución; desarrollar (pág. 417)

empire a large political unit or state, usually under a single leader, that controls many peoples or territories (p. 56)

imperio unidad política o Estado de gran tamaño, por lo general bajo el mandato de un solo líder, que controla muchos pueblos o territorios (pág. 56)

***enable** to make possible (p. 228)

***permitir** hacer posible (pág. 228)

encomienda a system of labor the Spanish used in the Americas; Spanish landowners had the right, as granted by Queen Isabella, to use Native Americans as laborers (p. 396)

encomienda sistema de mano de obra usado por los españoles en América; los terratenientes españoles tenían derecho, concedido por la Reina Isabel, de emplear a indígenas americanos como mano de obra (pág. 396)

***enhanced** improved (p. 800)

***aumentado** mejorado (pág. 800)

enlightened absolutism a system in which rulers tried to govern by Enlightenment principles while maintaining their full royal powers (p. 484)

despotismo ilustrado sistema en el cual los gobernantes trataron de dirigir siguiendo los principios de la Ilustración, pero en el que conservaban todas sus facultades reales (pág. 484)

***enormous** huge; vast; immense (p. 197)

***enorme** descomunal; vasto; inmenso (pág. 197)

***ensure** to make sure (pp. 141, 194)

***asegurar** garantizar (págs. 141, 194)

entrepreneur a person who finds new business opportunities and new ways to make profits (p. 528)

empresario persona interesada en hallar nuevas oportunidades comerciales y formas de obtener ganancias (pág. 528)

ephor one of the five men elected each year in ancient Sparta who were responsible for the education of youth and the conduct of all citizens (p. 83)

éforo uno de los cinco hombres elegidos cada año en la antigua Esparta, responsables de la educación de los jóvenes y de la conducta de todos los ciudadanos (pág. 83)

epic poem a long poem that tells the deeds of a great hero, such as the *Iliad* and the *Odyssey* of Homer (p. 79)

epopeya poema extenso que cuenta las hazañas de un gran héroe, como la *Iliada* y la *Odisea* de Homero (pág. 79)

Epicurianism a school of thought developed by the philosopher Epicurus in Hellenistic Athens; it held that happiness is the chief goal in life, and the means to achieve happiness was the pursuit of pleasure (p. 101)

epicureanismo escuela del pensamiento desarrollada por el filósofo Epicuro en la Atenas helenística; sostenía que la felicidad es la principal meta en la vida y que el medio para lograr la felicidad era la búsqueda del placer (pág. 101)

***erode** to diminish or destroy by degrees (p. 219)

***erosionar** disminuir o destruir algo poco a poco (pág. 219)

***erupt** to suddenly become active or violent (p. 549)

***estallar** entrar en actividad o tornarse violento repentinamente (pág. 549)

***establish** to set up permanently; to found (p. 703)

***establecer** instalar permanentemente; fundar (pág. 703)

estate a landed property with a large house (pp. 239, 601); one of the three classes into which French society was divided before the revolution: the clergy (First Estate), the nobles (Second Estate), and the townspeople (Third Estate) (p. 500)

latifundio propiedad de tierra con una casa grande (págs. 239, 601); una de las tres clases en las que se dividía la sociedad francesa antes de la revolución: el clero (Primer estado), los nobles (Segundo estado) y el pueblo (Tercer estado) (pág. 500)

***estimate** to make a rough determination (p. 48)

***estimate** to make a rough determination (p. 48)

eta Japan's outcast class whose way of life was strictly regulated by the Tokugawa (p. 458)

eta clase japonesa fuera del sistema de castas cuya forma de vida estaba estrictamente regulada por los Tokugawa (pág. 458)

***ethical** conforming to accepted standards of conduct; moral (p. 131)

***ético** de conformidad con los estándares de conducta aceptados; moral (pág. 131)

***ethics** moral principles; generally recognized rules of conduct (p. 96)

***ética** principios morales; reglas de conducta generalmente aceptadas (pág. 96)

***ethnic** relating to people who have common racial, religious, or cultural origins (p. 727)

***étnico** relativo a las personas que tienen un origen racial, religioso o cultural común (pág. 727)

Glossary/Glosario

ethnic cleansing a policy of killing or forcibly removing an ethnic group from its lands; used by the Serbs against the Muslim minority in Bosnia (pp. 685, 820)

limpieza étnica política que consiste en asesinar o sacar a la fuerza de sus tierras a un grupo étnico; la usaron los serbios contra la minoría musulmana en Bosnia (págs. 685, 820)

***eventually** in the end (pp. 486, 696)

***con el tiempo** al final (págs. 486, 696)

***evident** apparent (p. 838)

***evidente** aparente (pág. 838)

***evolve** develop; work out (p. 836)

***evolucionar** desarrollar; elaborar (pág. 836)

***exclude** to bar from inclusion or participation in (p. 192)

***excluir** impedir la inclusión o participación (pág. 192)

***exclusion** the act of excluding (p. 503)

***exclusión** el acto de exclusión (pág. 503)

***exclusive** limited to a single individual or group (p. 615)

***exclusivo** limitado a un individuo o grupo (pág. 615)

expedition a journey taken for a specific purpose (p. 61)

expedición viaje que se emprende con un propósito específico (pág. 61)

***exploit** to make use of meanly or unfairly for one's own advantage (p. 589)

***explotar** hacer uso de manera cruel o injusta para beneficio propio (pág. 589)

***export** to send a product or service for sale to another country (pp. 389, 589)

***exportar** enviar un producto o servicio para venderlo en otro país (págs. 389, 589)

***external** not intrinsic or essential (p. 363)

***exterior** no es intrínseco o esencial (pág. 363)

extraterritoriality living in a section of a country set aside for foreigners but not subject to the host country's laws (p. 614)

extraterritorialidad vivir en una sección de un país destinada a las personas extranjeras, pero que no está sujeta a las leyes del país anfitrión (pág. 614)

F

***factor** a contributing part (p. 311)

***factor** parte que contribuye a un resultado (pág. 311)

factory system a system of production where goods are manufactured by machines under one roof, with unskilled labor, using standardized parts (p. 529)

sistema de fábrica un sistema de producción en que se fabrica los bienes a máquina bajo el mismo techo, con obreros no cualificados, utilizando partes estandarizadas (pág. 529)

fascism a political philosophy that glorifies the state above the individual by emphasizing the need for a strong central government led by a dictatorial ruler (pp. 668, 853)

fascismo filosofía política que exalta al Estado por encima del individuo, poniendo énfasis en la necesidad de un gobierno central fuerte liderado por un dictador (págs. 668, 853)

federal system a form of government in which power is shared between the national and state governments (p. 492)

sistema federal forma de gobierno en la cual el poder se comparte entre los gobiernos nacional y estatal (pág. 492)

feminism the movement for women's rights (p. 567)

feminismo movimiento que lucha por los derechos de las mujeres (pág. 567)

feudal contract under feudalism, the unwritten rules that determined the relationship between a lord and his vassal (p. 230)

contrato feudal durante el feudalismo, reglas verbales que determinaban la relación entre un señor y sus vasallos (pág. 230)

feudalism political and social order that developed during the Middle Ages when royal governments were no longer able to defend their subjects; nobles offered protection and land in return for service (p. 229)

feudalismo orden política y social que se desarrolló durante la Edad Media, cuando los gobiernos monárquicos ya no podían defender a sus súbditos; los nobles ofrecían protección y tierras a cambio de servicios (pág. 229)

fief under feudalism, a grant of land made to a vassal; the vassal held political authority within his fief (p. 230)

feudo durante el feudalismo, porción de tierra concedida a un vasallo; el vasallo ejercía autoridad política dentro de su feudo (pág. 230)

filial piety the duty of family members to subordinate their needs and desires to those of the male head of the family, a concept important in Confucianism (p. 46)

piedad filial deber que tienen los miembros de una familia de subordinar sus necesidades y deseos a los del jerarca varón de la familia; un concepto importante en el confucianismo (pág. 46)

***final** the last in a series, process, or progress (p. 743)

***final** último en una serie, proceso o progreso (pág. 743)

***financial** relating to the management of funds (p. 157)

***financiero** relativo a la administración de fondos (pág. 157)

Five Pillars of Islam acts of worship every Muslim must perform; these include belief, prayer, charity, fasting, and pilgrimage (p. 209)

cinco pilares del islam actos de adoración que todo musulmán debe realizar. Estos son: creer, orar, practicar la caridad, ayunar y peregrinar (pág. 209)

***founder** one who founds or establishes (p. 101)

***fundador** quien funda o establece algo (pág. 101)

***founding** originating; beginning (p. 305)

***fundador** que origina; inicial (pág. 305)

free enterprise system economic system in which private businesses compete with little or no government control (p. 480)

sistema de empresa libre sistema económico en que los negocios privados se compiten entre sí con poco o ningún control gubernamental (pág. 480)

fresco painting done on fresh, wet plaster with water-based paints (p. 351)

fresco pintura elaborada sobre yeso fresco y húmedo con pinturas a base de agua (pág. 351)

***fundamental** basic or essential (p. 362)

***fundamental** básico o esencial (pág. 362)

G

***generation** a group of individuals born and living at the same time (p. 481)

***generación** grupo de individuos que nacen y viven durante la misma época (pág. 481)

genocide the deliberate mass murder or physical extinction of a particular racial, political, or cultural group (pp. 685, 728)

genocidio asesinato masivo o exterminio físico deliberado de un grupo racial, político o cultural específico (págs. 685, 728)

geocentric Earth-centered; a system of planetary motion in which the sun, moon, and other planets revolve around the Earth (p. 473)

geocéntrico con centro en la Tierra; sistema de movimiento de los planetas en el cual el Sol, la Luna y otros planetas orbitan la Tierra (pág. 473)

ghetto formerly a district in a city in which Jews were required to live (p. 372)

gueto antiguo distrito en una ciudad en el cual se obligaba a vivir a los judíos (pág. 372)

glasnost a Soviet policy permitting open discussion of political and social issues (p. 816)

glasnot política soviética que permitió el debate abierto de temas políticos y sociales (pág. 816)

globalization the movement toward a more integrated and interdependent world economy (p. 862)

globalización movimiento hacia una economía mundial más integrada e interdependiente (pág. 862)

***goal** an aim or a purpose (p. 775)

***meta** objetivo o propósito (pág. 775)

grand vizier the Ottoman sultan's chief minister who carried the main burdens of the state and who led the council meetings (p. 432)

gran visir primer ministro del sultán otomano responsable de las principales tareas del Estado, que encabezaba las reuniones del consejo (pág. 432)

greenhouse effect global warming caused by the buildup of carbon dioxide in the atmosphere (p. 871)

efecto invernadero calentamiento global ocasionado por la acumulación de dióxido de carbono en la atmósfera (pág. 871)

griot a special class of African storytellers who help keep alive a people's history (p. 306)

griot clase especial de narradores africanos que ayudan a mantener viva la historia de los pueblos (pág. 306)

guarantee to assure fulfillment of a condition (pp. 171, 493)

garantizar asegurar el cumplimiento de una condición (págs. 171, 493)

guerrilla tactics the use of unexpected maneuvers like sabotage and subterfuge to fight an enemy (p. 697)

táctica de guerrillas uso de maniobras inesperadas como el sabotaje y el uso de subterfugios para combatir a un enemigo (pág. 697)

gunboat diplomacy the practice of one state threatening another state with a nearby navy to force a treaty or unfair privileges (p. 587)

diplomacia de los cañones una práctica en que un estado amenaza a otro utilizando una armada cercana con la intención de imponer un tratado o privilegios injustos (pág. 587)

gunpowder empire an empire formed by outside conquerors who unified the regions they conquered through their mastery of firearms (p. 431)

imperio de la pólvora imperio formado por conquistadores extranjeros que unificaron las regiones que conquistaban gracias a su dominio de las armas de fuego (pág. 431)

H

hajj a pilgrimage to Makkah, one of the requirements of the Five Pillars of Islam (p. 208)

hajj peregrinación a la Meca; uno de los requisitos de los cinco pilares del islam (pág. 208)

hans approximately 250 domains into which Japan was divided under the Tokugawa (p. 457)

han aproximadamente 250 dominios en los cuales se dividía Japón bajo el dominio de los Tokugawa (pág. 457)

harem "sacred place"; the private domain of an Ottoman sultan, where he and his wives resided (p. 432)

harén "lugar sagrado"; dominio privado de un sultán otomano, donde este vivía junto a sus esposas (pág. 432)

heavy industry the manufacture of machines and equipment for factories and mines (p. 800)

industria pesada manufactura de maquinaria y equipo para fábricas y minas (pág. 800)

heliocentric sun-centered; the system of the universe in which the Earth and planets revolve around the sun (p. 473)

heliocéntrico con centro en el Sol; sistema del universo en el cual la Tierra y los planetas orbitan el Sol (pág. 473)

Hellenistic Era the age of Alexander the Great; period when the Greek language and ideas were carried to the non-Greek world (p. 99)

Era Helenística era de Alejandro Magno; período en el cual los griegos llevaron su idioma y sus ideas fuera del mundo griego (pág. 99)

helot in ancient Sparta, a captive person who was forced to work for the conqueror (p. 82)

ilota en la antigua Esparta, esclavo que era obligado a trabajar para el conquistador (pág. 82)

heresy the denial of basic Church doctrines (p. 281)

herejía rechazo a las doctrinas básicas de la Iglesia (pág. 281)

heretic one who does not conform to established doctrine (p. 404)

hereje persona que no acepta la doctrina establecida (pág. 404)

hieratic script simplified version of hieroglyphics used in ancient Egypt for business transactions, record keeping, and the general needs of daily life (p. 30)

escritura hierática versión simplificada de los jeroglíficos usados en el antiguo Egipto para realizar transacciones comerciales, llevar registros y para las necesidades generales de la vida diaria (pág. 30)

hieroglyphics "priest-carvings" or "sacred writings"; a complex system of writing that used both pictures and more abstract forms; used by the ancient Egyptians and Maya (p. 30)

jeroglíficos "tallas sagradas" o "escritos sagrados"; complejo sistema de escritura que combinaba imágenes y formas abstractas; usados por los antiguos egipcios y los mayas (pág. 30)

***highlighted** centered attention on (p. 612)

***destacado** algo sobre lo cual se centra la atención (pág. 612)

Hijrah the journey of Muhammad and his followers to Madinah in 622, which became year 1 of the official calendar of Islam (p. 208)

hégira viaje de Mahoma y sus seguidores a Medina en el año 622, que se convirtió en el año 1 del calendario islámico oficial (pág. 208)

Hinduism the major Indian religious system, which had its origins in the religious beliefs of the Aryans who settled India after 1500 B.C. (p. 105)

hinduismo principal sistema religioso de la India, que tuvo sus orígenes en las creencias religiosas de los arios que se establecieron en la India después del año 1500 A. C. (pág. 105)

Glossary/Glosario

HIV/AIDS human immunodeficiency virus/acquired immunodeficiency syndrome; any of the strains of HIV-1 and HIV-2 that infect and destroy the immune system's helper T cells causing a large drop in their numbers, and becomes AIDS when a person has 20 percent or less than the normal level of helper T cells (p. 777)

VIH/sida virus de inmunodeficiencia humana/síndrome de inmunodeficiencia adquirida; cualquiera de las cadenas de VIH-1 y VIH-2 que infectan y destruyen las células T cooperadoras del sistema inmunológico, lo que ocasiona una gran disminución de las mismas. Se convierte en sida cuando el número de células es igual o inferior al 20 por ciento del recuento normal de células T cooperadoras (pág. 777)

hominid humans and other humanlike creatures that walk upright (p. 6)

homínidos humanos y otras criaturas semejantes que caminan erguidas (pág. 6)

Homo sapiens sapiens "wise, wise humans"; a species that appeared in Africa between 150,000 and 200,000 years ago; they were the first anatomically modern humans (p. 6)

Homo sapiens sapiens "humano inteligente, inteligente"; especie que apareció en África hace entre 150,000 y 200,000 años; fueron los primeros humanos de anatomía moderna (pág. 6)

hostage system a system used by the shogunate to control the daimyo in Tokugawa Japan; the family of a daimyo lord was forced to stay at their residence in the capital whenever the lord was absent from it (p. 457)

sistema de rehenes sistema usado por el shogunato Tokugawa para controlar al señor daimio; la familia del daimio era obligada a permanecer en su residencia en la capital siempre que el señor no se encontraba allí (pág. 457)

humanism an intellectual movement of the Renaissance based on the study of the humanities, which included grammar, rhetoric, poetry, moral philosophy, and history (p. 348)

humanismo movimiento intelectual del Renacimiento basado en el estudio de las humanidades, que incluían la gramática, la retórica, la poesía, la filosofía moral y la historia (pág. 348)

I

icon a conventional religious image typically painted on a small wooden panel and venerated itself as sacred by Eastern Christians (p. 198)

ícono imagen religiosa convencional, por lo general pintada en un pequeño panel de madera venerada como sagrada por los cristianos orientales (pág. 198)

***ideological** based on a set of beliefs (p. 734)

***ideológico** que se basa en una serie de creencias (pág. 734)

***ideology** a set of beliefs (p. 139)

***ideología** conjunto de creencias (pág. 139)

idolatry the worship of a physical idol as a god (p. 199)

idolatría adoración de un ídolo físico como si se tratara de un dios (pág. 199)

imperialism the extension of a nation's power over other lands (p. 586)

imperialismo extensión del poder de una nación sobre otras tierras (pág. 586)

***imply** to express indirectly through reference or association (p. 82)

***implica** expresar indirectamente mediante una referencia o por asociación (pág. 82)

imperator commander in chief; the Latin origin of the word *emperor* (p. 161)

imperátor comandante en jefe; origen en latín de la palabra *emperador* (pág. 161)

***impose** to establish or apply (p. 463)

***imponer** establecer o aplicar (pág. 463)

indemnity the payment for damages (p. 617)

indemnización pago para compensar un daño (pág. 617)

indigenous native to a region (p. 594)

indígena nativo de una región (pág. 594)

indirect rule a colonial government in which local rulers are allowed to maintain their positions of authority and status (p. 589)

gobierno indirecto forma de gobierno colonial en la cual se permitía a los gobernantes mantener sus cargos de autoridad y su estatus (pág. 589)

***individuality** a total character that distinguishes an individual from others (pp. 137, 550)

***individualidad** carácter total que distingue a un individuo de otros (págs. 137, 550)

Glossary/Glosario

inductive reasoning the doctrine that scientists should proceed from the particular to the general by making systematic observations and carefully organized experiments to test hypotheses or theories, a process that will lead to correct general principles (p. 476)

razonamiento inductivo doctrina según la cual los científicos deben ir de lo particular a lo general haciendo observaciones sistemáticas y experimentos organizados cuidadosamente para probar hipótesis o teorías, un proceso que llevará a los principios generales correctos (pág. 476)

indulgence a release from all or part of punishment for sin by the Catholic Church, reducing time in purgatory after death (p. 363)

indulgencia exoneración total o parcial del castigo por un pecado que concede la Iglesia católica, la cual reduce el tiempo en el purgatorio después de morir (pág. 363)

industrial capitalism an economic system based on industrial production or manufacturing (p. 532)

capitalismo industrial sistema económico basado en la producción o manufactura industrial (pág. 532)

infidel an unbeliever; a term applied to the Muslims during the Crusades (p. 283)

infiel persona no creyente; término que se aplicó a los musulmanes durante las cruzadas (pág. 283)

inflation a rapid increase in prices (pp. 186, 407)

inflación aumento rápido de los precios (págs. 186, 407)

***insecure** uncertain, shaky; not adequately covered or sustained (p. 574)

***inseguro** incierto, flojo; que no está cubierto o sostenido adecuadamente (pág. 574)

***instability** the quality or state of being liable to change or alteration (p. 158)

***inestabilidad** ser susceptible al cambio o alteración (pág. 158)

***instituted** put into action (p. 141)

***instituido** puesto en práctica (pág. 141)

***institution** an organization for the promotion of a cause (p. 152)

***institución** organización que promueve una causa (pág. 152)

instruct to teach or to train (p. 331)

instruir enseñar o capacitar (pág. 331)

insulae Roman apartment blocks constructed of concrete with wooden beam floors (p. 170)

ínsulas bloques de apartamentos romanos construidos en concreto con pisos de vigas de madera (pág. 170)

***intelligent** having a high degree of understanding and mental capacity (p. 438)

***inteligente** que tiene un alto grado de comprensión y capacidad mental (pág. 438)

***intense** marked by great zeal, energy, determination, or concentration (p. 860)

***intenso** marcado por gran fervor, energía, determinación o concentración (pág. 860)

***intensity** extreme degree of strength, force, energy, or feeling (p. 579)

***intensidad** grado extremo de resistencia, fuerza, energía o sentimiento (pág. 579)

interdict a decree by the pope that forbade priests from giving the sacraments of the Church to the people (p. 279)

interdicto decreto expedido por el Papa que prohibía a los sacerdotes administrar los sacramentos de la Iglesia a las personas (pág. 279)

***intervention** the involvement in a situation to alter the outcome (p. 548)

intifada participación en una situación para alterar el resultado (pág. 548)

intifada "uprising"; a militant movement that arose during the 1980s among supporters of the Palestine Liberation Organization living in Israel (p. 771)

intifada "movimiento militante que se generó en la década de 1980 entre quienes apoyaban a la Organización para la Liberación de Palestina, y que vivían en Cisjordania y Gaza" (pág. 771)

***invention** a new idea, method, or device (p. 45)

***invento** idea, método o aparato nuevo (pág. 45)

***involvement** a commitment or a connection to (pp. 718, 720)

***participación** compromiso o conexión con algo (págs. 718, 720)

Islam monotheistic religion that emerged in the Arabian Peninsula during the seventh century (p. 208)

islam religión monoteísta que surgió en la península arábiga durante el siglo VII (pág. 208)

***isolate** to set apart from others (p. 76)

***aislar** separar de otros (pág. 76)

isolationism a policy of national isolation by abstention from alliances and other international political and economic relations (p. 718)

aislacionismo política de aislamiento nacional llevada a cabo absteniéndose de establecer alianzas y otras relaciones políticas y económicas internacionales (pág. 718)

isolationist a policy of national isolation by abstention from alliances and other international political and economic relations (pp. 451, 461)

aislacionista política de aislamiento nacional según la cual se evitan alianzas y otras relaciones políticas y económicas internacionales (págs. 451, 461)

issue a vital or an unsettled matter (p. 770)

asunto tema esencial o por resolver (pág. 770)

investor a person or an entity that commits money to earn a financial return (p. 701)

inversionista persona o entidad que compromete dinero para obtener un rendimiento financiero (pág. 701)

J

janissary a soldier in the elite guard of the Ottoman Turks (p. 430)

jenízaro soldado en la guardia principal de los turcos otomanos (pág. 430)

jihad "struggle in the way of God" (p. 210)

yihad "lucha en el camino de Dios" (pág. 210)

jurisdiction the limits or territory within which authority may be exercised (p. 836)

jurisdicción límites o territorio dentro del cual se puede ejercer autoridad (pág. 836)

justification the process of being justified, or deemed worthy of salvation, by God (p. 370)

justificación proceso mediante el cual Dios declara que alguien es justo o digno de salvación (pág. 370)

K

kaiser German for "caesar"; the title of the emperors of the Second German Empire (p. 543)

káiser en alemán, "césar"; título de los emperadores del Segundo Imperio Alemán (pág. 543)

kamikaze Japanese for "divine wind"; a suicide mission in which young Japanese pilots intentionally flew their airplanes into U.S. fighting ships at sea (p. 724)

kamikaze en japonés, "viento divino"; misión suicida en la cual jóvenes pilotos japoneses estrellaban sus aviones intencionalmente contra los barcos de combate estadounidenses que estaban en el mar (pág. 724)

karma in Hinduism, the force generated by a person's actions that determines how the person will be reborn in the next life (p. 110)

karma en el hinduismo, fuerza generada por las acciones de una persona, la cual determina cómo volverá a nacer esa persona en la siguiente vida (pág. 110)

khanate one of several separate territories into which Genghis Khan's empire was split, each under the rule of one of his sons (p. 256)

kanato uno de varios territorios separados en los cuales se dividía el imperio de Genghis Khan, cada uno gobernado por uno de sus hijos (pág. 256)

knight under feudalism, a member of the heavily armored cavalry (p. 229)

caballero durante el feudalismo, miembro de la caballería blindada (pág. 229)

L

labor people with all their abilities and efforts (p. 334); work performed by people that provides the goods or services in an economy (pp. 396, 528)

mano de obra personas con todas sus capacidades y esfuerzos (pág. 334); trabajo realizado por personas, que proporciona los bienes y servicios en una economía (págs. 396, 528)

laity regular church members (p. 181)

laicado personas que no pertenecen al clero (pág. 181)

laissez-faire the concept that the state should not impose government regulations but should leave the economy alone (p. 480)

laissez-faire concepto según el cual el Estado no debe imponer regulaciones gubernamentales, sino que debe haber libertad en la economía (pág. 480)

lay investiture the practice by which secular rulers both chose nominees to church offices and gave them the symbols of their office (p. 278)

investidura laica práctica según la cual gobernantes seculares escogían candidatos para cargos eclesiásticos y les entregaban los símbolos correspondientes (pág. 278)

***legal** relating to law; founded on law (p. 198)

***legal** relativo a la ley; basado en la ley (pág. 198)

Legalism a popular philosophy developed in China toward the end of the Zhou dynasty; it proposes that human beings are evil by nature and can only be brought to the correct path by harsh laws (p. 133)

legalismo filosofía popular que se desarrolló en China hacia el final de la dinastía Zhou; propone que los seres humanos son malos por naturaleza y solo pueden regresar al camino correcto mediante leyes estrictas (pág. 133)

***legislature** an organized body that makes laws (p. 684)

***Legislativo** cuerpo organizado que hace las leyes (pág. 684)

***libel** a written or an oral defamatory statement or representation that conveys an unjustly unfavorable impression (p. 286)

***libelo** declaración o representación difamatoria oral o escrita que presenta injustamente una imagen desfavorable (pág. 286)

***liberal** broad-minded; associated with ideals of the individual, especially economic freedom and greater participation in government (p. 514)

***liberal** de mente abierta; asociado con ideales de los individuos, en especial la libertad económica y una mayor participación en el gobierno (pág. 514)

liberalism a political philosophy originally based largely on Enlightenment principles, holding that people should be as free as possible from government restraint and that civil liberties—the basic rights of all people—should be protected (p. 518)

liberalismo filosofía política basada originalmente en los principios de la Ilustración, que sostiene que las personas deben estar tan libres como sea posible de las restricciones impuestas por el gobierno y que las libertades civiles, es decir los derechos fundamentales de las personas, se deben proteger (pág. 518)

liberate to free (p. 742)

liberar poner en libertad (pág. 742)

lineage group an extended family unit that has combined into a larger community (p. 304)

grupo de linaje unidad de familia extensa que se integra en una comunidad más grande (pág. 304)

longhouse an Iroquois house about 150 to 200 feet (46 to 61 m) long built of wooden poles covered with sheets of bark and housing about a dozen families (p. 323)

casa comunal casa de los iroqueses, de aproximadamente 150 a 200 pies (46 a 61 m), hecha de postes de madera cubiertos con láminas de corteza y que albergaba alrededor de una docena de familias (pág. 323)

Lutheranism the religious doctrine that Martin Luther developed; it differed from Catholicism in the doctrine of salvation, which Luther believed could be achieved by faith alone, not by good works; Lutheranism was the first Protestant faith (p. 365)

luteranismo doctrina religiosa desarrollada por Martín Lutero; se diferencia del catolicismo en la doctrina de la salvación, la cual según Lutero se podía alcanzar solo por la fe, no por las buenas obras. El luteranismo fue el primer credo protestante (pág. 365)

M

magic realism a form of expression unique to Latin American literature; it combines realistic events with dreamlike or fantasy backgrounds (p. 787)

realismo mágico forma de expresión propia de la literatura latinoamericana; combina sucesos reales con trasfondos irreales o fantásticos (pág. 787)

Magna Carta the "Great Charter" of rights, which King John was forced to sign by the English nobles at Runnymede in 1215 (p. 238)

Carta Magna la "Gran Carta" de derechos que los nobles ingleses obligaron a firmar al rey Juan en Runnymede en el año 1215 (pág. 238)

Mahayana a school of Buddhism that developed in northwest India, stressing the view that nirvana can be achieved through devotion to the Buddha; its followers consider the Buddha a divine figure (p. 265)

mahayana escuela budista que se desarrolló en el noroeste de India. Sostiene que el nirvana se puede alcanzar mediante la devoción a Buda. Para sus seguidores, Buda es una divinidad (pág. 265)

mainland states a part of a continent, as distinguished from peninsulas or offshore islands (p. 462)

Estados del territorio continental parte de un continente, en oposición a las penínsulas o islas mar adentro (pág. 462)

***maintain** to keep in an existing state of repair or efficiency (pp. 141, 807)

***mantener** conservar en buen estado de funcionamiento o eficiencia (págs. 141, 807)

maize corn (p. 330)

maíz elote (pág. 330)

major great; significant in size or importance (p. 26)

principal grande; de tamaño o importancia significativa (pág. 26)

mandate a territory temporarily governed by another nation on behalf of the League of Nations (p. 655)

mandato "territorio gobernado temporariamente por un país en nombre de la Liga de las Naciones" (pág. 655)

***manipulation** skillful or artful management (p. 870)

***manipulación** manejo hábil o astuto (pág. 870)

Mannerism an artistic movement that emerged in Italy in the 1520s and 1530s; it marked the end of the Renaissance by breaking down the principles of balance, harmony, and moderation (p. 420)

manierismo movimiento artístico surgido en Italia en las décadas de 1520 y 1530; marcó el fin del Renacimiento al romper los principios de balance, armonía y moderación (pág. 420)

manor in medieval Europe, an agricultural estate that a lord ran and peasants worked (p. 233)

heredad en la Europa medieval, propiedad agrícola a cargo de un señor feudal, que los campesinos labraban (pág. 233)

martial relating to, or suited for, war or a warrior (p. 141)

marcial relativo a la guerra o a los guerreros, o apropiado para ellos (pág. 141)

mass production production of goods in quantity usually by machinery (p. 571)

producción masiva producción de bienes en cantidad por lo general mediante el uso de maquinaria (pág. 571)

matrilineal tracing lineage through the mother rather than the father (p. 304)

matrilineal linaje que se traza teniendo en cuenta la línea materna, no la paterna (pág. 304)

***media** channels or systems of communication (p. 669)

***medios de comunicación** canales o sistemas de comunicación (pág. 669)

megacity a very large city (p. 787)

megaciudad una ciudad muy grande (pág. 787)

mercantilism a set of principles that dominated economic thought in the seventeenth century; it held that the prosperity of a nation depended on a large supply of gold and silver (p. 389)

mercantilismo conjunto de principios que dominaban el pensamiento económico en el siglo XVII. Planteaba que la prosperidad de una nación dependía de una abundante acumulación de oro y plata (pág. 389)

mercenary a soldier who fights primarily for pay (p. 343)

mercenario soldado que combate principalmente a cambio de un pago (pág. 343)

mestizo a person of mixed European and Native American descent (pp. 395, 547)

mestizo persona que desciende de un europeo y un indígena americano (págs. 395, 547)

***method** a systematic plan for doing something (p. 57)

***método** plan sistemático para hacer algo (pág. 57)

microchip also called an integrated circuit; a tiny assembly of electronic components and their connections that is produced in or on a tiny bit of material, usually silicon (p. 869)

microchip conocido también como circuito integrado; diminuto ensamblaje de componentes electrónicos y sus conexiones, producido en (o sobre) un trozo pequeño de material, por lo general silicio (pág. 869)

Middle Passage the forced voyage of enslaved Africans across the Atlantic Ocean to the Americas (p. 391)

travesía intermedia viaje obligado de los africanos esclavizados a través del océano Atlántico hasta América (pág. 391)

***migration** the movement of people from one country, place, or locality to another (p. 860)

***migración** movimiento de personas de un país, lugar o área a otra (pág. 860)

militarism the reliance on military strength (p. 542)

militarismo dependencia del poderío militar (pág. 542)

***military** relating to the armed forces or to soldiers, arms, or war (pp. 185, 635)

***militar** relativo a las fuerzas armadas o a los soldados, las armas o la guerra (págs. 185, 635)

minaret the tower of a mosque from which the muezzin calls the faithful to prayer five times a day (p. 221)

alminar torre de una mezquita desde la cual el almuédano convoca a los fieles a orar cinco veces al día (pág. 221)

***minimal** barely adequate (p. 795)

***mínimo** apenas adecuado (pág. 795)

ministerial responsibility the idea that the prime minister is responsible to the popularly elected legislative body and not to the king or president (p. 571)

responsabilidad ministerial idea según la cual el primer ministro es responsable ante el órgano legislador elegido popularmente y no ante el rey o el presidente (pág. 571)

missionary a person sent out to carry a religious message (p. 191)

misionero persona enviada para llevar un mensaje religioso (pág. 191)

mita a labor system that the Spanish administrators in Peru used to draft native people to work in the Spanish landowners' silver mines (p. 396)

mita sistema de mano de obra usado por los administradores españoles en Perú, que solían reclutar indígenas para trabajar en las minas de plata de los terratenientes españoles (pág. 396)

mobilization the process of assembling troops and supplies and making them ready for war (pp. 637, 722)

movilización proceso de reunir tropas y provisiones y prepararlas para la guerra (págs. 637, 722)

modernism a movement in which writers and artists between 1870 and 1914 rebelled against the traditional literary and artistic styles that had dominated European cultural life since the Renaissance (p. 576)

modernismo movimiento en el cual los escritores y artistas entre 1870 y 1914 se rebelaron contra los estilos literarios y artísticos tradicionales que predominaban en la vida cultural de Europa desde el Renacimiento (pág. 576)

monarchy government by a sovereign ruler such as a king or queen (p. 68)

monarquía gobierno de un dirigente soberano, como un rey o una reina (pág. 68)

monasticism the practice of living the life of a monk (p. 190)

monacato práctica que consiste en vivir la vida de un monje (pág. 190)

monk a man who separates himself from ordinary human society in order to dedicate himself to God; monks live in monasteries headed by abbots (p. 190)

monje hombre que se aparta de la sociedad humana común para dedicarse a Dios; los monjes viven en monasterios dirigidos por abades (pág. 190)

monotheistic believing in one God (p. 34)

monoteísta que cree en un solo Dios (pág. 34)

monsoon a seasonal wind pattern in southern Asia that blows warm, moist air from the southwest during the summer, bringing heavy rains, and cold, dry air from the northeast during the winter (p. 38)

monzón viento estacional del sur de Asia que sopla aire caliente y húmedo desde el suroeste durante el verano, y trae consigo fuertes lluvias y aire seco y frío del noreste durante el invierno (pág. 38)

***motive** a reason to take action (p. 620)

***motivo** razón para actuar (pág. 620)

muezzin the crier who calls the Muslim faithful to prayer from the minaret of a mosque (p. 221)

almuédano persona que convoca a los fieles musulmanes a orar, desde el alminar de una mezquita (pág. 221)

mulatto a person of mixed African and European descent (p. 395)

mulato persona que desciende de un africano y un europeo (pág. 395)

multinational corporation a company with divisions in more than two countries (p. 862)

empresa multinacional compañía con divisiones en más de dos países (pág. 862)

multinational empire an empire in which people of many nationalities live (p. 538)

imperio multinacional imperio en el cual viven personas de muchas nacionalidades (pág. 538)

Muslim a person who believes in Islam (p. 208)

musulmán persona que practica el islam (pág. 208)

N

nationalism the unique cultural identity of a people based on common language, religion, and national symbols (p. 515)

nacionalismo identidad cultural exclusiva de un pueblo que comparte su lengua, su religión y sus símbolos nacionales (pág. 515)

natural rights rights with which all humans are born, including the rights to life, liberty, and property (p. 412)

derechos naturales derechos con los cuales nacen los seres humanos, como el derecho a la vida, la libertad y la propiedad (pág. 412)

natural selection the principle set forth by Charles Darwin that some organisms are more adaptable to the environment than others; in popular terms, "survival of the fittest" (p. 552)

selección natural principio establecido por Charles Darwin según el cual algunos organismos se adaptan mejor que otros al medioambiente; en términos populares se conoce como "la supervivencia del más fuerte" (pág. 552)

Nazi shortened form of the German *Nazional,* or the National Socialist German Workers' Party; a member of such party (p. 673)

nazi abreviatura del alemán *Nazional*, relativo al Partido Nacional Socialista Obrero Alemán; miembro de ese partido (pág. 673)

neo-Confucianism a revised form of Confucianism that evolved as a response to Buddhism and held sway in China from the late Tang dynasty to the end of the dynastic system in the twentieth century (p. 258)

neoconfucianismo forma renovada del confucianismo que evolucionó en respuesta al budismo y predominó en China desde la dinastía Tang tardía hasta el final del sistema de dinastías, en el siglo XX (pág. 258)

***network** an interrelated or interconnected group or system (p. 462)

***red** grupo o sistema interrelacionado o interconectado (pág. 462)

neutrality the refusal to take sides or become involved in wars between other nations (p. 718)

neutralidad negativa a tomar partido o involucrarse en guerras entre otras naciones (pág. 718)

new monarchy in the fifteenth century, the government in which power had been centralized under a king or queen, i.e., France, England, and Spain (p. 294)

nueva monarquía durante el siglo XV, el gobierno en el cual el poder estaba centralizado en un rey o una reina, como en Francia, Inglaterra y España (pág. 294)

nirvana in Buddhism, ultimate reality, the end of the self and a reunion with the Great World Soul (p. 114)

nirvana en el budismo, realidad final, el fin del yo y una reunión con la Gran Alma Universal (pág. 114)

nongovernmental organization an organization that has no government ties and works to address world problems (p. 861)

organización no gubernamental organización que no tiene vínculos con el gobierno y que trabaja para tratar problemas mundiales (pág. 861)

***nuclear** being a weapon whose destructive power comes from a nuclear reaction (p. 847)

***nuclear** arma cuyo poder destructivo proviene de una reacción nuclear (pág. 847)

nuclear proliferation the spread of nuclear weapons production technology and knowledge to nations without that capability (p. 847)

proliferación nuclear expansión de la tecnología de producción y los conocimientos de armas nucleares a naciones que no tienen esa capacidad (pág. 847)

nun a woman who separates herself from ordinary human society in order to dedicate herself to God; nuns live in convents headed by abbesses (p. 191)

monja mujer que se aparta de la sociedad humana común para dedicarse a Dios; las monjas viven en conventos dirigidos por abadesas (pág. 191)

O

obsidian a dark natural glass stone formed by lava (p. 47)

obsidiana roca vítrea oscura formada por la lava (pág. 47)

***occupation** the military force occupying a country or the policies carried out by it (p. 728)

***ocupación** cuando las fuerzas militares se apoderan de un país; políticas derivadas de esta acción (pág. 728)

occupied held by a foreign power (p. 807)

ocupado en poder de una potencia extranjera (pág. 807)

oligarchy "the rule of the few"; a form of government in which a select group of people exercises control (pp. 82, 703)

oligarquía "gobierno de pocos"; forma de gobierno en la cual un grupo selecto de personas ejerce control (págs. 82, 703)

one-child policy China's effort, beginning in 1979, to control population growth; incentives such as education benefits, child care, and housing are offered to couples who limit their families to one child (p. 831)

política de un solo hijo iniciativa de China, que comenzó en 1979, para controlar el aumento de su población; las parejas que limitan sus familias a un solo hijo reciben incentivos como beneficios educativos, cuidado de los niños y vivienda (pág. 831)

Open Door policy a policy, proposed by U.S. secretary of state John Hay in 1899, that stated all powers with spheres of influence in China would respect equal trading opportunities with China and not set tariffs giving an unfair advantage to the citizens of their own country (p. 617)

política de Puertas Abiertas política propuesta por el Secretario de Estado estadounidense John Hay en 1899, según la cual las potencias con esferas de influencia en China debían respetar las mismas condiciones comerciales con ese país y no fijar aranceles que dieran una ventaja desleal a los ciudadanos de su país (pág. 617)

oracle in ancient Greece, a sacred shrine where a god or goddess was said to reveal the future through a priest or priestess (p. 92)

oráculo en la antigua Grecia, templo sagrado donde, según se decía, un dios o una diosa revelaba el futuro a través de un sacerdote o una sacerdotisa (pág. 92)

ordeal a means of determining guilt in Germanic law, based on the idea of divine intervention: if the accused person was unharmed after a physical trial, he or she was presumed innocent (p. 194)

ordalía forma de determinar la culpabilidad en la ley germana, basada en la idea de la intervención divina: si la persona acusada salía ilesa de una prueba física, se presumía su inocencia (pág. 194)

orthodoxy traditional beliefs, especially in religion (p. 436)

ortodoxia creencias tradicionales, especialmente religiosas (pág. 436)

ostracism in ancient Athens, the process for temporarily banning ambitious politicians from the city by popular vote (p. 89)

ostracismo en la antigua Atenas, proceso mediante el cual, por voto popular, se desterraba temporalmente de la ciudad a los políticos ambiciosos (pág. 89)

"out-of-Africa" theory also called the replacement theory; this theory refers to when *Homo sapiens sapiens* began spreading out of Africa to other parts of the world about 100,000 years ago and replacing populations of earlier hominids in Europe and Asia (p. 6)

teoría del origen africano se denomina también teoría del reemplazo; esta teoría señala que el *Homo sapiens sapiens* empezó a expandirse desde África hacia otras partes del mundo hace aproximadamente 100,000 años y fue reemplazando a las poblaciones de los primeros homínidos de Europa y Asia (pág. 6)

***overseas** beyond or across the sea (p. 380)

***de ultramar** más allá del mar o al otro lado del mar (pág. 380)

P

Pan-Africanism the unity of all black Africans, regardless of national boundaries (pp. 691, 776)

panafricanismo unión de todos las personas africanas negras sin importar sus fronteras nacionales (págs. 691, 776)

Pan-Arabism Arab unity, regardless of national boundaries (p. 770)

panarabismo unión de todos los pueblos árabes sin importar sus fronteras nacionales (pág. 770)

pandemic a widespread outbreak of a disease (p. 856)

pandemia brote generalizado de una enfermedad (pág. 856)

***parallel** having the same direction or course; similar (p. 774)

***paralelo** que tiene la misma dirección o curso; semejante (pág. 774)

Parliament in thirteenth-century England, the representative government that emerged; it was composed of two knights from every county, two people from every town, and all the nobles and bishops throughout England (p. 238)

Parlamento gobierno representativo que surgió en el siglo XIII en Inglaterra; lo integraban dos caballeros de cada condado, dos habitantes de cada ciudad y todos los nobles y obispos ingleses (pág. 238)

***participation** having a part in or sharing in something (p. 802)

***participación** que tiene parte en algo o comparte la propiedad de algo (pág. 802)

partisan a resistance fighter in World War II (p. 732)

partisano combatiente de la resistencia durante la Segunda Guerra Mundial (pág. 732)

pasha an appointed official of the Ottoman Empire who collected taxes, maintained law and order, and was directly responsible to the sultan's court (p. 432)

pachá funcionario del imperio otomano que recaudaba impuestos, mantenía la ley y el orden y era responsable directamente ante la corte del sultán (pág. 432)

pastoral nomad a person who domesticates animals for food and clothing and moves along regular migratory routes to provide a steady source of nourishment for those animals (p. 31)

nómada persona que domestica animales para alimentarse y vestirse y se traslada a lo largo de las rutas migratorias regulares para proporcionar una fuente estable de comida a sus animales (pág. 31)

paterfamilias in the Roman social structure, the dominant male head of the household, which also included his wife, sons, and their wives and children, unmarried daughters, and slaves (p. 169)

páter familias en la estructura social romana, varón dominante del hogar, que incluía a la esposa, los hijos y sus esposas e hijos, las hijas solteras y los esclavos (pág. 169)

patriarch the head of the Eastern Orthodox Church, originally appointed by the Byzantine emperor (p. 197)

patriarca jerarca de la Iglesia ortodoxa oriental, inicialmente nombrado por el emperador bizantino (pág. 197)

patriarchal dominated by men (p. 57)

patriarcal bajo el dominio de los hombres (pág. 57)

patrician a wealthy, powerful landowner (pp. 152, 236)

patricio terrateniente rico y poderoso (pág. 152, 236)

patrilineal tracing the lineage through the father (p. 304)

patrilineal linaje que se traza teniendo en cuenta la línea paterna (pág. 304)

peacekeeping forces military forces drawn from neutral members of the United Nations to settle conflicts and supervise truces (p. 847)

fuerzas de paz fuerzas militares conformadas por miembros neutrales de las Naciones Unidas para resolver conflictos y supervisar las treguas (pág. 847)

peninsulare a person born on the Iberian Peninsula; typically, a Spanish or Portuguese official who resided temporarily in Latin America for political and economic gain and then returned to Europe (pp. 394, 546)

peninsular persona nacida en la Península Ibérica; por lo general, un funcionario español o portugués que vivía temporalmente en América Latina para obtener beneficios políticos y económicos y luego regresaba a Europa (págs. 394, 546)

per capita per person (p. 829)

per cápita por persona (pág. 829)

***percent** a part of a whole divided into 100 parts (p. 508)

***porcentaje** parte de un todo dividido entre 100 (pág. 508)

perestroika the fundamental restructuring of the Soviet economy; a policy introduced by Gorbachev (p. 816)

perestroika reestructuración de los fundamentos de la economía soviética; política introducida por Mijaíl Gorbachov (pág. 816)

***period** an interval of time (pp. 252, 290)

***periodo** intervalo de tiempo (págs. 252, 290)

permanent revolution an atmosphere of constant revolutionary fervor favored by Mao Zedong to enable China to overcome the past and achieve the final stage of communism (p. 748)

revolución permanente atmósfera de fervor revolucionario constante promovida por Mao Tse-Tung para permitir que China superara el pasado y llegara a la etapa final del comunismo (pág. 748)

perspective artistic techniques used to give the effect of three-dimensional depth to two-dimensional surfaces (p. 351); viewpoint (p. 451)

perspectiva técnicas artísticas usadas para dar a las superficies bidimensionales el efecto de profundidad tridimensional (pág. 351); punta de vista (pág. 451)

phalanx a wall of shields created by foot soldiers marching shoulder to shoulder in a rectangular formation (p. 81)

falange barrera de escudos que formaban los soldados de infantería marchando hombro a hombro en formación rectangular (pág. 81)

pharaoh the most common of the various titles for ancient Egyptian monarchs; the term originally meant "great house" or "palace" (p. 27)

faraón título más común de los antiguos monarcas egipcios; el término originalmente significaba "casa grande" o "palacio" (pág. 27)

***phase** a part in the development cycle (p. 619)

***fase** parte en el ciclo de desarrollo (pág. 619)

philosophe French for "philosopher"; applied to all intellectuals during the Enlightenment (p. 478)

philosophe término francés para "filósofo"; se aplicaba a todos los intelectuales durante la Ilustración (pág. 478)

Glossary/Glosario

***philosopher** a person who seeks wisdom or enlightenment; a scholar or a thinker (p. 473)

***filósofo** persona que busca la sabiduría o la ilustración; académico o pensador (pág. 473)

philosophy an organized system of thought, from the Greek for "love of wisdom" (pp. 95, 131)

filosofía sistema organizado del pensamiento, del griego "amor a la sabiduría" (págs. 95, 131)

physical relating to the body (p. 28)

físico relativo al cuerpo (pág. 28)

pilgrim a person who travels to a shrine or other holy place (p. 119)

peregrino persona que viaja a un templo u otro lugar sagrado (pág. 119)

plague an epidemic disease (p. 185)

plaga epidemia (pág. 185)

planned economy an economic system directed by government agencies (p. 642)

economía dirigida sistema económico dirigido por agencias del gobierno (pág. 642)

plantation a large agricultural estate (p. 390)

plantación gran propiedad agrícola (pág. 390)

plateau a relatively high, flat land area (p. 302)

meseta área de tierra relativamente alta y plana (pág. 302)

plebeian in the Roman Republic, a social class made up of minor landholders, craftspeople, merchants, and small farmers (p. 152)

plebeyo en la República romana, clase social formada por los pequeños terratenientes, artesanos, comerciantes y pequeños agricultores (pág. 152)

plebiscite a popular vote (p. 543)

plebiscito voto popular (pág. 543)

pogrom the organized massacre of a minority group, especially Jews (p. 579)

pogromo masacre organizada de una minoría, especialmente los judíos (pág. 579)

***policy** an overall plan embracing the general goals and acceptable procedures of a governmental body (p. 406)

***política** plan general que comprende los objetivos generales y los procedimientos aceptables de un organismo gubernamental (pág. 406)

policy of containment a plan to keep something, such as communism, within its existing geographical boundaries and prevent further aggressive moves (p. 743)

política de contención plan para mantener algo, como el comunismo, dentro de los límites geográficos existentes y evitar movimientos radicales en el futuro (pág. 743)

polis the early Greek city-state, consisting of a city or town and its surrounding countryside (p. 80)

polis antigua ciudad-Estado griega, que constaba de una ciudad o un pueblo y sus alrededores (pág. 80)

polytheistic believing in many gods (p. 17)

politeísta que cree en muchos dioses (pág. 17)

popular culture entertainment created for a profit and for a mass audience (p. 826)

cultura popular entretenimiento creado con fines de lucro y dirigido a una audiencia masiva (pág. 826)

porcelain a ceramic made of fine clay baked at very high temperatures (pp. 259, 453)

porcelana cerámica elaborada con arcilla fina cocida a temperaturas muy elevadas (págs. 259, 453)

postmodernism an artistic movement that emerged in the 1980s; its artists do not expect rationality in the world and are comfortable with many "truths" (p. 826)

posmodernismo movimiento artístico surgido en la década de 1980; los artistas que lo practican no esperan encontrar racionalidad en el mundo y están a gusto con muchas "verdades" (pág. 826)

praetor an official of the Roman Republic in charge of enforcing civil law (p. 153)

pretor funcionario de la antigua República romana encargado de hacer cumplir las leyes civiles (pág. 153)

predestination the belief that God has determined in advance who will be saved (the elect) and who will be damned (the reprobate) (p. 370)

predestinación creencia de que Dios ha determinado de antemano quiénes se salvarán (los elegidos) y quiénes se condenarán (los réprobos) (pág. 370)

prefecture in the Japanese Meiji Restoration, a territory governed by its former daimyo lord (p. 624)

prefectura durante la Restauración Meiji en Japón, territorio gobernado por su antiguo señor daimio (pág. 624)

priest in early urban civilizations, an important and powerful person who supervised rituals aimed at pleasing the gods and goddesses (p. 15)	**sacerdote** en las primeras civilizaciones urbanas, persona importante y poderosa que supervisaba los rituales realizados para complacer a dioses y diosas (pág. 15)
***primary** most important (pp. 38, 169)	***primordial** lo más importante (págs. 38, 169)
***principle** a fundamental law or idea; when said of people (e.g., someone is highly principled), it means a devotion to high codes or rules of conduct (p. 439)	***principio** ley o idea fundamental; cuando se refiere a una persona (p. ej. alguien de sólidos principios), significa fidelidad a altos códigos o normas de conducta (pág. 439)
principle of intervention the idea that great powers have the right to send armies into countries where there are revolutions to restore legitimate governments (p. 518)	**principio de intervención** idea según la cual las grandes potencias tienen derecho a enviar ejércitos a países donde se presenta una revolución para restaurar los gobiernos legítimos (pág. 518)
principle of nonalignment Jawaharlal Nehru's refusal to align India with any bloc or alliance (p. 765)	**principio de no alineación** negativa del líder Jawaharlal Nehru a alinear India con ningún bloque o alianza (pág. 765)
privatization the sale of government-owned companies to private firms (p. 783)	**privatización** venta de compañías del gobierno a firmas privadas (pág. 783)
***proceed** to advance or move along a course (p. 284)	***continuar** avanzar o seguir un recorrido (pág. 284)
***process** a series of actions or operations necessary to meet a specified end (pp. 110, 456)	***proceso** serie de acciones u operaciones necesarias para lograr un fin específico (pág. 110, 456)
procurator in the Roman Empire, an official in charge of a province (p. 178)	**procurador** en el Imperio Romano, funcionario a cargo de una provincia (pág. 178)
***prohibit** to prevent or to forbid (p. 676)	***prohibir** evitar o impeder (pág. 676)
***projection** an estimate or a calculation (p. 860)	***proyección** estimación o cálculo (pág. 860)
proletariat the working class (p. 563)	**proletariado** clase trabajadora (pág. 563)
propaganda ideas spread to influence public opinion for or against a cause (p. 638)	**propaganda** ideas difundidas con el fin de influenciar a la opinión pública a favor o en contra de una causa (pág. 638)
protectorate a political unit that depends on another government for its protection (p. 588)	**protectorado** unidad política que depende de otro gobierno para su protección (pág. 588)
provincial local; of or relating to a province (p. 618)	**provincial** local; de una provincia o relativo a ella (pág. 618)
proxy war a war in which the powers in conflict use third parties as substitutes instead of fighting each other directly (p. 778)	**guerra subsidiaria** guerra en la cual las potencias en conflicto usan a terceros como sustitutos en lugar de combatir entre ellos directamente (pág. 778)
psychoanalysis a method by which a therapist and patient probe deeply into the patient's memory; by making the patient's conscious mind aware of repressed thoughts, healing can take place (p. 578)	**psicoanálisis** método por el cual un terapeuta y un paciente exploran en lo profundo de la memoria del paciente; se puede obtener una cura trayendo al consciente del paciente los pensamientos reprimidos (pág. 578)
***psychological** mental; directed toward the will or mind (p. 651)	***psicológico** mental; que se dirige a la voluntad o la mente (pág. 651)
***publish** to print for distribution (p. 370)	***publicar** imprimir para la distribución (pág. 370)
puddling the process in which coke derived from coal is used to burn away impurities in crude iron to produce high quality iron (p. 530)	**pudelación** proceso en el cual se usa coque derivado del carbón para quemar las impurezas del hierro bruto para producir hierro de alta calidad (pág. 530)

Puritans English Protestants who felt that the Church of England needed further reform and sought to simplify and regulate forms of worship (p. 409)

puritanos protestantes ingleses que sentían que la Iglesia de Inglaterra necesitaba una reforma más profunda y buscaban simplificar y regular las formas de culto (pág. 409)

***pursue** to follow up or proceed with (pp. 190, 279)

***perseguir** seguir o continuar con algo (págs. 190, 279)

Q

queue the braided pigtail that was traditionally worn by Chinese males (p. 452)

coleta mechón de cabello trenzado que usaban tradicionalmente los hombres chinos (pág. 452)

quipu a system of knotted strings used by the Inca people for keeping records (p. 333)

quipu sistema de cuerdas con nudos que los incas usaban para registrar información (pág. 333)

Quran the holy scriptures of the religion of Islam (p. 208)

Corán escrituras sagradas de la religión islámica (pág. 208)

R

racism the belief that race determines a person's traits and capabilities (p. 586)

racismo creencia de que la raza determina los rasgos y capacidades de una persona (pág. 586)

***radical** relating to a political group associated with views, practices, and policies of extreme change (p. 537)

***radical** relativo a un grupo político asociado con opiniones, prácticas y políticas de cambio extremo (pág. 537)

rationalism a system of thought expounded by René Descartes based on the belief that reason is the chief source of knowledge (p. 476)

racionalismo sistema de pensamiento expuesto por René Descartes, que se basa en la creencia de que la razón es la fuente principal del conocimiento (pág. 476)

realism a mid-nineteenth century movement that rejected romanticism and sought to portray lower- and middle-class life as it actually was (p. 553)

Realismo movimiento de mediados del siglo XIX que se oponía al Romanticismo y buscaba representar la vida de las clases baja y media tal como era (pág. 553)

real wages the actual purchasing power of income (p. 797)

salario real poder adquisitivo real de los ingresos (pág. 797)

redistribution of wealth the shifting of wealth from a rich minority to a poor majority (p. 700)

redistribución de la riqueza paso de la riqueza de una minoría rica a una mayoría pobre (pág. 700)

***regime** the government in power (pp. 139, 544)

***régimen** gobierno que está en el poder (pág. 139, 544)

reincarnation the rebirth of an individual's soul in a different form after death (p. 110)

reencarnación renacimiento del alma de un individuo en una forma diferente después de la muerte (pág. 110)

relic bones or other objects connected with saints; considered to be worthy of worship by the faithful (p. 282)

reliquia huesos u otros objetos pertenecientes a los santos; los fieles los consideran dignos de veneración (pág. 282)

***remarkable** worthy or likely to be noticed; being uncommon or extraordinary (p. 67)

***destacado** que vale la pena notarlo o que tiene la probabilidad de ser observado; poco común o extraordinario (pág. 67)

***remove** to eliminate (p. 279)

***quitar** eliminar (pág. 279)

reparation a payment made to the victor by the vanquished to cover the costs of war (p. 653)

reparación pago que el vencido hace al vencedor para cubrir los gastos de la guerra (pág. 653)

republic a form of government in which the leader is not a king and certain citizens have the right to vote (pp. 151, 343)

república forma de gobierno en la cual el líder no es un rey y algunos ciudadanos tienen derecho al voto (págs. 151, 343)

***require** to demand as being necessary (p. 676)

***exigir** demandar como algo necesario (pág. 676)

resident one who resides in a place (p. 332)

residente persona que habita en un lugar (pág. 332)

***resolve** determination; a fixed purpose (p. 718)

***resolución** determinación; propósito fijo (pág. 718)

***restoration** a bringing back to a former position or condition (p. 410)

***restauración** regreso a una posición o condición anterior (pág. 410)

***retain** to keep in possession or use (p. 265)

***retener** conservar la posesión o el uso (pág. 265)

***reveal** show; to make known (p. 41)

***revelar** mostrar; dar a conocer (pág. 41)

***revelation** a divine truth (p. 207)

***revelación** verdad divina (pág. 207)

***revenue** the yield of sources of income that a nation or state collects and deposits into its treasury for public use (pp. 261, 770)

***renta** producto de diversas fuentes de ingresos que una nación o Estado recauda y deposita en su tesoro para destinarlo al gasto público (págs. 261, 770)

revisionist a Marxist who rejected the revolutionary approach, believing instead in evolution by democratic means to achieve the goal of socialism (p. 563)

revisionista marxista que se oponía al enfoque revolucionario, y en cambio, creía en la evolución por medios democráticos para alcanzar los objetivos del socialismo (pág. 563)

***revolution** a sudden, radical, or complete change (p. 9); an overthrow of government (p. 645)

***revolución** un cambio repentino, radical o completo (pág. 9); derrocamiento de un gobierno (pág. 645)

***rigid** inflexible, unyielding (p. 113)

***rígido** inflexible, que no cede (pág. 113)

ritual a ceremony or a rite (p. 47)

ritual ceremonia o rito (pág. 47)

rococo an artistic style that replaced baroque in the 1730s; it was highly secular, emphasizing grace, charm, and gentle action (p. 482)

Rococó estilo artístico que reemplazó al Barroco en la década de 1730; altamente seglar, con énfasis en la gracia, el encanto y las acciones gentiles (pág. 482)

***role** a socially-expected behavior pattern (p. 767)

***conducta** patrón de comportamiento socialmente esperado (pág. 767)

romanticism an intellectual movement that emerged at the end of the eighteenth century in reaction to the ideas of the Enlightenment; it stressed feelings, emotion, and imagination as sources of knowing (p. 550)

Romanticismo movimiento intelectual surgido a finales del siglo XVIII como reacción a las ideas de la Ilustración. Ponía énfasis en los sentimientos, las emociones y la imaginación como fuentes de conocimiento (pág. 550)

Roundheads supporters of the Parliament in the English Civil War (p. 410)

cabezas redondas partidarios del Parlamento durante la Guerra Civil Inglesa (pág. 410)

S

sacrament a Christian rite (p. 279)

sacramento rito cristiano (pág. 279)

salons the elegant urban drawing rooms where, in the eighteenth century, writers, artists, aristocrats, government officials, and wealthy middle-class people gathered to discuss the ideas of the philosophes (p. 482)

salón elegante recinto urbano donde, durante el siglo XVIII, escritores, artistas, aristócratas, funcionarios del gobierno y personas acaudaladas de la clase media se reunían a analizar las ideas de los filósofos (pág. 482)

salvation the state of being saved (that is, going to heaven) through faith alone or through faith and good works (p. 363)

salvación salvarse (es decir, ir al cielo) a través de la fe solamente o por la fe y las buenas obras (pág. 363)

samurai "those who serve"; Japanese warriors similar to the knights of medieval Europe (p. 261)

samuráis "aquellos que sirven"; guerreros japoneses semejantes a los caballeros de la Europa medieval (pág. 261)

sanctions restrictions intended to enforce international law (p. 716)

sanciones restricciones cuyo propósito es hacer cumplir las leyes internacionales (pág. 716)

Sanskrit the first writing system of the Aryans, developed around 1000 B.C. (p. 41)

sánscrito primer sistema de escritura de los arios, desarrollado alrededor del año 1000 A. C. (pág. 41)

sans-culottes "without breeches"; members of the Paris Commune who considered themselves ordinary patriots (in other words, they wore long trousers instead of the fine knee-length breeches of the nobles) (p. 505)

sans-culottes "sin pantalón corto"; miembros de la comuna de París que se consideraban patriotas comunes (es decir, usaban pantalones largos en lugar de los finos pantalones hasta la rodilla que usaban los nobles) (pág. 505)

satellite state a country that is economically and politically dependent on another country (p. 743)

naciones satélite países que dependen política y económicamente de otro país (pág. 743)

satrap "protector of the Kingdom"; the governor of a province (satrapy) of the Persian Empire under Darius (p. 68)

sátrapa "protector del reino"; gobernador de una provincia (satrapía) del Imperio persa en tiempos de Darío (pág. 68)

satrapy one of the 20 provinces into which Darius divided the Persian Empire (p. 68)

Satrapía una de las 20 provincias en las cuales Darío dividió el Imperio persa (pág. 68)

savanna broad grassland dotted with small trees and shrubs (p. 303)

sabana amplia pradera con pequeños árboles y arbustos (pág. 303)

scholar-gentry in China, a group of people who controlled much of the land and produced most of the candidates for civil service (p. 254)

alta burguesía en China, grupo de personas que controlaba gran parte de la tierra y del cual surgía la mayoría de los candidatos para el servicio civil (pág. 254)

scholasticism a medieval philosophical and theological system that tried to reconcile faith and reason (p. 288)

escolástica sistema filosófico y teológico medieval que trataba de conciliar la fe y la razón (pág. 288)

scientific method a systematic procedure for collecting and analyzing evidence that was crucial to the evolution of science in the modern world (p. 476)

método científico procedimiento sistemático para recolectar y analizar evidencias, que fue fundamental para la evolución de la ciencia en el mundo moderno (pág. 476)

***sector** a sociological, economic, or political subdivision of society (pp. 605, 831)

***sector** subdivisión sociológica, económica o política de la sociedad (págs. 605, 831)

secularization indifference to or rejection of religion or religious consideration (pp. 482, 552)

secularización indiferencia o rechazo hacia la religión o las consideraciones religiosas (págs. 482, 552)

***security** freedom from danger or invasion; safety (p. 313)

***seguridad** cualidad de estar libre de peligro o invasión (pág. 313)

self-strengthening a policy promoted by reformers toward the end of the Qing dynasty under which China would adopt Western technology while keeping its Confucian values and institutions (p. 615)

autofortalecimiento política promovida por los reformistas hacia el final de la dinastía Qing, en la cual China adoptaba la tecnología occidental, pero mantenía sus valores e instituciones confucianos (pág. 615)

separation of powers a form of government in which the executive, legislative, and judicial branches limit and control each other through a system of checks and balances (p. 479)

separación de poderes forma de gobierno en la cual las ramas ejecutiva, legislativa y judicial se limitan y controlan entre sí mediante un sistema de equilibrio de poderes (pág. 479)

sepoy an Indian soldier hired by the British East India Company to protect the company's interests in the region (p. 597)

***cipayo** soldado indio contratado por la Compañía Británica de las Indias Orientales para proteger sus intereses en la región (pág. 597)

serf in medieval Europe, a peasant legally bound to the land who had to provide labor services, pay rents, and be subject to the lord's control (p. 233)

siervo en la Europa medieval, campesino atado por ley a la tierra, que debía prestar servicios de mano de obra, pagar rentas y someterse al control del señor feudal (pág. 233)

***series** a group of related things or events (pp. 47, 451)

***serie** grupo de cosas o eventos relacionados (págs. 47, 451)

shāh the ruler of Iran or Persia (p. 435)

sha gobernante de Irán o Persia (pág. 435)

shari'ah a law code drawn up by Muslim scholars after Muhammad's death; it provided believers with a set of practical laws to regulate their daily lives (p. 209)

sharia código redactado por los sabios musulmanes después de la muerte de Mahoma; comprende una serie de leyes prácticas para regir la vida diaria de los creyentes (pág. 209)

sheikh the ruler of an Arabic tribe, chosen from one of the leading families by a council of elders (p. 206)

jeque líder de una tribu árabe, escogido de una de las familias destacadas por un consejo de ancianos (pág. 206)

Shia a Muslim group that accepts only the descendants of Muhammad's son-in-law Ali as the true rulers of Islam (p. 213)

shií grupo musulmán que acepta sólo a los descendientes del yerno de Mahoma, Alí, como el verdadero líder del islam (pág. 213)

***shift** a change in direction (p. 795)

***desplazamiento** cambio de dirección (pág. 795)

Shinto "the Sacred Way" or "the way of the Gods"; the Japanese state religion; among its doctrines are the divinity of the emperor and the sacredness of the Japanese nation (p. 263)

sintoísmo "el Camino Sagrado" o "el camino de los Dioses"; religión oficial japonesa. Algunas de sus doctrinas son la divinidad del emperador y el carácter sagrado de la nación japonesa (pág. 263)

shogun "general"; a powerful military leader in Japan (p. 262)

sogún "general"; poderoso líder militar japonés (pág. 262)

Silk Road a route between the Roman Empire and China, so called because silk was China's most valuable product (p. 118)

ruta de la seda ruta entre el Imperio romano y China, llamada así porque la seda era el producto más valioso de China (pág. 118)

***so-called** commonly named; popularly termed (p. 302)

***llamado** denominado; conocido generalmente como (pág. 302)

social contract the concept proposed by Rousseau that an entire society agrees to be governed by its general will, and all individuals should be forced to abide by the general will since it represents what is best for the entire community (p. 481)

contrato social concepto planteado por Rousseau según el cual una sociedad accede a ser gobernada por su voluntad general, y todos los individuos deben ser obligados a acatar la voluntad general ya que esta representa lo que es mejor para toda la comunidad (pág. 481)

Social Darwinism theory used by Western nations in the late nineteenth century to justify their dominance; it was based on Charles Darwin's theory of natural selection, "the survival of the fittest," and applied to modern human activities (p. 579)

darwinismo social teoría de finales del siglo XIX con la cual las naciones occidentales justificaban su dominación; se basaba en la teoría de la selección natural de Charles Darwin, "la supervivencia del más fuerte", aplicada a las actividades humanas modernas (pág. 579)

socialism a system in which society, usually in the form of the government, owns and controls the means of production (p. 533)

socialismo sistema en el cual la sociedad, por lo general representada por el gobierno, posee y controla los medios de producción (pág. 533)

Socratic method the method of teaching used by the Greek philosopher Socrates; it employs a question-and-answer format to lead pupils to see things for themselves by using their own reason (p. 95)

método socrático método de enseñanza utilizado por el filósofo griego Sócrates; emplea un formato de preguntas y respuestas para llevar a los alumnos a ver las cosas por sí mismos usando su propria razón (pág. 95)

***sole** being the only one (p. 800)

***exclusivo** que es único (pág. 800)

***sought** made an attempt; tried (p. 67)

***pretendido** intentado; tratado (pág. 67)

***source** a document or primary reference book that gives information (p. 748)

***fuente** documento o libro usado como referencia primaria para aportar información (pág. 748)

soviets Russian councils composed of representatives from the workers and soldiers (p. 645)

sóviets consejos rusos conformados por representantes de los obreros y los soldados (pág. 645)

***sphere** any of the concentric, revolving, spherical transparent shells in which, according to ancient astronomy, the stars, sun, planets, and moon are set (p. 473)

***esfera** cualquiera de las capas concéntricas, giratorias, esféricas y transparentes en las cuales, según la astronomía antigua, están distribuidas las estrellas, el Sol, los planetas y la Luna (pág. 473)

spheres of influence areas in which foreign powers have been granted exclusive rights and privileges, such as trading rights and mining privileges (p. 615)

esferas de influencia áreas en las cuales se concede a las potencias extranjeras derechos y privilegios exclusivos, como derechos comerciales y privilegios para la explotación minera (pág. 615)

***stability** the state of being stable; strong enough to endure (p. 415)

***estabilidad** propiedad de estable; suficientemente fuerte como para resistir (pág. 415)

***stable** not changing or fluctuating; steady (p. 809)

***estable** que no cambia ni fluctúa; invariable (pág. 809)

state capitalism an economic system in which the central government plays an active role in the economy, establishing price and wage policies and subsidizing vital industries (p. 808)

capitalismo de Estado sistema económico en el cual el gobierno central desempeña un rol activo en la economía, estableciendo las políticas de precios y salarios, y subsidiando las industrias vitales (pág. 808)

stateless society a group of independent villages organized into clans led by a local ruler or clan head without any central government (p. 314)

sociedades sin Estado grupo de aldeas independientes organizadas en clanes dirigidos por un gobernante local o jefe de clan sin ningún gobierno central (pág. 314)

Stoicism the school of thought developed by the teacher Zeno in Hellenistic Athens; it says that happiness can be achieved only when people gain inner peace by living in harmony with the will of God and that people should bear whatever life offers (p. 101)

estoicismo escuela de pensamiento creada por el profesor Zenón en la Atenas helenística; sostenía que solo se puede lograr la felicidad cuando las personas consiguen la paz interior, mediante una vida en armonía con los deseos de Dios y que las personas deben soportar todo lo que la vida les depare (pág. 101)

***strategy** a plan or method (p. 91)

***estrategia** plan o método (pág. 91)

***structure** an arrangement in a definite pattern of organization (p. 181)

***estructura** organización en un patrón definido (pág. 181)

***style** having a distinctive quality or form (p. 351)

***estilo** que tiene un modo o una forma que lo distingue (pág. 351)

***submission** the act of submitting to the control or authority of another (p. 208)

***sumisión** acción de someterse al control o la autoridad de otra persona (pág. 208)

subprime investments investments based on loans that have an interest rate that is higher than a prime rate and is extended especially to low-income borrowers (p. 866)

inversiones de alto riesgo inversiones basadas en préstamos que tienen una tasa de interés más alta que la tasa preferencial y se otorgan especialmente a prestatarios de bajos ingresos (pág. 866)

***subsidizing** aiding or promoting with public money (p. 100)

***subsidiar** ayudar o promover con recursos públicos (pág. 100)

***subsidy** a government payment to encourage or protect a certain economic activity (p. 625)

***subsidio** pago del gobierno para estimular o proteger una actividad económica determinada (pág. 625)

subsistence farming the practice of growing just enough crops for personal use, not for sale (p. 313)

agricultura de subsistencia práctica que consiste en cultivar solo para uso personal, no para la venta (pág. 313)

***successor** one who follows, especially one who takes over a throne, title, estate, or office (pp. 56, 431, 485)

***sucesor** el que sigue, especialmente el que asume el trono o un título, una propiedad, o recibe una herencia o un cargo (págs. 56, 431, 485)

suffrage the right to vote (p. 567)

sufragio derecho al voto (pág. 567)

sultan "holder of power"; the military and political head of state under the Seljuk Turks and the Ottomans (pp. 214, 432)

sultán "quien posee el poder"; jefe político y militar de Estado durante los gobiernos de los turcos selyúcidas y los otomanos (págs. 214, 432)

Sunni a Muslim group that accepts only the descendants of the Umayyads as the true rulers of Islam (p. 213)

sunita grupo musulmán que solo acepta a los descendientes de los Umayyad como los verdaderos jerarcas del islam (pág. 213)

surrealism an artistic movement that seeks to depict the world of the unconscious (p. 666)

Surrealismo movimiento artístico que busca representar el mundo del inconsciente (pág. 666)

***survive** to remain alive or in existence (p. 7)

***sobrevivir** seguir vivo o existiendo (pág. 7)

sustainable development an economic development that does not limit the ability of future generations to meet their basic needs (p. 871)

desarrollo sostenible desarrollo económico que no limita la capacidad de las generaciones futuras de satisfacer sus necesidades básicas (pág. 871)

***sustained** supported or held up (p. 68)

***sostenido** apoyado o sustentado (pág. 68)

suttee the Hindu custom of cremating a widow on her husband's funeral pyre (p. 440)

satí tradición hindú de cremar a una viuda en la pira funeraria de su esposo (pág. 440)

***symbol** something that stands for something else by way of association; a visible sign of something invisible (p. 824)

***símbolo** algo que representa otra cosa por asociación; signo visible de algo invisible (pág. 824)

***systematic agriculture** the keeping of animals and the growing of food on a regular basis (p. 11)

***agricultura** sistemática cría de animales y cultivo de alimentos con regularidad (pág. 11)

T

taille an annual direct tax, usually on land or property, that provided a regular source of income for the French monarchy (pp. 294, 500)

talla impuesto directo anual, usualmente sobre la tierra o las propiedades, que proveía una fuente habitual de ingresos a la monarquía francesa (págs. 294, 500)

***target** something or someone marked for attack (pp. 640, 784)

***objetivo** algo o alguien marcado para un ataque (págs. 640, 784)

***technical** of or pertaining to a technique (p. 287)

***técnico** relativo a la técnica (pág. 287)

***technology** a manner of accomplishing a task using technical processes, methods, or knowledge (pp. 31, 232)

***tecnología** llevar a cabo una tarea utilizando procesos , métodos, o conocimientos técnicos (págs. 31, 232)

***temporary** lasting for a limited time; not permanent (p. 537)

***temporal** de duración limitada; que no es permanente (pág. 537)

tepee a circular tent made by stretching buffalo skins over wooden poles (p. 324)

tipi tienda circular que se hacía estirando pieles de búfalo sobre postes de madera (pág. 324)

***theme** a subject or topic of artistic work (p. 780)

***tema** materia o asunto de una obra artística (pág. 780)

theocracy government by divine authority (p. 18)

teocracia giobierno por autoridad divina (p. 18)

theology the study of religion and God (p. 288)

teología estudio de la religión y de Dios (pág. 288)

***theory** hypothesis or unproved assumption (p. 4)

***teoría** hipótesis o suposición sin comprobar (pág. 4)

Theravada "the teachings of the elders"; a school of Buddhism that developed in India; its followers view Buddhism as a way of life (p. 265)

teravada "enseñanzas de los mayores"; escuela budista que se desarrolló en India. Sus seguidores consideran el budismo una forma de vida (pág. 265)

totalitarian state a government that aims to control the political, economic, social, intellectual, and cultural lives of its citizens (p. 667)

Estado totalitario gobierno que intenta controlar la vida política, económica, social, intelectual y cultural de sus ciudadanos (pág. 667)

total war a war that involved the complete mobilization of resources and people, affecting the lives of all citizens in the warring countries, even those remote from the battlefield (p. 642)

guerra total guerra que implica la movilización total de recursos y personas, y afecta la vida de todos los ciudadanos de las naciones en conflicto, aun aquellas alejadas del campo de batalla (pág. 642)

trade embargo a policy prohibiting trade with a particular country (p. 783)

embargo comercial política que prohíbe comercializar con un país en particular (pág. 783)

***traditional** established; customary (p. 268)

***tradicional** establecido; acostumbrado (pág. 268)

***traditions** the established customs of a people (p. 595)

***tradiciones** costumbres establecidas de un pueblo (pág. 595)

tragedy a form of drama that portrays a conflict between the protagonist and a superior force and having a protagonist who is brought to ruin or extreme sorrow, especially as a result of a fatal flaw (p. 94)

tragedia forma de drama que representa un conflicto entre el protagonista y una fuerza superior y que tiene un protagonista que es llevado a la ruina or un dolor extremo, en especial como resultado de un error fatal (pág 94)

***transfer** to take over the control of (p. 755)

***traspasar** asumir el control (pág. 755)

***transformation** conversion; change in character or condition (p. 179)

***transformación** conversión; cambio de carácter o condición (pág. 179)

***transition** changeover; the move from one form, stage, or style to another (p. 562)

***transición** conversión; pasar de una forma, etapa o estilo a otra (pág. 562)

***transport** the moving of goods or people (p. 18)

***transporte** traslado de productos o personas (pág. 18)

trench warfare fighting from ditches protected by barbed wire, as in World War I (p. 639)

guerra de trincheras combatir desde zanjas protegidas por alambre de púas, como en la Primera Guerra Mundial (pág. 639)

triumvirate a government by three people with equal power (p. 159)

triunvirato gobierno ejercido por tres personas con el mismo poder (pág. 159)

tyrant a ruler who seized power by force from the aristocrats, gained support from the newly rich and the poor, and maintained power by using hired soldiers and fighting tactics (p. 82)

tirano mandatario que les quitaba el poder a la fuerza a los aristócratas, se ganaba el respaldo de los nuevos ricos y los pobres, y conservaba el poder valiéndose de soldados contratados y tácticas de combate (pág. 82)

U

ulema a group of religious advisors to the Ottoman sultan; this group administered the legal system and schools for educating Muslims (p. 432)

ulema grupo de consejeros religiosos del sultán otomano; este grupo administraba el sistema legal y las escuelas donde se educaban los musulmanes (pág. 432)

uncertainty principle the idea put forth by Werner Heisenberg in 1927 that the behavior of subatomic particles is uncertain, suggesting that all of the physical laws governing the universe are based on uncertainty (p. 666)

principio de incertidumbre idea planteada por Werner Heisenberg en 1927 según la cual el comportamiento de las partículas subatómicas es incierto, lo cual sugiere que las leyes físicas que gobiernan el universo se basan en la incertidumbre (pág. 666)

***uncharted** not mapped; unknown (p. 593)

***inexplorado** no cartografiado; desconocido (pág. 593)

***unification** the act, process, or result of making into a coherent or coordinated whole; the state of being unified (p. 541)

***unificación** acción, proceso o resultado de conformar un todo coherente o coordinado; estar unificado (pág. 541)

***unify** to make into a unit or whole; to unite (p. 830)

***unificar** hacer un todo; unir (pág. 830)

universal law of gravitation one of Newton's three rules of motion; it explains that planetary bodies continue in elliptical orbits around the sun because every object in the universe is attracted to every other object by a force called gravity. (p. 474)

ley de la gravitación universal una de las tres leyes del movimiento de Newton; explica que los cuerpos planetarios siguen órbitas elípticas alrededor del Sol porque todos los objetos del universo son atraídos entre sí por una fuerza llamada gravedad. (pág. 474)

universal male suffrage the right of all males to vote in elections (p. 537)

sufragio universal masculino derecho de todos los hombres a votar en las elecciones (pág. 537)

***unrestricted** having no restrictions or bounds (p. 641)

***irrestricto** que no tiene restricciones o límites (pág. 641)

utopian socialists individuals who believe that social ownership of the means of production can be achieved by the voluntary and peaceful surrender of property (p. 533)

socialistas utópicos individuos que piensan que la propiedad social de los medios de producción se lograr mediante la renuncia voluntaria y pacífica a la propiedad (pág. 533)

V

***valid** well-grounded or justifiable (p. 364)

***válido** bien fundamentado o justificable (pág. 364)

varnas the name given by Aryans in ancient India to a group of people in what was believed to be an ideal social structure of four groups (p. 108)

varnas nombre que los arios de la antigua India dieron a un grupo de personas en lo que se creía sería una estructura social ideal de cuatro grupos (pág. 108)

vassal under feudalism, a man who served a lord in a military capacity (p. 229)

vasallo durante el feudalismo, hombre al servicio de un señor feudal en una instalación militar (pág. 229)

Vedas the earliest known Indian literature, which contain religious chants and stories that were originally passed down orally from generation to generation and then recorded in Sanskrit after writing developed (p. 119)

vedas literatura india más antigua conocida, que contiene cantos religiosos e historias que al principio se transmitían oralmente de generación en generación y luego se registraron en sánscrito, después de la invención de la escritura (pág. 119)

vernacular the language of everyday speech in a particular region (pp. 289, 349)

vernácula lengua cotidiana que se habla en una región en particular (págs. 289, 349)

viceroy a governor who ruled as a representative of a monarch (p. 598)

virrey gobernante que regía como representante de un monarca (pág. 598)

***violation** a disregard of rules or agreements (p. 713)

***violación** desprecio de las reglas o acuerdos (pág. 713)

***visible** capable of being seen (p. 60)

***visible** que se puede ver (pág. 60)

***virtually** almost entirely; nearly (p. 152)

***prácticamente** casi por completo; por poco (pág. 152)

***vision** the way of seeing or believing (p. 259)

***visión** forma de ver o creer (pág. 259)

vizier a high government official in ancient Egypt or in Muslim countries (p. 213)

visir alto funcionario del gobierno en el antiguo Egipto o en los países musulmanes (pág. 213)

***volunteer** one who enters the military voluntarily (p. 689)

***voluntario** persona que entra al ejército voluntariamente (pág. 689)

W

war communism in World War I Russia, the government control of banks and most industries, the seizing of grain from peasants, and the centralization of state administration under Communist control (p. 648)

comunismo de guerra durante la Primera Guerra Mundial en Rusia, control gubernamental de bancos y la mayoría de industrias, la incautación de los granos y la centralización de la administración del Estado bajo el control comunista (pág. 648)

war of attrition a war based on wearing down the other side with constant attacks and heavy losses, such as World War I (p. 640)

guerra de desgaste guerra que consiste en desgastar a la contraparte con ataques constantes y pérdidas numerosas, como en la Primera Guerra Mundial (pág. 640)

***welfare** something that aids or promotes well-being (p. 117)

***asistencia** social algo que ayuda o promueve el bienestar (pág. 117)

welfare state a state in which the government takes responsibility for providing citizens with services such as health care (p. 795)

estado de bienestar estado en el cual el gobierno asume la responsabilidad de proveer a los ciudadanos servicios como la atención en salud (pág. 795)

wergild "money for a man"; the value of a person in money, depending on social status; in Germanic society, a fine paid by a wrongdoer to the family of the person he or she had injured or killed (p. 194)

indemnización "dinero a cambio de un hombre"; valor económico de una persona de acuerdo con su estatus social; en la sociedad germana, multa que pagaba un malhechor a la familia de la persona a quien este había herido o asesinado (pág. 194)

***whereas** although (pp. 164, 604)

***mientras que** aunque (pág. 164, 604)

***widespread** widely extended or spread out (p. 722)

***generalizado** muy ampliado o difundido (pág. 722)

women's liberation movement the renewed feminist movement of the late 1960s, which demanded political and economic equality with men (p. 799)

movimiento de liberación femenina movimiento feminista renovado de finales de la década de 1960, que exigía la igualdad política y económica con los hombres (pág. 799)

Y

yoga a method of training developed by the Hindus that is supposed to lead to oneness with Brahman (p. 110)

yoga método de ejercicio desarrollado por los hindúes que se supone lleva a la unidad con Brahmán (pág. 110)

Z

zaibatsu in the Japanese economy, a large financial and industrial corporation (p. 693)

zaibatsu en la economía japonesa, sociedad financiera e industrial grande (pág. 693)

zamindar a local official in Mogul India who received a plot of farmland (p. 439)

zamindar funcionario local durante el imperio mogol en la India, que recibía una parcela de tierra para la labranza (pág. 439)

Zen a sect of Buddhism that became popular with Japanese aristocrats and became part of the samurai's code of behavior; under Zen Buddhism, there are different paths to enlightenment (p. 263)

zen secta del budismo que se difundió ampliamente entre los aristócratas japoneses y pasó a formar parte del código de conducta de los samuráis. En el budismo zen existen diferentes caminos para alcanzar la iluminación (pág. 263)

Zionism an international movement originally for the establishment of a Jewish national homeland in Palestine and later for the support of modern Israel (p. 579)

sionismo "movimiento internacional en apoyo del establecimiento de un territorio judío en Palestina, donde se ubicaba el antiguo Israel, y luego en apoyo del Israel moderno" (pág. 579)

ziggurat a massive stepped tower on which was built a temple dedicated to the chief god or goddess of a Sumerian city (p. 17)

zigurat gran torre escalonada sobre la cual se construía un templo dedicado al dios o diosa principales de una ciudad sumeria (pág. 17)

The following abbreviations are used in the index: *m* = map; *f* = feature (photograph, picture, painting, cartoon, chart); *t* = table; *q* = quote.

A

C

Index

D

Index

Index

H

Index

I

J

Index

M

Index

N

O

Index

P

Index

S

Index

Index

T

U

V

W

Index

X

Y

Z